COMMAND OF OFFICE

ALSO BY STEPHEN GRAUBARD

British Labour and the Russian Revolution

Burke, Disraeli, and Churchill: The Politics of Perseverance

Kissinger: Portrait of a Mind

Mr. Bush's War: Adventures in the Politics of Illusion

SELECTED BOOKS EDITED BY STEPHEN GRAUBARD

Excellence and Leadership in a Democracy (with Gerald Holton)

A New Europe?

Historical Studies Today (with Felix Gilbert)

Edward Gibbon and the Decline and Fall of the Roman Empire
(with G.W. Bowersock and John Clive)

A New America?

The State

Generations

Eastern Europe . . . Central Europe . . . Europe

Exit from Communism

Toward the Year 2000: Work in Progress (with Daniel Bell)

A New Europe for the Old

COMMAND OF OFFICE

How War, Secrecy, and Deception
Transformed the Presidency from
Theodore Roosevelt to George W. Bush

STEPHEN GRAUBARD

BASIC
BOOKS

A Member of the Perseus Books Group
New York

Books published by Basic Books are available at special discounts for bulk purchases in the United
States by corporations, institutions, and other organizations. For more information, please contact
the Special Markets Department at the Perseus Books Group, 11 Cambridge Center, Cambridge MA
02142, or call (617) 252-5298, or (800) 255-1514, or e-mail special.markets@perseusbooks.com.

Designed by Brent Wilcox
Set in 11 point Adobe Garamond

Library of Congress Cataloging-in-Publication Data
Graubard, Stephen Richards.
    Command of office / Stephen Graubard.
      p.   cm.
    Includes bibliographical references and index.
    ISBN 0-465-02757-1 (alk. paper)
    1. Presidents—United States—Biography.   2. Presidents—United States—History—20th century.
3. United States—Politics and government—20th century.   4. United States—Foreign relations—
20th century.   5. Political leadership—United States—Case studies.   I. Title.

E176.1.G815   2004
973'.09'9—dc22

                                                                                    2004007706

04 05 06 / 10 9 8 7 6 5 4 3 2 1

For Margaret

Europeans often ask, and Americans do not always explain, how it happens that this great office, the greatest in the world, unless we except the Papacy, which anyone can rise by his own merits, is not more frequently filled by great and striking men. In America, which is beyond all other countries the country of a 'career open to talents,' a country, moreover, in which political life is unusually keen and political ambition widely diffused, it might be expected that the highest place would always be won by a man of brilliant gifts. But from the time when the heroes of the Revolution died out with Jefferson and Adams and Madison, no person except General Grant . . . reached the chair whose name would have been remembered had he not been President, and no President except Abraham Lincoln had displayed rare or striking qualities in the chair.

—JAMES BRYCE,
THE AMERICAN COMMONWEALTH

It is principally in relations with foreigners that the executive power of a nation finds occasion to deploy its skill and force. If the life of the Union were constantly threatened, if its great interests were mixed everyday with those of other powerful peoples, one would see the executive power grow larger in opinion, through what one would expect from it and what it would execute. . . . The President of the United States possesses almost royal prerogatives which he has no occasion to make use of, and the rights which, up to now, he can use are very circumscribed: the laws permit him to be strong, circumstances keep him weak.

—ALEXIS DE TOCQUEVILLE,
DEMOCRACY IN AMERICA

CONTENTS

PREFACE

This, the story of the American presidency in the years that began with Theodore Roosevelt, following the assassination of William McKinley, the third president so to be felled, is a tale of major institutional change, created in some measure by those who by accident, good fortune, or design came to hold that executive office, but also, more importantly, by the international circumstances that made the United States a world power. Increasingly seen today as an "empire," greater, some insist, than any that has existed since antiquity, since the fall of Rome, the book's title: *Command of Office: How War, Secrecy, and Deception Transformed the Presidency from Theodore Roosevelt to George W. Bush* emphasizes two factors that caused this political office to lose many of its most distinctive eighteenth- and nineteenth-century features. Wars, hot and cold, fought or feared, led to an unprecedented expansion of presidential power, as prophesied by a remarkable student of America's "political experiment," Alexis de Tocqueville, many decades earlier. Foreign policy assumed an importance in the life of the nation it had never previously claimed, and if those who came to the White House were not, as James Bryce, Europe's other great nineteenth-century commentator on the United States, understood, always "great" or "striking" men, the nation prospered, and not only in those periods when remarkable leaders came to the fore.

The tale of the twentieth-century presidency, which survives into the twenty-first, if George W. Bush is recognized as the disciple of Ronald Reagan, must dwell on all manner of political and moral restraints that atrophied, but also on weapons and intelligence, defined as the capacity for spying, that made war a very different thing from what it had been earlier in the century. Presidential leadership took many forms in the decades after Theodore Roosevelt and Woodrow Wilson, the principal tutors of Franklin D. Roosevelt, the century's incontestably greatest president assumed office, and no less major permutations occurred after the only general, Dwight D. Eisenhower, left the Oval Office. An analysis of the presidency that recognizes three great divides, the first that brought Theodore Roosevelt to the White House, following the assassination of William McKinley, the second that carried John F. Kennedy with a very slight popular majority into the Oval Office, and the third that ended two troubled decades, the 1960s and the 1970s, with the election of Ronald Reagan by a very wide margin cannot be said to follow the more conventional presidential chronologies. Nor, for that matter, does it see the first Roosevelt as simply a warrior and an imperialist, the tragically martyred Kennedy as an accomplished political leader who left the nation an intellectually important legacy, and Reagan, the actor, as someone who had his moment in the sun, without much relevance for the world of the twenty-first century.

If my analysis of the presidency as it has evolved over the last century has merit, then the portrayals of the individual presidents will be recognized to be something more than an *apologia* for either Democrats or Republicans who managed to climb the "slippery pole." An America that rebelled against the mother country, imagining it would have no further truck with kings, courtiers, or warriors, has since the beginning of the twentieth century known all, rarely so identified, but unmistakably recognizable as such. These eighteen Presidents, mortal bipeds, were on occasion powerful, sometimes inept, but increasingly subjected to national and international scrutiny, availing themselves of resources unknown to their nineteenth-century predecessors. The American democracy, transformed in the course of the long twentieth century, takes its form today in very considerable measure because of what these presidents elected to do but also what public opinion allowed them to do.

The question may well arise why the two epigraphs to this book are from Alexis de Tocqueville and James Bryce, the indisputable giants among those who wrote about the United States in the nineteenth century. Why should their works, written in 1835 and 1888, be thought relevant to a book concerned with the presidency since the time of Theodore Roosevelt? Three reasons may be given; first, both Roosevelt and Wilson, who did so much to enhance the power of the presidency, to make it more visible and internationally known, were learned men who read and wrote about both Tocqueville and Bryce. Their reflections on both, that of the politician but also of the academic transformed in middle life into a politician, cannot fail to have interest and importance. Second, and more significantly, perhaps, Bryce in the late nineteenth century wrote about American society, political parties, "bosses," corruption, and presidential nominating procedures in ways that continued to be descriptive of much that characterized political life in the United States through the time of Eisenhower. His book, more widely read during those many decades than Tocqueville's, became obsolete, a work of history for many only in the 1960s and 1970s. Finally, ironically, it was in the last decades of the twentieth century, that Tocqueville's work, descriptive of a society of not many millions overwhelmingly agricultural, that Bryce imagined as early as 1888 no longer existed, came to enjoy new renown. Tocqueville, not Bryce, offered reflections on war, race, patriotism, religion, foreign policy, and morality, treating values and opinion in an idiom that resonated for Americans living in the time of Reagan, Clinton, and the two Bushes. The brief Appendix to this book that considers Tocqueville and Bryce is an integral part of the work, as important as the chapters that deal with the individual presidents, their preparation for the high office they attained, and their performance in it, especially in foreign policy and defense.

THE PRESIDENCY

CHAPTER 1

Of a Republic Transformed by Kings, Courtiers, and Warriors

THOSE WHO FRAMED the U.S. Constitution were determined that the new republic should be deterred from pursuing the political policies and practices of the old country, abandoning royal power and the exaggerated deference it inspired, shunning war in all but very exceptional circumstances. Finding a proper way to address the president of the United States, giving him a title both dignified and simple, preoccupied men in George Washington's administration, and it is scarcely surprising that Thomas Jefferson, an ardent democrat, abandoned the practice of delivering in person his speeches to Congress, believing it reeked too much of the ways of George III.[1] American diplomats abroad shunned the elaborate uniforms so common with European diplomats, and served not in embassies but in more humble residences appropriately characterized as legations. The pomp and ceremony attendant on European power seemed virtually absent in the United States visited by Alexis de Tocqueville and James Bryce in the nineteenth century. Even following the assassinations of Abraham Lincoln and James Garfield, admission to the White House was never impeded by a small contingent of armed guards fearful that so horrendous a crime might be attempted a third time.[2] Simplicity, the theme of the nineteenth-century American republic, made the president the first citizen among equals, but these practices gave way in the twentieth century to a new kind of presidential office that vaunted itself on its simplicity, but showed unmistakable signs of having assumed the trappings traditionally bestowed on European heads of state.

By the end of the twentieth century, U.S. presidents, guarded by Secret Service agents in great number and pursued by hordes of journalists, attending their every excursion outside the White House gates, spoke of a condition that obtained in no other country in the world. American presidents, political icons, incontestably important, needed to be defended against those mad

3

enough to seek to do them harm. As leaders of the republic, their every action merited attention, and the country lived in the illusion it knew these men as it had never known those who had preceded them in more tranquil times. Few spoke of the presidents as kings, especially after World War I, when royalty ceased to exist in Germany, Russia, and Austria-Hungary, and when the limited monarchies of Europe's democratic societies claimed few prerogatives compara-ble to those enjoyed by the men who occupied the White House. Yet these American presidents were monarchs, admittedly of a new breed, increasingly attended by courtiers, scarcely resembling those once characteristic of royal Eu-rope. These new American kings fought wars constantly—many were warriors in all but name—and though the wars they waged scarcely resembled the U.S. military campaigns of the nineteenth century against native tribes or Latin American republics unable to defend themselves, the two great wars that began in 1917 and 1941 legitimated vastly expanded presidential authority. These two world wars, so different from those fought in Korea after 1950 and in Viet-nam after 1963, were still more unlike those initiated by Reagan, Bush the elder, Clinton, and Bush the younger.

Were this a book concerned only with the presidency in the twentieth cen-tury in strictly calendar terms it would open with a consideration of William McKinley, the Ohio politician who followed many others from his state into the White House, and end with Bill Clinton, the only Arkansas politician who managed to enter what all thought to be the nation's most honored precincts, which, in the minds of many, he then proceeded to defile. Why, then, does it not start with the assassinated McKinley, who lived on till September 14, 1901, but with Theodore Roosevelt, his vice president and constitutionally desig-nated successor? More surprisingly, what explains the decision to conclude not with Clinton, the only president in the century to be tried by the Senate after being impeached by the House, but with George W. Bush, the son of a former president, only the second such person in the history of the republic to succeed in winning the nation's highest office? The explanation is simple; my argument is that George W. Bush, inaugurated on January 20, 2001, is best understood as the most recent of the twentieth-century presidents. Though McKinley lived on to serve as president into the twentieth century, Americans always regarded him as a man of the nineteenth; so, also, with George W. Bush, though he serves in the twenty-first century, he is best seen as a man of the twentieth, po-litically the heir of Ronald Reagan, his father's principal tutor. That argument will have no appeal for those, perhaps in the majority today, who believe that September 11, 2001, inaugurated a new era in world history, and that the pres-ident's military and diplomatic initiatives since that fateful day suggest he is not simply the political clone of his father or of his father's chief patron.

To claim that he belongs to the twentieth century does not imply that George W. Bush is a latter-day Theodore Roosevelt, Woodrow Wilson, Harry

Truman, or Dwight Eisenhower any more than William McKinley, presiding over the nation's affairs in the same century as Thomas Jefferson, James Madison, James Monroe, Andrew Jackson, and Abraham Lincoln, was thought to resemble any of them. His is a late-twentieth-century presidency principally because it is redolent of Reagan's administration, at once patriotic, proud, rhetorical, and popular, not given to wearying citizens with complex explanations of arcane foreign policy and defense issues.[3] Until there is some understanding of how much the presidency changed between the time Theodore Roosevelt came to the office and Bill Clinton left it, it is difficult to appreciate the "silent revolution" that occurred in the course of the century. Though many astute politicians entered the White House after Theodore Roosevelt, able to cope with the novel foreign policy and defense issues that presented themselves, conducting the wars they felt obliged to wage, others, substantially less gifted, imagined themselves competent and were indulged in their illusions by those they chose to serve them. Many of these latter twentieth-century Cabinet and White House officials, boasting greatly inflated titles and egos to match, were men who lacked anything that could be mistaken for political experience. A good number, professional lawyers, had no experience of office. Chosen because they were trusted friends of the president or individuals highly recommended to him, in the last four decades of the century the White House staff grew to proportions inconceivable at any previous time. These were men and women purportedly selected for their intelligence and energy; the greatest number had never expected to enjoy such close proximity to a president of the United States. Awed by their newly acquired eminence and their near-presence to such incomparable power, they enjoyed perquisites that gave evidence of their importance. These might include chauffeured limousines, large staffs, and even occasional trips with the president in Air Force One. Obliged to work long hours to justify the grandiose titles granted them, even when their offices were not in the much coveted West Wing but across the street in the old State Department Building, appropriately renamed the Executive Office Building, they sensed their importance. This was no longer the presidency of Theodore or Franklin Roosevelt, dependent on miniscule White House staffs, with many Cabinet colleagues able to claim substantial congressional or federal executive experience.[4]

Theodore Roosevelt, an avid reader and an accomplished writer of U.S. history, sought to restore the presidency to what he imagined it had been in the heroic days of Washington and Lincoln.[5] His aim was to create a new presidency suited to a new century. To achieve that purpose, he created a persona for himself that spoke of power, informing Americans and the world abroad that a new generation, more ambitious than the old, had taken command. No one living in the first decade of the twentieth century, however loyal to McKinley's memory, could doubt that an elemental force had entered the White House.[6]

Can a comparable claim be made for George W. Bush? Have his words and actions since September 11 qualified him for comparable distinction, a new man for a new century, inaugurating a dramatically altered presidency? Some of his more ardent admirers will argue this, that he demonstrated after September 11 a resolve to take military, diplomatic, and political initiatives of a boldness and originality that none of his predecessors could have conceived or executed. His enemies, deploring many of his actions, may argue the same. Both exaggerate. The al-Qaeda success in using airplanes as missiles to destroy the two largest skyscrapers in New York and do great damage to the Pentagon in Washington, causing thousands of deaths and casualties, created political opportunities for the president that he used effectively, in the same way that Reagan did, responding decades earlier to more cosmic events attendant on the decay and ultimate dissolution of the Soviet Union. George W. Bush qualifies as the last of the twentieth century's presidents precisely because he expresses values espoused by Ronald Reagan, popular with millions, whose loyal courtiers embellished his reputation as someone who had left behind all the more timid earlier twentieth-century presidents, Democratic and Republican.[7]

The presidency of the first sixty years of the century, so largely fashioned by a handful of men, used very exceptional circumstances abroad to justify their greatly expanded claims to power. That presidency came to an end in the 1960s and 1970s—a soul-searing time of troubles—that witnessed a precipitous decline in the public's confidence in its elected leaders.[8] The argument that the U.S. presidency assumed new prerogatives and distinction in the first six decades of the century, was seriously challenged by domestic and foreign tragedies in the 1960s and 1970s, and became yet another kind of institution with the arrival of Ronald Reagan in 1981 may be thought a disguised version of a theme Woodrow Wilson first advanced in 1885, which James Bryce adopted in *The American Commonwealth* in 1888.[9] Their belief that the presidency attracted cultivated and astute political leaders in the last decade of the eighteenth and the first decades of the nineteenth century, lost such leadership before the start of the Civil War, and never regained it following the tragic assassination of Lincoln is not one that I intend to replicate for the twentieth century. Such, in fact, is not the leitmotif of this work; it argues quite different propositions, namely, that a new presidency was introduced by Theodore Roosevelt and Woodrow Wilson, interrupted by less accomplished presidents, including Warren Harding, Calvin Coolidge, and Herbert Hoover, sustained and vastly expanded by Franklin Roosevelt and Harry Truman, significantly altered in the time of John F. Kennedy, Lyndon Johnson, Richard Nixon, and Gerald Ford, that allowed a consummate politician, Ronald Reagan, to become president in 1981. We live in the shadow of the Reagan presidency today, and those who feel only disdain for the actor president are mistaken to ignore his continued influence.

Eric Hobsbawm, in his much admired work *Age of Extremes: The Short Twentieth Century, 1914–1991,* argued that the twentieth century was brief, a mere seventy-seven years; it was never that for the United States or for its most important political institution, the presidency.[10] The twentieth century for America was long, starting with Theodore Roosevelt and continuing till this day, a century of war, secrecy, intrigue, and scandal, that saw the White House become incontestably the most powerful organ of government. War was more generative than scandal, though the latter proved immensely diverting to men and women starved to know more about the foibles of the mighty. Secrecy became paramount, made necessary by the demands of modern war and the security hazards posed by atomic and thermonuclear weapons. In post–World War II America, even the prying media, with their eager investigative reporters, joined by large congressional staffs serving ambitious members of the House and Senate, learned relatively little of the secrets sedulously concealed by a succession of presidents preoccupied always with defending what they conceived to be the national interest.[11]

Because this book treats the American presidency, an eighteenth-century institution explicitly created to deny the need for kings, courtiers, and warriors, antiquated European forms disdained by the architects of the new American republic, it is curious that metaphorically speaking they figure so prominently in this work. Who, then, were the kings, courtiers, and warriors who insinuated themselves into a society purportedly distrustful of these outmoded and corrupt European role models? The words are intended to draw attention to major institutional changes in the presidency that legitimated novel assertions of constitutional authority, legitimated a vast expansion of the staffs recruited to serve overburdened chief executives, and in the process created new habits of subordination, subservience, and deference to them. A good number who bore the title commander in chief were warriors in every sense of the term, responsible for the nation's security in both hot and cold wars. Nuclear and thermonuclear weapons made the presidents who came after Franklin Roosevelt leaders of the free world, pledged to defend civilization against barbarians who threatened it.[12] The U.S. presidency became something it had never previously been, but the construction rested on foundations laid by Theodore Roosevelt and Woodrow Wilson, each in his own way a man determined to enhance the office granted them by a kindly fate.

Roosevelt developed a theory of stewardship to justify the unconventional policies he pursued, believing his actions legitimate precisely because they did not explicitly violate restrictions and prohibitions set by Congress.[13] It was Matthew Prior, the eighteenth-century poet and statesman who believed a king to be responsible for the care of his people, "a man condemn'd to bear the public burdens of a nation's cares."[14] Roosevelt, a monarch in that sense, cared for the nation but never thought the task a burden; for him, it was an unadulterated pleasure, a view he shared with his distant cousin, Franklin. Providence, working through the nation, had given them the presidency, and they proposed to enjoy it.

Theodore Roosevelt understood that his exaggerated ambitions for the office could never be realized by resisting powerful senators, men who enjoyed virtual life tenure in their six-year posts, constantly renewed by the state legislatures that elected them.[15] He searched for an area where he could be virtually supreme and discovered it in foreign policy. Confident he knew the subject as few others did, he saw it as a domain he could call his own, aware that neither the Senate nor the House could thwart him in fashioning day-to-day policy to make the United States a world power. Depicted by cartoonists as a war-loving imperialist, so different from the later peace-loving Woodrow Wilson, Roosevelt was never the warrior that cartoonists made him out to be. He was the first American to win the Nobel Peace Prize for his success in ending the war between Russia and Japan and never failed to emphasize all he had done to maintain peace.[16] A skilled manipulator of public opinion who courted popularity and used the press to advertise his incomparable qualities as a man of action, he worked persistently to project the image of the red-blooded American male, determined that those who trespassed on the rights of others should be punished, not least the so-called captains of industry who exercised their illegitimate claims to power through the monopolies and trusts they established.[17] Solicitous for the land, he cared greatly for the preservation of its natural beauty and resources and emerged as the steward who would abide no desecration of the nation's patrimony.[18] Roosevelt disdained the title of intellectual, thinking the breed timid and craven. He was a king who never sought to create a court, and the White House during the Roosevelt years was a Mecca thronged by men and women gratified to be in the presence of so elemental a force. There were no major wars during the time Roosevelt served in the White House, and whatever his admiration for military and naval power, they never led him into foreign wars.[19]

William Howard Taft could never be presidential in the Roosevelt manner. Lacking both his charisma and the exaggerated notions of the power that inhered in the office, no one spoke of Taft as the boss, and no one thought it dangerous to oppose him. His Yale education and years as a judge and governor of the Philippines did not greatly distinguish him from other late-nineteenth-century presidents who came from Ohio, served for a single term only, and left neither a political progeny nor a social program that commended itself to a later generation.[20] Taft, neither a king nor a warrior, never aspired to create a court in the White House. A family man, devoted to his ailing wife, children, and brothers, his girth became the symbol of his lethargy, although it did not begin to explain his political inadequacies, his failure to know how to treat with Congress or the public. His greatest misfortune was to follow Roosevelt into the White House, a place the former president missed and wished desperately to regain.[21]

Woodrow Wilson, a stubborn, articulate, and scholarly Calvinist who put no one in mind of the gregarious, joyous, and buoyant Roosevelt, owed his presidency to Roosevelt, to the unusual circumstances of the 1912 election that saw the former president declare war on Taft and the Republican Party for refusing to make him, the people's choice, as registered in a handful of primaries, the convention's nominee. Running as an Independent, Roosevelt, in effect, gave the presidency to Wilson, a man he distrusted, indeed despised.[22] Wilson never doubted he was the intellectual equal of Roosevelt and saw his task as marshalling his Democratic forces in Congress to pass domestic legislation to prove himself a more effective reformer than the bombastic Republican who had so recklessly disparaged him during the election campaign.[23] His accomplishments in pressing for major domestic reforms, especially during his first two years in office, greatly exceeded what Roosevelt had been able to do, and he sought comparable success in managing the nation's foreign affairs. Unable to acknowledge he knew less about the subject than Roosevelt, that his advisers were not in a position greatly to help him, his choice of William Jennings Bryan, the three-time defeated Democratic candidate for president, to be his secretary of state, virtually guaranteed his failure.[24] Not even the most ardent Democrat imagined Bryan the equal of John Hay or Elihu Root, the men who had served in the same post under Roosevelt.[25] Wilson was liberated of Bryan in 1915 when the doughty pacifist resigned, finding the president's message to Germany over the sinking of the *Lusitania* excessively severe. In his place, he chose Robert Lansing, an accomplished lawyer he neither cared for nor trusted.[26] Wilson proposed to be his own secretary of state, relying heavily on a confidante, Colonel Edward House, a courtier in all but name, on whom he had grown increasingly dependent from almost the day he entered the White House.[27] When war erupted in Europe, House became the president's principal emissary abroad, seeking to bring the Western Allies and the Central Powers to accept a negotiated peace.[28] Wilson aspired to be a peacemaker in the Roosevelt tradition but erred in two fundamental respects: he (and the Colonel) greatly exaggerated the willingness of any of the belligerents to make peace and substantially overestimated the role that even the most powerful neutral nation could have in that almost impossibly difficult mission.[29]

Although Wilson made valiant efforts to remain neutral, and was reelected in 1916 in some measure by his success in keeping the country out of Europe's war, he very reluctantly led Congress to declare war only six months later when Germany resumed its policy of unrestricted submarine warfare. Wilson failed as a diplomat, neither ending Armageddon nor maintaining the country's neutrality. His greatest success, surprisingly, came as a warrior, a war president given substantially new authority by Congress to mobilize the nation's resources, to dispatch rapidly the men, arms, industrial goods, and food that the war-weary Allies desperately needed. For a time, the presidency seemed impregnable; the war stimulated the nation's patriotism, and Wilson appeared the principal beneficiary of that belligerence. Still, he would be remembered not for these wartime accomplishments but for his diplomatic failure to make a lasting peace in Paris in 1919. Wilson suffered defeat at the hands of what disillusioned Americans insisted were the imperialist ambitions of more skilled and less principled European political leaders. The treaty he offered the Senate led to a second defeat, perhaps even more catastrophic to his reputation than the one he suffered abroad.[30] Senate Republicans, led by Henry Cabot Lodge, the most intimate friend of the recently deceased Theodore Roosevelt, rejected his proposed League of Nations, refusing to bow to what they conceived to be his ill-conceived measures to preserve world peace.[31]

An imperious president, very conscious of his constitutional prerogatives, a king in all but name, attended by one very active courtier whom he discarded only at the end, Wilson failed as a diplomat but succeeded as a warrior. Undone less by two wicked, old-fashioned European leaders, Lloyd George and Georges Clemenceau, than by his own arrogance and ignorance, he knew Europe less than he pretended. He greatly exaggerated what even a successful campaign to win over public opinion would have allowed him to do to meet the resistance of a Senate controlled since the election of 1918 by Republicans unwilling to give him the two-thirds majority vote required for the ratification of the treaty he had brought back from Paris.[32] Wilson, the victim of a stroke, a bed-ridden invalid for almost a year and a half, left the White House believing he harbored a vision of the world that would one day commend itself to men of intelligence and moral concern.[33] By his domestic successes and wartime accomplishments the presidency acquired an ascendancy it had never previously known—and would not know again until Franklin D. Roosevelt entered the White House in 1933.

No one ever thought of Warren Harding, Wilson's successor, as a king, though he won the 1920 election with an astonishing large popular vote, carrying with him massive Republican majorities in both the House and the Senate.[34] Harding's court, more of cronies than advisers, became sinister in the public mind only after his death when the extent of their peculations and crimes came to be known through congressional inquiry and newspaper publicity.[35] Calvin Coolidge, his successor, the second accidental president in the century, presided in a time of peace, prosperity, and harmony, a Puritan in a modern Babylon whose Vermont simplicity seemed to give the lie to those who believed the country soft and degenerate.[36] Had Coolidge sought another term in the White House it was his for the asking, but he preferred to retire, passing the baton to Herbert Hoover, who lacked any experience of elective office but was believed the most competent Republican since Roosevelt, boasting incomparable experience both at home and abroad. Hoover, defeated by the world economic Depression, was an honest and well-meaning president; he never aspired to be a warrior, could not think of himself as royal, and showed too great solicitude for his Cabinet subordinates to make them his courtiers. Coolidge and Hoover were chief executives in an older tradition, redolent of a day when the title commander in chief carried no special significance and when foreign affairs did not dominate public discussion.[37]

Franklin Roosevelt changed all this. Elected by a substantial majority of men and women frightened by what the Depression had done to deprive them of a security once taken for granted, he was at once the political heir of his kinsman and uncle by marriage, Theodore Roosevelt, but also of his Democratic Party patron, Woodrow Wilson.[38] Having observed both and learned from them, he intended to be a president in their expansive tradition, taking care to avoid the more serious mistakes they had made. Gregarious like his cousin, he courted the press, used radio to broadcast his inspirational messages, and made light of his polio affliction, never allowing the public to know the extent of his physical disability.[39] A magical figure, the incarnation of twentieth-century political influence and power, he created a court, appealing to many who had never previously thought to serve in Washington. Regal in bearing and manner, a patrician in the White House, he sought to make his presidency memorable, appealing to the very different expressions of political idealism he discovered in the only two twentieth-century predecessors he thought distinguished.[40]

While few who enjoyed access to him were designated courtiers by even the more hostile press, several qualified for the role. Gratifying the president's love of gossip, and competing for his favor, they sometimes exaggerated their influence, but all enjoyed the game he and they played together.[41] Roosevelt, secretive, sometimes described as feline, sat in his chair, rarely in his wheelchair, listened and laughed, but rarely showed his hand. The all-powerful Sphinx, a friend to all, an enigma for many, governed in a way that emphasized the importance of access, of being close to him, of having his ear. The Oval Office, the "King's closet" in all but name, became the site of confidential meetings, more important than any that took place in the Cabinet Room.[42] The first president to invite a woman, Frances Perkins, to serve in his Cabinet, and the first to select a Jew, Henry Morgenthau Jr., a friend and neighbor, to head a major department (Treasury), they were no less his courtiers than the dozens of others who crowded in, men like the Groton-educated Sumner Welles, who aspired to be his secretary of state, replacing the ill-used Cordell Hull, failing to realize the post was already filled, by the president himself, emulating his former chief, Wilson.[43]

Believing his long tenure as assistant secretary of the Navy gave him a unique geopolitical education, he aspired first to the role of Wilson, seeking to act as a mediator in Europe's disputes, and failing in that, turned to his

cousin's constant concern: the importance of naval and military preparedness.[44] While his diplomatic efforts to keep the peace in 1938 and 1939
foundered, scarcely more successful than Wilson's before 1917, his support of
Britain in its darkest hours, following on the fall of France in June 1940, gave
him a role Wilson never aspired to. Courted by British prime minister Winston Churchill, who before long became his principal foreign dependent, after
the Japanese attack on Pearl Harbor Roosevelt concentrated on the responsibilities that inhered in his position as commander in chief.[45] Harry Hopkins,
once one of many advisers on domestic policy, assumed a new role, becoming
in effect his major foreign policy confidante, his own Colonel House, the president's principal emissary to Churchill and Soviet leader Joseph Stalin.[46] In
Roosevelt's mind, Churchill was an incomparable war leader, but also an unreconstructed imperialist whose first concern was the preservation of the
British Empire. Like his principal tutors, Roosevelt and Wilson, the president
prided himself on his anti-imperialism, a sentiment he shared with other
Americans who never believed the United States was imperialist, knowing that
little of the world's map was colored red, white, and blue.[47] In his relations
with Britain and the Soviet Union, almost always correct, the president
showed a forbearance he rarely displayed with General Charles de Gaulle, the
leader of Free France. Roosevelt admired strength and felt a scarcely concealed
disdain for a country that had collapsed ignominiously. In his mind, the leader
of Free France was a pretentious poseur.[48] De Gaulle, in turn, never learned
the art of flattering the president that Churchill and Stalin in their very different ways practiced to perfection.[49]

Roosevelt, a successful war president, appreciated the importance of the
home front, realizing that maintaining civilian morale, understanding how
wage and price controls, rationing, employment regulations, taxation, and propaganda figured in a "total war" effort. Though the Executive Office of the
President was approved by Congress in 1939, allowing for the appointment of
"a small number of executive assistants who would be his direct aides in dealing with the managerial agencies and departments of government," Roosevelt
added negligibly to his White House staff.[50] Prepared to deal with a handful of
Cabinet officers and General George C. Marshall, his principal adviser on military strategy, he relied on a small company of friends but never on his vice
presidents. However much he might consult and take advice in domestic and
purely military matters, he took foreign policy to be his own special province
where he claimed exceptional proficiency and knowledge.[51] Abroad, at
Casablanca, Tehran, and Yalta, Roosevelt was diplomat in chief, trading on his
constitutional rights as commander in chief, able to make his influence felt on
any military or political issue he deemed crucial. He died before his plans for
the postwar world could be tested, but not before the extent of his presidential
power had been demonstrated both at home and abroad.

Harry Truman inherited a presidency fundamentally refashioned by his predecessor. Less articulate than Roosevelt, displaying nothing that could be mistaken for his grace or flair, Truman knew better than to try to imitate him, affecting his royal pretensions, establishing a court of intimates.[52] Because Roosevelt left neither a diplomatic nor a military road map to guide him after the defeat of the Axis powers, foreign policy innovation became the overwhelming challenge from almost his first day in office. Told about the atomic bomb by Henry Stimson, the secretary of war—the most closely guarded secret in the war—he learned also of the terrible U.S. casualties suffered at Guadalcanal, nothing compared to those anticipated from the planned invasion of the Japanese home islands.[53] To avert that catastrophe, he hesitated not at all in approving the use of the atom bomb against Japan.[54] Unlike Roosevelt and Coolidge, the century's earlier accidental presidents, Truman dismissed or quickly accepted the resignations of those who had served the dead president, replacing them with men he knew and trusted, unlikely to compare him with the remarkable leader so recently departed.[55]

Dean Acheson, his fourth secretary of state who followed Edward Stettinius Jr., James Byrnes, and General George C. Marshall into that office, chose *Present at the Creation* as the title of his autobiography, recognizing Truman's unique role as the creator of a bipartisan foreign policy committed to political and military objectives never previously contemplated. Truman, less imperious than Roosevelt, disinclined to surround himself with courtiers, never aspired to be the principal architect of the nation's foreign policy, believing that responsibility should be vested in his secretary of state, his principal Cabinet colleague. It was enough that he alone had the duty to decide when, if ever, to unleash the terrible weapon World War II had given the United States in its atomic bomb. The president, a Moloch of sorts, seemed almost disinclined to emphasize his own importance, to dwell on how powerful the United States had become in a world devastated by war. Loyal to the New Deal principles of the dead president, reelected in 1948 in an election no one expected him to win, he saw his own Fair Deal as extending the humane guarantees initiated by Roosevelt, believing his foreign policy innovations to protect the democracies of Europe simply replicated what America's only four-term president had also advocated.[56] Like both Roosevelts, Truman fought his 1948 election as a crusade of the people against the special interests and fended off two divisive attacks from within his own party; that of Strom Thurmond, who resisted the civil rights plank in the Democratic Party's 1948 platform, and of Henry Wallace, who thought the president excessively anti-Soviet.[57]

The election victory gave him only temporary respite from continuing Republican criticism that blamed him for losing China to the Communists, allowing the Soviets to develop its own atomic bomb many years before that development had been anticipated, and being soft on American Communists.[58]

When North Korea invaded South Korea, Truman saw it as an act of aggression that required the United States to fulfill its United Nations Charter obligations. His moment of triumph was brief, ending when General Douglas MacArthur disobeyed his explicit orders not to cross the Yalu River, an act that provoked the Chinese Communists to enter the war.[59] In dismissing General MacArthur, the president incurred the wrath of those who admired the hero of the Pacific War and who found credible his solution for resolving the Communist threat in Asia: bomb them into oblivion.[60] Truman, unlike Wilson and Roosevelt, failed as a warrior, knowing neither how to end the Korean War nor how to win it. Though his political enemies spoke of the power exercised by Missouri cronies in the White House, Truman governed with the advice of men he trusted in major Cabinet positions whose authority often extended into areas that had not existed before World War II.

Dwight Eisenhower resembled neither Roosevelt nor Truman, the presidents who advanced his military career and gave him the positions that guaranteed his fame.[61] Eisenhower found the White House a comfortable berth, rarely seeking to manipulate his subordinates in the way Roosevelt habitually did.[62] Richard Neustadt, one of America's leading authorities on the presidency, believed that Eisenhower aspired to be a twentieth-century George Washington, the president who united the country, stood above politics, a sordid game at best, and accepted to sacrifice himself for the good of all.[63] This may have been the pose; the reality was different. Unlike the Republican Roosevelt, Eisenhower had no desire to be a reformer. Democrats, including Harry Truman, never forgave his failure to defend General Marshall, his old colleague, mentor, and advocate, against the vicious attacks of red-baiting Senator Joseph McCarthy.[64] Eisenhower, more than any other previous president, was known abroad, especially by the British, and though politicians like Churchill desisted from committing to print their judgments of him, its leading military figures, including Generals Bernard Montgomery and Alan Brooke, were not equally reticent. Both, familiar with what they conceived to be Eisenhower's very limited command of military strategy, wrote what few Americans believed: Eisenhower, in their minds, lacked both political and military genius.[65]

With John Foster Dulles as his secretary of state, Eisenhower pursued a foreign policy that showed little originality, satisfied, despite occasional bursts of fierce anticommunist rhetoric, to leave matters much as they found them.[66] The New Look in defense policy that expressed the president's concern with the transformations wrought by transcontinental missile capability and the development of the hydrogen bomb—the latter aggressively initiated by Truman—changed the nature of war. In Eisenhower's determination to secure a bigger bang for a buck, always important for an economy-minded president, he acknowledged that the United States could never recruit and arm conventional forces to compete with those raised by the Russian and Chinese Communists.[67] Both the president and his secretary of state expected that covert operations conducted by the CIA, together with other forms of counterinsurgency, would greatly increase the country's intelligence capability, thereby substantially reducing the risk of war.[68] Timid where he might have been bold, Eisenhower, unlike Churchill, again in Number 10 Downing Street, saw no opportunities opened by Stalin's death and the arrival of a new leadership in the Kremlin. America's Soviet policy remained surprisingly static through Eisenhower's eight years in the White House, testifying to his ignorance of a Europe he pretended to know.[69]

In the autumn of 1956, just days before the presidential election, Anglo-French forces landed in the vicinity of the Suez Canal, claiming they were simply peacekeepers, seeking to prevent an extended Egyptian-Israeli war. This mad secret adventure, to which the prime minister, Anthony Eden, gave his consent in a truly reckless collaboration with both France and Israel, led to an Eisenhower rebuke that had two immediate consequences: the military operation was halted, and there was a catastrophic run on the pound that ended only when Eden accepted to leave Suez unconditionally.[70] As Eisenhower was to say later, "How can we possibly support Britain. . . if in doing so we lose the whole Arab world?"[71] Britain was indeed humbled, but Nasser was never won over; his collaboration with the Soviet Union continued after the 1956 debacle, and Eisenhower had no solution to that problem.[72] Nor did he and Dulles do more than jawbone when Soviet tanks invaded Hungary, routed the revolutionaries in Budapest, and tens of thousands were sent into exile.[73]

The president appeared invincible and won a second term easily over an ineffectual Adlai Stevenson, but the victory proved ephemeral. Embarrassed by the Soviet success in launching the Sputnik satellite, believed to be proof of its scientific and technological prowess, and humiliated by being obliged to lie about America's secret U-2 airplane downed by the Soviets that led to the collapse of his projected Paris summit meeting with Nikita Khrushchev, Eisenhower was simply too old for the presidency. Intellectually timid and too bound to the hierarchical habits he learned in his long military career to contemplate fundamental change, he lacked the political imagination that might have tempted him to exploit America's unique position in a world just beginning to emerge from its World War II trauma.[74] In his farewell address, where he warned of the dangers of the military-industrial complex, he sought to establish his credentials as a man of peace, and no one could fault him on that claim.[75] Yet his crucial political legacy was not this admonition to the nation but rather Richard Nixon, the vice president who supported him during his two serious illnesses, when it seemed possible that the oldest man in the century to reach the White House might not live long enough to leave it.

John F. Kennedy defeated Nixon in 1960 and assumed the presidency with the promise of bringing new ideas into government, congenial to those of his generation bored with the lethargy of a president too frequently ill or on vacation.[76] Though the promises Kennedy made were rarely fulfilled, his tragic death rendered a candid appreciation of his contributions to the presidency difficult.[77] His domestic achievements were minimal, not to be compared with those of his Democratic predecessors, Wilson, Roosevelt, and Truman.[78] In foreign policy, he enjoyed two incontestable triumphs—in the Cuban missile crisis and in the successful negotiation of a test ban treaty with the Soviet Union—but also one disaster at the Bay of Pigs, the brainchild of the CIA, planned originally while Eisenhower was in the White House.[79] In selecting his brother Robert to be the attorney general, he chose him for the same reason Franklin Roosevelt had appointed James Farley to be postmaster general—he could be of inestimable help to him politically—but no one equated the attorney general's post with that of postmaster general.[80] Inevitably, as the president's closest confidante, constantly intruding in areas he knew little about, including foreign policy, Bobby served to diminish the influence of others, not least Dean Rusk, the soft-spoken and self-effacing secretary of state. Kennedy's Cabinet, composed principally of men he scarcely knew, indeed in many instances had not met before his election, was said to be extraordinary by the media, prepared to extol the wizardry of Robert McNamara, his secretary of defense, and the wisdom of C. Douglas Dillon, his secretary of the treasury.[81]

The president's appointments to his White House staff, considered equally extraordinary, included McGeorge Bundy, dean of the faculty of arts and sciences at Harvard, summoned to be his national security adviser, Larry O'Brien, charged with handling congressional relations, and Pierre Salinger as press secretary. Gifted wordsmiths, ghostwriters in effect, Theodore Sorenson, Arthur Schlesinger Jr., and Richard Goodwin, were appointed as presidential assistants; they and others on the White House staff enjoyed easy access to the president, a privilege granted very few in the more starched Eisenhower era.[82] At the end of the day when the president flung open the door to the Oval Office, indicating the time had come for fun and gossip, he gave great pleasure to men who had never anticipated such intimacy with a president of the United States.[83]

With such incomparable talent, great accomplishments were expected; they never took place. Kennedy imagined himself expert in foreign policy; he deceived himself. The privileges he had enjoyed very early as the son of the ambassador to the Court of St. James, and later as a senator, scarcely compensated for what few at the time recognized to be his fairly conventional ideas about the nature of communism, the character of both the Soviet Union and Mao's China.[84] Neither he nor any of his close advisers recognized the importance of the Chinese-Soviet rift that made such a deep impression on de Gaulle, the French president, and Konrad Adenauer, the German chancellor. The growing evidence of division between Russian and Chinese Communists ought to have inspired a reconsideration of American policy in respect to both Moscow and Beijing, but such reflection never had very high priority among those who advised the president.[85] The administration's policies in South Vietnam, based on the idealistic proposition that a Western-style democratic regime could be established there, that the Americans would accomplish what the incompetent French colonialists had been unable to do, was doomed to failure.[86] Even the very secret operations that led ultimately to the assassination of South Vietnam's president—an incident that did credit to no one in the White House—helped the situation not at all.[87] The president and his advisers persisted in believing that all would work out for the best in the end.[88] In Europe, the president failed to devise a policy that commended itself either to the German chancellor or the French president when the East Germans built the Berlin Wall in 1961.[89] No one in the Kennedy entourage believed the West European leaders might have a more informed perception of the interests and policies of Nikita Khrushchev than those that came from their own intelligence sources. The administration's success in the Cuban missile crisis only confirmed the president and his aides in their belief that they knew more than the old men who presided in a Europe ignominiously defeated in World War II.[90]

When the president, gracious, young, and witty, an idol for many, was struck down by an assassin's bullet, the nation mourned, and the myth of Camelot was born.[91] The thousand days, represented as a time of unique accomplishment, of hopes only partially realized, became symbolic of a precious heritage to be protected, not least by the articulate and gifted men the president had summoned to the nation's capital.[92] The Kennedy court, loyal to the president, where the vice president had always been an outsider and where the attorney general exerted an influence that greatly exceeded the powers that attached to that office, lacked any record of concrete achievements abroad that compared with those registered under Roosevelt or Truman.[93] The administration's very limited efforts to address the complex problems of the Middle East, exacerbated by what Eisenhower imagined to be his boldness at the time of Suez and later in Lebanon, left no intellectual or institutional legacy that future presidents could build on.[94] As for the administration's more idealistic policies in providing aid to the newly independent states of Africa, the gains accomplished there proved disappointing, essentially ephemeral.[95] So, also, the Alliance for Progress, Kennedy's effort to restore Roosevelt's Good Neighbor policy in Latin America, produced few of the results hoped for.[96] No one could doubt that the president's advisers, in what became known familiarly as the Court at Camelot, so immensely taken with the president's charisma, sought to move the country away from the lethargy characteristic of the long supine Eisenhower era, but the promise of great domestic or foreign policy accomplishments were never fulfilled.

Lyndon Johnson, the beneficiary of the president's death, thought by many a crude and arrogant interloper, the antithesis of Kennedy, following the tradition set by the Republican Roosevelt, retained the whole of the assassinated president's Cabinet. He hoped by that gesture alone to indicate his fidelity to the liberal agenda left unfulfilled by the Dallas assassination.[97] Johnson's exceptional knowledge and command over Congress enabled him to pressure Southern Democrats known to be hostile to new civil rights legislation, allowing him to pass the Civil Rights Act, which exceeded any Kennedy might have secured.[98] Johnson saw himself not as Kennedy's heir but as beholden to a far greater president, Franklin Roosevelt. Even before his massive election victory over Barry Goldwater in 1964, he announced the War on Poverty and issued a call for a Great Society, to complete the reforms initiated by Roosevelt and Truman.[99] Johnson proved an incomparable reform president but failed as a warrior. Indeed, the war in Vietnam was his undoing, demonstrating that political talent honed on the home front did not always translate into competence in the handling of foreign relations.[100]

Johnson believed his patriotism and bravado could serve as the basis of a reasonable war policy and that no one would ever be able to charge him with losing Vietnam. He resorted to every kind of chicanery and subterfuge to defend the military policies he and his inherited team of advisers recommended and pursued.[101] Nothing was more disingenuous than the so-called Gulf of Tonkin Resolution that in effect gave the president a congressional blank check to pursue the war in Vietnam in whatever way he saw fit.[102] The information provided Congress by the White House and the Pentagon proved false, flawed, and exaggerated, not very different from that offered the general public.[103] While Johnson bullied those of Kennedy's advisers who consented to remain in his service, no one of them cautioned him of the dangers he ran in sending a force of more than half a million Americans into the jungles of Vietnam.[104] When Hubert Humphrey, the vice president, sought to warn the president, he was effectively banished from the White House court, and no one among the president's associates chose to argue his brief.[105] When McNamara and Bundy, two of his principal military and foreign affairs advisers, finally sought refuge outside the administration, with McNamara becoming president of the World Bank and Bundy president of the Ford Foundation, their replacements, Clark Clifford and Walt Rostow, were scarcely more effective in recommending a deescalation of the war, though the former argued from almost his first day in office that "the continued application of force did not promise ultimate success."[106]

Johnson, increasingly isolated and beleaguered, not least in the streets where students and others protested and rioted, recognized the incontrovertible evidence of his administration's disarray when two Democrats, Eugene McCarthy and Robert Kennedy, offered themselves as peace candidates in the early 1968 Democratic primaries.[107] Johnson saw no exit for himself except the one that pained him greatly. His surprise announcement that he would not seek another term as president, would end the bombing of North Vietnam, and would use his last months in office to achieve an early peace represented a bold effort on his part to redeem a reputation seriously compromised by all he had done in Vietnam.[108] Johnson, perhaps the greatest social reforming president of the century, compelled to rely on men whose knowledge and understanding of Vietnam was not significantly greater than his own, failed to win the popular support essential in a war that had become increasingly ugly and seemingly futile.[109] Kennedy's men proved less equal to the task the president set for them than those he appointed from his own Texas entourage that helped him secure the domestic legislation he and they deemed essential to the nation's well-being.[110]

Richard Nixon, the principal beneficiary of Lyndon Johnson's disasters, started with the same declared resolve to make peace in Vietnam, joined to a no less firm conviction, never as explicitly stated, that it could not be a peace based on capitulation to Communist military success. In his estimate of the world situation, any withdrawal perceived as an American defeat would only encourage further Communist aggressions.[111] The killings of both Martin Luther King Jr. and Robert Kennedy in April and June 1968, so profoundly shocking to the nation, served only to confirm the Republican charge that the country was hopelessly adrift, violent, and divided. That sentiment, as much as any other, allowed an individual known to be vindictive, furtive, and resentful—some would say paranoiac or worse—to win the presidency, doing so very narrowly, winning by only half a million votes in an election that saw more than 70 million Americans go to the polls. Few realized at the time that Lyndon Johnson, by his support of civil rights legislation, had permanently alienated the South, the bastion of the Democratic Party since the Civil War.[112] The electorate, disillusioned about Vietnam, increasingly denounced as Johnson's War, chose a president whose capacity for duplicity was known to be monumental. During the campaign, Nixon's references to the war were generally vague; it seemed easier for him to dwell on the need to restore law and order at home.[113]

In his first year in office, Nixon revealed little of his war exit strategy, though he substantially reduced the size of the U.S. forces Johnson had committed to the defense of South Vietnam.[114] The president's announcement on April 30, 1970, that he was sending troops into Cambodia, to prevent further infiltration of Vietcong and North Vietnamese armies into South Vietnam, caught the nation by surprise, confirming all the negative impressions of those who had long suspected his motives and never believed he intended to end the war.[115] Antiwar protests followed, and the killing of four students at Kent State University by National Guardsman escalated the turmoil that had existed for years, creating soul-searching in an older generation unable to understand either the values or the habits of the young.[116]

Though Nixon never made domestic policy his chief concern, he knew better than to ignore it, and with the support of men like Daniel Patrick Moynihan, one of his Harvard professorial appointees, his principal adviser on race relations, he offered himself as America's Disraeli, a convert to "Tory Democracy."[117] The self-styled attribution offended no one and had little meaning for a society that still imagined itself liberal.[118] For the president, the only issues that really mattered were those relating to war and peace. As a principal participant in the Eisenhower administration, and a not wholly objective observer of the Kennedy and Johnson administrations, he found little in any of them to impress him. Nothing would lead him to find fault with Eisenhower, the man who had given him the vice presidency, but he felt no comparable need to be silent about the shortcomings of the two Democrats who succeeded the general in the White House. Neither, in his mind, had developed a foreign or defense policy adequate to the world that had come into being since the death of Stalin.[119] Nixon aspired to be an innovator in foreign policy, hoping to use what he conceived to be his incomparable geopolitical knowledge to create a record for himself that would for all time establish his credentials as a superior president.

With National Security Adviser Henry Kissinger at his side, the two began to plan a diplomatic coup that the timid Eisenhower would never have considered, that no Democrat would have dared attempt. Their plan was to end the isolation of China, to seek a rapprochement with its Communist regime, persuaded that this projected opening to Mao Tse-tung would give the United States advantages it could realize from no other policy.[120] Nixon and Kissinger believed an understanding with China would frighten the Soviet Union, make it more amenable to arms control agreements they believed essential in the age of transcontinental missiles and thermonuclear weapons. In their imagination, it would also cause the North Vietnamese to become more reasonable, accepting peace terms the president and the American public would declare satisfactory.[121] Nixon, looking ahead to 1972, could only imagine that these spectacular diplomatic initiatives would greatly impress the voters and lead to a Republican Party victory comparable to the one Franklin Roosevelt had claimed in 1932.[122]

While his massive electoral victory over George McGovern in November 1972 could not be ascribed simply to his success in opening the door to improved relations with China, or even his pledge to end the war in Vietnam with his words, "peace was at hand," no Republican in the twentieth century could claim a victory comparable to his.[123] The Democratic Party, abandoned not in deference to a war hero, a second Eisenhower, but to a man dismissed as tricky Dick, deceitful and unstable, suffered a humiliating defeat. McGovern was un-

done by a strange, secretive, and insecure president who had succeeded in creating new constituencies and new support for the Republican Party. Nixon, ill
at ease with strangers, lacking anything that might be mistaken for wit or
charm whose courtiers scarcely resembled those of Camelot, had gathered
around him a new kind of White House staff, men who had helped him secure
the presidency, in many instances had known him in California, and were prepared to join him in his constant struggle against enemies, real and
imagined.[124] Nixon created his own electoral victories but also engineered his
own downfall, symbolized for all time in the single word: *Watergate*.[125] The
first president forced to resign, as late as the day of his departure on Air Force
One in August 1974, protested his innocence, acknowledging only much later
that he had made "errors of judgment."[126]

Remembered always as the congenital liar who lied even to himself, Nixon,
more than any other twentieth-century president, became the subject of what
passed for psychological analysis; the greater need was for political inquiry that
asked how a twentieth-century presidency that started with Theodore Roosevelt had degenerated into what it became only two years before the nation's
bicentennial. Had the presidential office become too powerful, and had those
who consented to serve him become too obsequious, craven, and servile? Had
war and the fear of war contributed to the creation of a presidency that led men
in high places to prevaricate, or was it only Nixon who had been unable to respect the traditions of the office, to exercise its powers, in the words first used
by Woodrow Wilson, "greatly" and "wisely"?[127] Nixon's disgrace nullified much
of what he did to give the country a new foreign policy. His accomplishments
in seeking to improve relations with the Soviet Union, opening a dialogue with
Communist China, launching arms control negotiations that led to the signing
of the Salt I Treaty, came to be disparaged, as much within his own party as
among the jubilant Democrats in Congress.[128] Prominent Republicans felt disgraced by the revelations that emerged, detailing the unsavory and illegal
money contributions given him.[129]

All that he had accomplished was impugned. His associates in the White
House, those he had brought with him from California, prosecuted and convicted, went off to serve prison sentences, in many instances protesting their
continued fidelity to him. His most intimate political advisers, including John
Mitchell, his attorney general, in their efforts to serve him, responded to his
paranoia by demonizing those who dared oppose him. Their crimes were not
venal, and the president's former chief of staff, H.R. Haldeman, may have expressed their feelings perfectly when he wrote that though he was never
"blinded to the dark spots" in the behavior of his chief, he believed them unimportant beside the unique opportunity offered him to "play a very special role
in what I firmly believed would be a drama of enormous success and accomplishment."[130] Men like Haldeman were prominent everywhere in the Nixon

administration; courtiers, servile and faithful to their chief, they bore no resemblance to those who had served earlier presidents, men like Colonel House and Harry Hopkins. These latter-day courtiers were essentially guards, intended to protect the president against his enemies, principally domestic, believed to be intent on his destruction.

Gerald Ford, who succeeded the disgraced Nixon, was the only accidental president in the century to fail to secure a second term.[131] An honest man, impugned by many who considered him dull, he made several serious political blunders, none more grievous than the one that led him to give Nixon a full, free, and absolute pardon, believing this would put Watergate out of the public mind, allowing the nation to address the more serious domestic and foreign issues that called for immediate attention.[132] Ford, compelled to treat the country's serious economic problems, including stagflation, a new malady that allowed inflation to soar without an accompanying rise in employment or consumer demand, was scarcely helped by a continuing oil crisis, produced by the foreign oil cartel's decision to punish the United States for its support of Israel during the Yom Kippur War.[133] The 1974 off-year congressional elections were a disaster for both the president and the Republican Party. While few thought to compare Ford's political problems with those Taft had encountered after 1910, confronted also with a hostile Congress and a powerful Republican competitor who sought to defeat him in the primaries, the similarities were striking. Ronald Reagan, the former governor of California, though scarcely resembling Theodore Roosevelt in any respect, posed a formidable challenge to the president.[134] In the first primaries where Reagan did exceptionally well, he condemned both Ford and Kissinger for their mistaken policy of détente and represented their subservience to the Soviet Union as threatening to make the United States a "second-rate power."[135] Though Reagan failed to take the nomination away from the president, and never considered running as an Independent, repeating the political mistake Roosevelt had made in 1912, he helped give the presidency to Jimmy Carter, the former governor of Georgia. It is impossible to know whether Carter's slim majority of a million and a half would have been secured in the absence of the immensely wounding primary battles waged by Reagan against Ford.[136]

Carter's administration, like Ford's, was a parenthesis between the two major Republican presidencies of the post-Eisenhower era, the disgraced and shelved Nixon, and the much-admired Reagan. Though Carter in his more grandiose moments imagined himself a latter-day Wilson, committed to democracy and human rights, few thought of him in such elevated terms.[137] Nor did many see him as a latter-day Kennedy, or as a Southern Democrat in the Johnson tradition.[138] Carter, yearning to be recognized as the outsider, the man from outside the Beltway who had no Washington connections, offered himself as the "plain man from Plains Georgia," a man of the people.[139] Modesty seemed his distinctive signature, and though he enjoyed large Democratic majorities in both the House and the Senate, he scarcely knew how to use them for his own or the country's advantage. Recognized very early by prominent Democrats as a provincial who understood less than he pretended, he seemed incapable of bringing the Democrats together to deal with the major problems of the day: the federal deficit, inflation, and mass unemployment.[140]

Carter, honest but inept, greatly exaggerated what Zbigniew Brzezinski, his national security adviser, and Cyrus Vance, his secretary of state, thought to be an incomparable team, could do to help him formulate and execute a moral foreign policy.[141] Their rivalry, said to replicate the earlier one of Kissinger and William Rogers under Nixon, was less important than many believed. Carter was not Nixon, knew infinitely less about foreign policy, and could never choose between the seemingly bellicose views of his national security adviser and the more cautious policies advocated by his secretary of state. Oscillating wildly between them, beginning his administration with hopes of making very substantial reductions in arms expenditure, his greatest success, undoubtedly, was to bring Egypt's Anwar Sadat and Israel's Menachem Begin together at Camp David to sign accords that seemed to carry the promise of Arab-Israeli cooperation.[142] His greatest failure, certainly, was to know how to react to the hostage-taking in Iran that led him to an abortive raid that ended in disaster.[143] Carter came at the end of a twenty-year time of troubles when the country seemed genuinely bewildered as to where it was heading and how to restore the national pride that had once seemed the country's most distinctive attribute. In 1980, Reagan beat Carter decisively, with almost 44 million votes against 35.5 million, not quite the victory Nixon enjoyed in 1972 over McGovern, but impressive nonetheless.[144]

The election of Reagan brought to an end two troubled decades that had witnessed a presidential assassination, other killings, social mayhem, and an unsuccessful war, characterized by an exaggerated belief in what American air power and ground forces would in the end achieve. Four administrations, two Democratic and two Republican, failed to acknowledge their hubris in believing a military solution attainable in a situation that called for historical, cultural, political, and diplomatic understanding of a kind none of them ever possessed. Vietnam became a Communist state, and Carter was the first president after Kennedy who had no need to concern himself with that problem. The failure of his administration, scarcely less great, however, showed a marked ignorance of the Middle East, *terra incognita* for a generation preoccupied principally with the Soviet Union, whose knowledge of both Iran and Iraq was negligible. The president's own very reasonable concern with a political goal, the rescue of American hostages taken by the mullahs in Iran, came to be exceeded in time only by the greater follies of Reagan and his courtiers. [145] Just as Americans never developed an adequate comprehension of Vietnam, despite the decades of being involved in that treacherous arena, it showed no greater capacity to master conditions in the Middle East, to devise policies adequate to a greatly altered geopolitical scenario created by the downfall of the shah. Carter and Reagan, together with those who advised them, never achieved the kind of understanding of Iran, Iraq, Saudi Arabia, or other Muslim republics and kingdoms of the region that informed American policy in respect to Europe. In the United States, Muslim studies remained massively underdeveloped through the whole of the twentieth century, in both the federal government and universities. The business deals, principally inspired by the substantial American oil interests, scarcely compensated for an ignorance already evident in the time of Eisenhower, that became no less conspicuous after he left office.

Reagan became the most successful Republican president of the century, rivaled only by Theodore Roosevelt.[146] He achieved what few would have thought possible; erasing all memory of the Nixon debacle, leading the nation to forget it was a Republican administration that had so recently disgraced the presidential office.[147] Nixon was a nonperson for Reagan. So, also, were all his distinguished predecessors—Eisenhower, Truman, and Roosevelt. Reagan felt no obligation to honor them, to exult over the advantages of bipartisanship in foreign policy, to dwell on what his predecessors had done to create and sustain international institutions that mattered. Reagan, an old man, arrived with the confidence and hubris characteristic of the much younger Kennedy, which both had the wisdom to conceal. Reagan insisted that the American people were distinctive, exceptional, like no other in the world, and this became the leitmotif of his very successful presidency.[148]

Democrats fretted over what they saw as possibly dangerous reductions in social welfare expenditures, and it is impossible to say how the president's budget might have fared had there been no attempt on his life.[149] Reagan's grace under fire, managing to joke while the would-be assassin's bullet was still lodged in his body, made him a hero to the media and the public.[150] Congress voted eagerly for his budget, with most Southern Democrats ready to join their Republican colleagues in registering their enthusiasm.[151] When the federal deficit soared to $100 million, twice what it had been when he assumed office, and unemployment rose to 10.8 percent, the highest since 1941, the president expressed no great alarm. His own quiet self-confidence, so little resembling the public anxieties of Presidents Johnson and Carter, served to calm the nation.

Meeting with the Pope in June 1982, the two discussed how covert U.S. aid to Solidarity might embarrass the Communist regime in Poland, and both were encouraged by the prospect of seeing a greatly diminished Soviet influence in the most rebellious of the satellite East European states.[152] Neither the destruction of the U.S. embassy in Beirut, leaving 63 dead in April 1983, nor the truck bomb explosion at the U.S. Marine headquarters in that city that killed

243, justified a military reprisal.[153] Reagan reserved that response for the inconsequential events in the tiny Caribbean island of Grenada, a member of the Commonwealth, where a claque of Marxists took control, and where he thought it expedient to take military action.[154] Though the intervention offended Margaret Thatcher, his friend and advocate, it carried no other penalties and did nothing to damage his reputation at home.[155] Responding to a reported Libyan terrorist attack in Berlin, he sent U.S. aircraft to bomb Tripoli, Libya's capital, showing again his characteristic military preferences—to undertake only fail-safe operations, none that risked the American public witnessing the return of body bags on its nightly news.[156] Such operations required no sacrifice from the country's civilian population and indeed no participation by them, though their enthusiasm for such military interventions was always welcome. America's aircraft and ships, equipped with the most modern missiles, could be relied on to do all that was required.[157]

To arrest the decline in America's military strength that Reagan saw as having begun in Nixon's first term, he employed arguments resembling those Kennedy used when he spoke of a missile gap. He recommended massive increases in defense appropriations, oblivious to how this would affect the federal budget or the national debt. Concerned only to demonstrate to the Soviet leaders in the Kremlin and the American public his firm resolve, he portrayed détente as a useless policy that served only to encourage Soviet aggression and provided no defense. Scrapping the Nixon-Kissinger program in favor of one that the men presiding over the "evil empire" would be compelled to respect—an arms buildup—he mocked the older Mutual Assured Destruction (MAD) doctrine that owed its beginnings to theories developed in the Kennedy administration. Reagan spoke forcefully and frequently of the only defense that he insisted would be impregnable, as contained in his Star Wars proposals, the Strategic Defense Initiative.[158]

Relaxed and self-confident, Reagan encouraged the same habits in his White House staff, under the direction of James Baker III, his able chief of staff, who worked efficiently to make life comfortable, not so much out of deference to his advanced years but because this so obviously gratified a president who had no wish to be involved except when absolutely necessary.[159] The photographs of Ronnie and Nancy setting off for a weekend at their California ranch or for another vacation seemed as characteristic of his administration as the daily walks of Harry Truman through the deserted streets of predawn Washington. Reagan saw no need to spend long hours in the Oval Office, to carry papers to his private quarters in the evening, or to seek public sympathy by dwelling on the hardships of the presidency. With Nancy at his side, these conditions did not exist.[160]

Any doubts about the president's popularity were laid to rest by his impressive victory in 1984 over Walter Mondale, Carter's vice president, thought by many to be the last of the faithful disciples of Roosevelt, Truman, and Johnson.[161] The nation craved neither a New Deal, a Fair Deal, nor a Great Society; the conservatism of California and Texas, as Reagan understood it, as Nixon, the nonperson in the years after his expulsion from Washington first practiced it, became the new national political orthodoxy.[162] Reagan managed this extraordinary metamorphosis with the help of those he brought with him from California, Michael Deaver, Ed Meese, and Lyn Nofziger, whom he installed in the White House, all subsequently charged with ethical misconduct. Were these men essentially different from those Nixon had recruited as his courtiers, Bob Haldeman and John Ehrlichman, among others, or were they simply more expert in knowing how to protect themselves and the president they served?[163] When one considers that a record number of those who served in the Reagan administration—138 in all—were indicted, convicted, or the subject of criminal investigation, it is extraordinary that the man dubbed the Teflon president by the media suffered not at all from his association with such individuals.[164] The White House was a tomb whose secrets were never shared with journalists or outsiders.[165] The Reagan court was a curious one, made so by his wife standing attentive guard, with all who served him knowing better than to cross her.[166] Reagan, for the public at large, was a regular guy, devoted to his wife, scarcely interested in his children—not a major offense in the America of the 1980s—who never ceased to flatter the American people. The new prosperous West, of California and Texas, vital and self-confident, immune to the intellectuality of a too effete and liberal East once crucially important in the Republican Party, saw itself in Reagan and exulted in his triumphs. A new Republican Party had been born, and the nation approved what its leader proposed, reelecting him with an impressive popular majority.[167]

That idyll was broken only in the president's second term when revelations of clandestine operations involving the secret transfer of weapons to Iran seemed for a moment sufficiently serious to threaten him.[168] The Iran-Contra scandal, an illegal scheme hatched in the National Security Council (NSC) intended to bring about the release of U.S. hostages held in Iran in exchange for the secret sale of arms to the government of the mullahs, was one the president claimed to have had no knowledge of.[169] Any suggestion that he would have approved of such a deal had to be strenuously denied by those who had long been his protectors and now emerged as his principal defenders against the media, inclined to doubt the information that came from the White House.[170] The president was saved less by his loyal associates than by Mikhail Gorbachev, the new leader in the Kremlin who desperately craved to end the Soviet Union's military rivalry with the United States, believing his own reform program, based on glasnost and perestroika, demanded an early accord with the Americans.[171] Reagan, meeting with Gorbachev, adamant he would never sacrifice his

Strategic Defense Initiative, gained worldwide publicity when he shouted in Berlin at the Brandenburg Gate, "Mr. Gorbachev, tear down this wall!"[172] As the Soviet leader felt increasingly compelled to make concessions, given the precariousness of his own position at home, Reagan's loyal courtiers represented the president as the man who had finally defeated Soviet communism, achieving a success none of his predecessors in the White House could claim.[173] That accomplishment in fact derived little from Reagan's abilities as a diplomat and even less from the strength of the U.S. economy. It gained credibility principally from the ability of the president and his advisers to disseminate myths persuasive to an American public sympathetic to the old man in the White House, able to weather the storm created by the Iran-Contra scandal, indeed virtually to extinguish all public memory of it.[174]

Implicit in this mythical representation of Reagan was the idea that the repudiation of the bipartisan foreign policy of earlier administrations was possible, that there was no greater need to pay deference to Nixon or Eisenhower than to Truman or Roosevelt. In the rendering of the president's political genius by his courtiers, he was represented as beholden to no one; he alone had destroyed the Soviet Union. The contributions of previous administrations might be given honorable mention, but the accomplishment, insofar as it was not the president's alone, owed a great deal to the efforts and heroic sacrifices of the American people.[175] In this fable, NATO and Europe scarcely figured.[176] Finally, and perhaps most important, those around Reagan knew that the vast additional defense expenditures gave the United States an unrivalled military capability—not an impregnable defense, explaining the continued need for the Strategic Defense Initiative—but the ability to punish all would-be aggressors, especially those known to have negligible military strength.[177] Korea and Vietnam belonged to a past never to be repeated; Reagan's successes in Grenada and Libya suggested that fail-safe wars were possible, that they need not issue in significant numbers of U.S. casualties.[178] Reagan never demanded sacrifices from the American people; his economic calculus told him that higher taxes would not be required to pay for the wars, never called that by someone who had no wish to be thought a war president.[179]

Reagan, surrounded by men who believed that the liberal elites of an earlier day, Democratic and Republican, had weakened the United States politically and morally, thought that only a revived patriotism could satisfy the vast numbers of middle-class men and women, white and black, who so little resembled the very different Americans Franklin Roosevelt had once appealed to.[180] These men saw themselves as the creators of a new Republican Party that might expect to retain the White House for decades. Reagan, their hero, existed on a pedestal shared with no one, and he left the Oval Office with his reputation intact, the most indefatigable and successful anticommunist warrior of the century who knew where to threaten, when to negotiate, and how to win.[181] The fact that he grasped few of the details of foreign policy and was most effective in setting a tone, confining his numerous radio and TV communications to a few simple sentiments, constantly reiterated, was ignored in the adulation awarded him by a public prepared to accept a man very much like themselves.[182]

Reagan, despite his rhetoric, was a cautious president who carefully avoided any military engagement that threatened significant numbers of Americans. More than that, he knew how to use others, never appearing superior, refusing to hector the public, a regular guy, a man of the people.[183] In fact, he was a cosseted old man who tired easily, repeated himself endlessly—telling the same jokes constantly—but the indisputable master of a White House that appeared at times to be little more than a very comfortable retirement home.[184] Reagan's greatest accomplishment was to restore the nation's pride in itself, giving the Republican Party a new patent on patriotism, the U.S. nationalism so frequently instrumental in justifying Americanism, never rendered as imperialism.[185] George Bush, his successor, learned from observing him over eight years as vice president but could never claim his charisma or common touch.[186] Bush, a one-term president, in many ways a latter-day Taft, also a Yale graduate, a member of the same Skull and Bones, the secret society that sent so many of its members into high places in the federal government, made his way through appointments given him by Nixon and Ford, feeling a greater indebtedness to the incomparable leader who had taken him on as vice president, and had not failed as president.[187]

Bush's great success came in the war he waged against a negligible foe, Saddam Hussein, the new late-twentieth-century Hitler, at least in the imagination of someone who found no reason to dwell on the strength of Germany and Nazism or the weakness of Iraq and Islam.[188] He claimed to be interested in establishing a new world order, but it never became anything other than rhetoric.[189] The policies he pursued following the liberation of Central and Eastern Europe lacked both the ambition and originality characteristic of what Truman managed in Western Europe in the years after 1945, though his accomplishment in securing the unification of Germany and the retention of its NATO membership showed foresight.[190] Bush lost the presidency to Bill Clinton in 1992, in the view of many Republicans and Democrats, because he betrayed his pledge not to raise taxes. Bush had lied to the public, and that was thought an unforgivable offense.[191] The explanation was too simple, not very different from those commonly given to explain his success in the Gulf War.[192] Bush's transgression was not that he had broken his word but that he lacked the essential political skills to appear something other than a New England stiff, pretending to be a Texan, compelled to compete with a boy from Arkansas, a born actor who knew how to cavort on a national stage, and would soon seek to use those same talents internationally.[193]

Clinton learned what to avoid by observing Bush; he learned much more by watching Reagan, a transcendent political personality. The presidency, as theater, decorous under Reagan, became raffish under Clinton, but behind those obvious changes were continuities of greater significance. Clinton, like Reagan, lacked any experience of war, knew less about foreign policy than he pretended, but saw that Reagan had been immensely successful in avoiding military adventures that could lead him into dangerous quagmires resembling Vietnam. Clinton made use of the military technology Reagan's large defense budgets had provided, especially air power; he confronted African terrorists from a safe distance and went on to bomb rogue states led by the likes of Saddam Hussein and Slobodan Milosevic, confident his actions would be approved by the American public, knowing they were in no sense hazardous.[194] Condemned by many as a draft-dodger, increasingly recognized as a sexually promiscuous liar, Clinton remained resilient under the most trying circumstances, even the Monica Lewinsky scandal that for a moment threatened his continued occupancy of the White House.[195] Like Reagan, he knew the power of the word, and his charisma, though essentially different from Reagan's, served him admirably as he pranced about from one crisis to another. The White House was porous; associates who left him told his secrets, but it seemed scarcely to matter.[196] He dreamed of instituting a vast new federal health scheme, concocted principally by his wife in association with one of his Oxford Rhodes Scholar friends, and when it went down to catastrophic defeat in Congress, bringing in its train a Republican domination of both the House and the Senate, he managed to live with the new situation. Indeed, he reinvented himself so that the Republicans appeared the irresponsible ones while he seemed to be in full control of the situation.[197] Clinton, the cool, saxophone-playing president, gained renown from a nation able to appreciate his remarkable capacity to pick himself up from the floor.[198]

The first overwhelmingly middle-class nation and the last major fundamentalist Christian nation resonated to arguments of presidents from California, Texas, and Arkansas, as an earlier generation had once responded to those made by more intellectually fastidious men from New York, New Jersey, and Massachusetts.[199] The twentieth-century presidency, inaugurated by success in a small war against Spain, a weak enemy, may have ended with the terrorist attacks on New York and Washington in 2001, but this verdict, so popular today, ought to be reconsidered.[200] In the wars George W. Bush launched, first in Afghanistan, later in Iraq, the most exaggerated tales were told of the terrifying hazards faced by the coalition forces he called into being, of the extraordinary risks the president was taking. Ronald Reagan lived on in both operations; there was never any possibility of either becoming the wars Wilson, Roosevelt, Truman, Johnson, and Nixon had found it necessary to wage.[201] Conducted against an insubstantial enemy by a Republican president who learned much from his father and his father's principal patron, he and his associates exaggerated the dangers and remembered always to credit the American people for their remarkable fortitude, knowing they had in fact asked nothing of them.[202] The American public responded with a patriotic fervor that exceeded even what had been common at the time of the Gulf War.[203] The most exaggerated pledges were made of the democracy that would soon descend on Iraq, stimulating popular democratic rule throughout the Middle East.[204] Bush, represented by journalists as determined and fully in charge, commanded the support of men who had served Reagan and his father, whose first experiences of government had been in the Nixon and Ford administrations.[205] When the war in Afghanistan went well and that in Iraq ended rapidly, these strong and determined men were thought to be incomparable. When it became apparent that the peace had not been won, that Iraq had not been pacified, their skills seemed somewhat less impressive. The greatest efforts were made, principally by journalists, to dwell on the policy differences between Secretary of State Colin Powell and Secretary of Defense Donald Rumsfeld, the influential views of Vice President Richard Cheney and the so-called Vulcans, the neo-cons who occupied positions just below the top. They believed against all the evidence that they had invented policies certain to lead to a decisive victory over terrorists in Iraq and elsewhere.[206]

In the constant mass media preoccupation with the warrior president, with those he commanded, never referred to as his courtiers, less attention was given to how little he or they resembled those who had governed in the United States before the Reagan era. Few emphasized the obvious fact that World War II had generated knowledge in the United States of its two principal enemies, Germany and Japan, and that this understanding in considerable measure contributed to the creation of America's alliances with those previously hostile and authoritarian states.[207] The Cold War had created comparable incentives for learning about the Soviet Union—"know your enemy" became almost the slogan of successive administrations—and this was accompanied by major intellectual efforts to understand the new weaponry and delivery systems that threatened a world thermonuclear disaster. No comparable intellectual effort was made after 1981 to learn about Islam, the Arab Middle East, or terrorism, though all three gave justified cause for alarm.[208] Where secrecy reigned, especially in respect to terrorist threats after September 11, it was difficult to know what to believe of the propaganda that issued out of the nation's capital, the White House, and the Defense Department. Discussion of real political alternatives was uncommon, and the tall tales, worthy of the Gipper, credible to many Americans, though substantially less persuasive to men and women abroad, enjoyed great currency.[209] The early-twentieth-century presidency virtually disappeared, but that of the late century lived on and prospered.

Though the incumbent president and his advisers never found it useful to heed the advice offered by Sir Michael Howard, one of England's premier historians, who recommended that they dub their Afghan operation a police action, not a war, they were confident that an aroused American public opinion would give them the only support they needed.[210] They showed comparable conviction in their war against Iraq, feeling no need to heed the warning Howard gave decades earlier, in 1979, when he sought to explain why large segments of the U.S. public and the world at large felt so little sympathy for America's Vietnam venture. Howard wrote then: "It was not simply the initiation and conduct of the war in Vietnam that caused such disquiet in the United States and elsewhere; it was the revelation of the clandestine activities, the domestic deception, and the oblique morality that the government of the United States believed were justified by that war and the circumstances that surrounded it" that explained the opposition to it.[211]

George W. Bush never read Michael Howard and would not have believed him had he done so. In his mind, the Taliban, like Saddam Hussein's Iraq, the sworn enemies of the United States, colluded together, and both had to be removed. Regime change, often contemplated by the United States through secret covert action, was to be achieved by a fail-safe war that the president and his advisers deemed necessary. Compelled to deal with a world they scarcely knew, confident that their operations would be successful, these were military engagements in the Reagan tradition, made to seem even more consequential by being called wars. They were represented as exceedingly dangerous, requiring great courage, and the president and his principal advisers adopted the pose of reluctant but determined warriors, anxious to shed that role to become peacemakers, bringing law and order to a region that had known only revolution and war for a century. The president's illusions were grandiose, befitting someone who lived with the kinds of myths so congenial to his principal political tutor, Ronald Reagan. No one informed the president that the United States might be more dependent on foreign public opinion, especially in Europe's principal democracies, than at any time since the end of World War II.[212]

Hubris, combined with ignorance, led Bush the younger to undertake adventures that concealed the more serious problems abroad, that ought to have concerned him.[213] Never a king in the manner of either Roosevelt, but a warrior in the Reagan tradition, he waged an easy war successfully but found peace elusive. Bush, compelled to rely essentially on a single ally, the United Kingdom, led by a prime minister equally innocent of history, the two together ignored several of their principal European allies, but also Russia and China, finding it necessary to exaggerate Saddam's military capabilities.[214] British participation in the Iraq War and the subsequent suicide of one of its principal investigators of weapons of mass destruction led to the disclosure of state secrets whose analogs were unlikely to be revealed in the United States for decades, if ever.[215] They told a melancholy tale, of the moral price paid for secrecy and deception, of the political consequences of relying too much on intelligence information that proved false. Worse, however, they raised questions about what representative assemblies like Congress and Parliament, lacking accurate information, could do to challenge the demands of a supposedly better-informed executive power. How, in a situation of admitted difficulty and danger, could the public be invited to intervene, and what resources could it command when rhetoric substituted for argument? The perils of exaggerated executive power were never more conspicuous than in the first years of the twenty-first century when the king, courtiers, and warriors domiciled in Washington, D.C., so little resembled those of other more perilous times.

CHAPTER 2

Accidental Presidents and
Vice Presidential Heirs Apparent

FOUR PRESIDENTS IN the nineteenth century died in office, two of natural causes, two by assassination. Of the four vice presidents who succeeded them, not a single one managed to win a second term—only one made the effort, fighting the election as the Know-Nothing candidate—and their names resonate not even for historians.[1] In the twentieth century, there were again four presidential deaths, two by assassin's bullets, and two as the result of illness. All four vice presidents who succeeded them fought to secure a term of their own and every one of them succeeded, winning sometimes by substantially larger majorities than those enjoyed by the men they succeeded. Only Harry Truman, despite his very remarkable and quite unexpected 1948 triumph, returned to the Oval Office with a smaller majority than the one Roosevelt had amassed in his unprecedented fourth-term victory in 1944. Lyndon Johnson, two decades later, defeated his Republican adversary, Barry Goldwater, by almost 16 million votes; John F. Kennedy, the president he succeeded, had barely managed to beat his adversary, Richard Nixon, winning by just over 100,000 votes.[2] Clearly, the argument Tocqueville made that White House occupants would be hard to dislodge seemed confirmed by much that happened in the twentieth century. Yet the advantages of incumbency did not seem to exist in the nineteenth century after Andrew Jackson left office in 1837. Not until Lincoln arrived in 1861 did another president manage to win a second term. After Ulysses S. Grant left the presidency in 1877, none of his successors till William McKinley in 1900 won a successive second term.[3] Why, then, did incumbency come to count so heavily again in the twentieth century, with two-term presidencies becoming the norm? What circumstances made it possible for four twentieth-century vice presidents to serve collectively in the White House for more than a quarter of a century? None of these accidental presidents, elevated to their positions by the death of their predecessors, were selected because they were deemed especially presidential. How, then, did their second-term victories leading to their long tenures reflect changed political conditions in the country?

When Theodore Roosevelt accepted the Republican Party's nomination to be vice president, feigning great reluctance to do so, seemingly torn between the sacrifice others were asking him to make in giving up a substantial post as governor of New York for the inconsequential role of vice president, no one thought he exaggerated the importance of Albany or denigrated the office that would make him the second man in the federal government.[4] Roosevelt fretted for months before making it apparent to the Republican National Convention that he accepted to be William McKinley's running mate. While Henry Cabot Lodge, his most intimate friend and confidante, urged him to do so and undoubtedly influenced his decision, so did Senator Thomas Platt, the powerful New York State Republican Party boss, who wished desperately to see him out of the governor's chair.[5] Roosevelt's acceptance of the party's nomination reflected nothing so much as his habitual political prudence. His ambition, recognized by all who knew him, was to be president of the United States. Because the New York governor enjoyed only a two-year term, any decision to remain in that post would require his winning two elections, that of 1900 and 1902, should he wish to remain a serious contender for the presidency in 1904. Because he had won the governorship in 1898 by an exceedingly slim margin, at a time when his fame as *the* Spanish-American War hero was at its height, the possibility of his being able to repeat that performance twice again was never very good. Henry Cabot Lodge understood that, and it explained his determination to see Roosevelt leave the powerful New York governorship for the inconsequential post of vice president.[6] Still, in his own dramatic rendering of the event, Roosevelt wished his acceptance of the vice presidential nomination to be seen as the sacrifice he made to serve the Republican Party and a president he esteemed. In this, as in so many other things, Roosevelt showed political astuteness, allied to his habitual lack of candor.[7]

Roosevelt had no reason to expect that McKinley, hale and hearty, would die in office, and the assassination of President James Garfield in 1881, carried out by an obviously insane man, was not an event he or others expected to be repeated. In the enthusiasm he showed during the 1900 election campaign when the president sat quietly at home in Canton, Ohio, receiving delegations of admiring Republican supporters, tending to the needs of his delicate and ailing wife, Roosevelt showed the fierce political appetite familiar to those who knew him well. William Jennings Bryan, the Democratic Party presidential candidate, an orator of exceptional gifts, defeated in his first presidential bid in 1896, proved an inviting target for a feisty Roosevelt, provoking his well-honed capacity for mockery and stimulating the feigned anger he seemed able to summon up at will. Bryan served Roosevelt's political campaign purposes admirably, losing to McKinley, doing substantially less well than in 1896. Both the president- and the vice president–elect knew how much the latter had contributed to the Republican victory, and in September 1901 an assassin's bullet gave Roosevelt the presidency he had long coveted.

Roosevelt accepted the vice presidency because he wanted it; he won a second term because he could not imagine leaving the White House, an incomparable haven, more enjoyable than any he had ever known. Never as self-confident as he pretended to be, he knew that many in the Republican Party distrusted him, had no use for all he had done as a trustbuster, a president insufficiently appreciative of the remarkable talents of America's captains of industry. Roosevelt disdained businessmen and had little use for intellectuals critical of his policies abroad, but knew the importance of advertising his many accomplishments so as to win the votes of the people, the only sovereign he respected. Roosevelt won the 1904 election easily, and did it largely by himself.[8] Though officially the Republican Party candidate, in fact an entrepreneur who sold the American public on his unique talents as the nation's leader, he won through his very remarkable efforts at self-publicity.

The story of Calvin Coolidge's elevation, the second of the century's accidental presidents, though less compelling, is equally significant for what it tells about American politics. Honest Cal, more familiarly known as Silent Cal, imposed by the Republican National Convention delegates in 1920 as Warren Harding's running mate, lacked both the charisma and the overweening ambition of Roosevelt. Harding, a first-term Ohio senator, secured his own presidential nomination on the tenth convention ballot when he defeated several more prominent Republicans, unable to secure the required majority to make any one of them the party's candidate. To avoid a deadlocked convention, Harding, a dark horse, chosen by a handful of influential senators who expected him to do their bidding, confirmed the belief, common to many skeptical Americans, that political bargains made in smoke-filled rooms were more significant than those reached by less-influential delegates on the convention floor.[9] Harding, considered "the best of the second-raters," was joined by Calvin Coolidge, equally conventional, scarcely more distinguished.[10] Henry Cabot Lodge, the senator from Massachusetts who had worked so effectively to destroy Wilson's plans for U.S. membership in the League of Nations, could never take Coolidge seriously. For a Boston Brahmin, proud of his own social position and intellectual attainments, Coolidge was a nobody, an insignificant politician, born and raised in rural Vermont, still showing the telltale traits of that hayseed society.[11]

Coolidge, a graduate of a tiny western Massachusetts college, remote from mighty Harvard, a small-town lawyer and the mayor of Northampton, a town of little significance for those who circulated in Boston, the state capital, had used his industry and craftiness to gain a seat in the state legislature—no very great accomplishment—but this was followed by two more important successes. Elected lieutenant governor, he went on to win the governor's chair in 1918 and gained considerable renown for breaking the Boston police strike in September 1919.[12] At a time when many feared anarchy—the dreaded foreign import, communism, was thought a real and present danger—Coolidge's bold action made him something of a national hero, attractive to Republicans concerned with the continuing threats to law and order.[13] A substantial number of convention delegates thought him one of their own, a man they could trust. Disgusted with the open display of power by a handful of vain and powerful kingmakers who discarded prominent nominees for the presidency, awarding it to Harding, a nonentity, these delegates supported Coolidge for the vice presidency. Theirs was a rebellion of sorts, a rebuke to those who gave so little heed to their concerns, who made their secret deals in hotel rooms, away from the convention floor.[14]

The contrast between the handsome glad-handing Harding and the plain, shy, and taciturn Coolidge suggested that the Republican Party was indeed ecumenical, with room under its ample tent for men of very different habits and temperaments.[15] Whether the two shared a common political philosophy—if so grandiose a term could be used to describe what either believed—no one could say, but that seemed scarcely to matter. The Republican Party electoral victory in 1920 was overwhelming, sinking not only James Cox, the Democratic Party's presidential nominee, but also Franklin Roosevelt, his running mate.[16] Indeed, the proportions of the landslide made it almost a unique event in the nation's history. Harding and Coolidge garnered more than 16 million votes; Cox and Roosevelt managed to receive just more than 9 million, mostly from states in the traditional South, the Democratic Party's secure post–Civil War stronghold.[17] When Harding died of an embolism in August 1923, less than two and a half years after he took over from the ill-fated and ailing Wilson, Honest Cal came into an office he had neither coveted nor imagined himself especially qualified for.[18]

Coolidge, never an intimate of the president, was no part of his poker-playing circle, and had no connection with the illegal deals that made the Harding administration after the president's death seem ridden with ill-begotten wealth, immortalized for a generation in the Teapot Dome scandal revelations.[19] Coolidge had no connection with any of this—it was as if he had not inhabited the same city as Harding—and this gave him his protection and indeed allowed him to seek reelection in 1924, opposing a Democrat, John W. Davis, who had secured the Democratic Party's nomination on the 103rd ballot, and Senator Robert La Follette, running as a third-party candidate. Coolidge's 1924 victory, with a popular majority over his Democratic opponent greater than even the one Harding boasted of in 1920, suggested he was not the insubstantial politician many imagined him to be.[20] Committed to thrift, believing that "economy is idealism in its most practical form," Coolidge was something of a cultural fossil in the exuberant American world of the 1920s, but a fossil that the nation took to its heart. Intellectuals, at home and abroad, were never able to understand why, vastly underestimating the craftiness of a man who seemed to win so effortlessly.[21] A second accidental president won a second term, achieving it by being neither Harding nor Roosevelt, but just a simple farmer's son from rural Vermont, committed to do-nothing political strategies that satisfied the country perfectly.[22]

The story of the third accidental president, Harry Truman, is in every respect more extraordinary. Because Henry Wallace, the incumbent vice president, was unacceptable to the majority of the Democratic National Convention delegates in 1944, and unpopular with many of President Roosevelt's intimates, he was clearly going to be set aside. All the principal Democratic Party bosses—the tribe so graphically described by Bryce almost half a century earlier—agreed that the nomination of Wallace would be a catastrophe. In their view, its repercussions might be serious enough to jeopardize the president's chances of winning a fourth term, and this was reason enough for dumping him.[23] Wallace's radical and purportedly pro-Soviet sentiments, never popular in the South, still the Democratic Party's principal bastion, were scarcely more acceptable to the leading trade unionists in the country, a crucially important Democratic constituency.[24] Loyal Democrats waited to hear whom the president wished to have as his running mate, but that information was very slow in coming.[25] Politically engaged Democrats could not fail to ask, even if only discreetly and privately, whether an aging Roosevelt, a polio victim, frequently ill with what were officially described as colds and bronchitis attacks, would be able to survive four more arduous years in the White House.[26]

While the prospects of the president's demise were speculated about, sometimes openly by Republicans and the press, only his physicians knew the full gravity of his medical condition.[27] Since late 1943, Roosevelt, suffering from very high blood pressure and heart disease, was at serious risk of early death. Death, his own, was not a matter Roosevelt chose to dwell on, and his almost instinctive dread of the subject guaranteed it would not figure in the few conversations he had with those who recognized the importance of reaching an early decision on whom he wished to have as his vice president. While there appeared to be no dearth of eligible candidates, the president showed little inclination to choose between them. Indeed, his silence rankled some, but no one was in a position to hasten his decision and in the end, it appeared that either Justice William Douglas, a recent appointee to the Supreme Court, or the longer-serving senator from Missouri, Harry Truman, would be acceptable to the president.

Roosevelt knew and liked Douglas and had seen a great deal of him when he served as chairman of the Securities and Exchange Commission, admiring him for his spirited attacks on Wall Street and appreciating his efforts as an ardent, committed, and loyal New Dealer.[28] He knew Harry Truman less well, though he valued what he did during the war as chairman of a special Senate committee to investigate graft and corruption in defense industries. The senator had saved the country hundreds of millions of dollars, and this had given him something of a national reputation.[29] Neither Douglas nor Truman boasted any significant familiarity with foreign policy questions, but the issue of their competence in this critical domain seemed scarcely relevant to the president. In the end, he chose Truman over Douglas, and it is impossible to know even now, more than half a century later why he settled on the senator from Missouri.[30] To the president's surprise and dismay, Truman announced he had no wish to be vice president, preferring to remain a senator. Truman's hesitations were not feigned; unlike both Roosevelts, he never set his sights on the White House and had no political ambitions that made him wish to leave the Senate. The president, reluctant to renew his search for another candidate, pleaded with Truman to accept, and the telephone conversation that led him finally to accede was revealing as much for what it said about an importuning president as for what it told about a genuinely reluctant senator.[31] The convention nominated Truman on the second ballot, and from that moment he knew he would almost certainly be Roosevelt's successor one day, but this was something never acknowledged openly. Truman's few encounters with the president during the campaign told him, if he did not already know it, that Roosevelt was not well, and if FDR's sudden death in April 1945 came as a shock, it was not a surprise.[32]

Truman lacked both Roosevelt's grace and knowledge; it was not modesty alone that told him how awesome a responsibility he had inherited, for which his years in the Senate offered only very slight preparation. Truman's presidency proved tempestuous and difficult, but the resilience and self-confidence he showed, qualities scarcely considered by Roosevelt when he selected him, guaranteed his survival. Few Democrats believed he could secure a second term, and looking always for a winner, they cast their eyes covetously on the country's World War II military hero, Dwight Eisenhower. Few bothered to ask whether he was in fact a Democrat or a Republican.[33] Truman, proud and self-confident, had no intention of renouncing his ambition for a second term, and knowing it would be difficult for the Democratic Party to deny him the nomination, went ahead to grasp it. In the minds of many, probably the majority, he was an all but certain loser. Without conspicuous Democratic Party support, crisscrossing the country by train, speaking before large and admiring crowds, Truman proceeded to win his own election, defeating Thomas Dewey, his Republican opponent, the expected winner, by more than 3 million votes. While Truman's victory compared only superficially with the more striking majorities registered in 1904 and 1924 by Roosevelt and Coolidge, it utterly confounded those who had prophesied his defeat.[34]

The story of Lyndon Johnson's ascent to the White House—the fourth of the century's accidental presidents—was more bizarre, at once comic and tragic. While neither Coolidge nor Truman ever hoped or expected to reach the White House by winning the presidential nomination in their respective political party conventions, these were never Johnson's sentiments, who expected to achieve that ambition one day. A powerful Minority and Majority Senate Leader—making more of the latter post than any of his predecessors—renowned for his manipulative talents and success in winning support for major Democratic Party programs, Johnson saw himself as a Texan with considerable potential appeal to delegates in any Democratic National Convention.[35] No more successful than Hubert Humphrey, defeated in the crucial West Virginia 1960 primary election that told the party that John F. Kennedy, a Catholic, could win in a predominantly Protestant state, Johnson fell before the powerful organization the junior senator from Massachusetts had created. Pulchritude, enhanced by ample funds from family, friends, and others, as well as a superb primary campaign organization, virtually guaranteed the young Kennedy the convention's blessing in 1960. Johnson felt aggrieved, considering all he had done for the party in the Senate, knowing how insignificant by comparison were Kennedy's own contributions.[36]

Kennedy, once assured of the nomination, recognized the need to mollify Johnson and imagined it might be done by appealing to his well-known vanity. In an election expected to be close, not least because of the religious issue, Kennedy knew that the retention of Texas in the Democratic fold could mean the difference between victory and defeat. He settled on a scheme that seemed foolproof; he would offer Johnson the vice presidency, knowing that the gift would flatter him, confident he would never accept so insignificant a post in exchange for the more considerable one he enjoyed in the Senate. Still, Johnson could not fail to be flattered by the offer, and this would certainly bring him to campaign actively for Kennedy in Texas. The possibility of his accepting the offer, exchanging his powerful position in the Senate for the insignificant role of presiding over that body, was unthinkable. In this instance, Kennedy guessed wrongly. Johnson, enigmatic even to those who pretended to know him, confounded the presidential nominee by accepting his offer. When Robert Kennedy, the candidate's brother and closest confidant, appalled by the prospect of a Kennedy-Johnson ticket, sought to retract the invitation, Johnson refused to go along.[37] The Kennedys had no choice but to accept his decision, knowing his name would almost certainly secure Texas for the Democrats even if it brought on to their team a man they neither cared for nor respected.[38]

Johnson never became one of the Kennedy crowd; denied a role in the mythic Court of Camelot, Johnson suffered all manner of indignities at the hands of those who reveled in Kennedy's thousand-day presidency, greatly exaggerating its importance even before its tragic end.[39] When Johnson became president after Kennedy's assassination in Dallas, he followed the example set by Theodore Roosevelt, hoping to inspire public confidence by retaining all of the slain president's Cabinet. Johnson never doubted that his command of politics greatly exceeded that of the less supple Kennedy, and his impressive victory over Goldwater in 1964, redolent only of what Roosevelt had achieved in 1936, convinced him that he had crafted his own victory. When one considers that Johnson beat Goldwater with slightly more than 43 million votes against the Republican's slightly more than 27 million, it was not simply the memory of a slain president that gave him so impressive a victory over an Arizona senator thought to be too right-wing, excessively ardent in his anticommunism, irrationally antagonistic to the New Deal that Johnson proposed to extend with his promise of a Great Society. Johnson, like the previous accidental presidents, Roosevelt, Coolodge, and Truman, intended to be his own man, making the necessary but very occasional obeisances to the memory of his dead predecessor, but striking out on his own.

These four accidental presidents, always professing loyalty to their party, and proud of their association with it, never imagined their role was simply to give heed to the commands that periodically issued from members of their party in Congress. Johnson, indefatigable in his legislative efforts, believed he existed to give direction to Congress, to use every weapon in his command to persuade the House and Senate to pass reform legislation even more fundamental than that of his two great Democratic presidential heroes, Roosevelt and Truman.[40] The Vietnam War, as he greatly expanded the commitment of U.S. forces, abetted by those in the Cabinet and White House who advised him— Kennedy's principal legacies—led him to political disaster. Johnson's second term was a galling time; there were few foreign policy successes, none to rival those Truman knew in even his most troubled days.[41] Those who became openly hostile to him, including the slain president's brother, explained their antipathy as stemming principally from policy differences; Johnson, the superficially self-assured president, knew they had never been able to accept him, in their eyes a Texas brute, lacking the grace, wit, and charm of his predecessor. Johnson, a keen judge of political talent, though an innocent in foreign policy, understood that Kennedy was never the accomplished leader his acolytes imagined him to be, and this knowledge served only to increase his frustrations and resentments, making him bitter and vulnerable, consumed by an anger uncommon in the White House in even the most tempestuous times.[42]

His was perhaps the most tragic presidency of the century, but it did not significantly diminish the authority vested in the office that several of his accidental predecessors had done so much to embellish. Johnson, like Roosevelt, Coolidge, and Truman, proud of the office they inherited, had no intention of leaving it diminished. Indeed, this was also the ambition of the last of the century's accidental presidents, Gerald Ford, but his was an administration that originated not in the death of a president but in a threatened impeachment that compelled him to resign. Ford arrived in the White House by a route never previously taken.[43] His elevation to the vice presidency followed on the forced resignation of Spiro Agnew, Nixon's combative vice president, accused of income tax evasion and illicit payoffs from construction companies during his term as governor of Maryland.[44] By the terms of the Twenty-Fifth Amendment to the Constitution, ratified in 1967, the president was required to nominate a candidate for the vice presidency should that position for any reason become vacant, and Congress would be required to give its consent to the proposed appointment. In the past, for thirty-eight years in all, following the death of a president or the resignation of a vice president—never, as in Agnew's case, brought on by charges of criminal behavior and corruption—the vice presidency was left vacant till the next quadrennial election. The 1967 constitutional amendment prohibited such lapses, and Nixon nominated Ford, the House Minority Leader from Michigan, to fill the post vacated by the disgraced Agnew.[45]

Ford, admired for his affability and generous nature, qualities conspicuously lacking in Agnew, was Nixon's choice because the president understood the importance of selecting a man who would have no difficulty in securing rapid congressional approval. It was politically important for the Republican Party to turn the page quickly to encourage the public to forget the crimes of someone many had once idolized; in Agnew's place, Nixon recommended an individual of undoubted integrity.[46] Some, suspicious of the president, imagined he chose Ford because he feared his own impeachment and believed it would never go forward if Congress knew his replacement would be the mild and seemingly ineffectual Ford.[47] Whatever his motives, Nixon guessed correctly; the nomination was enthusiastically ratified by a Congress scarcely aware they were selecting a future president of the United States. The earlier accidental presidents received the blessing of their respective parties in the conventions; Ford came by a different route and was the only accidental president who failed to win reelection, defeated as much by his initial difficulties in the Republican primaries with Ronald Reagan, the former governor of California, as by Jimmy Carter, the little-known Democratic former governor of Georgia who managed to defeat him by a very narrow margin.[48]

The ghost of Richard Nixon would not be laid. Among the many Nixon legacies, none was more important than the renewed suspicion of presidential power, voiced with growing enthusiasm and ever-greater effect by the nation's media—press, radio, and television. The country witnessed a resurgence of congressional power, redolent of what happened in the decades following Lincoln's demise, but it could not eradicate the increases in presidential authority that had become so conspicuous in the years that began with Theodore Roosevelt.[49] The Oval Office, especially after World War II, with the president in sole command of the nation's ultimate weapon, the atomic bomb, and later of thermonuclear weapons and missiles, gained a position that it never surrendered, not even when it appeared challenged by powerful members of Congress and influential figures in the media.[50] The presidency changed immensely in the first seventy years of the twentieth century; so, also, did the vice presidency, but for other reasons.

The attention given the greatly expanded powers of the presidency, beginning early in the twentieth century and continuing with minor interruptions to the end, has not been accompanied by a comparable interest in the transformed vice presidency. This latter development, significant in the second half of the century and intimately related to what a succession of presidents were willing to do to give new authority to an office long deemed inconsequential, has had important political consequences.

While no vice president after Martin Van Buren in 1837 ran for the presidency till Richard Nixon did so more than a century later in 1960, no fewer than four have attempted to make the same transition since. Only one, George Bush, succeeded; three others, all Democrats, Hubert Humphrey, Walter Mondale, and Al Gore, tried and failed.[51] How can one explain the sudden emergence in the second half of the twentieth century of an office long believed insignificant, so rarely coveted by ambitious men? To say that the vice presidency became a more visible post, made so by television but also by new duties awarded by a succession of presidents, is to state the obvious. Vice presidents since Nixon have enjoyed the kind of national publicity that no governor, senator, or congressman could hope to command.[52] This is not to suggest that the governor's chair has ceased to be a principal avenue to the presidency; only that it has a new rival in the vice presidents. A governorship in the late twentieth century, as before, remains a desirable political post from which to initiate a presidential campaign; the executive experience and training it provides make it seem a reasonable launching pad for would-be presidents, and the fact that the office gives limited foreign policy training is not considered a fatal handicap even in a day when foreign policy issues are known to be salient.[53]

Less noticed, in this connection, is the enhanced role of the Senate as a nursery for those who aspire to the presidency or accept to be nominated as vice presidents. While historians frequently noted the failure of nineteenth-century pre–Civil War senatorial giants, men as distinguished as John Calhoun, Daniel Webster, and Henry Clay, to realize their presidential ambitions, Warren Harding and John F. Kennedy—an unlikely pair—succeeded where their more renowned and distinguished predecessors had failed. Harding and Kennedy, never considered Senate luminaries in their day, moved directly from that chamber to a presidential nomination, and then to the White House. Nixon achieved the same success, going by the more circuitous route of the vice presidency. In this, as in so much else, he was followed, if not imitated, by three

Democrats—Humphrey, Mondale, and Gore—who would have repudiated any suggestion that they had learned anything from the Nixon example. Still, if someone with so many obvious character and personality flaws could translate his time as vice president into a credible claim for the presidency, why should others not seek to do the same? Each, in fact, did, making a similar transit from the Senate to the vice presidency, failing only to move a step higher, to the White House itself.[54]

Whether the American presidency became imperial, as Arthur Schlesinger Jr. suggested in describing the many unfortunate consequences of Nixon's traumatic and disastrous rule, his less advertised legacy was to make the vice presidency coveted, positively desirable.[55] Because the Republican Party during the second half of the twentieth century showed a certain proclivity for nominating and electing aged men to the presidency—Dwight Eisenhower and Ronald Reagan being the most conspicuous—it is scarcely surprising that each suffered grave illnesses when in office and that one of the results of their infirmity was the elevation of their vice presidents to an eminence they could not otherwise have known. While the gravity of the illnesses of two Democratic presidents, Woodrow Wilson and Franklin Roosevelt, were artfully concealed—an extraordinary accomplishment in both instances, but especially remarkable with Wilson, a White House invalid for well over a year—comparable concealment with Eisenhower or Reagan was impossible. Their illnesses required hospitalization and long periods of convalescence that could not fail to be publicized. In this one respect, at least, the late-twentieth-century presidency had become more transparent, the vice president more visible.[56]

When one considers that Charles Dawes, Coolidge's vice president, saw no reason as late as 1925 to retain his status as a member of the Cabinet, initially bestowed on Coolidge by Harding—the first vice president awarded even that modest distinction—one has some sense of the insignificance Dawes attached to the invitation to become a more influential member of the president's administration. Vice President Dawes saw himself as the presiding officer of the Senate, the sole responsibility granted him by the Constitution, and desired no other. Having no wish to preen himself as the principal colleague of the president, he saw himself essentially as a legislative figure.[57] Franklin Roosevelt had renewed the Cabinet invitation to his first vice president, John Nance Garner, and though it was accepted, there is no evidence that membership in the Cabinet gave Garner significant new authority or prestige. His value to the president came largely from his being a prominent Texas politician, in close touch with other influential Texans in the Senate, the House, and the administration more generally.[58] Texans were clannish, and Roosevelt recognized the importance of having in his entourage someone with easy access to them. When Garner, disappointed with the president's decision to break all tradition and seek a third term, effectively withdrew his support, the 1940 Democratic National Convention was theoretically free to choose his successor, but Roosevelt showed little interest in their views, offering the place to Henry Wallace, an unpopular choice even then.[59] Only the intervention of Eleanor Roosevelt, the president's wife, in a remarkably effective convention speech, swayed the delegates sufficiently for them to accept him, however reluctantly.[60]

Clearly, the vice presidency after World War II was not a significantly more exalted position than it had been decades earlier, when information about Wilson's grave condition was withheld from Thomas Marshall, his vice president, as much in the dark about conditions in the president's sick room as the Cabinet, journalists, and the general public.[61] Truman, never a Roosevelt confidante, determined he would not allow Alben Barkley, his vice president, elected with him in 1948, to be comparably uninformed and ignored, and insisted that the legislation passed in 1949 to establish the National Security Council, soon to eclipse the Cabinet in importance, should include provision for the vice president to be one of its permanent members. It was imperative, Truman believed, for the vice president to be kept informed of all critical national defense issues, necessarily secret, that he would know nothing about if denied admission to the NSC discussions. Barkley, with his long experience in Congress, acquired through more than three decades of service in both the House and the Senate, could be relied on to offer counsel and assistance. Because the minutes of the NSC are closed, it is impossible to know what influence Barkley exerted, but his NSC membership could not fail to make him a more prominent figure in the Truman administration.

We know nothing of what Nixon's presence in the NSC meant before September 1955 when the president suffered his first severe heart attack. Eisenhower, virtually incapacitated, asked Nixon to chair all meetings of the NSC and the Cabinet during his enforced absence. At a time when the president's own future was uncertain, and fears were expressed about whether his health would permit him to seek a second term in 1956, Nixon, known to be ambitious, was clearly a man to be watched. Many in the Cabinet, less than enthusiastic about him, feared he would use the accident of Eisenhower's illness to advance his claims for the presidential nomination in 1956 should the president find it impossible to run.[62] Eisenhower, knowing Nixon, aware of his strengths and frailties, knew he had no reason to fear him; any too-overt grasping for power could only harm him. However impetuous Nixon might appear at times, he was rarely foolhardy. In the months of his convalescence, Eisenhower had his first extensive experience of using the vice president as his political and administrative surrogate and found the relationship entirely satisfactory. Nixon never made the mistake of forgetting his subordinate status, showing always the degree of subservience that kept the president happy, satisfying also other members of the administration, including those known to be hostile to him. The aged general remained the man in charge, and that reassured those most instrumental in securing the presidency for him.

When, in November 1957, during his second term, Eisenhower suffered a minor stroke, less serious than his 1955 illness, he recognized the need to make more concrete the conditions that ought to obtain were he to become more seriously incapacitated. In a private letter to Nixon, Eisenhower set out the procedures he wished him to follow. Should he find himself disabled and be aware of his condition, he would inform the vice president, in effect transferring the powers of the presidency to him. If he became disabled and failed to recognize the extent of his infirmity, it would be the vice president's duty to consult with others, but the decision on whether to assume the prerogatives of the president would be his alone.[63] When Nixon claimed, years later, that "the Vice Presidency . . . is the only office which provides on-the-job training for the Presidency," he was not exaggerating; it proved to be that in his case.[64] Nixon reveled in his responsibilities, knowing, in effect, that he had become something of an assistant president, receiving public attention of a kind none of his predecessors had ever commanded. What some had feared earlier—that Nixon would seek the presidency in 1956 if Eisenhower found it impossible to run—became a reality in 1959 when Nixon made clear his wish to succeed him. Though other Republicans aspired to the nomination, Nixon started with advantages, not the least his experience of government at the highest levels that no governor, not even Nelson Rockefeller, was able to claim.[65]

Nixon's defeat, by a few thousand votes in an election that saw more than 68 million Americans troop to the polls, was a terrible experience for someone who recognized how much greater was his knowledge and experience of government than anything the junior senator from Massachusetts could claim. Nixon, having tasted the pleasures of the presidency, though in an obviously attenuated form, found intolerable the prospect of having to return to private life, resuming his practice as a lawyer.[66]

With Kennedy's inaugural in 1961 and the move of Johnson from the Senate to an office in the White House, yet another chapter in the history of the vice presidency was opened. While Kennedy advocates, including Arthur Schlesinger Jr., dwelled on all the president did to make the vice president feel a member of his team, Johnson knew that White House office space did not translate into influence. His privileges were irrelevant; Johnson, an insignificant figure in the Kennedy administration, recognized the superficial massaging for what it was.[67] When, after 1965, Johnson treated Humphrey more brutally, persecuting his vice president in ways Kennedy never thought to do, Johnson's ill temper, impatience, and violent outbursts were attributed to the extraordinary difficulties he faced in coping with an escalating war in Vietnam and growing political dissent and street violence at home. The vice president, Minnesota's most liberal and distinguished politician, gentle and self-effacing, different from the angry and foul-mouthed Texan who searched for enemies everywhere, bided his time, suffered the president's tantrums and rages, realizing the pressures under which he labored.[68] Always solicitous of Johnson, appreciating all he had done to ameliorate the condition of millions who suffered from racial persecution and economic and social disadvantage, Humphrey honored both the office and the man, recognizing very early the hazards of his Vietnam policies. Humphrey never received from Johnson the reward his loyalty entitled him to.[69] When he sought the presidency after Johnson announced his own withdrawal and Robert Kennedy's assassination, he faced an almost impossible dilemma—how to be loyal to a president he admired and still not be thought an advocate of his Vietnam policies.

Humphrey confronted in an even more acute form the problem Al Gore faced in the year 2000: how to identify with the president and still not appear his uncritical disciple.[70] Like Gore, Humphrey lost in a very closely fought election in which more than 72 million Americans went to the polls, and in which George Wallace, the American Independent Party candidate, a racist, was able to claim almost 10 million votes.[71] Nixon finally reached the home of his dreams, the White House, having used his vice presidency to make himself known, claiming a renown he could not have achieved by any other means. With the vice presidency becoming a possible route to the presidency—Nixon having done a great deal to make it that—another Minnesota Democratic liberal, Walter Mondale, Jimmy Carter's vice president, sought to unseat the conservative and immensely popular Ronald Reagan in 1984. His was a lost cause; Reagan defeated him easily and overwhelmingly.[72]

Though Reagan never credited Nixon with creating a new constituency for the Republican Party, pretending that the disgraced president left no legacy, he in fact left several, including one George Bush failed to acknowledge. Bush replicated in his relations with Reagan many of the practices Nixon developed in dealing with Eisenhower. The attempt on Reagan's life and his illnesses were a godsend to his less than charismatic vice president, who had limited experience of competing successfully for elective office but claimed a number of administrative appointments that purportedly made him a foreign policy and intelligence expert.[73] On March 30, 1981, when John Hinckley shot the president and Alexander Haig Jr., the secretary of state, made the mistake of pretending he was temporarily in charge of the government, Bush learned a lesson he never forgot. The influence he sought, in the company of the president's California cronies, Edwin Meese and Michael Deaver, and Bush's fellow Texan, James Baker III, the president's chief of staff, could be achieved only if their purposes were never revealed. These men became the president's handlers, who managed him and his affairs but knew better than to emphasize that anyone except the president was in charge. While the president's indolence was never a state secret, constantly reported by TV news programs and the press, even by those purportedly friendly to him, and while Bush knew everything about the sordid Iran-Contra deal from his former associates in the CIA over which he had once presided, he never questioned the president's policies in public or private.[74] A loyal subordinate, he did whatever was demanded of him, anything to lighten the president's burdens. While Reagan's prostate surgery in January 1987 never gave Bush the exceptional authority Nixon enjoyed under Eisenhower, the early signs of what later came to be diagnosed as Alzheimer's disease made it all the more necessary for Bush to cosset Reagan, to do nothing to offend his principal carer, his wife, Nancy. Reagan, an old man in the White House, required the support of men with greater energy, and Bush was one of many prepared to serve him, in a court as curious in its own way as the one created by the disgraced and rarely mentioned Nixon.[75]

Vice presidents, from Nixon to Gore, enjoyed an association with their presidents that none of their predecessors claimed or pretended to. By the last decades of the century, each was more than just a loyal associate. An iconoclastic observer from abroad, accustomed to speaking truths Americans had no wish to hear, might have described them as highly visible servants, lackeys in effect, prepared to do their masters' bidding. Such language, common in France for those who knew the conditions of service for someone as autocratic as Charles de Gaulle, would have been thought indecent in the United States, where presidents were thought to be more respectful of the feelings and dignity of their subordinates.[76] If the latter recognized the foibles and weaknesses of those who presided over their destinies, and in some instances knew themselves to be politically and intellectually superior to those they served, they wisely suppressed all such sentiment.[77] Given the publicity awarded vice presidents, newly minted celebrities, famous at home and abroad, habituated to observing if not sharing power, they recognized the importance of ingratiating themselves with their masters, recognizing that they were never free to become their critics.

Expected to show patience, they were, in effect, princes-in-waiting, a role unknown in the nineteenth or early twentieth century. After World War II, presidents, represented by the mass media as having their finger on the button, universally lauded as leaders of the free world, whether imperial or imperious, self-important or modest, presided over courts in which their vice presidents came to have an increasingly conspicuous place. In daily contact with presidential power, they could not fail to be affected by the spectacle. A foreign observer, a latter-day Tocqueville, might have found the play comic; few Americans did. The older simplicities of the republic, once described in sympathetic detail by friendly European visitors, were no longer in evidence. A vast bureaucratic machine had come into being, as conspicuous in the White House as in the rest of the federal government. The bosses had departed the political scene, and presidential primaries, fueled by unprecedented large campaign contributions, became the way public opinion registered its preference for those the political parties were then legally obliged to nominate.[78] Whether the opinion was educated or uninformed, whether it constituted the despotism of the majority Tocqueville had warned against, were issues politicians never discussed. The presidential nominations, taken away from those who met in smoke-filled rooms, gave way to what all purported to believe was a more democratic procedure. As for the vice presidential nominations, in the control of the party's presidential candidate, this, too, was thought appropriate. In effect, it made a single individual the arbiter of who would secure media attention, becoming a live candidate for the presidential succession. Governors from inconspicuous states, but also from others as important as Texas and California, might still aspire to the presidency, but they knew the competition was greatly altered from what it had been in the days of the Roosevelts.

Vice presidents, invited to become principal actors in the drama that saw the American democracy in potentially mortal combat with an alien and evil empire—the Soviet Union—viewed the world as only those with access to all the nation's intelligence secrets were in a position to do. Why, having learned so much about domestic and foreign policy, able to claim long years of experience as apprentices in the White House, having reached the second place in the federal hierarchy, should they not aspire also to the first? Only with the arrival of Richard Cheney, a certified heart attack–prone vice president in 2000, whose health record suggested he could never be a serious contender for the presidency, did the country enjoy a respite, perhaps temporary, from witnessing what the twentieth century had made so traditional: Presidents would yearn for and expect to serve two terms in the White House; their vice presidents, chosen by them, would think it only right that they should succeed them. That the accidental presidents, together with the others, heirs apparent, occupied the White House for slightly less than two-fifths of the century, a unique situation, allowed these men, particularly after 1939, to profit from the secrecy that war and the fear of war justified. Generally able to manipulate a hugely expanded bureaucracy and a mass media system partial to their claims to being the leaders of the free world, a number were burdened as many of their predecessors had not been, and all profited from the fact of their easy reelection.

The presidency, by the end of the twentieth century, was a vastly changed office from what it was in the beginning, with war and the threat of war, as much as the personality of the individual incumbents making it that. None of these men were tyrants in the classic sense of the term, but their powers greatly exceeded any contemplated by the Founders or even those exercised by Presidents Wilson and Roosevelt during the two world wars. Their prominence, greatly enhanced by the mass media, which came to have a vested interest in their daily activities, made even the more commonplace among them seem men of consequence, and their vice presidents gained immeasurably from being in such intimate association with them. While an occasional secretary of state, men of the stature of Henry Kissinger, might for a time rival the president in the media attention awarded them—a condition greatly resented by Nixon—even those who enjoyed that high Cabinet office rarely attained the prominence their elevation entitled them to. Many were quickly forgotten, recognized to be the servants of presidents who had become their own secretaries of state, who in the manner of Clinton imagined they understood foreign policy as only politicians could, as diplomats never did. In the later years of the twentieth century, the White House greatly overestimated its control of events abroad, mistaking its military might and purported intelligence capability for mastery of an international situation, making all who came into the presidential presence seem consequential, none more than the vice presidents who stood ready to serve and if called upon to succeed them. They were the true legatees of a political system that had become intensely personal, with political parties greatly reduced in their importance.[79]

CHAPTER 3

Let the People Speak:
No More Smoke-Filled Rooms

JAMES BRYCE, DESCRIBING the national nominating conventions that met every four years to select the party's candidates for president and vice president, wrote in 1888: "In every American election there are two acts of choice, two periods of contest. The first is the selection of the candidate from within the party by the party; the other is the struggle between the parties for the post."[1] This late-nineteenth-century method of presidential choice, as described by Bryce, remained recognizable in the 1920s and early 1930s when Harding, Coolidge, and Hoover presided over the nation's affairs. Indeed, those searching for explanations of how Roosevelt and Eisenhower in the 1930s and 1950s managed to secure their nominations and win their elections can do no better than consult Bryce's 1888 text. The quadrennial political party conventions, as he described them, were still very much in evidence when these last two presidents born in America's Victorian age secured their nominations. Politics changed dramatically only with the arrival of Kennedy, becoming more bizarre with the Nixon administration and his forced resignation, initiating a fin de siècle that allowed Reagan, a very accomplished political actor, to take the reins of power in 1981. These years witnessed the total triumph of the primary system, a method that allowed the voters in individual states to select the delegates to the nominating convention, requiring them to vote for the candidates they favored. Anyone proposing to revise the Bryce text today, to bring it up to date, would be obliged to change those particular sentences to read: "In every American election there are two acts of choice, two periods of contest. The first is the selection of the candidate from within the party by those voters who choose to vote in the individual state primaries, often doing so in very small number; the second is the struggle between the individuals so selected for the post." In theory, democracy has triumphed; candidates are no longer chosen by oligarchs, bosses, and others, meeting in private, negotiating between themselves on the individual they wish to represent the party in the presidential election.

The primary system, very gradually introduced in individual states in the course of the twentieth century, but virtually universal by the end, fundamentally changed the nature of the presidency. The quadrennial political party conventions, once the site of improbable but often exciting deals between influential politicians, became boring TV spectacles, coronation rites to confirm the selection of an individual already chosen through the primary election process.[2] The presidential nominees, political entrepreneurs more than servants of the party, had sold themselves through months of slogging through snow, mud, and rain to prove themselves attractive to thousands registered to vote in the state primaries. Insofar as they incurred debts through this grueling experience, it was not to the anonymous thousands who voted for them, but to the wealthy individuals and institutions who supported their campaigns financially and the men and women who advised them, generally expecting some kind of political reward for their labors. The political bosses of yesterday became an extinct species. Money became the essential fuel, increasingly important in the last decades of the century when the expense of TV advertising, together with those incurred through air travel, the hiring of consultants, and polling experts, compelled all who aspired to the presidency to raise unprecedented amounts, literally inconceivable in a pre-TV and pre-jumbo jet age.[3]

The rituals once conspicuous at political party conventions that made them occasions of fun, intrigue, hoopla, surprise, and outlandish rhetoric, became Hollywood-staged spectaculars, intended to give national publicity to the candidates whose success in the primaries guaranteed their nomination.[4] Elements of the earlier jamboree spirit prevailed, but only as staged spectacle; the conventions had become ratifying bodies, no longer selecting the nominees, but simply confirming the choices made by those who had chosen to vote in the individual state primaries. While the party convention still made the official investiture and might serve as the site where the presidential nominee indicated his choice for vice president, if that decision had not already been announced, all the traditional uncertainty had vanished. No one who attended either of the party conventions could doubt who would be the presidential candidate, who would deliver the address that promised the country a future more glorious than any it had ever known.[5]

The public, awarded the opportunity to choose the individual they wished to see compete for the presidency, a privilege denied their parents and grandparents, were disinclined to ask whether the changes led to the nomination of "great and striking men," the words James Bryce had first used in 1888.[6] It was enough for the greatest number to believe that citizens had been consulted, that the earlier political oligarchs had been routed. The proposition that the new system gave an advantage to skilled politicians who knew how to use it to advance themselves and that it simply created the potential for new mediocrity in the White House would have been thought irreverent, offensive to those who believed in the virtues of popular choice. Pulchritude and a pleasing TV presence, recognized as crucial in 1960 in the Kennedy-Nixon encounter, became ever more critical, as did the capacity to raise funds from all who imagined they would be advantaged by the victory of their candidate.[7] With the primaries becoming all-important, the presidential campaigns began in the year before the November elections, giving considerable advantage to those able to devote substantial time to the effort. In the new political arena, senators enjoyed an advantage denied to governors; congressional practice allowed them to absent themselves from Washington for long periods; it was more difficult for governors to leave their state capitals for extended periods of campaigning, though the prospect of becoming a presidential candidate generally encouraged the public to tolerate such absences.[8] Those who commanded fortunes of their own might give themselves wholly to the task of circulating among the party faithful for a year or longer before the primary season opened. Jimmy Carter, for example, a sufficiently well-to-do peanut farmer, spent almost two years following his retirement as governor of Georgia seeking the presidential nomination, and Ronald Reagan campaigned, though somewhat less strenuously, for years after completing his two terms as governor of California.[9]

To win an absolute majority of the delegates in the primaries became the sole object of the political game, and news reporters gloried in the task of estimating how the individual strategies were faring, what public opinion polls prophesied the results were likely to be. The earlier political rituals were replaced by breathless month-long marathons, detailing the daily successes and follies of those who managed to survive as credible candidates. The nightly TV news reports resembled nothing so much as the older Hollywood-staged *Perils of Pauline* serials except that they generally featured strident oratory, generally rendered in two-minute clips.[10] After the primary races bestowed the laurel on one successful contender, following the summer lull that ended on Labor Day, the first Monday in September, the candidates allocated vast sums to TV advertising, emphasizing their unique qualities, while denigrating those of their opponent. The new campaign amusement, the televised presidential debates— scarcely debates at all in the classic sense of the term but watched by tens of millions—permitted TV and press reporters to judge the candidates' performances, fortified in their views by opinion polls that told them who the vast TV audience believed had won. On rare occasions, the debates were declared a draw and sometimes were acknowledged to have been disappointing, a bore.[11]

Primaries, granting citizens the right to choose those they wished to see compete for specific public offices, were virtually unknown in the nineteenth century. Only a handful of states allowed relatively minor elected offices to be filled by those preselected in popular primaries, and this made the decisions of the Florida state legislature in 1901 and the Wisconsin state legislature in 1905 especially important. They were the first to mandate presidential primaries, and their example was quickly followed by a handful of other states.[12] In a decade when political reformers believed the people ought to become more actively engaged and given a greater role in choosing those who would govern them, various political innovations were recommended, all intended to guarantee the sovereign power of the people, to reduce the influence of bosses and trusts.[13] Reformers spoke enthusiastically of the benefits likely to be realized from the adoption of three basic reforms: the referendum, initiative, and power of recall. While none of these remedies ever achieved wide acceptance, another, never explicitly linked to them, made substantial headway. Presidential primaries seemed a reasonable political innovation for those who believed popular choice preferable to boss choice.[14]

Theodore Roosevelt played a critical role in emphasizing the democratic virtues of popular consultation. When he challenged William Howard Taft, the incumbent president for the Republican Party nomination in 1912, political primaries were uncommon, and Roosevelt believed he could wrest the nomination only if he entered all the primaries and won a substantial number. These victories, while not giving him anything like the delegate strength necessary for the nomination, were expected to tell the country that ordinary voters, faithful Republicans, when given the choice, preferred Roosevelt to Taft. In his mind, this would oblige the Republican National Convention to heed the popular will.[15] Making the primaries seem all-important, he triggered the political explosion at the convention that made Taft the Republican Party candidate and led Roosevelt to bolt the party, contesting the election as an Independent on the Bull Moose ticket. Believing that his primary election victories in California, Illinois, Maryland, Ohio, New Jersey, and Pennsylvania proved he was the candidate the Republicans preferred, Roosevelt represented the convention's decision to renominate Taft as a grave injustice to himself and to all who believed in democratic rule.[16]

Failing to persuade the majority of the delegates, and losing the support of some of his close friends, Roosevelt found the excuse he needed to form a new party, the Progressive Party, and offered himself as the people's candidate.[17] In the election that followed, Taft and Roosevelt rounded on each other in ways that would have been inconceivable before the start of the primary season, and Wilson, the Democratic candidate, emerged as the principal beneficiary of their mud-slinging quarrel.

In the Democratic Party, the battle for the 1912 nomination was scarcely less heated, though neither Wilson nor his principal rival, Champ Clark, the Speaker of the House, were thought titans comparable to those who battled for the Republican Party's presidential designation. Wilson and Clark, both winning five primaries, an insignificant number, recognized that only by their managers wheeling and dealing on the convention floor could they hope to gain the nomination. The Democratic National Convention rules required the nominee to win two-thirds of the delegate votes, and this alone guaranteed that the battle would be long and difficult. The convention, deadlocked for days in what newspapers represented as a struggle between the party's conservatives and progressives, on its forty-sixth ballot finally awarded the palm to Wilson, who earlier in the balloting had virtually abandoned hope of securing the nomination. Helped greatly by William Jennings Bryan, whose support proved crucial, but relying on others as well, Wilson, the only professor in the nation's history to win a presidential nomination in either party, achieved his success largely through the negotiating efforts of his team of convention-floor managers whose work he never adequately appreciated or acknowledged.[18]

By 1916, presidential primaries existed in twenty-five states, but no one assumed then or indeed for decades thereafter that the choice expressed by those who voted in the primaries should govern the decision reached by the party convention. Since the number of delegates elected in the primaries did not come close to giving the leading candidate a majority in the Republican Party, and nothing like a two-thirds majority in the Democratic Party, negotiation among the leaders on the convention floor, in corridors and hotel rooms, continued to be decisive.[19] While those who despaired of the system condemned the deals that determined the convention's choice, as evident in the nomination of Franklin Roosevelt in 1932 and in the more controversial choice of Woodrow Wilson in 1912, Roosevelt's nomination—perhaps the most important in the century—involved precisely the kinds of political deals described by Bryce more than four decades earlier. Roosevelt's claim to be considered for the office originated in his surprising success in winning the governorship of New York in 1928 in an election that saw Al Smith, the first Roman Catholic to seek the presidency, suffer a catastrophic defeat at the hands of Herbert Hoover. Roosevelt achieved what many considered a remarkable victory, winning the governor's chair in Albany, though by only a very slim margin.[20] His victory, made more newsworthy by Smith's defeat, gave him instant national celebrity, a potential major presidential Democratic Party contender in 1932. Journalists began to speculate whether his destiny was not to follow Theodore Roosevelt, moving from the Executive Mansion in Albany to the White House.

On January 23, 1932, Roosevelt surprised no one when he announced his intention to seek the Democratic Party's presidential nomination. Smith, furious, harbored the illusion that if the Democrats nominated him a second time, given the seriousness of the country's economic plight, he would certainly be victorious. Unwilling to give way to the man so recently his acolyte, Smith hoped to prove himself more popular than his rival by winning many of the key state primaries. This proved a hopeless political venture. Roosevelt entered all the major Democratic primaries and won in eleven states; Smith claimed only two, while other Democratic contenders managed to carry three. Roosevelt's principal rival at the convention was never Smith but John Nance Garner, the Speaker of the House, who came with two major assets: As the favorite son of Texas, he commanded the votes of that delegation; and his primary victory in California gave him the votes of the third-largest state in the nation. In California, Garner was greatly helped by the enthusiastic support of William Randolph Hearst, the newspaper tycoon, who thought the tobacco-chewing Texan, a populist in an older Democratic Party tradition, would have great appeal to the nation in its time of economic and social distress.[21]

Though Garner's total delegate strength was miniscule when compared with Roosevelt's, and no one believed his personality compared with that of the New York governor who radiated confidence and charm, concealing always the extent of his polio infirmity, Roosevelt had no hope of coming close to the required two-thirds majority unless he persuaded one or other of his competitors to release their delegates to him. In theory, Roosevelt might have hoped to win over some of Smith's delegates, but he knew this to be impossible. Smith would never release his delegates to someone he deemed a traitor, once a friend, now a sworn enemy. To avoid an impasse and the long days of indecisive balloting that all Democrats remembered from their recent past, Garner was clearly the man to be cosseted. Roosevelt's convention managers enlisted Hearst to do the actual negotiating with him and offered the Texan the vice presidency if he agreed to surrender his 90 delegates to Roosevelt. The deal was done, and Roosevelt became the party's nominee on the fourth ballot.[22] Though the primaries helped demonstrate Roosevelt's popularity, they did not secure the prize for him; the men who managed his campaign on the convention floor were responsible for his victory.

Not until 1952 did the nation witness again political party conventions where the final results seemed equally important and for a time comparably unpredictable. General Eisenhower, supreme commander of NATO in Europe, allowed his name to be entered in Republican primaries, appearing in the United States in the final week of the primary season. Only the convention could decide between the rival claims of an Ohio senator, Robert Taft, a dedicated Republican, intelligent and industrious, and a general universally lauded as a war hero. Because President Truman had failed to conclude the war in Korea, and was being condemned by Senator Joseph McCarthy and others for his failure to root out Communists at home and defeat them abroad, a Republican victory in 1952 was expected. For many delegates, Eisenhower appeared to be the candidate who could not possibly lose; Taft seemed more of a gamble, not least for the hostility he provoked in labor circles for the Taft-Hartley Act that had seriously curtailed trade union rights.[23] Eisenhower, by his pledge to bring peace in Korea, and because of his reputed diplomatic skills, important should any threat from the Soviet Union develop, enjoyed the additional advantage of being clean as a whistle, unlikely to countenance the kinds of corruption in the federal government that many Republicans insisted had become endemic in the Truman administration. Ike, irresistible to the delegates who gathered in Chicago in 1952, was a national hero who had demonstrated courage and restraint in World War II, never taken unnecessary risks, an incomparable soldier-statesman. Against such a rival, Taft was helpless; so, also, was Adlai Stevenson, the Democratic Party candidate.

The competition for the Democratic Party nomination in 1952 was somewhat more bizarre, but only because Senator Estes Kefauver of Tennessee, a clown to some, a man of the people to others, entered all sixteen of the party's primaries and emerged with 64 percent of the votes cast.[24] Because these victories did not give Kefauver the delegate strength sufficient to claim the nomination, the convention would have to decide between him and others who had failed to enter the primaries, including Adlai Stevenson, the governor of Illinois. Truman's decision not to seek another term in the White House, announced belatedly on March 29, 1952, when the primaries were already under way, left many party leaders aghast at the prospect of Kefauver emerging as the Democratic nominee. His primary successes failed to impress them and scarcely influenced the president, who felt an undisguised contempt for him.[25] Democratic Party chiefs, searching for a viable alternative able to derail what at that moment seemed a Kefauver bandwagon, embraced Truman's choice, Adlai Stevenson, who gave scant encouragement to those interested to have him as the Democratic Party nominee. The convention chose Stevenson, but the task of winning against Eisenhower exceeded the power of any Democrat. Stevenson's wit and elegance, qualities admired at home and abroad, offered little defense against a military hero no one ever accused of being witty, elegant, articulate, or political. Stevenson lost by a very wide margin in his contest with the popular five-star general, the first (and only) professional military figure to enter the White House in the twentieth century.

The 1960 struggle for the Democratic nomination was as different from 1952 as both were from the one that nominated Roosevelt in 1932. John F. Kennedy emerged victorious after an extraordinary campaign in which his large extended family participated, helped greatly by the ample fortune his father dipped into to guarantee his son's success. Kennedy's triumph derived not so much from a succession of primary victories—he entered only seven in fact—nor from his brother's acknowledged ability to manage the convention delegates but from a situation recognized by Norman Mailer, the novelist. However charismatic Roosevelt or Stevenson might have seemed for many Democrats, neither could claim to be in the same league as Kennedy. Mailer, with characteristic intuitive grasp, wrote of him: "The Democrats were going to nominate a man who, no matter how serious his political dedication might be, was indisputably and willy-nilly going to be seen as a great box-office actor, and the consequences of that were staggering and not at all easy to calculate."[26] The 1960 election opened a new era in American presidential politics, as much for Kennedy's victory as for Nixon's defeat.[27] Kennedy's successes in the Wisconsin and West Virginia primaries, correctly emphasized by Theodore White, the journalist who gave the campaign its most vivid analysis, never depended on his campaigning in the greatest number of states that held Democratic Party primaries that year. Kennedy, in fact, competed in less than half; his principal objective was to prove that he, a liberal Catholic, was more popular than Hubert Humphrey, his principal opponent. If a Catholic could win in West Virginia, 95 percent Protestant, this would finally lay to rest the ghost of Al Smith, that no one of the Catholic faith could hope to be elected president.[28] Kennedy won in West Virginia, and his supporters made certain that delegates understood the import of his victory. Kennedy was a winner, and the party would be well advised to make him its nominee. The party convention, acceding to that view, remained the powerful institution it had been for more than a century, nominating someone principally because it felt confident he would be victorious in November.

This was almost the last occasion when the Democrats, assembled in their quadrennial presidential nominating convention, would decide on the candidate, taking into account but feeling no compulsion to heed the message given by those who had voted in the still very limited number of primaries. Among the many political consequences of the violence outside the convention hall in Chicago that accompanied the selection of Hubert Humphrey to be the Democratic Party's candidate in 1968 was the decision taken by convention delegates to establish the Commission on Party Structure and Delegate Selection to prepare new rules to be in force by the time of the next election in 1972. That commission, chaired originally by Senator George McGovern of South Dakota, and later by Representative Donald Fraser of Minnesota, produced a report whose principal aim was to make delegate selection more democratic. By its provisions, all Democrats would be guaranteed the right to vote in state primaries, and delegates would be required to identify with a single candidate. Once elected as delegates, they would be legally bound to support the candidate in whose name they had competed in the primary. To make the delegate slates more representative, quotas were set as to age, race, and gender of those permitted to offer themselves, and no state party would be allowed to ignore these guidelines.[29] The changes wrought by the McGovern Commission proved immensely important. While only 3 percent of those who attended the 1968 convention as delegates were under age thirty-one, that number rose to 24 percent only four years later. More significant, perhaps, while women numbered only 13 percent of the delegates in 1968, their number escalated to 40 percent in 1972, and the black delegate contingent grew from 5.5 percent to 15 percent.[30] The 1972 primary season gave conclusive proof, if such was needed, that major changes had indeed been effected. There were fifteen Democratic state primaries in 1968; their number rose to twenty-three by 1972, and while McGovern garnered only 30 percent of the vote in these primaries, his vote greatly exceeded that of any of his opponents. McGovern conducted a one-issue campaign and recruited tens of thousands of college and university students to help spread the message about the evils of the Vietnam War.[31]

In 1972, fifteen Democrats offered themselves as presidential candidates, including Senators Edmund Muskie of Maine, Hubert Humphrey of Minnesota, Henry Jackson of Washington, and George McGovern of South Dakota, with Governor George Wallace of Alabama returning to the Democratic Party fold and Mayor John Lindsay of New York abandoning his earlier Republican Party allegiance to present himself as a Democrat. Muskie seemed the early favorite—public opinion polls suggested he would do extremely well in a presidential battle with Nixon—but his disappointing showing in the first of the primaries, in New Hampshire on March 7, receiving only 46.7 percent of the vote, shattered that illusion. If he could do no better in a state thought to be so much like his own, what hope could he have in other regions of the country?[32] McGovern surprised everyone by receiving 37.2 percent of the New Hampshire vote, a wholly unexpected result, and moved overnight from being virtually ignored by the media to become the political personality to watch. When Wallace, in Florida, a week later, made an equally impressive showing, with Jackson, Muskie, and Lindsay all doing badly, the race narrowed immediately. Candidates who lost in such a critical state could not expect to redeem their fortunes, not least because their financial supporters were unlikely to make new contributions to what the media represented as a lost cause. The race narrowed to three; Wallace, McGovern, and Humphrey. When on April 4, McGovern in Wisconsin emerged with 30 percent of the vote, Wallace with 22 percent, and Humphrey with only 21 percent, the so-called election pundits seemed mystified. How could Humphrey do so badly in a state that so closely resembled his own Minnesota? More important, how could a Southern racist fare so well in a liberal state famed for its tolerance, boasting a social reform record that compared with any in the nation? What, indeed, had the Democratic Party become? Was it no longer the party of Roosevelt and Truman? The primaries were having an effect few had dared prophesy when the competition started in the snows of New Hampshire. The Humphrey defeat, particularly galling to his supporters, saw him run well behind McGovern and lose to Wallace, confounding all who imagined they knew the Midwest. Wallace's victories in the South were explicable, but his showing in incontestably liberal Democratic strongholds made many realize he had become one of a trio who might just conceivably capture the Democratic Party's nomination through his primary victories. The battle between two Midwestern liberals and a Southern conservative gave proof of the political chasm that had opened in the Democratic Party, which some recognized had existed in a more attenuated form from the days of Roosevelt and Truman.[33]

While the media declared McGovern the frontrunner, the public's preferences were expected to be revealed in the next two primaries, scheduled for Michigan and Maryland. Media experts waxed eloquent in their consideration of the racing form of these three very different political steeds, but their ruminations and prophesies came to an abrupt halt when Wallace was shot and seriously wounded by a would-be assassin, determined to prevent the racist former Alabama governor from continuing his campaign for the presidency. While his wife and others in his camp insisted the fight would go on, this was a brave front that concealed a truth known to everyone: The governor, paralyzed from the waist down, was no longer a viable candidate. The California primary, scheduled for June 6, with its winner-take-all provisions, guaranteed that either McGovern or Humphrey would emerge as the party's candidate. Though McGovern beat Humphrey with a margin substantially smaller than the polls had predicted, he now commanded the delegate strength necessary to secure the nomination. The primaries had determined who the candidate would be.[34]

McGovern received his party's nomination on the first ballot, then went on to lose to Nixon in the November election by a margin of more than 17 million votes. When one considers how narrow Nixon's victory over Humphrey had been just four years earlier, this was a rout, greater even than the one the Democrats suffered in 1920 when Harding, profiting from the nation's disillusion with Wilson, gained his astonishingly large victory.[35] The primaries, in this instance, brought to the fore an articulate antiwar partisan from South Dakota who had scant appeal for the nation. Never in the country's history had a candidate from so inconsequential a state managed to win a presidential nomination; the bosses, professionals who knew their constituents, would never have consented to nominate such a candidate. They would have guessed that he would go nowhere. McGovern, familiar with the new primary election rules, and indeed largely responsible for framing them, showed his adeptness in using them to his political advantage. He taught other Democrats how to win primaries, and Jimmy Carter showed a proper respect for his skills when he acknowledged that McGovern's "intimate knowledge of the rules" and his "extraordinary organization" explained his success.[36]

Indeed, Carter's own success in winning the 1976 Democratic Party nomination and then going on to win the election must be accounted one of the more significant evidences of the transformation in the presidential selection process. When, as late as December 1974, the Gallup Poll surveyed Democratic Party voters, asking them to comment on 31 potential candidates, Carter figured not at all. Wallace led the list with 20 percent, Humphrey followed with

11 percent, trailed by Jackson with 10 percent, and Muskie and McGovern with 6 percent each. A racist led the list, and liberals of various hues followed, senators all, who collectively commanded only a third of the opinion poll vote. In this situation, a political entrepreneur, Jimmy Carter, still governor of Georgia, who described himself as "a farmer, an engineer, a businessman, a planner, a scientist, a governor and a Christian," saw an opportunity for himself.[37] Carter, before the year was out, even before his term as governor of Georgia had ended, sent out his first letter soliciting funds, announcing his intention to offer himself as a presidential candidate in 1976.[38] While both Wallace and Jackson were raising millions, Carter started more modestly, opening an office in Atlanta with a staff of three, and making his first visits to New Hampshire and Iowa, the states scheduled to have the first primaries. When Gallup polled the Democrats again in April 1975, less than a year before these primaries, Edward Kennedy, despite the Chappaquiddik disaster, led the list with 36 percent, Wallace followed with 15 percent, Humphrey with 9 percent, Jackson with 6 percent, and Muskie with 4 percent. With no one holding a commanding lead, Terry Sanford and Milton Shapp, governors of North Carolina and Pennsylvania, Lloyd Bentsen and Birch Bayh, senators from Texas and Idaho, and Stewart Udall, congressman from Utah, all thought to enter the race. With so many contenders, and none in obvious ascent, Carter pursued the McGovern strategy that became standard for all Democrats after 1976: declaring his presidential intentions early, giving special attention to the early primaries in New Hampshire and Iowa, knowing his performances there would be carefully observed by the media, and that their judgment would be influential in determining whether his candidacy survived or fell to the ground. For a candidate to have any hope of success, entering many primaries became essential. The Kennedy strategy in 1960 would never again succeed: The primaries were now the sole route to the nomination, and everyone accepted this new fact of American political life.

The Carter success in securing the nomination and ultimately the presidency diverted attention from another campaign, less successful but ultimately more important, waged by Ronald Reagan. The aging actor who made a new career for himself as a radio celebrity after leaving his eight-year stint as governor of California, aspired to the presidency but recognized his only hope of ousting the incumbent president—denying Ford the Republican Party nomination—was to enter many primaries and defeat him in a good number. Following the tradition set by Roosevelt in 1912 when he challenged Taft, but at a time when the primaries had become more numerous and significant, Reagan represented himself not as a conservative, certainly not as a politician, but as a constitutionalist determined to restore the country to its former greatness. When it became apparent, despite primary victories achieved through a vigorous campaign conducted against the president and his détente policies, that he lacked the votes in the Republican National Convention to defeat Ford, he withdrew, confident the Democrats would win the election, that his day would come in 1980. He guessed correctly; Ford lost the 1976 election, and Reagan led the list of eligible Republicans four years later, experiencing little difficulty in fending off George Bush, his one serious opponent, who for a moment only, winning the primary in Iowa, seemed formidable.

By the late 1970s, the political party convention system, as described by Bryce, had ceased to exist. Just as the primaries assumed a critical importance only after many decades, so, also, political fundraising, relatively modest in the first half of the century, took on wholly new dimensions following the Eisenhower presidency. Yet all histories of the subject must open with a consideration of McKinley's 1896 battle with Bryan, the Democrat many Republicans considered a threat to the economic system that had given the country its unprecedented post–Civil War prosperity. Marcus Hanna, the Ohio politician, McKinley's principal adviser and advocate, organized the financial campaign that gave McKinley some $7 million, a figure whose equivalent would not be reached again until 1936 when Roosevelt ran for his second White House term.[39] Hanna raised unprecedented sums—the equivalent of more than $150 million in twenty-first-century terms—because wealthy Republicans, genuinely frightened by the prospect of a Bryan victory, rallied to his call for help.

Hanna, very wealthy, concerned to help his closest Ohio friend, McKinley, contributed nearly $100,000 of his own money to the campaign he organized, expecting that others, alerted to the potential dangers of Bryan's program, would be equally generous. Given what he conceived to be the political interests of business, Hanna looked not only for large contributions from individuals but also from institutions, including banks he proposed to assess at one quarter of 1 percent of their capital, with other businesses contributing what they could to protect themselves against the Democrat who, if elected, would destroy them. Fear generated the exceptionally large funds collected for the McKinley campaign, making it possible for him to win easily against an accomplished popular orator who traveled more than 18,000 miles, making some 600 speeches in twenty-seven states.[40]

Hanna's political invention, raising corporate money to guarantee Republican success, though modestly experimented with earlier, became the preferred Republican method for raising substantial amounts to sustain a national campaign.[41] The Democrats, with their more populist ideology, unable to tap these same corporate sources, sought comparable funds elsewhere but were not equally successful during the early decades of the century. Because both parties relied on contributions from rich individuals, the Democrats, denied access to corporate wealth, became especially dependent on individuals who sympathized with their policies, men like August Belmont, father and son.[42] Their contributions, though substantial, never equaled those the Republicans enjoyed from their much larger stable of wealthy individual contributors that included, among others, John Jacob Astor, Jay Gould, and John B. Wanamaker.[43]

Because the Republicans were more successful in raising significant sums, Bryan supporters, very early, condemned all such solicitation as a new form of political corruption and began agitating in state legislatures to seek to control campaign expenditure. Though individual states, including several friendly to Bryan, began to pass restrictive legislation in the late 1890s, not till 1907 did the federal government bestir itself to pass a bill that prohibited the kinds of contributions Hanna had made popular. The Tillman Act made it illegal for federally chartered banks and corporations to contribute to political campaigns, but the law, lacking adequate enforcement mechanisms, proved largely ineffectual.[44] Given the importance of the primaries in the 1912 election, it is significant that the sums raised and spent by the leading candidates, in comparison with what became common decades later, were almost derisory. Roosevelt spent the most, $611,118, before the convention that rejected him; Taft spent $499,527. Democrats, less affluent, helped Wilson with a mere $219,104 in his campaign to win the nomination.[45]

While election expenses did not become prohibitively high, Congress, largely as a result of the scandal produced by the Teapot Dome revelations, passed the Corrupt Practices Act in 1925, the first moderately successful federal effort to control political campaign contributions.[46] The Teapot Dome investigations revealed that Harry Sinclair, the oil millionaire, had made substantial political contributions in nonelection years, and while these were not illegal under existing legislation, they were kept secret for obvious reasons—if revealed, they would provoke adverse publicity. The new legislation required disclosure whenever a contribution was made, and revised regulations were introduced to control the funds that might be made available to candidates in both Senate and House elections.[47] Until that time, the agitation for campaign contribution reform came principally from Democrats, anxious to prohibit or control the excessively large gifts made by well-to-do individuals to benefit the Republican Party. Beginning in 1939, the effort to control election expenditure came as much from Republicans and Southern Democrats concerned to staunch the funds pouring into the coffers of those sympathetic to Roosevelt's New Deal as it did from those traditionally interested in such legislation.[48] The Hatch Act, passed in 1939, banned all government employees from making political party contributions, rumors having long circulated that federal employees were being solicited to make contributions to support Roosevelt and other New Deal advocates.[49] In 1940 the Hatch Act was amended, making it illegal for federal contractors to make political contributions and for those employed by state agencies wholly or partially funded by the federal government to do so.[50] Because the trade unions, an increasingly important source of Democratic Party support, contributed significantly to the president's reelection campaign in

1936, Republicans in Congress began to agitate to control or outlaw such obviously politically inspired trade union support. Given the Republican weakness in Congress, such legislation could pass only if a sufficient number of Southern Democrats joined them. The Smith-Connally Act, passed in 1943, represented the triumph of that sort of coalition; it prohibited the trade unions from making contributions to political parties for the duration of the war.[51]

To circumvent this legislation, one of the major changes in political party financing came about with the creation of the first of the so-called political action committees (PACs). These committees collected money in separate accounts to support specific causes, and in the election of 1944 the CIO-PAC spent almost $2 million to support Democratic Party candidates friendly to specific legislation favored by the union.[52] In the decades that followed PACs proliferated, representing many very different kinds of economic, social, and political interest groups.[53]

As late as 1948, when Truman beat Dewey, the combined Republican and Democratic spending was the lowest since 1880; Truman never felt the need to spend his days as a fund-raiser. All this began to change in 1952, in great part because of the importance of television, an expensive medium that both parties recognized to be crucial for their political purposes. Advertising expenses escalated greatly in the 1960s, and unprecedented amounts had to be raised for successful presidential campaigns.[54] Voices were heard, even before Watergate, calling for some sort of federal legislative control of such solicitation. While individual candidates, as different as Barry Goldwater in 1964 and George McGovern in 1972, raised substantial amounts from small donors impressed by their messages, such contributions could never sustain a political campaign, certainly none that entailed both primary and presidential election expenses. The large donors remained the important ones, and they, together with the growing number of political action committees, provided the funding that candidates for both the presidency and Congress relied on. When one considers that W. Clement Stone, a Chicago insurance tycoon and his wife—scarcely household names at any time—gave some $2.8 million in 1968 to support Nixon's presidential election bid, this suggests the magnitude of the explosion in campaign spending that followed in the years after Eisenhower departed the White House.[55] These vast sums, obviously affecting the election campaigns, led to renewed demands both in and out of Congress for legislation to stem a process that appeared to be threatening new political corruption.

In 1966 Johnson had asked Congress to tighten the control of contributions, relating especially to their disclosure, and in 1968 the Twentieth Century Fund, a research institution that habitually selected critical issues for its widely disseminated studies, circulated the first report of its Committee on Campaign Costs in the Electronic Age. Two years later, in 1970, it published an even more important study, *Electing Congress: The Financial Dilemma*, the work of its Task

Force on Financing Congressional Campaigns. Both told essentially the same story: Modern electioneering costs were escalating—skyrocketing seemed not too exaggerated a term to describe the situation—and the earlier federal laws to limit contributions were obviously insufficient and unsatisfactory.[56] The demand for new regulation grew sufficiently intense for Congress in 1972 to pass the Federal Election Campaign Act, which replaced the old Federal Corrupt Practices Act, strengthening disclosure requirements and imposing severe penalties for improper disclosure. The accounting procedures for presidential elections required all monies from the opening of a campaign to its conclusion to be publicly declared. The act, passed before the events of the Watergate scandal led to the president's resignation, seemed even more necessary when the full extent of the secret contributions made to the Nixon campaigns became known. These included at least $10 million in illegal corporate gifts, including some $2 million from the dairy industry, as well as substantial individual contributions from individual donors, including $100,000 from Robert Vesco, the president's great friend.[57]

These revelations, coming at a time of growing disillusion with America's presidential excesses, justified the passage of Federal Election Campaign Act amendments in 1974 that created the first system of $1 voluntary campaign taxpayer write-offs to permit individuals to indicate on their income tax form a willingness to contribute that amount to the presidential election process. The other major innovation allowed presidential candidates to claim matching funds from the federal treasury once they had received $5,000 in contributions of $250 or less in each of twenty states. Clearly, the congressional intent was to make candidates less dependent on large contributions, legal or illegal, that Nixon had relied on.[58] These amendments, almost immediately challenged in court by several plaintiffs, including Senator James Buckley of New York, the American Civil Liberties Union, and the Libertarian Party, led the Supreme Court in *Buckley v. Valeo* to declare certain provisions of the law unconstitutional. The Supreme Court, in effect, denied the legality of provisions that imposed restrictions on total spending but also those that controlled candidate expenditure from their personal resources. The legislation, as amended and limited by the ruling of the Supreme Court, concerned with protecting freedom of speech, remains in effect today.[59]

While pressure has continued for further reform, most recently from Senator John McCain, few important changes have been made. Political campaign costs continue to soar, and this has given an advantage to incumbent members both in the Senate and the House, now regularly reelected with ease.[60] Contenders, considering whether to launch a campaign to dislodge incumbents, have been deterred, knowing the enormous amounts they would have to raise. The remark attributed to Will Rogers in 1931 seems more appropriate today than ever; "politics," he said in that seemingly innocent day, "has got so expensive that it takes lots of money to even get beat with."[61] For those who have no intention to be beaten, it is well to remember that George W. Bush spent almost $200 million to secure the presidency in 2000 and that Al Gore, hoping for the same prize, spent more than $130 million, sums that would have been inconceivable in post-World War II dollar equivalents in the time of Truman or Eisenhower.[62]

The efforts to control campaign expenditure went on in the last decade of the twentieth century, principally through the efforts of Senators John McCain and Russell Feingold in the Senate and Christopher Shays and Marty Meehan in the House of Representatives. The bills they introduced were never accepted, suggesting that the men and women already members of Congress felt no great dissatisfaction with the system that prevailed, but also that public opinion did not find the system as offensive or corrupting as those who advocated reform chose to believe.[63] Candidates for office hustled for funds, thinking it natural to do so, seeing it in no way unseemly, one of the many new requirements for those seeking election to public office. Made more confident by the *Buckley v. Valeo* Supreme Court decision that they were doing nothing more than exercising their First Amendment rights, seeking money not for their own private benefit but only to enlighten a public that required to be educated about pressing public issues, they saw it as not only a legitimate political obligation but also as an essential educational service.

The United States late in the twentieth century lived with the illusion that it had instituted a presidential primary system that gave power to the people, the only legitimate democratic sovereign. Critics, gazing at the political entrepreneurs who learned how to exploit the new methods of selection, recognized the growing importance of the media in American presidential politics, but also the influence of those prepared to contribute substantial sums to the campaigns of those they imagined might in one way or other recompense them for their contributions. Though no one recommended a return to the old-style convention system, with its smoke-filled rooms and deals made by powerful bosses and state politicians, it was not at all obvious that a system that allowed delegates to nominate men as different as Wilson, Roosevelt, Eisenhower, and Kennedy was clearly inferior to the primary system that brought men like Carter, Reagan, Clinton, and the Bushes to the White House.

THE PRESIDENTS

CHAPTER 4

To Be a King

THEODORE ROOSEVELT LOVED a good story, none more than those he himself told. His master tale was of himself, how through willpower alone he conquered illness and physical weakness and became the self-assured individual who very early impressed others with his vigor and determination. None of the tale was patently false, but it gave only a very partial portrait of a man, seemingly self-confident and bold, who kept secrets about himself he never revealed or shared. His hearty laughter concealed an inner uncertainty he knew it was hazardous to show. In a world where the "bitch Goddess" success was worshipped, failure was something to be hidden, dependence something to be denied. If Roosevelt perpetually dissembled, telling less about himself than those who remarked only on his juvenile antics and habits realized, mistaking him for an overgrown child, this was his most effective defense against those who might seek to learn more about the man he wished others to know only through his heroic self-representations of himself.

The son of a physically strong father and a somewhat delicate and sickly mother, the child of mid-nineteenth-century New York social privilege, the Roosevelts qualified as Old Money, able to claim seventeenth-century American origins.[1] Roosevelt could never associate his father with so crass a commodity as money. He was the best man he ever knew, "strong, courageous, tender and unselfish, intolerant of cruelty, idleness, cowardice, or untruthfulness, who taught his children the virtues of clean living," embodying all the qualities the young Theodore sought to emulate.[2] His father's failure to serve in the military during the Civil War, avoiding the draft by hiring another to take his place, was a detail Roosevelt left unmentioned. Equally important details about his mother, recalled as "a sweet, gracious beautiful Southern woman, a delightful companion, and beloved by everybody," made no mention of her hypochondria. Roosevelt saw himself as the heir of Northern vitality and Southern gentility, the legatee of a family that prized love and esteemed loyalty.[3] Aware that there was much amiss in late-nineteenth-century America,

Roosevelt declared very early his intention to redeem a political society that had become politically corrupt. Unlike Henry Cabot Lodge, his closest friend and confidante who lived in almost perpetual mourning for the lost glories of Boston, once the Athens of America, Roosevelt harbored no comparable feelings for an older New York. A romantic, he reserved his passion for the vigorous and untamed American West he came to know as an adult.[4]

Entering politics as a very young man in 1881, a recent graduate of Harvard College, he had lived until that time in a socially segregated male society that separated the sons of the wealthy and the wellborn from more recent arrivals. Roosevelt, at Harvard, belonged to the most exclusive undergraduate social club, the Porcellian, but spent much of his time in neighboring Brookline courting the young lady who became his first wife. While others of his social standing generally expected to follow their fathers into banking or law, seeing no need to excel in scholarly pursuits, Roosevelt, a voracious reader, elected to write an undergraduate thesis and chose the War of 1812 as his subject. It gave him his first familiarity with the Navy, a service he found endlessly fascinating. While the thesis showed his concern to master the technical details of the naval strategy that allowed the Americans to emerge victorious in their war with Great Britain, it provided him the opportunity also to express political views he retained for the rest of his life. Expressing little regard for Thomas Jefferson, who in his view had failed to prepare the country for the war that endangered the life of the infant republic, he reserved his praise for Alexander Hamilton, the advocate of a strong central government.[5] As for Andrew Jackson, whose military victory over the British at New Orleans in no way affected the war's outcome, Roosevelt scarcely considered him.[6]

Roosevelt's chosen profession—if it could be so dignified—was politics, not the vocation his Harvard classmates ever considered for themselves. When he competed for a seat in the New York State Assembly, to represent the wealthiest ward in the city, men he described as belonging to "the clubs of social pretension," mostly successful lawyers and businessmen, were unable to fathom his decision. Politics, they believed, was a low pursuit, with the party organizations no longer controlled by gentlemen but by "saloon-keepers, horse-car conductors and the like."[7] Roosevelt recalled telling those who questioned his choice "that if this were so it merely meant that the people I knew did not belong to the governing class, and that the other people did—and that I intended to be one of the governing class."[8] In Roosevelt's vivid imagination, he entered politics to bring men like himself back into public life, to redeem a calling that had once appealed to the best-educated and most public-minded citizens. Roosevelt, distrustful of the Democratic Party and contemptuous of Tammany Hall, the party's political machine in New York City, hoped to make his way in Albany, the state capital, by denouncing both. Others might think him a Republican dandy, a fop whose exaggerated speech and dress provoked laughter more than envy, but he saw himself as a man with a mission to root out political corruption. His years in the assembly confirmed his low opinion of Democrats and gave him no decidedly higher opinion of his Republican peers. Roosevelt recognized very early, both in Cambridge and in Albany, that only in very superficial ways did he resemble his contemporaries.[9]

Republicans in 1886, frightened by the prospect of Henry George, the radical single-tax advocate, succeeding in his campaign to become mayor of New York City, persuaded the young Roosevelt to enter the race against him.[10] Roosevelt's reputation in Albany as feisty, witty, and clean led some to believe he would be a formidable opponent, mocking George for his outlandish ideas, and denouncing Abram Hewitt, the Democratic Party's nominee, as the creature of Tammany Hall.[11] Hewitt, a wealthy and urbane Democrat, scarcely a minion of Tammany Hall, won the race easily, and Roosevelt came in a distant third, almost 30,000 votes behind Hewitt and more than 7,000 behind George. *Puck*, the humor magazine, wrote Roosevelt's political obituary, telling him he did not belong to that class of renowned young politicians, in no way resembling men like William Pitt, Alexander Hamilton, and Randolph Churchill. "You are not the timber of which Presidents are made," *Puck* declared.[12] Who had ever suggested that Roosevelt might one day be president? Two newspapers, the *Sun* in New York and the *Baltimore American,* had in fact raised that possibility before he was even constitutionally eligible for the post, a stripling of twenty-eight spoken of for an office that required candidates to be thirty-five. *Puck's* disdain reflected the disappointment it felt for someone who had initially opposed James Blaine for the Republican Party's presidential nomination in 1884, knowing he had been a corrupt Speaker of the House, but in the end accepted him and campaigned for him. Other Republicans, more faithful to their principles bolted the party and voted for Grover Cleveland, the Democrat who went on to win the election. Roosevelt cited private reasons for supporting Blaine, using code words many understood; Cleveland was said to be the father of an illegitimate child.[13] In Roosevelt's view, keeping the Democrats out of the White House justified any tactic, including those not commonly used by those who represented themselves as gentlemen, pledged to restore the politics of a more fastidious and discriminating age.[14]

Blaine lost the election, but Roosevelt told Lodge, his fellow loyalist, that their decision to support the Republican nominee had been right, "dictated by duty and unselfishness."[15] Had they bolted, he wrote Lodge, "we would have done an immense amount for ourselves." Roosevelt's capacity for self-deception was enormous; none of the bolters, the so-called mugwumps, ever achieved the success that came to those who remained loyal Republicans.[16] Separation from the political party of one's choice was suicidal, and both Roosevelt and Lodge as very young men understood this.[17] They knew also what neither cared to acknowledge—Roosevelt's political career that had started off brilliantly in 1881 was going nowhere. The election of Benjamin Harrison to the presidency in 1888 led both to hope that a major federal appointment might be in the offing, that James Blaine, appointed secretary of state and indebted to Roosevelt for campaigning in his behalf in 1884, would be prepared to help. Lodge approached Blaine, asking him to consider Roosevelt for the post of assistant secretary of state. Blaine's response, never shown to Roosevelt, who learned only that the secretary had spoken exceedingly well of him, read:

> My real trouble in regard to Mr. Roosevelt is that I fear he lacks the repose and patient endurance required in an Assistant Secretary. Mr. Roosevelt is amazingly quick in apprehension. Is there not danger that he might be too quick in execution? I do somehow fear that my sleep at Augusta or Bar Harbor would not be quite so easy and refreshing if so brilliant and aggressive a man had hold of the helm. Matters are constantly occurring which require the most careful concentration and the most stubborn inaction. Do you think that Mr. T.R.'s temperament would give guaranty of that course?[18]

Lodge, asked the same question on other occasions when he argued for a Roosevelt appointment, was generally prepared to give assurances that his friend's impetuosity would be controlled. With Blaine, he offered no such promise, realizing he would simply have to persevere in finding some other federal employ for him. President Harrison, though prepared to acknowledge Roosevelt's services during the election campaign, shared the hesitations of others who thought him too excitable. Only after considerable badgering by Lodge, recently elected to the House of Representatives, did he finally agree to appoint him a member of the Civil Service Commission. The post was a negligible one, but Roosevelt, as a longtime advocate of civil service reform, pretended it was precisely the one he craved. As someone who understood the art of self-promotion, and as an outspoken critic of the spoils system introduced half a century earlier by President Jackson, Roosevelt imagined great things might be achieved if he brought an otherwise somnolent commission to act. Roosevelt never asked himself whether the president wished this to happen, and his early decision to do battle with John Wanamaker, the postmaster general and one of the president's friends and major financial contributors to the Republican Party, showed a characteristic recklessness.[19] Neither Wanamaker nor Harrison saw any reason to accede to Roosevelt's demand that some twenty-five Baltimore postal employees, purportedly guilty of gross malfeasance, should be dismissed. Only in 1890, after the congressional elections gave the Democrats control of the House, did Roosevelt's complaints receive a sympathetic hearing.[20] President Harrison, however, had reason to wonder why he had ever gratified the young Lodge by agreeing to the appointment of his most intimate friend. While the Democrats used the political ammunition Roosevelt provided them in their 1892 presidential election campaign, no one ascribed Cleveland's decisive victory that year to the crusading efforts of an insignificant civil service commissioner who had discovered wrongdoing in the Baltimore post office.

Cleveland's decision to retain Roosevelt in his civil service post surprised those who recalled his earlier personal attacks on him. It reflected the quiet confidence Cleveland felt about a minor official who posed no threat to him and shared his concern to see the merit system prevail in federal civil service appointments.[21] Roosevelt, invited to remain in Washington in a position that gave him ample time to write and socialize, frequented an older generation of socially prominent Republican grandees whose memories went back to the Civil War and earlier. These men, beguiled by Roosevelt's youth, gregarious and boisterous manner, and intelligent and witty conversation, included Henry Adams, the grandson and great-grandson of two presidents, and John Hay, one of Lincoln's wartime secretaries, who had served in numerous diplomatic posts abroad.

In Washington, among the foreign diplomats Roosevelt came to know, none figured more prominently than his most intimate English friend, Cecil Spring Rice, who had served as best man at his second wedding in London.[22] Roosevelt moved in a capital society where politics vied with literature and history as principal intellectual entertainments.[23] An avid reader from the time he was a boy, Roosevelt devoured Alfred Mahan's book *The Influence of Sea Power upon History* when its three volumes appeared between 1890 and 1892, recognizing how much it confirmed and amplified ideas he had expressed more inchoately, and without the same wealth of learning, in his undergraduate essay on the War of 1812.[24] Mahan gave Roosevelt the empirical evidence he needed to support positions he had long advocated, emphasizing the importance of naval preeminence for any nation that aspired to be a great world power. Roosevelt's extensive travels in the West, still largely uninhabited, following on the tragic death of his first young wife in February 1884, led him to become acquainted with that region and gave him an early premonition of what the United States might one day become: a continental power linked by railroads joining new cities on the West Coast with the transformed older colonial cities in the East. The protection of the country's natural resources became an urgent matter for Roosevelt—conservation was his passion—stimulated by the recognition of how the insatiable demands of agricultural, industrial, and commercial development threatened a once-pristine continent.[25]

Because his duties as a civil service commissioner were in no sense arduous, he pursued the literary interests that had given him early recognition as a writer, exploring the Western wilderness few of his Eastern friends had any knowledge of. While he imagined the *Winning of the West*, a multivolume work, to be his magnum opus, it lacked the scholarly distinction of *The Naval War of*

1812. Still, it allowed him to voice his romantic sentiments, praising America's pioneers, "strong and simple, powerful for good and evil, swayed by gusts of stormy passion, the love of freedom rooted in their very heart's core." These men and women, courageous and hardy, scarcely resembled the effete Easterners he came increasingly to distrust and disparage. A New Yorker himself, Roosevelt refused to identify with those whose "warped, perverse, and silly morality" led them to argue for preserving the vast tracts of Western land for its original Indian settlers. In his mind, the natives' lives were "but a few degrees less meaningless, squalid, and ferocious than that of the wild beasts with whom they held joint ownership," and he insisted that only the arrival of white settlers had brought civilization to a world of virgin forests. Roosevelt celebrated what he termed "the spread of the English-speaking peoples over the world's waste spaces," and denying any racial, ethnic, or religious prejudice, felt no incongruity in declaring that it was "of incalculable importance that America, Australia, and Siberia should pass out of the hands of their red, black, and yellow aboriginal owners, and become the heritage of the dominant world races."[26] Without apology, in hyperbolic and sometimes brilliant narrative, Roosevelt sang the praises of white Americans who transformed a wilderness into a land fit for civilized men to live in. It is difficult to know what sceptical Republican intellectuals, including Henry Adams and John Hay, thought of such argument, but Adams, decades later, suggested that Roosevelt boasted "that singular primitive quality that belongs to ultimate matter—the quality that medieval theology assigned to God—he was pure act."[27]

Roosevelt's Western experiences as rancher and hunter gave him license to present himself as an all-American hero, adventurous and brave, never to be confused with the money-grubbing bankers of Wall Street, the goody-good professors of Harvard, or the politicians, craven and corrupt, who congregated around the village pump called Congress.[28] Roosevelt, aspiring to be seen as *sui generis*, was realist enough to know that membership on the Civil Service Commission was leading him nowhere. When, therefore, in May 1895, William Strong, the recently elected New York City reform mayor, a Republican businessman who had defeated the Tammany candidate, offered him a place on the New York Police Board, Roosevelt jumped at the opportunity. Strong expected the other commissioners to select Roosevelt as their president, and though that position would make him only primus inter pares, the mayor expected it would be taken as an augury of his firm intention to cleanse the city of its unsavory Tammany past.[29] Police headquarters on Mulberry Street became a Mecca for New York journalists, including Jacob Riis, a new friend who recognized Roosevelt's exceptional talents at once, happy to serve as his most devoted publicist.[30] The two men, in their late nocturnal rambles, searching for criminal activity, looking also for police sloth and corruption, became celebrated figures in a New York City melodrama. In no time at all, Roosevelt emerged as the hero of the city's tabloid press, a political reformer in fearless pursuit of virtue.

Roosevelt's exaggerated appetite for publicity, never easily sated, led him as in the past to go too far in his search for wrongdoing. Giving scarce thought to the mayor who had appointed him police commissioner, a politically inexperienced businessman, Roosevelt decided to increase his already glowing reputation by enforcing the so-called blue laws that required bars and saloons to close on the Sabbath. He knew, of course, that these regulations had been flouted for years by those who understood that the police had no interest in enforcing such antiquated social and religious controls, but he saw the opportunity to strike a blow for law and morality, reminding workingmen of their Christian obligation to join their wives and children in church on Sunday.[31] Few Irish Americans and not many German Americans, devoted to their drinking societies, welcomed this attempted regulation of their lives, and though Roosevelt knew the mayor wished him "to let up on the saloon," as he explained in a letter to Lodge, "impliedly threatening to turn me out if I refused," Roosevelt persisted in his determination to see the letter of the law obeyed. In the end, he was defeated as much by the ridicule he provoked as by the growing newspaper opposition to what many now claimed to be his authoritarian ways. As he told Lodge in a letter in December 1895, "It really seems there *must* be some fearful shortcoming on my side to account for the fact that I have not one New York City newspaper or one New York City politician on my side."[32] Roosevelt understood that only the presidential election of 1896 and the return of the Republicans to the White House could liberate him from what had become an untenable political situation.

Because it was clearly in his self-interest to help in the election campaign of William McKinley, the Republican candidate, but also because he relished the prospect of attacking William Jennings Bryan, in his mind a dangerous revolutionary, he rushed to offer his services to Marcus Hanna, the new chairman of the Republican National Committee and McKinley's most intimate political adviser. Roosevelt appreciated Bryan's strength in the West, the Midwest, and the South but believed he could be defeated even there if voters became aware of the danger he posed to the nation's prosperity and security.[33] Waging the 1896 battle for himself, McKinley, the Republican Party, and the endangered republic, he expected a political reward for his efforts. Lodge, always his friend and ally, rushed off to Canton, Ohio, soon after McKinley's decisive election victory to urge the president-elect to appoint Roosevelt assistant secretary of the Navy. Prominent Ohio Republicans, including Myron Herrick, a Hanna intimate, the Bellamy Storers of Cincinnati, major donors to the Republican Party, and William Howard Taft, a young and rising judge, were all recruited to help, along with John Hay and others, but Hanna seemed less than enthusiastic. While acknowledging that Roosevelt deserved recognition for what he had done during the campaign, he and others saw him as a dangerous jingo, unsuited to high office in the administration of President McKinley, a "man of peace." That, however, proved to be only one of the many impediments to his appointment. Tom Platt, the influential New York State Republican Party boss, actively disliked him, believing TR's crusade for righteousness in his short time as police commissioner had served only to endanger the Republican mayor, making a Tammany return to city hall more likely.[34]

When Lodge visited Platt to plead Roosevelt's cause, he received little more than a promise to consider the matter. In the end, Platt accepted him but only when Roosevelt ostentatiously withdrew his support of an old friend, Joseph Choate, who aspired to the seat in the United States Senate that Platt intended for himself.[35] That hurdle overcome, Roosevelt's candidacy risked opposition from another source, the Harvard-educated lawyer and former governor of Massachusetts, John Long, chosen by McKinley to be his secretary of the Navy. McKinley, in selecting members of his Cabinet, chose men he knew; merit, however defined, never entered into his calculations. Indeed, the most important post, secretary of state, went to John Sherman, aged and ailing, a seventy-four-year-old Ohio senator selected after William Allison, an Iowa senator, McKinley's first choice, refused him.

McKinley chose Sherman principally to create a vacancy in the Senate that Hanna, his loyal supporter, could then fill.[36] The president expected Sherman to be the nominal head of the department while William Day, the first assistant secretary, became the real power, and a career diplomat, Alvery Adee, the second assistant secretary, took up the slack. Day's habitual silences and Adee's deafness made for a strange supporting team as one diplomat recognized when he quipped: "The head of the Department knows nothing; the First Assistant says nothing; the Second Assistant hears nothing."[37] While none of McKinley's appointees claimed knowledge of foreign or naval policy to compare with Roosevelt's, it was impossible for Lodge to use this argument in pleading for his appointment. Only the suggestion that it was the single favor he would ask might move the president. McKinley had known Lodge when both sat in the House of Representatives, respected him for his intelligence, and knew the newly elected senator from Massachusetts could be an invaluable ally, but as late as the day of the president's inaugural, no appointment had been made, and Roosevelt was desperate.[38]

In a final appeal to Lodge to intercede with Long, Roosevelt made the most explicit promise of unconditional loyalty to the secretary. In unctuous and uncharacteristic language, he wrote: "I want him [Long] to understand that. . . I shall stay at Washington, hot weather or any other weather, whenever he wants me to stay there, and go wherever he sends me, and my aim should be solely to make his administration a success."[39] Roosevelt sent the message that Lodge could pass on to the secretary, confident it would satisfy him. Long, an aging

New Englander who cared little for the heat of Washington summers and wished only to be free during the tropical, humid months to enjoy his seaside retreat on Cape Cod in Hingham, Massachusetts, welcomed the offer. Roosevelt's no less crucial pledge—to be concerned only with the secretary's success and accept to be a loyal subordinate—gave him the position he craved. The elevation could not have come at a better time for Roosevelt. Though he and his admirers never acknowledged the depth of his despair in his final months as police commissioner, and greatly exaggerated what he achieved in that post, as they did in celebrating his service as a civil service commissioner, he had in fact been marking time for almost a decade, chafing at his failure to climb the political ladder.

Roosevelt's return to the capital coincided with a moment when foreign affairs were becoming increasingly critical, and both he and Lodge knew that their command of U.S. political, military, naval, and diplomatic history greatly exceeded that of all others in the administration and in Congress. Roosevelt's pledge to be discreet collapsed within seven weeks of his appointment. Asked to speak at the Naval War College in Newport, Rhode Island, he chose as his text George Washington's famous aphorism, "to be prepared for war is the most effectual means to promote peace," and praised war in terms that could not fail to offend the secretary. If, as he claimed, "all the great masterful races have been fighting races," with "cowardice in a race as in an individual. . . the unpardonable sin," his assertion that "no triumph of peace is quite so great as the supreme triumphs of war" could only rouse the hackles of those more pacifically inclined. So, also, his assertion that "diplomacy is utterly useless where there is no force behind it," and that "the diplomat is the servant, not the master of the soldier," were views anathema to Long.[40] While some might agree with Roosevelt that "there are many higher things in this life than the soft and easy enjoyment of material comfort," not everyone would proceed from that to argue that "it is through strife, or the readiness for strife, that a nation must win greatness." Roosevelt, though prepared to praise teachers, scientists, writers, and artists, portraying them as vital members of a civilized society, saw no incongruity in saying also that "there are educated men in whom education merely serves to soften the fiber."[41] Roosevelt, within weeks of his appointment, appeared to be the jingo his enemies had warned against.

Long, unprepared for the blast and unhappy about it, could do nothing to silence the assistant secretary. Scheduled to depart for a two-week vacation, prior to taking his much longer summer holiday, he made clear to Roosevelt that he "didn't like the address" and was "only lukewarm about building up the Navy," words Roosevelt used in describing the secretary's reaction to Mahan, his principal naval mentor.[42] The favorable comment on the speech in the *Washington Post* and the New York *Sun*, however, more than compensated for what was in effect an exceedingly mild rebuke. During Long's absence, Roosevelt served as acting secretary, and while he could do nothing to realize his hopes for a larger Navy, the president's decision to send a treaty annexing Hawaii to the Senate encouraged him to believe that the kinds of foreign policy objectives he and Lodge advocated might soon be realized.

When the Japanese protested the annexation, Roosevelt dismissed their argument with words he expected to resonate with the public. "The United States," he said, in a widely reported speech, "is not in a position which requires her to ask Japan, or any other foreign Power, what territory it shall or shall not acquire." Long, according to Roosevelt in a letter sent to Lodge, "gave me as heavy a wigging as his invaluable courtesy and kindness would permit," but such rebukes counted for little. In any case, these issues receded before another that quickly came to command the attention not only of Roosevelt but of the whole of the country's press. Revolt in Cuba against Spanish rule, long brewing, had reignited in 1897 following the dispatch of some 150,000 troops to the island, under the command of General Valeriano Weyler, christened "Butcher" Weyler by the New York City tabloid press. Weyler introduced detention camps on the island and incarcerated hundreds of thousands of Cuban peasants to prevent their helping revolutionaries with food, shelter, and recruits; many were reported to be dying of starvation or disease. The leading New York newspapers, including Hearst's *Journal,* Pulitzer's *World,* and Dana's *Sun,* published gruesome accounts of Spain's unspeakable barbarism.[43] Roosevelt, as early as August 1897, wrote Lodge of the need to take "firm action on behalf of the wretched Cubans," and in an even more explicit letter to Lieutenant Commander W.W. Kimball, author of the Navy's original war plan, recommended war against Spain in the name of humanity, but also to give the American people something to think about other than material gain.[44]

Roosevelt, months before rioting in Havana led the president to send the battleship *Maine* to Cuba as "an act of friendly courtesy," described what he conceived to be an appropriate American naval and military response to cope with the growing disorder on the island. Though his recommendations closely resembled proposals eventually adopted by the government, Roosevelt never went so far as to claim authorship of the military and naval strategies eventually decided on. The Cuban situation became grave with the sinking of the *Maine* on February 16, 1898, following an explosion that killed two officers and 264 others. Citizens waited impatiently to learn what the president's court of inquiry decided were the causes of the explosion. During this period, Roosevelt worked frantically to insist that only war with Spain offered a solution to the Cuban problem.[45] When the results of the inquiry, given to Congress on March 28, and made public almost immediately, attributed the *Maine* disaster to a submarine mine, war became inevitable. "Remember the Maine!" became the universal war cry, and Roosevelt fretted and complained that decisions were not being taken quickly enough to punish the Spanish aggressions.[46] His letters of the period reveal an almost hysterical fear that the president, "resolute to have peace at any price," might in the end refuse to wage war. If, as he believed, most members of Congress favored war, their opinion had to be set against the distressing fact, as Roosevelt saw it, that "the two biggest leaders, the President and the Speaker," both very powerful, were "almost crazy in their eagerness for peace, and would make almost any sacrifice to get peace."

Roosevelt wrote to Bryce of his fear that the "nation will not do its duty, chasing Spain from the new world, ending its policy of repression, reminiscent of the worst days of Alva and Torquemada."[47] For bankers, lawyers, and merchants who petitioned Lodge to vote against war, Roosevelt expressed only contempt, mincing no words in a message to a prominent New York corporate lawyer, Elihu Root, soon to be appointed secretary of war.[48] In an even more impassioned letter to Paul Dana, editor of the *Sun,* he accepted that while it was impossible "to analyse with perfect accuracy all of one's motives," and caring not to sound like a prig, he insisted that while he had no expectation of gaining military glory out of the war he felt it his duty to join in the fight. As he explained, "For two years I have consistently preached the doctrine of a resolute foreign policy, and readiness to accept the arbitrament of the sword if necessary; and I have always intended to act up to my preaching if the occasion arose. Now the occasion has arisen, and I ought to meet it." While the nation needed no encouragement to make money, he wrote, the example of men prepared to risk their lives in a "righteous" war told him that "although I have as much a dislike of death as anyone could have, and take as keen an enjoyment in life," even the claims of his family, a wife and six children, would never dissuade him from going to Cuba.[49]

The next hundred days were the most momentous in Roosevelt's life, giving him the fame he had long sought, and ultimately making him president of the United States. Never again as dependent on Lodge as he had been, knowing better than to consult his wife, he formed a volunteer cavalry regiment with Leonard Wood, an old friend serving as colonel, and himself as second in command with the rank of lieutenant colonel. In a military saga constantly repeated, Roosevelt led a cavalry charge up San Juan Hill outside Santiago, Cuba's second city, that made him the country's unrivalled war hero. Acquiring the glory he claimed to disdain, guaranteed by a patriotic and bellicose press that put all military units other than the Rough Riders in the shade, he expressed dismay with those in the effete East who dubbed the fighting the unnecessary war and complained of the country's imperialist expansion into the Caribbean and the Pacific.[50]

The Spanish-American War made Roosevelt governor of New York and led him ultimately to the vice presidency and then to the White House. Others might cavil, but Roosevelt knew he had proved himself a man of courage and principle who had taken risks, faithful to his creed, a belief in the nation as he imagined Lincoln had defined it.

Cecil Spring Rice, Roosevelt's oldest English friend, received a letter at once candid and disingenuous following his election as governor. Roosevelt wrote:

> I have played it in bull luck this summer. First, to get into the war; then to get out of it; then to get elected. I have worked hard all my life, and have not been particularly lucky, but this summer I *was* lucky, and I am enjoying it to the full. I am more than contented to be Governor of New York, and shall not care if I never hold another office; and I am very proud of my regiment, which was really a noteworthy volunteer organization.[51]

To James Bryce, in a letter written the same day, he indicated that the Republicans had nominated him because he was "straight," that he had made no promises to the "Machine," that "the professional Independents, like Carl Schurz, Godkin, Parkhurst, and the idiot variety of 'Goo-Goos'" opposed him because "they objected to my being for the war with Spain."[52] The electoral contest had been "close," he wrote, and the task ahead would be "hard," but since he did "not think that there is much in the way of constructive legislation to be done; at least, I do not see much that is needed," honest administration and a few changes in the state's civil service laws and enforcement of factory legislation would be his major concerns.[53] If there were no other challenges, why should Roosevelt have sought the governorship? Did he really believe that Albany represented the summit of his political ambitions?

Roosevelt's correspondence over the next two years is revealing for its constant preoccupation with whether he ought to seek the vice presidency in 1900, as Lodge and other of his friends insisted he do.[54] Second to this, and not wholly surprising, was his constant concern with foreign affairs, especially U.S. relations with Great Britain and Russia. For someone who purportedly had reached the summit of his ambition with his election as governor, these were unconventional interests. The Boer War fascinated him, as did reports out of Russia, a nation that in his view needed to "grow up."[55] While expressing the hope that the Russians would carry their "Slav civilization" to their most distant domains in Asia, he insisted they not seek to extend their influence beyond those frontiers.[56]

These were not the kinds of issues governors habitually concerned themselves with, nor did others write letters resembling the one he sent his old Navy friend, Lieutenant Commander William Kimball, where he said:

> I have always regarded Germany while the present Kaiser lives as our most probable serious opponent, and we are capable of such infinite folly in this country that we may not prepare as we should. I do hope that neither the na-

tion nor the navy accepts the war with Spain as anything but a warning. If we permit ourselves to relax in our exertions to bring the navy higher and higher, and if we do not build up the army and the forts, we should have a terrible time against Germany.[57]

If instead of Spaniards and Filipinos the Americans had been required to act against foes like the Boers, he wrote, "we should have eaten just such bitter bread as the English are now eating."[58] Roosevelt required an enemy to justify the large naval and military expenditures he deemed necessary, but why these issues should figure for someone concerned only with being a governor in Albany, Roosevelt never found it necessary to say.

What secrets, then, did Roosevelt keep that others only occasionally divined? All knew him to be ambitious, but only a few saw him as more cautious and, indeed, more fearful than he ever let on, and not only about his ability to win elections. His exaggerated preoccupation with masculinity, thought to be characteristic of his day, hid as much as it revealed about someone who wished to be seen as open, but was in fact more secretive, crafty, and politically cunning than many realized. An intellectual, more distinguished than many, he preferred to be seen as a warrior; a New Yorker who pretended to belong to the West, he was a boon companion to all prepared to venture with him into those vast unconquered spaces. His contempt for money, though somewhat exaggerated, reflected a sincere disdain for those who cared only for material things; Wall Street bankers could never be his heroes. A passionate political partisan, he used the Republican Party to advance himself, knowing there was no other route to the White House. A skilled mythmaker, he lauded the Lincoln accomplishment in preserving the Union, arguing that only the Republican Party could be trusted to carry the nation forward to a destiny greater than any it had ever known. Though his experience of office till the time he became assistant secretary of the Navy and governor had been inconsequential, he never allowed others to know that.

Self-advertisement became his distinguishing trait; it showed him a vain but creative politician who believed himself the intellectual equal of anyone who had preceded him in the White House. How he came to use his reputation as the hero of the Spanish-American War and how the assassination of William McKinley brought him to the presidency has already been told—instances of great good fortune—but one essential detail needs to be added. As in his earlier, less exalted posts, Roosevelt showed little interest in sharing power; he intended to be primus, knowing there was no one equal to him. He had learned, however, to be more cautious, to avoid making the kinds of mistakes that had so compromised his career as civil service commissioner and police commissioner. The bold president was also the cunning politician who had learned the necessity of compromise.

His very first presidential acts were revealing; at his Buffalo swearing-in, he insisted that some two dozen journalists be admitted to witness the ceremony. The man who knew how much his political career had been made by journalistic accounts of his heroic San Juan Hill exploits wanted the public fully informed about the simple but dignified ceremony that made him the twenty-sixth president of the United States. Barely installed in the White House, he summoned the managers of the three principal wire services, seated them around the Cabinet table, and told them that while he proposed to be accessible to them, he would expect discretion in what they reported. If any dared publish material offered on a confidential basis, the president would deny the story, "I'll say you are a damned liar," and the offending individual would never again enjoy access to him; his newspaper or press agency would suffer the same exclusion.[59] In effect, Roosevelt co-opted the press, acknowledged he would lie to protect himself, and made it clear he would permit reports only of those things he wished the public to know.

Roosevelt believed the bargain would be advantageous to both parties; if newspaper reporters cooperated, their reward would be the privilege of access to him. In the next seven and a half years, Roosevelt divided the press into two groups—insiders and outsiders—the latter a company of those who "betrayed" him—the term was his—who showed insufficient appreciation for the privileges granted them. Dubbed members of the Ananias Club by a president familiar with his New Testament, they would suffer the fate of the liar who fell dead when rebuked by Saint Peter for his falsehood.[60]

Because many in the Republican Party and the country thought Roosevelt dangerous and unreliable, distrusting him for his bellicosity, it was important that he prove himself a fit heir to the cautious, recently martyred McKinley. During his first months in office, he showed a reticence that even his most faithful friends were unprepared for. In retaining McKinley's Cabinet, but even more in seeking the views of powerful members of Congress on the State of the Union message he proposed to send, accepting their emendations and recommendations, he sought to prove himself a tamed politician, not the starry-eyed reformer or jingo his enemies traditionally denounced. Through the autumn and early winter of 1901–1902 Roosevelt enjoyed a political honeymoon that ended abruptly, however, as he knew it would, when late on February 19, 1902, his attorney general, Philander Knox, announced the government's intention to prosecute J.P. Morgan's Northern Securities Company for violations of the Sherman Anti-Trust Act.[61] The announcement, a shock to Roosevelt's Cabinet, with whom he never discussed the matter, but also to Morgan and the public, came after the stock markets had closed for the day. Roosevelt had no intention of creating panic on Wall Street. The president knew better than to discuss the matter with his secretary of war, Elihu Root, his most confidential Cabinet colleague, who would certainly have warned him against the move. Still, his decision to take on the world's most powerful capitalist suggested he knew the risks he was taking but also the political benefits he hoped to realize. The decision was a bombshell: Powerful capitalists, respected for their influence in Congress, were not habitually taken on by presidents. Those most surprised by his apparent recklessness had failed to take a proper measure of the man. Roosevelt intended to assert a truth few till that day dared believe: The president of the United States was a more powerful figure than the world's leading banker. More than that, Roosevelt expected the circulation-hungry press to advertise his courage, to remind their readers that this was not just another Republican president governing in the tradition set by his Ohio predecessor.

Had Roosevelt forgotten that Morgan had contributed $10,000 to his gubernatorial race in 1898, that he had made the contribution through Platt, a still powerful New York state boss and member of the Senate? Or did others pay insufficient attention to what Roosevelt had preached as governor when he questioned the alliance between party bosses and big business, what had begun to be described as America's invisible government? To take action against Northern Securities, the recently formed combination of the three major railroads in the Northwest—the Northern Pacific, the Great Northern, and the Burlington—was to seek the dissolution of the largest holding company ever established.[62] To prosecute the case as a combination in restraint of trade under the terms of the Sherman Anti-Trust Act was to do what McKinley would never have contemplated. While Roosevelt had no quarrel with Morgan's plans for industrial consolidation or for his hopes of U.S. domination of world markets, he acted to assert unmistakably the powers of the presidency, to express his dismay with what he conceived to be the arrogance of big business, the uncontrolled economic power. He would never have considered taking such action had he not believed it would profit him politically.

The Northern Securities case, tailor-made for someone of Roosevelt's political ambitions, involved celebrities presented by the Justice Department as villains. They included James Hill, famous for having built the only transcontinental railroad without substantial federal subsidies, and J.P. Morgan, renowned for his repeated interventions to bolster the stock market in times of financial adversity. These men and others like them, America's capitalist titans, imagined they were responsible for having created the nation's post–Civil War prosperity. Industrial and commercial buccaneers, they had challenged successfully an older established European dominance. Morgan visited the president almost immediately after the surprise announcement, accompanied by two of the Senate's most influential Republicans, Marcus Hanna and Chauncey Depew, to ask why no warning had been given of the government's intention to take action against Northern Securities. In Roosevelt's account of the meeting, Morgan reportedly said: "If we have done anything wrong, send your man

[Knox] to my man [Stetson] and they can fix it up." That could not be done, the president replied, and his attorney general chimed in, saying, "We don't want to fix it up; we want to stop it."[63] Whatever the political risk, Roosevelt deemed it negligible; the public would approve action taken against a foul monopoly, a trust created to limit competition, established by arrogant and ambitious men never previously held to account. Very early in his presidency, Roosevelt looked ahead to 1904, the year when he would seek reelection, knowing that no previous accidental president had ever succeeded in securing a second term. That became his prime objective, indeed his obsession. He expected the Northern Securities case to figure prominently in his claim to be a president who refused to defer to financial oligarchs able to hire large and expensive teams of lawyers to defend themselves against government attorneys whose only concern was to defend the public interest.

In a contest between the president and the richest man in America, the latter was bound to lose. Some such idea lurked in Roosevelt's mind, and he acted on it. When the United States Supreme Court announced its five-to-four decision on March 14, 1904, the president rejoiced in his judicial victory but knew it to be less than what he had hoped for. Oliver Wendell Holmes Jr., the justice the president had appointed in July 1902, largely on Lodge's recommendation, had voted in the minority, and this offended Roosevelt, made more galling by the brilliance of Holmes's soon-to-be-celebrated minority opinion. Roosevelt, Lodge, and Holmes, prominent Republicans and fellow members of Porcellian, all ardent admirers of Lincoln, the man of the people, were thought to be political allies. It was unthinkable that Holmes would wish to humiliate—Roosevelt preferred the word *betray*—those who had pressed for his appointment to the Court. Yet in a masterly dissent whose preamble gained greater attention than anything in the majority opinion, Holmes showed his independence of the two politicians who had elevated him to the high bench. His words, "Great cases like hard cases make bad law," were the most memorable of several the president found offensive.[64] Holmes had written: "Great cases are called great not by reason of their real importance in shaping the law of the future, but because of some accident of immediate overwhelming interest which appeals to the feelings and distorts the judgment."[65] Holmes, in effect, accused the majority on the Court of having allowed their feelings, their antipathy to Morgan and Hill, and their fears of big business to distort their judgment, encouraging them to voice their prejudices. Roosevelt, dumbfounded by what he considered Holmes's perfidy, threatened never again to permit him to cross the White House threshold. TR's anger subsided in time, but Holmes sometimes recalled what a senator had once said about the president: "What the boys like about Roosevelt is that he doesn't care a damn for the law." As Francis Biddle, one of Holmes's law clerks and later attorney general under Franklin Roosevelt, wrote, "The truth was that he [Theodore Roosevelt] could never forgive any-one who stood in his way." Biddle knew that Holmes secretly "despised the Sherman Act," believing it was "humbug, based on ignorance and incompetence, an absurd statute." In Biddle's words, "The theory of the act was that you must compete but you mustn't win the competition."[66]

Roosevelt, in seeking to distinguish between good trusts and bad trusts, created a distinction Holmes believed to be meaningless, finding neither merit nor legal justification in the arguments and tactics used by the government's lawyers. Many in the business community thought the president irresponsible for having initiated the action in the first instance, and some Republicans, incensed by what they regarded as Roosevelt's perfidy—his failure to take into account their financial interests—declared they would refuse to support him in his quest for renomination in 1904.

Lodge had served as Roosevelt's principal advocate in the first two decades of his political life; Root assumed that position after the Northern Securities case, notably among those bankers and lawyers increasingly vocal in their hostility to him. Addressing the Union League Club in February 1904, just before the Supreme Court announced its decision, Root described Roosevelt as "the greatest conservative force for the protection of property and of capital in the city of Washington during the years that have elapsed since President McKinley's death."[67] Root did not exaggerate; however much Roosevelt wished to appear the radical reformer, he was basically conservative. He knew that only the electorate could renew his mandate, and his principal concern was to choose words and adopt policies calculated to win their favor. Though he realized the Northern Securities case might hurt him in his effort to secure the Republican nomination, he expected it to help him greatly when he jumped that hurdle. Roosevelt placed a wager on his political popularity, and as he told George Courtelyou, his campaign manager, months before the election, "The Northern Securities suit is one of the great achievements of my administration. I look back upon it with great pride, for through it we emphasized in signal fashion, as in no other way could be emphasized, the fact that the most powerful men in this country were held to accountability before the law."[68] This was a campaign slogan of great value, and Roosevelt knew it.

The president, represented as the champion of the little fellow against big business, became known as a trustbuster. Few took account of the fact that of the forty-three other antitrust suits filed during his more than seven years as president, only one, against the beef trust, saw the government win a significant victory.[69] Yet his reputation as a friend of workingmen remained secure. Sensing that the country craved a strong presidency, one capable of resolving issues too long neglected, where he could act without congressional approval or consent, often exceedingly difficult to obtain, he showed himself a master political tactician. In May 1902, when some 140,000 miners voted to strike in the anthracite coalfields of Pennsylvania, John Mitchell, the president of the United Mine Workers of America, pleaded with his men not to resort to violence, believing their cause was just, and that it would compel the mine owners in time to accept their legitimate demands for higher pay. Mitchell deluded himself, scarcely knowing the opposition he faced in George F. Baer, of the Philadelphia and Reading Coal and Iron Company, and president of the Reading Railroad, an appointment he owed to J.P. Morgan. Baer told a clergyman that the "rights and interests of the labouring man" would be best protected "not by labor agitators, but by the Christian men to whom God in his Infinite Wisdom had given control of the property interests of the country," and refused to negotiate.[70]

As the price of coal rose steadily, going from $5 a ton in May to $30 a ton in October, Roosevelt became increasingly concerned, recognizing the dangers to himself and the Republican Party if the strike went on into the winter. Coal was the principal fuel for heating, and if it continued to be in short supply at greatly inflated prices, many families were bound to suffer. This was reason enough for Roosevelt to take action, but there was another, scarcely less compelling: The effects of a continued strike on the impending off-year congressional elections in November would certainly threaten Republicans seats in both the House and the Senate, and the election results could well be disastrous. Showing increasing impatience with the mine owners for what he considered their "wooden-headed obstinacy and stupidity," Roosevelt decided that only presidential intervention could avert a national and a Republican Party catastrophe; he decided to summon both the owners and the trade union leaders to meet with him in the White House to settle the dispute.[71]

While Mitchell agreed at once to the president's proposal to appoint an independent arbitration commission and to abide by its decision, Baer refused to "waste time negotiating with the fomenters of this anarchy." Only one solution appealed to him: The president in his capacity as commander in chief ought to act, mobilizing the U.S. Army to end the strike. When the miners, angered by the owners' dilatory tactics, voted to continue the strike, Secretary of War Elihu Root traveled to New York to consult with J.P. Morgan, the man who more than any other wielded influence in the coalfields. With Morgan's help, Root framed an arbitration agreement that the owners finally accepted; it provided for the appointment of an independent commission of five men to settle the dispute, an engineer, a judge, an "eminent sociologist," a military officer, and a mining expert.[72] Though Mitchell found some of the language in the agreement offensive, not least the reference to labor's "reign of terror," he agreed on condition that two additional mediators be appointed: a priest—most of the miners were Roman Catholic—and a trade unionist.[73] The owners refused to consider these changes, and for twenty-four hours it appeared that the accord would founder. Roosevelt then intervened with a solution that showed his unspoken contempt for the intelligence of the owners. He asked whether the eminent sociologist might not be a trade unionist and whether this would satisfy both parties, guessing correctly that it would. By October 23, just weeks before the elections, the strike was settled. Roosevelt wrote a profuse letter of thanks to J.P. Morgan for all he had done to avert a national disaster, and TR basked in his new reputation as a born negotiator.

The results of the off-year elections gratified the president; Congress remained safely Republican, and Roosevelt's reputation as a trustbuster and friend of the workingman augured well for the more important election still two years away. Whatever interest Roosevelt took in purely domestic issues, however much he claimed to be an innovator in that sphere, avoiding all unnecessary quarrels with influential members of Congress, his consuming interest could never be the internecine quarrels that formed an essential part of their daily life. Roosevelt came to the presidency with a more important mission—to realize and demonstrate the country's status as a great power—and he learned quickly that this ambition need not depend on congressional assent. He intended to be his own secretary of state, unofficially of course, paying appropriate deference always to Hay and the State Department, but providing the lead in every action he deemed important, by definition, vital to the nation's security and prestige.

In his first message to Congress, delivered within a month of his entering the White House, he sounded a note he never ceased to repeat, characterizing military intervention by the civilized among "barbarous and semi-barbarous peoples" as "a most regrettable but necessary international police duty which must be performed for the sake of the welfare of mankind."[74] In his second annual message, he reiterated this proposition and, after his reelection in 1904, proclaimed what came to be known as the Roosevelt Corollary to the Monroe Doctrine that had established in 1823 the principle that there could be no new European colonization in the Americas, no outside interference in the affairs of the independent Latin American states. Roosevelt, in his famous Corollary, told the world that

chronic wrong-doing, or an impotence which results in a general loosening of the ties of civilized society, may in America, as elsewhere, ultimately require intervention by some civilized nation, and in the western hemisphere the adherence of the United States to the Monroe Doctrine may force the United States, however reluctantly, in flagrant cases of such wrong-doing or impotence, to the exercise of an international police power.[75]

Given such declarations, it is scarcely surprising that many thought him bellicose, a jingo in the White House. Roosevelt refused to give any credence to such criticism, representing himself always as a peace-loving president whose one concern was to protect and sustain the interests of civilized states.

Roosevelt made foreign policy his preserve, and even when the younger Elihu Root succeeded John Hay as secretary of state, never ceded to him or to others the privilege of taking major foreign policy initiatives. Indeed, for the president, his foreign affairs decisions were the all-important ones he constantly advertised, proud that he alone decided what the route of the proposed Panama Canal should be. He never apologized for his role in abetting the revolution in Colombia that created the new state of Panama, which made the transit through the Isthmus of Panama possible. In his graphic and self-serving account of the origins of the Panama revolt, he saw it as provoked by Colombia's "corrupt and evil purposes" and "complete governmental incompetency."[76] The U.S. support of the rebellion, in his mind, was wholly legitimate, and the only opposition to it came from a "small body of shrill eunuchs" who lived principally in the Northeast.

In June 1904, as Root prepared to speak to support his renomination at the Republican National Convention, Roosevelt urged him to tell about "Panama in all its details."[77] Never doubting the correctness of what he had done to foment revolution in Colombia, and knowing the decision to construct the Canal through the isthmus was made without consultation with his Cabinet, he saw it as the most important act of his presidency.[78] But it was not the Panama Canal alone for which he claimed credit. In his letter to Root, instructing him about the things he would do well to emphasize in his speech to the Republican National Convention, the Northern Securities case and the settlement of the anthracite coal strike figured prominently. Both appeared as major items in a litany that emphasized the president's role in arranging for Cuban independence, the successful administration of the Philippines, the buildup of the Navy, the proper organization of the Army, and civil service reform. These were all represented as his personal achievements.

Roosevelt, determined to prove himself a president whose interest extended to every part of the country, wrote also of what he had accomplished in the area of forestry and irrigation, the incomparable benefits he brought to the states of the expanding West. To maintain the Open Door in China and enforce the Monroe Doctrine in Venezuela, using the International Court at the Hague to arbitrate that dispute and settle a disagreement with Mexico, he represented himself as a president committed to world order and peace.

In his boastful though not inaccurate self-portrayal, he emerged as the supreme architect of the nation's foreign and domestic policies.[79] There had been no president like him, certainly none in recent memory, and he saw no need to display false modesty before a Republican National Convention whose delegates intended to renominate him, making him the first accidental president in the history of the republic to compete for and win a second term in the White House.

On the race question that had become controversial partly because of his invitation to Booker T. Washington to dine with him in the White House, the first black person ever so honored, Roosevelt told Root: "I would suggest that the race question be treated simply incidentally by an allusion to show that I have set the same standard for black men and for white, just as for wageworkers and capitalists, for Jew and Gentile, for Catholics and Protestants."[80] He expected Root to have some difficulties with the tariff issue, and again his words suggest why some thought him the most accomplished politician of his day, always pretending to be bold, knowing when to be cautious, never acknowledging that circumstances might lead him to be that. In a telegram to Root, he said:

Speech admirable in every way. Have no suggestion to make except that instead of saying 'The tariff will presently need revision,' it might be better to say 'The tariff *may* presently need revision and if so it should receive it at the hands of the friends and not the enemies of the protective system.'[81]

However much Roosevelt might appear the reformer, he was not a president prepared to take on recklessly those in the party who differed with him. For such an individual, so accomplished in self-advertisement, victory in the 1904 election came easily, but even before that happy event Roosevelt revealed his constant preoccupation with foreign policy issues. To Cecil Spring Rice, his English friend, he wrote about the Russo-Japanese War, expressing sentiments that would not have been common to any other politician of his day:

I see nothing of permanent good that can come to Russia, either for herself or for the rest of the world, until her people begin to tread the path of orderly freedom, of civil liberty, and of a measure of self-government. Whatever may be the theoretical advantages of a despotism, they are incompatible with the growth of intelligence and individuality in a civilized people. Either there must be stagnation in the Russian people, or there must be what I would hope would be a gradual, but a very real, growth of governmental institutions to meet the growth in, and the capacity and need for, liberty.[82]

Reporting on a recent lunch with the Japanese minister to Washington, he told Spring Rice of their conversation: "I thought their chief danger was lest Japan might get the 'big head' and enter into a general career of insolence and aggression, that such a career would undoubtedly be temporarily unpleasant to the rest of the world, but that it would in the end be more unpleasant for Japan."[83] His Japanese guest expressed the fear that if the Russians succeeded in retaining Port Arthur, defeating the Japanese in their siege, this would give them the upper hand in Manchuria, allowing them to renege on their earlier pledges not to intervene there. Roosevelt sympathized with that view, saying that Russia had always pursued a "consistent career of stupendous mendacity, not only with Japan but with ourselves as regards Manchuria," and shared the Japanese worry that this might continue, that the autonomy of China in Manchuria would then be exceedingly difficult to guarantee.

In a long postscript to the letter, Roosevelt remarked that the "civilization of the Japs is very alien to ours," but he expressed the hope that each could learn from the other. "The Japs interest me and I like them," he wrote. "I am perfectly well aware that if they win out it may possibly mean a struggle between them and us in the future, but I hope not and believe not." The differences in race had no significance for him. As he told Spring Rice, "The Turks are ethnically closer to us than the Japanese, but they are impossible members of our international society, while I think the Japs may be desirable additions." This did not prevent him from adding:

> That there are large classes of the Japanese who will sometimes go wrong, that Japan as a whole will sometimes go wrong, I do not doubt. The same is true of my own beloved country. I do not anticipate that Tokyo will show a superior morality to that which obtains in Berlin, Vienna and Paris, not to speak of London and Washington, or of St. Petersburg. But I see nothing ruinous to civilization in the advent of the Japanese to power among the great nations.[84]

These were sentiments the president shared only with his intimates; they were not the sort he ever made public.

When he sat down to write his acceptance message to the Republican Party in the late summer of 1904 for having chosen him as its presidential nominee, one of the longest ever penned, he showed no reluctance to boast, emphasizing all he had done to make the world more peaceful. Dwelling on his accomplishments in Cuba, the Philippines, and Panama, and how he had defended the Monroe Doctrine, he emphasized also his efforts to protect persecuted minorities abroad, protesting against the Kishneff massacre in Russia, the treatment of Jews in Romania, and of the Armenians in Turkey. "No other administration in our history, no other government in the world," he said, "has more consistently stood for the broadest spirit of brotherhood in our common humanity, or has held a more resolute attitude of protest against every wrong that outraged the civilization of the age, at home or abroad." In his words, he "behaved towards all nations, strong or weak, with courtesy, dignity, and justice," and was "now on excellent terms with all."[85] The hyperbole of the message, intended as a political testament of sorts, gave the president the appearance of a man of peace who saw no contradiction between what he claimed to have achieved abroad with the U.S. Navy, "the most potent guarantee of peace," a force "formidable and ready for use," with what he had done to show his respect for the International Court at the Hague, to use it to effect important arbitration agreements.

Acknowledging that achieving an end to discrimination at home would be difficult, he nevertheless pledged himself to that purpose as he did to the struggle against human rights abuses in Turkey and Russia. In a peroration any number of his successors would also use, never acknowledging its source, almost certainly never knowing it, he said:

> We have striven both for civic righteousness and for national greatness; and we have faith to believe that our hands will be upheld by all who feel love of country and trust in the uplifting of mankind. . . . We hold ever before us the all-important end of policy and administration the reign of peace at home and throughout the world; of peace, which comes only by doing justice.[86]

Roosevelt's electoral victory in November 1904 was impressive. Though Judge Alton Parker, his Democratic opponent, proved a weak and ineffectual candidate, Roosevelt won a greater number of Electoral College votes than any of his predecessors, carrying thirty-three of the forty-five states, showing remarkable strength everywhere but in the South, the Democratic Party's only remaining political stronghold.

In a moment of high elation, he announced he would follow the example of George Washington and not seek an additional four-year term. His words—"Under no circumstances will I be a candidate for or accept another nomination"—were among the most ill-considered he ever made. What would a man of his energy and ambition, only fifty at the time of the next election, choose to do for the rest of his life? That problem seemed inconsequential in the exciting days of November 1904 but became increasingly serious as the years ran swiftly by. Roosevelt, in effect, made himself a lame-duck president at the moment of his great election victory and gained nothing from informing proud and self-willed senators and representatives that they would still wield power when another man sat in the White House. Roosevelt's success with Congress during his first administration was limited; senators, secure in their safe seats, aware of the influence they enjoyed through their long tenure, found little reason to accommodate him or defer to his wishes. With influential members of the House, led by the powerful Speaker, Joseph Cannon, he enjoyed no greater success, receiving only intermittent and very occasional support. If Roosevelt expected his decisive 1904 victory to change all this, the first few months of his second administration disabused him of that hope. Few in the Senate or in the House, habituated to exercising substantial power under a long succession of weak presidents, described so accurately by Woodrow Wilson in *Congressional Government*, were prepared to change their ways. Had Roosevelt been determined to win them over, to spend days, weeks, or even months cultivating them, negotiating deals with them, he might have enjoyed greater success. Lacking that interest, and openly contemptuous of a good many of those he would have had to propitiate, he came to rely increasingly on executive orders to achieve objectives Congress would never assent to.[87] Roosevelt, though obviously disappointed with what he achieved legislatively, complained constantly to his intimates about the vain men who presided in a Congress where his own Republican Party was ideologically divided. Knowing he could do little to change the situation, he accepted it, driven more than ever to occupy himself with foreign affairs where he knew that congressional intervention would be less likely and less effective.[88]

Like others who succeeded him in the White House, he found an agreeable refuge in foreign policy, where he claimed exceptional knowledge and expertise. While he continued to make bold and sometimes arresting observations on domestic issues, insisting on their importance, arguing, for example, that control of the big corporations of the country remained a very live political question, he recognized the limits of his influence. Writing to another of his English friends, the historian, Sir George Otto Trevelyan, on March 9, 1905, of "plenty of anxious times ahead" for the English-speaking countries of the world because of the continued drift to the cities and the radicalism it spawned, the war between Russia and Japan remained his principal concern.[89] Frustrated by senators, "wholly indifferent to national honor or national welfare," whom he saw as "primarily concerned in getting a little cheap reputation among ignorant people," in his words, "mischievous monkeys," he sought a role for himself where such men could neither touch nor harm him. He found it in what can best be described as "personal diplomacy," depending not on the ratification of treaties by a two-thirds approval vote in the Senate, always difficult to obtain, but on something more intangible, popular acclaim, nationally and internationally.[90] In what he elected to do through much of his second term, he hoped to gain for the presidency and the country recognition of a kind rarely given either. His overwhelming electoral victory in 1904 told him he was a popular president, chosen in his proud words by the same "plain people" who had rallied around Lincoln, a man of "resolution, courage, patience, gentleness, disinterestedness, and hard headed common sense."[91] Roosevelt aspired to become a world figure, a president whose commitment to peace would be universally recognized and applauded. He hoped to move into a higher and more interesting sphere, no longer thwarted by "fat-witted people" in the Senate, "headed by a voluble, pinheaded creature named Bacon from Georgia, a horrid instance of the mischief that can be done by a man of very slender capacity if he possesses great loquacity, effrontery, and an entire indifference to the national welfare."[92] Frustrated at home, aware he could do little to control the powerful financiers who scarcely understood how their obduracy served to bring moderates to join radicals in proposing legislation on interstate commerce inimical to their interests, Roosevelt settled on another agenda, one he could hope to control.

As early as April 1905, a month after his second inaugural, from a hunting holiday in Oklahoma, shooting wolves, Roosevelt wrote Taft, the acting secretary of state, temporarily replacing the ailing Hay, about a message he had just received from Kaiser William II, who asked Roosevelt whether the British government intended to "back up France in gobbling Morocco." The president, referring to the Kaiser's "pipe dream this week," told Taft he had no intention of becoming involved in the Morocco dispute, saying, ". . . we have other fish to fry and we have no real interest in Morocco." In any case, he could conceive of no benefit to the United States in its taking sides in any dispute between France and Germany. Indeed, as he explained to Taft,

> Each nation is working itself up to a condition of desperate hatred of each other from sheer fear of each other. The Kaiser is dead sure that England intends to attack him. The English Government and a large share of the English people are equally sure that Germany intends to attack England. Now, in my view this action of Germany in embroiling itself with France over Morocco is proof positive that she has not the slightest intention of attacking England. I am very clear in my belief that England utterly overestimates as well as misestimates Germany's singleness of purpose, by attributing to German Foreign Office the kind of power and of aim which it had from '64 to '71.[93]

In short, William II ought not to be mistaken for a second Bismarck, and Roosevelt never exaggerated either his abilities or his intentions; he recognized him to be a "nervous Nellie."

Roosevelt, showing all of his habitual caution but also his penchant for mockery, asked Taft to get in touch with the first secretary, the "fat-witted British intellect" in its Washington embassy, to learn precisely what Britain intended to do. He begged Taft to be diplomatic in his approach lest the British believe the Americans were "acting as decoy ducks for Germany." That suspicion was indeed raised by Taft's intervention, and Roosevelt learned that even King Edward VII believed the president had fallen under the influence of the Kaiser.[94] In a letter to Spring Rice on May 13, 1905, confident the information would be passed on to his superiors in the Foreign Office, Roosevelt said:

> There is much that I admire about the Kaiser and there is much that I admire about the German people. But the German people are too completely under his rule for me to disassociate them from him, and he himself is altogether too jumpy, too volatile in his policies, too lacking in the power of continuous and sustained thought and action for me to feel that he is any way such a man as for instance Taft or Root.[95]

If it proved possible to contribute to improved relations between Germany and England, Roosevelt would do what he could to help, but he had no illusions about the Kaiser or about his reputed friendship for the United States. As Roosevelt explained to Spring Rice,

> He respects us because he thinks that for a sufficient object and on our own terms we would fight, and we have a pretty good navy with which to fight. I shall hope that on those terms I can keep the respect not merely of Berlin, but of St. Petersburg and Tokyo both. I know that except on those terms the respect of any of the three cannot be kept. . . . I shall hope to keep on good terms with all, and to lend some assistance to Japan in the present war in which I think she is right.[96]

However interested Roosevelt might be in the Kaiser, in his erratic behavior, "jumpiness," and inability to have "long thought-out and deliberate purpose," his real concern was always with the more important issue, the Russo-Japanese War. As he made clear to Spring Rice, he believed the Russian fleet to be "materially somewhat stronger than that of Japan," but that advantage was offset by the "Japanese superiority in morale and training." His own interest, he told his British friend, was in peace, and he greatly regretted that the Japanese did not agree to negotiate after their military victory at Mukden, as he had recommended they do. "Just at the moment," he wrote, "Russia is riding a high horse and will not talk peace," but he expected the situation might soon change. In a letter to Lodge, written two days later, Roosevelt told him the Japanese were anxious for peace, indeed hoped he might intervene to bring it about. Worried that the impending naval battle might not bring them the victory they needed, the Japanese, according to the president, were showing a caution they had not previously displayed.[97] Moving away from his concern with the situation in Asia, Roosevelt expressed his disgust with those at home, principally in California and on the Pacific Slope, seeking to impose controls on Japanese immigration into the United States. In obvious anger, not least with congressmen and senators opposed to his requests for an expansion of the Navy, he wrote:

> It gives me a feeling of contempt and disgust to see them challenging Japanese hostility and justify by their actions any feeling the Japanese might have against us, while at the same time refusing to take steps to defend themselves against the formidable foe for whom they are ready with such careless insolence to antagonize. How people can act in this way with the Russo-Japanese war going on before their eyes I cannot understand. I do all I can to counteract the effects, but I cannot accomplish everything.[98]

If the Japanese were to win, and Roosevelt very early recognized that possibility, it would become a formidable power in the Orient, "a new force in eastern Asia." Roosevelt reflected on what that might mean for China, whether the two might become great "civilized powers," resembling those of the West, having started with very different ancestral traditions.

Following his reelection, Roosevelt alluded somewhat mysteriously in a letter to Spring Rice to "what I intend to do if circumstances permit, so far as this far eastern question is concerned," adding that it was impossible "to write my conclusions even to you."[99] He grieved that there was no one in the British embassy in Washington with whom he could discuss the matter freely. Clearly, even before the Japanese land and sea victories, before the tentative peace feelers from the Japanese, the president had begun to think of himself as a mediator. Roosevelt wrote as he did only to the few friends he trusted and did not think it inappropriate to express the doubts he felt to Spring Rice about whether the British government or its people could be relied on to take risks. In England, as in the United States, he believed that business interests were generally horrified at any policy that might "unsettle values," and this led them to prefer "softness" to decisiveness. Roosevelt reminded Spring Rice that in the Spanish-American War as in the Boer War,

> our generals and yours screamed with anguish over the loss of a couple of thousand men in the field; a sentiment of preposterous and unreasoning mawkishness, as is instanced by the fact that the actual mortality in the two wars, taken in the aggregate, did not equal the aggregate mortality in the two countries, during the same number of years, of the women who died in childbirth; nor, as regards my own country, of the men who were killed in private quarrels.[100]

Because he despised what he saw as this "softness and its attendant hysteria," he doubted that either the Americans or the English were prepared to take risks, least of all the risk of war.

Believing that "Russia for a number of years has treated the United States as badly as she has treated England, and almost as badly as she has treated Japan," he told Spring Rice that her diplomats had "lied to us with brazen and contemptuous effrontery." The Japanese, by comparison, were civilized, but he wondered whether

> the Japanese down at bottom did not lump Russians, English, Americans, Germans, all of us, simply as white devils inferior to themselves not only in what they regard as the essentials of civilization, but in courage and forethought, and to be treated politely only so long as would enable the Japanese to take advantage of our various national jealousies, and beat us in turn.[101]

Reporting on incidents brought to his attention that revealed Japanese insolence, he could only hope that this was a passing phase, a response to the racial intolerance shown by many Americans and Europeans to those of the yellow race. Whether Japan or Russia won, neither was likely to show a proper regard for the United States or England unless they knew them to be strong.[102]

Following the Russian retreat at Mukden on March 9, the situation inside Russia deteriorated rapidly. Still, the Czar and many of his advisers refused to accept that the country's situation had become desperate. They preferred to believe that all would be saved when the mighty Russian Navy defeated the Japanese at sea. Two months later, on May 26, before the Japanese destroyed the Russian fleet, Roosevelt prophesied in a letter to Spring Rice that they would win, but he acknowledged in a second letter sent on June 16 that he never expected the victory to be a "slaughter rather than a fight."[103] On June 8, inviting both belligerents to send representatives to the United States to negotiate a peace settlement, the president told Spring Rice what he imagined his intervention might accomplish. As he explained,

> My own policy is perfectly simple, though I have not the slightest idea whether I can get my country to follow it. I wish to see the United States treat the Japanese in a spirit of all possible courtesy, and with generosity and justice. At the same time I wish to see our navy constantly built up, and ships kept at the highest point of efficiency as a fighting unit. If we follow this course we shall have no trouble with the Japanese or anyone else. But if we bluster; if we behave rather badly to other nations; if we show that we regard the Japanese as an inferior and alien race, and try to treat them as we have treated the Chinese, and if at the same time we fail to keep our navy at the highest point of efficiency and size—then we shall invite disaster.[104]

Peace, he told Spring Rice, was in the interest of all mankind, including the two combatants. If the war continued for another year, Japan would drive Russia out of East Asia but would receive no indemnity. Believing the "terrific strain of an extra year's loss of blood and money" was something the Japanese could not easily bear, but also that the Russian expulsion from East Asia would be "a humiliating loss which a century could not repair," he saw the imperative need for an immediate peace. If peace could be negotiated, with Russia giving up Sakhalin and paying a reasonable indemnity while Japan retained what it had won, Russia would be in the situation it had enjoyed a dozen years earlier; in his words, "no unbearable humiliation and loss will have been inflicted upon her." While Roosevelt recognized all that Japan would have gained from the war, he did not believe it would be a threat to the United States. Were Japan to become a threat, the United States could save itself only by its own efforts, not by an alliance with others, a statement as remarkable as any that Roosevelt ever made. He hoped Britain would use its influence with Japan, its ally since 1902, to persuade her not to ask for impossible terms, which would only risk a continuation of the war.[105]

Spring Rice, replying to Roosevelt from London, told him he had communicated his letter to Lord Lansdowne, the foreign secretary, adding that "you probably don't realize the immense personal prestige and power which you exercise over here," and assuring him that his efforts for peace were greatly appreciated in England. He then went on to say, "But you yourself will be the first to recognize the claims of honour as the first interest of nations; and honour commands us to abstain from putting any pressure whatever on Japan."[106] In words that only raised Roosevelt's ire, Spring Rice told him that "American opinion will receive the fullest and friendliest consideration." A long disquisition followed on why the German menace remained the paramount one and why "England cannot allow France to be annihilated or turned into a province of Germany."[107] To all this, Roosevelt replied with an asperity he rarely used with his closest English friend. He wrote, "Now, oh best beloved Springy, don't you think you go a little needlessly into heroics when you say that 'claims of honor must be recognized as the first interest of nations and that honor commands England to abstain from putting any pressure whatever upon Japan. . . .'" Refusing to mince words, he wrote:

> . . . I wholly fail to understand the difference in position which makes it proper for France, the ally of Russia, to urge Russia in her own interest (that is, in Russia's interest) to make peace, and which yet makes it improper for England, the ally of Japan, to urge Japan in her own interest (that is, in Japan's interest) to make peace.[108]

To make even more explicit his disdain for the Foreign Office argument, Roosevelt added, "However, most of this talk as to what England ought to do is academic, because I think the Japanese have probably made up their minds just about what they will accept and what they won't." In short, Roosevelt had no need of British intercession with the Japanese, and the earlier American request for help was in effect withdrawn.[109]

Roosevelt, always courteous to his friends, had no wish to offend Spring Rice and injected humor in what was otherwise a calculated put-down. In words intended as much for the British foreign secretary as for Spring Rice, Roosevelt told of the last time he had met with John Hay, and of his remark that "the more I saw of the Czar and the Kaiser the better I liked the United States Senate; to which he was evidently inclined to respond that he drew no fine distinctions between them."[110] It is evident, Roosevelt wrote, ". . . that the Senate is a very poor body to have as part of the treaty-making power. But of course the business of an active politician is not to complain of defects which cannot be changed, but to do the best he can in spite of them." That, he told Spring

Rice, continued to be his policy with those in the San Francisco labor unions who seemed so determined to insult the Japanese. "They will not do one thing against them while I am President—I won't let them—but they may create an ugly feeling of distrust, and of course they are exactly the type which positively refuses to prepare for the trouble which they are willing to bring about." Roosevelt understood better than many of his generation why foreign and domestic policy did not exist in separate compartments.

In the end, peace between Japan and Russia was secured at Portsmouth, New Hampshire, but only because of the president's continued interventions. Life in Washington in the summer of 1905 might be tranquil, and Roosevelt, following his usual practice, spent July and August mostly at his home in Oyster Bay, Long Island, but he was more preoccupied than ever with foreign policy, taking delight in his growing correspondence with kings, emperors, foreign ministers, and ambassadors. Roosevelt had found his true vocation. By the end of August, he told his ambassador in St. Petersburg of the terms the Japanese were willing to accept, then passed the same information on to the German and French ambassadors in Washington, men he esteemed, whose governments he imagined could do a great deal to persuade the Czar to accept terms he deemed reasonable. Roosevelt enjoyed his role greatly, as was evident from the cordial and strategically important telegram he sent to the Kaiser on August 27 in which he outlined the terms he had been able to secure from the Japanese, described as having "assented reluctantly and only under strong pressure from me."[111]

By these terms, Russia would pay no indemnity but would receive back from Japan the northern half of Sakhalin for which it would pay the sum that a mixed commission decided on. Roosevelt told William II that these extremely moderate terms had not yet been presented to the Czar and hoped the Kaiser would agree to undertake that mission, saying: "I feel that you have more influence with him than either I or anyone else can have. . . . Can you not take the initiative by presenting these terms at once to him? Your success in the matter will make the entire civilized world your debtor."[112]

Roosevelt had learned many arts: how to pressure; how to flatter. The Czar, in fact, proved recalcitrant, insisting that no indemnity, even one artfully concealed, would be paid the Japanese. Within days, however, he relented, and on August 29 all the outstanding issues were settled. In the days that followed, Roosevelt received three telegrams of congratulation for the services he had rendered; they came from three emperors, of Russia, Japan, and Germany. Each felt beholden to the president for the peace he had secured.[113] Roosevelt, exulting in his Portsmouth triumph, soon to be repeated at Algeciras, where the Americans helped defuse the German-French quarrel over Morocco, became by these actions alone a major world figure, celebrated for his diplomatic accomplishments, and it seemed entirely appropriate that he should be the first American to receive the Nobel Peace Prize in 1906.[114] His renown abroad was unprecedented, but it did not translate into an effective control of Congress, an ability to persuade recalcitrant legislators to pass the kinds of domestic legislation that would have given even greater distinction to his presidency.

It is significant in this connection that Edmund Morris in his biography of Roosevelt, *Theodore Rex,* devoted almost twice as much attention to his first administration, a shorter one, than to his second. The reasons are not hard to find. The impressive triumph Roosevelt received at the polls in 1904, and his victories in managing to secure peace abroad, did not make his domestic policies more palatable either to Congress or the courts. Though he initiated antitrust suits against some of the most powerful corporate giants, including Standard Oil, Dupont, American Tobacco, and the Union Pacific Railroad, using the newly created Bureau of Corporations in the Department of Commerce and Labor to publicize their corporate malpractices, he enjoyed no victories in these presidential trustbusting efforts comparable to the one registered in the Northern Securities case.[115] Roosevelt recognized that modern industrial conditions made the process of combination inevitable, perhaps necessary, and told Congress in his 1906 State of the Union that the Sherman Anti-Trust Act, by seeming to forbid all combination, was unworkable.[116] In one of his more ardent personal letters to Jean Jules Jusserand, the French ambassador to the United States whom he greatly admired, he spoke of never being able to accept the Senate as anything but a "conservative body too much under the influence of the big corporations" when it was not "too much influenced by the craven demagogic fear of the mob."[117] Still, he felt proud of three legislative acts he successfully pressured Congress to pass in the last days of the Fifty-Ninth Congress—the Railroad Regulation Act, the Meat Inspection Act, and the Pure Food and Drug Act.[118] With the passage of that legislation, Roosevelt virtually exhausted the whole of his domestic reform agenda. If he intended to do more, he knew he lacked the Republican support in Congress to achieve such ends.

In August 1906, on his annual summer holiday at Oyster Bay, he learned to his dismay of an incident in Brownsville, Texas, where some armed colored soldiers ran amuck, killing at least one civilian and wounding a police lieutenant. The mayor of Brownsville, reporting the incident, told Roosevelt, "Our condition, Mr. President, is this: our women and children are terrorized and our men are under constant alarm and watchfulness. No community can stand this strain for more than a few days. We look to you for relief; we ask you to have the troops removed from Fort Brown and replaced by white soldiers."[119] After extensive investigations that lasted through the summer, Roosevelt dismissed 167 soldiers without honor and without trial. The decision proved to be a serious blunder; the evidence of guilt was negligible, and Roosevelt came to realize that too late, severely criticized both in Congress and by the press.[120] Two other serious racial problems commanded his attention during this period, and neither admitted of an easy solution. How ought he to react to the San Francisco school-board decision to segregate Japanese, Chinese, and Korean children in specially constructed Oriental schools? How ought he to treat the growing demands in Congress, spurred on by the trade unions, to exclude all Japanese laborers from coming into the country?[121]

With anti-Japanese sentiment increasingly strident, especially in California, trade union leaders agitated openly for strict immigration restrictions, and Roosevelt recognized the imperative need for a statement to reflect his own esteem for Japan, a nation that had "won in a single generation the right to stand abreast of the foremost and most enlightened peoples of Europe and America." The president believed it was in the American self-interest to treat Japan correctly and spoke in December 1906 of his determination to use all the federal authority at his command "to perform its own obligations to other nations." By the terms of the so-called Gentleman's Agreement, signed a few months later, the United States prohibited the immigration of Japanese laborers from Hawaii to the mainland, and Japan gave a verbal assurance that no passports would be granted skilled or unskilled workers who might seek entry to the mainland. Roosevelt, while recognizing the need to accommodate trade union sentiment in the matter, never retreated from his firm conviction that the exclusion of Oriental children from America's common schools was a "wicked absurdity."[122] At this stage, the president decided to send the U.S. battle fleet around the world, confident it would foster international goodwill and in no way offend Japan, a matter of constant concern to him.[123]

Roosevelt became an iconic figure for many Americans, moved by his eloquence, energy, and political oratory. Henry Adams, aware of his shortcomings and disinclined to discount them, recognized that the capital would never be the same without him and wrote in the last days of his administration, "I shall miss you very much."[124] Roosevelt was a dissembler, but not a fraud, a gifted and intelligent man, well-read and well-spoken, who gave the presidency a prestige and influence it had not previously known. He reminded the American public of all that a powerful personality in the White House could do to define the nation's agenda even if he did not always succeed in winning congressional approval for the measures he deemed important. His correspondence showed a command of foreign policy issues, a subtlety of analysis greater than that of almost anyone who had preceded him in the White House, and that few of his successors were able to rival.

Roosevelt, an international celebrity, made many in Europe and Asia aware that the United States had become a world power. Given that he derived his authority wholly from what he insisted was the will of the people—ordinary folk, in his mind—it is not surprising that he never accepted, as Tocqueville did, that there could be a tyranny of the majority and that this represented the most serious threat to the American democracy. Though he made a great deal of his hostility to bosses and rings, both were as conspicuous in the United States after he left office in 1909 as on the day he arrived in 1901. Disdainful of money, he did what he could to control those who had amassed vast fortunes, but his success was only very partial. Proud of the men of his social class he invited to join him in Washington, they were in fact few in number, and they did not contribute as much to his administration as those he inherited, not least Root, his favorite, and Taft, his heir.

Here was a king without courtiers, a man who insisted to his friend, Trevelyan, that "if it were not for the certainty of fools misunderstanding the terminology, and failing to see that a short-term elective King has nothing whatever in common with a hereditary King, I could best express to a foreigner the President's power by putting it in that form."[125] The president, Roosevelt suggested, never reigned as a hereditary monarch did but governed "most actively for four or eight years" as an "elective King."[126]

Though many emphasized Roosevelt's love of war and thought him a warrior manqué, the country experienced no major war on his almost eight-year watch, a record rarely mentioned by his enemies who represented him as always bellicose and belligerent. Roosevelt's facility for managing the country's foreign affairs drew on his unrivalled intuition, grounded in constant reading, greatly abetted by a never-ending correspondence with Americans and foreigners in a position to share their knowledge and opinions with him. Roosevelt came to the presidency with unusual credentials, created not by the high offices he occupied, few in number, but by his unusual intelligence, gleaned from an insatiable curiosity but also from a continuing dialogue with men able to recall an age he himself had not known. Roosevelt, as much as any of his successors, paid tribute to history, to what might be learned from studying the great administrations of an earlier day, those of Lincoln and Washington especially. Never remote figures, but presidents compelled to cope with dangerous conditions abroad, this in great part explained his fascination with them. In his mind, he lived more in succession to such men than to the one who by losing his life to an assassin had given him the presidency.

Roosevelt, sentimental and passionate, viewed his country as only a romantic could, glorying in its physical features, beautiful and sublime, but also in its remarkable past, its ability to ward off powerful European enemies initially, and then to restore itself as a united federal republic after the most serious threat to its existence during the Civil War. The president who refused to characterize himself as an intellectual knew many of the best minds of his generation. He vindicated all who believed that learning and passion mattered, making possible political innovation in an office too long occupied by more conventional minds.

CHAPTER 5

The Dauphin

WILLIAM HOWARD TAFT'S calling was the law, and he ought never to have abandoned it for politics, a vocation for which he was physically, emotionally, and intellectually unsuited. He came to the White House because Roosevelt wished him to be there, though TR would have greatly preferred for Elihu Root, his secretary of state, to be his successor. Because Root neither craved the office nor possessed the personality to compete for it, Roosevelt settled on his loyal secretary of war, clearly his second choice.[1] Taft's career to that moment greatly resembled his father's, Alphonso Taft, also a lawyer, frugal and self-effacing, who had made his way from rural Vermont to Yale University, in 1839 settling in Cincinnati, where after the dissolution of the Whig Party he quickly established a reputation as a staunch Republican. Appointed a superior court judge, President Ulysses S. Grant invited him to serve as secretary of war in 1876 in his second administration and then more briefly as attorney general. No one ever accused the God-fearing and God-loving Alphonso Taft of even a peripheral association with the more sordid political scandals that came to mar the reputation of the Grant administration, and Republican presidents after Grant sent him abroad to serve as minister, first to Austria-Hungary, then to Russia.[2]

His son's career seemed to replicate his own. Traveling the same road to Yale, first as an undergraduate and then to law school, he hoped one day to occupy a position on the bench that would lead to his appointment as a Supreme Court justice. Without an intimate friend like Henry Cabot Lodge to press for his federal advancement, it fell to Joseph Foraker, Ohio's governor, to serve as a surrogate. He secured an appointment for the twenty-nine-year-old Taft as a superior court judge in 1887. After the election of Benjamin Harrison in 1889 Taft began to dream of rising higher, becoming a Supreme Court justice. Why a young man, just past thirty, should have entertained such grandiose expectations is not easily explained, but during the years of the Ohio presidential ascendancy when connections were all-important, such a translation to the highest court seemed not impossible. Foraker, indeed, urged Harrison to consider Taft for a vacancy on the Court that had opened at the time Lodge was petitioning the president to secure almost any post for his unemployed friend, Roosevelt. Foraker described Taft to Harrison as a man "of positive convictions, fine address and in every way well adapted to fill the place with credit to yourself and your administration."[3] Harrison, the third in the post-Civil War Ohio Republican presidential dynasty, had already offered the post to another prominent Cincinnati lawyer only to have it refused, and he might have chosen Taft but saw no political advantage in doing so. Still, given the strength of Foraker's recommendation and the praise he heard from other prominent Ohio Republicans, he invited the young Taft to accept the position of solicitor general in his administration.[4]

Taft became, in effect, counsel to the attorney general, an office considerably more elevated than the one Lodge managed to secure for his protégé on the Civil Service Commission.[5] Taft enjoyed life in Washington, as did his socially ambitious wife, but neither frequented the exclusive political and intellectual society that congregated in the Henry Richardson-designed twin houses that Hay and Adams occupied on Lafayette Square, just opposite the White House. Still, as the son of Alphonso, the young Taft was noticed, and not only for his exceptional girth. Through the intervention of Senator John Sherman of Ohio, another patron, he became in March 1892 the U.S. circuit judge for the Sixth Judicial Circuit, returning to Cincinnati, more than ever settled on a judicial career. When in 1900 President McKinley invited him to visit in Washington, Taft failed to understand the summons, there being no Supreme Court vacancy at the time. What other reason might account for the invitation?[6]

Root, the secretary of war, and Long, the secretary of the Navy, were with the president when Taft came to see him and remained there to participate in the discussion that followed. McKinley told Taft he wished for him to be a member of the Commission for the Philippines, possibly its head, and Taft, recalling the interview in 1908 as president-elect, remembered his surprise at the offer and the doubts he expressed that he was the man for the post, telling the president, "I am sorry we have got the Philippines. I don't want them and I think you ought to have someone who is more in sympathy with the situation."[7] To this, McKinley reportedly answered: "You don't want them any less than I do, but we have got them and in dealing with them I think I can trust the man who didn't want them better than I can the man who did."[8] The United States had acquired the Philippines as the fruit of its victory over Spain in its short war in 1898 and confronted almost immediately a native insurrection led by Emilio Aguinaldo.[9]

The president, aware of the growing resistance in the United States to what many felt was a mistaken imperialist overseas venture, appealed to Taft's sense of duty and emphasized that the appointment need not interfere with the judicial career he had obviously set his heart on. Root, supporting the president, suggested that the Philippines appointment might advance his career, and McKinley went so far as to promise him a Supreme Court appointment with the words, "If I last and the opportunity comes, I shall appoint you."[10] Taft hesitated for some days but in the end, not surprisingly, accepted. The Philippines assignment did for Taft's career what the Navy appointment did for Roosevelt's—it made him a national figure.

Why did McKinley settle on Taft? He chose him principally because of his unblemished reputation. The designation of such an individual to head the commission almost guaranteed it would be increasingly difficult for the president's critics to characterize him as a secret imperialist, in thrall to colleagues known to favor U.S. expansion in the Pacific. Former President Grover Cleveland, together with other prominent Democrats, had characterized the administration's overseas policies as "dangerous perversions," policies of naked conquest and annexation, and these words had stung the president.[11]

By the terms of the Treaty of Paris, signed in December 1898, Spain had ceded the Philippine Islands to the United States for $20 million, and they were placed in the hands of General Elwell Otis. Aguinaldo, who had proclaimed Philippine independence in June 1898 and had helped the Americans to capture Manila, protested against this American claim to sovereignty and began an insurrection in February 1899. There were already some 7,000 regular United States Army troops in the islands, and General Otis, the governor of Manila and the commander of the Eighth Army Corps, estimated that some 30,000 to 40,000 U.S. troops might be needed to maintain peace on the principal island of Luzon alone. The dispatch of such a large force would have committed half the country's regular Army to the Philippines, not a prospect McKinley could view with equanimity.

With the capture of Aguinaldo, the leader of the rebels, in March 1901, shortly after McKinley's second inaugural, rebellion for all practical purposes ended, though skirmishes continued, and Taft, writing to Root from Manila, suggested the time had come to institute full civil government. This would effectively end the rule of General Arthur MacArthur, a man Taft found both rude and incompetent.[12] Root accepted Taft's proposal and spoke of his being appointed governor of the islands, a change that would take effect on July 4, 1901. The summer passed quietly, but September proved to be a miserable time for Taft, made so by the tragic news of McKinley's assassination. Writing to his brother, Henry, Taft expressed doubts about Roosevelt's "capacity for winning people to his support that McKinley had," and in a letter to a friend he wondered whether Roosevelt would be "able to retain the control over Congress which McKinley by reason of his long Congressional experience had succeeded in obtaining."[13] Still, the new president was a friend, though by no means an intimate, the two having met socially in Washington when both served there. Only days after the death of McKinley, on September 17, 1901, *Outlook* published an article written by the recent vice president in praise of Taft; Roosevelt's enthusiasm was unmistakable; he wrote:

> A year ago a man of wide acquaintance both with American public life and American public men remarked that the first Governor of the Philippines ought to combine the qualities which would make a first-class President of the United States with the qualities that would make a first-class Chief Justice of the United States, and that the only man he knew who possessed all these qualities was Judge William H. Taft, of Ohio. The statement was entirely correct.[14]

A greater tribute from the new president who had once envisaged the Philippines post for himself could not have been imagined.

Taft, in the United States in early 1902, recovering from major surgery following an attack of dengue fever complicated by abdominal and rectal disorders, had come home to recuperate, finding President Roosevelt and Secretary of War Root under serious attack. Both, according to the press and a number of congressional Democrats, had failed to control or halt atrocities purportedly committed by American soldiers in their efforts to quell the Philippine insurrection.[15] Root, on the defensive, admitted there had been forty-four cases of demonstrated cruelty, that thirty-nine soldiers had been tried and convicted in military courts, but insisted that this was a war characterized by "self-restraint, and with humanity, never surpassed, if ever equaled, in any conflict."[16] Root, carelessly and perhaps unintentionally, had misled Lodge, the chairman of the Senate Committee on the Philippines, claiming there had been no other violations of appropriate military conduct. He knew that Major Cornelius Gardener, governor of Tayabas, had reported the contrary in a document originally kept secret by Taft and then withheld by him for seven weeks. Because Taft doubted the accuracy of the Gardener report, he thought initially that it was unnecessary to share its findings with the War Department. Root learned only belatedly of the brutal behavior of American troops, goaded by what Gardener termed the Filipino "deep hatred toward us," exacerbated by the disdain U.S. officers and men felt for natives they spoke of and treated as "niggers."[17] Nelson Miles, commanding general of the Army, the nation's highest military officer, and no friend of the president, had managed to secure a copy of the Gardener report but knew better than to risk sharing it with Democrats in Congress. Still, he was not above letting some know that such a report existed. When he came to discuss the proposed reorganization of the Army before the Senate committee charged with considering the scheme devised by Root that called for the appointment of a chief of staff responsible to the secretary of war and ultimately to the president, he portrayed Roosevelt and Root "as executive upstarts who wished to create a monarcho-militarist court, like that of the

Kaiser in Germany."[18] These were not words normally used by high-ranking generals in discussing their civilian superiors.

The fat was in the fire, and Lodge as chairman of the Committee on the Philippines, pressured by adverse newspaper publicity, found it advisable to publish the Gardener report on April 11. The nation, profoundly shocked by its revelations, received even more startling news two days later when Major C.M. Waller, on trial in Samar, reported he had been ordered to "kill and burn" by the commanding general, Jacob Smith. A written order from General Smith included the words: "The interior of Samar must be made a howling wilderness."[19] Other witnesses told of American soldiers using the so-called water cure on Filipino prisoners, bound and gagged, with water poured down their throats, a cruel punishment devised originally by Spanish priests in the seventeenth century to chastise sinners who had failed to show sufficient reverence for the Holy Ghost.[20] With other reports circulating of "natives being flogged, toasted, strung up by their thumbs, and tattooed 'facially' for identification," the president recognized the need to act, to uncover all the facts.[21] Taft, in his own communications to Root, had given the secretary of war an exceedingly despairing view of the Filipino people. While constantly prating in public about "our brown brothers"—a much-favored Taft phrase—in letters to those he trusted, he described them as "the greatest liars it has ever been my fortune to meet," with the educated minority represented as "ambitious as Satan and quite as unscrupulous."[22] The peasants and tribesmen, more than 6.5 million, were obviously unfit for self-government, and Taft declared them inferior to "the most ignorant Negro." While he imagined they might in fifty or a hundred years learn to govern themselves, he had no expectation of more rapid progress.[23] Many who knew of Taft's performance in the Philippines respected and trusted him, but his life as governor was never easy. In 1902 and 1903 more than 100,000 Filipinos died of cholera, and he himself fell victim to amoebic dysentery. Resting in a mountain resort, Taft cabled Root: "Stood trip well. Rode horseback twenty-five miles to five-thousand elevation." The message received the only celebrated reply in their long and intimate correspondence; Root's response: "Referring to your telegram . . . how is the horse?"[24]

While Taft attended to his duties in the Philippines, Roosevelt considered him twice for elevation to the Supreme Court, initially in July 1902 when he appointed Oliver Wendell Holmes Jr., and again in October 1902 when another vacancy occurred. On both occasions Taft refused the offer, claiming his sudden departure from the Philippines would be misunderstood; there was too much unfinished business in Manila for him to abandon his post. Taft, more than a little disingenuous on the second occasion, knew that Root, in a conversation with his brother, Henry Taft, had spoken of the importance of his refusing any offer of a Supreme Court appointment. It was important for him to "reserve himself for another career," a remark that could admit of only one interpretation. Men who admired Taft in the nation's capital were beginning to speak of him as Roosevelt's successor in 1909. On February 14, 1903, Roosevelt wrote Taft again, saying "You will think I am a variety of the horse leech's daughter," but "the worst calamity that could happen to me . . . is impending because Root tells me that he will have to leave me next fall." Roosevelt asked whether Taft would be willing to succeed him as secretary of war if Root could be persuaded to remain for another year.[25]

Taft accepted the offer and assumed the post in 1904, succeeding a man renowned for his administrative and diplomatic talents who almost immediately rejoined the administration as secretary of state. Roosevelt, Root, and Taft became a Republican political troika, with the president very obviously in full command. Both Taft and Root, loyal and reliable, were worthy subordinates, prepared to serve their magnetic and ambitious leader, and it is scarcely surprising that Roosevelt thought of each as his possible successor in the White House. Justice Oliver Wendell Holmes Jr., at the time of Roosevelt's death in 1919, wrote a friend: "He [Roosevelt] was very likeable, a big figure, a rather ordinary intellect, with extraordinary gifts, a shrewd and I think pretty unscrupulous politician. He played all his cards—if not more. R.i.p."[26] Like Roosevelt, Taft was likeable and of course big, a corpulent giant beside the more lithe and athletic Roosevelt. Indeed, his exaggerated girth proved a handicap, making him a figure of fun to the press but, more important, contributing to a certain lassitude and lethargy.[27] Holmes's judgment that Roosevelt's intellect was rather ordinary would have been challenged by many of the ex-president's friends, but it described Taft's mind perfectly. As for extraordinary gifts, rarely claimed by Taft or even his devoted wife and brothers, no one ever thought to call him a shrewd and pretty unscrupulous politician. Indeed, many wished he had been something of both, or at least the first. Taft, when he followed four years later the most charismatic figure to have occupied the White House in half a century, showed almost immediately a political ineptitude that belied the advantages he had derived from family, education, and extensive judicial and administrative experience. He lacked precisely those poltical antenna that had made Roosevelt so exceptional.

Taft's greatest problem, however, came from being Roosevelt's successor, obliged to follow a president who had no desire to leave the White House, and recognized very quickly Taft's inadequacies as a politician.[28] By summoning a special session of Congress to honor the Republican Party's platform pledge to reduce the country's excessively high tariff, Taft made a fundamental error in his first months in office; he failed to understand why Roosevelt had never chosen to tangle with Congress on the tariff issue.[29] Because the Republican Party platform in 1908 declared "unequivocally for the revision of the tariff by a special session of Congress immediately following the inauguration of the new President"—a promise almost certainly encouraged by the country's experience in the 1907 financial panic when the excessively high duty on many imported goods kept prices artificially high—Taft felt duty-bound to honor that commitment, and explicitly agreed to do so when he accepted the Republican Party's presidential nomination.[30] Aware after his election that the Speaker of the House believed there was no need for major tariff revision, Taft, as president-elect, exploded in a letter to Root, saying:

> I am not . . . particularly averse to have Mr. Payne [Representative Serano Payne] and Mr. Dalzell [Representative John Dalzell], and Mr. Cannon [Speaker] understand that they cannot go ahead and fool the public without a protest from somebody and that protest seems to fall to me. If they do not pass a bill that is a genuine revision bill I will veto it, and if I find they are in a spirit of recalcitrancy I would just as lief have them believe that I am going in and fight.[31]

Except for the archaic language, Taft sounded as determined as Roosevelt, neglecting only to recognize that Roosevelt despised but never underestimated his congressional enemies, and rarely chose to give battle when he believed he might be defeated.

Taft knew his foes but forgot how Roosevelt had treated Cannon and Aldrich over the years. Neither the Speaker nor the senator from Rhode Island could be safely attacked in the absence of a very sure defense. "Uncle Joe" of Danville, Illinois, "the tightest wad and toughest talker in Congress," was not a man to be trifled with, any more than the former grocer who very early had shed his humble origins and become one of the richest and most powerful men in the Senate. Nelson Aldrich had served continuously in the Senate from 1881, and his formidable knowledge and memory guaranteed his position as the Senate's leading authority on tariffs and banking.[32] While Roosevelt might ridicule Lincoln Steffens for portraying Aldrich as "the boss of the United States," he never doubted his power, and he rarely crossed him. The newly elected president took on both the senator and the Speaker, or at least pretended to, and lost ignominiously to both. Taft might have won his tariff battle had he known how to deal with Congress, but he had learned little from serving under his more cunning predecessor.

In his own mind, as Taft explained after he lost the 1912 election, "our President has no initiative in respect to legislation given him by law except that of *mere recommendation,* and *no legal or formal method* of entering into the argument and discussion of the proposed legislation while pending in Congress."[33] Roosevelt had never viewed presidential authority in so restricted a way, insisting always that "executive power was limited only by specific restrictions and interpretations appearing in the Constitution." While Roosevelt recognized that he "did and caused to be done many things not previously done by the

President," he never believed that he had usurped power; all that he would acknowledge was that he had greatly broadened its use.[34] Taft, in his 1915 book,
The Presidency, characterized this as an "unsafe doctrine" that could "lead,
under emergencies, to results of an arbitrary character."[35] Believing this, he
never knew how to deal with Congress, when to resist and when to give way.

The revised tariff passed by the House—the House of Representatives always
dealt with money bills first—went next to the Senate, and on April 22, 1909,
barely seven weeks after assuming office, Taft learned something of senatorial
independence. Senator Aldrich rose in the upper house to say: "Where did we
ever make the statement that we would revise the tariff downward?"[36] Lodge,
scarcely less disingenuously, told his Senate colleagues on May 8 that nobody
"ever pledged me to revision downward, any more than to revision upward."[37]
Aldrich, asserting his traditional independence, altered the rates recommended
by the House substantially, and Root, the newly elected senator from New
York, purportedly the president's great friend, agreed with 104 of the proposed
changes, opposing only two dozen.[38]

Taft knew he was beaten, and as he confessed to his military aide, Archie
Butt, some time later: "Roosevelt would have come back at those preferring the
changes and would . . . have them on the run, but I cannot do things that way.
I will let them go on, and by and by the people will see who is right and who
is wrong. There is no use trying to be William Howard Taft with Roosevelt's
ways."[39] Taft, in the first weeks of his administration, showed a weakness that
long-serving legislators could not fail to notice and exploit. The president
mortgaged his reputation as an astute politician almost as soon as he entered
the White House.

Roosevelt would never have launched the tariff reform campaign in the first
instance. Had he done so and been humiliated by members of his own party,
he would have vetoed the bill that emerged from the Senate-House conference
where Aldrich and Cannon for all practical purposes decided the new rates.
The veto option held no appeal for Taft. Having long forgotten his brave words
to Root, he exulted that he was able to recommend a number of downward revisions when the differences between the House and the Senate versions were
in the last stages of negotiation. Taft believed his intervention important, saw it
as a personal victory, and treated it as such.[40] The Republican progressives in
both houses, dismayed by his ineptness and scarcely impressed by the inconsequential changes made, voted against the bill, believing the public would one
day punish those who had so cavalierly flouted the party's campaign promises.
The New York *World* published a "Roll of Honor," listing the ten Republican
senators who "voted for the people against privilege, plutocracy and the betrayal of the party faith," and an editorial in the Des Moines *News* read:
"Shades of Theodore Roosevelt! May ghosts of animals he has killed in Africa
ever haunt him for having foisted on the country this man Taft."[41]

Increasingly, the country came to see Taft as a prisoner of the country's capitalists, men Roosevelt had never trusted. In selecting so many wealthy corporate lawyers as his principal Cabinet colleagues, Taft made an error he compounded by deferring to what the press increasingly represented as the political interests of the more reactionary members of the House and Senate. These were not the principal reasons, however, for Roosevelt, in Africa on safari for a good part of 1909, to find fault with his successor.

By pressing for tariff revision Taft had obviously blundered, but not in such a way as to give offense to the former president, who understood instinctively why Lodge and Root, political animals, voted in the way they did, responding to what they conceived to be their constituents' economic interests. The tariff issue scarcely concerned Roosevelt; another crisis, however, involving the decision of the secretary of the interior, Richard Ballinger—one of Taft's many lawyer appointees—to dismiss Louis Glavis, a subordinate, did interest him. Glavis claimed that Ballinger, by reversing a decision of the Roosevelt administration to remove a million acres of public land from development, had in effect repudiated the conservation policies so strenuously defended by the former president.[42] Gifford Pinchot, a Roosevelt favorite, appointed as chief of the United States Forest Service in the Department of Agriculture, believed the Glavis charges and detected a "capitalist conspiracy" at the highest levels of government. Taft dismissed Glavis for what he and the Cabinet agreed was rank insubordination to his department chief, knowing he would thereby risk incurring Pinchot's wrath. Seeking to mollify him, in a letter of September 13, 1909, the president begged Pinchot not to "make Glavis's cause yours," aware that any difference with Roosevelt's protégé would be represented in the press and in Congress as a break with his predecessor's conservation policies.[43]

Would he, however, dare to take the next step and oust Pinchot, someone identified in the public mind with his fabled predecessor? In the end, Taft saw no alternative to doing so when Pinchot attacked him in a letter to Senator Jonathan Dolliver of Iowa.[44] The appeal of a senior government official to a senator could never be countenanced, and Root was one of many who urged the president to dismiss Pinchot. In doing so, Taft incurred the wrath of all the Republican progressives in Congress, a not inconsiderable company in both the House and the Senate, but also of reporters and editors who claimed he had betrayed the former president. Pinchot became a martyr of sorts, a victim of Republican reactionaries, still dominant in Congress, abhorred by all who proudly called themselves progressives.[45] The president, urged to dismiss Ballinger, refused to do so, seeing him as the victim of an "unjust conspiracy," knowing that a political price would be exacted for his retaining him, but refusing to be "a white-livered skunk."[46] Roosevelt sought to be fair to Taft and wrote Lodge in April 1910 that he was "not sure whether Taft . . . could have followed any course save the one he did."[47]

Clearly, the Ballinger-Pinchot affair did not by itself turn Roosevelt against Taft. Two other events, however, in the spring and fall of 1910, emphasized the distance between them. Roosevelt's return to the United States from Africa and Europe in June 1910, greeted by tens of thousands—100,000 by some estimates—proved to be something of a "royal progress," a personal triumph greater than what even his most ardent admirers had dared hope for.[48] An increasing number of progressive Republicans—those who believed that fundamental political and social reforms were imperative—began to speak openly of the need to set Taft aside, to persuade Roosevelt to become the Republican Party's presidential candidate in 1912.[49] When the off-year congressional elections proved a disaster for the Republicans in November, many blamed Taft for the party's huge losses. In the House, the Republicans lost control, and the Democrats emerged with an astonishing majority of fifty. In the Senate, the Republicans remained in the majority but lost eight seats, a considerable number in any off-year election.[50] These results boded ill for the Republicans in the 1912 presidential elections and were made to appear even more menacing by other Democratic gains that saw Henry Stimson, a Republican and great friend of Roosevelt, lose the governor's race in New York and Woodrow Wilson, a Democrat, succeed in winning in New Jersey.

While rumors had long circulated of the former president's displeasure with Taft for not being sufficiently faithful to his policies, the off-year election results made many Republicans pine openly for the "good old days of Teddy." The former president, idle in Oyster Bay, yearned to return to the White House but recognized the importance of concealing that ambition. The president, alive to the danger, made desperate efforts to mollify his predecessor, but nothing he or his friends said or did satisfied the man who had given him the presidency and now wished to reclaim it. While Taft's correspondence tells some part of the story of the rift, which would prove decisive in his defeat and in the election of Wilson, the published letters of Archie Butt, Taft's military aide, who had served in the same capacity under Roosevelt, remains *the* principal resource for understanding one of the century's more celebrated presidential rivalries.

The tale as told by Butt, sympathetic and loyal to both the former president and the incumbent, is instructive for what he saw as the differences between them, expressed as much in their personal as in their political behavior. While Butt esteemed Taft for his modesty and honesty, he knew that he lacked all sense of how to deal with the press. It was impossible for him to instill fear in those politicians who dared to cross him. During the height of the tariff struggle Taft told Butt that others were urging him "to make some headlines in the papers," and that "some wanted him to throw down the gauntlet to Congress and assert that the bill had to be this or that or else he would veto it," but he would never agree to such action. As he explained,

I realize as well as anyone else does that I could make a lot of cheap capital by adopting such a course, but what I am anxious to do is to get the best bill possible with the least amount of friction. I owe something to the party, and while I would popularize myself with the masses with a declaration of hostilities towards Congress, I would greatly injure the party and possibly divide it. . . . I wish to avoid this one thing.[51]

Roosevelt would never have uttered that sentiment, imagining that pursuit of popularity with the masses was something to be avoided, or that his greater loyalty lay with the Republican Party. Taft failed to understand American presidential politics, as they had been refashioned by Roosevelt. In an uncharacteristically philosophical moment, Taft spoke candidly to George Meyer, his secretary of the Navy, about the former president, and Butt reported the conversation, representing the president as having said:

I think this is an age of small men. I do not think either our House or Senate begin to have the big men of former years. . . . It seems to be true of legislative bodies throughout the world to-day. There are no great figures on the English political stage, or in Germany, or Austria, or any of the European countries. There is a pettiness about this immediate period which gives me some concern. I believe we are undergoing some change of which we are unmindful. It may be one of the periods which come frequently before some great epoch, the apparent stagnation which comes immediately before the crystallization of some great world thought or movement.

Taft, praising Roosevelt, noted that he not only impressed "rulers, potentates, and public men," but made a deep impression on ordinary men, saying:

The receptions which are accorded him in small obscure towns and hamlets are most significant. It illustrates how his personality has swept over the world, for after all no great event transpired during either of his administrations and no startling legislation was enacted into law. It is the force of his personality that has passed beyond his own country and the capitals of the world and seeped into the small crevices of the universe.[52]

Taft showed an extraordinary awareness of what his predecessor had accomplished. Roosevelt's legislative achievements, as we have noted, were indeed negligible; if the truth was told, unlikely to be uttered by an exceedingly modest Taft, they were not significantly greater than his own. Roosevelt's genius lay in his personality; he put one in mind of no other, especially at a time when there seemed to be a world shortage of outstanding politicians. When Meyer asked Taft what Roosevelt's permanent claim to greatness would be, the answer was instantaneous: "His rousing of public conscience."[53] Roosevelt, an accomplished politician who understood the importance of reaching out to the public, recognized that Taft had never acquired that essential political skill. Even when Joseph Cannon, the once all-powerful Speaker, was finally dislodged from his place—defeated by a combination of progressive Republicans and Democrats—Taft scarcely knew how to exploit his victory. He remained a political innocent, honorable, decent, and dull.

Only after the Republican electoral rout in 1910 did Taft seek to become somewhat less tentative, not by embracing the ideas of men sympathetic to Roosevelt but by making more explicit his alliance with the more conservative elements in the Republican Party. Three months before Senator La Follette announced his decision to seek the Republican's presidential nomination, and ten months before Roosevelt announced his own intention to do so, the president decided he would fight for the prize himself. Traveling extensively through the country, greeted by large crowds on his 13,000-mile trip, delivering many of his 330 speeches from the rear platform of his special train, he seemed suddenly energized. With Charles Hilles as his new secretary, charged with organizing the president's reelection campaign, both seemed confident of success. Hilles believed the president would win the Republican Party's nomination for two reasons: Taft partisans were certain to control the political machinery in a good number of states, and the strength of the insurgents was exaggerated, even in the purportedly rebellious Midwest.[54] Hilles knew, of course, that the president might fare badly in a number of the primaries, but the delegates selected by primaries would be few in number, insufficient to determine who would be awarded the nomination. What neither the president nor Hilles could have divined was that Roosevelt would claim that these were the only delegates elected by the popular will and that all the others, chosen by state committees, by what he chose to call the "machine," enjoyed less legitimacy and ought to be discounted.[55]

In his 1910 "New Nationalism" speech, delivered before a crowd of 10,000 in Osawatomie, Kansas, Roosevelt expressed his determination to "drive the special interests out of politics," to see the country's "swollen fortunes. . . put to public use by a graduated income tax and an inheritance tax." In that memorable address, Roosevelt argued for the direct primary, bolder conservation policies, currency reform, and the regulation of child labor.[56] These measures, he insisted, would greatly increase national efficiency, help to create the New Nationalism that would carry the country to an eminence it had never previously known. The Triangle Shirtwaist Company fire on March 25, 1911, added fuel to his demand that workers' safety and child labor figure prominently on the nation's political agenda, and on October 12 in New York he delivered a major address: "Conservation of Womanhood and Childhood," a choice of words and concepts that bore the distinctive Roosevelt signature, wholly alien to the man in the White House.[57] Attacking those opposed to the fifty-four-hour workweek legislation, he described the national government as "supine" and accused it of failing to cope with the destruction of family life engendered by inhumane labor practices. As Roosevelt continued to make speeches of this kind, the pressure for him to announce his candidacy grew, and on February 24 he told a reporter, "My hat is in the ring, the fight is on and I am stripped to the buff."[58] While many, originally prepared to support Senator La Follette, rushed to pledge their allegiance to Roosevelt, the former president's two closest friends in the Senate, Lodge and Root, found it impossible to do so. Neither could contemplate with equanimity abandoning the incumbent president, and both felt the Roosevelt challenge to be both injudicious and unnecessary.

Taft recognized very early the debt he owed Hilles, his secretary, whose grasp of the intricacies of the electoral situation in the individual states greatly exceeded his own. It appeared that Taft supporters controlled twenty-four state Republican Party organizations and that their combined delegate strength was 556, twenty-six more than the majority required for a first-ballot nomination.[59] This appeared to be the situation in late February 1912, less than four months before the start of the convention. On March 9 in Toledo, Ohio, Taft assumed the offensive and, without mentioning Roosevelt by name, ridiculed the proposition that judges should be subject to recall, that those found wanting might be dismissed by a vote of the electorate. In Taft's view, though judges were servants of the general public, they were not answerable for their decisions to the public. Those who argued that the public had the right to dismiss them were asserting a doctrine he found revolutionary and unconstitutional.[60] Responding to Roosevelt's oratory, Taft became increasingly hostile, suggesting that the former president was promoting class hatred and belonged to that company of "political emotionalists and neurotics" who menaced the nation's security. Newspapers friendly to Taft took their cue from him and began to circulate stories of Roosevelt's unreliability, some going so far as to dwell on his purported drunkenness, the vice of a man increasingly represented as a disguised "revolutionary."[61]

When Roosevelt fared badly in the first three state primary elections in North Dakota, Indiana, and New York, many in the president's camp relaxed, believing the Roosevelt boom had peaked. While Taft remained happily in the White House, Roosevelt campaigned more vigorously than ever in Illinois and Pennsylvania and won resoundingly in both states, going on to win also in Nebraska and Oregon, where La Follette came in second and the president trailed as a poor third. Where state conventions decided on the delegates, the president did substantially better, as, for example, in Texas, but Roosevelt partisans challenged the results there almost immediately. Because both saw the Ohio primary as absolutely crucial, they campaigned actively there for more than a week; Roosevelt emerged with thirty-four delegates, Taft with eight, and La

Follette with none. In Taft's home state, Roosevelt had carried sixty-nine of the eighty-eight counties, and his popular tally exceeded the president's by some 47,000 votes. While Taft had on one occasion announced that the primary in Ohio would decide the nomination, he conveniently forgot his words when the results were made known. The fight went on, with each hurling insults at the other, Roosevelt calling the president a "puzzlewit. . . behaving like a black-guard," and Taft responding that Roosevelt was guilty of "megalomania."

While each camp pretended it had the votes to win in the convention, nei-ther claim was believed by the press or the general public. Some 50,000 people turned out to greet Roosevelt in Chicago when he reached that Republican Na-tional Convention city, and many found his religious imagery deeply moving when he thundered: "We fight in honorable fashion for the good of mankind; fearless of the future; unheeding of our individual fate; with unflinching hearts and undimmed eyes; we stand at Armageddon, and we battle for the Lord." Be-cause 540 votes were required for the nomination, the Associated Press re-ported on June 10, a week before the start of the convention, that 201 delegates were instructed or uncontested and were expected to vote for Roosevelt; an-other 166 were uninstructed, and because 254 would certainly be contested, it was impossible to predict the outcome. When, however, the Republican Na-tional Committee, acting on the recommendation of the convention's creden-tials committee, awarded 238 of the contested seats to Taft, this virtually guar-anteed his first-ballot victory.[62]

None of the committee, in this obviously partisan vote, prophesied the sud-den appearance of an angry Roosevelt on the convention floor who de-nounced them and the president, vowing that if the convention failed to seat seventy-six of his contested delegates and Taft became the party's nominee, his supporters would refuse to accept their choice. Taft's supporters, assured of victory by the decision of the party national committee, saw him win the nomination on the very first ballot, knowing that Roosevelt's entry as an in-dependent candidate was now a certainty. The Progressive Convention, meet-ing in August, heard Roosevelt deliver his "confession of faith," accepting en-tirely the party's platform, its so-called Contract with the People to give the vote to women and protect trade unions in their efforts to organize. The plat-form called for an eight-hour workday, a six-day week, with promises of new federal unemployment and sickness insurance and provisions for old-age pen-sions, a social program that would not be realized for more than twenty years, under another Roosevelt.[63]

The Bull Moose candidate told those who came to celebrate his return to ac-tive politics,

> You are taking a bold and a greatly needed step for the service of our beloved country. The old parties are husks, with no real soul within either, divided on ar-

tificial lines, boss-ridden and privilege-controlled, each a jumble of incongruous elements, and neither daring to speak out wisely and fearlessly what should be said on the vital issues of the day.

Roosevelt described the Progressive Party platform as "a contract with the people," that he proposed to honor "as if it were actually enforceable under the penalties of the law." Describing government as "an efficient agency for the practical betterment of social and economic conditions throughout this land," he insisted that the only legitimate rule was that of the people. Presidential primaries and the popular election of U.S. senators were essential; so, also, were short ballots, corrupt practices acts, as well as the judicious use of the referendum, the initiative, and recall, all devices "to correct the misdeeds or failures of the public servants when it has become evident that these misdeeds and failures cannot be corrected in ordinary and normal fashion."[64]

Roosevelt claimed his aim was not to do away with representative government but to make it genuinely representative. The influence of special privilege in the business world, exercising its power through the political bosses, had too long thwarted the will of the people, and that situation had to be ended. Roosevelt called Taft's nomination a fraud, the old convention system hostile to primaries, a perversion of democratic rule. His beliefs, he insisted, were based not on study in the closet or the library—an early attack on Woodrow Wilson— but from experience in government over many years.[65] His fight, he insisted, was to guarantee that a greater use was made of governmental power to remedy industrial wrongs; his experience in office told him that "as a rule, I could secure the triumph of the causes in which I most believed, not from the politicians and the men who claim an exceptional right to speak in business and government, but by going over their heads and appealing directly to the people themselves." Roosevelt, no longer a Republican, spoke as if the people, the only sovereign power in the United States, could only trust him to be faithful to his promises.

Taft won the Republican nomination but knew as well as anyone the price he had paid for his victory. While the *New York Times* wrote editorially about the Progressives, "a convention of fanatics. . . managed by women and has-beens" that had preached socialism and revolution, seeking salvation in a renewed Roosevelt presidency, this was not how Wilson interpreted the Roosevelt phenomenon. Recognizing very early the importance of defeating the only candidate able to deny him the presidency, Wilson insisted that while there was no "indispensable man," only men who served as "instruments" to represent a "cause," he claimed to represent "the people's cause."[66] Roosevelt and Wilson became the chief protagonists in the 1912 election, each claiming to be concerned only with popular rule and the people's welfare. Wilson won the election with over 6 million votes, Roosevelt received more than 4 million, and Taft trailed with 3.5 million, carrying only two states, Vermont and Utah. As always, Roosevelt proved an aggressive and flamboyant campaigner while the president remained sedately in the White House, relying on Root and members of his Cabinet to campaign for him. Nothing Taft could have done would have reversed the nation's judgment. Roosevelt, finding political exile unbearable, aspired only to return to the White House.

Taft's problems, compounded by his political naïveté, and his appointment of a Cabinet with the late exception of Stimson substantially less distinguished than the one Roosevelt had chosen in 1905, included a lazy secretary of state—the president's own description of Philander Knox. Their so-called dollar diplomacy became a farce in Central and South America, dismissed as an unconvincing mask, an ill-fitting disguise for Yankee imperialism.[67] While Taft said that ". . . it was far better to use dollars than bullets as a means of achieving national goals," the world order he proposed to achieve through the growing economic interdependence of nations never materialized. The numerous arbitration agreements he entered into—only a few were ratified by the Senate, as recalcitrant with Taft's treaties as it had been with Roosevelt's—were less important than either the president or his secretary of state imagined.[68]

During Taft's single term in office foreign policy issues receded in importance. The Balkan crises that greatly preoccupied Britain, France, Germany, Austria-Hungary, Russia, and Turkey were largely ignored by the president and his secretary of state. Their interest was in Central America, specifically Honduras and Nicaragua, where military interventions were seen as a reasonable response to prevent their falling into the hands of irresponsible and uncivilized men. Taft and Knox spoke of the United States as having a "moral mandate" to intervene and a "duty to civilization"—terms appropriated from Roosevelt—but their expectations of what their policies might achieve exceeded what even the most generous loans by American bankers and financiers could do to guarantee the stability of a country like Nicaragua. The president genuinely believed that he helped maintain peace in Latin America by agreeing to sell warships to Argentina for $23 million; commerce, in his mind, was the cement that would establish good relations between states.[69]

Taft imagined himself an expert on the Far East, having served in the Philippines and visited Japan on several occasions. Because he lacked the geopolitical sense that made Roosevelt, a stranger to the region, more sensitive to its possible future, he showed none of his predecessor's grasp of the interests of other foreign powers in the region. Taft, surveying China, recently wracked by revolution, believed the United States could contribute to its peaceful political evolution by encouraging industrialization, and he pressed Americans to invest in the country.[70] Though some American businessmen feared the Chinese revolution would cause them to lose the benefits of dollar diplomacy, Taft entertained no such concerns, especially if other countries were quick to accept the new

Chinese republican regime. In his mind, the policies he proposed would go far to check the imperialist ambitions of the European powers, especially Russia, but also Japan, both anxious to profit from Chinese instability and disorder, looking always for special concessions.[71]

Roosevelt started with very different propositions about the Far East, never imagining that American businessmen could become his principal diplomatic agents, in effect helping to reduce imperialist rivalry in the region. A more critical interpreter of the political and economic imperatives that led stronger states to have designs on a weakened China, Roosevelt never accepted that these ambitions could be thwarted by American business investment. Taft lacked the almost intuitive feeling for foreign policy that Roosevelt boasted; more important, perhaps, he lacked the sense of how domestic policy related to foreign policy, why issues of race and national pride, not to speak of its concomitant, unreasonable, and unreasoning fear, figured so greatly in determining the foreign policies of the great powers. Roosevelt crafted a foreign policy he believed coherent, intended to establish the U.S. claim to be a great world power. Taft lacked any comparable vision. A pedestrian president not for lack of foreign policy opportunities, but for failing to understand what a president who followed a strong leader like Roosevelt could be, he fumbled badly in an arena where he might have pursued more ambitious objectives. Interestingly, Woodrow Wilson, who succeeded Taft, understood what Roosevelt had done to increase the power of the presidency and reflected constantly on policies he might pursue to make his own presidency more distinguished and distinctive. Taft never entertained such grandiose ambitions, almost instinctively understanding why they would be difficult to realize. He lacked, as did his lawyer-dominated Cabinet, those qualities of mind that made it possible for his predecessor so greatly to expand the prerogatives of the president. In the end, Taft saw no need to do so, believing that many of Roosevelt's initiatives expressed nothing so much as vanity, an almost contemptuous disregard for the constitutional provisions that limited the power of the presidency.[72]

CHAPTER 6

The Democratic Interloper

WOODROW WILSON, A child of the South, the son of a Presbyterian minister, was born in Staunton, Virginia, in 1856 and reared in humble parsonages in small Virginia, Georgia, and North Carolina parishes, still reeling from the ravages of the Civil War.[1] The romantic cavalier culture of the Old South familiar to Roosevelt from the tales told him by his mother formed no part of the education of this serious and devout Calvinist youth. Nor did Wilson ever seek to convert the story of his own childhood illnesses into a saga that dwelled on the triumph of will over physical weakness. Showing no unnatural fixation with bodybuilding, and claiming no accomplishments as a rider, hunter, or boxer, strenuous sport was wholly foreign to him. Wilson made light of his physical ailments and never acknowledged that ill-health proved to be something of a boon, compelling him to abandon his studies at Davidson, the small Presbyterian college in North Carolina he attended initially, and return home to recuperate. Never resuming his studies at Davidson, he enrolled as an undergraduate at Princeton, the eighteenth-century institution that sought to rival Harvard and Yale that still bore its original name, the College of New Jersey. As avid a reader as Roosevelt but less interested in the study of nature, he enjoyed writing, and his undergraduate essays on Bismarck and Pitt were published in the college journal, the *Nassau Literary Magazine*. Though he lacked the social advantages of Roosevelt, knowing neither wealth nor New York society, he aspired to the same political calling, imagining himself a future statesman, disdaining the more common term, politician. Gladstone, the Liberal Party prime minister, was his hero, the exemplar he proposed to follow. Taking the route traditional with many Americans who aspired to a political career, he enrolled at the University of Virginia to study law, imagining this would prepare him for the public offices he one day aspired to hold. The decision proved unfortunate, giving him neither the satisfaction nor the success he craved.

Searching for another profession to "afford him a moderate income, favorable conditions for study, and considerable leisure," and contemplating marriage, he quit Atlanta, Georgia, and went to Baltimore, Maryland, to seek a doctorate in history at the newly established Johns Hopkins University, apparently abandoning his political ambitions in favor of a career as a professor. Arriving in Baltimore in September 1883, having announced his engagement just days earlier to Ellen Louise Axson, the daughter of a Presbyterian minister, he set to work to establish himself as a serious scholar of history, looking for the economic security promised in those days by an academic post.[2] His revised doctoral thesis, *Congressional Government*, hastily prepared, was published in 1885 and praised by reviewers; it gave him modest celebrity in the small academic world he knew.[3] Wilson wrote easily, sometimes felicitously, rarely as brilliantly as Roosevelt, but with sufficient originality, clarity, and grace to give him his first teaching appointment in 1885 as an associate professor of history at an undergraduate woman's college, Bryn Mawr, in Pennsylvania. In 1888, a greater opportunity presented itself when the all-male Wesleyan College in Middletown, Connecticut, offered him a post at an appreciably higher salary, and by the end of that year Wilson had published his second book, *The State*, described by Arthur Link, his principal biographer, as "Wilson's probably greatest scholarly achievement."[4] His books sold well, and his industry was recognized as exceptional; few other professors claimed a comparable scholarly record at so early an age, and it is scarcely surprising that Princeton invited him to return there in 1890 as professor of jurisprudence and political economy. Wilson in the next decade became the most prominent member of the Princeton faculty, renowned for both his teaching and his scholarship, and no one expressed surprise when the trustees elected him university president in 1902, replacing someone forced to resign after losing the confidence of both the faculty and the trustees.[5]

Wilson, initially very successful as president, in eight short years became embroiled in university quarrels sufficiently grave to make his continued tenure precarious, perhaps even impossible.[6] Just as Roosevelt searched desperately for an early exit from his untenable position as police commissioner in 1896, so in 1909 Wilson sought to liberate himself from the servitude of the Princeton presidency and set his eyes, surprisingly, on the New Jersey governorship. He imagined that if he won that office, only slightly less important than that of neighboring New York, he might go from there to become the Democratic candidate for the presidency of the United States. This was an awesome ambition, the realization of which would have been an unprecedented triumph for an academic in the United States.[7] Wilson, relying on his undoubted intellectual and oratorical skills, and widely recognized as a close student of the presidency and the American political process, believed it to be possible.

Indeed, he felt that all he had done since his appointment as the first lay president of the university qualified him for this translation to an obviously higher political sphere. In his presidential inaugural address in 1902, entitled "Princeton for the Nation's Service," Wilson had spoken of the university's obligation to prepare men to serve, to assume responsibilities that would devolve on them when they entered the great world, leaving cloistered Princeton. Although he made no mention of either Harvard or Yale, Wilson clearly intended for Princeton to become their rival, not so much on the football field as in the great public and private offices its alumni would one day aspire to occupy.

Introducing plans for his so-called preceptorial system, never acknowledging any indebtedness to the tutorial traditions of Oxford and Cambridge, Wilson raised substantial sums from loyal alumni to make Princeton *the* American university committed to the life of the mind.[8] Lauded by both trustees and faculty, he began to think of even bolder academic ventures, abolishing the undergraduate eating clubs, introduced in the nineteenth century, that segregated the students, perpetuating social distinctions he believed iniquitous. Again, without referring to either Oxford or Cambridge, Wilson proposed the building of new residential quadrangles, with dining halls attached, each led by a resident master with his own group of preceptors.[9] While his first reforms aroused no opposition, his plan to abolish the eating clubs and raise funds for vast new residential construction provoked a debate that divided both students and alumni. Insisting that his scheme not be seen as an attack on the snobbery of the well-to-do, he offered it as an essential part of his program of educational reform.[10] In the end, the trustees, influenced by hostile alumni, voted to rescind their original approval of the quadrangle plan, and Wilson believed the trustees had "betrayed" him. Worse, however, was to follow. Wilson decided to appeal to the alumni over the heads of the trustees, imagining that their support would allow the plan to be revived; this proved a grievous mistake.[11]

Another university president, less confident of the moral and educational merits of his proposals, might have been willing to compromise with those who differed with him, but this was never Wilson's habit. Nor, for that matter, did he see any need to negotiate when his plans for the building of a graduate college clashed with those of the projected Dean and both faculty and trustees expressed reservations. What Arthur Link described as the battle of Princeton reached its climax in Wilson's speech to Pittsburgh alumni on April 14, 1910, when he threw aside all caution and represented the struggle as one between himself, the advocate of democratizing America's colleges, and those who showed no concern for social justice.[12] While Wilson came in time to regret the intemperance of these remarks, he never wholly disowned them. Indeed, he incorporated them into what soon became a more blatantly open political campaign, emphasizing not so much university reform as national revival. Wilson, increasingly spoken of as a possible Democratic candidate for governor of New Jersey, seized the opportunity to extricate himself from an impossible university situation, abandoning the parish politics of academe for the more interesting politics outside Princeton.

Wilson roused the hackles of many during his years as president of Princeton and had to habituate himself to hearing others describe him as an "arrant liar, narrow and bigoted," words only slightly less offensive than those used later by Hearst in his many newspaper attacks on him as a "modern Judas."[13] Wilson, a close student of Bryce's *The American Commonwealth,* knew that the New Jersey Democratic Party bosses, as powerful and venal as any in the country, had only one interest: to win elections. If they discovered a candidate likely to wrest the governorship from the Republicans, they would press for his nomination. Wilson believed his quarrels with the Princeton faculty and trustees had given him a national reputation as an educational leader committed to democratic principles. If the bosses could be made to see him as a viable candidate, a disinterested citizen beholden to no one, interested only in serving the state and the nation, they would choose him. Believing there were many roads to the White House and that years of political servitude in a state legislature or in Congress were not the only proper apprenticeships for high public office, he saw no reason to fear that voters would respond negatively to someone whose career had been made entirely in university teaching and administration. He set out to establish himself as the one Democrat who could win the New Jersey governorship, taking it away from the Republicans who had held it for too long.

Among those who had attended Wilson's Princeton inaugural in late 1902, a distinguished company that included J.P. Morgan, son of a Princeton alumnus, Booker T. Washington, the black educator, Mark Twain and William Dean Howells, America's most celebrated authors, was a less well-known New York editor and publisher, George Harvey. Wilson's inaugural address so impressed Harvey that he proceeded to read all his published works and concluded that Wilson was someone who might one day be elected president of the United States. In the years that followed, Harvey used *Harper's Weekly,* the magazine he edited, to advertise Wilson's many virtues, believing that any publicity that brought Wilson to the nation's attention would be grist for his own ambition to be a kingmaker, to realize the political miracle that would carry Princeton's president to the White House.[14] Wilson, though obviously gratified by the attention Harvey awarded him, understood that his support alone would never bring him the prize he coveted—the New Jersey gubernatorial nomination, a prerequisite to his becoming a Democratic presidential contender.

While the nomination for New Jersey was not in the gift of any individual, Wilson knew that James Smith Jr., Harvey's great friend and boss of the Newark-Essex Democratic Party machine, could greatly influence Democratic delegates to nominate any man that he settled on. Smith, a leading Catholic Irish American, together with his nephew, James Nugent, chairman of the New Jersey State Democratic Committee, were in a position to pressure other powerful Democratic leaders in the state to accept Wilson if they themselves were persuaded he was a winner. Wilson courted Smith assiduously, assuring him that if he received the nomination and was elected he would not "set about 'fighting and breaking down the existing Democratic organization and replacing it with one of [his] own.'"[15] What better proof could Smith have had that Wilson, though an academic, knew the rules of the game and was not entering the political fray with any intention of replacing him and others in their control of the Democratic Party in New Jersey?

Wilson, in words sufficiently ambiguous to allay concern, asked only that he be "left absolutely free in the matter of measures and men." These terms were acceptable to Smith and indeed were made even more appealing when Harvey assured him that Wilson, once elected governor, would become the obvious Democratic candidate for the presidency in 1912. The prospect of becoming the Marcus Hanna of the Democratic Party, doing for Wilson what Hanna had done for McKinley, greatly appealed to Smith. More than that, if the Democrats came to control the New Jersey State Legislature, Smith believed the governor would use his influence to support him in his own quest for a seat in the U.S. Senate.

Wilson refrained from making explicit promises but succeeded in his design to be the candidate proposed by the New Jersey Democratic bosses in 1910. The state Democratic Convention delegates accepted their recommendation, though some of the progressives worried that a man selected by the bosses, whatever his reputation for independence, might in the end become the captive of those who had engineered his nomination. Wilson reassured those who doubted him, saying untruthfully, "I did not seek this nomination. It came to me absolutely unsolicited."[16] Technically, Wilson told the truth, but those who knew the situation realized he had fudged the evidence. In any case, he made a more important promise when he said: ". . . I shall enter upon the duties of the office of Governor, if elected, with absolutely no pledge of any kind to prevent me from serving the people of the State with singleness of purpose."[17]

Wilson seemed to promise a new age for the Democratic Party in New Jersey, and this excited all who hoped for an end to the decades of boss rule. In the election campaign that followed, Wilson managed to satisfy the bosses while appealing also to the many progressives in his own party but also in the Republican Party. Even before Election Day a Democratic victory was predicted, but no one expected Wilson's vote to be a plurality of more than 49,000. Taft, two years earlier, in the presidential election had carried the state with a majority of more than 80,000, suggesting that the state was indeed safely Republican. Wilson's victory served to negate Taft's impressive showing in 1908, encouraging many to believe that the Republicans were indeed vulnerable and might lose the White House in 1912. No one doubted that a major new figure had emerged on the nation's political stage.

In the months that followed Wilson showed himself an accomplished politician. Determined to wrest control of the party from Smith, wholly ignoring the promises he had made, he rejected Smith's plea that he support him in the state legislature for the vacant U.S. Senate seat. Wilson had never promised to do this and in a letter to Harvey gave his reasons, saying:

> I have very little doubt that, if he [Smith] were sent to the Senate he would acquit himself with honour and do a great deal to correct the impressions of his former term. But his election would be intolerable to the very people who elected me and gave us a majority in the legislature. They would never give it to us again. . . . They count upon me to prevent it. I shall forfeit their confidence if I do not. All their ugliest suspicions dispelled by my campaign assurances will be confirmed.[18]

Wilson clearly intended for Harvey to share his letter with Smith, so that both would understand how he chose to interpret his 1910 victory. In his words, "It was no Democratic victory. It was a victory of the 'progressives' of both parties, who are determined to live no longer under either of the political organizations that have controlled the two parties of the State."

For Wilson, the capture of Republican votes had been all-important. As he explained to Harvey,

> If the independent Republicans who in this State voted for me are not to be attracted to us they will assuredly turn again, in desperation, to Mr. Roosevelt, and the chance of a generation will be lost to the Democracy: the chance to draw all the liberal elements of the country to it, through new leaders, the chance that Mr. Roosevelt missed in his folly, and to constitute the ruling party of the country for the next generation.[19]

The political strategy Roosevelt might have followed in his second term—to make the Republican Party a truly progressive party—was, Wilson thought, a failure the Democrats could capitalize on. The Democratic Party, for too long the party of the South, needed to become a national party, and it would achieve that goal only under the banner of progressivism.

Wilson saw himself as the architect of a new political coalition and refused to acknowledge any treachery in the political circumstances that compelled him to abandon Smith. After all, he had warned him from the beginning that he would demand "freedom on men and measures." Even before his inaugural, speaking in Jersey City, Wilson had used the formula Roosevelt made famous, condemning the "covert alliance between businessmen and politicians." Wilson told his enthusiastic audience that the electorate had "thrashed" the bosses at the recent election and that they were "going to stay thrashed," continuing with words more pregnant with meaning than his audience realized when he said: "God defend us against compromise! All weak men want compromise. . . . I'd rather be a knave than a coward."[20] With one eye always on Roosevelt, Wilson offered himself as a man of strength and principle.

With his Democratic majority in the New Jersey legislature, Wilson acted as if he had assumed the mantle of William Gladstone. He introduced legislation to reform the primary election process, guaranteeing that the popular will would be made paramount. While various corrupt-practices bills had been offered in previous sessions, none had passed; Wilson succeeded in pressing for legislation that made certain kinds of contributions illegal, ended false registration and the stuffing of ballot boxes, and made fraudulent voting more difficult. Determined to have the rates and services of public utilities and public service corporations closely monitored and regulated, he pressed for laws to achieve such surveillance, and he gained trade union support with legislation that provided for adequate workmen's compensation in the event of injury or illness.[21] While unable to persuade the legislature to ratify the Sixteenth Amendment to the U.S. Constitution that thirty other states had approved, allowing for the institution of a federal income tax, this was his only significant defeat.[22]

In two short years Wilson emerged with a greatly enhanced reputation, thought to be one of the leading progressive Democrats in the nation. He had displayed two unmistakable political talents: He knew how to engage the electorate when he believed their active intervention would help him, and he showed an uncanny ability to cobble together political coalitions in the legislature to accomplish purposes he deemed important.

What he had failed to achieve with the alumni and trustees of Princeton he accomplished with surprising ease with the electorate of New Jersey. The *New York Times* was not alone in representing the struggle as one between a determined individual, independent and fearless, and an antiquated political system.[23] The professor proved himself, and many thought his accomplishment remarkable. Not surprisingly, friends and acquaintances, mostly new, began to see Wilson as a potential president. Travelling through the West, the Midwest, the East, and the South in 1911 and 1912 with funds raised by men who wished to advance his chances as a Democratic contender for the presidency, he proved himself a progressive, not a radical, whose only concern was to persuade the Democratic Party to embrace his reform program.

A visit to Texas led to a new and important friendship, with Edward M. House—Colonel House—who first learned about Wilson through George Harvey, their mutual friend. House, a rich Texan—the military title was purely honorary—had long been active in Texas politics and had run the gubernatorial campaign of James Hogg as early as 1892. His hope was to groom a Democrat to become president of the United States, and he had seen great possibilities at one time in William Jennings Bryan, but he became increasingly disenchanted with the Nebraskan populist. Disappointed, the Colonel's meeting with Wilson told him that "he is going to be a man one can advise with some degree of satisfaction"; writing to his brother-in-law, Sidney Mezes, president of the

University of Texas, he added telling words: "Never before have I found both the man and the opportunity."[24] House had finally met the man he believed could be the first Democrat since Grover Cleveland to capture the presidency.

Wilson, the darling of the progressives but increasingly suspect to the more conservative elements in the Democratic Party, understood the difficulty of satisfying both. Compelled to choose, he offered himself as a reformer, knowing this would draw fire from Democrats hostile to progressive politicians, but it was the only strategy that commended itself. By early 1912, attacked by the New York *Sun*, a Republican newspaper, but also by the Hearst press, and more embarrassingly by Harvey, his old friend and early supporter, the Harvey dispute proved especially irksome. In November 1911, *Harper's Weekly* had printed on its editorial page masthead a notice that contained the words, "For President: Woodrow Wilson." While such an accolade coming from someone known to be a progressive would have been welcome, Harvey's reputation as a conservative Democrat made the endorsement dangerous. Progressives in the party, confused by such support, might be tempted to question Wilson's fidelity to their political principles. Harvey, noting Wilson's reticence, asked him point-blank in December whether "the support of *Harper's* is embarrassing your campaign." Wilson's reply, "I am sorry you asked me that," led Harvey to respond with "Let's have the answer anyway," and Wilson acknowledged that "some of my friends tell me it is not doing me any good in the West."[25] Wilson, certainly unintentionally, offended Harvey, and though he hoped to retain his support, Harvey felt betrayed, and "ingrate" was only one of many epithets he used to condemn Wilson for his treachery. With reports circulating of a break between the two, Harvey issued a statement on January 20, 1912, that read:

> The name of Woodrow Wilson as our candidate for President was taken down from the head of these columns in response to a statement made directly to us by Governor Wilson, to the effect that our support was affecting his candidacy injuriously. The only course left open to us, in simple fairness to Mr. Wilson, no less in consideration of our own self-respect, was to cease to advocate his nomination.[26]

The explanation said nothing of the circumstances that had led Wilson to make his remark, but it came as an enormous shock to many, especially those who knew how much he owed to Harvey. Was Wilson proving himself an ingrate once again, a charge made frequently by those who had observed him in Princeton and also those who recalled how he had abandoned Smith, a boss but also his benefactor?

William Jennings Bryan, thought by many to be the conscience of the party, rallied to Wilson and helped defuse the situation with his statement: "As soon as it became apparent that he was a progressive Democrat the predatory interests were shocked. . . . His former friends are now his bitter enemies and they are proving the sincerity of his present position by the violence of their attacks upon him."[27] Bryan could offer no greater compliment to the governor than to say that he "is the best modern example of Saul of Tarsus."[28] Many of the governor's advocates began to believe that a conspiracy existed to deny Wilson the presidential nomination. In their view, three of his rivals—Champ Clark, Hearst's favorite and Speaker of the House; Oscar Underwood, chairman of the House Ways and Means Committee; and Judson Harmon, governor of Ohio— had purportedly joined together in a "presidential trust," a sinister conspiracy to prevent the progressive candidate from becoming the Democratic Party's candidate.

Wilson, for all practical purposes, abandoned his duties as governor in 1912, spending his time mostly on the campaign trail. Early in the year, it appeared he would have the support of a majority of the convention delegates, but no one believed he could command initially the two-thirds majority required by Democratic Party rules for the nomination. Clark's overwhelming victory in the Illinois primary in April—his 218,483 votes greatly exceeding the 75,527 Wilson received—made many reconsider their prophecy that the New Jersey governor was unbeatable.[29] Clark emerged as the new favorite, and Wilson, even after his impressive primary showing in Pennsylvania, understood that any one of his three rivals might well emerge as the Democratic Party's nominee.

At the Democratic National Convention, the first nine ballots proved inconclusive, with Clark leading the pack, Wilson taking second place, and Harmon third, followed closely by Underwood. When, on the tenth ballot, Tammany shifted its support from Harmon to Clark, the latter for the first time enjoyed a majority of the votes. No Democrat in the past who had succeeded to that point had ever failed to go on to win the party's nomination. Wilson, believing his cause hopeless, instructed his floor manager, William McCombs, to release his delegates. William McAdoo, one of the governor's more ardent admirers and effectively his assistant floor manager, learning of the decision, phoned him in his New Jersey seaside retreat and begged him to countermand his order, not yet made public. In McAdoo's opinion, all was not lost. The governor agreed to say nothing, and the voting continued into its sixth day. Only on the fourteenth ballot did Bryan make the speech that many thought was the turning point in the convention, announcing that he and others in the Nebraska delegation were shifting their votes from Clark to Wilson. As a member of a progressive state, hostile to both Tammany Hall and Wall Street, their support of the conservative Clark rendered him unacceptable to proud Midwesterners.[30]

While some later believed that Bryan's speech guaranteed Wilson's nomination, it did not have that effect immediately. Indeed, only on the forty-sixth ballot did Wilson manage to secure the two-thirds vote required, an accomplishment that owed a great deal to the tireless activities of his floor managers.

Through their continuing negotiations with individual state delegations, they finally succeeded in pressing two very influential bosses, Roger Sullivan of Illinois and Thomas Taggart of Indiana, to persuade their delegations to cast their votes for Wilson.[31] While no satisfactory explanation exists of how Sullivan came to be won over, Taggart's support came from Wilson's decision to accept Thomas Marshall, Indiana's favorite son, once considered a presidential contender, to be his vice presidential running mate. Had Clark—a man James Bryce dismissed as vastly inferior—succeeded in winning the Democratic Party's nomination, the 1912 election would have become a contest between two conservative candidates and a single progressive, Theodore Roosevelt. Wilson's victory made that sort of race impossible. With Taft on the right and Wilson occupying the center of the political spectrum, Roosevelt could win only by proving himself *the* radical candidate. Stymied by the overly correct political behavior of both his opponents, Roosevelt disparaged Wilson as "the professor" and dismissed Taft as "a dead cock in a pit."[32]

Wilson, as we have seen, won the election easily, and for the first time since the Civil War the Democrats controlled both the Senate and the House, claiming fifty-one seats in the Senate to the Republicans' forty-four, with a single Progressive emphasizing the extent of that third party's rout. In the House, the Democratic Party's domination was even more visible—191 seats to the Republican Party's 127, with fourteen acknowledging allegiance to the Progressive Party. While the *New York Times* prophesied that Wilson would be a conservative president—little that he said during the campaign suggested otherwise—they mistook his intentions and underestimated what his large Democratic majorities in Congress would allow him to do.[33] Though Roosevelt had enjoyed almost comparable Republican majorities in Congress, his was a divided party, with many conservative members suspicious of the man who had succeeded the martyred McKinley. Wilson came with very different assets and credentials, having led the party to its greatest post–Civil War victory; his intention from the beginning was to lead the progressive Democrats in a legislative marathon that would effectively mock Roosevelt's 1901–1909 performance, making him the reformer Roosevelt claimed to be but, in Wilson's mind, never managed to be.

Roosevelt, within hours of learning of McKinley's death, insisted that journalists be admitted to witness his inaugural, indicating very early his interest in publicity and public relations. Wilson, on the day following his election, in a more private setting, showed a very different concern. Meeting with William McCombs, who had done a great deal to help him realize his presidential ambitions, but had also offended him by clashing with William McAdoo, the Wilson family favorite, soon to become his son-in-law, the president-elect, according to McCombs, opened with the astonishing words, "I wish it clearly understood that I owe you nothing," continuing with the even more extraordinary statement, "Remember that God ordained that I should be President of the United States."[34] Though McCombs felt keenly this apparent betrayal by Wilson and may have exaggerated in later years the events of that bleak November day, some such conversation undoubtedly took place. Wilson, perhaps offended by what he had learned of McCombs's exaggerated hopes for high office—he purportedly told Colonel House that he expected to be made secretary of state—showed the traits that would in the end destroy him: an insufficient regard for those who had helped him and a greatly exaggerated view of what he had done for himself. Wilson rarely showed gratitude to those who helped make his political ascent possible. Living always with recollections of a Princeton presidency damaged by what he imagined had been his excessively conciliatory attitudes toward those who opposed him, he promised House not to make the same errors in the White House.[35]

While he had no very high opinion of Bryan, respecting neither his knowledge nor his judgment, he realized the political necessity of appointing him secretary of state. To deny the man whom the Democrats on three occasions had nominated for the presidency would be an insult, made more serious by what many would interpret as rank ingratitude for all he had done to help his cause at the convention and during the campaign. For the second post in the Cabinet, secretary of the treasury, Wilson chose McAdoo, knowing this would offend McCombs, but telling House he expected to mollify him by offering him "a first-class ambassadorship."[36]

Wilson, in this instance as in others, greatly exaggerated his ability to retain the goodwill of those he no longer wished to have among his close associates. House approved of this decision as he did of the more painful one that led Wilson to deny Louis Brandeis the post of attorney general. Many of the president-elect's most ardent progressive supporters pressed for the appointment, and while Wilson appreciated the extent of his indebtedness to Brandeis, and not only for all he had taught him about trusts and competition, the opposition to the radical Massachusetts Jew was too intense for him to ignore.[37] The possibility of a Brandeis appointment as solicitor general was canvassed but also thought impolitic, and when the suggestion was raised that he be made secretary of commerce and labor, the hostility of virtually all those most powerful in the Massachusetts Democratic Party guaranteed that Wilson would not risk it.[38]

No one suggested that the choice of James McReynolds of Tennessee for attorney general or William Redfield, an anti-Tammany member of Congress, for secretary of commerce, were inspired appointments, and the selection of Franklin Lane of California to be secretary of the interior was made entirely on House's recommendation. Wilson did not know Lane and met him for the first time on the day of his inaugural. For the post of secretary of war, Joseph Tumulty, who had long served as Wilson's faithful secretary in the governor's office in Trenton, recommended Judge Lindley Garrison of New Jersey. Garrison, utterly confused by the offer, told the president-elect that as a lawyer he lacked all knowledge of the Army, had no experience of political life, and that he would do well to look elsewhere. Wilson, approaching inaugural day, and desperate to make an appointment—any appointment—insisted that Garrison accept.[39]

Though Josephus Daniels, of North Carolina, appointed secretary of the Navy, commanded no greater knowledge of that service he, at least, could claim friendship with the president. The Cabinet, in no sense distinguished, suffered particularly from the inexperience and ignorance of Bryan at State and the garrulousness of Lane at Interior. The latter, much to the president's disgust, regularly informed the press of confidential Cabinet discussions, and Wilson's solution for that problem was not to dismiss Lane but to make more limited use of the Cabinet, preferring to meet its members individually.[40]

Whatever problems Wilson encountered in making Cabinet appointments, they proved less embarrassing than the decision he confronted on whether to make Joseph Tumulty his presidential secretary. Wilson knew and appreciated Tumulty's qualities, valued his loyalty and judgment, and had reason to wish to appoint him, but as a Roman Catholic Tumulty was anathema to the more virulent Protestants in the country. They feared, as one Georgian expressed it, "that the secrets of state will always be made known by him to his Priest and then to the Papal Delegate."[41]

Others close to the president-elect thought Tumulty "too much the Irish ward–type of politician, lacking in breeding and grace," and for a time Wilson appeared to agree with them. When, however, Newton D. Baker, Wilson's first choice for the post, refused it, preferring to remain active as a progressive politician in Ohio, serving as mayor of Cleveland, House recommended Tumulty, persuaded he would perform well as the president's principal liaison with the press. Wilson had no option but to appoint him, lacking an alternative candidate for the post. Colonel House, at the president-elect's side during these crucial weeks, became the most influential figure in determining who would be asked to serve, and no one observing the relation between the two men could doubt the Colonel's influence.

Wilson, a very private person, boasted few long-term intimates, none from the academic world he had inhabited for almost the whole of his adult life. Though he shared with Roosevelt an intense loyalty to family, his wife and three daughters, he was less gregarious, less social, and showed very early his overweening ambition to prove himself a greater president than Roosevelt. Not given to displaying tolerance for those who disagreed with him, and disinclined to be interested in accommodating their views, he never lost the habits first revealed in his Princeton years, to be combative and self-regarding. Less the perpetual actor than Roosevelt, but a superb orator able to move vast crowds, he quickly came to dominate the American political scene as Roosevelt did and as Taft never could.

Wilson saw himself as a president able to act as a British prime minister might do when his party claimed a large majority in Parliament.[42] By directing and dominating Congress, providing leadership through the legislation he recommended to a Democratic majority prepared to do his bidding, he expected to achieve reforms of a kind Roosevelt never dared ask for with his own Republican Party divided between progressives and regulars, liberals and conservatives.

Though he began his administration by seeking to appeal to the press, adopting policies resembling Roosevelt's, going so far as to institute a semi-weekly news conference, he quickly abandoned these practices and limited himself to passing along largely inconsequential information.[43] Distrusting the press and showing little regard for journalists, he increasingly made himself available only to those in whom he had absolute confidence, who would never think to criticize him. With his large Democratic support in Congress, he felt less need for press approval and could be more than occasionally cavalier in his treatment of Cabinet members.[44] As early as 1913, expanding on ideas he had long held, Wilson described the president as "the leader of his party as well as the Chief Executive officer of the Government," but his more compelling observation was that the president "must be prime minister, as much concerned with the guidance of legislation as with the just and orderly execution of law." Not satisfied with even that ample description of presidential power, he described the president as "the spokesman of the Nation in everything, even in the most momentous and most delicate dealings of the Government with foreign nations."[45]

Not since Jefferson abandoned the practice of appearing in person before Congress, believing it smacked too much of the king's practice in opening Parliament, had any president chosen to come to Congress to address it, to press personally for legislation he favored. Yet Wilson did precisely that, addressing a joint session of Congress on April 8, 1913, taking seriously his obligation as leader of the Democratic Party to use his patronage to achieve his most pressing domestic policy objectives. The first of his many congressional triumphs came early in that same year. Unlike Taft, who began his administration by imagining he could bring his Republican colleagues in Congress to approve a reduction in the tariff—Roosevelt had understood the difficulties of effecting such a change—Wilson believed he had the Democratic votes to accomplish that. If he succeeded, and he never doubted he would, this would be the first major reduction in the tariff since before the Civil War, the last having been legislated in 1846. The large Democratic majority in the House guaranteed Wilson an easy victory there, but in the Senate, where the Democratic Party majority was only six, the results were not equally preordained. Though there was no one with the influence of Senator Nelson Aldrich—Taft's 1909 nemesis—in the upper chamber, the proposed lower duties on foreign imports were not acceptable to all Democrats, especially those from the South and West, actively solicited by powerful lobbyists to resist them.

Wilson made his first plea to those Democrats thought especially vulnerable to the propaganda of his Republican enemies, then proceeded to appeal to the country against a "lobby" he described as "numerous, industrious, and insidious." For a moment, the Republicans imagined he had overreached himself and demanded an inquiry into the activities of the so-called lobby that threatened his tariff legislation. Wilson welcomed the challenge, and though the investigation that followed never proved actual wrongdoing, it confirmed the existence of powerful agricultural and industrial interest groups determined to thwart the president. Wilson felt vindicated, and though the Republicans procrastinated, causing the debates to continue till the early days of September, Wilson carried the day; forty-four senators voted for the Underwood-Simmons bill, and only thirty-seven registered their opposition. Rates were lowered on sugar and raw wool, but also on woollen and cotton goods, and many food products were declared duty-free. Only two Democrats voted against the new tariff, and Wilson hailed his victory as a "fight for the people and for free business," achieved through the unity of the Democratic Party. Signing the legislation on October 3, 1913, Wilson quoted lines from Shakespeare's *Henry V*— "If it be a sin to covet honor, then I am the most offending man alive"—and went on to say that he did not covet the honor for himself alone but for those associated with him, "for the great party of which I am a member, because that party is not honorable unless it redeem its name and serve the people of the United States."[46] Wilson stood unchallenged as leader of the Democratic Party, but also as an unchallenged president.

This, indeed, was only the first of his legislative victories. Determined to reform the nation's antiquated banking and currency systems that dated from pre–Civil War days, Wilson in his electoral campaign, in outlining the principles of what he called the New Freedom, stressed the importance of creating a more elastic currency. Carter Glass, chairman of the House banking committee, responding to this clear presidential directive, proposed a bill to establish fifteen or more regional banks, owned and controlled by the member banks. A powerful Federal Reserve Board would be established at the summit with six public members and three bankers chosen indirectly by the regional bank directors. Bryan, the most influential member of Wilson's Cabinet, doubted the wisdom of the proposal and received support from his friend, Senator Robert Owen of Oklahoma, the powerful chairman of the Senate banking committee. Both opposed what they conceived to be the excessive influence of banker control in the proposed changes, as well as the proposition that the Federal Reserve notes should be a liability of the regional banks. Wilson consulted Brandeis and heard his friend argue for exclusive governmental control of the Federal

Reserve Board, with the Federal Reserve notes becoming the obligation of the federal government.

If the opposition to Wilson's tariff reforms seemed substantial for a time, it proved negligible when compared with the resistance to his banking and currency recommendations. Bankers, outraged by the proposed changes, joined with conservative businessmen and newspapers in their editorial control to represent the legislation as a belated triumph of Bryanism, panaceas they imagined McKinley had buried for all time. While Wilson agreed to give way on inessentials, he was genuinely surprised by the sudden eruption of opposition in the House of Representatives, where old-style agrarian radicals urged postponement of any consideration of banking reform. They argued that only the destruction of the so-called money trust—everything evil gained the distinction of being called a trust—would satisfy them. Wilson favored the changes proposed by Brandeis but would make no other concessions, recruiting Bryan to help defeat this unexpectedly fierce resistance in Congress.[47]

Though many small businessmen supported the changes, the continued opposition of bankers who saw the proposals as "communistic" guaranteed that the debate would go on and on. The House vote, in mid-September 1913, saw the Democrats stand solidly behind the president, with only three Democrats daring to oppose him. So striking a victory might have been thought sufficient to move the Senate also to approve the legislation, but it had no such effect. The banking opposition continued unabated, and Aldrich, from outside the Senate, and Root, from inside, loudly condemned the proposed changes. Again, the absolute unity of the Democrats in the Senate guaranteed the bill's passage; the final vote saw the Democrats joined by two regular Republicans, three progressive Republicans, and one Progressive. No one, for decades, had enjoyed a first year in the White House comparable to Wilson's, and though it came to an abrupt end soon thereafter, the legislative accomplishments were indeed substantial.[48]

Why, then, did the president not continue to press for other equally bold legislation? One theory, advanced by Arthur Link, Wilson's most eminent biographer, suggested that the progressives, a minority even within the Democratic Party, were Liberals in the nineteenth-century English tradition and not overly committed to the more radical proposals advanced by certain of their number. According to Link, "They wanted impartial government with a modicum of federal regulation, rather than dynamic, positive federal intervention and participation in economic and social affairs."[49] Wilson, Link argued, faithful to that tradition, made it possible for him to favor tariff, currency, and banking reforms and to advocate new policies in respect to trusts, but it did not encourage him to support the kinds of fundamental social and economic reforms that Roosevelt had proclaimed in his 1912 Progressive Party platform. Link believed also that the return of the Democrats to power in Washington signaled the revival of Southern values in the nation's capital, bringing with it a resolve to introduce into the nation's capital the segregation practices common in the states of the former Confederacy.

Wilson's own view of race relations resembled those of other Southerners who believed that separation and segregation served the interest of both races, and this attitude led Booker T. Washington to explode in anger, saying, ". . . I have never seen the colored people so discouraged and bitter as they are at the present time." When one considers Wilson's reluctance to appoint blacks to prominent federal government positions—the pleas of friends, Oswald Garrison Villard, owner of the *Nation* and the *New York Evening Post,* and Frank Cobb, of the *New York World,* notwithstanding—one has some sense of how much the president remained the child of Virginia, Georgia, and North Carolina manses, a devout Christian who saw no iniquity in racial segregation.[50]

On such issues as trusts, Wilson found it easier to satisfy the progressives in his party. Appearing before a joint session of Congress on January 20, 1914, he declared the antagonism between business and government a thing of the past and expressed the hope that the administration and Congress, "in quiet moderation, without revolution of any untoward kind," would together compose "the additional articles of our constitution of peace, the peace that is honor and freedom and prosperity."[51] The legislation that grew out of this pledge, the so-called Clayton bill, drawn up by Henry Clayton of Alabama, chairman of the House judiciary committee, sought not so much the breakup of industrial giants as the punishment of wrongdoers guilty of specific illegal trade practices, including price-cutting, that had done so much to destroy competition.

Wilson, a firm believer in the value of publicity, imagined that most businesses would never risk their being charged with illicit behavior. The act to establish the Federal Trade Commission, introduced on April 14, 1914, again in response to Wilson's urging, gave that newly created body authority to investigate corporate and business activity that violated the antitrust laws. Section 5 of the bill required the commission, modeled after the Interstate Commerce Commission, to investigate and prevent unfair competition, with the power to issue cease-and-desist orders, enforceable by the federal district courts; this provoked yet another massive resistance by conservative Republicans in Congress. Representative Frank Brandegee of Connecticut called it a "socialistic program," to be administered by an irresponsible agency with despotic powers, and others spoke derisively of the "inquisitorial powers" created by the legislation.[52] The bill, in the end, with amendments, passed easily in both the House and the Senate, and many saw it as the "beginning of a new era in constructive federal regulation of economic life."

Why, then, did this prove to be the end of the domestic reform road for Wilson? Why did he not proceed to demand legislation for child labor protection and a federal rural credits scheme, as many expected him to do? Link's explanation—that the business depression that began in late 1913 and continued into 1915 quelled the president's enthusiasm for further change—was undoubtedly important, but so, also, were other factors. Ellen Wilson's serious illness, first apparent in the winter of 1914, led to her death the following August and contributed to Wilson's diminished appetite for political struggle. The kinds of intervention with Congress he had once relished, calling for patience, energy, and resolve, no longer greatly appealed to him. His grief made him more passive, at times almost lethargic. More important, perhaps, though the crises in Mexico in the early years of his administration had required the president's close and constant attention, given the limited diplomatic skills of his secretary of state, they never consumed him in the way the war in Europe did after August 1914. Armageddon served as one of the excuses Wilson offered to explain his decision not to become involved in the off-year congressional elections of 1914 where the Democrats fared badly, its majority in the House reduced to twenty-five. Though the Democrats suffered no comparable losses in the Senate, the victories they had reaped in 1912 as a consequence of the split between Roosevelt's Progressives and Taft's Republicans no longer operated to their advantage.

Even had Wilson wished to resume his legislative forays, to demonstrate his prowess as a reformer, he would have had a more difficult time in 1915 and 1916 than in 1913 and 1914. He, in fact, lacked the ambition, and even before the election results were known, Wilson, writing to a friend, represented his legislative program as essentially completed. In a letter to William McAdoo, his son-in-law and secretary of the treasury, published in the *New York Times* a fortnight after the election, Wilson contrasted the spirit of contention characteristic of American life a decade earlier with the more pacific conditions, the marked absence of distrust and antagonism that had since come to prevail. In his mind, the change could be attributed largely to the legislative achievements of his administration.[53] Fundamental wrongs had been righted, and the president represented the future as bright with promise. When one considers the pledges Roosevelt and the Progressive Party had made in their 1912 platform, proposing new measures to protect workers, women, and children, the modesty of Wilson's political ambitions become clear. Still, no Republican, neither Roosevelt nor Taft, could claim to have accomplished legislatively what Wilson justifiably boasted of. Their Republican majorities in the House and Senate were never used as ruthlessly or effectively to promote economic change or to create new institutions intended to protect the public interest.[54]

Wilson, even before 1914, had assumed substantial control also of the conduct of foreign affairs, believing he would soon establish a reputation that would put Roosevelt's in the shade. Given his secretary of state's record in having opposed American imperial adventure in the Caribbean from the time of the Spanish-American War and the president's declared disdain for Taft's dollar diplomacy, his victory in 1912 seemed to carry the promise of a Caribbean and Latin American policy fundamentally different from that common to the Republicans. The early Wilson initiative to improve relations with Colombia, a country still smarting from Roosevelt's actions in fomenting Panamanian revolution, led to an agreement that seemed to carry the promise of finally settling that unseemly dispute. The United States agreed to pay an indemnity of $25 million to Colombia, but Roosevelt and the Republicans in Congress attacked the president for what they described as an "act of infamy."[55] The Senate, though controlled by the Democrats, showed little sympathy for any payment to Colombia, and it refused to agree to compensation even when the amount was reduced to $15 million.[56] Other Latin American initiatives fared no better. Plans for a Pan-American treaty, to create a hemispheric alliance for common defense that engaged the interest of Wilson, Bryan, and House, came to nothing, in part because of growing hostility in Latin America to the administration's policies in Nicaragua, but more especially in Mexico.

In neither place did Wilson seem prepared to abandon the kinds of intervention that had long characterized U.S. policy, as Republican business interests had purportedly dictated them. That a Democratic administration, pledged to moral principles constantly proclaimed during the election campaign, became involved in the internal affairs of Mexico, acting in ways that infringed on Mexico's sovereignty, came as a rude shock to many. Wilson inherited a problem that originated in 1911 and 1912 when the longtime Mexican dictator, Porfirio Díaz, was toppled by a coalition of reformers and revolutionaries. Francisco Madero, put in his place, was deposed and murdered by forces under the command of General Victoriano Huerta, who assumed the office of provisional president during Taft's last weeks in the White House. While most European governments quickly recognized the new regime, the United States refused to do so, abandoning its long-standing policy of giving de jure recognition to de facto governments. Though the U.S. ambassador in Mexico City, Henry Lane Wilson, urged recognition, and many in the State Department agreed, Wilson preferred to wait. In his mind, a popular constitutional government had been overthrown and its leader murdered by what he later called a "government of butchers." Knowing nothing of Mexico himself but seeking additional information on Huerta and his regime, he dispatched a friend, William Bayard Hale, in May 1913 to investigate the situation. Hale's dispatches represented Huerta as "an ape-like old man," a power-mad drunk who would certainly carry the country to inevitable bankruptcy and tyranny, and recommended that Wilson demand Huerta's resignation, call for free elections, and then recognize the newly elected government. That policy appealed to the president, though not to Great Britain and Germany, alarmed for their nationals in Mexico, and unable to understand what the president, preoccupied with his own internal political agenda, might be contemplating.

Both failed to understand why he imagined the United States had the right to interfere politically in the internal affairs of a sovereign state. Though the British Foreign Office believed free elections to be impossible in Mexico, the White House rejected that view. The president, supported by his secretary of state, saw an opportunity to be an arbiter in the Roosevelt tradition.[57] Appearing before a joint session of Congress on August 27, 1913, he explained his Mexican policy, claiming that its sole purpose was to help the Mexican people find peace and establish an "honest constitutional government." The Huerta government, he said, had brought only "war and disorder, devastation and confusion to Mexico," and it was the duty of the United States to offer its good offices. Wilson urged U.S. citizens to leave the country and forbade the export of munitions to any of the combatants. The American press heralded the administration's policy as one of "watchful waiting," and when Huerta agreed to new elections on October 26, 1913, accepting not to be a candidate himself, those who imagined Wilson to be as adept in foreign as in domestic policy rejoiced. Their pleasure was short-lived, however. The so-called Constitutionalists, opposed to Huerta from the start, breached his northern defenses, and when they threatened the capital itself Huerta arrested and imprisoned some 110 deputies, dissolved Congress, and assumed dictatorial powers.

Wilson, infuriated by Huerta's actions, and persuaded that the British supported him only because of the influence of Lord Cowdray, whose large investments in Mexican oil and railways were thought to explain British policy, imagined he could pressure the British to change their policy. Because Sir Edward Grey, Britain's foreign minister, had no wish to resist the Americans openly, he agreed to cooperate with Wilson in seeking to isolate Huerta.[58] Wilson, again, appeared to have understood the situation perfectly, but when the Constitutionalists bogged down in their offensive, he decided to help them by lifting the arms embargo, hoping this would spur them on. Huerta, still in office, was a thorn the president was determined to remove, and an incident in early April outside Tampico, Mexico's leading port city with Veracruz, gave him the excuse he needed to announce the start of large-scale U.S. military operations against Huerta. Appearing before a joint session of Congress to ask for punitive action, telling members that "the dignity and rights of the American Government" had been violated, the House, by a vote of 337–37, approved a joint resolution declaring that the president was "justified in the employment of armed forces . . . to enforce demands made on Victoriano Huerta."[59]

The president, together with his military advisers, planned an attack on both Tampico and Veracruz, and on the morning of April 21, 1,000 Marines and sailors landed at Veracruz. In the fighting that ensued, the Mexicans lost 126 dead and 195 wounded; the Americans suffered a loss of nineteen dead and seventy-one wounded.[60] The president had never anticipated casualties, imagining the dispatch of U.S. forces to Mexico would lead quickly to Huerta's collapse. Instead, he confronted a shocked American public, a hostile Mexico, outraged by its neighbor's aggression, and a world opinion that showed little sympathy for his actions. The president beat a hasty retreat, agreed to a mediation offer by Argentina, Brazil, and Chile, only to withdraw from that engagement when Huerta resigned in July and left for exile in Europe. U.S. troops remained in Veracruz for the next seven months, and while some imagined the Mexican imbroglio was over, it was in fact only beginning.

Wilson formulated the administration's Mexico policy even though he knew nothing about the country, and he gave no heed to the protests of the British and other Europeans who insisted that only de jure recognition of the Huerta government made sense. In relying on the views of the special envoys he sent to Mexico City who understood the situation scarcely better than he did, and in ignoring the recommendations of those in the State Department who counseled caution, Wilson revealed what some had quickly come to recognize as his undisguised contempt for America's professional diplomats. In a letter to Charles W. Eliot, the former president of Harvard whom he knew well, he said in September 1913:

> We find that those who have been occupying the legations and embassies have been habituated to a point of view which is very different, indeed, from the point of view of the present administration. They have had the material interests of individuals in the United States very much more in mind than the moral and public considerations which it seems to us ought to control. They have been so bred in a different school that we have found, in several instances, that it was difficult for them to comprehend our point of view and purpose.[61]

Wilson, from his lonely perch, disdainful of the State Department, suspicious of the Europeans, pursued a policy that led him to military action whose consequences he failed to anticipate, whose end he never foresaw. In his first major excursion into foreign policy, he showed himself arrogant, suspicious of those at home and abroad who questioned his strategy and tactics. By denying the Huerta regime recognition, Wilson, in effect, initiated the human rights policy that later presidents would also invoke to justify their military interventions against dictators.[62] He also gave legitimacy to the nonrecognition policy that was to govern relations with the Soviet Union till the arrival of Franklin Roosevelt in 1933. As Forrest McDonald, a historian not noted for his sympathy for Wilson, wrote:

> . . . despite the democratic rhetoric, Wilson proved to be as active an interventionist as his predecessors. His emphasis changed from dollar diplomacy to an insistence that America's southern neighbors govern themselves as stable democracies; whenever they did not, he governed them with American troops. After a year

of fruitless negotiations with Haiti, during which time the country had three regimes, Wilson sent in the marines and essentially adopted the place as an American protectorate. Relations with the Dominican Republic followed a similar course.[63]

Given the low opinion Wilson had of his secretary of state, it is scarcely surprising that he relied increasingly on unofficial advisers, Colonel House being the principal one. House, the ever-faithful counselor, could be relied on to show himself always sympathetic to the president's ideas. Wilson believed, even when they had known each other only for a very brief time, that "we have known one another always" and felt no comparable regard for those he sent abroad to serve as the country's ambassadors in the principal countries of Europe.

Indeed, unlike Roosevelt, he despised many of the men he dispatched to these posts, lacking all confidence in their judgment. James Gerard, a major contributor to the Democratic Party and a prominent Tammany politician, awarded the embassy in Berlin, was thought to be an "ass" by the president.[64] While he held Walter Hines Page, appointed to the Court of St. James, in somewhat greater esteem, Page's Anglophilia became so offensive to him that he left some of his dispatches unread.[65] The president believed only in himself and those men around him, who never dissented from his opinions. Arthur Willert, the *Times* of London correspondent, searching for the power behind the throne, believed he found him in Walter Lippmann, a young *New Republic* journalist who had become in his mind "second Assistant President," ranking just below Colonel House.[66] Willert exaggerated Lippmann's influence but, like many others in Britain, seeking to understand the president's mind, believed it derived from his accepting too easily the "obscurantist liberalism of Eastern intellectuals," those who wrote regularly for the *New Republic*. This was never the view of Spring Rice, Britain's ambassador in Washington, and Roosevelt's old friend, who knew that the complex man who directed America's foreign policy was not simply a Liberal in the *Manchester Guardian* tradition, though elements of that belief certainly insinuated themselves in a president he thought "intensely jealous" and "determinedly vindictive."[67]

When Bryan resigned in 1915, after what he considered Wilson's excessively aggressive statements following the German submarine sinking of the *Lusitania* on May 7, 1915, with more than 1,000 men and women losing their lives, 114 Americans among them, Robert Lansing took his place. Lansing had served as counselor in the State Department from 1914 to 1915, and Spring Rice described him as "a lawyer of no great importance personally or politically," a comment that might have been made of any number of Wilson's other Cabinet colleagues.[68] The president distrusted Lansing and remarked on one occasion that "he was so stupid he was constantly afraid that he would commit some serious blunder."[69] A hard taskmaster, Wilson never made Lansing a principal adviser and relied increasingly on his miniscule coterie of courtiers, none more conspicuous than Colonel House. With these men, including the secretary of the treasury, his son-in-law, Wilson on occasion shared confidences, but no one, including those recognized to be close to him, pretended to know him. They existed mostly to serve him, and someone like Colonel House showed no hesitation in accepting that role, recognizing the opportunities it offered him. Claiming none of the advantages (and disadvantages) of a Cabinet post, House understood Wilson's mind, and it took no great imagination for him to know following the outbreak of war in Europe in August 1914 that the president's overwhelming concern would be to prove himself a peacemaker, exceeding Roosevelt's accomplishment even in that sphere.[70]

As early as January 1915, the president dispatched House to Europe to meet with the principal belligerents to determine whether there was any possibility of the United States acting as a mediator in the war between the Western Allies and the Central Powers. Wilson saw himself as beholden to neither side and expected his good offices to be valued, believing the mission would initiate a process that would lead to peace. Though the president knew the Colonel well, he was almost certainly unaware of his bias in favor of the Allies and against the Central Powers. This became evident only after the sinking of the *Lusitania* when House sent a message he came to regret; the Colonel's cable read: "Our intervention will save rather than increase loss of life. America has come to the parting of the ways, when she must determine whether she stands for civilized or uncivilized warfare."[71] These were not sentiments the president cared to hear, least of all from his principal confidante. Determined to maintain the U.S. status as a neutral, Wilson did not at that moment choose to see the British as civilized, the Germans as barbarians. House suffered a real though temporary eclipse, redeeming himself only by never repeating such opinions again, but also, and more important, by advising the president on how best to disseminate the news of his impending engagement and marriage to Edith Bolling Galt, the woman who was soon to become his devoted second wife.[72]

By December 1915, House, restored to favor, embarked on his most serious effort to secure British consent to U.S. mediation in the war. His negotiations led to the so-called House-Grey memorandum, initialed by both men on February 12, 1916.[73] Under its terms, the British agreed to support an American mediation effort; should it fail, the United States promised to reassess its position on the war. House, in his London conversations, went so far as to suggest that the mediation effort was essentially a pretext to allow the United States to enter the war, information he of course never shared with the president. In his messages to Washington, he greatly exaggerated the British interest in the mediation proposal, and when it became apparent that this was not the situation at all, Wilson felt betrayed by what he interpreted as British perfidy.

The Cabinet at Westminster was scarcely less disconcerted by an American president it was unable to fathom.[74] While Wilson in his religious and moral fervor imagined the United States had been chosen by providence "to show the way to the nations of the world how they shall walk in the paths of liberty," this was not a view the British shared. When, in May 1916, the president in New York addressed the American League to Enforce the Peace, he reiterated his opposition to any American involvement in the war, insisting, however, that the United States had every interest to participate in a peace league after the war; Spring Rice told the Foreign Office that the peace league had become Wilson's obsession.[75] The president could not imagine that the United States, though a neutral, would be barred from participating in the peace settlement; the country's concern with moral principles entitled it to a place at the peace table.

The British disillusion with the president grew perceptibly, fueled by his Mexico policy but also by his seeming tolerance for continuing German submarine transgressions on the high seas. Wilson, pleased that Venustiano Carranza, the newly nonelected Mexican president, had defeated both his principal revolutionary rivals, Emilio Zapata and Pancho Villa, granted his government de jure recognition, believing the United States was no longer threatened by Mexican insurrection. Again, he misconstrued the situation; Villa, defeated inside Mexico, crossed the border into New Mexico on March 9, 1916, in a raid that cost nineteen American lives; the invaders lost sixty-seven of their own men. Wilson ordered General John J. Pershing to advance into Mexico to capture Villa, dead or alive.[76] Neither the president of Mexico nor the Mexican people looked with equanimity on this violation of their sovereignty, and though Pershing with his force of 15,000 men advanced quickly some 350 miles into Mexico, Villa continued to elude him, and Wilson appeared again to have blundered.[77] Because the Mexican military operation coincided with the sinking of the cross-channel steamer *Sussex* by a German U-boat, killing or injuring some eighty passengers, including four Americans wounded—the British hoped the president might use the incident to condemn the Germans and pull his troops out of Mexico. He did neither. The Germans, claiming the *Sussex* attack had been an error, promised that submarines would never again attack unarmed passenger or cargo ships and agreed to an indemnity.[78] Wilson begged the country to remain "neutral in thought as well as in deed," and the British were openly dismayed.

Spring Rice, seeking always to explain the president to the Foreign Office, wrote of him:

His standpoint seems to be that the world has gone mad and can only be saved by the few sane men who are left in it. As one of the madmen you will form your own opinion, no doubt a mad one, as to the claim of our sane Saviour. No one can doubt the President's perfect sincerity in his desire to help in the cause of peace. The high moral principles as well as enlightened self-interest point that way.[79]

The British ambassador understood that principle counted heavily with the president but that, as a political animal concerned with his reelection, he prized the American public's support of his neutrality policies; he would do nothing to jeopardize that favorable opinion. When the Democratic National Convention convened in 1916, Wilson's policies received enthusiastic support and the party's platform suggested the extent of his influence, nowhere better expressed than in the statement:

The circumstances of the last two years have revealed necessities of international action which no former generation can have foreseen. We hold that it is the duty of the United States to use its power, not only to make itself safe at home, but also to make secure its just interests throughout the world, and both for this end and in the interest of humanity, to assist the world in securing settled peace and justice. We believe that every people has the right to choose the sovereignty under which it will live; that the small states of the world have a right to enjoy from other nations the same respect for their sovereignty and for their territorial integrity that great and powerful nations expect and insist upon; and that the world has a right to be free from every disturbance of its peace that has its origin in aggression or disregard of the rights of people and nations; and we believe that the time has come when it is the duty of the United States to join the other nations of the world in any feasible association that will effectively serve those principles, to maintain inviolate the complete security of the highway of the seas for the common and unhindered use of all nations.[80]

The Democratic platform anticipated the whole of Wilson's proposed reform of the international system, as he imagined it in 1916, and as he sought to effect such changes two years later in Paris when he girded himself for battle with Europeans less than wholly convinced of the merits of his proposals.

In the Democratic Party's platform statement on Americanism, there was an early premonition of other policies the president would find it necessary to introduce after the declaration of war in April 1917, to "show itself not a nation of partisans but a nation of patriots."[81] Taking note of "conspiracies" that existed "for the purpose of advancing the interests of foreign countries to the prejudice and detriment of this country," the platform condemned all such disloyalty and in its "preparedness" recommendations spoke of the American people and their love of peace, emphasizing the need to maintain defenses adequate to any danger that might arise. The party, seeking to justify the president's policies in Mexico, implied that intervention, equated with military subjugation, was a concept revolting to the American people that would never be countenanced.[82] What then, had the administration done? Showing the "most scrupulous regard" for Mexico's sovereignty, only

> the want of a stable, responsible government in Mexico, capable of repressing and punishing marauders and bandit bands, who have not only taken the lives and seized and destroyed the property of American citizens in that country, but have insolently invaded our soil, made war upon and murdered our people thereon, has rendered it necessary temporarily to occupy, by our armed forces, a portion of the territory of that friendly state. Until, by the restoration of law and order therein, a repetition of such incursions is improbable, the necessity for their remaining will continue.[83]

There was nothing in the statement to suggest that the president would feel compelled to send armed forces into Mexico three more times in 1918 and on six occasions in 1919.[84]

Patriotism, one of the principal themes of those who gathered to renominate Wilson, coexisted with firm support for his policy of neutrality. When Senator James of Kentucky, the convention's permanent chairman, said of the president, "Without orphaning a single child, without widowing a single American mother, without firing a single gun, without the shedding of a single drop of blood, he wrung from the most militant spirits that ever brooded above a battlefield an acknowledgment of American rights and an agreement to American demands," pandemonium broke out in the hall.[85] Wilson, the man of peace, was the hero of his party, and Bryan joined all the others in praising him. Nominated by acclamation, with the vice president, Thomas Marshall, chosen in two minutes, the president who had "kept us out of war" prepared to open his campaign against Charles Evans Hughes, the former governor of New York who had resigned as associate justice of the U.S. Supreme Court to accept the nomination of a united Republican Party.

The summer and autumn of 1916 proved to be a difficult time for Wilson, less because of the Hughes campaign, and more because of what appeared to be a steadily deteriorating relation with the new British government, led by David Lloyd George. The president found it relatively easy to blunt Hughes's criticism of his Mexico policy, agreeing shortly after the Democratic National Convention to have a joint commission investigate the situation that had led to a clash between U.S. and Mexican troops, but it proved more difficult to counter Hughes's argument that the administration showed insufficient vigor in protecting the country's maritime rights. The British, on July 19, published a blacklist of eighty-seven American firms with whom British subjects were forbidden to deal, all suspected of trading with the Central Powers.[86] Wilson exploded at what he perceived to be this provocative and illegal act, telling

Colonel House he was at the end of his patience with the British and the Allies. "This black list business," he wrote House, "is the last straw," and he considered whether he ought not to go to Congress to ask for authority to forbid exports and loans to the United Kingdom. His anger was not feigned; it expressed his view that both the Allies and the Central Powers were guilty of violating international law in respect to neutral rights.

While the British Foreign Office ascribed Wilson's diplomatic actions during this preelection period principally to a concern to be victorious in the vote scheduled for the first Tuesday in November, they in fact expressed his larger political objective. Wilson, elected as a progressive Democrat in 1912, sought reelection as a president faithful to his reform principles, concerned as much with the need for new workmen's compensation protection as for new legislation to regulate child labor. His success in averting a national rail strike and winning support for the Adamson bill that mandated an eight-hour day for all railroad employees showed what presidential intervention in a major labor-management dispute could accomplish.

In making his continuing quest for peace a principal plank in his program, joining it to new proposals for domestic reform, Wilson hoped the two together would guarantee his victory in an election almost certain to be close. Hughes, though ineffectual as a political campaigner, gained immeasurably from the Republican Party's restored unity, and the president was not wholly surprised that the early election returns showed the Republicans carrying most of the large Eastern and Midwestern states. The *New York Times* shortly after 10 P.M. on election night declared Hughes the winner, but as returns from the West continued to pour in during the next day, Wilson's hopes revived. Not until late that evening did it become clear that he had in fact won, thanks to the crucial twenty-three electoral votes of California. Wilson's victory was exceedingly narrow; in the popular vote, his 9,129,606 votes barely exceeded the 8,538,221 Hughes claimed; in the Electoral College he boasted 277 votes against 254 for Hughes.[87] For the first time since Andrew Jackson in the early nineteenth century, a Democrat had managed to win a second consecutive presidential term, though only by the slightest of margins.

The six months that followed Wilson's reelection were the most important in his eight years as president. Spring Rice, the British ambassador, grasped the significance of his victory and, in a thoughtful dispatch to the Foreign Office on November 28, 1916, wrote:

> The president has now got all he can out of United States politics. He cannot play a war part for want of means and a peace part is indicated. At bottom his heart sympathized with Allies but we are unwilling to accept his mediation while Germany is willing. He may therefore wish to put pressure on Allies in form of embargo on loans and supplies.[88]

Spring Rice prophesied correctly; on the very day he sent his dispatch, the Federal Reserve Board issued a statement warning American investors to be wary of unsecured loans of the type the British and French were offering in the New York markets. Such purchases, the Federal Reserve indicated, were against the American national interest. While it was impossible for Spring Rice to know what role, if any, the president had in the matter, he correctly viewed it as ominous.[89]

When the German government, in the days that followed, sent Wilson a note blaming the Allies for continuing the war and refusing his efforts at mediation, indicating their own readiness to attend a peace conference, Wilson responded with a note of his own, sent on December 18 to all the belligerents.[90] The president dispatched his note, never suggesting in any way that it referred to what the Germans had recently asked for. He claimed that both sides appeared to be seeking the same ends: "to secure the futures of weak peoples and small nations; to protect their own countries; to prevent future wars of this kind from occurring; to protect their commercial rights and freedoms; and to establish a league to enforce the peace."[91] These were Wilson's ideas, not those of the Allies or the Central Powers, but the president pretended he was simply voicing the sentiments of the Europeans. Claiming his was neither a peace proposal nor an offer of mediation, he suggested "that soundings be taken in order that we may learn, the neutral nations with the belligerent, how near the haven of peace we may be for which all mankind longs with an intense and increasing desire."[92]

Balfour, who had taken over from Sir Edward Grey as foreign secretary, substantially less interested in humoring the president, believed with others in the Cabinet, including the prime minister, that peace could be achieved only by the defeat of the Central Powers. What Lloyd George had said in an interview in late September remained the government's fixed policy. No offer of help by the recently reelected president changed the prime minister's view that "the fight must be to the finish to a knock-out."[93]

Wilson refused to be dismayed by these evidences of recalcitrance and continued to preach for "a league of peace," adding a memorable phrase when he spoke of "peace without victory" on January 22, 1917.[94] The British, angered by the president ignoring the bill of particulars they had prepared to support their charges about Germany's aggressive behavior, found such words almost offensive. Spring Rice, in one of his last dispatches as ambassador—he was dying of Graves' disease—sought to explain why the president spoke and acted as he did, and wrote:

> The President is a transitory being. His glory is effulgent but brief. The temptation to play a great part before the authority is over is overwhelming. The Democratic Party for many years has not had consecutive terms of office. It is a one man

party. It is the permanent glory of the party in the person of its head. A man who was quite recently rejected by a local university and who becomes the arbiter of the destinies of the world, a partner with Pope and Kaiser, is naturally the object of admiration. . . . The President's great talents and inspiring character fit him to play a great part. He feels it and he knows it. He is already a mysterious, rather Olympian personage and shrouded by darkness from which issue occasional thunderbolts. He sees nobody who could be remotely suspected of being his equal should any such exist in point of intellect or character.[95]

Spring Rice, to the last, sought to explain the mysterious character who inhabited the White House, controlling the government as only Theodore Roosevelt had dared to do before him, a man the British knew they could not afford to ignore.

While the British pondered what policy to pursue in approaching this "rather Olympian personage," Germany rendered the problem moot by its own precipitous action. The German High Command, agreeing with the Kaiser, and ignoring the advice of Chancellor Bethmann-Hollweg, decided to renew unrestricted submarine warfare on February 1, 1917, ignoring its *Sussex* pledge. With Russia virtually out of the war, soon to be the victim of revolution, and the British Somme offensive having failed, William II's advisers believed a reversal of policy—a renewal of U-boat attacks on neutral and Allied shipping— would quickly lead to Britain's defeat and Allied surrender. The Germans understood that their policy carried some threat of war with the United States, but the risk, in the view of the High Command, seemed minimal. The Allies would be defeated long before American aid could reach them. Wilson learned of the German decision on January 31, 1917; unrestricted submarine warfare would begin the following day.

On February 3, Wilson appeared before Congress to announce the severance of relations with Germany, choosing not to represent that action as an intention to declare war. Germany, in his view, was led by "madmen," and this required the United States to show prudence, to seek to bring that distressed nation back to its senses.[96] Wilson refused at first to arm U.S. merchant vessels, preferring to pursue various diplomatic initiatives to impress the Germans with his resolve.

Initially, he hoped to persuade other neutral states to break off relations with Germany, and he approached both the Netherlands and Switzerland with that proposal, but neither showed great interest in it.[97] He then conceived the idea that Austria might be separated from Germany if offered a separate peace that guaranteed its original frontiers; he asked Lloyd George to support him in that initiative. The British prime minister delayed giving any answer, and nothing came of the plan. At this point, the British intercepted a telegram from Arthur Zimmermann, the German foreign secretary, to its Washington embassy for transmission to Mexico, offering an alliance with Mexico if war should break out between Germany and the United States. Zimmermann promised generous financial help to Mexico, together with "an undertaking on our part that Mexico is to re-conquer the lost territory in Texas, New Mexico, and Arizona."[98] The British pretended they had received the message through an agent in Mexico City; their ability to intercept transatlantic messages remained one of their most closely guarded secrets.[99] Wilson learned of the telegram on February 24 and expressed his outrage, concerned almost immediately about its authenticity. Once persuaded it was indeed genuine, he authorized its publication by the Associated Press on March 1. Americans, dumbfounded and shocked, learned two days later from the German foreign minister that the telegram was indeed authentic, and the press attributed its discovery to the work of American secret agents. The British were obviously delighted not to be discovered as the true messenger. On March 12, Wilson ordered an armed guard to be placed on all U.S. merchant vessels, ignoring what he called the opposition of "a little group of wilful men" in the Senate.[100] Bethmann-Hollweg, speaking to the Reichstag after Wilson agreed to the arming of U.S. merchant vessels, spoke of America's "subjection to English power and control" and of America's wish to "starve Germany and increase bloodshed."[101]

Wilson, profoundly shocked by these words, acknowledged there was no "peace party" in Germany, and while armed neutrality appealed to many in the country, the sinking of the *Laconia*, a Cunard liner, with three American dead, served to exacerbate the feelings of those who showed increasing impatience with what they characterized as the president's excessive timidity.[102] Bryce had once described Wilson's mind as "more twisted than a corkscrew," using Mark Twain's memorable phrase, and could only imagine he wanted to be absolutely certain that public opinion favored a declaration of war before he embarked on so dangerous a course.[103] With the reported sinking of three American ships on March 18, *City of Memphis, Illinois,* and *Vigilancia,* the inadequacies of a policy of armed neutrality became obvious. When Wilson summoned Congress to meet in special session on April 2, the world knew the call could have only one meaning—he intended to ask for a declaration of war against Germany. Wilson had waited for American public opinion to express itself, and he knew it had done so unmistakably by late March. His Cabinet, including men who had once counselled patience, accepted the necessity of war. The arguments used by the British from the early days of the war about the nature of the Kaiser's Prussian regime were finally accepted, by no means universally, but in ways wholly inconceivable five months earlier.

The Russian Revolution of March 1917, heralding the end of the autocratic regime of the czars, persuaded many Americans that the war had indeed become a war for democracy. As for the president, he clearly aspired to be a world leader in the cause for peace, and that ambition alone justified his coming to

Congress to ask for a declaration of war. William Wiseman, a British intelligence agent stationed in Washington who understood Wilson's distrust of subordinates, sought to explain the president to his superiors, and wrote:

> The President. . . has been long getting into the war but will not be in a hurry for peace. He will not approve peace until he is satisfied that (in his own words) 'the world is safe for Democracy.' He will be found to be just as stubborn and persistent in his dealing with Congress and his own people as in his dealings with the Allies and the enemy Governments.[104]

Was Wiseman issuing an accolade to Wilson or giving a warning to his government? His note admitted of either interpretation.

From almost the day the president declared war, he showed his determination to be a war president in the Lincoln manner. On April 7, he issued an executive order, never made public, that read:

> The head of a department or independent office may forthwith remove any employee when he has ground for believing that the retention of such employee would be inimical to the public welfare by reason of his conduct, sympathies, or utterances, or because of other reasons growing out of the war.[105]

The order was intended to be temporary, to be "withdrawn when the emergency is passed." Wilson issued the order in the exercise of power vested in him by the Constitution and by the resolution of Congress on April 5, 1917. According to Edward Corwin, whose book *The President, Office and Powers, 1787–1984* must be regarded as one of the major works on the presidency, Congress delegated to Wilson "the broadest discretion in dealing with a broadly defined subject in the furtherance of objectives equally broad." Whatever the infelicity of Corwin's phrase, Congress had felt it necessary to bestow on the president war powers that exceeded even those granted to Lincoln. Corwin, in a memorable paragraph, suggested how great were the powers invested in the president by the Food and Fuel Control Act, the Selective Service Act, the Espionage Act, the Priority Shipment Act, and the Trading With the Enemy Act, all of which gave him exceptional authority.[106]

Corwin distinguished between what he termed the "Lincolnian war dictatorship" and the one created by Wilson. The former, he believed, was based largely on the president's powers as commander in chief and the separation of powers principle; the latter relied on "the national legislative power and the minimization of that principle." Corwin chose to distinguish between Lincoln, a president who often felt compelled to act without congressional approval, and Wilson, who actively sought such approval, knowing he could secure it. Congress had become a negligible check on him, accepting to do what he insisted the war had made necessary. Corwin recognized that Wilson was also never slow in insisting on his rights as commander in chief; in his words, his creation of the "Committee on Public Information, the War Industries Board, and a War Labor Board rested exclusively on this basis, as did many of the vast powers exercised by these bodies in enforcing a so-called 'voluntary censorship' of the press and in 'co-ordinating' private industry." For Corwin, World War I was the "prologue and rehearsal" to World War II. The "emergency" created by the war gave Wilson wholly unprecedented powers, bestowed by an accommodating Congress, persuaded of the justice of the American cause. Wilson provided the example that Franklin Roosevelt would follow a quarter of a century later.[107]

The National Conscription Act passed by Congress in May 1917 allowed Wilson to promise Balfour that America's forces in Europe would number more than 1.5 million by the end of 1918.[108] This was an unprecedented expansion of the nation's military forces, again without any precedent since the time of Lincoln. Despite intensified U-boat attacks on Allied shipping, the most serious efforts were made to guarantee that Germany's intention to starve out Britain in five months, long before the Americans arrived in significant number, would never be realized. The defeat suffered by the Italians at Caporetto in the autumn of 1917 threatened the existence of that front, but the collapse of the Russian front upon the outbreak of the Bolshevik Revolution was the more grievous blow. When the Bolsheviks sued for a separate peace and published the so-called secret treaties, discovered in the czarist archives, Wilson announced that the territorial settlements in Europe and the Middle East promised by these secret engagements to which he had not been a party could never be the basis of the peace he sought. Wilson had learned of the agreements months earlier from Balfour when the foreign secretary led a British mission to the United States. Clearly incensed by these revelations, he wrote House at the time in uncharacteristic understatement, "England and France have not the same views with regard to Peace that we have by any means."[109] How, then, did he propose to deal with the situation? Wilson believed the time to argue would come later; he expected the United States, given its vital contributions to the final Allied victory, would be able to force the Europeans into line. Of one thing he was absolutely confident: Malign diplomacy, so characteristic of European leaders, would not be allowed to stand.

During the summer, other events intervened to make the issue of war aims increasingly urgent. The resolution passed by the German Reichstag, introduced by Matthias Erzberger, the Centrist Party leader, calling for a peace without "forced acquisitions of territories, forced requisitions and political, economic or financial oppressions" could be safely ignored but it proved more difficult to remain silent in response to the Pope's appeal for peace, made on August 1, 1917.[110] Wilson, addressing the Pope in a letter both conciliatory

and firm, condemned the Kaiser's government while at the same time repudiating any suggestion that the Allies might be considering a punitive peace. In
his words,

> Punitive damages, the dismemberment of empires, the establishment of selfish
> and exclusive economic leagues, we deem inexpedient and in the end worse than
> futile, no proper basis for a peace of any kind, least of all for an enduring peace.
> That must be based upon justice and fairness and the common rights of
> mankind.[111]

Clearly, Wilson intended to be the chief Allied spokesman in determining
peace terms and revealed his intentions very early by initiating with Colonel
House a study group, known as the Inquiry, with Walter Lippmann appointed
its first secretary, to gather material to help the president prepare for any projected peace conference.[112] It would almost certainly be the most important
peace conference since the one that had met in Berlin in 1878, and Wilson
clearly expected to attend.

The president, unwilling to share power with subordinates, refused to create
either a Cabinet department for munitions or a War Cabinet—both deemed
necessary by a number of his associates—showing his customary resolve to run
everything himself. With Colonel House as his only trusted adviser, he knew
that the British coveted Germany's African colonies and hoped for some sort of
control of Arabia. The Bolshevik demand for a peace of no annexations could
never be squared with these Allied ambitions. How, then, did he propose to intervene to make certain that decisions reached before the United States entered
the war would not be allowed to stand? Clearly, the time had come to speak
out, to make known to the Allies and to the Germans the kind of peace he contemplated. The British prime minister, under comparable pressure, created in
part by the foreign secretary's inability to quell the political storm raised by the
Bolshevik publication of the secret treaties, addressing a Trades Union Conference in London on January 5, 1918, offered terms not essentially different
from those Wilson was preparing to announce to the U.S. Congress.[113] Wilson,
in offering his Fourteen Points, hoped to blunt the support the Bolsheviks had
gained from their revelations about the secret treaties.

The proposition that the war was an imperialist venture, devoid of all moral
attributes, Wilson refused to accept, believing that providence had intended
him to intervene for quite other objectives. He offered his Fourteen Points as
an incentive for the German people to take action against their barbaric autocratic leaders who had dared to initiate unrestricted submarine warfare.
Though the Fourteen Points failed to incite the German popular revolt Wilson
hoped for, it accomplished another purpose, scarcely less important to him. He
had, in effect, announced his primacy among the Allied leaders.[114] Wilson of-

fered his Fourteen Points as a primer to inform the world what the United States proposed to do in its efforts to secure a just and enduring peace.

The president's aversion to criticism—to anything that smacked of disagreement—guaranteed that the Allies both in London and Paris would say nothing to indicate even the slightest doubts about his solemn declaration. The desperate need for U.S. troops on the Western Front in the early months of 1918 created an imperative reason to remain silent, but an even more compelling reason for reticence may have been that many in Great Britain and France welcomed Wilson's speech, believed it civilized and bold, statesmanlike in its denial of imperialism, uplifting in its promise of a new world order.

Yet within weeks of Wilson's declaration two events occurred that made him seem something of a naïve innocent. First, when the terms of the Treaty of Brest Litovsk were published on March 12, 1918, everyone recognized that the Germans had imposed on the Soviets a peace treaty of unprecedented severity. When, less than a week later, the Germans launched a new offensive on the Western Front, and appeared to be making progress greater than any made in the two preceding years, all illusions about a German desire for a negotiated peace evaporated. The British, covertly at first, became increasingly critical of the president, especially as the Allied military situation improved during the late summer. The Earl of Derby, reporting on a meeting of the European Allied leaders in October, wrote: "Lloyd George and Clemenceau vie with one another in scoffing at the President, and Sonnino [the Italian foreign minister] is almost openly apprehensive about allowing him to intervene in European politics."[115] Europe's Allied leaders were becoming increasingly restive about how the president might choose to respond to the German note of October 5, which some interpreted as a tentative request for an armistice.

After the second German note of October 12, Lloyd George's concerns became more acute, fearful that Wilson might accept the German offer of an armistice if a single condition was met—the evacuation of all the occupied territories. Alarmed that the president might negotiate with Germany without prior consultation with the Allies, and troubled by what appeared to be Wilson's "pure and simple" free-trade beliefs, Balfour, surveying all the exchanges, noted the president's failure to understand that "however successful the league," there had to be a transition period when Britain might be compelled to discriminate against Germany.[116] Wiseman, seeking to reassure the British that Wilson had no intention of making a separate peace with Germany, satisfied them on that point, but his comments on Wilson's proposed policy in respect to Russia were genuinely disconcerting. Wilson had told Wiseman: "My policy regarding Russia is very similar to my Mexican policy. I believe in letting them work out their own salvation, even though they wallow in anarchy for a while. I visualize it like this: A lot of impossible folk, fighting among themselves. . . ."[117]

Sir Maurice Hankey, the Cabinet secretary, in a diary entry made after lunching with the prime minister and Sir Eric Geddes, the First Lord of the Admiralty, following the latter's return from a visit with the president, wrote on October 24, 1918,

> Geddes is full of the point, which I have always suspected, that there is too much diplomacy and too little plain speaking with President Wilson. The glib-tongued Reading [who had replaced Spring Rice as ambassador] and the sycophant Wiseman merely flatter and turn their phrases to the President's ear. The President, Geddes says, golfs every morning, motors every afternoon, and goes to the picture palace every evening. He knows little of the war and was astounded when Geddes showed him the real comparative figures as regards British + American naval war effort. It is the same throughout the USA where it is universally believed that they are doing the whole thing. . . .[118]

Though Geddes exaggerated the president's ignorance and indolence, his views alarmed the Cabinet, not least when he told them of the president's intention to build a navy equal to that of Great Britain.[119] Wilson's failure to take more seriously the British government's misgivings about his policies on matters large and small reflected the greatly inflated opinion he had of his own superior understanding of the world situation, never doubting his own moral rectitude.[120]

More hazardous for the president, certainly, was his failure to take into account political events at home. For a time, the war could be represented as "Wilson's war," and even when it became the patriotic war of vast numbers of excited Americans, the president never understood how that transformation might threaten the kinds of peace policies he advocated. Though he took great pride in the legislation he pressed on Congress in April 1917 to create the Committee on Public Information to drum up support for the war, and was equally pleased with the Espionage Act, passed in June, intended to root out and defeat Germany's secret agents bent on sabotage, he never adequately reflected on how the surge of patriotic sentiment might in the long run affect his plans for world peace. So, also, in pressing Congress in May 1918 to pass the Sedition Act he acted as if he understood that collusion with the enemy was a hazard that could be met only with exceptional measures even if they threatened the civil liberties of citizens.[121] The president rarely considered how the rabid anti-German sentiment that infected the country, in considerable measure encouraged by him and his administration, would generate new suspicions about himself and make even his Fourteen Points hostage to the unflattering criticism of influential Republicans in both the Senate and the House. George Creel, the very efficient head of the Committee on Public Information, successful in making the American people believe the war was a crusade against evil, seemed scarcely concerned if members of the Socialist Party or the International Workers of the World were prosecuted for their antiwar activities. Wilson failed to understand the xenophobia that had taken root in the country that responded to the rhetoric of Republican notables like Roosevelt and Lodge, unsympathetic to his appeals for a peace of "justice and humanity."[122]

Less than a month before the Armistice, on October 25, 1918, the president issued an appeal to the country to show its support of his policies in the coming off-year congressional elections "by returning a Democratic majority to both the Senate and the House of Representatives." In his words,

> I have no thought of suggesting that any political party is paramount in matters of patriotism. I feel too deeply the sacrifices which have been made in this war by all our citizens, irrespective of party affiliations, to harbor such an idea. I mean only that the difficulties and delicacies of our present task are of a sort that makes it imperatively necessary that the nation should give its undivided support to the Government under a unified leadership, and that a Republican Congress would divide the leadership.

He went on to say:

> The leaders of the minority in the present Congress have unquestionably been prowar, but they have been anti-administration. At almost every turn since we entered the war they have sought to take the choice of policy and the conduct of the war out of my hands and put it under the control of instrumentalities of their choosing.[123]

While some believed the president erred in becoming so partisan, in asking for a vote of confidence his greater error was to ignore from almost the moment he secured congressional consent to the war in April 1917 the transformations in public opinion generated by the conflict. Just as an unwillingness to accept criticism prevented his allies in Europe from being candid with him, though some shared their misgivings with House who hesitantly communicated them, few Democrats felt secure enough to voice their misgivings about what many recognized to be his increasingly autocratic ways. Indeed, both before and especially after his remarriage, Wilson isolated himself from any criticism that might have led him to be more cautious, less overwhelmed with his undoubted ability to win congressional approval for the legislation he favored.

Neither from his Cabinet, American diplomats abroad, nor from his fellow Democrats in Congress did Wilson receive advice that might have told him that the American people, though scarcely disenchanted with his leadership, were not as overwhelmingly supportive as they had once been. When the results of the 1918 election were known, with the Democrats losing their majorities in both the Senate and the House, the president refused to see the vote as anything other than the traditional off-year losses that political parties invariably suffered.

The losses were in fact very serious; from a minority of six in the Senate, the Republicans emerged with a majority of two. In the House, their gains were spectacular; from being in a minority, the Republicans became a majority of forty-five. In the last days before the election the Republicans mounted a campaign to mock the president's search for a peace of "understanding," calling instead for "unconditional surrender by the accursed Huns." Only the generals, they argued, could make peace, and the "autocratic" president had no role to play in that delicate operation. In New York's Carnegie Hall, a rabid Roosevelt extolled "the triumph of the war spirit of America" and insisted that the Armistice "be obtained by machine guns and not typewriters." He declared the Fourteen Points mischievous, in his words, "greeted with enthusiasm by Germany and by all the pro-Germans on this side of the water, especially by the Germanized Socialists and by the Bolshevists of every grade."[124] Against such tirades, the president proved to be helpless. When, just a month later, in its famed Khaki election, held before the British armed forces were demobilized, Lloyd George spoke in scarcely less exaggerated terms, asking for the prosecution of the Kaiser for "wantonly planning and provoking the war," and indicated that "the Central Powers must pay the cost of the war up to the limit of their capacity," Wilson had a fair notion of the opposition he could expect to encounter at the peace conference. If Lloyd George avoided the graphic expression Sir Eric Geddes used, that England would "squeeze the German lemon till the pips squeek," he and others in the coalition government spoke in terms they would never have dared to use so long as they relied on American military assistance. Those days had passed, as the president ought to have recognized, but the rapture of the crowds that greeted his progress through the streets of London, Paris, and Rome in January 1919 blinded him to his political vulnerability both in Europe and at home.

A more cautious man, one less conscious of his moral authority, might have recognized the necessity of enlisting one or more prominent Republicans to join him in Paris as members of the American delegation. Taft or Root might have accepted to serve, even if it was unthinkable that he would consider including Lodge, the great friend of his old enemy, Roosevelt. Wilson never seriously entertained these possibilities. Taken with his own celebrity and his ascendancy as a world figure, he scarcely understood the Europe of 1919. The White House, during his time as president, had never been a place where diplomats and foreign guests congregated. Despite his acknowledged intellectual gifts, Wilson knew neither of his principal allies, Britain or France, and indeed, if the truth be told, no longer knew his own country, substantially transformed by the war. In his exaggerated idealism, he saw virtue only in what he himself proposed; those who opposed him, whether at home or abroad, were simply self-interested men he could neither respect nor listen to.

Only in 1919 did those who participated in the Paris Peace Conference come to observe closely the man whose character and opinions had for so long seemed incomprehensible. The president of France, Raymond Poincaré, and the French prime minister, Georges Clemenceau, according to the British, found Wilson amiable but "shockingly ignorant of the European situation."[125] Lloyd George, equally unimpressed by the president, greatly resented his failure to mention the British sacrifice in the war during the state dinner given in his honor by the king at Buckingham Palace. Still, these were matters of no great consequence, and his speeches in England were well received. Margot Asquith, the wife of the former prime minister, meeting him at the Mansion House, where he gave one of his more memorable speeches, confided to her diary opinions both shrewd and generous:

> The Republican Party in America stands for many things with which I am out of sympathy, but I cannot believe their dislike of the President is entirely political. From what I hear he is an Egotist; uncertain in his personal relations because he is not grateful; and a man who trusts few and mostly his inferiors. The last is what really counts; men who like their inferiors seldom achieve high purposes. Nevertheless President Wilson will go down in History as having produced the Great Idea of the War, and, after listening to one of the greatest speeches I had ever heard in my life at the Mansion House lunch, I said to myself: 'What is there that this man could not do, if his moral stature was comparable to his intellectual expression?'[126]

The president's oratorical gifts, while undeniable, proved to be of little use to him in Paris. There, negotiating skills were all-important, and while some pretended that the cunning Europeans, particularly Lloyd George and Clemenceau, constantly outwitted the rhetorical Wilson, the president's major problems were not created by his inexperience in these admittedly trying encounters. While the British and French prime ministers expressed views that coincided with those of their electorates, stemming from their tragic war experiences, reflecting a patriotism born of anger and a desire for revenge, Wilson ignored all such sentiment as he ignored the patriotic upsurge in his own country that had contributed to his party's defeat in the November elections, making him a prime minister without a majority in Congress. The Europeans, observing him in Paris, realized that while he appeared uncompromising at times he generally conceded in the end, even on supposedly crucial issues. Only on the League of Nations did he remain adamant, and on that issue Lloyd George found his views "quite unformed." The British, while prepared to humor the president on the League, never believed it the crucial or promising institutional innovation the president imagined it to be.

Lord Robert Cecil, one of those in the British delegation purportedly friendly to the president, confided to his diary in February 1919,

> Now that I have sat for two or three days with the President I am coming to the conclusion that I personally do not like him. I do not know what it is that repels me: a certain hardness, coupled with vanity and an eye for effect. He supports idealistic causes without being idealistic himself. . . . The President is exceedingly courteous to me, and I think listens to me more than any other member of the commission, also in 99 cases out of 100 we are agreed, but all the same, I do not like him.[127]

Lloyd George's feelings about the president were comparably ambivalent, but he chose never to share them, not even with his diary. On the contrary, he went out of his way to flatter the president, not least when conversing with his wife, knowing his every word would be repeated. Speaking to Edith Wilson at a luncheon, the prime minister said:

> We think your husband is the most wonderful man in every respect of them all. And we don't know what would come of our meetings in a moment of terrible tension, in this terrible crisis, when many of us feel the future is hanging by a thread—if it was not for his wonderful sense of humor that never fails to come to the rescue in the most trying time and in the most appropriate way. It gives a new breath of life to us all.[128]

When the terms of the Treaty of Versailles were finally announced on May 7, 1919, those who had once believed in Wilson's Fourteen Points were profoundly shocked. Many thought the treaty harsh, unworkable, and vindictive—a denial of all the principles the president purportedly supported.[129] Wilson defended the treaty, pretending it in no way violated promises he had made. Herbert Hoover, the U.S. food administrator, given a copy of the treaty just hours before its official release, and sufficiently distressed by its content to seek solace by walking in the predawn deserted streets of Paris, where he met both Jan Christian Smuts and John Maynard Keynes strolling about in comparable despair, said of this chance meeting at so unconventional an hour, "We seemed to have come together by some sort of telepathy. It flashed through our minds why each was walking about at that time of the morning. Each was greatly disturbed. We agreed that the consequences of many parts of the Treaty would ultimately bring destruction." Smuts, the South African representative, greatly distressed by the treaty, begged the president to intervene to change the terms, but to no avail.[130]

When Wilson returned to Washington from Paris on July 8—the Germans having been compelled to sign the treaty—his political tasks at home were formidable. The Democratic Party lacked a majority in the Senate; Lodge, Wilson's longtime enemy, secure in his position as chairman of the Senate Foreign Relations Committee, was certain to hound him, and not only out of deference to the memory of his great friend, Roosevelt, whose untimely death on January 6, 1919, he mourned. To secure a two-thirds vote in the Senate—the required majority necessary for treaty ratification—would be a severe test of Wilson's skills as a politician. There had been only one American architect in the peace-making process—the president himself—and when he met with the Committee on Foreign Relations, he insisted he would accept "reservations" to the treaty of an interpretative nature only, almost guaranteeing a standoff with Lodge and others in the Senate who argued for major revisions. Lodge, in an impassioned Senate speech earlier in the year, had pleaded for "facts, details, and sharp clear-cut definitions" and introduced what became known as the Round Robin resolution, signed by more than a third of the Senate, declaring unacceptable the constitution of the League of Nations as proposed in the treaty.[131] Lodge argued for the League question to be separated from the peace treaty, to be considered only after peace with Germany was formally ratified. Wilson rejected that suggestion: The Covenant of the League of Nations and the League itself were bound together inseparably in his mind; both had to figure in the final peace settlement.

Lodge did not recommend a policy of isolation. Such a program would have violated his fundamental principles, but as he gazed at the Wilson concessions on matters as different as Fiume, Danzig, and Shantung—denying Italy the city it most wished to have, creating a free city to give landlocked Poland a port, and taking the latter city from China as a gift to Japan—he could only believe the president lacked all understanding of the country's foreign interests. For Lodge, Germany remained the great threat to the future peace of Europe, and he feared any humiliation of Italy would lead to its becoming an ally of Germany. In his mind, as he wrote George Otto Trevelyan, Roosevelt's old friend, Wilson's intervention in the Fiume affair was simply "an illustration of the mistakes and troubles which are likely to arise from the United States undertaking to meddle with purely European questions in which they have no interest."[132] These doubts, however, were secondary to his major misgivings about article X of the League Covenant that guaranteed the political independence and territorial integrity of all League members when confronted with external aggression. By the terms of article X, League members were obliged to take action, including the use of military force should that prove necessary, to deter such aggression.

Had the United States accepted article X, it would have repudiated its long-standing policy not to intervene in disputes outside the Western Hemisphere and committed the country to maintain peace throughout the world. The Senate Foreign Relations Committee, chaired by Lodge, met with the president at the White House on August 19, 1919, to discuss the League Covenant and many of the questions relating to article X. Wilson insisted that the power of Congress to declare war would not be affected by article X and that in any case the article imposed only a moral obligation, not a legal obligation. When Warren Harding, a member of the Senate committee, asked whether article X had any meaning if it imposed only a moral obligation, the president replied: "Now a moral obligation is of course superior to a legal obligation, and, if I may say so, has a greater binding force."[133] These sentiments were unlikely to assuage critical Republicans like Lodge and Root, who had already indicated their unalterable opposition to article X. Root characterized the article as "not an essential or even an appropriate part of the provisions for a League of Nations to preserve peace" and feared it would "commit Americans to enter into foreign wars in faraway places where they would almost certainly not want to fight."[134]

Wilson, so often successful in appealing to the American public on domestic issues over the heads of its elected representatives in Congress, imagined he could do so again, rousing the public to reveal its unmistakable enthusiasm for the League. He opted for a high-risk strategy that began with an ambitious transcontinental train journey to allow him to bring his message to the people, confident they would support him in the end. While it is impossible to know for certain whether the plan could have succeeded—the omens were far from favorable—all his hopes were dashed by the massive stroke he suffered in Pueblo, Colorado, on September 25 that brought him back to the White House a seriously stricken invalid. Edith Wilson did what she could to shield her ailing husband from prying eyes, and the public could only guess about the extent of his disability. Rumors circulated that Colonel House was no longer a power in the administration, for obscure reasons never given, and that neither the vice president nor any member of his Cabinet exercised the authority once so jealously guarded by Wilson. While there was talk of a so-called junta having taken over, those who knew the situation realized this had not happened. The White House had ceased to be the nerve center of the nation, and Wilson's presidency, for all practical purposes, ended in the autumn of 1919, almost eighteen months before he left office officially. There had never been a comparable interregnum, and politicians no less than journalists were bewildered by the situation.

The president's plans for Senate approval of the peace of Paris lay in tatters. Lodge declared as early as October that "this treaty will never be ratified unless the Monroe Doctrine is finally and absolutely reserved from the jurisdiction of the League," and the following February he indicated he would "never assent to any change in principle in the two reservations relating to the Monroe Doctrine and Article X." This virtually guaranteed the Senate's rejection of both the

League Covenant and the treaty unless the president showed some willingness to compromise. Those who knew him best, who understood his imperious nature, knew how unlikely such a concession would be. The president, confined to his sick room, believed absolutely in the treaty he had brought back from Paris, and the most influential tract of the day, John Maynard Keynes's *Economic Consequences of the Peace*, published on December 12, 1919, in disparaging his handiwork, only gave political ammunition to his enemies.[135]

Keynes, in his highly unflattering portrayal of Wilson, represented him as neither a philosopher nor a prophet but as a slow-thinking, stubborn Presbyterian minister. Keynes made public what diplomats and politicians in Great Britain and the United States had long been saying in private, but rarely so scathingly. Indeed, some in England thought the judgment too severe, and Keynes felt some obligation to defend himself, saying "Attempts to humour or placate the Americans or anyone else seem quite futile, and I personally despair of results from anything but violent and ruthless truth-telling—that will work in the end, even if slowly."[136] When Lloyd George came to write *The Truth About the Peace Treaties* almost two decades later, he showed less contempt for the president, though finding no reason to deny that there was a "badly mixed" duality in him. In his words, "At once idealistic and a man of integrity, his personal hatreds, suspicions, and intolerance of anyone who dared to criticize him, made him ungenerous."[137] The former prime minister saw no need to add that it also made him politically vulnerable.

Unlike Roosevelt, the man he detested, Wilson had few friends, almost no intimates, and knew a great deal less about the world than he pretended. His knowledge of Britain came almost entirely from books, and of other parts of Europe he remained blissfully ignorant. Uninterested in surrounding himself with strong and independent individuals who might on occasion have corrected him, only in his recruitment of Newton D. Baker, appointed secretary of war in 1916, did he show great political acumen. Baker, perhaps more than any other of his Cabinet members, helped Wilson become an accomplished war leader, able to provide the Western Allies with the material assistance they relied on for their survival following the terrible military and diplomatic defeats suffered in 1917. Had Wilson followed House's advice and dropped Thomas Marshall as his vice president in 1916, recommending the convention to nominate Baker in his place, the history of the immediate postwar period might have been very different.[138] Wilson ignored House's advice, arguing that Baker was too good a man to be "sacrificed," relegated to the insignificant post of presiding over the Senate.[139] Had Baker been the vice president during Wilson's long convalescence, something of a copresidency might have been established, with Baker serving in a capacity no other vice president had ever aspired to.[140] Only an infirm Wilson would have agreed to share power with anyone, and he would never have considered doing so with Marshall.[141]

Wilson failed in his diplomatic initiatives, first in Mexico, then, more seriously, in Europe. Unable to maintain the country's neutrality, he set himself the formidable task of leading war-weary Europeans to the kind of peace he deemed moral and necessary. Concentrating his attention on national boundary issues, made critical through the disintegration of three multinational European empires—Germany, Austria-Hungary, and Russia—he joined with the leaders of Great Britain and France in imagining that new small republics carved out of those once-powerful monarchies would be able to retain their independence, never falling victim to their more powerful European neighbors. In his mind, the League of Nations guaranteed the independence of these infant republics. Schooled as a historian of the United States, he viewed Europe and his own country in a perspective that inhibited any understanding of why Europe had known peace for almost a century after the defeat of Napoleon, and why that peace had been shattered in the early twentieth century. Too many of his ideas about Europe rested on clichés that a more cultivated and cosmopolitan thinker might have shunned.[142]

If he knew Europe only slightly, his views on the rest of the world were even more primitive. Wholly uninvolved in the diplomacy that led Britain to receive the mandate to govern both Palestine and Mesopotamia (later Iraq), with France given the same responsibilities in Syria and Lebanon, these settlements were made in April 1920 at San Remo after the president had ceased to be active in European diplomacy. Though he showed intermittent sympathy for the Zionist cause, principally through the influence of Louis Brandeis, whom he elevated to the Supreme Court, and at one time a supporter of the Balfour Declaration, which promised the Jews the restoration of their homeland in Palestine, Wilson never claimed the kind of geopolitical grasp that had given such great advantages to Roosevelt. Lacking an awareness of the concrete conditions characteristic of a world he scarcely knew, he imagined he could be his own secretary of state, helped by an accommodating courtier, but the two together were unable to devise policies adequate to an international society that included China and Japan, the United Kingdom and France, Mexico and Brazil, Soviet Russia and Weimar Germany. The League of Nations became his idée fixe, an institution expected to provide the world the security it had forfeited through the mad policies of a nation charged with "war guilt."

Though his domestic policies during his first term showed daring and a remarkable capacity to lead his party majorities in Congress to pass the legislation he favored, Wilson showed no comparable skills as the architect of a new foreign policy. Contemptuous of too many in the State Department and in Congress, believing himself morally superior to the European leaders he felt obliged to deal with, his ideas about the international system were based on abstract principles. They found little resonance with leaders abroad, attentive to public opinion in their own countries. The absence of interlocutors and colleagues at home able to correct him, to question his foreign policy strategies and tactics, greatly handicapped him. He had no greater help from those abroad who viewed the world—its military, diplomatic, and moral history—in ways he never could. An isolated, self-absorbed, and vain scholar, greatly indebted to Tocqueville, Wilson failed to heed what he had read in the latter's nineteenth-century observations about the likely consequences of war for a democracy. Wilson courted democratic public opinion, helped create it, and in the end was destroyed by it. The patriotism he cultivated during the war proved more useful in Lodge's political armory than in his own. An accomplished war president, a warrior in everything but name, he disdained the distinction, preferring to see himself as a peacemaker. Wilson sought to rule alone, confident he could always control Congress, using public opinion as a final defense if it refused his entreaties. Like Roosevelt, he imagined public opinion would ultimately vindicate him, giving him the authority he sought, and he fatally misread that opinion.

There is no reason to believe that, even had a stroke not felled him, he would have accepted to compromise with the Republican majority in the Senate, that in the end he would have won the fight to protect his League Covenant. Yet for the years before his illness he showed the same appetite for power that Roosevelt had demonstrated and an even greater capacity to extend the powers of the presidential office, using the crisis created by war as his ultimate defense. Wilson left a legacy that a second Roosevelt, Franklin Delano Roosevelt, could never think to disparage or ignore, giving the presidency an authority and prestige FDR recognized to be invaluable. The office could never wholly revert to what it had been before Wilson entered the White House, though his immediate Republican Party successors seemed at times to yearn for a restoration of the more modest presidency that had existed in the time of McKinley. Whether Wilson had indeed "broken the heart of the world" in failing to win his battle for the League of Nations, as U.S. historian John Milton Cooper sought to argue, was indeed possible, though arguable.[143] A very crafty "King Franklin," prepared to honor Wilson's memory and indeed to resurrect the League of Nations in his own projected United Nations, knew the limits of all such international organizations and never made it the object of his secular political religion, more Machiavellian, less Calvinist.[144]

CHAPTER 7

Back to Normalcy

WARREN HARDING'S PRESIDENCY was brief, uneventful, and undistinguished. His unique accomplishment, if it may be called that, is that he succeeded in concealing the more salacious details of his private life during the time he occupied the White House. These emerged only after his death and titillated a generation that found tales of illicit sex diverting, made more compelling by the confessions of a former mistress recounting in detail the story of their relation and of the daughter he sired.[1] No comparable scandal had touched any of Harding's immediate predecessors; Theodore Roosevelt was always circumspect, and it would have been difficult for anyone to imagine William Taft as a lothario—his girth alone seemed to preclude such strenuous, illicit, and immoral behavior.

As for Woodrow Wilson, his one extramarital relation, never known during the time he occupied the White House, was a mild affair when compared with Harding's, and even the courtship of his second wife, characterized by one British wit as involving premarital sex that led the second Mrs. Wilson to fall out of bed when the president proposed marriage to her, was never known to the general public.[2] Not since the more anodyne revelations made about Grover Cleveland had there been serious suggestions of presidential sexual impropriety, let alone promiscuity. In the early twentieth century, as in the longer Victorian age, American politicians in the House and Senate might be venal, and money passed frequently between them and those prepared to pay for their services, but they were rarely represented as sexually immoral, then an obviously graver offense.[3]

Harding came to the presidency with negligible administrative experience, public or private. The first president born after the Civil War, in Blooming Grove, Ohio, the oldest of six children who survived, his middle name, Gamaliel, chosen by his devoutly religious mother, reflected her pride in a son who would bear the name of the teacher of Saint Paul, noted for his tolerant and pacific nature.[4] The family moved to Marion, Ohio, a town of about

4,000, where his father, originally a veterinarian, practiced homeopathy and where young Warren attended Ohio Central College, a modest institution that bore no resemblance to Princeton, Yale, or Harvard.

In 1891 he married a divorced woman, Florence Kling DeWolfe, five years older than himself, the daughter of the richest man in Marion. Harding acquired very early a considerable local reputation as the proprietor of the *Marion Star*, a mortgaged newspaper that he and two others had bought for $300 in 1884.[5] A handsome man of dark complexion—rumor suggested he was part black—only very partially explained Amos Kling's opposition to his daughter's marriage to a man who appeared to be going nowhere; not a drunkard like his first son-in-law, but hardly a man destined for great things.[6] He could not have been more mistaken.

An ardent Republican who constantly lauded the virtues of American businessmen, writing grandiloquent editorials about their incomparable achievements, the friend of Joseph Foraker, the former governor so influential in the early career of Taft, Harding set his eye on state office and managed to be elected a state senator and then to the more considerable post of lieutenant governor. Though he had every reason to expect to win the governor's chair in 1910, the Republican debacle in that year's elections, brought on in part by Taft's inadequacies as president, forced him to return to his earlier obligations as the proprietor of an increasingly influential newspaper in Ohio.[7]

In 1912, Harding, like all Republicans, was required to choose between Roosevelt and Taft; he had no difficulty in opting for the incumbent president. Indeed, still considered an influential Ohioan with a brilliant future, despite his loss of the governorship in 1910, Taft asked him to join other loyal Republicans in nominating him for reelection at the 1912 Republican National Convention. Harding, in characteristic oratorical flight, pretended to see no difference between the progressives and the regular Republicans, claiming that "progression" characterized the view of all Republicans.[8] The character of his argument and indeed of his mind may be suggested by his peroration where he said, with his usual penchant for alliteration,

> Progression is not proclamation nor palaver. It is not pretense nor play on prejudice. It is not of personal pronouns, nor of perennial pronouncement. It is not the perturbation of a people passion-wrought, nor a promise proposed. Progression is everlastingly lifting the standards that marked the end of the world's march yesterday and planting them on new and advanced heights today.[9]

In the election struggle that followed, Harding used mean and unflattering language to describe Roosevelt, proving again that he was a reliable company man, the enemy of all who dared to traduce the incumbent president or showed such irreverence by attacking the country's most powerful businessmen. Less than a decade later, Harding sought to forget these graceless attacks on the deceased and greatly mourned Teddy, now as much his hero as the greatly admired Ohio friend, former President Taft, whom he appointed chief justice of the Supreme Court soon after he entered the White House in 1921.

In 1914, with the Republican Party reunited, Harding ran for a U.S. Senate seat and won with a substantial majority, almost 100,000 votes, defeating his progressive Catholic Democratic opponent easily. In the first elections held after the ratification of the Seventeenth Amendment to the Constitution, requiring senators to be elected by the people and no longer by state legislatures, Harding ran against Timothy Hogan, once the state's attorney general. The campaign, characterized by its virulent anti-Catholic propaganda, gave early warning of a feature of American politics that would become increasingly conspicuous in the decades ahead.[10] Andrew Sinclair, one of the few biographers who has written sympathetically of Harding in recent decades, acknowledged that ". . . Harding was not fair enough to repudiate the campaign of hate against Hogan, part of which entailed the plastering of the walls and fences of Ohio with the slogan: 'Read the *Menace* and get the dope, Go to the polls and beat the Pope.'"[11] For the next six years, Harding sat in the Senate, missing many roll calls and making no great impression on his colleagues at a time when Lodge and Root, the distinguished figures of the Roosevelt period, figured among its most prominent Republican members. Harding, a Republican freshman senator in a body dominated until 1918 by the Democrats, joined his party colleagues in habitually voting against President Wilson's domestic legislative proposals.

How did so relatively insignificant a politician manage in 1920 to secure the Republican Party's presidential nomination, achieving what no senator in the nineteenth century, including men as eminent as Henry Clay, John Calhoun, and Daniel Webster, had done—moving from the Senate to the presidency? The Republican National Convention, enjoying its "roasting" of Wilson, the invalid president, was also the site of the coronation of the senator from Ohio on whom the delegates finally settled. The leitmotif of the party convention—the perpetual mocking of Wilson—allowed Chauncey Depew, former president of the New York Central Railroad and longtime senator from New York, to claim that the president had been taken in by the sharpest dealers in Paris, "the ablest men in the political game, in the diplomatic game, in the international game."[12] Depew, in what passed for humor, claimed that Wilson had been completely defeated by Lloyd George, who grabbed all the "German possessions in Africa just to settle the Negro question there," and by others in Paris who scarcely knew whether Fiume was "one of the Sandwich Islands or a fixed star."[13]

Myths of the perfidy of the Europeans and the simplicity and inadequacy of Wilson, first aired then, remained a part of the party's litany long after the former president was dead. Following these ritual condemnations of the Wilson administration and the start of the balloting, General Leonard Wood, Roosevelt's great friend, led the pack with Governor Frank Lowden of Illinois close behind, and Hiram Johnson, California's longtime senator, a distant third. In what became the classic account of the inanities of the 1920s, *Only Yesterday*, by Frederick Lewis Allen, Wood received a memorable portrayal as "a blunt soldier, an inheritor of Theodore Roosevelt's creed of fearing God and keeping your powder dry." In Allen's view, "he made a fairly good contrast with Wilson, but he promised to be almost as unmanageable."[14] Wood still led on the fourth ballot but had not come close to securing the majority required for the nomination. When a motion was made for the convention to adjourn for the night, Lodge, in his capacity as permanent chairman, called for a voice vote, and though the nays clearly won, Lodge declared the meeting adjourned till the next day. Through much of the night, prominent senators drifted in and out of a suite of rooms in the Blackstone Hotel discussing the problem created by the threat of a deadlocked convention.

The image of smoke-filled rooms in which influential bosses made the principal decisions the convention would then be expected to ratify took on new meaning during that memorable night. By morning, Harding's name was increasingly bandied about on the convention floor. Senator Frank Brandegee of Connecticut, who soon emerged as one of Harding's chief supporters, had no illusions about the senator and reportedly said: "This ain't 1880 or 1904; we haven't any John Shermans or Theodore Roosevelts; we've got a lot of second-raters and Warren Harding is the best of the second-raters."[15] George Harvey, Wilson's once erstwhile friend and supporter, purportedly summoned Harding to his hotel room to ask "whether there is anything that might be brought up against you that would embarrass the party, any impediment that might disqualify you or make you inexpedient, either as a candidate or as President." Harding asked for time to consider the matter and returned in ten minutes to say there was no impediment.[16] Whether Harvey's question was prompted by his having heard of Harding's affair with a married woman or having sired an illegitimate child by a younger woman, it is impossible to say. In any case, Harding lied, believing he would not be found out.[17]

The balloting continued on a sweltering Chicago summer day with the temperature in the convention hall rising to 102 degrees Fahrenheit.[18] By the eighth ballot, Lowden had forged ahead, closely followed by Wood, with Harding a distant third, and none of the three coming at all close to claiming a majority of the delegate votes.[19] Again, a motion was made for a recess, and Lodge for a second time ignored the overwhelming shouts of nay to declare the meeting adjourned till that afternoon.[20] On the ninth ballot, the Harding forces, winning the Connecticut delegation previously pledged to Lowden, and making inroads with other delegations, gave the senator a greater number of votes than any of the three principal contenders had managed to amass in the first eight ballots.[21] Harding's victory on the next ballot was a foregone conclusion.[22] Though Wood and his supporters called the nomination "theft," choosing never to use that word in public, the Republicans guessed they had nominated a winner. When some of the powerful senators responsible for the choice of Harding then sought to nominate Irvine Lenroot of Wisconsin for vice president, confident that the weary delegates would again accept their lead, a rebellion of sorts followed.[23] A delegate from Oregon placed Calvin Coolidge's name in nomination, and the governor of Massachusetts, the hero of the Boston police strike, won on the very first ballot.

Could the Republican National Convention in 1920 be thought unique, essentially different from others Bryce had described thirty years earlier? Not really, except that in this instance no collection of party bosses took charge; instead, a group of influential senators selected a man they knew to be pliable, easily controlled.[24] Frederick Lewis Allen, a decade after the events, wrote:

Wilson was a visionary who liked to identify himself with 'forward-looking men'; Harding. . . was as old-fashioned as the Indians which used to stand in front of cigar stores, 'a flower of the period before safety razors'; Harding believed that statesmanship had come to its apogee in the days of McKinley and Foraker; Wilson was cold; Harding was an affable small-town man, at ease with 'folks'; an ideal companion, as one of his friends expressed it, 'to play poker with all Saturday night.' Wilson had always been difficult of access; Harding was accessible to the last degree. Wilson favored labor, distrusted businessmen as a class, and talked of 'industrial democracy'; Harding looked back with longing eyes to the good old days when the government didn't bother businessmen with unnecessary regulations, but provided them with fat tariffs and instructed the Department of Justice not to have them on its mind. Wilson was at loggerheads with Congress, and particularly with the Senate. Harding was not only a Senator, but a highly amenable Senator. Wilson had been adept at making enemies; Harding hadn't an enemy in the world. He was genuinely genial. . . . Wilson thought in terms of the whole world; Harding was for America first. And finally, whereas Wilson wanted America to exert itself nobly, Harding wanted to give it a rest.[25]

Allen also noted what others frequently repeated: that Harding, in Boston, just weeks before the convention, added a new word, normalcy, to the language, when he said "America's present need is not heroics but healing; not nostrums but normalcy; not revolution but restoration; . . . not surgery but serenity."[26] Harding, in ways that Allen understood perfectly, appealed to a nation exhausted from what it conceived to be its herculean labors in the war, wanting only to return to a more tranquil existence.

Harding won the election easily, with more than 16 million votes as against the slightly more than 9 million registered for James Cox, the Democratic Party candidate who ran with Franklin Delano Roosevelt as vice president. The election, a rout, in effect, exceeded what the two Republicans, McKinley and Roosevelt, had managed to achieve. The Republican majority in the Senate soared from two to twenty; in the House, 233 Republicans were elected over 191 Democrats. With such majorities, redolent of those Wilson obtained in 1912, Harding was in a position to do almost anything. In fact, he did very little.

Arriving with no plans or programs for political or social reform, and seeing no need for such, he ignored the international institutions Wilson had placed his faith in, the League of Nations and the World Court. He knew better than to tamper with Wilson's domestic institutional creations, including the Federal Reserve Board that had proved surprisingly popular. His Cabinet, scarcely inferior to Wilson's—many would have argued it superior—included Charles Evans Hughes as secretary of state, caricatured as "a bearded iceberg" by Roosevelt, but claiming administrative experience as a former governor of New York of a kind William Jennings Bryan had never known. Andrew Mellon, secretary of the treasury, was a respected industrialist and banker and retained the post under the two Republican presidents who succeeded Harding, surrendering it only in 1932 when he went to London to serve as ambassador to the Court of St. James. In his day, Mellon seemed a figure of commanding authority, a banker of rare insight, an art collector of impeccable taste, a rival in every sense to the only other American whose reputation resembled his: J.P. Morgan.[27] Herbert Hoover, a self-made millionaire committed to public service, renowned for what he achieved in heading the Commission for Relief in Belgium, who had served as Wilson's food administrator after the United States entered the war, and thought to be imaginative, industrious, and ambitious, was appointed secretary of commerce and gave that relatively new Cabinet post a distinction it had not previously enjoyed and would never know again. Henry Wallace, believed to be one of the country's leading agrarian experts, not to be confused with his son, who served in Franklin Roosevelt's administration and later as vice president from 1941 to 1945, was appointed to head the Department of Agriculture, securing this highly sensitive post at a time when farmers were suffering severe economic distress. Harry Daugherty, who did as much as anyone to press for Harding's nomination at the convention—sometimes described by the press as the Marcus Hanna of his day—received his reward as attorney general. He, together with Albert Fall, senator from New Mexico, the president's poker-playing chum, appointed secretary of the Department of Interior, were the two Cabinet members later revealed to have been corrupt and venal. Though no one ever mistook Fall for a conservationist, that seemed scarcely to matter with TR dead and environmental issues having greatly receded since the days of the Ballinger controversy during the Taft administration.

The president established a schedule that allowed him to play golf at least two afternoons a week and poker in the White House or in one of the palatial mansions of his great and very wealthy friends, the MacLeans.[28] The so-called poker Cabinet—the president's boon companions—were reported to enjoy revels that some claimed were generously lubricated by liquor, a prohibited substance since the passage of the Eighteenth Amendment to the Constitution.

Walter Lippmann had prophesied that the Harding administration would come to be known as the "Regency of the Senate."[29] Senators, having given Harding the nomination, were expected to be the ones who would control him. Harding proved Lippmann mistaken; insisting always on his presidential prerogatives, he was popular with the press, able at times to make him seem an almost commanding presidential figure.[30] With so many new members of Congress, and few of the once prominent Republicans still active in the Senate, a power vacuum seemed to exist at both ends of Pennsylvania Avenue. Though no one pretended that this was a presidential rule redolent of either Wilson or Roosevelt, there was no return to the congressional government so characteristic of the late nineteenth century.[31]

Roosevelt and Wilson, presidents who had made foreign affairs their principal concern, were succeeded by an Ohio provincial who neither knew nor cared about the world abroad. He relied heavily on his secretary of state, Charles Evans Hughes, a distinguished lawyer who had served as governor of New York and associate justice of the Supreme Court. For Harding these were impressive credentials, and he could only imagine that all his appointees gained in stature from knowing he had succeeded in recruiting so illustrious a figure for the senior Cabinet position. Hughes, though not especially astute as a politician, understood how much the president stood to gain from being heralded as an advocate of peace and economy. He pressed for an arms limitation conference to be convened in Washington in July 1921 and in the next months of intense negotiations, helped to establish Harding's reputation as a statesman, able to persuade the Senate with its huge Republican majority to accept the two treaties he successfully negotiated. The secretary of state's achievement in bringing about naval reductions, establishing naval parity between the United States and Great Britain, and allowing Japan to become the third naval power in the world, was less remarkable than it appeared at the time, but the administration heralded it as an incomparable diplomatic victory.[32] Few noticed that the Senate, in accepting the so-called Four Power Treaty, showed itself no more willing for the United States to accept responsibility for guaranteeing the peace than when it had effectively thwarted Wilson in his League of Nations efforts. Still, Harding's success in this foreign policy venture seemed greater than any he enjoyed with comparably difficult domestic issues. There, continuing agricultural depression and massive industrial unemployment, conditions common also to Europe, confounded him, as they did all his principal Cabinet advisers.

With Mellon, the third-richest man in the country, installed as secretary of the treasury, businessmen knew they had a friend in court, and it was unthinkable that Harding, guided by Mellon, would challenge faithful supporters of the Republican Party in the way Roosevelt had done. The president's long experience as a newspaper proprietor, concerned always to defend business interests, guaranteed he would be friendly to those he regarded as the mainstay of the republic. Mellon quickly established his influence in the Cabinet and the country by advocating reduced taxes, intended to achieve two objectives: the restoration of business confidence, and the reduction of unemployment. Because federal expenditures had soared during the war, greatly increasing the national debt, Mellon insisted on government frugality; no unnecessary federal expense would be countenanced. If this involved a delayed payment of the so-called soldiers' bonus—eagerly anticipated by those who had fought in the war—this seemed a small price to pay for the restoration of the normalcy the president had promised.

No one in the Cabinet proposed other remedies to restore a lost prosperity, though Hoover, the indefatigable head of the Commerce Department, accustomed to innovation, seemed determined to find support for American business ventures abroad that gave promise of new commercial opportunities. Hoover, an administrative imperialist, constantly extended his domain, creating new agencies within his department to encourage foreign trade and convening an unemployment conference to find remedies for a seemingly insoluble problem that saw some 5,735,000 men and women out of work in August 1922.[33] Hoover believed that even the agricultural crisis would be greatly alleviated by making farmers more overseas-conscious, and it is hardly surprising that he became one of the president's Cabinet heroes, admired both for his industry and ingenuity.

While industrial unemployment and farm relief figured as priority problems for the president, one other commanded his close attention: immigration restriction. There, as in so many other things, Harding sought advice from Congress but never received it. Given the seriousness of the country's economic plight, it is scarcely surprising that the Republicans fared badly in the 1922 congressional elections, losing seven seats in the Senate and seventy in the House. When one considers the size of their 1920 victories, these losses were far from catastrophic, but newspapers, seeking to explain the Republican debacle, believed the president had erred in being too receptive to Mellon's advice, especially in refusing the veterans their well-deserved war bonus.

Many began to acknowledge, though much more tentatively, that the Volstead Act, passed in January 1920 to enforce the provisions of the Eighteenth Amendment to the Constitution, forbidding the manufacture, sale, or transport of intoxicating liquors, was being systematically flouted, and that the police and court measures put in place to prevent such infractions were wholly inadequate. While neither the president nor Congress dared admit this openly, fearing the wrath of the Prohibitionists, as ardent for their social experiment as ever, the growing disillusion with this unworkable system of social control could not be denied. The flouting of the law by millions, and the rumors circulating that the White House itself served liquor surreptitiously, did nothing to increase respect for Prohibition. Hypocrisy appeared to be in the saddle; neither the administration nor its critics knew how to cope with a situation where bootleggers and speakeasies were everywhere and the consumption of prohibited substances by growing numbers of men and women became the fashionable thing to do.[34]

Warren Harding came to the White House with many assets, including his election by an overwhelming majority and a Congress dominated by Republicans. A handsome president, good-humored and outgoing, he ought to have achieved a great deal, but his liabilities outweighed his assets. Harding's failure to be more innovative cannot be attributed simply to his provincial Ohio upbringing or the limits of his administrative experience. When one considers the sheer novelty and difficulty of the country's postwar problems, including those he refused to acknowledge, it is scarcely surprising that he accomplished so little. He appeared no more inadequate as a democratic leader than those in the two other principal World War I victor states, Great Britain and France. The early 1920s, as difficult a time for the victors as for the vanquished, brought forward politicians whose purchase on reality was slight, who appeared no more competent than those who claimed expertise as economists, sociologists, and political scientists.

After his death from an embolism on August 2, 1923, Harding's reputation plummeted, destroyed by the revelations about the corruption of members of his administration and by the sordid details that emerged about his private life. As the father of an illegitimate child and the long-term lover of a married woman, represented as a lecher, a poker-playing hypocrite who surrounded himself with cronies, untrustworthy criminals, mostly from Ohio, he appeared more pedestrian than even his longtime detractors had claimed.[35] While no one ever demonstrated that Harding profited from the illegal activities of those he appointed, the stories divulged in the ongoing Senate investigations and the press made "Teapot Dome" a household word, the quintessential expression of a widespread conspiracy to defraud the American public.[36] Teapot Dome, an area near Caspar, Wyoming, had been set aside as a naval oil reserve by Wilson in 1915 but had been transferred to the Department of Interior in 1921. Albert Fall, the president's great friend and secretary of the department, believed it legitimate to sell off these reserves, and one other in California, without competitive bidding. It was not very difficult for the Senate investigations that followed the revelation of these sales to demonstrate the corruption that the secretary and other of Harding's friends had engaged in.[37] William Allen White recalled what Harding had once said to him: "This is a hell of a job. I have no trouble with my enemies. . . . But my damn friends, my God-damn friends, White, they're the ones that keep me walking the floors nights."[38]

Bribery and corruption, as described by Bryce, considered the distinctive features of American political life in the nineteenth century, appeared to have taken on new life in the twentieth. "Back to normalcy" became a jest; Harding's critics proved more acute judges of his character, values, and abilities than those who served in his administration who continued to honor his memory.[39] A presidency transformed by Roosevelt and Wilson seemed to have reverted to what it had been before ambitious and learned men aspired to the office and managed to secure it. Harding appeared a throwback to an older America, less interested in the world outside, less committed to establishing its credentials as a great power led by a powerful chief executive.

CHAPTER 8

The Great Enigma

CALVIN COOLIDGE WAS thought to be a simple man, but those who believed this greatly underestimated him. Famed for his monumental silences and never renowned for his oratory, he had no illusion that he wished to be (or could be) another Theodore Roosevelt.[1] Without ever explicitly disowning Harding though never praising him as Hoover and Hughes did, his folksiness bore an authentic Vermont stamp very different from the Ohio variant that after 1923 seemed so greatly tarnished.[2] No one ever left Coolidge's presence feeling inferior to him; there was no dissembling or pretense. In his oath-taking, at his father's farm house in Plymouth, Vermont, he showed none of the public relations concerns that had so greatly preoccupied Roosevelt in his first days as a twentieth-century accidental president. While Roosevelt made certain that reporters in adequate number witnessed his swearing-in, Coolidge sought no comparable publicity, refusing to make it seem an event of cosmic importance. His modest account told of how a dutiful son, visiting his father to help with farm chores, was awakened by a messenger after midnight on August 3, 1923, to learn of the president's death and told to take the oath of office immediately. He asked his father, a notary public, to administer the oath, and in the simple darkened farmhouse that boasted no telephone, by the light of a kerosene lamp, he took the oath that made him president of the United States. Because an oath so administered, by someone who did not qualify as a judge, might be considered illegal, a second swearing-in was organized later in Washington by Harry Daugherty, the attorney general, but was never given much publicity. The simple ceremony in the Vermont farmhouse told a tale that suited Coolidge's political purposes.

Though Coolidge was never the hayseed politician Lodge and other more affluent and worldly Republicans imagined him to be, he recognized the political advantages of emphasizing his qualities as a frugal farmer's boy who had never lost touch with his Vermont roots. Considerably more crafty than many believed, socially prominent Washingtonians, including the ever-acerbic Alice

Roosevelt Longworth, the beautiful Princess Alice of old, celebrated in her father's day in the White House, may or may not have uttered the devastating comment that Coolidge was "weaned on a pickle," but others made equally unflattering remarks.[3] Though no one ever mistook his vivacious and witty wife, Grace Coolidge, for the Duchess—the imperious and vulgar Florence Harding who preceded her in the White House—Coolidge took pains to distinguish himself from his predecessor. The Harding poker parties became a thing of the past, as unthinkable as the drinking of hard liquor in the White House.

Coming to office when he did, Coolidge recognized the importance of being seen as a man of integrity and honor. Though lacking Harding's skills with the press, and having no journalistic experience, he intended to follow Harding's practice in scheduling regular press conferences, knowing that such publicity could only help him. Harding held two meetings with the press every week at different hours to accommodate both morning and afternoon newspapers, and he established rules acceptable to reporters and editors, never feeling the need to issue the kinds of threats Roosevelt used in guaranteeing protection against inadvertent disclosures. Harding's press conference rules required questions to be submitted in advance, with direct quotation prohibited. The phrase *according to a White House spokesman* originated with Harding, and Coolidge followed him in many of these innovations. He held more press conferences than any president before him and gave a greater number of speeches. Though many mocked him for his hackneyed verbiage, it never became as risible as Harding's, and the newly installed president achieved success in his first months in office greater than almost anyone had anticipated.

Following the precedent set by Roosevelt, he retained the whole of Harding's Cabinet, apparently committed to the domestic and foreign policies his predecessor had supported—strict economy in federal expenditure, maintenance of the high tariff, enforcement of the Volstead Act, refusal to give a soldiers' bonus, and continued restrictions on new foreign immigration.[4] Hostile to any proposals for Allied war-debt reduction, and refusing even to consider the possibility of recognizing the Soviet Union, he, like Harding, seemed prepared to have the United States accept the World Court, but any possibility of joining the League of Nations was excluded.[5] Coolidge showed no interest in establishing himself as an innovator in foreign or domestic affairs.

Although no one accused Coolidge of being in any way involved in the scandals that became major news stories in the fall of 1923 with the opening of the Senate's investigation of Teapot Dome and a separate Senate investigation of the Justice Department, the pressure to remove Henry Daugherty, the attorney general, grew steadily. Taft, years earlier, had referred to Daugherty as "one of the finest fellows I know," but the charges leveled against him in the Senate hearings were serious, and even Taft urged the president to ask for his resignation.[6] Many in the Cabinet, including Hoover, had never believed Daugherty's disclaimers and were delighted to see him go; others feared he had been treated too harshly. Coolidge put himself above the struggle and left it to others, including Hughes, his secretary of state, to remind Americans that all virtue did not reside in the Democratic Party and all vice in the Republican. While Hughes emphasized his concern that anyone found guilty of corruption should be punished, he found it useful to add: "There are crooks in every community and in every party. Now and then, one gets into office. Let wrongs be exposed and punished, but let not partisan Pecksniffs affect a 'holier than thou' attitude. . . . Guilt is personal and corruption knows no party." The president never uttered comparable words; in his characteristically cautious and terse manner, he ignored the stream of newspaper copy that gave daily accounts of the crime and corruption that had been a hallmark of the Harding presidency, and he acted as if he had been a very peripheral member of the Harding administration, which was true.

Coolidge's remoteness from Harding and indeed from his Cabinet gave him the protection he needed. Still, recalling the circumstances that had given him the vice presidential nomination, some hoped he might be replaced in 1924 with a stronger candidate, believing that Coolidge could not be certain of repeating Roosevelt's feat of 1904. The failure of Hiram Johnson and others who aspired to the presidency to deny him renomination in 1924 came less from the specific policies he advocated and more from the country beginning to enjoy what soon proved to be one of its more prolonged periods of national prosperity.[7] While Coolidge frequently found Congress difficult, with senators being especially obstreperous, and felt it necessary to use his veto to override legislation that gave the war veterans their promised bonus, these were minor defeats when placed beside the revival of America's business economy. What better proof could there be of success than the announcement during the week when the Republicans were meeting in Cleveland to choose their presidential and vice presidential nominees that the Ford Motor Company had just produced its ten-millionth automobile? Industry was reviving, unemployment declining, and consumers were showing a confidence they had never displayed during the Harding years.

The Republican Party platform, bland and brief, avoided any issue that might prove controversial. Its self-satisfied tone, set in the very first sentence, read: "We the delegates of the Republican Party in national convention assembled, bow our heads in reverent memory of Warren G. Harding." The party seemed scarcely embarrassed by the disclosures of the last year and a half. A huge portrait of the recently deceased president, flanked by smaller ones of Abraham Lincoln and Theodore Roosevelt, looked down on the assembled delegates, who found not the slightest incongruity in this linking of the three men.[8] The platform avoided any mention of the Ku Klux Klan, lest it offend Republicans in the South and elsewhere, but more significant, it omitted any plan for dealing with the agricultural depression, still a pressing problem for millions of farmers. Coolidge won the nomination easily, with all but thirty-four delegates voting for him on the first ballot. The vice presidential nominee, Charles G. Dawes, a banker and the first director of the Bureau of the Budget, beat Hoover on the third ballot; the secretary of commerce was still associated in many Republican minds with the hated Wilson administration in which he had served as food administrator. Hoover, though loyal and useful to Coolidge, received no endorsement from him, faithful to the proposition that the delegates should be free to choose his running mate, very much as they had done in 1920 when they had selected him.

The contrast with the Democratic National Convention, meeting in New York, could not have been more dramatic. While William McAdoo, Wilson's son-in-law who had served as secretary of the treasury in both of his administrations and as director of railways from 1917 to 1919, appeared to be the party's favorite, many were discomfited by his close association with Edward Doheny, the discredited oil magnate who had figured prominently in the Teapot Dome investigations. Many leading Democrats, including Colonel House, Josephus Daniels, and Bernard Baruch, though initially favorable to McAdoo, believed his candidacy to be fatally compromised by revelations of how he had profited from his association with Doheny and urged him to withdraw.[9] Others found ideological reasons to oppose him, the most important being a suspicion that the Ku Klux Klan supported him. McAdoo, vehemently denying these and other charges, saw himself as superior in every way to Oscar Underwood, an Alabama senator born in Massachusetts, and Al Smith, the quintessential New Yorker, elected governor of New York for a second time in 1923, a Catholic, and an outspoken opponent of Prohibition.

McAdoo did well in the Southern primaries, particularly in Georgia and Alabama, helped by Klan propaganda that represented Underwood as the "Jew, jug, and Jesuit candidate," and Smith as a Catholic from "Jew York."[10] While he gained substantially from appearing the advocate of the less affluent in the country, and profited from his condemnation of the policies of Coolidge's multimillionaire secretary of the treasury, his chief rival was Al Smith, the "poor boy from the Bowery," supported by America's Catholics, some 16 percent of the nation's population, the largest single minority in the country.[11] What were the Democrats to do, nominate a Catholic and risk the loss of the South, the Democratic Party's stronghold since the end of the Civil War, or nominate someone who might be expected to carry all the states traditionally loyal to the Democrats and many in the Midwest and West who retained their regard for Bryan and were not believed to be hostile to what Wilson had done in Paris? McAdoo, knowing that Smith was his only serious competitor, imagined he could defeat him by appealing to all in the country who considered New York a foreign place, scarcely resembling the pure and decent America that lay outside its borders. New York, as McAdoo represented it, was "the imperial city," the "city of privilege" created by Wall Street, "reactionary, sinister, unscrupulous, mercenary, and sordid"; in his spirited prose, it lacked "national ideals" and was "devoid of conscience." Warming to his subject, he saw New York as "rooted in corruption, directed by greed and dominated by selfishness."[12] Promising to repeal the tariff and develop foreign markets to absorb farm surpluses, he offered himself as a conservationist who supported all that was indigenously American. By caricaturing New York, and making its governor appear something he had never been, but avoiding the Klan effort to brand him a dangerous Catholic, he stigmatized the city as the place of sin and corruption, heaping praise on the other, more noble, America.

The Democratic Party platform, only slightly less innocuous than the Republican, sought to avoid all controversial issues. Though adherence to the League of Nations was discussed, the delegates omitted any platform plank that might have revived that contentious issue.[13] Indeed, the only question that stirred the convention related to the growing influence of the Ku Klux Klan. While all agreed on a general condemnation of intolerance and bigotry, most delegates preferred for the Klan not to be named as an organization explicitly committed to both. With a two-thirds vote required for the nomination, and many favorite sons retaining the votes of their state delegations, none of the principal contenders came even close to securing the 729 votes required. Vote followed vote, and no resolution of the divisions in the convention seemed possible. With unruly public galleries and ill-tempered delegates suffering from the excessive heat of an un-air–conditioned Madison Square Garden, McAdoo achieved his best showing on the seventieth ballot when he claimed the support of 528 delegates, still very distant from a two-thirds majority. Smith never received more than 368 votes, and the stalemate continued till the eighty-second ballot, when the convention agreed to accept Smith's proposal that delegates be liberated from their pledges to support specific candidates.

It was clearly time for one, the other, or both leading candidates to drop out, allowing someone to emerge as the compromise candidate. For a time, it appeared that Samuel Ralston, an Indiana senator, might be the convention's choice, but on the 103rd ballot the delegates chose John W. Davis, a Wall Street lawyer, the convention's third choice from the time the balloting started.[14] To make an already incongruous convention even more bizarre, the delegates selected Charles Bryan, governor of Nebraska and brother of William Jennings Bryan, to be their vice presidential nominee. A successful Wall Street lawyer was joined to a Nebraska radical, and this was considered a balanced Democratic Party ticket.

In the election that followed, Robert La Follette, the Progressive Party candidate, managed to secure 4,822,856 votes, more than half the number Davis received with his 8,386,503 votes, an extraordinary showing for a third-party candidate. But the true victor was Coolidge with his 15,725,016 votes, approximating Harding's remarkable achievement in 1920. How had this silent and unassuming Vermont farmer, translated into a Massachusetts politician, managed so impressive a victory over the Wall Street lawyer? Davis proved to be an exceptionally weak candidate, scarcely more articulate than the president, and not significantly less conservative. In only one respect did he challenge Coolidge, openly denouncing the Ku Klux Klan. Both Davis and La Follette pressed the president to join them in condemning an organization so obviously prejudiced against blacks, Catholics, and Jews, but Coolidge saw no political advantage in doing so and remained silent on this as on all other controversial matters. Silence proved to be his best defense.

Coolidge scored a remarkable victory, winning all the major states in the East and all in the West except for Wisconsin. His policy, predicated on an uncritical admiration for private initiative and a distrust of excessive federal intervention or expenditure—his federal outlays were only half those of Harding—expressed a philosophy of government fundamentally different from that of the man who had inaugurated the Republican Party's twentieth century, Theodore Roosevelt. In his military and naval policy, as in foreign policy, he showed neither the belligerence nor the enthusiasm that made Roosevelt appear the leader of a new world power Europe would do well to take note of.

In the Republican National Convention's choice of Charles Dawes as Coolidge's vice president, it showed respect for what he had accomplished with his Dawes Plan, which established a schedule of annual payments to guarantee Germany's ability to meet the reparations demands legitimated by the Treaty of Versailles. Dawes recommended to Germany the floating of a loan of 800 million marks abroad; $110 million of the loan in bonds, underwritten by J.P. Morgan and Company, and oversubscribed ten times, were sold in New York alone. Charles Kindleberger, the American economist and economic historian, noted that a $150 million loan was arranged that same year by J.P. Morgan to assist Japan, and a $100 million loan by the same bank helped stabilize the French economy.[15] America, again the world's banker, resumed the role it had enjoyed during the war, satisfying a president who wished not to imitate Roosevelt in the creation of a new navy but to model himself on Taft with his ideas of dollar diplomacy.[16]

Guaranteed a second term in the White House, Coolidge visited the Midwest for the first time in his presidency on December 4, 1924, delivering two major speeches in Chicago, addressed principally to business and commercial leaders. The *New York Times* headline, reporting the speech, read: "Coolidge Urges Cooperation for Peace, Declaring No Nation Can Travel Alone; Chicago Speeches Predict Prosperity."[17] Coolidge offered no thought on what he imagined the U.S. role in the world should be; indeed as the *New York Times* made evident, a good deal of the speech dealt with the country's agricultural problems that the Farm Board was expected soon to ameliorate. The audience, not surprisingly, responded enthusiastically to statements that "every prospect seems to indicate that we are starting on a new era," and that "there will be prosperity enough for all if we are willing to work for it and are willing to remain on a sound basis."[18] Coolidge sounded the same notes in a speech he gave to newspaper editors on January 17, 1925, when he said, quite simply, "The business of America is business." In his inaugural address, delivered on March 4, only a single sentence was recalled years later; from the steps of the Capitol the president told the nation: "Economy is idealism in its most practical form."[19]

Carrying the values of rural Vermont, Coolidge after his reelection, as before, emphasized toil as the sine qua non of prosperity. The federal government could do little to ameliorate the conditions of the less advantaged; self-help—the Victorian panacea for economic ills—was the only reliable remedy. Though parsimony became the hallmark of his administration, Coolidge saw the advantage of using the White House to entertain guests, issuing invitations to more guests than any previous White House occupant—and though the Volstead Act precluded the serving of wine or liquor, Grace Coolidge, always expensively and smartly dressed, seemed almost to compensate for the president's monumental silences. Making frequent use of the presidential yacht, the *Mayflower*, he invited influential Americans to join him for weekend cruises on the Potomac. Whatever evidence he showed of being old-fashioned, he greatly enjoyed movies and frequently entertained guests with previews. Though obviously dour and shy, as one of the few surviving members of his press corps said of him in 1967, "we kinda liked the old coot," and others felt the same way about him.[20]

What, then, did he choose to do as president? The short answer, very little; his legislative record was minimal in every respect. The Revenue Act of 1926 cut estate taxes and reduced the surtax on conspicuous wealth by 50 percent, repealed the gift tax, and greatly lowered income taxes across the board; a second tax bill in 1928 reduced corporate taxes still further, thereby encouraging the stock market speculation that had become a characteristic feature of the day. Coolidge saw no reason to worry, believing these measures served simply to perpetuate the prosperity that so obviously delighted the nation. He showed great confidence in his Secretary of the Treasury Andrew Mellon, whom he much preferred to Herbert Hoover, Harding's favorite. Coolidge, a fiscal conservative, took few risks, not even in the area that continued to dismay many Republicans: the condition of the nation's farm economy.[21]

He practiced the politics of silence as few of his predecessors had been able to do. When thousands of Ku Klux Klan members marched through Washington streets in 1925, at a time when the Klan claimed some 5 million members nationally, the president said nothing.[22] Nor did he choose to comment on the

Scopes trial, dealing with evolution, a sensitive issue for all who believed in a literal interpretation of the biblical story of creation.[23] Coolidge remained aloof from any matter that might conceivably offend any among the many millions who had voted for him. It seemed for a time that his marked reticence could only mean he intended to seek reelection in 1928, and that he proposed to do nothing to jeopardize his relations with any important segment of the electorate. When, therefore, he announced on August 2, 1927, five years after he first took the oath of office as president, that "I do not choose to run for President in 1928," the country was dumbfounded.[24] Everything seemed to be going well for him. Why should he voluntarily choose to leave the White House? The explanations generally given—that he was grieving for his son, who died of an infection from an injury suffered on the White House tennis court, that his own health and that of his wife had been impaired by that tragedy—satisfied only a few. Grace Coolidge implied that "papa" anticipated an economic depression and believed the prosperity could not last. This seemed as credible an explanation as any other.[25]

The president knew that he had been lucky, that his good fortune could not last. That, perhaps as much as any other factor, explained his decision not to seek another term. Though he administered the government well, working through the Cabinet he inherited but also the one he appointed, rarely interfering with decisions reached by his department heads, his failure to fashion policies appropriate to new conditions at home and abroad revealed the limits of his understanding of why it was not enough to make advantageous foreign loans or guarantee that the country enjoyed access to the oil and rubber its new automobile economy depended on. Whatever skills Coolidge showed in purely domestic politics, he lacked anything that could be mistaken for imagination in the realm of foreign policy. Europe remained a mystery to him, and he showed no greater appreciation of events in Asia, of the turmoil developing in that region. Having little interest in foreign affairs, unlike Roosevelt and Wilson, he left it to his secretary of state to handle these arcane matters. When he accepted Hughes's resignation in 1925, showing little remorse in the loss of someone many considered an outstanding statesman, and selected Frank B. Kellogg to succeed him, Washington was stunned. Rumors of Hughes's intention to resign had long circulated, and most informed Republicans expected that Hoover, given his vast experience in foreign policy, would succeed him. When, instead, the man almost universally disparaged as a dull lawyer received the senior Cabinet position, and the president ostentatiously set Hoover aside, retaining him at the Commerce Department, many asked whether it did not demonstrate conclusively the president's unwillingness to tolerate men of intellectual stature and independence.[26]

Nothing was more significant than the almost cavalier treatment by Coolidge of Charles Evans Hughes. While Hughes would later become a thorn in the side of a New Deal president, earning Roosevelt's ire, and though he somewhat exaggerated what he had achieved at the Washington Conference in Harding's administration, he was certainly the best secretary of state since Elihu Root. Coolidge never adequately recognized that it was Hughes who first saw the need for departing from what one German historian called "the ostrichlike [American] policy with respect to Europe, avoiding its postwar problems by turning their backs to the scene."[27] In a major address to the American Historical Association on December 22, 1922, Hughes had said: "We cannot dispose of these problems by calling them European, for they are world problems, and we cannot escape the injurious consequences of a failure to settle them."[28] Out of this speech came an initiative, led by Charles Dawes, later Coolidge's vice president, that settled on what Germany could be expected to pay in reparations and how she would pay them. The Dawes Plan was in many ways the Coolidge administration's only important foreign policy accomplishment, giving Germany the few years of stability she would know through what became a two-decade-long interwar time of strife, inflation, and ultimately the triumph of Nazism. Coolidge never made much of the Hughes achievement and could claim none that was even remotely comparable in his second term when Kellogg sat as secretary of state.

Coolidge failed to interest himself in European developments, seeing no significance in Joseph Stalin's final victory over Leon Trotsky in 1928, and showing scarcely greater concern with the continued economic instability in France that led Poincaré drastically to devalue the franc. In Germany where productivity and investment were lagging, wages were rising, and public finances were coming under increasing strain, the German economy had become heavily dependent on short-term U.S. loans. Neither the president nor his advisers saw dangers in this situation. When French foreign minister Aristide Briand, fearing the weakness of his country vis-à-vis Germany, approached the United States with a proposal that the two countries sign an agreement to renounce war and accept that all differences between them would be settled by peaceful means, Kellogg scarcely knew how to react. Because peace was so immensely popular a slogan, and because the proposed pact involved no engagement on America's part, he decided to accept it, urging the French to extend its excellent principles to include as many nations as possible.[29]

On August 27, 1928, just weeks before the election that would bring Hoover to the White House, the Pact of Paris, known more familiarly as the Kellogg-Briand Pact, was signed, with fifteen nations agreeing to renounce war as an instrument of national policy. The words were meaningless, made more so by the fact that many of the principal signatories, including France, Great Britain, and the United States, all added reservations of one kind or another to exempt themselves from its more stringent demands. The historian Denis Brogan captured the inanity of the pact when he wrote: "The United States, which had abolished the evils of drink by the Eighteenth Amendment, invited the world to abolish war by taking the pledge. The world, not quite daring to believe or doubt, obeyed."[30] The emptiness of Coolidge's policies were fully revealed on Armistice Day 1928, following Hoover's victory at the polls, when the president chose to say in his observance of that day: "Europe on the whole has arrived at a state of financial stability and prosperity where it cannot be said we are called on to help or act much beyond a strict business basis. The needs of our own people require that any further advances by us must have the most careful consideration."[31] In reaction, the American-born Lady Astor, speaking in the House of Commons, called the president a "narrow-minded little beast," but these were not remarks that greatly disturbed a president who gave little heed to foreign opinion.[32]

Coolidge never mastered the intricacies of disarmament negotiations and took little interest in them, showing a much greater concern with the war-debts issue. The American people expected the Allies to pay their war debts, and the president knew that Congress had no sympathy for states that had borrowed and then refused to honor their commitments. Whether or not he ever uttered the priceless sentence "They hired the money, didn't they?" the expression revealed the sentiment of a nation that felt cheated by crafty Europeans, treacherous in 1919, who could never be trusted. Neither in Congress nor among his Cabinet colleagues did he meet opposition that required him to revise the homespun homilies he derived from his Vermont boyhood. Like all the twentieth-century presidents before him, he lacked the knowledge of economics that might have made him distrust his own opinions, but the fact that he spoke as the people did—and as they expected him to—gave him self-confidence. He left office with the reputation of being a winner.[33]

Coolidge believed the country's continued prosperity depended on the intelligence, imagination, and innovation of America's industrialists.[34] Wall Street never figured as his enemy; Henry Ford and Thomas Edison were his major heroes, standing on pedestals only slightly lower than that reserved for the boy-aviator, Charles Lindbergh, the all-American hero. Coolidge believed Henry Ford a genius, not only for his invention of the low-priced Model T in 1908, but for introducing the moving assembly line in 1913 that had made the mass production of automobiles and many other industrial products possible.[35]

While Coolidge had no intention of recognizing the Soviet Union, he knew the Ford Motor Company exported more than a third of its tractors there in 1925 and that by 1927 some 85 percent of all tractors in the Soviet Union were produced in the United States by Ford.[36] That was good business, and for the president good business transcended any ideological contempt he might feel for the Bolshevik regime.[37]

In countries closer to the United States, particularly Canada, the United States virtually replaced Great Britain as the major economic power of influence. The United States export of capital and goods to Canada rose dramatically, and if this involved the destruction of Canada's automotive industry and the virtual control by General Electric of Canada's largest electric company, that seemed natural and legitimate. So, also, the growing U.S. influence in more distant markets, in Asia, both in Japan and China, but also in Latin America, meant that the United States had become the world's leading industrial and commercial power. In new industries, such as movies, in which the president took particular interest, he saw that this had become the nation's fourth-largest business enterprise with a capital investment of more than $1.5 billion. Such new industries offered incomparable opportunities for speculative investment, and by the time sound came to the movies in 1927 there were 20,000 movie houses in the country with a seating capacity of about 18 million.[38] Coolidge, admiring the country for its productive capacity, knew it had also become a society of avid consumers. How could he fail to be satisfied with what was happening? How could the nation fail to share his enthusiasms? The aspirations of both Roosevelt and Wilson for a more powerful presidency, more actively engaged in the world, were set aside in favor of a politics more redolent of the nineteenth century than of anything that had happened in the first two decades of the twentieth.

CHAPTER 9

The Engineer

HERBERT HOOVER, IN comparison with Calvin Coolidge, was an American cosmopolitan who had traveled the world. While he had never competed for elected political office before his nomination for the presidency in 1928, resembling William Howard Taft in this as in other ways, his energy, intelligence, and ambition, obvious from the time he enrolled as an undergraduate at the new Leland Stanford University in California, marked him as exceptional.[1] Born in West Branch, Iowa, a Quaker farming community in 1874, the first Quaker president, and the first born west of the Mississippi, he was also the first to be orphaned at an early age, losing his father, a blacksmith, when he was six and his mother two years later.[2] For the next two years he was cared for by an aunt and uncle, then told "thee is going to Oregon," to live with another uncle, his mother's brother, a country doctor who had just lost his only son. Henry Minthorn, in effect Hoover's surrogate father, pushed him to seek an education, and while he would have preferred for him to go to a Quaker college where a scholarship would have relieved the family of all financial obligations, the boy's interest in mathematics and science—disciplines little developed in Quaker colleges—made that option unreasonable. Though Stanford was a secular institution, and therefore had little appeal to either his uncle or his grandmother, they accepted the young boy's decision to enroll there as one of the university's first undergraduates. The choice could not have been more fortuitous; Stanford for Hoover—as Harvard for Roosevelt, Yale for Taft, and Princeton for Wilson—shaped his life, giving him the professional competences that lifted him very rapidly from the simple Quaker world into which he had been born.

Leland Stanford, the California senator who gave the land and the original endowment for the university to commemorate his dead son, declared his intentions for the university at the opening ceremonies when he said: "Remember that life is, above all, practical; that you are here to fit yourself for a useful career; also, that learning should not only make you wise in the arts and sciences, but should fully develop your moral and religious natures."[3] Those ideas, congenial to the young Hoover, led him to become the favorite student of Dr. John Branner, the head of the Department of Geology and Mining and, through his professor's influence, to find summer employ initially with the Geological Survey of Arkansas, and in the next two years with the United States Geological Survey, working in the High Sierras. At Stanford, Hoover met the woman who became his wife, Lou Henry, the daughter of a very successful Iowa banker, who shared his interests in geology and love of the outdoors. In the years that followed, in Australia but also in China, Hoover pursued his profession as a mining engineer, beginning as a very junior partner in an engineering firm, later achieving greater independence as a freelance engineer and consultant, making a very considerable fortune.[4] Living mostly abroad, spending almost as much time in London as in California, and traveling constantly to remote mining sites in places as different as Burma and South Africa, Hoover knew Asia, Africa, and Europe as few Americans did.[5]

Reading George Kennan's book *Siberia and the Exile System,* published in 1891, Hoover became interested in Russian mines in the Urals and was soon active in their development. Lecturing at Stanford and Columbia, incorporating his lectures into a book, *Principles of Mining,* published in 1909, where he expressed ideas unconventional in that day for anyone considered a capitalist entrepreneur, Hoover wrote:

> As corporations have grown, so likewise have labor unions. In general, they are normal and proper antidotes for unlimited capitalistic organization. . . . The time when the employer could ride roughshod over his labor is disappearing with the doctrine of *laissez-faire* on which it is founded. The sooner the fact is recognized, the better for the employer.[6]

Believing efficiency the key to profitability, Hoover wrote: "In these days of international flow of labor, commodities, and capital, the real controlling factor in wages is profitability."

Hoover never claimed to be an intellectual in the tradition of Roosevelt or Wilson but viewed himself as a professional engineer in the same way that Taft saw himself as a professional lawyer. Helped by his wife, the Latinist in the family, Hoover translated *De Re Metallica,* the sixteenth-century work of a German scientist, into English and showed a penchant for the kind of scholarship that characterized Taft's disquisitions on the law.[7] Although a self-made and well-to-do American, Hoover did not circulate in London in the company of the very rich, as did men like J.P. Morgan and others of their social position. Nor, for that matter, did he form close friendships with prominent British political, intellectual, and scientific leaders.[8] Only after the outbreak of the war in 1914, following his decision to organize the Committee for the Relief of Belgium, did Hoover come to the attention of men other than those he knew through his geological work and his continuing association with Stanford administrators and alumni.[9] A prominent philanthropist and humanitarian, he raised substantial sums in the United States to relieve hunger in Belgium, and Colonel House came to know him, indeed to consult him, when he went on his peace missions to Europe in 1915 and 1916.[10] Hoover, in his meetings with House and Walter Hines Page, the U.S. ambassador in London, never concealed his disillusion with the Western Allies and the Central Powers; neither seemed at all sincere in their quest for peace.[11] Given these views, so congenial to Wilson, and the experience he acquired in distributing food to the Belgians, the president asked him in 1917 to accept appointment to a newly established post, becoming what the press quickly heralded as the country's food czar.[12]

As the head of the Food Administration, Hoover hoped to avoid the draconian measures adopted both in Germany and the United Kingdom, relying instead on what he considered a better guarantee of fair distribution, the voluntary cooperation of the American public. With a new slogan—"Food Will Win the War!"—Hoover believed that meatless and wheatless days, together with new dietary habits, would make extensive rationing unnecessary.[13] A new verb entered the language—to *Hooverize* was to conserve. Hoover recognized the Allied problems to be grave, and the March Revolution in Russia and the downfall of the Czar disheartened him, leading him to say presciently to Will Irwin, one of his closest friends,

> The revolution will be difficult to stabilize. There have been centuries of oppression. There is no large middle class. There is almost total illiteracy in the people. There is no general experience in government. Russia cannot maintain a wholly liberal republic yet. Revolutions always go further than their creators expect. And in its swing, this one is more likely to go to the left than to the right.[14]

In London and Paris in July 1918, he conferred with Allied food controllers, and those meetings led to the establishment of the Allied Food Council under Hoover's chairmanship.[15] In a dinner to honor him, Lloyd George, the prime minister, made the flattering comment, "It seems to me, Mr. Hoover, that you represent not only the United States but also Merciful Providence. We are no longer aliens, foreigners to one another; we now disagree with the same violence and familiarity as if we were members of the same Cabinet."[16] Hoover may not have realized the full import of Lloyd George's words; even on so seemingly noncontroversial a matter as food, the Americans and the British did not always agree.[17] Hoover knew this, but his concern was to make certain that the American production of food remained high, that prices were kept down, and that supplies in sufficient quantity were sent abroad, both to the U.S. forces and the Allies. At home, citizens were expected to rally to his slogans, including "Wheatless days in America make sleepless nights in Germany."[18] By the publicity he generated, Hoover began to enjoy growing acclaim in the United States.

With the coming of the Armistice in November 1918, Hoover went abroad, to London and Paris, accompanied by his young secretary, Lewis L. Strauss, who would serve after World War II as the first chairman of the Atomic Energy Commission, and by his even younger legal counsel, Robert Taft, son of the president and later Mr. Republican, who would challenge Dwight Eisenhower for the Republican Party's 1952 presidential nomination. Hoover, dismayed by what he saw as the threat of starvation, especially serious in the former Austro-Hungarian Empire, on his return to New York spoke of famine as "the mother of revolution," and showed increasingly concern with the dangers posed by Bolshevism.[19] The Allies were insisting that all relief efforts be handled by a joint authority, but Hoover believed that since the Americans were supplying most of the food, they ought to control its distribution.[20] American farmers, encouraged to produce during the war, were harvesting bumper crops that Hoover wished to see made available both to former enemies and to neutrals.[21] An agreement negotiated in late 1918 by the Inter-Allied Supreme Council for Relief and Supply, on which Hoover served as director-general, with both John Maynard Keynes and Lord Reading representing Great Britain, accepted for the Germans to be supplied with 270,000 tons of food, but this was conditional on their handing over their merchant marine.[22] As James Patterson, Robert Taft's biographer, wrote, using both Hoover and Strauss as his sources, "The long struggle left Hoover forever convinced of the gulf between what he considered the idealism of America and the *Realpolitik* of Europe." America, he believed, should "retire from Europe lock, stock, and barrel," being "the only great moral reserve in the world today."[23] When the terms of the Treaty of Versailles were divulged, Hoover was as disgusted by them as were Keynes and Smuts. Hoover was one of those who believed Wilson had been taken in by wicked Europeans, and he returned to the United States disillusioned and angry with both the British and the French, optimistic only about what the United States might become if it stayed clear of European entanglements and realized its full potential as an industrial power.[24] Like Taft, his young assistant, he believed the diplomats had bungled the peace, that America had fought the war to promote international justice and that it had failed because of Europe's chicanery.[25] Hoover could see only one way forward for the United States: to follow an independent path, seeking its own prosperity in its own way. For Hoover, a geologist and a world traveler, trade seemed the only certain road to influence and prosperity.[26]

Hoover left Europe in September 1919 and wrote later of the many tributes he received for his work from presidents and prime ministers, the Pope, and the heads of the Greek, Lutheran, and Armenian churches. Meeting with

Georges Clemenceau, the aged French premier, Hoover heard him say: "There will be another world war in your time, and you will be needed back in Europe."[27] Keynes called Hoover "a weary Titan," and the phrase expressed perfectly his physical and psychological condition when he returned to the United States, to build a house in Palo Alto, in close proximity to his beloved Stanford University campus.[28] His many American admirers, including the young Robert Taft, hoped he might be considered for the presidency—in their minds he was the equal of anyone who had held the office in the twentieth century—and his name was put forward at the Republican National Convention in 1920. It received almost no support; a man who had served in a major position in the Wilson administration was not someone the Republicans who nominated Harding were likely to respect. Indeed, in the minds of many delegates, Hoover's credentials as a Republican were suspect, some doubting that he belonged to the party at all: His accepting to serve as vice chairman in late 1919 on a commission headed by the secretary of labor, William Wilson, appointed by the president to study labor relations, helped his reputation among Republicans not at all.[29] The report that issued from their three-month study, largely written by Hoover, seemed radical, at least to conservative Republicans unprepared to acknowledge that workers had the right to strike or that the commission's modest recommendations for old-age insurance were reasonable. When Harding first considered Hoover for a Cabinet position in 1921, several prominent Republicans made their negative opinions known to him.[30] Yet even before the publication in 1922 of Hoover's book, *American Individualism,* those who knew him best realized he was neither a radical nor a disciple of the Roosevelt of 1912.[31] An efficient administrator with great experience of the world abroad, he expressed views that emphasized the advantages the country derived from its productive capitalist system. Hoover may have been an advocate of collective bargaining and child labor laws, but he was also the champion of American business, believing in it as Roosevelt and Wilson never did.

Harding did not choose a radical when he selected Hoover to be his secretary of commerce. Hoover soon converted one of the lesser departments into one of the most important and was recognized as one of Harding's three principal Cabinet appointees, together with the secretary of state and the secretary of the treasury. Like Hughes and Mellon, Hoover achieved his ascent not by becoming an intimate of the president—one of his poker-playing and hard-drinking companions dismissed by the press as cronies—but as someone who could be relied on for probity, intelligence, and industry. Given Coolidge's enormous regard for business and business success, one might have expected him to share Harding's high regard for Hoover, but he never did. Coolidge failed to develop a close relation with him, neither before Harding's death nor after. On at least two occasions when Coolidge might have done a great deal to advance Hoover's career, appointing him secretary of state when Hughes re-signed, and later when his not very illustrious successor, Frank Kellogg, ap-peared to be interested in leaving, the president never seriously considered him for the post.[32] Why Silent Cal had so little regard for the boy wonder—his own unflattering name for Hoover—cannot be easily explained, but he al-most certainly resented him, found him domineering, aggressive, and self-serving, constantly seeking to extend his powers, too avid in advertising his many accomplishments.[33]

Whether in developing regulatory procedures for new industries like civil aviation and radio, or making certain he involved himself in settling such crises as the coal and rail strikes of 1922, Hoover appeared exceedingly bump-tious during the Harding years in ways that the more modest vice president may have found distasteful. Coolidge's was a characteristic Republican Party political career; Hoover's was that of a maverick. Coolidge had never traveled beyond Canada, going there only on his honeymoon; Hoover was a cos-mopolitan. Coolidge, to use Isaiah Berlin's famous distinction, was a hedge-hog; Hoover was a fox.[34] The president, though more than happy to use Hoover, had no interest in advancing him to higher office. By 1927, the evi-dences of coolness between the two were unmistakable. Until almost the mo-ment that Hoover received his party's nomination in 1928, he could never be certain that Coolidge would not reverse himself and choose to run again, or surprise the country by suddenly expressing his enthusiasm for some Republi-can other than himself.

Hoover had little reason to feel beholden to Coolidge when he won his elec-tion easily in 1928, defeating Al Smith decisively. Smith, the first Roman Catholic to seek the presidency, lost many of the Southern states until then loyal to the Democratic Party, and Hoover's 444 electoral votes as against Smith's 87 contrasted favorably with what Coolidge had managed to do in 1924 when he won with 382 electoral votes against 136 for Davis and 13 for La Follette. The 1928 election, unusual for the depth of the religious intoler-ance it revealed, provoked some to ask whether a Protestant Democrat, run-ning against Hoover, would have done equally badly. The question is unan-swerable, but 1928, like 1920 and 1924, were years when Republicans won easily, making the White House again a Republican Reserve, resembling what it had been almost continually after the Civil War. The ugly whispering cam-paign that helped destroy Smith would not have existed against a non-Catholic Democrat, and the theme of the Pope in the White House would not have been raised, but the prosperous, fun-loving, and self-satisfied society described by William Allen White in his perceptive biography of Coolidge, *A Puritan in Babylon,* was not one searching for political adventure.[35] The country was more than happy to remain with someone who promised continued prosperity and stability.

Had Coolidge chosen to run, he would have won; Hoover's victory reflected the confidence Americans felt in business success and acumen, in the administrative efficiency of a gifted engineer, a self-made man who had risen from poverty to become a millionaire. Americans in the 1920s respected efficiency; their unhappy experience with the Harding crowd gave them new respect for probity and integrity.[36] These qualities, shared by Hoover and Coolidge, made both acceptable. The young Robert Taft congratulated Hoover on his election, saying "I am looking forward to reading *Life, Time,* the *Nation,* and the *New Republic,* and seeing how they take the result. The discomfiture of the Eastern intelligentsia gives me as much pleasure as that of the radical farm leaders."[37] This, the authentic voice of Ohio, but also of the electorate in November 1928, suggested that men in the Wilson (or Roosevelt) tradition were unacceptable; conservatives, believing in individualism and capitalism, exemplified by Hoover, satisfied an electorate no longer attracted by the supposed virtues of progressivism or socialism.[38] Both seemed strangely anachronistic in the glitter of the Roaring Twenties. 1928 marked the end of an era when third-party candidates, despairing of the two traditional parties, appealed to substantial numbers of voters. Harding's election could be interpreted as a repudiation of Wilson; Hoover's was a denial of both Wilson and Roosevelt.

Hoover's Cabinet was not essentially different from the one Coolidge had appointed when reelected in 1924. He retained Mellon at Treasury, but his choice of Henry Stimson, Roosevelt's great friend and protégé, to be his secretary of state gave evidence of the importance he attached to a post Coolidge had never valued.[39] Aware of the continued dismay of farmers with their reduced income and constant threat of foreclosures and bankruptcies, Hoover persuaded the large Republican majority in Congress to join with a good number of Democrats to pass the Agricultural Marketing Act. In the creation of the Federal Farm Board, with a capital of $500 million to promote agricultural cooperatives and stabilization corporations to guarantee orderly markets in important farm commodities, Hoover appeared to be departing from the parsimony of the Coolidge administration. Less happy, certainly, was the passage in 1930 of the Smoot-Hawley tariff, intended to fulfill Hoover's campaign promise to impose higher duties on a wide range of imported agricultural commodities to help farmers cope with falling prices for their produce. Seen at the time as a serious blunder—what Sir Arthur Salter called a turning point in history—it seemed even more irresponsible after 1930 when the world economic Depression made it appear a positive disincentive to world trade.[40]

Walter Lippmann, America's most esteemed journalist, was even more severe; scathingly, he condemned the president for agreeing to the tariff: He "had surrendered everything for nothing."[41] Even before the full global dimensions of the Depression were apparent, Lippmann wrote of Hoover, "He gave up the leadership of his party. He let his personal authority be flouted.

He accepted a wretched and mischievous product of stupidity and greed."
Lippmann represented Hoover as exceptionally thin-skinned and bewildered,
unsuited to high office. How did this accomplished administrator, who had
recently stood so high in the public's esteem, come to fall so low? The answer,
very simply, is that Hoover's talent—an ability to organize for a specifically
limited purpose—proved useless in a situation of unprecedented disorder created by the world economic Depression of the 1930s. Where there were so
many disparate interests at home and abroad to be accommodated, and where
the president started with such grave suspicions of Europe, based on his experiences there during the war and at the peace conference, it was almost inconceivable that he would be inclined to consider remedies that went beyond
those used in the early Harding years.

It is significant, certainly, that less than a month before the New York Stock
Exchange crash, Hoover summoned a group of distinguished social scientists to
dine with him in the White House to launch an inquiry that three years later,
after he left the White House, was published as *Recent Social Trends,* the most
substantial investigation of how the country had changed since the beginning
of the century.[42] The "epoch-making events" listed in *Recent Social Trends* were

the Great War, mass immigration, race riots, rapid urbanization, the rise of great
industrial combines like U.S. Steel, Ford, and General Motors, new technologies
like power, automobiles, radios, and motion pictures, novel social experiments
like Prohibition, daring campaigns for birth control, a new frankness about sex,
women's suffrage, the advent of mass-market advertising and consumer financing.

Nothing Hoover had said during the election campaign suggested he understood how much American society had changed since 1914, since the time he
became a millionaire. The ideology of the oil engineer remained the ideology
of the Republican president. A social, cultural, and economic world essentially
different from the one Roosevelt, Taft, and Wilson had known had come into
being, and only in the political realm did the old institutions survive. Congress
still showed itself proud, difficult, and recalcitrant; the president continued to
rely on a Cabinet of predominantly middle-aged or aging well-to-do white
Protestant men, principally trained in the law, with a miniscule White House
staff, expected to cope with a public opinion shaped largely by newspapers and
political parties essentially unchanged from what they had been in the days of
McKinley.

These were the political resources available to the president, and they were
manifestly unequal to the problems that exploded dramatically on October
29, 1929, when stock market prices plunged, and the nation, investors and
speculators alike, habituated to seeing their market shares grow in value,
found it had lost some $26 billion. The stock market crash—an economic col-

lapse without precedent in U.S. history—was followed by a world economic Depression, effectively destroying Hoover's reputation for ingenuity and decisiveness. The president had spoken frequently of the dangers of excessive stock market speculation and was appalled by Coolidge's failure to address the problem, indeed exacerbating it by the optimistic and injudicious remarks he made just before leaving the White House. Hoover invented the term *depression* to define an economic catastrophe he scarcely understood, believing it was caused principally by errors the Europeans had made a decade earlier, little realizing how much American policy in the 1920s had contributed to the collapse.[43] Most Europeans believed the United States primarily responsible for the Depression, unwilling to write off the war debts, encouraging excessive stock market speculation that led to the stock market crash, following the two years of frenzied lending both at home and abroad in 1927 and 1928.[44] However the blame is apportioned between the two for the crisis that overwhelmed both, Eric Hobsbawm's severe judgment on why the British failed to avert the Depression or cope with its disastrous effects, saying that "never did a ship founder with a captain and a crew more ignorant of the reasons for its misfortune or more impotent to do anything about it," might just as properly have been said of the Americans.[45]

The president's intellectual resources proved to be limited; what passed for an economic philosophy—extolling the virtues of capitalism—seemed suddenly barren and strangely irrelevant. In Congress, he found no Republican majority prepared to recommend bold action, to formulate fiscal policies different from those employed in the immediate post–World War I economic depression. Neither his secretary of state nor his secretary of the treasury could greatly help him. Indeed, Stimson spent a considerable part of 1930 preparing for and conducting negotiations in London for a new treaty to deal with the size of the world's navies. Only much later did he acknowledge that what he did there was not "an important step toward disarmament and world peace."[46] Mellon persisted in believing the tested remedies, first proposed after World War I and that had borne fruit in 1923, were the ones to be relied on again. The times called for an imaginative leader with substantial economic knowledge; that man existed neither in the White House, the State Department, nor the Treasury Department.

The 1930 congressional election, while scarcely disastrous for Hoover, resembled other past off-year elections; the Republicans lost eight seats in the Senate, but with their forty-eight members, as against the forty-seven Democrats and the single Farmer-Labor member, they could still count on their Republican vice president to break any tie vote. In the House, the situation was more serious; there, the Republicans and Democrats each claimed 217 seats. Hoover understood that the statistics told only part of the story; in his view, a number of Republicans were irrevocably opposed to him, and he estimated he had the assured support of only forty senators.[47] Characterizing his Republican opponents as left-wing, he saw them as prepared to agree to federal assistance for the unemployed and to accept large budget deficits, propositions anathema to him and those who saw the remedies for economic recovery as he did. In the House, because thirteen members died before December 1931 when it first met in regular session, and because the majority of these were Republican, the Democrats assumed control.

Hoover recognized he had to act. His first impulse was to ask for new funds to construct public works, believing this would do something to alleviate the soaring unemployment. The president continued to see the problem as essentially domestic, to be resolved by actions taken at home. Only in 1931, the year Arnold Toynbee described as the *annus terribilis*, did he begin, however tentatively, to see the larger dimensions of the problem.[48] An American economic Depression had become a world Depression, and the solutions for it could not be found simply in legislation aimed at reducing domestic unemployment. The failure of foreign banks, first in Austria, then in Germany, sounded the alarm.[49] Ramsay MacDonald, the British prime minister, cabled the U.S. secretary of state to warn him that Germany was in a parlous situation, that only a moratorium on reparations together with the continued extension of credit could save its economy. Hoover, already considering an international moratorium on all war debts and reparations, took the plunge on June 20 and declared both temporarily suspended.

In September, Britain went off the gold standard, the pound fell, and commodity prices, bonds and stocks, production and consumption fell dramatically in all the major capitalist countries. Deflation became the universal economic malady, and Congress, reacting to these developments, could only believe that a balanced budget would ease the situation, a view common also with many in Europe. All to no avail: Investment shriveled, consumption fell, and unemployment skyrocketed. Between 1930 and 1932, 5,100 U.S. banks failed; in the absence of any system of deposit insurance, the losses suffered by individuals were catastrophic, estimated to exceed $3.2 billion. The president, desperate to reverse the situation, urged the revival of something like the War Finance Corporation of 1918.

In January 1932, he persuaded Congress to pass a bill creating the Reconstruction Finance Corporation (RFC), capitalized at $500 million, with power to borrow four times that amount, to assist banks, insurance companies, and railroads in distress. The RFC, considered one of Hoover's more imaginative institutional innovations, though enthusiastically endorsed by many, did nothing to reduce the army of unemployed, believed to be approaching some 13 million men and women.

Hoover, loyal to his belief that unemployment relief of the kind common to Britain would destroy American character and initiative, bringing in its wake a huge bureaucracy with all its attendant corruption and waste, could not imagine so drastic a measure for the United States. In the spring of 1932, tens of thousands of unemployed war veterans descended on the nation's capital to ask Congress to pay at once their promised war bonus, not due till 1945, but their demands were rejected. When many veterans proceeded then to occupy federal buildings on Pennsylvania Avenue, the District of Columbia authorities became convinced that they had no alternative but to evict them and called on the president for help. In the rioting that ensued, two bonus marchers were killed, and the president, through his chief of staff, General Douglas MacArthur, sent in infantry and cavalry, together with six tanks, to force the marchers to cross the river to their tent city in Anacostia, which was then burned to the ground. The country, shocked, outraged, and humiliated, believed all that was being said about heartless Hoover. The name once associated with philanthropy now came to be used to describe shanty towns, the disgraceful Hoovervilles visible in many parts of the country where the unemployed, evicted from their homes, sought shelter. The president, for millions of veterans—and for millions of others—was thought to have disgraced his office.

Under the most trying circumstances Hoover failed as a political leader. His domestic policies, lame and limited, gave scant satisfaction to a society reeling from the effects of mass unemployment and huge losses of income and savings. Though he had once boasted a great reputation as a publicist—able to advertise his own accomplishments—he appeared to have lost even that ability. The sheer magnitude of the nation's economic distress made all his accomplishments seem insubstantial. Thus, for example, his appointment of Benjamin Cardozo to succeed Oliver Wendell Holmes Jr. on the Supreme Court—an excellent choice—might once have been thought proof of his political acumen, but such achievement counted for little in scales that weighed only his all-too-obvious failures.

Even with an accomplished secretary of state at his side, he seemed powerless to check Japan's aggression against China, and when Manchuria was occupied and converted into a Japanese puppet state, Manchukuo, in March 1932, he could think of nothing to do. To join in the boycott of Japan recommended by the League of Nations seemed too dangerous.[50] When Stimson suggested the United States refuse to recognize Manchukuo, and seek to persuade other states to do the same—inventing the so-called Stimson Doctrine—both the president and his secretary knew the gesture was empty, but it seemed the only one available to them.[51] Stimson felt his failure keenly; Hoover rarely acknowledged it. Fearful and cautious, ultimately indecisive and unimaginative, he was not the man to lead the nation in a time of exceptional peril. That opportunity fell to his successor, Franklin Roosevelt, the Democrat who beat him decisively in 1932 with 22,821,857 votes as against Hoover's 15,761,841.

Felix Frankfurter may have said it all when he described Hoover "as a man of overweening ambition yoked to fear."[52] Coolidge had resented the ambition, but whether he also detected the fear is less certain. Others, however, equally unimpressed with Hoover, expressed their misgivings privately when Coolidge announced his intention not to run again. Thus, for example, Parker Gilbert, one of Hoover's brilliant undersecretaries at the Commerce Department, told Mellon, secretary of the treasury, that Hoover's nomination could destroy whatever hopes they had for closer relations with Europe. In his words, "He will be more subject than almost any other important candidate to being moved by his own personal prejudices and his own preconceived ideas," that "he would be about the *worst* possible president from the standpoint of foreign affairs, and that there would be real danger to our foreign policy if he should be elected."[53]

Mellon's reported response was that he himself would never appoint an engineer to run one of his businesses, believing that such men lacked understanding of the "human element."[54] Confronted with the most serious economic crisis in the nation's history, Hoover did no better (and no worse) than other heads of government abroad. The problems were simply too daunting, and Hoover's greatest weaknesses may have been his exaggerated self-esteem, an insufficient command of economics, and a naïve belief that his success as an oil engineer, businessman, and administrator qualified him to understand both domestic and foreign policy. Lacking interlocutors at home in his Cabinet or in Congress able to advise him, he showed his inadequacies, greatly exacerbated by the fact that he was not an especially astute politician.

CHAPTER 10

The Savior

FOR A GOOD many in the United States, perhaps for an even greater number in Europe, Franklin Roosevelt was the savior. Although he lacked the intellectual gifts of his two principal teachers, few who have written about him—an army of scholars and journalists—have emphasized sufficiently how much he learned and profited from observing and reflecting on the careers of Theodore Roosevelt and Woodrow Wilson. Theodore fascinated him, as he did so many others, and Franklin, in his late adolescence and early adulthood, could not fail to be beguiled by him, living a life so much more interesting than the one pursued by so many others of their social class, in law, banking, or business.[1] He admired Theodore's buoyancy, gregariousness, and wit, recognizing the pleasure TR took from exercising such unprecedented power, basking in the public's approval. Franklin saw what others more distant from his cousin only very occasionally appreciated. The president, to whom deception and secrecy were never wholly alien, knew the importance of maintaining a pose that he was open and available, candid and truthful, revealing everything, having nothing to conceal. It was a carefully cultivated pose that carried substantial political advantages, very congenial to a second Roosevelt who from an early age showed himself equally adept at creating fables about himself and scarcely less prone to secrecy. Woodrow, never so familiarly addressed by Franklin, his long-serving assistant secretary of the Navy (the one federal office he held before coming to the White House in 1933), taught him the importance of being cautious, preparing his ground carefully before embarking on any potentially perilous political adventure. In only one instance, exaggerating the political advantages he derived from his impressive victory in the 1936 elections, did Franklin show recklessness, and he paid a heavy price for that mistake. In his plan to increase the size of the Supreme Court, hoping thereby to defeat the "nine old men" who had so often thwarted him, he blundered badly. Never again would he make a comparable political mistake.

199

Franklin Delano Roosevelt, the scion of the Hyde Park Roosevelts, shared a way of life with the Oyster Bay Roosevelts, but this never led him to embrace the Republican Party enthusiasms of Uncle Ted.[2] Though the two resembled each other superficially—Harvard College undergraduate education, fathers they admired, loved, and lost in early adulthood, an upbringing that gave them all the advantages of wealth and position in New York society—they lived essentially different lives. Even in his youth, few thought the frenetic Theodore frivolous, but some considered this Franklin's most distinctive trait.[3] Books interested him only slightly; his passion was for sailing and to a lesser extent for riding.

Never an ardent letter-writer, he enjoyed collecting naval prints and postage stamps, skating, and clay-pigeon shooting. Big game hunting held no appeal for him. New York society, in the city and along the banks of the Hudson River, provided endless pleasures—dinner parties, balls, dances—the rituals faithfully attended by those who cared only to be among their own. Franklin, adored by his widowed mother, lived a life of ease and comfort, made more secure by his marrying someone who accepted the position New York society and her mother-in-law deemed appropriate to the wife of a "gentleman squire."[4] Eleanor Roosevelt, the dutiful mother of a rapidly growing family and the faithful helpmate of an exceedingly handsome husband, knew her husband's ambition was to follow her uncle into politics. He was elected to a seat in the New York state legislature very early, following his cousin's example, and like him clearly never intended to end his days in state politics in Albany.

Aware he had no wish to live his father's leisured life and that the law, the profession he halfheartedly chose, was uninteresting, he ran for the New York state senate in 1910 in a district where only one Democrat had been victorious over the last half-century. Dashing about in his open car at twenty miles per hour, hoping to reach as many voters as he could, he pressed the flesh and flashed his broad and winning smile, neither impressing nor frightening Republicans who saw him as a callow and ambitious youth, trading on his most celebrated attribute, the Roosevelt name.[5]

Receiving no support from the former president, who never thought to show preference for family over party, this mattered little in 1910, the year of Democratic Party triumphs that saw President William Howard Taft humiliated and the Democrats win twenty-six governorships. Roosevelt, in his county constituency, beat his Republican opponent with a respectable majority of 1,069 votes. As a state senator, he appeared at times to imitate the antics of the earlier Roosevelt, considered a well-to-do dandy in late-nineteenth-century Albany.[6] In accent and speech more redolent of Groton than of New York Democratic Party politics, Roosevelt denounced bosses and the machine, emphasizing always the virtues of good government.[7] Some of his senate colleagues distrusted him, thought him a shifty, hypocritical rich boy who pursued politics as a sport.[8] Known as "the un-Republican Roosevelt"—the Hyde Park Roosevelts had always been Democrats—he attended his first Democratic National Convention in 1912, learning there the importance of circulating among delegates and meeting the prominent Democratic elders who might one day be in a position to help him.[9]

Of such encounters, none proved more important than the one that brought him into touch with Josephus Daniels, a member of the Democratic National Committee, the editor of the Raleigh, North Carolina, newspaper, *News and Observer*, a longtime friend of William Jennings Bryan, and an ardent supporter of the Wilson candidacy. Daniels found Roosevelt "as handsome a figure of a man as I have ever seen" and later represented the friendship established there as "a case of love at first sight."[10] The association proved fortuitous for Roosevelt; it gave him less than a year later the office he most coveted, that of assistant secretary of the Navy. It had taken Theodore more than a decade and a half of political struggle to secure the same place; Franklin acquired it after a single two-year term in the state senate. FDR met with the president-elect in Trenton in January 1913 and was offered two desirable posts. Asked to choose between coming to Washington as assistant secretary of the treasury, and accepting a position as collector of the port of New York, he decided to accept neither. Roosevelt had set his heart on being appointed assistant secretary of the Navy, and when Daniels was named secretary of the Navy his hopes soared. On March 4, 1913, presidential inauguration day, in a story told many times, Daniels, meeting Roosevelt in the lobby of the Willard Hotel, asked him outright: "How would you like to come to Washington as Assistant Secretary of the Navy?" Franklin, in language redolent of Theodore's, replied: "How would I like it? I'd like it bully well. It would please me better than anything else in the world. . . ."[11] No one could fail to notice that the young Roosevelt was launched on the path that had led his namesake to the White House. Roosevelt's family delighted in his good fortune; so, also, did many of his legislative colleagues in Albany, happy to see him go. Franklin had been no more popular in Albany than Theodore.

The Navy appointment proved crucial in Franklin's career, as in Theodore's; given the opportunity to observe the federal government both in peace and war, he emerged from the sheltered cocoon his mother, always a formidable presence in his life, had long provided.[12] He learned much from the daily chatter of the secretary, who gave him invaluable instruction on the nature of the Democratic Party. Required to appear occasionally before congressional committees, he recognized quickly that Washington politics in only very superficial ways resembled those of Albany. Politicians took themselves more seriously in the nation's capital; the stakes were higher, and the interests fighting for influence were more aggressive. Roosevelt, in a position to observe closely a moderately complex federal bureaucratic system, with many in high places made more brazen and imperious by the war, sought favor with higher-ranking naval officers and their civilian superiors, both jealous of their prerogatives. Roosevelt revelled in his sudden prominence, in all the trappings of power; Navy rituals delighted him.

Like Theodore who demonstrated scant respect for John Long, his secretary, striving always to increase his influence while claiming to be a faithful and obedient servant, Franklin showed himself only slightly less devious or ambitious in respect to Daniels. The secretary's knowledge of the Navy and its ships, recognized to be limited, could not compare with what the young Roosevelt knew, proudly paraded before his admiring elders.[13] The Southern manners of Daniels, though superficially genteel, barely concealed what the young arrogant buck from New York saw as the face of a hillbilly.[14] Snobbery, never far below the surface with Franklin, led him to mock before family and friends the teetotaller, friend of Bryan, and unsophisticated journalist who never frequented his own more exclusive social circles. Roosevelt, in the company of admirals who appreciated his love of the sea, saw him as one of their own, unlikely to refer to ships as "boats" as Daniels habitually did. Wilson, in appointing Bryan secretary of state and Daniels secretary of the Navy, chose prominent Democrats who had helped advance his political career. Neither appealed to Roosevelt, unable to share their populist sentiments or pacifist inclinations; for him they were yesterday's men.

Just as the first Roosevelt had found President McKinley wanting, failing to respond quickly enough to the indignities perpetrated by the Spaniards, his cousin fretted over what he conceived to be Wilson's pusillanimous policies in respect to the European war. The president, asking Americans to demonstrate their neutrality by being "impartial in thought as well as action," demanded restraint of a kind the assistant secretary deemed inappropriate, but his native caution told him never to make his misgivings public.

Though he secretly favored the policies that leading Republicans, including Roosevelt and Lodge, advocated—larger naval and military expenditures and a greater concern with preparedness, including compulsory military conscription—Franklin never dared voice these opinions in public. Still, early in the war, he managed in five hours of testimony before the House Naval Affairs Committee to offer statistics to support his claim that the Navy was undermanned, that it was unprepared for war. Bryan's resignation from the State Department delighted him, something he felt free to acknowledge to friends, but it appalled Secretary Daniels, who regretted the departure from the Cabinet of his closest friend and ally. Daniels, more than ever, saw himself as the administration's conscience, the defender of the pacific policies Bryan had always argued for. Roosevelt, recognizing the political importance of showing himself active in support of the president's reelection campaign in 1916, spoke enthusiastically for him. Though his extensive speechmaking led to not a single Wilson victory in any of the states where he campaigned, Wilson received the most tangible evidence of his devotion and loyalty.

Following the declaration of war, Roosevelt's differences with Daniels grew more apparent. Increasingly disenchanted with the secretary's dilatory habits, he sent imperious memoranda to him, demanding immediate action of one kind or another. Keen observers, in and out of government, knowledgeable about naval matters, recognized Roosevelt's ambition to replace Daniels as secretary. Never backward in complaining secretly of the secretary's failings, Roosevelt found his subordinate status galling and thought many times of quitting, accepting an officer's commission in the Navy or the Army, following Theodore's brave example in 1898.[15] This never happened; an inspection trip abroad in the summer of 1918, principally to the United Kingdom and the front in France, was the closest Roosevelt ever came to military action. Though he regretted his failure to risk his life in combat, fearing it would one day be held against him politically, a matter of no small concern to him, the Armistice came too early for him to make amends. In later years he embellished his war record, greatly exaggerating his accomplishments as assistant secretary of the Navy.[16]

The *annus terribilis* for the Democrats—1919—witnessed race riots in many American cities, including the nation's capital. Wilson's physical collapse was a devastating blow to those who appreciated what he had done to secure the nation's military victory, and it dashed the hopes of all who shared his enthusiasm for the projected League of Nations. The president's refusal to accept the Lodge reservations guaranteed the Senate's rejection of his handiwork and made almost certain that the 1920 election would be a difficult one for the Democrats. Roosevelt, meeting with Louis Wehle, a fellow editor at the Harvard *Crimson*, heard him broach an idea he found intriguing. Wehle believed that if the Democrats nominated Herbert Hoover for president and Franklin Roosevelt for vice president, that ticket—embracing the two great states of California and New York—would be unbeatable. Even if the Democrats lost, Wehle told Roosevelt, as a young man he would live to run another time, and the campaign would give him invaluable political experience and national prominence.[17] Roosevelt, more than slightly interested in the proposal, recognized its difficulties; no one knew for certain whether Hoover was a Democrat and would consent to play the role so ambitiously planned for him by others. Hoover rendered the question moot when in March 1920 he declared himself a progressive Republican.[18]

Roosevelt knew that one potentially embarrassing situation had to be resolved before he could realize any grandiose political ambition. Since early 1919, an ongoing inquiry in Newport, Rhode Island, the site of a major naval station and one of the principal bases of the Atlantic Fleet, said to be a center of vice, had acquired a reputation for prostitution, the sale of drugs and illicit liquor, and flagrant and open homosexuality. When rumors spread of sailors, the so-called Ladies of Newport, soliciting new recruits in YMCA Saturday-night socials,

Daniels called for a court of inquiry to "clean the place up," and assigned Roosevelt the task of dealing with three problems: prostitution, drugs, and perversion. The creation of Section A, a special secret unit attached to the assistant secretary's office with powers to investigate, led to incidents that had serious potential for embarrassing Roosevelt. No one could say for certain whether he had approved plans to recruit sailors to entrap others, including civilians, and when Daniels appointed Admiral Herbert O. Dunn, a friend of Roosevelt's, to lead an inquiry into the scandal, he had no choice but to ask the assistant secretary to give evidence. Under severe attack in the Providence *Journal* for his actions in this highly secret operation, Roosevelt denied all responsibility.[19] Subjected to intense questioning on May 20, 1920, Roosevelt was asked, "Mr. Secretary, did you know that in nine instances, between the 18th of March and the 14th of April that certain naval [operatives] had permitted sexual perverts in the naval service to suck their penis for the purpose of obtaining evidence?" Roosevelt responded: "The answer is no."[20] He knew nothing of the methods used by the men attached to his office for securing the evidence they sought, and he had never asked about them. "Why not?" was the next question, to which Roosevelt answered, "Because I was interested merely in getting results. I was not concerned any more in finding out about their methods than I am concerned in finding out how the commanding officer of a fleet takes the fleet from New York to Newport. What I want to know is that he gets the fleet to Newport."[21]

Roosevelt handled himself with the deftness he habitually showed in such difficult situations and, with that ordeal surmounted, turned his attention to how he might advance his career at the Democratic Party Convention, scheduled for San Francisco. One of the leading presidential contenders, Al Smith, governor of New York, recognizing the advantage of recruiting Roosevelt to his cause, asked him to second his nomination, knowing it made sense for the "poor boy from the Bowery" to enlist the support of someone seen as a Hyde Park aristocrat, free of any association with the Tammany machine in New York City. In his vigorous and spirited speech, Roosevelt delighted delegates with his allusion to Harding, saying: "The nominee of *this* Convention will not be chosen at 2 A.M. in a hotel room," proceeding to give Smith the ultimate accolade when he awarded him honorary membership in the Navy with the words: "In the Navy, we shoot fast and straight. Governor Smith, in that respect, is a Navy man."[22]

Roosevelt did all Smith could have asked for, knowing he had also enhanced his own reputation. When James Cox received the presidential nomination on the forty-fourth ballot in that deadlocked convention, an Ohio–New York ticket held considerable appeal for those who believed Roosevelt's name and reputation as a vigorous political campaigner could only help Cox, a dark horse scarcely known outside Ohio. Roosevelt was nominated, seconded, and approved by acclamation, there being no need for a roll call of the individual state delegations. Daniels, Roosevelt's ever-faithful secretary, expressed his enthusiasm for the "clear-headed and able executive and patriotic citizen of New York" that the convention had so wisely chosen, saying ". . . when the war began, and he wished to go to the front, I urged him that his highest duty was to help carry the millions of men across and to bring them back. . . ."[23] No one could ever say that Franklin Roosevelt had shirked his duty; he, too, was a war hero, at least for Daniels.

Though President Wilson's notes of congratulation to Cox and Roosevelt were tepid, almost perfunctory, both saw the need to secure his blessing and went to the White House to meet with him, briefly, on July 18. Roosevelt, who had not seen Wilson for ten months, was shocked by his appearance and emerged to say that the fight to save the League would go on, that he and Cox would keep faith with the president's noble ambition.[24]

Given the magnitude of the Democratic defeat that followed, it is doubtful that any statement on international issues would have greatly altered the results. The country craved for the Republicans to return to the White House, its political animosity to Wilson and the Democrats made unmistakable in the large Republican majorities elected to both the Senate and the House. For Roosevelt, the experience was not an unhappy one; years later, he wrote, "I got to know the country as only a candidate for office or a travelling salesman can get to know it. . . ."[25]

No one in 1920 believed Roosevelt's career had ended. Yet less than a year later, that possibility loomed when he succumbed to polio and virtually lost the use of his legs. The story of his slow recovery, told many times as a tale of unexampled courage in a time of adversity, loses none of its courageous features by mention of other aspects of the struggle. First, the most strenuous efforts were made to conceal from the public the extent of Roosevelt's disability. At the time and later, Roosevelt and his family collaborated in minimizing the seriousness of his condition. Second, his long convalescence gave him an opportunity to reflect on his life as well as on the careers of the two presidents he had known.

Polio, by incapacitating him, made him reflective; despite the efforts of friends and family to bring others to him, he spent a great deal of time alone, with little to do except to think about himself, a privilege rarely granted any politician in the prime of life.[26] Finally, and perhaps most important, because his recovery was slow, coinciding with the death and posthumous disgrace of President Warren G. Harding, he was fortunate in not having his wartime romance with Lucy Page Mercer, once his wife's secretary, revealed. Relatives, including the Oyster Bay Roosevelts, and numerous friends knew of the affair and might have been tempted to reveal it, but this did not happen; reports of the relationship surfaced only after his death. Whatever effects it had on his marriage, it remained a closely guarded secret in the period when Roosevelt's political career would have been ruined by any public disclosure.[27] Whether his

penchant for secrecy was greatly exacerbated by the need to conceal this potentially damaging relationship, it is impossible to know, but he, even more than
the garrulous Theodore, pretending always to be open and candid, showed a
craving for privacy and secrecy that made intimacy with him virtually impossible. Both Roosevelts proved themselves master dissemblers.

For the next seven years, Roosevelt spent many months in Warm Springs,
Georgia, hoping its therapeutic waters would restore the mobility he had lost.
Living a very private life, principally in the company of a devoted secretary,
"Missy" Le Hand, the temptations to despondency during this prolonged convalescence were constant, but Roosevelt managed to conceal the sadness he
felt.[28] In 1924, when Al Smith approached him, asking him to place his name
in nomination at the Democratic National Convention, he realized the ordeal
would be a terrible one. Walking the few steps to the platform and managing to
appear erect, smiling and affable, would be physically and psychologically demanding, but Roosevelt knew the importance of making the effort. Looking not
for sympathy from those who watched and admired his fortitude, Roosevelt
sought a more important gain: to persuade the convention he was not a helpless
invalid but a vital politician able to make a memorable address. Concluding his
speech with the words delegates would long recall, calling Al Smith "the 'Happy
Warrior' of the political battlefield," his performance was exemplary. The speech
was acclaimed by many, including Tom Pendergast, the Kansas City boss influential years later in pushing Harry Truman into the Senate. Pendergast remarked
to a friend: ". . . Had Mr. Roosevelt. . . been physically able to withstand the
campaign, he would have been named by acclamation. . . . He has the most
magnetic personality of any individual I have ever met. . . ."[29]

When Smith, recalling his success, asked Roosevelt to place his name in
nomination for the presidency again in 1928, he agreed at once. No one who
had witnessed his performance four years earlier could doubt that his health
had improved yet further, and Smith could only feel gratitude for a speech that
represented him, the Happy Warrior, as ". . . a pathfinder, a blazer of the trail
to the high road that will avoid the bottomless morass of crass materialism that
has engulfed so many great civilizations of the past. . . one who has the will to
win—who not only deserves success but commands it."[30] Smith, observing the
self-confident and smiling Roosevelt, could only believe his own chances of
winning the presidency in November would be greatly enhanced if he persuaded him to accept the party's nomination to be governor of New York.
None of Roosevelt's intimates, neither his family nor his friends, wished him to
accept Smith's importuning and increasingly desperate requests; expecting him
to lose to Hoover, they had no wish to see Roosevelt brought down with him.

What would it profit him to help Smith in a hopeless cause? Roosevelt, in the
end, after protesting he could not accept the call, desperately seeking additional
time to recover his health, succumbed to the argument that the party needed

him. He knew Smith and his supporters would never forgive him if he refused to join them. In the election that followed Smith lost New York by 100,000 votes; Roosevelt won, but only after the initial returns suggested he too had been defeated. His margin of victory was small, a mere 25,000 votes out of more than 4.25 million cast, but it confounded all who imagined such a result impossible.

Roosevelt's long sojourns in Warm Springs were over. In his determination to be an effective governor, to do in Albany what Wilson had done in Trenton almost two decades previously, to prove himself a reformer whose credentials as a viable candidate for the presidency would be recognized by all, required him to be assertive, making it apparent that a new kind of Democrat was at the helm. In his efforts to reach out to the public, using the media, including radio, to broadcast his message, he proved himself an innovator, a worthy disciple of his two principal political tutors, Wilson and Roosevelt. The state Democratic committee agreed to buy radio time for him each month, and because he enjoyed the company of journalists—or at least pretended to—he manufactured the news that commanded the public's attention and became a highly publicized governor, very different from the crippled playboy depicted by his political enemies.[31] He attended the annual newspaperman's annual Gridiron dinner in April 1929, along with President Hoover and Chief Justice Taft, and heard himself serenaded with the words, "Oh, Franklin, Franklin Roosevelt/Is there something in a name?/When you tire of being Governor/Will you look for bigger game?"

As long as the state legislature was controlled by Republicans, Roosevelt had little hope for achieving a reform record comparable to what Wilson accomplished in his short two-year tenure in New Jersey, but the onset of the Great Depression in 1930, especially after 1931, allowed Roosevelt to show his scorn for a president who seemed helpless to alleviate the country's growing distress. In the area of unemployment relief, Roosevelt, through the influence of Frances Perkins, his industrial commissioner, received instruction from Professor Paul Douglas of the University of Chicago, experimenting in ways Hoover dared not follow.[32] In March 1931, he asked the legislature to appoint a commission to investigate unemployment insurance, and in August he secured the legislature's consent to establish the Temporary Emergency Relief Administration (TERA), which he placed under the direction of Harry Hopkins, a man he knew only slightly.[33] TERA provided relief to 10 percent of New York families, giving them an average of $23 a month, enough, in the words of Frank Freidel, one of Roosevelt's major biographers, "to prevent starvation."[34] In the words of a more recent biographer, Conrad Black, the TERA initiative "put Franklin Roosevelt ahead of any other politician or government executive in the nation in the struggle with the Depression and the scourge of unemployment."[35]

Roosevelt's four years in Albany—he won a second term easily in 1930—gave him the national publicity he sought, as well as an understanding of the economic and social problems he would certainly confront as president. The

Republicans, recognizing very early his political strengths, feared he would become the Democratic nominee and did what they could to discredit him, representing him as pusillanimous for refusing to take action against Jimmy Walker, the obviously corrupt mayor of New York City.[36] Early in 1932, Walter Lippmann published a scathing attack on him, saying: "Franklin D. Roosevelt is no crusader. He is no tribune of the people. He is no enemy of entrenched privilege. He is a pleasant man who, without any important qualifications for the office, would very much like to be President."[37]

On January 22, 1932, to qualify for the first of the primaries, scheduled for North Dakota, Roosevelt announced his candidacy for the presidency, and Smith followed suit a few days later. Though Roosevelt did well in the primaries and in many state conventions, showing greater strength than Smith, he fell substantially short of securing the two-thirds majority required by Democratic National Convention rules. Before the convention opened, it appeared that the battle would be principally between the two New York rivals, and that in a deadlocked convention the nomination might well go to a dark horse, as it did in 1920 and 1924. John Nance Garner, the Speaker of the House, having no wish to see the convention stalemated, and knowing that the Texas and California delegates pledged to him were crucial to a Roosevelt victory, released his delegates to him, giving FDR the nomination on the fourth ballot.[38] On the next day, in a move more unprecedented than even Wilson's decision to revive the tradition of the first presidents and appear before Congress personally, Roosevelt flew to Chicago to accept his party's nomination. In an extravagantly praised speech, he pledged a "new deal" for the American people, hoping the "period of loose thinking, descending morals, an era of selfishness among individual men and women and among Nations" had finally come to an end. His was to be a "crusade to restore America to its own people."[39]

The Democratic Party's 1932 platform, fashioned to a considerable extent by Roosevelt, was brief: Less than a fifth as long as the turgid document produced by the Republicans, it expressed the party's determination to do more than find fault with the lackluster and ill-fated Hoover administration.[40] The twelve years of postwar Republican presidential rule were in effect repudiated, and while no explicit mention was made of either Harding or Coolidge, the implication was clear: They, no less than Hoover, had failed the American nation. The platform opened with fundamentally revisionist sentiments:

> In this time of unprecedented economic and social distress the Democratic Party declares its conviction that the chief causes of this condition were the disastrous policies pursued by our government since the World War, of economic isolation, fostering the merger of competitive businesses into monopolies and encouraging the indefensible expansion and contraction of credit for private profit at the expense of the public.[41]

The country, because of Republican rule, had forfeited the advantages secured by its 1918 military victory. While there was no specific lauding of Wilson, it was impossible to misread the meaning of a statement that read:

Those who were responsible for these policies have abandoned the ideals on which the war was won and thrown away the fruits of victory, thus rejecting the greatest opportunity in history to bring peace, prosperity, and happiness to our people and to the world. They have ruined our foreign trade, destroyed the value of our commodities and products, crippled our banking system, robbed millions of our people of their life savings, and thrown millions more out of work, produced widespread poverty and brought the government to a state of financial distress unprecedented in time of peace.[42]

No more severe indictment of twelve years of Republican rule could have been crafted by Democrats proposing more than a mere change in political leadership. The American people, misled into electing Harding, Coolidge, and Hoover, were being invited to restore the party of Jefferson and Jackson with its belief in "equal rights to all; special privilege to none."[43] The platform, intentionally vague on many issues, explicitly promised to introduce new measures to cope with unemployment, assist farmers in their distress, and repeal the constitutional amendment that had introduced Prohibition, "the noble experiment" that had failed.

Its foreign policy plank, wholly conventional, expressed the party's faith in the arbitration of international disputes, announced its plans to adhere to the World Court "with reservations," and promised not to interfere in the internal affairs of other nations.[44] The Democrats avoided any suggestion that they proposed to relaunch Wilson's ill-fated League of Nations, knowing all too well the popular sentiment on that issue. Nor did the platform seem overburdened with specific ideas of how to resist the recent evidences of Japanese aggression or maintain world peace in a Europe plagued by economic distress, where the Nazis were making rapid strides in Germany. The nation's problems in 1932 seemed overwhelmingly domestic, and these were the ones the Democrats addressed, however imprecisely.

Roosevelt relished political campaigning, and in numerous motor cavalcades and meetings with local Democratic politicians once partial to Smith he showed the grace and humor that became the trademark of his buoyant self-confidence. The contrast with the president in the White House could not have been more striking. By early November, all expected him to win, but his margin of victory both in the popular vote and in the Electoral College proved greater than even he had dared hope for. Roosevelt achieved a victory that matched those of his immediate Republican predecessors, and was substantially more decisive than Wilson's 1912 and 1916 victories. Like Wilson in 1912, he entered office with a large Democratic majority in both houses of Congress, virtually guaranteeing the legislative marathon he intended—the famous Hundred Days after March 4, 1933—that had no parallel in the nation's history.

Before that, however, Hoover remained in charge, and the lame-duck Seventy-Second Congress that opened its final session on December 5, 1932, met in a virtual state of siege, protected by police, armed with tear gas and guns on the steps of the Capitol, deployed against the threat of riot. The so-called interregnum proved to be a difficult time for both men, with the banking crisis assuming proportions that compelled many states to order all banks to close their doors.

When Roosevelt arrived to take his oath of office, administered by Charles Evans Hughes, the chief justice, the country, fearful and bewildered, heard him deliver a message that seemed positively heroic, appropriate to what he chose to call "a day of national consecration." Roosevelt understood what his audience—listening by radio in every part of the country—needed to hear when he exclaimed: "Let me assert my firm belief that the only thing we have to fear is fear itself." Those words, as much as those that followed, asking for the nation's support—a theme he would constantly reiterate—were stirring: "In every dark hour of our national life," Roosevelt said, "a leadership of frankness and vigor has met with that understanding and support of the people themselves which is essential to victory." Roosevelt expected Congress to assist him in his efforts, but if this failed, "I shall ask the Congress for the one remaining instrument to meet the crisis—broad executive power to wage a war against the emergency, as great as the power that would be given to me if we were in fact invaded by a foreign foe."[45] Not for the first or the last time, Roosevelt used the metaphor of war, and some who heard him recognized this was not the traditional speech of a man recently elevated to the White House.[46] Roosevelt sounded a tocsin that the nation and Congress yearned to hear, but this did not lead all immediately to trust him or believe in his political remedies, still very imprecisely formulated. In the hundred days that followed, beginning with the president's proclamation on March 5 declaring a bank holiday, closing all the nation's banks—more accurately, the few that still remained open—an action confirmed by Congress on March 9, Roosevelt's bold move appealed to millions fearful that their bank deposits were at risk.

On March 12, in the first of his Fireside Chats, Roosevelt explained the banking crisis and the steps his administration had taken to resolve it, asking individuals not to withdraw funds greater than what they needed from the banks scheduled to reopen the next day. In his "my friends" salutation as in his concluding remarks, he made obvious his dependence on those to whom he spoke, saying:

> You people must have faith; you must not be stampeded by rumors or guesses. Let
> us unite in banishing fear. We have provided the machinery to restore our finan-

cial system, and it is up to you to support and make it work. It is your problem, my friends, your problem no less than it is mine. Together we cannot fail.[47]

The term *Fireside Chat*, invented by Harry Butcher of CBS in May 1933 and quickly adopted by all commentators, described a radio technique that Roosevelt originated and developed, one that he had first used in his years as governor, and it would be difficult to exaggerate its importance in making the president known to the country. As his cousin's disciple, Roosevelt appreciated the importance of the press and knew that winning its favor—pretending to take reporters into his confidence, amusing them with his wit and repartee—guaranteed he would have very powerful friends in court. When one considers that he held 337 press conferences in his first term in office and 374 in his second, that Hoover held only sixty-six during the four years he sat in the White House, one has some idea of the very different strategies each used in reaching out to the public. Roosevelt, without claiming the title, aspired to be the Great Communicator.

Two months after his initial fireside address, he spoke to the nation about his accomplishments and a month later did so again, emphasizing all that Congress had done in its hundred days, a phrase whose significance he fully grasped. In any listing of the congressional actions taken during this period, the Agricultural Adjustment Act and the National Industrial Recovery Act (NIRA) are generally given pride of place, but it is important to realize that these were but the tip of an iceberg that included the establishment of the Civilian Conservation Corps, the Federal Emergency Relief Act, the Emergency Farm Mortgage Act, the Tennessee Valley Authority Act, the Truth-in-Securities Act, the Home Owners' Loan Act, the Farm Credit Act, the Railroad Coordination Act, and the Glass-Steagal Banking Act. No president could claim a comparable record; no one had ever driven Congress in the way Roosevelt did; he showed himself a true disciple of Wilson.

His ability to do all this stemmed in great part from the country's incontestably grave condition, but it reflected also the extent to which he enjoyed overwhelming Democratic success in Congress, more than ready to see him experiment in ways Hoover had never dared to do. Roosevelt started with no fixed economic principles and nothing that could be called a fully articulated social doctrine, but he knew what his cousin had taught him: that bankers could be irresponsible and that the federal government existed to safeguard the well-being of millions too often ignored or indeed exploited by politicians.

In the Fireside Chat he delivered six weeks before the off-year November 1934 congressional elections, he lauded the N.R.A., under attack by many for its complex codes, as well as what some saw as its unfair price-fixing mechanisms and plans to control industrial production. Roosevelt asked that his effort to end employer-employee warfare, inaugurating an era of industrial peace, be given a fair trial. Of one thing he was absolutely certain: Unemployment, morally the greatest menace to the nation's social order, could never be countenanced. In words intended to appeal to voters soon to make their choice for one-third of the Senate and the whole of the House of Representatives, Roosevelt said:

> Some people try to tell me that we must make up our minds that for the future we shall permanently have millions of unemployed just as other countries have had them for over a decade. What may be necessary for those other countries is not my responsibility to determine. But for this country, I stand or fall by my refusal to accept as a necessary condition of our future a permanent army of unemployed. On the contrary, we must make it a national principle that we will not tolerate a large army of unemployed, that we will arrange our national economy to end our present unemployment as soon as we can and then to take wise measures against its return.[48]

These words were believed. And whereas most off-year elections saw the party in the White House emerge with significantly reduced numbers, Roosevelt achieved what few others had ever managed; the Democrats gained nine seats in the Senate and seven in the House. The Republicans, outnumbered in Congress three-to-one—a political situation with no precedent in the nation's history— saw the 1934 electoral verdict confirmed in 1936 by Roosevelt's decisive victory over Alfred Landon, where he emerged with 27,751,597 votes, almost 5 million more than the number he secured against Hoover; Landon gained less than 1 million votes over those Hoover claimed in 1932. In the Electoral College, the victory was no less decisive: Except for Maine and Vermont, with a combined electoral vote of eight, Roosevelt won in every state in the union.

By any criterion his first term had been an unqualified political success. While the economic condition of the country remained less than buoyant, the unemployment rolls were down, and workers and farmers, through congressional action, enjoyed protection of a kind they had never previously known. More important, perhaps, the fear that gripped the nation had largely disappeared; Roosevelt, by his personality as much as by specific policies, eliminated the despair that seemed universal in the months before his first inaugural. This did not mean that he had survived these four years without significant defeats; the Supreme Court's decision in 1935 to declare the N.R.A. unconstitutional and its decision a year later to disallow the Agricultural Adjustment Act greatly vexed the president and made him determined to bridle the "nine old men" who showed such scant respect for Congress and the popular will.

Had he demonstrated comparable resolve in handling the nation's foreign policy? Even Roosevelt's staunchest admirers would have been hard-pressed to claim this. In his 1933 inaugural address, he had stressed the primacy of domestic policy over foreign relations and made his priorities unmistakable when he said: "Our international relations, though vastly important, are in time and necessity secondary to the establishment of a sound national economy. I favour as a practical policy the putting of first things first." Roosevelt had been true to his word, giving very intermittent attention to foreign affairs during his first term. Cordell Hull, his secretary of state, a prominent congressional figure who had served in the House of Representatives from 1907, with one brief interruption, till 1931, and then in the Senate for two years, was known for his early advocacy of a federal income tax and support of lower tariffs. Not much versed in diplomacy, he was not the man likely to offer the president useful instruction on the dangers of Hitler's Germany or the hazards posed by Japan's continued aggressions against China. Indeed, at the World Economic Conference that opened in London on June 12, 1934, where Hull led the U.S. delegation, it was Roosevelt's message, sent on July 3, that proved the bombshell that virtually destroyed all hope of agreement. The president, in effect, rejected the attempts to stabilize currencies as "fetishes of the so-called international bankers," and while efforts were made to explain his ill-tempered cable—what some preferred to describe as ill-informed and illogical—Keynes, for one, initially supported him. He believed the president had been "magnificently right" in seeking to make national currency management his first order of business, but a more considered judgment led him to say later: "Roosevelt had about as much idea of where he would land as a pre-war pilot."[49] On international currency questions, the president was clearly out of his depth, and no one in his immediate entourage, neither the secretary of state nor the secretary of the treasury, could guide him.[50]

Roosevelt, preoccupied with grave domestic issues, showed a very limited concern with the deteriorating situation abroad, evident in 1935 and 1936 when Hitler marched into the Rhineland, Mussolini attacked Ethiopia, and civil war erupted in Spain. In Senate committee public hearings led by Senator Gerald Nye into the nefarious activities of American and European bankers and industrialists during the war, the public learned what it had long believed. The country had been inveigled into a war from which only munitions industry titans profited. Congress, reacting to the findings of the Nye committee, passed in 1935 the first of the so-called Neutrality Acts, prohibiting the sale or shipment of arms to all belligerents, instructing U.S. citizens that if they chose to travel on belligerent ships they did so at their own risk. Never again would the United States be tempted to enter a war so unnecessary and so little related to the interests of ordinary citizens; this was implicit in the action Congress had taken.[51] In this declaration of hostility to what the Wilson administration had done, Congress declared its determination to remain free of Europe's quarrels, to show its fidelity to the wise injunctions of its first president, as expressed in his farewell address.[52] Isolationism appeared to be in the saddle, and William Langer, America's most eminent diplomatic historian, noted that the president shared the common opinion that "the solution of America's problems would constitute the most effective contribution he could make toward a better world system."[53] This shortsightedness, never so characterized by Langer, who greatly appreciated Roosevelt's later foreign policy accomplishments, did not preclude his saying:

> It is true that the President commented adversely on the 'inflexible provisions' of the neutrality legislation of 1935–1937, but there is no evidence that he disapproved its general purpose. He was merely echoing the popular sentiment when he declared that his Administration was 'definitely committed to the maintenance of peace and the avoidance of any entanglements which would lead us into conflict.' Even though he might, from time to time, call attention to the dangers of the European situation, he drew no new conclusions with respect to American policy. As late as August 1936, he stated in his Chautauqua speech: 'We shun political commitments which might entangle us in foreign wars; we avoid connection with the political activities of the League of Nations. . . . We are not isolationists except in so far as we seek to isolate ourselves completely from war.'[54]

Roosevelt showed no greater grasp of the threats posed by Germany, Italy, and Japan than the heads of government in the democracies of Western Europe.[55] While they fumbled about, looking for solutions, the American president, together with his secretary of state, imagined it was enough to proclaim the need for more liberal trade policies, argue for disarmament, and propose the peaceful settlement of international disputes. Few in the United States advised Roosevelt that these were mere palliatives, no longer adequate to the dangers that existed; those who represented him in embassies abroad provided no greater guidance in a time of extraordinary international turmoil.[56]

The magnitude of his 1936 election victory allowed Roosevelt to become careless, to imagine he could defeat his enemies on the Supreme Court, a majority of the nine justices appointed for life who had declared important New Deal legislation unconstitutional. In words seen to be disingenuous, the president spoke of the need to improve the Court's performance, hastening its decisions, providing additional help to superannuated justices by increasing their number to fifteen.[57] The mail that descended on Congress, overwhelmingly unfavorable, told Roosevelt's friends that he had erred in making his proposal and would do well to offer a compromise, agreeing perhaps to add only two or three justices. Roosevelt would not hear of it and, when informed by Vice President Garner on July 20, 1937, that he lacked the votes to carry the Senate, he accepted his defeat gracefully, knowing he had waged and lost a costly political battle. Despite his large Democratic Party majority in the Senate, many sided with the Republicans in opposing his court-packing plan, and Roosevelt recognized he could never again take even its Democratic members for granted.

Worse, however, was yet to come. From August to October, the stock market fell precipitously, and many argued that the economic recovery of the last few years had been illusory. For the first time, Keynesian economics enjoyed a cetain appeal among advisers close to the president, though not with Henry Morgenthau Jr., his secretary of the treasury. Given the emphasis Roosevelt attached to the employment issue and the promises he had made, especially during the 1936 election campaign, the evidences of increased unemployment worried him greatly. That he had no solution to a condition he had once pretended resolved became evident in one of his least successful Fireside Chats, of November 14, 1937, when he urged the country to cooperate with the unemployment census to provide more accurate statistical data on the extent of the problem.[58] Five months later, on April 14, 1938, in his Fireside Chat that evening, the president described the message he had just sent to the special session of Congress summoned to deal with what everyone recognized to be a steadily deteriorating economic situation. While no one knew for certain the extent of the unemployment caused by the 1937 recession, some believed the number exceeded 4 million. Only a new economic policy could serve to restore confidence, and the president, without mentioning Keynes, indicated he had abandoned his earlier efforts to balance the budget, preferring to opt for a massive new infusion of public money to guarantee jobs for the millions of unemployed. All the work and relief agencies, including the Works Progress Administration, the Farm Security Administration, the National Youth Administration, and the Civilian Conservation Corps, were promised additional funds. To help business, additional credit would be made available to banks by the Federal Reserve Board, accepting also to reduce the reserves they would be required to hold.[59]

How could these vast additional requests for public expenditure be justified? According to the president, his chief concern was to protect the American democracy, not to allow it to fall victim to dictatorship. "History proves," he said, "that dictatorships do not grow out of strong and successful governments, but out of weak and helpless governments. . . . We are a rich nation; we can afford to pay for security and prosperity without having to sacrifice our liberties into the bargain."[60] In a speech delivered just a month after Adolf Hitler invaded Austria, and days after the Austrians voted by 99.7 percent for union with Germany, the president made no mention of this most recent German aggression but spoke instead of the economic conditions that had led to fascism in Italy in the 1920s and to Nazism in Germany in the 1930s. Appreciating the hazards created by mass unemployment, believing the threat to the United States from extremists on the left and the right to be real, he responded in the only way he imagined possible—dwelling on domestic turmoil as the nation's principal problem that called for exceptional federal expenditures.

Less than six months earlier, on October 5 in Chicago, the president had delivered his Quarantine Speech, the most explicit condemnation he ever made of the aggressor nations.[61] Why did this theme become paramount for him in 1937 and not before? Why, indeed, did he argue in Chicago for policies so different from those suggested during the election campaign? He said: "We shun political commitments which might entangle us in foreign wars. I have seen war. I have seen war on land and sea. I have seen blood running from the wounded. . . . I have seen the dead in the mud. . . . I hate war."[62] Was this mere political rhetoric, fashioned to offset the election promises of Landon, or was his Chicago speech a year later a belated reaction to events since 1933 in Europe, Asia, and Africa? Burned recently by the mistake he had made in seeking to pack the Supreme Court, why did he choose to risk himself again?

To ask this is to pose the most important question that can be raised about a president considered Machiavellian by his enemies who generally left himself a convenient exit if any of his proposals proved unexpectedly unpopular. The most memorable sentence in Roosevelt's Chicago speech read: "When an epidemic of physical disease starts to spread, the community approves and joins in a quarantine of the patients in order to protect the health of the community against the spread of the disease." Too few noted that he did not leave the matter there, but added: "It is my determination to pursue a policy of peace, to adopt every practical measure to avoid involvement in war."[63] When the reaction to the speech proved hostile, with many isolationists deploring its belligerent tone, he drew back, and the London *Times*, recognizing the imprecision of the speech, represented it as "defining an attitude and not a program."[64] The president dared not move too far ahead of public opinion, and the criticism of those most violently opposed to his Quarantine Speech warned him that he had done so.

Speaking privately with Harold Ickes, his secretary of the interior, Roosevelt characterized Japan, Germany, and Italy as "three bandit nations," but this did not lead him even to consider the positive use of sanctions against any of them.[65] That term, with its League of Nations connotations, anathema to many Americans, offered no solution that the president could contemplate with equanimity. He lacked anyone in his immediate entourage, including Sumner Welles, the undersecretary of state, able to think of foreign affairs in the geopolitical terms called for, and this led him increasingly to rely on his own intuition.[66] Heads of government in Europe, including those of the United Kingdom and France, scarcely understood his political situation at home, compelled to contend with a public opinion largely shaped by the imagined injustices the United States had suffered in the war, never adequately appreciated for all it had done to bring about the final Allied victory. The extent of America's suspicion of Europe was never recognized by those on the other side of the Atlantic who grossly miscalculated the options available to Roosevelt.

Because the president recognized the importance of appearing always buoyant, few of his Fireside Chats voiced sentiments that friends or foes might interpret as despair. Yet the one he delivered on June 24, 1938, as much as any other, revealed the disappointment he felt with recent events, more at home than abroad. While carefully avoiding any too-specific criticisms of the heavily

Democratic Party Congress elected with him in 1936, which "achieved more for the future good of the country than any congress did between the end of the World War and the spring of 1933," he knew that a small but articulate group in the country, constantly calling for a "restoration of confidence," ridiculed all that he had accomplished.[67] In the United States, he said, there were two principal schools of thought, the liberal and the conservative; the first accepted "that the new conditions throughout the world call for new remedies." The liberal, a believer "in progressive principles of democratic government and not the wild man who, in effect, leans in the direction of Communism, for that is just as dangerous to us as Fascism itself," differed from the conservative, he argued, in the latter's failure to "recognize the need for government itself to step in and take action to meet these new problems." Individual initiative and private philanthropy could never resolve them.[68] While Roosevelt did not explicitly ask all who heard him to vote only for Democrats—he would not make the mistake Wilson had made in 1918—he promised to fight for the liberal principles contained in the 1936 Democratic Party platform, supporting only those Democrats prepared to accept them. The president, as good as his word, in the months that followed spoke before several crucial state primaries, principally in the South, urging support of Democrats willing to challenge incumbent conservative Democrats. Neither in his efforts to unseat Walter George in Georgia, Millard Tydings in Maryland, nor Ellison "Cotton Ed" Smith in South Carolina did he succeed.[69] In the November elections, his defeats were even more striking. The Republicans gained eight seats in the Senate, eighty in the House, and Roosevelt, hampered when he enjoyed comfortable Democratic majorities, knew the day for major legislative innovations was over. The New Deal, for all practical purposes, was a completed project that could not be significantly added to. Only in the sphere of foreign policy, with continued new aggressions abroad, did he perceive opportunities scarcely apparent to him when the country was mired in the depths of the Depression.

In his 1939 State of the Union message to the new Congress, Roosevelt identified Germany, Italy, and Japan as aggressor nations, pursuing the argument he first made in his 1937 Chicago Quarantine Speech, suggesting there were many methods short of war and stronger than words for making aggressor nations respect the "aggregate sentiments of our own people."[70] Following the German occupation of Prague, in violation of the Munich Agreement reached with Great Britain and France, Roosevelt told a press conference that "the continued political, economic and social independence of every small nation in the world does have an effect on our national safety and prosperity."[71] Later that month, he addressed Hitler and Mussolini directly, asking them to give assurances that they had no intention of attacking thirty-one nations he specifically named. The dictators ridiculed his intervention, and there was little more the president could do or say.[72]

Indeed, the extent of his loss of influence in Congress can best be demonstrated by his failure to persuade the Senate Foreign Relations Committee to bring to the Senate floor a measure he favored to amend the country's Neutrality Act. Roosevelt hoped an amendment proposed by Elbert D. Thomas, senator from Utah, to modify that act would pass, giving the president authority to forbid the export of all supplies and raw materials, including arms, to all belligerents, but also the authority, with congressional approval, to lift the ban against states themselves the victims of aggression. With Senator Gerald Nye threatening a Senate filibuster if the administration tried "to repeal or emasculate" the existing legislation, the proposal died.[73] No less seriously, a bill that called for a major reorganization of the executive branch of the government, stripped through amendments in the previous Congress of many of its original features, was in such trouble that senators friendly to the president feared it would never pass. In providing the president with six administrative assistants, and in creating the Executive Office of the President, Roosevelt was guaranteed the kind of assistance he had never previously enjoyed. Knowing how desperately he needed the legislation, already passed by the House but waiting for Senate approval, with many crippling amendments passed or threatened, only the return of Senator Harry Truman from Missouri, traveling by plane through a dangerous snowstorm to register his vote, saved the bill.[74]

This was an unhappy time for Roosevelt, less because of Hitler's speech in which he ridiculed the president's proposal, and more because of attacks at home, including several from members of Congress, pleased to see the president humiliated by the German chancellor. Hiram Johnson, who had served California in the Senate since 1917, wrote in a letter to his son: "Hitler had all the better of the argument. Roosevelt put his chin out and got a resounding whack. I have reached the conclusion there will be no war. . . . Roosevelt wants to fight for any little thing. He wants. . . to knock down two dictators in Europe, so that one may be firmly implanted in America."[75] Johnson's longtime isolationism and hostility to the League of Nations did not by themselves explain his venom. Nor could Senator Nye's comments to the press be thought characteristic only of Midwestern political isolationism when he said: "Certainly nothing said by Hitler can be taken as an insult to the American people, and it might be that a reasonable approach to Germany by our government now would invite better understanding and bring rest to the world."[76] The antipathy to Roosevelt exceeded anything his cousin had known, rivaled only by the obloquy Wilson endured in 1918 and later. The president's spring, brightened by the visit of King George VI and Queen Elizabeth to Hyde Park and the White House, gave him almost his last moment of relaxation before Germany's invasion of Poland ended all hope that a second world war could be averted.

Through the long period of the phoney war in the last months of 1939 and 1940 when Germany and the Soviet Union, pursuing the terms of their secret pact, occupied the whole of Poland, and the Soviet Union attacked and over-whelmed "brave little Finland," Roosevelt worked indefatigably to achieve three objectives: to persuade Congress to revise the neutrality legislation to allow the Allies, on the principle of cash-and-carry, only loosely enforced, to buy and ship essential war material from the United States; to continue to con-fuse and bewilder politicians, journalists, and family members on whether he would seek a third term; and finally, most secretly, to initiate discussions that almost five years later issued in the dropping of two atomic bombs on Japan. These were months also when the German occupation of Denmark and the in-vasion of Norway, followed by massive land and air assaults on Holland, Bel-gium, and France, brought the president into touch with the first European statesman with whom he almost immediately established a close rapport.[77] Winston Churchill, the former naval person, on May 15, in a "most secret and personal message" to the president, showed no hesitation in asking for the "loan of forty or fifty of your older destroyers" and also "several hundred of the latest types of aircraft for which you are now getting delivery," along with anti-aircraft guns and ammunition, and the creation of facilities to expedite the pur-chase of steel and other materials should Britain no longer be able to pay for them. He hoped the Americans might send a United States squadron to Irish ports to prevent possible German parachute or airborne descents in Ireland, and finally, to dispatch whatever naval units were available "to keep the Japa-nese dog quiet in the Pacific, using Singapore in any way convenient."[78]

Roosevelt, in no position to grant any of these extraordinary requests imme-diately, replied in a way intended to mollify the beleaguered prime minister; he explained that even the transfer of overage destroyers would require congres-sional assent, that he could not be certain to secure it, and that the transfer could not in any case be made in less than six weeks.[79] Churchill found the reply disappointing and, as conditions on the Western Front deteriorated, sent an even more urgent request for help, saying on May 20, "Our intention is to fight on to the end in this Island and, provided we can get the help for which we ask, we hope to run them very close in the air battles." Were his government to go down, replaced by another obliged to "parley among the ruins," he could not guarantee the results.[80] Roosevelt made no reply to this note, but on May 16, the day he responded to Churchill's first message, he asked Congress for a $1.4 billion increase in defense appropriations, $732 million for the Army, $408 million for the Navy. The country, he informed Congress, needed to in-crease its military aircraft production from 12,000 a year to 50,000.[81] Many ridiculed his proposal, believing it vain propaganda. As the situation in West-ern Europe deteriorated and Italy joined in the war against France, the presi-dent became increasingly belligerent, expressing his disdain for Mussolini in one of his more memorable phrases—"the hand that has held the dagger has struck it into the back of its neighbor"—but his more important contribution was the dispatch of some 500,000 Enfield rifles to Britain, along with 900 75mm field guns, 50,000 machine guns, and great quantities of ammunition, bombs, and smokeless powder.[82]

Roosevelt, released from the torpor that had afflicted him from the time of the disappointing congressional elections in 1938, seemed almost a man possessed, with his energy and resolve restored to what it had been when he first became president in 1933. His correspondence with Churchill gave him an interlocutor on foreign policy issues, able to share information and confidences of a kind he received from none of his American courtiers. Welles, Hopkins, Ickes, Morgenthau, and others competed for his ear and sought to influence him, but none boasted the geopolitical intelligence of the former naval person, and the president, while not always agreeing with Churchill, understood very early the nature of the relationship, that of patron and dependent.[83]

Churchill's vitality gave Roosevelt the tonic he needed, the cure provided by no one else. The president, revelling in the knowledge he and few others shared, met secretly with Vannevar Bush, president of the Carnegie Institution, distinguished physicist and electrical engineer, on June 12, 1940, just a day before the Germans occupied Paris, and agreed then to establish a special committee to study the "possible relationship to national defense of recent discoveries in the field of atomistics, notably the fission of uranium." This, unquestionably the most momentous decision taken by the president in that tragic June, carried the promise of the development of a weapon more terrible than any previously known.[84]

During the summer, as if to emphasize the extent to which he needed to create a coalition government to gain support in Congress, and also to rid himself of two members of the Cabinet hostile to what they conceived to be his exaggerated determination to help Great Britain, Roosevelt appointed two prominent Republicans, Henry Stimson, Taft's secretary of war and Hoover's secretary of state, to be his secretary of war, and Frank Knox, the Republican Party's nominee for vice president in 1936, to be his secretary of the Navy. These appointments, announced just four days before the opening of the Republican National Convention, made it imperative for the delegates to select a candidate able to challenge a president who constantly surprised them. Their choice of Wendell Willkie, a dark horse, witty and well-informed, guaranteed that the race would be an interesting one, and Roosevelt, a shrewd judge of political talent, believed Willkie would be a formidable opponent. He had no difficulty in securing his own nomination, offending a number of prominent Democrats, including John Nance Garner, the vice president, and James Farley, the postmaster general, by breaking the two-term tradition that had existed from the time of George Washington.[85] While the president may at one time have considered the possibility of leaving—as some believed—it is questionable whether it was ever a very live option for him. When precisely he decided to run no one could say, but his campaign, punctuated by his "destroyer for bases deal," announced by the president to Congress on September 3, 1940, led many Republicans, including Willkie, to doubt whether he had the constitutional authority to act as he did. Roosevelt made no excuses for accomplishing this by executive order, thereby avoiding the need for congressional approval.[86]

Political campaigning, always a tonic for a president who relished any outing that gave him the plaudits of vast crowds, welcomed the opportunity to mock Republicans who had long sought to thwart him. "Martin, Barton, and Fish," three hostile Republican House members, became an unforgettable trio in a refrain his wildly enthusiastic Madison Square Garden audience responded to, their obvious mutual pleasure apparent to all who heard them. Roosevelt won the 1940 election easily.[87] A new political era opened in November 1940. The Republicans were forced to recognize that Roosevelt had retained his core support, had demonstrated once again his remarkable resiliency, confounding all those who believed the two-term tradition sacred.

Journalists and politicians, dwelling on the victory, paid little heed to what it might mean for the British in their stoic resistance to the German Luftwaffe. The president, deterred from too openly avowing the British cause as long as he sought a renewed presidential mandate, recognizing the strength of the antiwar sentiment in the country and its influence in Congress, felt suddenly liberated, able to pursue policies he would not have considered before. While the hundred days had become the standard phrase to celebrate his legislative accomplishments in 1933, few gave comparable attention to his 1941 foreign and defense policy innovations, achieved in some part by persuading Congress to act, but also by his bold and unprecedented executive actions.[88] In naming the four-man Defense Board almost immediately after his reelection and choosing William Knudson to head it, the president showed his determination to make America's defenses more secure and to hasten aid to the island whose civilian suffering under continuous Nazi air bombardment had become a principal concern, the subject of much press and radio commentary. Though Americans lauded the Royal Air Force for having defeated the Luftwaffe over the skies of rural England, saving the country from a late summer or early fall invasion, the blitz over London that began on September 7 and continued almost uninterruptedly until the onset of winter gave even more compelling evidence of the strength of British resistance. The bomb that fell on Buckingham Palace on September 13, which led to the much photographed visit of the king and queen to the East End of London, together with the bombardment of Coventry on November 14 and the virtual destruction of its Cathedral, became front-page news in the United States, but the great fire-raid on London on December 29 made the most lasting impression.

The virtual destruction of the City, of eight Wren churches, and of the Guildhall, not to speak of the thousands of burned offices and warehouses, with the port of London reduced to a quarter of its capacity, told a tale of woeful damage.[89] Still, the near miraculous saving of St. Paul's Cathedral, and the pictorial evidence of the great church enveloped in flames, hit by twenty-eight incendiary bombs, made an indelible impression on a country distant from the carnage but increasingly admiring of British fortitude, and especially of Winston Churchill's leadership.

While Joseph Kennedy, the retired ambassador to the Court of St. James, imagined he had issued a compliment to the British people when he said "I did not know London could take it," adding for the benefit of his Boston Irish friends that democracy in Britain was finished, and that the same fate might well await the United States if she foolishly entered the war, such opinion carried little weight with Americans responsive to Churchill's oratory.[90] Roosevelt, though never underestimating the strength of isolationist sentiment in the country and compelled always to take it into account, refused to share their dim view of Britain's war prospects. At the moment that St. Paul's and the City were burning, Roosevelt gave one of his most memorable Fireside Chats.[91]

The president, always cautious, knew better than to suggest that any of his recommendations might involve the country in armed conflict, but he refused to mince words about the dangers that existed. Informing the country of the threat posed by the Axis, an alliance formed by Germany, Italy, and Japan, on September 27, 1940, that pledged all three to take united action against the United States if it "interfered with or blocked the expansion program of these three nations," Roosevelt portrayed Germany as the leader in this "unholy alliance." His disdain could not have been more explicit when he said: "The Nazi masters of Germany have made it clear that they intend not only to dominate all life and thought in their own country, but also to enslave the whole of Europe, and then to use the resources of Europe to dominate the rest of the world." Were the British to be defeated, Roosevelt told the nation,

> the Axis powers will control the continents of Europe, Asia, Africa, Australasia, and the high seas—and they will be in a position to bring enormous military and naval resources against this hemisphere. It is no exaggeration to say that all of us, in all the Americas, would be living at the point of a gun—a gun loaded with explosive bullets, economic as well as military.[92]

The United States would be obliged to turn itself "permanently into a militaristic power," and even the broad oceans would give the country no defense. What, then, could be done to prevent this world conquest by those so obviously determined to destroy democracy? War was not the answer. An enhanced rearmament was urgently required, together with the sending of every "ounce and every ton of munitions and supplies that we can possibly spare to help the defenders who are in the front lines." Knowing his domestic enemies, Roosevelt said, "Let not the defeatists tell us that it is too late. It will never be earlier. Tomorrow will be later than today." Roosevelt told of what he had done just a few days earlier to create the Office of Production Management to coordinate the country's defense efforts and, in a passionate peroration, said:

> We must be the great arsenal of democracy. For us this is an emergency as serious as war itself. We must apply ourselves to our task with the same resolution, the same sense of urgency, and same spirit of patriotism and sacrifice as we would show were we at war. We have furnished the British great material support and we will furnish far more in the future. There will be no bottlenecks in our determination to aid Great Britain.[93]

Against those the president knew to be numerous, but without naming them, the president added,

> I believe that the Axis powers are not going to win this war. I base that belief on the latest and best of information. We have no excuse for defeatism. We have every reason for hope—hope for peace, yes, and hope for the defense of our civilization and for the building of a better civilization in the future.[94]

In this, as in so much else, Roosevelt spoke as much to the British as to the American people.

The Germans had planned their London raid to coincide with the Roosevelt speech, hoping it would deflect attention from anything the president said in what had been billed as a major address. Instead, the horror of the incendiary attack only made more imperative a fleshing out of an idea Roosevelt, in his most casual manner, had outlined in a press conference less than a fortnight earlier. On December 17, offering random thoughts on how the Americans might be able to help the British, he spoke of having the United States "either lease the materials or sell the materials subject to mortgage," and in one of his more inspired metaphors he went on to say:

> Now, what I am trying to do is to eliminate the dollar sign . . . the silly foolish old dollar sign. . . . Well, let me give you an illustration: Suppose my neighbor's house catches fire. . . if he can take my garden hose and connect it up with his hydrant, I may help him to put out his fire. Now, what do I do? I don't say to him before that operation, 'Neighbor, my garden hose cost me $15; you have got to pay me $15 for it.'. . . I don't want $15—I want my garden hose back after the fire is over. . . . In other words, if you lend certain munitions and get the munitions back at the end of the war. . . you are all right.[95]

When the idea was introduced as House Resolution 1776, it authorized the president to transfer munitions and supplies Congress had appropriated "to the government of any country whose defense the President deems vital to the defense of the U.S." Isolationists inside and outside Congress reacted violently; Senator Burton Wheeler claimed it would "plough under every fourth American boy," and Senator Taft called it "a kind of undeclared war all over the world."[96] Charles Lindbergh, in testimony before the House, termed it "another step away from democracy and another step closer to war."[97] Roosevelt, scarcely phased by those who called him a dictator or worse, pressed his allies in Congress to work for early passage of the bill and welcomed the support of Wendell Willkie, the defeated Republican presidential candidate, who agreed to testify in its behalf.[98] The majorities for the proposed legislation, 260–165 in the House, 60–31 in the Senate, gave evidence of the strength Roosevelt had mobilized through his reelection, but also the esteem many in Congress felt for the British and their indefatigable prime minister, who called it "the most unsordid act in the history of any nation."[99]

From March 11, the day the president signed the Lend-Lease Act, and December 7, the day Japan attacked Pearl Harbor, Roosevelt became his own secretary of state, taking risks of a kind he would not have considered a year earlier. Sometimes in secret, often by executive action, not always with the explicit consent of Congress, Roosevelt entered into what could only be called the status of a quasi-belligerent.

The foreign and defense policy decisions and actions taken in these months, as critical as those taken by the president on the domestic front in 1933, suggested that his 1940 electoral victory had been as decisive as the one that brought him into the White House initially. In nine extraordinary months, he prepared the nation for war while claiming always to be interested only in preserving the peace. On March 30, the government seized sixty-five Axis ships in U.S. ports, and on April 9, through an executive agreement with the Danish minister in Washington, the United States received permission to occupy Greenland, said to be necessary for the defense of the new world. A day later, the president declared the Red Sea no longer a combat area, allowing the shipment of supplies to British troops in the region without violating the terms of the Neutrality Act of 1939. On May 15, Roosevelt begged the French people to end their support of the Vichy regime, charged with collaborating with the Nazis. In an extraordinary Fireside Chat on May 27, following the Nazi conquest of Greece and Yugoslavia, and their rapid military advances in North Africa, Roosevelt declared "an unlimited national emergency," reasserting the "ancient American doctrine of the freedom of the seas and the solidarity of the twenty-one American republics and the Dominion of Canada in the preservation of the independence of the hemisphere." In blunt but ambiguous language, he added: "We in the Americas will decide for ourselves whether and when, and where, our American interests are attacked or our security threatened." On June 15, he froze all previously unfrozen assets of Germany and Italy, as well as those of countries controlled by the Axis.[100]

On June 22, at dawn, the Nazis invaded the Soviet Union, and Roosevelt confronted the problem of whether to support immediately the Bolshevik regime or delay, to see how their armies fared. While Cordell Hull and Harold Ickes favored giving all possible aid at once, Henry Stimson and Frank Knox, together with General Marshall and the general staff, believed the Soviets were likely to be defeated and had no wish to see U.S. supplies fall into German hands. Stimson argued that it was better to use "this precious and unforeseen period of respite" to press "with the utmost vigor our movements in the Atlantic theatre of operations," increasing the country's aid to England. When Roosevelt met the press on June 24, he said: "Of course we are going to give all the aid we possibly can to Russia," acknowledging he knew neither what the Soviets needed nor wanted.[101] Roosevelt, more than ever, wished to meet Churchill, believing the agenda for such a conference should be limited, that certain subjects could figure while others would go unmentioned. There was to be no discussion of economic or territorial deals, no talk about when the United States might choose to enter the war as an active belligerent.

Harry Hopkins, more than ever the president's confidante, was sent to London to learn Churchill's views on the Soviet Union's military prospects, as well as how the British proposed to prosecute their war in the coming months. He met for the first time many of those he would later deal with more extensively, greatly impressing the prime minister. As one of the principal architects of Lend-Lease, he understood the importance of securing accurate information on British needs, learning also what they believed the Soviets might require. Churchill told him that the Soviets had not responded to Britain's promise of material aid with very great enthusiasm, that Stalin seemed more preoccupied with discussing future frontiers and spheres of influence, a subject the prime minister claimed to have little time for.

The prime minister's principal concern was to involve the Americans in a more active and effective patrol of the North Atlantic sea-lanes, essential to the United Kingdom's economic survival. Hopkins, for his part, expressed the misgivings of the American Chiefs of Staff, though not of the president, with Britain's continuing preoccupation with the Middle East, of the vast resources being expended in that area. As he explained, ". . . You have got to remember that we in the United States simply do not understand your problems in the Middle East, and the interests of the Moslem world, and the inter-relationship of your problems in Egypt and India."[102] Though Churchill promised to justify Britain's commitment of nearly half its war production to the Middle East over the preceding eight months, he never wholly explained the rationale for these operations. Instead, he dwelled on the dangers posed by the Germans, including the possibility of their moving through Spain, bypassing Gibraltar, and occupying North Africa and West Africa, as far south as Dakar.[103] While Churchill doubted the Japanese would enter the war as long as the British were not beaten, if they did so, Singapore would prove impregnable, though both Austalia and New Zealand would be seriously threatened by the Imperial Japanese Navy.[104] More than ever, Hopkins saw the need to visit the Soviet Union, to learn how Stalin perceived the war, what he believed Hitler's next move might be.[105]

Securing the president's consent, and going as his personal emissary to deal with the "vitally important question of how we can most expeditiously and effectively make available the assistance the United States can render to your country in its magnificent resistance to the treacherous aggression by Hitlerite Germany"—the president's words—Hopkins went with a recommendation calculated to have great appeal to Stalin. Roosevelt told the Soviet leader he might treat with Hopkins as he would "with the identical confidence you would feel if you were talking directly to me," a message that encouraged Stalin to expatiate on the crucial importance of all nations accepting a common moral standard, making international coexistence possible.[106] The Germans knew no moral standards, Stalin told Hopkins; they were treaty-breakers, "an anti-social force in the present world." Concluding this homily, he listed the military materiel the Soviet Union required and suggested that it be sent through Archangel. Promising to be available to Hopkins every day from six to seven, in these four hours of conversation, Roosevelt's emissary found the Soviet leader intelligent, courteous, and direct. Reporting to the president, he said: "Not once did he repeat himself. He talked as he knew his troops were shooting—straight and hard. . . . He smiled warmly. There was no waste of word, gesture, nor mannerism. . . . Joseph Stalin knew what he wanted, knew what Roosevelt wanted, and he assumed that you knew."[107] How could Hopkins fail to be impressed by such courtesy, vigor, and forthrightness? Just as Hopkins's impressions of Churchill influenced the president, so his very full report on Stalin's opinions gave the president a sense that he knew the man, more confident than ever that in the end the Soviet Union would defeat Nazi Germany.[108]

A few days later, Hopkins joined Roosevelt and Churchill in their secret rendezvous off the coast of Newfoundland, officially announced to the world on August 14 when the Atlantic Charter was proclaimed, and the joint communiqué spoke of the two leaders having "discussed Lend-Lease and other problems of common defense." The Atlantic Charter, never thought of as a treaty, but only as a statement of common purpose, consisted of eight propositions; first, that both countries "seek no aggrandizement, territorial or other"; second, that they opposed territorial changes "that do not accord with the freely expressed wishes of the people concerned"; third, that "they respect the right of all peoples to choose the form of government under which they will live"; fourth, a guaranteed "access on equal terms, to the trade and to the raw materials of the world"; fifth, a desire to see "improved labor standards, economic advancement and social security"; sixth, that "after the final destruction of the Nazi tyranny. . . all the men in all the lands may live out their lives in freedom from fear and want"; seventh, "such a peace should enable all men to traverse the high seas and oceans without hindrance"; and eighth, "they believe that all of the nations of the world, for realistic as well as spiritual reasons must come to the abandonment of force. . . . pending the establishment of a wider and permanent system of general security, the disarmament of [aggressor] nations is essential."[109] A more Wilsonian document could scarcely have been conceived, but Churchill was led to agree to it by his desperate need to have an alliance, in all but name, with the man he recognized to be Britain's savior. The day that the Atlantic Charter was agreed to, the House of Representatives passed the draft extension bill by only a single vote, 203–202. As Conrad Black noted in his biography of Roosevelt, ". . . The isolationist dragon, though consistently confounded and defeated by the President, was not dead."[110]

Whether, as Black also noted, the Senate's vote, a more decisive one in favor of keeping conscription, more accurately reflected public opinion is impossible to know, but through the autumn Roosevelt acted as if he knew that he was in a position to take risks. In early October, following the *Greer* incident, an encounter between a U.S. destroyer and a German submarine, he issued orders to American warships operating in the Atlantic to destroy any German or Italian warships they encountered, and on October 17 the U.S. destroyer *Kearney,* torpedoed off Iceland, was later revealed to have engaged in a pitched battle with a German submarine.[111] On October 27—Navy Day—the president acknowledged "the shooting has started," and three days later the U.S. destroyer *Reuben James* was torpedoed and sank with the loss of 100 officers and men.[112] On November 6, the president declared the defense of Russia essential to American defense and asked Congress to appropriate $1 billion in Lend-Lease aid.[113] A week later, the House of Representatives, following action taken by the Senate, voted 212–194 to repeal all the restrictive provisions of the neutrality legislation passed in 1939.[114]

How had the president been able to do all these things in 1940 and 1941? How is one to account for his sudden daring? His reelection undoubtedly contributed to his sense of liberation from the restraints of a Congress still dubious of measures that might involve the United States in war. Roosevelt, at some time in 1940, reached several important conclusions, knowing that American public opinion, partly out of respect for British civilian and military courage but also because of its unqualified esteem for Churchill's leadership, accepted the importance and indeed the necessity of British survival. Roosevelt, like his cousin before him, preached the theme of military preparedness, knowing it entailed no political risk but only the Congressional appropriation of funds.[115] He propagated the theme Wilson had made paramount: that all measures taken were intended only to keep the country out of war. Any suggestion that he proposed to join the British as an active belligerent in the war would have exposed him to incalculable political dangers, and Roosevelt knew that neither

Congress nor the country believed that Nazi (or Japanese) aggression, however heinous, justified an American declaration of war. Just as he entered office in 1933 without fixed policies for remedying the nation's serious economic and social woes but showed a determined will to experiment, so in 1941 he moved in the foreign and defense policy arena without any reliable charts or compass, faithful to a single principle: Britain had to be helped to survive.

When the Soviet armies, contradicting the purportedly accurate and informed appraisals of most Western military observers, retreated from much of European Russia but did not collapse militarily, Roosevelt recognized the strategic advantage of dispatching the equipment Stalin so desperately needed. He ran no risk in doing this, none comparable to those he ran in sending U.S. warships into the North Atlantic. Whether the president ever believed that the British Empire and the Soviet Union alone would defeat Hitler under even the most favorable circumstances is impossible to say. Playing for time, he made aid to Britain his first priority, never averting his eyes from other dangers in the Far East, when Japan invaded and took Indochina and further incursions were feared. Though the secret codes of the Japanese, broken by the Americans in September 1940, told of the imminence of a Japanese attack, it was not clear what the object of that attack would be or whether the continuing talks between Hull and the Japanese ambassador might not avert it. When the blow finally came, on December 7, 1941, no one in the United States had anticipated a direct assault on Pearl Harbor.

Japanese aggression had been expected for months, but even in the last days of November the president and his close advisers knew nothing about the Japanese attack force that had slipped out of its harbor bound for Hawaii. Through MAGIC—the system that broke the Japanese code—Roosevelt learned on December 3 that the Japanese Foreign Office had instructed its principal embassies to destroy their code books, that Berlin had been informed that "war may suddenly break out between the Anglo-Saxon nations and Japan . . . quicker than anyone dreams."[116] On December 6, Secretary of the Navy Knox told the president of large Japanese convoys and fleets moving in the direction of Thailand and Malaya, and that same evening Roosevelt appealed directly to the Japanese emperor for peace. Less than sixteen hours later, news of the Japanese attack on Pearl Harbor made the president realize what he refused to acknowledge then or later: The United States had suffered its most serious naval and military disaster, the result of an intelligence failure as serious as the one that allowed the Soviet Union to become the victim of Nazi aggression.

While Roosevelt's enemies at home spoke of the president's treachery—of his having known of the imminence of a Japanese attack on Pearl Harbor, and of his secretly welcoming it—their voices scarcely resonated for tens of millions outraged by Japanese perfidy, on a day, in the president's memorable words to Congress, destined "to live in infamy." When Germany and Italy, faithful to their Axis Pact obligations, declared war on the United States on December 11, Churchill began immediately to prepare to leave for Washington. The damage to the British Navy was grave; two new battleships, the *Prince of Wales*, on which Churchill had traveled to his first meeting with Roosevelt, and the *Repulse*, both dispatched to Singapore, were sunk by Japanese aircraft off the Malay coast. The American losses were staggering: At Pearl Harbor, five battleships and three cruisers were either destroyed or seriously damaged, three other battleships were less seriously damaged, and some 177 aircraft were lost, destroyed as they sat on the ground. The casualties proved to be immense: 2,343 dead, 876 missing, and 1,272 injured.

In the days following the attack the Japanese took Guam, and Wake Island, occupied a fortnight later, increased the threat to the Philippines. The British losses, no less severe, saw Hong Kong fall on Christmas Day, and the Japanese advance steadily through Malaya. Both the president and the prime minister, seeking to exude calm, recognized the situation to be parlous, made more so by the news out of Russia. Leningrad, besieged since the first days of September, continued to hold out, but 3,000 men, women, and children were reported to be dying of starvation every day. In these circumstances, the question of where to concentrate one's military effort—against Japan or against Germany—became central. Churchill feared Roosevelt might opt for an Asia-first policy, but his concerns proved groundless. The president, like the prime minister, believed Germany posed the greater threat, that Hitler's defeat would be followed rapidly by that of Japan. In discussions that continued for more than a fortnight, often extending into the early hours of the morning, with the Chiefs of Staff of both countries meeting regularly, major decisions were made. While the British would have preferred to have two military committees, one based in Washington, the other in London, Roosevelt insisted on a single command centered in Washington to coordinate the military effort, with the Combined Munitions Board pooling the resources of the two principal combatants.

Roosevelt spent much time thinking about the duties that inhered in the president in his role as commander in chief, aware of all that had to be done to prepare the country for war. Here, again, his experience in World War I proved immensely useful. With Churchill still in Washington, the president created the War Labor Board to settle labor disputes and the War Production Board to coordinate industrial production.[117] Congress passed legislation quickly to create the Office of Price Administration, to enforce price controls, necessary to guard against hoarding, as well as to guarantee price stability. Roosevelt, donning his win-the-war mantle, spoke in grandiloquent terms of what the U.S. economy would soon produce—planes, tanks, and ships in unprecedented number. If he appeared sanguine in respect to American industrial capability, he knew better than to make light of the difficulties the Allies faced on the battlefield. In Asia especially the Japanese seemed invincible, taking Malaya,

Burma, the Philippines, and the Dutch East Indies. Yet in his Fireside Chat of February 23, 1942, he sounded no note of despair.

Offering the nation a geography lesson, he described a war the Allies were certain to win, never mentioning the decision he had taken three days earlier, by executive order, to remove and intern more than 100,000 Japanese Americans living on the West Coast.[118] Like many others, Roosevelt believed the Japanese Americans were a threat to the nation's security and that this justified initiating an action that the American Civil Liberties Union called "the worst single wholesale violation of civil rights of American citizens in our history." With memories of German sabotage in World War I, and greatly influenced by journalistic accounts of the effectiveness of the Nazi use of fifth columns in Europe, the president ignored the views of J. Edgar Hoover, the head of the FBI, who saw no need for an operation based on unreasoning public hysteria and political pressure in a single state, California.

In the months that followed, the battle situation in the Pacific improved slightly, but not so in Russia, where the Germans occupied Sevastopol after an eight-month siege, moved rapidly into the Caucasus, with its vast oil reserves, and encircled Russia's third city, Stalingrad. The most serious Allied defeat in this period, suffered by the British in Libya at Tobruk in June 1942, saw some 35,000 British officers and men surrender to a much smaller German force led by General Erwin Rommel. The U.S. naval victory some weeks earlier at Midway Island, achieved in great part by the Americans learning about the Japanese invasion intentions through a breaking of their code, a secret divulged by the *Chicago Tribune* to which the Japanese fortunately gave no attention, was rivaled only by the Americans sinking some 100,000 tons of Japanese shipping in the Coral Sea, almost certainly frustrating Japan's plans to invade Australia or the New Hebrides.

In these circumstances, it is scarcely surprising that the Soviets, desperate for help beyond the material assistance provided, should have argued strenuously for an early opening of a second front in Europe to relieve their own beleaguered forces. Roosevelt, sympathetic to their pleas, met resistance from Churchill, who believed there was no chance of the Allies succeeding in an invasion of Europe in the autumn of 1942, arguing instead for a landing in North Africa and an Allied occupation of Algeria and Morocco, then in the control of Vichy France. Roosevelt came in time to see the logic of Churchill's pleas, but Secretary Stimson, General Marshall, General Eisenhower, and Admiral King all resisted, seeing it as further evidence of Churchill's determination to protect Britain's imperial interests at the expense of others. In the end, they deferred to the president, and agreed to start preparations for TORCH, the military operation intended to make the Mediterranean an "Allied lake." Churchill appeared to have won, but his was a pyrrhic victory, quickly revealed as such.

While historians emphasized the importance of this first American-British collaboration in a joint military incursion into North Africa, concentrating on the instruction it provided in amphibious warfare, it had two other major consequences: It led to the elevation of Dwight Eisenhower to the supreme command, and it greatly influenced the president in his relations with Charles de Gaulle, the leader of the Free French, who was kept in the dark about the Allied plans. Just as important, perhaps, the president, though continuing to show regard for Churchill, always acknowledging his greatness, became increasingly suspicious of his motives and designs and began very gradually, almost imperceptibly, to move away from him.[119] However gratifying their hours of talk might be, Roosevelt recognized the gulf that separated them in their views about the kind of world each expected to issue from the Allied victory both thought inevitable. Roosevelt's hostility to de Gaulle was never concealed. His disdain for weakness, expressed in an almost Theodore Rex regard for strength, led him to underestimate the French, disappointed with their military performance in 1940, scarcely redeemed by de Gaulle's actions since. The Soviets, by comparison, seemed admirable, whose military and civilian courage and resilience could not fail to impress him. As Hopkins reported to Churchill, following the visit of Vyacheslav Molotov, the Soviet foreign minister, to Washington in the spring of 1942, the president projected a vision of a disarmed world, protected by "Four Policemen," all armed, and charged with enforcing the peace. Hopkins told Churchill: "Roosevelt had spoken to Molotov of a system allowing only the great powers— Great Britain, the United States, the Soviet Union, and possibly China—to have arms. These policemen would work together to preserve the peace." There is no record of what Churchill thought of the proposal.

We may be certain, however, that hearing or intuiting the president's views about empire, he would not have been surprised to learn that the president, speaking to his eldest son, Elliott, said: "When we've won the war, I will work with all my might and main to see to it that the United States is not wheedled into the position of accepting any plan that will further France's imperialistic ambitions, or that will aid or abet the British empire in its imperial ambitions."[120] De Gaulle, in his many references to Roosevelt in his *War Memoirs,* wrote disparagingly of the president's efforts to deny what France had done to secure the final Allied victory, ignoring her interests, and excluding her from the conferences intended to settle the fate of Europe.[121] Churchill never allowed himself comparable freedom in discussing the man who did so much to save England, but it was impossible for him not to sense the gulf opening between them. De Gaulle felt no need to be equally reticent.

Whatever esteem he may have once felt for the American president was extinguished by his conduct at the time of the North African invasion that he described in a chapter in his *War Memoirs* entitled "Tragedy."[122] The tragedy, in de Gaulle's mind, as explained to British ministers, lay in the moral turpitude displayed by the Americans in choosing to work through Admiral Jean Darlan, a servant of Vichy, a decision that dismayed him and all who thought as he did.[123] Speaking to Churchill and the foreign secretary, Anthony Eden, who argued the strategic reasons for the U.S. decision, de Gaulle said:

> You invoke strategic reasons, but it is a strategic error to place oneself in a situation contradictory to the moral character of this war. We are no longer in the eighteenth century when Frederick the Great paid the courtiers of Vienna in order to take Silesia, nor of the Italian Renaissance when one hired the myrmidons of Milan or the mercenaries of Florence. At least, we do not put them at the head of a liberated people afterward. Today we make war with our own blood and souls and the suffering of nations.[124]

Sharing telegrams he had received from France that revealed the extent of the disillusion with what the Americans were doing, de Gaulle told Churchill and Eden,

> Think of the consequences you risk incurring. If France one day discovers that because of the British and the Americans her liberation consists of Darlan, you can perhaps win the war from a military point of view but you will lose it morally, and ultimately there will be only one victor: Stalin.[125]

Churchill, after a difficult lunch, urged de Gaulle "not to confront the Americans head on" but to "be patient." In his words, "They will come to you, for there is no other alternative." "Perhaps," de Gaulle answered, but he went on to use words that no other person would have dared utter in the prime minister's presence, saying:

> But how much crockery will be broken in the meantime! And I fail to understand your own position. You have been fighting this war since the first day. In a manner of speaking you personally are this war. Your army is advancing in Libya. There would be no Americans in Africa if, on your side, you were not in the process of defeating Rommel. Up to this very moment, not a single one of Roosevelt's soldiers has met a single one of Hitler's soldiers, while for three years your men have been fighting in every latitude of the globe. Besides, in this African campaign it is Europe that is at stake, and England belongs to Europe. Yet you let America take charge of the conflict, though it is up to you to control it, at least in the moral realm. Do so! All of European public opinion will follow you.[126]

De Gaulle asked for the impossible; there was no way for Churchill to pursue policies in late 1942 of the kind he advocated. Great Britain had become dependent on the United States, and more than a sense of gratitude dictated its foreign policies. De Gaulle, with all the information available to him about Roosevelt, scarcely knew him and greatly overestimated Churchill's bargaining position. The president had found a new companion in arms, Stalin, who shared de Gaulle's reservations about American policy in North Africa only insofar as it might delay the opening of a second front in Europe. In short, 1942 was indeed a "hinge year" not only because, in Churchill's words, it represented a "turn from almost uninterrupted disaster to almost unbroken success," but also because it represented the assumption by President Roosevelt of the unquestioned leadership of the alliance, increasingly insisting on his interpretation of the war's necessities. Though he continued to learn from Churchill, and indeed on many occasions to accept his strategy, he felt America's contribution to the war made its claims preeminent.

Triumph and Tragedy, the title Churchill gave to the last volume of his World War II memoirs, almost certainly reflected (though few recognized it) his sense about a relation with the United States that had become less ardent on the American side—perhaps, if the truth be told, on both sides. It saw the president rely increasingly on what he perceived to be his excellent personal relations with Stalin, relegating his alliance with Britain to a somewhat secondary role. De Gaulle saw the war differently and followed his chapter on "Tragedy" with one entitled "Comedy" that told of the Casablanca Conference of January 17–27, 1943, that brought him and General Henri Giraud into the presence of both the president and the prime minister.[127] The assassination of Admiral Darlan on Christmas Eve compelled the Allies to search for a new French leader through whom they could operate in North Africa, and Giraud, amenable to taking orders from the Americans, was chosen as the reasonable replacement for Darlan. Roosevelt, recognizing the impossibility of excluding de Gaulle entirely, hoped the two might govern jointly. In what many described as a shotgun marriage, they were made to appear before the news cameras, solemnly shaking hands. De Gaulle rendered the scene memorably. Roosevelt, knowing de Gaulle's opposition to the arrangement, asked, "Will you at least agree to being photographed beside me and the British Prime Minister, along with General Giraud?" De Gaulle replied, "Of course, for I have the highest regard for this great soldier." Roosevelt then asked, "Will you go so far as to shake General Giraud's hand before the camera," to which de Gaulle answered, in English, "I shall do that for you." De Gaulle's irony, somewhat exaggerated, belied a more serious purpose. In the hours he had spent with the president, he reached certain conclusions about him, none very flattering.

Roosevelt, in his mind, depended on charm more than on reason to persuade others to accept what he had already decided on, an unacceptable trait in his view. Worse, writing as no other European dared to do, he said:

Franklin Roosevelt was governed by the loftiest ambitions. His intelligence, his knowledge and his audacity gave him the ability, the powerful state of which he was the leader afforded him the means, and the war offered him the occasion to realize them. If the great nation he directed had long been inclined to isolate itself from distant enterprises and to mistrust a Europe ceaselessly lacerated by wars and revolutions, a kind of messianic impulse now swelled the American spirit and oriented it toward vast undertakings. The United States, delighting in her resources, feeling that she no longer had within herself sufficient scope for her energies, wishing to help those who were in misery or bondage the world over, yielded in her turn to that taste for intervention in which the instinct for domination cloaked itself. It was precisely this tendency that President Roosevelt espoused. He had therefore done everything to enable his country to take part in the world conflict. He was now fulfilling his destiny, impelled as he was by the secret admonition of death.[128]

De Gaulle saw a greater and more calculated design in all that the president did than those who knew him more intimately. However exaggerated his opinion of Roosevelt's Machiavellian tendencies, he understood something few others were prepared to say openly. De Gaulle wrote:

But from the moment America entered the war, Roosevelt meant the peace to be an American peace, convinced that he must be the one to dictate its structure, that the states which had been overrun should be subject to his judgment, and that France in particular should recognize him as its savior and its arbiter.[129]

While the world imagined that Roosevelt showed his fidelity to Woodrow Wilson in his ardent support of the plan for a new international organization, the United Nations, realizing what the dead president had hoped to achieve with the League of Nations, de Gaulle saw him as a Wilsonian in a more fundamental sense; he sought to impose his ideas of an appropriate peace on Europe, states that had fought longer and no less courageously to preserve their freedom, whose views merited respect.

Anthony Eden, in one of his many conversations with de Gaulle, remarked, "Do you know that you have caused us more difficulties than all our other European allies put together?" "I don't doubt it," de Gaulle replied with a smile, "France is a great power."[130] Roosevelt refused to believe this. De Gaulle, in turn, could not simply fawn on the president as others did. He made no comment, for example, on Roosevelt's declaration to some fifty correspondents seated before him in Casablanca that the ". . . elimination of German, Japanese, and Italian war power means the unconditional surrender by Germany, Italy, and Japan."[131] Though these words did not appear in the final communiqué, they shocked Churchill, scarcely prepared for them, but unwilling to differ with him on a remark the president later told Hopkins had "popped into my mind" as he was speaking. Whether the words were intended to persuade the Soviets that there was no danger of the Americans or the British making a separate peace—a bogey that constantly figured—or whether they simply confirmed what many around the president knew—that he had no intention of discussing postwar plans till victory had been achieved—they almost certainly reflected the president's determination that there be no repetition of the German claim after 1918 that they had not been militarily defeated.

The year 1943 proved to be a tempestuous one for the president, though it had more than its fair share of military successes. Because the North African invasion had proved relatively easy, the president and the country exulted in their military success, and neither anticipated the events that followed almost immediately in Tunisia. There, in late February, the Germans, led by General Rommel, met the Americans at Kasserine Pass and inflicted a serious and humiliating defeat, taking many thousands of U.S. soldiers prisoner. It took the Allies only two months to reverse this disaster, effectively erasing all memory of it. In a brilliant campaign that saw American forces led by General George Patton, and British armies led by General Bernard Montgomery, traverse some 2,000 miles to encircle nearly 250,000 German and Italian troops, all taken prisoner, the Allies showed more than military daring.

Another success occurred in the same period, though it was less heralded. Through the breaking of the Japanese code, the plane bearing Admiral Isoroku Yamamoto, one of Japan's heroes who had planned the attack on Pearl Harbor, was brought down over the Pacific, and the president knew better than to dwell on how that feat had been accomplished.[132] When Roosevelt met with Churchill in May, much of their discussion centered on the impending invasion of Sicily and what should be done with those troops once the island was liberated. Roosevelt favored their being sent to England to prepare for the cross-channel invasion. Churchill preferred for them to be used in an invasion of Italy, and while the issue was not resolved, the two agreed to allow Eisenhower, the Allied commander in chief, "to plan such operations in exploitation of HUSKY [the Allied invasion of Sicily] as are best calculated to eliminate Italy from the war and to contain the maximum number of German forces." The very ambiguity of the resolution reflected the strength of feeling on both sides, with Churchill remaining faithful to his idea that an attack on the "soft underbelly" of Europe gave promise of both major political and military gains. The meetings, extending over a fortnight, were acrimonious, with Marshall depicting Churchill as acting like a "spoiled boy" and the president incensed over what he felt to be his friend's preoccupation with what he and the other Americans conceived to be purely British interests.[133]

While Roosevelt made his duties as commander in chief paramount during these months, he could not fail to give attention also to what many thought to be a deteriorating political situation at home, caused as much by labor shortages, trade union discontent, and administrative chaos in Washington as by a more restive public opinion.[134] On April 17, the War Manpower Commission banned some 27 million workers in essential defense industries from leaving their employ, but a strike by coal miners, ordered by John L. Lewis, president of the United Mine Workers, compelled Roosevelt to seize the mines, forcing the workers to return to work. The nation's anger with the miners was revealed unmistakably in the support given the Smith-Connally bill, hastily prepared and passed, that saw Congress impose severe penalties on any person encouraging a strike in government-owned plants. Roosevelt reflected long and hard on whether to veto this legislation, so obviously hostile to labor, and in the end decided to do so. His veto was quickly overridden—only the eighth time in ten years that this happened—allowing Stimson to call it "a bad rebuff and an unnecessary rebuff." The president appeared to have lost his taste and talent for domestic political combat, and his decision to create the Office of Economic Warfare, with James Byrnes as its head, superseding the old Board of Economic Warfare and assuming some of the functions of the Reconstruction Finance Corporation, suggested he knew he needed help.[135] Roosevelt had never acquired a reputation as an efficient administrator, and foreign affairs came to hold a fascination for him that domestic affairs could never compete with.

When one considers the delight Roosevelt took in being the first president to fly abroad on his long journey to Casablanca, and the first since Lincoln to visit U.S. troops in an active theater of war, one has some sense of how much he relished such activity—and how little interest he took in cajoling Congress. Abroad, Roosevelt was monarch of all he surveyed, and even the pinpricks of impossible men like de Gaulle scarcely affected him. When some 2,000 ships disembarked more than 160,000 men on the southern coast of Sicily, starting their invasion of that island on July 10, 1943, and the American, British, and Canadian forces advanced rapidly to take Palermo on July 24, Roosevelt could only exult. Days earlier, the Allies had bombed the railway yards of Rome, avoiding the Vatican and all other historical sites but achieving an objective they had not dared hope for: Mussolini's ouster by the king, his arrest, and replacement by Marshal Pietro Badoglio. In the next days, Roosevelt, obliged to decide how to treat the new Italian government, announced in a radio broadcast on July 28 that "our terms to Italy are still the same as our terms to Germany and Japan—unconditional surrender. We will have no truck with Fascism in any way, shape, or manner."[136] Roosevelt, scarred by his earlier dealings with Darlan, had no wish to repeat that experience with Badoglio. While he and Churchill exchanged notes on what to do next, Hitler moved his armies and occupied the whole of Italy. Churchill, arriving in Washington for yet another visit on August 12, on his way to Quebec, seemed to have guessed correctly. The conquest of Sicily had been relatively easy, and with the fall of Messina less than a week later, the Allies knew that their casualties numbered only 22,000 while the Axis had lost some 167,000 men; no less important, the Axis had lost some 1,691 aircraft, the Allies 274. Eisenhower, delighted by these results and empowered by the earlier agreement of the president and the prime minister, recommended an immediate attack on the Italian mainland, to begin on September 3. Roosevelt, once hostile to such a diversion, knowing a date had been set for the long-postponed invasion of France the following May, agreed to what had long been a Churchill obsession. Given that the projected cross-channel operation would involve a force with five times as many Americans as British soldiers, the selection of a U.S. commander for the operation seemed only reasonable. Churchill left the United States before the planned Allied invasion across the Strait of Messina led Badoglio to request an immediate armistice, granted by Eisenhower, knowing the Germans were pouring into Italy and would almost certainly soon occupy Rome.

An Allied military campaign began that had few of the characteristics originally envisaged by Churchill. The enemy was now Germany, not Italy, and while the rapid taking of Naples gave encouragement, winter and difficult mountain terrain soon halted the Allied advance on a line south of Cassino. It would take almost a year for the Allies to achieve what they had once imagined they might do in a matter of weeks. The Italian campaign never fully engaged the president's interests, more concerned during the summer and early autumn of 1943 with plans to meet with Stalin and Churchill in Tehran for their three-power conference. Roosevelt traveled by ship to Oran, then by air to Cairo, where he met with Chiang Kai-shek, his principal ally in Asia, but his great excitement came when he finally encountered Stalin for the first time.

The Tehran conference, which lasted from November 28 to December 1, 1943, ratified a change only the keenest observers might have noted a year earlier. Roosevelt showed increasing impatience with what he conceived to be the continued dilatory tactics of Churchill, who argued vehemently that the capture of Rome and the engagement of Turkey on the Allied side should be given the highest priority. Stalin cut short all such discussion, saying that Russia's only interest was in OVERLORD, the planned Allied invasion of France. In the new triangular relationship, Roosevelt used his undoubted charm to win what he imagined was Stalin's goodwill. If that involved mocking Churchill, which he showed no reluctance in doing, that seemed a small price to pay for what he thought would help cement a crucial new friendship.

Roosevelt, in his own words to Frances Perkins, "began to tease Churchill about his Britishness, about John Bull, about his cigars, about his habits." In his self-satisfied and somewhat juvenile account of the incident, the president reported:

> Winston got red and scowled, and the more he did so, the more Stalin smiled. Finally, Stalin broke out into a deep, hearty guffaw, and for the first time in three days I saw light. I kept it up until Stalin was laughing with me, and it was then that I called him 'Uncle Joe.' He would have thought me fresh the day before, but that day he laughed and came over and shook my hand. From that time on our

relations were personal. . . . The ice was broken and we talked like men and brothers.[137]

Stalin had every reason to be satisfied with Tehran. A firm commitment was made for an Allied invasion of France in the spring; the three agreed on the full demilitarization of Germany and the establishment of zones of occupation. Roosevelt raised no fundamental objection to Stalin's demand that the frontiers of Poland be moved westward, at Germany's expense, and appeared satisfied to allow the three Baltic states—Latvia, Lithuania, and Estonia—to remain within the Soviet Union. On the last occasion when there might have been a serious discussion of postwar aims, Roosevelt reveled in what he thought he had finally established—a firm friendship with the Soviet dictator, no longer recognizable as such.

1944 proved to be an even better year for the president. The U.S. Fifth Army entered Rome on June 5, liberating the first European capital from Axis domination. A day later, the invasion of Normandy began, and after the first few anxious hours both Roosevelt and Churchill knew that the thousands who had disembarked would not be thrown back into the sea. That, however, did not improve relations between them. Italy remained a point of contention, with Churchill demanding and failing to secure a promise that no troops would be withdrawn from that front to fight in the south of France. When, in August, Warsaw rose in rebellion against the German occupying forces as the Russians approached the city, Churchill begged Roosevelt to offer aid. Stalin denounced the resistance leaders as "power-seeking criminals" and denied permission for the Allies to land and refuel their planes behind Soviet lines. Roosevelt, having no wish to offend Stalin and believing he would need Soviet bases for the war against Japan, ignored Churchill's pleas. The Warsaw rising was ruthlessly crushed by the Nazis.

These, however, were minor concerns beside the one that became increasingly preoccupying to all who observed the president in 1944. Churchill was not alone in believing that his friend was very ill, and while Roosevelt's personal physician denied this, others—principally the physicians who examined him after his return from Tehran—knew it to be true.[138] While some wondered whether he would indeed seek a fourth term, whether he could possibly survive for another four years in the White House, the president seemed determined to continue. Indeed, his 1944 electoral victory over Thomas Dewey, only marginally less impressive than the one he had gained over Wendell Willkie four years earlier, told the world that he remained the powerful leader he had been from the time of his first election in 1932.

The final meeting of Roosevelt, Churchill, and Stalin, at Yalta in February 1945, a time when Roosevelt's mortal illness showed unmistakably in the grim photograph of the three seated together, saw the president largely preoccupied with what some in a later generation concluded were essentially peripheral issues. In his mind, two questions transcended all others: How could he be certain to win Soviet consent for voting arrangements that he believed essential to the success of the United Nations, soon to be formally established in San Francisco? More important, certainly, how could he guarantee that the Soviets would honor their Tehran commitment to help in the war against Japan? Yalta occurred before the atomic bomb had been tested, and all who advised Roosevelt, looking at the terrible casualties the Americans had suffered in taking a single island in the Solomons—Guadalcanal—could only imagine that any effort to invade Japan would involve many hundreds of thousands of deaths and casualties. To prevent that disaster, Roosevelt could only believe that Soviet military action, coinciding with the American, essentially replicating the strategy adopted at the time of the Allied invasion of France, could only serve to reduce greatly the risks to U.S. forces. If, at Tehran, Roosevelt had feared that a failure to mollify the Soviets, to launch the second front in 1944, might lead them to make a separate peace with the Nazis, this was no longer a danger. By the time of Yalta, Roosevelt felt he needed Stalin for the war against Japan as much as Stalin had once needed him for the war against Germany.

Though Stalin agreed to sign the Joint Declaration on Liberated Europe that promised free elections and the establishment of democratic governments in Eastern Europe, the Soviet definition of *democracy* was not one that either Roosevelt or Churchill would have recognized. In any case, Stalin knew what Roosevelt never chose to acknowledge: the Soviets, by occupying the area, with its armies liberating much of Eastern and Central Europe, would exert an influence there that neither the Americans nor the British would be in a position to challenge. Roosevelt, in the weeks before his death, becoming increasingly aware of Soviet actions in Poland that suggested their intention to flout the accords reached at Yalta guaranteeing free elections, and wrote pained letters to Churchill, but there was nothing either could do to alter the situation. The Soviet armies, the conquerors of all of prewar Poland, advancing rapidly into Germany, were showing an independence of their Western Allies never displayed as long as they were dependent on them.

Yalta became in Republican eyes the great diplomatic blunder that a president, near death, allowed a ruthless dictator to fashion, which led to a revision of Poland's frontiers and ultimately to his control of much of Central and Eastern Europe. Roosevelt saw Yalta as a triumph. In his words, it

. . . ought to spell the end of the system of unilateral action, the exclusive alliances, the spheres of influence, the balances of power, and all the other expedients that have been tried for centuries—and have always failed. We propose to substitute for all these a universal organization in which all peace-loving Nations will finally have a chance to join.[139]

The heir of Woodrow Wilson, Roosevelt created what he imagined were "the beginnings of a permanent structure of peace." Harry Hopkins, his Colonel House, was even more sanguine. As he told Robert Sherwood, his biographer,

> We really believed in our hearts that this was the dawn of the new day we had all been praying for and talking about for so many years. We were absolutely certain that we had won the first great victory of the peace—and by 'we' I mean all of us, the whole civilized human race. The Russians had proved that they could be reasonable and far-seeing and there wasn't any doubt in the minds of the President or any of us that we could live with them and get along with them peacefully for as far into the future as any of us could imagine. But I have to make one amendment to that—I think we all had in our minds the reservation that we could not foretell what the results would be if anything should happen to Stalin. We felt sure that we could count on him to be reasonable and sensible and understanding—but we never could be sure who or what might be in back of him there in the Kremlin.[140]

This idea—that there were others more terrible than the Kremlin dictator waiting to take over—would continue to bedevil U.S. analysis of the Soviet Union for years to come.

Hopkins, more than any other man, had the ear of the president, but others saw the situation as he did and said essentially the same things. Only George Kennan, writing from the U.S. embassy in Moscow to Charles Bohlen, the country's other leading Soviet expert, the diplomat who had accompanied the president to Yalta, expressed views of a fundamentally different kind. Kennan told Bohlen:

> I am aware of the realities of this war, and of the fact that we were too weak to win it without Russian cooperation. I recognize that Russia's war effort has been masterful and effective and must, to a certain extent, find its reward at the expense of other peoples in eastern and central Europe. But with all of this, I fail to see why we must associate ourselves with this political program, so hostile to the interests of the Atlantic community as a whole, so dangerous to everything we need to see preserved in Europe.[141]

Kennan's solution—to establish spheres of influence in Europe, one reserved for Russia, the other from which it would be excluded—seemed inconceivable to Bohlen. It would have been thought immoral by Roosevelt, who would have felt no greater sympathy for Kennan's reservations about the projected United Nations. Roosevelt, like Wilson, imagined he was creating a new world order, fundamentally different from the one that carried the seeds of war. Roosevelt came with very specific ideas about international affairs, more limited than those of his cousin, whose knowledge of history greatly exceeded his own, but both depended on intuition, a faculty that sometimes failed them.

In rescuing the country from its exaggerated fears after 1933, Roosevelt appeared as America's savior. In acting as he did in 1940 and even more in 1941, he gave England the courage to resist and may therefore be awarded recognition as the savior of Western Europe. However, in the end his vanity defeated him, as de Gaulle feared it would. Too self-confident, too isolated among the few who enjoyed access to him, he lacked the knowledge that might have made him more sympathetic to those—none in his immediate entourage—who understood that Stalin was not a democrat, resisting others in the Kremlin more hostile to the West.[142] In the end, Bohlen may have understood the situation best when he implied that the alliance forged during the war could not have survived the joint military victory. Roosevelt and Churchill were not Stalin's victims at Yalta; both profited greatly from the heroism of the Russian people who paid a terrible price for their decades of suffering under Bolshevik rule.

Roosevelt died in April 1945, unaware of what he had failed to accomplish. Too harsh with Churchill on occasion, but often prepared to follow his lead, immensely stimulated by him in the beginning, he accepted that relations with Stalin were crucial and may have shown his true character in his excessive impatience and contempt for de Gaulle.[143] Yet the shadow of Yalta cannot conceal an accomplishment as significant for the postwar world as any: Roosevelt's determination to build an atom bomb, to keep the research and development secret, fearing always that the Nazis were engaged in the same difficult scientific and technological enterprise.[144]

Cooperating with the British, accepting Churchill's formula, as outlined in a very secret agreement made in Quebec in 1943 that the two would never use the projected weapon against each other, or against third parties without the other's consent, and that neither would communicate information about atomic energy to third parties except by mutual consent, Roosevelt knew the British were the most reliable of his allies. Their economic distress, apparent long before the war ended, concerned him, and their differences, though important, never concealed what each did for the other. Neither Roosevelt nor Churchill boasted a truly imaginative view of how the Soviet Union might figure in the postwar world, both as a European and a world power. Roosevelt, as much a child of the late Victorian Age as Churchill, lived with many of the same fantasies, none more important than what G.M. Young called "the daily clamour for leadership, for faith, for a new heart or a new cause. . . ."[145]

Yet Roosevelt, building on the foundations laid earlier in the century, created a more powerful and more popular presidency, and though others who followed him, less able and crafty, might choose to ignore him or blame him for Yalta, a tragedy equated with the appeasement at Munich by George W. Bush, the presidency never reverted to what it had been in the days of Harding,

Coolidge, and Hoover. What, then, was Roosevelt's legacy? No less important, how are we to explain why so many hated and reviled him, refusing to acknowledge his greatness? What did he perceive that even the best of those who came after him sought to replicate but never wholly succeeded in doing? Why was he America's greatest president after Lincoln, and why has there been none since to compare with him?

To answer these questions is to dwell on circumstances insufficiently emphasized by even those who have made Roosevelt their hero. He came to the White House at a time of unprecedented economic, social, and political disorder. None of the economic recessions since have compared in any way with the conditions that prevailed in 1933. Though he failed to resolve all the economic problems created by the world economic Depression, with many settled only by the economic recovery stimulated by the war, he gave the nation hope at a time when very few enjoyed that luxury. The problems created by German and Japanese aggression, infinitely more serious than even those certain of his successors were compelled to cope with, allowed him to become an incomparable war leader, able to mobilize congressional and public opinion to accept innovations of a kind none of his predecessors had felt the need to recommend. While Roosevelt and Wilson had done much to enhance the president's role as the architect of the nation's foreign policy, World War II legitimated a greatly expanded role that has only very occasionally been challenged since and never permanently reduced.

Roosevelt's self-confidence drew on his constant appeal to the electorate. While influential men and women disparaged him, thought him a dictator and sought by every means to defeat him, they never recognized the president's strengths, his firm conviction, shared by both his cousin and his former commander in chief, so different in their political allegiances, that the strength of the country lay in its moral fiber, and in its economic and social potential. The word *reformer* was never uncongenial to either of his distinguished presidential predecessors, and became the badge Roosevelt showed particular pride in displaying. Though he lacked experience of actual combat, he recognized military valor and never imagined that the Soviet Union, after its heroic efforts in World War II, would be anything other than a great world power. While he exaggerated what China might become under Chiang Kai-shek's leadership and made fundamental mistakes about France's potential, he never doubted British resolve, questioning only Churchill's old-fashioned imperialist beliefs.

An incomparable war president, a warrior listed among the dead of World War II in Harvard's Memorial Church, Roosevelt had flair, knew it, enjoyed power, used it, and never wholly showed his hand. He was secretive, knew the importance of deception, and this too he left as a legacy to his successors.

CHAPTER 11

The Creator

HARRY TRUMAN, THE third of the twentieth century's accidental presidents and incontestably the most creative, bore only a very superficial resemblance to his predecessor, Franklin Roosevelt. Indeed, this may have been his greatest asset. No one mistook the plain man from Missouri for the so-called aristocrat of Hyde Park. Lacking Roosevelt's grace but also his guile, Truman accepted that he was following the political Moses of his day who had led his people to the promised land of peace and plenty, denied by his fatal illness the opportunity to enter into that long-promised paradise. It fell to Truman to end the war, first in Europe, then in Asia, and to begin the process that led the country to new eminence and power. Truman, recently a senator, a loyal New Dealer, by no means the most renowned, belonged to that large Democratic Party contingent whose confidence in the president, even when shaken, was never seriously in question. His initial entry into the Senate in 1934 had been scarcely noted; no one heralded it as a democratic breakthrough. The chosen candidate of Tom Pendergast's machine in Kansas City, Truman arrived with dubious political credentials for those in Congress who looked with suspicion on men lifted to important political positions by political bosses, still influential in many of America's leading cities. How did this young farmer become involved with Pendergast, a boss in the classic sense described so eloquently almost a half-century earlier by James Bryce?

David McCullough, Truman's most accomplished biographer, described him as a "son of the middle border," resembling thousands of others born in what was still then the "farmer's kingdom," a land of rich soil that promised ample rewards to those prepared to work long and hard.[1] Agriculture, as Alexis de Tocqueville correctly prophesied many decades earlier, had become a speculative and commercial business in the United States, carrying substantial monetary prizes but also very considerable risks.

John Truman, Harry's father, invested heavily in futures, guessed wrongly, and lost his farm in 1901, a tragedy for the whole family. Moderately prosperous Missouri farmers one day, bankrupt the next, father and son had no option but to seek work in Kansas City. Harry Truman, seventeen, expelled from his rural paradise in Independence, Missouri, hoped for an appointment to West Point, the country's principal military academy, but his poor eyesight made that impossible.[2] He worked first in the mailroom at the Kansas City *Star*, one of the city's leading newspapers, then as a construction timekeeper on the Santa Fe Railroad, and finally as a clerk and assistant teller in two banks.

In 1905, his father summoned him back to the land, to help the family maintain his grandmother's farm outside Grandview. For the next decade, Truman worked as a farmer, handling livestock, planting and harvesting crops, constructing fences, repairing tools, and also serving as the farm's accountant. When, in 1911, his younger brother, Vivian, married and moved away, Harry was made a full partner in the farm. By this time, Truman's romantic interest in Bess Wallace, whom he first knew at school in Independence, led him to consider marriage, but the formidable matron Wallace had no intention of allowing her beautiful daughter to marry the young farmer. Madge Gates Wallace was an imperious widow who had managed to suppress all memory of her late drunken and heavily indebted husband, who had committed suicide. Her marital ambitions for her only daughter were grandiose, and though Harry on his father's death in November 1914 assumed full responsibility for the farm, enjoying a greater income because the war in Europe created a substantial new market for American wheat, it did not provide enough to impress her. Truman, like his father, decided to speculate, not in land but in an Oklahoma zinc mine and in oil, and both ventures failed. Despairing, he wrote Bess in May 1916, "You would do better perhaps if you pitch me into the ash heap and pick someone with more sense and ability and not such a soft head."[3]

When war came less than a year later, in April 1917, Truman's only asset was his farm, but with land in Jackson County selling for $200 an acre, the farm's value was estimated at $100,000 or more. Had Wilson never declared war in 1917, Truman would probably have ended his days as a farmer, possibly marrying the "girl from Independence." Like many other young farmers, Truman responded enthusiastically to Wilson's call to enlist, not wishing to be thought a slacker. Rejoining the National Guard to which he had previously belonged, he organized an artillery battery, Battery F, in Kansas City, and the unit, following a long tradition of electing its officers, chose Truman, to his surprise and delight, to be a first lieutenant. After months of training in Oklahoma, he embarked for France, pleased to be joining the American Expeditionary Force under the command of General John J. Pershing, a fellow Missourian.[4]

Assigned to an artillery school near Chaumont, and promoted to the rank of captain, he learned in July that he would command Battery D of Second Battalion, 129th Field Artillery, in charge of 194 enlisted men, mostly Irish Catholic youths from Kansas City. Battery D, reputed to be undisciplined and unruly, was known to be disinclined to take orders from its officers. Truman acted promptly to assert his authority, making certain his slight appearance would not to be mistaken for physical weakness. He demoted several of the noncommissioned officers, and told the rest that "I didn't come over here to get along with you," making it clear that their problem "was to get along with him or face being 'busted.'"[5] Remarkably quickly, he established a close rapport with his men, and the battery's reputation improved markedly. Though Truman never exaggerated what the artillery accomplished in the Meuse-Argonne offensive, knowing that the infantry had been far more important in the operation, he believed that the soldiers under his command had conducted themselves honorably.

The war changed Truman's life, providing him with two great advantages: lasting friendship with his fellow officers and with those who served under him; and an understanding of his ability to lead others, not least in time of danger. Returning to Independence, he married Bess and moved in with her mother, believing the situation would be temporary; it lasted for the remainder of the old lady's long life. Indeed, Truman's marriage forced him to abandon farming. If the Trumans were to live with his mother-in-law in Independence, as his wife insisted, it was impossible for him to continue to farm in Grandview. Only by moving to Kansas City, within commuting distance of Independence, could he hope to enjoy any sort of family life. Retaining the farm but leasing it, his sale of cattle and farm machinery gave him $15,000 that he then invested in a "gents' furnishing" shop in partnership with his wartime friend, Eddie Jacobson. The shop opened for business in November 1919, and Truman believed that the profits from it, with the rent received from the farm, would be more than sufficient for his family's needs. But he never anticipated the severe economic depression of the early 1920s.

Though his political enemies later caricatured him as incompetent even in business, a mere "haberdasher," it was the agricultural depression in the immediate postwar years that caused Truman and Jacobson to fail. Like other Kansas City businesses dependent on farm families, the partnership fell heavily into debt, and while Truman chose not to file for bankruptcy, believing it immoral, he was still paying off a $35,000 debt some twenty years later when he sat in the Senate.[6]

Truman, a lifelong Democrat, held Harding and the Republicans responsible for the economic collapse. When, fortuitously, the powerful Democratic machine in Kansas City asked him to run for eastern judge of Jackson County—an administrative rather than a judicial post—he accepted with alacrity, knowing that the position would allow him to remain in Independence. As one of three judges authorized to oversee road construction and award contracts, it made him an influential man in the county.[7] The Pendergast machine chose Truman because of his unblemished reputation as a Mason, a war veteran, a

Baptist, and a recent farmer who understood the problems of his neighbors, an ideal candidate for the office with its $3,465 annual salary. Truman contended with three other Democrats in the party's primary election and won by some 279 votes in a contest that saw more than 11,000 Jackson County citizens troop to the polls.

In Missouri, victory in the primary election was tantamount to election, and on January 1, 1923, Truman became Judge Truman, a title he greatly prized. In 1926, when he ran to be presiding judge, a four-year post with a $6,000 annual salary, no one opposed him in the primaries, and he won the general election with a majority of 16,000. Four years later, again competing for the post, his majority rose impressively, to 58,000. Truman, a big fish in a small pond, respected for his honesty and industry, knew his fellow judges were profiting personally from their positions, that their habit of "shooting crap" behind the judge's bench while the court was in session, one of their more minor offenses, made him an honest man among thieves. Sometimes compelled, in his words, "to compromise in order to get the job done," he grew increasingly disillusioned and began to ask himself whether he ought not quit politics entirely.

With Roosevelt's election as president, Pendergast, as one of his principal supporters, pressed for the appointment of a Democrat to replace the Republican director of the federal employment service in Missouri, and Truman received the post. Having no wish to abandon his position as judge, he accepted it without pay, going twice a week for the next months to the state capital to secure federal jobs for some of the state's many unemployed.

Reporting in Washington to Harry Hopkins, the federal administrator of emergency relief, Truman began to consider a new career, possibly election to Congress. When a seat in the House became vacant, Pendergast, though aware of Truman's ambition, disappointed him, choosing another candidate, a circuit court judge, for the vacancy. A year later, however, in May 1934, to his great surprise, Truman learned that the boss wanted him to run for one of Missouri's two U.S. Senate seats. Pendergast had offered the nomination to others, but their refusal led him to think of Truman at a time when, in the words of one of his close associates, "Tom hasn't a field of world-beaters to pick from." Bearing the Pendergast imprimatur was an advantage to Truman but also something of a handicap, certain to be exploited by one or other of his opponents, already members of the House of Representatives, anxious to represent him as the creature of the Missouri boss. Truman surprised all the state politicians, winning with 40,000 more votes than his closest competitor.[8] It appeared that the Jackson County voters who knew Truman well had voted overwhelmingly for him, and though the outcome was a Pendergast victory, others saw it as a tribute to an honest man, not known to be committed to the traditions of boss rule.

Though a handful of senators embraced Truman from the beginning, many showed reserve, little interested in being too closely associated with the Pendergast nominee. Vice President John Nance Garner, who presided over the Senate, offered his friendship from the beginning, and though their social habits were different—Garner drank heavily, chewed tobacco, and spat the brown juice regularly into his private spittoon—as a Texan he recognized at once his kinship with the one-time Missouri farmer.[9] In a Senate still dominated by men with agrarian roots, Truman did not remain an outsider for long. On his modest $10,000 a year Senate salary, he lived a restricted social life, made more so by the frequent absences of his wife and daughter, tending to the needs of an aging Mrs. Wallace in Independence. Alone through the hot Washington summers, Truman suffered these separations in silence, rarely complaining, but occasionally alluding to his loneliness in his long letters home. Politics consumed him, and he believed very early that the president had made a fundamental error in his court-packing plan; that, however, never led him to ally himself with the more conservative Democrats in the Senate who became vocal critics of the president. Though Roosevelt never courted Truman, taking his loyalty for granted, the senator thought Roosevelt an incomparable leader who had saved the nation from disaster in 1933.

Truman, a member of the Appropriations Committee, took seriously the inquiry of one of its subcommittees into railroad finances that revealed a record of financial corruption and greed. Though it was not uncommon for a Missouri Democrat to be suspicious of Wall Street bankers and to show little esteem for the large New York and Chicago law firms that habitually defended them, Truman's disdain exceeded what was common at the time. In a memorable assault on both bankers and lawyers in a Senate speech on December 20, 1937, he spoke contemptuously of those who "worship money instead of honor," refusing to "see the dangers of bigness and of the concentration of the control of wealth."[10]

Truman, recently acquainted with Justice Louis Brandeis, was expressing what that old enemy of "bigness" had long preached. The speech gave him instant celebrity, but even this unexpected renown provided no protection against his critics when out of loyalty he defended Pendergast against those seeking to convict his old boss of mail fraud. Believing that federal judges, originally appointed by Harding and Coolidge, could not be impartial in any trial involving Pendergast, he used graphic language to condemn them, saying: ". . . A Jackson County, Missouri, Democrat has as much chance of a fair trial in the Federal District Court of Western Missouri as a Jew would have in a Hitler court or a Trotsky follower before Stalin."[11] Was it simply loyalty to an old friend and supporter that led him to such hyperbole?

When, in April 1939, Tom Pendergast, indicted for tax evasion, entered a guilty plea, was fined and sent to prison, Truman's stock fell.[12] Though no one accused him of wrongdoing, those who knew him understood why he had found it impossible to abandon the boss in his time of distress. Lloyd Stark, governor of Missouri, a leader in the move to indict Pendergast, heralded by the Missouri press as the state's moral leader, thought it a good time to challenge Truman for his Senate seat, believing that success there might one day lead him to be considered for the presidency. In these circumstances, Roosevelt's reaction to the Missouri race became all-important. Would he recognize the contributions Truman had made over the years in voting for New Deal legislation, or would he support Stark, an erstwhile Pendergast loyalist, who had recognized the political advantages of deserting him?

When, on February 3, 1940, Truman announced his candidacy for a second Senate term and indicated his opposition to the president seeking a third term for himself—Roosevelt had not yet made his decision known—many were dumbfounded, not least by his statement that he hoped Bennett Clark, his Senate colleague from Missouri, would seek the Democratic Party's presidential nomination. Why Truman, a New Deal Democrat, should support a known conservative, and an isolationist to boot, confused both his friends and his enemies. Like Garner, the vice president, Truman believed the two-term tradition sacred, and his constituents understood that, but his decision to support the senator who had opposed his own nomination in 1934 baffled them. Some thought it a political tactic, intended to win support in Missouri circles where Clark was popular.

Truman opened his primary campaign on June 15, 1940, the day following the German occupation of Paris. In the weeks that followed, many of his Senate friends, including Carl Hatch, Sherman Minton, Alben Barkley, and Hugo Black, came to express their support, and Senator Jimmy Byrnes, learning of Truman's dire need for campaign funds, persuaded the wealthy Bernard Baruch to contribute $4,000 to his reelection bid. The railroad unions, grateful for his help, offered $17,000, the largest contribution he received.[13] As for the president, he said nothing to indicate whether he preferred Truman, dismissed by Stark as a "Pendergast lackey," or would be content to see him go.[14] Just days before the Democratic National Convention that renominated Roosevelt, the Kansas City county court, controlled by the Republicans, foreclosed the mortgage on the Truman Grandview farm, and the 195 acres, belonging to his mother, were sold the next day at auction.

Truman saw the action as spiteful, intended to humiliate him, and grieved that his mother and sister, dispossessed of their property, would be compelled to seek refuge in a small rented house in Grandview. He fully expected a second blow when the primary results were announced, but his victory over Stark, winning by 8,000 votes in an election that brought out 665,000 voters, proved as much a surprise as his later presidential victory in 1948. His Senate friends could recall no election that had generated such interest, whose results were more favorably received. Despite the disadvantages he incurred in 1934 in being the chosen candidate of a boss, subsequently disgraced and jailed, Truman had retained the confidence of ordinary men and women in Missouri. Profiting from his friendship with influential figures in the Senate who valued his authenticity and integrity, they recognized him as one of their own, one of the boys.

Truman's reelection to the Senate led him in February 1941 to make a proposal that altered his political life. With defense expenditures escalating and many new military camps being constructed, Truman became aware of the excessive profits contractors were realizing; both big business and the labor unions were showing a greed that mocked their purported concern with the national interest. Relying on his early experience as a judge, where he had learned much about illicit practices that allowed contractors to defraud public authorities, he saw the need for a closer surveillance of companies awarded defense contracts. Truman's proposal to create the Senate Special Committee to Investigate the National Defense Program was accepted, with an initial appropriation of a derisory $15,000. The seven-man committee, with five Democrats and two Republicans, became Truman's platform, allowing him to tour the country, becoming aware of the waste and mismanagement that had greatly inflated all defense costs. Truman's hearings received adulatory treatment in national magazines, including *Newsweek* and *Time*, and on March 8, 1943, *Time* featured the committee on its cover, depicting it as the "watchdog, spotlight, conscience and spark plug to the economic war-behind-the-lines."[15] *Look* magazine named Truman one of the ten men in Washington most important to the war effort.[16] Only rarely had a second-term senator won such acclaim, but Truman by the work he did with his special committee became a national figure, and this made him one of several men considered for the vice presidency in 1944, a year when many knew Henry Wallace would not be renominated for the post.

Truman never claimed to be a Roosevelt intimate; he saw little of him during the election campaign and almost nothing after their joint inauguration. Like others who observed the president at the time, it was difficult to know what his ailments were, but his trembling hands, the dark shadows under his eyes, his pallor, and loss of weight—were too obvious not to be noticed. That Truman sometimes resented Roosevelt's coolness, interspersed with an almost exaggerated cordiality, was something he never chose to dwell on. Yet even after his election as vice president, Roosevelt never took him into his confidence and shared no information with him on the problems the country faced. The president, anxious to deny his mortality, must have felt that any too-close association with the man constitutionally mandated to succeed him would only serve to remind him of a condition he preferred not to confront.

Though Truman concealed his feelings about the president's failure to confide in him, he knew the man too well to be wholly surprised by his attitude; a senator who never acknowledged his suffering at the hands of an impossible mother-in-law could not be expected to speak candidly about the individual who in his mind had rescued the nation from disaster in 1933 and the world in 1940 and later. Truman's cardinal virtue, loyalty, had never been the characteristic strength of his chief, and the vice president certainly knew this.

Margaret Truman, in her idealized biography of her father—a work that merits attention despite its hagiographic bias—published two documents, a letter from Truman to his sister, and a desk calendar entry, both written in 1948 when Truman was trying desperately to establish himself as a viable candidate for a second term in the White House; each is immensely revealing. Truman, angered by the antics of two of Roosevelt's sons, Elliott and Franklin Jr., both opposed to his candidacy, wrote of those "whose definition of loyalty is loyalty to themselves . . . a one-way street." In his letter to Mary, he wrote: "Take the Roosevelt clan as an example. As long as Wm. Howard Taft was supporting Teddy he was a great man—but when Taft needed support Teddy supported Teddy. The present generation of Franklin's is something on that order."[17] His calendar note, written after he secured the Democratic Party nomination, was even more redolent of his Missouri origins; it included the words, "None of the smart folk thought I would call the Congress. I called 'em for July 26th, turnip day at home."[18] Truman, in accepting his party's nomination, had announced his intention to summon a special session of Congress to pass the legislation the Republicans in their platform claimed to support but had refused to accept during the regular session of Congress. Of his Republican opponent, he wrote: "Dewey synthetically milks cows and pitches hay for the cameras just as that other faker Teddy Roosevelt did—but he never heard of 'turnip day.'" Then, in words whose meaning could not be misinterpreted he wrote: "I don't believe the USA wants any more fakers—Teddy and Franklin are enough. So I'm going to make a common sense intellectually honest campaign. It will be a novelty— and it will win."[19]

This was the man who succeeded Franklin Roosevelt on April 12, 1945. Though many feared that this plain-spoken, seemingly prosaic individual, whatever his accomplishments as a senator, could not possibly succeed in resolving the many problems left unsettled by the war, Truman confounded the pessimists. Using his modesty to good effect, recognizing his strengths, particularly in the Senate, he courted his friends, joined them for lunch on his first full day in office, and after Roosevelt's funeral, in a brief fifteen-minute address to both houses of Congress, asked the country to help him defend the ideals of the late president. He promised to prosecute the war in a manner "unchanged and unhampered," that the nation's resolve to have its enemies surrender unconditionally would be respected. The press praised the speech, and the country found it reassuring. Truman spoke as the war against Germany was coming to an end, when Japan remained the sole surviving Axis power. Tokyo, he told Congress, "rocks under the weight of our bombs," and nothing in his speech suggested that this would not continue till final victory. Praising the nascent

United Nations, he expressed the hope it would be a "strong and lasting" instrument for keeping the peace, insisting that the United States would never again return to its mistaken isolationist policies.[20] Superficially, all went on as before; the changes, in fact, were substantial.

While Truman followed the precedent set by the two earlier twentieth-century accidental presidents, asking the Cabinet to remain in office, within months of his arrival all the principal Roosevelt appointees were retired, replaced by men who enjoyed Truman's confidence. Many were personal friends, individuals he knew in the Senate or in Missouri. In his *Memoirs*, he wrote with less than total candor of how Secretary of State Edward Stettinius Jr., Secretary of the Treasury Henry Morgenthau Jr., Secretary of War Henry Stimson, Attorney General Francis Biddle, Secretary of Labor Frances Perkins, Secretary of Agriculture Claude Wickard, and Postmaster General Frank Walker all came to be replaced. Though Stettinius had no wish to go, Truman had promised the post to Byrnes even before the president's funeral, never imagining that the elevation of so ambitious a politician would create problems for him. Morgenthau, the intimate friend and Hyde Park neighbor of Roosevelt, wished to be appointed a member of the delegation to accompany the president to Potsdam and threatened to resign when his request was refused. Morgenthau scarcely knew the man who had entered the Oval Office. Truman accepted the resignation at once, appointing a close friend, Fred Vinson, director of economic stabilization and later director of war mobilization, to take his place. Stimson, aged and ailing, asked to resign, and no one was surprised when Robert Patterson, his deputy, replaced him. Truman wrote admiringly of Francis Biddle, acknowledging he might not have been "as well satisfied with me as a liberal President as he had been with my predecessor," but the reasons for his departure were more mundane. The attorney general fancied himself a Philadelphia aristocrat, not someone calculated to appeal to the man from Missouri who expected Tom Clark, Biddle's recommended successor, to be more congenial. That Clark received strong endorsements, in Truman's words, "by the whole Texas delegation, including Sam Rayburn and Tom Connally, in all of whom I had the utmost confidence," mattered a great deal more than the Biddle recommendation. Frances Perkins, having served for twelve years—the first woman to hold a Cabinet appointment—expressed the wish to retire, and Truman chose Lewis Schwellenbach, an old Senate friend, to replace her.

These individual appointments acquired importance principally because the president intended to use these men as his predecessor had rarely used members of his Cabinet, especially after the outbreak of war. Truman believed that Roosevelt had "spent too much time doing the work that should have been delegated to the Cabinet" and did not imagine he exaggerated when he wrote: "He was his own Secretary of State nearly all the time he was President. He was his own Secretary of the Treasury. And when it came to the operation of military affairs, he was his own Secretary of War and Secretary of the Navy."[21] Truman had no wish to follow Roosevelt in these assertions of presidential authority. In his mind, the Cabinet existed to debate issues and make recommendations he would feel free to accept or reject, choosing between them. Once he had chosen, he expected all members of the Cabinet to support his decisions, reflecting what he believed were the legitimate powers of the "Chief Executive of the Republic and Commander-in-Chief of the Armed Forces."

When he left for Potsdam to meet with Joseph Stalin and Winston Churchill in mid-July, a conference that lasted from July 17 to August 2, 1945, he knew that the Senate was expected to ratify the United Nations Charter with only two negative votes—a decidedly different situation from the one Woodrow Wilson had confronted with the League of Nations in 1919. Truman, aware that he was profiting from a political honeymoon created in part by Roosevelt's sudden death, was beginning to enjoy the presidency, as was obvious from a letter he sent his mother and sister where he wrote: "I am getting ready to go see Stalin & Churchill, and it is a chore. I have to take my tuxedo, tails. . . preacher coat, high hat, low hat, and hard hat as well as sundry other things."[22] The pressures of the presidency had clearly not defeated him.

Though Truman wrote extensively about the Potsdam Conference in his *Memoirs,* a substantially less important encounter than the one the mortally ill Roosevelt attended half a year earlier at Yalta, he never thought to allude to anything that would in any way detract from the accomplishments of his predecessor. His own objectives appeared to be three: first, to convince Stalin that he was a friend, a president who could be trusted; second, to remind the Soviet leader of his promise to join the war against Japan once Hitler had been defeated, believing such a move could only hasten the Allied victory over the sole remaining member of the Axis; finally, to tell Stalin about the atom bomb. Churchill, before the results of the British election were made known, and Clement Attlee who succeeded him as prime minister, seemed almost incidental players at Potsdam, watching the president and his secretary of state navigate very rough waters with a Soviet leader who enjoyed the incomparable prestige secured through an impressive military victory achieved against very great odds.

Although it is impossible to know what Stalin thought of Truman's protestations of friendship—revelations from the former Soviet archives have yielded little evidence on this—the president walked through an open door when he insisted that the Communists honor the commitment they made at Yalta to enter the war against Japan. Stalin had every incentive to do so, given what the Allies had promised the Soviet Union in exchange for that military engagement.[23] As for the information given Stalin about the atom bomb, "a new weapon of unusual destructive force," the Soviet leader's seeming indifference to the news was thought to be evidence of his sangfroid. As the Americans were soon to learn, he had known about the bomb for months from his intelligence sources abroad.[24]

Charles Bohlen, present at the conference, mostly as an interpreter, did not think it a "vital conference," believing the results would not have been very different had Roosevelt been alive or had Churchill retained his place as prime minister.[25] Yet this was not what the president believed at the time or how Potsdam figured in the extensive account given in his *Memoirs,* published in 1955. For him, vital discussions on questions as different as those that touched Germany, Poland, Turkey, Italy, Spain, Iran, Lebanon, Syria, and Yugoslavia, war crime trials, and international control of internal waterways made it a seminal event.[26]

The American public showed less than overwhelming interest in any of these issues at the time, reserving their jubilation for VJ Day, when many felt great relief that the war was finally over, taking for granted that the wartime alliance would survive, guaranteeing peace for generations. Because the Potsdam Conference assigned to the Council of Foreign Ministers the task of drawing up the peace treaties that would then be presented to a peace conference, its first full meeting in London in September and October 1945 was considered an event of very great significance. Both Byrnes and Ernest Bevin, representing the United States and the United Kingdom, were surprised and dismayed by what they considered the truculent behavior of Vyacheslav Molotov, the Soviet foreign minister. They had simply taken it for granted that the American possession of the atom bomb would make the Soviets more amenable to compromise. Instead, they found them as difficult as ever, and the conference adjourned when it became evident that no progress was being made.[27]

Truman refused to believe that the differences were irreconcilable. At a Navy Day celebration in late October, soon after the collapse of the London meeting, he spoke of American foreign policy being "based firmly on fundamental principles of righteousness and justice," promising that "we shall not relent in our efforts to bring the Golden Rule [Do unto others as you would have done unto you] into the international affairs of the world."[28] Byrnes, more disheartened than the president, believed it imperative that the Americans and the British go to Moscow to repair the damage done in London. This time, the Soviets appeared more accommodating, accepting, for example, the suggestion that France be asked to join in the discussion of the peace treaties. A new date, in April 1946, was set for the next meeting of the full Council of Foreign Ministers, and Byrnes decided to ask James B. Conant, president of Harvard, so instrumental in fashioning the atom bomb, to accompany him to Moscow. Many American scientists, persuaded the United States would not retain its atomic monopoly for long, had communicated those concerns to Henry Stimson, and he had made the president aware very early that the creation of a system of national and international control was vital.[29] Truman, in his *Memoirs,* distinguished between what Byrnes told him at the time and what he had learned from Stimson, saying: "Byrnes had already told me that the weapon might be so powerful as to be potentially capable of wiping out entire cities and killing people on an unprecedented scale," adding that "the bomb might well put us in a position to dictate our own terms at the end of the war." Stimson, he wrote, "seemed at least as much concerned with the role of the atomic bomb in the shaping of history as in the capacity to shorten the war."[30] Byrnes had clearly misconstrued the probable effects of the bomb on Soviet behavior, and his anxiety to achieve some kind of understanding explained his determination to hold a hastily prepared Moscow meeting.

By inviting Conant to be part of the U.S. delegation, Byrnes hoped to demonstrate his concern that the control of nuclear weapons figure on the agenda. Not everyone in Washington welcomed Conant's participation; Senator Arthur Vandenberg, for example, feared that Conant's presence meant that the secretary of state intended to share atomic information with the Soviets, in his book a cardinal offense. Why, he asked, were college professors being recruited for so delicate a mission?[31] Vandenberg, soon to be feted as the leading Republican internationalist, scarcely knew Conant and had no idea that his suspicions of the Soviet Union exceeded even those of the secretary of state. Conant, wary of the Communists but persuaded that serious negotiations needed to be started, went along because he hoped the subject would finally receive the serious discussion it merited. Molotov, as in London, seemed little preoccupied with the issue but agreed to the creation of an atomic energy commission under the United Nations, along the lines suggested by the Americans, the British, and the Canadians a month earlier. The Moscow meeting produced what they imagined was a decisive breakthrough.[32] Yet Conant, speaking with Byrnes on Christmas Eve, left a memorandum of their conversation, unpublished at the time, that showed substantial disquiet with the secretary of state's policies. In a note to himself, Conant expressed the fear that Byrnes was "motivated more by ambition and public relations than by a genuine belief that progress with Moscow on the atomic bomb was either possible or even desirable."[33] Others, harboring similar misgivings about Byrnes, worried over what they interpreted as his overweening personal ambition, and the White House took offense with his failure to keep the president more fully informed about the Moscow talks. Indeed, the most important result of the Moscow meeting may have been the president's despleasure with his secretary of state.

Dean Acheson, undersecretary of state, saw that as its principal result.[34] Press and radio summaries of the conference, issued before the White House or the State Department received the full text of the final communiqué, caused Truman to be greatly annoyed. Disappointed that no progress had been made in settling any of the outstanding Balkan issues, the president expressed his fury that the secretary had cabled Acheson to arrange radio time for him on the evening of his arrival home to allow him to tell the nation about the Moscow meeting. He ordered the secretary to come at once to the presidential yacht, *Williamsburg,* and to schedule his talk for the following evening. The two left very different accounts of that fateful encounter; if Byrnes believed his own, he failed to understand that he had forfeited the president's confidence, that his days as secretary were numbered.[35] Writing of the report Byrnes submitted to him after his return from the Soviet Union, Truman said that the "message told him very little that the newspaper correspondents had not already reported from Moscow. . . . This was not what I considered a proper account by a Cabinet member to the President. It was more like a partner in a business telling the other not to worry."[36] When the final communiqué reached him, he became even more dissatisfied, writing: "I did not like what I read. There was not a word about Iran or any other place where the Soviets were on the march. We had gained only an empty promise of further talks."[37]

Truman published the full text of the letter he read aloud to Byrnes when he visited him in the Oval Office on January 5, repeating the criticism he had already made of how the secretary arrogated power to himself in Moscow, failing to keep the president fully informed. Now that he had read the documents left by Byrnes on his visit to the presidential yacht, he grew even more concerned. Truman told Byrnes he had no intention of recognizing the governments of Rumania and Bulgaria unless they were radically changed. As for the Soviet activities in Iran, he termed them an "outrage," given all that Iran had done during the war to allow the transit of goods from the Persian Gulf to the Caspian Sea. "Without these supplies furnished by the United States, Russia would have been ignominiously defeated," Truman said in the memo he read to Byrnes. "Yet now," he continued, "Russia stirs up rebellion and keeps troops on the soil of her friend and ally—Iran." Continuing in this vein, the president told the secretary, "There isn't a doubt in my mind that Russia intends an invasion of Turkey and the seizure of the Black Sea Straits to the Mediterranean. Unless Russia is faced with an iron fist and strong language another war is in the making. Only one language do they understand—how many divisions have you?"[38]

What, then, did he recommend?

I do not think we should play compromise any longer. We should refuse to recognize Rumania and Bulgaria until they comply with our requirements; we should let our position on Iran be known in no uncertain terms. . . and we should maintain complete control of Japan and the Pacific. We should rehabilitate China and create a strong government there. We should do the same for Korea. Then we should insist on the return of our ships from Russia and force a settlement of the lend-lease debts of Russia. I am tired of babying the Soviets.[39]

Byrnes later claimed no such letter was read to him; had such a dressing-down occurred, he would have resigned at once. Truman, in his own hand, wrote on the draft: "Read to the Sec. of State and discussed—not typed or mailed." Either the president or the secretary of state was lying. Truman, in his

Memoirs, suggested that Byrnes accepted the situation and agreed to stay on until the peace treaties stimulated by the Moscow negotiations were finally settled. Truman added:

> Throughout the remainder of 1946, however, it was understood between him and me that he would quit when I could designate his successor. I knew all the time whom I wanted for the job. It was General Marshall. But the general was on a vital assignment in China that had to run its course before the change in the State Department could be carried out.[40]

A quarrel of this dimension with his principal Cabinet colleague was of course important, but two others in 1946 that led to the resignation of the last of the Roosevelt appointees were even more telling for what they said about Truman's character. Ickes, Roosevelt's secretary of the interior from the beginning, resigned in February 1946, following his attack on Ed Pauley, Truman's nominee to be assistant secretary of the Navy. In Senate testimony on that nomination, Ickes claimed that Pauley had once promised to raise several hundred thousand dollars for the Democratic Party in California if the federal government abandoned its plan to have the tideland oil deposits brought into the federal domain. This was a serious charge, and the president, speaking to the press, suggested Ickes had been mistaken in what he had said. Ickes, furious with the president, who in effect had called him a liar, responded with a letter of resignation that Truman termed "not courteous."[41] Ickes told the president he would announce his resignation in six weeks; Truman responded that he accepted it, to take effect the next day.[42]

Ickes, like Morgenthau—a man he detested—did not know Truman; threats of resignation never frightened him. With Henry Wallace, the president was more patient. Truman knew that his secretary of commerce enjoyed considerable popularity with those who believed as he did that the president and the secretary of state were excessively hostile to the Soviet Union, so recently the country's trusted ally. When Wallace spoke truthfully but embarrassingly of the military advocating a "preventive war," and many at home and abroad believed him, Truman knew the time had come for him to go. Unlike Ickes, Wallace went quietly, continuing, however, to criticize the president for what he believed were his mistaken foreign policies. Truman had no difficulty in finding a successor to Wallace. Averell Harriman, the ambassador to the Soviet Union and once an erstwhile friend of Stalin's, seemed more than ready to return to Washington to replace Wallace as secretary of commerce.[43]

When one considers all these events, especially those relating to Byrnes, one question becomes paramount. How is one to explain Truman's vociferous anti-Soviet sentiments and his fears of new Communist aggressions, expressed as early as January 1946? Who led him to believe these things even before Stalin delivered his incendiary speech of February 9, 1946, in which he spoke of World War II having had its origins in a capitalist-imperialist monopoly that retained all its old influence? Because these forces were still so potent, the Soviet leader indicated that no new peaceful international order was possible. The Soviet Union had to be ready for any eventuality, and national defense would be its first priority. Stalin called for iron and steel production to be trebled, coal and oil production to be doubled, telling his Communist audience that civilian demands would also be satisfied, but at a later date.[44]

This speech gave George Kennan, then in the U.S. embassy in Moscow, one more reason to write his famous Long Telegram that circulated widely in Washington, urging the United States to prepare for a long struggle with the Soviet Union, in which the Communists would use every means to infiltrate, divide, and weaken the West.[45] In many traditional accounts of how Truman came to formulate the policies that initiated the Cold War, Kennan's Long Telegram figured prominently. It circulated in manuscript and was certainly read by Truman before he accompanied Churchill to Fulton, Missouri, where Churchill delivered his famous Iron Curtain Speech on March 5, 1946.[46] It is significant in this connection that Margaret Truman vociferously denied that Kennan's telegram, published as an essay anonymously (as the mysterious "X") in *Foreign Affairs* in July 1947, "profoundly shaped the thinking of the Truman administration." In her words, "I can say without qualification that such an assertion is nonsense."[47] Her father, she claimed, understood the Soviet Union long before he received instruction from Kennan; others in the White House, she claimed, would confirm this.[48]

On the Churchill address at Fulton, equally adamant, she quoted from a letter her father sent his wife and sister, saying that ". . . I think it did some good, although I am not yet ready to endorse Mr. Churchill's speech." Her own gloss on the speech included the words: "My father in no sense considered the speech a break with Russia, nor did he want one. In fact, he later invited Marshal Stalin to come to Missouri and deliver a speech, stating Russia's point of view on the various disputes that were imperilling the peace."[49] How is one to explain Margaret Truman's defensiveness? The answer, very simply, is that Churchill's speech provoked such a hostile reaction in some quarters in the United States that the president thought it expedient to disassociate himself from it. His daughter simply recorded opinions she heard him express. The president, perhaps dismayed by the adverse reaction to Churchill's speech, believed it impossible to approve of it in the way others, including Acheson, Harriman, and Leahy, did. To do so would be to run an unacceptable political risk.

Truman had learned from Roosevelt to be careful, not to proclaim policies that might provoke dissent in important sectors of public opinion. The Soviet Union, by the sacrifices of its people through four long years of war, had gained a reputation in the United States that no president, however irked by Stalin's words or actions, could safely ignore. Patience with the Communist regime in Moscow seemed the only reasonable policy. Though Margaret Truman, always the loyal daughter, argued as if her father's problems were caused principally by men like Senator Claude Pepper, who condemned Churchill's speech and warned against the United States becoming "a guarantor of British imperialism," this argument, frequently used during the war, did not explain Truman's hesitations. Though hostile to Pepper's plea for the United States to "destroy every atomic bomb which we have" to demonstrate the country's goodwill, Truman understood the importance of moving slowly in any overt public condemnation of the Soviet Union. The country was simply not ready for any open repudiation of its wartime ally, and the president knew better than to attempt to take foreign policy initiatives likely to create additional turmoil.[50]

Indeed, the president's political honeymoon, so conspicuous in April 1945 at the moment of Roosevelt's death, was virtually over by December of that year. The strike by the United Auto Workers against General Motors just before Christmas had ushered in a period of growing labor agitation. Workers, complaining of inadequate wages and failing to secure a sympathetic hearing from management for the increases they thought the continued inflation justified, followed their leaders' injunctions to join the picket lines. The year 1946, the first full year of Truman's presidency, saw some 4.6 million workers strike in many of the country's basic industries, including oil refining, steel, meatpacking, and electrical appliances. Almost one in every sixteen workers went out on strike during that fateful year.[51] When further strikes were threatened in the coal mines and on the railways, Truman asked Congress for legislation to allow the federal government to draft strikers into the military whenever their action threatened to create a national emergency. This unprecedented presidential initiative caused the railway strike to be called off, and much later in the year, after the off-year congressional elections, so disastrous to the Democratic Party, John L. Lewis, the miners' leader, capitulated to a federal judge who fined the union $3.5 million and Lewis personally $10,000. The president, victorious over the man he habitually referred to as a "racketeer" and a "son of a bitch," paid a heavy political price for his success, offending the trade unions, something his predecessor never thought to do.[52]

Less than two years after coming into the White House, Truman appeared to have lost a great deal of the trade union support that Roosevelt had so jealously nurtured and hoarded. No less ominously, the simple man from Missouri, once the admired president, now derided as a mama's boy surrounded by cronies, saw his popularity plunge to a low of 32 percent in public opinion polls. How to explain this mass disillusion? Why, indeed, did the Republican Party's 1946 congressional election slogan—"Had enough?"—seem so immensely attractive? Two conditions—inflation and continued shortages of basic consumer commodities—contributed to the president's problems, and while Sam Ray-

burn, the Speaker of the House, may have exaggerated when he prophesied a
"beefsteak election" that would allow citizens to show their contempt for an administration that had retained price controls, resulting in meat shortages, this
proved to be a relatively minor note in a Republican campaign that emphasized
other presidential delinquencies, including Truman's Pendergast past. Senator
Robert Taft, soon to become Senate Majority Leader, called his foreign policy
"futile and contradictory"; it had made the United States "the laughing stock of
the world."[53] A young Republican unknown, Richard Nixon, looking for a seat
in Congress, hit out at men in high places "who front for un-American elements, wittingly or otherwise." The Red Scare, so prominent in the last years
of the Wilson administration, surfaced again, this time more seriously, and the
president was caricatured as a "Bolshie appeaser."[54]

Why did Truman find it so difficult to refute these allegations, and why did
he fail so abysmally in his efforts to prove he was not soft on the Soviets? The
answer, in a word, is that he was sidelined, with his best friends, including Bob
Hannegan, who had helped secure the vice presidential nomination for him,
recommending that he not venture out on the campaign trail. Public opinion
polls confirmed the view that campaign appearances by the president on behalf
of Democrats seeking to retain their House or Senate seats would only hurt
them. When, in September, he announced that he had asked the British to
admit 100,000 Jewish refugees into Palestine, Thomas Dewey, New York's Republican gubernatorial candidate, dismissed the proposal contemptuously, saying it was politically inspired; he promised to work for a more generous admis-
sions policy.[55] The end of meat rationing, announced by the president in
October, received equal disdain, treated as a political gimmick.[56]

Democrats acted as if he no longer existed, and few were surprised when the
election results were announced. The Democrats suffered catastrophic defeats:
Both the House and the Senate, for the first time since before the Depression,
were again firmly in Republican Party control. In the House the Republican
majority was 246–188, in the Senate 55–41, and it was impossible to pretend
that this was simply the traditional off-year results for the party in the White
House. Many newspapers heralded the Republican victory as a repudiation of
the president and a final defeat of the New Deal. If the *Chicago Tribune* called
it the greatest victory for the country since Appomattox, the surrender of General Robert E. Lee to General Ulysses Grant that ended the Civil War, the president found more wounding the opinion preferred by William Fulbright, a
young Democratic congressman from Arkansas who recommended that he appoint Senator Arthur Vandenberg secretary of state and then resign, making
Vandenberg the new president.[57] (By the succession legislation then in effect,
in the absence of a vice president, the presidential office, following the death or
resignation of the incumbent, would pass to the secretary of state, the head of
the most senior department.) Truman, rightly offended, from that moment re-

ferred to Fulbright as "Halfbright," an epithet revived decades later to describe Madeleine Albright, Clinton's secretary of state.[58]

Truman's feelings about the 1946 Democratic debacle were nowhere revealed in his *Memoirs*; no mention was made of the election that more than any other single event created opportunities he exploited, making the last two years of his first term the most innovative in foreign policy in his almost eight years in the Oval Office. The large Republican majorities in the Eightieth Congress, dubbed the Do-Nothing Congress by Truman, gave him an advantage he used to good effect in his remarkable reelection campaign in 1948.

Before November 1946, Truman had to prove himself something other than a political usurper, a president faithful to all that Roosevelt had stood for. After the Democrats no longer controlled Congress, when Truman was finally free to be himself, when no one thought he could be elected to a second term, he showed his true mettle. Though Republicans had disparaged him throughout the off-year election campaign, he appeared not at all downcast when he delivered his State of the Union speech on January 6, 1947, telling Congress truths that had figured too little in the election campaign: Unemployment had virtually ceased to exist; national income was at an all-time peacetime high.[59] Now on the offensive, Truman spoke of the need to improve labor-management relations, to create a national health insurance program to provide child care and mental health benefits, and to encourage new hospital construction. Arguing for a "fair level of return" for farmers and help to veterans, constituencies he never neglected, he advocated an "aggressive" program to remedy the acute housing shortages in the country, to make good the losses suffered during the years of Depression and World War II.

Civil rights figured in Truman's speech in a way it never did in Roosevelt's time. Franklin, like Theodore, knew better than to tangle with influential elements in his party. If the first Roosevelt avoided the tariff issue, the second showed himself equally circumspect in respect to civil rights, all too aware of the influence of Southern Democratic senators and representatives, chairmen of powerful committees, whose opinions on that most sensitive subject could never be safely ignored. David McCullough noted that Truman's speech carried no mention of Franklin Roosevelt.[60] Truman, liberated at last, free as both the first Roosevelt and Coolidge were, as a later accidental president, Lyndon Johnson, could never be, used his freedom to announce the following evening that Byrnes had resigned as secretary of state, that General George C. Marshall would succeed him, and that the general was already on his way home from China.

From January 1947 to November 1948, in many ways Truman's golden age, as distinctive as 1940 to 1942 for Roosevelt, the president collaborated closely with his secretary of state to achieve objectives that gave the country a new international standing. If Roosevelt's most striking foreign policy innovations were made immediately before and after his success in winning a third presidential term, Truman's were fashioned in the years following the most serious Democratic Party congressional defeats at the polls in decades. The Truman foreign policy innovations showed a new appreciation of both the strengths and the weaknesses of the United Kingdom, America's principal ally, to whom too little attention had been awarded by Roosevelt in his last years in office and Truman in his first. The abrupt cancellation of Lend-Lease on August 17, 1945, for example, which both surprised and offended the British, forced the president to use rather lame arguments in a press conference to defend his position, claiming that Lend-Lease was a "weapon of war, and after we ceased to be at war it is no longer necessary." Somewhat defensively, he added: "I happened to be Vice-President at the time the law was extended, and I made such a promise. I am merely living up to the promise I made as Vice-President of the United States."[61] Truman's later defense of the $3.75 billion loan to the United Kingdom, negotiated by John Maynard Keynes and Lord Halifax, the British ambassador, as given in his *Memoirs,* proved equally lame. He wrote: "At the close of the Anglo-American financial talks there was some misgiving expressed on both sides of the Atlantic. There was criticism that the loan was insufficient and criticism that it was extravagant, and Uncle Sam was cartooned both as Santa Claus and as Shylock."[62]

Truman signed the legislation to effect the loan on July 15, 1946, blissfully unaware of how Britain's chief negotiator viewed his experience in negotiating the loan. Keynes had written his mother: "They [the Americans] mean us no harm—but their minds are so small, their prospects so restricted, their knowledge so inadequate, their obstinacy so boundless and their legal pedantries so infuriating. May it never fall to my lot to have to *persuade* anyone what I want, with so few cards in my hand."[63] British-American relations continued to be uneasy through early 1947, with neither side choosing to reveal the extent of its disenchantment with the other. No books comparable to what Keynes wrote about Wilson in *The Economic Consequences of the Peace* appeared; indeed, Truman remained relatively immune to British criticism, but the British ambassador, Lord Halifax, understood the situation perfectly when he said: "Because since 1939 we have had to seek and accept American assistance, and because lately we have seemed to be pleading poverty, the Americans have gotten too much into the habit of regarding us as weak."[64]

That weakness seemed more apparent on February 3, 1947, when the British announced they were withdrawing half their depleted military force in Greece, already reduced from 80,000 to 16,000 men, with the Labour government recognizing that it could no longer maintain even that level of military involvement. The chancellor of the exchequer, knowing the precariousness of the country's finances, believed further cuts would have to be made, and Ernest Bevin, the foreign secretary, agreed, reluctantly, that an appeal should be made to the United States to assume responsibility for defending Greece and

Turkey.[65] Great Britain, the Americans were informed, would be unable to provided military or civilian assistance to either beyond March 31.

The Truman administration, shocked by this unexpected disclosure, had scarcely six weeks to prepare a policy to win congressional support for a commitment that had no precedent. Given that the United Kingdom had already indicated its intention to make other military withdrawals from India, Burma, and the Middle East, the Americans realized they were confronted with a challenge to assume burdens they imagined the British would never willingly abdicate. Would Congress approve such intervention, making the large appropriations that would prove necessary? No less seriously, would the American public accept such a vastly expanded commitment? Both the president and the State Department recognized the seriousness of the situation, and Undersecretary of State Dean Acheson told the Cabinet on March 7, "If we go in we cannot be certain of success in the Middle East and Mediterranean. If we do not go in there will be a collapse in these areas."[66]

Because Congress was disinclined to approve any intervention unless the argument could be made that a Communist threat existed, Truman included that danger as an integral part of the message he delivered to a joint session of Congress on March 12, 1947. In asking for a $400 million appropriation to help Greece and Turkey, proclaiming what became known as the Truman Doctrine, he said:

> At the present moment in world history nearly every nation must choose between alternative ways of life. The choice is too often not a free one. One way of life is based upon the will of the majority. . . . The second . . . is based upon the will of a minority forcibly imposed upon the majority. It relies upon terror and oppression; a controlled press and radio; fixed elections and the suppression of personal freedom.[67]

What, then, did the president propose? In words that could admit of only a single meaning, he said: "I believe it must be the policy of the U.S. to support free people who are resisting attempted subjection by armed minorities or by outside pressure. I believe that we must assist free peoples to work out their own destinies in their own way."[68]

Congress reacted warmly to what it heard, and a good part of the press seemed persuaded by the argument. Walter Lippmann approved of the proposal to help Greece but disapproved of what he feared the policy portended. In his view, this was a "vague global policy which sounds like the tocsin of an ideological crusade," and he worried it would not be controlled; its effects could not be predicted.[69] Others, including conservative and liberal senators, fretted about the costs of the proposal, as well as about its effect on any hopes for an early reconciliation with the Soviet Union. Still, when the Senate voted on the bill, it approved the measure overwhelmingly, 67–23; the House major ity was equally convincing, 287–107. The president's priceless asset was his ability to meet and defeat Robert Taft, the Majority Leader, on foreign policy issues, enjoying the same success when he secured the appointment of David Lilienthal to be the new head of the Atomic Energy Commission, against those, including Taft, who charged Lilienthal with being a Communist.[70]

The Communist issue had figured prominently in the 1946 congressional elections, and there had been much talk of disloyalty in high federal offices. The president, believing there was little truth in these accusations, realized they would not be silenced as long as congressmen and others saw political advantage in pressing that argument. This led him, reluctantly, to issue Executive Order No. 9835, which established the Federal Employees Loyalty and Security Program.[71] Again, there was no precedent for such an action in peacetime, and Truman approved the measure, with all that it implied for loyalty checks and the like, only because he knew that resistance would make him politically vulnerable in 1948.

The Republicans seized on an issue he knew they would not soon abandon. The president, to prove his own serious commitment to rooting out espionage, chose to issue an order that sanctioned FBI investigations, legitimating the dismissal of those thought to be disloyal. Whatever the president's misgivings about the order, he felt compelled to issue it. Still, it suggested—to those searching for new evidences of American hostility to both the Soviet Union and communism—the president's growing aggressiveness, never previously demonstrated so openly. In fact, the incentives to issue Executive Order No. 9835 were very different from those that now led the president to undertake foreign policy initiatives that made him seem more determined than ever to challenge the Soviet Union, to make certain its aggressions in Europe would not continue. General Marshall, Truman's recently appointed secretary of state, attending his first meeting of the four foreign ministers, those of the United States, the United Kingdom, France, and the Soviet Union in Moscow in March 1947, expressed the hope that Germany, still occupied and divided into four zones, would be treated as an economic entity and that the ministers would resist any policies that contributed to a divided Germany and a divided Europe. When he visited with Stalin on April 15, at a time when the conference appeared stalemated, the secretary, with his habitual candor, explained why he believed relations with the United States had deteriorated, how Soviet policies were contributing to new doubts about Soviet intentions.

In Marshall's view, the Soviet Union did not appear at all interested in negotiating a treaty for a united and disarmed Germany, and he intended to communicate that message to the president. Going beyond the specifics of the conference, Marshall made clear that while Americans accepted that individual states should be free to choose the political and economic system they wished to live under, the United States intended to offer assistance to all democracies threatened with economic collapse, believing such aid would serve to stabilize their governments. Stalin listened to Marshall and in response spoke of the differences being only "the first skirmishes and brushes of reconnaissance forces" that would eventually lead to compromise. Patience was required.[72]

Marshall, in reporting to the American people on the Moscow meeting, quoted Stalin's remarks but added:

> I sincerely hope that the Generalissimo is correct in the view he expressed and that it implies a greater spirit of co-operation by the Soviet Delegation in future conferences. But we cannot ignore the factor of time. . . . The recovery of Europe has been far slower than had been expected. Disintegrating forces are becoming evident. The patient is sinking while the doctors deliberate. So I believe that action cannot wait compromise through exhaustion. New issues arise daily. Whatever action is possible to meet these pressing problems must be taken without delay.

The plight of Germany was extreme, and Marshall, conferring with Bevin in Moscow, knew that some plan for a general European recovery had to be worked out. The first general outlines of such a plan were made by Marshall at the Harvard Commencement on June 5. The Marshall proposals for substantially increased aid to the democracies of Europe had been anticipated by others in the administration, including Will Clayton and Dean Acheson, but it was the secretary's speech that galvanized the British foreign secretary into action, allowing Bevin to see the possibilities raised by one sentence in Marshall's Harvard address, which read: "The initiative, I think must come from Europe."[73] Almost a year later, speaking at the National Press Club in Washington, Bevin said,

> . . . it was like a lifeline to sinking men. It seemed to bring hope where there was none. The generosity of it was beyond our belief. It expressed a mutual thing. It was 'Try and help yourselves and we will see what we can do. Try and do the thing collectively, and we will see what we can put into the pool.' I think you understand why, therefore, we responded with such alacrity and why we grabbed the lifeline with both hands.[74]

The single most important sentence in the Harvard speech, perhaps, read:

> our policy is directed not against any country or doctrine, but against hunger, poverty, desperation and chaos. Its purpose should be the revival of a working economy in the world so as to permit the emergence of political and social conditions in which free institutions can exist.[75]

The president and the secretary of state recognized the importance of not excluding the Soviet Union from participating in the plan, but both knew from the two principal Soviet experts in the State Department, George Kennan and Charles Bohlen, that they did not expect Stalin to accept the offer.[76] They were proved right, of course, and both Truman and Marshall felt relieved that the Soviets did not choose to join in what came to be known as the European Recovery Program, calculated to help the democracies of Western Europe.

Congress was asked to approve appropriations that eventually amounted to $17 billion, and Vandenberg again had the greatest role in persuading Republicans in the Senate to vote for these large appropriations in April 1948, almost a year after the Marshall Plan was originally proposed. Truman exulted in his victory, always giving much of the credit to Marshall, who toured the country, seeking wide public support for the measure. Truman, ecstatic with his success, wrote in a private note,

> In all the history of the world, we are the first great nation to feed and support the conquered. We are the first great nation to create independent republics from conquered territory, Cuba and the Philippines. Our neighbors are not afraid of us. Their borders have no forts, no soldiers, no tanks, no guns lined up.[77]

Despite the hyperbole, Truman had reason to be gleeful, even if the true significance of the Marshall Plan could never be acknowledged. Until the summer of 1947, the Soviet Union had never been checked. Many, both in the Communist world and in the West, took for granted that the Soviet successes in Eastern Europe would soon be followed by equal victories in the West, where economic distress threatened even the most stable of governments. This did not happen principally because the Marshall Plan gave hope where none had existed previously. Western Europe began to recover, and Stalin's reaction—to impose even stricter command of the Communist Parties that controlled the governments established by the Soviets in Eastern Europe—made the Iron Curtain a reality in a way it had not been when Churchill delivered his initial warning in Fulton.[78] Indeed, Stalin's response to the events of 1948 led him to engage in kinds of brinkmanship he had not previously attempted.

Beginning in March 1948, the Soviets blocked Allied road access to Berlin, claiming the interruptions were caused by the need to repair the highway. General Lucius Clay, in Berlin, reporting to Washington, described "a new tenseness in every Soviet official with whom we have official relations" and expressed the fear that war could come "with dramatic suddenness."[79] The blockade continued through the spring, and by June the Western sectors' food supply was down to thirty-six days, and its coal supply to forty-five days. Clearly, only an airlift could relieve the city, but Clay estimated that the combined Allied air forces could only supply some 700 tons per day compared with the 4,000 tons needed.

The prudent course seemed to be for the Allies to withdraw from the city, but neither Clay nor Bevin believed this to be the solution; the Soviets, in their view, were testing the Allies, and they would do well to remain firm. When the Western Allies on June 18 announced a new currency in the three western zones of Germany, a reform under discussion for two years, the Soviets responded four days later with the announcement that only east zone currency would be acceptable in all sectors of Berlin. In the days that followed, all rail and road links between Berlin and the West were cut, and the supply of electricity to the western sectors from the eastern sector and the east zone were terminated. On June 26, a very modest airlift was inaugurated, and two days later Truman ordered a full-scale airlift. That same day, he sent two squadrons of B-29s to Germany, the same aircraft used in dropping the atom bombs on Japan.[80]

By September, at the start of the 1948 presidential campaign, Truman having won renomination, Bevin informed the House of Commons that some 200,000 tons of supplies had been airlifted to Berlin, 60 percent by the Americans, 40 percent by the Royal Air Force. Both had come to believe that the Soviet intention was to seal off the east zone of Germany, end the four-power occupation of Berlin, and make the city the capital of a new Communist-controlled German state. Whether the Allied airlift could prevent this was by no means certain, but with the Americans introducing their C-54s, capable of carrying four times the load of the B-29s, Bevin believed Berlin would have all the supplies it required through the winter.[81] Truman never underestimated the gravity of the situation but chose not to exploit it for his own political advantage. As he explained in a letter to Churchill, written in early July,

> We are in the midst of grave and trying times. You can look with satisfaction upon your great contribution to the overthrow of Nazism and Fascism in the world. 'Communism'—so called—is our next great problem. I hope we can solve it without the 'blood and tears' the other two cost.[82]

Truman, in the two crucial years, 1947 and 1948, demonstrated a remarkable capacity to innovate in the area of foreign policy. His accomplishments reflected the successful synergy that developed between him and his secretary of state, helped also by the active collaboration of Britain's foreign secretary, Ernest Bevin.[83] In one crucial negotiation, however, involving the recognition of the state of Israel, Truman traveled a road that isolated him from both, as well as from many in the State Department, and from James Forrestal, his secretary of defense.[84] On no other foreign policy issue did he experience greater pressure; on no other did he receive some 100,000 letters and telegrams when the United Nations debated the issue and voted for partition by a narrow margin, a result accomplished in great part by the pressure exerted by the United States delegation. Bevin greatly resented Truman's interference and ordered the

British delegation to abstain from the vote. In the House of Commons debate that followed the United Nations decision, Bevin said quite simply:

> I think that the Arab feeling in this question has been underestimated. It has got to be assessed at its correct value by everybody, or we shall not get a peaceful settlement. It is because I want it assessed at its proper value that I do not want the Arabs to be dismissed as if they were nobody.[85]

Comparable opinion existed in the United States, though it was more politically dangerous to voice it. Truman, receiving information from his newly created Central Intelligence Agency that partition would not work, and that the whole plan ought to be reconsidered, heard the same thing from his secretary of state. Marshall believed the United States was "playing with fire while having nothing with which to put it out." Sensitive to the need for Middle East oil supplies should there be a war in Europe, Marshall saw the danger of offending the Arabs. As rumors circulated of growing opposition to the partition plan, Warren Austin, the U.S. ambassador to the United Nations, announced before the UN General Assembly on March 19, 1948, that the United States recommended abandoning the partition plan and substituting for it a temporary UN trusteeship over Palestine. The president, abused in the press and in Congress, represented as having sold out to the enemies of the Jews—oil being his sole interest—was dismayed.[86] The *New York Times* joined other prominent newspapers in disparaging the administration for its sudden and inexplicable reversal, saying: "A land of milk and honey now flows with oil, and the homeland of three great spiritual religions is having its fate decided by expediency without a sign of the spiritual and ethical considerations which should be determining in that part of the world."[87]

Truman, furious, believed that individuals in the State Department hostile to the establishment of an Israeli state had sabotaged him, and he fumbled to explain the inexplicable. On his calendar, he wrote: "This morning I find that the State Department has reversed my Palestine policy. The first I know about it is what I see in the papers! Isn't that hell? I am now in the position of a liar and a double-crosser. I've never felt so in my life."[88] In the final days before the British were scheduled to leave Palestine, debate raged in the administration about whether or not to recognize the new state of Israel immediately after the British departure. Clark Clifford, a successful lawyer who had recently joined the White House staff, argued vigorously for recognition, claiming that any postponement, as recommended by the State Department, would not be tolerated by the Jews, clearly referring to the Jewish vote at home. A Jewish state was inevitable, and the United States had every reason to accept it.[89] Marshall, responding to Clifford, refused to accept his reasoning. In one of his few major differences with the president, he indicated that domestic political considerations ought never to govern foreign policy decisions. If the president followed Clifford's advice and recognized the state of Israel immediately, he would himself feel obliged to vote against the president in November.[90] Truman's associates, the few who knew of these White House discussions, realized how serious any breach between the president and his secretary of state would be and, fearing that Marshall might resign his post, worked to persuade him not to make his differences with the president public. Marshall, always loyal, agreed in the end and phoned Truman to say that though he did not approve of immediate recognition he would not make his views known in public.[91] Truman was now free to do what he had long intended; he offered de facto recognition on May 14, the day the new state of Israel was proclaimed in Jerusalem. Many in the State Department expressed outrage; others abroad were dumbfounded. But Truman achieved what he had long considered just. His decision helped him also achieve what had once seemed unlikely: his reelection.

The Truman Doctrine, the Marshall Plan, the beginning of the Berlin airlift, and de facto recognition of Israel, independently of any other foreign policy action, would have established Truman as a major innovator in foreign policy, establishing precedents destined to have major consequences over many decades. However, his activities were never limited to such novel interventions. On February 26, 1947, a bill introduced into Congress that with amendments became law on July 26—the National Security Act—established the new Department of Defense, and a jubilant Truman wrote of it, "For the first time in the history of the nation an over-all military establishment was created."[92] Though the Army, Navy, and the more recently established Air Force retained their separate identities and their department secretaries, all were placed under the jurisdiction of a single Department of Defense. The act also created the National Security Council, which Truman viewed as "the place in the government where military, diplomatic, and resources problems could be studied and continually appraised." Finally, under NSC direction, the Central Intelligence Agency was established "for the purpose of coordinating the intelligence activities of the several government departments and agencies in the interest of national security." Years later, in retirement, Truman claimed that "I never had any thought when I set up the CIA that it would be injected into peacetime cloak and dagger operations."[93] The president, disingenuously, concealed his very early approval of covert action in Italy that allowed the Christian Democrats to defeat the Communists, retaining power there for more than a generation. NSC 1/1, the first numbered document of the National Security Council, citing the weakness of the Italian government and the threat posed by the Communist Party, recommended an "effective U.S. information program and by all other practicable means, including the use of unvouchered funds."[94] The CIA laundered some $10 million from captured Axis funds to help Alcide de Gasperi, the Christian Democratic prime minister, in his election campaign. In August 1948, before starting his transcontinental election campaign, Truman approved NSC 20, drafted by Kennan, that authorized guerrilla operations behind the Iron Curtain. While Kennan explained that "it is not our peacetime aim to overthrow the Soviet Government," he believed that covert action could help create "circumstances and situations" that would make it difficult for the "present Soviet leaders. . . to retain their power in Russia."[95] Truman, in these matters, exercised an authority no previous president had considered necessary in time of peace. Covert action had become a major option for presidents to consider.

Relying on bipartisan support for foreign policy initiatives that required the consent of Congress, the president enjoyed no comparable success with either the Senate or the House in respect to domestic legislation. There, Republican control proved absolute and was made more effective by the support offered by the more conservative Southern Democratic members. Truman's most serious defeat, certainly, came with the passage of the Taft-Hartley Act in 1947 that he tried unsuccessfully to veto.[96] The object of the bill, according to its proponents, was not to deny trade union rights but to limit trade union power, to protect the public against actions taken by large and powerful unions of the kind that had proved so disruptive in recent years. Its more fundamental purpose, scarcely concealed, was to weaken the rights guaranteed the trade unions by the National Labor Relations Act of 1935, the so-called Wagner Act. By the provisions of the new bill, secondary boycotts that allowed workers to boycott the goods of allegedly antilabor companies were declared illegal, and the president was given authority to call for an eighty-day cooling-off period before any strike that might affect the national interest was permitted; closed shops were specifically banned. Workers could no longer be compelled to join a union at the time they were hired, and states, encouraged by this provision, passed right-to-work laws that in effect blocked union shops.

While the trade unions protested vehemently against what they deemed an infringement of powers granted them by New Deal legislation, the bill received overwhelming congressional approval. Truman, though prepared to accept legislation "to prevent certain unjustifiable practices, such as jurisdictional strikes, secondary boycotts, and the use of economic force by either labor or management to decide issues arising out of existing contracts," felt that the Taft-Hartley legislation went too far. In his veto message, he spoke of the bill being "a clear threat to the successful working of our democratic society." His veto, quickly overridden, saw the Senate vote 68–25 in favor of the new restrictions, but his veto guaranteed him labor's support in the 1948 election.

Like the decision he made with respect to the early recognition of the state of Israel, Truman understood the political profit he was likely to realize, but it is difficult to prove conclusively that electoral considerations alone determined his policy. With both Israel and Taft-Hartley, Truman represented the issue as one of "justice." While he could not hope in the domestic sphere to overcome Republican and conservative Democratic Party opposition, losing out constantly to those prepared to undo much that Roosevelt had accomplished, in the foreign sphere he remained unchallenged; the decisions were his to make.[97]

Harry Truman, a proud man for all of his undeniable humility, had no wish to leave the White House as the accidental president unable to win a term on his own. When Henry Wallace announced in 1947 that he would seek the presidency, running as the candidate of the Progressive Citizens of America, Truman's foreign policy, including the Truman Doctrine and the Marshall Plan, became the principal object of his attacks.[98] By early 1948, public opinion polls suggested that Wallace would receive at least 6 percent of the vote, principally from individuals who had once voted overwhelmingly for Roosevelt. Truman risked an even more serious loss in the traditional South, where many considered him unreliable because of his advocacy of civil rights reforms.[99] A Democrat who favored federal intervention to alter race relations was unacceptable to someone like the governor of South Carolina, Strom Thurmond, who told Senator J. Howard McGrath, chairman of the Democratic National Committee, in February 1948 that the president's proposed civil rights laws "would be unconstitutional invasions of the field of government belonging to the states." Thurmond made it clear that if the president persisted in advocating controversial civil rights legislation he would be creating problems for the party, and his warning carried weight because the 56 percent approval rate Truman received for his presidential performance in October 1947 had dropped to 36 percent by the following April.

Prominent among the many prepared to dump the president was an anticommunist liberal organization, Americans for Democratic Action, formed in January 1947.[100] Leading Democrats, judging the president a sure loser and, interested only in supporting a winner, hoped to persuade war hero Dwight Eisenhower, the great World War II general, despite his disclaimer of any interest in competing for the presidency, to run as a Democrat. No one, in fact, knew where Eisenhower's political sympathies lay, but all knew him to be famous and charismatic, sufficient reason for a number of Democratic Party city bosses, Southerners, and liberals to argue for his nomination.[101]

In his 1948 State of the Union message, Truman had called for a major civil rights program that included federal protection of the right to vote, an end to public interstate transport regulations that segregated the races, the creation of a Fair Employment Practices Commission to prevent unfair employment discrimination, and the institution of federal laws to outlaw lynching.[102] Truman, aware of the political dangers created by his proposals, understood the need to be wary. Still, he accepted that his name—associated as much with these civil rights measures as with support for labor in its battle against Taft-Hartley and with Jews in their struggle to give early recognition to the state of Israel—

would stand him in good stead with blacks, trade unionists, and Jews. In several crucial states, he looked for their support to compensate for the losses expected from white Southerners, liberals who questioned his policies on the Soviet Union, and those who simply thought him a loser.[103] Hubert Humphrey's success in securing at the Democratic National Convention a civil rights plank more radical than any the president favored virtually guaranteed that Senator Thurmond would enter the race as an independent, which would certainly result in the loss of several Southern states.[104]

The president, once nominated, remained optimistic. In a speech that stirred the assembled delegates, its great surprise was his announcement that he would summon Congress into special session on July 26 to press for the passage of legislation that would halt rising prices, meet the housing crisis, and provide for federal aid to education, a national health program, and civil rights protection—all matters the Republican Party platform claimed to support. Truman proposed to test the terrible Eightieth Congress, a Congress the nation could not afford to see perpetuated.

Truman's reelection campaign seemed positively inspired. On the very day Congress reassembled, the president issued an executive order to end racial segregation in the armed forces.[105] That he saw the potential uses of this executive order in securing black votes cannot be doubted, but as his campaign progressed, other features of his strategy became more important. Truman spoke as if the whole of his predecessor's New Deal was in jeopardy; Taft-Hartley was simply a harbinger of what the Republicans intended to do to deny workers the rights they had come to enjoy. The Eightieth Congress became the president's political football. Thomas Dewey, his opponent, was made to appear ridiculous—a man of platitudes who refused to discuss real issues. Knowing that the Republicans were making much of the supposed infiltration of his administration and that of his predecessor by Communists, he denied the charge, claiming the Communists supported Wallace because they craved a Republican victory, hoping its "reactionary policies" would "lead to the confusion and strife on which communism thrives." Arguing that his foreign policies had checked the Communist tide, he saw no need to credit the Republicans with having helped him achieve those worthy objectives.[106] Dewey, believing in the public opinion polls, saw no need to refute Truman's charges; with some 65 percent of the nation's press supporting his candidacy, he could afford to be sanguine.

As the campaign progressed, neither Wallace nor Thurmond seemed to be seriously challenging the two principal candidates, but this did not alter the conventional opinion that this was a Republican year, that Dewey would be the next president. When the votes were counted, the country and many abroad were astonished to learn that the president had won with 24,105,812 popular votes against Dewey's 21,970,065; in the Electoral College, he had 303 votes against Dewey's 189.

How had this come to pass? While all agreed that the pollsters had failed, and that the president had been as effective a campaigner as anyone in the century, two other factors claimed attention. First, both Wallace and Thurmond performed less well than expected, splitting some 2.3 million votes almost equally. Wallace won in not a single state; his pro-Soviet speeches failed to move the nation. More impressive, certainly, was Truman's labor support; because of his Taft-Hartley veto, he emerged as the principal defender of the New Deal and retained his hold on that all-important constituency. While he did less well with Jewish voters than FDR, no one doubted that his support of Israel had given him votes he might not otherwise have claimed. So, also, with the black vote, both in the North and the South; as a civil rights advocate, he had generated immense enthusiasm. His farm support exceeded Roosevelt's; farmers in the Midwest recognized him as one of their own and knew they could rely on him to defend their interests. Dewey's personality helped him not at all: Stiff, cold, and complacent, he ran a campaign that never caught fire. Truman won the White House, and Democrats emerged victorious in Congress, an extraordinary reversal in party fortunes. In the Eighty-First Congress, the Democrats outnumbered the Republicans 263–171 in the House and 54–42 in the Senate.

Truman triumphed as the heir of Roosevelt, a staunch supporter of all that the New Deal had done to change the nation. Though he did not greatly emphasize the Roosevelt connection, mentioning his name only once in his acceptance speech at the Democratic National Convention, reminding delegates that labor had no better friend than Roosevelt, Republican "misrule and inaction" became the principal components of his message, as they were in 1932. Truman mocked the Eightieth Congress, the incarnation of everything the country associated with Republican reaction. When addressing the farmers of Iowa, he spoke of big corporations, Wall Street, reactionaries, privilege, and reaction much as Roosevelt did. "In this century," he said, "every great step forward has come during Democratic administrations of the National Government. Every movement backward has come under Republican auspices, and it is the people who have paid dearly for these reactionary moves."[107]

In populist rhetoric made familiar by a whole succession of presidents, Truman claimed that only the Democratic Party's success could guarantee peace and progress. Wisely choosing not to concentrate his attention on Henry Wallace, who offered himself as the peace candidate, Truman ignored the challenge set by him early in the campaign when Wallace had said:

The bigger the peace vote in 1948, the more definitely the world will know that the United States is not behind the bipartisan reactionary war policy which is dividing the world into two armed camps and making inevitable the day when American soldiers will be lying in their Arctic suits in the Russian snow.[108]

Nor did he think it necessary to refute Wallace when he said: "We are restoring western Europe and Germany through United States agencies rather than United Nations agencies because we want to hem Russia in. We are acting in the same way as France and England after the last war and the end result will be the same—confusion, depression, and war."[109] Truman acted as if Wallace did not exist, and showed no greater concern with Thurmond's challenge.[110]

Truman's inaugural was joyous, very different from the gray January day in 1945 when he was sworn in as vice president. Then, the president, obviously ailing, gave a brief and uninspired speech from the rear porch of the White House, helped to his feet by his son, revealing by the way he grasped the lectern and his general demeanor the infirmity that would take his life less than three months later.[111] The crowd was small; there was no inaugural parade; the country was at war, and the hoopla characteristic of other inaugurals was clearly out of place.

In 1949, Truman and the country celebrated in the traditional fashion what all knew to be a remarkable personal victory. Though the president had reason to be worried by foreign and domestic developments, none more serious perhaps than the rapid conquest of China by the Communists, led by Mao Tsetung, to which the corrupt Chiang Kai-shek regime had given most inadequate resistance, and, on a lesser plane, by the recent indictment of Alger Hiss for perjury, nothing in his inaugural address suggested that Chinese communism or American communism figured among his major concerns. At the Capitol, in the first televised inaugural ceremony, he spoke to the nation not of domestic matters but only of foreign policy. Though he made no specific mention of the Soviet Union, it was impossible to mistake his meaning when he said that "the actions resulting from the Communist philosophy are a threat to the efforts of the free nations to bring about world recovery and lasting peace."[112] He represented communism as a false doctrine, dependent on violence and deceit, never to be confused with democracy, the "vitalizing force" in the world.

He pledged continued loyalty to the United Nations and promised that the efforts to rehabilitate Europe through the Marshall Plan would continue. He spoke very generally of a new defense arrangement that would bring the North Atlantic democratic community together, pledged to a common defense, able to resist any threat to their security. The reference was vague but the intent was clear: The rationale for NATO had been broached. So, also, he called for a "bold new program" to make the benefits of American science and industry available to underdeveloped countries—the seed of what later became the Point Four Program. Clearly the president viewed the Marshall Plan as only the beginning of a more intensive American engagement abroad. Earlier in the month, addressing the new Congress in his State of the Union speech, he spoke of the Fair Deal he hoped to secure for the country, achieving the social benefits the Eightieth Congress had refused to accept.[113] Both by what he said at his inaugural but also in his address to Congress, Truman described policies he knew to be distinctive, that he hoped his newly appointed Cabinet would help him realize.

Marshall, his esteemed secretary of state, had indicated his firm desire to leave office, and Truman replaced him with Dean Acheson, a man he had come to admire. In the Defense Department the situation was less happy; Secretary of Defense James Forrestal, acting strangely, almost incoherent at times, had found it increasingly difficult to deal with the complex problems created by the union of the three military services. He clearly had to be replaced. The president, though not knowing the full seriousness of the secretary's mental condition, recognized the time had come for him to go and, in the most delicate manner, requested his resignation, choosing Louis Johnson to succeed him. That appointment would cause him great grief, but this was not obvious when he selected Johnson, a former assistant secretary of war, invaluable as a fundraiser in his election campaign. Because Tom Clark, his attorney general, had never been wholly satisfactory, Truman sought another place for him and appointed him a justice of the Supreme Court. In neither office did Clark show the ability Truman expected; indeed, he spoke of him years later as his "greatest mistake," in his words, a "dumb son of a bitch. . . about the dumbest man I think I've ever run across."[114] While he never said comparable things about Howard McGrath, whom he appointed in his place, a former chairman of the Democratic National Committee, he proved scarcely more able. In his last year in office, Truman fired McGrath for failing to do the cleanup job that he had asked for in the Bureau of Internal Revenue.[115] Truman's appointments were, with the single exception of Acheson, substantially less inspired than those he made in his first term.

That, however, was not apparent in the early months of his second administration, when he enjoyed the fruits of his surprising victory. The Soviet decision to end the blockade of Berlin on May 12 could only be viewed as a triumph for the president, and he exulted in it. Though the news from China was less encouraging, with the Communists crossing the Yangtze River and Chiang Kai-shek losing his last foothold in China, Truman did not immediately recognize the political hazards these developments posed for his administration. He believed a corrupt Nationalist (Kuomintang) regime had brought the catastrophe on itself and that nothing the United States could have done would have averted it. For him, the signing of the NATO Treaty in April 1949, and the recognition of the Federal Republic of Germany (West Germany) the following month, were supreme foreign policy accomplishments, an augury of even greater successes for Acheson in his new role as secretary of state.

Acheson, in his autobiography, *Present at the Creation,* suggested that three problems seemed paramount to him at the time: the defense of Europe and the rehabilitation of its economies; a peace treaty with Japan; and, less important, the situation in Southeast Asia.[116] When Truman asked Congress in July for $1.4 billion to sustain the NATO engagements it had accepted, Vandenberg and Taft, as well as other Republicans and a good number of Democratic senators, questioned the wisdom of making so large an appropriation for the infant organization.[117] More ominous, when Acheson issued his 1,000-page report on China at the end of July, complaints were heard about the administration's neglect of China and a too great cosseting of Europe. Indeed, in a private lunch in August, Secretary of Defense Johnson was reported to have said: "The UK was finished, and there was no sense in trying to bolster it up." In his words, "As the empire disintegrated we should write off the UK and continue cooperation with those parts of the Empire that remain useful to us." Acheson, committed to the Anglo-American "special relation," refused to be dismayed by these reports, but his difficulties with the secretary of defense became the subject of daily newspaper speculation. Clearly, Acheson did not enjoy the almost universal acclaim given to Marshall.[118] And then, on September 23, came the announcement that created new and seemingly insuperable problems for the administration. The president distributed a release to the White House press that contained the ominous words: "We have evidence that within recent weeks an atomic explosion occurred in the U.S.S.R."

Less than a year after his inaugural, Truman found himself in serious difficulty. Though there had been a general expectation that the Soviets would one day manufacture and detonate an atomic bomb, no one anticipated their success to come so early.[119] Indeed, an intelligence report, made available to the president in July 1948, spoke of mid-1950 as a possibility, adding, however, that "the most probable date is mid-1953."[120] Almost immediately after the Soviet achievement was known, discussions were opened at the Atomic Energy Commission looking to the creation of a thermonuclear or hydrogen weapon—a superbomb. On January 31, in a brief statement of 125 words that he never embellished till the end of his presidency, Truman announced that the United States would proceed with the development of a hydrogen bomb.[121] McGeorge Bundy, in his magisterial work *Danger and Survival: Choices About the Bomb in the First Fifty Years*, wrote:

Harry Truman's decision is second in importance only to Franklin Roosevelt's commitment of October 1941; it led straight on, with no second thought by the president, to the world's first full-scale thermonuclear explosion, on November 1, 1952. For the human race there was no turning back. The first Soviet device was tested less than a year later.[122]

Lest these observations be thought an acknowledgment by Bundy that Truman's action stimulated the Soviet response, he explicitly denied this. There was ample evidence that the Soviets were at work on their own hydrogen bomb before the president made his own decision to proceed, and Bundy recognized that both governments were equally responsible for what followed. Those who retained their admiration for Truman recognized his traditional decisiveness in his hydrogen bomb decision; those who derided him expressed shock by the Soviet communist atom bomb success, coming as it did on the heels of the announcement by Mao Tse-tung of the establishment of the People's Republic of China. The administration, since the unsuccessful Marshall mission to China, had feared this development, and Acheson wrote: "The unfortunate but inescapable fact is that the ominous result of the civil war in China was beyond the control of the... United States. . . . It was the product of internal Chinese forces which this country tried to influence but could not."[123]

Truman began his second term with a promise of a Fair Deal, a program of domestic legislation to equal what Roosevelt had achieved in the 1930s. These hopes were never wholly realized. The Hiss conviction, the Soviet atom bomb explosion, and the fall of China became a political mantra for Republicans, especially the previously obscure senator from Wisconsin, Joseph R. McCarthy, who spoke increasingly of America's decline, caused less by Soviet achievement than by the presence of Communist traitors within the Truman administration. This became McCarthy's principal message after February 1950 when he claimed to have "here in my hand" the names of 205 "known Communists" in the State Department. Within a month, he changed the number to 57 "card-carrying Communists," and on the Senate floor his count went up to 81.[124] The secretary of state became his principal target, but Truman was himself represented as the "prisoner of a bunch of twisted intellectuals." Truman's initial inclination—to dismiss McCarthy as a demagogue, not to be taken too seriously—was a mistake; it became impossible for him to argue this after 1950 as the McCarthy attacks became the daily fare of the mass media.

Even before the full blast of McCarthyism, the president ordered the secretary of state and the secretary of defense to conduct a "re-examination of our objectives in peace and war." A team, led by Paul Nitze, who had succeeded George Kennan as the head of the State Department's Policy Planning Staff, produced what became the single most important study produced by the National Security Council to that date. NSC 68, not yet declassified when Acheson wrote *Present at the Creation*, saw him acknowledge that while some liberals and Kremlinologists questioned the Nitze analysis, he himself never doubted its quality.[125] With the document now declassified, it is possible to see that it went considerably beyond what X published in *Foreign Affairs*. Alarmist in a way Kennan had never been, NSC 68 claimed that the Kremlin had a master plan "for the complete subversion or forcible destruction of the machinery of government and structure of society in the countries of the non-Soviet world and their replacement by an apparatus and structure subservient to and controlled from the Kremlin."[126]

The Nitze group, lacking accurate data on what Stalin's eventual intentions might be, chose an incendiary and exaggerated rhetoric to describe what it believed justified the vastly increased defense budget it recommended; in its words, "building up our military strength in order that it may not have to be used."[127] Whereas Kennan's recommendations on containment might be thought wholly defensive, NSC 68 posited a more aggressive stance to "induce a retraction of the Kremlin's power and influence and. . . foster the seeds of self-destruction within the Soviet system. . . ." How was this to be accomplished? In the words of NSC 68, through "operations by covert means in the fields of economic warfare.[128] The appeal of NSC 68 to the president justified his request for a greatly expanded military budget, a matter made even more urgent for him after the start of the Korean War, where a major intelligence failure—as serious as the one that led to Pearl Harbor—gave him a new awareness of the need for more accurate information on Communist intentions, in Asia as much as in Europe.[129]

Another important document, NSC 64, issued before the start of the Korean hostilities, had described the threat in Southeast Asia as grave. If Indochina fell, Burma and Thailand would certainly follow, and "the balance of Southeast Asia would be in grave hazard." While South Korea was not considered in comparable danger, when the armies of North Korea suddenly invaded that country on June 24, and began their rapid advance on Seoul, the capital, the president ordered the Air Force and the Navy to give all-out support to the South Koreans, for the moment confining their activities to the south of the 38th Parallel.

Even before Truman officially asked the United Nations to join in the fight against North Korean aggression, he represented the invasion as part of the single global threat posed by the Communist powers to destroy the world's democracies.[130] Senator Taft found that view unacceptable; speaking in the Senate on June 28, he claimed the Truman administration had been derelict in accepting the division of Korea and then had done too little to arm South Korea, had lost China to the Communists, and had allowed the secretary of state to be so careless in a speech made some months earlier as virtually to invite the North Korean attack. The president, Taft argued, ought to have sought congressional approval before he embarked on any military action.[131] Truman shared none of Taft's misgivings and believed his secretary of state had handled the situation admirably, not least in calling for the UN Security Council to convene in immediate emergency session.

The war's consequences for the president proved enormous, providing an incentive for larger military appropriations and the rapid conclusion of a peace treaty with Japan. In Europe, it gave an excuse for the rearmament of Germany, believed more necessary than ever to thwart the possibility of an imminent Soviet attack. The question of what the Americans proposed to recommend to the United Nations when the North Koreans were pushed back to the 38th

Parallel was not an academic one. General Douglas MacArthur's plan—to out-flank the enemy and land substantial forces at Inchon, though recognized to be a high-risk military operation—received the president's approval in the end. The attack, by totally surprising the enemy, leading to a quick and decisive victory, made the president more receptive to another MacArthur proposal; to cross the 38th Parallel and to pursue the fleeing North Korean armies to the borders of China and the Soviet Union.

MacArthur, warned to desist from pursuing the North Korean forces if either the Chinese or the Russians appeared to be engaging their armies, ignored this explicit prohibition, believing that he understood the situation better than those who sent orders from Washington. China, through its foreign minister, Chou En-lai, gave notice that Chinese armies would intervene to help the North Koreans if the Americans crossed the 38th Parallel, but MacArthur thought the threat an empty one. The president, believing a UN victory was imminent, announced his intention to fly to an undisclosed site in the Pacific—soon revealed as Wake Island—to confer with MacArthur on the final phase in Korea.

The president made a fundamental error—not so much in choosing to visit MacArthur on Wake Island but in being so beguiled by the general's military success at Inchon as to believe his assurances that the Chinese would not move. MacArthur, never a very perceptive political analyst, knew much less about China than he pretended and managed to persuade a president who knew even less.[132]

Truman accepted a military strategy that, in Kissinger's words, "traded a 100-mile-long defensive line located a considerable distance from the Chinese border for the necessity of protecting a 400-mile front right next to the main concentrations of Chinese communist power."[133] Though Washington ordered MacArthur not to approach the Yalu River with non-Korean forces, MacArthur deemed the order impractical and ignored it. The Chinese reacted by moving armies into the country, causing the American troops to panic and make a hasty retreat, losing Seoul for the second time. Though the president insisted his only purpose was to establish peace and independence for a South Korean state that had been viciously attacked, the Chinese found these statements unconvincing. The administration claimed initially that its only interest was to repel aggression; by crossing the 38th Parallel, it appeared to be seeking the unification of Korea—the objective many Republicans believed the administration ought to have been aiming for even before the North Korean invasion.

Truman knew he had made an error and insisted in the days and weeks that followed that unification was not his war aim, that he wished to leave the question open for the United Nations to resolve in later negotiations. When, on November 28, the National Security Council met, all recognized that the MacArthur promises of a quick victory were unlikely to be fulfilled; the boys would not be home by Christmas. The question, obviously, was to decide what the Americans intended to do next. Was this a war against international communism, or one fought against a single Communist state? Acheson doubted that the Americans could defeat the Chinese in Korea, and if the United States extended the war into Manchuria, the Soviets would certainly enter the conflict. On only one issue did the president seem adamant: In no conceivable circumstance would the United States agree to abandon Korea. Nor would he join in the chorus condemning MacArthur for his action. In a press conference where all these issues were thrashed out, Truman said: "We will take whatever steps are necessary to meet the military situation just as we always have." The next question, "Did that include the atomic bomb?" led to the quick response: "There has always been active consideration of its use. I don't want to see it used. It is a terrible weapon, and it should not be used on innocent men, women, and children who have nothing whatever to do with this military aggression. That happens when it is used."134

While the last two sentences might be read to suggest he had no intention of using the atom bomb, the news media reported only that its use was under consideration. Never before had Truman made so serious a gaffe; only the precariousness of the U.S. military position, and his own sense of being in some measure responsible for it, having accepted MacArthur's strategy, led him to make remarks that caused British prime minister Clement Attlee to hurry across the Atlantic, fearful of what the president might be intending. Walter Bedell Smith, the recently installed director of the CIA, met with the congressional leadership to explain how developments in Korea related to those in the Soviet Union. In his view, the Korean War demonstrated that the Soviet Union was engaged in an "experiment in war-by-proxy."

Many in Europe and Asia, genuinely frightened by what the administration seemed to be intending, could only fear the worst, but Attlee learned almost immediately on his arrival in Washington that the chances of the Americans using the atom bomb in Korea were virtually nil. Attlee's conversations with the president and the secretary of state dealt largely with the British concern that the United States negotiate with China and that it even consider an action that many in the world favored: the admission of China to the United Nations.135 Truman dismissed such a policy as appeasement, believing that neither Congress nor the American people would ever accept it. Indeed, the president found it incongruous that the British should press for such a policy at the moment when the American forces in Korea had suffered a grievous defeat. Acheson considered this a time when all the president's advisers, both military and civilian, failed him. No one came forward to propose any policy different from the one being pursued.

MacArthur showed himself increasingly belligerent and recommended the dispatch of an ultimatum to China demanding an immediate cease-fire, with a declaration of war threatened if it failed to comply. At other times, he urged the bombardment of Chinese bases in Manchuria, the institution of a naval blockade against China, and the acceptance of Chiang Kai-shek's proposal to send Chinese troops from Taiwan to join in the battle. MacArthur vastly exceeded his authority as a theater commander, but no one in daily touch with the president dared reprimand or silence him. Only in the spring of 1951, when U.S. troops under the command of General Matthew Ridgway began to push back the Chinese, recapturing Seoul, and were again at the 38th Parallel, did Truman begin to argue that the time had come for negotiation, that a cease-fire proposal should be prepared. MacArthur, furious with this decision, issued a proclamation of his own, in effect an ultimatum to the Communist Chinese, threatening them with an extension of the war. Acheson thought it "insubordination of the grossest sort," and General Bradley, the chief of staff, long disenchanted with MacArthur, called it an "unforgivable and irretrievable act." In his *Memoirs,* Truman wrote:

> This was a most extraordinary statement for a military commander of the United Nations to issue on his own responsibility. It was an act totally disregarding all directives to abstain from any declarations on foreign policy. It was in open defiance of my orders as President and as Commander in Chief. This was a challenge to the President under the Constitution. It also flouted the policy of the United Nations. . . . By this act MacArthur left me no choice—I could no longer tolerate his insubordination.[136]

Though furious with General MacArthur, Truman knew his dismissal would create turmoil both in Congress and in the country. The Cabinet recognized the seriousness of the situation and warned him of its dangers; in the words of Acheson, "you will have the greatest fight of your administration." Truman seemed prepared for it, and hearing all his advisers, civilian and military, recommend action, he proceeded to issue orders for MacArthur's recall. The popular outcry exceeded what even the most pessimistic of his advisers had feared. The general returned to the United States in triumph, made a historic speech before both houses of Congress, and appeared to have reduced the president's prestige beyond anything he had known in even the worst days of his first administration.

Yet MacArthur's triumph proved short-lived, largely destroyed when the Senate opened hearings on his proposed remedies for the Korean stalemate. General Bradley knew that only one solution made sense—the one MacArthur had rejected. In his view, the United States ought to "try to fight it out in general where we are now without committing too great forces." Truman and the general staff accepted the prospect of a stalemate, little realizing the political consequences of their decision. The Republicans would make this, Truman's war, a principal object of their attack; the death and injury of almost 150,000 Americans would be represented as the needless sacrifice the nation had made in response to the actions of an incompetent president. From the time Truman dismissed MacArthur to the end of his days in the Oval Office, the Korean War hung as an albatross around his neck that neither he nor his loyal associates were able to dislodge. As rumors circulated of the sleaze that characterized the administration, Truman's Pendergast past became a staple of Republican criticism, and Senator McCarthy—more insidious than ever in his attacks on the president—made it difficult for even Truman's friends to defend him. The last year of the administration, chaotic and unhappy, made more so by the Supreme Court declaring the president's action in seizing the steel plants unconstitutional, suggested that the Fair Deal was indeed dead, killed by the war more than by congressional hostility or public disapproval.[137]

Acheson, always defended by the president, had reason to be beholden to him and wrote what he believed to be an objective analysis of his presidency. While acknowledging that the "misconceptions of the state of the world around us, both in anticipating postwar conditions and in recognizing what they actually were when we came face to face with them" created the turmoil of the president's second term, he insisted that he would rank as one of "the few who in the midst of great difficulties managed their office with eminent benefit to the public interest."[138] Acheson represented Truman as vital, energetic, and cheerful, who gave and expected loyalty from his associates. He saw him as decisive, a man who "restored the health and strength of our allies," was able to enlist the help of the country's former enemies, and showed an abiding commitment to democratic values and institutions. Acheson, determined to laud Truman, neglected to consider his two principal failures: to negotiate an acceptable exit from the Korean War; to counter the tactics employed by McCarthy and those who supported him. Both failures reflected Truman's inability to be the Machiavellian prince his predecessor had been.

Truman, one of the most honest of the twentieth-century presidents, seemed helpless before Republicans who resented his 1948 victory and wished only to destroy him and those who served him. Hyperbole became the order of the day, gratifying a new generation of politicians different from those who had sought power in the more innocent and carefree days of the two Roosevelts.

Truman created institutions that survived: the Department of Defense, the National Security Council, and the Central Intelligence Agency. The atom bomb had contributed to the creation of a new state, what Peter Hennessy, the English historian, looking at his own country, described as the "secret state."[139] That state gave vast new authority to the president, and though Truman used the CIA and covert action less than his successors did, war and secrecy greatly enhanced presidential power. Truman governed in a new age but lived in a state of dependence on men whose knowledge of the world rested principally on what they had learned from Europe's tragic history in the 1930s and America's more happy experiences in World War II. Their understanding of Europe allowed them to be immensely creative in that sphere; in Asia, their innocence led to disasters, made more grave by their failure to understand the Soviet Union, "not merely, like Nazi Germany, a totalitarian dictatorship engaged in power politics, but a unique and abnormal member of international society inspired by a dynamic ideology with a strong international appeal."[140] Those words, used by the Joint Intelligence Committee in Great Britain in 1947, resembled others George Kennan had employed in his X article, but they scarcely replicated what Paul Nitze and his colleagues had argued in NSC 68, a document that greatly influenced Truman and the presidents who succeeded him, leading them into an Asian morass they never learned how to escape. Truman was left no blueprint for the postwar world by Roosevelt; he created one and established institutions that remain extant today. His was the most creative presidency of the post–World War II period.

An innate modesty precluded his ever adopting the swagger of certain of his successors, and Truman never emphasized his real and very substantial military record. He never claimed to be the education president, but the passage of the GI Bill during the last year of Roosevelt's presidency gave him the opportunity to offer veterans of World War II, and later of the Korean War, education benefits that did as much to transform the lives of those generations as any other single act of Congress.[141] In making higher education available to millions, the GI Bill created the incentive for a vast expansion of colleges and universities, establishing their preeminence with several unrivalled by any abroad.

Truman came into the presidency as the leader of a nation of workers and farmers. Much that he did contributed to the founding of a large new middle class, prosperous and educated, that would soon become the model for the world, first in Western Europe, then in Asia. He left a legacy that even Dwight Eisenhower, wary of federal expansion and pledged to control it, could not wholly ignore.[142]

CHAPTER 12

The General

DWIGHT D. EISENHOWER, born in Abilene, Kansas, on October 14, 1890, started life in a farming family that resembled Harry Truman's. Like his predecessor, a devoted son, especially close to his mother, Eisenhower suffered from his father's bankruptcy, the victim of a cheating partner who absconded with all the cash and much of the goods from a clothing store they owned jointly. The family, close-knit, resembled its neighbors in frugality but also in their simple religious devotion. David Eisenhower, the father, dour and preoccupied, obliged to work long hours, though incontestably head of the family, allowed his wife to take charge of the boys—soon five—and they lived much as other ordinary Midwesterners did, socially unpretentious, avoiding any pleasure deemed sinful or vain. Unlike the Roosevelts, neither Truman nor Eisenhower pretended to belong to what those unfamiliar with Tocqueville imagined was an American aristocracy; New York might claim to breed aristocrats, but neither Missouri nor Kansas ever did. Though the Eisenhowers lived in town, the country lay just outside, and the boys enjoyed hunting and fishing, cooking, and card-playing. Their religious beliefs made drinking and smoking sinful, but cards did not figure as a prohibited activity. David Dwight—his names were later reversed—an excellent student, interested in history, especially military history, worked at odd jobs during the school year, full-time during the summer. His passion for sports, especially football and baseball, made him consider enrolling at the University of Michigan, renowned for its exceptional teams.[1] A sports scholarship would have spared the family the expense of a university education, but his friendship with Everett "Swede" Hazlitt, planning to study at the U.S. Naval Academy in Annapolis, Maryland, told him of other possibilities. Eisenhower hoped his senator would sponsor his appointment—a privilege enjoyed by members of Congress—but having already promised the place to another Kansas youth, it was impossible for him to make a second nomination. Another option—to secure admission by scoring well in the written examinations given annually in each state—gave Eisenhower the entry he sought, not to Annapolis, but to West Point, the military academy. The young Eisenhower, athletic and strong, disciplined and motivated, joined a company of youths not very different from himself.

There is no evidence that the academy's rote learning—the heavy emphasis placed on memorization—proved uncongenial to him, but his passion for sports, frustrated when a knee injury barred him permanently from the academy's football team, depressed him for a time. Though the role of cheerleader and coach lifted his spirits, they never compensated for what he felt he lost when his hopes of becoming one of the academy's nationally famous football stars evaporated.[2] Among the 164 cadets who graduated in 1915, Eisenhower ranked sixty-first, accepted service in the infantry, knowing the cavalry, his preferred branch, was closed to him because of his knee injury.[3] Though he hoped for assignment to the Philippines, he was posted to Fort Sam Houston, outside San Antonio, Texas, where he met the young woman, Mamie Dowd, who became his wife.

Socially, Mamie ranked above the man she married, and her father consented grudgingly to the marriage, reminding the young lieutenant that his daughter was accustomed to certain luxuries; her own maid, and a generous allowance.[4] Mamie's father withdrew both after the marriage, and only the birth of his first grandson led him to relent, giving the young couple an automobile and a $100 monthly allowance. Life for a junior officer in the Army, though frugal, scarcely resembled the existence Truman knew as a farmer in Missouri. From the day Eisenhower entered the Army, he lived in a military ghetto, among his fellow officers and their wives, guaranteed adequate housing and other perquisites, enjoying the congenial company of men and women able to spend time together socializing, dining, playing cards, and gossiping, with the men engaged in all manner of sports.

The approach of war in 1917 told Eisenhower what every other West Point graduate also understood: Military service abroad would create advancement opportunities unlikely to be won by those who remained at home. Anxious to be posted overseas but denied the opportunity, and assigned to be the commander at Camp Colt in Gettysburg, Pennsylvania, Eisenhower felt he missed out on the greatest war in history through no fault of his own and envied his more fortunate classmates.[5] Following the rapid demobilization of the conscript armies, by January 1, 1920, only 130,000 men remained on active duty. The Army was again a backwater, and though Eisenhower's military assignments took him to Panama, Washington, Paris, and Manila, with no battles to fight and no victories to claim, promotions came slowly.[6] Stephen Ambrose, describing life in the late Coolidge era when Eisenhower lived in the nation's capital and studied at the nearby Army War College, wrote:

> These Army officers, all captains and majors, kept to themselves. They had neither social standing nor prestige in rank-conscious Washington. They wore mufti

on orders from the Chief of Staff, who wanted to reduce their visibility in a capital given over to isolationism. . . . The prejudices against them made them even more tight-knit than they would have been anyway. They knew one another intimately; everyone knew everyone else's habits, salaries, preferences in food and drink, hobbies (generally golf for the men, bridge for the women), and prospects. They exchanged birthday greetings, sent formal messages of congratulations on appropriate occasions. . . . Being part of that scene was like being part of a large, happy, close family.[7]

It did not introduce Eisenhower to the Republican political world he would later come to know that gave him advantages of a very different kind. In 1928 Eisenhower was offered the chance either to join the general staff or to go to France as a member of the Battle Monuments Commission. He opted for the latter, mostly because Mamie insisted on it. Again, their friends were other U.S. Army officers, stationed in France or passing through; they associated little with the French, learning neither their language nor anything of their culture. It was a restful time for both, living in a beautiful city, not yet threatened with the disasters that lay ahead in the 1930s and 1940s. When they returned to their Washington apartment in November 1929, the Wall Street crash scarcely figured as a major event in their protected circle. Assigned to the office of the assistant secretary of war, Eisenhower performed duties he found neither arduous nor interesting. When Douglas MacArthur became chief of staff in the fall of 1930, and Congress decided to create the War Policies Commission to study policies to be pursued in the event of war, Eisenhower became one of the officers on whom he relied.[8]

Though rumors circulated years later of tension between the two, Eisenhower persistently denied this, claiming that "there must be a strong tie for two men to work so closely together for seven years."[9] While acknowledging that MacArthur was a "peculiar fellow," he saw him as "a hell of an intellect," grateful for all he did to give him the administrative experience that proved so useful during World War II. Whatever Eisenhower learned while serving MacArthur, doing his bidding and holding his tongue, he derived other lessons from watching a proud martinet prone to excess and very rarely cautious. Eisenhower, observing his performance in putting down the bonus-marchers, dismissed as Communist agents and dupes, knew he could do nothing to control him. In a bombastic press conference, MacArthur justified the whole operation with the words: "That mob down there was a bad-looking mob. It was animated by the essence of revolution."[10] Eisenhower knew this was nonsense but said nothing, accepting the unwritten rules of his profession.

In February 1933, a month before Franklin Roosevelt entered the White House, MacArthur appointed Eisenhower his personal assistant. No one pretended that the country boasted a modern fighting force, and while MacArthur

argued for these conditions to be remedied, his words had no effect on a president with more pressing priorities. MacArthur, like other of his fellow officers,
including Eisenhower, had little esteem for the president's domestic policies and
none whatever for his foreign policies.[11] Neither the promise of independence to
the Philippines, the recognition of the Soviet Union, nor the Good Neighbor
policy in Latin America expressed their view of what U.S. foreign policy should
be, though none showed great imagination in defining what it might be. Eisenhower, a lowly major more than twenty years after graduating from West Point,
knew Europe and Asia superficially, aware that American civilians rarely thought
of their professional Army, were massively disinterested in it.

In 1935, MacArthur's term as chief of staff ended, and the new commonwealth government in the Philippines—scheduled to be granted full independence in 1946—asked the general to come to Manila to organize and train
what would soon be its own independent army. Eisenhower, invited to join
him, felt little excitement at the prospect of going, and his wife seemed even
less resigned to his accepting the assignment, but the opportunity to continue
working with the country's leading general could not be refused. For the next
four years, Eisenhower lived a boring life, made more difficult by a deteriorating relation with MacArthur. Eisenhower's unhappiness, like Mamie's, never a
secret from those who knew them well, made them anxious to leave, but there
was no possibility of doing so. MacArthur needed Eisenhower and would never
agree to his transfer.

With the outbreak of war in Europe in September 1939, it became more important than ever for Eisenhower to return to Washington. In a perceptive letter to his brother, Milton, he wrote:

> It's a sad day for Europe and for the whole civilized world—though for a long
> time it has seemed ridiculous to refer to the world as civilized. If the war. . . is. . .
> long-drawn-out and. . . bloody. . . then I believe that the remnants of nations
> emerging from it will be scarcely recognizable as the ones that entered it.[12]

Communism, anarchy, crime and disorder, the loss of personal liberties, and
abject poverty would be the afflictions of the postwar European world. He saw
Hitler as a "power-drunk egocentric . . . criminally insane . . ." and thought
that Germany, if defeated, would have to be dismembered.[13]

Although there is no evidence to suggest that Eisenhower derived these ideas
from the hundreds of hours he spent in MacArthur's company, it is difficult to
know from what other source they would have come. Eisenhower, never an
avid reader, knew few civilians who might have instructed him in European affairs.[14] Leaving Manila on December 13, 1939, to return home, he spurned the
offers of the Philippine government to remain. His separation from
MacArthur, though superficially amicable, led MacArthur years later to speak

disparagingly of him, referring to him as a "clerk, nothing more."[15] Eisenhower, no less critical of MacArthur, once reportedly said: "Oh yes, I studied dramatics under MacArthur for seven years."[16] Whatever the accuracy of these accounts, they expressed certain truths: Eisenhower was a clerk of sorts, very useful to his chief; MacArthur was an actor. Both displayed other attributes, less in evidence during the years they spent together.

Theodore Roosevelt's ascent to the presidency would have been unlikely in the absence of the Spanish-American War; Eisenhower's elevation would have been inconceivable without World War II. A minor military officer, a lieutenant colonel in 1940 in a service whose reputation at home and abroad was negligible, he moved from total obscurity to world renown only after the Japanese attacked Pearl Harbor, and General George C. Marshall, the chief of staff, recognizing the country's precarious situation in the Pacific, not least in the Philippines, asked what Eisenhower, familiar with the situation, would recommend. Returning after a few hours of reflection, Eisenhower told Marshall that the Philippines could not be saved but should not be abandoned at once, given the shock such a loss would have for China, the Dutch East Indies, and others in the area. Every effort had to be made to hold the islands, but the more important initiative, in his view, required the United States to establish Australia as a principal base of operations. Marshall, impressed, responded by placing Eisenhower in charge of the Philippines and Far Eastern Section of the War Plans Division. In the months that followed, the Philippines fell, and MacArthur blamed the president, but also the chief of staff and Eisenhower for failing to do more.[17]

These months were crucial for Eisenhower's career; Marshall, observing him closely, decided he was one of the Army's most talented officers. The esteem proved to be mutual, and Eisenhower advanced rapidly to become head of the War Plans Division. While he craved a command in the field, scarcely relishing the prospect of spending a second war away from the front, Marshall needed him at home and saw no reason to transfer him out of Washington. Through the winter and early spring of 1942, Eisenhower worked on plans for an early Allied invasion of Europe. The British, in Washington and London, found his proposals fanciful; any early invasion of France would result in the decimation of the Allied forces. The British preferred campaigns along the periphery in Norway, Greece, and North Africa, looking to a cross-channel operation at a much later date.[18] Eisenhower, like other of his fellow American officers, rejected the British recommendations, reflecting what he and they believed to be excessive timidity, linked to what they saw as unacceptable arrogance.[19] The British, unable to take the American military proposals seriously, learned to their dismay that both the president and his chief of staff believed them feasible and that plans for ROUNDUP, the name chosen for the operation, were going forward.

In the end, nothing came of all this, partly because of British resistance, but principally because the ships, the manpower, and the will to take such risks when the U.S. forces in Britain numbered a mere 55,000 officers and men made such an operation inconceivable.[20] Eisenhower, visiting England in the spring of 1942, recognized the problem but took no position on what could be done. Instead, he recommended to Marshall that a European theater of operations be established in London and that the man chosen to head it be given full authority to organize, train, and command all the U.S. ground, naval, and air forces assigned to the theater. Marshall accepted the idea, believing that only Eisenhower could fill the role.

During his first months in London, Eisenhower came to appreciate the gulf that separated the British from the Americans, and when General George C. Marshall, Admiral Ernest J. King, and Harry Hopkins descended on London, their unhappiness with the British resistance to the American plan for an early invasion of the continent became apparent. Both Marshall and King expressed a strong preference for a military invasion of France, in 1942 if possible, but no later than 1943. In their view, this was the only way to help the Russians, whose military situation was desperate. The British counterproposals for a North African invasion satisfied none of them initially, and King began to speak of the need for an operation in the Pacific to defeat Japan.[21]

Eisenhower was not present at these crucial meetings, having received no invitation to attend, but found it incomprehensible that his colleagues abandoned the idea of an early invasion of France, accepting instead the British proposal to launch an attack in North Africa. He believed that "the prize we seek. . . to keep 8,000,000 Russians in the war" justified all risks and failed to understand British reasoning. Their argument—that the chances of an Allied success were negligible, that an invasion with a small force, even if successful, would not help the Russians, and that Germany's military strength in France was greatly underestimated by the Americans—led to heated discussions that ended with the Americans accepting the British argument, agreeing that the supreme commander of the operation should be American, his deputy British. No one thought that the Americans would select Eisenhower as supreme commander; the best evidence of his insignificance at the time is that Churchill's invitation, on July 25, 1942, to Marshall, King, Hopkins, and Harriman to dine and spend the night at Chequers, along with the three British chiefs of staff and General Alan Brooke, did not include him.[22]

Eisenhower believed the decision in favor of TORCH, the invasion of North Africa, precluded a European offensive, essential in his mind to keeping the Russians in the war. July 22, the day on which the decision was taken, might well go down as the "blackest day in history," he wrote, scarcely realizing that the operation would give him the opportunity he had long sought: to lead troops into battle.[23] General Marshall, together with Admiral King, decided that Eisenhower was the only reasonable candidate to plan TORCH and command an offensive that would not be danger-free. The possibility that the French would resist and that Spain would seize that moment to enter the war on the side of the Axis gave them cause to be uneasy. Marshall fretted and worried and left to Eisenhower the decision of when to invade, with the president hoping it would take place before the off-year congressional elections, scheduled for November 3. Roosevelt, like Churchill, never doubted that the operation would succeed.[24]

The amphibious operation, though technically successful, encountered problems more serious than those anticipated by either the military planners or the politicians. Churchill's expectations that the Allies would be masters of French North Africa by D-Day plus twenty, that Eisenhower would then attack and occupy Tripoli in Libya, and that the British Eighth Army would defeat Rommel in Egypt, clearing the whole of North Africa's shore by the end of the year, proved wildly optimistic. An operation expected to take weeks, months at the most, took a great deal longer.[25] Fierce fighting at Oran and Casablanca told the Americans and the British that the French forces loyal to Marshal Philippe Petain showed no interest in responding to the plea made by General Henri Giraud, asking them to end all resistance and lay down their arms. The decision to engage Admiral Darlan, who had served in the Vichy government as navy minister, vice president of the Council of Ministers, and secretary of state for foreign affairs, to do what Giraud had failed to do satisfied Eisenhower's craving to bring the fighting to an end, to minimize American casualties. Eisenhower met with Darlan, and while he felt no enthusiasm for the admiral, claiming to be fatigued by "the necessity of dealing with little, selfish, conceited worms that call themselves men," he shared with Roosevelt and Churchill the idea that such men could be useful.[26] This more than justified their collaborating with a man of Vichy.[27]

On November 10, the American deal seemed to bear fruit when Darlan's call for a cease-fire was obeyed by the French forces. A few days later, on November 15, when Darlan proclaimed that all the measures taken had been "in the name of Marshal Pétain," de Gaulle expressed disgust, and his emissaries, visiting with the president a week later, hinted at their disappointment with him. According to the report sent de Gaulle, Roosevelt, "annoyed at their protests. . . shouted at them," saying: "Of course I'm dealing with Darlan, since Darlan's giving me Algiers. Tomorrow, I'd deal with Laval, if Laval were to offer me Paris."[28] Though Marshall invariably praised Eisenhower as the accomplished general who commanded TORCH brilliantly, the advantages expected to follow from Darlan's support never materialized. The hopes of securing the French fleet for the Allies evaporated when the greater part of the fleet was scuttled in Toulon Harbor as the Germans were preparing to board and capture the ships. Three battleships, seven cruisers, and 167 other ships that Churchill and Roosevelt desperately wanted were lost, and the Allied advance in Tunisia was made no easier by the French refusal to fight the Germans who then occupied the country.

The year 1943 opened inauspiciously for the Allies, still bogged down in Tunisia, with Montgomery's armies unable to reach them from the east. The differences between the British and the Americans—barely hinted at in the communiqué that followed the Casablanca meeting between Roosevelt and Churchill in January 1943, attended by Eisenhower for only a single day— dealt mostly with the military operations that would follow the end of the North African campaign. Churchill's military and civilian advisers argued for an invasion of Sicily or Sardinia, leading to Italy's rapid defeat, a plan the Americans found unattractive, Marshall being especially hesitant about further operations in the Mediterranean, believing they were doing less to defeat the Germans than the British claimed.[29]

Admiral King suggested the Allies change their priorities entirely, giving attention first to the defeat of Japan.[30] Alan Brooke, Britain's commander-in-chief of the General Staff, confided to his diary highly unflattering observations about Eisenhower—"deficient of experience, and of limited ability."[31] Given that opinion, never seriously altered, he urged the appointment of British officers as Eisenhower's principal deputies: General Sir Harold Alexander, to take charge of the land forces, Admiral Andrew B. Cunningham, the naval units, and Air Marshall Sir Arthur Tedder, the air forces. In his diary, he wrote:

> We were pushing Eisenhower up into the stratosphere and rarefied atmosphere of a Supreme Commander, where he would be free to devote his time to the political and inter-allied problems, whilst we inserted under him . . . our own commanders to deal with the military situations and to restore the necessary drive and coordination which had been so seriously lacking.[32]

Brooke's reservations about Eisenhower were scarcely more serious than those about other of the U.S. chiefs of staff, including Marshall, as well as King and General Henry H. Arnold. Though in the end he believed the British succeeded in getting "practically all we hoped to get when we came here," this did not cause him to revise his opinion that the Americans, however charming, were exceedingly difficult to work with.[33]

When the last of the Axis forces surrendered in Tunisia on May 13, 1943, with some 275,000 taken prisoner, a number larger than those captured by the Russians at Stalingrad just a few months earlier, Eisenhower began preparations for the Sicily invasion. Recognizing that the price the Allies paid for their North African victory had been heavy—71,810 casualties, with 10,820 dead—he planned a campaign that would be more sparing of Allied men. The invasion of Sicily, scheduled for early July, called for the assembling of a vast armada, some 2,000 vessels carrying more than 160,000 men from Montgomery's Eighth

Army and Patton's Sixth, expected to lead to a quick and relatively casualty-free victory. It proved to be the first, but not the second. The Allies suffered some 22,000 casualties on the island before they crossed the Strait of Messina to land in southern Italy on September 2. Though the Allies rejoiced in the overthrow of Mussolini by Marshal Pietro Badoglio on July 25 and delighted in the armistice the new regime agreed to on September 3, Eisenhower felt uneasy over the size of the German armies sweeping into Italy, understating the gravity of the situation when he cabled Marshall, "there is more than a faint possibility that we may have some hard going."[34] Marshall, for almost the only time in their relationship, found fault with Eisenhower, acknowledging disappointment that he had failed to use the Eighty-Second Airborne Division to seize Rome and that the Allied advance from the beaches in the Italian toe had been so slow.[35] Marshall, wary always of Churchill's plans, feared a long and difficult campaign, not at all what the Americans had bargained for.[36]

Still, when Roosevelt met with Churchill and Stalin in Tehran from November 28 to December 1, Italy scarcely figured on their agenda. Indeed, with the Italian front stabilized, all attention focussed on the coming second front in France, OVERLORD, scheduled for the spring. On the last day of the Tehran Conference Roosevelt informed Stalin he had chosen Eisenhower to command that operation, and Eisenhower spent the winter preparing for what would be the largest amphibious assault in history.

The excitement of the first hours following D-Day, the June 6, 1944, landings, concealed initial fears that some of the invading forces might be pushed off the beaches or taken prisoner, encouraging all who had planned the operation, but the advances proved painfully slow. Though Eisenhower praised Generals Montgomery and Omar Bradley for their accomplishments, others were less satisfied; Montgomery had promised to take Caen on the first day and had not done so by the end of the month. The press had anticipated much more rapid advances, and if Eisenhower showed little sympathy for what he resented as uninformed criticism, the Normandy campaign, like that in North Africa, did not proceed as rapidly as originally hoped. Meanwhile, the first of the German V1 rockets fell on London, attacks that began on June 12, that made even more imperative the capture of the bases from which they were being launched in France and Belgium. On August 1, the situation became desperate when the first of the V2s descended on England. In his memoirs, *Crusade in Europe,* Eisenhower wrote of the serious damage to morale that followed the introduction of these weapons, virtually inaudible, invisible, and not easily intercepted, suggesting that had they been introduced six months earlier OVERLORD might not have been possible.[37]

Meanwhile, in France, Montgomery launched an attack, GOODWOOD, taking Caen, though at great cost, with 401 tanks lost, and the British forces suffering heavy casualties. Eisenhower complained of a too impetuous Montgomery when he and Churchill lunched together in July, and both Brooke and Bedell

Smith did what they could to improve steadily deteriorating relations between the two.[38] The American press, Brooke confided to his diary, insist "that the British are doing nothing, and suffering no casualties, whilst the Americans are bearing all the brunt of the war!!" To express his dismay with the whole situation, he added: "I am tired to death with and by humanity and all its pettiness! Will we ever learn to 'love our allies as ourselves'??!! I doubt it!"[39] Repeating judgments he made earlier, he added:

> There is no doubt that Ike is out to do all he can to maintain the best of relations between British and Americans, but it is equally clear that Ike knows nothing about strategy and is *quite* unsuited to the post of Supreme Commander as far as running the strategy of the war is concerned! . . . With that Supreme Command set up it is no wonder that Monty's real high ability is not always realized.[40]

Eisenhower saw no need to think in broad strategic or geopolitical terms. For him, the problems were tactical. How, for example, should he act in respect to the taking of Paris? Eisenhower, essentially sanguine, wrote "we were substantially on the line that had been predicted before D-Day as the one we would attain three or four months after our landing," but by the end of November the British were again criticizing him.[41]

Brooke told his chiefs of staff of his growing concerns about the military situation, writing in his diary:

> I then put before the meeting my views on the very unsatisfactory state of affairs in France, with no one running the land battle. Eisenhower, though supposed to be doing so, is detached and by himself with his lady chauffeur on the golf links at Rheims—entirely detached from the war and taking practically no part in the running of the war! Matters got so bad lately that a deputation of Whiteley, Bedell Smith and a few others went up to tell him that he must get down to it and RUN the war, which he said he would. Personally, I think he is incapable of running the war even if he tries.[42]

By the end of the year, with Field Marshal Gerd von Rundstedt attacking in what came to be known as the Battle of the Bulge, a counteroffensive Montgomery had long feared, the German armies were finally stopped, largely by Montgomery, who claimed all credit for the success, greatly offending Eisenhower.[43] In March, with the war clearly coming to an end, Brooke breakfasted with Eisenhower in London and found one more occasion to comment in his diary on Eisenhower's lack of strategic sense, his failure to understand Montgomery.[44] Later that month, on March 29, he leveled more serious charges against him, writing in his diary,

A very long COS meeting with a series of annoying telegrams. The worst of all was one from Eisenhower direct to Stalin trying to coordinate his offensive with the Russians. To start with he had no business to address Stalin direct, his communications should be through the Combined Chiefs of Staff, secondly he produced a telegram which was unintelligible, and finally what was implied in it appeared to be entirely adrift and a change in all that had been previously agreed on.[45]

Eisenhower, increasingly distressed with Montgomery, decided to take the Ninth Army away from the Twenty-First Army Group and give it to Bradley to allow him to advance on Dresden. In a telegram to Stalin, Eisenhower informed him of his plans, suggesting that the Red Army meet the Americans near Dresden, and asked what the Russians proposed to do.[46] In response, Stalin said he intended to send only secondary forces to capture Berlin since it had lost its military significance, grossly deceiving Eisenhower. More than 1.25 million Red Army soldiers had been dispatched to take the city, accompanied by more than 22,000 pieces of artillery. The British, recognizing the importance of the German capital, greatly resented Eisenhower's opting for Dresden, and the British chiefs protested directly to Marshall who, not surprisingly, supported Eisenhower.[47] In a complaining note, Eisenhower for the first time expressed his disdain for British advice; he told Marshall:

The Prime Minister and his Chief of Staff opposed 'Anvil'; they opposed my idea that the Germans should be destroyed west of the Rhine. . . Now they apparently want me to turn aside on operations in which would be involved many thousands of troops before the German forces are fully defeated. I submit that these things are studied daily and hourly by me and my advisors and that we are animated by one single thought which is the early winning of the war.[48]

Churchill tried again to persuade Eisenhower to move toward Berlin, saying:

If the enemy's resistance should weaken, as you evidently expect and which may well be fulfilled, why should we not cross the Elbe and advance as far eastward as possible? This has an important political bearing, as the Russian armies of the South seem certain to enter Vienna and overrun Austria. If we deliberately leave Berlin to them, even if it should be in our grasp, the double event may strengthen their conviction, already apparent, that they have done everything. Further, I do not consider myself that Berlin has yet lost its military and certainly not its political significance. The fall of Berlin would have a profound psychological effect on German resistance in every part of the Reich. While Berlin holds out great masses of Germans will feel it their duty to go down fighting. The idea that the capture of Dresden and junction with the Russians there would be a superior gain does not commend itself to me.[49]

Churchill quoted this message in the last volume of his memoirs, *Triumph and Tragedy*, but neglected to quote his last paragraph, in which he indicated his wish for the British to get to Berlin first, if possible. Such a solution, he wrote, "avoids the relegation of His Majesty's Forces to an unexpected restricted sphere."[50] Eisenhower, offended by this explicit criticism of his strategy, replying to Churchill, insisted he had not changed his plan, that the Twenty-First Army Group would seal off the Danish Peninsula and keep the Russians out of Denmark. He thought this an important objective, and added, "I am disturbed, if not hurt, that you should suggest any thought on my part to 'relegate His Majesty's Forces to an unexpected restricted sphere.' Nothing is further from my mind and I think my record over two and a half years of commanding Allied forces should eliminate any such idea."[51] By the closing weeks of the war, Eisenhower had lost the confidence of Churchill and of Britain's principal military commanders. But these matters scarcely concerned him.

In the next fortnight, the opportunity for the Americans to take Berlin presented itself again. Fifty miles outside Berlin while the Russians were much more distant, General William H. Simpson, commanding the Ninth Army, asked Bradley's permission to advance on the city. Bradley consulted Eisenhower, who refused to be deflected from what he considered more important objectives. He believed that taking Lubeck in the north and the Alpine region to the south were tasks "vastly more important than the capture of Berlin."[52]

On April 17, only days after the death of Roosevelt, Eisenhower flew to London to persuade Churchill that his strategy had indeed produced the results intended. Although Churchill, in his memoirs, made no mention of this visit, Stephen Ambrose, Eisenhower's biographer, suggested that Ike totally persuaded the prime minister of the correctness of a strategy, which in the north saved Denmark from Russian occupation and in the south guaranteed that the German atomic research facilities would not fall into the hands of the advancing French.[53] One last difference between the British chiefs and Eisenhower followed from the issue of whether to advance into Czechoslovakia if that operation did not delay the final German defeat. Marshall, responding to this British recommendation, told Eisenhower, "Personally, and aside from all logistic, tactical, or strategical implications I would be loath to hazard American lives for purely political purposes."[54] Eisenhower found no flaw in Marshall's reasoning; neither showed any understanding of the relation between military and political objectives.

In his book *At Ease*, written in 1967, Eisenhower made claims he never alluded to in *Crusade in Europe*, suggesting that he told Roosevelt early in 1944 that he expected trouble from the Russians and that Roosevelt had chosen not to listen. He claimed to have told Brooke even earlier that if the Allies did not get to Europe soon, the Soviets would overrun it. Again, Brooke paid no attention to his warnings.[55] Ambrose, with some understatement, wrote: "It was noticeable that in both cases he had made his point in private, and in both cases the man he made it to was dead."[56] Ambrose suspected he was fabricating, as he did again in 1948 when the Soviets initiated their blockade of Berlin and Eisenhower pretended, especially with the Republican Party faithful, that he had not taken the city only because the operation would have been militarily difficult.[57] When Eisenhower came to write his own memoirs in 1948, he scarcely hinted at these differences with his British colleagues, suggesting only that he objected principally to the British insistence on three commanders, one for ground, one for air, one for the navy. Writing about Montgomery, who showed certain "eccentricities," Eisenhower mentioned only one, the tendency "to separate himself from his staff."[58] Montgomery, when he came to write his own memoirs, showed no comparable forbearance, but Eisenhower's account of the "crusade," deliberately sanitized, sold widely and made him independently wealthy, never hinting at the substantial differences on strategy that had plagued British-American relations from the first days of the war, which only became more serious as the war proceeded.[59]

Eisenhower showed equal reticence in his statements about Charles de Gaulle, whose "many fine qualities" he appreciated, finding fault only with his "hyper-sensitiveness and an extraordinary stubbornness in matters which appeared inconsequential to us."[60] A man capable of concealing so much scarcely resembled the president he had followed into the White House who showed no comparable restraint. Truman, interviewed many years later by Merle Miller, when asked what he thought of Eisenhower's memoirs, gave no answer, and Miller wrote: "That was the only time in all our conversations that Mr. Truman didn't respond at all to a question."[61] Asked whether he had read Bradley's *A Soldier's Story*, Truman replied, "Yes, I have, and that is a very good book," going on to say: "Bradley was perhaps our greatest field general in the Second World War, and in his book. . . so far as I can make out, he hasn't told a single lie. Of course he's a Missourian, so maybe I'm prejudiced." No one reading those passages could fail to understand Truman's meaning. Bradley was an honest man; Eisenhower was not.

Other exchanges, even more damning, led Miller to ask the former president, "Were you surprised when Eisenhower finally did become a Presidential candidate in 1952?" and heard him reply:

No no. I could see it coming a long way back. I told you. Once the bug bites a man, there are very few, generals or not, who can resist. And I never thought Eisenhower was one of those who could. He had. . . a very high opinion of himself. Somewhere along the line he seemed to forget the fact that he was just a poor boy from Kansas.[62]

Asked whether he had anticipated Eisenhower's 1952 victory, he said: "When I saw the way the fellow that was running against him acted, I did. That fellow didn't know the first thing about campaigning, and he didn't learn anything either. He got worse in 1956."[63] Still, Truman had helped Stevenson. Why? The answer,

Yes, I did. After Eisenhower got his picture taken with that fella from Indiana—what's his name—the one that called General Marshall a traitor [Senator William Jenner]. He got his picture taken with him, and then when he was in Milwaukee. . . he was going to pay a tribute to General Marshall, but he took it out rather than stand up to McCarthy. It was one of the most shameful things I can ever remember. Why, General Marshall was responsible for his whole career. When Roosevelt jumped him from lieutenant colonel to general, it was on Marshall's recommendation. Three different times Marshall got him pushed upstairs, and in return. . . Eisenhower sold him out. It was just a shameful thing.[64]

Truman, asked to compare Eisenhower with General Ulysses Grant, the post–Civil War president, said:

For one thing, Grant was a hell of a lot better soldier than Eisenhower. What they never seem to say about Eisenhower is that he was. . . very weak as a field commander. . . Bradley was a great field soldier, but Ike wasn't. That job he had over there in London and in Paris, what he was, what he did, he presided at meetings mostly, and he approved strategy that had been drawn up by other people, but he never did *originate* anything. General Marshall was just the kindest man that ever was or ever will be, but he told me that Eisenhower had to be led every step of the way.[65]

Asked whether he had offered Eisenhower the presidency in 1948, Truman answered that he had not done so. "In the first place, it wasn't mine to offer. What happened, before he retired as Chief of Staff to go up there to Columbia we had a talk, and again he assured me he had no intention whatsoever of going into politics. I told him I thought that was the right decision, and it was."[66] Truman then continued: "But I wouldn't have ever supported Eisenhower under any circumstances for President even if I. . . hadn't known about his personal life." To that, Miller responded: "I'm sorry, sir. What do you mean about his personal life?" Truman replied: "Why, right after the war was over, he wrote a letter to General Marshall saying that he wanted to be relieved of duty, saying that he wanted to come back to the United States and divorce Mrs.

Eisenhower so that he could marry this Englishwoman." Miller, remarking that "it took me a moment to recover from that one," then said: "Do you mean Kay Summersby, who I believe was his jeep driver?" Truman replied: "I think that was her name, yes. But I don't care what her name was. It was a very, very shocking thing to have done, for a man who was a general in the Army of the United States." He then continued:

Well, Marshall wrote him back a letter the like of which I never did see. He said that if. . . Eisenhower even came close to doing such a thing, he'd not only bust him out of the Army, he'd see to it that he never for the rest of his life would be able to draw a peaceful breath. He said it wouldn't matter if he was in the Army or wasn't. Or even what country he was in. Marshall said that if he ever again even mentioned a thing like that, he'd see to it that the rest of his life was a living hell. General Marshall didn't very often lose his temper, but when he did, it was a corker.[67]

Miller, reporting on the conversation, wrote: "Mr. Truman was silent for a moment, and then said: 'I don't like Eisenhower; you know that. I never have, but one of the last things I did as President, I got those letters from his file in the Pentagon and I destroyed them.'" Miller added: "That was the first mention and the last of Miss Summersby and the exchange of letters between Generals Marshall and Eisenhower."[68] Ambrose dismissed the story as "untrue," suggesting that Truman "was approaching senility," a gratuitous insult.[69]

Everything Truman said to Miller confirmed what the British had also said about him, a man they knew as they had never known any previous president. Their views contradicted the conventional American opinion about the general, represented as a remarkable military and political strategist, who sought the presidency only to prevent the nomination of Senator Taft, to save the nation from a grave isolationist threat. Ambrose believed that at the end of the war, "Eisenhower's personal desire was for a quiet retirement with perhaps a bit of writing and lecturing" and that only the nation's insistence that he was the "only man" who could do the job, together with his sense of duty kept him from pursuing a "quiet retirement."[70] This was a canard, useful for Eisenhower's reputation, that made him appear a twentieth-century Cincinnatus.

Eisenhower's acceptance to be head of the American Occupation Zone in Germany and then chief of staff in 1945, retiring then to become president of Columbia University in 1947, and finally supreme commander of NATO in late 1950—steps that led him eventually to the White House—suggests a concern to do something more than a "bit of writing and lecturing." At Columbia, following the ancient Nicholas Murray Butler in his forty-three-year presidency, Eisenhower, chosen by the trustees for his name and fame, made clear he had no intention of serving as the university's principal fund-raiser. Except for creating the American Assembly, with its periodic conferences at the old Harriman estate on the Hudson River, he achieved little in his brief time on Morningside Heights, and as one disillusioned alumnus explained, he "was not a bad president because he was no president at all."[71] When Truman offered him the NATO position, he accepted with alacrity, taking a leave of absence from Columbia, but only because the trustees still imagined he planned one day to return there.

A momentous year for Eisenhower, 1951, opened with Senator Taft delivering a 10,000-word speech on the Senate floor on January 5 that inaugurated the media's so-called Great Debate on foreign policy.[72] Taft, fearing that Truman intended to send some 300,000 U.S. combat troops to Europe and possibly twice that number of support personnel, believed such a commitment would greatly strain the country's resources, and worse, would encourage the Europeans to become dependent on the United States when the only reasonable policy was to compel them to look after their own defense. Truman's plans were unconstitutional, Taft argued; the president had no right to send U.S. troops abroad in time of peace without the explicit prior approval of Congress.

Eisenhower returned from Europe to explain the administration's policies, and though he appeared to support at least some of Taft's reservations, believing, for example, that the dispatch of American troops would neither deter nor defeat the Russians, he expected it would raise Europe's morale, making Europeans more willing to spend of their own resources to improve their military capability. Europe, Eisenhower insisted, was indeed essential to America's defense.[73] In Washington, he met with Taft privately and purportedly asked the senator whether he and his congressional associates would "agree that collective security is necessary for us in Western Europe—and will you support this idea as a bipartisan policy?" Had Taft answered yes to that question, Eisenhower claimed that he intended to spend his next years in Europe carrying out that policy. If his answer was no, this would be a serious setback for NATO, and he would probably return to the United States.

In Eisenhower's version of the meeting, Taft refused to commit himself, and this "aroused my fears that isolationism was stronger in the United States than I had feared." The explanation, entirely acceptable to his admirers, men and women prepared to believe that Eisenhower entered the contest only because he feared the nascent isolationism of influential men like Taft, gained credibility from Eisenhower's suggestion that he carried a statement with him that evening he proposed to issue if Taft had answered yes. It would have said quite simply: "I want to announce that my name may not be used by anyone as a candidate for President—and if they [sic] do I will repudiate such efforts." James T. Patterson, Taft's biographer, casting doubt on Eisenhower's account of the meeting, wrote:

Eisenhower's story may have claimed too much. It was not entirely clear from his retrospective account (Taft left none) exactly when the meeting occurred, or who the aides were who allegedly witnessed the destruction of the statement. Could he really have expected Taft, who was leading the debate, to make a commitment to collective security in Europe, let alone involve his colleagues in it? If he had hoped for such a promise, why did he not actually tell Taft he would issue his statement that very night? Finally, how unequivocal would the statement have been? Given Eisenhower's enormous popularity, it was doubtful that his avid supporters, who later refused to be discouraged, would have paid much attention to it. It was also not surprising, given the magnitude of the request, that Taft was (as Eisenhower phrased it) 'a bit suspicious of my motives,' or that he refused to bind himself to a policy Republicans had been questioning in the Senate. Thus Taft's response was neither a blunder nor—the reverse—an act of political integrity.[74]

Eisenhower himself never gave this encounter with Taft the importance others attached to it. For him, the pleas of Henry Cabot Lodge Jr., the grandson of Wilson's nemesis, were more influential in causing him to become a candidate. Lodge came away from his discussions persuaded that Eisenhower would run, accept a draft, but not actively seek the nomination. This certainty allowed Lodge on January 5, 1952, to declare that the general was a Republican and that he was entering his name in the New Hampshire primary. Eisenhower confirmed he was a Republican but emphasized he would not "seek nomination to political office."[75] This, scarcely a Coolidge-like statement, provided the green light to all Republicans who wished to see him as the party's candidate.

When Eisenhower won decisively against Taft in New Hampshire, receiving 46,661 votes against the Ohio senator's 35,838, he responded with: "Any American who would have that many Americans pay him that compliment would be proud or he would not be an American."[76] Eight days later, in Minnesota, where Harold Stassen was the favorite son, and Eisenhower was not even listed as a candidate, he received 108,692 write-in votes as against Stassen's 129,076. Eisenhower claimed to be astonished, adding: "The mounting number of my fellow citizens who are voting. . . [for] me. . . are forcing me to re-examine my present position and past decision."[77] On April 11, attention temporarily diverted from the primaries by the president's dismissal of General MacArthur, led both Senators William E. Jenner and McCarthy to call for the president's impeachment, and that same day, Eisenhower asked to be relieved of his duties by June 1, allowing him to return to the United States in time for the Republican National Convention. Four days later, Eisenhower won the New Jersey primary with 160,000 votes more than Taft.[78]

In the weeks that followed, both contenders won some primaries, lost others, and in Abilene, Kansas, on June 2, the town celebrated Eisenhower's return, allowing him to give the first of his many homilies on the greatness of

America. He told his fellow citizens: "In spite of the difficulties of the problems we have, I ask you this one question: if each of us in his own mind would dwell more upon those simple virtues—integrity, courage, self-confidence, an unshakeable belief in the Bible—would not some of these problems tend to simplify themselves?"[79] That evening, in a nationwide radio address, he warned of four threats to American life: disunity at home, inflation and swollen federal spending, the federal bureaucracy, and communism abroad.[80] Expressing confidence "in the future of the United States," he then set out to win support in states as different as Texas, New York, and the Midwest he knew so well from his childhood.

Despite his protests, Eisenhower became an active candidate, and when the convention opened on July 6 in Chicago, Taft, though believed to have the greater number of pledged delegates, was compelled to compete with a general the public opinion polls continued to show would defeat any Democrat. As the convention proceeded, it became increasingly apparent that Eisenhower's managers were in control and that on crucial issues, including the all-important one of the seating of contested delegations, Eisenhower's friends were winning. The so-called liberal Republicans of the Eastern Seaboard, led by the twice-defeated Republican candidate Thomas Dewey, were determined to deny Taft the nomination. Dewey became the chief enemy of the senator's supporters and was denounced as the mastermind of the Eisenhower campaign, "the most cold-blooded, ruthless, selfish political boss in the United States today."[81] When Senator Everett Dirksen, a Taft advocate, pointed at Dewey and told him he had "the habit of winning conventions and losing elections," charging him with taking "us down the path to defeat," and warning against taking "us down that road again," pandemonium broke out in the hall.[82] Such demonstrations did nothing to prevent the delegates from voting for the candidate they believed would win. Eisenhower secured the nomination on the first ballot.[83]

Taft, seeking to understand his defeat, blamed it on New York financiers, certain influential Republican newspapers, and his failure to win support from key Republican governors. He would have been happy to accept the vice presidency, but Eisenhower's supporters rejected that possibility, urging the general to choose Richard Nixon, a junior senator from California, the scourge of Democratic Party liberals, a rabid anticommunist, a foe of corruption, who offered the attractiveness of youth, energy, and an incomparable political record for having defeated the liberal Helen Gahagan Douglas, and very early denounced Alger Hiss as a Communist spy. Eisenhower scarcely knew Nixon but accepted the recommendation of those familiar with the requirements of American politics. Because the Republicans were so obviously divided, Eisenhower recognized the need to win Taft over and achieved that purpose after a celebrated breakfast in New York on September 11 when the two, in a joint statement, appeared to agree on fundamental questions, including the all-important one that "liberty against the creeping socialism in every domestic field" was the defining issue of the 1952 electoral battle.[84] Eisenhower committed himself to a budget of $60 billion in 1954–1955, substantially below the one the president had proposed, and promised also to reduce taxes, pledging full support to the main features of Taft-Hartley. On foreign policy issues, Taft and Eisenhower's disagreements were totally ignored, represented in their joint statement as simply "differences of degree."

Taft campaigned for Eisenhower, denounced Democratic nominee Adlai Stevenson as a man prepared to "surrender to Communist policy," and warned that his election "would mean a continuation of the wavering, unstable, pro-Communist philosophy that has almost brought this country to destruction."[85] Aware of the general's inadequacies, Taft confided to one of his newspaper friends, Eisenhower "doesn't understand what the issues are," but these reservations were never made public.[86]

However intellectually appealing Stevenson might be to died-in-the-wool New Dealers and to segments of the press at home and abroad, he scarcely knew how to confront a World War II military hero who seemed the incarnation of all the things the country most valued. Eisenhower won handily, his 33,936,234 popular votes greatly exceeded Stevenson's 27,314,992; in the Electoral College, he had 442 votes against Stevenson's 89.[87] The Republicans gained control of both houses of Congress, the Senate by a very small majority, 48–47. With Taft elected as Majority Leader, Eisenhower had every reason to propitiate him but consulted him scarcely at all on his principal Cabinet appointments. Nevertheless, the new president pleased him in two ways: By appointing John Foster Dulles as secretary of state, he denied the position to Thomas Dewey, who desperately craved it.[88]

Dwight Eisenhower came to the presidency with the most extensive military experience of anyone who held the position in the twentieth century, and many, not only Republicans, believed that with an accomplished secretary of state at his side, the two would conduct a vigorous foreign policy that would gain bipartisan support. All accepted that Eisenhower's command of domestic political and policy issues was somewhat limited, and Taft, though prepared to help him, told friends that he "showed the quality which he is accused of having, an inability to make up his mind."

The death of Stalin on March 5, 1953, seemed to recommend some reconsideration of U.S. policy in respect to the Soviet Union, and Churchill, once again in Number 10 Downing Street, having returned there in 1951, believed this might be a propitious time for three-power talks. Neither Eisenhower nor Dulles welcomed the idea.[89] Though the president treated the prime minister with the respect due Britain's incomparable World War II hero, he saw no reason to go along with what he considered an old man's fancy, seeing Churchill's proposal as his way to retain power, to keep Anthony Eden, his heir-apparent, out of Downing Street. In a diary note, he wrote: "Winston is trying to relive the days of World War II. In those days he had the enjoyable feeling that he and our President were sitting on some rather Olympian platform with respect to the rest of the world, and directing world affairs from that vantage."[90] This implicit criticism of both Churchill and Roosevelt, written by someone who believed that very little was accomplished by "summitry," reflected his judgment that "such a relationship is completely fatuous, and that it was time for Churchill to hand over leadership to younger men."[91] He, in his mid-sixties, believed himself young; Churchill, by comparison, was an old man simply clinging to office.

In response to a message from Churchill on March 17, 1953, asking him not to miss any chance "of finding out how far the Malenkov regime are prepared to go in easing things up all around," Eisenhower told his old wartime ally to wait for a speech he planned to deliver to the American Society of Newspaper Editors on April 16 that would give his thoughts on the matter. In that speech, Eisenhower, making no mention of the Churchill intervention, repudiated any idea that "Cold War" tensions could be relieved by anything other than a Korean armistice, an Austrian peace treaty, and "an end to the direct and indirect attacks upon the security of Indochina and Malaya." For him, as for Dulles, Soviet and Chinese Communist aggression were irrevocably linked, and this was a time not for words but for deeds. America would respond only when Communists in Europe and Asia began to behave properly and ceased to be obstructive.[92] Churchill tried again, but to no avail. Eisenhower had no interest in summit meetings with the new masters in the Kremlin.

When on June 16 and 17, first in East Berlin, then in other East German cities, including Halle, Jena, and Leipzig, riots broke out, it appeared for a moment that the German Communist regime was seriously threatened, and Eisenhower spoke of the uprising as "an inspiring show of courage." Nothing he said indicated a willingness to consider exploiting the situation, using it to wrest concessions from the Soviets or the East German Communists. Charles Bohlen later suggested the Soviets considered giving up East Germany at the time, that acceptance of the Churchill proposal for a meeting with the Soviets might have advanced that possibility, leading "to a radical solution in our favor on the German question," but neither Eisenhower nor Dulles deviated from their fixed policy of responding to all communist developments with the exaggerated rhetoric that had become habitual to them.[93] Lavrenti Beria's ousting and execution in 1953, like the assumption of power by two members of the Politburo, Georgi Malenkov and Nikita Khrushchev, had little meaning for an administration persuaded that Stalin's death and the arrival of new leaders changed nothing in the Soviet regime. Even the Soviet explosion of a hydrogen bomb in August, accompanied by the realization that the Communists possessed a bomber force capable of reaching the United States, did not unduly alarm the president who had anticipated these developments.[94] Much of the president's attention focused on the truce recently signed in Korea, which promised the end of the war, the fulfillment of his election promise.[95]

On October 30, 1953, less then a year after entering the White House, the president approved a statement of national security policy that included the words: "In the event of hostilities, the United States will consider nuclear weapons to be as available for use as other munitions."[96] Eisenhower understood the import of the statement and was not led to it by a bellicose secretary of state. Indeed, he made clear that the policy should not be made public till the National Security Council had given it further study.[97] Its importance derived from the fact that it announced a New Look in defense policy, predicated on two principal presidential beliefs: the nation could safely reduce its total military expenditures, understanding that there would never again be a conventional war; the nation's newly created strategic nuclear forces were the only sure defense.

Eisenhower believed that conventional forces, like those used in Europe in World War II and in Korea, were useless. Europe, he imagined, could be defended only by the threat of a nuclear attack on the Soviet Union should the Communists ever seek to penetrate NATO ground defenses.[98] Dulles made the president's views very explicit on January 12, 1954, before the Council on Foreign Relations, when he spoke of the need to have the "further deterrent of massive retaliatory power," to allow the "free community to be willing and able to respond vigorously at places and with means of its own choosing."[99] The concept of massive retaliation was born. The critical sentences, uttered by Dulles, were largely drafted by Eisenhower.[100]

Churchill, who met with Eisenhower in Bermuda in December 1953, together with Joseph Laniel, the French prime minister, was not greatly surprised by these statements. Churchill's dismay with Eisenhower, carefully concealed, had existed from the day he was elected president. On the Sunday after the election, in a conversation with Sir John "Jock" Colville, his secretary and confidante, he said: "For your private ear, I am greatly disturbed. I think that this makes war much more probable."[101] Eight months later, Colville reported Churchill as "very disappointed in Eisenhower whom he thinks both weak and stupid."[102] In Bermuda, Dulles expressed the view that if there was a "deliberate Communist offensive" in Korea, the United States "would feel free to use the atomic bomb against military targets, whenever military advantage dictated such use."[103] Churchill, shocked by these remarks, expressed his opposition to any such military operation, explaining that Britain "was a small crowded island; one good nuclear bombing could destroy it, and recklessness might provoke such a catastrophe."

Eisenhower assured Churchill he had no intention of acting rashly but would not be prevented from acting because of the objections of an ally. As he explained, "I merely wanted our friends to know that past limitations on our actions, in the event of a heavy attack on us, would not necessarily be observed."[104] This was not a chance remark; the president repeated it in a meeting with congressional leaders the following month.[105] If the Communists were to reopen the war, he would "hit them with everything we got."[106] In his concern to meet the demands of his Republican colleagues for a reduction in the defense budget, and because he believed the Truman appropriations excessive, his New Look was intended to provide strategic nuclear capability, lodged in long-range bombers under the control of the Strategic Air Command, that would guarantee the security both of the United States and its European allies.[107] Nuclear weapons were no longer to be thought of as exceptional; they were an additional arm, to be used only in self-defense.

Many, alarmed by what they heard, wondered what it would mean when the next crisis arose. They did not have to wait long. On March 13, 1954, in Vietnam, some 200 miles west of Hanoi, a French garrison was besieged by Communist guerrillas at Dien Bien Phu, and the question arose at once of what the United States would do militarily to help the French, whose armies at that point they were supporting only financially.[108] With a five-power conference planned to consider several crises, Vietnam among them, scheduled to begin in Geneva on April 26, the Communist attack on Dien Bien Phu was clearly timed to increase the chances of their securing more favorable terms. As early as January, the president had approved a paper whose first sentence read: "Communist domination, by whatever means, of all Southeast Asia would seriously endanger in the short term, and critically endanger in the longer term, United States security interests."[109]

Vietnam was thought the most vulnerable Communist target at the time, and the president began to talk of Vietnam as a domino whose fall might threaten any number of other countries in the region. The question of whether he should respond favorably to the French plea for military help became increasingly urgent.[110] When Dulles visited London on April 11, hoping to secure united action, to involve Britain in helping France militarily, Eden made it clear that while the government would support plans for a collective security system for Southeast Asia—the seeds of what later became the Southeast Asia Treaty Organization (SEATO)—it could not agree to do anything in Indochina until after the Geneva conference.[111] Churchill, meeting with Admiral Arthur Radford, chairman of the Joint Chiefs of Staff, was more emphatic, saying: "Since the British people were willing to let India go, they would not be interested in holding Indochina for France."[112]

Neither Churchill nor Eden believed there was a major Communist threat to Southeast Asia; both thought the French would be well advised to seek a compromise solution and hoped it would be provided by the Geneva conference. Churchill, more than ever, doubted Dulles, whom he characterized privately as "the only case of a bull I know who carries his China closet with him."[113] Eisenhower and Dulles did not receive from Churchill or Eden the kinds of support Truman and Acheson had come to rely on from Attlee and Bevin. When the journalist James Reston asked the president on June 30 if he was willing to accept a partition in Vietnam that enslaved millions of people, Eisenhower replied: "I won't be a party to a threat that makes anybody a slave; but to make such a statement doesn't mean you are not going to study every single region, every single incident that comes up, and decide what to do at the moment."[114] Clearly, the president was less hostile to what the new French prime minister, Pierre Mendès-France, had concluded needed to be done than his secretary of state. On July 21, agreements were signed at Geneva that established a cease-fire, partitioned Vietnam, called for national elections within two years, and created an independent Laos and Cambodia.[115]

Eisenhower, more or less resigned to that solution, knew that his secretary of state had no wish for the United States formally to accept the Final Declaration, and in the end the administration's refusal to sign it caused all the others to refuse as well.[116] Without a firm commitment on the part of the Americans to enforce the agreement, neither the Soviets nor the Chinese were prepared to do so, and the Americans agreed merely to take note of the agreements.[117] While Eden, for Great Britain, and Mendès-France, for France, believed the conference had been successful, largely through their efforts, noting what they interpreted as the reasonableness of both Molotov and Chou En-lai, Dulles interpreted the developments differently. The president also appeared to worry, fearing that the Geneva Agreements, already being violated by the North Vietnamese, might figure in the off-year congressional elections scheduled for November, affecting the Republicans adversely.[118]

Eisenhower relaxed during the summer and autumn and left it to his vice president to mount the hustings in support of Republicans contesting House and Senate seats. Nixon, delighted to be Eisenhower's surrogate, thought ahead to the day when he might need help from these same Republicans in seeking the presidential nomination for himself. In his vigorous campaigning, he showed all his characteristic habits, blaming the Democrats for the loss of China and the war in Korea, condemning the "Acheson policy" for ignoring the dangers that lurked in Indochina. In a forty-eight-day tour of thirty-one states, he charged the Democrats with having misunderstood or ignored the Communist threat at home, having "covered up rather than cleaned up" the Communists' infiltration of government.[119] Adlai Stevenson, irked by these attacks, saw Nixon as "McCarthyism in a white collar," and Sam Rayburn called him "the next thing to McCarthy in the United States," a man with "the meanest face I've ever seen in the House."[120] Lyndon Johnson, in private, referred to him as a "fascist," but the president, revelling in Nixon's attacks on those who advocated the "socialization of American institutions," wrote in late September a note of congratulations and thanks for "the result of your intensive—and I am sure exhaustive—speaking tour." Having done almost no campaigning himself, he added: "Please don't think that I am unaware that I have done little to lighten your load."

In the last weeks of the campaign, warned that the Democrats might make substantial gains in Congress, Eisenhower bestirred himself and traveled some 10,000 miles to speak for Republican candidates, but to no avail.[121] Nixon's harsh words and Ike's own laid-back presidency did not translate into victory for the Republicans, who lost control of both houses of Congress; in the Senate the Democratic majority was small, but it was substantial in the House.[122] Conservatives in the Republican Party blamed Eisenhower for the defeat, arguing that he had not been aggressive enough in his first twenty-two months in office.

In the period that followed, some Republicans pressed him to launch an atomic attack on China, in response to the Communist shelling of Quemoy and Matsu, two tiny islands off the Chinese coast.[123] Others begged him to be more aggressive in relations with the Soviet Union, still seen as "an implacable enemy whose avowed objective is world domination." In a report submitted to Eisenhower on the CIA, increasingly used by the president in covert operations, his investigating committee told him: "We must. . . learn to subvert, sabotage, and destroy our enemies by more clever, more sophisticated, and more effective methods than those used against us."[124] Because of the difficulties of introducing agents into the Soviet Union, Eisenhower came to believe that aerial reconnaissance offered the best prospect of meaningful discoveries. To prevent a surprise Soviet attack on the United States, Eisenhower agreed, in the greatest secrecy, to the construction of a new high-altitude plane, later christened the U-2, capable of using new photographic techniques to discover from very high altitudes vital information on the ground. The president approved the construction of these aircraft in late 1954, and the first successful test-flight took place the following July. The program was so secret and potentially so dangerous that Eisenhower accepted personally to review and approve every mission.[125] Intelligence by technology became increasingly important as the administration sought to learn more about the Soviet Union's military capabilities.

The Kremlin's agreement to the Austrian peace treaty encouraged many to believe a Soviet thaw was in the making, and both British and French pressure persuaded the president, apart from his own growing concern with Soviet missile development, that a meeting with the new leaders of the Soviet Union might prove useful. Leaving for the summit meeting in Geneva on July 15, 1955, he addressed the nation, speaking without notes, emphasizing his determination to bring about a new era in American-Soviet relations. Eisenhower's words—"I say to you, if we can change the spirit in which these conferences are conducted we will have taken the greatest step toward peace, toward future prosperity and tranquillity that has ever been taken in the history of mankind"—may have been hyperbolic, but the stage was set for a meeting that could not fail.[126] Eisenhower, for the first time in his presidency, enjoyed universal acclaim, as much from the foreign as from the American press.[127]

Germany, disarmament, and the development of East-West contacts figured as the important items on the summit agenda, and while agreement on German unification could not be reached—the Soviets refusing to accept free elections until all foreign troops, meaning the Americans, left Europe—few considered this a major setback. The president, in lecturing Khrushchev on the need for increased U.S.-Soviet trade and a "free and friendly exchange of ideas and of people," helped create what the media dubbed the "spirit of Geneva."[128] In this new atmosphere, where everyone seemed cordial and civil, it became difficult to believe that either side would ever be so irresponsible as to use its thermonuclear weapons. Eisenhower emerged as the celebrated man of peace, gaining new prestige for himself, telling congressional leaders that Khrushchev was clearly the boss, but that both he and Bulganin, "amateurs in diplomacy," took direction always from the old hand in the game, Molotov.[129]

Eden, now prime minister, and Harold Macmillan, his foreign secretary, shared the same impression that the Russians "wanted to be loved," but the imponderable leader for Macmillan was Khrushchev, of whom he wrote: "How can this fat vulgar man, with his pig eyes & his ceaseless flow of talk, really be the head—the aspirant Tsar—of all those millions of people & their vast country."[130] Eisenhower made no comparable comments, surprised only that the Soviet leaders appeared to have internal problems; though they were dictators, their constant refrain, "We can't go home with that statement or agreement" fascinated him.[131]

The summer of 1955 was a relaxed time in East-West relations, broken only by the startling news in late September that the president had suffered a severe heart attack.[132] When fears for his life subsided, many doubted that given the state of his health he would be able to run for a second term in 1956. The prospect of a Nixon candidacy filled many both at home and abroad with dread. Eisenhower, heralded as the man of peace, enjoyed a distinction he could never share with this dark, brooding individual suddenly catapulted into a position of prominence. Almost three years into his presidency, Eisenhower took credit for all that he had accomplished in Geneva, as well as for his victories over the Iranian rogue, Mohammed Mossadegh, forcing him out of power and returning the shah to Tehran, but also for a victory closer to home in Guatemala, where he defeated the Communists. That both were largely CIA accomplishments did not prevent his listing them among his proudest achievements in his first televised news conference in January 1955.[133] The CIA, together with the armed forces, seemed almost immune to criticism in what became the general's second political honeymoon as president.[134]

Indeed, the event in 1954 that more than any other commanded the attention of the nation—the decline and fall of Senator Joseph McCarthy—was achieved entirely without the president, principally through the work of the Senate. The public, transfixed for the thirty-six days of Senate hearings, all televised, saw McCarthy humbled by Joseph Welch, the Army's special counsel, determined to clear General Ralph Zwicker of charges the Wisconsin senator had recklessly made.[135] On September 27, the Senate committee appointed to judge their fellow senator voted to condemn him for breaking Senate rules and abusing the general.[136] Not till after the election did the Senate vote to censure McCarthy, but the hearings played heavily in the 1954 congressional elections and did something to diminish the fear of Communists at home.[137]

By the time of Eisenhower's heart attack, a new power had come to the fore in the Senate: Lyndon Johnson, the Democratic Majority Leader, who seized the occasion to seek legislation to increase the minimum wage, provide public housing, and extend Social Security benefits.[138] Johnson, persuaded that Eisenhower would not dare veto such obviously popular legislation, joined the president in pressing for a $33 billion appropriation for the construction of an interstate highway system, believing such collaboration with the administration would never hurt the Democrats at the polls.[139]

When the Republicans gathered in 1956 to renominate Eisenhower—gratified by his recovery—they made his foreign policy achievements seem all-important, showing an almost equal concern to take credit for what Congress had done in the domestic field. The Republicans, led by an aging president, recently incapacitated by an ileitis attack that required major surgery only two months before the start of the convention, represented themselves as "the party of the young"— one of the more exaggerated statements in a platform distinguished principally for its hyperbole.[140] The Republicans, gleeful that Eisenhower would lead them again but divided on whether they cared to have Nixon as his running mate, found the president heartily supporting his vice president, grateful for all he had done during his illness.[141] This did not deter Harold Stassen from suggesting that he be replaced by Christian Herter, the less controversial liberal Republican governor of Massachusetts, but the dump Nixon movement failed when Senator Jacob Javits of New York expressed his support of Nixon, and 180 Republican members of Congress joined in insisting he not be replaced.[142] The Republican ticket in 1956, unchanged from what it was in 1952, saw Stevenson, again the Democratic nominee, do what he could to portray Eisenhower as a "part-time leader."[143] While the issue of the president's health figured in the campaign, nothing the Democrats said or did seemed to diminish his appeal.

Stevenson's references to the heir-apparent had no impact on those who went to the polls. Nor did his comments on a president often ill-informed, frequently away on holiday, golfing or shooting, seem to distress voters. If, in his words, "the Eisenhower system just doesn't work," precisely because his Cabinet, all "hired hands," could never take the place of the man elected to "run the store," the election showed the president immune to all such criticism. His victory, the greatest of any candidate since that registered by Roosevelt in 1936, was a landslide, but the Republicans failed to capture either the Senate or the House—only the fourth time in the history of the republic that a president started his term without his party controlling one or both houses of Congress.[144]

There was no evidence that many had taken interest in the two foreign crises in Suez and Budapest that vied for national attention during the last weeks of the campaign. Neither the president nor his secretary of state understood either crisis, in part because each knew too little of how the situation in both the Middle East and Eastern Europe was changing under the growing dominance of two men—Gamal Abdul Nasser in Egypt, and Nikita Khrushchev in the Soviet Union.[145] On Nasser, Eisenhower received a warning as early as March 15 from Eden, based on what the British prime minister claimed was intelligence "of whose authenticity we are entirely confident," that the Egyptians were determined through covert action to overthrow the pro-Western ruling families of Iraq, Jordan, and Libya, establishing "purely Arab republics in Tunisia, Algeria, and Morocco."[146] Egypt, according to this information, intended to remove King Saud of Saudi Arabia, seeking to establish a union of the Arab republics under Egyptian hegemony.[147] Eisenhower, concerned that Egypt might one day cleave to the Soviet Union, recognized the importance of finding someone other than Nasser capable of acting as a prospective leader of the Arab nations, and he showed a decided preference for King Saud.[148]

This, as much as anything, revealed the president's innocence about the Middle East, its history and prospects.[149] Eden seemed prepared to sanction covert action to assassinate Nasser, but Eisenhower rejected that solution, and when Nasser nationalized the Suez Canal Company on July 25, the British prime minister pressed Eisenhower to agree that some sort of action was imperative. The Suez Canal, literally Britain's lifeline, with most of its oil passing through its locks, made Eisenhower aware of the extreme danger of the situation. He sent Dulles to London, hoping to calm Eden, to arrange for a conference of Canal users to negotiate with Nasser for terms satisfactory to all.[150] When nothing came of this, Eisenhower pressed for covert action against Nasser; anything, in his mind, was better than an outright British attack on his regime.[151] Eden, dissatisfied, contemptuous of Dulles, entered secret talks with the French, hatching a plan that would see the Israelis attack Egypt across the Sinai desert, allowing the French and British to intervene purportedly to separate the forces, thereby safeguarding the Canal.[152] Macmillan, having recently visited Eisenhower, told Eden, "I don't think there is going to be any trouble from Ike—he and I understand each other—he's not going to make any real trouble if we have to do something drastic."[153] He proved mistaken; Eisenhower, acting on slender information secured from the CIA, sent U-2s to spy on his allies—a situation he did not relish—to learn more about the French, British, and Israeli military intentions.[154]

Meanwhile, equally disconcerting events occurred in Budapest. Reports from the CIA told of 250,000 people in the streets, calling for free elections and the withdrawal of Soviet troops, and a day later, of Russian tanks entering the city to crush the "counter-revolutionary uprising." As intelligence findings reported some 5,000 Hungarian civilians killed by the Soviet troops, Eisenhower campaigned in New York City, denouncing the Soviet aggression and speaking warmly of the "renewed expression of the intense desire for freedom long held by the Hungarian people."[155] The rising did not end, however, and reports reached Eisenhower that a reformist Hungarian, Imre Nagy, had taken over as prime minister and that the crowds were continuing to demonstrate, appealing for American help. The president, alarmed by a situation that could lead to general war and confounded by the Soviet action, had never understood the significance of the secret speech Khrushchev delivered to the Twentieth Party Congress in February 1956, in which he denounced Stalin for his crimes against the Russian people and spoke bitterly of the "cult of personality" too long dominant in the Soviet Union.[156]

The president hoped the speech gave promise of an early relaxation of Communist controls within the Soviet Union and in its East European satellites, but neither he nor Dulles ever anticipated that the speech, once it became known in the Communist satellite states of Eastern Europe, would incite rebellion there. Neither thought to associate the speech with the risings in Poland that had preceded the Hungarian Revolution and were as surprised by one as by the other. Indeed, the CIA, having secured a copy of the speech, asked Eisenhower's consent to offer it to the *New York Times,* believing its publication could only redound to America's credit.[157]

Stalin, finally revealed for what he was, not by a foreigner but by a fellow Soviet Communist, did not lead many in the State Department or the White House to ask why Khrushchev had spoken as he did. No one recognized what Adam Ulam, a Soviet expert, said years later:

> But in 1956, American foreign policy, and not only in regard to Russia, was stymied and incapable of major initiatives or probes for a new approach. . . . American foreign policy. . . was well suited to counteract Soviet misbehaviour, to isolate and contain a Russia of the Stalinist model. But it was ill-prepared to deal with *intermittent* Soviet behaviour combined with appeals for friendship and eulogies of coexistence. The formulas and policies of 1952–3 had served their purpose, and they were useless in coping with the new opportunities.[158]

Though Ulam wrote principally of Eisenhower's policies in respect to the Soviet Union, he might as well have been describing the administration's reactions to events in the Middle East. As the U-2 flights in the region revealed heavy Israeli mobilization and substantial new British bomber strength on Cyprus, the president concentrated mostly on the first, wiring the Israeli prime minister, David Ben-Gurion, saying: "I must frankly express my concern at reports of heavy mobilization on your side."[159] When the Israelis invaded, the Americans still lacked information of what the British and French intended to do. Only when Eden spoke in the House of Commons did the Americans learn their intentions: to issue an ultimatum to both Israel and Egypt, insisting they withdraw ten miles from the Canal within twelve hours, allowing British and French forces to occupy strategic points along the Suez Canal, thereby effectively separating the forces.[160] Eisenhower was outraged at what he considered Eden's treachery; his first words to him on the telephone were sufficiently harsh to cause the prime minister to break into tears.[161]

When the British and French began to bomb Egyptian airfields on October 31, a U-2 surveillance plane estimated the damage, and Eisenhower decided at once he could not support Britain and France, believing that to do so would mean the loss of the Arab world. More than ever concerned not to give the Soviets an opportunity to make inroads in the Middle East and incensed by what his Allies had done, he instructed the secretary of state to introduce a resolution in the UN General Assembly calling for an immediate cease-fire. In the vote that followed on November 2, the Americans won wide support for their motion, with only Australia and New Zealand prepared to sanction the British, French, and Israeli military action.[162] Had the British and the French acted quickly, Eisenhower might have ignored their transgression. As it was, they did not land paratroopers in the Canal Zone till November 5, and Eisenhower worried that the Russians might use their aggression to launch a direct attack on Great Britain and France. The fact that the Soviets on the preceding day had sent 200,000 troops into Budapest along with 4,000 tanks, greatly stretching their own resources, did nothing to diminish his fears.[163]

On Election Day, November 6, a run on the pound and a heavy fall in Britain's gold reserves forced the United Kingdom to seek American support for an International Monetary Fund loan. The Americans responded immediately; there would be no help for the pound unless a cease-fire was declared by midnight.[164] The Eden government, humiliated and embarrassed, had no choice but to comply. The operation, a foolhardy one from the beginning, led to the most serious rebuff that the United States had ever inflicted on two of its major European allies.

While the British-French-Israeli operation had been a fiasco, the United States bore some responsibility for what they had done. The administration had hoped initially that the United States and Great Britain might win Egypt's favor by helping Nasser to construct the new Aswan Dam. That decision, made originally in December 1955, was an attempt to mollify Nasser and win his support; it suggested that neither the president nor the prime minister came close to understanding the man they were dealing with.[165] When the Soviets, in June 1956, sent an emissary to Cairo with an offer to finance and construct the Dam, Egypt thought to play the two superpowers off against each other; Dulles, angered by their duplicity and even more by Egypt's recognition of Communist China, decided the Americans ought to withdraw their offer to help build the dam. That decision led to consequences Dulles failed to foresee. Nasser's reply came on July 26 when he told a vast rally in Alexandria that Arab nationalism, on the march, would not be halted by the imperialists. The battle in Algeria between the French and the Muslim masses was Egypt's battle, he told the delirious crowd, ending his speech with the announcement that: "At this moment as I talk to you some of your Egyptian brethren. . . have started to take over the canal company and its property and to control shipping in the canal—the canal which is situated in Egyptian territory, which. . . is part of Egypt and which is owned by Egypt."[166]

Eisenhower, refusing to assent to the use of force, miscalculated the extent of British and French anger that made Eden write despairingly to him that had he not acted "Nasser would have become a kind of Moslem Mussolini and our friends in Iraq, Jordan, Saudi Arabia and even Iran would have gradually been brought down."[167] Indeed, Eden could see Egypt taking over the whole of North Africa.[168] The French, no less distressed, realized that Eisenhower had given too little heed to their plight in Algeria, where Egyptian assistance was contributing to what Guy Mollet, the French premier, believed was a principal incitement to Muslim rebellion.

Eisenhower's policies made the Europeans aware for the first time of the distance that separated them from the United States, and it is significant that the German chancellor, Konrad Adenauer, generally the most ardent admirer of Dulles, in a conversation with Christian Pineau, France's foreign minister, on November 6, said:

France and England will never be powers comparable to the United States and the Soviet Union. Nor Germany, either. There remains to them only one way of playing a decisive role in the world; that is to unite to make Europe. England is not ripe for it but the affair of Suez will help to prepare her spirits for it. We have no time to waste: Europe will be your revenge.[169]

If Germany and France saw Europe as the answer to the need for a diminished dependence on the United States, Britain interpreted the American rebuff as justified, anxious never again to separate itself from its protector. More than at any time since World War II, Suez led Britain to interpret its special relationship with the United States as the most reliable and necessary anchor of its foreign policy. Under Harold Macmillan, Eden's successor, the United Kingdom realized as never before that it could not afford, politically or economically, major responsibilities outside Europe.

The speed of decolonization in the years that followed exceeded what anyone had anticipated before Suez. At the same time, the Soviet Union's success in crushing the Hungarian Revolution served only to make Khrushchev increasingly reckless. Having demonstrated his ability to split the alliance, to frighten its principal members—the United Kingdom and France—with his threats, he imagined himself invincible.[170] Eisenhower, feeling no guilt for having denounced what his Allies had so stupidly done, used his victory to ask the new Congress to approve what became known as the Eisenhower Doctrine—a program of economic aid and military assistance, with the promise of protection against Communist aggression to all Middle East states.[171] The resolution, an extension of the Truman Doctrine of 1947, promised aid "to protect the territorial integrity and political independence of such nations requesting such aid, against overt aggression from any nation controlled by International Communism."[172] Congress passed the resolution, scarcely aware that the real danger to the Arab world came not from international Communist aggression but from internal social and political instability, nationalism exploited by Nasser, seeking to spread his doctrine of pan-Arabism.

In his State of the Union address in January 1953, Eisenhower committed the United States to defend the entire free world, a pledge never previously made. His words, expressive of a *hubris* inconceivable before Suez, informed Congress, "First, America's vital interests are worldwide, embracing both hemispheres and every continent. Second, we have community of interest with every nation in the free world. Third, interdependence of interests requires a decent respect for the rights and the peace of all peoples." He spoke as if Hungary had never happened, as if all of the secretary of state's fine talk about the liberation of enslaved peoples had been in no way compromised by what the administration dared not even consider doing in the first days of November. If Eisenhower and Dulles never understood Nasser, they showed no greater understanding of Khrushchev, the man who gained immeasurably from Suez and Budapest. Months after the Soviet suppression of Hungary, Dulles justified the U.S. failure to act with the words, "There was no basis for our giving military aid to Hungary. We had no commitment to do so, and we did not think that to do so would either assist the people of Hungary or the people of Europe or the rest of the world."[173] The United States had no legal obligation to help Hungary; this was a characteristic lawyer's defense. In Suez, the country demonstrated its moral virtue; this was the Christian believer's defense. Both ignored the fact that the crises allowed the Soviets to secure their bases in Eastern Europe and to gain new influence in the Middle East. The new Soviet leader, an accomplished actor, a genius at dissembling, knew how to use propaganda to achieve his ends; Eisenhower, tired, ill-informed, and indolent, lacked all those gifts.

This became apparent during the last months of 1957 when the Soviets launched their Sputnik satellite. Congress, the press, and the public, alarmed by what they interpreted as new evidence of Soviet superiority in missile development and in scientific education, demanded some response. Eisenhower, striving to restore calm, insisted that the American lead in intercontinental ballistic missiles was secure, but many, convinced the United States was vulnerable to Soviet missile attack, refused to believe him.[174] Indeed, the lethargy of a White House dominated by what Eisenhower's critics were now bold enough to call a semiretired golfer showed conclusively that the second-term administration's brief political honeymoon had ended. When, on November 3, the Soviets launched a second Sputnik, a much heavier satellite carrying a dog, the Democrats called for an impartial Senate investigation of the country's defense capabilities.

The hearings went on for two months and proved conclusively, at least to the Democrats' satisfaction, that the administration had failed in its efforts to create an effective missile and space program.[175] When, during these hearings, an unsuccessful attempt was made to launch a U.S. satellite, Lyndon Johnson expressed the common view when he said: "How long, how long, oh God, how long will it take us to catch up with the Russians' two satellites?" On January 7, 1958, speaking before the Democratic caucus, Johnson declared an effective space program to be imperative. "Control of space means control of the world," he said, and described Sputnik as the greatest challenge to America's national security in its history, hyperbole characteristic of that day.[176] Johnson, collaborating with Senator Styles Bridges, introduced legislation in April 1958 to create the National Aeronautics and Space Administration (NASA). The president, initially opposed to the creation of a separate space department, thought the idea of a lunar probe useless, but pressure from Democrats, the press, and prominent scientists told him to give way, pretending always, of course, that he had in no way surrendered.[177]

Because Sputnik was taken as evidence of America's backwardness in scientific instruction, proposals were made for what became the National Defense Education Act, passed on September 2, 1958. Again, Eisenhower began by rejecting the premises of the legislation, believing the federal government should not involve itself in education.[178] Compelled by Congress and public opinion to accept the need for some sort of federal assistance, he wished it to be limited; the $1 billion appropriation, finally approved, was to be spent over seven years, intended to improve instruction in science, math, and foreign languages, all declared essential to the country's defense. This legislation, passed at a time when the country was experiencing a mild economic recession, found the Democrats arguing for greater expenditures also for public housing and unemployment relief, proposals anathema to a president who believed in a balanced budget. The country's sentiments about the second Eisenhower term were revealed unmistakably in the off-year congressional elections when the Democrats gained fifteen seats in the Senate, going from a slim 49–47 majority to the really astonishing 64–36 edge. Rarely had any party been able to win so many seats in a single off-year election, and in the House the situation was scarcely less dramatic. The Democrats claimed 282 seats to the Republicans' 153. A more explicit repudiation of the president and his policies could not have been registered.

That, however, was not the way Eisenhower saw the situation, believing he had patched up his difficulties with the British in March in Bermuda, where he had met with his old World War II colleague, Harold Macmillan. While the prime minister agreed with the president that the Soviet menace in the Middle East called for close attention, he found the "legalism and pedantry" of the Americans disconcerting, deploring their weakness in addressing the continued Israeli occupation of the Gaza Strip and Sinai, both occupied at the time of Suez.[179] In his diary on February 19, a month before he met Eisenhower, Macmillan wrote with undisguised contempt,

> President Eisenhower, who has been on holiday for the last month or two, golfing and quail-shooting, has returned to Washington. The situation regarding the Israel-Egypt dispute over Gaza and the Gulf of Aqaba is getting more and more confusing and dangerous. . . poor Foster Dulles is foundering more and more. . . .[180]

Other diary entries of the period included references to the administration having "ratted again" and having "re-ratted." Finally, just before the Bermuda meeting, the Israelis, under considerable pressure, decided as an act of faith to abandon Gaza and the Gulf of Aqaba.[181] Of all this, Macmillan wrote, "it looks as if the American passion for being liked by everybody has got them into the position of being trusted by nobody. . . ."[182] His other diary entry, more meaningful than he realized, spoke of the delight the president felt in being able to "have somebody to talk to! In America, he is half King, half Prime Minister. This means he is rather a lonely figure, with few confidants. He told me very frankly that he knew how unpopular Foster Dulles was with our people and with a lot of his people. But he must keep him. He couldn't do without him."[183]

This indeed was Eisenhower's tragedy. He lacked an interlocutor who knew the Middle East, who could counsel him when crises erupted in the region. In May 1958, just months after Bermuda, President Camille Chamoun of Lebanon asked the British and American governments whether they would be prepared to provide military assistance within twenty-four hours if such an appeal was made. Nasser, it seemed, was preparing a military campaign against Lebanon, with Russian arms introduced from Syria, hoping to force Lebanon to join the Egyptian-Syrian state. Macmillan feared that were this to happen, Iraq would be the next to go. Iraq, the most pro-Western of the Arab states, was led by Nuri-al-Sa'id, ardent in his pro-British sympathies. On July 14, the British learned there had been a revolution in Baghdad, led by army units, that King Feisal had been murdered, together with his uncle, the Regent, and his cousin, Hussein of Jordan. Prime Minister Nuri al-Sa'id had escaped, only to be detected by a mob who then murdered him. The Baghdad Pact, signed in 1955 by Iran, Iraq, Turkey, Pakistan, and Great Britain, providing for their common defense, was dead, explicitly repudiated by Iraq in 1958.[184] The administration's hopes of making Iraq the defender of two weaker Middle East states, Jordan and Lebanon, were effectively dashed.[185]

Eisenhower, acting quickly, sent the U.S. Sixth Fleet to Beirut, and landed the Marines there, hoping this dramatic move would save Lebanon.[186] Jordan, under increased pressure from Syria, appealed to Britain for help. All that Britain could offer were two battalions of paratroopers, to be sent from Cyprus. A telegram from Khrushchev arrived, with the same warning he had given at the time of Suez. It read: "At the present historical moment the world is on the verge of a military catastrophe and the slightest careless step may entail irremediable consequences."[187] In the end, Lebanon was saved by the U.S. action, Jordan by that of Britain, but privately Macmillan feared that American policy in the Middle East "seemed to be becoming all the time more fitful and uncertain."[188] The Eisenhower Doctrine had purportedly worked, but Adam Ulam was not the only scholar who asked whether "the barn was half locked after the most valuable horse (Iraq) was lost, and again not to 'International Communism.'" Ulam stated the dilemma for Washington when he wrote: "Internal anarchy, abetted by the Arab-Israeli conflict, had created opportunities for Soviet influence to move into the vacuum created by the British withdrawal. Western influence could not be recouped through Congressional resolutions."[189]

Eisenhower never perceived the problem in these terms. Nor did he know how to counter Soviet propaganda, not least the claim made at the Seventh Congress of the Bulgarian Communist Party on June 4, 1958, by Khrushchev, when he said: "We are firmly convinced that the time is approaching when socialist countries will outstrip the most developed capitalist countries not only in tempo but also in volume of industrial production."[190] While many in Washington detected the bombast in these words, the Soviet Union's undoubted strides in military development blinded them to the Kremlin's weaknesses. More seriously, almost no one recognized the importance of the growing antagonism between the Soviet Union and China.[191] The administration continued to speak of the threat of international communism and acted as if the Soviet Union and China were Siamese twins, bound irrevocably together. Expressions of concern by the Chinese Communists about the Soviet Union's fidelity to Marxist ideology were very largely ignored. Indeed, when China declared 1958 the year of the Great Leap Forward, outlining its ambitious plans for rapid industrial development, no one in the administration believed that such changes could be realized as quickly as Chinese Communist propaganda suggested.[192] The question few asked was whether this was not a declaration by the Chinese of their determination to free themselves of their earlier dependence on the Soviet Union.

Hence, when the Chinese began to threaten two offshore islands, Matsu and Quemoy, no one in the administration doubted that this was done with Soviet support and that Beijing's ultimate aim was to take Taiwan. Indeed, when Dulles threatened the Chinese with nuclear retaliation, Khrushchev, in a letter to Eisenhower, wrote: "To touch off a war against People's China means to doom sons of America to certain death and to spark off the conflagration of a world war." The White House found the letter intemperate and returned it to the Soviet embassy. As the crisis deepened, and the policies of the secretary of state came under increasing attack both at home and abroad, Dulles, on September 30, repudiated much of what he had previously argued, insisting, of course, that there was "no intention of modifying our policy." In fact, he modified it substantially, saying that the United States had no legal commitment to defend Quemoy and Matsu, "no commitment of any kind" to assist Chiang Kai-shek to return to the mainland, and hoped a "reasonably dependable" cease-fire could be arranged. The Americans had backed down, all too obviously, and the Chinese Communists, gratified, announced a one-week cease-fire in the Taiwan Strait out of "humanitarian considerations."[193]

During a year when Americans were preoccupied with Sputnik, Lebanon, and Quemoy, the Supreme Soviet announced its plans to suspend unilaterally its atomic and hydrogen bomb tests, asking the other nuclear powers to do the same.[194] In these months it sought also to have the so-called Rapacki Plan accepted to create a nuclear-free zone to embrace West and East Germany, as well as Poland and Czechoslovakia.[195] The administration, fearing the plan's ultimate aim was to guarantee the division of Germany, rejected the idea. So, also, when the Soviets issued warnings against the placing of intermediate-range ballistic missiles in West Germany, the Allies could only believe that the Soviet intent was one day to use their superior conventional forces to conquer West Germany. What other explanation could there be for such threats?

On March 27, Nicolai Bulganin resigned as premier and Khrushchev took over that position, retaining also the office of secretary of the party.[196] When, on November 10, 1958, Khrushchev delivered a speech demanding an end to Berlin's four-power status, as agreed to at Potsdam, and followed this on November 27 with a note to the United States, Great Britain, and France declaring the four-power agreement null and void, saying that Berlin must be transformed into a demilitarized free zone, all recognized this as a serious crisis. If no agreement was reached within six months, the Soviet Union planned to sign a peace treaty with East Germany and turn over its occupation rights and access routes to the German Democratic Republic.[197] Adenauer, understandably shaken, refused to see it as Macmillan did: a threat that concealed an invitation to negotiate. Macmillan, desperately seeking an invitation to Moscow, was "cock-a-hoop" when he received it. During his eleven-day visit he saw Khrushchev alternate between being reasonable and flying into rages, making it clear that "the consequences would be very grave" if any violation of East Germany should occur after the conclusion of the peace treaty. Macmillan saw Khrushchev as a "curious study" and described him as

> impulsive, sensitive of his own dignity and insensitive to anyone else's feelings; quick in argument, never missing or overlooking a point; with an extraordinary memory and encyclopaedic information at his command; vulgar, and yet capable of a certain dignity when he is simple and forgets to 'show off'; ruthless, but sentimental—Khrushchev is a kind of mixture between Peter the Great and Lord Beaverbrook. Anyway, he is the boss, and no meeting will ever do business except a Summit meeting. . . .[198]

This became his constant plea with de Gaulle, Adenauer, and Eisenhower. The French president found Macmillan's arguments unconvincing, having no faith that exploratory talks with the Soviet Union would produce satisfactory results. In his mind, the Soviet Union was fundamentally fragile, its inferior political system concealed largely by the façade of military power.[199] De Gaulle, determined to prove himself Adenauer's friend, seeking closer Franco-German relations, wished to wean the chancellor from what he regarded as a too-great dependence on the United States. Eisenhower gave too little heed to these developments, as indeed he did to the establishment a year and a half earlier in March 1957, by the terms of the Treaty of Rome, of a common market. The joining of six continental West European states, France, Germany, Italy, Belgium, the Netherlands, and Luxembourg—three of them inconsequential for a president who concentrated all his attention on the antics of the Soviet leader—was a nonevent for him. Eisenhower had no idea of how much his victory at Suez had transformed the situation in Europe.[200]

Khrushchev's visit to the United States in September 1959, his Berlin deadline having been conveniently forgotten, proved to be the diplomatic event of the year for the president. The Soviet leader received a tumultuous welcome in the streets of Washington. Meeting with Gordon Gray, Eisenhower's national security adviser, Khrushchev heard Gray express views that he found wholly congenial, saying, "We must remember that Berlin is an abnormal situation; that we had found it necessary to live with it, and that it had come about through some mistakes of our leaders—Churchill and Roosevelt."[201] Gray told Khrushchev that "the time was coming and perhaps soon when we would simply have to get our forces out," ideas unlikely to commend themselves to either Adenauer or de Gaulle, fearful that Eisenhower almost certainly harbored comparable thoughts.[202] The president, after the Khrushchev visit, warmed to the idea of a summit, believing that it would indeed serve the interests of both the United States and its allies.

While many joined him in his euphoria over the thaw in U.S.-Soviet relations, others worried about the so-called missile gap, concerned that the American deterrent might not be effective in preventing a Soviet surprise attack on the United States. In the last year of his presidency, Eisenhower made the negotiation of a test-ban treaty, to be followed by significant disarmament, his principal policy objectives, believing they would have many beneficial results, not the least important being a substantial reduction in the size of the federal budget.[203] He hoped these ends might be achieved at a Paris summit with Khrushchev; meeting with de Gaulle and Adenauer in March and April, he won their agreement to make disarmament the main subject of the summit.

Two weeks before the start of the meeting, Eisenhower learned that a U-2 plane had been shot down over the Soviet Union. Khrushchev immediately denounced the United States for sending a "bandit flight" over his country and charged Eisenhower with not knowing what was going on in his administration, where "aggressive imperialist forces" were working to destroy the summit.[204] The president's initial silence, followed by the lame excuse issued by NASA that a research plane studying meteorological conditions was missing, having strayed off course, was made substantially more embarrassing when the wrecked plane was photographed, together with its pilot, acknowledged to be alive.[205] The State Department's determination to protect the president, suggesting he knew nothing of the flight, now led to another lie: The president claimed to know nothing of this particular flight. The summit, inevitably, was a disaster, with the president humiliated, made to appear a fool by the man many considered a buffoon.

As the nation turned to the nominating conventions, less was heard of the president, and few knew of the CIA plans made during his last months in office to oust Cuban rebel leader Fidel Castro. Eisenhower told Macmillan in August 1960 that if Castro survived for another year, "most of the governments in this Hemisphere. . . run the risk of being overtaken by revolution."[206] Believing a paramilitary operation against Cuba would succeed, and forgetting that an earlier one against Indonesia had failed abysmally, Eisenhower imagined the operation could be kept secret and was appalled when the *New York Times* on January 10, 1961, just ten days before the end of his term, published a story describing the training of anti-Castro guerrillas. Covert action, heartily approved by Eisenhower from the beginning of his first term, which had successfully toppled an impossible leader in Iran, was still his preferred policy for ridding himself of an equally offensive man in Cuba.[207] The Caribbean legacy he bequeathed proved a misfortune to his successor, John F. Kennedy.

Eisenhower's more serious failure—rarely acknowledged by those who continued to admire him—was his inability to understand the world abroad, as it had evolved since he had served as commander of the NATO forces in Europe. While some blamed his bombastic and self-righteous secretary of state for the errors made, Eisenhower as much as Dulles ignored the opportunities offered, starting with the death of Stalin and continuing into Khrushchev's ascendancy. He neglected to develop a Middle East policy that took account of what had changed after Britain left that troubled scene and was as ideological in misunderstanding Communist China as those who prattled on about how the Democrats had lost China. He never understood the Europe he pretended to know and failed utterly to comprehend how his policies were influencing both Adenauer and de Gaulle.

As a man who knew war and detested it, he kept the country at peace, and this was his signal achievement, but it was secured at a heavy price: the creation of the illusion that the United States could be the world's policeman, keeping totalitarian forces at bay everywhere. Eisenhower, the famed military alliance–builder in World War II, failed as a civilian. Men expected him to be an innocent with respect to politics and domestic policy, but his Kansas-bred belief in frugality, exacerbated by his Army-induced exaggeration of the values of an organized hierarchical staff, blinded him to anything that might be mistaken for a social vision. Reared in a military ghetto, granted perquisites, housing, and a guaranteed income by the federal government that were denied to tens of millions who had to weather the Depression, he lost touch with the Kansas world he was born into.[208] His intimate association with the very rich, his constant attendance on them on the golf links, were insignificant blemishes beside one other, rarely mentioned: his isolation from men able to instruct him, those in a position to offer constructive criticism of his policies. Only the British, who had come to know him well during World War II, anticipated his failure to conceive and execute a foreign policy adequate to the times.[209] Neither a savior nor a creator, he was, quite simply, a five-star general out of his depth in the White House.

CHAPTER 13

The Boy Wonder

JOHN F. KENNEDY, succeeding Dwight D. Eisenhower on January 20, 1961, delivered an inaugural address as memorable as the one Franklin Roosevelt gave in the depths of the Great Depression. Who could possibly forget Kennedy's first sentence: "Let the word go forth from this time and place, to friend and foe alike, that the torch has been passed to a new generation of Americans—born in this century, tempered by war, disciplined by a hard and bitter peace, proud of an ancient heritage."[1] Kennedy, just forty-three, the first president born after America's Victorian Age, had no need to remind his audience that his predecessor, seated behind him, was born in 1890. Nor did he need to say that the world's leaders were all ancient, Nikita Khrushchev and Harold Macmillan, sixty-six, Konrad Adenauer, eighty-five, Charles de Gaulle, the same age as Eisenhower, seventy, Jawaharlal Nehru, seventy-one, David Ben-Gurion, seventy-four, and Pope John XXIII, eighty.[2] The concluding words of Kennedy's speech—"ask not what your country can do for you—ask what you can do for your country"—was a proper patriotic ending for an inaugural address in which God received three mentions, Catholicism none.[3] Eisenhower, even with the aid of speechwriters would never have been bold enough to say:

> Now the trumpet summons us again—not as a call to bear arms, though arms we need—not as a call to battle though embattled we are—but a call to bear the burden of a long twilight struggle, year in and year out, 'rejoicing in hope, patient in tribulation'—a struggle against the common enemies of man: tyranny, poverty, disease and war itself.[4]

Nor would the general have been so immodest as to conclude: "With a good conscience our only sure reward, with history the final judge of our deeds, let us go forth to lead the land we love, asking His blessing and His help, knowing that here on earth God's work must surely be our own."[5]

Who, hearing these words, would have been so ungenerous as to suggest they expressed the sentiments of the boy wonder, the term Coolidge used to disparage Hoover?

Kennedy, young and handsome, arrived with the promise of leading the country out of its lethargy. Appealing to men and women, children of the twentieth century, Kennedy imagined he had discovered the constituency that would serve him as racial, ethnic, and religious minorities, trade unionists, farmers, and workers had helped Roosevelt, creating a solid Democratic base, guaranteeing him two terms in the White House. While the press and television dwelled on the beauty of the occasion and the uniqueness of the event, Kennedy was feted as the first Roman Catholic to reach the White House. Conspicuous for his wit and appearance, complemented by the beauty of his young wife, he boasted an exuberantly large and affluent family, all fit and athletic, much in evidence as he took the oath of office. Kennedy, other than Harding, was the only man to move directly from the Senate to the White House—a highly unconventional route, a detail left unmentioned—that led no one to compare his Senate career, one of modest distinction, with Lyndon Johnson's, the man sworn in as vice president.

No earlier twentieth-century president could claim a father remotely like Joseph Kennedy, a self-made millionaire and the great patron of his son. The Roosevelts, well-to-do and socially prominent, were rich, but as old-money Americans they never flaunted their wealth in the way the Kennedys did. Joseph Kennedy, an outsider in the Brahmin Protestant world of Boston, had made his way through the use of his intelligence and craftiness, never underestimating the importance of elbows. An expert in knowing how to profit from the stock market boom of the 1920s, and when to make an exit from that highly volatile market before the crash came in 1929, a rich man after World War I and very rich after the world economic depression, he had invested wisely in stocks and bonds, making a fortune in the new film industry.[6]

While his activities as a bootlegger during Prohibition were rarely dwelled on—Doris Kearns Goodwin's euphemism, referring to his having been in the liquor trade—they scarcely described the life of an entrepreneur whose extramarital affair with Gloria Swanson, one of the leading actresses of her day, was widely known. Entranced by Hollywood and New York, greatly preferring both to staid Boston, Joe Kennedy moved his growing family to a New York suburb in 1927 to escape Boston's anti-Catholic and anti-Irish prejudice, buying a house in Riverdale and a summer home on Cape Cod at Hyannis Port. A business mogul in many ways resembling the Gatsbys of his age, immortalized by F. Scott Fitzgerald, he soon owned a third house, a magnificent villa in Palm Beach, Florida, designed by Harry Mizner, the most celebrated architect of that affluent region.[7]

Successful and ambitious, Kennedy began to consider politics as his next conquest, believing that "the people who run the government will be the biggest people in America."[8] Franklin Roosevelt, the patrician he scarcely knew, influenced him greatly, and as a wealthy Democrat with a substantial fortune Kennedy was in a position to make significant contributions to the Democratic Party, the party of the Boston Irish in which his wife's father had been influential as mayor of that city. He contributed generously to Roosevelt's campaign in 1932, expecting some tangible reward, but Louis Howe, Roosevelt's closest confidante, distrusted him as a dangerous speculator and advised the president against offering him a place in his administration.[9] Roosevelt, in the end, appointed him head of the newly established Securities and Exchange Commission, arguing that it "would take a thief to catch a thief," believing that Kennedy knew Wall Street as few others did.[10] Having no illusions about his character, Roosevelt's choice dismayed many of his New Deal associates, but Kennedy recruited an able staff that included two young lawyers, William O. Douglas and Abe Fortas, who later served as justices of the Supreme Court.

Conscientious and industrious, he warned the president he would remain on the job only as long as necessary to get the commission fully operating. After only fifteen months, he resigned, expecting that a more important appointment would come his way, perhaps at the Treasury. None was offered, and Kennedy returned to his business activities, increasing his fortune, and contributing generously to the president's election campaign in 1936. Again, he received a disappointing reward for his ample support; offered the chairmanship of the Maritime Commission, scarcely the post he had set his heart on, he accepted, believing it might lead in time to something more prestigious.[11] Good fortune pursued him in December 1937 when the president invited him to become U.S. ambassador to the Court of St. James, a post generally reserved for socially prominent men, never before offered to someone still dismissed by many as Boston Irish.[12] Neither Kennedy, his wife, nor any of his jubilant children could have guessed that the appointment would end disastrously, destroying his friendship with the president, and giving him a permanent reputation as an appeaser who doubted that Britain could emerge victorious in any war with Nazi Germany, and that the only rational policy for Neville Chamberlain was to seek an accommodation with Hitler.[13]

With the approach of war, the ambassador's pessimism separated him from many of his English friends, and his defeatism, greatly resented by Winston Churchill when he became prime minister in 1940, guaranteed that he would always be persona non grata in England. That stigma attached to none of his children, neither his first son, Joseph Jr., killed in the war, nor his second, John Fitzgerald, nor his daughter who married the Marquess of Hartington, heir to the Duke of Devonshire, also killed in the war. Joseph Kennedy's London post gave the family a social standing it could have secured in no other way, allowing it to move in circles never previously entered by an Irish American.

Joseph Kennedy imagined his first son would one day be president, helped to that eminence by what he himself proposed to do with his substantial fortune.

After his eldest son's tragic death, he transferred that ambition to his second son, John—known universally as "Jack"—wealthy and handsome, famed for his heroism during the war, whose social grace and educational attainments made him seem a part of the WASP elite in everything but religion. While the boarding school Jack attended, Choate, in Connecticut, did not compare with Grottlesex—the Protestant Episcopal schools of greater renown—and while he never expected to be invited to join Porcellian, the Harvard club Theodore Roosevelt belonged to and from which Franklin, much to his chagrin, was blackballed, Spee served as an adequate substitute, a club for the sons of the well-to-do who in many ways resembled him.[14] Understanding and taking advantage of the perquisites that came from being the son of a wealthy and much sought-after American ambassador, Jack, unlike his parents, paid no price for his Catholic belief.[15] While the Protestant ladies of Cohasset on Cape Cod in an earlier day might look down on the daughter of Honey Fitz, Jack's mother, and refer to Joe Kennedy as "the son of Pat, the barkeeper," such sentiments were rarely expressed about the next generation of Kennedys, young men and women of privilege.

Jack Kennedy's undergraduate thesis at Harvard, completed in the spring of 1940, a 150-page paper entitled "Appeasement at Munich," exonerated both Chamberlain and Stanley Baldwin for their failure to halt Hitler, placing the blame on the country's slow-moving democratic system. The ambassador declared the product "swell" and asked his friend, Arthur Krock, a *New York Times* columnist, whether it might not be converted into a publishable book. With Krock's help, carrying the title he recommended, *Why England Slept,* the book appeared in July 1940, making Kennedy an instant celebrity. In the book's foreword, Henry Luce, the owner of *Time* and *Fortune* and a great friend of Jack's father, said: "I hope 1,000,000 Americans will read this book. They won't. But 100,000 citizens may well read this book. In doing so they will have performed an act of national preparedness quite as valuable as the easy flip-flapping of another appropriation bill through Congress."[16] Expressing the hope that "Mr. Kennedy will now proceed to give us a book on the relations between American policy and the near-collapse of civilized order throughout the world," Luce made extraordinary demands of a recent Harvard undergraduate who had written a fairly pedestrian account, a cut-and-paste exercise that pretended to explain why Britain had failed to rearm early enough, and why Munich was the penalty paid for that transgression.[17] As between the undergraduate thesis and the published book, the differences were substantial; with less emphasis given to the blamelessness of Baldwin and Chamberlain, democracy, conceived in the thesis as possibly an "unaffordable luxury," came to be represented in the published book as the ultimate good.[18] Kennedy, with help and advice from his father but also from Krock, ended with the words: "We should profit by the lesson of England and make our democracy work. We must make it work right now. Any system of government will work when everything is going well. It's the system that functions in the pinches that survives."[19] These juvenile sentiments resonated for the 40,000 who bought the book, and Joe, delighted with its success, wrote his son, "You would be surprised how a book that really makes the grade with high class people stands you in good stead for years to come. . . . You have the brains and everything it takes to go somewhere, so just get yourself in good condition so you can really do things."[20]

Excessively generous in the comments he made to his son, Joe Kennedy showed foolhardiness in what he said, presumably off the record, to Louis Lyons and two other journalists shortly after Roosevelt's election to a third term.[21] Pessimistic both about democracy and the war, Kennedy told the reporters: "I'm willing to spend all I've got left to keep us out of the war. There's no sense in our getting in. We'd just be holding the bag. . . . People call me a pessimist. I say, what is there to be gay about? Democracy is all done. . . . Democracy is finished in England. It may be here." He spoke of the queen of England and of Eleanor Roosevelt, highly flattering about the first, corrosive in his comments about the second. Of Queen Elizabeth, he said: "Now, I will tell you when this thing is finally settled and it comes to a question of saving what's left of England, it will be the Queen and not any of the politicians who will do it. She's got more brains than the Cabinet." On Eleanor Roosevelt, he said: "She's another wonderful woman. And marvelously helpful and full of sympathy. . . . she bothered us more on our jobs in Washington to take care of the poor little nobodies who hadn't any influence than all the people down there together. She's always sending me a note to have some little Susie Glotz to tea at the embassy."[22] When the interview, even in its sanitized version, appeared, Kennedy had burned his bridges with the president and the prime minister, as well as with many others in the United States and in Great Britain. Joe had submitted his resignation as ambassador weeks earlier, and the interview changed nothing in respect to his career, but on the day after it became official, he wrote a friend: "Having finished a rather busy political career this week, I find myself much more interested in what young Joe is going to do than what I am going to do with the rest of my life."[23]

The ambition that had once led him to concentrate on himself, he now transferred to his eldest son. Jack, at that point one of his greatly loved but troublesome nine children, was having an affair with a Washington reporter, Inga Arvad, suspected by the FBI of being a spy. Jack, working in the Office of Naval Intelligence with access to secret information, aroused FBI interest, and their investigation confirmed that he had indeed been "playing around" with Inga, "apparently spending the night" with her.[24] When Walter Winchell, the gossip journalist, alluded to the affair in a column on January 12, 1941, basing his information on an FBI source, the Navy transferred Kennedy to Charleston, South Carolina, where he remained for six months before receiving orders to report to the United States Naval Reserve midshipmen's school in Chicago to prepare for duty at sea on a recently invented small ship, the PT boat.[25]

Understanding Jack's determination to serve abroad, his father intervened with his friend, Senator David Walsh of Massachusetts, to make that possible, and the young lieutenant reached the remote Solomon Islands in the Pacific in late March 1943, taking command of PT 109.[26] Kennedy saw action almost immediately, and the destruction of his vessel by a Japanese destroyer established his reputation as a war hero. The collision caused the PT to break in two; Kennedy, stranded in the half that remained afloat, and realizing it would soon sink, swam to shore, an arduous five-hour effort that led to his rescue after six harrowing days. Joe Sr., first told that Jack was missing in action, learned later that he was alive and safe, and the story of PT 109, greatly embellished by John Hersey and others, made young Jack a hero.[27]

The family rejoiced for only a brief time; in the months that followed, Jack's older brother and his English brother-in-law, the son of the Duke of Devonshire, were both killed in action. Joe Kennedy, devastated by the death of his eldest son, transferred the ambitions he once held for him to his second son, and in a letter written on August 22, 1945, soon after Japan's defeat, indicated that Jack "is becoming quite active in the political life of Massachusetts," adding: "It wouldn't surprise me to see him go into public life to take Joe's place."[28] When, in November 1945, James Michael Curley ran for mayor of Boston and his seat in Congress became vacant, Jack, against the advice of his father, who wished him to campaign to become lieutenant governor of the state, chose to run in Curley's Eleventh Congressional District. His father took control of Jack's campaign, providing funds, and all the family joined in the Democratic Party primary battle, with only his sister, Kathleen, excluded. As the widow of a Protestant, a marriage disapproved of in a devout Irish Catholic constituency, it seemed better for her to remain uninvolved.[29] Kennedy achieved a remarkable 40 percent vote in a primary with ten candidates, and as the Democratic nominee in a district where the Republicans were vastly outnumbered, his election in November was assured; indeed, he won that election in a landslide, and his father wrote a friend: "I find myself with a new occupation—that of furthering young Jack's political career."[30]

No one ever claimed that Kennedy achieved very much in his time as a member of the House. In ill health a certain amount, suffering from back and other ailments, never adequately diagnosed or disclosed, Kennedy belonged to the Democratic contingent that lost its majority in 1946.[31] Harry Truman, president for the whole time Kennedy sat in the House, never referred to him once in his *Memoirs,* though Jack supported both the Truman Doctrine and the Marshall Plan, as most other Democrats did.

As a very junior member of the House, lacking political clout, Jack knew this was not the place in which he cared to remain for very long, and he began to think of competing for a seat in the Senate. Henry Cabot Lodge Jr., the grandson of Woodrow Wilson's nemesis, a principal aide in the effort to make Eisenhower the Republican presidential candidate in 1952, seeking reelection that year, had every reason to believe that both he and the much-admired Ike would win. Jack's father saw the situation differently, believing Lodge vulnerable, calculating that if his son ran against him and won, particularly in a year when the Republicans regained the White House, he would become a national figure instantly.[32] Lodge, respected for his integrity and industry, a senator from 1937 to 1944 and again from 1947, a Protestant Brahmin in a state where Catholics were in the majority, was supported by Republicans who admired his efforts on Eisenhower's behalf, but had to contend also with some in the party who were ardent Taft supporters.

Eisenhower, traveling to Boston on election eve to help Lodge, urged the crowd in the Boston Garden and the larger audience that heard him on radio to reelect the man who had first recommended him to "undertake this great crusade," characterizing him as "a man of courage and conviction, a vigorous opponent of the menace of Godless Communism."[33] Eisenhower, making a powerful plea to the tens of thousands of Massachusetts Catholics who figured among the more ardent supporters of Senator Joseph McCarthy, failed to persuade them to choose his Brahmin hero. In an election that saw 2,353,231 voters cast their ballots, Kennedy won with a majority of more than 70,000 votes; Democratic presidential nominee Adlai Stevenson lost to Eisenhower by more than 200,000 votes; and the Democratic governor, Paul Dever, lost to his Republican opponent, Christian Herter, by 14,000 votes.[34]

How had Jack managed to win? While his younger brother, Bobby, his campaign manager, deserved some of the credit, the lion's share went to the candidate himself, told by his college roommate, Torby MacDonald, that he owed his victory to his appeal to minorities, the newly arrived men and women of the state, no longer prepared to bend the knee to old-line Yankees.[35]

The young Kennedy, elected as much for his heroism, pulchritude, and Catholicism as for his father's willingness to spend vast sums to advance his political career, entered a chamber where seniority counted greatly. As a freshman senator, Jack was appointed to the Labor and Public Welfare Committee, a post not calculated to give him prominence; his father bestirred himself to see whether a more conspicuous assignment, to Appropriations, Foreign Relations, or Finance, might not be arranged. While no one wished to keep the young Kennedy down, few saw any reason to lift him to eminence, particularly after 1954, when he was the sole Democrat in the Senate not to vote to censure McCarthy. Absent from the Senate on that day, preparing for back surgery in a Boston hospital, he offended many of his liberal friends, but not Arthur Schlesinger Jr., his ever-loyal advocate, who noted he was "gravely sick in the hospital" at the time, adding, as if in further exoneration, that he "never gave the slightest support to McCarthyism."[36] Eleanor Roosevelt, less forgiving, showed no sympathy for him when his ambitions for the presidency became more apparent, saying: "I feel that I would hesitate to place the difficult decisions that the next President will have to make with someone who understands what courage is and admires it, but has not quite the independence to have it."[37] This condemnation by the former First Lady of the author of *Profiles in Courage* stung Kennedy, fearing its possible influence on his political prospects.[38]

Although it is difficult to know what attention, if any, Lyndon Johnson, the Majority Leader in the Senate, gave to the junior senator from Massachusetts, Joe Kennedy, watching Johnson attentively, believed he had presidential ambitions and might well become the Democratic Party's candidate in 1956, running against Eisenhower. Would it not make sense for the Texan to choose his Massachusetts son as his running mate?

Thinking always of Franklin Roosevelt's political career, unable to dismiss him even though he detested him, Joe believed FDR's 1920 campaign as vice president had helped to make him a national figure. Even if a Johnson-Kennedy ticket lost to an Eisenhower-Nixon ticket—and the older Kennedy was never persuaded it would—Jack would receive priceless publicity, and as a senator not obliged to run for reelection till 1958, he would retain his seat even if the Democrats failed to unseat the incumbent president. Approaching Tommy Corcoran, who had served Roosevelt and was now an intimate of Johnson, and bringing his younger son, Robert, along with him, Joe Kennedy asked Corcoran to carry a simple message to Johnson: If Johnson announced his candidacy for the presidency in 1956 and agreed privately to have Jack as his vice president, the old man promised to arrange financing for the campaign.[39] Corcoran carried the proposal to Johnson, who turned it down flatly. Unprepared to announce his own intentions, and seeing no advantage in making them known to the Kennedys while all others were kept guessing about them, Johnson refused to consider the offer. According to Corcoran, "Young Bobby. . . was infuriated. He believed it was unforgivably discourteous to turn down his father's generous offer."[40] Jack, knowing all about the plan, approached Corcoran himself to find out why Johnson had responded as he did. According to Corcoran, the senator, scarcely less blunt than his father and brother, said: "Listen Tommy, we made an honest offer to Lyndon through you. He turned us down. Can you tell us this: Is Lyndon running without us? . . . Is he running?" Corcoran answered: "Does a fish swim? Of course he is. He may not think he is. And certainly he's saying he isn't. But I know God damned well he is. I'm sorry that he doesn't know it."[41] Joe Kennedy, learning of the conversation, called Johnson to ask point-blank whether he proposed to be a candidate and heard him say he was not.[42]

As the 1956 Democratic Party convention approached, and as it became increasingly apparent that Stevenson would be the party's nominee again despite Truman's warning he could not possibly win, the Kennedys discussed whether

Jack would do well to pursue the vice presidential nomination, as recommended by many in the Boston press. When Stevenson won the nomination and declined to name his running mate, allowing the decision to be made by the convention, what Johnson later called "the goddamned stupidest move a politician could make," Kennedy knew he had only twelve hours to fight for the nomination if he indeed wanted it. His father, in the south of France, persuaded that Stevenson would lose despite Eisenhower's recent attack of ileitis, warned his son against attaching himself to a falling star.[43] While no such scruples existed when he thought Johnson a possible nominee, imagining then that the election might be close, he knew that outcome was impossible with Stevenson.

Jack, in this instance, decided to ignore his father's advice, allowed his name to go forward, and emerged with a surprising 304 votes on the first ballot, trailing Estes Kefauver, the senator from Tennessee, who claimed 483 and a half votes.[44] On the second ballot, Kennedy surged ahead with 618 votes to Kefauver's 551 and a half. The great surprise of this ballot was not New York declaring itself for Kennedy but Texas doing so, led by Lyndon Johnson, in its resounding cry: "Texas proudly casts its fifty-six votes for the fighting sailor who wears the scars of battle."[45] Kennedy needed only 33 and a half votes to win the nomination, but his managers failed to find them. On the third ballot, when several Southern states switched their votes to Kefauver, the nomination went to the man in the coonskin cap. Kennedy captured the imagination of millions who watched him on television, a handsome and vigorous senator, scarcely showing either the scars of battle or the effects of illness and surgery, arriving on the rostrum to ask the convention to vote to accept Kefauver by acclamation. James Burns, the historian, wrote: "In this moment of triumphant defeat, his campaign for the presidency was born."[46]

Burns understood the situation perfectly. Joe Kennedy wanted his son to be president; Jack wanted to be president. From the family's Thanksgiving dinner at Hyannis Port that year till the spring of 1960, nothing else interested them. No earlier campaign for the presidential nomination resembled the one fashioned by the Kennedys.[47] As Johnson recalled years later,

All of a sudden Joe Kennedy bombarded me with phone calls, presents and little notes telling me what a great guy I was for going with Jack during the vice-presidential fight. But I knew all along there was something else on his mind, and sure enough one day he came right out and pleaded with me to put Jack on the Foreign Relations Committee, telling me that if I did, he'd never forget the favor for the rest of his life. Now, I knew Kefauver wanted the seat bad and I knew he had four years seniority on Kennedy. And I would have preferred showing preference for Tennessee over Massachusetts. But I kept picturing old Joe sitting there with all that power and wealth feeling indebted to me for the rest of his life, and I sure liked that picture.[48]

Not surprisingly, Kennedy received his appointment to the Senate Foreign Relations Committee on January 8, 1957, using his position almost immediately to denounce France for its policy in Algeria. As he explained in a widely acclaimed speech, "colonies are fruit which cling to the tree only until they ripen," making it imperative that France recognize "the independent personality of Algeria" and seek to make peace with those fighting for a new status.[49] It took no great political courage for a U.S. senator to show disdain for the Algerian policies of the dying Fourth Republic, but many thought the young Kennedy had shown his true mettle.[50]

In Jack's battle to be reelected to the Senate in 1958, his father spent some $1.5 million, and the results showed the money was spent wisely: Kennedy won with 73.6 percent of the vote, a majority never previously registered in any Massachusetts senatorial race. Rose Kennedy, Jack's mother, active in his 1952 race, participated not at all in this campaign, knowing she was not needed. As she wrote at the time, "Shall await the big putsch—1960." While some imagined Stevenson might seek the nomination again in 1960, repeating what Bryan had done earlier in the century—a two-time loser who hoped to be victorious on his third try—most Democrats expected the two principal rivals to be Hubert Humphrey and Jack Kennedy, though no one discounted the possibility that Lyndon Johnson himself would carry off the prize.

Among liberals, and not only because of his father, Kennedy enjoyed very mixed reviews. When Eleanor Roosevelt issued her attack, she hoped it would be lethal; Kennedy, a "trimmer" who refused to take political risks, however brave he had been on a single occasion in the war in the Pacific, was not the person she yearned to see in the White House.[51] She was not alone in that sentiment; the liberal disaffection in the party worried Kennedy, but he hoped to compensate for it with an appeal to all those ethnic and other constituencies that had voted so decisively for him in 1958. On January 20, 1960, announcing his candidacy in the Senate Caucus Room, he believed the only issue that might defeat him was his Catholicism. Uncertain whether the country had changed sufficiently since 1928 to elect a Roman Catholic, he relied greatly on his brother Bobby, chosen as his campaign manager, to devise the strategy that would give him the prize. With his brother-in-law, Steve Smith, appointed schedule coordinator, and his "kid" brother, Teddy, assigned to organize victory in the Rocky Mountain states, he called on his mother to carry the torch for him in New Hampshire, the first of the primary states. Rose proved a superb campaigner; unafraid to be sentimental, she reminded audiences that "Jack knows the sorrow, the grief, the tears and the heartbreaking grief and loneliness that come to a family when a mother has lost her eldest son and a young bride has lost her bridegroom. So I know that Jack will never get us into war."[52]

Kennedy won in New Hampshire easily, a New England state with a large Catholic population, and no one expressed surprise at this victory. The next major primary battle, in Wisconsin, would be more difficult. When, on the Sunday before the Tuesday primary, the *Milwaukee Journal* published a map of the state, distinguishing between the predominantly Protestant areas and those where Catholics were in the majority, and when the election results showed that Kennedy had won narrowly, losing all the Protestant areas to Humphrey but winning overwhelmingly in Catholic areas, the religious issue became central. Only a victory in a predominantly Protestant state could demonstrate to Democratic Party leaders that a Catholic could be safely nominated. West Virginia, a poor state, one of the smallest, overwhelmingly white and Protestant, where coal mining and other extractive industries sustained a largely ill-educated population, became the pivot state. The media helped to create the impression that this was the make-or-break primary for both the leading candidates, Kennedy and Humphrey.[53]

Joe Kennedy, genuinely fearful, left in his private papers a cartoon from a Baptist West Virginia paper, entitled "Big John and Little John," showing the senator, with Pope John XXIII's hand on Kennedy's head, saying: "Be Sure to Do What Poppa Tells You."[54] Because FDR had enjoyed almost saintly status in the impoverished mining towns of West Virginia, where the New Deal did so much to alleviate the worst conditions of the 1930s, Joe Kennedy urged his son to recruit Franklin D. Roosevelt Jr. to speak on his behalf. Roosevelt scarcely helped him with his ill-considered charge that Humphrey had been a draft-dodger, a canard Kennedy felt obliged to repudiate, but the campaign became unpleasant for other reasons as well, made more so by Bobby, who acted as a man possessed, believing that any political tactic guaranteeing his brother's victory was legitimate.[55] Kennedy won, and Humphrey withdrew from the race, saying in a rare moment of anger, "You can't beat a million dollars. The way Jack Kennedy and his old man threw the money around, the people of West Virginia won't need any public relief for the next fifteen years."[56]

Kennedy went on to new victories in the Nebraska, Maryland, and Oregon primaries and had 550 delegates pledged to him when the Democratic National Convention opened in Los Angeles. Some liberals, fearing both the senator and his father, hoped to persuade Stevenson to run again. Johnson, recognizing that the twice-defeated Democrat would probably not succeed, looked to the possibility of emerging as the compromise candidate. At a meeting of the Washington State caucus, Johnson, throwing caution to the wind, denounced Joseph Kennedy in words he had never previously thought to use, saying: "I wasn't any Chamberlain umbrella-policy man; I never thought Hitler was right."[57]

Senator Eugene McCarthy, nominating Stevenson, caused the galleries to explode and for a moment Adlai appeared in serious contention for the prize, but this was a delusion, rapidly extinguished when Mayor Richard Daley of Chicago announced that Illinois would give 59 and a half votes for Kennedy, and only two for Stevenson. A first-ballot Kennedy victory was certain, and the only remaining question was who he would choose as his running mate. Despite what the Democratic Majority Leader had said of his father, he opted for Johnson—a safe bet from his point of view because he never expected Johnson to accept the offer. Kennedy knew the Senate Majority Leader less well than he imagined.[58]

Campaigning vigorously, traveling through the country promising "to get the country moving again," his greatest victory, perhaps, came in his first televised debate with Richard Nixon, the Republican candidate, on September 25, 1960. While no one declared it an outright victory for Kennedy, his charm and charisma showed on screen to great advantage; Nixon, nervous and awkward, using makeup to conceal his heavy beard and jowls, sweated profusely through the ordeal. Kennedy, as skillful with television as Roosevelt had been with radio, a Prince Charming beside the man seeking to hide his five o'clock shadow, was seen by some 70 million Americans, and the debate set the tone for the campaign that followed.[59]

One of Kennedy's many charges, one that had stung Eisenhower acutely, suggested he had given insufficient attention to the country's missile development, and that a serious missile gap existed. In the tale, as told by Kennedy, the United States was falling behind the Soviet Union in its military capability because of unnecessarily severe budget restrictions, and until that changed, negotiations with the Soviet Union would never succeed. Nixon, seeking liberal Republican support, especially that of Nelson Rockefeller, New York's governor, issued a joint statement with him, saying among other things: "The United States can afford and must provide the increased expenditures to implement fully this necessary program for strengthening our defense posture."[60] Eisenhower could only believe that Nixon had betrayed him, appeasing Rockefeller to win his support.[61] When in a press conference the president was asked to give an example of a major idea proposed by Nixon that his administration had adopted, his answer was: "If you give me a week, I might think of one, I don't remember." Though not an intended insult, this made the vice president seem to lack even the president's imprimatur.[62] Such gaffes, though important, counted for little in an election in which Kennedy's vigor, gaiety, charm, and glamor contrasted with the more pedestrian qualities of an aging president and an awkward vice president. Kennedy defeated Nixon with a bare majority of the popular vote but with a comfortable majority in the Electoral College, which some Republicans claimed was secured largely through fraudulent returns in Texas and Illinois.[63] Nixon, hurt and angry, wisely chose not to challenge the official count.

A Democrat with as limited experience of administration as any twentieth-century president with the possible exception of Warren Harding moved into the White House, and the nation rejoiced, believing a new generation had indeed taken over. The victory was Kennedy's alone, his and that of his devoted extended family, principally his younger brother, who had worked indefatigably for it. While Woodrow Wilson, grateful to William Jennings Bryan for all he

had done to secure his nomination, rewarded him with his appointment as secretary of state, Kennedy felt no obligation to Adlai Stevenson, often mentioned
for the post. Nor did he feel any need to appoint any member of the Senate or
House, where his friends were few and where none had proved especially helpful. William Fulbright of Arkansas would have welcomed the State Department
appointment, but Kennedy saw no reason to favor him; he chose Dean Rusk, a
former assistant secretary of state, whom he scarcely knew. As secretary of the
treasury, after approaching several others, he settled on C. Douglas Dillon, a distinguished banker, expected to enjoy wide support in the business community.

For secretary of defense, he chose Robert McNamara, president of the Ford
Motor Company, recommended to him by one of his chief talent scouts, Harris
Wofford.[64] Deborah Shapley, McNamara's biographer, suggested that Kennedy
wanted to have one or two Republicans in his Cabinet, and while McNamara
hardly qualified as a prominent Republican, he claimed other distinctions: a
young and prominent businessman who had been to the Harvard Business
School, supported the American Civil Liberties Union, and read Teilhard de
Chardin—these were all considered very substantial assets. In what must figure
as one of the more amusing sentences in Shapley's biography, she wrote of
McNamara's "coyness," suggesting it did not much daunt the president-elect.
In her words, "On the contrary, the Kennedy brothers had been steeped in classical literature, and according to Wofford, fancied that their government would
be like Plato's Republic, where the most worthy citizens would be reluctant to
serve."[65] One can only assume that Shapley quoted Wofford accurately, that he
really believed the Kennedys were "steeped in classical literature," an idea that
would have seemed grotesque to anyone who knew the true situation, but then,
decades later, two prominent Harvard historians, beguiled by the legacy of the
then-dead president, referred to him as a historian, as if *Why England Slept* and
Profiles in Courage gave him that distinction.[66] In any case, McNamara accepted the post, and another individual unknown to the president became a
prominent member of his Cabinet.

When Eisenhower came to the White House, scarcely knowing political
Washington, it was taken for granted that he would rely on those who had
pressed him to run, men like Henry Cabot Lodge Jr. Kennedy, after just a little over a decade in the House and the Senate, knew Washington no better, and
having achieved his election through his own efforts and those of his family,
felt beholden neither to Democratic Party political leaders nor to former colleagues in Congress. He showed his independence most conspicuously in his
decision to appoint Robert Kennedy to be attorney general. Though there was
no record of comparable presidential nepotism in the past, only a few voices
were raised to question the appointment of someone who lacked the credentials
traditionally thought important for that legal appointment. Kennedy wanted
tough men in his entourage, and no one doubted that his brother qualified on

that score.[67] How the appointment would affect other members of the Cabinet and how it might distort their relations with the president scarcely figured in a situation where Kennedy clearly needed one intimate in his immediate entourage, on whom he could rely absolutely.[68]

While newly elected presidents generally enjoyed a political honeymoon, Kennedy's proved exceedingly short, principally because of the disastrous Bay of Pigs invasion, planned by the CIA during the last months of the Eisenhower administration. Still, Kennedy started with one incontestable advantage, made even more remarkable by his extraordinary inaugural address. Represented by the media as a political genius, surrounded with men no less able, Dean Rusk at State, Robert McNamara at Defense, McGeorge Bundy as national security adviser, and Adlai Stevenson at the United Nations, these men were all thought exceptionally brilliant and talented.

The second team, according to the media, was no less remarkable and included, among others, Walt Rostow, William Bundy, George Ball, Paul Nitze, John McNaughton, Arthur Schlesinger Jr., Bill Moyers, and others, in some instances less known but no less promising. Not till 1969, when David Halberstam published *The Best and the Brightest,* did anyone dare suggest that many were no more able and scarcely more accomplished than those who had served under Truman or Roosevelt. James MacGregor Burns, one of the first to ask whether the hyperbole was not excessive, wrote of the president:

> He is not only the handsomest, the best dressed, the most articulate, and graceful as a gazelle. He is omniscient; he swallows and digests whole books in minutes; his eye seizes instantly on the crucial point in a long memorandum; he confounds experts with superior knowledge of their field. He is omnipresent; no sleepy staff member can be sure that he will not telephone—or pop in; every hostess at a party can hope that he will. He is omnipotent; he personally bosses and spurs the whole shop; he has no need of Ike's staff apparatus; he is more than a lion, more than a fox. He's Superman.[69]

Superman surrounded by supermen—that was the initial judgment of the mass media, and even the vice president, Lyndon Johnson, seemed prepared to share that view. Praising the new Cabinet to his old friend, Sam Rayburn, he heard the Speaker reply: "They may be every bit as intelligent as you say, but I'd feel a lot better about them if just one of them had run for sheriff once."[70]

While the Bay of Pigs disaster dented the president's reputation for sagacity, it did little to destroy it. Indeed, his willingness to assume responsibility for the failed intelligence and military operation created sympathy for him, at home and abroad. Still, it was impossible to avoid the question of how the president could have been so naïve as to accept such flawed plans for a covert invasion of Cuba. Christopher Andrew, author of *For the President's Eyes Only,* believed that neither the president nor any of his close advisers knew very much about the CIA when they took office.[71] The director of central intelligence, Allan Dulles, instructing the secretary of state, the secretary of defense, and the attorney general on January 22, hours after the inaugural festivities ended, informed them that the plan to hold "a beachhead long enough for us to recognize a provisional government and aid that government openly" seemed feasible.[72]

The president, recognizing the enormity of the political risks, preferred small guerrilla operations to a major invasion and specifically asked that there be no overt U.S. air support. The obsolete B-26 planes given to the rebels would be flown by American contract pilots, and McGeorge Bundy, drafting NSAM 31 (National Security Action Memorandum) in early March, expressed the president's readiness to "authorize U.S. support for an appropriate number of patriotic Cubans to return to their homeland" but complained that the "best plan" for doing so had not yet been offered. The CIA, responding to this explicit criticism, changed the plan for the site of the landing, and Bundy informed the president that the CIA had "done a remarkable job of reframing the landing so as to make it unspectacular and quiet, and plausibly Cuban in its essentials."[73] With these minor changes the president seemed satisfied and approved the proposal, concerned only that he be able to deny any U.S. involvement should it fail. The original plan to establish a provisional government on the beachhead was dropped, the assumption being that a general uprising would follow in Cuba if the invasion succeeded; if it failed, guerrilla activity on the island would be stimulated by those who had landed.

As rumors spread of the impending invasion, and stories appeared in the American press, even in the *New York Times,* the president grew increasingly apprehensive, determined to go ahead, but to do so with a minimum of aircraft and men.[74] Early on April 17, 1,400 men landed, and as Bundy told the president the next day, "the Cuban armed forces are stronger, the popular response is weaker, and our tactical position is feebler than we had hoped."[75] Nikita Khrushchev, denouncing the invasion and urging the United States to stop an operation "fraught with danger to world peace," seemed for a moment to frighten the president, but the mood passed; believing "he'd rather be called an aggressor than a bum" he appeared resolute again, deciding later to return those still on the beachhead. Even that effort failed; 140 of the invaders were killed, 1,189 taken prisoner.[76]

Kennedy, having gambled and lost, despairing but never doing so in public, emerged with the memorable words, "victory has a hundred fathers and defeat is an orphan."[77] Kennedy blundered as badly in Cuba as the British prime minister Anthony Eden had done in Suez, stopped not by outraged allies but by his unwillingness to risk a greater defeat, possibly a Soviet attack on Berlin.[78] Surprisingly, Kennedy saw his popularity at home soar to 83 percent approval.

"The worse you do, the better they like you," he said, knowing that in the first major crisis of his administration he had failed abysmally. In the White House, tempers flared, unmentioned by Arthur Schlesinger Jr., who together with Chester Bowles had opposed the plan, and secret talks were opened on the possibility of assassinating Fidel Castro. On October 5, in NSAM 100, Bundy asked Rusk for a plan for a "particular Cuban contingency."[79] The contingency, never mentioned explicitly but communicated orally, would have had Castro "in some way or other. . . removed from the Cuban scene."[80] Clearly, as Lawrence Freedman, one of the more sympathetic of those who wrote about the president and the Bay of Pigs operation, said: "It seems reasonably clear that Kennedy had asked for the plan."[81] The State Department answered that the elimination of Castro would only bring his brother, Raul, to power, that a reign of terror would follow, and that the successor regime would destroy "any hope of U.S. intervention short of a massive assault." In Freedman's words, "The United States would be blamed for the death, and this would be generally believed throughout Latin America."[82]

The Board of National Estimates made an equally grim forecast. Castro's death, by "assassination or natural causes, would certainly have an unsettling effect, but would probably not prove fatal"; the regime would survive. Indeed, Castro as a martyr might prove more useful to a Communist regime than Castro alive. In November, the president, as if to close an issue the public knew nothing about, said quite simply: "We cannot as a free nation, compete with our adversaries in tactics of terror, assassination, false promises, counterfeit mobs and crises."[83] The Bay of Pigs episode seemed closed, and the president turned his mind to more urgent matters—specifically, how to deal with Khrushchev's increasing belligerence, and what attitude to adopt in respect to the growing Soviet threats to Berlin.

Those threats became even more preoccupying following Kennedy's encounter with Khrushchev in Vienna in June.[84] The president's days in Paris before that fateful meeting, allowing him to use his charm to flatter the French president, gave him one reward, compliments more effusive than any granted other American leaders. De Gaulle, praising the young Kennedy for his energy, drive, intelligence, and courage, in a dinner to honor the president and his wife, expressed views not repeated to his colleagues later, where he spoke of Kennedy "suffering the drawbacks of a novice."[85] While the discussions ranged over many subjects, including NATO, Berlin, Laos, and Vietnam, de Gaulle warned Kennedy against any intervention in Southeast Asia, claiming it would be "a bottomless military and political quagmire."[86] No substantive agreements were reached in Paris, and Kennedy spoke privately of the general caring for nothing except the "selfish" interests of his country, taking it as a given that he, as president of the United States, had more universal interests.[87]

Averell Harriman, advising him before he encountered Khrushchev, told him to go to Vienna, but don't be too serious, have some fun, get to know him a little, but don't let him rattle you; he'll try to rattle you and frighten you, but don't pay any attention to that. Turn him aside, gently. And don't try for too much. Remember that he's just as scared as you are. . . he is very aware of his peasant origins, of the contrast between Mrs. Khrushchev and Jackie. . . . His style will be to attack and then see if he can get away with it. Laugh about it, don't get into a fight. Rise above it. Have some fun.[88]

Harriman gave the president a script that he found impossible to follow. In a discussion of the relative virtues of the capitalist and communist systems, the president sought to reassure the Soviet leader, accepting the reality of Soviet strength, and dwelling on its numerous accomplishments, stressing always the importance of mutual understanding for the preservation of peace. Khrushchev seemed more interested in scoring points, telling his colleagues later that the president, young and intelligent, was also a weak man.[89] The president hoped to reach an agreement with Khrushchev on a nuclear test ban, but no progress was made, and the Soviet leader's insistence that he would soon sign a peace treaty with both the Federal Republic of Germany and the German Democratic Republic to prevent their unification greatly disconcerted Kennedy. If only the latter agreed to sign, Khrushchev warned, access to Berlin by air and road through East Germany would be suspended.[90] Prepared to wait till December to achieve his objective, but no longer, the president left Vienna a shattered man, looking for solace in London with Prime Minister Macmillan.[91]

Once again in Washington, in a major televised address, Kennedy described the crisis, insisting the choice was not "between resistance and retreat, between atomic holocaust and surrender. . . . Our response to the Berlin crisis will not be merely military or negative."[92] What, then, would it be? When the East Germans threw up barriers that blocked access from East to West Berlin on August 13, the first steps in the construction of what soon became the Berlin Wall, the president and his advisers, increasingly despondent, saw their confusion grow with the unexpected announcement that the Soviets planned to resume nuclear testing.[93] On August 28, 1961, McGeorge Bundy, in a memorandum to the president, wrote: "The main line of thought among those who are now at work on the substance of our negotiating position is that we can and should shift substantially toward acceptance of the GDR, the Oder-Neise line, a non-aggression pact, and even the idea of two peace treaties."[94]

Konrad Adenauer, the German chancellor, exploded when a newspaper report on September 22, clearly inspired by the White House, suggested that West Germany would have a better chance of achieving German reunification "by talking to the East Germans" instead of ignoring them.[95] Bundy imagined he improved the situation in December when he told Bonn it would never have any "legitimate cause to regret their trust in us," adding that "we cannot grant—and no

German statesmen have asked—a German veto on the policy of the West. A partnership of free men can never move at the call of one member only."[96]

When Kennedy phoned de Gaulle on December 12, suggesting a new approach to Khrushchev, the French president showed scant sympathy for his proposal, explaining that he would never participate in talks with the Soviets as long as the Berlin Wall existed. De Gaulle, in this transatlantic call initiated by Kennedy, asked what the "heart of the problem was" and proceeded to answer his own question, claiming that the Soviet leader sought "the neutralization of Germany, which would be followed by the neutralization of Europe," and that France would never consent to either.[97] In the general's mind, the only relevant question—whether the Europe he and the chancellor wished to see established would be European or Atlantic—admitted of only a single answer, one he guessed the president had no interest in.[98]

Another crisis, less dangerous but nonetheless preoccupying, led the president to send General Maxwell Taylor and Walt Rostow, his assistant national security adviser, to South Vietnam, to make recommendations for American policy in that recently created state, threatened by both internal and external Communist aggression.[99] Taylor and Rostow, after a fortnight's visit, returned to urge that the United States become more actively involved in the country's economic, political, and military operations. In their words, "Only the Vietnamese could defeat the Viet Cong; but at all levels Americans must, as friends and partners—not as arm's length advisors show them how the job might be done—not tell them or do it for them."[100]

The two advisers suggested a U.S. military task force of 6,000–8,000 men to raise South Vietnamese morale and "conduct such combat operations as are necessary for self-defense."[101] These troops, the president was told, could be dispatched under the fiction of helping the Vietnamese to recover from a devastating flood in the Mekong Delta.[102] Accepting that the existing Ngo Dinh Diem regime was a "cauldron of intrigue, nepotism, and corruption joined to administrative paralysis and steady deterioration," they made no recommendation for any effort to dislodge Diem; such a policy would be too dangerous.[103] While those who advised the president believed that the small military force would be helpful to the South Vietnamese, they never imagined it would be sufficient to defeat the North Vietnamese or the Vietcong; the latter were deemed immensely dangerous, and an imminent takeover by them was not thought impossible. Kennedy hesitated but in the end agreed to send troops, telling Diem, in effect, that they were not to be used in combat.[104] Kennedy, however reluctantly, had taken the first step on the slippery slope that would lead in time to a war more terrible than any he or his advisers imagined in his first year in the White House.

The year 1961 had not been the extraordinary period he and his colleagues had envisaged, and the situation improved scarcely at all in the following

Theodore Roosevelt standing before a globe (Photo Courtesy of the Library of Congress, LC-USZ62–7220)

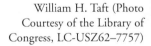

William H. Taft (Photo Courtesy of the Library of Congress, LC-USZ62–7757)

Woodrow Wilson and wife riding in the backseat of a carriage to his second inauguration, March 5, 1917 (Photo Courtesy of the Library of Congress, LC-USZ62–22737)

Warren Harding with his pet dog, Laddie (Photo Courtesy of the Library of Congress, LC-USZ62–65041)

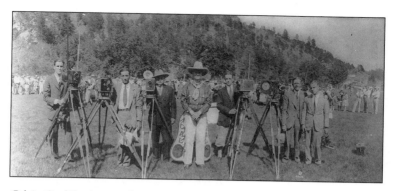

Calvin Coolidge in a cowboy outfit, standing with photographers (Photo Courtesy of the Library of Congress, LC-USZ62–29740)

Herbert Hoover (Photo Courtesy of the Library of Congress, LC-USZ62–92155)

Franklin D. Roosevelt signing the declaration of war against Japan (Photo Courtesy of the Library of Congress, LC-USZ62–15185)

Harry Truman at his desk
(Photo Courtesy of the Library
of Congress, LC-USZ62–70080)

Truman at Potsdam with
Clement Attlee and Joseph
Stalin (Photo Courtesy of
the Library of Congress,
LC-USZ62–11988)

Dwight D. Eisenhower (Photo
Courtesy of the Library of
Congress, LC-USZ62–84331)

John F. Kennedy and Robert Kennedy (Credit: Associated Press. Photo Courtesy of the Library of Congress, LC-USZ62–120981)

Lyndon B. Johnson (Photo Courtesy of the Library of Congress, LC-USZ62–94417)

Richard Nixon (Photo Courtesy of the
Library of Congress, LC-USZ62–13037)

Gerald Ford (Photo Courtesy of the
Library of Congress, LC-USZ62–13038)

Jimmy Carter (Photo Courtesy of the
Library of Congress, LC-USZ62–13039)

Ronald Reagan (Photo Courtesy of the Library of Congress, LC-USZ62–13040)

George H.W. Bush (Photo Courtesy of the Library of Congress, LC-USZ62–98302)

Bill Clinton at his desk (Photo Courtesy of the Library of Congress, LC-USZ62–124945)

George W. Bush on the flight deck of the USS *Abraham Lincoln* in a pilot suit, May 1, 2003 (Credit: Corbis)

spring, though this was not apparent to Kennedy. McNamara echoed what other administration officials also told the president, claiming after a two-day visit to South Vietnam that he saw "nothing but progress and signs of further progress," that the United States was winning, and that there would be no need for the introduction of combat troops.[105] General Taylor, visiting the country a second time in September 1962, was equally optimistic and spoke of the great success of the strategic hamlet program that "had resulted in some 5,000 hamlets being fortified or in the process of fortification."[106] Secretary of Defense McNamara expressed the hope he would be able to withdraw the last 1,500 U.S. troops by 1968, reducing military assistance to $40.8 million, less than a quarter of what was being spent in 1962.[107] That opinion scarcely reflected what press and TV commentators in Vietnam were reporting, but the president chose to believe what his secretary of defense and chairman of the Joint Chiefs of Staff told him.

During the summer, for reasons never adequately explained, the president ordered the installation of a secret taping system to record conversations in the Cabinet Room, the Oval Office, and the Library. The president, by simply pressing a button, would be able to record any conversations he wished to preserve. Ernest May and Philip Zelikow, the editors of these tapes, first published in full in 1997, while acknowledging that it was impossible to know what motivated the president to wish to install such a system, believed that "as both a reader and a writer of history, he may have been looking forward to future memoirs."[108] The same argument, used later to explain President Richard Nixon's decision to install a more complex taping system, though reasonable, was never wholly convincing, and May and Zelikow, somewhat uncomfortable with their own explanation, thought it necessary to add that the "practice had precedents," citing Franklin Roosevelt having "recorded a few conversations by means of a Dictaphone hidden in his desk."[109]

Kennedy, like several of his predecessors, also authorized wiretapping and bugging by the FBI—neither illegal at the time—details offered to exonerate what might otherwise appear to be presidential behavior of dubious legality and morality. The Kennedy tapes provided incomparable information on what proved to be *the* great event in the Kennedy administration: the Cuban missile crisis. Because Robert Kennedy's *Thirteen Days: A Memoir of the Cuban Missile Crisis,* published originally in 1969 and republished in 1971, with an afterword by two Kennedy School of Government professors, Richard Neustadt and Graham Allison, recounted the epic of these thirteen days that guaranteed the "survival of civilization," it, more than any other document, served to laud a president of extraordinary ability, aided by an incomparable group of advisers, whose actions spared the country and the world the ultimate catastrophe: thermonuclear war.[110]

Neustadt and Allison, editing and interpreting the tapes, understood that it was not enough to accept the Robert Kennedy view of how the crisis that

threatened a nuclear holocaust was finally averted. They recognized the importance of mentioning that "some men near the Ex Comm [the Executive Committee of the National Security Council] but not of it—mainly military officers
advising in subordinate capacities"—believed from the moment the president
broadcast his awareness of the Soviet missile installation and insisted on their
removal, that this, in effect, ended the crisis.[111] Neustadt and Allison rejected
the view of these "mainly military officers," claiming that it presumed "ratio-
nality" on the part of the Soviets, a belief that they were "cool calculators" and
"assured controllers, orchestrating every act of their bureaucracies."[112] Noting
the absence of any prominent member of Congress in the Ex Comm deliberations, and explaining why certain officials had to be engaged, given their responsibilities, the editors wrote admiringly of the so-called president's men, his
brother, of course, as well as Theodore Sorenson, his special counsel, who were
always present. It was they who warned the president against those, including
members of the Joint Chiefs of Staff, who recommended quick military action,
"a clean surgical air strike."[113] In the end, after prolonged discussion, the president made the decision that preserved the peace and saved the world from
thermonuclear war. The tale that Robert Kennedy told was wholly acceptable
to the editors of the book.

While there was some truth in the story told by the president's late brother
and in the commentary prepared by Neustadt and Allison, they ignored the
salient point made by the lower-ranking military officers: Once the president
announced in public the Soviet missile placement in Cuba and his resolve not to
allow them to remain, he had taken all the steps necessary to stop Nikita
Khrushchev.[114] That argument, questioned by Neustadt and Allison, replicated
precisely the view taken in London by the Joint Intelligence Committee in its
October 27, 1962, assessment ("Possible Responses to a U.S. Decision to Bomb
or Invade Cuba"), made available to Number 10 Downing Street. Though
Prime Minister Harold Macmillan continued to fret and lose sleep, putting
Britain's V-bombers on fifteen minutes' readiness at the end of their Lincolnshire
runways, the Joint Intelligence Committee told the prime minister that
Khrushchev, in deciding to turn back the Soviet missile-carrying freighters, had
already suffered "a considerable climb down" and "loss of face," and that there
was no longer any threat to Berlin.[115] To acknowledge all this was to take away
some of the credit from Kennedy for his remarkable sangfroid, and none of
those anxious to protect his reputation as an incomparable political strategist
cared to entertain that proposition. Indeed, Robert Kennedy refused even to acknowledge that there had been a quid pro quo for the Soviet action, a secret acceptance by the president to remove the Jupiter missiles from Turkey.[116] In this,
as in so much else, the Kennedy brothers deceived the American public but also
their European allies, and while some leaders in Europe knew this, it was not information generally available in the United States.[117]

May and Zelikow, writing more than three decades after these events, having access to Soviet and other archives, believed that Khrushchev alone made the decision to place the missiles in Cuba and acted more from instinct than calculation, and that his instincts were "disciplined by relatively little experience or knowledge," obviously different from the more rational moves orchestrated in Washington.[118] In their description of Khrushchev, they represented him as someone who lived with a "simplistic version of Marxism-Leninism," had a "narrow experience of the outside world," and was greatly influenced by the Suez-Hungary crisis of 1956 and internal Kremlin politics, exacerbated by an agricultural crisis; they emphasized that he "seriously needed some success to offset a string of losses."

Fidel Castro, increasingly fearful of an American invasion, believing the rumors of new CIA plots to depose him, insisted on Soviet help by installing the missiles. Khrushchev simply obliged him. This, May and Zelikow argued, was the genesis of the crisis; as for its denouement, they gave all credit to what they described as "the finest hours of John F. Kennedy's public life," saying:

> To us he seems more alive to the possibilities and consequences of each new development than anyone else. He remains calm, lucid, and is constantly a step, or several steps, ahead of his advisers. He is the only one in the room who is determined not to go to war over obsolete missiles in Turkey. Yet he fully understands and is trying to work around the large consequences of appearing to sell out the Turks. We can understand why, after celebrating Khrushchev's announcement that the missiles would be withdrawn from Cuba, Kennedy kept Rusk behind and privately, but witheringly, dressed him down for not having better planned to cope with Khrushchev's predictable move.[119]

To deny the importance of the president's role in the Cuban missile crisis would be historically inaccurate, an almost churlish equivalent to a denial of the role Roosevelt played in guaranteeing Britain's survival in 1940 and 1941 and ultimately in helping secure the Allied military victory in 1945 he did not live to see. Yet, the two events are of very different historical import, and this has become increasingly evident with the passage of time. Although the missile crisis may still figure as Kennedy's "finest hour," revelations in recent years tell a tale that must somewhat tarnish his reputation, and even more that of his brother. Both, interested in foreign policy—the issues that really mattered—and imagining themselves more gifted in this domain than the State Department and its too-gentlemanly secretary, set themselves objectives they were never able to achieve. We know now, not only from Soviet sources revealed since the disintegration of the Soviet Union, of the extraordinary efforts the administration made to destroy the Castro regime, all the while protesting their friendship for Khrushchev if not for his Caribbean ally. The story is not wholly edifying.

As late as October 4, less than a fortnight before a U-2 discovered the Soviet missile installations in Cuba, Robert Kennedy, in his habitual arrogant and assertive manner, berated John McCone, the head of the CIA, for his failure to move ahead more rapidly with OPERATION MONGOOSE. That very secret operation, intended to "help Cuba overthrow the Communist regime," from the start an administration objective of the highest priority, allowed the attorney general to express the president's anger that greater progress was not being made.[120] He repeated his complaint, perhaps less peremptorily, a week later when he told McCone: "We'll have to do something drastic about Cuba." Clearly, Castro's fears about the administration's intentions, constantly communicated to Khrushchev, were not fanciful. The president was indeed pressing the CIA to develop plans to overthrow the Castro regime, and his brother was carrying the message, neither recognizing the dangers such a policy posed to his declared program of improving American-Soviet relations.

His brother, always the president's principal protector, believed he had an "authentic friendship" with Georgi Bolshakov, a Soviet intelligence agent operating as the head of the Washington bureau of Tass, the Soviet news agency. The two met periodically to talk confidentially, hoping thereby to "short-circuit the ponderous protocol of official diplomacy."[121] So confident was Robert Kennedy of the importance of this "authentic friendship" that he imagined it would serve the president's interest for him to tell Bolshakov:

> Goddamn it, Georgie, doesn't Premier Khrushchev realize the President's position? Doesn't the Premier know that the President has enemies as well as friends? Believe me, my brother really means what he says about American-Soviet relations. But every step he takes to meet Premier Khrushchev halfway costs him a lot of effort.

Robert Kennedy, when making this plea, intending it to be communicated to the Soviet leader, had no notion how someone like Khrushchev would respond. Khrushchev, no better informed about the United States than the Kennedy brothers on the Soviet Union, when told about the fears Kennedy had expressed to Bolshakov, could only say: "They can't mean it. Is he the President, or isn't he? If he is a strong President, he has no one to fear. He has full powers of government, and his brother is Attorney-General in the bargain."[122] Neither of the Kennedys understood the Kremlin leadership, and neither showed great skill in dealing with it. How could they have known that Khrushchev had never gotten over his idea that the president was weak, encouraging him to believe that he could steal a march on the Americans, install the missiles in Cuba, and not be found out? Once they were installed, he could not imagine that the president, averse to risk-taking, would approve of military action to press for their removal. If Khrushchev had not anticipated the U-2 flight that would discover the installations before they were fully operational, Kennedy's mistake was no less great. He never understood that Khrushchev was no more a gambler than he was. The idea that he would risk thermonuclear war to protect Castro (or his missiles) showed insufficient appreciation of the mentality of a shrewd politician mistaken by some of Kennedy's well-born colleagues to be only a crafty and bumptious peasant. If, indeed, they had appreciated the native intelligence, wiles, and ambitions of this man who had pushed his way to the top, they might have been less surprised and alarmed by what he had done. Regrettably, empathy was never the Kennedy family's most recognizable trait, and it is significant certainly that they showed as little appreciation of the motives that had led Khrushchev to his action than they did in their efforts to comprehend the policies of their allies, notably those of de Gaulle and Adenauer. The truth that could not be uttered in the United States after the president's success in the Cuban missile crisis, that neither the president nor the attorney general had a firm grasp of foreign policy issues, was one that would have seemed heretical to their loyal friends, colleagues, subordinates, and admirers.

May and Zelikow, studying the White House transcripts, write: "It is not far-fetched to characterize the missile crisis as the Pearl Harbor *and* Midway of the Cold War. Never again, even in the crisis years of 1979–83, would the Soviet challenge or the Western response be so direct and so intense."[123] Unintentionally perhaps, they used the argument Henry Kissinger advanced in *Diplomacy*, published in 1994, in which he had written: "The Berlin crisis—together with its culmination in the Cuban missile crisis—marked a turning point in the Cold War, though it was not perceived as such at the time," going on to say what few of those who concentrated only on the Cuban crisis cared to acknowledge. Though Kennedy did indeed humble Khrushchev, and ultimately contributed to his downfall, his actions gained him no new favor either in Paris or Bonn. In Kissinger's words, "Had the democracies not become so consumed by their internal disputes, they might have interpreted the Berlin crisis for what it was—a demonstration of latent Soviet weakness."

Kissinger saw the Berlin crisis as all-important, giving attention to the Cuban missile crisis, of course, but never choosing to make it central.[124] That position, taken also by Percy Cradock, British diplomat and head of the Joint Intelligence Committee, political adviser to two Tory prime ministers, as given in his book, *Know Your Enemy*, published in 2002, allowed Cradock to say:

From the Western viewpoint, the [Cuban missile crisis] victory loses a quantity of gloss when judged in the light of later knowledge. It was less an outright win than a bargain, a compromise: Cuban missiles for Turkish missiles. Without informing many of his closest advisers and in disregard of NATO obligations, the President, it seemed, had shown himself ready unilaterally to bargain away installations of great importance to Turkey in order to secure greater safety for the US mainland. At the same time he had been giving a very different impression to his allies. In his personal message to the Prime Minister of 27 October, explaining his rejection of Khrushchev's message proposing a missile trade, he said, 'I do not feel that this country should allow itself to become engaged in negotiations affecting the individual security interests of our NATO allies. Any initiatives, in this respect, it seems to me, should appropriately come from Europe.'[125]

Cradock wrote: "If the secret understanding had become known at the time it would have been very harmful to Kennedy personally in the United States. And among the NATO allies the effect would have been to cast serious doubt on American reliability in times of acute crisis."[126] Why was all this important? For one reason, principally: While it cannot be conclusively demonstrated that the president, buoyed by his success in the missile crisis, became more self-confident, persuaded he could manage the situation in South Vietnam, this seemed to happen in 1963. Kennedy and his associates greatly exaggerated their first foreign policy success and then proceeded to take unnecessary risks in Southeast Asia.

While Roger Hillsman, director of the State Department's Bureau of Intelligence and Research, very early said his intention was to reduce the Vietcong to "hungry, marauding bands of outlaws devoting all their energies to staying alive," no one in the United States as late as April 1962 was prepared to say openly what the Joint Intelligence Committee had told the prime minister: that for the Americans to defeat the Vietcong the dispatch of at least 100,000 combat troops would be necessary.[127] Indeed, the president refused to acknowledge that such a commitment would be required as late as 1963. As the head of an administration whose knowledge of Vietnam was minimal, with not a single person in a responsible position in Washington knowing even the language, Kennedy lived with the illusion he could teach Diem to be democratic, prepared, in return for a promise by Diem to become responsible, to offer substantial economic aid, going beyond anything previously granted. This was conditional, however, on Diem's agreeing to place Americans in advisory roles at all levels of government, a request he never accepted.

When, on May 8, 1963, Diem's soldiers killed a number of Buddhist demonstrators, and the immolation of individual Buddhists continued—photographed and seen on American TV screens by millions—the president felt a strict warning to be in order. The news, as reported in the *New York Times* by David Halberstam, worried Kennedy greatly.[128] Was the campaign against the Vietcong going as badly as Halberstam claimed when those who reported to the president and the secretary of defense argued the contrary? When Henry Cabot Lodge Jr., the newly appointed U.S. ambassador to Vietnam, arrived in Saigon on August 22, he discovered that Diem, contrary to his promises, had organized a nationwide campaign to crush the Buddhists. The president, outraged by this, sent instructions to Lodge to make it clear to Diem that unless he removed his brother, Ngo Dinh Nhu, from his position as head of the country's security forces, the United States would be compelled to "face the possibility that Diem cannot be preserved."[129]

Diem understood the nature of the warning; Kennedy and McNamara had issued comparable threats before, though in a more muted form. In these late summer days Kennedy hesitated, fearing he might be starting something that would end badly, another Bay of Pigs. As the pressure inside Saigon for a coup against Diem grew, Kennedy's principal concern was the one he showed in the Bay of Pigs invasion, that the American involvement had to be carefully concealed. Lodge told the president that "any course is risky, and no action at all is the riskiest of all," going on to say, "we are launched on a course from which there is no respectable turning back: the overthrow of the Diem government."[130] Still the president hesitated, and a visit by McNamara and Taylor in early October served only to increase his doubts, with their reports of "great progress" on the military front joined to the frank acknowledgment of the difficulties of the political situation.[131] Neither seemed ready to see the Americans participate in a coup, and the president and other of his advisers felt comparable reservations.[132]

With a number of high-ranking Vietnamese officers continuing to plan a coup, Diem was overthrown on November 1 and killed the following day, along with his brother. The president, genuinely shocked, could not avoid blaming himself for what had happened. He wrote:

I feel that we [at the White House] must bear a good deal of responsibility for it, beginning with our cable of early August in which we suggested the coup. In my judgment that wire was badly drafted. It should never have been sent on a Saturday. I should not have given my consent to it without a roundtable conference at which McNamara and Taylor could have presented their views. While we did redress that balance in later wires, that first wire encouraged Lodge along a course to which he was in any case inclined.[133]

The contrition was genuine, and while there is no way of knowing what Kennedy would have done had he not been assassinated later that month, two characteristics of his administration merit attention. First, constantly preoccupied with foreign policy issues, he imagined he understood them, greatly exaggerating his grasp of their complexity. Second, because he and his brother took foreign policy questions to be critical, they looked for those who viewed the world as they did, ignoring the opinions of old men, like de Gaulle, who warned them against certain dangers.[134]

The missile crisis success and the later administration accomplishment in securing a test-ban treaty with the Soviet Union did not cancel out the more conspicuous failures, in Cuba and Vietnam, as well as in deteriorating relations with major European allies, including those seen to be the most difficult, de Gaulle and Adenauer. The president's excellent relations with Prime Minister Macmillan scarcely compensated for the differences he had with his two principal European continental allies. Because his domestic accomplishments were equally insubstantial, in no way comparable to those of his three twentieth-century Democratic presidential predecessors, his thousand days were largely barren of legislative accomplishments, and this could never be admitted by those who took such pleasure in serving him.

While his efforts to secure an increased minimum wage and more substantial federal aid to education were made much of, cited as proof of his ambition to be a liberal reformer, both were relatively minor accomplishments. Though the Democrats controlled the House and the Senate, Kennedy found the resistance of Southern conservative Democrats, influential for more than two decades, an insuperable barrier to plans to go beyond the modest civil rights revolution that Truman had initiated.

Overly concerned with his reelection prospects, knowing how narrowly he had won in 1960 against a candidate who lacked both charisma and charity, he feared defeat in 1964 if he seriously offended the South. Because of the growing agitation for civil rights legislation, both he and his brother appreciated the importance of emphasizing their attachment to the black cause, and his decision to dispatch federal troops to escort James Meredith, a black student, on to the campus of the University of Mississippi, barricaded by those hostile to racial integration, was given immense publicity.[135] While a significant gesture, it scarcely compensated for what many saw as the president's dilatory attitude in ending racial discrimination in federal housing, a pledge he had made frequently during the 1960 election campaign. Not till November 1962, after the congressional elections of that year, did he issue an executive order to redeem that promise, doing it in a way that gave minimum publicity to his action. The president, having good reason to fear white Southern Democratic backlash, moved warily.[136]

While the Justice Department, pressed by his brother, urged black and white political activists in the South to work together to register black voters, believing the ballot box would ultimately be decisive, finally ending the disgraceful Jim Crow system of segregation, it was politically imperative that the agitation remain peaceful. Violence, with its attendant hazards, would certainly create problems both at home and abroad and had to be avoided. The president wishing always for his concern with racial integration to be recognized, insisted that civil rights advocates show patience. While blacks, following the advice of their greatly admired charismatic leader, Reverend Martin Luther King Jr., were committed to nonviolence, the whites who opposed them showed no comparable restraint, and when King led what he hoped would be peaceful antisegregation protests in April 1963 through the streets of Birmingham, Alabama, the police reacted violently.

Police beatings of unarmed men and women and the use of dogs and pressure hoses both alarmed and horrified the millions who watched it all unfold on national television.[137] That scene, followed only days later by another, less violent, but scarcely less disconcerting, saw George Wallace, governor of Alabama, seeking to thwart integration in his state, announce his intention to defy a federal court order compelling the state to admit two black students to the all-white University of Alabama in Tuscaloosa. Wallace waited to see how the president and the attorney general would react, informing the press that "I will be present to bar the entrance of any Negro who attempts to enroll."

Kennedy could not ignore this challenge, and when Wallace personally blocked the entry of students and federal marshals, the president federalized part of the Alabama National Guard.[138] When the Alabama soldiers appeared on the scene, the governor beat a hasty retreat; the two black students were registered, and Kennedy knew that this was the moment to exploit his victory. Accepting what Theodore Roosevelt had preached decades earlier, which he knew to be true—that the White House was a bully pulpit—he spoke eloquently that night in a nationally televised broadcast on a single theme: civil rights. While he had addressed the issue on other occasions, he had never spoken of it as he did that evening.

"It ought to be possible," he said,

for American students of any color to attend any public institution without having to be backed up by troops. It ought to be possible for American consumers of any color to receive equal service in places of public accommodation, such as hotels and restaurants and theatres and retail stores, without being forced to demonstrations in the streets, and it ought to be possible for American citizens of any color to register and vote in a free election without interference or fear of reprisal. . . . In short, every American ought to have the right to be treated as he would wish to be treated, as one would wish his children to be treated. But this is not the case.[139]

What, then, did he propose to do? In the next week, he promised to ask Congress to make a firm commitment to the proposition that "race has no place in American life or law."[140] On the night Kennedy spoke, Medgar Evers of Mississippi, a leader in that state's National Association for the Advancement of Colored People (NAACP), was shot dead.[141] Kennedy had spoken none too soon, and when his proposed legislation came to Congress on June 19—incontestably the most substantial civil rights law ever presented to that body—the president could not be certain how much of it would pass, but the country knew of his firm commitment to change. When black leaders, led by Martin Luther King, insisted on going forward with their plans for a massive march on Washington, the president worried whether the demonstration would help him in his legislative battles. The August 28, 1963, March on Washington saw nearly 250,000 men and women, black and white, from every part of the country, congregate at the Lincoln Memorial. The event was peaceful, deeply moving for those who attended and the millions who watched it on television. Kennedy could only hope that it had helped his legislative cause.[142]

The president's assassination, less than three months later, made it impossible to know how his civil rights legislation would have fared had he lived. James Patterson, the historian, suggested years later that his "record in the realm of domestic policies was hardly stellar" and attributed the modesty of the achievement to "uninspiring leadership," disdain for liberals dismissed as "honkers," and refusal to court members of Congress, adding one other reason—foreign affairs was the only thing that interested him.[143] Patterson reported Kennedy as once having said to Nixon, "Foreign affairs is the only important issue for a President to handle, isn't it. . . . I mean, who gives a shit if the minimum wage is $1.15 or $1.25, compared to something like Cuba?"[144]

Kennedy imagined he understood foreign policy and that those he chose to assist and advise him were exceptionally able. He lived with these illusions till the last day of his life. In no sense, however, was he a creator in the Truman tradition, nor could his performance as a war leader, revealed in the Bay of Pigs or in South Vietnam after 1961, appear especially stellar. As a diplomat he failed abysmally, incapable of developing a policy in respect to the Berlin Wall that gained the respect of either his allies or his enemies. The Alliance for Progress, praised by certain of his biographers and hagiographers, proved largely an exercise in rhetoric; during his short thousand days, there were military coups in Argentina, Peru, Guatemala, Ecuador, the Dominican Republic, and Honduras, and the administration that pretended to know how to bring democracy to South Vietnam did not realize that its ten-year, $220 billion plan to create friends in Latin America, while generous, was wholly inadequate to the region's needs.

More serious, certainly, was the failure of those who advised the president to understand the social structure of Latin American societies, imagining that its emerging middle class would be sympathetic to their reforms, causing the old landowning elites to capitulate. Neither of these things happened; agrarian reform, as the Americans practiced it, did not prove to be the economic panacea that those most influential in Latin America were hankering for.[145] With foreign policy accomplishments in Latin America, Asia, and Europe, less striking than his admirers pretended, the president's handling of the Cuban missile crisis became his principal claim to fame. In this, as in other things, the accomplishment, when seen in the perspective of time, however remarkable, is not the epic tale imagined by those who served him.

Interestingly, McGeorge Bundy, one of the president's principal admirers, thought it important to single out for praise John McCone, the director of the CIA, one of the first to suspect that the Soviets intended to install missiles in Cuba, who warned Bundy of the possibility before it happened.[146] Percy Cradock in Britain was even more effusive, saying: "Cuba was a major test for the United States. On the intelligence side it was passed narrowly, thanks to the imagination of John McCone and highly effective aerial photography."[147] No comparable appreciation of McCone was made by May and Neustadt, who dismissed him as an early advocate of military action, siding with Acheson, Dillon, and Nitze, with Rusk represented as leaning in their direction.

In the May-Zelikow comments on the tapes, McCone figures as an inconsequential figure, not to be compared with McNamara or the president's brother. This same reticence showed itself in what friends and former colleagues of the president chose to say about him in the months following his assassination. Schlesinger and Sorenson, leaving the White House soon after Kennedy's death, rushed into print what they hoped would be measured eulogies of an incomparable national leader.[148] Decades later, Bundy and McNamara, still carrying the torch for the slain president, absolved him of all blame for Vietnam. Both wrote as if they knew for a fact that he would have ended U.S. involvement had he lived to enjoy a second term as president.[149]

While revelations abounded in the years that followed relating to his sexual habits (in the words of a sympathetic British critic, "a private life somewhat at odds with a public life dominated by charm, wit, and intellect"), and while there was much written about his "insatiable sexual appetite and dubious associations," many of the most serious charges, such as those made by Seymour Hersh in *The Dark Side of Camelot,* seemed excessive, the work of ambitious journalists seeking to titillate an audience finally liberated from the trauma it had experienced at the time of his assassination.[150]

Recently, however, as a new generation of historians have come to the fore, with less reason to laud or blame, a more critical literature has developed. In *Virtual History,* edited by Niall Ferguson and originally published in 1997, an essay by a young historian, Diane Kunz, appeared, resembling none previously published. She said, quite simply:

Fairy stories are necessary for children. Historians ought to know better. In fact, John F. Kennedy was a mediocre president. Had he obtained a second term, federal civil rights policy during the 1960s would have been substantially less productive and U.S. actions in Vietnam no different from what actually occurred. His tragic assassination was not a tragedy for the course of American history.[151]

While such an interpretation goes considerably beyond anything hinted at here, it raises issues implicit in many of the accounts written about Kennedy in recent years. Was he indeed as accomplished as he and his friends pretended? Did his capture of the Democratic Party's presidential nomination, so skillfully engineered by him with substantial financial and other assistance from his extended family, bring into the White House a callow and ambitious senator who accomplished considerably less than any of his twentieth-century Democratic Party predecessors? Did de Gaulle, with his somewhat jaundiced view of American presidential claims to honor and principle, have a better measure of the man than Macmillan, overly impressed by his wit and bearing, an "aristocrat" in all but name? Was a president prepared to make his brother a principal member of his Cabinet, guilty of nepotism? Did he not exaggerate what a president, once installed in the White House, might legitimately do? Was his contempt for Congress not excessive, matched only by his suspicion of the military he imagined he knew from his naval service in the war? Did his own brief congressional service, both in the House and the Senate, give him experience at all comparable to what Truman boasted? Having never held an executive position, having no experience of serving as an elected governor or an appointed official in some conspicuous public or private capacity, did this not make him more of a stranger in the capital than he pretended to be? Did it explain his need to choose so many in his Cabinet he had never previously met or known?

A sophisticated and well-traveled man of wealth, endowed with wit and charm, an incomparable public speaker, he seemed a latter-day incarnation of both Roosevelts. Was it possible that he resembled neither and that, as the son of a twentieth-century tycoon prepared to use the family fortune to elevate a favorite son to the White House, he started with advantages he used to the full, keeping secret the one condition that might have impeded his rise—his serious health problems: Diagnosed very early as suffering from Addison's disease, which left him permanently in pain, and addicted to varying cocktails of drugs, Kennedy showed a stoicism that marked him as exceptional, though not as intellectually gifted or politically astute as his courtiers, in his vastly expanded White House staff, imagined him to be.[152]

CHAPTER 14

The Texan

LYNDON B. JOHNSON scarcely resembled John F. Kennedy; indeed, only as ambitious fellow Democrats, preoccupied with their quest for personal influence and power, could they be seen as inhabiting the same political universe. While journalists and others at the time of Kennedy's death thought to compare the appearances of the two—one unprepossessing, lumbering, and awkward, appearing many years older than his chronological age, the other handsome and graceful, the perfect image of a vital and healthy young American—a more probing examination would have revealed more significant differences, prefiguring a Johnson presidency as different from Kennedy's as Theodore Roosevelt's was from McKinley's. It could not have been otherwise.

No one familiar with bumptious Texans, proud of their Southern and Western roots, planted in a soil that spoke of war with Mexico and the state's early existence as an independent republic, could ever mistake Texas culture for that of twentieth-century Massachusetts, liberated from its once confining Puritan heritage, but managing still to see itself as harboring the learned institutions that made it the Athens of America.[1] The grinding rural poverty of Johnson's childhood and adolescence shaped a personality essentially different from that of the New England youth who knew only substantial comfort, granted him through wealth whose origins neither he nor others inquired into. The Padernales River bore no resemblance to the Charles, and the vast open spaces outside Johnson City seemed a world away from Cape Cod and the urban splendors of New York City and its affluent suburbs.

It would be interesting to know whether Johnson as a boy ever heard of a place in Cambridge called Harvard University; Kennedy, enjoying the social life of London, certainly never heard of Texas State Teachers College at San Marcos, Johnson's alma mater. If genealogy meant anything, Johnson was FFT—belonging to the first families of Texas—his forbears having come to the state and prospered there, at least for a time, before the Civil War.[2] His father served in the state legislature and met Sam Rayburn there, later one of Lyndon's great friends and early patrons. The Kennedys, by comparison, were newcomers to ancient Boston, lace-curtain Irish to Protestant neighbors disdainful of their religion and the island from which their forbears had emigrated; they carried no regional identity comparable to the one proudly exhibited by the man who hailed from the Lone Star State. No one gazing at the Irish aristocrat and the Texan cowboy—ludicrous terms used by journalists to describe both— would have guessed that only nine years separated Johnson, born in 1908, from Kennedy, born in 1917.

While both were children of the Coolidge era, with Johnson accepting many of its pieties, as Doris Kearns Goodwin, his biographer, suggested when she described "small town Texas" as a world where "success was a reward for virtuous effort, ambition was an admired good, and there was little room for cynicism," these were not the values of New York or Hollywood, as Kennedy's philandering father knew and practiced them.[3] Nor were they conspicuous in the life of the young Kennedy; his letters to friends at school and college, filled with boasts of sexual conquests, reveal a proud and juvenile raunchiness, scarcely kept in check by the Catholic belief of his mother, with its emphasis on sin and absolution. Johnson, obliged to work from a very early age, teaching first in an elementary school in Cotulla, Texas, described by him as "a little dried-up. . . dying" place, "one of the crummiest little towns in Texas," and later in a more salubrious high school in Houston, knew nothing of the privileged wealthy American existence of Kennedy.

The Great Depression, like World War II, changed Johnson's life, as it did most other Americans of his generation. By comparison, as we have seen, the Depression touched Kennedy not at all; his father's wealth gave him the protection that Johnson and Texans of his social class never enjoyed. The war made Kennedy a hero and gave him new status with his father; Johnson enjoyed no comparable war bonuses, though it exacerbated his highly developed capacity for fabricating tales about himself and exaggerating greatly his combat experiences.[4] Roosevelt, the nation's principal war hero for Johnson, could never fulfill that role for Kennedy, especially after his father's break with the president following FDR's third-term reelection in 1940.

Kennedy lived with one principal patron, his father; Johnson had none except for his devoted mother, who believed him exceptional, and an uncle who stimulated his interest in politics—Democratic Party politics—the only politics that mattered in Texas.[5] Uncle George, a child of the nineteenth century, instructed his young nephew in the incomparable achievements of two great populist leaders, Andrew Jackson and William Jennings Bryan, figures more alive for him than Calvin Coolidge or Herbert Hoover, the Republican defenders of wealth and privilege.[6] Johnson never imagined that teaching would be his eventual profession; politics was his passion from the time he was an adolescent, and his life changed dramatically in November 1931 when he became the secretary to a recently elected congressman from Houston, Richard Kleberg, whom he had never met.

Kleberg, victor in a special election for the Fourteenth Congressional District following the death of the Republican incumbent, was an immensely rich member of the family whose share of the King Ranch was some 20 percent.[7] Johnson, despite the humble nature of his appointment, was led into a world he would otherwise never have known, inhabited largely by influential Democratic Texans. Introduced to John Nance Garner just weeks before Garner became Speaker of the House, the prize of the party's substantial 1930 off-year election victories that brought more than a hundred new Democratic members into Congress, Johnson soon met the Texas chairmen of some of the most influential House committees.[8] Roosevelt's election to the presidency and Garner's to the vice presidency allowed Johnson to believe that some appointment greater than that of secretary to a not especially important member of the House might be in the offing.

When, in the summer of 1935, Roosevelt issued the executive order establishing the National Youth Administration, Johnson lobbied his Texas friends to recommend him for the post of Texas state director. Though exceedingly young for such a major administrative post, twenty-seven at the time, he received the appointment largely through the influence of the bachelor Rayburn, already the Democratic Party Majority Leader and later to become Speaker of the House, who had virtually adopted Johnson as his son.[9]

The youngest state director in the National Youth Administration, Johnson was responsible for a state where some 125,000 Texans between the ages of sixteen and twenty-five were unemployed, on relief, with many enrolled in the small colleges having no visible means of support. Johnson's problems were greatly exacerbated by the exceptionally large number of uneducated and unskilled black and Mexican youths, more conspicuous than ever before. Working sixteen- and sometimes eighteen-hour days in Austin, Johnson believed it his responsibility to find jobs and secure other federal benefits for those in such obvious distress, victims of farm foreclosures and mass unemployment.

Johnson's friends in Washington and Austin, impressed with his energy and resolve, urged him to seek election to Congress and, as with Kleberg, the death of an incumbent created an opening he imagined he might win. Election as representative for the Tenth Congressional District, centered in Austin, would make Johnson, only twenty-eight, the youngest Texan in the U.S. House of Representatives; indeed, only two House members among the 435 were comparably young.

Though he enjoyed a modest reputation as the Texas state director of the National Youth Administration, his name was little known to the greatest number of those eligible to vote in the Democratic Party primary, and according to Johnson's most caustic and accomplished biographer, Robert Caro, it was Alvin

Wirtz, Johnson's friend from Austin, who provided him with the strategy that gave him his victory. In Caro's astringent account, "It could be summed up in three words: Franklin Delano Roosevelt."[10] Johnson defended the president in everything, including his "court-packing" proposal and made it the centerpiece of his commitment to the New Deal. In the Tenth Congressional District, victory in the Democratic primary was tantamount to election, and Johnson emerged an easy victor with 8,280 votes, his nearest opponent claiming a mere 5,111 votes.

His father's words—"Now get up there, support FDR all the way, never shimmy, and give 'em hell"—expressed perfectly the credo he and Sam Rayburn believed and practiced. At a time when numbers of Southern Democrats were abandoning Roosevelt, refusing to support many of his domestic policies, Johnson offered himself as an aggressive New Dealer whose only concern was to help the president struggling with the forces of reaction. Some among the president's close advisers thought him the "best New Dealer from Texas." In refusing to support Garner and Rayburn in their effort to persuade Roosevelt not to seek a third term, he showed that in any contest between his Texas friends and the president, FDR would always be the victor. For Johnson, Roosevelt was indispensable, made more so by the tragic events in Europe. Understanding that war might be imminent, Johnson found Roosevelt's arguments on foreign and defense policy wholly persuasive, as commendable in every way as those he had once used in his struggle for social and economic reform.

In April 1941, the sudden death of Senator Morris Sheppard, the senior senator from Texas, gave Johnson the opportunity he had sought from almost the day he entered the House: to compete for a Senate seat. His most formidable rival was "Pappy" O'Daniel, the Democratic governor of Texas, unsympathetic to Roosevelt's New Deal but immensely popular with those who knew him as a celebrated radio commentator. Johnson concentrated his campaign on his record as an unqualified supporter of the president.[11] Roosevelt, recalling all that Johnson had done to support him since 1937, reciprocated with his habitual enthusiasm, leading two journalists, Joseph Alsop and Robert Kintner, to say: "As much as any candidate in recent years Johnson is running under the White House banner." Though Johnson waged an effective campaign, amply funded, he lost in an election marked by ballot fraud and violations of campaign finance laws on both sides.[12] O'Daniel won by a mere 1,311 votes, but the governor, with his hillbilly band and appeal to ordinary folk, men and women like himself, managed to organize a more effective campaign for a Senate seat than the distant president, necessarily preoccupied with many other things.

The Pearl Harbor disaster compelled the ambitious Johnson to confront the problem young Roosevelt had faced in 1917. Would he advance his political career by remaining in Washington, D.C., or would he do better to join the tens of thousands of other Texans of his generation flocking to the colors? Would it not be held against him if he sought safety at home when others risked their lives in combat? Johnson resolved the dilemma characteristically by seeking an appointment in the Navy, using the president's influence to send him to the Southwest Pacific to report on the morale of the U.S. forces stationed there.[13] In New Zealand and later in Australia, where he met General Douglas MacArthur and the general's staff, ordered to give "Congressman— not Lieutenant Commander Johnson—V.I.P. treatment," MacArthur viewed Johnson as someone who could argue his case with the president for a larger commitment of resources to the Pacific war.[14]

MacArthur agreed to have Johnson accompany a mission to bomb Japanese bases on New Britain Island and New Guinea. The operation almost ended in disaster: the B-26 in which Johnson flew, was hit several times by Japanese fire, and managed only barely to return to its base. Other adventures, equally hazardous, followed, but Johnson's participation in the dangerous mission over Lae gave MacArthur the excuse to award him a Silver Star, a medal he pretended not to want yet never failed to cite in his later political campaigns.[15] Robert Dallek, one of Johnson's biographers, wrote: "It is difficult not to suspect political back scratching. Lyndon went home with a 'war record' and a medal and MacArthur had a new vocal advocate in Washington with some access to the President and more to Congress and the press."[16]

Such adventures, however exciting, never deluded Johnson into believing that his military contribution to the war effort was as important as what he might do in Congress, and when the president issued a directive ordering all congressmen in the armed forces to return to Congress, four of the eight, including Johnson, did so. Still, he thought it necessary to seek Rayburn's assurance that his return to Congress would not be misconstrued in Texas, that he would not be criticized.[17] His own defense was simple; "I have been ordered out of uniform and back to Washington by my Commander-in-Chief," an argument no one could contradict.

Johnson had no battle experience to compare with Kennedy's, no war record redolent in any way of Eisenhower's; his wartime contributions in the House did not compare with those of Truman in the Senate. Yet these years were critical in his later ascent, if only because they led to his becoming a millionaire, largely through the purchase of a virtually defunct Austin radio station, KTBC, bought for a miniscule sum by his wife, about which questions were periodically raised, with no one ever conclusively proving malfeasance.[18] Though there were occasions late in the war when he differed with the president, he never appeared to Texans or to fellow congressmen as anything other than a committed New Dealer, the loyal supporter of the man leading the country to victory. When Roosevelt died, Johnson was devastated, literally taking to his bed, grieving for his lost commander in chief.[19]

Johnson, aware of all that had happened to Texas during the war, recognizing it was no longer the pre–1937 New Deal state, remained loyal to Roosevelt's memory but felt no comparable bonds to his successor. Although Johnson and Truman shared an almost uncritical esteem for Rayburn, proud of their friendship with him, the two were never close and did not become so after Roosevelt's death. Truman, observing Johnson in his relations with Rayburn, pretending to be his dutiful son, thought him an untrustworthy flatterer. As Richard Bolling, a Missouri House member, saw the situation, "He [Johnson] tried to play Truman the way he played Rayburn but Truman had watched him doing it with Rayburn. So when Lyndon started doing it with him, he knew exactly what Lyndon was doing, and it didn't work."[20]

Johnson's closest friend in the Roosevelt Cabinet was Harold Ickes, and when Truman accepted his resignation as secretary of the interior in 1946, this severed Johnson's last vital link with the White House.[21] The final divorce, however, came when Johnson accepted the Taft-Hartley Act and voted in 1947 to override Truman's veto of the bill.[22] Aspirations for a Senate seat compelled Johnson to recognize that Texas had become more "conservative," with numerous "new-money" voters prepared to support only those candidates who shared their values. In an interview at the time, Johnson went out of his way to suggest that the term *New Dealer* was a misnomer; he himself believed in "free enterprise," in not having the government do "anything that the people can do privately." Expressing those views in 1947, he lost entrée to the White House, but that seemed a small price to pay for someone who believed, as most other Democrats did, that Truman would no longer be its occupant after 1949.[23]

Rayburn remained Johnson's friend and did what he could to give him committee assignments that gave promise of prestige, including appointment to the House and Senate Joint Committee on Atomic Energy, but these counted for less after 1946 when the Republicans became the majority party in the House.

Johnson's prospects dimmed appreciably during these years, and he knew that only a successful fight for a Senate seat in 1948 could restore his reputation. To engage in that battle was exceedingly dangerous; should he lose in his second try for the Senate in a regular election when he would be unable to run for his House seat, he would be a political casualty with no prospects for the future. His likely opponent, Coke Stevenson, the governor who had succeeded Pappy O'Daniel when he defeated Johnson in the special election in 1941, and then went on to win it for himself the following year, was a formidable campaigner, and Johnson never underestimated the difficulties he faced. Johnson won by a mere eighty-seven votes, which led him to be derided as "Landslide" Lyndon, and even that slight edge in votes, according to his enemies, was secured by fraudulent means.[24] Johnson made it to the Senate with scarcely any help from the victorious Truman, who never once mentioned him in his *Memoirs*.

Johnson's membership in the Club—his own affectionate name for the institution he treasured—gave him the promise of a renown he could never have hoped for in the House. Unable to establish close relations with Truman but fancying himself a conscientious worker in the Fair Deal vineyard, he supported the president in his programs to erase poverty, extend Social Security benefits, provide additional low-rent public housing, maintain rent control, and increase the minimum wage.[25]

While disagreeing with the president on the civil rights bill he offered in 1949, and differing with him on Taft-Hartley revisions, he vigorously endorsed Truman's recommendations for a larger federal commitment to education.[26] Johnson, increasingly aware of the conservative sentiments of many of his Texas constituents, whether the issue was oil or the dangers of Communist subversion, concealed his earlier New Deal enthusiasms—yesterday's passion—and was unprepared to fight in 1949 or 1952 for what he had conscientiously supported in 1937 and 1940. His task, as he saw it, was to be faithful to the Democratic president but also to listen sympathetically to the views of his Texas constituents, supporting the president's decision to send troops to resist North Korea's incursion into South Korea, seeing it as part of the Soviet design to secure world domination. He joined other Democrats in approving the principal foreign policy and defense innovations favored by the president, and when he became the Senate Democratic Party Whip, in January 1951, created a subcommittee with himself as chairman, modeled on the one Truman had headed in World War II.[27] Johnson hoped its work would benefit the nation through a more efficient use of military manpower, publicizing the need for a more rapid military buildup, especially in aircraft production.

Though believing that a final showdown with the Communists was inevitable, he had no trouble in deciding between MacArthur and Truman when the latter fired the general for insubordination. In hearings conducted jointly by the Senate Foreign Relations Committee and its Armed Services Committee, chaired by Senator Richard Russell, one of Johnson's closest friends, the two worked together to discredit the general for his biased and unsound opinions about the war.[28] Johnson gained new prestige as an effective interrogator, helping the president in a difficult time, but this counted for little with many of his Texas constituents.

In the 1952 election, he supported Adlai Stevenson unenthusiastically, feeling certain he would lose, but knowing better than to appear to favor Eisenhower. In his mind, a Democratic victory would guarantee the federal activism that had given the party its strength under Roosevelt; a Republican victory would mean stagnation. Scarcely surprised by the results, he took no pleasure in the Democratic losses in the Senate that made them the minority party, but with the Minority Leader post open, he decided to compete for it; with the help of Russell, he secured it against the opposition of a handful of liberal Democrats with whom he immediately made peace.[29]

Unity within the Democratic Party seemed the only solution for a situation that would otherwise serve the interests of Republicans, led by Robert Taft, the Majority Leader. Eisenhower, believing bipartisan support of his foreign and defense policies essential, saw Johnson as the Democrat who might serve him as Arthur Vandenberg, a Republican, had once helped Truman.[30] It suited Johnson to appear the president's accomplice in putting down reactionary Republicans, isolationists in all but name. Bipartisanship became Johnson's principal strategy, hoping it would have appeal for conservative voters in Texas. While he never became an advocate of all of Eisenhower's policies, differing with him on Hawaiian statehood, agricultural price supports, and Taft-Hartley, he showed his independence most conspicuously in his support of the Supreme Court's *Brown v. Board of Education* decision of May 1954, which mandated the desegregation of schools. That position was a dangerous one for Johnson to take, but he saw no way to avoid it. Education had long figured as a chief concern, and he knew too much about Texas and the South to believe that a continued policy of segregated schools would ever lift the blacks out of poverty.

At the polls in 1954, Johnson beat his weak opponent by an extraordinary margin—883,000 votes against 354,000.[31] His liberal stands on desegregation of schools and on other social issues had not hurt him, and he felt free to help deliver the coup de grâce that finally humiliated Joseph McCarthy. In Johnson's mind, McCarthy had disgraced the office of senator—a matter of great consequence to someone who valued the dignity of the upper chamber—and would never accept to see its reputation sullied. McCarthy fell before the onslaught of the Senate subcommittee, and Johnson could only revel in all that the Democrats had done to destroy him. The official censure by the Senate—the last stage in an operation that engaged Johnson from the beginning—set him apart from Jack Kennedy, the liberal senator from Massachusetts who, as we have seen, played no role in the proceedings. In his determination to make the condemnation of McCarthy bipartisan, to persuade the nation that anticommunism was not the monopoly of right-thinking Republicans, as the vice president wished the nation to believe, Johnson sought to erase the stigma that had for too long attached itself to the Democrats. Their success in the 1954 congressional elections, gaining seventeen seats in the House, gave them a majority that allowed Rayburn's return as Speaker; in the Senate, with Wayne Morse's earlier decision to declare himself an Independent, the Democrats enjoyed a 49–47 majority; Johnson, at forty-six, moved from being Minority Leader to become the youngest Majority Leader in Senate history.[32]

The years that followed were the best in Johnson's life. As Majority Leader, he showed an almost uncanny capacity to wheel and deal, persuading others to go along, in effect to do his bidding. No one in living memory had been able so successfully to mobilize his party supporters. A serious heart attack in the summer of 1955 slowed him for a time, but friends and enemies knew that he loved power too much to stay away from the Senate for very long. By mid-1956, some spoke of him as a possible Democratic nominee for the presidency, and while the prospect of a race between two recent heart-attack victims never materialized, Johnson hoped to make so distinguished a record during Eisenhower's second term as to become the Democratic Party's presidential nominee in 1960.

After the 1958 off-year congressional elections, in which the Democrats scored impressively both in the House and the Senate, Eisenhower knew he had to rely on the collaboration of Johnson. By seeking to prove himself a moderate, concerned with a balanced budget, Johnson competed with someone who made such economic orthodoxy almost an article of religious faith.[33] In these encounters, the president's cards, better than those held by the Majority Leader, led some Democratic liberals in the Senate to distrust Johnson, criticizing him for what they interpreted as unnecessary concessions made to an excessively cautious president. A number shared Hubert Humphrey's view that Johnson, in seeking to propitiate the South, knowing that no presidential nomination could come without their support, went too far in accommodating them.[34]

Johnson's greatest problem—the prospect of a Kennedy candidacy—led George Reedy, his closest political adviser, to argue early in 1960 that the time had come to do a hatchet job on that largely absent senator.[35] Reedy proposed that the attack avoid all reference to Kennedy's religion and youth and dwell only on his father. As he explained in a memorandum to Johnson that he asked him to destroy immediately after he read it, "Americans would bitterly resent the concept that the White House is a plaything to be handed out as a Christmas present."[36]

Johnson, too late, sought to boost Humphrey's campaign in West Virginia, recognizing it to be the only way to derail Kennedy, but their common adversary was not so easily put down. After Kennedy's West Virginia primary victory, Johnson made further efforts to persuade influential Democrats that Kennedy would lose against a strong Republican adversary, arguing that his youth and religion would be held against him.[37] The idea that "Sonny Boy," Johnson's derogatory name for Jack, would fall before this belated onslaught proved wildly optimistic. Even the U-2 debacle, which Johnson hoped would help his own campaign, emphasizing why a seasoned and experienced leader was more acceptable in a time of danger than a callow youth, served him scarcely at all.

Announcing his candidacy only on July 5, he and his supporters lashed out at the arrogance of someone whose greatest skill appeared to be that of concealment. Kennedy, they said, had no wish to have his record as Senator revealed; it would only emphasize the extent of his absenteeism and his failure to be critical of Senator McCarthy.[38] Kennedy supporters, having raised the question whether a recent major heart-attack victim was suited to the presidency, heard Johnson's defenders ask whether Kennedy did not conceal his own health problems, whether they were not more serious than those commonly acknowledged.[39] All such efforts to stop Kennedy came to naught; at the 1960 Democratic National Convention Kennedy captured the nomination with 806 delegate votes on the first ballot; Johnson trailed far behind with support from only 409 delegates.

The circumstances that led Kennedy to offer Johnson the vice presidency, expecting it to be refused, and the dismay his brother and others felt at not being able to retrieve the offer, suggests how little they knew either the man or his wiles. The dangers of serving as vice president were obvious: Johnson had known Garner and Barkley too well not to realize that the second position was greatly inferior to the first, but even Garner had exercised power, not least in respect to appointments. Truman, who had made the greatest efforts to engage his vice president, a former senator from Kentucky, insisted that the legislation creating the National Security Council include the vice president as one of its permanent members. Might Kennedy not show comparable wisdom, recognizing the importance of seeking Johnson's counsel, in respect to appointments, but also more generally with regard to domestic policy? Johnson, always the realist, believed there was much he could bring to a Kennedy administration; these considerations, as much as any others, led him to seek what had been offered him.[40]

The Democratic Party's presidential nominee and his brother certainly miscalculated when they offered Johnson the vice presidency; Johnson made a no less serious mistake in imagining the young Kennedy would need him, seek his advice, and make him a key member of his administration.

Johnson's thousand days as vice president were among the unhappiest in his long political life. Though efforts were made to appeal to his vanity, known to be gargantuan, he was never the fool some in the administration imagined him to be.[41] Johnson felt acutely his exclusion and marginality; his views counted for little; the assignments given him were substantially inferior to those he had hoped for. Once able to dispense political gifts, to offer committee chairmanships and the like, Johnson had built a secure network of Senate friends on whom he relied. In his new role—as the outsider thrown a crumb from time to time—he was never awarded the attention he sought. No one had ever doubted that vanity was one of his weaknesses; others had played to it; Kennedy and his crowd failed to understand how to do so.

As president, Johnson knew Congress as few men of his generation did and secured passage of some of the most radical reforms of the century.[42] Neither FDR nor Truman could claim a record of domestic legislative achievement to compare with his. In foreign policy and military affairs, where those skills counted for less, he failed abysmally, making grave errors from almost the day he entered the White House. Understanding how to persuade Congress to pass civil rights and social legislation promised by the Democrats from the day they surrendered the White House to Eisenhower in 1953, Johnson lacked the same sureness of touch when it came to deciding between alternative strategies for treating with enemies abroad, especially in Asia.

His initial decision to retain the whole of the dead president's Cabinet, following the precedent set at the start of the century by Roosevelt after McKinley's assassination, made sense; his later decision not to make significant changes after his massive electoral victory in 1964 showed an exaggerated regard for "the brightest and the best," those summoned by Kennedy to serve him.[43] The first decision, with its promise of continuity, assured a stricken nation that things would go on as before, with Johnson using the tragedy of the president's death for his own political purposes—to make civil rights reform the nation's most fitting memorial to him. Johnson, understanding how insubstantial Kennedy's legislative record had been, and incensed never to have been taken into his confidence, knew he had gained little from being his vice president, but he also recognized how much he stood to profit in public esteem from showing loyalty to his memory. In this, as in so much else, Johnson showed himself an astute politician.

He hoped to use the remarkable men Kennedy had brought to Washington to serve in his administration. At least one principal member of the Cabinet, Robert Kennedy, could never accept Johnson as his brother's legitimate heir, resenting him, seeing him as an interloper. While others, feeling the obligation to continue to serve in a time of national distress, tried to adjust to someone of very different habits and temperament, few ever became the new president's confidantes.[44] They were not his men; his wit scarcely resembled that of their slain hero, and his manner and language appeared positively brutish when compared with the grace and elegance once common at the court of Camelot.[45] Only Dean Rusk, the secretary of state, a Southerner and the least of Kennedy's Cabinet intimates, often set aside in an administration where the president and his brother posed as foreign policy experts, came close to becoming a friend to the new president.[46] The more self-conscious of the so-called intellectuals who had served Kennedy, including Robert McNamara and McGeorge Bundy, unknown to Johnson before he became vice president but admired for their quickness of mind, were either put off by his bombastic manner or frightened by it. Neither, despite their incontestably important roles as foreign policy and military advisers, ever served as the critics the president desperately needed.[47]

Lacking credible interlocutors, Johnson remained blissfully ignorant of the limits of his own understanding of foreign policy issues. Imagining that his years of service on the House Naval Affairs and Armed Services Committee, and later on the Senate Armed Services Committee, together with his expert interrogation of General MacArthur and influence as one of the architects of the nation's space program, gave him ample instruction, more than Kennedy or Truman started with, he misconstrued his weaknesses and fumbled badly, rarely aware that his policies were inconsistent and often self-defeating. In choosing a White House staff, very different from the one selected by Kennedy, Johnson showed his strengths; concerned principally with a domestic policy agenda, he chose individuals he knew, including Walter Jenkins, Bill Moyers, Jack Valenti, Horace Busby, and George Reedy. He believed that he and they, working together, could press Congress to accept the legislative innovations that would make the Johnson presidency memorable. These men, prepared to accept total subservience to him, tolerating his tantrums, were rarely looked to for advice on foreign policy issues, which remained the domain of Kennedy's original appointees.

Only in domestic policy did Johnson show his extraordinary talent. In one of his first acts, he pressed for the $11 billion tax cut that Kennedy had proposed but that had never been enacted. Johnson, though doubting the wisdom of so drastic a reduction in federal income tax, recognized that his reputation as Kennedy's political heir would be damaged if he did not secure its passage. He gave the measure the highest priority and, in less than four months achieved what Kennedy had been unable to do in almost a year, knowing how to pressure influential members of Congress to recognize the wisdom of the policy. Coming to believe that tax relief might indeed stimulate the economy and help reduce unemployment—Johnson never accepted the reduction simply as a way to honor his predecessor's memory—he gained overwhelming approval for a bill he personally negotiated with members of Congress.[48]

Tax reduction, however appealing, could never move the president in the way his celebrated War on Poverty did. That effort to lift the nation's poor became Johnson's principal preoccupation in the early months of his administration, and he chose Sargent Shriver, the late president's brother-in-law, believed to be less than friendly to his other brother-in-law, the attorney general, as the man to direct it. The War on Poverty became one of the principal planks of the Great Society, a label fashioned by Richard Goodwin that figured in a speech Johnson gave at the 1964 University of Michigan Commencement.[49]

That speech, as much as any other, outlined the program the president fought for in his election battle with Republican presidential nominee Barry Goldwater in November 1964. The recommendations for rebuilding America's cities, with provision for better housing and new and more efficient transportation systems, were offered as programs to end the urban decay that blighted the nation's man-built landscape. Equally concerned to protect the country's natural resources, guaranteeing Americans again the unpolluted air and clean water, the forests and beaches they had once known and enjoyed, Johnson called for a conservation program reminiscent of the one advocated by Theodore Roosevelt. His principal plea—to sponsor an educational revolution that would see the federal government become actively involved in a domain once exclusively within the jurisdiction of the states—would require Congress to appropriate funds for the building of schools in every part of the country, making it possible for all children, including millions still handicapped by poverty, to enjoy the advantages only education could provide. The president crafted a program intended to have universal appeal, as much to America's growing middle class as to the millions trapped in the slums of its decaying cities.[50]

In his mind, he was fulfilling FDR's mission; Kennedy was wholly incidental to the project. In securing the passage of the Economic Opportunity Act, overwhelmingly approved by the Senate and winning House approval by a comfortable margin in the summer, the president announced triumphantly: "For the first time in all the history of the human race, a great nation. . . is willing to make a commitment to eradicate poverty among its people."[51] Neither the president nor Congress knew precisely how the program would work, but the pledge they made in the summer of 1964 seemed important. With civil rights, Kennedy in his last months in office had indicated the road to take, and Johnson intended to follow it, imagining he would be "the President who finishes what Lincoln began." Johnson knew the risks he was taking, not least in his own state, in becoming so forceful an advocate of civil rights, but he saw no way to avoid the issue, regarding it as a moral test of the nation's will to redress the most serious social problem that had plagued the country for centuries, dividing the South from the rest of the nation, making it a pariah in the eyes of the world. Achieving a success in the House greater than anticipated, he knew that the more difficult struggle would be in the Senate. There, however, with the help of Hubert Humphrey, he managed his greatest victory in his first months in office; after seventy-five days of debate on the proposed civil rights legislation, the Senate voted closure, and the bill passed by a comfortable margin. Segregation, as the South had known it for centuries, was at an end, and Johnson had caused it to happen.

He had good reason to be satisfied, but his gnawing self-doubts would be relieved only by winning the 1964 election against Goldwater overwhelmingly, not as Kennedy had won against Nixon, but as Roosevelt had won against Landon in 1936. Achieving that remarkable feat, Johnson claimed 61 percent of the nation's vote; Roosevelt, in his greatest triumph, had managed 60.7 percent.[52] Whether it reflected the weakness of Goldwater's campaign, the country's concern to honor the memory of its dead president, or the view many held of Goldwater as a frightening extremist, Johnson achieved what he most wanted: a decisive victory for himself and the Democratic Party.

While the Republicans launched their crusade for traditional American principles, embodied in the slogan, "In Your Heart You Know He's Right," the

Democrats had the wit to construct a sure defense with their jeer, "In Your Guts You Know He's Nuts."[53] Roosevelt's extraordinary success in his 1936 victory had led him astray, tempting him to pack the Supreme Court, not realizing the opposition he would encounter in Congress; Johnson never made the same mistake. He knew his victory had brought in a more solidly Democratic Congress than the one that had passed his civil rights legislation, and like Woodrow Wilson more than half a century earlier he intended to press Congress to introduce reforms that even Roosevelt and Truman would never have dared to contemplate.

Though events during the campaign—the attacks on the U.S. destroyers that led Congress to pass its Tonkin Gulf Resolution, the ousting of Khrushchev in the Soviet Union, and the Chinese explosion of their first atomic bomb—might have told the president that his attention ought not to be given exclusively to domestic affairs, that foreign policy issues could not be neglected, he never considered an issue that ought to have preoccupied him— a wholesale revamping of his foreign policy team. For Johnson, habituated to think mostly in congressional terms, the Great Society was not simply a slogan but a pledge that needed to be redeemed. Johnson expected to control the Eighty-Ninth Congress, knowing that he alone, building on his friendships there, and relying also on his loyal White House staff, could give daily attention to the vain and self-seeking men he had known from the day he first won his seat in the House of Representatives. His years in the Senate, honing his legislative talents, had made him an expert negotiator with men prepared to provide favors in return for favors given. In his mind, there was nothing demeaning or improper in these political tactics; unlike so many in the Kennedy crowd, he did not see congressmen "as archaic buffoons with tobacco drool running down their shirts." He wanted to work with them and was confident that he knew how to do so.

He made his influence felt first in seeing that the three most critical House committees—Appropriations, Rules, and Ways and Means—would be dominated by men friendly to his programs. He left nothing to chance, for this was not a president prepared to see his major programs defeated by committees hostile to legislation he favored. He and his aides, while prepared to listen to recommendations for changes in the laws they proposed showed little tolerance for those who refused to consent to the principles he advocated. Independence had its price, and no one ever doubted that Johnson's memory for legislative rebellion was flawless.[54]

After 1964, he made education his first priority, believing the future of the country depended on the federal government intervening in an area traditionally the prerogative of individual states, knowing he would have to overcome the hostility of those who insisted that federal engagement would mean federal control. He recognized that he had to expect opposition from those who feared that Catholic schools would become eligible for federal assistance, destroying the separation of church and state that many thought a cardinal protection guaranteed by the U.S. Constitution. As aides prepared the Elementary and Secondary Education Act, which proposed to give help to individual students and not to their schools, with title 1 of the act appearing as an essential part of his antipoverty program, every effort was made to show that the legislation aimed not at rescuing a single class—poor, black, or otherwise disadvantaged— but with helping all children. The act passed the House easily with a 263–153 vote, and the Senate voted approval even more emphatically, 73–18.[55]

Congress, in effect, gave the federal government authority and funding to assist the individual states in their efforts to improve the educational opportunities of the young. In November 1965, Johnson enjoyed a second victory only scarcely less important; by the terms of the Higher Education Act, particularly its title 4, federal scholarships and loans were made available to all students for the first time. This legislation, as revolutionary as the GI Bill—an educational benefit to veterans—made higher education an option for millions of young men and women previously unable to consider going beyond high school.[56]

Johnson's second priority was medical care. Unlike the major democracies of Europe, the United States had no system of health care to guarantee access for all, including the aged and the poor, or that gave adequate support to hospitals and laboratories conducting research on the three major causes of death: heart attack, cancer, and stroke.[57] Johnson, determined to make "the wonders of modern medicine available to all," started by believing that a campaign waged against the major killers would be enough but soon expanded his view, recognizing that only a system of federally guaranteed insurance, proposed but defeated in the past, would satisfy the needs of those, especially the aged, who lacked the resources for their own health care.

Medicare became his cause, and Wilbur Mills, the chairman of the House Ways and Means Committee, initially hostile to the proposal, became his principal collaborator.[58] To avoid the complaint that the president was introducing socialized medicine, the Medicare legislation made no provision for paying doctors' fees but guaranteed sixty days of hospital care, 180 days of skilled nursing home care, and 240 days of home health visits to all Social Security recipients aged sixty-five and older. In committee, Mills refined Johnson's proposals, making them even more generous, and the bill that eventually emerged included provisions for reimbursing physicians as well as hospital costs; also significant, it created a special program for the indigent— Medicaid—to be administered by the states.[59] Medicare, after the most difficult negotiations in the Senate, with some 500 amendments proposed and discussed, became a reality on July 28, 1965.[60] Again, it is inconceivable that such legislation would have passed without the president's constant interventions. Though its costs escalated eventually beyond those originally projected, Medicare provided services for senior citizens more important than any mandated by earlier federal legislation.[61]

One other great legislative reform effort had to be made, and it was not an easy one for Johnson, a Southerner, to launch. Despite the guarantees given blacks by the civil rights legislation of 1964, in many Southern states they remained for all practical purposes disenfranchised. In several states, Mississippi and Alabama most conspicuously, few blacks appeared on the voting rolls. Clearly, a voting rights act was called for. Johnson was uncertain whether Congress would consent to legislation on a matter that previously lay wholly in the province of states; it was only the violent response of Alabama state troopers to peaceful marchers, seeking to walk from Selma to Montgomery, the state capital, recorded on television, with clubs, tear gas, and whips used against the protesting men and women, that forced the president's hand.

Appearing before Congress, giving what many believed his greatest speech, he compared Selma to Lexington and Concord, to Appomattox, a "turning point in man's unending search for freedom."[62] The rhetoric was moving, and the political intent was clear; Johnson told Congress: "The command of the Constitution is plain. There is no moral issue. It is wrong—deadly wrong—to deny any of your fellow Americans the right to vote in this country. There is no issue of States rights or national rights. There is only the struggle for human rights."[63] Again, he made certain that the bill, when presented, would pass overwhelmingly, as it did in the Senate by a vote of 77–19; the House passed it 333–85. The legislation dramatically increased the number of blacks allowed to vote in the South and encouraged blacks to seek elective office at every level— local, state, federal.

Johnson, in his efforts on behalf of children, older people, and blacks, gave concrete meaning to his hopes for a Great Society, making it something more than rhetoric, but his expectations for massive public acceptance of many of his reforms did not survive the long summer of 1965, which opened with black rioting in Watts, a suburb of Los Angeles, in which thirty-four men and women lost their lives and property damage was estimated at $35 million.[64] The promise of better conditions for blacks, eloquently expressed by the president just two months previously at Howard University's commencement exercises in the nation's capital, had done little to staunch the despair of those compelled to live in black enclaves, whether in California or New York, exposed to exceptionally high levels of unemployment, juvenile delinquency, and crime. Watts, a setback for all who counseled patience, created fear of further black outbreaks and contributed in some measure to the establishment of the reputations of conservatives like Ronald Reagan, never mistaken for racists but increasingly outspoken in their insistence that the liberal measures of the Texan president were failing to achieve the results promised.[65] After the summer of 1965, many ordinary white citizens never felt the enthusiasm for civil rights common at the time of Selma. The president, resolute in his aim to improve further the condition of blacks, used the ample powers given him by recent legislation but understood that the opposition to his racial policies, once restricted largely to the South, had become much more widespread in the country. Fear had generated disenchantment, and both contributed to end the peaceful revolution once promised but only partially fulfilled.[66]

Johnson worried about the white backlash and had good reasons for his concern, imagining that by showing his hostility to black rioters, whom he represented as no better than Ku Klux Klansmen, he would be able to contain white anger. Civil rights, once major legislation was passed, inevitably, became a less urgent matter for him, and he gave greater attention to other elements in his Great Society program, including the appropriation of larger funds for his War on Poverty, the inauguration of a new educational program, Head Start, to help disadvantaged preschool children, and changes in the unjust and highly discriminatory immigration laws that had their origin in 1924 when Coolidge sat in the White House. In establishing a new Department of Housing and Urban Development, he hoped to do more than obliterate the slums of the country. As he saw the problem, it was not enough to build new public low-cost housing; attention had to be given also to transportation, recreation, and social services—all essential to city-dwellers who yearned for something more than a brutish existence. The environment remained a prime concern, expressed as something more than the quest for clean water and unpolluted air; his Highway Beautification Act, though not one of his principal reforms, expressed his determination to have billboard advertising controlled and landscaping introduced, intended to make motorists aware again of the rare beauty of the countryside too long befouled.[67]

No other twentieth-century president could claim a legislative record to compare with Johnson's in his first two years in the White House. Although Wilson, Roosevelt, and Truman established credible records that gave proof of their ability to collaborate with Congress, to secure passage of the domestic legislation they insisted on, none was master of the arts of persuasion in the way Johnson proved to be in 1964 and 1965. But he lived with the premonition he would never be credited for his remarkable achievements, and not because those who carried the torch for the dead president resented his successes or wished to diminish them.

Johnson—the most tragic president of the century—ruined his reputation by mistakes he made in foreign policy, particularly in respect to the war in Vietnam. There, his vaunted political talents counted for little; his knowledge of Texas and Washington, D.C., helped him not at all in dealing with societies abroad he neither knew nor understood. Habituated to giving orders, issuing instructions after listening to his advisers, scarcely aware that their understanding of the situation abroad was not significantly greater than his own, there was never an intentional betrayal of the trust he reposed in the Kennedy appointees he retained, but their cockiness and self-confidence led them all astray.

Though he never explicitly said so, Johnson's aim was to save Asia in much the way that Truman, by his policies, had saved Europe. In his autobiography, *The Vantage Point: Perspectives of the Presidency, 1963–1969,* he communicated four truths he thought incontrovertible: first, that his Vietnam policy simply continued what his predecessors had also accepted, a determination to protect Southeast Asia, and to be faithful to the obligations the United States assumed in establishing SEATO, that had led Kennedy to recognize the need to send some 16,000 U.S. troops to South Vietnam before his death; second, that he went beyond this very limited commitment, beginning with selective bomb-ings of North Vietnamese targets, only when the Communists in Hanoi, de-termined to test American will, started ruthlessly to attack and kill U.S. sol-diers, supply the Vietcong with arms, and send troops of their own into the country to frighten the population and destabilize the South Vietnamese regime; third, that his aim was only to halt this aggression, and that he agreed several times to bombing halts, believing this would test the goodwill of the North Vietnamese, but their responses were invariably disappointing; and fi-nally, that he accepted very reluctantly the recommendations his advisers made for a major U.S. troop commitment on the ground when they persuaded him that the bombing was not deterring the North Vietnamese, that the South Vietnam regime was precariously close to collapse, and that the consequence of that failure would be a Communist takeover of all Vietnam and, ultimately, of all Southeast Asia.[68]

Johnson always emphasized that his decisions were invariably made with full discussion in the National Security Council, that he depended primarily on the advice (and consent) of his three principal foreign policy advisers, Rusk, McNa-mara, and Bundy, and that Congress, through its principal leaders, was always kept fully informed of what he proposed to do. He never failed to indicate the resistance, occasional and tentative, of some in his administration, including George Ball, the undersecretary of state, and Hubert Humphrey, the vice presi-dent. He was always concerned to demonstrate that he consulted widely, at least among those in the nation's capital, on the many escalations he felt obliged to order. Johnson represented himself as the commander in chief prepared to order action, but only after the most deliberate consultation with others.[69]

Though the names of those who came to question and in some instances op-pose his policies in Vietnam included men as influential as Senators William Fulbright and Mike Mansfield, as well as Walter Lippmann, America's most es-teemed journalist, and numerous leaders abroad, including Charles de Gaulle and Harold Wilson, the British prime minister, no one reading Johnson's Viet-nam tale could have guessed the nature of their misgivings and even less the policies that they advocated.[70]

While Johnson represented his responses to North Vietnam, including his later bombings of Hanoi and Haiphong as the necessary responses to their acts of aggression, comparable to those taken against the North Koreans in 1950, he believed he was avoiding the mistakes Chamberlain and others had made in the 1930s—seeking peace through a mistaken policy of appeasement.[71] Words like *napalm*, so frequently mentioned by those who opposed the war, expressing their horror at the pictorial evidences of U.S. military action, never appeared in his account. Johnson wrote self-righteously of what he and his advisers did, never admitting error, but never seeking to shift the blame to those who served as his principal collaborators.

From the time he used the attacks on the U.S. destroyer as the excuse for securing the Tonkin Gulf Resolution from Congress, which authorized him to take "all necessary measures" to "repel armed attacks against the forces of the United States and to prevent further aggression," the president told only very partial truths.[72] Senator Wayne Morse, one of only two senators to vote against the resolution, insisted that the *Maddox,* the destroyer in question, had been escorting South Vietnamese patrol boats in their raids on North Vietnam, but Senator Fulbright categorically denied the truth of the allegation, as did McNamara. In fact, it was true.[73] So, also, a reported second North Vietnamese attack on the destroyer never occurred, and the president knew this but said nothing; it was acknowledged decades later, in 1995, by Robert McNamara.[74]

It is impossible to know what role, if any, these incidents and the Tonkin Gulf Resolution played in bringing the North Vietnamese to dispatch troops into South Vietnam, but in the president's mind only one thing mattered: The House, by accepting the Tonkin Gulf Resolution by a vote of 416–0, in effect granted him virtual carte blanche to do whatever was necessary to defeat the aggressors. That approval, he imagined, legitimated his first limited air strikes on North Vietnamese targets, and as the situation in South Vietnam deteriorated, with the Vietcong became more aggressive, using mortars to kill eight American soldiers and wounding 125 at a U.S. helicopter base and barracks at Pleiku in early February, just weeks after the president's inaugural, he gave orders for 132 carrier-based jets to attack North Vietnamese targets. The president, perpetually worried he might one day be accused of losing Vietnam as Truman had been accused of losing China, saw no alternative to ordering a more sustained bombing of North Vietnam. OPERATION ROLLING THUNDER, never mentioned by Johnson in his autobiography, was ordered to begin on March 2.

North Vietnam, in the decade that followed, survived bombings that exceeded in intensity all the bombings of World War II, but these more extended bombing raids, modest in the beginning, were made to appear as simply extensions of earlier policy. When, on April 7, the president spoke at Johns Hopkins University, he called for an independent South Vietnam, "securely guaranteed and able to shape its relationships to all others—free from outside interference—tied to no alliance—a military base for no other country." He called for an immediate start of "unconditional negotiations." Walter Lippmann, shown a draft of the speech before its delivery, called it a "disguised demand for capitulation" and urged Bundy to persuade the president to offer a "carrot," an "unconditional" cease-fire.[75] The Communists reacted as Lippmann expected they would, and Johnson could only express dismay that they had not recognized his good intentions, that Beijing denounced the speech as "full of lies and deceptions," that Moscow dismissed it as "noisy propaganda."[76]

Just days before, on April 1, secretly, the president authorized the sending of 18,000–20,000 additional troops to Vietnam, in the words of a memo Bundy prepared for his files, "to permit their more active use."[77] The National Security Council on that day agreed "to change the mission of our ground forces in South Vietnam from one of advice and static defense to one of active combat operations against the Viet Cong guerrillas."[78] This policy, maintained through the spring of 1965, interrupted only by a coup in the Dominican Republic that Johnson saw as Communist-inspired, allowed him to live in the illusion that only by a commitment of U.S. forces could the North Vietnamese, the Vietcong, and other Communists be made to understand that he would never abandon any "free society" to their rule.[79]

During the summer, Johnson wrote in his memoirs,

> I came to the painful conclusion that an independent South Vietnam could survive only if the United States and other nations went to its aid with their own fighting forces. From then until I left the Presidency, we had three principal goals: to insure that aggression did not succeed; to make it possible for the South Vietnamese to build their country and their future in their own way; and to convince Hanoi that working out a peaceful settlement was to the advantage of all concerned.[80]

Johnson, wildly optimistic at the time, believed that nations other than the United States would come to the aid of South Vietnam, and he showed his secretive side in failing to mention that three options were offered to him in late June, dramatically different ones, by McNamara, Ball, and William Bundy, McGeorge Bundy's brother. McNamara, on June 26, submitted a memorandum that recommended a substantially increased U.S. military commitment, the dispatch of some 200,000 troops immediately, together with a tripling of bombing sorties over North Vietnam and a naval blockade of its ports.[81] Ball, in a memorandum sent on June 28, urged the president to "cut our losses" and withdraw from Vietnam. The alternative, he wrote, would require the president to send U.S. troops into a war "they are ill-equipped to fight in a non-cooperative if not downright hostile countryside." Their casualties would be enormous, and the end would be "national humiliation."[82] William Bundy, transferred from the Defense Department to become assistant secretary of state, argued in a memorandum, intended in part to be an answer to Ball's, that the best policy for the moment was to maintain U.S. forces at their current level but to use more in ground combat to see how well they would fare in Vietnam's difficult terrain.[83]

Just as the president failed to mention the alternative policies offered him, so he said nothing of the meeting of the so-called Wise Men, which included Dean Acheson, John McCloy, Robert Lovett, General Omar Bradley, and others—the old men who had served in earlier administrations—whom he summoned to meet with him in the White House on July 8–9 to discuss Vietnam. Acheson, writing to Truman of that experience, described it in terms that would make sense only to someone who knew Johnson, both his strengths and vulnerabilities.

The president, meeting with a small group over drinks, according to Acheson, felt only pity for himself; in his words,

> We were all disturbed by a long complaint about how mean everything and everybody was to him—Fate, the Press, the Congress, the Intellectuals and so on. For a long time he fought the problem of Vietnam (every course of action was wrong; he had no support from anyone at home or abroad; it interfered with all his programs etc. etc).

Finally, Acheson told Truman he could stand it no longer, "I blew my top and told him he was wholly right on Vietnam, that he had no choice except to press on, that explanations were not as important as successful action." The others, Acheson reported, soon joined in, and the president was given a green light for going ahead.[84] His decision to do so three weeks later did not reflect simply his acceptance of their call to action but an unwillingness to hear what very few dared to tell him, that Acheson knew to be true, that "if we take over the war, we defeat our purpose and merely take the place of the French."[85] Acheson used these words when he met with Erik Boheman, a former Swedish ambassador, the day after he urged Johnson to go ahead.[86] Johnson's Cabinet and White House staff failed him, something Acheson chose not to say. They understood the situation less well than they pretended but intuited correctly that he greatly feared the consequences of not acting, of losing Vietnam, and were therefore prepared to argue for policies they knew to be hazardous, that they believed he wished to pursue. The blind led the blind into a quagmire, and Johnson courted catastrophe.

Because the difficulties in Vietnam were recognized by all who had any appreciation of the situation there, and because of growing domestic and foreign pressure, Johnson agreed to halt the bombings of North Vietnam over the

Christmas holidays, a respite that continued for the whole of January. In his State of the Union message, delivered on January 12, 1966, he urged the North Vietnamese to come to the conference table, to negotiate a peace that would honor the Geneva accords of 1954 and 1962. Ho Chi Minh, Johnson complained in his memoirs, responded by calling the offer "deceitful and hypocritical," leading the president to say:

> Throughout the pause in the bombing, Hanoi continued to rush men and supplies toward the demilitarized zone and into the supply lines through Laos, which were known as the Ho Chi Minh Trail. North Vietnam's actions, and its words, once again said 'no' to peace. It was obvious that nothing 'good' had happened, as diplomats friendly to Hanoi had forecast; nor was anything good going to happen. After consulting with leaders of Congress and with the National Security Council, I decided to resume bombing on January 31.[87]

Johnson argued, as he invariably did, that his only interest was peace and that only the North Vietnamese refusal to negotiate caused the war to continue, insisting that he never adopted policies except those discussed and approved by both his National Security Council and congressional leaders. What greater legitimacy could he ask for? That certain journalists and politicians abroad did not accept those policies was made to appear insignificant.

When McGeorge Bundy left office as national security adviser in early February 1966, the president, furious with what he conceived to be desertion, replaced him with Walt Rostow, in his mind no less an intellectual than Bundy, whom he expected to be even more amenable to the kinds of policies the administration had pursued in the last years.[88] By the end of 1965, U.S. casualties in Vietnam numbered 1,636 killed and 7,655 wounded. In the first two months of 1966, the Americans suffered an additional 4,300 casualties, but none of this led the administration to change its policies; on the contrary, it only reinforced the view that the search-and-destroy missions recommended by General William Westmoreland were depleting the ranks of the Vietcong even if they were also laying waste the countryside and forcing tens of thousands of peasants into the cities, facts never admitted. By the end of 1966, a year when the Democrats suffered substantial losses in both the House and the Senate, managing, however, to retain control of both, the United States had some 400,000 troops in South Vietnam. The war seemed no closer to being won, but Johnson took comfort from polls in the spring of 1967 suggesting that only 19 percent of the American public favored withdrawal from Vietnam, almost 40 percent supported what they considered to be Johnson's policy of limited war, and 30 percent would have had him escalate further, making it a major war.[89] With opinion still so favorable to the war, Westmoreland recommended for the U.S. troop commitment to be increased even further, though he did not reveal this in his speech before Congress, in which he spoke of being certain America's forces would "prevail."[90]

McNamara, increasingly skeptical of these claims, wrote a single-spaced, twenty-two-page memorandum for the president on May 19, 1967, that went considerably beyond anything he had dared to say previously. He told the president, in effect, that to continue the current policy would not end the war and would not bring the North Vietnamese to the peace table, if only because they were already looking forward to a possible change of the American government in November 1968.[91] However, to escalate the war would risk either China or Russia coming to the aid of their North Vietnamese ally. At home, the war was increasingly unpopular and had left many disenchanted and confused as to why the country had allowed itself to become so heavily engaged.[92] The memorandum, in its pessimism, contrasted greatly with what the secretary of defense continued to say in his public utterances.

Years later, McNamara explained to his biographer, Deborah Shapley, that he kept his misgivings concealed, intentionally understated, because most of the president's close advisers, including his new national security adviser, Walt Rostow, not to speak of the Joint Chiefs of Staff, had no wish to hear such views expressed.[93] Indeed, William Bundy, expressing the contempt he felt for the defeatist memo, called it "a fig leaf cover for withdrawal."[94] Nothing that McNamara submitted to the president diminished the more intense bombings of Hanoi that continued through the summer, making it seem increasingly likely that an all-out war was indeed in prospect.

The secretary of defense, aware that this was a no-win war, sent a Harvard professor, Henry Kissinger, whom he had come to know, to Paris to negotiate with French interlocutors believed to have influence in Hanoi; any measure likely to hasten the opening of negotiations seemed a reasonable option to him.[95] Once an ardent advocate of the war, McNamara had come to doubt his initial optimism but found it impossible to say so in public. The president and others in his entourage would have regarded such a statement as treason.

When some 50,000 antiwar demonstrators marched on the Pentagon in late October, McNamara, obviously shaken, realized perhaps for the first time the depth of the nation's discontent with the war. At the meeting of the so-called Wise Men with the president on October 31, Generals Earle C. Wheeler and Creighton W. Abrams spoke as if the enemy was losing, that the South Vietnamese forces were showing remarkable resilience, that only the press in the United States believed the Tet Offensive had been a success for the enemy. McNamara found it impossible to show equal optimism and years later acknowledged he told the group that perhaps everything he and Dean Rusk had tried to do since 1961 had been a failure. At lunch, he was even more specific, saying that "continuation of our present course in Vietnam would be dangerous, costly in lives, and unsatisfactory to the American people."[96]

When McNamara the next day suggested in a note to the president that his policy should be to keep the U.S. forces at their current level of 525,000, that more of the fighting should be left to the South Vietnamese, that the bombings over North Vietnam should cease at once, not least because they were not having their desired effect, the president showed little sympathy for his view, thought to be defeatist.[97] McNamara's days as secretary of defense were numbered. No longer able to conceal his differences with the president, in revealing them he had only incurred Johnson's displeasure; exhausted and frustrated, McNamara found the prospect of an appointment as president of the World Bank very appealing, and because the nomination required presidential approval, it was never clear whether McNamara was pushed from office or simply presented the president an opportunity to be rid of him.[98] The Kennedy foreign and defense policy entourage, gradually but obviously, had begun its exodus.

The year 1968 proved to be even more difficult for Johnson than 1967. With Clark Clifford's appointment as secretary of defense, the president found himself dealing with someone unsympathetic to the military's demand for an additional 205,000 men. Clifford refused to believe that these additional forces, if granted, would produce an outcome substantially different from what had been happening throughout 1967, especially at the time of the Tet Offensive. As he explained to the president, "I see more and more fighting on the U.S. side, and no end in sight."[99] While Rostow and Rusk continued to urge the president to "hang in there," the damage to the president's reputation grew constantly, and his increased anger and nervousness were evident to all who witnessed his rages. The military's demand for additional men, leaked to the press on March 10, only two days before the president won the New Hampshire primary, the first in the 1968 season, by only the slightest margin, saw him barely defeat Senator Eugene McCarthy of Minnesota, whose sole election promise was to end the Vietnam War.[100]

On March 14, to no one's surprise, Robert Kennedy announced his intention to seek the Democratic Party's presidential nomination, a challenge Johnson had long feared, and that he responded to in his characteristic way, calling three days later for "a total national effort to win the war."[101] Clifford knew something had to be done, and urged Johnson to summon his Wise Men again, to hear their recommendations. Among those who attended this meeting were Acheson, Ball, Bundy, Dillon, Vance, and Generals Bradley, Ridgway, and Taylor. Generals Wheeler and Abrams gave their customary roseate view of the situation, with Wheeler arguing that he saw no reason for "all the doom and gloom we see in the U.S. press," Abrams claiming that the South Vietnamese had fought well during the Tet Offensive, as effectively as the South Koreans in the 1950–1953 Korean War.[102] McGeorge Bundy, asked to summarize the views of the group, indicated there had been a marked shift in attitude since their last meeting in November.

The earlier hopes for slow but steady progress, shaken by Tet, had made several doubt the prospect of any imminent military success; in these circumstances, Acheson recommended that steps be taken to disengage.[103] Ball, Dillon, and Vance all supported Bundy and Acheson, with Ball recommending that the president halt the bombing in the next six weeks, that a world figure, possibly the Pope, be asked to propose a moratorium. Generals Bradley and Taylor refused to share the pessimistic views of their colleagues, and the president, summing up what he heard, suggested that "six advisers suggested some form of disengagement, one was in between, and four were opposed." Bundy, according to the president, saw it as less clear-cut than that, believing the group was recommending "a shift of emphasis," transferring more of the fighting to the South Vietnamese to see what results would follow from a halt in the bombing. In the president's words, "I thanked the advisers for their views and their counsel and asked them to continue to be available to me." Speaking to Rusk and Clifford after the meeting, he used less polite language confiding to Humphrey that he "remained convinced that the blow to morale was more of our own doing than anything the enemy had accomplished with its army. We were defeating ourselves."[104]

There is no reason to believe that this meeting alone moved the president to make his announcement on March 31 that "I have ordered our aircraft and our naval vessels to make no attacks on North Vietnam, except in the area north of the demilitarized zone, where the continuing buildup directly threatens allied forward positions and where the movements of their troops and supplies are clearly related to that threat." He expressed the hope that the North Vietnamese, impressed by this action, would show equal restraint, that all the bombing could end, and that the two sides could sit down together to make peace.

Then—surprising all who never imagined he would abandon his hope to serve for another term in the White House—he added: "I shall not seek, and I will not accept the nomination of my party for another term as your President." Writing about this in his autobiography, the president said:

> I wanted Hanoi to know that Lyndon Johnson was not using this new move toward peace as a bid for personal political gain. Maybe now, with this clearest possible evidence of our sincerity thrown into the balance, North Vietnam would come forward and agree to a dialogue—a genuine communication dedicated to peace. Those who doubted me and disliked me, those who had fought my struggle for men and women who had for so long suffered injustice, might now be willing to adjust their rigid view and seek to fashion a workable formula for peace in the streets.[105]

He hoped the days of "criticism and cynical speculation" were over. But to the end, he failed to understand the tragedy that had made so many see Vietnam as Johnson's War, convincing millions, both at home and abroad, of its injustice and cruelty.

The last nine and a half months of Johnson's presidency were anticlimactic. At his regular Tuesday lunches, the distance between Rostow, Rusk, and the military on one side, and Clifford on the other, never narrowed. Rostow, especially, believed with the Joint Chiefs of Staff that victory in Vietnam was still possible; Clifford knew it to be a dream.

While the talks on peace negotiations seemed to go nowhere, and the killing continued, the country became increasingly preoccupied with other matters, initially the primary election campaign in the Democratic Party, but then the assassination of Martin Luther King Jr. on April 4 and of Robert Kennedy on June 5.[106] Johnson, who had never cared for Bobby Kennedy but wished the public to believe he felt no enmity, that in their last White House meeting they had expressed mutual respect, used his death to write in his autobiography an elegy for a vanished era as much as for a slain leader. Johnson wrote:

> Robert Kennedy's death seemed to symbolize the irrationality that was besieging our nation and the world. The summer months of 1968 brought no easing of disorder and unrest. Our Ambassador to Guatemala, John Gordon Mein, was machine-gunned to death by local guerrillas. Soviet troops marched brutally into Czechoslovakia on August 21 and stamped the heavy boots of oppression on the first serious shoots of freedom that had appeared on Czech soil in twenty years. When the Russians made this move, they slammed the door on the missile talks we had painstakingly worked out and planned to announce the next day, August 22. That same week, fighting between police and students at the Democratic National Convention in Chicago proved to every television viewer in America how deep the cleavage was in our society, how intense the hatreds, and how wide the gulf between law enforcers and those who had nothing but contempt for the law. These conflicts also exposed the ugly side of the so-called New Politics, in spite of its claims of idealism.[107]

President Johnson had achieved remarkable legislative victories and seemed a titan as long as he remained free of foreign engagements. It is scarcely surprising that his Cabinet, before his departure from office, presented him with a scroll showing the "Landmark Laws of the Lyndon B. Johnson Administration," year by year. The most casual glance at these items can only reveal that after 1966, following the party's election reverses of that year, the yield was less rich than it had been. The president still maintained his majorities in Congress, but the country was no longer greatly impressed with his command of the situation either at home or abroad. He might wax eloquent on all he achieved on July 1, 1968, when more than fifty nations signed the Treaty on the Nonproliferation of Nuclear Weapons, or what he accomplished a year earlier in his summit meeting with Alexsei Kosygin in Glasboro, where he sought to use Soviet influence to press the North Vietnamese to join him in peace negotiations, but these and other comparable victories weighed little in the scales American newspapers and TV programs traditionally used. They, in common with millions of ordinary men and women, believed his venture in Vietnam foolhardy, thought the military showed unacceptable cruelty in their search-and-destroy operations, and felt shame at the havoc, destruction, and loss of civilian lives wrought by the air strikes.

It became increasingly difficult to detect the gains realized by any of these operations, and the president, acutely aware of the growing number of casualties, could only agree to capitulate, taking the only exit that appeared to exist. His administration, so fertile in its realization of domestic reform, ended in foreign policy failure. Johnson was seen then and is thought even today to have been the perpetrator of a war he knew neither how to win nor how to end. Few subscribed to the opinion Charles de Gaulle expressed when he heard of his decision to end the bombing and not to seek another term: He called it "courageous," a term few chose to use then or have thought to use since.[108]

Yet Lyndon Johnson, this highly complex individual, vain and insecure, a master politician able to persuade Congress to accept major domestic reform, fumbled badly when circumstances abroad required him to be a warrior. He never understood Vietnam or the Vietnamese, and none of his advisers knew that world any better. Johnson, aware of all that Truman had suffered at the hands of the Republicans for having lost China, was determined not to lose Vietnam. This led him to prevaricate and dissemble, flaws common to him throught his life, both fatal to his reputation.

CHAPTER 15

The Villain?

RICHARD NIXON REMAINS today the most controversial of the twentieth-century presidents. In the many biographies written of him, few represent him as other than infamous.[1] It is well to remember that many more than 45 million Americans voted for him in 1972 as against the slightly more than 28 million who preferred George McGovern, his Democratic opponent; but he lost that support very largely as a consequence of the Watergate revelations. If Johnson is one day rehabilitated, principally for what he achieved domestically, a comparable restoration of Nixon for his foreign policy accomplishments is also probable.[2] In decades that saw a number of very strange men occupy the White House, Richard Nixon was perhaps the strangest. Secretive, scheming, devious, and insecure, Nixon excelled in all these unattractive attributes, and it is scarcely surprising that he is often seen as the presidential villain of the century.

Nixon, born into a humble California Quaker family on January 9, 1913, the second president after Hoover to claim Quaker origins, betrayed few evidences of conscious fidelity to the pacifist principles of that seventeenth-century religious sect. The Harvard Club of California, recognizing his academic qualities, awarded him a scholarship in 1930 for being the best all-around student, but the family's strained financial circumstances kept him from going East; he remained at home, attending Whittier College, the modest local Quaker institution.[3]

Second in his class, he received a $250 full-tuition scholarship to the law school at Duke University in Durham, North Carolina, where he excelled as a student, lived frugally, and hoped his superior academic performance might recommend him for a position with one of the more prestigious New York law firms.[4] That dream unrealized, he was obliged to return home to Whittier, where he found employ, doing probate law, in Wingert and Bewley, a small firm whose two principal partners were Quakers. Nixon, partial to the evangelism common in Southern California at the time, was ardent in his Republican

Party sympathies and abhorrence of "that man in the White House," a sentiment initially revealed at Duke, that led him in 1940 to make speeches before small local audiences on what he called "Nine Young Men," an ironic attack on FDR's court-packing plan.[5] These faint stirrings of political ambition led nowhere, and in the 1940 presidential election, Nixon campaigned, as tens of thousands of others did, for Wendell Willkie, the dark horse Republican nominee. The war liberated Nixon from his small-town lawyer's existence, leading him to the nation's capital, where he became one of a small army of lawyers, some 177 in all, who served in the Office of Price Administration (OPA).[6]

Nixon, though learning something of the bureaucratic struggles characteristic of World War II Washington, aspired to a political career and realized that service in some military capacity was a sine qua non. In explaining later how he came to join the Navy in April 1942, his wish to serve his country figured prominently; so also did his desire to be free of "some of the remnants of the old, violent New Deal crowd" so conspicuous in the OPA that included, in his description, a good number of intellectuals and Jews.[7] He attended naval officer candidate school in Rhode Island, where he met William Rogers, who became a friend and, decades later, his secretary of state. Nixon claimed no wartime exploit comparable to Kennedy's, but the abundant time to read, play poker, and write daily letters to his wife in his "honorable but unheroic" war—the judgment of one of his many unflattering biographers—allowed him to rise to the rank of lieutenant commander.

A family friend, associated with the Whittier branch of the Bank of America, recognizing his political ambitions, recommended that he run against Jerry Voorhis, the incumbent New Deal Democrat who had held his House seat for a decade, thought by many to be invulnerable. In a vicious campaign, Nixon represented Voorhis as a "tool of the Communists," an explosive accusation in 1946 in Southern California; by the last days of the campaign, the original charge was converted in anonymous telephone calls to voters to the flat statement that he *was* a Communist.[8] Widely distributed flyers characterized Voorhis as a spokesman for the Jews who protected "the subversive Jews and communists. . . in the interests of international Jewry," had "solidly voted the PAC-CIO program. . . to destroy Christian America and our form of government."[9] Whether those who financed and managed Nixon's electoral campaign were as sinister as many have argued is almost incidental to a larger fact: The young and articulate war veteran won in an off-year election where the Democrats did badly everywhere, losing seats in both the House and the Senate.[10]

Nixon boasted few accomplishments during his four years in the House, but his early attacks on Alger Hiss, later indicted and imprisoned for perjury, having lied about transmitting secret state documents to Whittaker Chambers, a *Time* editor, who had been an agent for an international Communist spy ring. The disclosure gave Nixon a national reputation, especially among

Republicans fearful of the much-advertised Communist infiltration into the federal government.

Capitalizing on his fame as an enemy of the Commies, Nixon set his eyes on the Senate, to replace Helen Gahagan Douglas, a former Broadway star and opera singer, an avid New Deal Democrat, and a friend of Eleanor Roosevelt. Through her marriage to Melvyn Douglas, one of Hollywood's leading movie stars, Helen Gahagan had moved from being a well–born New Yorker, Republican, and Episcopalian, to become a Broadway and Hollywood celebrity with great appeal to the war president, who had pressed her to run for the Senate in 1944, a seat she won easily. A "political gypsy" to her enemies, not a true Californian, too involved with leftist causes, she constantly questioned Truman's foreign policy, believing that the use of the United Nations might be a more reasonable way to curb Soviet aggression than the forging of foreign alliances.[11] Her opposition to the activities of the House Un-American Activities Committee gave her national publicity, not least among those partial to Henry Wallace's political arguments, but in the 1950 senatorial contest, she proved no match for Nixon.

Dubbed the "Pink Lady" by the Los Angeles *Daily News,* with more than half a million pro-Nixon and anti-Douglas flyers, printed on pink paper and distributed, Douglas fought back by talking of "young men in dark shirts"—an allusion to the fascism of Mussolini and Hitler—but such responses proved ineffectual against the thousands of anonymous phone calls that characterized her as a Communist.[12] The tactics Nixon had used against Voorhis four years earlier worked equally well in a statewide election when the war against North Korea commanded public attention and Communists at home and abroad were seen as the enemy to be beaten. From the day Nixon defeated Douglas so decisively, he bore the epithet tricky Dick, and though he felt some slight remorse at the tactics he used, implicit in remarks he purportedly made to David Astor, the British newspaper publisher, years later ("I want you to understand. I was a very young man"), the words he used led him to a seat in the United States Senate.[13]

Nixon was a virulent anticommunist at a time when that attribution carried many advantages, not least in Southern California. He became a person to watch for those who imagined that the nonpolitical general, Dwight Eisenhower, might need a running mate who satisfied the more traditional elements in the Republican Party, offended that their true champion, Robert Taft, had failed to secure the nomination. While Eisenhower might have invited Taft to be his running mate—and there is reason to believe that he would have accepted the call, as Johnson did less than a decade later with Kennedy—the general and his sponsors had no wish to reach out to someone so clearly identified with isolationism. It was easier for them to press for Nixon, whom Eisenhower scarcely knew, enthusiastically recommended for his youth and vigor.

In the campaign that followed, the corruption purportedly endemic in the Truman administration, together with its failure to comprehend or deal with the Communist menace at home and abroad, figured prominently in the speeches of the forty-year-old Nixon. All seemed to be going well for him until mid-September, when news broke that carried the threat of a major political scandal: Well-to-do Californians had purportedly supported Nixon secretly, providing him with funds to supplement his meager salary as a senator. A crisis more serious than any Nixon had ever confronted in his six-year political career led him to make his famous Checkers speech, perhaps his most successful TV appearance.[14]

The fund had never been a secret, Nixon told the nation, and was used only to offset political expenses; no one who contributed to it had ever profited from doing so. Not rich himself, unable to offer his wife who sat at his side a mink coat—she wore only a "respectable Republican cloth coat"—a middle-class family beset with high mortgages, able to afford only a 1950 Oldsmobile, not the vehicle of the rich, Nixon spoke of the one gift, the cocker spaniel, Checkers, black and white, sent to his daughters by a Texan at the time of his election to the Senate that he had no intention of returning. In his words, "Regardless of what they say, we are going to keep it."

A man of the people scarcely resembling Eisenhower's opponent, Adlai Stevenson, born to wealth, Nixon claimed no log cabin in his background but trusted the Republican National Committee to recognize that he was blameless. In his remarkable peroration, he said:

> I am going to continue this fight. I am going to campaign up and down America until we drive the crooks and the Communists and those that defend them out of Washington. And remember, folks, Eisenhower is a great man. Folks, he is a great man, and a vote for Eisenhower is a vote for what is good for America.[15]

Eisenhower responded with "you're my boy," and the crisis was over. While Walter Lippmann dismissed the Checkers speech as "the most demeaning experience my country has ever had to hear," this was not the view of ordinary folk. President Truman might denounce Nixon as a "shifty, goddamn liar" who had traduced him—as well as Acheson and Stevenson—but no one knew for certain what Eisenhower really thought about his devious and sharp-tongued running mate. Though Nixon never became an Eisenhower intimate, the president's illnesses gave him a prominence he could not have otherwise claimed. Used as a stand-in, what those hostile to the vice president referred to as his errand boy, Nixon gained a legitimacy from his association with Eisenhower greater than any obtainable from any other source.

Nixon yearned to be president and spent many of his waking hours, starting as early as 1956, touring the country to guarantee that he rather than Nelson Rockefeller, New York's popular Republican governor, would be the party's nominee in 1960. His so-called Kitchen debate with Nikita Khrushchev in the summer of 1959 at an American exhibition in Moscow, a slugfest that began in the Kremlin with the Soviet leader denouncing Congress for its Captive Nations Resolution, saying: "It stinks like fresh horse shit, and nothing smells worse than that," found Nixon responding with, "I am afraid the Chairman is mistaken. There is something that smells worse than horse shit, and that is pig shit."[16]

These words, never heard by the American public, still shielded from such obsenities, learned only that the vice president had bested the Soviet leader in their Kitchen debate where the vice president, sweating profusely, went "toe-to-toe"—Nixon's words—with the chairman and scored impressively.[17] When the Rockefeller presidential campaign stalled, ending almost before it started in reaction to public opinion polls that told him he had no chance of winning in key primaries, the vice president was virtually guaranteed the nomination. In late December 1959, Rockefeller's words, "I am not, and shall not be, a candidate for the nomination for the Presidency," that "this decision is definite and final," ought to have ended the hopes of those who persisted in believing that he still might be drafted, bringing the Nixon bandwagon to a halt.

Because antipathy to the vice president persisted among liberal Republicans—scarcely less virulent than among Democrats—Nixon recognized that the party's nomination would be worthless unless he brought Rockefeller into his camp. Only an understanding with the New York governor could create the political alliance that would defeat the Democrats in 1960. Nixon won Rockefeller's support by embracing the governor's program, greatly offending conservatives in the party and, more seriously, the president.[18] Eisenhower, disconcerted by the so-called Nixon-Rockefeller accord, with its implied criticism of his own administration, had no option other than to continue to support him; the alternative, Senator Barry Goldwater of Arizona, was not a Republican he could embrace.

Nixon chose Henry Cabot Lodge Jr., Eisenhower's initial supporter, as his running mate, proving again his political astuteness; a friend of both the president and the governor, he offered himself as a politician committed to Republican unity. In a rousing convention acceptance speech, Nixon answered the Soviet claim that the future of the world would be Communist with the declaration, "When Mr. Khrushchev says our grandchildren will live under Communism, let us say his grandchildren will live in freedom."[19]

Nixon knew he had a formidable opponent in Jack Kennedy but imagined his own extensive executive experience, acquired in eight years as vice president, together with his record of having impressed millions with his TV spectaculars—his still-remembered Checkers speech and his more recent celebrated encounter with Khrushchev—would stand him in good stead.[20] The four televised debates between the candidates, watched by some 70 million viewers, established Kennedy as the more effective campaigner. And while commentators differed on who won the first debate in late September, few doubted that Nixon had lost ground.[21] Appearing haggard at the first debate from a recent hospital stay, uncomfortable and ill-at-ease beside the suave, self-confident, and vigorous senator from Massachusetts, the next three debates were no more decisive but had the effect the Democrats intended: Television established itself as the medium any aspirant to the presidency would be obliged to master. Kennedy's simple message—"to get this country moving again"—thwarted a more experienced candidate who knew more but could never match Kennedy's celebrated pulchritude and charm.

The election results greatly distressed Nixon; in the popular vote, he lost by less than 120,000 votes in an election that saw almost 69 million Americans go to the polls. In the Electoral College, Kennedy won more decisively, with precisely the same number of votes, 303, that Truman had secured in his remarkable 1948 victory. In five states, Illinois, Missouri, Nevada, New Mexico, and Hawaii, Kennedy's margin of victory was small, less than 12,000 votes, and Nixon never doubted that in two states, Illinois and Texas, Kennedy won through fraud.

Had Nixon challenged the Kennedy vote in Illinois, where he lost by only 4,480 votes, he would have had to prove either that the boss of the Chicago machine, Mayor Richard Daley, had tampered with the vote or, as some charged, that the Mafia had used its celebrated strong-arm methods to guarantee that voters chose Kennedy over Nixon. Both charges, though frequently made, could not have been easily sustained, and many believed that Eisenhower, though genuinely distressed by the results, counseled acceptance of the final tally.[22]

Nixon lost what he had most coveted, but never imagined this would be his last chance to win the presidency. If Democrats, including Adlai Stevenson, were offered a second chance, and William Jennings Bryan three, with Thomas Dewey chosen twice by the Republicans, Nixon had good reason to believe he would succeed in winning the Republican Party nomination in 1964. The problem, however, was to secure an office in the interim that would guarantee his continued national prominence. A four-year retirement into a high-paying position as a partner in a prestigious law firm would not be the ideal platform from which to launch a new presidential appeal.

Nixon decided to seek election as governor of California, the second-largest state in the union, the state that had given him the House and Senate seats that had catapulted him into the vice presidency. Assembling a team he would later carry with him into the White House, including Bob Haldeman and John Ehrlichman as campaign aides, Nixon hoped to unseat the Democratic governor, Pat Brown, and it is impossible to know what the results would have been had Khrushchev and Castro not collaborated to give Kennedy his great Cuban missile crisis victory, a triumph that led to many Republican defeats in November, including Nixon's. Losing by some 297,000 votes out of 6 million cast, Nixon's fury at losing to Kennedy in 1960 paled beside the anger he felt in 1962, berating reporters with an unforgettable phrase: "You won't have Nixon to kick around any more because, gentlemen, this is my last press conference."[23] The *New York Times* believed his political career was over, declaring him "un-elected and unmourned, an unemployed lawyer."[24]

Unemployed only very briefly, he joined a New York law firm renamed Nixon, Mudge, Rose, Guthrie, and Alexander, abandoned California, and became a Manhattan resident, buying a luxurious apartment in the building Nelson Rockefeller also lived in. It was Kennedy's death that reinvigorated Nixon's interest in politics, making him realize he need not be a Republican has-been, that he could revive his political fortunes if he offered himself as a "new Nixon," chastened and reformed.[25]

He knew better than to present himself in 1964 when the public's memories of 1960 and 1962 were fresh, when he would almost certainly lose to Goldwater in key Republican primaries. Confident that Goldwater's brand of Republicanism would never win in a national election, he learned from the Republican 1964 election debacle that the road to a second nomination in 1968 was open if he offered himself as the candidate able to bring the party together—conservatives of the Goldwater persuasion as well as liberals partial to Rockefeller. Nixon campaigned actively for Goldwater in 1964, expecting him to lose but knowing the importance of proving himself a loyal Republican, and was even more active in the congressional off-year 1966 elections, when he visited some three dozen states to help Republicans recover seats they had lost. The election results in both the House and the Senate delighted him: With many of the Democratic gains made in 1964 erased, Nixon knew he had earned the respect of those he had campaigned for and that memories of his own 1960 and 1962 defeats were fading fast.

In 1967, taking a calculated risk, he declared a one-year sabbatical from politics, proposing to travel and write. Instead of maintaining the frenetic pace he set for himself in 1965 and 1966, appealing to Republicans everywhere in his rabid denunciations of the Johnson administration, he waited for the 1968 primary season to open, knowing who his adversaries were likely to be and believing he would defeat them all. George Romney, the governor of Michigan, proved no match; Romney explained his initial support of the Vietnam War with his startling revelation that he had been "brainwashed" by American briefing officers in Vietnam, thereby virtually destroying his candidacy.[26]

With Romney dropping out of the New Hampshire primary at almost the last moment, leaving Nixon as the sole contender, the country waited to see whether Rockefeller would take up the challenge. While the New York governor desperately wanted the nomination, he doubted that he could win in Republican primary battles with Nixon and, to the amazement of his supporters, declared on March 21 that "I am not a candidate campaigning directly or indirectly for the presidency of the United States."[27] In answer to a reporter's question, he acknowledged he would accept a draft, then added: "I expect no call and will do nothing to encourage such a call." Asked whether the decision to withdraw did not virtually guarantee Nixon's nomination, he replied: "I think that is a fair conclusion."[28] Then, following the assassination of Martin Luther King Jr. on April 4, and riots in the nation's capital and a hundred other cities where some thirty-seven men and women lost their lives, witnessing property damage that escalated into the hundreds of millions of dollars, a traumatized nation heard Rockefeller announce on April 30, barely six weeks after his original statement, that he had reentered the race.[29]

The assassination of Robert Kennedy on June 6 transformed the race in the Democratic Party. It also led some Republicans to ask whether a Nixon candidacy at so parlous a time made political sense. Rockefeller, recognizing the importance of not being dismissed as a party-wrecker, having been charged with that offense once before for his lukewarm support of Goldwater in 1964, resisted making direct attacks on Nixon. Instead, he used his ample fortune to invest heavily in newspaper and TV advertising—a campaign that in the end cost him $4.5 million—confident that its effects would become obvious when the public opinion polls registered the undeniable fact that he alone was a sure winner against any Democrat.

How could Republican National Convention delegates fail to respond to such evidence of potential success? Governor Ronald Reagan in California, an undeclared candidate, followed a different strategy, traveling extensively through the South, seeking support there for his conservative policies. Neither strategy proved successful; the polls on the eve of the Republican National Convention indicated that Nixon was likely to win in a battle with either Humphrey or McCarthy.[30] It appeared, if the polls could be believed, that the New York governor would do less well than Nixon and that the governor of California, despite his oratorical successes in opposing forced school integration, trumpeting the importance of law and order and condemning Johnson for his failure to win the war in Vietnam—positions that had great appeal in the South—lacked the support to defeat the former vice president.

Nixon, on the first ballot, won the nomination, with 692 votes, twenty-five more than the necessary majority. As his running mate, he chose Spiro Agnew, governor of Maryland, a newcomer to politics, little known to the public, originally a Rockefeller supporter.[31] Nixon, in his acceptance speech, spoke to the "forgotten Americans," the hard-working men and women "who suffered acutely from inflation and high taxation, knew that the war in Vietnam had been badly mismanaged, and were dismayed by the violence that had erupted in America's cities."[32] He promised to bring "new leadership" to the country and "an honorable end to the war in Vietnam," to "re-establish freedom from fear in America and freedom from fear in the world."[33]

While the divisions within the Democratic Party, greatly exacerbated by the TV images of police and 10,000 antiwar protestors fighting in the Chicago streets outside the convention hall, with tear-gas canisters exploding and clubs being used indiscriminately, dimmed Humphrey's victory, his real problems began only after his nomination. How could he show himself loyal to the president without seeming to approve of the Vietnam War as Johnson and his colleagues had conducted it?[34]

Nixon, knowing how poorly he himself had performed in 1960, recognized the importance of avoiding new presidential debates and initially opposed them because he refused to consent to a three-way debate in which the racist governor of Alabama, George Wallace, the nominee of the American Independence Party, would participate. When Wallace finally agreed not to insist on his right to participate, Nixon claimed it was too late for him to change his schedule to allow for a debate with Humphrey alone. Both Nixon and Wallace imagined they were doing well in September, and only Humphrey seemed to be in trouble. When, over the protest of hecklers, he promised some sort of withdrawal of U.S. forces from Vietnam in late 1968 or early 1969, both the president and the secretary of state, in effect, repudiated him, with Johnson, speaking to the American Legion, suggesting that "no one can predict" when Americans could begin to leave Vietnam.[35]

The Chicago violence, repeated wherever Humphrey spoke, saw both Nixon and Wallace gain in the polls, and on September 30, in Salt Lake City, Humphrey, increasingly desperate, said, quite simply, "As President, I would stop the bombing of the North as an acceptable risk for peace."[36] In Nashville, a day later, he called Wallace a "charlatan" and a "demagogue" and spoke with disdain of Nixon's "perfumed" and "deodorized" campaign.[37]

While Nixon always expected the Wallace vote to decline as the day of the election approached, and imagined himself the principal beneficiary of that decline, the October polls suggested that in the North and Midwest, where Wallace had been strong, he was weakening, but the expected Wallace vote was going not to Nixon but to Humphrey.[38] Nixon, previously low-key and calm, became excitable in the last days of October, accusing the administration of allowing a serious "security gap" to develop, with the United States lagging behind the Soviet Union.[39] Once elected, Nixon claimed, he would restore "clear-cut military superiority." Clark Clifford, the defense secretary, immediately challenged Nixon on his facts, and Humphrey deplored this "needless and mortally dangerous escalation of the arms race."[40] Even before these exchanges, the president summoned the three candidates to tell them that the talks in Paris between the Americans and the North Vietnamese had led to a tentative but promising development; a peace agreement might soon be reached.[41]

On October 25, Nixon responded to all this with an extraordinary statement:

In the last 36 hours I have been advised of a flurry of meetings in the White House and elsewhere on Vietnam. I am told that top officials in the Administration have been driving very hard for an agreement on a bombing halt, accompanied possibly by a cease-fire, in the immediate future. I since learned these reports are true. I am also told that this spurt of activity is a cynical, last-minute attempt by President Johnson to salvage the candidacy of Mr. Humphrey. This I do not believe.[42]

All of Nixon's foes, long familiar with the stratagems of tricky Dick, saw that he had once again set up a strawman—Johnson's collusion in a campaign to win the election for Humphrey—only to suggest that he, for one, refused to believe the president capable of such chicanery.[43] In the days that followed, Saigon expressed its opposition to meeting with the North Vietnamese, and the president learned that the pressure on the South Vietnamese to refuse to meet had originated with Anna Chennault, the Chinese-born widow of a U.S. Air Force general, cochair with Mamie Eisenhower of the Women for Nixon-Agnew Committee.[44] Suspicions, never proved, suggested that Nixon had urged Anna Chennault to intervene, and Johnson, calling Nixon to verify whether he had promised the South Vietnamese a better deal if they refused the administration's offer, heard him say that he knew nothing of the matter.[45]

Humphrey, informed of all this by Johnson, decided not to use the information in the last forty-eight hours of the campaign.[46] Whether he would have gained sufficient votes had he been less circumspect, no one can say. In any case, Nixon won by an exceedingly narrow popular majority, 31,783,783 votes to Humphrey's 31,266,006; Wallace received 9,898,543 votes, principally in the South. This was a slim victory, comparable to Wilson's in 1912 in another three-way contest, and it registered the South's defection from the Democratic Party. Even Al Smith's loss in 1928 had not been equally devastating; Humphrey lost every Southern state except Texas, five going to Wallace, seven to Nixon. Outside the South, the Democrats held their ground, but this proved insufficient to guarantee their victory in the Electoral College. Humphrey, honest and honorable, lost to someone known to be neither, and Nixon began his presidency with his party in control of neither the Senate nor the House.

Although there had been other close elections in the twentieth century, Wilson's and Kennedy's being the obvious examples, Nixon's was different in that the two Democrats never promoted the anger felt by those who despised Nixon. He arrived a hated man, offensive to millions for what he had done politically since his first days in Congress; he entered the White House, wounded and angry, still smarting from what he felt had been an unjustified denial of the presidency in 1960.

All this was artfully concealed in his inaugural address, in which he promised a "spiritual revival," anticipated by the remarks of Billy Graham, the noted evangelist, his longtime friend, whose invocation included the words:

The whole world is watching to see if the faith of our fathers will stand this hour. Too long we have neglected thy word and ignored thy laws. Too long have we tried to solve our problems without reference to thee. Too long have we tried to live by bread alone. We have sown to the wind and are now reaping a whirlwind of crime, division and rebellion.

The newly inaugurated president sounded the same note. Recalling Franklin Roosevelt's problems created by the Great Depression, he contrasted the material needs of that day with those he confronted, saying, "Our crisis today is in reverse. . . . We are caught in war, wanting peace. We're torn by division, wanting unity. We see around us empty lives waiting fulfilment. We see tasks that need doing waiting for hands to do them. To a crisis of the spirit we need an answer of the spirit." In words that seemed to mock the whole of his tempestuous political career, he added: "When we listen to the better angels of our nature, we find that they celebrate the simple things, the basic things—such as goodness, decency, love, kindness."[47] Though the theme of spiritual revival dominated the occasion, the president spoke also of more mundane matters—the need for full employment and better housing, the rebuilding of the nation's cities, protection of the environment—all issues his predecessor had made central to his presidency. On the crucial issue of the Vietnam War, he borrowed from Saint Francis of Assisi, saying, "Let us take as our goal where peace is unknown, make it welcome; where peace is fragile, make it strong; where peace is temporary, make it permanent." Quoting from the liberal poet Archibald MacLeish, he ended with: "Our destiny offers not the cup of despair, but the chalice of opportunity."[48] The rhetoric was not stirring in the Kennedy tradition, but it suggested a wish to be thought something other than a red-baiting firebrand.

The Cabinet he appointed, neither less nor more distinguished than the one chosen by Kennedy, included William Rogers, his longtime friend and adviser, as secretary of state. No one foresaw that the rivalry between Rogers and a Harvard professor of government, Henry Kissinger, chosen as the president's national security adviser, would soon cause Rogers to lose much of his authority, suffering the same indignities experienced by Rusk under Kennedy, compelled to compete for the president's ear with Bundy and the president's brother. Nixon, like Wilson, Roosevelt, and Kennedy, intended to be his own secretary of state, consulting and using only those he believed might contribute to his success. For him, as for Roosevelt, the State Department could offer little. Imagining himself extraordinarily endowed as an expert in foreign affairs, knowing but never acknowledging the ineptitude of Eisenhower, whom he had observed closely, and having little regard for Kennedy or Johnson, he found only one interlocutor, the man he scarcely knew, Kissinger, as the person to consult with. Nixon simply perpetuated the control of foreign policy in the White House that his Democratic predecessors had initiated.[49]

As attorney general, he chose the dour John Mitchell, another old friend who resembled Robert Kennedy only in his total commitment to the president, ready to do anything to assist him, the ever-reliable adviser, useful in numerous roles other than those that fell strictly within his Department of Justice jurisdiction.[50] In the White House, with a greatly expanded National Security Council staff, Nixon relied heavily on two political confidantes, Robert Haldeman, appointed chief of staff, and John Ehrlichman, counsel to the president and chair of the Domestic Council. Both, influential in Nixon's earlier election campaigns, were more than ready to protect him against any of his many foes. They became his courtiers, faithful servants he berated, but never failed to depend on, who felt honored to serve him.[51]

From Harvard, he recruited to serve as his assistant on urban affairs Daniel Patrick Moynihan, who purportedly introduced him to the idea he might be America's Disraeli, a "Tory with liberal principles."[52] On the all-important issue of race, Nixon intended no major innovations; having won the presidency with only 12 percent of the black vote in a substantially expanded black electorate, he saw the blacks as unnecessary to Republicans able to craft their electoral victories without them.[53] Using the issue of law and order to his advantage, he discerned an electoral map fundamentally different from the one that had led Democrats to their presidential victories. The white citizens of the country, many for all practical purposes having shed their ethnic affiliations, were clearly disenchanted with what they saw as New Deal and Great Society programs intended to help only the poor, the unemployed, and those on welfare. These men and women were searching for a party that would sustain them in their newly acquired middle-class status and ambitions, making their interests all-important. Nixon, like FDR before him, aspired to use the crisis of his day to transform the party he led and imagined himself the architect of a new Republican Party, shorn of the simple pieties of his former chief, Eisenhower, as well as those that had led the party to nominate a loser like Barry Goldwater.[54]

Nixon's domestic reform proposals, insignificant beside those initiated by Johnson, left no permanent institutional legacy but established him as an astute politician seeking to appeal to upstanding white citizens. His Family Assistance Plan, for example, his solution to the problem of poverty, represented as workfare, was an incentive scheme to compel men and women to seek employment, taking millions off the welfare rolls, and satisfying an electorate who believed that welfare cheats were destroying the moral fiber of the nation.[55] He accepted that some expansion of the Food Stamp program might be necessary and was even prepared to introduce affirmative action, though on a very modest scale, but his most radical proposals stemmed from a resolve to control the dangerous inflation that had become endemic since the last years of the Johnson administration.[56]

In August 1971, the president introduced price and wage controls, an emergency measure to be retained for three months only. Inflation, more serious than at any time since the 1940s, could well threaten his reelection in 1972, and Nixon, never one to take risks with his political future, initiated what he termed phase two of his New Economic Program—providing for selective wage and price controls in major industries.[57] These efforts scarcely improved the situation and, by the end of 1973, following his reelection, were unceremoniously interred.[58]

Still, in seeking to prove himself a Tory Democrat, he showed a concern to treat issues that Eisenhower and other Republicans of comparably sanguine views ignored. By establishing the Environmental Protection Agency in 1970, he donned the Theodore Roosevelt mantle of conservationist, but this never led him to support memorable legislation or to take administrative actions that mattered greatly. He disparaged the efforts made by Johnson in his celebrated War on Poverty, eliminated the Office of Economic Opportunity, and greatly weakened the Community Action program, espousing the New Federalism that diminished the role of the federal government and returned some measure of authority to the individual states.[59] In his revenue-sharing plan, states received block grants from federal agencies, allowing them to spend federal funds without the restrictions traditionally imposed.[60] To make the Supreme Court again a conservative tribunal, he thought to replace liberal justices with men more sympathetic to his own political creed; in this effort, he failed twice, first with Clement Haynesworth, then with G. Harrold Carswell.[61] The Southern Democrats, though prepared to sustain him in his battles for welfare reform, had no interest in supporting the appointment of men recognized to be incompetent and undistinguished.

In his pledge to restore law and order, he claimed extraordinary successes. Though the antiwar demonstrations continued, the race riots of the Johnson years virtually ended. While Nixon never pretended to be interested in extending black voter participation, he showed some concern to enforce the Supreme Court's desegregation decisions, ready to claim credit for the fact that in 1968 some 68 percent of black children in the South attended all-black schools and that their number had dropped to 8 percent by 1974.[62] Carl Rowan, a black journalist, thought Nixon's record on civil rights "respectable" and wrote:

> It just may be that the Nixon administration is not too bad in the field of civil rights, but you can get hooted out of any Negro audience in America by saying so. Yet it is Nixon's team that has given the Chicago school system two weeks in which to end racially discriminatory practices in assigning and transferring teachers. Lyndon B. Johnson is rated a great civil rights president, but he would never let the Justice Department do anything in Chicago that might upset Mayor Richard Daley.[63]

Only a minority accepted that judgment, believing that in engaging Moynihan as his principal urban affairs adviser Nixon accepted the Harvard professor's argument that "benign neglect" was the best solution for the race problem.[64] Stephen Ambrose, who published biographies of both Eisenhower and Nixon, described his desegregation policies as politically inspired: "Nixon had to be hauled kicking and screaming into desegregation on a meaningful scale, and he did what he did not because it was right but because he had no choice."[65]

Why did he have no choice? For one reason, principally: Many of his closest advisers, including Leonard Garment and Ray Price, argued that any policy that identified him with the racist views of George Wallace would give the Democrats new strength outside the South.[66] Electoral politics demanded restraint and required that Nixon prove himself a moderate, a president who heeded the Supreme Court's mandates. Still, there were limits to the deference he thought it necessary to give to judicial decisions.[67] Though the Supreme Court in April 1971 authorized busing to desegregate Southern schools, obliging Northern schools to follow suit, the president, knowing how unpopular busing was with his white supporters both north and south of the Mason-Dixon line, bought TV time during the 1972 primary season to express his serious doubts about the policy.[68] The mail that flooded the White House told him he had taken no risk in doing so.

For four years, Nixon courted the votes of white men and women, traditional Republicans but also dissident Democrats who had lost their faith in the conventional liberal panaceas. Nixon captured the mood of a nation disillusioned with Johnson, still reluctant to disparage Kennedy but no longer in his thrall. Nixon proved himself an acute critic of liberalism, knowing the political advantages that would follow from his insistence that the Republican Party would no longer subscribe to the domestic policies of his Democratic predecessors.

Yet domestic policy—however important to Nixon in helping to create an electoral coalition he hoped to use—never figured as his principal interest. Foreign policy consumed him as domestic issues never could, except as they related to winning votes from blocs of disenchanted voters. Believing himself uniquely qualified to conduct foreign affairs, he imagined himself a master of geopolitics and, with Kissinger at his side, conceived foreign policy initiatives that others would not have considered. While claiming, as Eisenhower did in respect to the Korean War, that he had come to the White House with a plan to end the fighting in Vietnam, he had none; the war went on, and it fell to the president to explain why. This involved him in an intensive campaign to persuade the American electorate of his good intentions, and he succeeded to an extent that few of his detractors dared to acknowledge. The industrious and hard-hitting president, so different from Eisenhower, the man responsible for his initial elevation, would never concede defeat, searching always for popular approval, sustained by public opinion polls that suggested hostility to his Vietnam policies was never as great as his critics claimed.[69]

In his view, three reasons accounted for the ongoing war: First, the North Vietnamese, unwilling to settle on terms other than those he deemed shameful, demanded that he renege on promises made to the leaders of South Vietnam since the time of Kennedy; second, any abandonment of South Vietnam would lead to disastrous consequences elsewhere in the world, inviting new Communist aggressions and greatly diminishing U.S. influence everywhere, especially in Asia; and finally, dismissing the demonstrations at home that criticized him for seeking a "just peace," he represented those who supported such protests in Congress and in the media as partisan and uninformed, ignorant of the issues at stake.[70] The Nixon (and Kissinger) explanations, in their fusion of political, geopolitical, and moral argument to support their insistence on the importance of sustaining the South Vietnamese government, though with substantially reduced numbers of U.S. soldiers, enjoyed no credibility whatever with those who saw the continued bombings as immoral, the casualties, American and Vietnamese, military and civilian, as unnecessary.

Johnson, by pledging a bombing halt and voluntarily withdrawing from the presidential race, imagined these actions alone would suffice to extricate the more than 500,000 Americans from a war in which some 700,000 South Vietnamese were also engaged, confronting at least 250,000 North Vietnamese and an equal number of Communist guerrillas. Nixon, adopting the strategy some dubbed Vietnamization, favored also by a number of Johnson's advisers, believed a gradual withdrawal of U.S. forces could be made if the South Vietnamese accepted to make a larger military commitment to their own defense and if the Americans agreed to send military advisers and equipment in sufficient quantity to compel the North Vietnamese to recognize they would never win the war. They had to be persuaded that negotiation was the only reasonable course.[71]

Kissinger doubted that the gradual withdrawal of U.S. troops would bring the North Vietnamese to the peace table; in his mind, it would only encourage them to go on in the hope that Americans' disenchantment with the war, what he described as the country's "psychological defeat," would in the end force the country to withdraw all its forces leading to the collapse of the South Vietnamese resistance.[72] Because the administration lacked any military plan to compel a North Vietnamese military withdrawal, the president and his national security adviser, in secrecy, without consulting others, decided that only the opening of private discussions with the North Vietnamese in Paris carried any prospect of an early peace. Such discussions had taken place during Johnson's time, with Harriman as the principal negotiator, but they now became more frequent, and there were six such encounters, lasting over many days, all conducted in great secrecy between Kissinger and the North Vietnamese in the two years after 1970.[73]

During this period, Nixon reduced the U.S. military forces in Vietnam from 550,000 to 260,000, and casualties fell from 16,000 in 1968 to 600 in 1972, but peace did not follow, and the Americans persisted in their bombing campaign. Students continued to demonstrate throughout 1969, culminating in the vast outpouring at Kent State University in early May 1970 following the president's announcement on April 30 that the North Vietnamese were using sanctuaries in Cambodia from which they were receiving men and material and that these had to be wiped out. Once the sanctuaries were eliminated, Nixon promised to withdraw from Cambodia. In a characteristic statement, he added: "If when the chips are down, the world's most powerful nation, the United States of America, acts like a pitiful, helpless giant, the forces of totalitarianism and anarchy will threaten free nations and institutions around the world."[74]

Such statements, traditional with the president, on this occasion carried an additional pledge when he said: "I would rather be a one-term President and do what I believe was right than be a two-term President at the cost of seeing America become a second-rate power."[75] Nixon, in this instance as in others, lied; he never intended to be a one-term president, and he never expected this to be the consequence of his Cambodia decision.

As surprised as the governor of Ohio and the general public by the Kent State tragedy, in which members of the National Guard opened fire on students, killing four and wounding nine, the Presidential Commission on Campus Unrest later characterized the "indiscriminate firing" as unnecessary, unwarranted, and inexcusable.[76] With student demonstrations and strikes following at some 350 colleges and universities, involving at least 2 million participants, greater than any previously known, when *Newsweek* polled the country on how it regarded the Kent State catastrophe, only 11 percent thought the National Guard acted excessively; 50 percent expressed approval of Nixon's invasion of Cambodia.[77] These polls persuaded Nixon that it was safe to continue with the policies he had initiated, but such polls carried little influence with the increasingly vocal Democratic opposition in Congress.[78]

On January 1, 1971, Congress explicitly forbade the use of U.S. ground troops in Laos and Cambodia, but not the use of airpower in either country. That same month, Harvard professor Matthew Messelson claimed that the U.S. Army's defoliation program had destroyed 250,000 acres of mangrove forest in South Vietnam, a claim the Department of Defense immediately denied.[79] A few days later, Reverend Philip Berrigan, already serving a six-year term for destroying draft records, was indicted with five others for conspiring to kidnap Kissinger and to blow up the heating tunnels in federal buildings in Washington. The Harrisburg Six, as they came to be known, dismissed the charges as an attempt by the government to destroy the peace movement.[80] On

January 21, sixty-four Democratic congressmen introduced a resolution to deny money for air and sea support to military operations in Cambodia.[81] The lines on both sides—those who favored the administration and supported its policies and those most ardent in their denunciation of its immoral policies—became increasingly taut. Beginning in February and continuing through April, South Vietnamese troops, supported by U.S. airpower and artillery, crossed into Laos, seeking to close the Ho Chi Minh Trail, the supply route for much of the material reaching the North Vietnamese and the Vietcong. The bloodiest fighting followed, with the operation failing in the end. President Nixon, in his first major news conference since the start of the Laotian offensive, said on February 17 that he would put no limit on the use of U.S. airpower, barring only the use of tactical nuclear weapons.[82]

These and similar remarks persuaded many in the antiwar movement that Nixon had no serious intention of making peace. In April, the radical group Mayday threatened to "shut the government down," and when their protests led to lie-ins on the bridges and main thoroughfares of the capital, the police reacted, arresting some 12,000 men and women.[83] The verdict on Lieutenant William Calley in March 1971, found guilty of murdering civilians at My Lai and sentenced to serve a life sentence at hard labor, hardened opinion in antiwar circles when the president chose to release him from the stockade and confine him to quarters at Fort Benning while his case was being reviewed.[84] All these events, especially the murders at Kent State, provoked new demonstrations, with construction workers in New York City, the so-called hard hats, taunting and battling with antiwar protestors at city hall. The president, seeking to build support for his policies and to prove their popularity, seemed ready to risk additional riots, believing it in no way unseemly to accept an honorary hard hat from the head of the New York City construction workers, calling it "a symbol, along with our great flag, for freedom and patriotism to our beloved country."[85]

Worse, however, was yet to come when the *New York Times* published in June 1971 the *Pentagon Papers*, a 7,000-page collection of top-secret documents, originally commissioned by Robert McNamara, that described the war as the United States had fought it until 1967 under Kennedy and Johnson. Since these documents dealt not at all with Nixon, the president might have been wise to ignore them.[86] Kissinger, however, learning that one of his own appointees as consultant to the National Security Council, Daniel Ellsberg, was responsible for the leak, and fearing others would follow, urged the president to seek a Supreme Court injunction to prevent further disclosures. When the Supreme Court refused to condemn the *New York Times* for publishing the papers, and voted 6–3 that publication did not violate national security, Nixon pressed Ehrlichman to find other ways to stop the leaks.[87] The Special Investigation Unit established in the White House—the Plumbers—broke into Ellsberg's psychiatrist's office, hoping to find incriminating evidence to prevent such infractions of national security in the future.[88]

All this, however, was very secondary to a grandiose plan the president and his national security adviser were fashioning, an initiative to reverse U.S. policy in respect to Communist China and create an understanding between the two countries that no Democrat would have dared to contemplate. The Republican president, having never been thought soft on communism—having indeed gained his initial fame through charging Democrats with that heinous offense—felt free to explore a diplomatic approach no Democrat would have dared consider.

Nixon expected his opening to China would have at least two immediate beneficial results: It would almost certainly make the North Vietnamese more amenable to accepting reasonable peace terms; and it would distress the Soviet Union, China's Communist adversary, sufficiently to make the Kremlin more responsive to compromise on various arms control and comparable issues that he believed could be negotiated.[89] The president, abetted by a national security adviser who also thought in geopolitical terms, greatly exaggerated the benefits likely to be realized. In their more optimistic moments, they developed the concept of linkage, imagining the repercussions likely to follow from the world realizing that the United States and Communist China were no longer enemies. A more reasonable Soviet policy on Berlin and reduced tensions in the Middle East were only a few of the many benefits confidently prophesied.[90]

The president's commitment to a reconsideration of U.S.-China relations was of long standing. In October 1967, before he became president, he had written an essay in *Foreign Affairs* that spoke of the need to reconsider these relations, saying: "Taking the long view, we simply cannot afford to leave China forever outside the family of nations, there to nurture its fantasies, cherish its hates and threaten its neighbors. There is no place on this small planet for a billion of its potentially most able people to live in angry isolation."[91] In February 1971, in his annual foreign policy report, Nixon expressed his administration's policies on both China and the Soviet Union unmistakably when he wrote: "We are prepared to establish a dialogue with Peking. We cannot accept its ideological precepts, or the notion that Communist China must exercise hegemony over Asia. But neither do we wish to impose on China an international position that denies its legitimate national interests." Because China and the Soviet Union were quarrelling in public, and because many feared that war might result, Nixon made clear his intention to remain neutral in the event of an outbreak of hostilities. His report read:

> We will do nothing to sharpen that conflict—nor to encourage it. It is absurd to believe that we would collude with one of the parties against the other. . . . At the same time, we cannot permit either Communist China or the USSR to dictate

our policies and conduct toward the other. . . .[W]e will have to judge China, as well as the USSR, not by its rhetoric but by its actions.[92]

Given these statements, it is surprising that Kissinger's secret visit to China in July 1971 was not anticipated. Clearly, both the president and his national security adviser believed that improved relations with China were possible, that they would inevitably influence the Soviet Union and the world more generally, inaugurating a period when the habits and practices of the Cold War were gradually abandoned. Kissinger's secret visit to Beijing opened the door to an official presidential visit in February 1972, and the Nixon-Mao conversations led to the Shanghai Communiqué, which Kissinger summarized in his book *Diplomacy*:

> Stripped of diplomatic jargon, these agreements meant, at a minimum that China would do nothing to exacerbate the situation in Indochina or Korea, that neither China nor the United States would cooperate with the Soviet bloc, and that both would oppose any attempt by any country to achieve domination of Asia. Since the Soviet Union was the only country capable of dominating Asia, a tacit alliance to block Soviet expansionism in Asia was coming into being (not unlike the Entente Cordiale between Great Britain and France in 1904, and between Great Britain and Russia in 1907).[93]

There is no reason to doubt that Nixon understood the extraordinary achievement he and his national security adviser had fashioned. In their minds, they had done more than rectify a condition that had existed for decades, created in part by the Republican search for the Democratic scapegoats who had lost China. Their policy represented a shrewd effort to do what the Democrats would never think to do—befriend China as a way of checkmating the Soviet Union, and encouraging the Soviets to enter into even more basic agreements with the United States.

Nixon's long-held views, that there had to be "some relationship between political and military issues" and "that crisis or confrontation in one place and real cooperation in another cannot long be sustained simultaneously," seemed to have been confirmed. Though prepared to acknowledge that earlier negotiations that led to agreement on "numerous bilateral and practical matters such as cultural or scientific exchanges" were important, neither the president nor his national security adviser believed these altered the fundamental conditions that made for international discord.[94] Kissinger was an academic who, together with Bernard Brodie, Klaus Knorr, Oscar Morgenstern, and Thomas Schelling, had contributed significantly to the development of the strategic thinking important in the arms control and military plans instituted by McNamara during the Kennedy administration, based essentially on the principle of deterrence.[95] Mc-

Namara, like Kennedy, accepted that U.S. strategic policy had to be based on the concept of having sufficient military power "to inflict unacceptable damage upon any single aggressor or combination of aggressors at any time during the course of a strategic nuclear exchange, even after absorbing a first strike." This, for McNamara, qualified as America's "assured-destruction capability."

In his very first press conference, Nixon had indicated his policy on strategic arms limitation talks when he said:

> What I want to do is to see to it that we have strategic arms talks in a way and at a time that will promote, if possible, progress on outstanding political problems at the same time—for example, on the problem of the Mid East and on other out-standing problems—which the United States and the Soviet Union acting to-gether can serve the cause of peace.[96]

Reviewing during the next months what the two previous administrations had done in proposing the Strategic Arms Limitation Talks (SALT), Nixon de-cided that too many of the decisions had been made by middle-ranking bureau-crats; these were issues that demanded the active involvement of the president and his most trusted colleagues. While the Pentagon feared the Soviet installa-tion of an ABM system around Moscow, and pressed the administration to make comparable arrangements to protect America's cities, the president de-cided very early, hoping to stimulate negotiations with the Soviets, that there should be a limited deployment only around selected missile sites. As he ex-plained in March 1969, there was no way to provide the American people "with complete protection against a major nuclear attack, but a moderate deployment of ABMs around missile sites, clearly defensive, would tell the Soviets that the Americans were serious in wishing to initiate strategic arms limitation talks." The SALT talks finally got under way in November 1969, and Senator Henry Jackson, soon to become a thorn in the president's side, seemed enthusiastic about the administration's arms control policies as late as March 1971.[97]

Kissinger, working through secret back channels, pushed for the resolution of arms limitation differences to allow Nixon and Leonid Brezhnev to settle all remaining differences, and they finally met in Moscow in May 1972, just months before the presidential election. The ABM Treaty, signed there, con-fined both nations' defenses to two sites and 200 missile launchers, with a sep-arate five-year interim agreement guaranteeing that both would freeze all strategic forces at agreed-upon levels. The SALT I agreements, though wel-comed by many, were almost immediately denounced by others, especially those who saw the doctrine of mutually assured destruction (MAD) as mad, and so described it.[98]

The objections made by Senator Jackson rested on the proposition that Nixon had made a serious error in accepting land-based Soviet missiles in greater number than those allowed to the United States. The fact that the U.S. would have a larger missile capability through its bomber and submarine fleets, that it would have MIRVs (multiple independently targeted reentry vehicles) long before the Soviets possessed a comparable capability, did not assuage Jackson. While he could not defeat the interim agreement in the joint resolution passed by Congress, he succeeded in adding an amendment that expressed his concern about retaining U.S. superiority; it read: "[Congress] urges and requests the President to seek a future treaty that, *inter alia,* would not limit the United States to levels of intercontinental strategic forces inferior to the limits provided for the Soviet Union."[99] McGeorge Bundy recognized that Senator Jackson, advised by his able assistant, Richard Perle, had in effect disparaged the Nixon accomplishment, but the Jackson-Perle view did not unduly disconcert a president for whom the whole year had been one of notable foreign policy accomplishments, expected to give many advantages in the November elections.[100]

Nixon, by his foreign and domestic policies, had created a political coalition that robbed the Democrats of votes they had depended on from the time of FDR. Ethnic support among Irish, Italian, and Polish voters no longer went automatically to Democrats; more than that, Nixon's views on race, even when not explicitly stated, were highly congenial to blue-collar workers, and not only those trapped in the decaying cities of the country. Just days before the election, in a paid political broadcast, Nixon addressed the nation in a speech that contrasted greatly with the one delivered by McGovern a day later. As much as anything, it suggested why McGovern could not win and why Nixon achieved a victory that exceeded even those Eisenhower had managed in 1952 and 1956. The president spoke of a "free people, in a free nation, a nation that lives not by handout, not by dependence on others or in hostage to the whims of others, but proud and independent—a nation of individuals with self-respect and with the right and capacity to make their own choices, to chart their own lives." He indicated that a "major breakthrough" had been made in the peace negotiations but that certain details remained to be worked out. Why, he asked, were the details important? "My study of history convinces me," he said, "that the details can make the difference between an agreement that collapses and an agreement that lasts." He was not going to make the mistake of 1968, "when the bombing halt agreement was rushed into just before an election without pinning down the details."[101] Having disparaged Johnson without naming him, he went on to say: "We want peace—peace with honor—a peace fair to all and a peace that will last. . . . I am confident that we will soon achieve that goal."

Hanoi was watching the U.S. election, he said, to see whether the results would bring "peace with honor or peace with surrender." Emphasizing the improved relations with both China and the Soviet Union, and expressing his determination to see the restoration of "the religious faith, the moral and spiritual values that have been so basically a part of our American experience," he spoke of having reduced inflation greatly, almost by half, of workers enjoying "record numbers of jobs," and making great gains in "real spendable earnings," with levels of violence down, and the tide turning in the fight against crime. The children of America in a generation or a century would be able to say that

> America in the 1970s had the courage and the vision to meet its responsibilities and to face up to its challenges—to build peace, not merely for our generation but for the next generation; to restore the land, to marshal our resources, not merely for our generation, but for the next generation; to guard our values and renew our spirit, not merely for our generation but for the next generation.

He wanted the "next 4 years to be the best 4 years in the whole history of America."[102]

McGovern answered the president the following night and told of promises made by Nixon, all broken. It had been "a campaign marked by falsehood, sabotage, secret funds, special-interest deals, and criminal activity," and the claim that Nixon craved peace was "the worst deceit of all." Truth, he said, was more precious than victory; Nixon and those around him, incapable of telling the truth, cared only to win the election, deceiving the electorate with promises of imminent peace, concerned only to remain in power. Nixon and his men were "tricksters," and McGovern claimed to be "tired of answering the same old lies." The president had always supported the war; he, by contrast, had always opposed it.

If elected, McGovern promised to disengage from Vietnam and bring all the men home in the ninety days following his inaugural. Tuesday, Election Day, was a "day of reckoning," he said, when the nation would be asked to decide between war and peace. While some in the nation believed him (slightly more than 28 million), more than 45 million did not. Nixon enjoyed a success comparable to the one Johnson achieved in defeating Goldwater, but what followed from his victory differed dramatically from the events of 1964–1965. Johnson had used his triumph to proclaim the need for new legislation, achieving congressional support that compared with what only one other twentieth-century president, Franklin Roosevelt, had managed to do. Nothing comparable followed Nixon's victory; indeed, from almost the moment of his triumph, he seemed more isolated, remote, and troubled than at any time since his arrival in the White House.

Henry Kissinger, the most authoritative source on the strange happenings of the days that followed the president's reelection, told of how on November 8, within hours of the celebrations that accompanied victory, the whole White House staff, assembled in the Roosevelt Room, heard a "grim and remote"

president thank the group "in a perfunctory manner" and leave after five minutes, learning then from Haldeman that the president wished all members of
the White House staff to submit their resignations, and that the president intended to announce his personnel decisions for the coming term within a
month. Kissinger wrote: "The audience was stunned. It was the morning after
a triumph, and they were being, in effect, fired. Victory seemed to have released
a pent-up hostility so overwhelming that it would not wait even a week to surface; it engulfed colleagues and associates as well as opponents."[103] Members of
the Cabinet heard the same message an hour later. Kissinger termed it "political butchery" for which there was no obvious explanation.[104]

Nixon, even in his best days, had not been an easy man to work under, and
it is unlikely that even a premonition of the disasters that awaited him from the
Watergate break-in, whose links to the White House were still unknown to the
press, wholly explained this strange vindictiveness, though it may have accounted for his growing remoteness in the weeks that followed.

When the talks in Paris between Kissinger and Le Duc Tho stalled, failing to
achieve the settlement that had once seemed so imminent, the president and
his national security adviser, together with General Alexander Haig, his soon-
to-be-appointed chief of staff, agreed that only a massive bombing campaign
would bring the North Vietnamese to become serious about the negotiations.
They had to be made to realize that the Americans were not prepared to wait
around indefinitely for a resumption of talks.[105] A decision was made to resume the bombing of North Vietnam on December 18, and the president saw
no need to go before the public to explain why that had become necessary.[106]
Kissinger, given the responsibility for explaining it to the press, put the blame
entirely on the leaders in Hanoi.[107] The so-called Christmas bombings, initiated then, continued for ten days and ended only when North Vietnam, in effect, decided to return to the conference table.[108]

The public outrage in the press, on television, and among members of Congress was intense.[109] As Kissinger wrote, "indiscriminate carpet bombing of
heavily populated areas" was the most common accusation; believing the
charge false, he penned what even today must stand as the most spirited defense of Nixon's postelection decisions:

No foreign policy event of the Nixon Presidency evoked such outrage as the
Christmas bombing. On no issue was he more unjustly treated. It was not a barbarous act of revenge. It did not cause exorbitant casualties by Hanoi's own figures; certainly it cost much less than the continuation of the war, which was the
alternative. It is hard to avoid the impression that a decade of frustration with
Vietnam, a generation of hostility to Nixon, and — let me be frank — frustration
over his electoral victory coalesced to produce a unanimity of editorial outrage
that suppressed all judgment in an emotional orgy. . . . Nixon chose the only

weapon he had available. His decision speeded the end of the war; even in retro-spect I can think of no other measure that would have.[110]

Kissinger wrote this knowing that the president was unhappy with him at the time, that he could be "ruthless, fierce, and devious in defending his turf," always remaining superficially gentle on the surface. Ultimately, Kissinger saw Nixon as having "revolutionized international diplomacy," accomplishing this through his intelligence and daring. Not many others saw him in this way, and even the final conclusion of peace on January 23, 1973, caused few to alter their views on the B-52 bombings. While Kissinger could see both the good and the bad in the president, the contradictions that made him resemble no other figure in public life, this was not how most Americans saw him, particu-larly after the revelations of Watergate linked him to an incontestably criminal break-in that had taken place in June 1972 at the Democratic Party's national headquarters.

The publication of the *Pentagon Papers*, which led the White House to cre-ate the Plumbers, had produced a break-in at the offices of Daniel Ellsberg's psychiatrist, where none of those responsible for the crime had been appre-hended. On June 17, a comparable break-in was attempted at the Watergate complex, and this time, James McCord, chief of security for Nixon's Commit-tee to Re-Elect the President (CREEP), was discovered by a guard and arrested along with two of his accomplices. While no one ever discovered conclusively why CREEP launched this operation, and what precisely they were hoping to find by rifling through papers and installing a tap in Democratic Party head-quarters, these questions became secondary to others of far greater importance. Did the president himself know of the plan before it was hatched and, if so, what was his complicity in it? The discovery of the name of E. Howard Hunt, a one-time Plumber and CREEP activist, in the address book of two of those arrested led to his being charged as a coconspirator, and as early as June 23, Nixon told Haldeman to instruct the CIA to stop any investigations of the break-in. The order—illegal, of course—could only be thought a patent ob-struction of justice.

Watergate literally destroyed Nixon as no previous event had ever crushed any predecessor. His major problems stemmed not from what others did to him but from what he did to himself, not least in having instituted a taping system that in the end told the world he had known about Watergate from al-most the day it happened. Nixon knew he was not the first president to record messages secretly, but no one had ever established a system as elaborate as his. Johnson, in his years as president, secretly recorded more than 10,000 tele-phone conversations, and used the FBI to observe activities of potential oppo-nents during the 1964 Democratic National Convention, feeling no com-punction about planting bugs in embassies and private residences to monitor

Nixon's activities in 1968. In the Oval Office, Johnson introduced a taping system that could be activated only by the president and thus was, by definition, used selectively.[111]

Nixon, when he entered the White House in January 1969, ordered Johnson's recording system dismantled, but two years later, in February 1971, told Haldeman to reinstate a more sophisticated system. For some time, only the president, Haldeman, and one of Haldeman's aides, Alexander Butterfield, knew about the system, originally installed only in the Oval Office but soon extended to the president's hideaway in the Executive Office Building, Camp David, the Cabinet Room, and the White House and Camp David telephones. Butterfield, in testimony before the Senate Select Committee investigating Watergate on July 16, 1973, first told senators of the existence of this elaborate system. As he explained, "The President is very history-oriented and history-conscious about the role he is going to play, and is not at all subtle about it, or about admitting it."[112] The senators knew that if they gained access to the tapes they would have a full record of what the president knew about the Watergate break-in and whether he was in any way himself involved.

These events, coming so early in Nixon's second term, immediately after his unprecedented victory over McGovern, guaranteed he would protest total innocence, that it was not a matter that greatly concerned him, claiming he was spending his days, as always, consumed with critical foreign policy issues. In this hastily prepared political scenario, he appeared as the master of the White House, working closely with Kissinger, still national security advisor but soon to be elevated to secretary of state. Many in Washington suspected this was a myth to give the impression that the president had nothing to fear, that all was well. In fact, he had become increasingly agitated and preoccupied with a single issue: to devise strategies to defeat the growing congressional and public pressure for full disclosure of what he had known about the Watergate break-in. Though Nixon pretended still to be in charge at the White House, Kissinger and Haig emerged as the true managers of a perplexed president uncertain about how to proceed to defeat those in Congress and in the media he feared were intending the destruction of his presidency.

The questions Senator Howard Baker posed at Senator Sam Ervin's Select Committee to investigate Watergate became the preoccupying ones: What did the president know, and when did he know it? For the press and television, a no less important question was whether the Watergate break-in was in some way related to the reported burglary of papers in the office of Daniel Ellsberg's psychiatrist. John Sirica, the U.S. district judge who tried the men involved in the Watergate burglary, all found guilty early in 1973, indicated he would delay sentencing until March, hoping the accused would cooperate in naming the higher-ups who had given them the orders for the break-in. In the interim, Senator Ervin, together with Senate Majority Leader Mike Mansfield, gained support for the creation of a select committee to conduct hearings on campaign finances. When John Dean, the president's counsel, told Nixon of a "cancer on the presidency" on March 21—an allusion Nixon pretended not to understand—and when the president and Haldeman continued to pay hush money to keep individuals from speaking out, both imagined they had found a scapegoat in Dean. He would be made to appear the one who had arranged it all.

Before this, however, in one of the more remarkable late-night conversations with Kissinger, on April 17–18, when the president's alarm over the situation was unmistakable, Kissinger sought to reassure him, telling him he had "saved this country" and that "the history books will show that, when no one will know what Watergate means."[113] Nixon's own words revealed his distress, as well as the incoherence of his thought at the time; he told Kissinger:

> Of course, [Leonard] Garment, as you know, was having the idea that I should get up and announce that I'd fired Haldeman, Ehrlichman, and Dean without waiting until they get up to the main—the real culprit is Mitchell, [the attorney general] of course. He's in charge of the whole Goddamn thing, and John Mitchell should step up like a man and say, 'Look, I was in charge; I take the responsibility,' period.[114]

Kissinger replied: "Exactly. All the more so, as doing the opposite won't help him any."[115] Later in the conversation, the president made clear that he would not fire Haldeman until he had absolute proof of his complicity; in his words, "I'm not going to fire a guy on the basis of a charge made by Dean, who basically is trying to save his ass and get immunity, you see."[116] As the situation deteriorated, and the president wrestled with having to ask Haldeman and Ehrlichman to leave, he became more preoccupied with whether he would be able to save himself, whether the country realized what would be lost if he was impeached and Agnew came into the presidency. No one could wish that, he said, alluding often to his crucial importance for the peace of the world.[117] With Ron Ziegler, his press secretary, on April 27, he spoke of himself as the man on whom "the whole hopes of the whole Goddamn world of peace. . . rest right in this damn chair."[118]

On April 30, 1973, Nixon announced the resignations of both Haldeman and Ehrlichman, "two of the finest public servants it has been my privilege to know," and also of the dismissal of John Dean, Ehrlichman's assistant. The president, speaking with Haldeman after his speech, was gratified to hear his ever-faithful former chief of staff say he had done well, to which he answered: "Well, it's a tough thing, Bob, for you and for John and for the rest, but, Goddamn it, I'm never going to discuss the son-of-a-bitching Watergate thing again—never, never, never, never."[119] He then informed Haldeman that though the speech had been delivered a full fifty minutes earlier, only one Cabinet member, Casper "Cap" Weinberger, had called to tell him he had done well. After a "hmm" from Haldeman, he continued, "All the rest, you know, are waiting to see what the polls show. Goddamn strong Cabinet, isn't it?"[120] Haldeman suggested they might not know how to reach him, but these words did not wash with an angry president, who replied: "They know, they know," but "I just wanted you to know that Cap called and he was all the way."[121]

Following this extraordinary exchange, Nixon protested his love for Haldeman and Ehrlichman, going on to say, "I love you, as you know," and after hearing an "okay," adding: "Like my brother."[122] Minutes later, he heard from Rogers, telling him he had been trying to reach him, without success, saying that the speech was "terrific, really superb." The president's answer—"Don't give me that shit, you know"—only elicited further compliments and the assurance that he had indeed been trying to get through, as he expected other members of the Cabinet had, but that the "Goddamn system" had not been working properly.[123] Elliot Richardson, named in his speech as the new attorney general, also called to tell him how great the speech was—in his words, "in a real sense your finest hour."[124]

The president may have believed the worst was over, that his appointment of Richardson and the scuttling of Haldeman and Ehrlichman had saved his administration, and that he need never again consider the possibility of being impeached. Though he told Richardson, "I'm innocent. You've got to believe I'm innocent. If you don't, don't take the job," and while Richardson may have believed him that day, he grew increasingly worried as Haig, the newly appointed temporary chief of staff, tried to rein in Archibald Cox, the man Richardson had appointed as special prosecutor. Kissinger in warning the president against Cox, had called him a "liberal fanatic Democrat," and wished Richardson had settled on someone like John McCloy, always reliable. But the attorney general had acted, and there was nothing the president could do to change the situation, obviously fraught with danger for him.

In early May, Dean shocked the White House with his revelation that he had removed certain documents from his office in the White House before leaving, that they were in a safe-deposit box, and that he intended to turn the key to the box over to Judge Sirica. Less than a week later, the White House announced the appointment of J. Fred Buzhardt as special counsel to the president for Watergate. With the nationally televised Senate Watergate hearings opening on May 22, and the *New York Times* and the *Washington Post* announcing on June 3 that Dean's testimony would almost certainly reveal that the president was himself involved in the cover-up, the president prepared to meet Soviet leader Leonid Brezhnev in Washington and to take him to San Clemente. On June 3 and 4, alarmed by what Dean might reveal, Nixon began to listen to his tapes, confident that Dean would say nothing to link him to the break-in.[125]

For a moment he seemed euphoric, but nothing changed the fact that this was an unpropitious time for a U.S.-Soviet summit. Even the most loyal Nixon supporters could not imagine the meeting would divert attention from what had now become the nation's obsession. Was he guilty or not guilty? In the circumstances, it is scarcely surprising that the president was not at his most effective in his discussions with the general secretary, and Kissinger, though trying to minimize the difficulties of the occasion, found it impossible to suggest that very much had been accomplished.[126]

Indeed, as the summer of 1973 progressed, the president found it increasingly difficult to give his attention to anything other than Watergate. On June 25 to 29, Dean testified before the Watergate committee and made several explicit charges against the president. Two weeks later, in an interview with members of the Senate committee, Alexander Butterfield revealed the existence of the taping system. That same day, July 16, Nixon informed his lawyers that they might not listen to any of the tapes, and the elaborate taping system was disconnected two days later. Cox, on July 23, subpoenaed the tapes of nine presidential meetings, and the president, claiming executive privilege, refused to turn them over.[127] On August 29, Judge Sirica ruled that the president had to turn over the tapes, and the White House responded with a declaration that it would appeal the judgment.[128]

Given all these circumstances, exceptional in every sense, it is scarcely surprising that neither the president nor the media gave much attention to the military coup in Chile that brought down the Salvador Allende government in September.[129]

Even the Kissinger appointment to be the new secretary of state failed to interest the media, transfixed by the scandal. Their interest was in one issue only: What new Watergate revelations would emerge, that is, when and if the tapes were released? How the scandal was affecting the country's foreign policy, what friends or enemies abroad thought of the matter, seemed scarcely relevant. Nixon, traumatized by Watergate, vulnerable as he had never previously been, lost interest in foreign affairs and gave Kissinger authority such as he had never enjoyed during his first term. Kissinger, in the second volume of his memoirs, *Years of Upheaval*, in discussing how Watergate changed the administration, gave particular attention to how he came to be appointed secretary of state.[130] While his original intention had been to leave the White House after a decent period in the second term, Watergate made that impossible since he would appear to be abandoning a sinking ship.[131] But, more significant, the president's attitude toward him changed after early 1973. In his words,

Nixon no longer insisted in keeping me in the state of insecurity that he had fancied was essential to my sense of proportion. He had never been willing to engage personally in the petty harassment by which this strategy was implemented, and with Alexander Haig installed as chief of staff he now lacked subordinates prepared to do it for him. Nor did Nixon retain the nervous energy to play the little games that so delighted him, designed to exploit, and if necessary to generate, tensions between Rogers and me, so that both of us had to appeal to him or Haldeman for support. Nixon's attention span for foreign policy was also declining. He would sign memoranda or accept my recommendations almost absentmindedly now, without any of the intensive underlining and marginal comments that in the first term had indicated he had read my papers with care. He stopped engaging me in the long, reflective, occasionally maddening conversations that were his means of clarifying a problem in his own mind. Increasingly, he went through the motions of governing, without the bite or the occasional fits of frenzy with which in more normal times he had driven issues to decision and steeled himself for a characteristic act of courage.[132]

In these circumstances, Nixon needed Kissinger, no longer harassed him, and showed less resentment of his growing celebrity. While Kissinger claimed he tried on every occasion to urge both Garment and Haig to press the president to acknowledge all he knew of Watergate, this never happened. Where the White House no longer harbored anyone able to claim institutional memory, with the exception of press secretary Ron Ziegler, the president, with what Kissinger called his "Walter Mitty tendencies. . . endowed wishful thinking with the attributes of truth."[133] On August 15, he repeated the claims he had made earlier: He had learned of malfeasance only late in the day, after he had ordered a full investigation on March 12.[134] In Kissinger's words, "Nixon was torn between shifting the blame to his subordinates and avoiding so antagonizing them that they would turn on him."[135] No longer defended by others, he said nothing of whether he would agree to make the tapes available.

Watergate led to the elevation of Kissinger to the first post in the Cabinet; it led also to the elevation of General Haig, whose career had been largely made as Kissinger's chief assistant. He now became Nixon's chief of staff in the White House, and in the months that followed, these two, more than the president, conducted the country's affairs. Kissinger, not Nixon, handled the crisis that followed the outbreak of the Yom Kippur War between Israel, Egypt, and Syria, coinciding with the days when Agnew resigned the vice presidency and the president recommended Gerald Ford to succeed him.[136]

The story of the Middle Eastern war, revealed in Kissinger's book *Crisis,* told of a president virtually out of the loop, with Kissinger in daily conversations with heads of state, foreign ministers, ambassadors, the secretary-general of the United Nations, the secretary of defense, senators, and members of the press. Kissinger, seeking to keep the Soviet Union faithful to its promise not to intervene to help its Arab allies, Egypt and Syria, who had initiated the surprise attack on Judaism's most holy day, hoped in the beginning to create a cease-fire while keeping the Soviet Union faithful to its interest in maintaining good relations with the United States. The Israelis, though successful in resisting the attack, suffered very heavy losses in men and equipment, and became increasingly demanding of the military supplies that only the United States could provide. Kissinger, pressed by the powerful Israeli lobby in Washington but also by senators and the press concerned with the threat to Israel's existence, did what he could to speed the delivery of essential materials to the Israelis, at the same time working for a cease-fire. When the Israelis struck back, crossing the Suez Canal into the Sinai and making inroads against Syria, its armies moving rapidly toward Damascus, Brezhnev demanded that Israel return to the lines that had existed on October 6, the day the war started, and asked for both Soviet and U.S. troops to be sent to the scene to enforce that demand.[137]

The Brezhnev message to Nixon, telephoned by his ambassador in Washington, Dobrynin, to Kissinger, read: "If you find it impossible to act jointly with us in this matter, we should be faced with the necessity urgently to consider the question of taking appropriate steps unilaterally." The message, received late at night, led Haig to decide the president should not be awakened. Kissinger agreed, having heard him just a few hours earlier, "as agitated and emotional as I had ever heard him," concerned not about the war in the Middle East but about what the media would soon describe as the Saturday Night Massacre—his decision to fire Archibald Cox, which led to the resignation of Elliot Richardson and the deputy attorney general, William Ruckelshaus.

With Kissinger in the chair, and James Schlesinger, the secretary of defense, sharing his views, decisions were taken and executed by the chairman of the Joint Chiefs of Staff, Admiral Thomas Moorer, just before midnight to order a military alert, Defense Condition III. The Eighty-Second Airborne Division was put on alert, aircraft carriers in the Mediterranean were moved, and sixty B-52 bombers were ordered to return from Guam to the mainland.[138] These decisions had the desired effect; the Soviets made no unilateral move, and Egyptian president Anwar Sadat, recognizing the reasons for the American action, agreed that the international force should include neither Soviet nor U.S. troops. Kissinger, in addition to providing the text of innumerable telephone conversations in *Crisis,* told of the reply to Brezhnev delivered to Dobrynin at 5:40 A.M. in Nixon's name—he had in fact not participated in the conversations at all—that rejected all the Soviet demands.[139]

The next day, the president and the secretary of state, meeting with congressional leaders, found them, in Kissinger's words, "at once supportive, rudderless and ambivalent," saying:

> They approved the alert; they were enthusiastic about our refusal to accept a joint U.S.-Soviet force. But their support reflected more the Vietnam-era isolationism than a strategic assessment. They opposed a joint U.S.-Soviet force because they wanted no American troops sent abroad; the *American* component of the proposed force bothered them a great deal more than the Soviet one. By the same

token, they would object to the dispatch of American forces even if, in our view, they were needed to resist a unilateral Soviet move.[140]

Kissinger wrote of the "cynicism" that characterized much of the reaction to the alert. As he explained, "Two kinds of questions were put forward: whether Soviet actions had been caused by our domestic disputes; and its opposite, whether we had generated the crisis for domestic rather than foreign policy reasons. . . ."[141] Many believed the Watergate crisis had led the administration to issue the alert.

On November 1, Leon Jaworski, the prominent Texas lawyer chosen to succeed Cox as special prosecutor, began his work, and two days later the president's principal lawyers, Buzhardt and Garment, flew to Key Biscayne, Florida, to recommend that he resign. Nixon guessed what their mission was and chose not to see them. On November 12, a new and more startling revelation emerged that made the president appear the unreconstructed villain, capable of a thousand tricks. It was now revealed to Judge Sirica that the tape of the president's conversation with Dean, central to Dean's charges but also to Nixon's defense, was missing. Only a week before, according to the president's lawyer, the tape had been looked for and not found. On November 21, Sirica made public the fact that eighteen and a half minutes of the tape were missing.[142] Few believed it had simply been lost through Rose Mary Woods, the president's secretary, accidentally erasing it. On March 1, the grand jury indicted Haldeman, Ehrlichman, and Mitchell, the president's principal guardians, along with Charles Colson, a presidential aide, and others for the cover-up. In information kept secret, the president was named as a coconspirator.

After renewed requests for additional tapes, the president on April 30, 1974, supplied some 1,254 pages of transcripts, making clear he would provide no more. On May 24, Jaworski appealed to the Supreme Court for a ruling on his subpoena requesting sixty-four additional presidential tapes, conversations he deemed essential to his inquiry. The Supreme Court, in a unanimous 8–0 decision on July 24, indicated that the special prosecutor was justified in his demand for the additional tapes and ordered them to be handed over. Three days later, the House Judiciary Committee passed by a 27–11 vote the first article of an impeachment resolution, charging the president with obstruction of justice, seeking to cover up the Watergate crime. The vote gained significance from the fact that six Republicans joined all the Democrats in voting for impeachment.

By the end of the month, two other articles of impeachment were voted, and the House began to prepare to debate the issue. On July 31, John Ehrlichman was sentenced to twenty months to five years in prison for conspiracy and perjury, and that same day Kissinger learned from Haig that the so-called smoking gun had been found. A tape of an Oval Office conversation between Nixon and Haldeman on June 23, less than a week after the Watergate break-in, suggested that the president, in Kissinger's words, "was familiar with the cover-up"; indeed, as Kissinger said, "he may in fact have ordered it."[143]

The two men closest to the president now understood that impeachment was certain, conviction virtually guaranteed. The president had lied once too often. By August 6, the end of what Kissinger chose to call "a surrealistic world" was in sight, but the president, meeting with his Cabinet, acted as if his removal from office was in no sense inevitable.[144] Kissinger, reporting on the Cabinet meeting, described the president, alluding to other difficult times he had gone through, wondering whether he would do the presidency great harm if he resigned in response to congressional pressure.[145] Would he not, he asked, be turning America's presidential system into a parliamentary system? Kissinger saw the preposterousness of the suggestion; as he explained in his memoirs, "Impeaching a President was not the same as a parliamentary vote of no-confidence."[146]

It fell to the vice president, Gerald Ford, to answer Nixon, doing so with the kindness habitual to him, acknowledging he was a "party in interest," but knowing there would be an impeachment in the House and that it was impossible to know what the judgment of the Senate would be. Seeking to buoy the president, but knowing there was no possibility of his remaining in office, Ford said: "You have given us the finest foreign policy this country has ever had. A super job, and the people appreciate it. Let me assure you that I expect to continue to support the Administration's foreign policy and the fight against inflation."[147] While the president took up the inflation issue, acting as if he had heard nothing of what the vice president had said about Watergate, George H.W. Bush, chairman of the Republican National Committee, sought to bring the Cabinet back to reality with the argument that the party was in deep trouble, that the coming off-year elections could be disastrous. Watergate had to be ended at once. The message was unmistakable: There was no solution to the problem other than presidential resignation.[148]

The Cabinet had in effect rebelled against its chief. Nixon could not fail to understand that no option remained except that of resignation, and he accepted the inevitable on August 7. A day later, after a very emotional televised farewell to the nation, Vice President Ford was inaugurated as president.

Not since the days of the McCarthy hearings had there been a political spectacle to compare with the one that finally ended in these hot August days when many Americans, on vacation, watched in wonder as the first president ever to be forced from office announced his resignation. Till the very last, Nixon pretended he was still fully in charge, visiting the Middle East for more than a week in June, capitalizing on the successes of his secretary of state in that region, and going to the Soviet Union in late June and early July for a summit to tell the world that détente was still alive.

Nixon acted as if nothing had changed; he remained the commander; others simply took instruction from him. No one close to the White House believed this. Gravely wounded, he played the role, delighting in the honors shown him when abroad, unable at home to appear in public without risking incidents. The Senate and the courts found his actions reprehensible; he committed crimes he sought in vain to deny, which in the end compelled him to go. He left, angry and resentful, believing he had been betrayed by others. In fact, he brought disaster on himself, not only by his perpetual lying but also in the suspicions he harbored that led him to speak in a way that made loyal subordinates imagine he wished for an operation like Watergate to reveal Democratic Party secrets he could then make use of. He never practiced fair play in his political life and could not develop habits in the White House that differed from those he had used for decades against Democrats as well as against any others who might seek to thwart him. He searched always for enemies, at home and abroad.

His one incontestable talent had been his ability to defend himself. He used that talent most effectively in his Checkers speech in 1952 when he appeared to be threatened with removal from the Eisenhower-Nixon ticket. Had he failed at that time, his aspirations for the presidency would have ended. His ability to emerge from that ordeal unscathed, as with his recovery from his 1960 loss to Kennedy and the more grievous gaffes he made when he failed to become governor of California in 1962, gave proof of great political resilience, as well as a remarkable capacity to dissemble and constantly to reinvent himself.

There never was a new Nixon, and the proof of that came in 1974, when he used every device to prove himself innocent, lied consistently, and allowed others to pay a price for the crimes he in some sense had led them to commit. His ranting and raving, rages, and foul language led others to imagine they were simply carrying out his political orders—to humiliate the Democrats through the discovery of incriminating documents in the Watergate complex.

When the operation failed and the thieves were apprehended, he sought to divert attention from himself by collaborating with his close associates in bribing the burglars to keep them silent. In earlier difficult situations, the president had been fortunate, but in 1974 his luck ran out. Nixon, who so frequently benefited from accidents—Eisenhower's illness, Kennedy's death—was never renowned for truthfulness; only after Watergate did Congress and the nation come to believe they understood the man. They deceived themselves, and only an account like Kissinger's revealed Nixon's true strangeness.[149] No other presidential aide had ever been comparably candid; none had ever told so much about both the achievements and follies of the president they served.

It took Nixon some time after his resignation to recover his equilibrium, but once he managed to do that, he set out on a long campaign to vindicate himself, doing so in exile through innumerable books and speeches.[150] Some believed him and found his arguments convincing, but most did not.[151] Still, by the end of his life, he deluded himself into believing he had been restored in the public's esteem; that, too, was an illusion.

Yet the realities that Nixon's loyal national security adviser and secretary of state sought to emphasize were never wholly believed, either. Thus, for example, McGeorge Bundy, though accepting that the most "conspicuous moment of superpower tension after Cuba was in the last moments of the Yom Kippur War," never believed that the military alert deterred the Soviets, saying it "played a bigger part in American public debate than in the resolution of the international crisis."[152] Bundy, like so many others who served in the Kennedy administration, could never accept that Kissinger was not simply "posturing"— the word he used—in what he said and did.[153]

More serious than such pinpricks, however, were those who accepted the arguments of Senator Jackson, who thought détente a mistaken policy, who in Kissinger's words hoped "to return to the original premises of containment and to wait behind strong defenses for the transformation of the Soviet system." Kissinger characterized Jackson's nightmare as "strategic vulnerability"; Nixon's nightmare, he wrote, was "geopolitical vulnerability." In his mind, Jackson's concern was always "the balance of military forces"; Nixon's interest was "the global distribution of political power," and this interest led him to develop his ideas on linkage, never accepted by those who always distrusted him.[154]

Nixon, Kissinger wrote, sought to "encourage moderation in Soviet *international* conduct by making restraint in Soviet foreign policy the litmus test of increased trade with America," but Jackson and those who thought as he did hoped "to use trade as a means of producing *domestic* upheaval in the Soviet Union." Kissinger recognized the irony in a situation where Nixon, "a Cold War Warrior four years earlier," was "now castigated for being too soft and trusting toward the Soviet Union—surely the first time that this particular charge had been levelled against the man who had started his political career in the anticommunist investigations of the late 1940s."[155]

The full price for supporting détente was never exacted from Nixon; the price was paid by Ford, his successor. Nixon left the presidency a greatly weakened institution, but its influence and power could not be long denied. With the arrival of Ronald Reagan in the White House in 1981, the memory of Richard Nixon was erased; it was as if he had never been in the White House, that the crimes committed during his watch had never occurred.

CHAPTER 16

The Innocent

GERALD FORD, THE last of the century's accidental presidents, came to the White House by Richard Nixon's choice, first to succeed the disgraced Spiro Agnew, forced to resign in October 1973 at the height of the Yom Kippur War, and then to take his own place when Congress threatened presidential impeachment. Ford, resembling Nixon not at all, seemed almost a throwback to the first decade of the century, to the time when William Howard Taft occupied the presidential office.

A child of the Midwest like Taft, though from Michigan rather than Ohio, a lawyer by profession, trained at Yale Law School, Ford differed from Taft in having spent almost the whole of his adult life as a congressman, never in high federal appointive office. He entered the House of Representatives in 1949; elected Minority Leader in 1965, Ford looked forward to the day when the Republicans enjoyed a majority in the House—and he would be the most likely candidate for Speaker.[1] That day never came, not even after Nixon's overwhelming victory over George McGovern in 1972, when the Republicans failed once again to capture the House. A dismayed Ford gave serious thought to making a midlife career change, abandoning Congress for some other more promising profession. Though he was not Nixon's first choice to succeed Agnew as vice president, the Watergate scandal made it imperative that the president choose someone trusted and respected by Congress. Wisely, he settled on Ford, popular with both Republicans and Democrats, and he became vice president in December 1973, serving in that office for only eight months.

Nixon, preoccupied with Watergate and unable to contemplate his expulsion from a White House he had so greatly yearned for, found little time for Ford and had no interest in instructing him in the duties that might one day fall to him. Isolated and frequently alone, secreted in his hideaway in the Executive Office Bulding that had once housed the State Department, or meeting with lawyers, Nixon spent endless hours reading the voluminous tran-

413

scripts of the tapes that the courts or the Senate committee investigating Watergate demanded to see. Ford, like Truman, came to the presidency with negligible administrative experience but with one incontestable asset: his many friends in Congress.

Following the Theodore Roosevelt precedent, he retained the whole of his predecessor's Cabinet, and after the political tempests of August 1974, the first week of September seemed positively tranquil, almost normal, but the season of goodwill ended abruptly on September 8 when Ford announced his intention to grant a "full, free, and absolute pardon" to Nixon. The new president, having no wish to see his predecessor hounded through the courts, suffering perhaps for as long as a year before a formal indictment could be made, believed that the national interest would be served by an early closure of the Watergate debacle.[2] The pardon, coming so soon after Nixon's disgrace, represented by the media as a deal between the two men, seemed a grave infraction of justice to ordinary citizens unable to find any excuse for so partisan a treatment of a man many considered a criminal. Ford's public approval ratings fell from 71 percent to 49 percent in a matter of days, and his hopes that the decision would lead the country to concentrate on fundamental domestic and international issues—rising unemployment, continued inflation, and Soviet incursions into Latin America and Africa—were effectively dashed.[3]

Ford made a genuine effort to bring the country together, in Lincoln's words, "to bind up the nation's wounds," imagining his offer of a limited amnesty to Vietnam War deserters and draft-evaders would help to serve that purpose. Again, he miscalculated; the nation, in a more generous mood, might have applauded the gesture, but the circumstances of 1974 made such tolerance unlikely.[4]

His decision to nominate Nelson Rockefeller to be his vice president was an error of a different sort.[5] Failing to understand the political risks he ran in nominating a prominent Eastern liberal Republican, anathema to all Goldwater partisans still grieving their hero's catastrophic 1964 presidential defeat, Ford incurred the wrath also of powerful Democrats in both the Senate and the House, who disdained Rockefeller as a rich plutocrat, excessively belligerent in his foreign policy views.[6] For Democrats anxious to remind an unelected president of the limits of his executive power and seeking to reassert a congressional authority too long sacrificed to the whims of the White House, the Rockefeller nomination offered a too-inviting target. The congressional hearings on the Rockefeller nomination dragged on for months, and the president learned how much he had risked in recommending him.[7] A wiser decision would have been to select a less controversial figure, someone more like himself, acceptable to a Republican Party greatly transformed by Barry Goldwater's 1964 defeat and Nixon's 1972 victory. Congress in the end voted to accept Rockefeller, but the lengthy and acrimonious nomination hearings told Ford he had erred in choosing him.

The Democrats, not surprisingly, given the repercussions to Watergate and the presidential pardon, registered substantial gains in both the Senate and the House in the off-year 1974 elections. Recognizing the president's vulnerability and exploiting the public's contempt for a discredited Nixon administration, Democrats sought to capitalize on their good fortune by new investigations to reveal the extent of the Republican chicanery. No target could be more inviting than Nixon's covert intelligence operations, especially to Democratic senators thinking ahead to 1976, developing strategies intended to increase their chances of winning their party's presidential nomination. Ford, who had long served on the Intelligence Subcommittee of the House Appropriations Committee and knew a great deal about the subject, more than his detractors imagined, recognized the challenge of these proposed congressional inquiries and decided to resist or at least to contain them.

On the very day he pardoned Nixon, the *New York Times* had published a story that suggested the extent of American involvement in the overthrow of the Allende government in Chile, a covert action previously concealed. In a press conference on September 16, the president, asked whether it is "the policy of your administration to attempt to destabilize the governments of other democracies," responded defensively, suggesting that the U.S. involvement in Chile was nothing more than an effort to prevent Allende from squelching opposition to his regime. The American interest, he insisted, involved nothing more than helping opposition newspapers and political parties—the essential components of any democratic society.[8] With the media concentrating their attention on the presidential pardon, the Allende issue received only slight attention at the time but resurfaced later when more troubling questions were raised about CIA covert activities.

On December 22, in the *New York Times,* Seymour Hersh published a lead article that began: "The Central Intelligence Agency, directly violating its charter, conducted a massive illegal domestic intelligence operation during the Nixon administration against the antiwar movement and other dissident groups in the United States, according to well-placed Government sources."[9] Though CIA director William Colby minimized the extent of these illegal operations, it was impossible for him to deny that some had taken place, and on December 30, in an amendment attached to the Foreign Assistance Act, it became obligatory for the president to authorize every covert action and to inform the appropriate congressional committee of its scope and why it was important to national security.[10] This modest harbinger of congressional intervention soon gave the coming year, 1975, its reputation as the Year of Intelligence.[11]

Ford, anxious to avoid appearing to be an uncritical defender of the CIA, decided to establish the Commission on CIA Activities Within the United States, appointing the vice president as its chair and Ronald Reagan, the former governor of California, one of its members. The commission, limited in its inquiry to CIA domestic misbehavior, had no mandate to investigate the agency's activities abroad. Indeed, the full extent of that foreign involvement, particularly its assassination attempts, was unknown at the time and became a major issue only later in the year. On January 27, 1975, the Senate had established its Select Committee to Study Governmental Operations with Respect to Intelligence Activities, under the chairmanship of Frank Church, and the House created its own Select Committee on Intelligence a month later. Both initiatives coincided with a serious gaffe made by the president at a meeting with the publishers and editors of the *New York Times* on January 16. Ford spoke then of intelligence files that contained material it was not in the national interest to reveal; in his words, it would "blacken the reputation of every President since Truman." When the editors asked, "like what," the answer came, "like assassinations," which the president indicated immediately should be treated as an off-the-record comment.[12]

Such a revelation could not be kept secret for long, and once senators on the Church Committee learned of it, they proceeded to inquire into what many believed had been a CIA plot to poison Patrice Lumumba, the leader of the Congo.[13] When this information became known, the president hoped to staunch his self-inflicted wound by asking the Rockefeller Committee to extend its inquiry to include assassination plots. The president never suggested that any of these had been successful; only that plans had existed, and it became politically expedient for him to claim that these operations never originated in the White House, but came only from the CIA.

Both assertions were dangerous; neither was true. Ford retreated again, implying there had been "good intelligence covert activity," never mentioning the bad, denying that presidents were in any way complicit in such activity.[14] These revelations coincided with the renewal of fighting in Vietnam and Cambodia. Partly as a result of growing congressional suspicion of the administration's policies abroad the president's pleas for renewed help to the South Vietnamese were ignored, making North Vietnam's military victory inevitable.[15] As the president knew, and as Henry Kissinger insisted, a U.S. defeat in Vietnam could only bring the country's allies everywhere to question American resolve, and this seemed to happen after the last of the Americans were removed from the roof of the embassy in Saigon, memorialized on television, in the last days of April 1975.

The Vietnam adventure, once believed in, had ended in disaster, and the country's humiliation grew with the announcement that a American merchant vessel, *Mayaguez*, had been seized in international waters by Cambodian gunboats. The president, recognizing the serious threat to his authority, approved a rescue plan that he represented as a great success—another fiction; forty-one Americans died in the rescue operation, and another fifty were wounded.[16]

In seeking to quiet growing public discontent over intelligence activities, the administration decided to give the Rockefeller Commission's findings very wide publicity. Though the report acknowledged illegal domestic surveillance, "initiated or ordered by Presidents either directly or indirectly," these were represented as few in number; on the more serious issue of presidential involvement in assassination plots, the commission remained silent. Senator Church, hoping to be the Democratic Party's presidential nominee in 1976, seized the opportunity to exploit the issue, knowing he had to avoid saying anything that might lead the public to realize that many of the major transgressions had occurred during the Kennedy era. For him, only a single culprit existed—the CIA. Representing the agency as a "rogue elephant," Church began his investigations at a time when the president hoped to initiate new covert operations in Angola to prevent that African country from falling into Communist hands. The CIA expected its support of two rival groups to lead quickly to the defeat of the Communist-led forces, and while the Church Committee knew nothing of these operations, in its open hearings it publicized the $3 million the CIA had spent over the last eighteen years in developing poisons and biological weapons. The victim of these spectacular televised hearings was not the president so much as Director of Central Intelligence William Colby. Ford felt he had to be replaced and decided to recall George Bush from his assignment in China, knowing he was achieving little there, and believing his appointment might staunch the Church Committee's quest for CIA villains.[17]

Just as the Popular Movement for the Liberation of Angola was increasing its hold in Angola, despite the vast expenditure of CIA funds to prevent its victory, Seymour Hersh published in the *New York Times* on December 14, 1975, a full account of the Angola intervention.[18] The Senate, angered by these latest revelations, decided by a vote of 54–22 to cut off all funds for covert operations in Angola.[19] For the first time, Congress had halted a covert operation, and the president fumed at what such congressional intervention was doing to his foreign policy.

In his State of the Union address in January 1976, profiting from the dismay many felt at the assassination of the CIA station chief in Athens, the president made his first outright attack on those he depicted as seeking to cripple the country's foreign intelligence services. In words that could only be interpreted as explicit criticism of the Church Committee in the Senate and the Pike Committee in the House, Ford said:

Without effective intelligence capability, the United States stands blindfolded and hobbled. In the near future, I will take actions to reform and strengthen our intelligence community. I ask for your positive cooperation. It is time to go beyond sensationalism and ensure an effective, responsible and responsive intelligence capability.[20]

When the Pike Committee report, leaked to the *Village Voice,* a New York weekly, appeared under the headline, "The Report on the CIA That President Ford Doesn't Want You to Read," Ford went on national television to denounce the "irresponsible and dangerous exposure of our nation's secrets" and described the reorganization of the intelligence community he intended to institute at once.

Ford spoke as if U.S. presidents had never abused their power, hoping that the creation of a joint intelligence committee, with members from both the Senate and the House, would satisfy both Congress and the public.[21] Senator Church, not so easily mollified, concluded in his committee's final report that congressional oversight had been inadequate and that closer surveillance was necessary.[22] No one reading his report could doubt that the CIA had become an "arm of the presidency," used to achieve objectives, often of dubious legality. That Church used the Senate hearings to advance his own political career was true, but the more important truth was that Congress, sensing the weakness of the presidency, accepted this as a favorable time to reassert an authority it had once claimed and lost.

The president, though aware of his problems, remained loyal to Kissinger, his secretary of state, never doubting that Kissinger's fears about the damage inflicted through the Senate and media disclosures about CIA transgressions were in no way exaggerated. Kissinger, unable to admit the harm that Nixon had done to established institutions, betraying the trust essential to their legitimacy, saw Senator Church as simply an ambitious politician who showed too little regard for the nation's security.

Neither he nor the president understood how disillusioned the country had become with the assertion of presidential prerogatives and what seemed all-important to them—the national interest, as they interpreted it. Both failed to recognize that the media attacks on Ford, emphasizing his clumsiness and dullness, reflected their continuing ambition to retain the influence they had acquired through their successful investigative reporting during the Watergate crisis. The media, in insisting that Ford was a legitimate object of their criticism, persisted in the habits that had become habitual with them, almost unthinkable in the time of Eisenhower or Kennedy. Their attacks hurt the president, causing him to divert his attention from the serious and complex issues he might otherwise have addressed, many relating to the country's serious economic plight. Inflated energy costs, greatly exacerbated by the Yom Kippur War and the punitive actions taken by OPEC, the oil cartel, had stifled many of the country's basic industries, a situation greatly worsened by growing foreign competition, principally from Japan and Western Europe.

When Ford entered the White House inflation stood at 12 percent, and the president, like other of his Republican predecessors, imagined the solution to the problem would be a strict control of federal expenditures, the elimination of the budget deficit, and the imposition of a tight monetary policy by the Federal Reserve.[23] Though stagflation, a condition that combined three features that had never previously coincided—a stagnant economy, rising unemployment, and dangerous levels of inflation—confounded his economic advisers, Ford accepted that his economic remedies, intended principally to control and reduce inflation, would lead to higher unemployment. Still, those who pretended to understand the problem could offer no alternative solutions for a situation that perplexed them as much as it did the president. As a Midwesterner, Ford knew only too well the suffering in his region of the country, the Rust Belt, that threatened many of its once prosperous industries, mocking all Republican claims of a restored national prosperity.

In pressing for his less than ambitious policies, Ford provoked strenuous opposition from the Democrats, in full control of Congress, and during his brief presidential tenure—865 days—he vetoed sixty-six bills, not a record, but substantially higher than normal.[24] Determined to avoid the federal government assuming any additional obligations, he seemed prepared to see New York City descend into bankruptcy before finally, and very reluctantly, agreeing to offer the city limited federal assistance.[25] His programs for fighting inflation, never acceptable to Congress, led him to institute a public anti-inflation campaign with the acronym WIN, for Whip Inflation Now; satirists represented him as a stumbling former football hero who had obviously lost sight of the ball.[26]

Within months of Ford assuming office, the country's recession became the president's greatest problem, and his solution, a tax cut, though obviously gratifying to Congress and the country, giving consumers greater purchasing power, did little to remedy a situation that seemed impervious to all such traditional palliatives. Congressional hostility guaranteed that his legislative achievements would be meager; except for bills introduced to reduce energy consumption, acceptable to the Democrats, he accomplished little. While his Cabinet came to include a number of renowned professors, including Edward Levi, professor of law and former president of the University of Chicago as attorney general, and John Dunlop, professor of economics and former dean of the faculty of arts and sciences at Harvard as secretary of labor, in addition to the two holdovers, Henry Kissinger at State and James Schlesinger at Defense, his major administrative appointment was to recall Donald Rumsfeld from his position at NATO to become chief of staff in the White House in everything but title.[27] Rumsfeld, hard-driving, intelligent, and de-

vious, purportedly interested only in orderly administration, was not a politician likely to defer for very long to Nelson Rockefeller, the vice president,
who soon became his principal rival.[28] Ford's surface amiability could never
conceal the fact that he had no ambition be an activist president and lacked
any plans for major domestic reform.

While Rumsfeld introduced a tracking system that made it easier for the
White House staff to monitor the follow-up actions required to implement the
president's decisions, he was never the adviser who could advance proposals for
radical domestic policy changes. Indeed, no one in the president's entourage
did this, and Congress, dominated by the Democrats, though tolerant of Ford's
inactivity, rarely thought to assist him. Ford's term as president was barren of
major domestic policy innovations; only in the area of foreign policy—and
even there less conspicuously than before—did there appear to be movement.
Kissinger remained the president's major confidante even after his forced resignation as national security adviser; Ford's continued confidence in him guaranteed that his ideas and proposals would be listened to. In any account of what
happened during the slightly more than two years when Ford occupied the
White House, Kissinger's third volume of his autobiography, *Years of Renewal,*
a vast tome, must figure as a major source. Indeed, his last chapter, "Reflections," merits attention, less for its reports on the specific crises the administration confronted and more for what it says about the period, as well as the views
that he and the president shared.[29]

The Kissinger "Reflections" dwell not on OPEC's decision to punish the
United States for its support of Israel in the Yom Kippur War, or the determination Congress showed to punish the Turks for their invasion of Cyprus, ignoring the president's plea that such a policy could entail the loss of vital U.S.
bases in Turkey, or even the congressional refusal to grant South Vietnam additional military and economic aid, thereby guaranteeing that regime's collapse.[30]
These developments, together with full accounts of U.S. relations with the Soviet Union and the efforts made to sustain détente and to negotiate SALT II, as
well as the administration's policies in China, Africa, the Middle East, and
Latin America, and its European alliance problems figure prominently in a
book of more than 1,000 pages. Yet none of the details that Kissinger gives in
the body of the book on the Helsinki Accords, the abortive plans for a Year of
Europe, and the constant frustrations created for the president by Senators
Jackson and Church convey the message communicated in his final chapter,
which is nothing less than a eulogy of the president.[31] Ford, so obviously different from Nixon, is represented as a president who bore no grudges and never
sought to "shift blame for setbacks to his associates."

For Kissinger, Ford remained the president who brought the nation together,
whose "lack of guile became a part of the healing process." The nation, "close
to chaos" when Ford entered the White House, was rescued by a president able

to replace Nixon's "idiosyncratic style. . . with a more transparent, less personal method of government."[32] In short, Kissinger represented Ford's administration as "a period of renewal," a view that never came to be accepted, either by Republicans or Democrats. In their view, Ford's administration, like Jimmy Carter's, became a brief and relatively insignificant parenthesis between the two major presidencies of Nixon and Reagan. What then, did Kissinger, unquestionably close to the scene and an interested party, fail to perceive about the period that has become more obvious since?

Essentially, Kissinger failed to understand that the opposition to Ford, particularly in Congress, expressed a fundamental fear of the Soviet Union that lingered, that summit meetings could never wholly extinguish. More seriously, perhaps, Kissinger may have confused the intellectual opposition to himself—a combination of ideological and personal disdain mixed with envy—and the opposition to Ford. He believed incorrectly that the radicals of the left, important during the time of Johnson and Nixon, still mattered, that they remained influential. In fact, their political force was greatly spent, diminished as a consequence of the end of the Vietnam War. The new political power in the country—neoconservative—created in substantial part by Nixon, was important precisely because it had survived his disgrace and was becoming the dominant element in the Republican Party. Its influence was registered in its ability to compel the president to acknowledge he could not hope to win the nomination or the election if he retained Rockefeller as his vice president.

The challenge confronting Ford was to tame that neocon element, as important in the new post–Nixon Republican Party as the Robert Taft element had been in the earlier Eisenhower period. Had he taken a page out of Truman's book and recruited a major Democrat to cooperate with him, as Truman did in co-opting Arthur Vandenberg, a reasonable bipartisan foreign policy might have been constructed and defended. His failure to keep his Democratic critics in check derived from his mistaken belief that they were all beyond redemption, political disciples in one sense or other of Senator Church. Ford allowed the Republican Party to become dangerously monolithic in its disdain for East Coast Republican internationalists, once so influential as political ballast in a party dominated by more provincial interests.

The professors who served in Ford's Cabinet, though competent in their individual departments, were amateurs in a situation where professionals were needed to help build political constituencies to sustain the specific foreign policies Ford believed in. The Republican Party during his administration was split, as it had often been in the past, and Ford knew neither how to bring it together nor which wing he cared to be identified with. Faithful to Nixon's policies on détente, he could never make way against the substantial Republican Party resistance to it, personified by Reagan. In this as in others ways, Ford resembled an earlier Taft, another one-term twentieth-century Republican president who knew neither how to represent himself to the larger American public nor how to unite the Republicans in Congress to support his policies.

Ford's failure can be recognized across a broad spectrum of issues, including civil rights. Like other Republicans, he came quickly to sense the popular hostility to busing and could accept the practice reluctantly and only as a last resort. Though he welcomed blacks into the White House and showed a sympathy for their plight greater than any ever shown by Nixon, this never led him to make serious concrete proposals for reform that went beyond what Johnson had accomplished. When, for example, he agreed to address the annual conference of the NAACP (National Association for the Advancement of Colored People) in 1975, a gesture Nixon would never have made, he failed to capitalize on the goodwill created by his decision.[33]

Nixon knew he had achieved his overwhelming victory in 1972 without substantial black support, and Reagan believed he could do the same. Ford never challenged that proposition, realizing perhaps that it was true. When the issue of civil rights emerged during the primaries, largely because of Reagan being more vociferous in his antibusing stance than Ford, the president knew of no way to meet the challenge except to suggest that the distance between them was not very great. His decision to dump Rockefeller, described by one historian as "the last great fighter for civil rights in the Party," showed his willingness to accommodate Reagan, who believed that white people were being victimized, losing out to blacks both in employment and education.[34] While Reagan harped continually on the importance of his opposition to affirmative-action quotas, intended to benefit blacks, Ford's response to such argument was feeble. Beating a hasty retreat, going so far as to speak in Indiana of the federal courts "practically running our school boards," that sentiment gained him applause in certain Republican circles, and the president knew it was one more issue where he could not afford to separate himself from the more conservative elements in his party. Even his choice of Senator Robert Dole to run as vice president in 1976 showed his weakness, his inability to stand up to Reagan's supporters. He might have chosen someone like Senator Howard Baker of Tennessee, but Richard Cheney, Ford's last chief of staff, indicated he would do well to choose Dole. As John Osborne, in the *New Republic* wrote,

> It was not, I'm sure, that the President let Ronald Reagan dictate the choice or veto some other choice in any explicit way. It was simply that there would be no risk of trouble at the convention from Reagan delegates, trouble that would impair or even wreck the impression of success in Kansas City.[35]

Ford, an unelected president, compelled to deal with an overwhelmingly Democratic Congress, confronting an opponent in his own party as determined as any in the opposition, knew of no way to counter the Reagan argument that "this nation has become Number Two in a world where it is dangerous—if not fatal—to be second best." This, a version of the argument John Kennedy had used to disparage the Eisenhower administration, led Ford, honorable and decent, thought by many to be dim and malleable, to win his party's nomination but to lose the election to a Democratic unknown, Jimmy Carter, the former governor of Georgia, whose only pledge was that he would always tell the truth.

Ford was a political victim of the Nixon transgressions, as well as of his own failure to prove himself adept in meeting the opposition within his own party. He was beaten by a Democrat who knew how to present himself as the anti-Nixon. The shadow of the disgraced president lurked long after he bade the country a final farewell. Ford's defeat, Carter's victory, and Reagan's much more conspicuous success in 1980 may all be counted as the price the nation paid for electing Nixon over Humphrey in 1968. The other very important Ford legacy, too rarely noted, is that those he elevated to high places in his administration—George Bush, Donald Rumsfeld, Richard Cheney, Brent Scowcroft, and James Baker III—became powerful Republican figures in the last third of the century, and that none of them might have reached that eminence but for the decisions he made in what journalists chose to call the 1975 massacre.[36]

While November 2 and 3, 1975, have never figured as conspicuous dates in the history of the Ford administration, certainly not to be compared with September 8, 1974, when he pardoned Nixon, their long-range significance may have been no less great. In firing James Schlesinger as secretary of defense, whom he had never much cared for, replacing him with Donald Rumsfeld, a man he had known in Congress, he brought into the Cabinet one of his more articulate, ambitious, and Machiavellian friends. Rumsfeld wanted the Cabinet position, hoping perhaps it would give him the chance to replace Rockefeller as Ford's running mate in 1976.[37] The president's decision to dismiss William Colby as director of the CIA, blaming him for errors he was himself partly responsible for, gave a huge boost to George Bush, appointed to succeed him, rescuing him from exile in Beijing, where his diplomatic mission was accomplishing little at a time when Mao Tse-tung, a dying man, clung to power.[38]

In depriving Kissinger of his post as national security adviser and retaining him as secretary of state, but appointing Brent Scowcroft, his deputy, to succeed him, he gave new prominence to one of the many accomplished men Kissinger had recruited for the National Security Council. Ford's appointment of James Baker as his new chief of staff, to succeed Rumsfeld, and of Richard Cheney as his deputy, brought two other new faces into his administration, men who would assume far greater responsibility under President Reagan, going on then to serve the Bushes, father and son. Those who had served earlier Democratic presidents, Truman, Kennedy, and Johnson, had not remained in the federal service for long; those chosen by Ford in 1975 were destined to remain powerful for the next quarter of a century and longer. This was as much Ford's legacy as anything he accomplished in foreign or domestic policy.[39] The man who had learned about politics through long years of service in the House of Representatives showed himself less than a consummate politician when translated to the more astringent world of the presidency, suggesting that honesty and goodwill were not sufficient guarantees of success in a post that called also for craftiness and cunning.

CHAPTER 17

The New Georgia

JIMMY CARTER, MORE than any other twentieth-century president, learned the art of winning primaries and used the newly created Democratic Party rules to replicate Senator George McGovern's success in 1972. Carter was a political entrepreneur, the only president to come out of the Deep South in 128 years, the first since Zachary Taylor in 1848 to be nominated by a major party whose credentials included a twentieth-century version of the log-cabin myth.

Reared in rural America, the son of a farming family, just plain folks from Plains, Georgia, they lived without electricity or indoor plumbing before World War II. Carter entered the U.S. Naval Academy at Annapolis in 1942 and secured there the training his family would not otherwise have been able to afford; he served as an officer in the Navy's submarine fleet from 1946 to 1953.[1] World War II gave many of the white farmers of Georgia incomes they had never previously known, and young Carter returned to Plains in 1954 to manage what had become a thriving agricultural business, his family's peanut farm. Because neither nuclear-powered submarines nor farming could long engage the interest of someone who saw politics as a more attractive calling, Carter sought election to the Georgia Senate in 1962 and, after only four years, imagined himself ready for the governorship. Though defeated in his first campaign for the governor's chair in 1966, his large and prosperous peanut business gave him abundant time to pursue politics, and in his second try, in 1970, he won the governor's seat.[2] He served only a single term, and a month before leaving office in 1974 announced his intention to seek the presidency in 1976. Outside Georgia, Carter was an unknown Democrat, and "Jimmy who?" became the jibe of those who could not imagine that this Southern provincial could defeat the many other more prominent Democrats who aspired to the office, all believing that the Republican incumbent, Gerald Ford, contending with divisions in his own party, would be a weak candidate if he indeed managed to take the nomination away from Ronald Reagan, his principal challenger.

Carter sought the presidency as he had once sought the governorship—giving all his time to the effort, realizing that he enjoyed several advantages over those who were better-known. The country, still suffering from the trauma of Vietnam and the disillusion of Watergate, would almost certainly welcome a candidate who could claim truthfully no involvement with either, who promised a return to the politics of a more innocent day when Washington insiders did not run the country. His principal opponent appeared to be Senator Henry Jackson of Washington, known for his violent anti-Soviet views, who had used the Communist restrictions on the emigration of Jews as a principal argument for being cautious in the pursuit of détente. A liberal Democrat on domestic issues, Jackson had accepted the Vietnam War as necessary; representing a state heavily dependent on aircraft production, he recognized very early the importance of supporting higher defense expenditures. Carter's other Democratic rivals included Lloyd Bentsen, a recently elected senator from Texas, and Senator Birch Bayh of Indiana, as well as liberals of one stripe or another; Representative Morris Udall of Arizona and R. Sargent Shriver, former director of the Peace Corps under John Kennedy and the head of the antipoverty program under Lyndon Johnson. George Wallace, who had secured 10 million votes in 1968 as an Independent, had seemed a promising candidate in 1972 until he was shot and seriously wounded that spring. Partially recovered, though confined to a wheelchair, he elected to run again as a Democrat in 1976, hoping to win wide support in the South and also in the North from those hostile to what many whites regarded as the excessive concessions made to black voters. All the Democratic candidates except for the two Southerners, Wallace and Carter, were New Deal, Fair Deal, and Great Society Democrats.

How, then, could Carter hope to distinguish himself from these other so-called Democratic liberals, including Jackson, especially on the contentious issue of forced busing? Carter had won the governorship with negligible black support, but his record in office showed him sympathetic to the plight of black citizens in a Southern state where rednecks remained conspicuous. Believing himself the incarnation of the New Georgia, a more tolerant Georgia, he emphasized all he had done to show sympathy for blacks, appointing them to high state offices, recommending the celebration of Martin Luther King Jr.'s birthday as a state holiday, and pressing for the portrait of the martyred civil rights leader to be hung in the statehouse.[3] Would he choose to display comparable political proclivities in the primaries, compelled to compete with another Southerner, a known racist?

In his preprimary statements, Carter showed almost excessive caution in approaching delicate domestic issues, and though endorsing racial equality he seemed determined to avoid the more contentious race issues, including busing, quotas, and affirmative action. Dwelling instead on his opposition to welfare spending and welfare fraud, taking a page out of Richard Nixon's political primer, he showed interest also in public housing and prisons, issues he believed ordinary citizens were concerned about, that other politicians generally chose to ignore.[4] Carter said nothing to disabuse Southern primary voters of the conviction that he was essentially conservative on questions of race. Indeed, carefully avoiding any too-close identification with Johnson, Kennedy, Truman, or FDR, though never explicitly repudiating any of them—it would have been foolhardy to do so—he made great efforts to show himself something other than the traditional old-line, big-spending Democrat. While the country scarcely knew him as late as December 1975, his announcement on the popular *Meet the Press* Sunday TV program that he intended to run in every state primary made him an instant celebrity of sorts.

No previous Democrat (or Republican) had ever aspired to engage in such a national campaign, and it confirmed Carter's populist image as someone concerned only with the people's vote, never with the good opinion of powerful Democratic Party politicians. Because 70 percent of the delegates would be chosen in the primaries, Carter believed that victories in a good number of states would quickly give him the media attention he needed. He placed great store on doing well in the New Hampshire primary, knowing that a victory there would surprise the media and give him the publicity essential for comparable success elsewhere. In the Iowa caucus, Birch Bayh beat him easily, a result in no way surprising given the senator's Midwestern appeal. It made the February 24 New Hampshire primary, always regarded as important, absolutely critical for Carter. When more than 23,000 men and women voted for him, 28.4 percent, as against Udall's 22.7 percent, Bayh's 15.2 percent, and Shriver's 8.2 percent, it was obvious that a new Democratic star had appeared.

In the week that followed, Carter's picture appeared on the covers of the country's two principal newsmagazines, *Time* and *Newsweek*; more important, his TV news coverage exceeded that of all his opponents by three times, and newspapers awarded him four times the attention they gave all the other candidates. Some 23,000 Americans in an untypical New England state had given an unknown former governor of Georgia national and international recognition.

Only a week later, the Carter express seemed momentarily halted. In the Massachusetts primary, the only state that had failed to give its electoral votes to Nixon in 1972, busing remained a potent issue, and Jackson and Wallace expressed hostility to the policy; both did exceedingly well as a result. Udall came in third, and Carter took fourth place, blaming his defeat on Jackson for having exploited the busing issue, something he would never do.[5] The Florida primary was the next crucial test, and Carter knew he had to do well against Wallace, who had carried 42 percent of the vote in 1972. If he, a Southerner, managed to defeat another Southerner in a state geographically linked to the

South, though only superficially resembling Georgia or Alabama, he would appear the racial moderate who had challenged successfully Wallace's reputation in the region. With many of the principal liberal Democrats agreeing not to enter the race so as not to dilute the anti-Wallace vote, Carter relied on the black vote but also on support from the United Auto Workers union, determined to deny Wallace a Florida victory that would only increase his popularity in the upcoming Michigan primary.

The primary results showed that Carter had gained 34.3 percent of the vote against the 30.6 percent received by Wallace; Jackson trailed far behind with 23.9 percent.[6] After the Florida victory, the media decided Carter would be the Democratic candidate, and when he beat Wallace in North Carolina on March 23 with a convincing 53.6 percent of the vote against Wallace's 34.7 percent, his hold on the South seemed firm. Only one question remained: Would he do equally well in the North, in the New York primary, scheduled for April 6? The answer was discouraging. Jackson took 38 percent of the vote; Udall 25.6 percent; and Carter 12.8 percent, with 23.7 percent remaining uncommitted to any candidate.[7] Interestingly, the media gave less attention to this defeat than to Carter's victory in Wisconsin by 271,220 votes over Udall's 263,771, a margin of only 7,449 votes.[8]

Both the defeat and the victory were made more significant by the flap created some days earlier when Carter, speaking to a reporter of the New York *Daily News,* acknowledged he saw "nothing wrong with ethnic purity being maintained" in public housing. In his words, "I would not force a racial integration of a neighborhood by government action. But I would not permit discrimination against a family moving into the neighborhood."[9] Asked to clarify the statement by a CBS correspondent, he seemed only to dig a deeper hole for himself, saying he opposed governmental programs "to inject black families into a white neighborhood." Indeed, expressing himself as being in no way hostile to ethnics and blacks seeking to maintain the ethnic purity of their neighborhoods, he found it natural that they should wish to do so. With Carter initially disinclined to withdraw his statement, both his wife and one of his principal black supporters, Congressman Andrew Young, insisted he do so, and he complied in a characteristic way when Dr. Martin Luther King Sr., at a rally in downtown Atlanta on April 13, came forward to insist there had been a mere slip of the tongue; the words Carter used did not represent his thinking at all. He, the father of the martyred civil rights leader, forgave the erring former governor of Georgia.[10]

The Republicans around Ford were not equally forbearing. Arthur Fletcher, one of the few blacks in the White House who had served as deputy assistant for urban affairs, called the comment "race-baiting" and went on to say: "The votes in Indiana and Michigan are so important that Carter felt he had to say to middle-class blue collar voters that 'I won't let the blacks break your neighborhood up.'"[11] The comment, offered at a time when Wallace was virtually eliminated from the race, and when the Pennsylvania, Michigan, Texas, Indiana, and Missouri primaries loomed, revealed the undeniable fact that Carter could not fail to be interested in securing the votes of white citizens who might otherwise have voted for Wallace. Udall believed the Carter statement was not a slip of the tongue, that it was intended to win support from white Southerners and Northern ethnics hostile to blacks. A Republican pollster estimated that the comment, intentional or not, had achieved its purpose: For every black vote lost, Carter gained four white votes.[12]

On April 27, in Pennsylvania, he received 37 percent of the preferential vote against Jackson's 24.6 percent, Udall's 18.7 percent, and Wallace's 11.3 percent. Again, the media declared he was the only Democrat who could win the nomination. With both Bayh and Shriver out of the race, and Jackson having run out of funds, Udall remained as Carter's only viable opponent. Though California's governor, Edmund "Jerry" Brown entered the race late, as did Senator Frank Church of Idaho, they were never considered serious contenders. By the first days of May, it was difficult to see how Carter could be stopped. On May 1, he beat Bentsen, running as a favorite son in Texas, capturing 92 out of the 98 delegates. On May 4, he registered even more impressive victories in Indiana with 68 percent of the vote and in his own Georgia with 83.4 percent. He carried Tennessee overwhelmingly two days later with 77.6 percent of the vote. The *New York Times* reported he had slightly more than one-third of the votes needed for the nomination, but *Time* magazine suggested that while some 39 percent of Democratic Party voters wished for him to be their party's nominee, some 59 percent hoped it might be someone else.[13] Beginning on May 11, Carter suffered some reverses but made slight of them. Though he lost to Church in Nebraska, and to Brown in Maryland, he did better in Michigan, beating Udall narrowly, 43.4 percent to 43.1 percent. But for the votes that went to Shriver, Udall might well have won in that state. When one considers that Carter had the support of both Leonard Woodcock, the president of the United Auto Workers, the most powerful union in the state, and Coleman Young, the black mayor of Detroit, the victory was not impressive. Indeed, his loss of Oregon and Idaho to Church, and Nevada to Brown, might have suggested that his victory in the convention was far from assured. But for every defeat, there were also victories.[14]

By entering all the primaries, inevitably losing some but winning many more, Carter had 1,117 delegates pledged to him; nomination required him to win fewer than 400 additional delegates to reach the magical figure of 1,505. In the days after the last of the primaries, all the other candidates released their delegates, expecting they would go to Carter, and his first-ballot victory was assured. In his acceptance speech he spoke of his pride in being in a succession that included Roosevelt, Truman, Kennedy, and Johnson and went out of his way to declare himself a populist, determined that "special influence and privilege" would have no place in his administration.

Carter had done the apparently impossible—an outsider without links to the more powerful leaders in the Democratic Party, he had managed to win support from workers and blacks, moderates and liberals, from those in the South and elsewhere who wished for Wallace to go away. He had skirted all the most sensitive issues, choosing to be neither a McGovern nor a Goldwater, knowing that respectability was his strength, that he could represent himself as "a farmer, an engineer, a businessman, a planner, a scientist, a governor, and a Christian," but never a politician. Refusing to label himself either liberal or conservative, pretending to know blacks as Martin Luther King did, precisely because both, reared in the South, recognized the importance of race, his religion purportedly explained his concern to heal a nation that had seen its reputation sullied by presidential actions, illegal and ill-advised. Like Woodrow Wilson, Carter was self-righteous, concealing his arrogance by pretending to be concerned only with others. A consummate actor, he offered himself as an ordinary American resembling millions of others. He became the candidate in some measure because of the mass media, opting for someone not an insider able to claim an unsullied political reputation. As party bosses had once searched for winners, the media now showed the same appetite.

President Ford, believing himself better informed than his opponent, knowing a great deal more about both domestic and foreign policy, imagined he could overcome the losses he suffered in his bruising primary battles with Reagan by pressing Carter to accept nationally televised debates, the first held since 1960, when Nixon met Kennedy. Though Carter proved less than scintillating in these encounters, Ford seemed positively inept. Unable to take advantage of Carter's gaffe in his September *Playboy* interview, in which he acknowledged that he often looked at women with "lust in his heart," using words like "screw" and "shack up," unlikely to win favor with fundamentalist Christians, the president was too nervous to strike a telling blow.[15] Both, indeed, seemed uncomfortable in their TV roles, and the power failure that interrupted the first debate for twenty-seven minutes helped neither. When the debate was over, the *New York Times*/CBS poll declared Ford the winner by 37 percent to 24 percent, but 39 percent were reported as undecided, and few seemed in any way excited by what they had heard.[16]

In the second debate, Carter sought to put Ford on the defensive and repeated Reagan's arguments about Henry Kissinger's flawed shuttle diplomacy and America's decline vis-à-vis the Soviet Union. His accusations that the Ford administration had participated in the overthrow of the legitimate government of Chile, and had wanted to start a new Vietnam War in Angola, angered the president sufficiently to cause him to strike out, condemning Carter for his readiness to cut defense spending.[17] Then, in a disastrous mistake, when asked about the Helsinki Pact, Ford said: "There is no Soviet domination of Eastern Europe, and there never will be under a Ford administration."[18] The error cost Ford dearly; he had misspoken, and Zbigniew Brzezinski, later Carter's national security adviser, saw the advantage his Democratic friend had gained from the gaffe.[19]

In the final debate, Carter argued simply that Ford was a good and decent man but could never provide the leadership the country required. His final questions were politically effective; he asked the audience: "Can you think of a single program that he's put forward that's been accepted? Can you think of a single thing?"[20] Ford, apparently defeated in the TV debates, counterattacked in the final weeks of the campaign, arguing that Carter "will say anything, anywhere, to be President." Few who heard Ford found him exciting; many who listened to Carter believed him a small man excessively pretentious in his claims to virtue, boasting of all he would do but generally shying away from specific policy recommendations. Some thought him weird, but others worried about more substantial flaws that could not be ascribed simply to Southern provincialism.

When the returns came in, Carter won narrowly with 40.8 million votes against Ford's 39.1 million. Had Eugene McCarthy's name been allowed to remain on the New York ballot—his eligibility as an Independent candidate had been successfully challenged—Ford might have won there, and that would have given him an Electoral College majority. As it was, Carter's Electoral College victory was narrow, 297 to 240, the smallest since Wilson's victory over Charles Evans Hughes in 1916. The effects of Watergate, obvious in the congressional elections, where the House remained overwhelmingly Democratic, 292–143, and the Senate showed a Democratic majority of 62–38, gave Carter the opportunity to win support for whatever policies he favored.[21] In his inaugural address, in effect proclaiming his independence of all his immediate predecessors, he made clear that he came to the presidency with no grandiose intentions. Pretending always to modesty, he declared: "We have learned that 'more' is not necessarily 'better,' that even our great nation has its recognized limits, and that we can neither answer all questions nor solve all problems."[22]

For the first months after his inaugural, determined to establish a mood, to prove himself a man of the people who shunned the Kennedy chic but also the Nixon pomp, he decreed that simplicity would be the order of the day. Disdaining limousines, he walked from the Capitol to the White House to observe the inaugural parade; hand-in-hand with his adoring wife, decked out not in furs but in a plain Georgia-designed wool coat, he seemed truly a man of the people.[23] In his first televised fireside chat, he appeared in a cardigan, as any other middle-aged, middle-class American might dress in the privacy of his home. In short, the imperial presidency described by Arthur Schlesinger Jr. had ended, and the nineteenth-century presidency of devout men like McKinley who treasured their wives and cosseted them, never thinking to cheat on them, was restored. Carter, no philanderer in the tradition of Kennedy, neither a liar nor a crook in the fashion of Nixon, had no specific complaints about his immediate predecessor but simply believed him dim. Purity in the White House was reestablished; the stables, too long filthy, were said to have been finally cleansed. Believing that the White House staffs had proliferated too greatly since the end of World War II, Carter reduced them, believing this to be a significant economy worthy of note.

Though his majorities in Congress were immense, in theory enabling him to do what Wilson had accomplished in 1913, Roosevelt in 1933, and Johnson in 1965, the Democratic congressional leaders soon developed a marked distaste for him, suspicious of his barely concealed arrogance and pretended sagacity. Exaggerating the value of information he claimed to command, showing a prosaic side only intermittently apparent earlier, he thought himself uniquely qualified to deal with domestic issues, particularly those that affected the nation's economy.[24] Secretary of the Treasury Michael Blumenthal, a former chief of Bendix Corporation, failed to inform him that the tax reforms he advocated would occur only following deliberate and sustained negotiation with influential House members and the chairmen of powerful committees.

Members of Congress, more than ready to assert their authority, had little use for Carter, to whom they felt no special obligation, knowing that their own elections owed nothing to him. The large Democratic majority elected in 1974 because of Watergate had survived virtually intact, and Illinois representative Dan Rostenkowski, one of the most influential Democrats in the House, warned Carter that "I don't see Congress playing dead," but the president, confident of his command of politics, scarcely heard his message.[25] Nor did he seem more receptive to the words of the House Speaker, Tip O'Neill, who gave him comparable advice. Carter knew Washington not at all; indeed, he scarcely knew the Democratic Party as it existed in Congress, split as it had been since 1937 between a liberal majority and a solid Southern conservative minority. He deluded himself that he would appeal to both as Johnson did and as Roosevelt after 1937 was able to do only in respect to foreign policy and defense issues.

What some termed Carter's symbolic politics—the reduction of the White House staff by a third, the order to Cabinet members to drive their own cars, the sale of the presidential yacht, and the prohibition of the playing of "Hail to the Chief" at his public appearances—cut little ice with long-serving Democrats who looked for more tangible evidences of serious political intentions. Nor were they greatly impressed by the Georgian friends Carter brought with him to Washington. Neither Bert Lance, appointed director of the budget, nor the president's principal White House aides, Hamilton Jordan and Jody Powell, seemed wholly at home in a capital city still dominated by men and women who had gained their prominence first in the days of Kennedy. Democrats in Congress came increasingly to think of the Georgians and their leader as provincials, pretending to understand the political process, showing ignorance and arrogance when competence and modesty were called for. To show himself a healer, one of the president's first acts was to pardon most of America's Vietnam draft-evaders, doing this by executive order. When, however, he acted as if Congress simply represented special interests whom he had no need to consult, and submitted proposals that dealt with energy conservation, government reorganization, immigration and social welfare, Food Stamp reform, and changes in election procedures, believing he would enjoy a hundred days reminiscent of Franklin Roosevelt's, he was quickly disabused of that illusion.

The incentives for even a Congress dominated by fellow Democrats were few, and though a very watered-down version of his economic stimulus package finally passed, and a Department of Energy was created, with James Schlesinger, the former secretary of defense, appointed as its head, the legislative accomplishments were in fact meager when compared with those of either Roosevelt or Johnson, other presidents who enjoyed large Democratic congressional majorities.

Carter lacked the skill to drive Congress to do the things he wanted, and no one in his entourage could serve as his surrogate. Worse, he inherited an inflation problem that confounded him and his secretary of the treasury as much as it did his predecessor. Johnson's policy of fighting the Vietnam War without increasing taxes had created the problem, but it became worse in 1978 when inflation rose to 9.6 percent. The greatly increased price of oil, together with a poor harvest, compounded the problem, reflected in the dramatic fall of the dollar against major world currencies. Carter, the technician who thought himself an economist, was as bewildered as his secretary of the treasury, a Princeton Ph.D. in economics. He saw his popularity plummet; in April 1978, a *New York Times*/CBS poll suggested that 63 percent viewed inflation as the nation's principal problem; only 32 percent thought the president's record on the economy was satisfactory.[26]

In foreign policy, he showed no greater success. Abetted by his national security adviser, Zbigniew Brzezinski, who looked back always at Henry Kissinger, believing himself more moral and intellectually adept, the administration made human rights a major component of its foreign policy. As Brzezinski wrote in his memoirs,

I had long been convinced that the idea of basic human rights had a powerful appeal in the emerging world of emancipated but usually nondemocratic nation-states and that the previous Administration's lack of attention to this issue had undermined international support for the United States. . . . I felt strongly that a major emphasis on human rights as a component of U.S. foreign policy would advance America's global interests by demonstrating to the emerging nations of the Third World the reality of our democratic system, in sharp contrast to the political system and practices of our adversaries. The best way to answer the Soviets' ideological challenge would be to commit the United States to a concept which most reflected America's very essence.[27]

Because Brzezinski believed that "détente was not the panacea many thought it to be," and because Congress seemed to agree, accepting the Jackson-Vanik and Stevenson Amendments to the Trade Act of 1974 that imposed restrictions on the Soviet Union until it treated its dissidents more generously and allowed Jews to emigrate, he saw these as expressions of the "widespread dissatisfaction with an American foreign policy that dealt primarily in terms of power."[28] This not-too-subtle dig at Kissinger, America's advocate of realpolitik, contrasted with what the Carter administration hoped to advance in its proclaimed defense of human rights.

The Brzezinski apologia for himself and Carter was never wholly convincing and was seldom voiced by others who knew the president well. Sol Linowitz, for example, the lawyer who helped the president negotiate the Panama Canal Treaty, one of the administration's major accomplishments in foreign affairs, recognized both the president's strengths and weaknesses when he wrote:

> He learned by gathering details and putting them together, but there wasn't always time to learn that way. . . . He lacked the surefootedness he thought he should have, and he was uncomfortable about relying on others for things he thought he should know and be able to do himself. He had an unusually strong grasp on what he wanted to accomplish but an uncertain hold on how to go about it.[29]

Hedley Donovan, the former editor of *Time*, brought into the White House as a special adviser to the president, wrote even more perceptively that Carter was "a man of decency and compassion, yet also capable of petty and vindictive behaviour. . . a tendency to impute unworthy motives to those who crossed him. . . almost meek in his arrogance. . . with a surprising weakness for hyperbole and an odd lack of a sense of history."[30] These were serious flaws, the last perhaps being the most serious, rendering Carter an amateur as much in domestic as in foreign policy. Lacking both the knowledge and the experience to cope with inflation, and tempted to meet the problem with many of the same remedies introduced by Ford, he imagined for a time that voluntary wage and price controls might work; when that failed, he opted, as Ford did, for a budget cut. With stocks losing value every day and the dollar declining precipitously, he sounded the old Republican Party cry: In time of economic adversity, the government would do well to spend less and reduce taxes. No one told the president his responses to the recession resembled what Hoover sought to do in a much more parlous time.

The Republican gains in the off-year congressional elections—twelve House and three Senate seats—were certainly significant but by no means catastrophic; the Democratic majority in both chambers, still profiting from Nixon's disgrace, remained substantial. The success of Proposition 13 in California, which mandated lower state taxes, suggested to the president that he would do well to pursue that same policy nationally even if it offended liberal Democrats distressed to see their favorite social programs cut. With two very powerful liberal Massachusetts Democrats in Congress, Speaker Tip O'Neill and Senator Edward Kennedy, no president, least of all Jimmy Carter, could hope to pursue that policy without criticism. Unable to control the two factions in the Democratic Party in 1977 during the months of his presidential honeymoon, and even less successful in 1979 when he was in deep trouble, Carter knew of no way to negotiate with or accommodate the factions in his own party. Lacking all experience of massaging powerful members of Congress, showing too little regard for their opinions and complaints, he incurred the contempt of those who believed he lacked all understanding of the rules of the political game.

The situation became more parlous for him after the 1978 elections when the vastly increased energy costs, exacerbated by the overthrow of the shah and the arrival of the mullahs in Tehran, saw the price of foreign oil increase dramatically. Any further increase in prices or any shortage in supply could only create problems for the country whose dependence on foreign oil had risen from 35 percent to more than 50 percent. The president, recognizing he had to do something in the early summer of 1979, when gasoline prices were escalating and pumps were running dry, sought to restore confidence with an impassioned address to the nation that included promises of major legislative action.

The sentiment about Carter at that critical juncture may be suggested by one account given by an English historian, Steven Gillon, who wrote with scarcely concealed irony:

With public anger reaching a boiling point, the president cut short a vacation and rushed back to Washington to address the nation. Prodded by Patrick Caddell's suggestion [one of his White House aides] that the nation's inability to address the energy problem was symptomatic of a deep crisis of the American spirit, the president abruptly cancelled his televised address and retreated to Camp David for eight days of meeting with religious leaders, politicians, poets and psychiatrists. On Sunday evening, July 15, the president descended from the mountain to give his long-awaited speech to a curious and concerned nation. After describing the 'crisis of confidence' that 'strikes at the very heart and soul of the national will,' the president proposed a new energy plan that included development of alternative energy sources, higher oil and natural gas taxes, and tougher automobile fuel-efficiency standards. The public reacted warmly to the president's speech and to his proposals, but the mood soured a few days later when Carter dismissed half his Cabinet. The public viewed the firings as the desperate act of a president unable to control his own administration. Within a week of the Cabinet purge, Carter's popularity plummeted, dropping to 74 percent negative, the lowest for any president in modern times.[31]

This comment suggested only disdain for a very unconventional president and scarcely exaggerated the surprise many felt at his dismissal of the secretary of the treasury, the attorney general, the secretary of health, education, and welfare, the secretary of commerce, the secretary of housing and urban development, the secretary of transportation, and the secretary of energy.[32] The president hoped to start anew with a new team, in fact no more distinguished than his first, but no longer identified with the mistakes he had made in his first two and a half years in office.

Only in foreign affairs did he retain his original team, and there conditions deteriorated even further from what they were in his first fumbling efforts to create a new moral foreign policy. Believing he understood foreign policy issues, greatly exaggerating his competence in this as in the economic sphere, neither his national security adviser nor his secretary of state exercised a decisive influence on him.[33] His greatest success, bringing Menachem Begin and Anwar Sadat together at Camp David to sign what became the first peace treaty between two major Middle East combatants, Israel and Egypt, seemed for a moment to augur further comparable developments in relations between the Jewish state and other Muslim governments in the Arab world, but this promise never materialized.[34] Carter showed exemplary patience in these negotiations, but his knowledge of the Middle East, which owed so much to his Christian beliefs, made him only very superficially familiar with a world that scarcely resembled that of ancient Babylon or Persia. He knew less about twentieth-century Islam than he pretended and never saw the need to learn more.[35]

Carter's success in settling the Panama Canal controversy, greatly praised by Brzezinski in his account of what he conceived to be a remarkable administration, was purportedly made even more noteworthy by the even greater triumph in securing the recognition of Communist China.[36] The record, as compiled by Carter's national security adviser, gave little space to persistent failures, most conspicuously in Afghanistan and Iran. In Brzezinski's tale, his own disagreements and conflicts with Cyrus Vance, the secretary of state, figured prominently, and while neither McGeorge Bundy nor Henry Kissinger had found it necessary to explore the reasons for the influence they acquired at the expense of Secretaries Rusk and Rogers, Brzezinski imagined his conflict with Vance for the president's ear had seminal importance.[37]

Because Carter arrived in the White House determined to lead the country in a moral reformation, making Congress less subservient to special interests, with allies and others abroad given instruction in their responsibilities, and human rights figuring as a key foreign policy innovation, he had proclaimed in his inaugural address the hope of eliminating all nuclear weapons.[38] To demonstrate his bona fides, he ordered the immediate withdrawal of U.S. nuclear weapons from Korea, the postponement of plans to develop a new bomber, the B-1, and a halt in the efforts to create a neutron bomb. Within six months of coming to the White House, he traveled to Vienna to sign SALT II, which established strategic parity between the United States and the Soviet Union.[39] Could better proof be offered that a new kind of president with bold and novel ideas had taken charge of foreign and defense policy? These actions, all intended to reassure the Kremlin, had none of the results anticipated. The Soviet buildup in conventional arms continued, and the Kremlin became ever more active in support of Communist movements abroad, particularly in southern Africa, making use of Cuban troops as surrogates.

By late 1978, Carter felt obliged to abandon his earlier promises, adopting a vocabulary he had never previously used, arguing for military preparedness. Plans for military cuts were set aside, and the president appeared before Congress to propose increased military spending, a strengthening of NATO, the installation of intermediate-range cruise missiles and Pershing missiles in Europe, and the creation of a new missile—the MX—to be housed in a complex system of underground tunnels. Even the development of a neutron bomb was no longer deemed inappropriate.[40] All the promises of perpetual peace were forgotten in a sudden concern not to appear vulnerable to what he knew was coming: a presidential election in which the Republicans would find him wanting. Even on Carter's vaunted achievement with Panama, Republicans demonstrated their hostility, with thirty-eight senators claiming his foreign policy was one of "incoherence, inconsistency and ineptitude."[41]

Worse, however, was yet to come. In October 1979, in response to the White House decision to allow the deposed shah to come to the United States for medical treatment, Iranian nationalists stormed the U.S. embassy in Tehran, taking fifty-three U.S. diplomats and soldiers hostage. Helpless before this threat, Carter suffered an even greater setback on Christmas Day when the Soviets invaded Afghanistan, took Kabul, destroyed the existing Afghan regime, and replaced it with one of their own. The president, not knowing where the Soviets might strike next, proclaimed the Carter Doctrine, telling the world that "an attempt by any outside force to gain control of the Persian Gulf region will be regarded as an assault on the vital interests of the United States of America, and such an assault will be repelled by use of any means necessary, including military force"[42] The Soviet invasion meant that SALT II would never be ratified. More important, Carter consented to the kinds of covert action he had never previously approved, traveling a path that soon led him to intervene in Angola, Ethiopia, Mozambique, and South Yemen, all quasi-Marxist states sustained by the Soviet Union.[43] Admiral Stansfield Turner, head of the CIA, who had long pressed the president to be more aggressive, wrote: "Thus it was that the Carter administration, despite its dedication to human rights and its considerable reservations about the morality of covert actions, turned easily and quickly to covert devices."[44] Robert Gates, Turner's successor at the CIA, said quite simply: "Jimmy Carter laid the foundations for Ronald Reagan."[45]

An administration that opened with such fair promises of innovation was by April 1980 so desperate about the hostages taken in Tehran that the president, against his secretary of state's objections, gave his approval to EAGLE CLAW, a military operation to rescue the hostages that ended in failure when two helicopters crashed in a sandstorm and eight soldiers were killed.

The president's indecisiveness, demonstrated by his inability to develop a policy to counter the Soviet Union's invasion of Afghanistan other than his program of covert action, restriction of grain sales, and a boycott of the Olympic Games in Moscow, as with his timid response to Iraq's invasion of Iran, suggested the limits of his geopolitical understanding. With so many foreign policy failures, the talk of America's decline grew louder, and Ronald Reagan knew how to exploit issues that made the Carter administration seem feeble. With inflation soaring into double digits, even the most strenuous efforts of Paul Volcker, the newly appointed chairman of the Federal Reserve, seemed incapable of keeping the interest rates from reaching unprecedented levels. Auto sales plummeted, and the Dow Jones index fell precipitously.

Carter was in a hopeless situation when he met Reagan in two televised encounters. Reagan's question, addressed to his vast TV audience—"Are you better off than you were four years ago?"—showed he had taken the measure of the opponent he would beat decisively in November. Till almost noon on January 20, 1981, Carter sat by the White House telephone hoping to hear that the Iranians had finally released their hostages, imagining that history might still judge his administration a success, that no fatal errors had been made on his watch. This was self-deception, innocence, and arrogance by a president who claimed only to be modest and virtuous.

Brzezinski, carrying the torch for the man who had admitted him to his very strange White House court, dominated by men from Georgia who would never again hold high federal office, could only believe that Iran, inflation, and the opposition of Senator Kennedy had doomed the president to defeat at the hands of Reagan. He was sustained in that opinion by a conversation he had with Richard Nixon in 1982 that led him to write: "In my view, these three factors together resulted in Carter's decisive defeat; the subtraction of any one of the three would have made for a close election; and in all probability he would have won quite strongly if handicapped by only one of the three."[46]

A much more objective judgment was offered by a less biased observer, Daniel Yergin, who understood the inadequacy of Carter's policies in Iran and dwelled on the mistakes he made in ridding himself of so much of his Cabinet in the summer of 1975, especially Secretary of the Treasury Michael Blumenthal and Secretary of Health Joseph Califano. Hamilton Jordan and Jody Powell, the ever-loyal men Carter had brought with him from Georgia, persuaded the president that these two Cabinet officials had been disloyal to him and that he would do well to dismiss them. Yergin wrote:

> Altogether, five people left the Cabinet, some fired and some resigning. The aim was to bolster presidential leadership. It had quite the opposite effect. The sudden news of the departures sent tremors of uncertainty throughout the country and the Western world. Over lunch that day, the national editor of the *Washington Post* muttered darkly that America's central government had just collapsed.[47]

That was an exaggeration; the more important truth was that few foreign leaders, including Chancellor Helmut Schmidt and President Giscard d'Estaing, felt any respect for him and had no confidence in his leadership or judgment.[48] Denis Healey, chancellor of the exchequer in the Callaghan government, may have given the most damning indictment of the president when he dubbed him a "moral puritan and an economic profligate," but that was nothing compared to the contempt Schmidt felt for Carter, an innocent in the field of defense.[49]

Carter, manifestly unsuited to lead the United States at a time when the Soviet Union, sensing his weakness, took advantage of his inexperience and exaggerated rhetoric, and when leaders in Iran and Iraq conducted a war whose significance he failed to understand, proved to be the least-effective Democratic president in the long American twentieth century. He left neither a foreign policy legacy nor a political progeny.

His most remarkable achievement, perhaps, was his ability to invent new activities for himself following his defeat in 1980, proving that there is a life for former presidents even after their departure from the White House. The large adulatory work written by Douglas Brinkley, *The Unfinished Presidency,* is revealing of what Carter sought to do in the two decades after his defeat to promote peace in the Middle East, restore democracy in Haiti, and supervise free elections in all manner of places including some as unpromising as Zimbabwe.[50]

If Herbert Hoover, another one-term president, moved from philanthropy to politics, Carter took the reverse route, seeking new satisfaction after his failed political career in a new kind of philanthropy, using his base at the Carter Presidential Center in Atlanta, near the flourishing Emory University, to organize good works. Though Brinkley's account of these activities is in many ways arresting, its greatest contribution may be in reminding us of Carter's difficulties with other politicians, both Democratic and Republican. The chapter "Carter vs. Clinton" tells a distressing story, documenting Clinton's contempt for Carter, going so far one time as seriously contemplating to refuse even to issue an invitation for the former president to attend his inaugural.[51] Clinton instructed his secretary of state, Warren Christopher, one of the few in his administration who had served under Carter, to limit his relations with the former president, to do nothing to assist him in what he saw as efforts to promote himself. Even when Carter returned from Haiti with what many presumed was his greatest success, having helped establish what passed for a democratic government in that impoverished island, many in the Clinton administration could only regard it as one more effort at self-publicity, "'unconscionable' glory-hogging on CNN."[52]

These and other more serious Clinton criticisms and snubs were of course wounding, made scarcely more tolerable by the contempt Reagan showed for Carter, failing to invite him and his wife on even a single occasion to a White House dinner. Carter simply did not exist for Reagan. Nor did the supposedly disgraced Nixon, making his own efforts to prove himself, have a good word to say for Carter. In *The Real War,* one of the many books Nixon wrote in his enforced retirement, he showed a barely concealed disdain for what Carter had tried to do in fashioning new defense and arms-control policies.[53] Carter was a president who never earned the respect of his political peers, neither in Congress during his years as president nor in the one Democratic administration that followed his, an unmentioned wound that could not fail to fester.

CHAPTER 18

The Actor

RONALD REAGAN, THE third Californian to enter the White House, bore no resemblance to the two Republicans who preceded him, Herbert Hoover and Richard Nixon. Indeed, if the truth be told, Reagan put one in mind of no earlier American president, though admirers wished to imagine him the ideological descendant of Theodore Roosevelt, the most distinguished of the large Republican tribe who occupied the presidency after the death of Lincoln.[1] If Reagan scarcely resembled Roosevelt as an intellectual—reading was not his habit, and writing was never a principal pleasure, though his wife would have denied this—patriotism and a post–World War II disdain for Democrats, together with constant play-acting and a talent for dissembling and prevaricating, showed him to be an accomplished self-invented hero who knew how to sell himself to a public avid for something other than the greyness of Carter and Ford.

Like the first Roosevelt, Reagan pretended to be bold, acting in ways inconceivable to cautious men, but his words were substantially more aggressive than his deeds. This was a president reluctant to take risks, but the country was invited to believe the contrary. The first divorced man to enter the White House, the son of a drunken Catholic father and a devout mother who took her obligations as a member of the pietistic Disciples Church seriously, he seemed the quintessential Californian, a Hollywood matinee idol, handsome and gregarious, concealing the Midwestern Illinois traits that made him a child of small-town Middle America, redolent of the world Truman and Eisenhower had been born into.[2] Reagan, loyal to his mother's religion, studied at Eureka College, founded by the Disciples, where dance and drink were prohibited, compensated somewhat by the encouragement given to athletics and dramatics. Dutch—the nickname he and his friends favored, first given him by his father, perhaps in tribute to his plumpness as a baby, a Dutchman in infancy—won recognition in two sports and served as a cheerleader in others, appearing in seven plays, their names lost to history. President of the Eureka Booster Club and of the College Senate, he wrote for the school newspaper and yearbook and

managed to pay his own tuition, largely through summer earnings as a life-
guard. Within the small world of Eureka, no one mistook him for a scholar,
but many granted him a far greater distinction: They thought him a regular
guy. Reagan graduated in the depths of the Depression; and with no member
of his family fully employed, all dependent on federal largesse of one kind or
another, he took his place as an ardent Democrat, aware of all Roosevelt had
done to cope with the mess left by the Republicans.

Unlike others of his generation who remained unemployed for years, Reagan
used his rich baritone voice to win a job in radio as a broadcaster in Davenport,
Iowa, and then in the state capital, Des Moines, where he gained local renown
as a sports commentator, specializing in the all-American sport, baseball. By
June 1937, ambitious for greater adventure, he secured a six-month movie contract with Warner Bros. and headed for California, the Mecca that held great
appeal for many from the Midwest. Reagan, a Hollywood booster, defended his
new home against those who represented it as the capital of sin and sex, finding it significant, in his words, that "it leads the nation in church attendance on
a per capita basis, that its schools are among the best in the nation; that the divorce rate in Hollywood is far below the national average," a moral citadel in
every sense of the term.[3]

Although his career in Hollywood was often rendered as undistinguished,
portrayed as an actor who appeared principally in B movies, never achieving
the fame of other leading stars, that judgment greatly understated the success
he achieved with *King's Row,* a film released in 1942, after he had been called to
duty as an Army reservist. *King's Row* gave Reagan a new contract with a salary
only slightly below that of the more renowned male film celebrities of his day.[4]
Because the sexual implications of Henry Bellamann's best-selling novel were
carefully excised before being made into a film, it is unlikely that Reagan
grasped the bisexual and homosexual character of Drake McHugh, the male
lead he delighted in playing.

His marriage to actress Jane Wyman, in what Louella Parsons, the gossip
columnist, his great patron and friend, characterized as "innocent young sweet-
hearts, in love for the first time and the last," conveniently obliterated all mention of Jane's earlier marriage.[5] The Reagans belonged to Hollywood's aristocracy, an elite created by their acknowledged fame and not by genteel birth. A
captain in the Army Air Force First Motion Picture Unit, *This Is the Army* was
his principal propaganda film. As innocent of the real war as Johnson was, but
no less inclined to tell stories of all he had done, his imagination substituted for
fact.[6] The war was a happy time for Reagan, followed by a more stressful postwar. Jane Wyman's film success greatly exceeded his own, reaching its climax in
1948 in *Johnny Belinda,* in which she played a deaf mute, a role that won her
an Academy Award. In 1949 the couple divorced, and it was impossible for
Reagan not to regard that year as an *annus terribilis* when he lost a wife and

found himself no longer a matinee idol. His 1948 film with Shirley Temple, *That Hagen Girl,* like his first Technicolor picture, *It's a Great Feeling,* did little to enhance a reputation, gradually but obviously falling, as apparent to him as to Warner Bros., his employers.

While Reagan remained sympathetic to the Democratic Party in the immediate postwar period, by 1946 he had become somewhat disenchanted with what he now saw as "the seamy side of liberalism." In his words, "Too many patches on the progressive coat were of a color I didn't personally care for." He claimed much later that the liberals' "ideological myopia" prevented them from seeing Communists as they were and that this greatly influenced his growing disaffection with Democrats.[7] Unable to support the strikes that erupted in the movie industry in the early postwar years, he ostentatiously crossed the picket lines set up around the Warner Bros. lot, but this did not prevent his election as president of the Screen Actors Guild in November 1947, an office he held for five consecutive one-year terms.[8]

Appearing as a friendly witness in the House Un-American Activities Committee's investigation of Communists in Hollywood in 1947, Reagan insisted he saw no reason to blacklist those who had once been members of Communist organizations, a view he later changed. Jack Warner, his employer, an early convert to the Republican Party, was angered by the strike action taken against his studio and may have influenced the young Reagan to question his own Democratic loyalties. Still, as late as 1950 Reagan supported Helen Gahagan Douglas in her Senate battle with Richard Nixon, as much perhaps out of friendship as out of party loyalty.[9] While he expressed doubts about Truman's tax policies and the efforts the president made to close certain loopholes that had left Hollywood celebrities immune to higher tax rates, his growing obsession with communism came increasingly to define his political attitudes. By late 1951, he was speaking in an idiom that soon became conventional for him, saying: "Scratch a Hollywood Communist—especially the 'intellectual'—and you find a person afflicted with some kind of neurosis."[10]

In 1954, Reagan abandoned his film career to become a TV star, the host of *General Electric Theater,* a Sunday-night show that made him more famous in that medium than he had ever been in Hollywood. His youthful appearance, spontaneous manner, courtly relations, and gentle repartee with his many famous guests made him an appealing TV personality, familiar to millions of viewers. According to Edward Langley, a member of GE's public relations team, Reagan began at that time to accept invitations to speak to GE staffs throughout the country, and in the next eight years he visited some 135 plants in thirty-eight states, meeting with 250,000 employees and giving some 9,000 speeches to staff and community groups. Langley, graphically describing this period, wrote: "Reagan was steeped in, saturated with and overpowered by Middle America. . . . No-one has been that saturated—marinated—in Middle

America, not even William Jennings Bryan. . . . Giving endless talks to the Elks, the Moose, the American Legion, and soapbox derby contestants it changed him."[11] He became a confirmed Republican, patriotic, anticommunist, an ardent free-enterprise advocate.

Writing Nixon, his fellow Californian in 1960, to whom he had become increasing attached, Reagan said:

> Shouldn't someone tag Mr. Kennedy's *bold new program* with its proper name? Under
> the tousled boyish hair cut is still old Karl Marx—first launched a century ago. There
> is nothing new in the idea of a Government being Big Brother to us all. Hitler called
> it his 'state socialism' and way before him it was 'benevolent monarchy.'[12]

Reagan, lauded by Californians who loathed the New Deal and the Fair Deal, persuaded that Communists had successfully infiltrated the government and were serving the Soviet Union in disarming America, found his speeches persuasive. Making some 200 speeches during Nixon's 1960 presidential campaign, by 1961 *Time* magazine heralded him as a "remarkably active spokesperson for conservatism." His growing fame as a public speaker made it possible for him to command as much as $10,000 for a single speech, adding to his already substantial TV income. As he showed himself more strident in his oratory, however, he became something of an embarrassment to his GE employers, who in early 1962 asked him to limit his remarks to company promotions, finding unacceptable some of his criticism, especially of the Tennessee Valley Authority, a major GE customer. Reagan refused to be bridled; two days later, by coincidence or design, the company cancelled *General Electric Theater*.[13]

By this time Reagan, without ever holding any public office, had become a leading Republican figure, sought after by those who believed that Barry Goldwater was the man best suited to succeed Lyndon Johnson in the White House. Reagan worked hard to secure the nomination and election of Goldwater and in the final days of the 1964 campaign delivered a nationally televised address, "A Time for Choosing," that brought some $600,000 into the Goldwater coffers. Using the apocalyptic language that had become common with him, he said:

> So we have come to a time for choosing. Either we accept the responsibility for
> our own destiny, or we abandon the American Revolution and confess that an in-
> tellectual belief in a far distant capital can plan our lives for us better than we can
> plan them for ourselves. You and I have a rendezvous with destiny. We can pre-
> serve for our children this, the last best hope of man on earth or we can sentence
> to take the first step into a thousand years of darkness.[14]

In his dictated memoirs, written largely by his collaborator, Richard Hubler, and published in 1965 with the title *Where's the Rest of Me?*, Reagan represented himself as a modest but combative Republican. Expressing his appreciation for those of his fellow citizens who wished him to seek political office as governor or senator, he refused to consider either possibility, saying: "For me, I think that the service is to continue accepting speaking engagements, in an effort to make people aware of the danger to freedom in a vast permanent government structure so big and complex it virtually entraps Presidents and legislators."[15] Big government and federal bureaucracy were the principal enemies to be beaten, and Reagan intended to do battle with both.

Goldwater, decisively defeated by Johnson, could never be Reagan's longtime hero. Never the man to carry the torch for someone who had lost so ignominiously, Reagan gave increasing thought to his own political prospects. By 1965, conservative Californians had organized Friends of Reagan to campaign for his election as governor under the slogan "The Creative Society," a deliberate play on Johnson's Great Society. Reagan, with no apparent reluctance, accepted the call to serve. How could he resist such importuning demands from so many upstanding California citizens? In a score of speeches, he emphasized the evils of big government, welfare handouts, and high taxes, seeing himself as the "great liberator" who would free private enterprise to do those things it alone could do. His message was one of optimism, emphasizing all that California could be if it once accepted limited government and an unfettered marketplace. Reagan, a gifted and accomplished TV celebrity, informal and dignified in the Hollywood movie tradition, witty and smiling, used his famous one-liners to great effect and won easily, securing some 58 percent of the vote in a state where Johnson had triumphed overwhelmingly just two years earlier.

Those who supported Reagan in 1966, principally Goldwater adherents angry that their hero had been so roundly defeated in his battle with Johnson, saw Reagan as the governor who would redeem the conservative Republican standard in the 1968 presidential elections. Even a short two-year term was expected to make him a powerful contender for the party's presidential nomination, but this was not to be, for two reasons no one had anticipated. First, Nixon, considered out of the running after his 1962 gubernatorial election disaster, managed a comeback no Reagan supporter had imagined possible. Second, though Reagan won the governorship in 1966 with a majority of more than 1 million, his first term proved to be something of a political disaster.

Democrats had left the California state treasury empty, and Reagan recognized very early the need to ask for a substantial tax increase. The man who campaigned as the enemy of big spending and campus radicals, of all who had thrived under the permissive rule of weak and feckless Democratic leaders in Sacramento and Berkeley, had promised a vastly reduced state budget. Unable to redeem his pledge, even with a substantial Republican majority in the state legislature, he raised taxes, and his situation seemed unenviable in 1970 when he sought reelection against Jesse Unruh, a powerful Democrat.[16] Those who believed the election would be a cliff-hanger were proved wrong; Unruh was no match for the actor-turned-politician. Again Reagan won easily, profiting from the support given him by President Nixon in Washington but achieving the victory mostly by his own efforts and those of his loyal staff.[17] By the end of his second term, he had in place a team that worked efficiently, aware that their man in the governor's chair had no intention of ending his days in Sacramento. Though the California state budget had risen from $4.6 billion to $10.2 billion during his governorship, this was never acknowledged by Reagan, who insisted he had fulfilled all his pledges to keep government small. If the state's taxes were higher and the budgets larger, these were pesky details that did not much preoccupy a governor who imagined he had brought new fiscal responsibility to a state sorely tried by his Democratic predecessors.

In 1970, Reagan expected Nixon to win a second term and imagined that Spiro Agnew, Nixon's gregarious and hard-hitting vice president, would be the Republican Party's presidential candidate in 1976. By 1974, neither was in office and Reagan, advised by John Sears, once active in recruiting convention delegates for Nixon, learned what he most wished to hear: Ford, the newly installed president, would be vulnerable if the governor challenged him in the Republican primaries. Because the early primary election results proved somewhat discouraging, Reagan found it necessary to become more strident, sounding notes he had not previously thought to use, emphasizing how much the Ford–Nixon policy of détente with Russia and the de facto recognition of China were mistakes that had led the United States to become a second-rate power. Reagan, increasingly confident of finding support for such propositions in a society profoundly disillusioned by Watergate, became even more aggressive in the Florida primary where he received wild applause for his words protesting any cession of the Panama Canal to Panama. His disdain for what President Ford appeared to be interested in doing, reaching some sort of accommodation with Panama, led him to utter one of his more memorable phrases: "We bought it; we paid for it, it's ours, and we aren't going to give it away to some tinhorn dictator!"[18]

Though his attacks on Ford and Kissinger grew increasingly violent, they did not give him the delegate strength he required for the nomination. Still, his campaign was sufficiently effective to deny Ford the votes he needed for his nomination. In the end, it was in the nonprimary states that the governor and the president competed for delegates, and as in 1912 with Taft, the president beat his challenger. The results in 1976 were not too different from those of 1912; Reagan's battle, like Roosevelt's, contributed to the victory of a Democrat. Unlike Roosevelt, he did not bolt the convention but gave a gracious speech following his defeat, encouraging many to see him as the Republican who would be the principal contender for the 1980 nomination.

Though Reagan did not actively oppose Ford and nominally campaigned for him, he expected him to lose, hoping to be the principal beneficiary of that defeat. Following the primary season, while the election campaign was still proceeding, Reagan began to broadcast almost weekly on radio, continuing this practice through the Carter years and into his own two terms as president. These broadcasts, composed not by a team of ghostwriters, provide remarkable testimony about the mind of an actor-politician who proved considerably more astute than his enemies realized. None of these radio talks was more revealing than the one he delivered on September 1, 1976, in the midst of the Ford reelection campaign, when he described to his audience what he imagined the world might look like in a century, in September 2076. His remarks prefigured the political role he envisaged for himself, saying:

> The choice we face being continuing the policies of the last 40 years, that have led to bigger & bigger govt, less & less liberty, redistribution of earnings through confiscatory taxation or trying to get back on the original course set for us by the Founding Fathers. Will we choose fiscal responsibility, limited govt, and freedom of choice for all our people? Or will we let an irresponsible Congress set us on the road our English cousins have already taken? *The road to ec. Ruin and state control of our very lives?*[19]

At a time when Reagan was theoretically supporting Ford in his effort to retain the White House, he spoke disparagingly of the last forty years, of the time since Franklin Roosevelt, when all his Democratic and Republican successors forsook the path of the nation's Founders, threatening liberty and prosperity. Reagan never imagined that Ford could depart from that road, so long taken; he reserved that role for himself.

Once Ford was out of the way, Carter became Reagan's principal target, thought to be as vulnerable as his predecessor on the Panama Canal issue. Arguing that the Canal was vital to the country's security and economy, that any concession to the Panamanian dictator would only confirm the world's opinion that the United States was showing unnecessary weakness, Reagan challenged the newly elected president, only to see Carter win support for his treaty, securing its ratification by a single vote in the Senate. In the next four years, in innumerable broadcasts, Reagan cast Carter as the ineffectual president, unable to devise a satisfactory defense policy, demoralizing the nation's intelligence services, failing to deal adequately with the Soviet Union, and making a grievous error in officially recognizing the People's Republic of China.[20] As Kennedy once used flawed arguments about Eisenhower's failure to match the Soviet Union's missile capability, so Reagan now spoke of the awesome power of the Soviets that had left the United States vulnerable.

With no other prominent Republican candidate able to challenge him for the 1980 nomination, though several tried initially—George H.W. Bush proved to be an easily defeated rival—Reagan showed his strength as a political campaigner, relying on his few well-worn panaceas for ending the American decline. His acceptance speech at the Republican National Convention—a coronation of sorts—confirmed what many felt had been the inadequacies of the Carter presidency. Reagan, in his most ingratiating manner, asked the delegates:

> Can you look at the record of this administration and say, 'Well done'? Can anyone compare the state of our economy when the Carter administration took office with where we are today and say, 'Keep up the good work'? Can you look at our reduced standing in the world today and say, 'Let's have four more years of this'?[21]

The Carter record may have been poor; Reagan made it appear dismal, convincing the TV audience that he knew to be more influential than the delegates who heard him.

In the election that followed, Reagan won 51 percent of the vote to only 41 percent for Carter; Independent candidate John Anderson managed to win 7 percent. In the Electoral College, Reagan's triumph was overwhelming, claiming 489 electoral votes to Carter's 49. For the first time since Dwight Eisenhower's election in 1952, the Republicans gained control of the Senate. Among the seven liberal Democratic senators who went down to defeat, George McGovern, the party's presidential candidate in 1972, was the most conspicuous. Did the country by this overwhelming vote for Reagan suggest it had turned conservative, favoring his remedies for curbing double-digit inflation and his recommendations for becoming tough with the Soviet Union, abandoning the namby-pamby policies of Ford and Kissinger? In his inaugural address, Reagan repeated the refrains that had become common with him as the enemy of big government. In his words, "It is my intention to curb the size and influence of the federal establishment. It's not my intention to do away with government. It is rather to make it work—work with us, not over us; to stand by our side, not ride on our back."[22] The rhetoric scarcely concealed the poverty of his thought; if many were relieved to learn it was not his intention to do away with government, they saw surprisingly little evidence of concrete proposals to curb the size of the government, or indeed to give the individual states greater authority, to limit the "influence of the federal establishment."

Nor did he demonstrate, in his first months in office, a determination to pursue a foreign policy more belligerent than that of Carter, who by the end of his term had become wholly committed to substantial increases in military expenditure. Yet Reagan showed a political acumen that Carter never revealed. In response to the Soviet invasion of Afghanistan, Carter imposed an embargo on grain shipments that undoubtedly hurt the Russians but also adversely affected American farmers.[23] Reagan lifted the embargo, ignoring the advice of Alexander Haig, his secretary of state, who wished it used as a bargaining chip with the Kremlin, at a time when the Soviet Union was substantially helping its

Communist allies in Poland who had recently felt compelled to impose martial law to counteract the growing influence of the Solidarity movement.

Indeed, Reagan did little in his first hundred days—never called that—to suggest he was fulfilling his campaign promises to strike new and radical foreign policy poses. He did nothing to discontinue arms-control talks—the unratified SALT II Treaty was never violated during his first term—and he seemed quite satisfied to accept the official relations with Communist China that Brzezinski had so proudly inaugurated. Belligerence with respect to the Soviet Union figured scarcely at all in his first months in office, and when Haig recommended an incursion into El Salvador, a Central American republic purportedly being supplied with arms by Fidel Castro's Cuba, the president saw no reason to support so aggressive a proposition.[24]

When his advisers recommended cancellation of the Law of the Seas Treaty, seven years in the making, he accepted their arguments, knowing this would please businessmen who detected opportunities for mining mineral rights in international waters. This was an issue scarcely calculated to stir great interest in the country. So, also, in appointing Jeane Kirkpatrick, whom he had first met in 1979, as ambassador to the United Nations and making her a member of the Cabinet, he signaled his approval of someone he knew to be feisty, unlikely to tolerate the anti-American sentiments increasingly heard in UN General Assembly debates. His decision to withdraw from UNESCO and cut off U.S. support for the UN Fund for Population Studies, and his apparent interest—never consummated—to leave both the Food and Agricultural Organization and the International Atomic Energy Commission, alarmed some Democrats but gave no offense to the tens of millions who had voted for him.

Whereas Nixon might have reacted to the Soviet imposition of martial law in Poland, the shootdown of a Korean airliner, and the support given Syria in Lebanon's war with Israel, Reagan did nothing.[25] Though he continued to use rhetoric about the Soviet Union that Carter never employed and shunned any association with the human rights community that Carter had found so appealing, the fundamental difference lay in his decision to subordinate foreign policy to domestic policy, recognizing that political gains might be realized by doing so. Reagan, at least during his first term in office, attended largely to domestic ills, having no compelling or original ideas for dealing with events abroad.

His policies to revive the economy, end double-digit inflation, and increase employment received constant rhetorical emphasis during his first months in office. With a staff quickly put in place in the White House to guarantee he would not be unnecessarily burdened, boasting James Baker III, the Texan intimate of the vice president, as his chief of staff, cooperating with Edwin Meese and Michael Deaver, reliable seconds, who had long served him in California, Reagan created the troika that could be relied on to protect him. For his principal economic adviser, he selected the whiz kid, David Stockman, making him director of the Office of Management and Budget. Stockman, a very junior Michigan member of Congress, had helped Reagan prepare for his televised debates with Carter and Anderson, delighting him with his impersonations of both. With these men as his trusted aides, Reaganomics, or supply-side economics, became the principal remedy for achieving his three promised campaign goals: the lowering of taxes, the maintenance of essential defense expenditures, and the avoidance of drastic cuts in existing social programs.

Having bought into the simple theory that reductions in taxes and diminished government regulation would allow the entrepreneurial talents of the nation to flourish, restoring a lost prosperity, the president appeared before a joint session of Congress on February 18 to unveil his program. He proposed cutting some $41.4 billion from the Carter budget and promised a 30 percent income tax reduction over three years. Rapturously received by a Congress where Republicans of his ideological persuasion figured more prominently than at any time in the past, Reagan recognized that because the House remained Democratic, his success would depend ultimately on winning support from Southern Democrats. Knowing the history of every presidential administration since 1937, he had every reason to be confident of this backing and left the capital on the first of his many California holidays knowing he had inaugurated his presidency with a domestic program that appealed both to politicians and the media.

How the president's budget would have fared had there been no attempt on his life a month later, it is impossible to say. Many Democrats, alarmed by his attacks on specific social welfare programs they favored, would almost certainly have resisted certain of his proposed budget reductions. But the attempted assassination by John Hinckley made it almost unthinkable that any criticism would be made of a president who had shown such grace under fire, able to joke even when the would-be assassin's bullet was still lodged in his body. Reagan, in characteristic fashion, called Hinckley "a mixed-up young man from a fine family" and confided to his diary, "Whatever happens now I owe my life to God and will try to serve him in every way I can."[26] Indeed, his rapid recovery led almost no one to ask whether a man of his years had not suffered more permanent damage to his health than his physicians acknowledged. Reagan proved a fighter, and if anyone doubted that, his instant dismissal of the air-traffic controllers, who went out on strike during the summer, demonstrated this was not a president to be tampered with.

Congress passed his budget with alacrity in May, and many in the country welcomed a tax bill that reduced personal income tax by almost a quarter and the capital gains tax from 28 percent to 20 percent. The euphoria lasted through the summer but had begun to wane perceptibly by early 1982, with the federal deficit soaring, and unemployment rising to 10.8 percent—more than 9 million men and women—the highest since 1941. Another president would have found the situation distressing; Reagan showed no alarm and kept smiling. The recession, he insisted, was exacerbated not by anything he had done but by "the failed policies of the past." He knew the rate of inflation was falling, however slowly, as a consequence of Paul Volcker's recommendations as the head of the Federal Reserve Board, and if tight money policies did little to reduce unemployment or diminish the number of bankruptcies, it helped end the stagflation that had plagued the country from the time Ford had entered the White House. After years of railing against budget deficits, Reagan seemed prepared to believe those who argued that they might serve as an additional stimulus to take the country out of its recession. Accepting Volcker's advice that inflation was the major problem to be resolved, and that other benefits would follow when that malady was attended to, he faced resistance from some in his entourage, including James Baker and Secretary of the Treasury Donald Regan. Both opposed the reappointment of Volcker to head the Federal Reserve for a second term.[27] Reagan ignored their advice, reappointed the man originally chosen by Carter, and insisted in his weekly radio address in early February 1983 that his economic program was succeeding.

While Reaganomics was not the name he chose for his policy, saying "it sounds like a fad diet or an aerobic exercise," he took credit for all that happened in the manner that became customary with him.[28] Reagan started his presidency believing that budget cuts and tax reduction would bring the country out of the recession Carter had allowed to fester. When these remedies failed to produce the anticipated results, he changed course and adopted policies, not of his own invention, largely initiated by Volcker, that in the end helped produce the results he had hoped for.

In foreign policy, he started with a few comparable axioms and showed the same talent for abandoning them. Like every president since Eisenhower, Reagan recognized that nuclear war would have devastating effects on all the belligerents, and though he never pretended to understand the technicalities of arms control—few in fact did—he saw the importance of reducing nuclear arms, always doubting that the treaty arrangements made by previous administrations were adequate. For him, foolproof systems of verification were the only guarantee that the Soviets would not cheat. Disdaining the doctrine of mutual assured destruction, MAD, the official strategic policy for decades, but believing that the Soviet Union was "an implacable foe," the "center of an evil empire," he argued that America's advantage lay in its superior economy. If the United States upgraded its military capability, the Soviets would seek to do the same, but they would fail in that endeavor; and this remained his firm conviction from which he never deviated. Though pretending to be uninterested in any dialogue with the Soviet Union, he showed considerably more appetite for such discussions than either Haig or Cap Weinberger, his original secretaries of state and defense.

As early as April 1981, while still recovering from his gunshot wound, he wrote a letter to Leonid Brezhnev, the Soviet president, which Haig then converted into what Deaver disdainfully called "typical bureaucratise." Deaver, one of Reagan's most loyal White House courtiers who had followed him from California, told the president to discard the Haig version and to send his own. In his mind, the State Department and the National Security Council had been "screwing up for a quarter of a century," and there was no need to defer to them.[29] Reagan in the end sent his own letter, reminding the Soviet leader of their earlier meeting, when both expressed the hope that the peaceful aspirations of people everywhere could one day be realized. Reagan, in characteristic idiom, told Brezhnev that the peoples of the world "want to raise their families in peace without harming anyone or suffering harm themselves," then went on to say: "Government exists for their convenience, not the other way around. If they are incapable, as some would have us believe, of self-government, then where among them do we find people who are capable of governing others?" With brutal candor, he wrote:

> Is it possible that we have permitted ideology, political and economic philosophies, and governmental policies to keep us from considering the very real, everyday problems of peoples? Will the average Soviet family be better off or even aware that the Soviet Union has imposed a government of its own choice on the people of Afghanistan? Is life better for the people of Cuba because the Cuban military dictate who shall govern the people of Angola?[30]

The letter showed a beguiling faith in what the Soviet leader might be prepared to do to accommodate the wishes of an American president, and if it produced no result, this scarcely offended someone who never thought the Soviet leadership inspired or politically supple.[31]

Reagan came to the White House with negligible experience in foreign policy but with a few very firm convictions. While his subordinates in State and Defense indulged him in his homilies, imagining that the real problems had to do with whether the Europeans would allow the United States to deploy cruise and Pershing missiles to counter a growing Soviet threat, and whether it was indeed in the American national interest to do so, these were not the preoccupying questions for the president. Nor did he seek initially to interfere with Haig, his secretary of state, never admired or trusted by the troika at the White House—Deaver, Meese, and Baker—or by Bush, the vice president. Haig, so influential in the last months of Nixon's presidency, did not fall under the ban that excluded other Nixon appointees from high places in the Reagan administration, but the president scarcely knew him and chose him mostly because he liked his bearing and admired what he had done as commander of NATO.[32] When Reagan came to dismiss him in the spring of 1982, he wrote of differences they had and alluded to the impression Haig gave some members of Congress that "if it were up to him, he'd deal with some of our problems in Central America and Cuba with a bombing run or an invasion."[33] Reagan did not exaggerate when he wrote that Haig was "utterly paranoid with regard to the people he must work with," never identifying them as his loyal White House staff.[34] Nor did he choose to mention all that Haig had tried to do in fashioning a new Middle East policy. In fact, he scarcely knew the man he had appointed to head the State Department, though he saw correctly that "Al didn't want anyone other than himself, me included, to influence foreign policy while he was secretary of state." This was what led Reagan and his White House team ultimately to turn against the man who aspired to become a greater Henry Kissinger, achieving in the Middle East the permanent peace between Israel and the Arab states that had so far eluded successive administrations.[35] If he proved able to advance the peace process and improve the lot of the Palestinians, Haig imagined he would achieve what no previous secretary had accomplished.

Because Iran after the fall of the shah had become irrevocably hostile to the United States, with only Egypt and Jordan among the Arab states remaining friendly to U.S. initiatives in the region, Haig searched for new friends to rely on. Saudi Arabia, long courted for its oil, appeared as the most reasonable candidate for that role. Carter in his last months in office had agreed to sell the Saudis a weapons system they coveted, that the Israelis were determined they should not have. Both Haig and Weinberger saw many advantages in making the Airborne Warning and Control System (AWACS), important for its ability to detect other planes at a range of up to 350 miles, available to the Saudis. While recognizing the importance of the Israeli lobby's opposition in the United States to any such sale, they were prepared to ignore such protests. Haig believed that terrorism, Islamic fundamentalism, and Soviet penetration of the Persian Gulf were causing growing anxiety in Saudi Arabia and imagined that the sale of AWACS would do a great deal to cement relations between the two countries, help create a new security system in the region, replacing the one lost with the overthrow of the shah.

The arguments for the sale were many; moderate Arab states like Saudi Arabia and Kuwait would be tempted to forgive Egypt for the crime it had committed in making peace with Israel; the anticipated $8.5 billion sale would be advantageous to a still-ailing American economy. At a time when the Iranian Revolution was thought to be on the verge of collapse—an opinion common in the early Reagan years—this seemed a golden opportunity for the United States to forge new alliances, thwart the Soviet Union, and influence Israel to negotiate seriously, to return land for peace.

Haig, greatly influenced by Anwar Sadat, Egypt's president, accepted the idea that the Soviets had a two-crescents policy in the Middle East and Africa, with the first running through Iraq, Syria, the Yemens, Somalia, and Ethiopia, the second concentrating on southern Africa, principally in the former Portuguese colonies. Both thrusts, he believed, might be defeated if the Americans bestirred themselves.[36] Though the AWACS sale could be thwarted by Congress refusing to agree to it, Haig hoped that Republican control of the Senate would in the end guarantee acceptance. On October 29, he registered his first success: A motion to prohibit the sale was defeated in the Senate by a vote of 52–48, and while the so-called alliance with Saudi Arabia never materialized, Haig tended to ignore the more important Middle East issue of the day: the Iran-Iraq War. In the weeks when Reagan was recovering from his gunshot wound, Haig seemed all-powerful, but the hostility he provoked among other of the president's associates, not only because of his policies in the Middle East and his abrasive personality, but also because of his indiscretion at the time the president was wounded, claiming that he was "in charge," guaranteed he would not long survive as secretary of state.

While the arrival of a more cautious and crafty secretary of state, George Shultz, in July 1982 did not immediately provide Reagan with new foreign policy ideas different from those he had long espoused, and did little to compensate for weaknesses in his White House staff, the president felt comfortable with Schultz, a Ph.D. in economics from MIT who had served as secretary of labor and secretary of the treasury under Nixon. The internecine wars within his administration continued, but the president, always aloof from such mundane political squabbles, gave scant attention to the fact that there was no love lost between his newly appointed secretary of state and the secretary of defense. Cap Weinberger's stable of bright young men, led by Richard Perle, made some in the media refer back to the geniuses who had once surrounded McNamara, though Perle and others of his conservative persuasion despised the radicals introduced into the Pentagon decades earlier in the Kennedy administration. However ardent some of these seconds in command were in recommending more aggressive action against the Soviet Union, the president had no intention of doing anything that might create trouble. It was enough to speak boldly, and this he did with growing frequency and enthusiasm.

In almost the last days of his life, Brezhnev spoke of the Americans pursuing a policy of "adventurism, rudeness and undisguised egoism" that threatened "to push the world into the flames of nuclear war."[37] Given Reagan's address to the British Parliament in June 1982, these words seemed legitimate. A more careful reading of Reagan's speech, however, might have told the Soviets that the president had indeed been rude, but there was no suggestion of adventurism in what he had said. Unlike Khrushchev, he never suggested that the United States would bury the Soviet Union; on the contrary, he told the British and the world that the Soviets were in the process of burying themselves. In his words, a "great revolutionary crisis" had come to the Communist world; in Poland, for example, only martial law held the nation in thrall to its Soviet masters. Reagan minced no words when he said: "It is the Soviet Union that runs against the tide of human history by denying human freedom and human dignity to its citizens."[38] Borrowing from CIA estimates available to him, but knowing better than to mention his source, he spoke eloquently of the Soviet Union's economic difficulties, saying

> The rate of growth in the national product has been steadily declining since the fifties and is less than half of what it was then. The dimensions of this failure are astounding. A country which employs one-fifth of its population in agriculture is unable to feed its own people. . . . Over centralized, with little or no incentives, year after year the Soviet system pours its best resources into the making of instruments of destruction. The constant shrinkage of economic growth combined with the growth of military production is putting a heavy strain on the Soviet people. What we see here is a political structure that no longer corresponds to its economic base, a society where productive forces are hampered by political ones.[39]

No other American president had ever spoken so explicitly of the fact that the Soviet system was doomed. The words gave no hint of any need to act; the Soviets were defeating themselves. The president's contempt for their economic performance could not have been more explicitly stated.

Indeed, in his more moralistic speech to the National Association of Evangelicals, delivered in Orlando, Florida, on March 8, 1983, in which he spoke of the Soviet Union as an evil empire, his purpose was less to warn the Soviets of what he intended to do to bury them and more to beg his sympathetic audience not to be taken in by those who claimed that the arms race was a giant misunderstanding. In the president's mind, it was nothing less than a conflict between good and evil.[40] Believing this, he could only imagine that building a defense system to make the United States invulnerable was a responsibility he could not evade.

On March 23, 1983, with the economy recovering, he announced his plans for the Strategic Defense Initiative (SDI), dubbed Star Wars, the program that many in the scientific community in the United States thought fanciful, a view shared neither by Congress nor by the Soviet leadership. Yuri Andropov, Brezhnev's successor as the Soviet leader, thundered against the American president, "blinded by anticommunism," who had embarked on a "crusade against Socialism," prepared to risk atomic war to achieve his objectives. These words scarcely affected the president.[41] When, on September 1, 1983, a Korean Air Lines jet was shot down, ostensibly because it had wandered into Soviet airspace, with sixty-one U.S. citizens among the 269 dead, Reagan called the action a "crime against humanity" but saw no need to issue threats.

The vote less than three months later by the Bundestag to permit the deployment of U.S. Pershing II and cruise missiles in Germany seemed further proof of more aggressive American anti-Soviet policies, but the president saw all these innovations as simply defensive. Believing the Nixon policy of MAD an insufficient guarantee of U.S. safety, he dreamed of a more certain system of protection. SDI, like the missile deployments, were thought to be reinsurance policies. The Soviet Union found it difficult to accept so benign a view of what the Reagan administration was planning, and U.S. policies in Central America suggested the president was determined to destroy Communist governments wherever he could do so without risk of war.

Speaking from the Oval Office on May 9, 1984, as the nation prepared for the presidential nominating conventions, Reagan told of how the Sandinistas had promised a truly democratic government in Nicaragua in 1979, but instead, with their Cuban advisers, had instituted a "Communist reign of terror," repressing all democratic groups, showing itself both anti-Semitic and anti-Catholic, forcing many, once sympathetic, to take up arms against them. These men, the Contras, were "freedom fighters," and it was inconceivable that the United States, with its obligation to help freedom's friends and resist freedom's enemies, would not wish to help them.[42] As the president told the nation, "If the Soviet Union can aid and abet subversion in our hemisphere, then the United States has a legal right and a moral duty to help resist it." Both strategic and moral considerations dictated that the country not allow "peace-loving friends depending on our help [to] be overwhelmed by brute force if we have any capacity to prevent it." He implied that he proposed to do nothing more than what Harry Truman had done decades earlier in saving Greece from Communist subversion—to give economic aid.[43]

Though journalists began to write of a Reagan Doctrine, the president avoided all such hyperbole, satisfied he had led the nation to see the Contras as freedom fighters.[44] Behind the scenes, conflict raged as to what the United States should do to help the Contras, but the president distanced himself from all the contending factions, acting as if he knew nothing of what was going on. Just as the president revealed a remarkable capacity to make declarations on the situation in the Middle East and then ignore them, so he now opened with a striking declaration of hostility to the Sandinista regime but saw no need to follow through with any call for specific action.[45] The president's habit was to speak loudly and carry a very light stick. Years earlier, he had revealed this same tendency in respect to the Middle East. When Israel destroyed Iraq's Osirak nuclear reactor, located just ten miles outside Baghdad, a detail unmentioned in Reagan's autobiography, the president and his advisers were dismayed but could think of nothing to do except delay the shipment of F-16 fighters to Israel.[46] Many believed the president secretly supported the Israeli decision to eliminate Iraq's nuclear capabilities, and only a month later, when the Israelis bombed Beirut, killing hundreds in its effort to destroy the headquarters of the Palestine Liberation Organization (PLO) in that city, the president, distressed, not least by the televised images of mass killing and destruction, instructed his special envoy, Philip Habib, to arrange a cease-fire between Israel and the PLO.[47] This was accomplished, with some help from the Saudis, and the president showed no further interest in the area until almost a year later, on June 6, 1982, when the Israelis invaded Lebanon in force, claiming this was the only way to destroy the PLO, responsible for continuing terrorist attacks inside Israel.[48] Reagan showed an extraordinary ability to appear the warrior while in fact avoiding any action that might endanger the lives of American troops.

Though the Isreali military action went well initially, leading to the virtual destruction of the Syrian air force and the elimination of much of the PLO, Israel's persistent bombing of West Beirut, in the president's words, virtually "shattered the fragile political consensus in Lebanon." Before leaving for one of his many holidays, Reagan announced that "the United States was committed to a Lebanese government of national unity, security for Israel's northern border and expulsion of the PLO from Lebanon."[49] During this period, before Shultz had taken charge at the State Department, the president committed himself to sending U.S. forces to Lebanon to participate in a multilateral peacekeeping force that would be kept in place for no more than thirty days. By August 25, the first contingent of 800 U.S. Marines arrived on a mission whose purpose was never made very explicit. Because the removal of Syrian and Palestinian forces from West Beirut proceeded with extraordinary speed, the Marines withdrew on September 10, two weeks before the thirty-day limit originally set. The administration imagined it had achieved a remarkable success, and the election of the Phalangist leader, Bashir Gemayel, as president of Lebanon encouraged them to believe that the worst was over. When, however, Gemayel was assassinated on September 14, and the Israelis responded with a new military operation in Lebanon that they claimed was intended to protect Palestinian civilians against those who blamed them for President Gemayel's death, the White House said nothing.

In a secret order issued by Israel's general staff that explicitly forbade its troops to enter the two principal Palestinian refugee camps at Sabra and Shatila, believed to contain remnants of the PLO forces, the Israelis created the justification for their doing nothing that might involve them in combat. The order read quite simply: "Searching and mopping up the camps will be done by the Phalangists and the Lebanese Army." What followed was a catastrophe that saw the Gemayel militia enter the two Palestinian refugee camps at Sabra and Shatila, massacring some 700 people, women and children among them, and the scenes of slaughter, as revealed on television, were searing.[50]

The president expressed "outrage and revulsion over the murders" and announced the creation on September 20 of a new multinational force to keep the peace. In explaining his policy to Congress, he said that his sole purpose was to protect the territorial integrity and political independence of Lebanon. The Marines would go as peacekeepers, to remain in Lebanon for a short time only.[51] Again, for a moment, the introduction of U.S. troops seemed to create some semblance of order, but in March 1983 five Marines were injured in a terrorist attack.

Worse followed in April when a delivery truck exploded on the grounds of the U.S. embassy in Beirut, killing sixty-three, among them twenty-three Americans. One of the dead was Robert Ames, the chief CIA analyst for the Middle East. Shultz made it clear that the United States would not be deterred by this terrorist attack from maintaining its determination to achieve peace in Lebanon.[52]

The Americans knew what Israeli intelligence had already told them—that Syria was behind the murder of Gemayel—as well as what became more obvious after the attack on the U.S. embassy—that Shiite terrorists, sent from Iran, were now cooperating with Syrians in the Bekaa Valley to harass Israelis and to frighten Americans. Hezbollah, the Party of God, with its promise of jihad, holy war, had become a major combatant in Lebanon. Indeed, Syria was now the principal enemy of both Israel and the United States, and the material losses it suffered in Israel's initial attacks were largely compensated for by a massive Soviet resupply of weapons, estimated to exceed $2.5 billion in value.[53] The administration, seeking to support Lebanon's new president, the younger brother of the slain Gemayel, imagined the Marines might help him to create an army that would eventually guarantee a free and united Lebanon. Shultz traveled in May 1983 to the area to negotiate what he chose to see as a just agreement between Israel and Lebanon but that others in the administration, including Secretary of Defense Weinberger, ridiculed. In Weinberger's words, "It was nothing, not even an agreement. It gave the Syrians a veto power and they exercised it. From then on, I argued that the Marines should be brought back to the ships."[54]

This, however, did not happen. Though the administration gradually lost confidence in the Lebanese president, recognizing that his sole interest seemed to be to maintain the domination of the Christian minority in the country, no one close to the president advised him that the Marine presence was doing little to promote peace, and was not even very effective in creating a viable Lebanese army. On August 29, 1983, two U.S. Marines were killed and fourteen injured in a battle between the Lebanese Army and its Muslim enemies, and on September 1, precisely a year after he had made his original plea for peace in the Middle East, the president ordered an additional 2,000 Marines into the Mediterranean, in the waters outside Beirut.

As U.S. warships bombarded Syrian garrisons in the hills around Beirut, the Syrians warned of retaliation if the attacks continued. The French urged the Americans to desist, but to no avail. No one in Congress complained; few in the country realized what was happening. Then, on October 23, 1983, when 241 U.S. servicemen were killed in a suicide attack on a Marine barracks in Lebanon's capital, the nation's attention was riveted on that country as never before.[55] The president denounced the attack as "vicious and cowardly" and insisted the Americans would not be driven from Beirut. Again, he was posturing.

The Syrians became more active than ever in Lebanon, and the PLO leader, Yasser Arafat, returned to Beirut, establishing his headquarters in the downtown area. A fortnight after the attack on the Marine barracks, Palestinian guerrillas destroyed the Israeli headquarters in Tyre, with some sixty killed and thirty wounded. The Israelis retaliated immediately, shelling Palestinian positions outside Beirut. Later that month, the new Israeli prime minister, Yitzhak Shamir, meeting with Reagan in Washington, agreed to establish a joint committee to coordinate their military activities in the area. In the months that followed, the Americans attacked Syrian positions in Lebanon, losing two planes in the operation, but there was no incentive to go beyond these relatively fail-safe operations.

The president, increasingly pressed by members of his Cabinet and White House staff to withdraw the Marines from Lebanon, recognizing they were accomplishing little and might be further endangered, understood the importance of doing so before the November elections.[56] Though his secretary of state argued that any such sudden departure would damage U.S. standing in the area, Reagan found little merit in that argument. Lebanon was no more stable in 1984 than in 1983, and it made little sense to continue the intervention. Though the president had approved of the intervention, Thomas Friedman, one of the more acute critics of the operation, recognized that he was only one of many responsible for the catastrophe. Friedman, in his passionate jeremiad *From Beirut to Jerusalem,* wrote that the Marines were the "victims of the ignorance and arrogance of the weak, cynical, and in some cases venal Reagan Administration officials who put them into such an impossible situation," claiming that Reagan, Shultz, McFarlane, Weinberger, and Casey "will have to answer to history for what they did to the Marines."[57]

The president engaged in military operations only when confronted with obviously inferior forces and had no larger concept for achieving strategic objectives. He knew the Middle East not at all, and no one in his immediate entourage understood its tragic complexities. The president's capacity to do nothing, to shun off what might have been thought a serious setback, was best demonstrated in his decision to order the invasion of the tiny island of Grenada, a member of the Commonwealth, just two days after the carnage at the Marine headquarters in Beirut.

Arguing that the assassination of that island's Marxist prime minister, Maurice Bishop, by a renegade Communist faction threatened the breakdown of law and order, and that some 800 Americans on the island might be in danger, Reagan ordered the dispatch of a small task force to restore peace to the troubled island.[58] Prime Minister Margaret Thatcher, his friend and confidante, outraged by his action, complained in a BBC World Service broadcast that "many peoples in many countries would love to be free of Communism, but that doesn't mean we can just walk into them and say now you are free."[59] Always solicitous of her friend, her criticism was mild, and the president boasted of having saved the island from a formidable foe, thought to be preparing an invasion of Jamaica, Barbados, St. Vincent's, St. Lucia, Dominica, and Antigua.

The administration revealed once again its capacity for spin control, scarcely acknowledging that a number of American soldiers were killed or wounded through mistakes incurred by friendly fire, and the Democrats in Congress dared not mock Reagan's Caribbean adventure.

The presidential campaign of 1984, memorable principally for Reagan's runaway victory over Walter Mondale, winning with more than 54 million votes against Mondale's more than 38 million, saw the president achieve a victory greater than Eisenhower's in 1956, though not as great as Nixon's in 1972. How had he managed this extraordinary political feat? Did the weakness of his opponent explain his monumental triumph, or had there been a mass conversion of the electorate, rather like what Johnson achieved with his victory over Goldwater in 1964? Neither, in fact, wholly explained Reagan's phenomenal success. He owed his triumph principally to a capacity, honed over many years, to simplify issues, reiterating a single patriotic message that resonated for Americans wishing to believe in their national virtue and uniqueness.

Reagan never found it necessary to apologize for what he had done during his first four years in office. The country, as he saw it, had lost self-confidence, its most precious asset in the tragic 1960s and 1970s, and regained that priceless advantage only through the policies he advocated. While the Democrats might mock Star Wars and speak disparagingly of inflated defense budgets, the Republican Party platform, echoing the president, accepted that he intended to create a defense system that would make the country invulnerable to foreign attack.

Dangers persisted, of course, not least in Central America, but the Republicans knew that the president, alive to the hazards of Communist infiltration in the country's backyard, accepted that "the entire region. . . is gravely threatened by Communist expansion, inspired and supported by the Soviet Union and Cuba," and the party platform pledged "continued assistance to the democratic freedom fighters in Nicaragua."[60] The Democrats, incapable of framing an equally succinct statement to express their policy for the region, spoke of the need to end American support of the Contras and other paramilitary groups but couched its demand in the kind of liberal jargon the president found easy to ridicule. The Democratic platform read: "We need to develop relations based on mutual respect and mutual benefit. Beyond essential security concerns, these relations must emphasize diplomacy, development and respect for human rights."[61] Reagan never made the mistake of speaking in such inflated political jargon. Indeed, in accepting his party's nomination, he spoke as he always did, in brief sentences that gained authority from their simplicity. Reagan roused his Republican audience with the words:

We promised we'd reduce the growth of the Federal Government, and we have. We said we intended to reduce interest rates and inflation, and we have. We said we would reduce taxes to provide incentives for individuals and businesses to get our economy moving again, and we have. We said there must be jobs with a future for our people, not government make-work programs. And, in the last 19 months, six and a half million new jobs in the private sector have been created. We said we would once again be respected throughout the world, and we are. We said we would restore our ability to protect our freedom on land, sea and in the air, and we have.[62]

This was vintage Reagan, and some of it was true. When he used the same sort of argument in the first of his televised debates with Mondale, the latter imagined he was responding to him by protesting that while the wealthy were better off, citizens of middle income were about where they were in 1980, and those of modest income were in fact worse off. Mondale believed such argument would sway significant numbers of voters, allowing him to capitalize on what he represented as the president's follies. Mondale asked:

Are we better off with this arms race? Will we be better off if we start this 'Star Wars' escalation into the heavens? Are we better off when we de-emphasize our values in human rights? Are we better off when we load our children with this fantastic debt? Would fathers and mothers feel proud of themselves if they loaded their children with debts like this nation is now, over a trillion dollars, on the shoulders of our children? Can we be—say, really say, that we will be better off when we pull away from that basic American instinct of decency and fairness?[63]

To prove his sincerity, he added: "I would rather lose a campaign about decency than win a campaign about self-interest. I don't think this nation is composed of people who care only for themselves."[64] The rhetoric did not do for Mondale what Reagan did for himself in answering one of the questions put to him in the second debate when asked about his age, a supposedly delicate subject. In his characteristic jocular way, the president provoked laughter even from Mondale when he replied: "I want you to know that also I will not make age an issue of this campaign. I am not going to exploit for political purposes my opponent's youth and inexperience."[65]

Reagan won in 1984 less for his concrete accomplishments and more for his ability to make light of his defeats—indeed never mentioning them—dwelling only on a perpetual celebration of the remarkable American people. An accomplished actor who pretended to be an activist, in fact a laid-back politician, cautious and crafty, indolent and aged, he understood the game of American politics as few others did. While his Electoral College victory almost rivaled that of Roosevelt in 1936, his popular vote put him in that ambiguous company of other landslide victors that included Republicans and Democrats as different as Harding, Roosevelt, Johnson, and Nixon.

But his was a personal victory that did not translate into major congressional gains for the Republican Party. Indeed, the Republicans lost two seats in the Senate, their majority reduced from 53 to 47. Their fourteen-seat gain in the House still left them as the minority party in that chamber; the Democrats remained firmly in control with 253 seats against 182. The impressive victory Nixon had registered in 1972 was repeated by Reagan in 1984. He appealed largely to the same voters, winning 72 percent of the white vote in the South, and enjoying substantial support from Christian fundamentalists, Catholics, and antiabortion advocates throughout the country.[66] Mary McGrory, the journalist, noted the irony of Geraldine Ferraro, the Democratic vice presidential candidate, being attacked for her views on abortion while the president received praise for being pro-life. McGrory wrote:

> Here she is, a lifelong Catholic, a product of Catholic schools and colleges. She goes to Mass every Sunday, and the hierarchy of her church is acting like an army of the Reagan re-election committee. Ronald Reagan, who never puts a foot inside a church, is acclaimed as the nation's spiritual leader, introduced by cardinals and invited to ring monastery bells.[67]

The president had emerged as the spiritual leader of the country, made so largely by his rhetoric, and not only in respect to a single issue, abortion. Reagan called for a moral renaissance, constantly referring to family values, making little of his own divorce or the very superficial interest he took in his children.[68] This consummate actor appeared as the nation's moral leader, contending with welfare queens and poverty pimps at home, with an evil empire abroad.

Unless Reagan's anticommunism is understood as the quintessential expression of his determination to protect an America threatened by the Soviet Union and its satellites, his oratory loses much of its force. The worldwide Communist conspiracy, in Reagan's mind, needed to be constantly guarded against by a people prepared to reconstruct its military defenses, to act decisively when foreign dangers lurked. Reagan preached this message incessantly after the Marine tragedy in Lebanon, representing the country's intervention in Grenada as part of a larger campaign to halt Communist expansion wherever it appeared. As he explained in a televised speech to the nation:

> The events in Lebanon and Grenada, though oceans apart, are closely related. Not only has Moscow assisted and encouraged the violence in both countries, but it provides direct support through a network of surrogates and terrorists. It is no coincidence that when the thugs tried to wrest control over Grenada, there were thirty Soviet advisers and hundreds of Cuban military and paramilitary forces on the island.[69]

Reagan's ability to link the Middle East to events on an insignificant Caribbean island showed what critics might ruefully dismiss as a professional actor's political ingenuity. The price of this fable, so expertly constructed, proved to be high; it contributed to the American failure to assess correctly the transformations occurring in an increasingly volatile Middle East, to recognize them as something other than crises produced by the machinations of men obeying orders emanating from Moscow.

None of this, however, seemed to matter during Reagan's lucky first term in the White House. If many expected his massive electoral victory in 1984 to issue in an even more successful second term, they were mistaken. Indeed, the abysmal history of the 1960s and 1970s seemed almost to be repeating itself when, soon after his second inaugural, Reagan began to experience difficulties reminiscent of those Johnson and Nixon encountered after their own impressive electoral triumphs. The president's decision to lay a wreath at the Bitburg cemetery in Germany proved embarrassing when it was discovered that some forty-nine SS soldiers were buried there, but this was nothing compared to what followed, as details of Iran-Contra came to light.

Because terrorism and Central America had figured so prominently in the president's mind before the fall election, both were high on his action agenda after his 1984 reelection triumph. He represented Iran and Nicaragua as members of "a new international version of Murder, Incorporated," linked with Libya, North Korea, and Cuba, all described as "outlaw states run by the strangest collection of misfits, Looney Tunes, and squalid criminals since the advent of the Third Reich."[70] After a rash of Shiite kidnappings of Americans in Beirut, where Iranians were clearly implicated, three taken hostage in 1984 and four in 1985, the president expressed his determination to find and release the captives, refusing all suggestions that he treat secretly with their kidnappers, possibly even offering them a ransom. As he proclaimed on June 30, 1985, a few weeks before he entered the hospital for the removal of a large intestinal polyp, "The United States gives terrorists no rewards. We make no concessions. We make no deals."[71] Like many of the president's declarations, his rhetoric gave no hint of the concern in both the CIA and the National Security Council about Iran, the extent of the Soviet influence there, the stability of the Ayatollah Khomeini regime given the age of its leader, and what the final outcome of the Iran-Iraq War might be.[72]

The president never concealed his concern about the hostages in his daily meetings with Bud McFarlane, his national security adviser, giving almost equal attention to the fate of the Contras in Nicaragua. As he explained to McFarlane, he wished for these freedom fighters to be protected "body and soul," knowing this would be difficult in the Democratic-controlled House, where the majority showed itself reluctant to offer further assistance.[73] Everyone in the White House understood that these were the issues that greatly preoccupied the president, and when McFarlane told him in the hospital "that we had

had a contact from Iranians whom we had reason to believe had reasonably good connections within Iran but who were on the outside and this had come primarily as a result of Israeli connection with the Iranians," the president showed immediate interest in the matter. In his mind, an operation that opened the possibility of a release of hostages had much to commend it; his words—"Open it up"—were taken to indicate his agreeing to negotiations not with the kidnappers but with those who enjoyed access to them.[74]

Whether he understood that a price would have to be paid, that the price would be the sale of arms to Iran, was less clear. This, however, was never in doubt after August 6 when the president, meeting with Bush, Shultz, Weinberger, McFarlane, and Donald Regan, his newly appointed chief of staff, agreed to allow the shipment of 100 antitank TOW missiles (tube-launched, optically tracked, wire-guided antitank weapons) to Iran in exchange for the release of four hostages.[75] Shultz opposed the sale from the beginning, calling it "a very bad idea," arguing that "we were just falling into the arms-for-hostages business and we shouldn't do it."[76] Weinberger also opposed the sale, believing it would give the Iranians an advantage in their war with Iraq, never concealing his contempt for the Iranians or his wish to see Iraq triumph over the fanatics who had humiliated the Americans in 1979. Though Bush said nothing at the meeting, he was known to support in private whatever the president wished. Regan told McFarlane to "go slow," to "make sure we know who we are dealing with before we get too far into this." The president made no comment at the meeting but telephoned McFarlane a few days later to tell him he authorized the Israeli sale to Iran of modest quantities of "TOW missiles or other spares." The United States undertook to replenish the Israelis for any materials sent. Later, the president implied he had not given prior approval to the sale but in the end suggested he could not recall when he had given his assent.

On August 20, ninety-six TOW missiles were sent by Israel to Iran, which now escalated its original demand, asking that another 400 be sent; as a token of good faith, a single hostage was released. In public, Reagan continued to describe Iran as a major source of terrorism in Lebanon and Europe; in private, he accepted to supply missiles to Iran, using Israel as his conduit. The Iranians ignored their promise to release four additional hostages, but when they asked for 150 HAWK missiles, there was no disposition to deny the request, and the HAWKs, sent from Israel, reached Iran by way of Portugal. In Geneva, on November 19, the first day of the president's summit meeting with Gorbachev, McFarlane gave the president full details of the operation, and Regan, present at the meeting, wrote in his own memoir, "This was certainly the first time the President had heard the whole scenario. It was not in his character to be especially interested in the nuts and bolts, and he asked no probing questions."[77]

While it is impossible to doubt that he understood that HAWKs were being sent, and that hostages were not being released, McFarlane, increasingly dismayed by the whole operation, wished only to be relieved of his duties. He was replaced by Admiral John Poindexter as national security adviser, with Oliver North appointed as his deputy. North recognized the need for additional sales and was prepared to see Iran receive 3,300 TOWs and fifty HAWKs, delivered in increments to coincide with the liberation of individual hostages.

At the last meeting chaired by McFarlane in the White House family quarters on Saturday, December 7, attended by Reagan, Shultz, Weinberger, Regan, and Poindexter, as well as by John McMahon, sitting in for William Casey, the head of the CIA who was traveling, the vice president was absent, preferring to adhere to his original schedule and attend the Army-Navy football game.[78] Lou Cannon, one of Reagan's principal biographers, said of the vice president: "Bush avoided expressing himself on a critical issue on which he knew the president to have strong feelings."[79] Shultz claimed the initiative would "negate the whole policy" of not making deals with terrorists and predicted the whole plot would become public, shaking moderate Arabs when they learned that the United States was "breaking our commitment to them and helping the radicals in Tehran fight their fellow Arab Iraq."

Weinberger, even more hostile to continuing the policy, emphasized the illegality of the action, claiming it violated the U.S. embargo on the sale of arms to Iran, ignoring the restrictions on third-country transfers, as contained in the Arms Export Control Act.[80] Believing the scheme would become known, he insisted that "we had no interest whatsoever in helping Iran in any military way, even a minor way, and that in every way it was a policy that we should not engage in and most likely would not be successful." Don Regan joined the two in arguing for the plan to be abandoned, a view supported also by McMahon. As for the president, responding to Weinberger, he said that "the American people will never forgive me if I fail to get these hostages out over this legal question."[81]

Reagan, advised to desist, spurned the counsel of his principal Cabinet officers. The occasion was ripe for the newest of his courtiers to take over: Oliver North, deputy to Poindexter, a Marine colonel, knew what the president cared about—the return of the hostages. He felt it was impossible to turn back; to do so would only risk the lives of the hostages. While the United States might continue to send TOW missiles to Iran through Israel, believing this policy would lead eventually to the release of the prisoners, he saw another opportunity—a bolder one—that carried even greater promise. Why should the United States not send the missiles directly to Iran, then use the funds acquired through the sale to finance the Contras in Nicaragua? Thus, two of the president's most cherished foreign policy objectives would be realized. While no firm decision was made on whether to continue to use Israel as the conduit, or whether to ship the arms directly, both actions were illegal, violating the terms of the Arms Export Control Act. That technicality scarcely worried North, who, like everyone else in the White House, knew the president's wishes in the matter and cared only to gratify them. Weinberger continued to doubt the reasonableness of the policy and became "Dr. No," while Shultz, more aloof, though hostile to the plan, chose a path that made him "Dr. I Don't Want to Know."

What the president understood of the plan remains a contested issue, but by January 6 he signed papers that made it obvious he wished arms to be sent directly to Iran. On that day, in his diary he wrote: "I agreed to sell TOWS to Iran."[82] By agreeing to the sale, the president violated his promise never to negotiate with terrorists. More important, by engaging in secret sales that gave major arms to Iran for its war with Iraq, supplemented by the intelligence the CIA provided the Iranians on Iraqi military deployments, the president hoped his hostage objective would be achieved. George Shultz, observing that no hostages were being released, said later that the "United States was being taken to the cleaners," but he saw no way to intervene to halt the operation. Both Shultz and Weinberger might have considered resigning, but neither did. Major Cabinet officers were not in the habit of resigning when presidents resisted their advice, Vance being the sole exception in the Carter administration. North, satisfied that the money realized from the sales was being used to help the Contras, was wholly content with what he conceived to be a splendid operation. While these illegal measures were pursued, the president continued to speak of never countenancing terrorism and to demonstrate his resolve ordered the bombing of Tripoli and Benghazi in retaliation for a Libyan bombing of a West Berlin disco where an American soldier had been killed.[83] More than ninety 2,000-pound bombs were dropped in a perfectly fail-safe operation intended to demonstrate the president's firm resolve.

While France's president, François Mitterand, objected, saying "I don't believe you stop terrorism by killing 150 Libyans who have done nothing," Reagan knew that the country approved of what he had done; he was standing tall—and that mattered. On August 27, he signed a new antiterrorism law that banned all military sales to nations, including Iran, that supported terrorism, acknowledging that while legislation could never end terrorism, the nation "must remain resolute in our commitment to confront this criminal behavior in every way—diplomatically, economically, legally and, when necessary, militarily." Reagan imagined he was doing all these things, and his presidential approval ratings were never higher than in the spring and summer of 1986. The sales to Iran remained secret, and on the eve of the congressional off-year elections, only two hostages had been released. However popular the president might be, his popularity did not extend to the Republicans fighting to retain control of the Senate. Six of the twelve Republicans who entered the Senate in 1980 on Reagan's coattails were defeated, and the Democrats now enjoyed control of both houses of Congress.

Just days after the off-year elections, the story broke in the American press, based on a speech given by Iran's leader, Ali Akbar Hashemi Rafsanjani, that gave the first hint of the secret negotiations that had been ongoing for more than a year. The president understood the need to remain silent—to give no credence to the rumors flooding newspaper offices throughout the country. While Poindexter sought to persuade both Shultz and Weinberger that the whole policy aimed at a "long-term strategic relationship with Iran," and that its sole purpose was to strengthen Iranian moderates and halt terrorism while of course also freeing the hostages, both the secretary of state and the secretary of defense recognized the lies in all these rationalizations of a failed policy. Shultz blamed the Israelis for pressing the sale in the first instance but knew that the president approved it—he had sold arms for hostages.

The president, confronted with a hostile Congress, took to his favorite medium, television, to explain himself to the nation. In his November 13 address, he pretended that Iran was a strategic bulwark against the Soviet Union and that this fact alone explained the arms sale, so negligible, they "could easily fit into a single cargo plane."[84] That disclosure, wholly untrue, barely concealed other equally false claims that the administration communicated to the media. The president, increasingly on the defensive, seemed suddenly vulnerable, and Shultz, restive and uncertain, sought to create some distance between himself and the president, incurring the wrath of those who cared only to protect the Gipper, with Donald Regan emerging as his principal run-blocker.[85] In a news conference on November 19, the president, asked whether the United States had in any way been involved with Israel in its sales of arms to Iran, replied that this was an outright lie; in his words, "We, as I say, have had nothing to do with other countries or their shipment of arms or doing what they're doing." When another reporter contradicted him, reminding him that his chief of staff, Regan, had spoken of a shipment of arms by Israel before the release of one of the hostages, the president lied again, saying: "Well, no, I've never heard Mr. Regan say that, and I'll ask him about that."

In the president's mind, the operation had not been a mistake; it had led to the release of three hostages, and those releases would have continued had the media not intervened, wrecking a well-conceived plan. But worse was to come when Edwin Meese, now attorney general, sought additional information on the arms sale and discovered a memo that told of the diversion of funds from that sale by Oliver North to the Contras in Nicaragua. Meese told the story to the president, sparing him none of the sordid details.[86] It appeared that the Iranians had been charged $30 million for $12 million worth of missiles, and no one could account for what happened to the missing $18 million. Meese, persuaded that the president knew nothing of this plan, heard Regan quickly invent the story that the diversion of funds to the Contras was done wholly without his knowledge. Poindexter, told he would have to resign, did so on November 25, with the president announcing that he had also dismissed North. The president took only a single question at his next news conference, saying he had not made a mistake in sending arms to Iran, but that he was "deeply troubled that the implementation of a policy aimed at resolving a truly tragic situation in the Middle East has resulted in such controversy."

Meese, preparing the president's defenses, suggested that North was alone responsible for everything, that the president knew nothing of the excessive charges, or of the transfer of funds to the Contras. The president, angry only at the media for its disclosures, continued to think of North as a national hero who had failed only in not telling him everything. It was impossible for the country to believe the president's protestations of innocence, and within days of these disclosures, a *New York Times*/CBS poll suggested that his approval rating had fallen from 67 percent to 46 percent, a fall even more grievous than the one Ford suffered after his Watergate pardon of Richard Nixon. While no one could prove that the president had lied about knowing nothing of the diversion of funds, some, especially in the media, talked of impeachment, but few in Congress cared to repeat for a second time the ordeal of 1974. The Democrats, controlling both houses of Congress, might have pushed for more intensive inquiry, but few saw any advantage in doing so.

After publication of the *Tower Commission Report* on the whole affair in February 1987, a commission that included the conservative former senator from Texas, Brent Scowcroft and Edmund Muskie, former Maine senator and Carter's secretary of state, the president's flawed memory no longer figured as an explanation of his persistent lying; it was the failure of his chief of staff to keep him informed that explained his having known nothing of the actions taken. Regan was made the scapegoat; in the words of the *Tower Commission Report*,

> He [Regan] was personally active in national security affairs and attended almost all of the relevant meetings regarding the Iran initiative. He, as much as anyone, should have insisted that an orderly process be observed. In addition, he especially should have ensured that plans were made for handling any public disclosure of the initiative. He must bear primary responsibility for the chaos that descended upon the White House when such disclosure did occur.[87]

In the speech the president gave on March 4, in effect acknowledging that mistakes had been made, he would never go so far as to admit that he had made them. Still, this was enough for the *Washington Post* to say editorially that he had given "the right speech last night."[88] When he came to write his memoirs, Reagan said quite simply, "It was as if Americans were forgiving me for something I hadn't done."[89] The stupidity and illegality of the operation was never acknowledged; the vacuity of the administration's Middle East policies was never admitted. The president had lied, but the nation forgave him. This was how the country's media chose to represent the issue, and Reagan's quick move to deflect attention from Irangate to the collapsing Soviet Union meant that his last years in office were successful, represented by Republicans as monumental in their accomplishments.[90]

Reagan's second term—indeed his reputation—was saved by Mikhail Gorbachev. The new Soviet leader, canonized first in early 1985 by another renowned conservative, Margaret Thatcher, as a man with whom business could be done, recognized it was impossible for the Soviet Union to sustain the policies abroad pursued since the death of Stalin. It was essential for the country to reduce its military expenditures and to abandon some of its more ambitious far-flung foreign ventures.[91] If he could secure American friendship by agreeing to reduce the Soviet Union's thermonuclear weapons arsenal, expecting equivalent reductions to be made by the United States, persuading the president to go slow on Star Wars, this would be a bargain advantageous to both countries.

When Reagan met with Gorbachev in Geneva for the first time in July 1985, before Irangate became a running political sore, he was impressed with the Soviet leader but unable to accept his assurances that the Soviet Union had no aggressive intentions. As for the idea that he might be induced to abandon SDI in exchange for Soviet concessions on missile development, this was a proposition inconceivable to him. In that initial meeting, little was accomplished except that both agreed to meet again at future summits. Gorbachev failed to secure an agreement from the president to halt Star Wars planning, and the Chernobyl nuclear plant disaster on April 26, 1986, told Reagan that the Soviet leader would almost certainly be more amenable to compromise. In his memoirs, the president wrote:

> Gorbachev must have realized it could no longer support or control Stalin's totalitarian empire; the survival of the Soviet Union was more important to him. He must have looked at the economic disaster his country was facing and concluded that it couldn't continue spending so much of its wealth on weapons and an arms race that—as I told him in Geneva—we would never let his country win. I'm convinced the tragedy at Chernobyl a year after Gorbachev took office also affected him and made him try harder to resolve differences with the West.[92]

Reagan proposed to make no concessions on SDI, saying it "might one day enable us to put in space a shield that missiles could not penetrate, a shield that could protect us from nuclear missiles just as a roof protects a family from rain."[93] In the months that followed, the president showed a willingness to extend the ABM Treaty for another five years, but when the Soviet Union arrested Nicholas Daniloff, the Moscow correspondent for *U.S. News & World Report,* in retaliation for the arrest of a Soviet spy working at the United Nations in New York, relations froze again.[94] The October 1986 Reykjavik summit in Iceland failed to bring the two leaders any closer together, but many in the country believed the president had done well, and both Reagan and Gorbachev shared an interest in maintaining that illusion. It was obvious after Reykjavik that Reagan would never give way on SDI, and it appeared that Gorbachev would not reduce Soviet strategic forces substantially unless such a promise was forthcoming.

In these circumstances, progress depended on the Soviet readiness to destroy intermediate-range and short-range missiles if the United States agreed to do the same. When it emerged that the two leaders were prepared to agree on an Intermediate-Range Nuclear Forces (INF) Treaty, and that Gorbachev would agree to sign such an accord in Washington, the president could not fail to be delighted by the prospect. His tour of Europe, in the spring and summer of 1987, further to deflect attention from the continuing inquiry into Irangate, proved to be a great personal success, made so principally by the memorable speech he delivered at the Brandenburg Gate. There, Reagan praised the "reform and openness" that had become increasingly apparent in the Soviet Union, then went on to say:

> There is one sign the Soviets can make that would be unmistakable, that would advance dramatically the cause of freedom and peace. General Secretary Gorbachev, if you seek peace, if you seek prosperity for the Soviet Union and Eastern Europe, if you seek liberalization: come here to this gate! Mr. Gorbachev, open this gate! Mr. Gorbachev, tear down this wall.[95]

Gorbachev's Washington visit, a striking success for him but also for the president, led to the signing of the INF Treaty that in the next three years led to the destruction of 859 U.S. missiles and 1,836 Soviet missiles with a range of 300–3,400 miles. This figured as the high point of a visit that saw the American media celebrate the arrival of a new kind of Soviet leader.[96] Though some in the Defense Department worried over whether the INF Treaty did not create new dangers for Europe, there was never any doubt that it would be ratified.[97] Reagan strongly supported it, suggesting in an Oval Office interview with network anchormen in December that those opposed to the treaty were "ignorant of the advances that had been made in verification," unwilling to accept that war was not inevitable and had to be avoided. In his words,

> I think that some of the people who are objecting the most and just refusing even to accede to the idea of ever getting any understanding, whether they realize it or not, those people basically down in their deepest thoughts have accepted that war is inevitable and that there must come to be a war between the superpowers.[98]

Reagan proved to be the best salesman for the INF Treaty, and few were surprised when the Senate approved it overwhelmingly in May 1988, just days before Reagan met Gorbachev for his last summit in Moscow. In Moscow, he achieved a success scarcely less remarkable than the one Gorbachev had experienced in Washington. In a series of speeches, with material provided him by two of the country's leading Soviet experts, the U.S. ambassador to the Soviet Union, Jack Matlock, and Librarian of Congress James Billington, the president enjoyed numerous photo opportunities, making speeches that were among the best he ever delivered.[99]

At the Danilov Monastery, he expressed the "hope for a new age of religious freedom in the Soviet Union" and at the U.S. embassy spoke to ninety-six Soviet dissidents, declaring his human rights agenda to include freedom of religion, freedom of speech, and freedom of travel. In his remarks, he linked these freedoms to economic growth, quoting Aleksandr Pushkin at the end, "It's time, my friend, it's time." Speaking beneath a gigantic bust of Lenin at Moscow State University, he said:

> Your generation is living in one of the most exciting, hopeful times in Soviet history. It is a time when the first breath of freedom stirs the air and the heart beats to the accelerated rhythm of hope, when the accumulated spiritual energies of a long silence yearn to break free. . . . We do not know what the conclusion will be of this journey, but we're hopeful that the promise of reform will be fulfilled. In this Moscow spring, this May 1988, we may be allowed that hope: that freedom, like the fresh green sapling planted over Tolstoy's grave, will blossom forth at last in the rich fertile soil of your people and culture. We may be allowed to hope that the marvellous sound of a new openness will keep rising, ringing through, leading to a new world of reconciliation, friendship and peace.[100]

In preparing the text of the final communiqué of the Moscow summit, Gorbachev suggested there be some reference to the fact that military means could never resolve the world's problems, with some suggestion made of what he called the principle of peaceful coexistence.[101] Neither the secretary of state nor the secretary of defense, Frank Carlucci, accepted the phrase; it smacked too much of Soviet Cold War propaganda. General Colin Powell, Reagan's newest national security adviser, was no less opposed, believing that Gorbachev hoped to "trick him [Reagan] into a backdoor commitment" to halt giving assistance to rebel forces in Afghanistan.[102] The phrase was never inserted. At the Guildhall, in London, on June 3, Reagan spoke of the new "worldwide movement toward democracy" certain to usher in "an era of peace and freedom for all."[103]

Was this not Reagan's finest hour? Had he not realized his most ardent ambition—to see the Soviet Union, in its earlier Bolshevik definition, for all practical purposes destroyed? Had his demands for increased military expenditures not achieved what he most hoped for? Did the Soviet Union not collapse in the time of his successor because of the policies he had initiated? The short answer to the last two questions must be a resounding no.

Reagan's presidency, the most successful Republican administration since that of Theodore Roosevelt, succeeded for one reason principally: Reagan was a popular and canny monarch who made admirable use of his courtiers and knew when to cross them. His ideas were few, but in domestic as in foreign policy, he knew how to persevere, when to change course. A superb orator, he gave the impression of being brave, even reckless, but in fact he took negligible risks, engaged in bombings in Libya and Lebanon, fail-safe operations that could never be thought dangerous; Grenada was a military comedy. If both Roosevelts, together with Wilson, gave the country a new presidency, Reagan did something of the same, establishing his rule by effective oratory, an accomplished actor who comforted the nation with the idea it was once again strong, that its enemies had been vanquished. He left a terrible legacy in the Middle East, and there were few critics in his immediate circle or in the larger society prepared to recognize that he and those who advised him had limited understanding of the region.

Reagan never pretended to be anything other than an ordinary American, supremely confident of his own virtue and that of his fellow citizens. He left a progeny; Bush and Clinton, though only the first ever acknowledged the full extent of his indebtedness. If a new, more photogenic presidency was introduced with the Camelot court established by Kennedy, a second more important transformation took place with the arrival of the true believers prepared to serve in the court of Reagan. They were neither critics nor sycophants, accepting to serve as a supporting cast in a play, never rendered as a comedy, directed by a master stage producer, happy about his country, content in his marriage, faithful to his simple mottoes and slogans.[104]

Reagan created no new institutions, did nothing to increase the country's knowledge of the world abroad, least of all in the Middle East, but took pride in having never succumbed to an exaggerated notion of the strength of the Soviet Union. He warned of its dangers constantly but never felt really threatened. A master dissembler both in the beginning and at the end, luck never deserted him. His laid-back manner, like his simple oratory, resonated for a society that had no wish to be preached to, that responded to his homilies with the enthusiasm he welcomed.

More than any other president in the twentieth century, he used stories— narratives he mastered—to bring himself closer to ordinary men and women. He was equally at home on television and radio; the country believed him to be just an ordinary American, a distinction it was harder to ascribe to his guardian, Nancy, his ever-watchful wife and constant companion. Lou Cannon, one of his many biographers, showed rare inspiration in the title he chose for his book, *President Reagan: The Role of a Lifetime*; it described the man and his accomplishment perfectly.[105]

CHAPTER 19

The Connecticut Yankee in Disguise

GEORGE H.W. BUSH, the privileged son of a Connecticut senator, a WASP who married into a family whose lineage included a former president of the United States, the long-forgotten Franklin Pierce, attended all the right schools, Phillips Andover Academy and Yale, was a member of Skull and Bones, and served in the Navy as a combat pilot during World War II. He made a substantial fortune in oil speculation in Texas by practices never too closely inquired into. Like so many other New Englanders of his social class who maintained summer homes in Maine, courted Smith College girls, relished sailing and riding, and were always aware of the advantages they enjoyed as heirs of what passed for an American aristocracy, Bush was a gentleman who made a great deal of being a regular guy with roots in both Texas and Maine.

His political career, in respect to elective office, was unspectacular, though he was never shy about seeking entry to Congress, believing it appropriate that he follow his father there. He competed for a Texas Senate seat in 1964, a fatal year for Republican hopefuls, and lost badly. Setting his sights somewhat lower, he ran next in 1966 for a House seat and won, serving there for only two terms. Like other congressional freshmen, subordinated in a seniority system that gave all substantial power to those who had served for longer periods, Bush made no impression then but kept his eye always on graduating to the higher chamber, seeking a seat in the Senate.[1]

In 1970, he ran again but lost a second time, beaten decisively this time by a more aggressive Democrat, Lloyd Bentsen. At this juncture, President Nixon, a man he scarcely knew, came to his rescue, appointing him ambassador to the United Nations to replace Charles Yost, a diplomat and old-time State Department hand, known to be unhappy with Nixon's autocratic ways.[2] The UN post, which once commanded the services of eminent politicians, including two very prominent Democrats, Adlai Stevenson and Arthur Goldberg, had lost much of its luster under a Republican president, jealous of his authority, who intended all major foreign policy decisions to be made in the White

House.[3] Nixon, in appointing Bush, chose someone he expected to be loyal, do his bidding, and create no problems for him. In the Nixon White House, with both the president and his national security adviser taking a dim view of the United Nations as a peace-keeping organization, the UN ambassadorship counted for little.

Nevertheless, for Bush, the appointment was a godsend. The disgruntled Yost retired to write a mildly critical book, *The Conduct and Misconduct of Foreign Affairs,* published in 1972, that told how the State Department under William Rogers had been shunted aside, but Bush arrived with no comparable grievances, grateful to the president for having selected him.[4] Nixon, seeking always to have some in his administration who qualified as well-born Eastern Republican gentlemen, chose Bush for that reason among others, confident he would never ally himself with those despised striped-pants diplomats in the State Department he abominated. Nixon guessed correctly about Bush, who knew his place and faithfully executed the orders that came from the White House. A loyal player on the Nixon team, Bush would have been content to remain as UN ambassador, enjoying a sumptuous Waldorf Astoria apartment, membership in the Cabinet, and other comparable perquisites, but circumstances within the Republican Party took him away from that safe haven to another that proved more hazardous but in the end more advantageous to his career.

When the president, despite his success in winning so overwhelmingly in 1972 against George McGovern, found it difficult to persuade influential Republicans to accept the post of Republican national chairman, he settled on the man he knew he could control. Bush, never one to refuse a presidential summons, accepted the call, scarcely aware that it was a hazardous leap into a political fire created by the Watergate break-in, just then beginning to command public attention.

Because Republicans had begun to realize the potential disaster that threatened from rumors circulating about possible links between the White House and the Watergate break-in, Bush's position as chairman of the Republican National Committee took on an importance no one had foreseen. While Bush did what he could to make it appear that the president was in no way involved or endangered by Watergate, the Republican National Committee's decision in 1973 to appropriate $20,000 to assure the success of a presidential rally in Phoenix, Arizona, suggested that party leaders recognized Nixon's vulnerability and wished to create an occasion to demonstrate his continued popularity among the Republican faithful.[5] Nixon used the Phoenix rally to say that "the time has come to put Watergate behind us and to get on with the business of America"; he promised "to stay on the job" and received tumultuous applause in response to his declared intention to defeat those who had so wrongly traduced him.

Bush, too well-informed to be wholly persuaded by this mock display of self-confidence, recognized the dangers and understood very early that the Republican triumph of 1972 might soon prove ephemeral. These were difficult days for a Nixon loyalist, and on at least one occasion Bush thought of resigning, but in the end he battled on. While neither he nor Vice President Ford ever went so far as to use the word *resignation* in the final meeting of the Nixon Cabinet in August 1974, his role as chairman of the Republican Party allowed him to say what everyone in the Cabinet knew to be true: The party was in desperate straits and risked losing catastrophically in the off-year November elections if the Watergate problem was not quickly resolved.[6] Days later Nixon resigned, understanding that the alternative would be a trial in the Senate and almost certain conviction.

President Ford, soon after reaching the White House, relieved Bush of his thankless task as Republican Party chairman and appointed him chief of the United States Liaison Office in Beijing, representing the United States in Mao's China. Bush spent less than a year there and accomplished very little, through no fault of his own. If Ronald Reagan later complained of Kremlin leaders constantly dying on him, preventing him from doing much to improve U.S.-Soviet relations, Bush faced the opposite problem in China. Mao, the hero of the revolution, refused to die, and as long as he held on, bold American initiatives of any kind were impossible. Bush passed an agreeable-enough time in China, emerged as something of an expert on the country, but no one who looked at the record imagined he had achieved anything of consequence.

Again, neither success nor failure accounted for the presidential summons that brought him back to Washington in November 1975 to become CIA director. Bush received the appointment because Donald Rumsfeld, Ford's chief of staff, recommended it.[7] Indeed, the Bush appointment was the least important of the changes that led the president to drop Rockefeller as the prospective Republican nominee to run with him as vice president in 1976, to relieve Kissinger of his duties as national security adviser, retaining him as secretary of state, and to dismiss James Schlesinger as secretary of defense, replacing him with Rumsfeld, who coveted the position and had become a principal confidante of the president.[8]

Ford's dissatisfaction with Colby as head of the CIA grew out of his displeasure with gaffes he had made in testimony given before the Church Committee in the Senate. Ford believed that a new director, with no previous links to the agency, would dampen the media's enthusiasm for the ongoing investigations and keep the lid on the agency till after the 1976 elections. Bush did not disappoint Ford, accepting the appointment with alacrity, and in the short year that elapsed before Carter's arrival managed to keep a low profile, saying and doing nothing to embarrass a beleaguered White House. Bush, indeed, would have accepted to stay on at the CIA after Ford's defeat, believing the post should be regarded as nonpolitical, but Carter had no wish to retain him. Returning to Texas, he began to plan with James Baker III, his intimate friend and the unsuccessful manager of the president's reelection campaign, their joint return to Washington. Both understood that Reagan, given his stellar performance at the 1976 convention, would be a formidable contender for the Republican nomination, but neither believed his victory was certain; each could imagine circumstances that would allow them to serve in the next Republican administration, whoever its leader might be. Like Reagan, they expected Carter to be a one-term president, recognizing him for what he was—an ineffectual leader out of his depth.

When the primary season opened in 1979, Reagan was seen to be the principal Republican contender, but three others, John Connally, Howard Baker, and George Bush, were all considered potential rivals. Baker, a senator from Tennessee, and Connally, briefly Nixon's secretary of the treasury, were considered stronger contenders than Bush, but the latter's victory over Baker in a straw vote in Maine and Reagan's victory over Connally in a straw vote in Florida led the media to argue that the race might well turn out to be between the former governor of California and the *faux* Texan who had never held a comparably important elected position.

When Bush surprised many by defeating Reagan in the Iowa primary, the media touted the upcoming New Hampshire primary as all-important. If Reagan won there, he would probably go on to become the party's candidate; if Bush emerged the victor, the race would become closer. In the end Reagan won, in part because Bush refused to debate on television if all five of the Republican contenders were allowed to join the fray. By insisting on a televised debate between the principals only—himself and Reagan—Bush showed his New England primness, scarcely resembling the self-confidence that seemed second nature to the laid-back actor from California. While Bush then went on to win in Connecticut, his father's home state, he lost crucial primaries in New York and Pennsylvania, and even his victory in Michigan did not compensate for his loss of Oregon to Reagan. Lacking adequate funds to continue to wage an active campaign, Bush wisely decided to surrender, guaranteeing the convention's anointment of Reagan. Only one issue remained unresolved: Who would Reagan choose to be his vice presidential running mate?

The media speculated endlessly on those considered eligible, principally Bush, Baker, and Rumsfeld, as well as Reagan's closest friend in Congress, Senator Paul Laxalt of Nevada. Surprisingly, it appeared that Reagan was giving serious thought to asking Gerald Ford to run with him.[9] His interest in the former president reflected his belief that the choice would encourage many moderates, Republicans and Democrats, to vote for him. Unenthusiastic about Bush, whose testy performance in New Hampshire had not greatly impressed him, the Ford possibility remained a live one until, in a televised interview with Walter Cronkite on CBS News, Ford insisted he "would not go to Washington. . . and be a figurehead Vice President."[10] Cronkite, replying, asked whether Ford was thinking of "something like a co-presidency" and heard him say: "That's something Governor Reagan really ought to consider." Those words told everyone in the Reagan camp that the dream team was impossible, and they felt great relief when Ford, pressed for a final decision, declined the offer. Reagan, free to offer the vice presidency to anyone, chose Bush, the only serious contender in the primaries; he was not greatly surprised when he accepted.[11]

Had this been the hoped-for Texas scenario from the beginning? Did both Bush and Baker understand very early that it would be virtually impossible to defeat Reagan, to take the nomination away from him, and was their strategy calculated to guarantee both a prominent place in his administration? While it would be difficult to prove such political astuteness, Bush showed the political talents as vice president he had carefully nurtured when he held lesser posts under Nixon and Ford—at once servile, deferential, and anxious to please.

While not a member of the original White House troika that included James Baker, Edwin Meese, and Michael Deaver—the men who micromanaged the president's daily life in his first term, guaranteeing against egregious errors being made—Bush proved less impetuous than Haig, the secretary of state, knowing better than to pretend he was in charge when a would-be assassin's bullet felled the president and for a moment seemed to threaten his life. Later, at the time of Irangate, as the individual who stood most to gain from a successful impeachment of the president, it was incumbent he say and do nothing that would give the media any hint of his knowledge of the true situation. Indeed, discretion, Bush's most distinctive political trait, endeared him to Reagan and explained his active support of the vice president's campaign to succeed him in 1988.

Whatever misgivings Dwight Eisenhower may have had of Richard Nixon, Reagan felt none about Bush, whose attacks on Michael Dukakis, his Democratic opponent in 1988, seemed entirely acceptable, in no way transgressing normal campaign practices. While Reagan himself might have employed a somewhat lighter touch in belittling Dukakis, the diminutive Greek American Massachusetts governor, Bush, the old-money Yankee, born to the Republican purple, saw no need to conceal his contempt for the son of recent European immigrants. Nor did he disdain to exploit the Willie Horton case that allowed a black first-degree murderer to be granted a weekend furlough, in accordance with Massachusetts state penal practice, who then proceeded to commit a stabbing and a rape.[12]

Bush's feigned anger with the permissiveness of a state and a candidate too greatly steeped in an outmoded liberalism showed him a worthy acolyte of his principal political tutor. How much these and comparable attacks accounted

for Bush's substantial victory in 1988, it is impossible to know, but his victory
was decisive; 49 million votes for Bush as against 42 million for Dukakis. The
regard the president felt for his vice president may be suggested by the message
he left in the Oval Office on a printed pad that bore the ineffable heading
"Don't Let the Turkeys Get You Down." Reagan wrote, "Dear George, You'll
have moments when you want to use this particular stationery. Well, go for it.
George, I treasure the memories we share and wish you all the very best. You'll
be in my prayers. God bless you and Barbara. I'll miss our Thursday lunches.
Ron."13

Only in the last decade, in stories told by Bush's biographers but also by Reagan's, has this tale of mutual regard begun to lose some of its credibility.
Michael Beschloss and Strobe Talbott, in *At the Highest Levels,* a study of the
Bush presidency published in 1993, opened with a story that could only have
originated with Mikhail Gorbachev.14 The Soviet president, driving with Bush
to the airport on December 10, 1987, after his highly successful first visit to the
United States, was said to have been told by the vice president that "he had
something on his mind and would prefer that Gorbachev never publicize what
he was about to say." According to the authors, Bush's words were: "There's a
good chance that I'm going to win the presidential election next year. Dole
looks pretty dangerous right now, but I think I'll get the Republican nomination. If I'm elected—and I think I will be—you should understand that I want
to improve our relations."15 While there was nothing in that remark that would
not bear publication, his additional comments were much more incendiary. If
the authors can be trusted, and there is no reason to doubt them, Bush claimed

> that during his seven years as Ronald Reagan's vice president, he had to keep his
> moderate views to himself. He explained that Reagan was surrounded by 'mar-
> ginal intellectual thugs' who would be delighted to seize on any evidence that the
> vice president was a closet liberal. Therefore, during the 1988 campaign, he
> would have to do and say many things to get elected. Mr. Gorbachev should ig-
> nore them.16

According to the authors, "Gorbachev said that he understood" and, continuing in the same vein, "recalled this conversation as the 'most important
Bush and I ever had.'" The final gloss on the conversation included the words,
"Over the next four years, each time the Soviet leader's close aides complained
that Bush was pandering to Republican conservatives, Gorbachev reminded
them of their talk in the limousine, saying, 'Don't worry. His heart is in the
right place.'"17

Who were the marginal intellectual thugs who surrounded the president? If
they existed, and if the vice president had reason to fear them, what did this
prevent him from saying or doing? Did that situation, so fraught with danger,

explain his almost perpetual silences in Cabinet and National Security Council meetings? Did he communicate anything to the president in their private Thursday lunches that contradicted what the intellectual thugs were telling him? These were not questions Beschloss and Talbott chose to pursue in speaking with Bush or others who served him during his term as President. Nor, for that matter, did Edmund Morris in his more controversial biography of Reagan, *Dutch,* published in 1999, ask the kinds of probing questions about relations in the Reagan crowd that would have illuminated the tensions in that diverse and servile company. Yet a handful of paragraphs in the Morris biography, especially those that reported on a conversation he had with the president-elect and his wife on Christmas Eve 1988, told a great deal of what Bush felt when finally liberated of the need to defer to his "master."

Morris wrote: "I go round to the president-elect's house to interview him. Barbara sits in, knitting dangerously *a la* Madame Defarge. They clearly have something to get off their collective chest about their eight years as 'the help,' but Bush's preppy politeness keeps moderating her fury." Capturing what may best be described as Bushspeak, Morris heard the president-elect say: "Gotta tellya, I really love that guy, he's such a terrific fellow. Only one thing kinda bothered me, whichistersay, just never been able to understand—guy never seemed to *need* anybody. Except Nancy, says BB, needles *accelerando.*" Morris then asked another question, "Anything else about the president bother you?" To which Bush replied: "Listen, he was a prince of a feller. I'd never say anything against him. Nancy neither." Morris noted a pause, with the Bushes exchanging glances, and then heard him say: "Well, something. . . I kinda wished they'd shown—y'know, a little appreciation. Didn't seem to want us upstairs in the White House."[18]

Continuing in this vein, Morris quoted Barbara Bush as saying: "We would always thank them for their gifts," to which her husband replied: "Guess they didn't always thank us. Gave him, of such a *neat* present for his seventy-fifth birthday, took a whole lot of trouble customizing it to the right measurements, borrowed his boots so it would stand up real pretty. . . ." Morris, bewildered, heard Bush say, "Lemme show you. We had a duplicate made. He escorts me to a bathroom upstairs, outside of which stands the single most terrifying piece of kitsch I have ever seen. It would not be out of place at Auschwitz. There, standing and booted, are *Dutch's feet and lower legs,* supporting, like some dwarfish torso, an embroidered seat with the presidential seal *au centre.* Reflecting on it, Morris could only add: "While I marvel, as so often before, at the aesthetic perversity of well-born WASPS, Bush shakes his head, and says in the same hurt voice, 'Not a word of thanks.'"

This was not the George Bush who less than a month later took the oath of office as president and spoke in ways that honored the prince of a feller who sat behind him. In words that might have been uttered by Reagan, penned by

Peggy Noonan, who had helped craft Reagan's farewell address, Bush quoted an unnamed saint, saying: "I take as my guide the hope of a saint: In crucial things, unity—in important things, diversity—in all things, generosity."[19] The speech, sparing in detail of any projected domestic or foreign policy initiatives, represented the totalitarian era as a thing of the past, "its old ideas blown away like leaves from an ancient, lifeless tree."

The world's destiny, Bush told the millions who heard him on television, was one of "free markets, free speech, free elections and the exercise of free will unhampered by the state." Faithful to all the old Reagan slogans, Bush spoke of a country, "proud, free, decent, and civil," that understood why material goods were of small account. Children, he said, needed to be taught "what it means to be a loyal friend, a loving parent, a citizen who leaves his home, his neighborhood and town better than he found it." Because America was never great except when committed to high moral principle, he urged that it "make kinder the face of the nation and gentler the face of the world." The modern scourges—homelessness, drug addiction, and crime—would not be overcome by the old-fashioned remedies. Taking another leaf from his master's book, he said: "The old solution, the old way, was to think that public money alone could end these problems. But we have learned that is not so. And in any case, our funds are low: We have a deficit to bring down. We have more will than wallet: but will is what we need."[20] Describing the new activism he advocated, he spoke of "harnessing the unused talent of the elderly and the unfocused energy of the young" to create "a thousand points of light" that would fully engage the community organizations of the country. "Duty, sacrifice, commitment, and a patriotism that finds its expression in taking part and pitching in" was what America was all about.[21] The speech might have been delivered by Reagan; intended not to spell out a program, even less to give a lead to Congress, it was an inspirational address, meant to be uplifting. Somehow, in Bush's mouth it sounded stilted and unconvincing, lacking the conviction it would have had if given by his more accomplished predecessor.

Bush won the presidency with the promise to remain faithful to Reagan's legacy. In his mind, that committed him to four principles: levy no new taxes; reduce the size of government; maintain the country's defenses; uphold family values. Loyal always to Nancy Reagan, whom he courted as assiduously as her husband, and knowing her principal cause was drug abuse, he moved quickly to establish in the White House an office to develop and supervise a national drug control policy. January 20, the day of his inaugural, declared a National Day of Prayer, allowed religion and patriotism to become the twin icons of a revitalized Americanism.

His Cabinet appointments, in no instance surprising, included his most intimate friend, James Baker, as secretary of state; another f.o.g., "friend of George," Nicholas Brady, a Wall Street banker, installed to head the Treasury in late 1988 at Bush's urging, was retained, as were Richard Thornburgh, attorney general, and Lauro Cavazos, secretary of education, others Bush had pressed on Reagan during his last months in office. To head the Department of Defense, he hoped to appoint former Senator John Tower of Texas, so helpful to Reagan during the Irangate crisis, but the Senate, made aware during the confirmation hearings of the extent of Tower's drinking and womanizing, refused to accept him.[22] No previous president had been comparably rebuffed during his first months in office in seeking a specific individual to occupy a high Cabinet position, but Bush had no recourse but to appoint another in his place.

His choice fell on Richard Cheney, Ford's former chief of staff, launching the Wyoming member of Congress on the career that would eventually give him the vice presidency in 2001. The most important appointment, though little remarked on by the media, was General Brent Scowcroft as national security adviser. Scowcroft, who had served as Kissinger's deputy and taken his place when Ford relieved him of his White House post, was one of the few in the Bush entourage who could claim major foreign policy experience.[23] In the first months of the new Bush administration, when Gorbachev experienced growing difficulties at home, the president might have been tempted to carry out his limousine promise to improve U.S.-Soviet relations, but they remained so static that Gorbachev felt compelled to complain to Margaret Thatcher when he visited her in London of the president's "pause," which he found "intolerable."[24]

In Washington, disagreement over how secure Gorbachev was and whether glasnost and perestroika had fundamentally changed the Soviet state inhibited the administration from taking bold initiatives. The words the Soviet leader used in his speech to the United Nations during his visit in the last days of the Reagan administration were in effect ignored. In New York, Gorbachev had announced dramatic unilateral military cuts, 500,000 men and 10,000 tanks, including half the Soviet tanks that confronted NATO, promising also a reorganization of the Soviet forces in Central Europe so that they might be used only for defensive purposes. To reassure China, he pledged the withdrawal of the major portion of Soviet troops in Mongolia, hoping the United States and Europe would take note of these unilateral moves, and make comparable reductions in their forces.

In fact, there was little incentive to place much confidence in Gorbachev as long as many in Washington during the first months of the Bush administration believed that his hold on power was precarious. The American news media, increasingly critical of Gorbachev, dwelled on the horrors of the nationalist demonstration in Georgia that had ended with Soviet soldiers killing at least twenty demonstrators in Tbilisi. The massacre of June 1989 at Tiananmen Square in Beijing, coinciding with Gorbachev's arrival in China, the first visit of a Soviet leader to Communist China in thirty years, served only to raise further doubts about the likely political evolution of these two troubled Communist societies. Though the president himself remained firmly committed to Gorbachev, believing as he insisted in a speech at Texas A&M that he wished to move "beyond containment," that sentiment failed to resonate for many of his associates.[25]

The summer and fall of 1989 saw the virtual disintegration of Soviet influence in Central and Eastern Europe, with the Communist regimes collapsing in Warsaw, Budapest, and Prague, and the Baltic republics declaring their independence from the Soviet Union. In October, more than 100,000 demonstrators marched through the streets of Leipzig in East Germany, and on November 9 East Germans began to dismantle the Berlin Wall. This—certainly the most momentous event in the first year of the Bush administration—seemed to mark the end of the era that had its origins in World War II.

While Bush and Baker revelled in these extraordinary and largely unanticipated events, neither knew how to exploit them. In the months that followed, Baker and his opposite number in Moscow, Eduard Shevardnadze, met frequently, looking to advance the START negotiations to limit strategic long-range nuclear systems, initially proposed during Gorbachev's visit to Washington in the last months of the Reagan administration. Events were moving rapidly, and some of Bush's principal colleagues, including Vice President Dan Quayle, worried that the secretary of state might be acting too precipitously, accepting Gorbachev's protestations of friendship when the evidence remained inconclusive.[26] All the Baker talk of partnership with the Soviet Union had little resonance for Quayle, who in a TV interview raised the question whether Gorbachev was not a "master of public relations," whether perestroika was not simply a form of Leninism. Quayle reminded his audience that the Soviets were "still making mischief" in Afghanistan, North Korea, Cambodia, and Central America, and while Scowcroft did not go that far, he, too, worried that the Soviets were sending mixed signals on START and asked whether it was not too early to say that real progress was being made, whether Gorbachev and Shevardnadze might not simply be "reshuffling the chairs on the *Titanic*."[27]

The secretary of state, offended by the vice president's interventions, persuaded officials in the State Department to express their displeasure with this internal bickering, and the president, in good Reagan fashion, acted as if he was above the fray, seemingly interested only in meeting with Gorbachev at a summit conference. That event finally took place in December 1989 on ships outside Malta in the midst of a terrible winter storm that captured the attention of the media much more than the specific proposals each brought to the table. Indeed, the events of that December, including the execution by a mob of the most ruthless of the Communist leaders, Nicolae Ceauşescu of Romania, on

Chrismas Day, and the election of Václav Havel to the presidency of the Czech parliament, suggested that the events of 1989 were irreversible, that the Cold War was indeed over.

By the time Bush and Gorbachev met for their second summit in Washington on May 30, 1990, certain facts could no longer be disguised: The Soviet empire had disintegrated, not because of specific U.S. policies but because the peoples of the Communist bloc in Europe were in full rebellion against the Soviet Union. Gorbachev, however unwittingly, by perestroika had in effect encouraged rebellion, and though many in Europe and the United States honored him for his role within the Soviet Union, he was increasingly challenged by a formidable rival, Boris Yeltsin.[28] Given Gorbachev's weakness at home, it was impossible for him to resist what the president and the secretary of state both knew to be the firm resolve of German chancellor Helmut Kohl—not only to unify Germany but to insist that the Soviet Union accept for the new Germany to retain its membership in NATO.[29]

While both the British and the French had serious initial reservations about German unification as conceived by Kohl, the formula developed principally by the secretary of state and his associates in the State Department could not be long resisted; it was too hazardous for either the United Kingdom or France to oppose a solution that commended itself both to the Germans and the Americans. Whether the accomplishment merited the accolade Philip Bobbitt in his book, *The Shield of Achilles*, gave Baker and his team is debatable; to compare this with "Acheson's skilful creation of NATO and the Marshall Plan," as Bobbitt did, was almost certainly an exaggeration, but no one could deny that the resolution of the German question figured as one of the significant foreign policy accomplishments of the Bush administration.[30]

In *A World Transformed*, the 1998 book jointly written by Bush and Scowcroft, the latter told of the decision reached early in the administration that "a full-blown NSC gathering was not always the place for a no-holds-barred discussion among the President's top advisers." As Scowcroft explained, "Some might be inhibited from expressing themselves frankly with staff present and the constant possibility of leaks."[31] He believed that a small group, meeting informally in the Oval Office, preceding the meetings of the NSC would be desirable; and the only members would be the vice president, the secretary of state, the secretary of defense, the director of the CIA, the deputy secretary of state, Lawrence Eagleburger, the president's chief of staff, John Sununu, and himself. Scowcroft wrote:

The President liked the suggestion, and it worked. This marked the beginning of a new pattern for top-level meetings (the 'core group') during the rest of the Administration. While we continued to hold formal NSC meetings, the informal group became the rule rather than the exception for practical decision-making.[32]

Seven men became the president's principal foreign policy advisers; the only two highly qualified among them, Scowcroft and Eagleburger, were individuals Kissinger had brought into the White House who had risen because of his influence. What Quayle and Sununu contributed to these discussions Bush never revealed, but he spoke highly of them, saying, "Both were bright and very interested in arms control, and over the years their advice would prove extraordinarily helpful." It would be interesting to know what either contributed, especially in respect to arms control, a highly technical subject, but the president seemed happy to issue the accolade.

The decisions reached in improving U.S.-Soviet relations, including those that related to the reduction of nuclear weapons stockpiles, the prohibition of the further production of chemical weapons, and, most important for the Soviet Union, the normalizing of trade relations, were all vital, clearly the accomplishments of the president and his secretary of state, but none produced great excitement in the country. After decades of the Cold War, when no progress with the Soviet Union seemed possible, the new thaw seemed almost to obliterate all memory of earlier days. So, when at the Conference on Security and Cooperation in Europe, meeting in Copenhagen in the spring of 1990, Shevardnadze surprised the other foreign ministers with his startling announcement that the Soviets were prepared unilaterally to remove all their tactical nuclear weapons from Europe, this seemed of a piece with all that had been going on in the Soviet Union for almost a year. Days later, the Warsaw Pact members, meeting in Moscow, announced they no longer viewed the West as an ideological enemy, and NATO's leaders, meeting in London, reciprocated with their London Declaration, proposing that the Warsaw Pact and NATO issue a joint statement declaring the end of their adversarial relationship.[33] President Gorbachev and the other Warsaw Pact leaders were invited to visit NATO headquarters in Brussels to "establish regular diplomatic liaison with NATO." The Cold War had passed into history, or so at least it seemed. Gorbachev, a great favorite in the United States, received an astonishing 73 percent American approval rate in the weeks before his arrival for the Washington summit, but there was no evidence to suggest that very many outside the administration understood the precariousness of his political situation in the Soviet Union.

The media reported Yeltsin's election as president of the Russian parliament days before the summit meeting, but that development sounded no alarm in the White House. Nor, for that matter, did the president seem excessively disconcerted when the CIA, soon after the Washington meeting, gave its most pessimistic forecast about Gorbachev's prospects for survival. Its report read: "President Gorbachev is losing control of the political process. . . . The continuing drift toward crisis could produce growing pressure for traditionalist elements for an attempt to reimpose authoritarian controls. They could conspire to take action on their own, moving against Gorbachev in the process."[34] In early July, a comparable warning, uttered by Yeltsin at the meeting of the Twenty-Eighth Congress of the Soviet Communist Party, led him to speak of the hard-line forces on the offensive and of Gorbachev's failure to neutralize them. When he later stormed out of the hall, announcing his resignation from the party, the news seemed scarcely to resonate for George Bush.[35] Summer had come to Washington, and no threatening clouds appeared on the horizon—none comparable to those that had once existed. Indeed, even after the CIA reported on July 17 that a crisis appeared to be developing in the Middle East, with some 30,000 Iraqi soldiers moving toward the Kuwaiti border, and later reports gave more specific detail on the character of Saddam Hussein's war preparations, the president remained sanguine.

Bush was accustomed to telephoning friendly heads of state, imagining them more reliable than the information passed on by the CIA. In one such conversation, President Mubarak of Egypt assured him that Saddam was bluffing; there was no prospect of his invading Kuwait. King Hussein of Jordan told him the same.[36] Still, thought had to be given to the possibility that war might break out, and on August 1 Robert Gates, the CIA director, brought the president a draft, approved by his senior advisers, that set out U.S. aims in the event of a war in the Persian Gulf. According to Gates, it omitted any mention of a regime change in Iraq because "we weren't sure we could bring it about."

Gates thought it a historic document, but the president gave scant attention to it. In an interview Gates gave years later, he reported that "Bush glanced at it and signed it without comment."[37] Later that evening, Scowcroft arrived with the news that Iraqi troops had crossed the border into Kuwait. Had the president seriously considered this threat?[38] Had he realized that Iraq, by the eight-year war it had waged with Iran, had become the most formidable military power in the Gulf? Despite intelligence reports that told of Saddam's brutal repression of all dissent within his country and a policy that allowed him to support terrorism abroad, the administration showed little alarm. Even Saddam's incendiary speech of April 1, 1990, in which he posed as the leader of the Arab world and boasted of his stockpile of chemical weapons, warning that "we will make the fire eat up half of Israel if it tries to do anything against Iraq," the president managed only to say that the statements were "bad," and that he had urged Iraq never to use chemical weapons.[39] In his words, "I don't think it helps peace in the Middle East."

While intelligence reports suggested that Iraq possessed a missile capacity capable of reaching Tel Aviv, the president, his national security adviser, and the director of the CIA all believed that Iraq was weaker than its despotic ruler pretended and that his threats need not be taken too seriously.[40] All were proved wrong on August 1. On the following day, the president seemed uncertain what the crisis would require the United States to do. In his first words to reporters, he announced: "We're not discussing intervention," and nothing suggested that the National Security Council, meeting that morning, had recommended so drastic a course of action. Later that day, flying to Aspen, Colorado, where he and Margaret Thatcher were scheduled to give speeches, the president heard her say that any policy of appeasement would have dire consequences. While one of her advisers suggested "the Prime Minister performed a successful backbone transplant," the president never thought to mention her influence at all.[41] Still, when he returned to Washington, he showed a resolve scarcely apparent just a few hours earlier. In the NSC meeting on August 3, Bush learned from the CIA that the Iraqi leader intended to become an Arab superpower; it would take the Iraqi forces only three days to move from Kuwait to Riyadh in Saudi Arabia, and his victory there would make him the virtual dictator of all the oil in the Gulf.[42]

Scowcroft, according to evidence provided by Christopher Andrew in *For the President's Eyes Only*, argued for a two-track policy, that the "United States make clear that it was prepared to use force to stop Iraqi aggression," and to "embark also on a covert operation to overthrow Saddam."[43] According to Andrew, "Bush ordered the CIA to begin immediate planning for covert action to destabilize the Iraqi regime, strangle its economy, provide support for Saddam's opponents inside and outside Iraq, and identify alternative leaders."[44] Meeting with reporters after a weekend of conferences at Camp David, the president announced: "This will not stand, this aggression against Kuwait." Some of his closest advisers, including General Colin Powell, now chairman of the Joint Chiefs of Staff, were surprised by his sudden vehemence; there had been no anticipation of such resolve in the first days. Bush represented Saddam as the new Hitler; in his own mind, he was the new Churchill.[45]

The first priority was to persuade King Fahd of Saudi Arabia that his country was in imminent danger, a task assigned to Cheney, the secretary of defense, who rushed to Riyadh to show aerial photographs to persuade the king that Iraqi troops were indeed massed on his border, preparing to attack.[46] It was imperative for the king to allow U.S. troops to be airlifted to Saudi Arabia to prepare the country's defenses, the first requirement for the operation soon to be designated DESERT SHIELD. A no less important achievement, certainly, followed Bush's meeting with Gorbachev in Helsinki on September 8–9 when Iraq's longtime Soviet ally accepted the proposition that Saddam had illegally invaded Kuwait and joined the president in demanding an immediate and unconditional withdrawal.[47] Baker, vastly encouraged by this happy Gorbachev compliance, later spoke of the Soviets as "very reliable partners." The Americans gave no special reward to Gorbachev for his condemnation of the Iraqis; the communiqué that followed the Bush-Gorbachev summit simply took note of the Soviet interest in Arab-Israeli peace efforts and suggested that the Soviet Union would be invited to participate in any international negotiations on the subject.[48]

By late October, Bush, preparing to activate the National Guard and the Army Reserve, appeared more determined than ever, certain his actions would secure him the place in history that other opponents of aggression by dictators had laid claim to. Baker began the difficult task of negotiating what some soon described as the greatest alliance in history, presumably greater than the one that had defeated the Nazis in World War II. Hyperbole became the order of the day, and Baker, as aware as the president of the need for financial support, told King Fahd that the United States expected Saudi Arabia to contribute funds to help defray the huge costs of its intended military mobilization.

The Saudi kingdom, once so generous in helping finance Iraq's war with Iran, was solicited to help an American president whose budgetary problems were also severe. Bush had no intention of meeting the exceptional expenses incurred by his decision to defend the Saudis with the imposition of new taxes on an already burdened American public. Nor would he consider the World War II expedient of borrowing to meet the essential costs of the military deployment of large forces. The king agreed to provide $500 million a month to help support the U.S. military engagement in the Gulf, and Baker received a further promise of financial help from the Kuwaitis.[49] Japan, dependent on Gulf oil, was expected to make an equally generous contribution, and when it chose to approve a sum substantially below what many had hoped for, Congress expressed dismay, scarcely more impressed by Germany's paltry contribution, a mere $2 billion. The excuse Germany offered—that it was making substantial contributions to the rehabilitation of the East European economies and could afford no larger gift—seemed unconvincing to those who believed that if the United States stood ready to sacrifice its youth, its allies ought to be willing to donate funds to the cause of freedom. War rhetoric took hold, carefully orchestrated by a very accomplished, media-conscious administration.

The president, appearing before a joint session of Congress on September 11, promised that "Saddam Hussein will fall."[50] This seemed to go considerably beyond earlier pledges that emphasized only America's determination that Iraq leave Kuwait. Bush, using the occasion to speak as Reagan might have done, saw a new partnership of nations emerging, a new world in the making. In his words, "Out of these troubled times. . . a new world order can emerge: a new era, freer from the threat of terror, stronger in the pursuit of justice, and more secure in the quest for peace. An era in which the nations of the world, East and West, North and South, can prosper and live in harmony." This, he told Congress, was a vision he shared with President Gorbachev, both having the same objective: "Iraq must withdraw from Kuwait completely, immediately, and without condition."[51]

A few days later, in New York, at the United Nations, Shevardnadze confirmed what the president had said: The Soviet Union would support UNapproved military action against Iraq. The UN Security Council, by a vote of 14–1, voted to extend the existing embargo of Iraq to include all airborne traffic.[52] Meanwhile, Great Britain and France, actively solicited by the president to help, indicated they would send troops and military equipment to Saudi Arabia to assist in any military operation.[53] Bush, addressing the UN General Assembly, looking for additional Arab support, implied that the Iraqi pullout from Kuwait might provide the opportunity "to settle conflicts that divide the Arabs from Israel."[54] A very wide coalition was being fashioned, and the president and his trusted secretary of state took charge as its principal architects.

In these circumstances, the president might have expected Congress to support him for what he proposed to do in Iraq, but many Democrats, thinking back always to Vietnam, were unprepared to give him what they saw as a blank check to do whatever he thought necessary in a war that could result in tens of thousands of American casualties.[55] Their confidence in the president, never very great, had been compromised further by the continuing fallout stemming from the failure of some 722 savings and loan associations, threatened with imminent collapse.[56] By the terms of the Financial Institutions Reform, Recovery, and Enforcement Act, passed the previous August, Congress had agreed to appropriate an amount not to exceed $120 billion to rescue those institutions, and when it became apparent that the federal government's deficit, as recommended by the Bureau of the Budget for the coming year, would be greatly exceeded by these additional expenses, the Democrats in Congress pressed the president to abandon his pledge never to raise taxes.

The alternative, they feared, would be a major recession, and this worried them almost as much as the imminent military action against Iraq. Bush, using language that carefully avoided the terrible term *tax hikes,* acknowledged the seriousness of the country's financial situation and agreed, in principle at least, to a tax increase.[57] The congressional 1990 off-year elections suggested that his decision had compromised his reputation for truth-telling; Republicans attributed their loss of nine seats in the House to his having reneged on his pledge never to raise taxes.[58]

The president's reaction to all this, as rendered in *A World Transformed,* written jointly with Brent Scowcroft, was that the "budget battle dominated everything, dividing the Congress and the Administration, increasing tensions and unpleasantness."[59] As he explained, when he said in what he now chose to describe as convention rhetoric—"Read my lips, no new taxes"—he had failed to anticipate the 1990 situation. Given the mood of Congress in the last days before it recessed for the off-year elections, he appeared to have broken his word, especially to those on the Republican right, but he saw his choice as a "compromise on taxes or literally to shut down the government." In that situation, he did what Reagan had also been compelled to do, in his case having to "raise revenues many times." Acknowledging that "Read my lips" was "rhetorical overkill," that "when push came to shove and our troops were moving overseas, we needed a fully functioning government." It was imperative that he "hammer out a compromise to keep the government open." For that compromise, he wrote, "I paid a terrible price."[60]

Iraq seemed almost to provide a release from these domestic difficulties. In late November, the UN Security Council gave Saddam Hussein a January 15 deadline to withdraw all his forces from Kuwait, and the president indicated he would send his secretary of state to Baghdad to meet with the Iraqi president at any time between December 15 and January 15 to discuss the issue, making it clear that "I am not suggesting discussions that will result in anything less than Iraq's complete withdrawal from Kuwait, restoration of Kuwait's legitimate government, and freedom for all the hostages."[61] In his news conference, he made it clear that "should military action be required, this will not be another Vietnam."[62]

A debate raged in Congress on whether to vote affirmatively on the president's request for a resolution to support his planned intervention. Edward Kennedy feared that another blank check, comparable to the Tonkin Gulf Resolution, was being asked for, and only after days of debate did the Senate vote 52–42 to sanction military operations; in the House, the vote approving the administration's proposed intervention was more emphatic, 250–83. In a declaration signed by the president on January 14, the existence of "Iraq's conventional, chemical, biological, and nuclear weapons and ballistic missile programs" were cited as "a grave threat to world peace."[63]

With United Nations and congressional support, the president had the authority he required to begin bombing Baghdad in the early hours of January 16, 1991. Bush, speaking to the nation, made it clear he would never appease Saddam as others had once appeased Hitler. The initial attack came from the air, from bombers and missiles launched from unidentified bases and ships. While Saddam announced the start of the "mother of all battles," and called the president a "hypocritical criminal," the president remained calm, with Cheney, his secretary of defense, warning the nation that the war "is likely to run for a long period of time."[64] Given the disparity between the U.S. forces and those available to Iraq, this seemed unlikely, but the administration recognized the importance of persuading the public that the operation would be immensely hazardous, but that victory was certain.

Although the attacking forces were predominantly American, a great effort was made to demonstrate that this was a Coalition war, with British Tornados, Saudi F-15s, and Kuwaiti bombers all prominently featured. The Dow Jones, with its dramatic rise of 114 points, and the fall in oil prices to $10 a barrel registered what all businessmen knew to be true: This was going to be neither a long nor a difficult war. While the SCUD missile attacks on Israel gave reason for concern, the nation remained sanguine, watching the war on its TV screens, made memorable for the painful display by the Iraqis of seven Coalation airmen shot down, three Americans, two Britons, a Kuwaiti, and an Italian.

The *New York Times,* though congratulating the administration on its remarkable air victories, expected the war would never be won by bombing alone and that U.S. infantry would be obliged to meet the awesome Republican Guards, said to be one of the great fighting forces in the world. While television took on the character of a visual tabloid, emphasizing sentimental tales that made the war seem something of a soap opera, the more responsible press, as exemplified by the *New York Times* and its principal Washington correspondent, James Reston, dwelled on the dangers of a land offensive; it was better to go after Saddam himself, using the smart bombs known to be available to find and destroy the tyrant.[65]

Reston, praising the "courage of patience" that Dwight Eisenhower had always displayed, warned Bush against those in the Army and the Marines, seeking glory comparable to that already claimed by the Air Force and the Navy, begging the president to resist their pressures. It was not in the U.S. interest, he wrote, to make Iraq a wasteland, open to "Iran's and Syria's tender mercies."[66] With American flags and yellow ribbons displayed everywhere, tangible proof of the nation's support of its courageous president, the occasional TV images of antiwar protests in Germany or elsewhere counted for very little.

More disconcerting, certainly, was the *New York Times* revelation that while blacks constituted only one in eight in the nation, they figured as one in four among those sent to fight in the Gulf War.[67] Its front-page story, headlined "Blacks Wary of Their Big Role as Troops," spoke of the "deep well of resentment and anger in some blacks who fear that their community will pay disproportionately for a war that many of them do not support."[68] With the chairman of the Joint Chiefs of Staff being black, the administration felt it had a compelling answer to the son of the assassinated Reverend Martin Luther King Jr., who urged black soldiers not to fight, arguing that "every black soldier ought to say: 'You all do what you want to. I'm not going to fight. This is not my war.'"[69]

In his State of the Union message, delivered on January 29, Bush pressed the Munich analogy. In his words, "Together we have resisted the trap of appeasement, cynicism and isolation that gives temptation to tyrants." A nation that had "done the hard work of freedom" was prepared to "lead the world in facing down a threat to decency and humanity." The "indomitable" American character could be relied on to overcome all difficulties, at home and abroad.[70] On February 24, the ground offensive began and proved to be a walkover, but this could never be admitted by the administration. Herbert Parmet, Bush's principal biographer, sought to explain why Americans had so greatly overestimated Iraq's military capabilities, and wrote:

They [the Iraqis] had the largest army in the Gulf, the fourth strongest in the world. Saddam, in the past, had shown no hesitation about going to extremes. His Republican Guard operated from the rear, where they stood ready to kill those who refused to advance into enemy fire. To a degree that was not appreciated until later, however, they were being salvaged, moved to the north, even beyond Baghdad, together with some of the best T-72 tanks.[71]

Four days later, after the Iraqis were ousted from Kuwait, Bush, consulting with General Powell, agreed the time had come to declare victory, to end a war the administration had never imagined would lead to many American casualties. As the president acknowledged in *A World Transformed,* the military casualty estimates were always "below 2,000," far from the 30,000 predicted by Robert McNamara and the 50,000 prophesied by George McGovern.[72]

Because the decision to stop the war was later questioned, General Powell, in his autobiography, *My American Journey,* defended the advice he tendered to the president. Quoting General Norman Schwarzkopf, the commanding general on the ground, he emphasized Schwarzkopf's view, as expressed in his book, *It Doesn't Take a Hero:*

My gut reaction was that a quick cease-fire would save lives. If we continued to attack through Thursday, more of our troops would get killed, probably not many, but some. What was more, we'd accomplished our mission: I'd just finished telling the American people that there wasn't enough left of Iraq's army for it to be a regional military threat. . . . we'd kicked this guy's butt, leaving no doubt in anybody's mind that we'd won decisively, and we'd done it with very few casualties. Why not end it? Why get somebody else killed tomorrow? That made up my mind.[73]

Powell found the argument convincing, saying: "Schwarzkopf was absolutely right. Yet, it is still hard to drive a stake through charges that the job was left unfinished," and he thought it important to add: "While the belief that Saddam pulled off some sort of Dunkirk at the end of Desert Storm may have a superficial attraction, I want to cut it off and kill it once and for all."[74]

The Americans had defeated the Iraqi army, leaving it less than half of what it had been, and had fulfilled all the objectives set by the United Nations. Why, then, Powell wrote, "Didn't we push on to Baghdad once we had Saddam on the run? Why didn't we finish him off? Or, to put it another way, why didn't we move the goalposts?" Answering his own questions, he added, "What tends to be forgotten is that while the United States led the way, we were heading an *international* coalition carrying out a clearly defined UN mission. That mission was accomplished."[75] Powell continued with two other defenses, explaining that the Arab states, as members of the Coalition, had no wish to see Iraq dismembered into separate Sunni, Shia, and Kurdish political entities. And then, in a remarkable paragraph, possibly written by Joseph Persico, his coauthor, the general added,

> Of course, we would have loved to see Saddam overthrown by his own people for the death and destruction he had brought down on them. But that did not happen. And the President's demonizing of Saddam as the devil incarnate did not help the public understand why he was allowed to stay in power. It is naïve, however, to think that if Saddam had fallen, he would necessarily have been replaced by a Jeffersonian in some sort of desert democracy where people read *The Federalist Papers* along with the Koran. Quite possibly, we would have wound up with a Saddam by another name.[76]

Powell mentioned the accolade accorded DESERT STORM by John Keegan, "probably the world's foremost contemporary historian," who wrote: "The Gulf War, whatever it is now fashionable to say, was a triumph of incisive planning and almost faultless execution." It fulfilled the highest purpose of military action: "the use of force in the cause of order."[77] In *Time*, Hugh Sidey wrote even more extravagantly of what President Bush had achieved, and Powell found his view in no way exaggerated; in Sidey's words, "Never before has an American President stood so grandly astride this capacious world as George Bush does these days. Historians scratched their heads . . . and looked for something comparable. There was nothing."[78] Seven months after the end of the war, Powell noted, the president's approval rating stood at 66 percent. Could there be better proof of his success?[79] After the victory parades described by Powell, with the Kurdish and Sunni massacres left unmentioned, later to figure prominently in all accounts that made the U.S. triumphs seem less untarnished, the president appeared before Congress to celebrate the nation's victory.

In his March 6, 1991, speech, he heralded the defeat of "the darker side of human nature" and promised to defend the nation's vital interests in the Gulf, giving that "special vigilance" to Iraq that the world's concern with the need to "control the proliferation of weapons of mass destruction and the missiles used to deliver them" clearly required.[80] He hoped Israel and the Arab states, so recently allied against a common enemy, would seek peace, understanding the need for compromise.[81] Calling for a new world order, one faithful to Churchill's belief in the "principles of justice and fair play" to "protect the weak against the strong," he saw the possibility of the United Nations, finally liberated from the Cold War stalemate, fulfilling the historic mission of its founders, to guarantee perpetual peace. Of the United States, "transformed" by its victory, using words that again might have been uttered by Reagan, Bush said: "We hear so often about our young people in turmoil; how our children fall short; how our schools fail us; how American products and American workers are second-class. Well, don't you believe it. The America we saw in Desert Storm was first-class talent."

That the president, admired and lauded, should have been unable to maintain his popularity in the long period that followed as he prepared to beat whoever the Democrats nominated was most often explained by two phenomena: his egregious mistake in accepting a tax hike, violating his pledge never to do so; and the remarkable gifts of Bill Clinton, the Arkansas governor, who won the Democratic Party nomination easily and proved a more formidable campaigner than anyone had imagined. Both factors, while incontestably important, need to be seen in a larger context, and three others, one mentioned by Powell, also figured.

Dan Quayle, Bush's vice president, proved a drag on the Republican ticket, and it is scarcely surprising that a number of prominent members of the party wished he could be replaced with Powell. Had such a change been engineered, the president would certainly have been helped. But he would still have had to overcome other obstacles: The DESERT STORM victory came too early, and he had a full twenty months to create a record after that event to give him additional strength; neither he nor his associates had any idea of what to do either at home or abroad to achieve that end. It was as if their luck had run out, that there were no new situations abroad they could exploit to the president's advantage. Finally, and perhaps most important, in his efforts to imitate Reagan, his master and model, Bush showed that he lacked both his charisma and his guile. A stiff Connecticut Yankee in Texas boots, he never boasted the geopolitical or historical interests of his distinguished Republican predecessor, Theodore Roosevelt.

Philip Bobbitt, an admirer of Bush and Baker, refused to believe that better leadership would have given the United States a more adequate foreign policy. Still, one must acknowledge surprise at Bobbitt's comment, appended to his praise for the administration's efforts to unify Germany and expel Iraq from Kuwait, that "the predecessor to the Clinton administration had no better answers to Haiti, North Korea, Somalia, Yugoslavia, or Ukraine, all of which it made modestly worse by not having a policy and bequeathing acute problems that became chronic to its successor."[82]

Why, then, did Bush and his associates have no better answers? Did he lack in himself and in his devoted Texan secretary of state, the talented professing Christian lawyer whose foul speech would have made John Foster Dulles blanch, intellectual resources that made Kissinger such an invaluable interlocutor for Nixon? Did Baker lack the education, as well as the domestic and foreign experience acquired in years of public and private life, that made Shultz, Reagan's secretary of state, more qualified, ready to resign when "subjected to a low-level guerrilla warfare from the White House staff"? Shultz, for all his admiration of Reagan, knew that his foreign policy had "refused to lift and soar," that "the United States held the winning hand, but it was proving a difficult hand to play."[83]

Neither Bush nor Baker understood that this had become the situation again after 1990. Helmut Schmidt, in May 1982, had said to Shultz: "The superpowers are not in touch with each other's reality. The Soviets can't read you. More human contact is needed."[84] Baker, in his close relations with Shevardnadze, sought to create that greater human contact but both he and Bush tended to rely too much on their personal relations with foreign leaders, ignoring the importance of a command of geopolitics that might have placed the crises of their day in a larger perspective. François, Mikhail, Hosni, and Jack, like the much-esteemed Margaret, were thought to be the president's friends—perhaps Bush's most overused expression—but that friendship scarcely compensated for a lack of ideas for major foreign policy innovations.[85]

The opportunities that presented themselves to the president after 1989 were immense but too little perceived and too little taken advantage of. Bush seemed satisfied to revel in his public relations triumphs, none more consequential than his Gulf War victory, but even that success never led him to devise a coherent new Middle East policy. Unlike Reagan, he never enjoyed political combat and found the experience unpleasant and bewildering. Boris Yeltsin, who came to admire him, wrote of the "severe stress" he was under during the 1992 election campaign and, learning he would "sit immobile for several hours staring into space. . . called him to try to cheer him up."[86]

Bush, as much as Carter, lacked the skills of a natural politician that made Reagan popular even with those who knew him to be aged and indolent. Like Reagan, Bush used rhetoric to substitute for action that involved risk, and though pretending to cope with terrorism, never initiated policies calculated to make that issue salient for the nation.[87]

CHAPTER 20

The Rake's Progress

BILL CLINTON WILL always be remembered as the president who came within a hair's breadth of being ousted for lying about his sexual liaison with Monica Lewinsky. While a later generation may wonder how an administration that started with such promise could have ended so ignominiously, many will find abundant evidence to support whatever conclusions they reach in the telltale accounts of those who served him.[1] While a certain number continued to admire him, grateful for all he did to advance their careers, others have felt the urge to tell all, and in doing so, did much to diminish him.[2]

Clinton, a serial prevaricator, and not only in respect to his sexual exploits, was as faithless to some who helped him climb the greasy pole as they were to him, who had introduced them to the delights of celebrity and power. George Stephanopoulos, one of many who served him, absorbed for years the president's frequent explosions of anger and invective but was too ambitious not to realize what he stood to gain from telling tales of the president's foibles and frailties. In 1999, when letting it all hang out was no longer thought treacherous, Stephanopoulos wrote the story of the president's first term, remarking that before the Lewinsky scandal he had thought to write a memoir "shaped like a human comedy." After the affair and the impeachment proceedings, he was tempted "to think of the Clinton story as a tragedy," but try as he would, he could never find in Clinton the "grandeur of a tragic hero."[3] Correct in both judgments, even if the account of a disordered and agitated presidency, rendered as comedy, might have offered some welcome relief to a too-solemn America, it was a measure of the Stephanopoulos maturity, perhaps his Greek American birth, that told him not to represent the president as a tragic figure. What, then, was the Clinton story? A skilled editor might have urged Stephanopoulos to render it as farce; that, however, would have been *lèse-majesté*, inappropriate for a president, even for one who was a congenital liar.

495

Stephanopoulos wrote of the difficulty of understanding how a "president so intelligent, so compassionate, so public-spirited, and so conscious of his place in history" could have acted "in such a stupid, selfish, and self-destructive a manner."[4] Confounded by the thought that the man he had served faithfully would have had "a sexual affair with a twenty-two-year-old intern"—one wonders who would have been an acceptable candidate for consensual sex with a president not wholly ignorant of Kennedy's remarkable record in this regard—Stephanopoulos presented Clinton as a "popular president presiding over an America prosperous and at peace."[5] This was precisely the description that might have been made seventy years earlier of the administration of Calvin Coolidge, but the praise on this occasion went to someone who had "outsmarted his enemies, out-hustled his adversaries, and overcame his failings and those of his team to help our country and achieve what no Democrat has done since Roosevelt—two full terms in office and a successful presidency."[6]

Joe Klein, the erstwhile anonymous author of *Primary Colors*, a fictitious account of Bill and Hillary Clinton, published *The Natural: The Misunderstood Presidency of Bill Clinton* in 2002, which approached Stephanopoulos in its accolades to a man of rare intelligence and political skill.[7] The once-subtle satirist who had written of his hero's genius in "pressing the flesh" and "flattering you with the illusion of conspiracy," pretending to share real secrets but never doing so, abandoned such trivia to write that

> Bill Clinton conducted a serious, substantive presidency; his domestic achievements were not inconsiderable and were accomplished against great odds. He rescued the Democratic Party from irrelevance and pursued a new philosophy of governance that made public-sector activism plausible once more, even in a time of national apathy and skepticism. Moreover, he performed the most important service that a leader can provide: He saw the world clearly and reacted prudently to the challenges he faced; he explained a complicated economic transformation to the American people and brought them to the edge of a new era.[8]

The impeccable prose concealed a flawed argument. Clinton's domestic achievements, when placed beside those of other Democrats, including Roosevelt, Truman, and Johnson, certainly, and Wilson, arguably, were negligible. He rescued the Democratic Party not from irrelevance but from candidates like George McGovern and Michael Dukakis, more principled men but substantially less photogenic and calculating. If he had a new philosophy of governance, if the New Covenant and the Third Way merit that distinction, they scarcely resembled the New Deal, the Fair Deal, or the Square Deal. The proposition that he "saw the world clearly and reacted prudently to the challenges he faced" might just as reasonably have been said of Ronald Reagan, whom he observed attentively, or even of George Bush, for whom he and his acolytes felt an exaggerated contempt.

Clinton was cautious, concerned always that no body bags return from foreign fields of battle while he occupied the White House. In Africa as in Europe, he showed himself more indecisive than his spin doctors allowed the public to believe. In matters of war and peace, so crucial in giving the twentieth-century presidency its distinctive character, Clinton left no record that showed either innovation or imagination. Unlike certain of his Democratic predecessors who created institutions and policies that survived them, Clinton showed only the most superficial grasp of foreign policy, and never brought into his company men or women able to lead him to take initiatives of the kind fostered by Wilson, Roosevelt, and Truman. That he scarcely understood the extent of the threat posed by terrorism and showed little appreciation of the opportunities created by the demise of the Soviet Union, was as true of him as of the two Republicans who preceded him.

In foreign policy, more than in domestic policy, he showed himself an amateur, able to demonstrate an articulate command of any agenda presented in the summit meetings of the Big Seven, yet unable to give either the American public or his opposite numbers abroad any sense of how much the world had changed since the demise of the Soviet Union. Against those like Klein who argued that Clinton brought the American people "to the edge of a new era," it is important to consider whether he did not simply perpetuate the late-twentieth-century world that another journalist, Elizabeth Drew, described in her book *The Corruption of American Politics: What Went Wrong and Why,* published in 2000.[9] Drew dwelled on what she called "the debasement of American politics over the past twenty-five years," in short since the time of Nixon, writing of "the decline in statesmanship and leadership, civility and quality, and the growth of partisanship."[10] Her theme was "corruption: the expanding corruption of money in all its pervasive ways, some of them novel, and including the corruption of the Washington culture—and the inability of the system to reform itself."[11] This was *fin de siècle* America as one journalist saw it.

Drew, in her severe indictment of Clinton, claimed he had "laid waste to two of the office's most important elements: its mystique and its power to influence the public and the Congress."[12] His presidency, "a squandered opportunity" by a man of "formidable political skills and exceptional brain," led him, in her view, to be preoccupied with self-preservation rather than leadership, and this had been true even before the Lewinsky scandal.[13]

If a proclivity for self-preservation was Clinton's fundamental weakness, did it derive from his experience as the child of a rackety Arkansas family whose father, William Jefferson Blythe, a traveling salesman, was killed in a motor accident before his birth? His mother, remarried in 1950—Bill was born on August 19, 1946—brought into the family a reckless and foul-mouthed drunk, Roger

Clinton, often unemployed, whose physical abuse of his wife, son, and stepson was a tale Clinton never tired of telling.[14] Indeed, it formed part of the late-twentieth-century heroic story he reveled in—how he took the surname of his bullying father, implicitly forgiving him for his violence, bravely challenging him when he attacked his mother, knowing her to be the self-sacrificing woman who had helped him escape from an intolerable family situation. While neighbors might recall his mother principally for her passion for the racetrack and love of nightlife, her somewhat bizarre appearance and frequent violent arguments with the man she divorced and later remarried, her son knew her as his generous benefactor, the woman who worked long hours as a nurse to save money to make his education outside Arkansas possible.[15]

Clinton's Arkansas, poor and raw, resembled only superficially the more genteel Arkansas that Senator William Fulbright, who preceded him at Oxford as a Rhodes Scholar, had known. These two Oxford careers could not have been more different; while Fulbright emerged as an Anglophile, and went on to serve for decades in the Senate, resisting presidents, including those of his own party, Truman and Johnson, Clinton never risked separating himself from the party that had given him his career.

A good boy, a loving son, a serious student, a churchgoing Baptist, he first visited the nation's capital in 1963 as a representative of Boy's Nation, a youth organization sponsored by the American Legion, a visit made memorable by his meeting President Kennedy and being photographed shaking his hand in the White House. While Clinton's high school contemporaries rarely attended university, a few made their way to the University of Arkansas–Fayetteville, but why the young Clinton, a devout Baptist, chose to attend Georgetown University, a Jesuit college attractive mostly to the sons of affluent Catholics, has never been fully explained. Why, indeed, he enrolled in the School of Foreign Service, whether he intend a career as a diplomat, or had simply learned of the school's fame, established decades earlier by Father Walsh, its leader and something of a celebrity in the time of Franklin Roosevelt, remains a mystery.[16]

Georgetown, once a gilded ghetto for privileged Catholic boys, had opened its doors to Protestants and Jews in the early post–World War II years, and Clinton came from a region little represented in a university seeking recognition as a national and international institution. With low tuition and the promise of a modest scholarship, together with funds sent by his mother, Clinton had no need to earn money during his years at Georgetown, but studies alone could never satisfy his growing ambition. Not surprisingly, he sought employ, part-time and necessarily menial, in the office of Senator Fulbright and had his first experience there of seeing Washington from the inside—a very humble inside.[17]

From Georgetown, Clinton proceeded to University College, Oxford, in 1968, the recipient of a Rhodes Scholarship, winning in a six-state region that included Texas that never boasted the competition common in other parts of the country.[18] While attention later in his career centered on how he managed to avoid conscription, engaging Fulbright and others to write his draft board to secure exemptions for him—details generally concealed or embroidered by Clinton—the more compelling story, told with comparable exaggeration and omission, related to his active engagement abroad in the campaign to denounce a war in Vietnam that he and many of his American friends believed to be immoral. Though later charges of draft-dodging proved embarrassing, as did his purported drug use, he showed considerable originality in claiming he never inhaled in his experiments with marijuana, prefiguring the argument he would later use in the Lewinsky affair—that a sexual encounter without penetration was obviously not sexual in the literal meaning of the term.

Though rumors spread, decades later, of his purported Communist sympathies during this time, symbolized by his visit to the Soviet Union, these were charges easily refuted.[19] A more accurate account of his two Oxford years would have dwelled on the extent to which he knew principally other Americans who shared his opinions and had only the most limited experience of either Harold Wilson's England or of the Europe that lay across the narrow English Channel. University College would later honor him, proud to claim an American president among its alumni, but none of the English who knew him at Oxford thought him remarkable or indeed thought about him at all. He made little impression on his tutors and left Oxford without the B.Phil. degree that most other Rhodes Scholars carried away. In his next academic incarnation at Yale Law School, again a marginal figure little noticed, unlike his more studious contemporaries, he did not after graduation claim a clerkship in the chambers of a prominent judge or, as with others of exceptional legal ability, receive an invitation to serve as a clerk to a justice of the Supreme Court. Still, he had gained a valuable credential, the Yale law degree, and this allowed him to launch his political career in his native Arkansas.

In Hillary Rodham, who became his wife, one of the first women to graduate from Yale Law School, he courted someone as ambitious as himself, thought to be no less articulate and, as events increasingly showed, no less devious. Indeed, their passionate commitment to politics separated them from the greatest number of their contemporaries; both were political junkies in the most literal sense of the term, addicted to politics as others were to wealth or work.

Neither emerged in any way scarred by the tempestuous events of the 1960s; neither believed the political road was one best not taken. Clinton's advantage lay in his Arkansas roots, and in 1974, in the election following the resignation of Richard Nixon, when so many Democrats did exceptionally well, he risked very little by running for Congress in a traditionally Republican district. His opponent, John Paul Hammerschmidt, a four-term incumbent, the only

Arkansas Republican in the House, defeated him easily. At the Democratic Party state convention at Hot Springs in September 1974, Clinton made something of a name for himself by vigorously attacking President Gerald Ford for his pardon of Richard Nixon, a common criminal. Gazing at the six years of recent Republican rule, Clinton detected only failure—in his words, "record interest rates, record prices, record budgets, record deficits, and recession."[20] Clinton failed to win the election in November, but many in the Arkansas Democratic Party, impressed by his energy, saw him as a young man with a future in a largely one-party state where winning a primary was virtually tantamount to winning office.

After his defeat, Bill married Hillary, and the partnership, previously unofficial, which saw both live in separate apartments, became the talk of Fayetteville when the newly appointed female member of the law school faculty announced she had no intention of assuming her husband's name and would continue to be Ms. Hillary Rodham. Clinton's next move, proof of his political astuteness, led him to look away from a congressional career, recognizing that achieving fame in the House of Representatives carried little promise of substantial prizes quickly gained. He detected greater opportunities in competing to become the state's attorney general, expecting to use that office as a springboard to the governorship. He campaigned vigorously and won easily, with some 60 percent of those who voted showing their preference for him in the state's primary. Facing no opposition in the general election in November, he devoted his time and energy to the presidential race, helping Jimmy Carter, a fellow Southerner, win the White House for the Democrats.

That task successfully accomplished, he returned to Arkansas, hoping to establish a record as attorney general that would make him a major contender for the governorship in 1978. With funds provided in part by Hillary's law firm—she had done well in her legal practice with Rose's, one of the principal Little Rock partnerships—he collected $600,000, an unheard-of sum for a gubernatorial race in Arkansas. Not surprisingly, he defeated four less-financially endowed opponents, a rural judge, a lawyer, a state legislator, and a turkey farmer. Clinton, barely past thirty, the youngest governor in the nation, of a small, poor, backward, and ill-educated state, was hailed by the *New York Times* as the thirty-one-year-old whiz kid of Arkansas politics.[21] Hillary continued to pursue her legal career in Little Rock, establishing her own reputation and fortune, and more than $100,000 in a commodities deal destined later to cause them both considerable embarrassment.

Clinton, observing Carter closely, knew that all was not going well for the president. In a speech prepared for a Connecticut audience in 1980, he spoke in an idiom familiar to those who listened to Ronald Reagan, at that time campaigning for the Republican Party nomination. Clinton wished for the people to gain greater control of their daily lives, dwelling on the greatness of a nation he knew to be both good and just.[22] Ignoring Carter, too greatly preoccupied with what he conceived to be the country's diminished spiritual state, Clinton showed little respect for those policies on which the Georgian president laid such great store—his energy program and recommendations for environmental protection. Without explicitly finding fault with either, Clinton suggested the former needed to be made more "realistic," the latter more "sensible."[23] Clinton used Connecticut to rehearse for his far more important engagement in New York, where he spoke for the Democratic Governors' Association at the party's presidential nominating convention.[24]

Friends of Carter might have been excused for asking whether the governor of Arkansas, in his very effective speech, offered useful advice or simply challenged a president he was obviously disenchanted with. Clinton told the convention that Carter could not win "by putting together the old elements of the Democratic coalition and repudiating Ronald Reagan."[25] The "cheap energy, abundant natural resources, and lack of foreign competition on which the stability and prosperity of the country had depended for years" were all gone, and Clinton expected them never to return. In 1974, he had been satisfied to speak of six years of Republican misrule, those of Nixon; in 1980, he spoke of the last ten years, no longer distinguishing between Ford and Carter when "our economic system has been breaking down," characterized by "high unemployment, high inflation, large governmental deficits, loss of our competitive edge."[26]

How might all this be changed? Clinton recalled the year 1936 when the Depression had not yet ended, and when Franklin Roosevelt had a vision, the country's most urgent need at that moment and scarcely less important in 1980.[27] Reagan, he told the convention, was strong, and it would be dangerous to underestimate him. In his words, "His voice is clear, consistent, and committed."[28] By inference, Carter could claim none of these talents. Reagan's remedies—reduced taxes, increases in federal defense spending, and a balanced budget—calculated to end inflation and reduce unemployment, would produce none of these results, Clinton told his fellow Democrats. What, then, ought they to do? In his words, their mission was to give the people a sense of "our vision."[29]

In 1980, outlining policies he knew Carter incapable of initiating, he spoke of living in a "time of transition, a difficult and painful one" where the imperative need was for an economic revitalization of the country, unlikely to be achieved by Reagan's remedy, a big tax cut for big business. Clinton spoke of the need to redefine the relationship between the federal government and big business, leading to a revitalization of the country's basic industrial structure. Only greater risk-taking and a commitment to job creation, not least in the new and growing businesses of the country, would end the economic stagnation that had bewildered so many for so long.

In calling for a good environmental policy, together with a more deliberate search for alternative energy sources, he touched on policies Carter imagined were his own, but the president had never been as explicit as Clinton in dwelling on the importance of the middle class for the Democratic Party.[30] That class, if brought to vote in great number for Democrats, would register what everyone knew to be true—"the country is still the finest in the world." That message would bear constant repetition, and Clinton recognized its importance. In the end, however, it proved easier for him to preach to Democrats assembled in New York than to win his own gubernatorial election in Arkansas. In 1980, the year when Reagan showed the country the strength of Republican sentiment and made the Nixon debacle a thing of the past, Clinton lost to a Republican, Frank White, characterized by one *New York Times* reporter as "an affable, unimaginative Republican with a blustering style and an aversion to syntax." How had the whiz kid, after only two years in the governor's chair, managed to lose to a former Democrat, an Annapolis graduate, a successful banker who accomplished what few had imagined possible—a Republican gubernatorial victory in Arkansas, only the second time in the century when that had happened?

The condition of the state's economy certainly hurt Clinton; so also did Carter's decision to resettle some 20,000 Cuban refugees at Fort Chaffee, leading to a riot quelled only by state troopers and National Guardsmen.[31] The campaign that had seen a booming White denounce the never-silent Clinton for raising gasoline taxes and license fees to fund his highway program hurt the governor, but the more serious threat came from his thinly veiled misogynist thrusts at Hillary, the woman who would not change her name, who sat at the governor's elbow running the show. White won by some 32,000 votes in an election that saw an unprecedented 77 percent, more than 800,000 of eligible voters go to the polls.

If anyone believed the defeat spelled the end of Clinton's political career, they were rapidly disabused of that idea. Within months of leaving the governor's mansion, Clinton, hurt, angry, and blaming everyone except himself, began to plan his return to office. In February 1982, in a thirty-second TV clip, repeated throughout the week, he begged the citizens of Arkansas to forgive him for mistakes he had made as governor, especially in respect to the license fees. He asked for another chance and assured those who watched him that this time he would listen to them.[32] Clinton came out first in the primary race, with 41.7 percent of the vote, but this required him to engage in a runoff that he won easily.[33] The general election that followed was as fierce as any Clinton ever engaged in, realizing that a second defeat by White would end his political career. Clinton represented White as the candidate of big business, a governor who had doubled the price of prescription drugs for Medicaid recipients, given additional tax exemptions to the very rich, and boosted private utility company profits by some 50 percent. Indefatigable in his campaigning, he beat White decisively, managing to secure some 55 percent of the vote.[34]

Though once again governor in 1982, Clinton never imagined his future lay in Arkansas. In the speech he delivered in San Francisco, at the 1984 Democratic National Convention where Walter Mondale, Carter's vice president, was officially nominated, with Mario Cuomo, the governor of New York, and Jimmy Carter the principal speakers, Clinton gave a speech in praise of Harry Truman. Following the showing of a film on the last incontestably great Democratic Party president on the occasion of the centennial of his birth, Clinton waxed euphoric in lauding a man so different from those who searched only for "glamour and charisma."[35]

Truman's one concern, he told his enthusiastic audience, was to be "a good citizen," to believe in change, in new ideas, in the future. In staccato sentences, Clinton said:

> If he were here today, he'd give a speech that would take our hides off. He'd speak from the heart, not the teleprompter. He'd say again that a 'statesman is a dead politician.' He'd remind us that 1948, like 1984, was a time of change, when new realities required new ideas and a willingness to stand up to interest groups both within and outside our party when the public interest demands it.[36]

Then, giving much the same spiel he had given four years earlier, he spoke of the need for greater productivity and better jobs, adding details on the need for affordable health care, an invigorated education system, and a strong defense to reduce the hazards of nuclear war.[37] Though only a recent supporter of Mondale's candidacy, he felt great enthusiasm for a man prepared to select a woman to run with him as vice president.[38] His final words, "The real way to honor Harry Truman is to wage a campaign that would make him as proud of us as we are of him," almost suggested he thought Ronald Reagan might be beaten.

Clinton never believed that. His 1984 speech was intended to alert delegates to his availability in 1988, when he expected his several terms as a reform leader in Arkansas and his reputation as the education governor would give him the nomination that had once gone to Democratic governors of more influential states, New Jersey and New York. In fact, Clinton expected Reagan to win easily and may have suspected that the vice president, George Bush, his loyal and obedient servant, would be the Republican Party's presidential candidate in 1988. The prospect of meeting that stiff scion of good family and breeding who had only very rarely succeeded in his efforts to win elective office must have seemed an attractive prospect to someone who knew his own strengths.

In 1988, the accident that destroyed Gary Hart's candidacy, the leading Democratic Party contender, also spelled the end of Clinton's hopes that he might emerge as the party's nominee. The *Miami Herald*, pursuing the rumor that

Hart was having an illicit relation with a twenty-nine-year-old woman, Donna Rice, and proving its allegation with photographic evidence of her leaving the senator's Washington townhouse, was made substantially worse by tales and photographs of a weekend tryst of the two on the island of Bimini.[39] That kind of scandalous behavior, dangerous in James Bryce's day and scarcely more acceptable a century later, had another effect, little noted at the time. After the Hart revelations, only a squeaky-clean candidate could be nominated in 1988, and no one who knew Clinton even superficially imagined he qualified in that respect. Michael Dukakis, the reform governor of Massachusetts, was duly nominated, with his name placed before the delegates by Clinton, his friend and fellow governor. The speech Clinton delivered proved a disaster; droning on for far too long, he read a speech he later claimed the Dukakis campaign managers had imposed on him, prohibiting his changing even a single word.[40] Like so much that Clinton said, it was impossible to know what truth, if any, lay in the allegation. In any case, the speech helped his reputation not at all; seen by many as insipid and dull, it served as news for a day but was soon forgotten in a campaign made memorable mostly by the Willie Horton affair, the Republican Party's use of race and crime to emphasize its purity, that sent the Dukakis campaign into a freefall from which it never recovered.[41]

Clinton, again in Arkansas, contemptuous of the man he had nominated, sat out the election; after his convention performance, no one cared to involve him, and he was just as happy to be removed from the scene of what he knew would be a Democratic Party disaster. Always active in the Democratic Leadership Council, an organization he had helped found in 1985, he continued to represent himself as a moderate Democrat, pledged to restore "the hopes of the forgotten middle class," never acknowledging how much he had borrowed from Reagan in calling for smaller government and welfare reform.

In 1992, after Bush's impressive Gulf War victory, a number of leading Democrats believed the president unbeatable and, recalling their family obligations, showed little interest in entering their names in a growing list of Democratic Party sacrificial lambs. Still, a number, including Clinton, guessed that Bush was not as invulnerable as he appeared to be. Ready to see whether he might not oust a president less charismatic and more insipid than Reagan, Clinton announced his candidacy on October 3, 1991, starting preparations immediately for the first of the primaries, scheduled for New Hampshire in February. Before that crucial first test, seeking publicity for his ideas, he gave two speeches at his alma mater, Georgetown University, intended to show his command of an area where he believed Bush vulnerable—economic policy—and one where he thought him strong—defense policy.

In the first speech, heralded as "A New Covenant for Economic Change," Clinton promised to cut income tax rates for the middle class, estimating that the average family's taxes might be reduced by as much as 10 percent. How the federal government would compensate for this income loss, certain to exacerbate the budget deficit, was simple, according to Clinton; the taxes of the rich, those who earned over $200,000 a year, would be raised. Using rhetoric that had given him renown in Arkansas, Clinton called his campaign "a crusade to restore the forgotten middle class."[42] It was time, he said, to "lay George Bush off, put America back to work, and our problems will go away."[43]

Telling stories of recent encounters with suffering individuals—a device he used constantly and effectively—he attributed the country's wage and productivity decline to the Republicans, but the blame was not theirs alone. Clinton chastised also those Democrats in Congress who "forgot about real people," allowing a tripling of the national debt and a constant increase in the deficit.[44] "For twelve years of this Reagan-Bush era," he said,

the Republicans have let S&L crooks and self-serving CEOs try to build an economy out of paper and perks instead of people and products. It's the Republican way: every man for himself and get it while you can. They stacked the odds in favor of their friends at the top, and told everybody else to wait for whatever trickled down.[45]

A "radically different direction" was called for, requiring a departure from the "Republicans' failed experiment in supply side economics" but also a "move away from the old Democratic theory that says we can just tax and spend our way out of any problem we face."[46] "What America needs," Clinton told the Georgetown assembly, was "a president with a radical new approach to our economic problems that will give new life to the American dream."[47] He offered himself as that person, neither liberal nor conservative but both, different from what the country had endured for too long.

Everyone had to be "empowered," from the preschool child to the adult seeking to learn, from the poor to the tax-burdened middle class, all brought to understand that government could be made "an engine of opportunity again, not an obstacle to it."[48] A revolution in the workplace, changes to affect both workers and businesses, would bring new prosperity and new independence. His was a "new radical approach to economics," he said, calculated to unify the country, so that the ideas of Robert Kennedy, whom he had brought to address Georgetown students twenty-five years earlier as president of his class, might again be realized. America needed to be renewed; "social and spiritual renewal" would follow from his crusade.[49] The speech prefigured a message that became increasingly crucial, represented in the unforgettable words never uttered in public—"It's the economy, stupid!"—that theoretically won Clinton the 1992 election.

Because Bush enjoyed a reputation as a heavyweight in foreign policy, Clinton saw the need to prove he was something other than an innocent from the hills of Arkansas. In his speech "A New Covenant for American Security," delivered again at Georgetown two weeks later, he proclaimed the "new era that had opened with America's victory in the Cold War." Unlike Republicans who never tired of giving their two presidents, Reagan and Bush, prime billing for that remarkable achievement, Clinton dwelled on the "unstinting courage and sacrifice of the American people" that had led to this happy ending. Because a "new vision" for national security was called for, Clinton offered the proposition that "foreign and domestic policy are inseparable in today's world" and that if "we're not strong at home, we can't lead the world we've done so much to make."[50] Though Clinton reminded his audience that he had supported Bush in "his efforts to kick Saddam Hussein out of Kuwait," and congratulated him for his "masterful job in pulling together the victorious multilateral coalition," admiring him for not turning his back on NATO, continuing to seek peace in the Middle East, and fashioning a free-trade agreement with Mexico, he found him wanting on other grounds.

In his view, the president, too greatly concerned with political stability and personal relations with foreign leaders, too little committed to "a coherent policy of promoting freedom, democracy, and economic growth" in the "dynamic new era" just opening, the objective should be "not to resist change but to shape it." Vision was needed if the collapse of communism was to be seen not as an isolated event but as part of a worldwide march toward democracy. Individual liberty, political pluralism, and free enterprise, were they to take root everywhere, would lead to a "grand new era of reduced conflict, mutual understanding, and economic growth."[51] Because all danger had not evaporated, Clinton spoke of the country's need to restructure its military forces and regain its economic strength. In a characteristic Clintonism, he said: "We cannot afford to go on spending too much on firepower and too little on brainpower."[52] Ideas would rule the world in the new Information Age, and he spoke of the role of "television, cassette tapes, and the fax machine" in bringing down the Berlin Wall.[53]

Finally, on the environment and other global issues, survival depended on the United States taking the lead. Pretending to understand the defense needs of the country, he recommended making the new post–Cold War military structure "smaller," with a "more flexible mix of capabilities."[54] B-2 bomber production should be ended, saving the country $20 billion by 1997; Star Wars had already cost the nation $26 billion; a more "realistic and attainable goal" had to be pursued, "defending against very limited or accidental launches of ballistic missiles." This would allow R&D on missile defense to continue within the framework of the ABM Treaty. Every effort had to be made "to stop the threat of weapons of mass destruction from spreading."[55] U.S. forces in Europe could be reduced; a 21 percent cut in military spending through 1995 might be contemplated, assuming always that the Soviet

Union remained intact. In short, he imagined a $100 billion saving beyond anything proposed by Bush.[56] More of the costs and risks of maintaining the peace had to be borne by America's allies. The United Nations had begun to assume the responsibilities Roosevelt and Truman had envisaged for it, and Clinton hoped this would continue, contributing to America's greater purpose, to promote democracy around the world. Because democracies "don't go to war with each other" and do not "sponsor terrorist groups," they represented the hope of the future.

Bush, he said, erred at the time of Tiananmen Square, coddling China when he ought not to have done so, showing too little support for Yeltsin before the Moscow coup that brought him to power. The president, he said, "is wrong to use pressure tactics against Israel," though he accepted that his aim was to bring Israel and its Arab enemies to negotiate. In Africa, the United States had to align itself with the rising tide of democracy, not least in South Africa. Demilitarization of the Soviet Union had to be given a high priority, with Ukraine granted its independence, and private American investment in the former Soviet empire encouraged. The time was ripe for the creation of a Democracy Corps, to "send thousands of talented American volunteers to countries that need their legal, financial, political expertise." Addressing the need to restore America's economic leadership, he spoke of all that greater free trade would do to create more jobs at home. A new bipartisanship was called for, like that of the Truman age, to move the country into the new era.[57]

Clinton's speech, intended to demonstrate his understanding of foreign and defense policy issues, was more revolutionary in its rhetoric than in its recommendations. It said nothing that departed greatly from what others were saying at the time, including many serving in the Bush administration. Still, it suggested that the Arkansas governor was not as incapable of making major pronouncements on foreign and defense policy as some of his more worldly detractors wished to believe.

On January 23, in *The Star,* a supermarket tabloid, a story appeared as hazardous to Clinton's presidential bid as the Donna Rice story had been to Hart's four years earlier. Gennifer Flowers, a former Arkansas TV reporter, told of a twelve-year affair with Clinton, supported days later by tapes of her conversations with the governor in which he specifically asked her to deny any sexual relation with him.[58] Clinton, appearing on the CBS program *Sixty Minutes,* Hillary at his side, admitted to having caused "pain" in their marriage, adding that most Americans would "get it," while denying the truth of the allegations.[59] Hillary suggested, however implicitly, that if she did not mind his philandering, why should others be so concerned?[60]

The act, perfectly staged, appeared to end the risk that Clinton's infidelity would do him irreparable damage in New Hampshire. Then, on February 6, the *Wall Street Journal* published a potentially more damaging story that told of how he had manipulated the draft laws to gain an exemption from military service. In a state like New Hampshire, with its reputation for patriotism, this was an exceedingly serious charge, but on February 18, when the primary election returns were broadcast, Clinton had managed to receive 25 percent of the vote, only 8 percent behind the frontrunner, Paul Tsongas of Massachusetts, New Hampshire's neighbor. How had he accomplished this? Stephanopoulos, surprised by the results, could only say "he was by far the best politician I'd ever met."[61] Given Stephanopoulos's age and limited acquaintance with politicians, the accolade counted for little, but his other comment, about the man he saw "with flaws as profound as his gifts," showed a certain prescience; he wrote that Clinton "had more ideas than anyone in the race, his heart was in the right place, and he refused to quit."[62]

The third was true; the second, believed by many who knew Clinton less well, was a useful myth; the first was false. Clinton had no more ideas than a number of those who opposed him. He won in New Hampshire and went on to win primaries elsewhere because no one of his three principal senatorial opponents, Paul Tsongas, Bob Kerrey, and Tom Harkin, or the loquacious and long-serving governor, Mario Cuomo of New York, appeared to be as hungry for the presidency, or if the truth be told, as devious. No one of the three senators had access to money in their home states that Clinton, after a decade as governor of Arkansas, commanded. Cuomo, for reasons never made apparent, seemed intermittently interested in entering the race but never dared to do so.

When the Flowers revelations and the draft accusations surfaced, it appeared for a time that the media might succeed in derailing the Clinton bandwagon, but the attacks on the Arkansas governor scarred him scarcely at all.[63] When, on Super Tuesday, he won eight primaries, principally in the South, it was apparent that no one from any other region of the country could match his appeal. By early April, his victories in New York, Michigan, and Illinois told the country what it ought to have realized earlier—using techniques originally developed by Jimmy Carter in 1976 and understanding the primary system as none of his opponents did, Clinton emerged as the indisputable choice of those who cared to vote in Democratic primaries.[64]

The Democratic National Convention in New York City simply confirmed what the primaries had registered: Clinton, an accomplished campaigner, attractive even to many who suspected him to be a liar, would be the party's nominee, running with Al Gore, senator from Tennessee. November would see a *faux* Texan, a Connecticut Yankee, together with J. Danforth Quayle of Indiana, known as moral Dan, oppose two sons of the South. Earlier traditions that had emphasized the importance of balanced geographical tickets seemed less compelling by 1992 when the nation appeared to be of a piece and when a Southern affiliation had become positively advantageous. The contest was unequal, and Clinton may have intuited this as early as the New Hampshire primary when Pat Buchanan challenged the president in that state's primary and emerged with 37 percent of the vote. Buchanan fell by the wayside early in the race, but J. Ross Perot took his place, running as an Independent, an enemy as much of Bush as of Clinton.

Perot, a rich Texan egotist, was prepared to spend from his own ample fortune to propagandize for the change he thought imperative. He claimed a vast following everywhere, but few were able to gauge the degree of his appeal to the larger public. In the three televised presidential debates that followed in close succession in October, the president showed his limits as a campaigner.[65] Bush, lacking experience of electoral politics, and not naturally attuned to a medium where he competed with someone able to dive into the audience in the second Town Hall Meeting to take questions and talk easily with just plain folks, suffered from being old money, stiff and awkward. Clinton, proclaimed a supreme communicator by the media in a phrase frequently used about Reagan, showed the talents increasingly recognized as crucial for anyone aspiring to the presidency, rivaling John F. Kennedy's memorable performances.

Clinton finished with slightly less than 45 million votes in the November election against Bush's slightly more than 39 million and Perot's almost 20 million. Superficially, the election seemed a comic repeat of 1912, but few thought to make the comparison. America in 1912 was ancient history, and Clinton was no Wilson, Perot no Roosevelt, but some might have been forgiven for thinking that Bush, with his Yale background, was a slim, latter-day Taft Republican, lifted to eminence by having faithfully served a more charismatic leader.[66] A born number-two who aspired to grasp the presidential ring a second time and fell to the hard tarmac below, Bush's greatest problem may have been less the formidable opponent he confronted in Clinton than his inability to show qualities made famous by the supreme actor, Ronald Reagan.

That said, no one could deny that Clinton had run an extraordinary campaign. Though few of the Democrats who came to control both the House and the Senate felt especially beholden to him, his calls to reduce the taxes of an overburdened middle class, to create new jobs, support educational opportunity, and protect the environment appealed to many. How all this might be accomplished while effecting major reductions in the federal deficit, few were able to say.

The size of the projected federal deficit, when studied closely by those chosen to prepare the new budget, was expected to exceed what even the president-elect and his supporters had feared.[67] Clinton, the New Democrat, as disdainful of old time Democrats in Congress as Carter had been, started with many of the same handicaps, recognized only belatedly. As a Southerner lacking experience of political life inside the Beltway, he imagined this to be an advantage, but the problems tested even his acute and acknowledged political intelligence.

With Hillary at his side, coaching and coaxing, he placed the task of selecting his principal Cabinet aides in the hands of a transition team headed by two successful lawyers, Vernon Jordan, black and socially well-connected in the nation's capital, famed for his civil rights work in an earlier day with the National Urban League, joined by the less charismatic Warren Christopher, the second man in the Carter administration State Department.

When Kennedy came to the presidency, transition teams did not exist; it was assumed that he, with his friends and acquaintances, would recommend candidates for the principal Cabinet and agency posts and that the task would be completed by the day of his inaugural. Such casual procedures no longer sufficed. In 1992, Jordan and Christopher were expected to recommend individuals the president-elect and his wife would then meet, interview, and accept or reject, a good number previously unknown to either.

While a Cabinet appointed by this process would not necessarily be inferior to that common in the more relaxed days of FDR or Eisenhower, the criteria for selection had changed substantially. Because no one could tell the president-elect that he knew less about foreign policy than he pretended and would almost certainly be vulnerable in his role as commander in chief, not least because of the professional military's disdain for a man many considered a draft-dodger, three appointments were obviously crucial, that of secretary of state, secretary of defense, and national security adviser. For the first, Clinton chose Warren Christopher, who desperately wanted the position, disappointed at not having been named secretary by Carter when Cyrus Vance resigned over the Iranian hostage rescue fiasco. Jordan, knowing Christopher's yearning for the appointment, pressed his case, scarcely aware that he was doing neither the president nor his friend a favor in promoting his candidacy.

If, indeed, Clinton believed a new era called for a new foreign policy, the California lawyer, modest, unassuming, honest, and honorable, was not the man to conceive such a policy or to bring it into being. In choosing Les Aspin to be secretary of defense, Clinton made an even more egregious error. Aspin, intelligent and driven, disorganized and garrulous, a member of the House of Representatives, understood defense policy and arms-control issues as few others in Congress did, but if his command of the subject qualified him for the post, his lack of experience in running a vast bureaucracy ought to have disqualified him. Aspin could never hope to win support from Pentagon subordinates, military and civilian, searching for someone, starched and disciplined, who might be a foil to a president recognized to be neither. For national security adviser, the transition team recommended Tony Lake, a man of impeccable anti-Vietnam War credentials who resigned from his post with the National Security Council in Kissinger's day principally because of his dismay with Nixon's secret decision to bomb Cambodia. He had served as director of policy planning in Vance's State Department, where he acquired an enviable reputation for his concern with human rights issues, especially in Africa. These were the men the president would rely on in the all-important area of foreign and defense policy; it was not the best team he might have chosen.

Given the emphasis he awarded economic issues throughout his campaign, believing his presidency would be made or broken by his success in dealing with those matters, his choice of Lloyd Bentsen to be secretary of the treasury seemed positively inspired. Bentsen, wealthy, poised, articulate, and self-confident, a longtime Democratic senator and chairman of the influential Senate Finance Committee, remembered for having defeated George Bush in 1970 for the vacant Senate seat in Texas, had starred again in 1988 when, as the Democratic Party's vice presidential nominee, he humiliated the bumptious Dan Quayle in their only TV encounter, reminding him that he was "no Jack Kennedy." Bentsen was the elder statesman Clinton desperately needed, not least to complement the others, including Robert Reich, appointed secretary of labor, his longtime Rhodes Scholar friend whose books had greatly influenced him, and who provided ideas on the crucial importance of education and job training in the development of the country's most vital resource—its workforce.

While Reich might have aspired to almost any post related to the economy given his closeness to Clinton, he opted for the Labor Department, imagining perhaps that he would make of that department in a Clinton administration what Herbert Hoover had accomplished with an even less promising Commerce Department in the business administrations of Harding and Coolidge. With Ron Brown, the black Democratic Party chairman who had long been partial to Clinton's presidential aspirations, awarded the commerce post, and Leon Panetta, a highly regarded member of Congress, appointed as his budget director, Clinton imagined he had the economic team to enable him to realize the most important of his campaign promises. Even his appointment of Richard Riley, the virtually blind former governor of South Carolina, to be secretary of education, could be seen as contributing to his ambition to be an education president as he had once claimed to be an education governor. Clinton came into the White House having promised to make fundamental domestic reform, to get the country moving again.

While he desperately hoped that Vernon Jordan would accept to become his attorney general, that was not to be. To have had a black man, almost a boon companion, in that sensitive position would have helped Clinton enormously, and he made the most strenuous efforts to persuade him to accept, all to no avail. Those unfriendly to Jordan, whether out of envy or malice, dismissed him as an oreo, black on the outside, white on the inside, and could only imagine he refused the offer because he preferred to retain his position as one of the most highly paid lawyers in Washington. The reasons were almost certainly more complex, but Jordan never chose to reveal them.

The transition team, aware of the First Lady's interest in having women appointed to high places in her husband's administration, expected she and others to be gratified by the nomination of Zoe Baird, a gifted lawyer who had made her way in a profession only recently opened to significant numbers of women, to become the country's attorney general.[68] Baird's name was sent to the Senate, but background checks quickly revealed that she had failed to pay Social Security taxes for her household help, illegal immigrants.[69] While Baird claimed she had not withheld this information from the transition team, insisting that Christopher had been informed, it was inconceivable that the Senate would approve the appointment of someone as attorney general, in charge of the Justice Department, who had flouted the law.[70] The press and television delighted in what they called the administration's nanny problem, but sympathetic Democratic senators were unlikely to find humor in the situation.

Clinton's next choice for the post, Kimba Wood, proved no more acceptable; it quickly emerged that she, too, had a Zoe problem, having used an illegal immigrant for child care. With both Baird and Wood rendered ineligible, Clinton considered for a moment appointing an old friend, Judge Richard Arnold of Arkansas, but in the end selected Janet Reno of Florida, a woman less gifted than Baird or Wood, to occupy the most senior Cabinet post ever held by a woman. Pressed by his wife to show himself the feminist he always claimed to be, he appointed Donna Shalala secretary of health and human services, and Hazel O'Leary secretary of energy. No previous president had ever appointed so many women to his Cabinet, and none had ever placed them in such prominent posts.

With the selection of Henry Cisneros, a Hispanic, as secretary of housing and urban development, the president appeared to have touched all the gender, racial, and ethnic bases believed essential to Democratic Party success. No one looking at his administration, so markedly different from those of Bush and Reagan, could claim it was dominated by rich white men, though neither Christopher nor Bentsen qualified as men of modest fortune. On the subcabinet level, the president's concern with gender, race, and ethnicity was even more apparent, but the White House staff itself spoke more of Arkansas than of the country. There, the so-called FOBs—friends of Bill—were everywhere, men from Arkansas, known and trusted by the newly elected president. Vincent Foster, Mack McClarty, David Watkins, Webster Hubbell, and William Kennedy—just a few of many who joined him—might not be names known to those steeped in capital lore, but then few had ever heard of any of those Jimmy Carter had brought out of Georgia sixteen years earlier.

Clinton detested Carter—"I'm not Jimmy Carter" said it all—and he could never make that most recent Democratic president his model. Johnson, though more appealing, posed other difficulties for him, not least because of what he had done to continue the country's involvement in Vietnam. Though Clinton resembled Kennedy superficially, able to claim comparable charisma and a no less active libido, he had never risked his life in combat, had never served in Congress, House or Senate. Indeed, the assassinated president's brother, Ted, the last of the political Kennedys, had figured little in Clinton's life and played no role in facilitating his political ascent.

Clinton imagined himself a latter-day Truman, a risk-taking and courageous man of the people. He awarded Truman's miraculous 1948 electoral victory too much attention and his other qualities—loyalty to friends and colleagues, modesty, and a remarkable facility for recruiting able men, not least in the crucial area of foreign policy—too little. It was apparent within days of Clinton's entry into the White House that his gifts did not include those central to the domestic successes of three earlier Democratic presidents, Wilson, Roosevelt, and Johnson. He knew neither how to reach out to Congress nor how to make friends in either chamber whom he could rely on for his legislative program.[71] Influential senators like Daniel Patrick Moynihan, who owed nothing to the newly elected president, needed to be courted and cosseted, not least because of his crucial role as the new chairman of the Senate Finance Committee, but the president had no inkling of what he needed to do to win the confidence of someone who thought himself his intellectual equal, whose vanity was legendary.[72]

Ranting and raging within the White House, if Stephanopoulos's account of the first weeks may be believed, Clinton worried about the leaks to the press that had once sent Nixon into a fury, never realizing that such behavior would have been unthinkable in even the worst days when Truman and his Democratic predecessors suffered comparable obloquy. Clinton, from the start, felt sorry for himself, and his wife joined him in that sentiment, looking for enemies everywhere, persuaded that the press, as exemplified by the *Wall Street Journal*, would never give him his due, that unfriendly Republican members of Congress resented his victory and would do what they could to destroy his administration.

While no overwhelming crisis attended the president's first weeks in office, he acted as if beleaguered, with too few prepared to compliment him for his courage in repeating his campaign pledge to end discrimination against gays in the military. Neither his secretary of defense nor any of those he appointed told him of the risks he ran in giving that pledge such high priority. Worse, however, was to follow.

In recommending Lani Guinier to head the Office of Civil Rights in the Justice Department, he neglected to anticipate the hostility a black woman with radical ideas about minority representation in government would provoke. When it became obvious that she would never be accepted by the Senate—the president did little to defend her during her confirmation hearings—she was unceremoniously dropped.[73] Guinier, a Yale friend of many years of both Clintons, felt betrayed. In May, a more bizarre episode opened when seven career employees of the White House Travel Office were summarily dismissed. It appeared that the First Lady and Vince Foster, the president's counsel, believed an Arkansas-based travel company, headed by several of Clinton's friends, could provide better service.[74] The media had a field day with what quickly became known as Travelgate, and only the threat of a congressional investigation, joined to disdain by a public outraged by such imperious behavior, guaranteed that the fired employees would be reinstated in their White House posts. The whole affair proved to be a debacle for the president, an unnecessary one.

Before the election, Clinton had spoken airily of the importance of relieving the neglected middle class of their excessive tax burdens, but the size of the impending budget deficit told him within days of reaching the White House that any such gift was not in his power to give. As discussion proceeded in the Senate about the president's proposal for a $500 billion budget cut over five years, it became increasingly clear that Clinton and a good number of senators were divided on what tax increases could be contemplated, what appropriations might be substantially reduced. Clinton proposed a $16 billion job stimulus bill, incorporating ideas advanced by Reich, but saw that figure quickly reduced, with only $4 billion retained in unemployment relief.

That, however, proved to be only the beginning of a humiliating process that revealed the president's inadequate understanding of how to press Congress to do those things he wanted. To carry his own Democratic majority with him, he modified his bold plan for proposed energy taxes with a more modest and limited tax on gasoline. In the end, Congress accepted tax increases on couples earning more than $180,000 a year and single individuals earning more than $140,000, but in the House, the bill passed by only the slightest margin, 218–216. The appropriations bill passed the Senate by a vote of 51–50, with Vice President Gore casting the decisive vote.[75] The new president, enjoying what often passed in earlier administrations for a political honeymoon—his first months in office—failed to show the skill that had made Roosevelt's hundred days a household word in a much more serious time of economic disorder.[76]

Still, the legislation that emerged carried some features that bore recognizable Clinton signatures. Thus, for example, the taxes imposed on those he denominated rich, a class of men and women he felt no need to propitiate, together with his earned income tax credit plan, guaranteeing supplemental income to working families compelled to live on inadequate wages, carried his unmistakable stamp. These triumphs, real but relatively minor, could scarcely compensate for what became his greatest defeat, guaranteeing disaster for the Democratic Party in the off-year 1994 congressional elections.

In selecting his wife, helped by Ira Magaziner, his Rhodes Scholar friend, to fashion a comprehensive health care reform scheme, Clinton showed his characteristic arrogance and innocence. Hillary knew less than she pretended of a system more complex than any she had experience of, and while Ira might know how to force a weak Brown University president to capitulate to his undergraduate demands, neither understood how to win congressional or popular approval for a radical revision of the nation's health care system. Both, wildly ambitious, conceived a plan they imagined would be acceptable to all the critical constituencies: the working- and middle-class public searching for affordable health care; the millions who had no insurance at all; the considerable army of health care professionals, doctors and nurses, and those who administered hospitals in what had become a trillion-dollar industry; and the politicians, local, state, and national, who understood the gravity of the problem but did not necessarily approve of the solutions proposed by the president's wife.

For decades, prominent senators, including Ted Kennedy, had been arguing for basic reforms in Medicare and Medicaid to extend the benefits that many had come to enjoy through legislation passed during the Johnson administration. For the president's wife, these appeared palliatives only, believing a bolder plan would win overwhelming public support and make her husband as memorable a reformer as anyone who had occupied the White House in the century.[77] In greatly underestimating the opposition she was likely to encounter from both the health care and the health insurance industries, she worked for months to produce a 1,300-page report of baffling complexity, intended to meet almost every conceivable health care contingency. In theory, she had covered all her bases; in fact, she had failed to consider that neither she nor Magaziner knew how to do battle in a political arena where the effort to make the struggle appear to be one between entrenched privilege, as represented in the pharmaceutical and insurance industries, as against those concerned only with the public welfare, would appear simplistic and excessively ideological.[78]

The president's original decision, to entrust his wife with this critical initiative, had been a mistake; no one so closely associated with him, known for her exaggerated pride and intolerance of those who dared to differ with her, could negotiate successfully in an area where so many interests had to be accommodated. The secrecy she practiced and found congenial, seeking expert advice from some, ignoring others, could not be compensated for by even the most effective presidential intervention in a splendid speech to Congress late in 1993. Clinton did what he could to protect the hard nine months of labor endured by his ambitious and gifted wife, but her failure to insist on a more continuous and open political dialogue, not least with those who would finally have to approve the financial provisions of so extensive a health care reform, guaranteed the defeat of a plan few in the general public ever understood.

In a White House where nameless right-wing groups were thought to be compassing the president's political destruction, effectively thwarting the will of the millions who had elected him, any suspicion that attached to either the president or his wife could always be dismissed as politically inspired. When Vince Foster, the president's longtime personal attorney, committed suicide, and it became known that papers had been taken from his office immediately after his death, the media speculated on what these papers contained, whether they did not relate to certain Clinton financial dealings in Arkansas that had already become the subject of public discussion. While some believed the death had not been a suicide but a murder, this was not a view either the president or his principal aides would even consider. For the Clintons, as for Stephanopoulos and others in the White House, Foster's death was self-inflicted, a "mystery" that could not be explained. This was never the view taken by the media. Stephanopoulos stated the situation succinctly when he wrote:

> His suicide raised suspicions; the suspicions spawned scrutiny; the scrutiny sparked resentment and resistance; and the inevitable 'cover-up' charge that followed, in the 'irresistible logic' of a modern Washington scandal, led to the appointment of an independent counsel. The rest, as they say, is history.[79]

The Stephanopoulos account, too abbreviated and excessively protective of the president and the First Lady, made no allusion to the fact that in the 1992 election, when Clinton's candidacy became a serious possibility, the *New York Times,* in its most discreet manner, had raised questions about possible Clinton financial impropriety in the Whitewater Development Corporation decision in 1978 to exploit some 220 acres of riverfront property in northern Arkansas for recreational purposes.[80] Those charges, sufficiently vague at the time to encourage the Clintons to believe that no attention need be given them, gained credibility only when the Foster suicide brought the issue to the fore again.[81] While it was only one of several factors that made Republicans believe Hillary Clinton had been less than forthright in telling the story of her involvement in Whitewater, the talk that circulated in the capital of a cover-up led Janet Reno, the attorney general, to ask a three-judge appeals court to appoint an independent counsel to investigate Whitewater and related charges.

It is doubtful that Vernon Jordan, had he been the attorney general, would have thought such a move necessary. In any case, Reno's decision led to the appointment first of James Fiske, and then of Kenneth Starr, the latter having served as solicitor general in the Bush administration. Reno scarcely guessed when she made the original appointment what it might eventually lead to. Having almost certainly consulted with the Clintons, and learning there was no combustible material in Whitewater, it was impossible for her to foresee that the inquiry would lead to charges that threatened for a second time in the century the impeachment of a president.

The question frequently asked during all four administrations of Franklin Roosevelt—"Why do they hate him so?"—was no less relevant to Clinton's time in the White House. With Roosevelt, a successful first term led him to make many enemies, not least among bankers, lawyers, and businessmen, whom he never ceased to berate for all they had done to bring on the Depression. Many thought him a traitor to his social class and could neither forgive nor exonerate what they considered his impetuous and illegal actions, creating an America very different from the one they were born into and treasured. Roosevelt's acknowledged electoral strength generated additional animosity that he felt secure enough to ignore, placing a proper value on the unmistakable verdicts given by the electorate in 1936, 1940, and 1944.

The contempt for Clinton derived not from his strength but from his weakness. A superb political campaigner, once installed in the White House, he fumbled badly and constantly. The stories that issued from 1600 Pennsylvania Avenue told of administrative chaos, indecision, high-flown rhetoric, and botched policies. Hillary, his loyal accomplice, became something of a figure of fun for those who saw her as a twentieth-century Lady Macbeth, constantly interfering, excessively haughty, insufficiently deferential to the social customs of a city that still prized a certain decorum and modesty.

The extent of the president's failure in his first two years in office was made manifest in the off-year 1994 congressional elections. The Republicans gained control of both the Senate and the House for the first time since 1954—they had not enjoyed such influence even in the halcyon days of Reagan—and their victories in twenty-four of the thirty-six governors' races told the Democrats they had not suffered a comparable debacle in living memory, indeed not since 1920. For those with longer historic memories, it appeared that Clinton had blundered as Taft did in 1910, and it seemed almost inconceivable that a president held responsible for such catastrophic Democratic Party losses could recoup his political fortunes and go on to win a second term.

The Democratic electoral defeats in 1994, to an extent few had anticipated, gave the president a new lease on power. While he could never blame himself or his wife for what had happened, believing the trouble grew out of "those kids who got me elected," he thought belatedly that he should "never have brought anyone under forty into the White House."[82] Had he continued in that morbid state of mind, failing to understand how much he and his wife, and not the kids, were responsible for the debacle, there would have been no second term. The Republican victory had been too overwhelming and more dangerous for those who now chose Newt Gingrich as Speaker of the House than they or he realized.

Gingrich, like Clinton, was reputed to be an expert hardball player—the phrase much favored by the media—and was remembered for having ousted Jim Wright, an earlier Democratic House Speaker, for ethics violations. He posed as a conservative revolutionary who would never mollycoddle the poor and those others habituated to feed at the Democratic Party trough. Gingrich, an intellectual tough, met his match in Clinton, no less garrulous, but substantially more shrewd. Gingrich's vaunted Contract with America, with its promise of tax cuts and higher defense expenditures, made possible in great part by major cuts in Medicare and Medicaid, as well as in federal support of student loans, crime prevention, and environmental protection, allowed the president to represent him as the incarnation of all that was most vicious in the Republican Party.

As Nixon had used his 1962 defeat in California to reinvent himself, Clinton did the same three decades later, emerging as a New Democrat, something he had long claimed to be. Shedding the last of his so-called liberal beliefs and becoming, though never openly, the disciple of Reagan, he appealed to an increasingly affluent middle class, took a page out of Truman's book and made the Republican reactionaries in Congress, led by Newt Gingrich, his principal foes.

No longer fighting a health care industry, having lost any incentive to spend his time disparaging doctors, insurance companies, and pharmaceutical giants for their selfishness, Clinton did what Roosevelt so effectively accomplished when he mocked Martin, Barton, and Fish, isolationists who scarcely understood the world of the 1940s. Clinton personalized the 1990s struggle with Congress, making it appear a fight between himself and Newt Gingrich, a hopeless Georgia reactionary who was leading an army of Republican congressional lemmings to a sea that would soon engulf them. Recognizing that there would be no new universal health care legislation, that the almost unanimous opposition of Republicans in Congress and the serious divisions within the Democratic Party made that a lost cause, he wisely decided to cut his losses. Gingrich, in several highly publicized confrontations, including the virtual shutdown of the federal government in 1995 and early 1996, caused by the Republican majority's refusal to provide interim funding until a new budget was approved, showed himself reckless. The president, by comparison, took on the qualities of a statesman, a role he vastly enjoyed.

As rumors continued to fly about his sexual excesses, with Paula Jones filing a sexual harassment lawsuit against him, it became more important than ever to insist that these charges, encouraged by Republican zealots determined to destroy him, would never deter him from being the people's president. In his 1996 State of the Union speech, he declared that "the era of big government is over," sounding all the notes already made familiar by Reagan and Bush, but he promised not to sit idly by, allowing the Republicans to savage major social legislation, including the Aid to Families with Dependent Children, which had existed for decades.[83] While he rejected the Republican plans for workfare, and vetoed two bills that would have allowed individual states to determine eligibility for federal welfare payments, in the end he accepted to cut the Food Stamp program, reduce benefits to legal immigrants, and make other concessions to a Congress determined to clean up the welfare mess.

Clinton, in signing the welfare reform bill that placed strict limits on how long people could remain on the dole, gave eloquent testimony to his concern to be thought a centrist, disillusioned with Republican extremists but unwilling to become a hostage to their propaganda. As Hillary was to write,

> The legislation was far from perfect, which is where pragmatic politics entered in. It was preferable to sign the measure knowing that a Democratic administration was in place to implement it humanely. If he vetoed welfare reform a third time, Bill would be handing the Republicans a potential political windfall.[84]

While many in Clinton's Cabinet, including Shalala, Reich, and Cisneros, urged him to veto the bill, Clinton, the New Democrat, knew better; his interest was to make welfare yesterday's issue, one that would no longer have any appeal to aggrieved middle-class voters.[85]

In his election contest with Robert Dole, the Republican Party's presidential nominee in 1996, Clinton met for a second time a Republican considerably less charismatic than himself. Dole, knowing his party, had always sought to promote some sort of compromise between the more reactionary of his colleagues, whose support he knew he needed, and those who shared his own more reasonable political preferences. This had become very apparent in the long struggle over health care reform. Dole knew that the escalating costs of health care and the inadequacy of medical coverage required some action to be taken, but he understood also that many in his party would never accept a plan that required every citizen to arrange his or her own health insurance, precisely as they did with auto insurance. Compelling employers to be responsible for the expenses incurred by their employees would be even more unwelcome to orthodox Republicans.

In the end Dole had no proposals for major health care reform, and fell back during the election campaign on the same issues Bush had used in his efforts to defeat Clinton—he felt compelled to dwell on the president's character. The suit filed by Paula Jones, with its charge that the president had made crude sexual advances in an Arkansas hotel room in 1991, and that her rejection of him had led to a loss of promotion and mental distress, were matters the president made light of, that the media were not equally ready to ignore. Still, in the TV debates and in his stump speeches, Dole never managed to challenge the president, to administer the knockout blow that would have made the election interesting. November 1996 proved again that Clinton was the comeback kid, winning with an even larger popular vote than in 1992. Perot, running a second time, lost more than half the votes he had garnered in

1992, and both he and Dole appeared political innocents beside the acknowledged political master.

How, then, is one to explain this remarkable presidential success, following so many catastrophic earlier failures? Incumbency undoubtedly helped, though it had never served to give Carter an advantage against Reagan, but then Dole never pretended to be a second Reagan. The more significant detail, certainly, was that though Clinton achieved a remarkable personal victory, testimony to his extraordinary talent as a political campaigner, his coattails were not long enough to bring great numbers of Democrats into the Senate or the House, wresting control of either chamber from the Republicans.

Clinton, a consummate actor, almost in Reagan's class, traded on many of the same attributes; laid-back and folksy, he guessed correctly that the liberal policies of an earlier day would never suffice to give him victory. While he could never acknowledge that he was a Reagan Democrat—any such admission would have been fatal to his cause—he learned much from observing his presidency. Reagan, thought by many to be an ideologue, had never made the mistakes of Gingrich; he appealed to middle-class Americans who imagined themselves overburdened by excessive taxes. Clinton came to the White House with the same conviction, and though unable to realize initially the campaign promises he had made in 1992 because of the size of the federal deficit, he never wholly abandoned the hope that one day he could show the Americans a middle way, very distant from the one proposed by Gingrich in his Contract with America.

If Clinton's domestic accomplishments in his first term resembled those of Reagan more than of Johnson, this was even more evident in matters of foreign policy. Though he spoke of a new age and promised a new foreign and defense policy suited to the opportunities created by the demise of Soviet communism, this never happened. Neither he nor others in his administration ever dared question the wisdom of what George Bush and his associates had done in bringing the Gulf War to an early end, condemning thousands of Kurds to extinction by Saddam Hussein's forces. All that seemed ancient history for Clinton, a closed chapter that need not be reopened. His greater failures were in Bosnia, Rwanda, Srebrenica, and Kosovo, tragedies on his watch, events he understood no better than Carter did the turmoil in Iran and Afghanistan.

Dole, more knowledgeable about the Yugoslav tragedy than the president, having seen something of Serbian atrocities in Kosovo as early as 1990, never attempted to make foreign policy a major part of his election campaign. Clinton was allowed to set the agenda for the 1996 election, and it contained little that related to foreign policy. The first Clinton administration, except for its success in negotiating the Dayton Accords, achieved largely through the efforts of Richard Holbrooke, showed itself ineffectual in the Balkans and scarcely less so in Africa, but all this mattered little to a society persuaded that the great danger to its security had passed, that the time had come once again to enjoy a well-earned prosperity, too long deferred.

Why, then, was the president unable to address the problems that surfaced abroad, that recommended a major reconsideration of the policies pursued by his two Republican predecessors? The short answer is that Clinton, like Bush and Reagan, feared any engagement that carried substantial risk, defined as the return of American body bags. Both his first secretary of state, Warren Christopher, and his second, Madeleine Albright, knew this, and so also did his national security advisers, as well as those who served him as secretary of defense. In Yugoslavia, particularly in Bosnia, he inherited a problem Bush had neglected, knowing that the Serbs were committing atrocities against their Muslim neighbors, imprisoning many in detention camps, latter-day concentration camps, but seeing this as a civil war, not a quarrel that the United States need become involved in.

James Baker's deathless prose, "We don't have a dog in this fight," and Bush's periodic insistence, "Tell me again what this [is] all about," expressed the innocence of American leaders whose knowledge of the Balkans was miniscule. Lawrence Eagleburger, who succeeded Baker in the last months of the Bush administration as secretary of state and had served as ambassador in Belgrade, knew more, but he, too, recommended abstention from any policy that might lead to the engagement of U.S. troops.[86] The Yugoslav legacy bequeathed to Clinton was not one he was especially interested in or competent to deal with. He much preferred to negotiate with ol' Boris, the Russian leader he imagined he could influence.[87] While he had taken note of the many reported Serbian atrocities during his 1992 election campaign, it never became a major concern. As he put it in one of his speeches, "I want us to be focused on the problems of people at home. I'm worried about kids being killed on the streets here at home."[88] In his mind, the Yugoslav debacle was something for the United Nations to handle.

The secretary of state, Warren Christopher, deeply troubled by the Balkan imbroglio, aware that as many as 100,000 had been killed since the dissolution of the Yugoslav state, saw no way for the United States to intervene to end the "ethnic cleansing" that had become characteristic of a civil war that confounded the Europeans as much as it did the Americans. What Samantha Power later described as "mass murders, systematic beatings, and the rape of Muslims and others, prolonged shellings of innocents in Sarajevo and elsewhere, forced displacement of entire villages [and] inhuman treatment of prisoners in detention camps," though shocking in their pictorial representations, admitted of no solution that secured any wide support in the administration, even among those who recognized its tragic human dimensions.[89]

In May 1993, the president sent Christopher to Europe to win support for a new policy he and his advisers had decided on; "lift and strike" called for a lifting of the arms embargo against the Bosnian Muslims and a bombing of the Serbs, but the secretary of state never believed in the policy he was dispatched to advocate, and the Europeans remained unconvinced of its efficacy. A new policy was then proposed by the UN Security Council, to create safe areas in the Muslim-held enclave of Srebenica, Sarajevo, and four other cities, with some 30,000 troops dispatched out to defend them. The Americans refused to contribute to such a force, and the Europeans showed themselves equally reticent.

With Clinton's military advisers arguing against intervention, and the president himself uncertain that the public favored his risking American lives in any Balkan engagement, he seemed satisfied to say that "the U.S. should always seek an opportunity to stand up against—at least *speak out against*—inhumanity," but such words were no substitute for a policy.[90] As for the secretary of state, he found it not at all incongruous to call the Bosnian War "a humanitarian crisis a long way from home, in the middle of another continent."[91] Dick Morris, Clinton's leading pollster, told the president, "You don't want to be Lyndon Johnson, sacrificing your potential for doing good on the domestic front by a destructive, never-ending foreign involvement."[92] When it appeared that Sarajevo would fall to the Serbs, Christopher would say no more than that the "United States is doing all that it can consistent with its national interest." Clinton had no wish to risk American lives in an effort to prevent ethnic cleansing and genocide, and in June 1995, he and Vice President Gore appeared on *Larry King Live*, a popular TV show, to defend their policy. Gore believed it was a tragedy "unfolding for a long time, some would say for 500 years," and the president thought the enmities were of even longer date, going back "almost a thousand years."[93] In any case, United States policies had not failed; some 130,000 people had been murdered in 1992; that number had declined to 3,000 in 1994. "That's still tragic," Clinton said, "but I hardly think that constitutes a colossal failure."[94]

These remarks, made just weeks before the Serbs seized the so-called safe area of Srebrenica, where some 40,000 Muslim men, women, and children had sought refuge, resulted in the killing of some 7,000 Muslim men and boys, the worst slaughter Europe had known for over half a century. The U.S. Senate, prodded by Senator Dole, voted 69–29 on July 26, 1995, to lift the arms ban in Bosnia, and almost all the Republicans and twenty Democrats challenged the president's do-nothing policies. Clinton, refusing to accept any blame, criticized the United Nations for failing to call for NATO air strikes.[95] In his words, "This distribution of responsibility all grew out of a decision made prior to my Presidency—which I am not criticizing. I say again—to try to say: 'O.K., here's a problem in Europe. The Europeans ought to take the lead.'"[96]

Many of the leading newspapers in the country refused to accept these excuses for inaction, and the *Washington Post* mocked Clinton's "big mouth, no stick administration."[97] Zbigniew Brzezinski, perhaps taking revenge on a president never friendly to Jimmy Carter, penned a presidential speech that might have been given "if the post of Leader of the Free World was not currently vacant."[98] Beginning on August 30, 1995, following a second attack on a Sarajevo market where many were killed, NATO bombers attacked Serb targets, communications centers, ammunition dumps, and other military targets, continuing the assault for three weeks.[99] The president, belatedly, approved of the kind of action that in no way threatened him.

It was inconceivable that many in the United States, knowing the terror the Serbs had inflicted, would oppose the president in his bombing campaign. When Senators Dole and John McCain pressed the Senate to approve the deployment of U.S. troops to Bosnia, sixty senators gave their consent, and only thirty-nine expressed their opposition. While there was always a hazard that this land operation would in the end cause deaths and casualties, with body bags returned—Clinton's perpetual nightmare—it was never as dangerous as some wished to pretend. As with the Gulf War, the illusion had to be created that the operation was fraught with danger; it was not, and the president knew it.

Meanwhile, a different crisis opened on April 6, 1994, in Africa when an airplane carrying the Rwandan president, Juvénal Habyarimana, and the Burundian president, Cyprien Ntaryamira, was shot down in mysterious circumstances, and the secretary of state, made aware by the assistant secretary of state, Prudence Bushnell, that their deaths threatened a mass outbreak of violence in both countries, scarcely knew how to respond.[100] The United States had never been much preoccupied with Rwanda; within hours of the air tragedy Hutus began to seek out and kill Tutsis, and in the next hundred days some 800,000 Tutsis and politically moderate Hutus were murdered. While the *New York Times* and other newspapers reported on the mass killings, and the Red Cross suggested as early as April 26 that "at least 100,000 but possibly as many as 300,000 Rwandans had been killed," with Oxfam claiming some days later that 500,000 people were reported "missing," the Tutsis begged the United Nations to do something to prevent a genocide that threatened to take on the proportions of the Holocaust. The UN dared not do anything that would put their own civilian forces at risk, and in the United States, neither in the State Department nor in the Pentagon was there any pressure to make any commitment that might prove dangerous. The White House showed no wish to press them to do so.[101] Rwanda was very far away; the off-year elections were imminent, and Clinton imagined he had already risked enough in consenting to the NATO bombings of Serbia to prevent further aggression in Bosnia. The president, cautious in the Reagan tradition, lacking all sensitivity for foreign policy issues, even those that touched human rights, and having no one in his entourage prepared to differ with him, opted to do nothing.[102]

Because the NATO bombings had made the Serbs aware of the need to negotiate some kind of settlement, they agreed to receive Richard Holbrooke, the president's emissary, in September 1995, knowing that he was intent on establishing an independent Bosnia. The Dayton Accords, negotiated in November 1995 and heralded by the president, created a single Bosnian state in which the Serbs were 31 percent of the population, occupying 49 percent of the land, the Croats were 17 percent with control of 25 percent of the territory, and the Muslims, the largest group, 44 percent of the population, controlled roughly 25 percent of the country.[103] At no time in the past had an independent Bosnia existed.

The earlier Vance-Owen plan that had called for a loose confederation had been rejected by the Americans in 1993. Now, this multiethnic, multireligious new state was created with the president's blessing, largely engineered by Holbrooke, his very able special envoy. Holbrooke, courting the president assiduously, dreamed of becoming the Henry Kissinger of the Clinton presidency, pledged not to *realpolitik* but to human rights, and his accomplishment must figure as the great diplomatic triumph of Clinton's first administration, though not quite comparable to what Bush and Baker had achieved in their negotiations for a united Germany, firmly anchored in NATO. In this instance, neither the president nor his secretary of state played any significant role in the negotiations; the achievement remained that of an intelligent and tough Holbrooke, a worthy adversary to a rogue, Slobodan Milosevic, expecting his reward might come in the second administration when Clinton, following the expected resignation of an exhausted Christopher, might appoint him secretary of state. This was not to be; Madeleine Albright received the presidential nod, gaining the highest post ever awarded a woman.

Because Serb aggression against the Albanian Muslim settlers in Kosovo continued through much of the president's second term, by early 1999 the United States and its allies, losing all patience with Milosevic, realized that only by making a credible threat could they hope to control him. Meeting at Rambouillet, the United States and its European allies issued a warning to the Serbs to remove their troops from Kosovo, grant virtual autonomy to its Albanian residents, and allow 25,000 armed peacekeepers to be sent to Serbia. The Americans agreed to provide 4,000 of these troops, and Serbia was warned that if it resisted these terms NATO would begin a bombing operation. Receiving no satisfactory response, the bombing started on March 24, 1999.

The Serbs responded by effectively expelling the whole of the Albanian population from Kosovo, denying that they were doing so, and on June 9, after seventy-eight days of consecutive bombing, Milosevic surrendered, accepting an agreement that obliged the Serb army and police to leave Kosovo, still an integral part of Serbia, with the rights of its Albanian residents to return guaranteed. Clinton, overjoyed, visited Kosovo as a hero, the president who had said no to a terrible dictator, accomplishing it without American casualties. The operation in Serbia was in fact fail-safe, in the tradition of Reagan's Grenada and Libya, though on a vastly greater scale. Clinton appeared to be enjoying foreign policy successes in his second term that exceeded what he had accomplished in his first years in office, and he reveled in his success.

His undersecretary of state, Strobe Talbott, a Rhodes Scholar friend from Oxford, a journalist whose command of the Russian language qualified him as an expert on that troubled society, wrote an admiring account of Clinton's many feats in dealing with Yeltsin, ol' Boris, the drunken and ailing Russian leader Clinton both courted and patronized. *The Russia Hand,* Talbott's eulogy of Clinton, narrated the purportedly remarkable presidential accomplishments that followed from his eighteen meetings with Yeltsin, a record number of American encounters with his opposite number in the Kremlin. Talbott never asked whether Clinton might have done well to see Yeltsin less, to give heed to other foreign policy issues, to be somewhat less beguiled with all that would follow from an expansion of NATO to include the former Communist states of Eastern Europe.

In a work that lacked any memorable observation by the president on any foreign policy issue, though it faithfully recorded his self-serving and simple analyses of the Russian situation, Clinton lived with the illusion that he was saving Russia from a red communist resurgence or a brown fascist takeover. Like Reagan, he wished to be an innovator, beholden to none of his predecessors, and looked for the slogan that would define his administration, never wholly satisfied that he had discovered it. For a moment, he imagined he found it in "Partnership for Peace," a phrase forgotten within a year of its invention. Clinton, according to Talbott, disdained any effort to suggest that his ideas for NATO expansion simply sought to "consolidate the gains of his predecessors" and told his people "he never wanted to see it in a speech draft again." What, then, was he aiming for? In his words, we shouldn't be "telling people who are already bored that their mission is to put icing on the cake someone else has baked."[104] He would start anew, knowing that Roosevelt and Truman deserved recognition for their "instincts" that "they just made it up as they went along."[105]

Failing to understand what his two illustrious Democratic predecessors had done, what he might have learned from them, he proposed to be an innovator, and his courtiers were more than ready to give him the same prime billing as an architect of a novel foreign policy that Reagan's servants so readily accorded him. Putin, who met him only in his last months in office, recognized him for what he was, an amateur, a poseur, what French president Jacques Chirac probably also guessed, that the British prime minister, Tony Blair, equally concerned with finding a middle way, never understood.

If his accomplishments in foreign affairs were in fact negligible, the same could not be said of his skills as a politician or of his victories on the domestic front, especially conspicuous at the start of his second term when the Congressional Budget Office projected the first federal budget surplus since 1969. By early 1998, unemployment had fallen to its lowest levels since the time of Nixon, and the president, trading on his success, persuaded Congress in August 1997 to pass a budget that showed no deficit, regarded by many as an incomparable political feat. The perilous federal fiscal conditions of the Bush and Reagan years, like those of Carter and Ford, seemed to have vanished, leaving the nation rich and contented, living in a slightly frenetic 1990s version of the Coolidge era, with the stock market registering spectacular gains and new industries booming in Silicon Valley and elsewhere. Middle-class taxes, as Clinton had promised before his first election, were substantially reduced, and the robust economy allowed new federal appropriations to be made in support of education. Clinton, anxious to shed the tax-and-spend image that the Republicans had fastened on all Democrats since FDR, made it clear that he would oppose further tax cuts until he could be absolutely certain that the Social Security system was invulnerable.

An experienced and accomplished political leader at home more than ever, he wished to prove himself a statesman abroad. In this latter area where he had achieved so little in his first years, he dispatched George Mitchell, the respected Democratic senator from Maine, to try to settle the continued fighting between Protestants and Catholics in Northern Ireland. His voluble and ambitious new secretary of state, together with Richard Holbrooke, worked diligently in the fall of 1998 to secure a peace accord between the Israelis and the Palestinians in negotiations at Wye Mills, Maryland. When terrorists attacked U.S. embassies in Kenya and Tanzania, the president ordered a bombing of their known camps. So, also, when Iraq refused the UN demand to inspect its suspected nuclear, chemical, and biological warfare capabilities, Clinton seemed initially prepared to negotiate but in the end ordered air attacks to compel compliance. These operations achieved little, but they helped establish his reputation as a president who would not allow the country's security to be threatened by terrorists or rogue states. Reagan and Bush had frequently warned the country against both, and Clinton showed himself no less committed to their extinction, having no idea of how to do so except to bomb them into submission.

In the midst of this near euphoria, Kenneth Starr, the independent counsel, received information suggesting that the president, though continuing to deny any guilt in the Paula Jones affair, had in fact been involved in another sexual relationship with a soon-to-be-celebrated Monica Lewinsky, a twenty-two-year-old White House intern.[106] The Paula Jones charges had created a new bimbo crisis for the president, but in May 1997, the Supreme Court decided unanimously that Jones could not sue the president in court as long as he remained in office, and it appeared that he would be immune from prosecution until he departed the White House on January 20, 2001. At this point, knowing his guilt, and having no interest in seeing the case revived after he forfeited his presidential immunity, Clinton instructed his lawyers to enter discussions with Jones's lawyers, looking to a monetary settlement. In the end, they offered $700,000 in compensation for the damages Jones purportedly suffered, which only led to a new Jones demand—this time, for a formal apology by the president. Clinton refused to give one, and in January 1998, in a formal deposition, explicitly denied the truth of several of her allegations, also vigorously repudiating the suggestion, when cross-examined by her lawyers, that he had been involved in a sexual affair with a White House intern.

Monica Lewinsky, in an affidavit submitted in the Jones suit, denied ever having a sexual relation with the president, but Jones's lawyers had reason to doubt the truth of her statement. Starr, having failed to that point to prove presidential malfeasance in Whitewater or Travelgate, saw his opportunity, knowing that Linda Tripp, another White House employee, had secretly taped Lewinsky's account of her affair with the president. He now asked for and received permission from Janet Reno, the attorney general, to expand his investigation, looking into the possibility that the president had committed perjury in his testimony and might be guilty of obstructing justice. Reno, without informing the president, consented to Starr's proposal for an expanded inquiry, and rumors flew of what the president had said in his meeting with Jones's lawyers, of what his associates in the White House had been doing to find employ for Lewinsky outside Washington, D.C. When news of the affair exploded in the media on January 21, 1998, the president, supported by his wife, denied the truth of the charges, insisting they were all part of a right-wing conspiracy to discredit him.[107]

Clinton acted as if he had nothing to hide, gave a vigorous State of the Union address a few days later, and his friends rallied around, accusing Starr of conducting a vendetta against an innocent man. But there was no possibility of the crisis ending there. Lewinsky, appearing before a grand jury, having been assured of immunity from further prosecution, gave a full account of her relations with the president, providing the semen-stained dress that proved her charge. On August 17, 1998, Clinton, summoned by the federal grand jury, acknowledged an "inappropriate, intimate relationship" had existed and, in an emotional TV appearance, begged the American people to forgive him for having "misled" them.[108] Refusing to provide additional details, and insisting he had done nothing illegal, he watched as Starr moved to prepare and send to the House of Representatives an eleven-point charge of indictable offenses that merited the president's impeachment.

By a vote of 258–156, with thirty-one Democrats voting with the majority, the House accepted to initiate impeachment proceedings. Those Democrats who remained loyal to the president accepted he had acted immorally but refused to see his offenses as the high crimes and misdemeanors that the Constitution declared were the only ones that justified impeachment, removal from office. Although many in the country, and not only Republicans, called for the president's resignation, the Democrats both in the House and the Senate felt overwhelmingly that he should be censured but allowed to complete his term. Indeed, the midyear elections, which gave five new seats to the Democrats in the House, suggested that the country took a somewhat less grave view of the president's transgressions than those who thought it a disgrace that such a man should continue to occupy the White House.

When the House finally voted on Starr's recommendations, it accepted two of his original articles; the president was charged with perjury for having lied to the federal grand jury and for obstructing justice in the Jones case. The vote on the first charge was 228–206, with all but three Republicans agreeing; on the second charge, the vote was 221–212. The Senate spectacle, broadcast in its entirety on television, captured the nation's attention as no other political event had since the congressional and media investigations of Nixon. With a two-thirds vote required for conviction, and the Democrats having forty-five seats in the Senate, it was inconceivable that the president would be convicted. The nation watched the acrimonious debates, not wholly surprised when not even a majority could be found to convict the president.

His private behavior was reprehensible, but a president who had restored the nation's prosperity, never taken the country into war, and done so many of the things that had made Reagan popular was not going suddenly to be dismissed from office. In the midst of the impeachment trial, Clinton went before Congress to deliver his State of the Union address. No one observing him that day could doubt that he was cool, able to ignore the charges of his enemies, telling Congress and the nation all that he intended to do with part of the federal government's budget surplus to improve education and health care, to provide new monies for defense, and rescue the nation's imperiled Social Security system. While Republicans might rile at his having abandoned his earlier beliefs, not a New Democrat any longer, but one more big-time Democratic Party spender, the nation knew it was prosperous and at peace; that was enough to guarantee acclaim for the supreme communicator.

In his last months in office, Clinton sought to resolve the Israeli-Palestinian conflict, imagining he could end his administration with an incomparabe foreign policy victory, capping what he and many of his admirers imagined he had achieved at Dayton with Bosnia. He failed in this, not for lack of trying but because he never understood either Yasser Arafat's problems as leader of Palestine or Ehud Barak's as prime minister of Israel. What Theodore Roosevelt understood almost intuitively in mediating the Russo-Japanese War, Clinton never grasped, failing to understand that so delicate a negotiation would not succeed simply because an American president wanted to leave his mark on history.

Clinton's understanding of foreign policy was always primitive; the world abroad was not one he knew at all well, though his colleagues in the Seven, observing his performances at their meetings, accepted that he was both articulate and intelligent. He promised a new foreign policy for a new age but failed to provide one, not least because he never understood how the world had changed since the time of Ronald Reagan, since the end of the Cold War and the collapse of the Soviet Union.

He saw problems in isolation, imagining at one time that Haiti required his attention, at another that he ought to support the North American Free Trade Agreement, never understanding how these several initiatives might serve as components in a larger conceptual framework. He lacked strategic vision, never reconsidered how American alliances were likely to fare in a world where the Soviet Union no longer existed and where Communist China no longer appeared to be a major threat. He failed to satisfy the minority in the country who wished him to be bold in protecting human rights, to prevent genocide in Serbia and Rwanda, but this was a small failing compared to the larger one, never admitted or recognized.

Clinton failed to tell a self-satisfied and prosperous nation that its security was still at risk, that history had *not* ended, that Bush's victory in Iraq was less monumental than the Republicans claimed, that democracy, as represented by free elections and a market economy, was not on the march everywhere. Much of the world continued to be governed by authoritarian rulers; billions lived in dire poverty in Asia, Africa, and Latin America; terrorist threats were unlikely to be met by the fail-safe measures the president opted for.

Finally, and perhaps most crucially, in his long eight years he did nothing to advance the country's understanding of the vast and complex Muslim world that had been seething from the time his despised predecessor, Jimmy Carter, failed to recognize the significance of the Iranian Revolution. Clinton, following in the tradition of Reagan, failed to create that greater appreciation of the external world that Roosevelt and Truman had done so much to foster, which led them to support educational and political initiatives that gave the country a new understanding of societies previously too little known, including the Soviet Union, Germany, and Japan.

Retiring from politics to become an elder statesman at an exceptionally early age, passing the political baton to his wife, the successor to Daniel Patrick Moynihan as the senator from New York, Clinton remained prominent, feted wherever he went, not least in the United Kingdom, where his great buddy, Tony Blair, purportedly his disciple, held sway.[109] Together or separately, the Clintons were celebrities wherever they travelled, abroad as much as at home.

"My story," as told by Hillary Rodham Clinton, was the tale of a president universally regarded as a great communicator in the Roosevelt-Reagan tradition, who had been able to fashion impressive electoral victories against powerful, wicked, and irresponsible Republican enemies. The task of demonstrating the president's unique diplomatic talents fell to others, in time especially to one who had served Clinton as his very successful secretary of the treasury. Robert Rubin knew the president to be fallible, as all mortals were, but he saw him also as courageous, innovative, and dedicated.[110]

In *In an Uncertain World,* Rubin's autobiography, he represents the president as prophetic and far-seeing, willing and able to listen to others, prepared to risk himself in seeking support of the Mexican peso, rescuing the Mexican economy when it was faltering, showing equal resolve later when several of the Asian economies teetered on the edge of collapse. Clinton, intelligent and informed, understood the repercussions such a monetary disaster might have for the American economy and, presiding in his second term at a time of almost unprecedented national prosperity, raised taxes appreciably, achieving a vast reduction in the national debt.[111] This, an undoubted accomplishment for any president, especially for a Democrat, was not the remedy all his Democratic Party colleagues favored. Robert Reich, for example, secretary of labor in his first administration, had joined the Cabinet because he believed Clinton would pursue policies to lift the poor and the disadvantaged out of their misery.[112] Reich, unmentioned by Hillary Clinton, airbrushed out of her *Living History* for having written critically of the president after he left his administration, figured in the Rubin autobiography as one whose books on social policy had once greatly influenced the president. Reich, a populist in Rubin's mind, was characterized as "unwise economically," the ultimate political sin.[113]

Rubin's professional training as an investment banker told him that economic issues were all-important, a seemingly obvious truth that almost precluded his understanding the political problems that plagued the Clinton White House. His testimony to Clinton's sagacity showed little grasp of the diplomatic and security issues that made it impossible for Clinton to be creative in the Truman tradition. It is significant that the only Truman mentioned in the Rubin autobiography is one Ted Truman, and one may well ask, without undue rudeness, "Who he?" Rubin, like his chief, certainly read history but showed excessive tolerance for a president who could not possibly be creative in the Harry Truman tradition.[114]

In Rubin's autobiography, as in those written by Hillary Clinton and Madeleine Albright, there is the same failure to consider in depth those subjects that came to preoccupy the mass media in the years after September 11, 2001. Terrorism and Islam figured only peripherally in these books, backburner issues for a president who believed with his very successful secretary of the treasury that globalization was the world's inevitable destiny, and that this required "effective governance." In their minds, only the United States could provide such guidance, and only the president could be looked to for leadership.

Clinton did indeed have a "vision," the quality the first Bush mistakenly disparaged, but it was not one calculated to prepare the country for the twenty-first century. In those who served Clinton, happy to praise him, their ignorance of history was disconcerting, not least of the century into which they had been born. In their overwhelming concern to tell the stories of their own rise to eminence, they neglected to suggest why states and societies different from the one they knew best were unlikely to view the world as they did. While no one could fault Rubin for saying that "we are living in a time of great geopolitical and economic change, when the choices we make can have huge consequences," these words scarcely hinted at what those geopolitical changes were—and why they might be significant.

Clinton, less provincial than Carter, and infinitely more politically astute, lacked the knowledge and the will to break out from the foreign policy fictions and paradigms established by Reagan, meekly and ineffectually copied by Bush.[115] Indeed, he scarcely recognized how much he showed himself loyal to both, depending on a team that referred back constantly to Munich, the last great event in Madeleine Albright's conceptually impoverished history of the twentieth century. Roosevelt had been a savior, Truman, a creator; Clinton was neither. When Strobe Talbott told the president of George Kennan's remark that the administration should content itself with a "thoughtful paragraph or more, rather than trying to come up with a bumper sticker" to encapsulate its policy vis-à-vis Russia, Clinton replied, "Well, that's why Kennan's a great diplomat and scholar and not a politician."[116] Averse to doing the "old business," Clinton looked for new maps but never found them, and while the men he elevated to positions they had never expected to hold, as with Talbott, declared him a hedgehog, using Isaiah Berlin's famous description to celebrate those who knew one great thing—how to outwit the fox—Clinton performed principally as an accomplished dissembler. He was lucky Bill, who never understood how much had changed as a consequence of America's more than forty-year struggle to contain and defeat a powerful adversary, the Soviet Union.[117]

This is nowhere more evident than in *My Life*, Clinton's hilarious *apologia* that so many critics have found wanting. Anne Applebaum, an American, reviewing the book in the English *Sunday Telegraph*, may have delivered the most devastating verdict on its inadequacies when she writes: "*My Life* is not just hard to read; it's unreadable." In two succinct paragraphs, she alludes to some of the principal defects of his maudlin tale, intended to be a celebration of a life and a presidency that in fact fails to celebrate either. Applebaum writes: "In fact, other than the personal issues that interest the former president—the putting to rest of his 'demons,' the healing of his 'self-inflicted wounds'—there are no real themes in this book at all, unless you count his battle with the 'forces of reaction and division' that wanted to impeach him." She goes on to say: "For all Clinton's vaunted interest in policy solutions, it is hard to glean anything like a 'big idea' from the mass of detail. For all his faith that he is on 'the right side of history,' he doesn't much engage, intellectually, with his political opponents at all, or even acknowledge that they have any arguments worth engaging with."[118]

A third complaint might have been added; Clinton vastly exaggerates his presidential accomplishments and nowhere shows the command of the international situation as it existed during his years in the White House that justifies his perpetual self-praise. He imagines he has made an acute observation when he speaks of our having "moved from the industrial age into the global information age," and that learning to live in this new "interdependent" world is the principal policy imperative of our day. Having only the most conventional sense of history, he shows no imagination in considering what the United States or others, less militarily and economically dominant at this moment, may be tempted to do in the new era, and how they are likely to perceive the options open to them. Clinton, in his romantic self-serving tale, as in his constant adulation of the country that allowed someone like himself to rise, a life, in his words, "that would have been impossible anywhere but America," may have written unwittingly the most telling verdict on his own political career but also on that of the man who succeeded him, George W. Bush.[119]

CHAPTER 21

Reagan's Boy

GEORGE W. BUSH, president of the United States by the grace of a U.S. Supreme Court decision, was the first president since 1877 to gain admission to the White House by an Electoral College majority that nullified the loss he suffered in the popular vote.[1] More significant, perhaps, he was the only president since 1825 to be elected to the office his father had held. A more historically minded generation might have been tempted to dwell on both these phenomena, reflecting on how Rutherford Hayes had come to defeat Samuel Tilden, and how John Quincy Adams had beaten three opponents, Andrew Jackson, Henry Clay, and William Harris Crawford. But all this was ancient history for a society that had lost its earlier passion for political and diplomatic history, that had come to rely on the mass media to explain how Albert Gore, the vice president, somewhat tarnished by his too-close association with a promiscuous and louche president, came to lose the election to George W. Bush, the Texas governor, once an alcoholic who had discovered God and forsaken liquor. A less grave age might have found comic elements in the tale, and might even have thought to explore the affinities between Bush and Adams, sons who followed their fathers into the White House.[2] John Quincy Adams came to the presidency almost a quarter of a century after his father, the only president in the republic's first four decades to fail to win reelection. George W. Bush succeeded his father, another one-term president, after an interlude of only eight years, made memorable more by Bill Clinton's sexual transgressions than by any specific domestic and foreign policy innovations.

Shortly after the 2000 election, when David McCullough's celebrated biography of John Adams appeared, a comparison of the political careers of the two one-term presidential fathers would have made for an illuminating essay, but such an account would have been thought politically motivated, documenting a twentieth-century presidential decline redolent of the deterioration Woodrow Wilson and James Bryce had noted in the nineteenth century.[3] Nor would it have been seemly to contrast the two presidential mothers, the remarkable Abigail Adams and the more hard-bitten though very maternal Barbara Bush.[4] Indeed, the failure to reflect on the Adams dynasty, to compare it with that of the Bushes in the twentieth-century—grandfather, father, and sons—may have reflected a more serious reluctance to contrast George W. Bush's education and career with that of the cosmopolitan and worldly John Quincy Adams. Such a comparison would have deepened the mass media analyses that dwelled on how much the younger Bush resembled his father, following him to Phillips Andover Academy and Yale, a Skull and Bones man, a bona fide Texan oil entrepreneur who also enjoyed the same privileges of wealth and social position that had so greatly facilitated his father's ascent. It might even have suggested that George W. Bush, though genetically the son of George H.W., was best understood as the political son of Ronald Reagan, whose successes he emulated and whose strategies he adopted. Though some admirers thought to discover Theodore Roosevelt in the second Bush, especially after September 11, he no more resembled Roosevelt, a learned president, than he did John Quincy Adams, both representatives of an extinct political America.

Adams, fluent in seven languages, accomplished in both science and mathematics, took pride in the cultivation he had acquired through years of living in close proximity to his gifted and influential father, benefiting from his schooling in Paris and service as a very young man as an additional secretary to the American negotiators that ended the war with Britain. A student at the University of Leiden and Harvard, Adams opted for the career his father had also chosen—the law—but George Washington recognized his potential, a talented well-born gentleman, and appointed him minister to the Netherlands when he was only twenty-six. Two years later he went to Lisbon as minister to Portugal, but his father, succeeding Washington as president, transferred him to the more important post in Berlin, the capital of Prussia, which had become increasingly powerful in the reign of Frederick the Great.

Adams, returning to the United States after the election of Thomas Jefferson to the presidency, served first in the Massachusetts senate and then in the United States Senate. Never an admirer of Alexander Hamilton, the leading Federalist politician of his day, Adams, though officially a Federalist, supported Jefferson frequently, enthusiastically advocating his Louisiana Purchase, as well as the embargo that Jefferson hoped would guarantee U.S. neutrality in the European wars initiated by Napoleon's aggressions. Because these prohibitions on trading so adversely affected the economic interests of New England, Adams lost his Senate seat and spent the next three years as Boylston Professor of Rhetoric and Oratory at Harvard.

In 1809, Madison, Jefferson's successor, dispatched Adams to be U.S. minister in Russia and in 1814 appointed him a member of the commission to negotiate peace between Britain and the United States following the War of 1812. Appointed minister to the Court of St. James, he served for two years in London, returning to America when President Monroe appointed him secretary of state. In that post, remarkable for its distinguished late-eighteenth- and early-nineteenth-century incumbents, Adams excelled, contributing to the negotiations that led to the acquisition of Florida from Spain and, no less important, to the proclamation of the Monroe Doctrine, as much his creation as that of the president he served.[5]

Almost nothing in the career of George W. Bush, except for the advantages he derived from being the son of a former president, compared with those enjoyed by John Quincy Adams. The second Bush, who made a great deal of his authentic Texan roots, rarely thought to emphasize his family's association with Connecticut, Maine, and Washington, D.C., their long-term homes. He traveled little, knew neither foreign languages nor the world abroad, and boasted the conventional education of American boys of his social class. He ranked 114th in a class of 238 at Phillips Andover Academy and excelled in no sport, but he elected himself High Commissioner of Stickball, rare evidence of intentional humor. He made no very great impression either on his teachers or his fellow students at Andover and was almost equally inconspicuous at Yale, where he was admitted as a legacy, accepted not for his academic or athletic accomplishments but as the son of a famous father and grandfather, both Yalies.

His reputation at college was that of a heavy drinker, known to enjoy a good party, a not especially distinguished member of Skull and Bones, the most socially exclusive of the secret societies. A future Bonesman, visiting Yale at the time, wrote of him: "I must have seen George W. five times that weekend, totally, completely drunk," and went on to say: "On a Sunday morning, at five A.M., I saw him raving drunk, holding on to the back of a garbage truck in a three-piece suit, singing and carrying on and helping the garbage guys put the garbage in the truck. He was known in those days as an affable drunk."[6]

Bush, a conventional well-to-do Yalie, a member of the class of 1968, participated in none of the student demonstrations inspired by the Vietnam War. A party boy who never pretended to be a scholar, his mediocre academic performance at Yale proved to be no impediment to his admission to Harvard Business School, having been previously rejected by the law school at the University of Texas.

Just as Yale in that period admitted graduates of Phillips Andover almost automatically, paying little heed to their academic records, so the Harvard Business School showed equal tolerance for undistinguished Yale graduates who boasted good family connections and might be expected, through their fathers, to pursue successful business careers. George W., unlike other Bonesmen, including William Howard Taft, never worshipped mother Yale, thought little of the college, and condemned it for what he called its "intellectual snobbery."[7] Returning to New Haven as the nation's president in 2001, he mocked the institution in the address he delivered, knowing it had done little to provide him with an education that in any way contributed to his political ascent.[8]

George W. was never one to acknowledge indebtedness, but his overwhelming debt was in fact to his father, whom he followed into the Texas oil and gas business, intending to add to an already substantial Bush family fortune. When he created Arbusto Energy Inc. (*arbusto* is Spanish for "bush") in 1977, he received invaluable help from an uncle who interested other venture capitalists in investing in the Bush enterprise, confident that their $565,000 investment would in time realize substantial returns.[9]

Though the younger Bush sought a seat in Congress, representing the Nineteenth Congressional District in Texas, he proved no more successful in his first try for public office than his father and retired temporarily to earn more money, becoming a principal owner of the Texas Rangers, an American League baseball club.[10] By investing in a failing oil company that he then sold to Harken Energy, the young Bush, in an astute business move, gained stock valued at $530,000 plus $200,000 in loans, allowing him to buy yet additional stock. When he sold his Harken stock, just before its financial collapse in June 1990, some accused him of using inside knowledge to make a financial killing, but the SEC investigation that followed found no evidence of wrongdoing.[11] Barbara Bush thought George the smartest of her four sons, and Jeb, a Florida land developer, later governor of that state, the most serious. She almost certainly recognized what others, looking only at his business career, failed to note; wealthy and well-connected, able and ready to exploit his inherited personal and material assets, Bush learned how to use others to advance himself. Money, however, never shaped his character quite as much as the event in 1986 that led to his religious conversion.

Meeting Billy Graham, the noted evangelist, Bush, in the account he gave of this seminal event in his autobiography, *A Charge to Keep*, published in 1987, told of how he became a born-again Christian.[12] The Graham visit with his family in Maine in 1986—when his father was vice president, a detail left unmentioned—"sparked a change in my heart," and in his words, "Over the course of that weekend, Rev. Graham planted a mustard seed in my soul, a seed that grew over the next year. He led me to the path, and I began walking. It was the beginning of a change in my life."[13] Bush, aged forty, left his parents' more fashionable Episcopal Church for the Methodist Church of his wife, influenced by her also to abandon liquor, the dangerous substance threatening to make him just one more easily recognizable Texas drunk. Teetotallers in an earlier age had often been the object of derision; they were that no longer in fin de siècle twentieth-century America, where such self-denial and self-discipline accorded perfectly with a fundamentalist religious belief that the United States was a Christian nation, that men like Bush, converted to the true faith, could lead others to tread the same path to righteousness.

Bush's conversion led him to think again of a political career, following in the footsteps of his father and grandfather. In 1994, in a distinctly unfavorable political year for the Democrats, when Clinton demonstrated his political ineptitude by pressing for and failing to achieve major health care reform, Bush sought and won election as governor of Texas, trading on his father's name. Having never previously held elective office, resembling in this one respect only a more successful and worldly businessman, Herbert Hoover, Bush understood that the governor's chair in Austin could catapult him into the presidency as the governorship of lesser states, in Atlanta and Little Rock, had served to elevate two Democrats, Carter and Clinton. Bush won the Texas governorship in 1994 and for a second time in 1998, when the Monica Lewinsky affair was breaking and the Clinton presidency seemed imperiled. Emerging as a moral leader who believed in God and bore no resemblance to the rake who occupied the White House, his political base allowed him to compete for the presidency in 2000, replicating what Carter had done in 1976, though starting with more ample funds and incomparably greater name recognition.

Bush's strategy in many ways resembled Carter's; it required him to distance himself from the ineffectual Democratic incumbent much as the Georgian Christian had once insisted he bore no resemblance to the Republican Ford, in thrall to a strange and foreign Machiavellian.[14] Like Carter, Bush profited from having no influential competitors in his own party, and his purity appealed to a society sated with the antics of a philandering president. Bush, like Clinton and Carter, lacked any significant experience of foreign policy, and once he gained the nomination through primary victories, he delivered only two speeches that touched on foreign affairs or defense issues. Though he advanced no very original arguments in either, Bush understood what Reagan, his father's mentor, had taught him: to feign originality, to show no deference to the past, and to pretend to be striking out on new and bold paths, an almost sure recipe for political success.

His foreign policy address, given appropriately enough at the Ronald Reagan Presidential Library, promised to "defend America's interests in the Persian Gulf and advance peace in the Middle East, based upon a secure Israel."[15] Those conventional sentiments might have been uttered by any presidential aspirant in the previous quarter century, but his more startling words, explicitly critical of Clinton, suggested that the Democrats had been too accommodating in respect to China, a "competitor," never to be mistaken as a "strategic partner." Bush, using the Reagan strategy, distanced himself from an administration too congenial with its Communist enemies, too uncritical of their policies. Though Bush's battle was with the Democrat Al Gore, he saw the advantage of making it appear a political struggle with a corrupt Democratic administration, feckless, craven, and defeatist, led by Clinton.[16]

In his defense policy speech, even more explicit in its contempt for the man who occupied the White House, he exploited the country's low opinion of its draft-dodging incumbent and promised to "renew the bond of trust between the American president and the American military." Committing himself "to begin creating the military of the next century," he pledged a pay rise and spoke disdainfully of the "open-ended deployments and unclear military missions" that had led Clinton to send American soldiers abroad to participate in questionable peace-keeping operations. Arguing that "an orderly and timely withdrawal from places like Kosovo and Bosnia" was imperative, he spoke of reforming the defense establishment, saying:

> I will begin an immediate, comprehensive strategy review of our military—the structure of its forces, the state of its strategy, the priorities of its procurement—conducted by a leadership team under the Secretary of Defense. I will give the Secretary a broad mandate—to challenge the *status quo* and envision a new architecture of American defense for decades to come. . . . The real goal is to move beyond marginal improvements—to replace existing programs with new technologies and new strategies.[17]

A gifted ghostwriter had given Bush words to make him appear more than just the critic of a draft-dodging president, a Republican candidate who promised a fundamental reform of the military establishment. The fact that he himself had no experience of combat, had never served in Vietnam or elsewhere, was irrelevant to a larger fact—he promised to introduce innovation through a strong leadership team led by an effective secretary of defense.

As Michael Lind, author of *Made in Texas: George W. Bush and the Southern Takeover of American Politics,* has written, Bush was not the first Texas president but the first Texas conservative to make his way to the White House.[18] In this highly contentious work that emphasized the extent of the Southern domination of the Republican Party—Texas had always boasted Southern elements and had become for all practical purposes a Southern state—Lind wrote that "the party of Lincoln had become the party of Jefferson Davis," once president of the Confederacy.[19] The hyperbole of that argument could not conceal certain incontrovertible facts that Lind dwelled on: The Republican Party had come to rely on the votes of white voters, male and female; while Gore received 90 percent of the black vote, 62 percent of the Latino vote, and 55 percent of the Asian vote, with 95 percent of black Texans and more than 60 percent of Latino Texans preferring him to Bush, these scarcely compensated for the losses he suffered in being rejected by white voters at every economic level.[20]

The new Republican Party created by Nixon, that Reagan had perpetuated, giving them such impressive electoral victories in 1972, 1980, and 1984, relied on an unremitting hostility to liberal Democrats. Though the younger Bush was theoretically much beholden to the advice he received from neoconservative intellectuals, he owed a greater allegiance to bible-believing Christians, not a majority in the country, but a constituency large enough to give him the fundamentalist votes he needed. The polls, though predicting a close election, never prophesied one that would give Gore a popular majority and Bush the presidency when the decision of the Supreme Court gave him the contested Florida votes, guaranteeing his Electoral College majority.

For over a month the nation and the world were treated to a political spectacle neither edifying nor comic, that some chose to see as tragic. As long as it was impossible to know who the next president of the United States would be, everything depended on whether a recounting of votes by hand in three Florida counties would be sanctioned by the courts. Though the Republican governor of the state, Jeb Bush, the legislature, and all the principal Florida state officials, including Katherine Harris, the Florida secretary of state, could be relied on to support the claims of George W. Bush, none of them controlled the decision of the Florida Supreme Court in Tallahassee. When that court decided to allow the recount, James Baker III, former secretary of state and great champion of the Bush family's political interests, recruited to be the second Bush's principal defender, erupted into a mock or genuine show of hysteria. As Lewis Lapham wrote in his acerbic *Theater of War,*

> The expression in his [Baker's] face—pinched, vengeful, and mean—I could assign to a choleric temperament or a display of tactical emotion on the part of a clever bully. . . . The man apparently believed what he was saying, a rich lawyer inveighing against the rule of law, inciting the Florida legislature to overturn (by a fiat more to Mr. Baker's liking) the judgment of the court.[21]

Lapham, like others, believed the Republicans were convinced that "unless we win, it's illegal"; they were the true "patriots," and opposed to them were "partisan hacks," in Lapham's inimitable prose, "by definition crooked and self-serving, slum-dwelling perps accustomed to stealing elections and cars."[22] In the end, the Supreme Court decided the issue on December 16, and while some, outraged by the decision, dismissed it as wholly political, Gore accepted the verdict and Bush began to name his Cabinet, choosing General Colin Powell, a black, to occupy the highest position ever awarded any member of his race. With another black, Condoleezza Rice, appointed national security adviser, no one could accuse the president of racial bias. By 2001, appointment of blacks to high places in the federal government seemed so normal, indeed so inconsequential, that the newly elected president felt scant need to allude to its significance.

Powell, who had served as national security adviser under Reagan and chairman of the Joint Chiefs of Staff under George H.W., joined Rice as the two most influential members of the new president's foreign policy team. In earlier administrations, they might have been thought the principal architects of whatever new foreign policy initiatives the president decided on, but in this instance they were expected to share power with others, including Dick Cheney, the vice president, who had served the older Bush as secretary of defense, and previously as Ford's chief of staff, as well as Donald Rumsfeld, appointed secretary of defense. Rumsfeld, who had figured prominently in the short Ford administration, initially as chief of staff and later as secretary of defense, had been denied a role in Bush the elder's administration, according to journalist Bob Woodward, because he had taken a dim view of Bush's political abilities. Woodward, in his *Bush at War,* written as a eulogy of the president who had showed such courage and daring after September 11, suggested that during their years together in the House of Representatives Rumsfeld found the elder Bush a lightweight, more interested in friendships, public relations, and public opinion polls than in substantive policy.[23] In his view, he "avoided controversy and sweat, except in the House gym," and appeared to suffer from the "Rockefeller syndrome," defined as "available, wanting to serve, but not having clear goals."[24] To make matters worse, Woodward, a journalist still highly regarded for his Watergate disclosures, suggested that Rumsfeld believed Bush had been a weak CIA director "who seriously underestimated the Soviet Union's military advances and was manipulated by Secretary of State Henry Kissinger."[25] Clearly, for the younger Bush, such earlier differences with his father mattered not at all. An observer wishing to psychoanalyze the newly elected president might have been tempted to suggest that the appointment reflected Bush's determination to declare independence from his father, but a more reasonable explanation was that he respected Rumsfeld's character as a bruiser and wanted such men close to him.

No less interesting, certainly, were Bush's appointments to major secondary foreign policy and defense posts, principally neoconservatives, who included Deputy Secretary of Defense Paul Wolfowitz, Deputy Secretary of State Richard Armitage, and U.S. Trade Representative Robert Zoellick.[26] The president's team, experienced, articulate, and committed, seemed formidable, old hands who had never held back from expressing their grave misgivings about a Clinton foreign policy they deemed seriously flawed. Indeed, in 1998, Rumsfeld, Wolfowitz, and Armitage had sent a joint letter to Clinton that Andrew Bacevich, author of *American Empire: The Realities and Consequences of U.S. Diplomacy,* described as "denouncing the policy of containing Iraq as flaccid and insisting that removing Saddam Hussein from power was now 'the only acceptable strategy'"[27] A similar message, delivered in London by former Secretary of State Baker that same year at the Institute of United States Studies, led him to speak of "rogue states like Iraq," whose "flouting of UN resolutions. . . should be met by force," and "not of the 'pin-prick' variety." In Baker's words,

I fear we have just missed an opportunity to do that at a time when Saddam had badly overplayed his hand. I do not doubt for one minute that there will be another time—and probably soon—when we will have to back up rhetoric with resolve—or further lose credibility. I only wish that I were certain that we would have the necessary political will to act when that time comes.[28]

That moment appeared to come almost as soon as Bush arrived in the White House when U.S. airplanes bombed targets in the vicinity of Baghdad. Again, like Reagan's bombings, and Clinton's, these were fail-safe military operations, but the newly installed president insisted they would continue as long as there was a need to enforce the Iraqi no-fly zones, and the British joined the United States in air strikes that affected Saddam Hussein hardly at all.

Too few have chosen to see Bush as Reagan's disciple, starting with the same declaration of contempt for the policies pursued by his predecessor, declaring his hostility to all those actions that Clinton had purportedly favored. The Kyoto Accord on global warming, so enthusiastically embraced by many states abroad, like the support given the proposals to create the International Criminal Court, seemed positively dangerous to a president who believed that these were not the issues that the United States ought to be advocating. Indeed, in Bush's first months in office, even the Democratic presidential efforts to bring Israel and Palestine to reach a peace accord, what Clinton, following in the Carter tradition, imagined had been his most serious foreign diplomatic endeavor, seemed suddenly suspect, scarcely worthy of emulation or praise.

Instead, acting as if he had heard the voice of the people, a citizenry suffering from excessive taxation, Bush began his presidency with a proposal that replicated what Reagan had achieved, on a somewhat more modest scale, two decades earlier. Though he made no use of Reagonomics, the theory that had lost whatever validity it had once enjoyed, he flattered the electorate with the same traditional Republican arguments that his purpose was to reduce a tax burden that had become positively oppressive. Though his ten-year proposed tax cut, agreed to by an enthusiastic Congress, gave the most considerable advantages to those with annual incomes of $200,000 or more, all citizens were expected to benefit, and the economy, already vigorous, was expected to become even more so.[29]

These happy auguries were never realized, but the president acted as if the nation had given him a mandate to introduce major reforms in environmental, health, and education policy. Before September 11, the president appeared preoccupied entirely with domestic issues, happy to install officials friendly to his conservative values in the high offices where his power of appointment gave him the opportunity to clear Washington of the Clinton gang, men and women he despised. The new administration seemed to take almost perverse pleasure in moving away from initiatives once favored by Clinton, a man they abominated. The Republican hostility to Clinton, superficially reminiscent of feelings once expressed about both Roosevelt and Truman, took on additional venom because the president from Arkansas seemed so much the incarnation of the permissiveness of a society these more self-righteous men distrusted. Even the evaporation of the hopes once entertained for America's blue-chip corporations, as reflected in dramatic stock market declines, like the later, more spectacular collapse of the Houston-based Enron Corporation, so intimately linked to the president, his family, and advisers, did nothing to tarnish the reputations of men who seemed oblivious to all such dangers.[30] As late as May 2001, the secretary of state found it "hard to avoid a permanent state of optimism and glee," seeing no insoluble problems in the world abroad that cried out for immediate attention.[31]

With September 11, the situation changed entirely. The newly declared war president, ministering to a nation in deep shock, traumatized by the al-Qaeda aggression, profited from a political event almost unique in the history of the republic. Not even the Japanese attack on Pearl Harbor in December 1941 had produced such an outpouring of support for the commander in chief, a president suddenly rendered invulnerable to all criticism. Bush became the hero of the nation, with no one in Congress and the media prepared to question his policies. The White House, a tomb even before September 11, became a fortress to which only a privileged few were admitted, generally to learn of the president's resolve that those who had perpetrated the atrocity would be taken, dead or alive. Such presidential rhetoric suited the gait of a man who seemed the quintessential American macho male, invigorated by the threat that others before him had ignored, that could no longer be denied.

Recognizing that the country had been traumatized by the pictorial evidences of death and desolation inflicted by al-Qaeda's assault, the president emerged as a man determined to destroy the Taliban in Afghanistan and to capture Osama bin Laden. While some abroad, including the historian Sir Michael Howard, urged the president to see the terrorist challenge as requiring police action, resembling what the British had long found it necessary to do in Ireland and what other European states, comparably threatened, chose to do when confronted by terrorists, that policy held no appeal for the suddenly energized Bush.[32] Seeing the attack as legitimating war, certain to be long and difficult, it became civilization's fight, one that obliged all states and individuals to choose. His memorable phrase—"Either you are with us or against us"—summed up what he and others saw as the new foreign policy and defense imperative.[33] The world, initially sympathetic to America's plight and prepared to follow the president's lead, found little to object to when Rumsfeld insisted this was a war like no other where exit strategies could not be immediately fashioned.[34]

In an all but unanimous vote, Congress gave the president authority to use all necessary and appropriate force against those responsible for the attack and those who had helped them. Appearing before Congress, Bush gave the inspirational address the tragic circumstances called for. Feeling no need to review the conditions that had created the Taliban and al-Qaeda, and none that would ask why the attack had not been anticipated by U.S. intelligence services, he spoke only of why the terrorists hated America so, claiming that they hate "our freedom of religion, our freedom of speech, our freedom to vote and assemble and disagree with each other."[35]

In the fortnight after the attack, no one could fault the president for seeking to make the war against terror appear a latter-day version of the war fought against Nazi Germany. ENDURING FREEDOM, the operation to destroy the Taliban and capture bin Laden, started on October 7, 2001, and the administration used its effective propaganda machine to emphasize the extreme dangers of the operation, as well as the certainty of eventual triumph.[36] A military offensive that in fact was never dangerous, that involved only limited U.S. special forces on the ground, greatly resembling the wars Reagan and Clinton had fought with their superior airpower, had to be rendered by the White House as exceedingly hazardous. With access to the Pentagon, CIA, and foreign intelligence archives closed, and unlikely to be opened for decades, it is impossible to know what those responsible for the war in Afghanistan expected, but there is reason to believe, as with the Gulf War against Iraq, that significant American military casualties were never anticipated.[37]

Overwhelming U.S. airpower almost guaranteed an early defeat of the Taliban, and the small contingents of commandos, American and British, given some assistance by the indigenous Northern Alliance, led to the rout of al-Qaeda forces in a matter of weeks, failing, however, to capture bin Laden and many of his armed supporters. A newly established government in liberated Kabul told the world that a vicious enemy had been vanquished, but there was little incentive or disposition in Washington to relax. al-Qaeda, an international terrorist organization, might strike again at any time, threatening New York, London, and any other city and government friendly to the country that had declared terrorism its principal enemy. Members of Congress, fearing new terrorist attacks, dared not criticize what the mass media, especially in the United States, represented as the president's remarkable Afghan accomplishment.

In the United States, September 11 appeared to have transformed the nation, with patriotism displaying itself as rarely before; flags flew everywhere, from factories, office buildings, apartment houses, and private dwellings, on cars, trucks, and buses, in the buttonholes of every political leader of note and the millions happy to follow their proud example. Public opinion polls told the country that the president enjoyed wide support; citizens approved of his policies, and the almost nightly TV news programs featured his appearance before massed flags, addressing crowds enthusiastically responding to his simple message that the terrorists had to be taken, dead or alive.

In Congress, a new law, strangely entitled the United and Strengthening America by Providing Appropriate Tools Required to Intercept and Obstruct Terrorism Act (a/k/a the USA Patriot Act), passed easily.[38] No one, conscious of the patriotism that had become the nation's most distinctive trait, dared question the excessive controls on aliens, noncitizens who might one day be discovered as undercover terrorists. Whatever opposition to the president and his administration had once existed, stemming from the very exceptional circumstances that attended his coming into office, virtually disappeared. As long as no one could know whether the Golden Gate Bridge, the Holland Tunnel, and the White House itself might not figure as the object of the next terrorist attack, no one dared make light of the dangers, let alone question the intelligence findings that periodically raised ever-increased national alert signals.

In these circumstances, homeland defense became a principal administration concern, and Congress responded to the nation's disquiet with the creation of the new Department of Homeland Security. As the country in an earlier period, frightened by the prospect of Soviet nuclear attacks, had taken to building air-raid shelters, preparing for the unthinkable, so now, in the age of terrorism, it became transfixed by a growing preoccupation with the weapons of mass destruction that terrorists might avail themselves of.[39] Even a body as circumspect as the Council on Foreign Relations, never known for sounding unnecessary alarms, published a special task force report that declared the country "dangerously unprepared" for the new terrorist dangers. In the words of the report, the country's emergency responses were "drastically underfunded," manifestly inadequate to cope with biological, chemical, radiological, and nuclear threats.[40]

These, the more sober reflections of a traumatized America, fearful of what the next terrorist action might be, suggested that September 11 heralded an age of unprecedented danger. This was not simply the substitute of a new enemy for an old one, resembling what Noel Annan had described in 1995 in his book, *Changing Enemies,* where he wrote of how the "defeat and regeneration of Germany" gave way to a four-decade Cold War with the Soviet Union.[41] Nor did it replicate the gratifying story John Dower told in *Embracing Defeat,* his 1999 account of how Japan transformed itself after Hiroshima, becoming a democratic society essentially different from the militaristic empire it had recently been, an ally of the United States.[42]

In the American September 11 saga, as represented by the president in his State of the Union speech on January 29, 2002, in which he spoke of Iraq, Iran, and North Korea, as an "axis of evil," he gave warnings of a kind of warfare that seemed to make all earlier twentieth-century history irrelevant. Doctrines of containment and deterrence, fashioned by earlier administrations that had once enjoyed considerable repute, greatly eroded by Reagan and his successors, were in effect relegated to the ashbin of history.[43] Bush, like Reagan, his mentor, imagined himself embarking on a new voyage of discovery that owed nothing to presidents who had defeated their enemies, reacting to specific acts of aggression, managing with the help of others abroad to establish new and stable democracies in places where totalitarian regimes had once flourished. All this earlier twentieth-century history seemed suddenly superseded.

At West Point, on June 1, 2002, Bush made his strategy most explicit when he said: "We must take the battle to the enemy. . . and confront the worst threats before they emerge. In the world we have entered, the only path to safety is the path of action. And this nation will act."[44] In September 2002, the White House issued *The National Security Strategy of the United States of America,* which made the new Bush Doctrine even more concrete:

> Given the goals of rogue states and terrorists, the United States can no longer solely rely on a reactive posture as we have in the past. The inability to deter a potential attacker, the immediacy of today's threats, and the magnitude of potential harm that could be caused by our adversaries' choice of weapons, do not permit that option. We cannot let our enemies strike first.[45]

Every detail of the proposed remedy—to protect the nation against terrorism—was mistakenly represented. The threats posed by terrorists and rogue states—the administration chose to link the two—were unlikely to be as immediately threatening to the survival of the United States as those posed by Nazi Germany and the Communist Soviet Union. Those earlier threats had been defeated not by preemptive American action but by a calculated policy, developed over time, that engaged others, principally allies, critical to the final defeat of those recognized to be dangerous.

In the novel scenario developed by Bush, many, especially in Europe, believed he greatly exaggerated the dangers and opted for a do-it-yourself policy that boded ill for peace in the world. Whether because of political considerations, a belief that his policy would win favor with millions impressed by the country's reinvigorated American patriotism, or out of a more long-range interest to assert U.S. hegemony, what his critics disdainfully dismissed as the nation's determination to be the new Rome, the president viewed himself as a bold innovator. Critics, especially abroad, thought him a reckless gambler, departing from traditions that had given the United States its unique position among the world's democracies.

Though it was impossible to know for certain what the president intended— the White House had become a tomb from which few secrets ever emanated— journalists, the sole source of purportedly accurate information, regaled the public with stories of the president's resolve and of the tensions that existed between the warriors, Rumsfeld and Cheney, vying for influence with a determined president, and the secretary of state, who counseled caution. Whether the differences between Powell and the others were as substantial as journalists wished to make them appear, whether Powell's insistence that new opportunities be given to Hans Blix, the UN weapons inspector, to continue his search for weapons of mass destruction in Iraq effectively pitted him against the vice president and the secretary of defense, it became increasingly clear that the president interpreted the original UN vote of September 2002 as a sufficient sanction for war against Iraq.

Ignoring the opposition of France, Germany, and Russia to an early military assault on Iraq, the administration took special pains to condemn the French for their perfidy in seeking to win support from the nonpermanent members of the UN Security Council. Bush led a new coalition—magnified to appear more than a military alliance of essentially the United States and Britain—into war with Iraq. Again, the effort was made to suggest that the war would be long and difficult, that it would take months before Baghdad fell, almost certainly requiring American foot soldiers to win the city in terrible street by street combat. Whether British or U.S. intelligence ever believed this, we are unlikely to know for many years.[46] The president, joined by his national security adviser and others, believed the destruction of the tyrannical Saddam regime essential, arguing that would lead to a democratizing of Iraq, greater American influence throughout the Middle East, and issuing in a final peace settlement between Israel and Palestine.[47]

The United States, with its vastly superior military technology, won easily in a war where the Saddam forces offered no significant resistance. But as many had expected, bringing peace to the conquered nation proved much more difficult. The weapons of mass destruction were never found; Saddam was finally captured and taken prisoner in mid-December 2003, but the Iraqis did not appear greatly to exult in the U.S. military triumph. Guerrilla activity continued to claim the lives of American and British soldiers, as well as civilians, Iraqi and foreign, many of the latter sent by the United Nations or other organizations to help restore some semblance of order in Iraq.

As for the connection between al-Qaeda and the Baathist Iraqis, an additional reason offered to justify America's military intervention, this, too, appeared to be a myth artfully disseminated by those in the administration to justify the actions they had taken. If the Americans expected to be greeted as liberators, they grossly mistook the sentiments of a people long subjected to Saddam's tyrannical rule, who never accepted the idea that the American purpose was simply to restore Iraq to a democratic rule it had never known.

Bush proved himself an effective war president, able to use the weapons sanctioned by Congress over many decades to defeat a regime whose military capabilities he greatly exaggerated. As a peacemaker he failed utterly, with none of his close associates able to offer the advice needed to allow for reasonable post-war planning. Relying principally on Reagan's political tactic—patriotic rhetoric—when a more global political and diplomatic strategy was called for, Bush seemed almost oblivious to the damage he was doing to long-standing relations with allies. It was as if he, like others in his Cabinet and in Congress, no longer imagined such criticism mattered.

The lies told by the vice president, the secretary of state, and the secretary of defense, intended always to sustain the president in his own exaggerated rhetoric, concealed the condition comprehensible only to those who recalled Reagan and Irangate. The president's closest advisers were no longer independent individuals who yearned only to return to their peacetime pursuits, for whom service in Washington was a sacrifice made in the public interest. None even remotely resembled those who had once congregated around presidents, Republican and Democratic, who bore the name Roosevelt.

These men and women, courtiers and mock warriors, served a monarch whose authority rested on a contested election, who acted as if the nation had invested him with exceptional powers, which for a moment it did. Only very slowly did the realization grow that war, with its secrecy and deception, risked the very survival of the freedoms the president claimed to be defending, that his very simplistic notions of the character of the enemy scarcely accorded with what many abroad believed to be true. The president's defenders were as ardent as his critics; neither knew how to transform the debate from what it had become—a paean of praise of the American people, exceptional in every way, the guardian of the world's peace.

Europeans, especially those critical of the president, spoke of the irreparable damage done to the Atlantic Alliance, NATO, and the European Union. Bush, abetted by his secretary of defense, refused to view European opposition as anything but a failure to recognize a real and present danger, expressing their barely concealed contempt for those who dared to question the administration's policy. In Congress, only a few voices were raised initially, following the easy military victory over Iraq; most representatives and senators, looking ahead to 2004, remained silent or supportive of the war, even after it had ended, joined by a preponderant segment of the mass media.

Europeans, initially equally ardent in their support of the United States after September 11, never believed there was a link between the religious fundamentalist terrorist bigots in al-Qaeda and the Baathist regime in Baghdad. They knew too much about Saddam and were too aware of his perverse and destructive appetites to underestimate the ways in which he had used twentieth-century technology to maintain himself in power. Many, genuinely bewildered by the Bush administration's haste to make war, took almost secret pleasure in seeing the president embarrassed by the escalation of guerilla violence after the war's official end. At a time when few in the president's court spoke with any-thing that could be mistaken for candor, it was impossible to know how the world's reaction was interpreted, what shame, if any, registered with those obliged by the end of 2003 to go with their begging bowls to seek interna-tional support for the rehabilitation of an economy and a society they had helped to destroy.

Though the administration spoke constantly of the coalition, this was largely a figment of their imagination. The war in Iraq, essentially a U.S.-British mili-tary operation, resulted in a substantial weakening of the esteem the British public felt for their prime minister, Tony Blair, seen increasingly as the only major European leader who, wittingly or unwittingly, accepted the president's arguments, greatly exaggerating the threats posed by Iraq. In telling Parliament that Saddam possessed weapons of mass destruction he would be able to release in forty-five minutes, Blair made a fundamental error: justifying a war by an in-telligence finding he would in the long run find impossible to defend. In the absence of an effective opposition in the Tory Party, Blair clung to office, but the public opinion polls told an unmistakable story—the prime minster was no longer believed. While no comparable disdain for the president existed on the other side of the Atlantic, voices began to be raised there, especially in Demo-cratic Party ranks, expressing doubts about the veracity and judgment of some-one who had strutted about so confidently just months earlier, but Bush's White House courtiers were as loyal to him as they had been to Reagan.

The most remarkable aspect of the Bush presidency may have been his suc-cess in hermetically sealing off the White House, so that the information that came out of that fortress reflected only what he wished for the public to learn and believe. Though a book by Richard Clarke, the former counterterrorism chief, told how the president repeatedly ignored his warnings in the spring and summer of 2001 of the threat posed by Osama Bin Laden and his al-Qaida net-work, caused something of a stir, especially when Clarke appeared before a con-gressional committee, the equally damaging testimony published by Ron Suskind, narrating the travails of Paul O'Neill, Bush's first secretary of the trea-sury, received less attention. Yet, the second book, as much as the first, told of the president's obsession with Iraq months before September 11 and of his firm conviction that Saddam's weapons of mass destruction constituted a threat to the United States it would be foolhardy to ignore.[48] These works, like all the journalistic accounts that reported on the administration's feeble explanations for why Iraqi resistance continued and why the preparations for the postwar reconstruction were so inadequate, could never compete with the exciting rev-elations made by Bob Woodward in his two quick studies, the first on the Afghan war and the second on the American preparations for the war against Iraq. Woodward, who had done so much to bring down Nixon, wrote *Bush at War* and *Plan of Attack* as eulogies of a president who knew his mind, controlled those he had appointed to high places, and never wavered in his conviction that he had pursued the right policy in seeking to overthrow a hated dictator who oppressed his people and was preparing to attack the United States.[49] Woodward, delighted to have been given so much time with the president, never considered the possibility that he had been taken in, sold a bill of goods, and used for White House propaganda purposes, or that his portrayals of all the president's seconds-in-command, his loyal courtiers—Cheney, Rumsfeld, Powell, and Rice—were partial, incomplete, and self-serving in the best sense of the word.

The major combat operations in Iraq ended in military victory, but there was nothing resembling the intellectual ferment that followed World War II. Then, especially after the start of the Cold War, substantial efforts were made to understand the awesome weapons created by the war, but also the Soviet Union, a new foe, as well as the old enemies, Germany and Japan. No comparable efforts were made after September 11 or the coalition military success in Iraq to foster analogous understanding of terrorism or Islam. The triumphal rhetoric of the first days following the U.S. victories in Afghanistan and Iraq, though later muted, never gave way to a more sober estimate of the gains and losses of what the administration had seen as fail-safe military operations.

This was true even after the embarrassing images of torture of imprisoned Iraqis made the American military occupation appear somewhat less benign than it had seemed to those prepared to view the war as simply an operation whose sole purpose was to liberate a people of its oppressor. The doubts expressed earlier by tens of millions in Europe and elsewhere, unwilling to accept the White House analysis of the danger posed by Iraq, grew many times, almost as much at home as abroad. Newspapers like the *New York Times*, once ready to accept the president's view of a real and present danger, saw its ombudsman, its so-called public editor, declare that its reporting had been deeply flawed, that it, like many others, had "missed the real story," that the "hunger for scoops," the "front-page syndrome," together with its "hit-and-run journalism" and "coddling [of] sources" had allowed that venerable newspaper, so proud of its independence, to be used by those determined to propagate false stories about Iraq's "weapons of mass destruction." Daniel Okrent, in his outspoken criticism, asked not for "further acts of contrition or garment-rending, but a series of aggressively reported stories detailing the misinformation, disinformation and suspect analysis that led virtually the entire world to believe Hussein had W.M.D. at his disposal."[50] Such an investigation was even more imperatively called for in the federal bureaucracy, not simply to apportion blame but to suggest how the White House had become the chief purveyor of myth and falsehood, and why the president was no longer controlled by either Congress or the huge bureaucracy that in theory existed to instruct him. There had been a massive display of presidential ignorance and arrogance, and a failure of intelligence at every level. Never in the long twentieth century had so fundamental a foreign policy error been made and rarely had so much been promised and so little achieved.

The continuing turmoil in Iraq and the Islamic world more generally merited the attention the president and his associates, clinging to outworn perceptions, gave to those problems, but their solutions for the continued instability proved shallow. Worse, by dwelling only on terrorism, they greatly underestimated other changing conditions in the world, in the European Union, as well as in Asia, Latin America, and Africa, that challenged many of the older conventional foreign policy shibboleths. Their cavalier dismissal of those they believed weak or impotent showed the same arrogance Reagan's courtiers had demonstrated, though less overtly, when they represented him as the sole hero responsible for the decline and fall of the Soviet Union.

Those who served George W. Bush, schooled in the lessons of the Cold War, displayed few of the creative gifts that historians associate with the names of the more distinguished of the country's twentieth-century leaders. Indeed, the predominant number were ideologues who lacked the political subtlety of both Roosevelts, the idealism of Wilson, and the authenticity of Truman. They perpetuated myths that derived mostly from their political experiences in the last two decades of the twentieth century, a barren time in the country's history, when neither intelligence nor reason flourished.[51] They, like the president, imagined that the war to defeat Saddam would be easy, given the military superiority of the United States, even if it was politically important to pretend the contrary. They believed they knew how to win the minds and hearts of the Iraqi people, and in this, they greatly deceived themselves. Bush imagined that he could imitate Reagan, speak boldly while taking negligible risks, and pretend that he was the savior of the world, the president who had won the war against terrorism as Reagan had won the war against Communism. It was all a fable, calculated to give political advantages that in the end served principally to create international turmoil. These veterans of the "Cold War," would-be warriors, showed themselves vain and inept, lacking the political suppleness that allowed Reagan to retire from the presidency as a victor, eliciting a vast outpouring of sentiment decades later, at the moment of his death.

Whether these men have done lasting damage to the United States in its relations with others abroad, whether their invasions of civil rights and privacy at home, legitimated by terrorist threats, will long prevail, depends to a considerable extent on whether a new presidency comes into being early in the twenty-first century, as creative as the one that gave the United States its undisputed primacy in the twentieth. This is something that is impossible to prophesy.

EPILOGUE

Alexis de Tocqueville, more than any other European or American in the nineteenth century, prophesied correctly the evolution of the American presidency in the twentieth century. Recognizing that a growing concern with foreign affairs and a larger engagement in wars abroad would change the presidential office, vastly increasing its powers, Tocqueville was silent on whether there would be an accretion also of congressional or judicial power. In his prophesies about the presidency, he showed remarkable acumen. Americans, faithful to their belief in heroes, though no longer subscribing by the end of the twentieth century to the exaggerated views expressed by Thomas Carlyle in the nineteenth, knew the arrival of accomplished accidental presidents like Theodore Roosevelt, Harry Truman, and Lyndon Johnson were significant events. Even with less influential leaders—Calvin Coolidge and Gerald Ford, for example—it was difficult to believe that it mattered little whether one man or another occupied the White House.

For Tocqueville, war, patriotism, and religion carried great political consequences, never to be underestimated. His achievement was to make Americans and Europeans aware that the republic across the Atlantic was a new experiment in government, different from any known to Europe. If he lauded much that he discovered in the American democracy, it was impossible for him to conceal his concern about the tyranny of the majority, the conformity he found in a people passionate for equality but not always as wholeheartedly committed to liberty, showing at times insufficient regard for the views of minorities.

Though Tocqueville neither foresaw nor dwelled on the secrecy and deception that became defining features of American presidential politics in the twentieth century, these developments would not have greatly surprised him given his familiarity with Europe's kings and courtiers. He recognized very early the royal attributes of the presidential office, and would not have found wholly bewildering the display and deference that attended those who became elected monarchs in all but title.

While it is perhaps gratuitous to argue that there has been no twentieth-century observer of the American political and cultural scene who has demonstrated equal prescience in analyzing the likely evolution of the presidency into the twenty-first century, this is a truth that bears reflection. Because TV and newspaper reporters have become immensely influential in disseminating the views Americans and others abroad hold of individual presidents, they are today the principal source for information on an office as renowned for its accomplishments as for its foibles and follies. Access to the White House has become all-important, and investigative reporters, unabashed in their courting of those behind the presidential gates able to grant them information otherwise unavailable, are prepared to persevere in a task at once delicate and dangerous. They have become snoops, but few are so self-critical of what they do as to believe that their efforts are in any way demeaning. How else is the public to be kept informed of what kings and courtiers prefer for them not to know?

The presidential autobiographies, together with those of their courtiers, now so lucrative, often commanding publication advances of millions, are rarely noted for their candor; they have become commercial products intended to sell to a public that craves to be titillated. In these circumstances, those from the media prepared to search for secrets in a White House increasingly hermetically sealed perform a public service, doing combat with the political professionals, accomplished in manufacturing spin, concealing both the motives and the policies of those enjoying a power most had never anticipated. Because American political and diplomatic history have declined substantially as major fields of study, replaced by greater emphasis on social and cultural developments, only very rarely linked to the political in the Tocqueville tradition, the Oval Office is known increasingly not by what scholars write but by what the media choose to report.

Where so many abroad have reason to be concerned with the United States and presidential power, one would expect a very substantial published literature on both. No such literature exists. It would be difficult, indeed, to cite a single French, German, Japanese, Italian, Spanish, or Russian study that compares with those written more than a century ago by Tocqueville or indeed by James Bryce. Yet British scholars, more than others abroad, often seduced into settling in the United States by the attractive offers they receive from eminent American universities, have become the principal foreign critics whose works on the United States are read, known, and appreciated. In 1986, following what this book has characterized as America's "time of troubles," Paul Kennedy paraphrased George Bernard Shaw's quip, "Rome fell; Babylon fell; Scarsdale's turn will come," prophesying the inevitable decline of the United States as a hegemon.[1] An even more original British judgment on the future of the American democracy was issued by Niall Ferguson when he wrote in 2003 that the

United States was an empire "that dare not speak its name," an "empire in denial."[2] In Ferguson's words,

> [The] empire that rules the world today is both more and less than its British begetter. But it is an empire that lacks the drive to export its capital, its people and its culture to those backward regions which need most urgently and which, if they are neglected, will breed the greatest threats to its security.[3]

These British commentators, together with many others preoccupied with the decline and fall of their own empire, write in an elegiac tone congenial to those who believe that terrorism, rivaled perhaps only by poverty, are the incendiary materials likely to set off new conflagrations in a world no longer dominated by Communists. Having no personal experience in their own blessed isle of the recent rule of despots or tyrants, having lost an earlier fascination with the history of ancient Greece and Rome that educated men of Tocqueville's and Bryce's generation boasted, few worry greatly about the tyranny of the majority, though there is growing concern about the new powers vested in political executives in much of the democratic world, including a more presidential Downing Street. The complexities of modern life seem to make such government necessary, and the concept of a polity of discussion, so congenial to Walter Bagehot and other Victorians, belongs to a largely forgotten past when Parliament mattered profoundly.

Whether billions of Chinese and Indians believe these same things, whether their experience of the twentieth century has made them equally accepting of such ideas are issues not generally considered. Nor is it common to ask whether a billion Muslims in the Middle East, Africa, and Asia see America's destiny as George W. Bush and Tony Blair do, and whether their misgivings may not be more significant for the twenty-first century than what a disgruntled French president and German chancellor thought of the American-British coalition war against Iraq, or even what a canny Russian leader, Vladimir Putin, expected it might lead to.

Few in the nineteenth century prophesied the civil war that destroyed traditional Europe in the twentieth century; it is impossible to know whether new wars, equally unpredictable, may not have equally cataclysmic consequences in the twenty-first. In the nineteenth century, Britain saw its economic supremacy lost first to imperial Germany and then to the United States, a country recently wracked by Civil War. Whether America's current economic supremacy will be equally challenged, and by whom, are issues that command only limited attention at a time when terrorist threats are thought to be all-important, when they give the president his new legitimacy and his greatly extended powers.

America's twentieth-century record of being able to respond to new challenges, emanating from powerful European and Asian states but also from a number that counted for little when Theodore Roosevelt occupied the White House, is not a historical development that greatly preoccupies Republican or Democratic politicians today. The interest of the former, to retain control of the White House, perpetuating the dominance of the party that managed to rule almost uninterruptedly for decades after the Civil War, is not substantially different from that of those seeking to pry their way into that citadel. If memories of the Civil War created a party able to assert political supremacy for over half a century, why should the threat of terrorism not do the same?

While journalists continue to ply their trade, catering to publics hungry for novelty and suspicious of complexity, new worlds are being fashioned that show no overwhelming concern to follow the American example. It is difficult, indeed almost impossible, for most Americans to believe this, or to acknowledge the truth Tocqueville insisted on: that a new political science was needed for a world itself new, which he and others of his intellectual persuasion believed would be comprehensible only to those who knew the past and showed some regard for it. Yet, as the twenty-first century opened, nothing seemed so obsolete as political history; the past had ceased to be prologue, to use the words emblazoned on the pediment of the United States Archives building.

George W. Bush, faithful to Ronald Reagan, his father's politically astute ideological patron, recognized the importance of insisting that we live in a time like no other, unprecedented for its dangers, a myth ingeniously crafted to satisfy an age wedded to hyperbole. Whether intellect, accepting the reality of these new dangers, will be able to place terrorist threats in perspective and learn to cope with them, recognizing other hazards, more substantial and serious, is part of a larger question that remains unanswered: When, if ever, will the presidency come again to attract learned men, and what will the consequences of such individuals, men and women, entering the White House be?

Will new elites, as different from the WASP elite of yesterday—still extant in a diminished form for all the reports of its purported death in the 1960s—come to enjoy influence in the United States, and what ideas will they propound for a democracy jaded with today's prosaic and simplistic political rhetoric? Will these new elites show an understanding of the world in the Middle East, Asia, Africa, Latin America, and Europe that has not been much in evidence in recent decades? The twentieth-century presidency fashioned by Wilson, Roosevelt, and Truman survives—in however attenuated a form—reflecting changes made by the wars they felt compelled to wage, as well as by the traditions of secrecy and deception they initiated, that their successors perpetuated and made considerably more noxious. The history of the twentieth-century presidency will always have to make room for the antics of the disgraced Nixon and the much-lauded Reagan, and it is legitimate to ask whether the latter's shadow does not lurk in the White House today.

The American presidency, as it evolved in the twentieth century, bestowed powers on that office never conceived by those who invented it in the eighteenth. Its achievements are incontestable; so, also, are its failures. Whether that influential office will command greater respect in the future depends principally on whether those who cleave to it and are prepared to serve it come only as courtiers, or whether their intelligence and goodwill encourages their chiefs to accept them also as critics. James Bryce, more than Tocqueville, saw that very ordinary men were coming to occupy the White House; this was as true in the late twentieth century as in the late nineteenth. It matters profoundly whether it will be equally true in the twenty-first, or whether they and those they select as their subordinates will arrive with intellectual capital greater than what has been common of late. Because so much of what Americans know about their twentieth-century presidents, based on accounts, historical, biographical, autobiographical, and journalistic, produced by men and women who write in English, giving scant heed to views expressed in newspapers, journals, and books written in other languages, we do not always appreciate how much our view of the American presidency derives principally from American and British sources. If there has been a "special relation" in this century, making the United Kingdom the major ally of the United States, that alliance has existed also in the intellectual realm. Inevitably, we see our institutions as American and British commentators see them, as they choose to write about them. If these twin perspectives, so often distinctive, provide valuable insights, and who would be foolhardy enough to deny that they do, they can also be imprisoning, making us too unaware of the tragic histories of other societies that have known the terrors of modern war as the United States and the United Kingdom have not. In these circumstances, it becomes important to consider what can be learned from the histories of these two societies, the American and the British, that can in fact explain why their institutions have developed as they have, why they are what they appear to be today. The English historian G.M. Young, gazing on his own society in the grim, dark 1930s, wrote with admiration of the Victorian age as it had existed in its greatest days. Though Young's work is unknown to many Americans who still honor the memories of two Roosevelts, not to mention Wilson and Truman, his words are eerily relevant to the American nation and its presidency as both exist today. Young, in 1936, wrote:

> Compared with their fathers, the men of that time [the late Victorians and Edwardians] were ceasing to be a ruling or a reasoning stock; the English mind sank towards that easily excited, easily satisfied, state of barbarism and childhood which press and politics for their own ends fostered, and on which in turn they fed.

He went on to say: "But the great age is not so far behind us that we must needs have lost all its savour and its vigour."[4] Is it simply nostalgia to suggest that this may be one of several legitimate verdicts on the character of the American political experience in the last century deserving of serious consideration?

Are we so far from the age of the Roosevelts, Theodore and Franklin, to have forgotten what Republican and Democratic presidents were once able to do, what despite their human frailties, they aspired to be? One need not be nostalgic for a lost innocence to believe that the last decades have not brought to the White House men of that quality. How, then, are we to explain the presidency as it has evolved since the age of Truman? Does G.M. Young, mourning a Britain that no longer existed in the "locust years" of the 1930s provide clues that need to be pursued by Americans searching for an explanation of their present discontents? What has the failure been? Can it be ascribed to those elected to lead the country, and to those they selected to advise and serve them? Or must it be seen as a failure of the American mind, "too easily excited" and "too easily satisfied"?

APPENDIX

Bryce's and Tocqueville's America: A Prefiguring of Twentieth-Century America?

The two most celebrated nineteenth-century studies of American politics, society, and culture were written not by Americans but by Europeans. Alexis de Tocqueville's *Democracy in America,* published in 1835 and 1840, and James Bryce's *The American Commonwealth,* published in 1888, were works noted and commented on by both Theodore Roosevelt and Woodrow Wilson. That would be reason enough to cite their opinions of the two studies, suggesting how these two *learned* presidents, so different from each other, viewed American politics. There is, however, another, perhaps even more compelling reason for doing so. Bryce's work, *the* classic that Americans consulted when Roosevelt and Wilson occupied the White House, is scarcely read today. The decline in Bryce's reputation in the last half-century, and the growing reputation of Tocqueville, especially since the time of Kennedy, Johnson, Nixon, Reagan, and the two Bushes, cannot be an anomaly. Tocqueville's study, descriptive of Jacksonian America, an agrarian United States that has long since disappeared, resonates for Americans as Bryce's more sanguine study of a confident and expanding industrial America no longer does.[1]

How to explain this phenomenon? Why was Theodore Roosevelt, an astute politician, so greatly impressed by Bryce's rendering of American politics and society, and why did Wilson, able to admire the work and to praise it, recognize it to be inferior to Tocqueville's? No less important, why has the Wilson judgment been so massively confirmed in recent decades?[2]

Roosevelt, writing to Bryce soon after the book's publication, expressed his enthusiasm for it in the exaggerated terms common to him, telling him that his study had "all of De Tocqueville's great merits, and has not got, as his book has, two or three serious and damaging faults."[3] Roosevelt gave no hint of what these faults were, but given his opinions then and later, one may guess that he found unacceptable Tocqueville's proposition that a tyranny of the majority existed in the United States, inhibiting free speech and independent thought. Wilson, commending Bryce's work for the information it contained, knew it lacked the profundity and grace of Tocqueville's study. Admirable for its description, an "invaluable store-house of observations on comparative politics," it offered little instruction on what Wilson believed to be all-important, the "guiding principles of politics."[4] Wilson, concerned with what a "mature American democracy" might one day become, found Bryce's observations on such matters not very compelling.[5] Roosevelt felt no comparable reservations, delighted that Bryce had made extensive use of his own ideas, of how post–Civil War political bosses had come to grasp power from the gentlemen who had once made politics their calling, and why that condition called for immediate remedy.

Roosevelt's contribution to *The American Commonwealth* lay principally in what he taught Bryce about bosses and rings, the whole paraphernalia of post–Civil War state and local political corruption that extended even to the selection of presidential candidates. Roosevelt's article, "Machine Politics in New York City," informed much of what Bryce wrote about the bosses who so greatly disfigured the late-nineteenth-century American scene. Roosevelt, passionate and articulate, made corruption his major theme, writing that the direction of political affairs in New York City, as in many other American cities, lay "in the hands of a class of men who make politics their regular business and means of livelihood," allowing them as skilled organizers to bring out the voters and guarantee the election of their friends to public office. These men, dubbed professionals by Roosevelt, gave all their time to politics and transformed what had once been a gentleman's sport dominated by amateurs into a game that promised substantial rewards to those who played it.[6] Roosevelt, disdaining the wealthy middle class whose only concern was money, refusing to bestir themselves to do something about a wretched political condition, showed scarcely greater regard for intellectuals who drew back from battle, disdaining the coarseness of political life, shunning their obligations as citizens.[7]

Wilson's preoccupations were of a very different kind. Looking back to a time when Washington and his Cabinet "commanded the ear of Congress and gave shape to its deliberations," he asked why that situation no longer prevailed.[8] In his view, Congress had wrested power from those awarded it by the Constitution, and "the perfection of selfish party tactics" explained the political deterioration that had occurred since. Writing as only a scholar could, as Roosevelt, the politician, never dared to do if it obliged him to criticize the post–Civil War Republican presidents and the Republican Party, Wilson called for a revitalized presidency. The political parties and Congress, in divesting the executive of many of its constitutionally mandated powers, had destroyed the eighteenth-century political system in a way the bosses could never have done. This was Wilson's implicit and explicit message.

Bryce borrowed from Wilson's *Congressional Government*, but only selectively, and failed to see the import of his more original observations. Thus, for example, Wilson emphasized the role of political parties in making "expediency and availability the only rule of selection." In his words, "When the presidential candidate came to be chosen, it was recognized as imperatively necessary that he should have as short a political record as possible, and that he should wear a clean and irreproachable insignificance."[9] When he wrote that a "decisive career" was a "positive disability for the presidency," or that the "shoals of candidacy can be passed only by a light boat which carries his freight and can be turned about readily," his prose was not only more felicitous than Bryce's; it also carried a more disconcerting message.[10] Wilson, persuaded that the increased centralization of government made continued congressional domination dangerous, and that the political parties could no longer be trusted with the powers they had grasped, intended to sound an alarm. Bryce neglected to hear it. So, also, when Wilson insisted that public opinion be made more influential in exerting pressure on Congress, and that it become better informed, neither of these imperatives greatly preoccupied the more sanguine Bryce.

Wilson, reviewing *The American Commonwealth*, noted that Bryce's concern was to explain "democracy *in* America" when the more compelling subject was to explain "democracy *by* America." Why, he asked, has democracy "been a cordial and a tonic to little Switzerland and to big America, while it has been as yet only a quick intoxicant or a slow poison to France and Spain, a mere maddening draught to the South American states?"[11] Decades before Wilson led the United States into a war "to make the world safe for democracy," he craved to know "why England approached democratic institutions by slow and steady stages of deliberate and peaceful development, while so many others passed to democracy through constant revolution?" Why, he asked, has "democracy existed in America and Australia virtually from the first, while other states have utterly failed in every effort to establish it?"[12] These were fundamental questions for Wilson; democracy was "neither a body of doctrine nor a form of government," he wrote, but a "stage of development," created not by "aspiration or by new faith" but "built up by slow habit."[13] Wilson emphasized what Tocqueville had argued decades earlier when he wrote: "America has democracy because she is free; she is not free because she has democracy."

Wilson believed that the reform of American politics presupposed an acceptance of the fact that congressional procedures and political party practices militated against the most able men opting for a political career. Bosses did not keep them out; traditions of organization and debate in Congress discouraged them, and these had to be changed.[14] Wilson was persuaded that the British parliamentary system nourished talent in a way that the

American congressional system did not, and as long as that remained the situation, those entering the White House would always be inferior to those who made their way to Number 10 Downing Street. Bryce did not wholly disagree with him.[15]

Wilson, a serious student of Walter Bagehot's works, accepted his notion that the prime ministerial system excelled over the presidential, but Wilson never thought that the former would replace the latter in the United States. More ardently even than Roosevelt, he looked for better men to enter politics, but refused to embrace the idea that the extinction of bosses and the end of the spoils system would achieve that end. Bryce's study became the political bible for his generation of Americans, and the book went through many editions and sold in tens of thousands of copies on both sides of the Atlantic. When, as late as 1920, a group of distinguished American historians considered whether the study ought to be revised—Bryce was too old to do it himself—they decided the classic ought to remain unchanged from its last edition. Though a great deal had changed in the United States between 1888 and 1920, the election of Warren Harding seemed only to confirm what Bryce had written about why great men were neither nominated nor elected to the presidency. Indeed, as late as 1960, much that Bryce had written about presidential politics, and indeed about politics more generally, still seemed relevant. The party conventions retained their old jamboree flavor, and the bosses, though less powerful, were very much in evidence. Only in the decades that followed did Bryce's 1888 work seem suddenly dated, made so by the total triumph of the primary system and by the new and growing influence of the mass media, especially television. In these changed situations, Tocqueville's 1835 study suddenly claimed a relevance it had never previously known. Americans living in a society greatly transformed by an intellectual, social, economic, and political revolution, read *Democracy in America* in wholly new ways.

Though Tocqueville shared the enthusiasm Americans almost automatically awarded the Founders—the creators of the Constitution—his interpretation of their accomplishment was in many respects different from theirs. Emphasizing the independence of the revolutionary generation, saying that "they spread their brilliance over the nation and did not borrow [their brilliance] from it," he admired the *"virile candor and manly independence of thought"*—using italics to emphasize the importance of these qualities—that made it possible for a small group of gifted men to frame an extraordinary Constitution.[16] While Tocqueville never explained when these political habits came to be lost, why they were no longer in evidence in the United States he visited in the mid-1830s, he criticized President Andrew Jackson for courting the electorate, always seeking its favor, and never aspiring to lead it.[17]

Had Tocqueville been alive to read Bryce's observations on American politics in the late 1880s, he would have noted the continued absence of that kind of political independence, and it is doubtful that he would have ascribed it simply to the power of the bosses, the professional politicians. Conditions basic to democracy where politicians accepted to be subservient to mass opinion—the only sovereign power—had produced two unfortunate results: Minorities were virtually silenced, and politicians ceased to be independent. The condition to be remedied, in Tocqueville's mind, was not that imperfect political institutions were being exploited by ambitious and craven individuals searching for wealth and power but that elected officials looked only to win the support of uninformed voters. Wilson, in his admiration for William Gladstone, saw him as a democratic leader who did not wait to be instructed by the nation but took the initiative to lead it. He imagined himself a political leader in that tradition.

Tocqueville, consorting with Americans as socially and intellectually distinguished as those Bryce encountered a half-century later, noted their habit of never expressing in public the opinions they dared to voice in private. Such views, sometimes highly unflattering to the practices of the American democracy, might be shared with a foreigner—someone like Tocqueville, a stranger passing through—but were never intended for public consumption. Tocqueville knew from the American reaction to what other European visitors had written about the United States that they did not welcome criticism from foreigners. While many of the early European travel accounts had dwelled on American rudeness, crude manners, and the perpetual habit of exaggerating the nation's virtues, Tocqueville's reservations were of a different kind. In a disturbing and disconcerting paragraph, he wrote: "If these lines ever come to America, I am sure of two things: first, that readers will all raise their voices to condemn me; that many among them will absolve me at the bottom of their consciences."

Tocqueville proved correct in both prophesies; Americans had no wish to hear their country's political habits criticized, and a minority, perhaps larger at the time of the Vietnam War than in any earlier period, recognized the validity of his concerns. The proposition that majority opinion was not easily criticized, that those with contrary views were often silenced and derided, would not have been thought an outlandish view when Richard Nixon was president.

Tocqueville suggested that the president had only a "temporary, limited, and dependent power, with no great prizes to distribute to his friends." Unlike European heads of state, the president enjoyed no conspicuous wealth, nothing that could be mistaken for glory. His influence was generally too feeble to counteract that of Congress.[19] The weakness of the office was guaranteed by the absence of external enemies; when that situation changed and foreign affairs became salient, the powers of the president would grow appreciably.[20] This was Tocqueville's signal contribution to an understanding of the presidency, more significant certainly than Bryce's recognition of why the office so often attracted only mediocre men. Tocqueville, gazing at a relatively weak institution, the presidency, prophesied one of greatly expanded power, coincidental with war and the nation's expanded foreign engagements.

In considering the presidency, Tocqueville raised a question that neither Roosevelt nor Wilson ever considered: Were those who framed the Constitution right to permit the reelection of the president? At the time of Tocqueville's visit, all presidents save one, John Adams, had been reelected. Understanding why Americans had no wish to dismiss someone who had governed well, who might be needed in a time of crisis, that reasoning had little appeal for him. Tocqueville expected that anyone seeking the presidency from the outside would intrigue for it, but there were limits to what such an individual might be able to do. "When, on the contrary," he wrote, the "head of state puts himself in the running, he borrows the force of government for his own use. In the first case, it is one man, with his feeble means; in the second, it is the state itself, with its immense resources, that intrigues and corrupts."[21] Tocqueville returned to his constant theme, not that power corrupts, but that currying favor with the multitude is corrupting, the danger a democracy needs constantly to guard against.

Had the president been ineligible for reelection this would not have rendered him independent of the electorate; he would still have wished to be responsible, but there would have been no incentive to bend his will to conform to popular demands, becoming, in Tocqueville's words, "a docile instrument in the hands of the majority." In describing the man who cared only to renew his White House tenancy, Tocqueville showed his contempt for anyone prepared to sacrifice his independence to gain the applause of the crowd. In his words,

He loves what it loves, hates what it hates; he flies to meet its will; anticipates its complaints, bends to its least desires; the legislators wanted him to guide it, and he follows it. Thus, in order not to deprive the state of the talents of one man, they have rendered those talents almost useless; and in order to provide a resource for extraordinary circumstances, they have exposed the country to dangers every day.[22]

Tocqueville recognized that ousting a president after a single term would be difficult; the temptation to use the power of the state to influence the election, to shape opinion, would be overwhelming, and it would generally be successful—a prophesy amply fulfilled in the twentieth century.

In several long chapters ("On the Three Races that Inhabit the Territory of the United States"), Tocqueville contrasted the sorry plight of the Negro and the American Indian with that of the white man. For Bryce, writing a half-century later, the Negro scarcely existed; a threat to no one, not even a preoccupying national problem, his condition could be safely ignored. There was even less reason to be concerned with the American Indian. Viewing both as many of the "better people" in America did, an opinion shared by his British contemporaries who saw the United States as the work only of Anglo-Americans, Bryce agreed with them that they were the sole creators of American civilization. Bryce saw slavery as yesterday's problem, settled by the Civil War. Tocqueville was never so sanguine, saying, "I perceive slavery receding, the prejudice to which it has given birth is unmoving" and argued that this was as true in the North as in the South.[23]

Bryce made no such observations. Race relations, defined as black-white relations, were unimportant to him as they were for both Roosevelt and Wilson, though each made race, defined as *ethnicity*—in the Anglo-Saxon jargon of their day—a major component of the American national character. Are these the reasons, then, for Tocqueville's restored prominence after World War II, when civil rights issues came to the fore? Or were there more compelling reasons for his revived reputation?

Tocqueville's book, controversial in its own day because of what it said about the tyranny of the majority, and genuinely alarming because it virtually prophesied the Civil War, could never be mistaken for a jeremiad. The country appealed far too much to the young French visitor not to receive his praise, but he never felt any need to succumb to the exaggerated enthusiasms of those who praised it unstintingly. It was easy for a post–World War II generation, especially after the 1950s, to acknowledge that the tyranny of the majority was not a figment of Tocqueville's lively imagination or a throwback to an America that had existed in the time of Jackson that had since disappeared.

The facile optimism of the early twentieth century, only superficially interrupted by the Great Depression, did not survive the Vietnam War, the political assassinations, and the social mayhem of the 1960s. The country, in Johnson's time and in Nixon's, began to ask questions about presidential authority never previously posed so insistently by so many.

What role, if any, did public opinion have in legitimating the presidents' war policies, and why were they able so effectively for such long periods to ignore the views of vocal minorities? More than that, did the wars they initiated and fought coarsen American society, creating levels of distrust never previously registered? Had war and the threat of war served to fuel a White House propaganda machine that allowed these men and those prepared to serve them to stifle dissent, making resistance to majority opinion seem immoral and unpatriotic?

Nothing that Bryce wrote in 1888 or in his revised editions of *The American Commonwealth* prepared the country for the events of the latter decades of the twentieth century. Tocqueville's *Democracy in America,* with its critical appraisal of the power of the multitude, became meaningful when public opinion legitimated vast extensions of presidential power, said to be necessary to protect society against foreign and domestic enemies. The presidency became suspect when certain of its most characteristic modern features—covert intelligence, deception, and unprecedented military expenditures—established themselves as essential components of government policy. Tocqueville spoke to a generation that believed itself deceived and abused, kept in a state of not very blissful ignorance.

Tocqueville treated issues of war and peace in a way that repudiated the notion that war ought to be seen as the illicit pursuit only of monarchs and aristocrats, that democracies could be relied on to shun war and avoid its terrors. These were utopian visions for him. Tocqueville saw war as "an accident to which all peoples are subject, democratic peoples as well as others," and while he accepted that citizens in a democracy might crave peace, their "proletarian armies," no longer commanded by the aristocrats of old, were more addicted to war.[24] Because Tocqueville believed that "the wealthiest, the best instructed, the most capable citizens" in a democracy rarely chose a military career, he felt no awe for that "separate little nation" of soldiers that did not greatly impress him by its intelligence. In one of his more prescient observations, he wrote: "There are two things a democratic people will always have trouble doing, beginning a war and ending it."[25]

War, in his mind, always put freedom at risk, not so much in creating the possibility of victorious generals establishing their rule over the people, as Caesar and other of the ancients did, but in its tendency to increase the prerogatives of civil government which "inevitably centralizes the direction of all men and the employment of all things in its hands."[26] Though never a pacifist himself, he thought war an exceedingly dangerous pursuit for democratic societies. As he explained, "All those who seek to destroy freedom within a democratic nation ought to know that the surest and shortest method of succeeding at this is war. This is the first axiom of the science."[27] No such ruminations or warnings were issued by Bryce; they were wholly outside his ken.

Five years after the publication of his first volume of *Democracy in America*, Tocqueville wrote a second, thought by many to be inferior to his 1835 study. Meditating always on his chosen theme, the "tyranny of the majority," he acknowledged that though his fears on that subject had in no way diminished, he had come to see the matter in a new light. While he saw no possibility of a despotism like that of ancient Rome coming to America or to any other modern democracy, he feared another kind of domination that neither of the traditional terms—tyranny or despotism—adequately described.[28]

This new control, he wrote, would be "more extensive and milder," and "would degrade men without tormenting them." This "tutelary power," different from any that had previously existed, would guarantee citizens their enjoyments while watching over them and infantilizing them. In a memorable passage, Tocqueville wrote:

It is absolute, detailed, regular, far-seeing, and mild. It would resemble the paternal power if like that, it had for its object to prepare man for manhood; but on the contrary, it seeks only to keep them irrevocably fixed in childhood. It likes citizens to enjoy themselves provided that they think only of enjoying themselves. It willingly works for their happiness, but it wants to be the unique agent and arbiter of that; it provides for their security, foresees and secures their needs, facilitates their pleasures, conducts their principal affairs, directs their industry, regulates their estates, divides their inheritances; can it not take away from them entirely the trouble of thinking and the pain of living?[29]

While some in the twentieth century chose to interpret these words as a prophesy of what the welfare state would one day do to assume responsibilities once claimed by individuals and families, Tocqueville's purpose was a quite different one. He saw his contemporaries as "incessantly racked by two inimical passions. . . the need to be led and the wish to remain free, they were unable to eradicate either instinct."[30] This made them vulnerable to the wiles of men who flattered them incessantly. Tocqueville's indignation expressed itself in the proposition that this was a base currying of favor with the least instructed, unable to see how they were being manipulated and used.

Bryce never imagined that a later generation of Americans, initially elated but then scarred by wars he had not anticipated and by a world economic Depression more terrible than any he had known, would discover that their country, mired in the violence of the 1960s and 1970s, would find little virtue in his liberal political nostrums. Tocqueville's study, undoubtedly more speculative but also more compelling than Bryce's, purportedly scientific, empirical, and objective text, saw the nation's problems as moral and intellectual, only very incidentally political. In 1835, Tocqueville wrote:

What I most reproach in democratic government, as it has been organized in the United States is not, as many people in Europe claim, its weakness, but on the contrary, its irresistible force. And what is most repugnant to me in America is not the extreme freedom that reigns there; it is the lack of a guarantee against tyranny.[31]

Many Americans, living in the age of Johnson and Nixon, might have thought that criticism excessive. Did the public in the end not rise up against both, compelling Johnson to withdraw his candidacy for another presidential term, literally chasing Nixon from the White House for his political excesses? The humiliation of Johnson and Nixon, most often represented as triumphs of American democratic procedures, will seem to many convincing refutations of Tocqueville's exaggerated fears. Yet the invention of the term *political correctness*, coincidental with this troubled period, signifying the limits of tolerated discourse, would seem to support Tocqueville's astonishing statement, "I do not know any country where, in general, less independence of mind and genuine freedom of discussion reign than in America."[32]

Was this true? Did the investigative reporting of journalists, together with the many highly publicized congressional hearings into all manner of dubious governmental activities, not guarantee full discussion of all critical questions? Or were there, indeed, a greater number of prohibited subjects after 1960 than before? Had war and the fear of war contributed to the creation of a climate of secrecy that made information on many subjects virtually unobtainable? Were the silences of most Americans on all manner of sensitive matters more telling than the noise that periodically issued from Congress and from the nation's TV screens?

Because the Reagan presidency boasted so many mythic elements, greatly influencing the office as it evolved in the last decades of the century, it is important to consider Tocqueville's views on patriotism and religion, the revived sacred subjects of latter-day America. On patriotism, Tocqueville wrote: "There is nothing more annoying in the habits of life than this irritable patriotism of the Americans. A foreigner would indeed consent to praise much in the country; but he would want to be permitted to blame something, and this he is absolutely refused." Continuing in this vein, and becoming more ironic, he added:

> America is therefore a country of freedom where, in order not to wound anyone, the foreigner must not speak freely either of particular persons, or of the state, or of the governed, or of those who govern, or public undertakings, or of private undertakings; or, finally, of anything one encounters except the climate and the soil; and still, one finds Americans ready to defend both as if they had helped to form them.[33]

Patriotism, an exaggerated sentiment in the United States in the nineteenth century, conspicuous in both World War I and World War II, enjoyed an even greater revival in the days of Reagan. The president's managers, anxious always to extol him, ignoring much of what his predecessors had done to weaken the Soviet Union, made him appear the remarkable leader of an incomparable people, both exceptional in every way. While others abroad, divested of their empires, were less partial to such patriotic excess, the United States, before the Gulf War and after, under Bush, father and son, exulted in what it conceived to be its unique prowess. In this, though few thought to make so wounding an analogy, the country resembled many of the newer states of the world, an infant republic still proud of its undeniable virtues.[34]

Tocqueville, no less profound in his discussion of American religion, wrote: "Religious zeal constantly warms itself at the hearth of patriotism. You think that these men act solely in consideration of the other life; but you are mistaken; eternity is only one of their cares." Tocqueville noted that the philosophers of the eighteenth century imagined that religious zeal would weaken as freedom and enlightenment grew; America, he said, both enlightened and free, disproved that theory. Greatly impressed by the "religious aspect" of the country, he dwelled on the "great political consequences that flowed from these new facts" and wrote:

> Christianity has therefore preserved a great empire over the American mind, and what I especially want to note is that it reigns not only as a philosophy that is adopted after examination, but as a religion that is believed without discussion. In the United States, Christian sects vary infinitely and are constantly modified, but Christianity itself is an established and irresistible fact that no one undertakes either to attack or defend.[35]

Believing Christianity to be central to American culture, he returned to his favorite theme, the tyranny of the majority, giving it yet another dimension, saying:

> In the United States, the majority takes charge of furnishing individuals with a host of ready-made opinions, and it thus relieves them of the obligation to form their own. There are a great number of theories on matters of philosophy, morality or politics that everyone thus adopts without examination, on the faith of the public; and if one looks very closely, one will see that religion itself reigns there much less as revealed doctrine than as common opinion.[36]

Reagan, even more than his predecessors, paid heed to this common opinion, not only in how he reacted to the evil empire, the Soviet Union, but also in how he treated such issues as abortion, busing, and crime, matters of great concern to the religious right, a political force that Franklin Roosevelt never had to contend with. The old American religious quarrels between Protestants and Catholics were adjourned; new ones, between born-again and fundamentalist Christians, politically influential in the South and West, but not as conspicuous in the East, became all-important.

A new political agenda took shape under Reagan, first articulated by Nixon, and all who followed them knew better than to ignore it.[37] Tocqueville had greater relevance for the America of Ronald Reagan and George W. Bush than he did for that of Andrew Jackson. One of the greatest of France's nineteenth-century intellectuals spoke to Americans in the last decades of the twentieth century and in the years after September 11 as few of its politicians dared to do. An American presidency, crafted in the first two decades of the twentieth century, which experienced unprecedented turmoil and dangers during World War

II, came to an end in the 1960s and 1970s. Another was created following those tumultuous decades that survives today. Tocqueville's concern with the tyranny of the majority, and also with the hazards of war for a democracy concerned to retain its liberty, has lost none of its resonance.

Whatever Woodrow Wilson may have learned from Tocqueville, whatever pleasure Theodore Roosevelt derived from knowing that Bryce had adopted many of his notions of what ailed the republic, becomes almost secondary to three new facts rarely explored by journalists. Minority opinion, especially at home, enjoys little credence or influence among those prepared to serve the new-style monarchs. Foreign opinion counts for even less. Patriotism is in the saddle, and while it is offered as balm to millions, frightened by the prospect of new terrorist attacks, it provides no solution to a world situation scarcely comprehended by either the elected monarch or his chosen courtiers. Both, of late, have been excessively aggressive and self-willed, fearing little resistance from Congress, but few in the world today are greatly impressed by either their intelligence or their learning. The learned presidency of Roosevelt and Wilson appears to be extinct, perhaps for a time only.

So long as journalists continue to seek to pry open the gates of a barricaded White House, depending on the self-interested tittle-tattle of those inside, their revelations will provide amusement and sometimes provoke anger but will never explain what Tocqueville, a great admirer of the United States, knew when he committed his thoughts on "What Kinds of Despotism Democratic Nations Have to Fear." In his words, "Men who live in the democratic centuries we are entering have the taste for independence naturally. They naturally tolerate rule with impatience. . . . They love power; but they are inclined to scorn and hate whoever exercises it. . . . These instincts will always be found because they come from the foundations of the social state, which will not change. For a long time they will keep any despotism from being able to settle in, and they will furnish new arms to each new generation that wants to struggle in favor of men's freedom. Let us therefore have that salutary fear of the future that makes one watchful and combative, and not that sort of soft and idle terror that wears hearts down and enervates them."[38]

NOTES

CHAPTER 1 (Of a Republic Transformed)

1. See Gordon S. Wood, *The Creation of the American Republic, 1776–1789* (University of North Carolina Press, 1969) for discussion of monarchy, democracy, and aristocracy as the Founders viewed these institutions.

2. See Alexis de Tocqueville, *Democracy in America* (University of Chicago Press, 2000), translated and edited by Harvey C. Mansfield and Delba Winthrop, pp. 115–118 for comparison of presidency and monarchy.

3. Cf. infra, Chapter 18, "The Actor."

4. Edward S. Corwin, *The President: Office and Powers, 1787–1984* (New York University Press, 1984), 5th rev. ed. by Randall W. Bland, Theodore T. Hindson, and Jack W. Peltason, pp. 135–136. The editors, adding postscripts to the classic work written by Corwin emphasize the "dramatic increase in size in both the Executive Office of the President and the White House office," emphasizing the "precipitous decline" of the Cabinet, with the exception of State, Treasury, Defense, and Justice.

5. See Edmund Morris, *Theodore Rex* (Random House, 2001). A less celebrated biography, in many ways complementing the Morris volume, is Kathleen Dalton, *Theodore Roosevelt: A Strenuous Life* (Alfred A. Knopf, 2002). The "Reagan Court," so different from what was common earlier in the century, receives its most penetrating analysis in Lou Cannon, *President Reagan: The Role of a Lifetime* (Simon & Schuster, 1991), especially in what he says about James Baker and Michael Deaver; see pp. 429–436.

6. None of Theodore Roosevelt's contemporaries ever doubted this.

7. These affinities merit closer study.

8. The 1960s and the 1970s need to be seen as America's "Time of Troubles."

9. James Bryce, *The American Commonwealth*, new ed., 2 vols., published originally in 1888 (Macmillan, 1928); Woodrow Wilson, *Congressional Government* (Transaction, 2002), published originally in 1885.

10. Eric Hobsbawm, *Age of Extremes: The Short Twentieth Century, 1914–1991* (Michael Joseph, 1994). Hobsbawm argues that the collapse of the Soviet Union brought the twentieth century to an end; others have suggested that September 11, 2001, by its effects on the United States, ought to be seen as ending the twentieth century. I argue that the twentieth century lives on to this day, with George W. Bush pursuing strategies redolent of those common to Ronald Reagan.

11. The term, increasingly used after World War II, legitimated the secrecy and subterfuge believed necessary for national defense.

12. Wilson, even more than Roosevelt, ascribed his securing the presidency to the workings of Divine Providence. Both, more than their predecessors, sought to legitimate what they knew to be their vastly expanded authority. See Woodrow Wilson, *Constitutional Government in the United States* (Columbia University Press, 1908), pp. 54–71; also, Theodore Roosevelt, *An Autobiography,* with a new introduction by Elting E. Morison (Da Capo, 1985).

13. Ibid., for Roosevelt's discussion of "stewardship," see p. 372.

14. Matthew Prior, English poet and Tory statesman, wrote this in 1718.

15. Popular election of senators began only in 1913 with the passage of the Seventeenth Amendment to the Constitution.

16. Roosevelt, *Autobiography,* p. 558.

17. Ibid., pp. 575–589.

18. Ibid., pp. 408–436.

19. Ibid., pp. 516–519. Roosevelt made no reference to the sporadic fighting that continued in the Philippines during the first year of his administration.

20. James Chace, *1912: Wilson, Roosevelt, Taft and Debs—The Election That Changed the Country* (Simon and Schuster, 2004).

21. Dalton, *Roosevelt,* p. 414. Dalton discusses why Roosevelt chose to write his autobiography, believing it would prove "he was not a power-hungry fake."

22. Ibid., p. 409. After the election, Dalton writes, "TR still wrote about Wilson in tempered language," thinking Taft "a plain fool" and Wilson "not a fool." That tolerance did not survive for very long.

23. Arthur S. Link, *Wilson: The Road to the White House* (Princeton University Press, 1947), pp. 475–476.

24. Arthur S. Link, *Wilson: The New Freedom* (Princeton University Press, 1956), p. 97. Wilson "made a valiant effort to maintain good relations" with Bryan, Link wrote, defending him against "hostile editors [who] lampooned the Nebraskan for neglecting his duties and for alleged social gaucheries." His more serious lack, certainly, was a deep understanding of foreign policy issues.

25. Wilson needed an able secretary of state more than Roosevelt did. Neither Bryan nor Lansing could claim that distinction.

26. John Milton Cooper Jr., *Breaking the Heart of the World: Woodrow Wilson and the Fight for the League of Nations* (Cambridge University Press, 2001), p. 200. The president's relations with his secretary of state, unsatisfactory before his illness, disintegrated further following his stroke.

27. Link, *New Freedom,* pp. 5–19.

28. Charles Seymour, *The Intimate Papers of Colonel House* (Houghton Mifflin, 1926), chapters xii–xiv.

29. Ibid., p. 470. Seymour writes: "The mission of Colonel House had not accomplished the miracle of peace, which in 1915 was a practical impossibility."

30. Cooper, *Breaking the Heart* is the best account of Wilson's failure to move the Senate to approve the treaty he brought back from Paris.

31. William C. Widenor, *Henry Cabot Lodge and the Search for an American Foreign Policy* (University of California Press, 1980) remains the most sympathetic and authoritative account of how Lodge and his Republican allies perceived the League of Nations issue.

32. Ibid., pp. 300–348.

33. Michael Mandelbaum, *The Ideas That Conquered the World: Peace, Democracy and Free Markets in the Twenty-First Century* (Public Affairs, 2002). A characteristic early-twenty-first-century eulogy of Wilson, whose first chapter is entitled, very appropriately, "Wilson Victorious."

34. Harding's congressional victories were virtually unprecedented.

35. Andrew Sinclair, *The Available Man: The Life Behind the Masks of Warren G. Harding* (Macmillan, 1965), pp. 296–299. An unconventional biography of Harding that argues he was

a "shrewd and competent politician" whose reputation was "blasted more by writers of fiction than of fact."

36. Arthur Schlesinger Jr., *The Crisis of the Old Order, 1919–1933* (Houghton Mifflin, 1957), p. 58. Schlesinger, commenting on White's characterization of Coolidge, writes: "His frugality sanctified an age of luxury, his taciturnity an age of ballyhoo. He was the moral symbol the times seemed to demand."

37. The president's role as commander in chief is rarely mentioned by those who write about Harding, Coolidge, or Hoover.

38. This indebtedness is central to any understanding of Franklin Roosevelt's presidency.

39. Press photographers cooperated with Roosevelt in concealing the extent of his infirmity; no such forbearance is conceivable today.

40. Mandelbaum, *Ideas*, p. 41. Mandelbaum argues that Wilson lacked Franklin Roosevelt's guile; he also lacked Roosevelt's sense of fun and love of intrigue.

41. *The Secret Diary of Harold L. Ickes: The First Thousand Days, 1933–1936* (Simon and Schuster, 1953) suggests that this was true from the beginning, before the hazards of war led the president to be more secretive in his relations with Cabinet colleagues.

42. The depreciation of the Cabinet's importance became apparent first in FDR's time.

43. Frank Freidel, *Franklin D. Roosevelt, A Rendezvous with Destiny* (Little, Brown, 1990), p. 474. A succinct account of the quarrel between Hull and Welles that led the president to feel compelled to ask for Welles's resignation.

44. This was an instance where Roosevelt clearly pursued policies redolent of those advocated decades earlier by both his principal political tutors.

45. Roosevelt greatly relished this title, and used it extensively during the war.

46. Robert E. Sherwood, *Roosevelt and Hopkins, An Intimate History* (Harper, 1948).

47. Freidel, *Roosevelt,* pp. 456–457; Roosevelt, like Wilson, strongly believed in self-determination, and never concealed his disdain for colonialism.

48. Ibid., pp. 596–597. The president's relations with de Gaulle never improved, and were as bad at the end of the war as at the beginning.

49. De Gaulle never sought to accommodate or mollify the president, believing him hostile to France's legitimate aspirations.

50. He never chose to take full advantage of the legislation that created the Executive Office of the President.

51. In this, again, he showed himself a disciple of "Uncle Theodore."

52. Truman's enemies spoke of his "cronies," installed in the White House, but they were never a "court" in the Franklin Roosevelt tradition.

53. Elting E. Morison, *Turmoil and Tradition: A Study of the Life and Times of Henry L. Stimson* (Houghton Mifflin, 1960), p. 632. Morison, citing evidence of the United States Strategic Bombing Survey, accepts that "Japan would have succumbed without invasion and without the atom bomb to aerial bombardment by conventional means," but this was not the view of those who advised Stimson in July 1945 that the use of the bomb would shorten the war by months and possibly years.

54. Harry S. Truman, *Memoirs: Year of Decisions,* vol. 1 (Doubleday, 1955), p. 419. Truman wrote: "I regarded the bomb as a military weapon and never had any doubt that it should be used. The top military advisers to the President recommended its use, and when I talked to Churchill he unhesitatingly told me that he favored the use of the atomic bomb if it might aid to end the war."

55. Ibid., pp. 323–328.

56. Truman never said this explicitly, but made great efforts to avoid any suggestion that his policies deviated from those pursued by FDR.

57. Harry Truman, *Memoirs: Years of Trial and Hope,* vol. 2 (Doubleday, 1956), pp. 183–87 for a very candid evaluation of Thurmond and Wallace, and their challenges to him in the 1948 election.

58. Ibid., pp. 270–277.

59. Max Hastings, *The Korean War* (Simon and Schuster, 1987), pp. 200–207. An illuminating account, not least for what it says about the British attitude toward MacArthur's actions and policies. A more authoritative account of the war itself is provided by Clay Blair Jr., *Forgotten War: America in Korea, 1950–1953* (United States Naval Institute, 2003).

60. Ibid., p. 202. Hastings expresses admiration for Truman's political courage and his surprise that so many Americans "recoiled" from the Administration's policies.

61. Eisenhower was never one to acknowledge what others did to elevate him to the positions that gave him his reputation as a superb military strategist.

62. Richard E. Neustadt, *Presidential Power and the Modern Presidents: The Politics of Leadership from Roosevelt to Reagan* (Free Press, 1990), p. 7.

63. Ibid., p. 139.

64. Merle Miller, *Plain Speaking: An Oral Biography of Harry S. Truman* (Gollancz, 1974), p. 341. Truman, remarking on an Eisenhower campaign speech in Milwaukee, Wisconsin, on October 3, 1952, said of him: ". . . he was going to pay a tribute to General Marshall, but he took it out rather than stand up to McCarthy. It was one of the most shameful things I can ever remember. Why, General Marshall was responsible for his whole career. . . . Three different times Marshall got him pushed upstairs, and in return . . . Eisenhower sold him out. It was just a shameful thing."

65. Alanbrooke, *War Diaries, 1939–1945* (Weidenfeld and Nicolson, 2001), p. 575. Alanbrooke wrote in his diary on July 27, 1944, "There is no doubt that Ike is out to do all he can to maintain the best of relations between British and Americans, but it is equally clear that he knows nothing about strategy and is *quite* unsuited to the post of Supreme Commander as far as running the strategy of the war is concerned." Miller, quoting Truman, in *Plain Speaking,* p. 365, heard him give the same negative opinions of Eisenhower as a general, saying, "What they never seem to say about Eisenhower is that he was . . . very weak as a field commander. . . . Bradley was a great soldier, but Ike wasn't."

66. The Dulles rhetoric led some to believe that the country's foreign policy changed substantially under Eisenhower; it did not, though world conditions changed greatly.

67. Stephen E. Ambrose, *Eisenhower: The President* (Simon and Schuster, 1984), vol. 2, p. 171 defines the "New Look" defense policy as comprising "fewer conventional forces, more atomic power, less cost." It called for "an expanded strategic air force and a much reduced conventional force on land and at sea."

68. Ibid., pp. 285–286.

69. Adam Ulam, *The Rivals: America and Russia Since World War II* (Viking, 1971), pp. 244–245. Ulam characterizes Eisenhower's foreign policy as "one of waiting for events, of reactions rather than initiatives," in a word, of "torpor."

70. D.R. Thorpe, *Eden, The Life and Times of Anthony Eden, First Earl of Avon, 1897–1977* (Chatto and Windus, 2003), pp. 529–531.

71. Ambrose, *Eisenhower: The President,* p. 377. Ambrose wrote: "Eisenhower recognized that one of the fundamental truths the Suez crisis taught was that the Arabs were more important to the West than the West was to them. . . . " In speaking to "Old Guard China Lobby Republicans," he said: "Formosa, if lost, is a blow, but not a major world defeat." If the West lost the Middle East, it would be "major."

72. Ulam, *The Rivals,* pp. 278–280.

73. Ibid., p. 265. Ulam characterized United States policy of doing nothing in respect to the Hungarian uprising as "humane and realistic" on one level, but "impolitic and shameful" on another. To censor the "actions of its friends and allies [over Suez] while transgressions by the other side remained unchecked after a resolution or two was hastily passed by the world organization" showed the ineptness that Ulam, like others, believed characteristic of the Eisenhower/Dulles policies.

74. Eisenhower never understood the consequences of what he did in 1956; if it bound Britain more closely to the United States, determined never to repeat the Suez error, it had no comparable effects in France, laying the basis for the closer collaboration with Germany and ultimately the exclusion of Great Britain from the Common Market.

75. Ambrose, *Eisenhower: The President*, pp. 612–613. Ambrose wrote of the speech, and its warning of the dangers of "the military-industrial complex" as that of "a soldier-prophet, a general who had given his life to the defense of freedom and the achievement of peace."

76. Kennedy promised "activity," and the media exulted in his pledge.

77. The nation, traumatized by the assassination, had to wait for almost a decade before moderately objective assessments of the Kennedy presidency appeared.

78. An assertion rarely made, but incontestably true.

79. These were the three defining foreign policy moments in the Kennedy years.

80. The appointment received relatively little criticism at the time or since.

81. This was again the typical mass media reaction to his appointments.

82. These were the "loyalists" who after the president's assassination helped create the myths that have remained current to this day about Kennedy's exceptional qualities.

83. As with Franklin Roosevelt, those who served Kennedy revelled in telling tales of their association with a president they believed incomparable.

84. A view not commonly held by Americans.

85. This was as true of Rusk as of Bundy, of the president as of his brother and McNamara.

86. Robert Dallek, *John F. Kennedy: An Unfinished Life, 1917–1963* (Allen Lane, 2003), pp. 166–168, 185–187. Kennedy's dubieties about the French in Indochina were long-standing, expressed when he was in the House, as well as when he was in the Senate. Like Roosevelt, he distrusted "old-fashioned European imperialists," and wished to align himself with the emerging nations.

87. H.R. McMaster, *Dereliction of Duty: Lyndon Johnson, Robert McNamara, the Joint Chiefs of Staff, and the Lies That Led to Vietnam* (HarperCollins, 1997), pp. 40–41. Kennedy, according to McMaster, seemed ambivalent about helping to engineer a coup against Diem, and in the end "declared indecisively that he would 'discourage' a coup only if Lodge, on whom he depended to generate Republican support for his policy, shared Taylor's and Robert Kennedy's misgivings." McMaster added: "On October 31 McGeorge Bundy instructed Lodge that 'once a coup under responsible leadership has begun. . . it is in the interest of the U.S. government that it should succeed.' Diem's fate was sealed."

88. Ibid., p. 41. McMaster, critical of both Kennedy and Johnson, wrote: "John Kennedy bequeathed to Lyndon Johnson an advisory system that limited real influence to his inner circle and treated others, particularly the Joint Chiefs of Staff, more like a source of potential opposition than of useful advice."

89. Dallek, *Kennedy*, pp. 426–429.

90. Kennedy's attitudes toward Adenauer and de Gaulle have never been adequately studied; while he imagined he could placate them, his differences with both were fundamental.

91. Seymour M. Hersh, *The Dark Side of Camelot* (Little, Brown, 1997). This, the most damning book written about the deceptions perpetrated by the president and his brother, to which others in the administration also contributed, needs to be read with caution.

92. The president was fortunate in the people he brought to work for him in Washington. None ever betrayed him in the way subordinates of other presidents did.

93. Hersh, *Camelot*, pp. 225–226, 291–292, 363–364. These pages, along with many others, carry interesting details on how both Schlesinger and Sorenson contributed to the perpetuation of myths about the president, his intentions, and his policies.

94. This is too rarely acknowledged, especially by those who remain faithful to the Kennedy legend.

95. Dallek, *Kennedy*, p. 320. The appointment of former Governor G. Mennen Williams to be assistant secretary of state for Africa was believed important, but nothing in Dallek's long biography of the president suggests that much was accomplished by him or by others in that vast impoverished and politically unstable continent.

96. Peter H. Smith, *Dynamics of U.S.–Latin American Relations* (Oxford University Press, 2000), pp. 150–154.

97. This was a characteristic example of Johnson's political adeptness.

98. Even the greatest admirers of Kennedy would acknowledge this.

99. Lyndon Baines Johnson, *The Vantage Point: Perspectives of the Presidency, 1963–1969* (Holt, Rinehart and Winston, 1971), pp. 322–346. A full expression of what Johnson hoped he might achieve with his "Great Society."

100. This was something Johnson could never admit.

101. McMaster, *Dereliction*, pp. 317–322. These pages recount but a small part of the lies and deceptions practiced by Johnson and those who advised him.

102. Ibid., pp. 124–132.

103. Ibid., pp. 133–136.

104. Ibid., pp. 234–236.

105. Ibid., pp. 241–242.

106. Ibid., pp. 287–288.

107. Johnson, *Vantage Point*, pp. 539–542. This, Johnson's account of his last meeting with Robert Kennedy prior to his assassination, emphasizes its cordiality.

108. Ibid., p. 550. Johnson believed that North Vietnamese recalcitrance in 1968, together with "the prevailing mood of frustration and conservatism in the nation" weighed heavily with the electorate, contributing to Humphrey's defeat.

109. Ibid., p. 538. He found it significant that he received a 49.5 percent write-in vote in the New Hampshire primary when he was not a candidate as against Eugene McCarthy's 42.4 percent vote who ran as the so-called peace candidate.

110. Few who have written about Johnson have emphasized sufficiently how much his domestic team succeeded while his inherited team of foreign policy experts failed.

111. This was the standard argument that Nixon used repeatedly.

112. This was perhaps the most important and lasting political consequence of Johnson's efforts to achieve the civil rights "revolution" through a legislative program more radical than any proposed by his Democratic Party presidential predecessors.

113. Nixon showed his habitual political acumen in emphasizing this issue.

114. The reduction in U.S. forces was larger than Nixon's foes were ever prepared to acknowledge.

115. Nixon's reputation almost guaranteed that he would not be believed.

116. The generational split was thought most significant by the media.

117. Godfrey Hodgson, *The Gentleman from New York, Daniel Patrick Moynihan, A Biography* (Houghton Mifflin, 2000), pp. 159–160.

118. Alan Brinkley, *Liberalism and its Discontents* (Harvard University Press, 1998), pp. 277–297. Brinkley reflects on why liberalism has figured so prominently in studies of American twentieth-century politics while conservatism has not received comparable attention.

119. This observation draws on a conversation with Henry Kissinger.

120. Henry Kissinger, *Diplomacy* (Simon and Schuster, 1994), pp. 713–732.

121. Ibid.

122. Nixon, like all twentieth-century presidents in their first terms gave close attention to preparing his reelection campaign, to make certain of victory.

123. The size of his 1972 electoral victory is too rarely commented on.

124. Bruce Mazlish, *In Search of Nixon: A Psychohistorical Inquiry* (Basic Books, 1972), pp. 84–85, where he writes of Nixon's "paranoid fear" of international communism.

125. Stanley I. Kutler, *Abuse of Power: The New Nixon Tapes* (Free Press, 1997), p. xxiii. Kutler writes: "These tapes reveal anew his tragic quality of self-destruction, and they remind us all too clearly of who and what Richard Nixon was."

126. See especially David Greenberg, *Nixon's Shadow* (W.W. Norton, 2003), pp. 338–347, a chapter entitled "Nixon as Comeback Artist."

127. These characteristic Wilsonian values, expressed in all his works, including his biography of George Washington, reflected his understanding of the qualities supposed to inhere in all who aspired to the presidency.

128. Greenberg, *Nixon's Shadow,* pp. 270–303. This negative image was never shared by Nixon loyalists and foreign policy experts who deemed his foreign policy performance in many ways exceptional. Greenberg's chapter, "The Foreign Policy Establishment" must be read by those who continue to believe that these accomplishments were negligible.

129. Kutler, *Abuse,* p. 2. Kutler notes that in the year preceding the Watergate break-in the tapes reveal Nixon's plans to use the Internal Revenue Service "for his political and personal purposes," and also the efforts he made "to undermine the candidacy of others," including both Senators Muskie and Kennedy.

130. H.R. Haldeman, with Joseph DiMona, *The Ends of Power* (New York Times Books, 1978). The book starts with an appreciation that concludes with the words, "And to President Nixon, who made possible what was despite its ending, the mountain-top experience of my life."

131. The best evidence of how incumbency in the twentieth century almost guaranteed a second term, with only a very few failing to secure one.

132. This draws on a conversation with General Brent Scowcroft.

133. Henry Kissinger, *Crisis: The Anatomy of Two Major Foreign Policy Crises* (Simon and Schuster, 2003), pp. 7–13. This is the best account of the diplomacy pursued by the United States and the Soviet Union in the international crisis created by the Egyptian/Syrian attack on Israel in October 1973.

134. Few have thought to compare the 1912 election with that of 1976. Much is to be learned from doing so.

135. Garry Wills, *Reagan's America: Innocents at Home* (Doubleday, 1987), pp. 330–331.

136. Ibid., p. 331. Wills writes: "Reagan accepted his defeat with equanimity, campaigned loyally for Ford, and began to plan his own race in 1980, when he would be sixty-nine years old." Not everyone in the Ford camp would accept the idea that Reagan "campaigned loyally for Ford," but all would accept the accuracy of the other statements.

137. Zbigniew Brzezinski, *Power and Principle, Memoirs of the National Security Adviser, 1977–1981* (Farrar, Straus, Giroux, 1983), p. 520. Brzezinski believes that Carter "thirsted for the Wilsonian mantle," a thirst never wholly quenched.

138. Carter made strenuous efforts to claim no affiliation with either.

139. A latter-day populist who bore only slight resemblance to William Jennings Bryan who carried the same distinction earlier in the century.

140. Few doubted Carter's native intelligence; many questioned his command of the subjects he pretended to know.

141. This, more than anything, defined what Carter hoped to achieve as president.

142. Brzezinski, *Power,* p. 288. A spirited and merited eulogy of the president's performance at Camp David, it neglects only to acknowledge that its long-term results were in the end disappointing.

143. Ibid., Brzezinski claims, incorrectly in my view, that the president's actions in Iran "succeeded in preserving both lives *and* our national interest, but at the cost of his Presidency."

144. Cf. supra, p. 448.

145. Ibid., pp. 463–465.

146. With Vietnamese studies, the difficulties of the language militated against very many Americans seeking to become competent in it. With Muslim studies, political considerations made universities and independent research organizations wary of embarking on projects that many deemed sensitive, provocative to those in the United States who held very strong opinions on the Arab-Israeli conflict. In both instances, an opportunity to learn more was lost. The research sponsored by the oil companies, whose quality one can only guess at, could never be made public, not least because of growing sensitivity in the Arab world to anything that might be deemed critical of their societies. As for the secret research sponsored by the CIA and other federal agencies and departments, that, too, remained unavailable.

147. It is well to reflect that America's most popular twentieth-century Republican president came into office with a majority substantially smaller than the one Nixon had secured just two years before he was compelled to resign.

148. Reagan, pretending to be an innovator, in fact embraced more of Nixon's policies than he ever chose to acknowledge. His courtiers in the White House worked diligently to promote this image of his presidency.

149. Cannon, *Role,* p. 126. "Tip" O'Neill, Speaker of the House, said of Reagan: "There's just something about the guy that people like. They want him to be a success. They're rooting for him, and of course, they're rooting for him because we haven't had any presidential successes for years. . . ."

150. Ibid., p. 142. Cannon writes of his behavior at the time he was recovering from the assassination attempt, saying "Reagan's sense of humor proved his saving grace."

151. Ibid., p. 251. Only when Reagan, on the advice of David Stockman, his director of the budget, sought to reduce Social Security benefits, did Congress reject the proposal, a rare defeat for him in his first months in office.

152. *Reagan, In His Own Hand,* edited with an introduction and commentary by Kiron K. Skinner, Annelise Anderson, and Martin Anderson (Free Press, 2001), pp. 176–177. Reagan characterized the Pope, one of his great heroes, in a radio address given on June 29, 1979, as "a leader of such courage and such uncompromising dedication to simple morality—to the belief that right does not make might." A slip of the tongue?

153. Cannon, *Role,* p. 443. He did nothing, but made a passionate speech outside the south portico of the White House, that seemed to imply the Americans would not be driven out of Lebanon by those of "bestial nature" whose deeds he abominated.

154. Ibid., p. 445. Many Democrats, including the Speaker, O'Neill, believed mistakenly that the Grenada invasion was a response to the Lebanese tragedy.

155. Ibid., pp. 448–449. Cannon writes: "Fortunately for Reagan, the invasion of Grenada would overshadow the disaster in Beirut throughout the 1984 campaign. This was Reagan's doing. . . . Viewed strictly in political terms, Reagan's nationally televised speech of October 27, 1983, was a masterpiece."

156. Ibid. Reagan was expert in concealing casualties—19 dead and 115 wounded—in the Grenada operation.

157. Two later presidents, Bush, father and son, learned from him.

158. Cannon, *Role*, pp. 325–329.

159. Ibid., p. 717. Cannon suggests that Reagan was unable ever to accept the proposition that he was "ignorant or distanced from crucial decisions."

160. Reagan, *In His Own Hand*, p. xv. Nancy Reagan is quoted as saying: "He worked a lot at home," adding, "Nobody thought that he ever read anything either—but he was a voracious reader. I don't ever remember Ronnie sitting and watching television. I really don't."

161. Brinkley, *Liberalism*, p. 263. Writing of the 1984 Democratic National Convention, Brinkley says: "At the end of the final night, after an acceptance speech whose most memorable line was Mondale's disastrous pledge to raise taxes, the convention orchestra did not play the Democratic party's traditional closing refrain, 'Happy Days Are Here Again,' the music that every Democratic candidates since Franklin Roosevelt had heard as he stood on the podium waving to the crowd. Instead, it played 'Celebrate,' a contemporary soft-rock song that was a favorite of bands at weddings and bar mitzvahs in the mid-1980s."

162. Cannon, *Role*, pp. 73–87. An interesting discussion by Cannon of Nixon's influence on Reagan, too rarely considered.

163. *The Reader's Companion to the American Presidency*, edited by Alan Brinkley and Davis Dyer (Houghton Mifflin, 2000), pp. 498–501. Gil Troy, in his essay on Reagan, writes of the more prominent scandals characteristic of his years in the White House.

164. Cannon, *Role*, pp. 217–218. Cannon argues that the phrase "Teflon President" contains only "a small kernel of truth in the rather large grain of Teflon theory."

165. In this, as in so many other ways, Reagan anticipated the George W. Bush administration.

166. No one who observed Nancy Reagan in the White House ever doubted her influence.

167. The victory seemed almost to extinguish all memory of the Nixon debacle.

168. Cannon, *Role*, pp. 589–652. This superb account of the "Iran-Contra" affair is given in a chapter appropriately entitled "Darkness at Noon."

169. On January 17, 1986, Reagan wrote in his diary: "I agreed to sell TOWs to Iran, the only acknowledgment that he understood what others purportedly proposed to him."

170. Suspicion by the media of information disseminated by the White House had never been wholly overcome in the aftermath of Watergate.

171. Ronald Reagan, *An American Life* (Hutchinson, 1990), pp. 702–703. Reagan in his autobiography argued that perestroika was communism's epitaph; it signalled the triumph of capitalism over communism.

172. Ibid., pp. 680–683.

173. Reagan's courtiers avidly propagated the myth that celebrated his unprecedented deeds.

174. Reagan's debt to Gorbachev is rarely sufficiently emphasized.

175. To praise the American public is always good politics, as Reagan knew.

176. No prominent European found it advantageous to puncture this myth.

177. Neither Reagan nor any of his successors accepted or sought conflict with a major military adversary.

178. Memories of Vietnam casualties, dead and wounded, figured prominently for all who entered the White House after 1974.

179. George W. Bush was the first president after Reagan to call his military actions a "war," though a highly unconventional one.

180. The term "neo-cons," neo-conservatives, came to be increasingly used beginning with Reagan, though the company had begun to gain its renown in the time of Nixon.

181. There had been no "victor" in the White House for decades before Reagan and his associates awarded him that distinction.

182. Reagan's genius was to be a "good Joe," no different from millions of others who valued their wives. They appreciated the sentiment he scrawled in his autobiography, "To Nancy. She will always be my first lady. I cannot imagine life without her."

183. Reagan was a latter-day "populist," but not in the tradition once common in American politics.

184. Reagan, a very aged president, chronologically, mentally, and physically, concealed these attributes almost to the day he left the White House.

185. Reagan restored the good repute of patriotism, making it again fashionable.

186. Bush was stiff, never wholly able to overcome what he and others took to be his patrician birth.

187. Like Taft and Hoover, two other one-term Republican presidents, Bush boasted little experience of elective office and made his way through political appointments by presidents who valued his loyalty.

188. It would not have served his political interest to acknowledge this.

189. Bush, though an ardent disciple of Reagan in the grandiloquent promises he made, never enjoyed the same success in realizing them.

190. The German settlement, so ardently desired by Kohl, Germany's chancellor, may have been Bush's greatest foreign policy achievement.

191. If lying was a cardinal offense, punishable with the denial of a second term in the White House, no president in the twentieth century would ever have been reelected.

192. The war was never a true contest, though it had to be represented as one.

193. Clinton, like Reagan, a born actor, was also an accomplished dissembler.

194. In this, as in other ways, Clinton learned much from observing Reagan.

195. This threat was real, and Clinton showed great imagination in thwarting it.

196. The Reagan White House was a "tomb"; no one ever claimed the same distinction for a Clinton administration of novices, elevated to high office, who never tired of telling secrets about their garrulous chief.

197. The Republican domination of Congress, lost in the time of Roosevelt, was won again in the time of Clinton, and has never since been surrendered.

198. He was the "comeback kid" in the best sense of the term.

199. The most decided geographic shift occurred in the last decades of the twentieth century when the East and the Middle West lost their once prominent place as the political base of men who succeeded in making their way to the White House.

200. This proposition is too rarely considered today by politicians or journalists.

201. This is another reason for emphasizing the distinctiveness of the Reagan administration and what has followed since.

202. That enthusiasm appears to have survived, though somewhat compromised by the disappointments of the Iraq War, the failure to find the celebrated weapons of mass destruction, and the revelations of military tortures.

203. This was true only at the beginning; by the summer of 2004 it had begun perceptively to wane.

204. A proposition little believed in outside the United States.

205. The principal figures in the recent Bush administration, almost all aging men, have been in and around Washington for decades, a situation very different from those who came to serve Clinton.

206. Bob Woodward, *Bush at War* (Simon and Schuster, 2002). Woodward was one of the first journalists to argue that Bush is his own master, little beholden to those who serve him, a tireless fighter for his principles, served by men and women who know better than to resist him. See also Ivo H. Daalder and James M. Lindsay, *America Unbound: The Bush Revolution in Foreign Policy* (Brookings, 2003), pp. 22–31, which emphasizes, however obliquely, the limits of the power enjoyed by the "neo-cons," believed by others to be very influential.

207. The knowledge spawned by the Cold War, by what the universities and the "think tanks" did to create an understanding of the world abroad, has been too little considered by those who rarely ask whether comparable information is being generated today about conditions thought to be even more threatening to the security of the United States.

208. These were indeed "locust years," a term used by Winston Churchill to describe other wasted decades.

209. The gulf between American and foreign opinion about the so-called Bush Doctrine—preemptive war—is recognized to be great, but it is difficult to know whether this is the fundamental reason for the growing expressions of distrust in many quarters about U.S. intentions and policies.

210. War was a compelling argument for an administration that understood why the call for police action against terrorists would never generate the patriotic fervour required to justify vast expenditure and the dispatch of large military forces to Iraq.

211. Michael Howard, "War and the Nation-State," *Daedalus,* Journal of the American Academy of Arts and Sciences, Fall 1979, p. 105.

212. Few in the United States believed this; few in Europe dared to say it.

213. Iraq, terrorism, and weapons of mass destruction virtually obliterated all American interest in other foreign policy issues. Even at the height of the Soviet threat, there was never such a total ignoring of other major foreign policy issues.

214. The provincialism of American thinking on foreign policy is today replicated in Great Britain where neither the Labour government nor the Tory opposition shows any disposition to reflect creatively on other critical issues; all have receded.

215. The British information, gleaned from the Hutton Inquiry, is substantially greater than anything available to Americans to explain how and why the Bush administration took the decision to wage war on Iraq. Whether there was comparable flawed intelligence in Washington is a matter unlikely to be revealed for many years, decades perhaps, though Richard A. Clarke, *Against All Enemies: Inside America's War on Terror* (Free Press, 2004) has generated a debate whose final influence is still to be determined.

CHAPTER 2 (Accidental Presidents)

1. The nineteenth century presidents who died in office were William Henry Harrison, Zachary Taylor, Abraham Lincoln, and James Garfield.

2. Eisenhower, elected just before Kennedy, won his second term with a majority of over 9 million.

3. Grover Cleveland was the only president to enjoy two nonconsecutive terms, from 1885 to 1889, and from 1893 to 1897. See Allan Nevins, *Grover Cleveland: A Study in Courage* (Dodd and Mead, 1932).

4. The nineteenth-century vice presidents, with the exception of several who served in the early years of the republic, Thomas Jefferson, Aaron Burr, George Clinton, and John Calhoun, were scarcely conspicuous even in their own day.

5. Roosevelt's correspondence for the period is replete with expressions of doubt and uncertainty about whether he ought to seek the vice presidency.

6. Ibid. The Roosevelt-Lodge correspondence during this period merits close study. For a very long time, Roosevelt acted as if he had to offer excuses to Lodge for not accepting his constant advice to seek the vice presidency.

7. Roosevelt, an accomplished dissembler, never really explained when he finally decided to seek the post and why he did so.

8. Elting E. Morison et al, *The Letters of Theodore Roosevelt,* 8 volumes (Harvard University Press, 1951–1954). Look at vol. 4, pp. 1343–1345 where the editors have compiled a chronol-

ogy for where Roosevelt spent his time in the period January 1, 1901, till August 31, 1905. There was nothing for a vice president to do in Washington when the Senate was not in session, and it is scarcely surprising that Roosevelt spent it mostly in Oyster Bay ruminating on what his future life might be, as is evident in his *Letters,* vol. 3.

9. Edmund Morris, *The Rise of Theodore Roosevelt* (Ballantine Books, 1979), pp. 721–722. In 1900, Roosevelt pretended not to seek the vice presidential nomination; no such pretense existed in 1904 when he fought strenuously to prove that accidental presidents would not be turned away when they sought a second term.

10. The "smoked-filled room" metaphor gained greater currency because of the deals made in the Chicago hotel suite that gave Harding his nomination. See Francis Russell, *President Harding: His Life and Times* (Eyre and Spottiswoode, 1969), chapter xv, entitled "The Dark Convention."

11. No Republican of any prominence pretended that either of the nominees was a political figure of exceptional ability or quality. It was not simply Lodge's snobbery that made it impossible for him to see Coolidge as his social or intellectual equal.

12. His actions in the police strike gave him his renown outside Massachusetts.

13. See Arthur M. Schlesinger Jr., editor, *History of American Presidential Elections 1789–1968* (Chelsea House, 1985), vol. vi, p. 2403 for the Republican Party Platform of 1920 which opened with the words, "The Republican Party . . . affirms its unyielding devotion to the Constitution of the United States, and to the guarantees of civil, political, and religious liberty therein contained. It will resist all attempts to overthrow the foundations of the government or to weaken the force of its controlling principles and ideals, whether those attempts be made in the form of international policy or domestic agitation."

14. Coolidge took pride in the manner of his nomination and refused to choose his own vice president in 1924 when he ran for re-election.

15. Both were self-made men.

16. Franklin Roosevelt, at 38, was even younger than Theodore Roosevelt, 42, when he ran as vice president.

17. Ibid., p. 2375. In an essay written by Donald R. McCoy, he explains that Coolidge, unlike Roosevelt, lacked all appetite for campaigning, and sought to limit his few forays outside Massachusetts to New England, claiming that his duties as governor required him to be in Boston.

18. This was the Democratic Party's most catastrophic presidential defeat in almost a century, since Andrew Jackson was elected to the presidency in 1828.

19. No one ever thought to accuse Coolidge of dishonesty.

20. Frederick Lewis Allen, *Only Yesterday, An Informal History of the 1920's* (John Wiley, 1997), a reprint of the work originally published in 1931 by Harper's. This is a spirited analysis of the three Republican administrations of the 1920s. Its two chapters, "Harding and the Scandals" and "Coolidge Prosperity" merit close attention.

21. Many underestimated Coolidge; he was both canny and careful, qualities not always discernable in other twentieth-century presidents.

22. Arthur Schlesinger Jr., *The Crisis of the Old Order, 1919–1933* (Houghton Mifflin, 1957), p. 58. Schlesinger writes: "To some his [Coolidge's] aphoristic self-confidence represented homely folk wisdom; to others, intolerable smugness. To some his inaction was masterly restraint; to others, it was complacent emptiness of a dull and lazy man. To some his humor was innocent fun; to others, it was sadistic meanness. To some his satisfaction with his purpose represented 'character'; to others, it seemed a bankruptcy of mind and soul. To some he was the best in the American middle class. To others he was almost the worst. William Allen White called him 'a Puritan in Babylon.' His frugality sanctified an age of waste, his simplicity an age of luxury, his taciturnity an age of ballyhoo. He was the moral symbol the times seemed to demand." Allan, *Only Yesterday,* p. 137. Allan said it somewhat differently, noting that Coolidge "did not have a jutting chin, a Powerful Personality, or an irresistible flow of selling talk. If you had come from

Timbuctoo and found him among a crowd of Chamber of Commerce boosters, he would have been the last man you picked as their patron saint. . . . Almost the most remarkable things about Coolidge Prosperity was Coolidge himself."

23. See Edward J. Flynn, *You're the Boss* (Viking, 1947), p.179.

24. Roosevelt courted trade union leaders assiduously, and won the confidence of many who became his most ardent supporters.

25. Franklin Roosevelt, frequently dilatory when compelled to deal with what others knew to be difficult issues, showed that propensity markedly in 1944.

26. Though there were occasional newspaper references to Roosevelt's age and health, the public had no notion of the gravity of his medical condition.

27. Dr. Howard Bruenn, a young Navy cardiologist, brought in to examine the president on his daughter's insistence, unhappy with the attention he was receiving from Dr. Watson, the resident White House physician, diagnosed extreme hypertension and congestive heart failure. Though many of his recommendations could not be followed—prolonged bed rest, for example—Dr. Bruenn's careful monitoring of the patient's condition and other recommendations he made undoubtedly prolonged Roosevelt's life. Conrad Black, *Franklin Delano Roosevelt: Champion of Freedom* (Weidenfeld and Nicolson, 2003), p. 933. His son, Elliott, seeing his father after an absence of some months, and visibly shocked at his appearance, heard him say: "Well, what did you expect?"

28. David McCullough, *Truman* (Simon & Schuster, 1992), pp. 306–307. The story, frequently told, is that Robert Hannegan, the Missouri "boss," prevailed on the president to name his preferred vice presidential candidates, and that the short note he penned, possibly prepared by Hannegan beforehand, named both Bill Douglas and Harry Truman. Hannegan, according to stories never confirmed, reversed the names when the letter was typed out, so that Truman would appear to be the preferred candidate. The letter read: "Dear Bob, You have written me about Harry Truman and Bill Douglas. I should, of course, be very glad to run with either of them and believe that either one would bring real strength to the ticket."

29. Ibid., pp. 259–267.

30. Ibid., p. 307. McCullough claims that Hannegan played "an extremely deceitful game," and that there is reason to wonder whether Truman was the president's preferred candidate.

31. Ibid., pp. 314 and 308. This account of the telephone conversation between the president and the senator confirms Truman's sincerity in not wishing to be nominated; he capitulated only very reluctantly to Roosevelt's importuning demand. A reporter, speaking to him just days earlier, indicated that the office might one day lead to his becoming the president. Truman, according to McCullough, replied: "Hell, I don't want to be President," and in his biographer's words, "described the failures and scorn experienced by every Vice President who had succeeded to the highest office, beginning with John Tyler." McCullough noted that he overlooked "the most obvious example to the contrary, Theodore Roosevelt."

32. Roosevelt's fame at home and abroad exceeded greatly that of even the two presidents who must be regarded as his principal political mentors, and Truman never underestimated the difficulties that followed from succeeding such a man.

33. Bryce's view that the convention cared only to nominate a "winner" showed itself in the genuine reluctance with which the Democrats, unable to nominate the famed World War II general, finally agreed to accept Truman, believing he could not possibly win but finding it difficult to turn him aside.

34. McCullough, *Truman*, p. 710. McCullough writes: "He had won against the greatest odds in the annals of presidential politics. Not one polling organization had been correct in its forecast. . . . Every expert had been proven wrong, and as was said, 'a great roar of laughter rose from the land.' The people had made fools of those supposedly in the know." The 1948 Truman victory remains the most surprising election result in the century. If Truman's triumph was the most

important event for the nation, the defection of the South proved to be the most ominous political development for the Democratic Party. The Democratic Party would never again be able to rely on the South as the bastion of its national strength. Truman, however, had crafted his own victory and other of his successors sought to do the same, making the political parties less important in determining the election results. The gradual decline of the political party as the force described by Bryce in 1888 may be said to have its origins in the 1948 election.

35. Texas had become a key state for Democrats to win, given the number of its electoral votes. As much a Southern as a Western state, its loyalty to the Democratic Party could no longer be taken for granted.

36. Johnson never developed much esteem for Kennedy, neither in his dealings with him in the Senate nor as a result of his experiences as vice president.

37. Robert Dallek, *John F. Kennedy: An Unfinished Life, 1917–1963* (Allen Lane, 2003), p. 270. Dallek writes: "Kennedy doubted that Johnson would accept an invitation to join the ticket. Johnson had declared: 'I wouldn't want to trade a vote for a gavel, and I certainly wouldn't want to trade the active position of the greatest deliberative body in the world for the part time job of presiding."

38. Ibid. Dallek's explanation of why Johnson accepted the vice presidency is plausible; he writes: "In fact, Johnson wanted the vice presidency. By 1960, his control of the Senate as majority leader had begun to wane; the election of several liberals in 1958 had undercut his dominance. He also assumed that if Kennedy won the White House without him, the White House would set the legislative agenda and he would be little more than the president's man in the Senate. Moreover, if Nixon became president, he would have to deal with a Republican chief who would be less accommodating than Eisenhower and less inclined to allow Johnson to exercise effective leadership. "

39. No twentieth-century president was more faithfully served by those he selected than those Kennedy chose as his subordinates.

40. Roosevelt and Truman were the two presidents Johnson hoped to emulate; Kennedy never figured as a presidential model.

41. While both Roosevelt and Eisenhower were capable of exploding in anger when provoked, neither resembled Johnson in his increasingly furious outbursts.

42. Johnson literally frightened his subordinates, and few felt at all comfortable in his presence.

43. He was never nominated to the office by the Republican Party.

44. Agnew resembled Nixon in one very important attribute; he made the most exaggerated appeals to the patriotism of the country, and never hesitated to lambaste Democrats and any others who dared to criticize the administration.

45. He was the first vice president compelled to resign.

46. Ford was much esteemed by colleagues in the House.

47. Suspicion of Nixon's motives figured in this presidential decision as in so many others made by someone who was never trusted.

48. Reagan's role in bringing about Ford's defeat has been insufficiently studied. Reagan, more than Carter, made the president seem inadequate, pursuing the flawed policies of Nixon, still employing Kissinger, the purported disciple of Metternich and Bismarck.

49. Given the continued gravity of the international situation, greatly exacerbated by domestic economic turmoil, it was impossible for Congress to recover the authority it had enjoyed in the last decades of the nineteenth century.

50. Both figured greatly in the efforts to render Ford as ineffectual, an irresolute president.

51. That two Republicans converted their fame as vice presidents to claim serious consideration for the presidency and succeeded in their design is as significant as the fact that three Democrats sought to do the same, and failed. Except for Carter and Clinton, no Democrat has occupied the White House since Johnson left the office in 1969, a situation redolent of what followed the Civil War when the presidency became virtually a Republican preserve.

52. The Senate remains an especially attractive launching pad for Democrats, somewhat less so for Republicans.

53. Men from relatively small states with few electoral votes were never nominated until very recently when political party presidential conventions became mere ratifying bodies, nominating those who had emerged as winners in the primaries. Almost no president selected by the voters in the primaries could claim substantial experience in foreign policy, though George Bush made the claim, a dubious one in my view.

54. A senator has one advantage over a governor in seeking the presidency; it is relatively easy for him to absent himself from his public duties.

55. Arthur M. Schlesinger Jr., *The Imperial Presidency* (Atlantic Monthly, 1973).

56. The role of illness in affecting the presidency, beginning with Wilson and Roosevelt, but continuing through Eisenhower and Reagan remains an insufficiently studied matter. The exception in recent decades was of course Kennedy who managed to conceal the seriousness of his ailments, created by his suffering from Addison's Disease but also from the back injury he incurred during the war. Robert Dallek's *Kennedy* is illuminating for what it tells about the president's illnesses but also about the "cocktail" of drugs he relied on throughout his time in the White House.

57. Charles Dawes, the first director of the budget, appointed by Harding in 1921, and responsible for the plan devised in 1924 for settling Germany's reparations problems, valued his role as Coolidge's vice president after 1925 but refused to see himself as a member of the executive branch of the federal government.

58. The influence of Texans had already become evident in the Wilson administration with the president's choice of Colonel House as his most intimate personal adviser. The Roosevelt administration showed an even greater receptivity to the appointment of Texans to high governmental places. Vice President Garner hoped he might himself be considered for the presidency in 1940, but this was not his principal reason for opposing Roosevelt in his decision to seek a third term.

59. Schlesinger, *Elections,* vol. vii, p. 2396. See the excellent study of the 1940 election by Robert E. Burke.

60. No presidential wife has ever exercised comparable influence with a party convention.

61 Phyllis Lee Levin, *Edith and Woodrow: The Wilson White House* (Scribner, 2001), pp. 338–343. Levin is most informative on the authority Mrs. Wilson assumed following her husband's second stroke, building on an influence she had asserted even earlier.

62. Many who supported Nixon's nomination as vice president, believing he would relieve the general of onerous duties in the election campaign and add strength to the Republican Party ticket had no wish to see him in the White House.

63. Ambrose, *Eisenhower, The President,* p. 440.

64. Schlesinger, *Imperial Presidency,* pp. 471–499. See especially his appendix on the vice Presidency, a highly original analysis of the office, together with a radical proposal for its reform.

65. It is not at all obvious that Rockefeller or those who supported him understood this.

66. This was an exceedingly painful transition for someone who had not practiced law for decades, and harbored only a single wish—to seek the presidency again.

67. Johnson never exercised great influence as vice president.

68. Humphrey showed exemplary patience in all his dealings with the president, suffering abuse and never complaining.

69. Humphrey's political career, like Johnson's, must be seen as among the more tragic of the 1960s.

70. Gore's problem was an easier one than Humphrey's, but he handled it with no conspicuously greater skill.

71. The 1968 election was one of the most shameful in the century, revealing the potency of race as an electoral issue.

72. Reagan claimed some 10 million more votes in 1984 than in 1980 when he ran against Carter, a Southerner who appealed to voters in that region as Mondale, a liberal Midwesterner, never did.

73. In my view, always a very dubious claim.

74. Bush was always the soul of discretion, showing these qualities as much when he served under Nixon as under Reagan.

75. A comparison of the Nixon White House court and that established by Reagan would demonstrate differences that have been too rarely commented on, reflecting Reagan's more astute use of Texans, Baker and Bush, principally, appreciating their gentility, mixing them with the somewhat more raunchy types who had accompanied him from California.

76. No president would have dared to be imperious in the manner of de Gaulle, if only because it would have made him the subject of mass media ridicule.

77. Vice presidents knew the importance of being discreet and obsequious, showing great regard for their chiefs. Not one of them, except for Humphrey, ever differed fundamentally with their presidents, and he paid a heavy price for daring to be his critic.

78. This was certainly the major revolution in the nominating procedures, deemed a triumph of the popular will.

79. See Michael Novak, *Choosing Our King: Powerful Symbols in Presidential Politics* (Macmillan, 1974), p. 3. Novak writes: "Every four years Americans elect a king—but not only a king, also a high priest and prophet."

CHAPTER 3 (Let the People Speak)

1. Bryce, *American Commonwealth*, vol. 2, p. 176.

2. In theory, three candidates might emerge from the primaries with votes insufficient to make any one of them the party's nominee, and the task of choosing between them would again devolve on the convention delegates. That has not been the situation in recent decades when in both parties one candidate has been the clear winner, and the others have dropped out.

3. Television advertising expenses have escalated greatly since the early 1960s, becoming the principal reason for the candidates being obliged to raise unprecedented sums to keep their campaigns alive.

4. A comparison of the 1948 convention, specifically the Republican one I attended in Chicago that chose to nominate Eisenhower rather than Taft, and the one that selected George W. Bush in 2000 is the story of a ritual that changed from being an exciting political game with unpredictable results to a Hollywood-staged coronation rite of someone already preselected by the primaries.

5. The rhetoric remains inflated, but its purpose is now to introduce the victor to the nation, to demonstrate the delegates' enthusiasm for him.

6. Bryce, *American Commonwealth*, vol. l, p. 77. Bryce's words were exceedingly powerful; he wrote: "Europeans often ask, and Americans do not always explain, how it happens that this great office, the greatest in the world, unless we except the Papacy, to which anyone can rise by his own merits, is not more frequently filled by great and striking men."

7. The "bosses" and "trusts" that purportedly dictated presidential choices in the past are now extinct; today's political demonology makes money, solicited as campaign contributions, the dangerous element, very imperfectly controlled by federal legislation.

8. The Bill Clinton and George W. Bush candidacies are the two most recent examples of governors able to absent themselves frequently from their state during the primary and election campaign seasons, confident that their constituents would approve of their absences, wishing only to see them translated to a higher political sphere.

9. See Kevin Phillips, *Wealth and Democracy: A Political History of the American Rich* (Broadway Books, 2002), pp. 407–408. Both Bill Bradley in the Democratic Party and John McCain in the Re-

publican Party, unsuccessful in their efforts to win their party's nominations, sought to capitalize on the Theodore Roosevelt tradition of condemning vast concentrations of wealth. Neither Carter nor Reagan felt any necessity to do this. Each, independently wealthy, could argue that they were the creators of their own fortunes, scarcely resembling Nelson Rockefeller who had inherited wealth.

10. See Michael Schudson, "News Conventions in Print and Television," *Daedalus,* Journal of the American Academy of Arts and Sciences, in Fall 1982 issue entitled "Print Culture and Video Culture," p. 98.

11. Jeffery Auer, "The Counterfeit Debates," in Sidney Kraus, editor, *The Great Debates: Background, Perspectives, Effects* (Indiana University Press, 1962), pp. 142–149. Auer's essay on the 1960 debates between Kennedy and Nixon is one of the more compelling essays written about presidential debates, expressing the hope that later debates might not be equally counterfeit. That hope was never realized. Harold Lasswell, in his introduction to the volume, writes: "Even the title of the present publication—for reasons obvious to people who pass on titles— uses the conventional cliche of calling the programs 'debates,' and 'great debates' at that. Fortunately and wisely, the symposium has an article by Auer that challenges this usage."

12. Lewis L. Gould, *America in the Progressive Era, 1890–1914* (Longman, 2001), p. 39. Robert M. La Follette used the primary to battle his way into the governorship of Wisconsin. On the national level, the presidential primaries were so unimportant before 1912 that Bryce gave scant attention to them in the revised editions of *The American Commonwealth,* published in the early twentieth century.

13. Ibid.

14. Ibid., p. x. Gould writes: "By 1914, devotion to parties had receded. Independent voters had become a major element in national elections, and suspicion of partisanship had become commonplace. Such innovations as the 'direct primary' to choose candidates for elections, the 'initiative' to propose legislation, the 'recall' to oust unpopular officials, and the 'referendum' to put specific issues before the voters, had all sapped the power of the parties to set the political agenda." These reforms did not produce the results anticipated. As Gould perceptively observes, "One of the notable features of the progressive spirit was the actual decline it produced in the involvement of Americans in their government and public life. That development proved to be one of the important unintended consequences of an age of reform."

15. Cf. infra, Chapter 4, "Theodore Rex."

16. See George E. Mowry, "Election of 1912" in Schlesinger, *American Presidential Elections,* vol. VI, pp. 2144—2147.

17. Dalton, *Roosevelt,* pp. 395–408.

18. Cf. infra, Chapter 6, "The Great Interloper."

19. Bryce, *American Commonwealth,* vol. 2, pp. 186–203 in Chapter lxx entitled "The Nominating Convention at Work."

20. Franklin Roosevelt's New York gubernatorial victory in 1928 was even narrower than Theodore Roosevelt's in 1898.

21. Black, *Roosevelt,* p. 219–220. Hearst, in a front-page editorial lambasted both Roosevelt and Smith as "Wilsonian internationalists," and argued that only Garner could be trusted. Col. House and Joseph Kennedy, father of the later president, were among those who begged Hearst to reconsider his views of Roosevelt, as did James Farley who insisted that the governor's views on the League had "evolved." Hearst reacted violently to Farley's approach, asking Roosevelt to stop playing political "shell games," and to announce publicly that he was no longer an internationalist if that was indeed his position.

22. Ibid., p. 237. Black writes: "Lost in contemporary (and most historic) analysis was the fact that if Roosevelt had not placated Hearst as he did in his 'shabby' address to the New York Grange in April, and even in his support of Hearst's candidate for U.S. Senator from New York in 1922 . . . he could have lost the 1932 nomination."

23. The most controversial bill passed by the Republican-dominated Congress in 1947, the Labor-Management Relations Act, sought to control the trade unions more closely through outlawing jurisdictional strikes, secondary boycotts, and closed union shops. It allowed the federal government to obtain an 80-day injunction against any strike that threatened to endanger the national health or safety.

24. Barton J. Bernstein, "Election of 1952" in Schlesinger, *American Presidential Elections*, vol. viii, pp. 3234–3237.

25. Ibid., p. 3235. Truman's hostility to Kefauver reflected his disdain for a senator he could never take seriously, as well as his contempt for someone who had argued for giving the Chinese Communists a truce deadline and then carrying the war into Manchuria if the deadline was not respected. Worse, Kefauver appeared to have accepted the Republican charge that the administration was riddled with corruption, an unforgivable offense to the president.

26. Quoted by Michael Kazin in his essay "John F. Kennedy" in Alan Brinkley and Davis Dyer, editors, *The Reader's Companion to the American Presidency* (Houghton Mifflin, 2000), p. 424.

27. Theodore H. White, *The Making of the President, 1968* (Atheneum, 1969), pp. 539–540. White recognized this when he wrote: "It takes years to evaluate any President; and we will probably sit longer in judgment on Richard Nixon than any other President of recent times." Carrying the torch for John F. Kennedy, his hero, White wrote in the hyperbolic terms still common in the years immediately after the president's assassination, saying: "To the surge of black revolt, he offered clear openings; to the stagnant economy he offered new management that set it on course to prosperity; in the stalemate of cold-war confrontation, he offered, first, resolution in the missile crisis, and, next, a détente with our then greatest adversary, Russia; and to a newly educated people he offered a quality of beauty and elegance that met an unrecognized hunger."

28. Dallek, *Kennedy*, p. 239. Dallek writes: "Because there were only sixteen state primaries, the road to the nomination in 1960 principally involved winning over state party leaders."

29. Kathleen E. Kendall, *Communication in the Presidential Primaries: Candidates and the Media, 1912–2000* (Praeger, 2001), pp. 37–44; also, p. 50. Kendall writes: "Both in 1912 and in 1972, those advocating change in the presidential selection rules wanted to remove decision-making power from the metaphorical 'smoke-filled back room' of party leaders and bring it into the open, where the 'voice of the people' could speak. The reformers were disappointed with the results in 1912. Finally, in 1972, the number of presidential primaries surged, voter turnout in the primaries grew, and the revised rules assured that primary victories would bring delegate votes. The winner of the primaries actually secured the nomination. . . . But right from the start, reformers could see that the primaries produced a candidate-based system rather than a party-based system, they knew the primaries would weaken the party, and they actively sought this change."

30. Ibid.

31. Ibid., p. 38.

32. Ibid., p. 42. Kendall prints the Theodore White observation, "They can't open up this political party *only* to the reformers; it has to be open for George Wallace to voice those sentiments for which he stands," and Kendall notes that "Wallace's great success came as a shock to the party regulars." She adds, p. 72, "Senator George McGovern of South Dakota was anything but fuzzy in image; he made the antiwar issue his central theme for much of the primary period. What he called the 'centerpiece' of his campaign was the idea of returning to 'the enduring ideals with which the nation began,' a turning away from war and militarism, and a return to a society where people cared about each other and about the needy."

33. Arthur T. Hadley, *The Invisible Primary* (Prentice-Hall, 1976), pp. 237–238. Hadley, describing Wallace's oratory, writes: "It's a speech against things. It's against the 'intelligentsee' and

the 'bureaucrats with briefcases who make more than the working man.' It's against Washington, 'hypocrisy city' where the bureaucrats make laws during the day telling the working man how he and his children shall live and then go home to Virginia so 'they' don't have to obey their own laws. It's against *The New York Times,* which has bankrupted New York City. It's against big government, elitists, all of the 'theys' who do bad things to you who are good."

34. 1972 was the year when the primaries became all-important.

35. Few wish to recall how great was Nixon's victory in 1972. Even fewer choose to note that only Harding scored a comparable victory, though both Eisenhower and Reagan were other Republican candidates who won with impressive majorities.

36. Clinton learned a great deal from observing closely the primary campaigns of both McGovern and Carter.

37. Hadley, *Primary,* p. 214.

38. Ibid., p. 215. Georgia law prevented a governor from succeeding himself, and Carter, appointed in 1974 to be the head of the Democratic National Committee's Campaign Committee, made certain that he spent a great deal of time in New Hampshire, Iowa, and Florida, all states with early primaries.

39. See Gilbert C. Fite, "Election of 1896," in Schlesinger, *Presidential Elections,* vol. v, p. 1817. There are discrepancies about how much money the Republicans raised for their 1896 campaign, but no one doubts that the sums were unprecedented. Fite writes: "The Republicans, fortunately, experienced no shortage of funds. Not only did wealthy party members contribute, but rich Democrats as well poured thousands of dollars into McKinley's campaign. Cornelius Bliss contributed $50,000; Standard Oil gave $250,000 and the four big meat packers $100,000 each."

40. Herbert Croly, *Marcus Alonzo Hanna: His Life and Work* (Macmillan, 1912), p. 214. There had never been a campaign like Bryan's, and it became a model for others later in the twentieth century when traditions mandating decorous behavior for politicians seeking the presidency ceased to have any relevance.

41. Hadley, *Primary,* pp. 98–105. It has remained so to this day, though contributions from individuals, given through dinners and other fund-raising events, have remained crucial. Hadley believed in 1976 that fund-raising by such practices would soon lose favor, but he recognized that the passage of the Federal Election Campaign Act of 1972, like the passage of the Reform Act of 1974, greatly influenced by the Watergate revelations, had effects few in Congress had anticipated. Hadley writes: "When the bill became law, the liberals slowly began to discover what a look at the history of campaign financing would have told them: the chief beneficiaries were Republicans and right-of-center Democrats. The chief losers: liberal Democrats. The reason is that both Republicans on the far right and Democrats on the far left depended for funds on what in the political trade is known as 'ideological money,' or less politely, 'bucks for bullshit.' This is particularly true of left-wing Democrats who have a few extremely rich supporters who can give them several hundred thousand dollars but not many middle-income supporters who can give $100 to $1,000. Up until June 1972, George McGovern was actually getting more large gifts than President Nixon."

42. Bradley A. Smith, *Unfree Speech: The Folly of Campaign Finance Reform* (Princeton University Press, 2001), p. 23.

43. Ibid., p. 21.

44. Ibid., pp. 24–25.

45. Hadley, *Primary,* p. 97.

46. Ibid., p. 98.

47. Smith, *Speech,* pp. 25–26. Smith, arguing that Teapot Dome "had little to do with campaign contributions," notes that Harding was not a "big money" candidate, that he raised only

$113,000 for his campaign, that his rivals for the Republican nomination raised a great deal more.

48. Ibid., p. 27.

49. Ibid., p. 28. Again, the act had unintended consequences, and Smith notes that it actually increased "labor union involvement by institutionalizing a system for political giving—the PAC—and by focusing labor's attention even further on politics."

50. Ibid.

51. Ibid.

52. Ibid., p. 56.

53. Ibid.

54. Hadley, *Primary,* p. 104. In 1960, candidates spent $14 million for TV time; by 1968, that figure had risen to $40 million, and by 1970, a year of congressional elections, it stood at $50 million.

55. Smith, *Speech,* p. 30.

56. See Susan B. King and Robert L. Peabody, "Control of Presidential Campaign Financing" in Harvey C. Mansfield, *Congress Against the President* (Praeger, 1975), p. 186. King and Peabody write: "Campaign reform might well have abated had it not been for the revelations flowing from the Watergate break-in, including the discovery of some 'laundered' contributions in the possession of the arrested burglars."

57. Smith, *Speech,* p. 32.

58. Ibid., pp. 32–33.

59. Ibid., pp. 34–36. Smith, unsympathetic to this new legislation, but aware of its effectiveness, writes: "Despite the Supreme Court's evisceration of spending limits, the fact is that the Court upheld most of the act, including what many reform advocates considered to be the most crucial part of the law—contributions limits. By the 1976 elections, the United States had entered a period of unprecedented regulation of political speech in federal elections. No individual could contribute more than $1,000 to a single candidate in a federal election, nor more than $25,000 total. No group of individuals, or PAC, no matter how many people it represented, could contribute more than $5,000 in any election."

60. Ibid., p. 36. Smith says that once again this legislation, intended to control expenditures, failed to have its intended effect, especially in state campaigns involving the election of senators and representatives. In his words, "Incumbent reelection rates began to rise, reaching record levels in the late 1980s and setting off a nationwide craze for term limits. . . . Total spending on congressional campaigns continued to rise, by nearly 400 percent from 1976 through 1978, and candidates began to spend more time, rather than less, raising money for campaigns. Special interests, instead of declining in influence, actually seemed to grow in influence and importance."

61. See David M. Kennedy, *Freedom From Fear: The American People in Depression and War: 1929–1945* (Oxford, 1999), p. 31, for the even more amusing Will Rogers quip: "I don't belong to an organized party. . . I'm a Democrat."

62. See Charles Lewis and the Center for Public Integrity, *The Buying of the President, 2004: Who's Really Bankrolling Bush and His Democratic Challengers—And What They Really Expect in Return* (HarperCollins, 2004), pp. 5–6. This work, like others that Lewis has written, argues "that in *every* presidential election since 1976, the candidate who has raised the most money at the end of the year preceding the election, and has been eligible for federal matching funds, has become his party's nominee for the general election." He goes on to say: "Prior to the 2000 campaign, no single presidential candidate has found more than roughly 19,000 donors contributing the maximum $1,000 contribution. That all changed in 1999–2000, when George W. Bush received 59,279 donations of $1,000, more than *triple* that of any previous contender."

63. Smith, *Speech,* pp. 176–180.

CHAPTER 4 (To Be a King)

1. Nelson Aldrich, *Old Money: The Mythology of Amercas Upper Class* (Knopf, 1988), p. 283. This is an arresting and original study that treats the Roosevelts, Theodore and Franklin, sympathetically, but is less generous to George Bush who sought to conceal his "old money" origins that carried no great cachet in late-twentieth-century America.

2. Roosevelt, *Autobiography,* pp. 7–10.

3. Ibid., pp. 11–15.

4. Ibid., p. 94. There is no romanticizing of New York City in his *Autobiography,* but a perpetual tribute to the Wild West, "the West of Owen Wister's stories and Frederick Remington's drawings."

5. Ibid., p. 67. Alexander Hamilton and Abraham Lincoln were Roosevelt's heroes, along with George Washington. He had no use for either Jefferson or Jackson.

6. Roosevelt represented the War of 1812 as an American victory, made so by the brilliant exploits of its Navy. Jackson's military campaign and victory at New Orleans held no interest for him.

7. Roosevelt, *Autobiography,* p. 57.

8. Ibid.

9. Ibid., pp. 58–93. Roosevelt gives arresting profiles of the men, Republican and Democrats, he encountered in Albany during his years in the New York State Assembly.

10. Roosevelt, never one prepared to acknowledge his defeats, made no mention of his fight for the mayoralty of New York in his *Autobiography.*

11. Abram Hewitt, a wealthy and public-spirited New Yorker, never a "tool" of the Tammany machine, fought strenuously for Samuel Tilden's right to the presidency when Tilden won the election with a popular majority in 1876 but lost in the Electoral College by a single vote to Rutherford B. Hayes.

12. Henry F. Pringle, *Theodore Roosevelt: A Biography* (Blue Ribbon Books, 1931), p. 115.

13. Allan Nevins, *Cleveland: A Study of Courage* (Dodd, Mead, 1944). This is incomparably the best study of Grover Cleveland's public career and is equally candid about his personal life.

14. Roosevelt's capacity to ignore the purportedly "gentlemanly" habits of his day, evident throughout his life, showed itself whenever he stood to gain politically.

15. Morris, *Roosevelt,* p. 279. Roosevelt sought to buoy up Lodge, knowing he was depressed, and actually snubbed in the streets of Boston, finding all of the so-called Massachusetts "intellectual and Boston aristocracy" bolting the Republican Party to vote for Cleveland.

16. Many of the Bostonian "bolters," never contemplating a political career for themselves, acted as conscientious citizens, offended by the aura of corruption that surrounded the Republican candidate, James Blaine.

17. Both Lodge and Roosevelt, shrewd politicians, understood that separation from the Republican Party would gravely endanger their political prospects.

18. Morris, *Roosevelt,* p. 392.

19. Roosevelt underestimated the risk, believing that securing a reputation for himself and the Civil Service Commission more than compensated for any damage he might do the wealthy Wanamaker and his great friend, the president.

20. This was one of the relatively rare off-year nineteenth-century post–Civil War elections when the Democrats gained control of the House.

21. Cleveland was a longtime advocate of civil service reform.

22. David H. Burton, *Cecil Spring Rice: A Diplomat's Life* (Dickenson University Press, 1990), p. 26. Spring Rice became Roosevelt's most intimate English friend, the two having met first in December 1886.

23. There has been no such society in Washington since the death of Roosevelt in 1919, neither in Republican nor in Democratic administrations.

24. Morris, *Roosevelt*, p. 424. Morris makes important observations on what Mahan added to Roosevelt's understanding of "the intricate relationships between political power and sea power, warfare and economics, geography and technology," but is almost too hyperbolic in his rendering of the importance of Mahan's work.

25. Roosevelt, *Autobiography*, pp. 408–436.

26. Roosevelt, "Winning of the West," *Works*, vol. vii, pp. 3–7; also, Morris, *Roosevelt*, p. 410. Morris writes of the enormous success of the book on both sides of the Atlantic, remarking that Roosevelt "was hailed as a historian of model impartiality," praised by many historians of his day, including Frederick Jackson Turner.

27. Henry Adams, *The Education of Henry Adams* (Modern Library, 1931), p.417.

28. Roosevelt disdained Wall Street, had scant regard for professors and so-called intellectuals, and never imagined that Congress was anything but an institution blighted by the mediocrities in its corridors.

29. Morris, *Roosevelt*, pp. 481–492.

30. See Jacob A. Riis, *Theodore Roosevelt: The Citizen* (Macmillan, 1904). Roosevelt attracted many ardent admirers who could not conceal their awe for him. The Theodore Roosevelt Collection at Harvard University, including many of his unpublished letters, all of his published works, and a fair selection of the books written by those who knew him suggests why there has been no president since who begins to resemble him.

31. Ibid., pp. 305–306.

32. Roosevelt, *Letters*, vol. 1, p. 503.

33. Roosevelt, characteristically, exaggerated the threat posed by Bryan as did most other Republicans.

34. For Roosevelt's relations with Thomas Platt, the New York State Republican Party "boss," see Morris, *Roosevelt*, pp. 516–526. The most authoritative study of Platt is by Harold F. Gosnell, *Boss Platt and his New York Machine: A Study of the Political Leadership of Thomas C. Platt, Theodore Roosevelt and Others* (University of Chicago, 1924). The introduction by Charles Merriam, America's leading political scientist at the time, is perceptive for what he says about Theodore Roosevelt's *Autobiography* where his defeats in the New York mayoralty race in 1886 and the presidency in 1912 go virtually unmentioned.

35. Pringle, *Roosevelt*, p. 169.

36. Margaret Leech, *In the Days of McKinley* (Harper, 1959), pp. 99–102.

37. Ibid., pp. 152–153.

38. Without Lodge's constant interventions on his behalf, Roosevelt would never have been made assistant secretary of the Navy.

39. Roosevelt, *Letters*, vol. 1, p. 589.

40. Morris, *Roosevelt*, pp. 569–572.

41. Ibid., p. 570.

42. Roosevelt, *Letters*, vol. 1, pp. 622–623.

43. See David Nasaw, *The Chief: The Life of William Randolph Hearst*, pp. 125–142, a chapter entitled "How Do You Like the *Journal's* War?" which is especially interesting for what it tells about Joseph Pulitzer's efforts to compete with the Hearst press in treating what both considered the greatest crisis since the Civil War.

44. Roosevelt, *Letters*, vol. 1, pp. 638 and 717.

45. Pringle, *Roosevelt*, pp. 175–180.

46. Roosevelt, *Letters*, vol. 2, p. 803. Writing to his brother-in-law, William Sheffield Cowles on March 29, 1898, Roosevelt said: "I am utterly disgusted at the present outlook in foreign re-

lations. I can only hope that the Senate, under the leadership of men like Lodge, will rise to the needs of the hour and insist upon immediate independence for Cuba and armed intervention on our part. Nothing less than this will avail. Shilly-shallying and half-measures at this time merely render us contemptible in the eyes of the world; and what is infinitely more important in our own eyes too."

47. Ibid., pp. 805–807. With so prolific a correspondent, some repetition was a constant hazard, and Roosevelt made the same points about Alva and Torquemada in a letter to William Pierce Frye, the Republican Senator from Maine. The two letters, written on the same day, March 31, 1898, show significant differences, however, not least in the reference Roosevelt makes to the fact "that this fight will be of great advantage to the nation, both from the moral lift it will give us, and because it will mean we shall acquire both St. Thomas and Hawaii."

48. Ibid., pp. 812–814.

49. Ibid., pp. 816–818.

50. Ernest R. May, *Imperial Democracy: The Emergence of America as a Great Power* (Harper Torchbooks, 1961), p. 220–221. The war, more than any other event, made Roosevelt contemptuous of those who deemed it an "unnecessary war," anticipating a comment Winston Churchill was to make many decades later about the Second World War.

51. Roosevelt, *Letters,* vol. 2, p. 888.

52. Ibid.

53. Ibid., pp. 888–889.

54. That issue, not surprisingly, dominated his correspondence during this period. See especially, Ibid., vol. 2, pp. 1101, 1107–1108, 1112, 1119–1120, 1122, 1140, 1156–1157, 1159, 1162–1163, 1169, 1276–1278, 1290, and 1302, letters all written to Lodge.

55. Roosevelt's letters, beginning in 1900, suggest the close attention he gave to the Boer War and its lessons for the United States.

56. Ibid., vol. 2, p. 1128. On January 2, 1900, when still governor, Roosevelt wrote to Spring Rice: "I suppose that what I am about to say is a dream, but I do wish that Russia could grow fast enough in civilization to make it possible to co-operate with her and let her have her own way in working up Slav civilization in her part of Asia, provided she did not interfere elsewhere."

57. Ibid.

58. Ibid., pp. 1130–1131.

59. George Juergens, "Theodore Roosevelt and the Press" *Daedalus,* Fall 1982, "Print Culture and Video Culture," p. 113.

60. Ibid., p. 114.

61. William Letwin, *Law and Economic Policy in America: Evolution of the Sherman Antitrust Act* (University of Chicago, 1981), pp. 182–237. This is the most judicious study of the Sherman Anti-Trust Act and the *Northern Securities* case.

62. Ibid., p. 182. Letwin writes: "It was the first antitrust case in which those cast as villains were celebrities. On the other side the personalities were less vivid, although behind the Government's attorneys lurked the romantic and excitable figure of Theodore Roosevelt, partly stage manager and script writer, partly protagonist."

63. Pringle, *Roosevelt,* p. 256.

64. Letwin, *Sherman Antitrust,* pp. 234–235. To Sir Frederick Pollock, the English jurist and great friend, Holmes wrote: "I enforce whatever constitutional laws Congress or anybody else sees fit to pass—and do it in good faith to the best of my ability—but I don't disguise my belief that the Sherman Act is a humbug based on economic ignorance and incompetence. . . ."

65. Ibid., p. 235.

66. Francis Biddle, *Mr. Justice Holmes* (Scribner's, 1943), p. 118.

67. Letwin, *Sherman Antitrust,* pp. 237 and 201.

68. Roosevelt, *Letters,* vol. 4, p. 886.

69. Forrest McDonald, *The American Presidency: An Intellectual History* (University of Kansas, 1994), pp. 288–289.

70. Morris, *Theodore Rex,* p. 137.

71. Ibid., pp. 157–163.

72. Ibid., p. 166. The operators would have wished for a very different group of commissioners.

73. Ibid., pp. 164–167. It was Root's idea to involve J.P. Morgan in the negotiations, a man he appropriately styled "Pierpontifex Maximus," known to have great influence with the mine operators.

74. *New York Times,* December 4, 1901, p. 6.

75. Ibid., December 7, 1904, p. 3.

76. Roosevelt, *Autobiography,* pp. 553–571.

77. Pringle, *Roosevelt,* p. 330.

78. Ibid. At the University of California in March 1911, after he had left office, Roosevelt said: "I am interested in the Panama Canal because I started it. If I had followed conventional, conservative methods, I should have submitted a dignified state paper of approximately two hundred pages to the Congress and the debate would have been going on yet, but I took the canal zone and let Congress debate, and while the debate goes on the canal does also."

79. See letter to Root, *Letters,* vol. 4, pp. 810–814.

80. This was a recurrent theme for Roosevelt.

81. Roosevelt, *Letters,* vol. 4, p. 833.

82. Ibid., vol. 4, p. 829. Roosevelt wrote on this letter, "Be very careful that no one gets a chance to see this."

84. Ibid., pp. 832–834.

85. Roosevelt, in his extraordinarily long statement to J.G. Cannon, chairman of the committee notifying him of his nomination, delivered on September 12, 1904.

86. Roosevelt always insisted that his only concern was with peace and justice.

87. Roosevelt, *Letters,* vol. 4, pp. 1028–1029. The editors of the *Letters* suggest that on the issue of tariff reform, Roosevelt regarded the matter as one of "expediency." He looked upon tariff discussions as a "useful weapon" against those in Congress, including the Speaker of the House and Senator Aldrich in the Senate, who feared he would call a special session of Congress to debate the issue. In return for his not doing so, they were willing to support his railroad "reform" proposals.

88. Roosevelt, *Autobiography,* p. 367. Roosevelt is wholly candid about his efforts to get on with Cannon and Aldrich, and with Senator Hale, another very powerful Republican. He writes: "I made a resolute effort to get on with all three and with their followers, and I have no question that they made an equally resolute effort to get on with me. We succeeded in working together, although with increasing friction, for some years, I pushing forward and they hanging back. Gradually, however, I was forced to abandon the effort to persuade them to come my way, and then I achieved results only by appealing over the heads of the Senate and House leaders to the people, who were the masters of both of us."

89. Ibid., pp. 521–524. Roosevelt, with unusual candor, tells how he decided to intervene in Santo Domingo, without asking for prior senatorial consent. He writes: "Nine-tenths of wisdom is to be wise in time, and at the right time; and my whole foreign policy was based on the exercise of intelligent forethought and of decisive action sufficiently far in advance of any likely crisis to make it improbable that we would run into serious trouble."

90. Roosevelt, *Letters,* vol. 4, pp. 1132–1135.

91. Ibid., p. 1133. That Roosevelt's disdain for Wall Street did not originate with his 1912 defeat is evident from his 1905 statement: "In all these matters I have to do the best I can with the Congress. I have just as much difficulty in preventing the demagogues from going too far as in

making those who are directly or indirectly responsive to Wall Street go far enough. In foreign affairs I have considerable difficulty in getting the Senate to work genuinely for peace, and also in making it understand, and indeed in making our people understand, that we cannot perpetually assert the Monroe Doctrine on behalf of all American republics, bad and good, without ourselves accepting some responsibility in connection therewith."

92. Ibid.

93. Ibid., p. 1162.

94. Ibid., pp. 1177–1179.

95. Ibid.

96. Ibid., p. 1178.

97. Ibid.

98. Ibid., pp. 1177–1179.

99. Ibid., pp 1180–1181. In this letter, Roosevelt wrote: "It always amused me to find that the English think that I am under the influence of the Kaiser. The heavy-witted creatures do not understand that nothing would persuade me to follow the lead of or enter into close alliance with a man who is so jumpy, so little capable of continuity of action, and therefore, so little capable of being loyal to his friends or steadfastly hostile to an enemy. Undoubtedly with Russia weakened Germany feels it can be fairly insolent within the borders of Europe. I intend to do my best to keep on good terms with Germany, as with all other nations, and so far as I can keep them on good terms with one another; and I shall be friendly to the Kaiser as I am friendly to everyone. But as for his having special influence with me, the thought is absurd."

100. Ibid.

101. Ibid., pp. 1082–1088. This letter, written on December 27, 1904, one of the longest Roosevelt ever sent to his most intimate English friend, is remarkable as much for his ruminations on American politics, on the nature of the Democratic Party, as for his thoughts about foreign policy, in respect to Japan, Russia, Germany, and the United Kingdom. It would be difficult to find any letter of Roosevelt's presidential successors that would compare with this for its insights on diplomatic strategy and for its use of historic examples to explain what he conceived as possible future outcomes.

102. These several quotations from Roosevelt's long post-Christmas letter to Spring Rice only vaguely suggest his uncanny ability to formulate striking observations on the condition of the world when inspired by his recent election victory he found the time to spend hours at his desk writing unselfconsciously to his favored English friend.

103. Ibid., pp. 1194–1195. In his letter of May 26, Roosevelt told Spring Rice, always fearful of German aggression against England, "As you know, I cannot believe that the Kaiser has any deep-laid plot against England. That he may have dreamed at times of such movement, is possible. His actions and words in reference to Russia and France during the last few months are in my judgment incompatible with any serious purpose on his part to get these two countries actively or passively to support him in the war with England. . . . I don't believe he has the Bismarckian continuity of policy and resolution of purpose."

104. Ibid., pp. 1233–1234.

105. Ibid., p. 1234.

106. Stephen Gwynn, ed., *The Letters and Friendships of Sir Cecil Spring Rice*, 2 vols. (Constable, 1929), vol. 1, pp. 474–475.

107. Ibid., pp. 474–478. These statements, characteristic of Spring Rice at the time, received short shrift from Roosevelt who found it impossible to see the European situation in this light in 1905.

108. Roosevelt, *Letters*, vol. 4, pp. 1283–1287. This, perhaps the harshest letter Roosevelt ever wrote to Spring Rice, was filled with acute observations about the Japanese and the Russians.

109. Ibid., p. 1285.

110. Ibid., p. 1286.

111. Ibid., p. 1317.

112. Roosevelt, often garrulous, showed in his telegram to the Kaiser that succinctness had virtues and flattery carried rewards.

113. There is no evidence in the *Letters* that King Edward VII sent a comparable accolade.

114. The Nobel Peace Prize recipients before Roosevelt included no one of equal reputation. Though Baroness Bertha von Suttner was known for her antiwar novel, *Lay Down Your Arms,* and for her passionate efforts to make pacifism influential, neither Jean-Henri Dunant, Frederick Passy, Elie Ducommon, Charles Albert Gobat, or Sir William Cremer were household names with an international resonance. All who received the peace prize before Roosevelt were pacifists in one sense or another. Roosevelt never pretended to be that, though he saw himself as an ardent peace advocate, a claim his foes could never accept.

115. McDonald, *Presidency,* pp. 288–289.

116. Letwin, *Sherman Antitrust,* pp. 245–247.

117. Roosevelt's two great ambassadorial friends in Washington were Jules Jusserand, the French ambassador, and Hermann Speck von Sternberg, the German ambassador. With both he maintained a considerable correspondence, as replete with literary and historical allusions as with those that touched more purely diplomatic and political issues. None of Roosevelt's presidential successors could claim comparable friendships with the ambassadors of France and Germany. The few who cultivated foreign diplomats generally chose to establish intimacy with Great Britain's ambassador, as was the case of John F. Kennedy with David Ormsby Gore.

118. McDonald, *Presidency,* p. 358. McDonald writes: "Sometimes the legislation was a supposed reform that others sponsored and Roosevelt took credit for."

119. Pringle, *Roosevelt,* p. 366.

120. Morris, *Theodore Rex,* pp. 464–465. Roosevelt summoned Booker T. Washington to meet with him to discuss the crisis. Morris writes: "He [Washington] had just been in Atlanta, and sensed that Roosevelt was making a terrible mistake. American blacks would have trouble understanding why 'our friend' (as Washington always called him) should rush to judgment at such a time, without giving a single man of the Twenty-fifth Infantry a chance to testify in court."

121. Charles E. Neu, *An Uncertain Friendship: Theodore Roosevelt and Japan, 1906–1909* (Harvard University Press, 1967). This treatment of the complexities of American-Japanese relations in Roosevelt's second administration is illuminating for its observations on the domestic and foreign policy implications of the problems that came to agitate so many during this period.

122. Ibid., pp. 299–303.

123. Ibid., pp. 122–144, a chapter entitled "A Summer of Uncertainties."

124. Pringle, *Roosevelt,* p. 494.

125. Roosevelt, *Letters,* vol. 4, p. 1045.

126. Ibid.

CHAPTER 5 (The Dauphin)

1. Few presidents were ever able to impose their successors on their party conventions in the way that Roosevelt did; Taft was indeed his *dauphin.*

2. Scandal never touched the Taft name; the family's reputation for integrity was its greatest asset.

3. Henry F. Pringle, *The Life and Times of William Howard Taft: A Biography,* 2 vol. (Farrar Strauss, 1939). Pringle wrote biographies of both Roosevelt and Taft, and one of the few who studied the careers of both, obviously preferred the latter. Elihu Root, who served Roosevelt but

remained loyal to Taft in 1912, greatly regretted Roosevelt's decision to run against him, but could never have given Taft the compliments he bestowed on Roosevelt following his death. In *Men and Policies, Addresses by Elihu Root*, edited by Robert Bacon and James Scott (Harvard University Press, 1924), p. 5, Root said of Roosevelt that he loved and cultivated literature, was a perpetual reader who "scorned the meretricious and the decadent," and had a genius for friendship. He spoke of him as "the most advisable man I ever knew, and the most independent and fearless in acting upon his final conclusions." Calling him "great hearted," he emphasized his "saving grace of abundant and ever-present humor."

4. Pringle, *Taft*, vol. l, pp. 106–107.

5. Taft's ascent was substantially more rapid than Roosevelt's; no one ever accused him of being foolhardy, a potentially dangerous demagogue.

6. Pringle, *Taft*, vol. 1, pp. 159–160.

7. Ibid.

8. Theodore Roosevelt was one of those who would have gladly accepted the Philippines post had the president offered it to him. Could McKinley have been thinking of Roosevelt when he made this statement?

9. The administration never anticipated native resistance, believing that the American occupation would be greeted with glee.

10. Taft had made his ambition for a judicial appointment known to all prominent Republicans, and the president, undoubtedly advised by Root, understood the importance of offering this pledge.

11. Nevins, *Cleveland*, pp. 742–746.

12. Pringle, *Taft*, vol. 1, pp. 195–198 and 168–169.

13. Ibid., p. 211.

14. Ibid., p. 199.

15. Ibid., pp. 218–219.

16. Philip C. Jessup, *Elihu Root*, 2 vol. (Dodd, Mead, 1938), vol. 1, pp. 338–339.

17. Morris, *Rex*, p. 98.

18. Ibid.

19. Ibid., p. 99–100.

20. Ibid., p. 100.

21. Ibid., pp. 100–101.

22. Pringle, *Taft*, vol. 1, pp. 235–236.

23. Ibid., p. 243.

24. Ibid., pp. 252–253. Whereas hundreds of tales exist about the reactions of others to Roosevelt's adventures, many of them humorous and telling, this is almost the only one relating to Taft that shows wit.

25. Roosevelt, *Letters*, vol. 3, p. 425.

26. Biddle, *Holmes*, p. 118.

27. It would be difficult to overstate the extent to which Taft's girth contributed to his sedentary ways. His sole recreation was golf, and his military aide sought to encourage him to exercise, to do something other than take long rides in the presidential limousine.

28. It is possible to argue, though few have done so, that Taft failed to recognize his political inadequacies; he was a born "second man," ready and able to serve others.

29. Roosevelt understood the deep divisions in the Republican Party on the tariff question, and saw no possibility of legislating significant changes.

30. See "Election of 1908" by Paolo E. Coletta in Schlesinger, ed., *Presidential Elections*, vol. 5, p. 2103 for the explicit Republican promise to revise the tariff.

31. Pringle, *Taft*, vol. 1, p. 422.

32. Nathaniel Wright Stephenson, *Nelson W. Aldrich: A Leader in American Politics* (Scribner's, 1930), the only substantial biography of this powerful United States senator. See also, Aldrich, *Old Money*, pp. 11–12, where he discusses his grandfather's social origins, saying that the senator's "mother told him what Somebodies were in the New World. He was descended from two of them, she said: from John Winthrop, the first governor of Massachusetts, and from Roger Williams, the founder of Rhode Island."

33. Pringle, *Taft*, vol. 1, pp. 424–425.

34. Roosevelt, *Autobiography*, pp. 377–381. Roosevelt defended his theory, said to originate with Jackson and Lincoln, against the one Taft espoused.

35. William Howard Taft, *Our Chief Magistrate And His Powers* (Columbia University Press, 1916), pp. 144–147. Taft challenged Roosevelt explicitly. In Taft's mind, he, not Roosevelt, was the true disciple of Lincoln.

36. Stevenson, *Aldrich*, p. 351. He represents the battle as one between the majority Republicans and the "Progressive die-hards," members of the La Follette bloc. Stevenson writes: "No tariff has had a more interesting concealed history than the tariff of 1909." For a full description of this contentious issue, see Richard Cleveland Baker, *The Tariff Under Roosevelt and Taft* (Democrat Printing Co., 1941), pp. 191–198. Baker, denigrating Roosevelt and finding much to commend in Taft, argued that Taft accepted the tariff bill and signed it "not because he was pleased with the law itself, but rather because it was the best he could obtain under the circumstance and also because he did not want to lose the concessions it gave to his 'little brown brothers' in the Philippines."

37. *Congressional Record*, May 8,1909, p. 1911.

38. Jessup, *Root*, vol. 2, p. 217.

39. Archibald Butt, *Taft and Roosevelt: The Intimate Letters of Archie Butt*, 2 vols. (Doubleday Doran, 1930), vol. 1, pp. 201–202 and 246. Butt served as military aide both to Roosevelt and Taft, and his observations on both are arresting. Comparing Taft to Roosevelt, he wrote: "I have never known a man to dislike discord as much as the President. He wants every man's approval, and a row of any kind is repugnant to him. If by saying the word publicly that would defeat Cannon, I believe he would say it, so sincere is his dislike of the Speaker, but he does not feel that he is strong enough to say it, and so he takes the opposite tack, hoping to aid in his defeat by private innuendo. But the Speaker is too wily for him. I saw how he maneuvered to get the President in constant opposition to himself and how he made use of that position to further his own ends. He gave several openings which would have afforded Roosevelt, for instance, many opportunities to kill him politically, and which Mr. Roosevelt would have taken advantage of, too, by the way. But the President let them go by, leaving the impression that he actually endorsed the old vulgarian." Writing of Aldrich, Butts said: "I feel that the Rhode Islander is the most sinister influence around the President. The President thinks he has captured Aldrich and can make him do anything he wants of him, but I fear it is the case of the wolf in sheep's clothing."

40. Baker, *Tariff*, pp. 191–192. In his denial of Roosevelt's qualities, Baker cites the recent researches of Allan Nevins who has been doing "yeoman work in tearing away the halo which has so long enshrined Roosevelt's brow."

41. Mark Sullivan, *Our Times* (Scribner, 1936), vol. 4, p. 371.

42. All biographies of Taft's presidency give a great deal of attention to the Glavis-Ballinger controversy, and to the position taken by Pinchot, but none is more interesting than the one written by Secretary of the Interior Harold Ickes, in 1940. Harold Ickes, *Not Guilty: An Official Inquiry Into the Charges Made by Glavis and Pinchot Against Richard A. Ballinger, Secretary of the Interior, 1909–1911* (Government Printing Office, 1940). Ickes writes that he came to Washington thinking Ballinger "guilty of more than bad administration, that he was a co-conspirator with the Guggenheims and the Cunninghams in a movement to defraud the United

States of valuable forest lands." His study of all the relevant documents led him to change his mind; nothing like the Ballinger affair had captured the attention of the country "since the scandals that shook the Grant administration," and Ickes saw that it was Pinchot who hounded Ballinger, doing so even after his death. Ickes, the Progressive, was unprepared to allow that, to make Glavis appear an American Dreyfus, and to have the Department of Interior unjustly condemned. For a more unbiased but less spirited interpretation, look at James L. Penick Jr., *Progressive Politics and Conservation: The Ballinger-Pinchot Affair* (University of Chicago, 1968).

43. Pringle, *Taft,* vol. 1, p. 491.

44. Ibid., pp. 508–514.

45. Ickes, as a young man believed as most "progressives" did, that Ballinger was guilty. In his 1940 tract, he confessed his error.

46. Pringle, *Taft,* vol. 1, pp. 504–505.

47. Roosevelt, *Letters,* vol. 7, p. 69.

48. Taft, wisely, stayed away from New York at the time, sending a warm message of greeting to the former president through his military aide, Archie Butt.

49. Butt, *Taft and Roosevelt,* p. 403. Writing about Roosevelt's triumphant return, Butt said: "I don't think Nick [Nicholas Longworth] has the slightest inkling what his father-in-law intends to do—and I don't think anyone else has either. I was with him [Roosevelt] most of the day, and he never said a word that could be construed one way or the other. . . . His old associate, Secretary Wilson [secretary of agriculture] had quite a long talk with him. He repeated it to me word for word when we got to the hotel where we were both stopping, and he thought that the silence of Mr. Roosevelt was most ominous."

50. Pringle, *Taft,* vol. 2, p. 579.

51. Butt, *Taft and Roosevelt,* vol. 1, pp. 143–144.

52. Ibid., pp. 331–332.

53. Ibid., p. 332.

54. Pringle, *Taft,* vol. 2, pp. 756–774. Pringle seeks to be objective on Taft's campaign to win the nomination, but a more compelling analysis, less friendly to the president, is provided by Norman M. Wilensky, *Conservatives in the Progressive Era: The Taft Republicans of 1912* (University of Florida Press, 1965).

55. Mowry, "Election of 1912" in Schlesinger, *Presidential Elections,* vol. vi, pp. 2144–2146.

56. Dalton, *Roosevelt,* pp. 366–367.

57. Ibid., p. 419. It is interesting to note that years earlier, in February 1905, Roosevelt spoke to the National Congress of Mothers in a quite different idiom. At that time, he said: "No piled-up wealth, no splendour of material growth, no brilliance of artistic development will permanently avail any people unless the average man possesses honesty, courage, common sense and decency, unless he works hard and is willing at need to fight hard; and unless the average woman is a good wife, a good mother, able and willing to perform the first and greatest duty of womanhood, able to bear and bring up children as they should be brought up, healthy children, sound in body, mind and character, and numerous enough so that the race shall increase and not decrease."

58. Few politicians would have thought to use so graphic a description to announce their candidacies.

59. Taft depended on control of the state delegations.

60. Taft found many of Roosevelt's proposals offensive, but none alarmed him more than his suggestions for judicial reform.

61. Dalton, *Roosevelt,* p. 410. In a small-town newspaper, *Iron Age,* a staunch Republican, George Newett, wrote: "Roosevelt lies and curses in a most disgusting way; he gets drunk, too, and that not infrequently, and all his intimates know about it. All who oppose him are wreckers

of the country, liars, knaves and undesirables. He alone is pure and entitled to a halo. Rats. For so great a fighter, self-styled, he is the poorest loser we ever knew."

62. Mowry, "Election of 1912," p. 2146. Mowry writes: "Possibly, the Roosevelt delegates added to La Follette's might have been numerous enough to have stopped Taft's nomination on the first ballot. In that contingency there is little question that Roosevelt would have been eventually nominated. But the National Committee, supported by past precedents, was determined to allocate enough delegates to the President to assure his nomination. Once that objective was realized, the Taft men quickly organized the convention, selected the temporary chairman, Elihu Root, wrote the platform, and renominated Taft and his Vice-President, James Sherman, by a vote of 561 to 107 for Roosevelt, and 41 for La Follette. Many Roosevelt delegates (344) refused to participate, thereby characterizing the proceedings as fraudulent and raising the question of their future relations with the party."

63. Ibid., pp. 2185–2197. The text of the Progressive Party platform, in its plank on "Peace and National Defense," faithfully expressed Roosevelt's values; it read: "The Progressive party deplores the survival in our civilization of the barbaric system of warfare among nations with its enormous waste of resources even in time of peace, and the consequent impoverishment of the life of the toiling masses. We pledge the party to use its best endeavors to substitute judicial and other means of settling disputes. We favor an international agreement for the limitation of naval forces. Pending such an agreement, and as the best means of preserving peace, we pledge ourselves to maintain for the present the policy of building two battleships a year."

64. Ibid., pp. 2220–2226. Roosevelt's remarks, as given in his so-called "confession of faith," delivered before the Progressive Party convention in Chicago, expressed his political philosophy as he had come to define it in 1912.

65. Roosevelt recognized that Wilson was his only real foe; the nomination of Taft, as he represented it, was "a fraud upon the rank and file of the Republican party" whose right to choose had been denied."

66. Ibid., pp. 2227–2236. Mowry writes: "Woodrow Wilson projected himself in his acceptance speech as a progressive southerner, with a gentlemanly concern for the public weal. Less specific and more reserved than Roosevelt, Wilson nonetheless struck the same moral note."

67. Peter H. Smith, *Talons of the Eagle: Dynamics of U.S.-Latin American Relations* (Oxford University Press, 2000), pp. 56–57. Taft's interventions in Nicaragua may be thought representative of what passed for "dollar diplomacy." Also, look at P. Edward Haley, *Revolution and Intervention: The Diplomacy of Taft and Wilson with Mexico, 1910–1917* (MIT Press, 1970).

68. Knox, an effective attorney general under Roosevelt, who was a strong president, scarcely impressed anyone at home or abroad when he served as secretary of state under Taft.

69. Pringle, *Taft*, vol. 2, p. 699.

70. Akira Iriye, *From Nationalism to Internationalism: U.S. Foreign Policy to 1914* (Routledge and Kegan Paul, 1977), pp. 228–229.

71. Ibid., p. 229. Iriye writes of the vast opportunities that Taft saw in closer relations with China, but adds: "Most of these projects were to be left to the succeeding administrations, and Taft and Knox did not even accomplish the cherished object of recognizing the new Chinese government as they failed to obtain the concurrence of other countries."

72. *Cowboys and Kings: Three Great Letters by Theodore Roosevelt* with an Introduction by Elting Morison (Harvard University Press, 1954). It is difficult to render the genius of Theodore Roosevelt in designing a foreign policy, a competence that Taft lacked, but these three letters suggest why Roosevelt, always outspoken, but a close observer of those he met, dared to voice opinions to his friends of a kind never uttered by a more cautious and less acerbic Taft. Visiting Egypt in late 1911, Roosevelt wrote to his English friend, George Otto Trevelyan, of his impressions of that society. "In Cairo and Alexandria," he said, "many of the noisy leaders of the Nationalist movement were merely Levantine Moslems in European clothes, with red fezzes;

they were of the ordinary Levantine type, noisy, emotionally rather decadent, quite hopeless as material on which to build, not really dangerous to foes, although given to loud talk in the cafes and to emotional street parades. . . . The real strength of the Nationalist movement in Egypt, however, lay not with these Levantines of the cafes but with the mass of practically unchanged bigoted Moslems to whom the movement meant driving out the foreigner, plundering and slaying the local Christian, and a return to all the violence and corruption which festered under the old-style Moslem rule, whether Asiatic or African." (pp. 30–31) That Roosevelt was not simply unsympathetic to those of the Muslim faith, that he could be equally critical of Catholic Rome, is suggested in a second letter in which he tells of the Pope's rejection of any plan for Roosevelt to visit him because he refused to make a pledge not to meet with the Methodists while he was visiting Rome. Roosevelt wrote of Merry del Val, the papal secretary of state to Pope Pius X, using a "servile tool of his, the head of the so-called American College in Rome . . . whose predecessor was a second scoundrel named O'Connell, now Archbishop of Boston, who had been an open champion of Spain when we were at war with her" to refuse Roosevelt the audience (p. 37). His remarks on his visit with the Italian prime minister and the mayor of Rome, both Jews, were equally interesting. He wrote: "The Prime Minister and his colleagues struck me as upright men, sympathizing with liberal and progressive ideas, and anxious to do justice, and also on the whole as cultivated men, well read, and in short, good fellows, but they did not strike me as possessing very great force" (pp. 41–42). In a letter to David Gray, he wrote of his visit in London, saying, "I dislike Winston Churchill and would not meet him, but I was anxious to meet both Lloyd George and John Burns and I took a real fancy to both." He found Lloyd George the most powerful statesman in England, "*the* man of power." As for Gray, while he was not as brilliant as Balfour or a born leader like Lloyd George, he thought him "the kind of high-minded public servant, as straight in all private as in all public relations whom it is essential for a country to have." On London newspapers, while he found them "not as vicious and degrading as ours are, at least as fatuous" (pp. 105–108). It is inconceivable that Taft could have made these observations, or that most presidents in the twentieth century, confronted with comparable evidence, would have done so. They express quintessentially the pride and prejudice that made Roosevelt distinctive.

CHAPTER 6 (The Democratic Interloper)

1. Link, *Road,* pp. 1–35. Biographies of Wilson are legion, but none compare with Arthur Link's, a magisterial work, reliable and measured, a five-volume history, of which this is the first.

2. Academic salaries, though miniscule, gave the promise of an adequate income, not assured in the more hazardous private practice of law.

3. This guaranteed his academic advancement, a substantial boon at that time in his career.

4. Link, *Road,* pp. 21, 29–30. Link notes that Wilson was a prolific writer in the next decade, publishing nine books and thirty-five articles from 1893 through 1902 when he assumed the presidency of Princeton. Link writes: "The more books Wilson wrote, however, the more his scholarship deteriorated," and while his books gave him additional income, they were not equal to those he wrote earlier.

5. Ibid., pp. 37–57.

6. Ibid., pp. 59–91. Link's chapter, "The Battle of Princeton" is essential reading for anyone concerned to understand Wilson's complex personality, his inability to brook criticism, to compromise with those he conceived to be his enemies.

7. John Quincy Adams was the only president before Wilson to hold an academic appointment, if only briefly, but no one thought of him as a professor.

8. Wilson knew Oxford only very slightly, but his interest in English history guaranteed he would esteem the university that William Gladstone, his great political hero, had attended.

9. The term was Wilson's; it had no precise equivalent in either of England's two ancient universities.

10. Wilson aspired to the same reputation as an academic innovator that had made the name, Charles William Eliot, president of Harvard, universally known.

11. Some may wish to see this as a harbinger of what Wilson would seek to do decades later when the possibility of Senate rejection of the League of Nations Covenant made him launch his appeal to the nation.

12. This may be taken as an early example of Wilson's penchant for investing a contentious issue with moral implications.

13. Nasaw, *The Chief,* p. 228. Hearst's *Magazine* published what Nasaw describes as a "scathing exposé" of Wilson.

14. Link, *Road,* pp. 98–104. Harvey's efforts in Wilson's behalf were never ending; at one time, he conceived the idea of pressing for Wilson's appointment to be senator, a "step toward achieving the presidential nomination in 1908 or 1912."

15. Ibid., p. 143.

16. Ibid., p. 167.

17. Ibid.

18. Ibid., pp. 212–213.

19. Ibid., p. 213.

20. Ibid., pp. 205–237. The struggle over the Smith nomination was important, and so indicative of Wilson's political skills that Link devoted a whole chapter to the subject, awarding it the title, "The First Battle." Wilson, by preventing the Smith nomination in a legislature dominated by the Democrats, established himself as the incontestable leader of the Democratic Party in New Jersey. More important, though Wilson lost the support of the New Jersey "bosses" who no longer trusted him for betraying Smith, one of their own, it increased his reputation among the "progressive" elements in the party throughout the country.

21. Wilson used his New Jersey governorship to establish his credentials as a "reformer," what Franklin Roosevelt also did two decades later.

22. The record was indeed remarkable, considerably more impressive than any Theodore Roosevelt achieved in his two years as governor of New York.

23. Link, *Road,* pp. 273–274.

24. See Philip Bobbitt, *The Shield of Achilles: War, Peace and the Course of History* (Allen Lane, 2002), pp. 367–368. Wilson's friendship with House was the most important of his life. Bobbitt refers to it as a "friendship unique in twentieth-century American history."

25. Link, *Road,* pp. 359–361.

26. Ibid., pp. 362–365.

27. Ibid., p. 373.

28. Ibid.

29. Ibid., pp. 412 and 399. Clark, one of Bryan's most loyal disciples, had been a member of the House of Representatives since 1892, and was elected Speaker in 1911 after the Democratic Party off-year election victories in November 1910. Link described him as an "old-fashioned Democrat, a strict party man, a free trader, and of course an inveterate opponent of civil service reform; on one occasion he had even advocated the abolition of the diplomatic corps."

30. Ibid., p. 401. Clark's so-called conservatism was almost certainly exaggerated, and Link is persuasive in arguing that "if he was something of a party hack . . . he could at least point to a more consistent progressive record than Wilson or any other Democratic candidate could claim."

31. Ibid., pp. 458–459.

32. Mowry, "Election of 1912" in Schlesinger, *Presidential Elections,* vol. vi, p. 2156.

33. Ibid., p. 2165.

34. William F. McCombs, *Making Woodrow Wilson President* (Fairview, 1931).

35. See *The Intimate Papers of Colonel House,* edited by Charles Seymour (Houghton Mifflin, 1926), vol. 1, pp. 89–90. Wilson's discussions of possible Cabinet appointees, principally with Col. House, continued till November 16 when he sailed for Bermuda for a brief holiday. Few firm decisions had been made by that date, the problem undoubtedly exacerbated by the fact that no Democrat had served in a high federal office since Cleveland had left the White House in 1897.

36. Wilson offered McCombs the Paris embassy, which he refused.

37. Bryan supported the Brandeis appointment, but to no avail.

38. House, *Intimate Papers,* vol. 1, p. 104. House visited with Bryan in Florida in late January 1913, and wrote the president-elect, "He is very earnest in his advice that a Catholic, and perhaps a Jew, be taken into the family. I told him T[umulty]'s appointment as Secretary would cover the one, but he thought not."

39. Link, *New Freedom,* pp. 19–20.

40. Ibid., p. 75. Also, see House, *Intimate Papers,* vol. 1, pp. 108–109 where he said that the "President-elect had never met Lane and knew him only through me." More interesting, perhaps, was his comment that the post of attorney general was offered to A. Mitchell Palmer, but that the opposition to him was so great that Wilson offered him the secretaryship of War instead. Palmer, a Quaker, refused that post, and Wilson made him attorney general years later in 1919, when he became the scourge of all suspected of disloyalty to the United States.

41. Link, *New Freedom,* pp. 20–21.

42. The British example that greatly influenced Wilson when he served as governor, that retained its influence when he occupied the White House.

43. Wilson never developed the rapport with the press that the Roosevelts, Theodore and Franklin, managed to achieve.

44. Except for William McAdoo, the secretary of the treasury who became his son-in-law, no Cabinet member pretended to be a presidential intimate; none enjoyed the president's confidence in the way that Col. House did.

45. Link, *New Freedom,* pp. 63–65. Both these statements might have been made by Theodore Roosevelt, describing his own notion of the powers that inhered in the presidency, but Wilson was no Roosevelt, as Link never explicitly stated but made very evident. Link explained that after his assumption of the Princeton presidency in 1902, "his serious reading" virtually ceased. "It is little wonder," he wrote, "that he was often ignorant of the currents of economic, political, and social thought that was revolutionizing scholarship in the social sciences after the 1890s, and that he derived such knowledge as he had of these developments secondhand." Link recognized the "curious limitations in Wilson's intellectual processes," arising from his interest in ideas "chiefly to the degree to which they could be put to practical use and hardly at all for their own sake." Because "his thinking was pragmatic rather than philosophical, he had little interest in pure speculation and tended to judge public men, both historical and contemporary, not by their thought but by their actions; he was rarely an original thinker." Link saw also how much Wilson's religion affected his thinking, writing "Faith in God and submission to the Christian ethic underlay most of Wilson's political assumptions and fired his ambition to serve the Almighty by serving his fellow men." Wilson, Link wrote, once said "The way to success in America is to show you are not afraid of anybody except God and His judgment." Without that belief, Wilson acknowledged, it would have been impossible for him to believe in democracy or popular government. Roosevelt would have been incapable of making such statements.

46. Link, *New Freedom,* p. 182. In Link's view, ". . . the objective of the Underwood bill was not free trade but rather the destruction of the special privileges and the undue advantage that

Republican protectionist policy had conferred upon American producers; relief for the mass of consumers in such basic items as food and clothing; and the placing of American producers in a genuinely competitive condition with regard to European manufacturers."

47. Wilson was genuinely surprised by the character and extent of the outrage expressed by many Republicans when he sought to introduce the Federal Reserve system.

48. Because it is easy to exaggerate the importance of this legislation, it is useful to recall what Alfred D. Chandler Jr., has written in *The Visible Hand: The Managerial Revolution in American Business* (Harvard University Press, 1977), pp. 494–495. Chandler says: "Prior to the depression and World War II, the impact of the state and federal government on the modern corporation was primarily through taxes, tariffs, and regulatory legislation. . . ." Wilson, more than his Republican predecessors, gave these prime attention, able to do so because of his large congressional Democratic Party majorities.

49. Link, *New Freedom,* pp. 241–243.

50. Ibid., pp. 243–254.

51. Ibid., p. 425.

52. Ibid., pp. 439–440.

53. Ibid., pp. 469–471.

54. Ibid., p. 471. That, however, was not the way most Progressives viewed Wilson's achievement. Herbert Croly, the editor of the *New Republic,* asked "How can a man of his [Wilson's] shrewd and masculine intelligence possibly delude himself into believing the extravagant claims which he makes on behalf of the Democratic legislative achievement. . . ?" In even more caustic terms, he wrote: "Any man of President Wilson's intellectual equipment who seriously asserts that the fundamental wrongs of a modern society can be easily and quickly righted as a consequence of a few laws passed between the birth and death of a single Congress, casts suspicion either upon his own sincerity or upon his grasp of the realities of modern social and industrial life. Mr. Wilson's sincerity is above suspicion, but he is a dangerous and unsound thinker upon contemporary political and social problems. He has not only, as he himself has said, 'a single track mind,' but a mind which is fully convinced of the ever-lasting righteousness of its own performances and which surrounds this conviction with a halo of shimmering rhetoric. He deceives himself with these phrases, but he should not be allowed to deceive progressive popular opinion."

55. Roosevelt refused to sanction any action that seemed to legitimate Colombia's claims that an injustice had been done them at the time of the revolution that created the state of Panama.

56. Widenor, *Lodge,* p. 184.

57. See House, *Intimate Papers,* vol. 1, p. 283. This remained Wilson's unacknowledged goal from almost the day he took office, as is evident in his Mexico policies and in his attitudes toward the war in Europe.

58. Viscount Grey of Fallodon, *Twenty-Five Years, 1892–1916* (Frederick Stokes, 1925), vol. 2, pp. 98–100. Grey wrote: "President Wilson's policy, as explained to me by Page [the United States Ambassador] was to bring about a better state of affairs in Mexico. The precedent of Cuba was quoted. . . . The policy was altruistic; it was not being pushed for material interests; it was a policy of using the influence of the United States to lift a backward country on to a higher plane. . . . Our conversations about Mexico were not always very sympathetic. I made it quite clear that we should look passively on with acquiescence in whatever policy the United States thought fit to pursue about Mexico, but I could not be enthusiastic about the prospect."

59. Widenor, *Lodge,* p. 181. Wilson's decision to ask Congress to authorize hostilities by explicitly naming Huerta as the enemy, Lodge regarded "as an unwarranted and undignified declaration," ignoring "the real and only truly justifying international grounds for war." Lodge had no wish to see the United States "pick and choose between the factions which tear Mexico asunder," and had no doubt that the American military intervention would be resisted.

60. Ibid., p. 182. Though Lodge blamed Bryan mostly for the disastrous policy that led to the military action at Veracruz, his remarks on Wilson suggest that he knew the president had blundered badly; he wrote: "We found Mr. Wilson in a state of great agitation and very much disturbed. He had never meant to have war. Owing to his misinformation he was taken completely by surprise by the fighting at Vera Cruz and he was thoroughly alarmed. . . . What struck me most in the conversation was the President's evident alarm and his lack of determination as to his policy. He evidently had not thought the question out or in any way determined beforehand what he would do in certain very probable contingencies. . . . It must have been clear to everybody that armed resistance was likely to occur; but it was only too obvious that the President had made no preparation in his own mind for this most probable event."

61. Woodrow Wilson, *Papers,* vol. 28, p. 280.

62. Walter Russell Mead, *Special Providence: American Foreign Policy and How It Changed the World* (Knopf, 2001), pp. 75–77. It is significant that the phrase human rights never figured with Wilson, a president generally adept at inventing phrases. See also Mandelbaum, *Ideas,* p. 195. Mandelbaum writes: "The protection of human rights was more important to Americans (judging, at least, from their political rhetoric) than to other people. And the country had a long tradition of criticizing the non-liberal practices of others."

63. McDonald, *Presidency,* p. 397.

64. Link, *New Freedom,* pp. 101–102. Link wrote that "Henry White told Edith Bolling Wilson that Gerard gave some $120,000 to the Democratic campaign fund of 1912, most of which was sent to local leaders without being officially reported." Needless to say, such details do not appear in James W. Gerard, *My First Eighty-Three Years in America* (Doubleday, 1951).

65. The Walter Hines Page collection of letters at the Houghton Library at Harvard merits attention because of its flagrant and scarcely concealed Anglophilia.

66. G.R. Conyne, *Woodrow Wilson: British Perspectives, 1912–21* (Macmillan, 1992), p. 98.

67. Ibid., pp. 98–99.

68. Ibid., p. 48.

69. Lansing was scarcely more complimentary to Wilson; see his very acute analysis of the president in Link, *New Freedom,* pp. 611–618.

70. House, *Intimate Papers,* vol. 1, p. 283. How could Wilson fail to feel fondness for someone able to write, as House did on August 5, 1914, "My heart is full of deep appreciation for your letter of August 3. I never worry when I do not hear from you. No human agency could make me doubt your friendship and affection. That my life is devoted entirely to your interests, I believe you know, and I never cease from trying to serve you."

71. Ibid., pp. 433–435.

72. Levin, *Edith and Woodrow,* p. 11. Levin writes of the "idealized, sanitized, and indeed invented" history that the second Mrs. Wilson offered in her own autobiography, and promises to provide one that "is darker and more devious, and more astonishing, than previously recorded."

73. Grey, *Twenty-Five Years,* vol. 2, pp. 127–128. Grey prints the memorandum, which with the single word change made by Wilson, read: "Should the Allies accept this proposal, and should Germany refuse it, the United States would *probably* enter the war against Germany."

74. Ernest R. May, *The World War and American Isolation, 1914–1917* (Harvard University Press, 1959), pp. 355–357. May writes that after the sinking of the *Sussex,* House "sought to warn the British that if they wanted American help, they had best seek it by inviting mediation." But despite these warnings, the Allies did not respond.

75. Conyne, *Wilson,* p. 66.

76. A Wilson phrase with some resonance in the age of George W. Bush.

77. Frederick Palmer, *John J. Pershing, General of the Armies: A Biography* (Military Service Publishing Company, 1948), pp. 67–69.

78. Wilson regarded this as a signal victory.

79. Conyne, *Wilson*, p. 65.

80. Link and William M. Leary Jr., "Election of 1916" in Schlesinger, *Presidential Elections*, vol. vi, p. 2274.

81. Ibid., pp. 2272–2273.

82. Ibid., p. 2275.

83. Ibid.

84. McDonald, *Presidency*, p. 397.

85. Link and Leary, "Elections," p. 2254.

86. May, *American Isolation*, pp. 329–334.

87. House, *Papers*, vol. 2, pp. 361–363. Charles Seymour, the editor, publishes the interesting memorandum prepared by the Colonel for the president in which he outlined on June 20, 1916, the election campaign plan that he would do well to follow. Dividing the states into three categories, those where a maximum effort needed to be made, those that called for a strong effort, and those who he could safely ignore, House placed California in the second category, little realizing that victory in California would ultimately give Wilson the election.

88. Conyne, *Wilson*, p. 83.

89. Ibid., pp. 84–87.

90. Laurence W. Martin, *Peace without Victory: Woodrow Wilson and the British Liberals* (Yale University Press, 1958), pp. 120–121.

91. Ibid., Martin notes that House objected to the statement that both sides were seeking the same ends, but to no avail.

92. Ibid., p. 123. To House, Wilson declared, "This country does not intend to become involved in this war. . . . It would be a crime against civilization for us to go in!"

93. Ibid., pp. 34–35. Grey, no longer foreign secretary, privately regretted the new prime minister's use of such "intemperate language," but agreed with him in public that this was not the time to open negotiations with Germany.

94. Ibid., pp. 124–125. Wilson's words were significant; he said: "Victory would mean peace forced upon a loser, a victor's terms imposed upon the vanquished. It would be accepted in humiliation under duress, at an intolerable sacrifice, and would leave a sting, resentment, a bitter memory upon which terms of peace would rest, not permanently, but only as upon quicksand. Only a peace between equals can last."

95. Conyne, *Wilson*, p. 95.

96. House, *Papers*, vol. 2, p. 442. The president, in this speech, said: "I refuse to believe that it is the intention of the German authorities to do in fact what they have warned us they will feel at liberty to do. . . . Only actual overt acts on their part can make me believe it even now. . . . We wish to serve no selfish ends. . . . These are the bases of peace, not war. God grant we may not be challenged to defend them by wilful injustice on the part of the Government of Germany."

97. Martin, *Wilson*, p. 127.

98. House, *Papers*, vol. 2, pp. 451–452.

99. Ibid., pp. 453–454.

100. Ibid., pp. 456–457. Also, May, *American Isolation*, p. 425. May notes that too little attention has been given to what Wilson said in his second inaugural address on March 4, 1917. While House saw it as "a replica of his address of January 22," and thought to comment mostly on the weather on inaugural day, "dark and gloomy, with high winds and floods of rain," May saw it as an important statement, superficially "following the fashions of Jefferson and Lincoln," but having distinctive features in its ardent plea for national unity.

101. See Gordon A. Craig, *Germany 1866–1945* (Oxford University Press, 1945), pp. 366–386 for a sympathetic but critical appraisal of Bethmann Hollweg's performance and fate.

102. Arthur S. Link, *Wilson The Diplomatist: A Look at His Major Foreign Policies* (Johns Hopkins University Press, 1957), p. 81. As late as January 4, 1917, Wilson told House "This

country does not intend to become involved in this war. We are the only one of the great white nations that is free from war to-day, and it would be a crime against civilization for us to go in."

103. Conyne, *Wilson,* p. 100.

104. Ibid., pp. 111–112.

105. Corwin, *President,* pp. 429–430.

106. Ibid., pp. 269–272.

107. Ibid. Corwin calls World War I a "prologue and rehearsal" to the Second.

108. Blanche E.C. Dugdale, *Arthur James Balfour, 1906–1930,* (Putnam's, 1930), vol. 2, p. 140. Balfour, asking Walter Hines Page, the American ambassador, why the British were so unpopular in the United States, heard him say: "Among other reasons our official people on both sides steadfastly refuse to visit one another and become acquainted. Neither he, nor Lord Grey, nor Mr. Asquith, nor Mr. Lloyd George, had ever been to the United States . . . and not a single member of the Administration was personally known to a single member of the British Government."

109. House, *Papers,* vol. 3, pp. 42–51. It is certain that both House and Wilson learned of the "secret treaties" from Balfour when he visited in late April 1917. In this connection, comments by Charles Seymour are especially important. Seymour writes, "House did not urge Balfour to give him complete details of the secret treaties, nor being a private citizen, would he wish to ask for copies of the texts," but Wilson learned of "the character of the secret treaties and was entirely aware of the difference between his own peace programme and that of the Allies." Seymour went on to say: "At the time of the Balfour Mission he may have expected that in the end American influence at the Peace Conference would be sufficient to eliminate the treaties as practical factors in the settlement. Writing to Colonel House, a few weeks later, President Wilson intimated strongly that American economic power would be such that the Allies must perforce yield to American pressure and accept the American peace programme: England and France, he wrote, "would not have the same views with regard to peace that we have by any means. When the war is over we can force them to our way of thinking."

110. Ibid., pp. 157–158. From Magnolia, Massachusetts, House wrote Wilson on August 19, 1917, "The Russian Ambassador is with me today. He is very much disturbed over the Pope's peace overture and how you will reply to it. . . . He would like you to take the lead and let Russia follow. He hopes you may be willing to say that the United States will treat with the German people at any time they are in a position to name their representatives. He thinks that is the crux of the situation. . . . I believe you are facing one of the great crises that the world has known, but I feel confident that you will meet it with that fine spirit of courage and democracy which has become synonymous with your name."

111. Wilson, *Papers,* vol. 44, pp. 57–59.

112. Lawrence E. Gelfand, *The Inquiry: American Preparations for Peace, 1917–1919* (Yale University Press, 1963).

113. John Grigg, *Lloyd George, War Leader, 1916–1918* (Allen Lane, 2002), pp. 379–383.

114. Ibid., pp. 383–384. Grigg, quoting Colonel House, wrote that Wilson was depressed by Lloyd George's speech, fearing he had stolen his thunder, but House argued the contrary, insisting that "he would so smother the Lloyd George speech that it would be forgotten and that he, the President, would once more become the spokesman for the Entente, and indeed . . . for the liberals of the world."

115. Conyne, *Wilson,* p. 140.

116. Ibid., p. 141.

117. Ibid., p. 142.

118. Ibid., p. 143.

119. Ibid.

120. Grigg, *Lloyd George*, pp. 384–385. Grigg, decades later, chose to say of the Fourteen Points what few in Britain dared to say during the war, showing the "absurdity" of Point I, the inadequacy of Point II, mocking the "courage" Wilson showed in promulgating "equality of trade" for a protectionist country. On Point VI where Wilson said, "The treatment accorded Russia by her sister nations in the months to come will be the acid test of their good will, of their comprehension of her needs as distinguished from their own interest, and of their intelligent and unselfish sympathy." Grigg wrote: "But Wilson's commitment to the Russians, apparently regardless of their regime or their willingness to fight, is surely indefensible in principle and an insult to fellow democracies which had made, and were still making, enormous sacrifices for the common cause." See, also, Grigg's extensive discussion, in his Afterword, of Lloyd George's reaction to the 14 Points (pp. 619–640).

121. McDonald, *Presidency*, p. 438. McDonald calls Wilson a "skilful, ruthless, and frightening propagandist," who believed that to fight the war properly, the people had to be infected by a "spirit of ruthless brutality." George Creel, who headed his Committee on Public Information, "enlisted ministers, college professors, and hordes of wordsmiths to write and distribute anti-German hate literature, distort history and current events, harangue audiences, and maintain a steady barrage of propaganda. High schools and colleges quit teaching German, orchestras stopped playing Wagner and Beethoven, teachers scoured high school and college history texts and literally cut out all favorable references to Germany."

122. Merle Curti, *The Roots of American Loyalty* (Columbia University Press, 1946), pp. 198–199 and p. 232. Curti wrote that Wilson, however reluctantly, came to accept the Theodore Roosevelt concept of force as necessary in international relations. Curti recognized, however, that Wilson could never satisfy Roosevelt who thought Wilson's League of Nation a surrender of national values and interests to a "vague, sentimental humanitarianism."

123. Wilson, *Papers,* vol. liii, p. 381.

124. Roosevelt had begun to refer to "Peace-God" Wilson and his League.

125. Conyne, *Wilson*, p. 148.

126. Ibid., pp. 150–151. Her husband, Herbert Asquith, in his *Memories and Reflections, 1852–1927* (Little Brown, 1928), vol. 2, p. 196, wrote in his diary on November 16, "President Wilson is coming after all, and is expected to arrive here about our polling date, December 14. I confess he is one of the few people in the world that I want to see and talk to. . . . Gilbert Murray, who was here this morning and knows him, thinks that I should like him." In a more telling comment, he wrote, "President Wilson was unwise enough at this time to slip down from his oracular tripod at Washington, and to rub shoulders with European diplomacy at Paris and Versailles. I had an interesting talk with him as he passed through London: among other topics, on the difference between the position and authority of the Cabinet in the United States and here. On one rather critical occasion during the Civil War, Lincoln (he told me) summoned his Cabinet, which contained some exceptionally able and distinguished men, and asked them their opinions as to what ought to be done. They were unanimous in favour of a particular policy, and the President took the unusual course of calling for a division. When they had all voted 'aye,' he said curtly, I think the noes have it." (pp. 197–198) The tale, told by Wilson, said as much about him and his perceptions of the presidency as it did about Lincoln.

127. Conyne, *Wilson*, p. 161.

128. Ibid., p. 164.

129. The literature on the Paris Peace Conference is vast, but no earlier book is more important than that published by Margaret MacMillan (*Peacemakers: The Paris Conference of 1919 and its Attempt to End War* [John Murray, 2001]). Its uniqueness derives from the fact that it does not concentrate, as so many other histories do, on the decisions made in respect to Germany, or even on those relating to the creation of new Balkan states and an independent Poland. Its pages on

Japan and China are critical, but even more important is the very large Part VII, appropriately entitled "Setting the Middle East Alight," providing material as relevant to the international situation today as anything written in the interwar period when historians concentrated their attention on the reparations question and Germany. Only on Russia, is MacMillan less thorough, and here two older and considerably more controversial works need to be consulted, Arno J. Mayer, *Wilson vs. Lenin: Political Origins of the New Diplomacy, 1917–1918* (Meridian Books, 1964) and his *Politics and Diplomacy of Peacemaking: Containment and Counterrevolution at Versailles, 1918–1919* (Vintage Books, 1969). Because the Paris Conference led to a break between Wilson and House, the most compelling analysis of that still controversial subject may be Alexander L. George and Juliette L. George, *Woodrow Wilson and Colonel House, A Personality Study* (Dover, 1964). Phyllis Levin adds new material on how Wilson's wife helped destroy the relation between the president and his Texas intimate. See also Robert Lansing, *The Peace Negotiations: A Personal Narrative* (Houghton Mifflin, 1921), a defense of his own performance in Paris against those, including the president, who doubted his loyalty. No twentieth-century secretary of state has ever been comparably critical of his president. An even more important source is by Allan Nevins, *Henry White, Thirty Years of American Diplomacy* (Harper, 1930), the only Republican in the delegation, that offers a more sensitive analysis of Wilson's problems both in Paris and after his return to the United States.

130. Keynes and Smuts became close friends during the Paris Conference; Wilson scarcely knew either.

131. John Milton Cooper Jr, *Breaking the Heart of the World: Woodrow Wilson and the Fight for the League of Nations* (Cambridge University Press, 2001). Chapter 2, "Round Robin and Revision," pp. 55–108 provides a searching analysis of why and how the two leading Republicans, Lodge and Root, came to oppose Wilson on the League issue, and the role Taft and Knox played in the crisis. All these men, so important in Theodore Roosevelt's administrations, came forward as the "elder statesmen" critical of Wilson's creation.

132. Widenor, *Lodge*, pp. 326–328.

133. Cooper, *Breaking the Heart*, p. 143.

134. Jessup, *Root*, vol. 2, p. 400.

135. John Maynard Keynes, *The Economic Consequences of the Peace* (Harcourt, Brace and Howe, 1920). Keynes, after his death, was attacked in France by Pierre Mantoux in *The Carthaginian Peace or the Economic Consequences of Mr. Keynes*, published in 1946, which claimed that Keynes's tract, in discrediting the Versailles Treaty and finding numerous supporters for his views, did much to bring on World War II. Keynes, in fact, was only one of many in England dismayed by Wilson's performance, and though others who wrote about his performance at the Paris Peace Conference, including Harold Nicolson, *Peacemaking, 1919* (Grossett and Dunlap, 1965), p. 198, did not resort to the same irony, they were scarcely more generous. Nicolson wrote: "The spiritual arrogance which seems inseparable from the harder forms of religion had eaten deep into his soul. It had been confirmed in the course of many battles with the Faculty of Princeton. His vision had been narrowed by the intensive ethical nurture which he had received; he possessed, as he himself admitted, 'a one-track mind.' This intellectual disability rendered him blindly impervious, not merely to human character, but also shades of difference. He possessed no gift for differentiation, no capacity for adjustment to circumstances. It was his spiritual and mental rigidity which proved his undoing. It rendered him as incapable of withstanding criticism as of absorbing advice. . . . The profound, rigid, and quite justified conviction of his own spiritual rectitude; the belief that God, Wilson and the People would triumph in the end led him to look upon his own inconsistencies as mere transient details in the one great impulse towards right and justice."

136. Robert Skidelsky, *John Maynard Keynes: Hopes Betrayed, 1883–1920* (Macmillan, 1983), pp. 376–402.

137. David Lloyd George, *The Truth About the Peace Treaties*, 2 vols., (Victor Gollancz, 1938), vol. l, pp. 221–242.

138. Cooper, *Breaking the Heart,* pp. 211–212.

139. Ibid.

140. Ibid.

141. Ibid., pp. 210–211. As Cooper makes clear, Marshall was a more considerable person than Wilson believed; he understood how much pride and jealousy undermined all that the president hoped to achieve.

142. Many who met Wilson in Europe were unimpressed with him, but only in England did there develop a literature of memoirs and histories that explored his insufficiencies as a diplomat and thinker.

143. This statement is not intended to denigrate Cooper's work, a study of the greatest value. It is simply to suggest that Americans, especially in recent years, have been more prone to mourn Wilson's defeat, evident in the writings of Michael Mandelbaum and any number of others, than is true of Europeans or Asians. Wilson was a hero for some English during World War I, rarely a hero since, and, despite the avenue that bears his name in Paris, always suspect to many French. Even Germans have refused to give him his due.

144. Cooper, *Breaking the Heart,* pp. 405–406. Cooper avoids making any statement like this, which is more characteristic of Conrad Black in his recent biography of Roosevelt. Cooper, commenting on a letter Franklin Roosevelt sent to Ray Stannard Baker, Wilson's friend and biographer, writes: "This statement revealed the basic lesson that FDR had learned from the League fight—that 'public psychology' and 'human weakness' could not stand too much talk about deep matters." Cooper adds, significantly: "He also lauded Theodore Roosevelt for having succeeded where Wilson had failed 'in stirring people to enthusiasm over specific individual events, even though these specific events may have been superficial in comparison with the fundamentals.'" For Cooper, Roosevelt's great gift was to know how to "manipulate public debate about foreign policy." Wilson never mastered that art.

CHAPTER 7 (Back to Normalcy)

1. Nan Britton, *The President's Daughter* (Elizabeth Ann Guild, 1927). The book carried the inscription: "The first edition of The President's Daughter was hindered and trodden upon by interests which did not want to see this mother's true story given to the world."

2. Levin, *Edith and Woodrow,* pp. 399–406.

3. This had been true through much of the nineteenth century, as Bryce indicated in *The American Commonwealth.*

4. H.L. Mencken was one of several who satirized Harding, referring to his prose as "Gamalielese."

5. Andrew Sinclair, *The Available Man: The Life Behind the Masks of Warren G. Harding* (Quadrangle Paperback, 1969), pp. 14–15. Sinclair writes: "The success of Harding with the *Star* was certainly in the model of Horatio Alger. He started with nothing, and through working, stalling, bluffing, withholding payments, borrowing back wages, boosting, and manipulating he turned a dying rag into a powerful small-town newspaper."

6. Ibid., p. 36.

7. Ibid., pp. 47–48.

8. Ibid., pp. 49–50.

9. Ibid., p. 50.

10. Ibid., p. 55. Sinclair writes: "This campaign marked the beginning of the flood of nativist hatred that was to supersede progressivism and persecute aliens during the First World War and

rise to an apex of disgrace in the Red Scare of 1919. The forces of nativism and nationalism always helped Harding, who quickly learned how to gain their support."

11. Ibid., pp. 54–55.

12. Francis Russell, *President Harding: His Life and Times* (Eyre and Spottiswoode, 1969), pp. 369–370.

13. Ibid., p. 370. See also Donald R. McCoy, "Election of 1920," in Schlesinger, *Presidential Elections*, vol. vi, p. 2357. This remark, typical of many made at the Republican 1920 Convention, allowed McCoy to write: "Altogether the 1920 platform was the most conservative document written by a Republican convention in two decades. It reflected not only the dominance of conservatives in the party, but also the weakening of liberal impulses among many progressive Republicans."

14. Frederick Lewis Allen, *Only Yesterday* (John Wiley, 1997), p. 29. This, a reprint of the book published in 1931, had an immense success during the Depression years.

15. Russell, *Harding*, p. 383.

16. Ibid.

17. George Harvey, offended by Wilson in 1912, had become an ardent Republican.

18. McCoy, in Schlesinger, *Presidential Elections*, pp. 2358–2359.

19. Ibid., p. 2359.

20. Russell, *Harding*, p. 389.

21. Ibid., pp. 392–393.

22. Ibid., p. 394.

23. Ibid., p. 396.

24. Ibid.

25. Allen, *Only Yesterday*, pp. 29–30.

26. Ibid., p. 30.

27. One waits with interest to see the new biography of Andrew Mellon, being prepared by David Cannadine.

28. The McLeans were thought to belong to the "top drawer" of the new postwar Washington society. Ned McLean, the proprietor of the *Washington Post* and his wife, the proud owner of the Hope Diamond, were both great friends of Harding.

29. Ronald Steel, *Walter Lippmann and the American Century* (Vintage Books, 1981), p. 168. Lippmann wrote contemptuously that Harding "was put there by the Senators for the sole purpose of abdicating in their favor." In his words, "The Grand Dukes have chosen their Weak Tsar in order to increase the power of the Grand Dukes," and this would mean "the substitution of government by a clique for the lonely majesty of the President."

30. Harding, familiar with newspapers, proud of his having owned one, held regular press conferences that he greatly enjoyed.

31. Lippmann, in this prophecy as in many others made through his long career as a journalist, was proved mistaken.

32. Samuel Flagg Bemis, *A Diplomatic History of the United States* (Henry Holt, 1942), rev. ed., pp. 694–710. Bemis, perhaps the country's leading historian of U.S. diplomatic history at the time, wrote of Hughes's efforts in Washington, saying: "Secretary Hughes opened the negotiations with the trump card of high naval strength, actual and potential, backed by undoubted support of the Republican Senate. He proposed that 'preparations for offensive war stop now.' He then offered an itemized plan for the reduction of armaments according to an agreed ratio finally fixed at 5–5–3–1.7–1.7, corresponding generally to the existing ratio before the conference, which involved the sinking or scrapping of designated ships, built or building, of the three great naval powers, and a naval holiday in the construction of capital ships, with only limited replacements of superannuated ships thereafter." According to Akira Iriye, in his book *After Imperialism*

(Harvard University Press, 1965), pp. 14–21, the Japanese government was seen in the State Department as "an oligarchy of military clansmen and their adherents, all alike imbued with the same materialistic political philosophy, differing among themselves only in the degree to which their nationalistic aspirations are tempered by considerations of prudence in dealing with the rest of the world." In this situation, the United States wished to "demolish the existing system of imperialist diplomacy." How was this to be accomplished? Iriye writes: "This involved the annulment of all deals and agreements among the powers and the enunciation of new principles to govern their conduct in the Far East. The former led to the abrogation of the Anglo-Japanese alliance and its replacements by the Four-Power Treaty, while the latter objective was embodied in the Nine-Power Treaty and other agreements." The Nine Power Treaty was intended to govern the relations of the great powers with China, and Iriye writes that "it condemned spheres of influence, upheld the principle of equal opportunity, and solemnly confirmed the 'sovereignty, the independence, and the territorial and administrative integrity of China.'" Calling these "abstract principles," Iriye says that they made no commitment to respect China's diplomatic independence, and "did not mean that imperialism was gone." In his words, "China did not emerge as a nation with all the attributes of sovereignty. To the delegates of the Washington Conference the country seemed to lack essential characteristics of a modern state."

33. *Cf. infra*, Chapter 9, "The Engineer."

34. Brogan, *Introduction to American Politics* (Hamish Hamilton, 1954), p. 186. Brogan, very perceptive on Prohibition as a political issue, wrote: "The old conflict that had flared up, from time to time, between the 'old Americans' and the Germans and Irish, was now a permanent and open war. That the saloon was always in politics and always a source of evil in politics was an axiom in the more moralistic circles. But the saloon had gone and the liquor business was more in politics than ever. If it had paid to vote dry before now, more and more it paid to vote wet. The Democratic party in the cities began to win friends, as the Republican party was in office and was the instrument of tyranny, although, in many regions, the zeal of the federal law-enforcement officers could hardly have been more tepid. The question of prohibition was one of the underground forces undermining the old party alignments from 1922 to 1932."

35. Harding's reputation never recovered from the revelations that followed his death. Indeed, they became so identified with his administration that no accomplishments were ever acknowledged. They were, in fact, few in number, and even the foreign policy success of his secretary of state now appears insignificant. Harding, unlike Roosevelt and Wilson, never sought to win fame through legislation, and the little that attached to his administration suggested a very limited ambition to move Congress toward new objectives. He relished the presidency, was almost certainly surprised to have achieved it, and did little to embellish the office.

36. An excellent older work, J. Leonard Bates, *The Origins of Teapot Dome: Progressives, Parties, and Petroleum* (University of Illinois, 1963), is especially valuable.

37. These were the largest scandals in more than half a century, and both the press and the Congress showed themselves avid to explore them.

38. William Allen White, *The Autobiography of William Allen White* (Macmillan, 1946), p. 619.

39. The proof that even clearly inferior presidents never die is perhaps best suggested by Robert K. Murray, *The Harding Era: Warren G. Harding and His Administration* (University of Minnesota, 1969).

CHAPTER 8 (The Great Enigma)

1. The only contemporary biography of Coolidge that may be said to have some merit is by Robert Sobel, *Coolidge: An American Enigma* (Regnery, 1998). A more useful volume, certainly, is by John Earl Haynes, ed., *Calvin Coolidge and the Coolidge Era* (Library of Congress, 1998).

2. William Allen White, *A Puritan in Babylon: The Story of Calvin Coolidge* (Macmillan, 1938), is the most arresting study of his life.

3. White, *Puritan*, p. 222. See also Donald McCoy, *Calvin Coolidge: The Quiet President* (Macmillan, 1967), p. 164.

4. These, the signal contributions of the Harding administration, continued essentially unchanged in the time of Coolidge. When the Republican-dominated Congress sought, on rare occasions, to go beyond what had become common in Harding's day, Coolidge was apt to veto the bills. He enjoyed the distinction of seeing his veto of four bills all repudiated on a single day. See McDonald, *Presidency,* p. 353.

5. The possibility of joining the League was never seriously discussed. See Joseph Schumpeter, *Capitalism, Socialism, and Democracy* (George Allen and Unwin, 1950), 3rd ed., p 402 where, following World War II, he wrote: "In Stalinist Russia, foreign policy is foreign policy as it was under the tsars. In the United States, foreign policy is domestic politics. . . . There is no tradition and there are no organs for playing the complex game of any other foreign policy." This was certainly true in the time of Coolidge, and some may be tempted to say that it is still true.

6. Pringle, *Taft,* vol. 2, p. 1022. Taft had been appointed chief justice of the Supreme Court by Harding in 1921.

7. See Joseph A. Schumpeter, *Business Cycles: A Theoretical, Historical and Statistical Analysis of the Capitalist Process* (McGraw-Hill, 1939) for one analysis, by no means universally accepted, of the "booms" and "busts" characteristic of twentieth-century capitalism.

8. David Burner, "Election of 1924" in Schlesinger, *Presidential Elections,* vol. vi, p. 2505. The platform, in its eulogy of Harding, included the words: "We nominated him four years ago to be our candidate; the people of the nation elected him their President. His human qualities gripped the affections of the American people. He was a public servant unswerving in his devotion to duty. A staunch republican, he was first of all a true patriot, who gave unstintingly of himself during a trying and critical period of our national life. His conception and successful direction of the limitation of armaments conference in Washington was an accomplishment which advanced the world along the path toward peace."

9. Ibid., p. 2468.

10. Ibid., p. 2469.

11. No other religious, ethnic, or racial minority could claim comparable numbers.

12. William G. McAdoo, *Crowded Years* (Houghton Mifflin, 1931), pp. 240–242. His image of Wall Street is that of a "malign collective entity."

13. Burner, "1924," vol. vi, p. 2491. The Democratic Party platform, after its ritual statement of "profound homage to the memory of Woodrow Wilson," stated its commitment to "equal rights to all and special privilege to none," and included the words, "The republican party is concerned chiefly with material things; the democratic party is concerned chiefly with human rights. . . . The democratic party stands for remedial legislation and progress. The republican party stands still."

14. Arthur M. Schlesinger Jr., *The Crisis of the Old Order, 1919–1933* (Houghton Mifflin, 1957), p. 100. Schlesinger, no friend of Coolidge, Harding, or Hoover, wrote approvingly of Davis, saying that "few men were better qualified for the Presidency than the man it [the Democratic Party] eventually chose."

15. Charles P. Kindleberger, *The World in Depression, 1929–1939* (University of California Press, 1973), pp. 31–82. The first chapters of this seminal work, dealing with the 1920s, are an incomparable resource for anyone wishing to study the economic policies pursued by the Coolidge administration.

16. See Steel, *Lippmann,* pp. 236–239. Lippmann, an ardent critic of Coolidge's "dollar diplomacy" in both Mexico and Nicaragua, had only contempt for Frank Kellogg who succeeded

Hughes as secretary of state in 1925. Coolidge became sufficiently angered by the barrage of press criticism that he demanded reporters to clear their stories with the White House on Mexico before printing them. This led to a Lippmann outburst that eventually caused Coolidge to retreat. Lippmann wrote: "There is a name for the kind of press Mr. Coolidge seems to desire. It is called a reptile press. This is a press which takes its inspiration from government officials and from great business interests. It prints what those in power wish to have printed. It suppresses what they wish to have suppressed. It puts out as news those facts which help its masters to accomplish what they are after. . . . It makes no independent investigation of the facts. It takes what is handed to it and does what it is told to do."

17. *New York Times*, December 5, 1924, p. 1.

18. Ibid. In this speech, significantly, he said: "We cannot hope indefinitely to maintain our country as a specially favored community, an isle of contentment lifted above the general standards of humanity." He called for a better accord with our "partners," the other world powers.

19. Halford Ryan, ed., *The Inaugural Addresses of Twentieth-Century American Presidents* (Praeger, 1993), pp. 69–80.

20. Daniel J. Leah, "Coolidge, Hays, and 1920 Movies," in Haynes, *Coolidge*, p. 101.

21. The farmers' plight never improved markedly even in the days of Coolidge prosperity.

22. Nancy MacLean, *Behind the Mask of Chivalry: The Making of the Second Ku Klux Klan* (Oxford University Press, 1994), p. 133.

23. Edward J. Larson, *Summer of the Gods: The Scopes Trial and America's Continuing Debate Over Science and Religion* (Harvard University Press, 1998).

24. White, *Puritan*, p. 360.

25. Ibid., p. 361. At the time of the announcement, Grace Coolidge claimed to have had no advance warning of it.

26. McCoy, *Coolidge*, pp. 281–282.

27. Erich Eyck, *A History of the Weimar Republic: From the Collapse of the Empire to Hindenburg's Election* (Athenaeum, 1970), vol. I, p. 291.

28. Ibid., pp. 292–293. The British collaborated importantly in making these agreements possible.

29. David Bryn-Jones, *Frank B. Kellogg: A Biography* (G.P. Putnam, 1937), pp. 171–173.

30. D. W. Brogan, *The French Nation from Napoleon to Pétain: 1814–1940* (Harper and Row, 1963), p. 267.

31. *New York Times*, November 12, 1928, p. 1.

32. Stephen A. Schuker, "American Foreign Policy," in Haynes, *Coolidge*, p. 303.

33. Coolidge's own account of why he did not seek another term, as given in his *Autobiography*, pp. 240–241, and p. 247 in a chapter entitled "Why I Did Not Choose to Run," is exemplary for its simplicity but also for its candor. Coolidge wrote: "Although my own health has been practically perfect, yet the duties are very great and ten years would be a very heavy strain. It would be especially long for the mistress of the White House. Mrs. Coolidge has been in more than usual good health, but I doubt if she could have stayed there for ten years without some danger of impairment of her strength. . . . It is difficult for men in high office to avoid the malady of self-delusion. They are always surrounded by worshippers. They are constantly, and for the most part sincerely, assured of their greatness. They live in an artificial atmosphere of adulation and exaltation, which sooner or later impairs their judgment. They are in grave danger of becoming careless and arrogant. My election seemed assured. Nevertheless, I felt it was not best for the country that I should succeed myself. A new impulse is more likely to be beneficial. It is therefore my privilege, after seeing my administration so strongly indorsed by the country, to retire voluntarily from the greatest experience that can come to mortal man. In that way, I believe I can best serve the people who have honored me and the country which I love."

34. In this, as in so many other ways, Coolidge bore no resemblance to the Republican Roosevelt or to his immediate predecessor.

35. Warren. I. Cohen, "America and the World in the 1920s," Haynes, *Coolidge*, pp. 240–241.

36. Ibid.

37. Ibid.

38. Leah in Haynes, *Coolidge*, p. 103.

CHAPTER 9 (The Engineer)

1. Herbert Hoover, *Memoirs* (Macmillan, 1952), are three vast volumes, very different from the slight volume written by Coolidge. Even more surprising, perhaps, are the three volumes written by George H. Nash, *The Life of Herbert Hoover* (Norton, 1983). We are still waiting for the fourth volume.

2. Hoover, the only Quaker other than Richard Nixon to enter the White House, a president different from him in every respect, demonstrated, if proof was needed, that religious affiliation may lead an individual to be something of a pacifist or, as in Nixon's case, a would-be warrior.

3. George T. Clark, *Leland Stanford* (Stanford University Press, 1931), pp. 408–414.

4. Engineering, especially in oil, became a lucrative profession only in the twentieth century though a number of Europeans and Americans began to make substantial fortunes earlier by their successful explorations. See Daniel Yergen, *The Prize: The Epic Quest for Oil, Money, and Power* (Free Press, 1991).

5. Though Hoover would have disdained the label "cosmopolitan," he resembled in no way the true son of the manse, the "provincial" Coolidge.

6. Herbert C. Hoover, *Principles of Mining, Valuation, Organization, and Administration* (Hill Publishing Co., 1909), pp. 167–168.

7. Neither Taft nor Hoover was an intellectual; neither was seen as such by those who knew them but both were deemed competent in their respective professions, though few thought Taft an especially distinguished chief justice.

8. Hoover, *Memoirs*, vol. 1, pp. 124–130.

9. Though Roosevelt maintained fairly close relations with Harvard, and Taft even closer ties to Yale, they compared scarcely at all with Hoover's relations with Stanford where he figured as the university's most prominent alumnus.

10. As a Quaker, Hoover showed great sympathy for what Wilson proposed to do in seeking an early negotiation between the Allies and the Central Powers. Their common interest in promoting peace undoubtedly led to their close association.

11. Hoover, *Memoirs*, vol. 1, pp. 212–215.

12. House, *Papers*, vol. 3, pp. 17–18. House ardently recommended Hoover to Wilson, writing: "I trust Houston will give him full powers as to food control. He knows it better than any one in the world and would inspire confidence both in Europe and here. Unless Houston does give him full control, I am afraid he will be unwilling to undertake the job, for he is the kind of man that has to have complete control in order to do the thing well."

13. Hoover, *Memoirs*, vol. 1, pp. 260 and 244.

14. House, *Papers*, vol. 3, p. 409. Hoover was an excellent prophet in respect to Russia, and after the November Revolution when the Allies discussed whether to pursue a policy of military intervention, especially after the Germans imposed the Treaty of Brest Litovsk on the Bolsheviks, House recommended that a Russian Relief Commission be appointed, and that Hoover be made its head. In his letter to Wilson on June 13, 1918, House said: "The Russians know Hoover and Hoover knows the East. If he heads 'The Russian Relief Commission' it will typify in the Russian mind what was done in Belgium, and I doubt whether any Government in Russia, friendly or unfriendly,

would dare oppose his coming in. . . . Hoover has ability as an organizer, his name will carry weight in the direction desired, and his appointment will, for the moment, settle the Russian question as far as it can be settled by you at present." Nothing came of this proposal, but in a very long letter to Wilson, written on March 28, 1919, Hoover gave an extraordinarily acute appraisal of the Bolsheviks and their probable intentions. Excerpts are to be found in Herbert Hoover, *The Ordeal of Woodrow Wilson* (McGraw-Hill, 1958), pp. 117–119, but the full text is available in Arno Mayer, *Politics and Diplomacy of Peacemaking: Containment and Counterrevolution at Versailles, 1918–1919* (Vintage, 1969), pp. 24–29. Mayer's commentary on the text is relevant; he writes: "In this letter Hoover brilliantly summarized the key tenets of the Wilsonian view of the Bolshevik problem: Russian Bolshevism was a condition to be cured rather than a conspiracy to be destroyed; there were considerable sources of Bolshevik contagion outside Russia; the spiritual appeals of the Bolshevik ideology were far from negligible; the reactionary consequences of a military crusade against Bolshevism could not be ignored; and a military truce combined with economic aid was most likely to redirect the revolutionary currents into reformist channels in Russia."

15. Hoover, as the result of his work in seeking to prevent mass starvation in war-ravaged Europe, became one of the best-informed Americans on the condition of that unhappy continent, threatened with revolution and disorder.

16. Hoover relished compliments of this sort, and never neglected to cite such accolades in his *Memoirs*.

17. The differences between the British and the Americans may have been even more fundamental than those that divided the French from the Americans.

18. Hoover, *Memoirs*, vol. 1, pp. 249–250.

19. Hoover's network of those helping him to feed the hungry of the defeated powers, principally Austria and Hungary, gave him unique access to information on how these people were being subjected to propaganda and pressure by local Communists friendly to the Bolshevik regime in Russia.

20. Hoover was never one who cared to share authority, and in this instance believed he had no reason to do so.

21. This reflected Hoover's continuing commitment to his Quaker ideals, as well as his shrewd political opinion that only such a policy could stabilize Europe and stem the Communist tide.

22. Robert Skidelsky, *John Maynard Keynes: Hopes Betrayed, 1883–1920* (Macmillan, 1983), p. 358.

23. James T. Patterson, *Mr. Republican: A Biography of Robert A. Taft* (Houghton Mifflin, 1972), p. 76.

24. Mayer, *Politics and Diplomacy*, p. 25. Hoover never faltered in his high opinion of American industrial capacity; in his long letter to Wilson on Bolshevism, he wrote: "It is not necessary for Americans to debate the utter foolishness of these [Communist] economic tenets. We must all agree that our processes of production and distribution, the outgrowth of a hundred generations, in the stimulation to individual initiative, the large equality of opportunity and infinite development of mind and body, while not perfect, come about as near perfection as is possible from the mixture of avarice, ambition, altruism, intelligence, ignorance and education, of which the human animal is today composed."

25. This became a staple of the Republican criticism of the Treaty of Versailles, the work of European politicians who hoodwinked a naïve president.

26. In this regard, as in most others, Hoover resembled Taft more than Roosevelt.

27. Hoover, *Memoirs*, vol. 1, p. 482.

28. The house would eventually become the residence of the president of Stanford University.

29. The extent of the hostility to Hoover in Republican circles, precisely because he had accepted to serve under Wilson, cannot be overstated.

30. Sinclair, *Available Man,* pp. 184–185. Though Harding scarcely knew Hoover, he insisted on having him in his Cabinet over the opposition of Senator Lodge who finally accepted him in return for the president-elect's promise to appoint Andrew Mellon as secretary of the treasury. Sinclair believes that Harding's choice of Hoover, "the most popular administrator in the country," was "a slap at the Senators, who had expected to control him." Hoover, in his *Memoirs,* reported the president as having told Lodge: "Mellon and Hoover, or no Mellon." For a longer explanation of this "deal," see Hoover, *Memoirs,* vol. 2, p. 36.

31. Herbert Hoover, *American Individualism* (Doubleday, 1922).

32. Whether the country's foreign policy after 1926 would have been substantially different, given Hoover's contempt for the Europeans, it is impossible to say, but he would certainly have brought to the post of secretary of state an intelligence and experience that Kellogg lacked.

33. These were all legitimate charges, reasonable grievances.

34. Isaiah Berlin, *The Hedgehog and the Fox* (Simon and Schuster, 1953), p. 1. Berlin, using the concept first developed by the Greek poet, Archilochus, writes, "The fox knows many things, but the hedgehog knows one big thing," how to escape capture by the fox. Hoover, Harding's favorite, never enjoyed the same success with Coolidge.

35. White's *Puritan in Babylon* must figure, along with Allen's *Only Yesterday,* as the two most entertaining accounts of the United States in the 1920s, an era tailor-made for those who appreciated the necessity for wit and satire.

36. Both Hoover and Coolidge shared this distinction, but so, also, did Roosevelt, Taft, and Wilson.

37. Patterson, *Mr. Republican,* p. 141. It is interesting to note that those Taft believed would be chagrined by Hoover's victory included *Time* and *Life,* both owned by Henry Luce, considered by many a Republican, as well as the left-leaning *New Republic* and *Nation.*

38. Both "progressivism" and "socialism," still seemingly vital in 1924, were no longer robust, indeed barely alive in prosperous 1928.

39. Stimson was certainly Hoover's most inspired appointment, his performance at State was never stellar, rarely acknowledged by his many ardent admirers, though more or less admitted by one of his principal biographers. See Elting E. Morison, *Turmoil and Tradition: A Study of the Life and Times of Henry L. Stimson* (Houghton Mifflin, 1960), p. 450.

40. Kindleberger, *World Depression,* p. 134.

41. Steel, *Lippmann,* pp. 287–288. Lippmann wrote: "Everything he touches seems to sour on him. And yet I cannot quite bring myself to condemn him completely. For underneath all his failures, there is a disposition in this administration to rely on intelligence to a greater degree than at any time, I suppose, since Roosevelt. Hoover seems to be the victim partly of bad luck, partly of a temperamental weakness in dealing with irrational political matters, and partly of bad advice in matters where he has no personal experience."

42. President's Research Committee on Social Trends, *Recent Social Trends in the United States* (Greenwood, 1970), p. 1, a 1,500-page report, originally published in 1933, stands as a testament to what a group of distinguished social scientists were able to do to analyze major social and economic transformations. Coming out when it did, it offered no help to Hoover in resolving the problems created by the world economic Depression.

43. Hoover never overcame his suspicion of Europe or his contempt for what Europeans tried to do in 1919.

44. Hoover, while recognizing the hazards of the excessive speculation of the late 1920s, was helpless in seeking to warn against such practices.

45. Hobsbawm, *Age of Extremes,* pp. 85–108. "Into the Economic Abyss," chapter 3, of this imaginative but tendentious study, merits careful study by all who seek to understand what is implied in his words: "The Great Slump confirmed intellectuals, activists and ordinary citizens in

the belief that something was fundamentally wrong with the world they lived in. Who knew what could be done about it? Certainly few of those in authority over their countries, and certainly not those who tried to steer a course by the traditional navigational instruments of secular liberalism or traditional faith, and by the charts of the nineteenth century which were plainly no longer to be trusted."

46. Henry L. Stimson and McGeorge Bundy, *On Active Service, in Peace and War* (Harper, 1947), p. 188. Few statements in this book are more interesting than those made in explaining how and why Secretary Stimson came to close down the so-called Black Chamber, the State Department's code-breaking office. The relevant passage reads: "In 1929 the world was striving with good will for lasting peace, and in this effort all nations were parties. Stimson, as Secretary of State, was dealing as a gentleman with gentlemen sent as ambassadors and ministers from friendly nations and, as he later said, 'Gentlemen do not read each other's mail.'"

47. Hoover, *Memoirs,* vol. 3, p. 101.

48. Piers Brendon, *The Dark Valley: A Panorama of the 1930s* (Knopf, 2000), p. 85.

49. Ibid. Toynbee saw "the world crisis of 1931. . . as comparable to the World War of 1914."

50. See Stimson and Bundy, *Service,* p. 258.

51. Ibid. Because both the president and the country were opposed to sanctions, Stimson saw as his only course the "moral" one, hoping "it would lay a firm foundation of principle upon which the Western nations and China could stand in a later reckoning."

52. Robert Skidelsky, *John Maynard Keynes: The Economist as Savior, 1920–1937* (Macmillan, 1992), p. 489.

53. Schuker, *Foreign Policy,* in Haynes, *Coolidge,* p. 304.

54. Ibid.

CHAPTER 10 (The Savior)

1. Few presidents have been as fortunate in the historians who have written about their early lives as Franklin Roosevelt. Geoffrey C. Ward, *Before the Trumpet, Young Franklin Roosevelt, 1882–1905* (Harper and Row, 1985) may be the best biography written about the childhood, adolescence, and early adulthood of any American president.

2. Eleanor Roosevelt, though written about abundantly, has never had an historian of Ward's ability to comment on her life. Many of the more recent books, filled with conjecture about her purported sexual preferences, mostly conjectural, do not add much to our understanding of the most remarkable twentieth-century president's wife. See, for example, Blanche Wiesen Cook, *Eleanor Roosevelt* (Penguin Books, 1992), vol. 1, for the numerous references to Eleanor's relations with Lorena "Hick" Hickock whose correspondence stimulated the writing of the book. Cook's own perspective is admirably stated on page 13 where she writes: "In the case of her demonstrated ardour for Lorena Hickock, the denials have been high-strung and voluble; and ER's romantic love for her younger friend Earl Miller, which began when she was forty-five and he thirty-two, has been dismissed without hesitation. And yet it is now clear that ER lived a life dedicated to passion and experience. After the 1920s many of her closest friends were lesbian women. She honored their relationships, and their privacy. She protected their secrets and kept her own."

3. The "featherduster" was one of many unflattering characterizations of young Franklin.

4. A term that still had some meaning in early twentieth-century America.

5. Franklin Roosevelt was the first president to trade on the name of his distinguished and highly regarded presidential predecessor. John Quincy Adams made no comparable effort to profit from his association with his father, John Adams, the second president of the United States.

6. Theodore Roosevelt would have abominated the notion of being thought a "dandy," especially as that term came to be used in the nineteenth century. For an original and witty treatment of the subject, consult George Walden, *Who Is A Dandy?* (Gibson Square Books, 2002).

7. In this, as in many other ways, Franklin Roosevelt replicated the arguments first used by his distant cousin.

8. The same charge had been levelled at Theodore Roosevelt.

9. Franklin Roosevelt, in time, created his own court. When young, he assiduously courted others, those in a position to help him.

10. Geoffrey C. Ward, *A First-Class Temperament: The Emergence of Franklin Roosevelt* (Harper and Row, 1989), pp. 216–218. This book, which carries the Roosevelt story through his governorship, is no less stimulating though somewhat less compelling than his first.

11. Ibid., p. 200. When one considers the difficulties "Uncle Theodore" had in securing the same post, one can only say that Franklin seemed to live a charmed life. See also Frank Freidel, *Franklin D. Roosevelt: The Apprenticeship* (Little, Brown, 1952), p. 155.

12. The story of Roosevelt's relations with his mother, told in every biography, are nowhere more sensitively treated than in Ward's *Before the Trumpet.*

13. Ward, *Temperament,* p. 217.

14. Ibid., p. 217.

15. An ambitious politician, both young and vigorous, who chose to avoid military service might incur a heavy penalty with a patriotic electorate, and Roosevelt, aware of this, sought to avert the danger.

16. Conrad Black, *Franklin Delano Roosevelt: Champion of Freedom* (Weidenfeld and Nicholson, 2003). This massive biography, partial to Roosevelt as a political leader, is deliberately provocative and contentious. Black makes no effort to conceal Roosevelt's penchant for telling lies, a calculated dissembler in the tradition of his Roosevelt predecessor, a point Black does not choose to make.

17. Ward, *Temperament,* pp. 470–471.

18. Black, *Roosevelt,* p. 119. Black writes: "Given Hoover's espousal of the League, it is hard not to attribute his adherence to the Republicans to rank political opportunism." That charge, in my view, is not substantiated by the evidence.

19. Ward, *Temperament,* p. 487.

20. Ibid., p. 488.

21. Ibid., pp. 488–489.

22. Ibid., p. 509.

23. Ibid., pp. 511–512.

24. There can be no question that Roosevelt remained loyal to the Wilson ideal for the League of Nations, believing in it profoundly in 1920.

25. Black, *Roosevelt,* pp. 131–132. Roosevelt pretended not to be downhearted by his defeat; it was only a pose.

26. So far as I know, this point has never been made by any of Roosevelt's biographers, but it may have been as important in shaping his life as the explanations that dwell, correctly, on how his suffering changed his character and personality.

27. Had the news of Roosevelt's "affair" leaked at the time when Harding's sexual activities became the prime subject of a prying press, this would have been a catastrophe for the bed-ridden Roosevelt, and would have ended his hopes for a political career.

28. Even the best of Roosevelt's biographers find it difficult to describe the despair Roosevelt must have felt at this time, a strong virile man in the prime of life reduced to the condition of an invalid, wholly dependent on others.

29. Ward, *Temperament,* p. 699.

30. Ibid., p. 785.

31. Roosevelt, like his cousin, drew fire from those who chose to underestimate him, believing he would be wounded by their criticism. More than Theodore, Franklin developed a thick skin very early.

32. The best account of his years as governor is to be found in Kenneth S. Davis, *The New York Years, 1928–1933* (Putnam, 1972).

33. Frank Freidel, *Franklin D. Roosevelt: A Rendezvous with Destiny* (Little, Brown, 1990), p. 61. Arthur Schlesinger called the Freidel volume "the best single-volume biography of our greatest President." That accolade, still valid today, is challenged only by Black's more tendentious and passionate study.

34. Ibid., p. 62.

35. Black, *Roosevelt*, p. 216.

36. Ibid., p. 213–214.

37. Steel, *Lippmann*, p. 292. To Newton Baker, he wrote an even more devastating critique in November 1931, saying: "I am now satisfied. . . that [Roosevelt] just doesn't happen to have a very good mind, that he never really comes to grips with a problem which has any large dimensions, and that above all the controlling element in almost every case is political advantage."

38. See Frank Freidel, "Election of 1932" in Schlesinger, *Presidential Elections*, vol. vii, pp. 2728–2729. These volumes, edited by Arthur Schlesinger Jr. have many excellent individual essays, none better than that written by Freidel.

39. Ibid., pp. 2729–2730. Some nineteen other parties challenged the Democrats and Republicans in 1932. Freidel writes: "All of these were insignificant side-shows, attracting little attention and fewer votes."

40. Ibid., pp. 2741–2744. The Republican Party platform, more than five times as long, (pp. 2744–2762), opened with an accolade to Hoover that read: "We have had in the White House a leader—wise, courageous, patient, understanding, resourceful, ever present at his post of duty, tireless in his efforts and unswervingly faithful to American principles and ideals" (p. 2745).

41. Ibid., p. 2741.

42. Ibid.

43. Ibid., p. 2743.

44. These were the conventional foreign policy ideals of the period.

45. Black, *Roosevelt*, pp. 270–271. Black notes that "400,000 spectators, more than half the population of greater Washington, covered forty acres of greensward beside the Capitol."

46. Ibid., p. 271. Black writes: "Many businessmen and people from similar backgrounds to the President's would shriek with outrage at his demagogy and what they saw as his dishonorable desertion of his own peers. They were unaware, as businessmen often are, especially in America, of the subtleties of politics—that Roosevelt had spared them the status of scapegoats hated and reviled by 80 percent of the population; that Roosevelt had made the country safe again for the wealthy."

47. *FDR's Fireside Chats*, edited by Russell D. Buhite and David W. Levy (Penguin Books, 1993), pp. 12–17. The whole of this fireside chat merits rereading; it suggests how early Roosevelt developed the radio technique that served him so well in the next twelve years.

48. *Fireside Chats*, p. 61.

49. Robert Skidelsky, *Keynes*, vol. 2, pp. 481–482.

50. A.J.P. Taylor, *English History, 1914–1945* (Oxford University Press, 1965), p. 335. Taylor, the distinguished English historian, always a curmudgeonly critic of prevailing opinion, saw no reason to criticize Roosevelt for what he had done. He wrote: "On 5 July President Roosevelt killed the conference by refusing to stabilize the dollar, which he had previously taken off gold and devalued as part of the New Deal. After some lamentations, the conference adjourned for ever. The age of pious platitudes, as MacDonald once called it, was running down."

51. Black, *Roosevelt*, pp. 361–362. When Roosevelt signed the Neutrality Act of 1935, he praised the "wholly excellent" purpose of the legislation, but warned that its "inflexible provisions might drag us into war rather than keep us out."

52. Felix Gilbert, *To the Farewell Address: Ideas of Early American Foreign Policy* (Princeton University Press, 1961), p. 135. This, the most imaginative study ever made of Washington's ad-

dress, led Gilbert to write: "The political separation of America from the European power struggle was strengthened by changes which took place in Europe. Nationalism and industrialism shifted the interests of the European powers, and the competition among them into new channels. Thus, in the nineteenth century, conditions came into existence under which America's foreign policy could become a policy of isolation."

53. William L. Langer and S. Everett Gleason, *The Challenge to Isolationism, 1937–1940* (Harper, 1952). It would be difficult to overstate the value of this volume by Langer and Gleason, and of the one that followed, *The Undeclared War, 1940–41* (Harper, 1953). Indeed, when one looks at foreign policy studies published since, one can almost say that these two volumes spell the end of diplomatic history as that discipline had been developed by scholars in the United States like William Langer and in the United Kingdom by Sir Charles Webster. Langer and Gleason, profiting from their service during the war in the Office of Strategic Services, the predecessor to the Central Intelligence Agency, were able to secure full access to the documents of the State Department, but also, enjoying the confidence of the major figures who served Roosevelt, profited greatly from their disclosures.

54. Langer and Gleason, *Isolationism*, p. 16. Though immensely respectful of what Roosevelt sought to accomplish once domestic affairs no longer claimed all his attention, gazing at the administration's performance at the London Economic Conference of 1933, they call it "a case of almost unpardonable bungling."

55. This point is too rarely made.

56. Langer and Gleason, *Isolationism*, p. 17. This is not the view of Langer and Gleason who write: "Secretary Hull, perusing daily the many well-informed and discerning telegrams that flowed into the State Department from American representatives abroad, was probably more keenly aware than the President of the evil omens over Europe and perhaps more fully convinced that the United States could not stand wholly aloof. But the Secretary had no more thought than the President of committing this country to any positive course of political or military action. His concern was largely with the moral content and principles of international relations and how these could be saved from complete destruction."

57. The plan to "pack" the Supreme Court, the words used by Roosevelt's critics, and by a good segment of the press, may have been his major political blunder during his more than twelve years in the White House. The most authoritative study of the issue is by William E. Leuchtenberg, *The Supreme Court Reborn* (Oxford University Press, 1995).

58. *Fireside Chats*, pp. 106–110.

59. Ibid., 112–121.

60. Ibid., p. 118.

61. Black, *Roosevelt*, pp. 460–461.

62. *New York Times*, August 15, 1936, p. 4.

63. *New York Times*, October 6, 1936, p. 1.

64. *Times* (London), October 6, 1937, p. 15.

65. *The Secret Diary of Harold L. Ickes: The Inside Struggle 1936–1939, vol. 2* (Simon and Schuster, 1954), p. 213.

66. Langer and Gleason, *Isolationism*, pp. 1–10. This introduction is an incomparable analysis of Roosevelt's habits, why he took so few men into his confidence, and why, in their words, his attitude toward the State Department could scarcely be termed "gracious." Resembling the earlier Roosevelt, unmentioned by Langer and Gleason, "he did not, in the pre–Pearl Harbor years, take Congressional leaders into his confidence so far as foreign relations were at issue (p. 8)." Following in the tradition set by both Roosevelt and Wilson, again unmentioned in this connection, "his practice . . . was to appeal not to the good sense of Congress, but to that of the country at large."

67. *Fireside Chats*, pp. 125–135.

68. Ibid., pp. 133–135.

69. Black, *Roosevelt*, pp. 458–459. Roosevelt's foes spoke of his effort to "purge" his enemies, hoping, in Black's words, "to assimilate his behaviour to that of Hitler and Stalin."

70. *New York Times*, January 5, 1939, p. 16.

71. The official statement, issued over Sumner Welles's signature—the acting secretary of state in Hull's absence—was even more hostile in its condemnation of "acts of wanton lawlessness and of arbitrary force . . . threatening world peace and the very structure of modern civilization." Kenneth S. Davis, *FDR, Into the Storm, 1937–1940, A History* (Random House, 1993), p. 426. Davis referred to the statement as "a predictable, ritualistic, impotent condemnation."

72. Black, *Roosevelt*, pp. 515–519. As an intended snub to Mussolini, who was not officially head of state, the letter to Mussolini went over Hull's signature, and was declared "absurd" by Il Duce who had no use for "messiah-like messages." Hitler responded in a two-hour-long speech, ridiculing the letter, saying privately that he was reluctant to answer a "communication from a creature so contemptible as the present President of the United States."

73. Davis, *FDR*, pp. 427–428.

74. Ibid., pp. 420–421.

75. Ibid., p. 440.

76. Ibid.

77. Winston S. Churchill, *The Gathering Storm* (Houghton Mifflin, 1948), p. 440. Roosevelt wrote to Churchill on September 11, 1939, just days after the outbreak of war, expressing his pleasure that Churchill was again back in the Admiralty. Roosevelt said: "Your problems are, I realise, complicated by new factors [different from those that existed in the First World War] but the essential is not very different. What I want you and the Prime Minister to know is that I shall at all times welcome it, if you will keep me in touch personally with anything you want me to know about. You can always send sealed letters through your pouch or my pouch." It is inconceivable that Wilson would have sent such a letter to any English politician in August, 1914.

78. Winston S. Churchill, *Their Finest Hour* (Houghton Mifflin, 1949), p. 24.

79. *Churchill and Roosevelt: The Complete Correspondence*, edited with Warren F. Kimball, 3 vols. (Princeton University Press, 1984), vol. 1, pp. 37–39.

80. Martin Gilbert, *Winston S. Churchill: Finest Hour 1939–1941* (Heinemann, 1983), p. 368.

81. Langer and Gleason, *Isolationism*, p. 474.

82. Ibid., pp. 520–521. Langer and Gleason describe the differences within the War Department on whether such a transfer could be safely made, given their possible need for America's defense, with the secretary of war, Harry Woodring, soon to be replaced, supported by General Marshall, chief of staff, objecting strenuously to any transfer of destroyers.

83. John Charmley, *Churchill: The End of Glory—A Political Biography* (Hodder and Stoughton, 1993), p. 440. Charmley, accepting that Churchill seemed to be "the essential man in May and June 1940," suggests that he was no longer that a year later. A growing number of people, he argued, believed that it was "certainly better to be an American rather than a German protectorate," but "given that the war was being fought to preserve Britain's independence and a balance of power, that reflection was of little comfort to many Englishmen."

84. McGeorge Bundy, *Danger and Survival: Choices About the Bomb in the First Fifty Years* (Random House, 1988), p. 39.

85. See Robert E. Burke, "Election of 1940" in Schlesinger, *Presidential Elections*, vol. vii, pp. 2933–2937. James Farley's decision to oppose the third term and to seek the nomination himself ended a relation that had been politically advantageous to both. With historical hindsight, it is difficult to imagine Farley, the postmaster general and national chairman of the Democratic Party, in the White House during World War II.

86. Langer and Gleason, *Isolationism*, pp. 742–776, a chapter entitled "The Destroyer Deal," an excellent example of the scholarship that made their research so exemplary. They wrote: "From the standpoint of both friend and foe, then, the destroyer deal was a milestone in the development of American policy. The United States had obviously abandoned neutrality, and though Americans refused to recognize the new-fangled Fascist term, 'nonbelligerency,' had entered upon a status of 'limited war.'" (p. 775) Roosevelt caused all this to happen, acting more in the tradition of his cousin than of Wilson.

87. This speech, broadcast, utterly delighted the vast audience that heard it.

88. Corwin, *President*, pp. 232–234. Corwin, in these pages, gives a telling list of the actions taken by the administration, beginning with the passage of the Lend-Lease Act on March 11, 1941, and ending with the repeal on November 13 of all the restrictive clauses of the Neutrality Act of 1939 that allowed the United States to become a "quasi-belligerent" in the war.

89. Philip Ziegler, *London at War, 1939–1945* (Sinclair-Stevenson, 1995).

90. Doris Kearns Goodwin, *The Fitzgeralds and the Kennedys* (St. Martin's Press, 1987), pp. 614–617. Goodwin gives an arresting account of the Kennedy interview that caused him such difficulties.

91. *Fireside Chats*, pp. 163–173. This radio address, delivered on December 29, 1940, soon after his third-term election, introduced the idea of the United States as "the arsenal of democracy," and first broached, though in very general terms, the concept of "lend-lease."

92. Ibid., p. 166.

93. Ibid., p. 173.

94. Ibid. This, the most important foreign policy "fireside chat" Roosevelt ever gave, suggests the extent of Roosevelt's sense of liberation following his 1940 electoral victory.

95. Black, *Roosevelt*, pp. 605–606.

96. Patterson, *Taft*, pp. 242–244. Taft claimed that Roosevelt's words "were smoother than butter, but war was in his heart."

97. Black, *Roosevelt*, p. 614. Black writes: "He [Lindbergh] declined to express any preference or recognize any moral distinction between Britain and Germany. This pleased the galleries, which were filled with isolationists."

98. Ibid., pp. 609–610. Black notes: "Apart from Willkie, whose support of Lend-Lease was powerful and unwavering, most leading Republicans opposed Bill 1776, including Hoover, Landon, Dewey, Vandenberg, and Taft. The McCormick and Hearst newspapers were as shrill as they had been at their most frenzied during the New Deal, but the *New York Times*, the *Herald Tribune*, the *Christian Science Monitor*, and many other influential newspapers supported the administration."

99. Churchill, *Finest Hour*, p. 569.

100. Langer and Gleason, *Undeclared War*, pp. 537–547. These were among the most aggressive actions taken by Roosevelt before December 7, 1941.

101. *New York Times*, June 25, 1941, p. 1.

102. Robert E. Sherwood, *Roosevelt and Hopkins: An Intimate History* (Harper, 1948), pp. 314–315.

103. Ibid., pp. 316–317.

104. Ibid.

105. Ibid., p. 318.

106. Ibid., pp. 321–322.

107. Ibid., pp. 333–343. Sherwood prints large portions of the report Hopkins sent to Roosevelt on these conversations, of what Stalin said about the military problems the Soviet Union confronted and of its needs. Part III of his report, originally kept secret, "for the President only," expressed Stalin's view that only the entry of the United States into the war could bring about Hitler's defeat.

108. No one can seriously doubt that Hopkins greatly influenced Roosevelt in his views on Stalin, greatly reinforced by the president's deep regard for the bravery and suffering of the Russian people.

109. See Winston S. Churchill, *The Grand Alliance* (Houghton Mifflin, 1950), p. 435. Churchill prints a facsimile copy of the Atlantic Charter with his own corrections, as incorporated in the final version.

110. Black *Roosevelt,* p. 656.

111. Ibid., p. 660.

112. Ibid., p. 667.

113. *New York Times,* November 7, 1941, p. 1.

114. This action, coming when it did, suggested how much isolationist sentiment in Congress had subsided.

115. Roosevelt, like many of his successors, discovered that persuading Congress to appropriate funds for national defense was never very difficult.

116. Christopher Andrew, *For the President's Eyes Only: Secret Intelligence and the American Presidency from Washington to Bush* (HarperCollins, 1995), pp. 114, 119–120. Andrew cites Roberta Wohlstetter in her book, *Pearl Harbor: Warning and Decision* (Stanford University Press, 1962), calling it "a failure not of intelligence collection but of intelligence analysis." Andrew says that the Wohlstetter argument was mistaken, that more recent research suggests that "not a single Japanese decrypt available in Washington pointed to an attack on Pearl Harbor." He writes: "Since no mission abroad was given advance notice of the attack, Magic [the code-breaking mechanism] made no mention of it."

117. In these, as in so many other ways, Roosevelt showed his indebtedness to Wilson's First World War administrative inventions.

118. Black, *Roosevelt,* pp. 720–725. This action, described by Black as "one of the most discreditable episodes in the entire Roosevelt era," was not initially proposed by either J. Edgar Hoover, head of the F.B.I, or Francis Biddle, the attorney general, but by the Army. Black wrote: "In his memoirs, Stimson whitewashed the episode by dumping it onto Roosevelt, McCloy and the generals, and taking refuge in the legitimisation by the Supreme Court." Black, while seeking to absolve Roosevelt of blame, recognized that the action "did him no credit."

119. Churchill never suggests this in his own World War II histories, and the principal Roosevelt biographers, equally silent on the matter, generally ascribe the "cooling of relations" to a later period.

120. Elliott Roosevelt, *As He Saw It* (Duell, Sloan, and Pearce, 1946), pp. 15–16.

121. Charles de Gaulle, *The Complete War Memoirs: 1940–1946* (DeCapo Paperback, originally published by Simon and Schuster, 1946). For a very different view of Roosevelt's policy toward Free France, Vichy, and Darlan, see William L. Langer, *Our Vichy Gamble* (Norton, 1947), p. 398.

122. De Gaulle, *Memoirs,* pp. 349–381.

123. Ibid., pp. 349–350. Churchill, responding to de Gaulle's complaints, said: "We have been obliged to go along with them in this," and added, "Rest assured that we are not revoking any of our agreements with you."

124. Ibid., p. 361.

125. Ibid.

126. Ibid., p. 362.

127. Ibid., pp. 382–418. This must certainly figure as the most amusing chapter in de Gaulle's *Memoirs,* as well as one of the most serious.

128. Ibid., p. 392.

129. Ibid.

130. Ibid., pp. 230–234. On both Eden and Churchill, de Gaulle wrote perceptively, saying that Eden was "the favored child of English traditions," who showed "an openness of mind and

a sensitiveness that were European rather than insular, human rather than administrative." Of Churchill he said: "Though he felt, more than any other Englishman, the awkwardness of Washington's methods, though he found it hard to bear the condition of subordination which the United States aid placed the British Empire, and though he bitterly resented the tone of supremacy which the President adopted towards him, Mr. Churchill had decided, once and for all, to bow to the imperious necessity of the American alliance."

131. This was the first mention of "unconditional surrender" by Roosevelt.

132. Andrew, *President's Eyes Only*, pp. 137–138. This book must be regarded as one of the most sober treatments of how Roosevelt used secret intelligence during the war. He ran a great risk that the Japanese might learn from U.S. military actions that their codes had been broken.

133. By this time, the divergences were recognized by all who participated in the negotiations, though they were still unknown to the general public.

134. The situation, a growing fatigue with the war, that developed in World War I under Wilson asserted itself also under Roosevelt, and was to be increasingly conspicuous in all the wars the United States engaged in after 1945.

135. Black, *Roosevelt*, p. 822. Franklin, like Theodore, did not easily forgive those who crossed him. Commenting on the president's conflict with the leader of the miners, Black wrote: "It had become a personal grudge match between Roosevelt and Lewis, to which Roosevelt brought his full bag of tricks, including renewed harassment of Lewis from the Internal Revenue Service."

136. Ibid., pp. 926–927. Black writes: "The Joint Chiefs of Staff had urged Roosevelt to amend his unconditional surrender policy, because they thought it was serving the Nazis by encouraging a more tenacious resistance."

137. Frances Perkins, *The Roosevelt I Knew* (Viking, 1946), pp. 84–85.

138. Freidel, *Roosevelt*, pp. 512–514. Dr. Howard Bruenn, a Navy cardiologist, brought in by Anna Boettiger to investigate her father's obviously deteriorating health, was the first to recognize the gravity of his condition. His intervention almost certainly extended the president's life for a year.

139. *New York Times*, March 2, 1945, p. 12.

140. Sherwood, *Roosevelt and Hopkins*, p. 870. A much more sober account of the "constant military understandings and inconstant diplomatic compromises" reached at Yalta is available in Herbert Feis, *Churchill, Roosevelt, Stalin: The War They Waged and the Peace They Sought* (Princeton University Press, 1957).

141. David Mayers, *George Kennan and the Dilemmas of US Foreign Policy* (Oxford University Press, 1988), pp. 94–97. See, also, Charles E. Bohlen, *Witness to History, 1929–1969* (Norton, 1973), pp. 175–177, which gives part of the text of Kennan's letter and also Bohlen's reply, which ended with the words, "Either our pals intend to limit themselves or they don't. I submit, as the British say, that the answer is not yet clear. But what is clear is that the Soyuz [Soviet Union] is here to stay, as one of the major factors in the world. Quarrelling with them would be so easy, but we can always come back to that."

142. Bohlen, *Witness*, pp. 178–179. Roosevelt at Yalta, in a situation very different from that in Tehran, enjoyed a "State Department staff of about a dozen officers to back him up," but Bohlen notes that "as the conference progressed, it became obvious that Roosevelt had not studied the 'black books' as much as he might have . . . " Harry Hopkins, still his principal adviser, "was quite ill . . . and too ready to grant concessions in return for what he mistakenly thought were Soviet retreats."

143. Ibid., p. 201.

144. Bundy, *Danger and Survival*, p. 113. This is an essential text for those who seek a critical appraisal of Roosevelt's role in deciding to press for the development of the atom bomb, who seek to understand his refusal "to examine such questions of policy—or let others examine them—one step further than was immediately necessary."

145. G.M. Young, *Portrait of an Age* (Oxford University Press, 1936), p. 164.

CHAPTER 11 (The Creator)

1. David McCullough, *Truman* (Simon and Schuster, 1992). Truman, like Roosevelt, has been uncommonly fortunate in his biographers. No recent president has received a comparably judicious treatment by those who have set out to describe their lives and times.

2. This was also Eisenhower's dream, in his case fulfilled. Had Truman gone to West Point, his life would have been wholly different. He was the only twentieth-century president never to have gone to any university, although the institutions Harding and Johnson attended were very modest, and not only by "Ivy League" standards.

3. McCullough, *Truman*, p. 99.

4. Truman, always proud of his native state, placed great value on General Pershing's Missouri origins, as he did years later with General Omar Bradley.

5. McCullough, *Truman*, pp. 117–118. McCullough correctly gives great attention to Truman's military service; it made him the man he became.

6. Most other small businessmen, confronted with comparable problems, would have declared bankruptcy. Truman, a child of Victorian America, would never consider such action, believing it disgraceful.

7. Truman was the first (and only) twentieth-century president to have this sort of local political experience.

8. McCullough, *Truman*, pp. 208–209. Truman ran an exceedingly hard campaign, and Bennett Clark, Missouri's senator, the son of "Champ" Clark, Wilson's 1912 opponent, complained it was one of "mendacity and imbecility," that Truman never expected to win, and that his real interest was to secure a good county job when he retired as "judge" of Jackson County. Though Truman never forgot these insults, it did not prevent his supporting Clark when he considered running for president in 1940.

9. The Senate, as late as 1934, was filled with men who had started their lives on farms, always aware of the differences between them and "city folk."

10. McCullough, *Truman*, pp. 231–234.

11. Ibid., p. 237.

12. Ibid., pp. 239–240.

13. The sums are significant, very different from what became common in senatorial contests in the 1960s with the arrival of television.

14. McCullough, *Truman*, p. 241. McCullough writes: ". . . Roosevelt gave no endorsement or even encouragement, no help at all except to let the senator know in roundabout fashion that he would be glad to appoint him to a well-paid job on the Interstate Commerce Commission. 'Tell them to go to hell,' Harry responded. If he couldn't come back as a senator, he didn't want to come back at all."

15. Ibid., p. 285. To be on the cover of *Time* was no small distinction in the 1940s when that weekly boasted a large and influential readership.

16. Ibid., p. 286. *Look,* the rival to *Life,* Henry Luce's weekly, was never a serious competitor, but the honor awarded Truman by a vote taken among Washington correspondents was another no mean achievement.

17. Margaret Truman, *Harry S. Truman* (William Morrow, 1973), p. 9. It is significant that this letter, written in 1948, figures so prominently in the first pages of the book. Truman never deceived himself about either of the Roosevelts or about Franklin's children, but felt very differently about Eleanor.

18. Harry S. Truman, *Memoirs,* vol. 2, entitled "Years of Trial and Hope" (Doubleday, 1956), pp. 207–208. Truman referred to his announcement to recall Congress into "special session" before the 1948 election as his "trump card," confident that the "do nothing" Congress would perform as he claimed it always did.

19. Truman, *Truman,*, pp. 14–15. Needless to say, these remarks were reserved for his desk calendar; he would never have been so indiscreet as to make them public.

20. Harry S. Truman, *Memoirs,* vol. l, entitled "Year of Decisions" (Doubleday, 1955), pp. 41–42. The speech, a brief one, ended with the words: "I ask only to be a good and faithful servant of my Lord and my people."

21. Ibid., vol. 1, pp. 328–329. This was a characteristic though understated expression of Truman's intention to avoid the Roosevelt example, having no wish to intervene in all departments, greatly reducing the importance of the Cabinet.

22. Ibid., p. 331.

23. Bundy, *Danger and Survival,* pp. 61–62. Roosevelt, persuaded by Stimson and Marshall that American casualties in any campaign to subdue the Japanese homeland would be enormous, made it seem reasonable to make major concessions to Stalin to assure his entry into the war immediately after Hitler's defeat.

24. Stimson, as secretary of war, informed Truman about the bomb days after his assumption of the presidency, a secret kept from him until then.

25. Bohlen, *Witness,* p. 240.

26. Truman, *Memoirs,* vol. 1, pp. 332–412. The Potsdam Conference received more attention in Truman's *Memoirs* than any other single subject, though his observations on the meeting were neither very original nor at all self-critical.

27. Hugh Thomas, *Armed Truce: The Beginnings of the Cold War, 1945–46* (Hamish Hamilton, 1986). This volume, expressing considerable skepticism about the new foreign policy team in Washington, led by Truman, was especially caustic about James Byrnes, his secretary of state.

28. Truman, *Memoirs,* vol. 1, pp. 537–538.

29. James G. Hershberg, *James B. Conant: Harvard to Hiroshima and the Making of the Nuclear Age* (Knopf, 1993), pp. 251–257.

30. Truman, *Memoirs,* vol. 1, pp. 415–419. Truman never denied that he was alone responsible for the decision to bomb Hiroshima.

31. Hershberg, *Conant,* p. 251.

32. Ibid.

33. Ibid., p. 257.

34. Dean Acheson, *Present at the Creation: My Years in the State Department* (Norton, 1969), p. 135.

35. Ibid., p. 136. Acheson wrote: "Driving from the airfield to the Department with the Secretary, I broke to him gently the President's displeasure. He was disbelieving, impatient, and irritated that Mr. Truman had sailed down the Potomac on the *Williamsburg,* leaving word for him to follow. . . . Afterward both men gave me accounts of their meeting. The President's report was even more vivid than the one published in his memoirs. . . . Mr. Byrnes's account could not have been more different. To him the discussion was informative on his side and pleasant on the President's. They parted with affectionate mutual good wishes for the new year. Mr. Byrnes thought me an imaginer of trouble where none existed. Both impressions were quite possibly entirely genuine. On most occasions Mr. Truman's report of his bark vastly exaggerated it."

36. Truman, *Memoirs,* vol. 1, pp. 547–549.

37. Ibid., p. 549.

38. Ibid., pp. 551–552. Truman published the whole of the memorandum he purportedly read to Byrnes, clearly wishing his readers to know how profound was his disenchantment with the Soviet Union, and how very early he registered his complaints about their behavior with his secretary of state.

39. Ibid., p. 552.

40. Ibid.

41. Ibid., p. 554.

42. Ibid., pp. 553–555.

43. Ibid., pp. 555–560. To his sister and mother, the president wrote: "Well I had to fire Henry today, and of course I hated to do it. . . . Henry is the most peculiar fellow I ever came in contact with."

44. This was as aggressive a speech as any that Stalin had made since the start of the war in 1941.

45. George Kennan, *Memoirs, 1925–50* (Pantheon, 1967), pp. 547–559. The full text of the telegram, dated February 22, 1946, is published here.

46. Roy Jenkins, *Churchill* (Macmillan, 2001), p. 813.

47. Truman, *Truman*, p. 309.

48. Ibid.

49. Ibid., p. 312.

50. Ibid., pp. 313–315. Margaret Truman, showing scant sympathy for either Henry Wallace or Claude Pepper, condemned both for their attacks on her father's foreign policy, saying that "Wallace lacked what the French called *mesure* and what Missourians call common sense."

51. See McCullough, *Truman*, pp. 480–482 and 492–506, for a full discussion of the strikes and how they affected the president's morale and his standing in the country.

52. Ibid., p. 506. McCullough writes: "He was denounced as the country's number one strikebreaker, called a Fascist, a traitor to the union movement."

53. Patterson, *Mr. Republican*, p. 313.

54. Ibid. Taft, rarely a rabble-rouser in the manner of Nixon, said that Truman sought the "support of . . . the Communists in the November election," and looked for a Congress "dominated by a policy of appeasing the Russians abroad and of fostering Communism at home."

55. McCullough, *Truman*, p. 520. Dewey, McCullough writes, made this plea "on the eve of Yom Kippur, the Day of Atonement, what struck many as a bald play for the Jewish vote in New York. . . ."

56. Ibid., pp. 520–522. These pages, admirable for their description of the 1946 off-year election campaign, document the obloquy heaped on Truman by the Republicans and of the growth of public anxiety about "Reds" and "parlor pinks."

57. Ibid., p. 523.

58. This insult became common again when Albright first served as the American ambassador to the United Nations.

59. McCullough, *Truman*, pp. 531–532.

60. Ibid., p. 532.

61. Truman, *Memoirs*, vol. 1, p. 476.

62. Ibid., pp. 479–480.

63. Robert Skidelsky, *John Maynard Keynes, Fighting for Britain 1937–1946* (Macmillan, 2000), p. 438.

64. Ibid., pp. 403–458. The negotiations were grim, described in great detail by Skidelsky, but they inspired at least one memorable ditty,

"In Washington, Lord Halifax
Once Whispered to J.M. Keynes,
'It's true they have the money bags,
But *we* have all the brains!'"

65. Alan Bullock, *The Life and Times of Ernest Bevin*, vol. 3 (Heinemann, 1983), pp. 368–369.

66. Acheson, *Creation*, p. 221. Acheson stresses the rapidity with which all the major decisions were made about the appropriations that would be asked for.

67. *New York Times*, March 13, 1947, p. 1.

68. Louis W. Koenig, editor, *The Truman Administration: Its Principles and Practice* (New York University Press, 1956), p. 299.

69. Steel, *Lippmann,* pp. 438–439. The administration resented Lippmann's criticism, and Steel reports that he and Acheson argued furiously about the wisdom of the policy at a dinner party where Acheson accused Lippmann of "sabotaging" American foreign policy. Interestingly, there was some division in the State Department as well about the wisdom of the policy. See Bohlen, *Witness,* p. 261. Bohlen wrote: "The Soviet Union was not mentioned by name, but there was no question that the basic aim of the doctrine was to stop Soviet efforts to undermine the free nations through subversion. It seemed to General Marshall and to me that there was a little too much flamboyant anti-Communism in the speech. Marshall and I felt that Truman was using too much rhetoric. Marshall cabled our thoughts back to Washington. He received a reply that in the considered opinion of the executive branch, including the President, the Senate would not approve the doctrine without the emphasis on the Communist danger."

70. Patterson, *Mr. Republican,* pp. 344–345. Taft characterized Lilienthal as a "typical power-hungry bureaucrat," who had run the T.V.A. in a "secretive and arbitrary manner," and was "soft on the subject of Communism." Taft lost his battle to deny Lilienthal his confirmation.

71. Corwin, *President,* pp. 118–123. Corwin writes that the order "was not improbably designed in part to head off more drastic action by Congress itself."

72. Bohlen, *Witness,* p. 263. Bohlen accompanied Marshall on his visit to Stalin, and a full account of the conversation was sent to the president. Marshall, deeply troubled by what he had heard, viewed it as the sort of crisis that communism thrived on. In Bohlen's words, "All the way back to Washington, Marshall talked of the importance of finding some initiative to prevent the complete breakdown of Western Europe. On our return, Marshall instructed the new Policy Planning Staff, which he had set up under George Kennan, to take on as its first task an examination of European recovery and the role the United States could play in the process."

73. Forrest C. Pogue, *George C. Marshall: Statesman, 1945–1959* (Viking, 1987), p. 217.

74. Bulloch, *Bevin,* vol 3, p. 405.

75. Pogue, *Marshall,* p. 213.

76. Bohlen, *Witness,* p. 264. Bohlen wrote the greater part of the speech.

77. McCullough, *Truman,* p. 583.

78. See Truman, *Truman,* p. 343. Truman biographers have reason to wonder when Truman first became suspicious of the Soviet Union, and how much his advisers contributed to his education in that regard. In this connection, a letter sent to Margaret, written on March 13, 1947, must be thought significant; his daughter called it "one of the most important letters my father ever wrote me." In characteristic Truman prose, he wrote. "I knew at Potsdam that there is no difference in totalitarian or police states, call them what you will, Nazi, Fascist, Communist or Argentine Republics. You know there was but one idealistic example of Communism. That is described in the Acts of the Apostles. . . . The attempt of Lenin, Trotsky, Stalin, et al., to fool the world and the American Crackpots Association, represented by Jos. Davies, Henry Wallace, Claude Pepper and the actors and artists in immoral Greenwich Village is, just like Hitler's and Mussolini's so-called socialist state. Your pop had to tell the world just that in polite language."

79. Adam Ulam, *Expansion and Coexistence: The History of Soviet Foreign Policy 1917–67* (Praeger, 1968), p. 452.

80. W. Phillips Davison, *The Berlin Blockade* (Princeton University Press, 1958). This is still the best book on the blockade that seemed so threatening at the time.

81. Bulloch, *Bevin,* vol. 3, pp. 606–607.

82. McCullough, *Truman,* pp. 874–875. Churchill returned the compliment, when once again prime minister he visited Washington in January 1952. At a dinner on board the *Williamsburg,* he said: "The last time you and I sat across the conference table at Potsdam, Mr. President, I must confess, sir, I held you in very low regard then. I loathed your taking the place of Franklin Roosevelt." Pausing, he added: "I misjudged you badly. Since that time, you more than any other man, have saved Western civilization."

83. Though Truman felt no special esteem for Britain's prime minister, Clement Attlee, both he and Acheson greatly valued Bevin's assistance and counsel.

84. Yergin, *Prize*, pp. 406–407. Yergin writes: "Forrestal was one of the first senior policymakers to conclude that the United States had to organize itself for a protracted confrontation with the Soviet Union. Oil held a central place in Forrestal's strategy for security in the postwar world. . . . The largest known oil reserves outside the United States were in the area of the Persian Gulf. . . . The State Department should work out a program to substitute Middle Eastern Oil for American oil . . . and use its 'good offices' to promote the expansion of United States holdings abroad, and to protect such holdings as already exist, i.e., those in the Persian Gulf area."

85. Hansard, House of Commons Debates, 12 December 1947, col. 1395.

86. Truman, *Truman*, pp. 384–385. Writing a vigorous defense of her father's policy in respect to Israel, vehemently denying that politics played any role in his decision, Margaret Truman cited many of her father's letters, none more interesting than the one he sent to Eleanor Roosevelt on August 23, 1947. He wrote: "The action of some United States Zionists will eventually prejudice everyone against what they are trying to get done. I fear very much that the Jews are like all underdogs. When they get on top they are just as intolerant and as cruel as the people were to them when they were underneath. I regret this situation very much because my sympathy has always been on their side."

87. *New York Times*, March 21, 1948. The article was entitled: "The Switch on Palestine."

88. Truman, *Truman*, p. 388.

89. Clark Clifford, with Richard Holbrooke, *Counsel to the President: A Memoir* (Random House, 1991), pp. 3–25. Clifford opens his more than 700-page memoir with a chapter entitled "Showdown in the Oval Office," documenting his quarrel with Marshall over the issue of Palestine and the recognition of the state of Israel. He notes that Marshall was supported by almost all those who later came to be known as the "Wise Men," including Lovett, Acheson, Bohlen, Kennan, Forrestal, and Rusk (p. 4).

90. McCullough, *Truman*, p. 616.

91. Ibid., pp. 617–618. See also, Pogue, *Marshall*, p. 377. Marshall felt so strongly about the Clifford intervention that he never forgave him and never spoke to him again, indeed never mentioned his name.

92. Truman, *Memoirs*, vol. 2, pp. 51–52.

93. Merle Miller, *Plain Speaking: An Oral Biography of Harry S. Truman* (Berkley Medallion Books, 1974), pp. 419–420. Miller, asking Truman what he thought of the creation of the CIA, for which he was responsible, heard him say: "I think it was a mistake. And if I'd known what was going to happen, I would never have done it. . . . But it got out of hand. The fella . . . the one that was in the White House after me never paid any attention to it, and it got out of hand. Why, they've got an organization over there in Virginia now that is practically the equal of the Pentagon in many ways. And I think I've told you, one Pentagon is one Pentagon too many. Now, as nearly as I can make out, those fellows in the CIA don't just report on wars and the like, they go out and make their own, and there's nobody to keep track of what they're up to. They spend billions of dollars on stirring up trouble so they'll *have* something to report on. . . . They don't have to account to anybody. That's a very dangerous thing in a democratic society and it's got to be put a stop to. The people have got a right to know what those birds are up to."

94. Andrew, *President's Eyes Only*, pp. 171–172. Acheson, in *Present at the Creation*, makes no mention of the efforts to influence the Italian elections, and the CIA figures scarcely at all in his account, very different from that given by Andrew.

95. Ibid., p. 173. David Mayers, in his laudatory study of Kennan, makes no mention of NSC 20, but emphasizes Kennan's opposition to NSC 68 which alleged an imminent Soviet threat to the United States.

96. Harry A. Millis and Emily Clark Brown, *From the Wagner Act to Taft Hartley: A Study of National Labor Policy and Labor Relations* (University of Chicago, 1950). This book, though more than half a century old, remains one of the best introductions to issues relating to both Democratic and Republican policies on labor issues.

97. He profited greatly from having the support of Senator Vandenberg and other Republicans who rarely shared Senator Taft's views on foreign policy.

98. See H. Stuart Hughes, *Gentleman Rebel* (Ticknor and Fields, 1990), p. 207. The supporters of the Wallace candidacy proved to be fewer in number than many expected. Stuart Hughes, a Harvard professor at the time, and grandson of the former chief justice, gives eloquent testimony of his disenchantment with Wallace, whom he initially supported.

99. McCullough, *Truman,* pp. 586–587. Truman delivered a civil rights message to Congress on February 2, 1948, based on the findings of his Civil Rights Commission. McCullough says that it was "the strongest such program that had ever been proposed by a President."

100. Arthur M. Schlesinger Jr., *The Vital Center: The Politics of Freedom* (Houghton Mifflin, 1949). This may be the best expression of A.D.A. philosophy at the time, anti-Communist and fervently loyal to the "New Deal."

101. Few thought to compare this elevation of the World War II military hero with those who had once opted for Herbert Hoover, the great humanitarian figure of World War I, hoping he might prove to be a Democrat.

102. McCullough, *Truman,* p. 587.

103. Ibid., pp. 589–590. Nothing that Truman wrote or said ever indicated how he weighed the importance of these several constituencies, but Clark Clifford, for one, was persuaded that his civil rights' stance would help him; it was morally and politically the right policy to pursue.

104. Richard S. Kirkendall, "Election of 1948" in Schlesinger, *Presidential Elections,* vol. viii, pp. 3099–3145. This is an extraordinarily perceptive essay on the 1948 election by a professor of history at the University of Missouri. It informs much of what I have written on the election.

105. McCullough, *Truman,* p. 651. He issued another executive order that day, guaranteeing fair employment in the civil service. McCullough writes: "His reception when he appeared before Congress the next day was noticeably cool. (As a show of their resentment, some members did not even rise from their seats as he entered.)"

106. He offended a number of Republicans, including Senator Vandenberg, by never acknowledging all they had done to support his foreign policy.

107. McCullough, *Truman,* pp. 660–668. McCullough is expert in giving extracts from many of Truman's feisty speeches during the campaign that made such a deep impression on those who heard them.

108. Richard J. Walton, *Henry Wallace, Harry Truman, and the Cold War* (Viking, 1976), p. 181.

109. Ibid., p. 182.

110. McCullough, *Truman,* p. 680. McCullough writes: "With his headlong lambasting of Wall Street and 'the special interests,' the constant harkening to grim memories of the Depression, he sounded often as if he were running against Herbert Hoover."

111. Having witnessed the small Roosevelt inaugural at the White House with one of my war veteran friends, Ben Paul Noble, invited to attend by Mrs. Roosevelt, his report to me of the Truman inaugural—I was abroad, studying in England at the time—suggested that the two events could not have been more different. Margaret Truman had been enormously helpful to us in securing her father's support for our efforts to create a veterans' organization at George Washington University.

112. McCullough, *Truman,* pp. 729–730.

113. Ibid., p. 726. McCullough writes: "On Wednesday, January 5, 1949, he went to the Hill to deliver his State of the Union message to the 81st Congress, calling again for the same progressive social measures he had championed the year before, except he now had a new name for

his domestic program, 'the Fair Deal,' a name he had coined himself, and unlike January 1948, when almost no one was listening, everyone now paid close attention." Two days later, in an emotionally charged news conference, he announced the retirement of Marshall.

114. Miller, *Plain Speaking*, pp. 242–243.

115. McCullough, *Truman*, p. 894.

116. Acheson, *Creation*, pp. 254–263. This chapter, entitled "The World That Lay Before Us" recounts how the world appeared to Acheson when he became secretary of state. More interesting, is his chapter, "A Reappraisal of Policies," (pp. 344–353) that comes immediately before the most personal chapter in the book, "The Attack of the Primitives Begins," (pp. 354–361) that tells of McCarthy's initial attacks on the State Department. These attacks all preceded the outbreak of war in Korea.

117. Acheson from almost his first days in office experienced difficulties considerably more serious than any faced by Marshall.

118. McCullough, *Truman*, pp. 741–742. McCullough wrote that "Louis Johnson was possibly the worst appointment Truman ever made."

119. Bundy, *Danger*, p. 199.

120. Ibid.

121. Ibid., pp. 197–235. In this very perceptive chapter, "To Have Thermonuclear Weapons—and Other Truman Choices," Bundy makes clear that the final decision was Truman's alone, following the advice offered by others.

122. Ibid., p. 197.

123. Acheson, *Creation*, pp. 355–356. These remarks were made by Acheson in a National Press Club speech, delivered on January 12, 1950, entitled "Crisis in China—An Examination of United States Policy."

124. McCullough, *Truman*, pp. 769–770. Originally, Truman refused the request of the Tydings Committee, a special subcommittee of the Senate Foreign Relations Committee, to come to the White House to look at the files of the 81 named by McCarthy, but when he relented and allowed them to come, hoping this would end the Republican calumny that he was "covering up" evidence, this only resulted in many believing that the president, like so many others, had capitulated to McCarthy.

125. James Chace, *Acheson: The Secretary of State Who Created the American World* (Simon and Schuster, 1998), p. 277. Chase writes: "The State Department contingent was united in its support of the paper. . . . Acheson, while he harbored some doubts as to the value of the document, favored the study. . . . Both Charles Bohlen and George Kennan were highly critical of the scant attention paid to Soviet intentions rather than Soviet capabilities. Both men found the description of Soviet aims oversimplistic, and thought it would lead to the conclusion, as Bohlen put it, that 'war is inevitable.'"

126. Mayers, *Kennan*, p. 181. After the start of the Korean hostilities, Kennan's hostility to NSC 68 became even more intense. Mayers writes: ". . . Kennan—unlike Acheson, Nitze, and many in the Defense Department—never viewed events in Korea as preliminary to generalized Soviet military incursions either in Europe or the Far East. Contrary to the majority view, he also maintained that the underlying assumptions in NSC 68 were not confirmed by Korea and that the Soviets were merely taking advantage of a specific target of opportunity; they still lacked the desire and material wherewithal to expand the scope of Korean hostilities into something approximating a third world war."

127. Both George Kennan and Walter Lippmann, from their very different perspectives, criticized NSC 68.

128. Henry Kissinger, *Diplomacy* (Simon and Schuster, 1994), pp. 462–463. Kissinger describes NSC 68 as "America's official statement on Cold War strategy," and suggests that despite

its "ostensibly hardheaded realism," it was essentially a statement of moral principles. The country, having "convinced itself that it was relatively weak militarily," a fiction in fact, accepted the NSC 68 recommendations to build up its military potential.

129. The administration's grasp of Asian affairs was always weak.

130. Kissinger, *Diplomacy*, p. 474. Korea had been declared "outside America's defense perimeter" just a year earlier.

131. Ibid., p. 475. Kissinger explains that it was not strategic considerations that led Truman to act as he did; he saw himself as fulfilling the country's moral obligation to resist Communist aggression.

132. The knowledge about Korea was minimal; the president knew little; Acheson knew scarcely more; and the president never had in his entourage anyone who could advise him on the subject. For Taft and many Republicans critical of Truman, the issue was essentially political.

133. Kissinger, *Diplomacy*, pp. 478–481. Kissinger writes: "America thus found itself in a limited war for which it had no doctrine and in defense of a distant country in which it had declared it had no strategic interest. Beset by ambivalence, America perceived no national strategic interest in the Korean peninsula; its principal aim was to demonstrate that there was a penalty for aggression." On MacArthur, he said: "Although MacArthur was a brilliant strategist, he was less perceptive as a political analyst" (p. 480).

134. McCullough, *Truman*, pp. 820–821.

135. C.R. Attlee, *As It Happened* (Viking Press, 1954), pp. 280–282. Attlee made no mention of Truman's press conference in his autobiography but wrote: "There was considerable support in America for an extension of the war. Some people were anxious for a showdown with Russia. MacArthur was a Republican and a possible future candidate for the Presidency, and this, I think, led to insufficient control of his activities. . . . Our view had always been that the Far Eastern war should be confined to Korea and that it would be a great mistake to have large forces committed to a major campaign in Asia. We also realized how important it was that a contest between the forces of the United Nations and aggressor states should not become a fight between Europeans and Asiatics. We had recognized the Chinese Republic as being the real and effective government of China, but the Americans continued to support the discredited government of Marshal Chiang Kai-shek and to protect his forces in Formosa."

136. Truman, *Memoirs*, vol. 2, pp. 446–450. Truman wrote: "The kind of victory MacArthur had in mind—victory by the bombing of Chinese cities, victory by expanding the conflict to all of China—would have been the wrong kind of victory."

137. The Korean War, unlike the later war in Vietnam, has not generated a significant scholarly literature, certainly none that expresses the kind of political criticism common during Truman's time in the White House. I have relied largely on two books, Clay Blair, *The Forgotten War: America in Korea, 1950–1953* (United States Naval Inst., 2003) and Max Hastings, *The Korean War* (Simon and Schuster, 1987).

138. Acheson, *Creation*, pp. 725–737. This is an affectionate and almost uncritical eulogy of a president who always protected his secretary of state against his critics.

139. Peter Hennessy, *The Secret State: Whitehall and the Cold War* (Penguin, 2003).

140. Ibid., p. 1.

141. The World War II veterans, more than those who fought in Korea and Vietnam, took advantage of the GI Bill to secure an education that would otherwise have been denied them. The legacies of these three wars, in this as in so many other ways, were very different.

142. For especially acute observations on Truman's national security policies, see Melvyn P. Leffler, *A Preponderance of Power: National Security, The Truman Administration, and The Cold War* (Stanford University Press, 1992).

CHAPTER 12 (The General)

1. The only substantial biography of Eisenhower, written by Stephen E. Ambrose, is somewhat uncritical, excessively adulatory, representing Eisenhower as "great and good," one of the "outstanding leaders of the Western world in this century." Ambrose, *Eisenhower*, vol. I, p. 10.

2. Football, more than any other West Point sport, carried the possibility of national fame at that time and for decades thereafter.

3. It is interesting to speculate whether Eisenhower would ever have achieved his later military position had his injury not prevented him from being made a cavalry officer.

4. Eisenhower resembled his younger brother, Milton, to whom he was devoted. Like him, he married above his social station, and profited greatly from the hospitality Milton was able to provide in Washington, D.C., during the years he served in the Department of Agriculture.

5. Promotion counted for a great deal in the Army, providing higher salaries, of course, but other perquisites as well, none more important than housing.

6. Those who went abroad achieved higher rank earlier, though these promotions were awarded on a temporary basis only.

7. Ambrose, *Eisenhower*, vol. I, p. 85.

8. Ibid., p. 91. The commission, created in 1930, with Secretary of War Patrick J. Hurley as its chairman, was told "to study and consider amending the Constitution" so as to take the profits out of war, the overwhelming bugaboo of congressmen who persisted in believing that America had been inveigled into World War I by rapacious individuals, whose one interest was to acquire wealth.

9. Ibid., pp. 93–96. Ambrose suggests, correctly, that Eisenhower was never a MacArthur protégé, that he observed him closely but never accepted his political opinions.

10. Ibid., p. 97.

11. Such differences, while figuring in private conversation with fellow officers, were of course never expressed in public. Even MacArthur, to whom the press gave considerable attention, showed discretion in his political pronouncements at that time.

12. Ambrose, *Eisenhower*, p. 116.

13. Ibid.

14. There is no evidence to suggest that Eisenhower before his dispatch to England in 1941 claimed many European friends or acquaintances.

15. Ambrose, *Eisenhower*, pp. 138–141. The jealousy on MacArthur's part, watching his subordinate rise above him, largely because of the influence of Marshall, is scarcely surprising.

16. Ibid. As was evident later with Montgomery, Eisenhower could never abide criticism; he deeply resented MacArthur's implicit and explicit denial of his talents.

17. Ibid., pp. 138–139. MacArthur believed that Marshall and Eisenhower could have done a great deal more to support the U.S. forces isolated on Bataan, a charge that offended Eisenhower who confided to his diary, "In many ways MacArthur is as big a baby as ever. But we've just got to keep him fighting."

18. A.J.P. Taylor, *English History, 1914–1945* (Oxford University Press, 1945), pp. 553–554. Taylor writes: "Most American leaders, including Marshall, chief of the army staff, and Stimson, the secretary for war, had no interest in the British policy of nibbling at the edges. They wanted a direct assault on Germany, and their advocacy was strengthened in May 1942 when Molotov, the Soviet foreign minister came to London and Washington with an urgent demand for a second front. Churchill dared not go directly against the Americans. If he did, they might turn their backs on Europe and concentrate on the Pacific war. On 14 April therefore the British and American staffs agreed to prepare for a large-scale landing in France. The Americans admitted that this could only be ready in 1943."

19. Neither Marshall nor Eisenhower ever understood what the British interest in the Mediterranean was, and could only believe that it reflected Churchill's penchant for protecting his country's imperial interests.

20. Why neither Marshall nor Eisenhower perceived this remains something of a mystery even now.

21. Admiral King, always suspicious of the British, and aware of how crucial the Navy would be in any effort to defeat Japan, was one of the more ardent advocates of a policy to give the Pacific war priority.

22. Eisenhower had landed in England only a month earlier, and Churchill, in failing to invite him to Chequers, did not deliberately snub him.

23. These words, spoken to Mark Clark, were recorded by Harry Butcher, Eisenhower's unofficial public relations officer, his great friend and confidante, in a diary entry on July 23, 1942.

24. See Robert E. Persico, *Roosevelt's Secret War: FDR and World War II Espionage* (Random House, 2001), p. 208. Marshall, seeking to understand why the president pressed for a campaign in North Africa that his military chiefs opposed said later "that the leader in a democracy has to keep the people entertained. That may sound like the wrong word, but it conveys the thought."

25. Ibid., pp. 209–215. Roosevelt's intelligence sources, including that provided by the Office of Strategic Services (OSS) under the leadership of William ("Wild Bill") Donovan, predicted a "cakewalk," but the invasion proved to be anything but that. The Americans lost some 1,500 men, killed, wounded, or missing in the first days of the operation. Roosevelt, having resisted the advice of his military advisers, saw the action as a military success, and took great pride in having placed such trust in Donovan and the OSS.

26. See Robert Murphy, *Diplomat Among Warriors* (Doubleday, 1964), pp. 164–166.

27. Stephen E. Ambrose, *The Supreme Commander: The War Years of General Dwight D. Eisenhower* (Doubleday, 1970), p. 130. Churchill's tolerance for collaborating with men sympathetic to Vichy never included Admiral Darlan, a man he considered detestable.

28. Jean Lacouture, *De Gaulle: The Rebel, 1890–1944* (Norton, 1990), p. 406.

29. Forrest C. Pogue, *George C. Marshall: Organizer of Victory, 1943–1945* (Viking, 1973), pp. 21–22.

30. Alanbrooke, *War Diaries, 1939–1945* (Weidenfeld and Nicolson, 2001), pp. 315 and 359. King had long argued for a "Pacific first" policy, but it was only at Casablanca that the extent of his disagreement with the policies favored by the British became fully apparent. Alanbrooke, writing in his diary of Marshall's disagreement with the British proposal for a landing in Sicily, said: "I then asked them to explain their views as to the running of the Pacific War. Admiral King then did so, and it became clear at once that his idea was an 'all-out' war against Japan instead of holding operations. He then proposed that 30 per cent of the war effort should be directed to the Pacific and 70 per cent to the rest. We pointed out that this was hardly a scientific way of approaching war strategy."

31. Ibid., p. 343. Alanbrooke's comments on Eisenhower were always scathing, never more so than when he wrote in one of the addenda to his diary: "It must be remembered that Eisenhower had never even commanded a battalion in action when he found himself commanding a group of armies in North Africa! No wonder he was at a loss as what to do, and allowed himself to be absorbed in the political situation at the expense of the tactical. I had little confidence in his having the ability to handle the military situation confronting him, and he caused me great anxiety." A very detailed refutation of Brooke's views and of the other British officers critical of Eisenhower is provided by Eric Larrabee, *Commander in Chief: Franklin Delano Roosevelt, His Lieutenants, and Their War* (Harper & Row, 1987).

32. Alanbrooke, *War Diaries*, p. 365.

33. Ibid., p. 367. Alanbrooke regarded the Casablanca Conference as very satisfactory from the British point of view; in his diary, he wrote: "I wanted first to ensure that Germany should continue to be regarded as our primary enemy and that the defeat of Japan must come after that of Germany. Secondly that for the present Germany can best be attacked through the medium of Italy in the Mediterranean, and thirdly that this can best be achieved with a policy directed against Sicily. All these points have been secured, and in addition many minor ones connected with Turkey, command of operations in Tunisia and at home, etc."

34. Ambrose, *Eisenhower*, p. 264.

35. Ibid. Eisenhower was furious with Marshall for making this criticism.

36. Ibid., p. 265. Churchill, unlike Marshall, congratulated Eisenhower for "running risks," and Eisenhower proudly passed the message on to Marshall.

37. Dwight D. Eisenhower, *Crusade in Europe* (William Heinemann, 1948), pp. 283–285.

38. Alanbrooke, *Diaries*, p. 575.

39. Ibid.

40. Ibid. See also Ambrose, *Eisenhower*, p. 360 where he writes of the contempt Montgomery felt for Eisenhower, and the increasingly bitter disputes between them, with Montgomery expressing his negative sentiments openly. Eisenhower, replying to him by letter, wrote: "I most definitely appreciate the frankness of your statements, and usual friendly way in which they are stated [sic], but I beg you not to continue to look upon the past performances of this great fighting force as a failure merely because we have not achieved all that we could have hoped."

41. Eisenhower, *Crusade*, p. 389. Eisenhower made no mention of these criticisms, writing only of a telegram he received from Marshall, referring to "articles in certain London papers proposing a British deputy commander for all your ground forces and implying that you have undertaken too much of a task yourself." Marshall wrote: "My feeling is this: under no circumstances make any concessions of any kind whatsoever. I am not assuming that you had in mind such a concession. I just wish you to be certain of our attitude. You are doing a grand job, and go on and give them hell." Eisenhower, replying, said: "You need have no fear as to my contemplating the establishment of a ground deputy."

42. Alanbrooke, *Diaries*, p. 628.

43. Ibid., p. 644.

44. Ibid., p. 669. Alanbrooke, in his diary, wrote: "Breakfast with Ike and another long talk with him. There is no doubt that he is a most attractive personality and at the same time a very limited brain from a strategic point of view. This comes out the whole time in all conversations with him. His relations with Monty are quite insoluble, he sees only the worst side of Monty and cannot appreciate the better side." Needless to say, such conversations with Brooke figured not at all in what Eisenhower wrote in *Crusade in Europe*, but in his one effort to portray him (p. 185), he wrote that he was "adroit rather than deep, and shrewd rather than wise." Comparing him with Marshall, he noted that "he lacked that ability . . . to weigh calmly the conflicting factors in a problem and so reach a rock-like decision." Still, he was "easy to work with," a "brilliant soldier."

45. Ibid., p. 679.

46. Eisenhower, *Crusade*, p. 436. Eisenhower provides no information on the texts of these telegrams to Stalin in his *Crusade in Europe*, saying simply, "This general plan was presented to Generalissimo Stalin."

47. Ibid., pp. 436–440. Eisenhower gave almost complete texts of his telegraphic exchanges with Marshall, saying: "May I point out that Berlin itself is no longer a particularly important objective. Its usefulness to the Germans has been largely destroyed and even his government is preparing to move to another area."

48. Ambrose, *Eisenhower*, p. 394.

49. Ibid., pp. 394–395. Ambrose, determined to defend Eisenhower's decision, offered only a tiny segment of the correspondence, omitting all the most crucial arguments. For the fuller text, one must consult Winston Churchill, *Triumph and Tragedy* (Houghton Mifflin, 1953), pp. 405–411.

50. It was this phrase that greatly offended Eisenhower.

51. Ambrose, *Eisenhower*, p. 395.

52. Ibid., p. 397.

53. Ibid.

54. Ibid., p. 398. See also, Eisenhower, *Crusade*, p. 440. Marshall, in his telegram to Eisenhower on March 31, indicated that his "single objective should be quick and complete victory," and that he "should continue to communicate freely with the Commander-in-Chief of the Soviet Army," explicitly repudiating the British suggestions that he had no right to do so.

55. Dwight D. Eisenhower, *At Ease: Stories I Tell to Friends* (Doubleday, 1967), pp. 264 and 268.

56. Ambrose, *Eisenhower*, p. 403. This is one of the few instances when Ambrose, however obliquely, suggested that Eisenhower may have been less than wholly truthful.

57. Ibid., pp. 403–404.

58. Eisenhower, *Crusade*, pp. 313–314.

59. *Crusade in Europe* sold exceedingly well, and Eisenhower became a rich man, having written a book that celebrated the achievements of a great military alliance. While his British military colleagues showed no reluctance to deny their differences with him, the politicians were much more reticent.

60. Eisenhower, *Crusade*, p. 453.

61. Miller, *Plain Speaking*, pp. 340–341.

62. Ibid., p. 341.

63. Ibid.

64. Ibid.

65. Ibid., pp. 337–340.

66. Ibid., p. 339.

67. Ibid., p. 340.

68. Ibid.

69. Ambrose, *Eisenhower*, p. 415.

70. Ibid., pp. 409–410.

71. Ibid., pp. 480–489. Eisenhower clearly found the Columbia presidency boring, and Ambrose dwells on why the faculty thought him "hopelessly naïve," and why he found them so unsatisfactory, seeking only to produce "exceptional scholars" when his concern was to make students "better citizens." For an interesting critique of Eisenhower's short time at Columbia, see Travis Beal Jacobs, *Eisenhower at Columbia* (Transaction, 2001).

72. Patterson, *Mr. Republican*, pp. 477–478.

73. Ibid., pp. 483–484.

74. Ibid., p. 484.

75. Ambrose, *Eisenhower*, p. 522. Ambrose acknowledged Eisenhower's coyness in refusing to "confirm Lodge's claim that he was a Republican," while admitting that "he did vote for that party." Without explicitly approving what the "Citizens for Eisenhower" were doing to place his name on the primary ballot in New Hampshire, he spoke of all Americans being free to "organize in pursuit of their common convictions," making it clear he would not ask for release from his duties at NATO "to seek nomination for political office."

76. Barton J. Bernstein, "Election of 1952" in Schlesinger, *Elections*, p. 3227.

77. Ibid.

78. Ibid., p. 3228.

79. Ibid., p. 3229.

80. Ibid.

81. Ibid., p. 3230.

82. Ibid.

83. Ibid., p. 3231.

84. Patterson, *Mr. Republican,* pp. 576–578.

85. Ibid., pp. 578–579.

86. Ibid.

87. D.W. Brogan, *An Introduction to American Politics* (Hamish Hamilton, 1954), p. 76. Brogan makes the interesting observation that "the states, the classes, the individuals that went for General Eisenhower in 1952 were not the states, the classes, the individuals (by and large) that went for Governor Thurmond. They were much more like the Hoovercrats of 1928." Brogan saw that a two-party system was in the making in the South, in Texas, Virginia, and Georgia, and recognized that "these conservative Democrats would be forced into their true home, the Republican Party."

88. The Dulles appointment was the most significant made by Eisenhower, and it is well to remember that Dulles, in the words of William Leuchtenberg, was "a man who disliked Roosevelt, whom Roosevelt detested." See the chapter on Eisenhower in William E. Leuchtenberg, *The Shadow of FDR: From Harry Truman to Ronald Reagan* (Cornell University Press, 1983), pp. 41–62, especially pp. 55–57.

89. Patterson, *Mr. Republican,* p. 578.

90. Stephen E. Ambrose, *Eisenhower: The President,* vol. II (Simon and Schuster, 1984), p. 19.

91. Ibid. In the war, Churchill and Roosevelt, Eisenhower believed, "had frequently been more of a hindrance than a help, and what they were able to accomplish was only possible because of the dedicated staff work of thousands of others." Ambrose recognizes that Eisenhower saw himself as one of those others.

92. Townsend Hoopes, *The Devil and John Foster Dulles* (Little, Brown, 1973), pp. 172–173. The speech contained numerous passages that spoke of Eisenhower's idealism, asking for a peace "throughout Asia as throughout the world. . . that is true and total." In the president's plea for disarmament, he hoped that "a substantial portion of the savings achieved" through that policy might be used to create "a fund for world aid and reconstruction." It is scarcely surprising, given the presence of such statements, that the *New York Times* called it a "magnificent and deeply moving" peace initiative.

93. Bohlen, *Witness,* pp. 371–372.

94. John Lukacs, *Churchill: Visionary, Statesman, Historian* (Yale University Press, 2002), p. 82.

95. McGeorge Bundy, *Danger and Survival* (Random House, 1988), pp. 238–239. Bundy notes that both Eisenhower and Dulles "believed that clear indications of a greater readiness to use nuclear weapons would increase the chances of an acceptable truce."

96. Ibid., p. 246.

97. Ibid.

98. Ibid., p. 253. Bundy's observations on "The New Look and its Nuclear Import" describe a president who "held to the view that any war between the Soviet Union and the United States would in fact be a nuclear war, and if that war ever came, he knew what he intended to do."

99. Ibid., pp. 255–257.

100. Ibid., p. 256.

101. John Colville, *The Fringes of Power: Downing Street Diaries 1939–1955,* (Hodder and Stoughton, 1985), p. 654.

102. Ibid., p. 672.

103. Bundy, *Danger*, p. 244.

104. Ibid.

105. Ibid.

106. Ibid.

107. Ibid., p. 247. Eisenhower believed he understood the significance of nuclear weapons as others, civilians, did not. Any large-scale attack in Europe would be met by strategic nuclear attack on the Soviet Union.

108. Ibid., p. 260.

109. Ibid., p. 261.

110. See Raymond Aron, *The Imperial Republic, The United States and the World* (Winthrop, 1974), p. 180. Aron, citing what Eisenhower wrote in 1963, that if Vietnam fell, the catastrophe whould be enormous, suggested that the "domino theory" was "designed for consumption by an ill-informed public."

111. Bundy, *World*, p. 265.

112. Ibid., p. 271.

113. Dominique Enright, *The Wicked Wit of Winston Churchill* (Michael O'Mara Books, 2001), p. 73. See also Lord Moran, *Churchill: Taken from the Diaries of Lord Moran: The Struggle for Survival, 1940–1965* (Houghton Mifflin, 1966), p. 380. Though this is the most witty of Churchill's comments on Dulles, his contempt for him knew no bounds, and the Moran diaries are filled with his criticisms of a secretary of state he depicted as "a dull, unimaginative, uncomprehending, insensitive man; so clumsy, I hope he will disappear."

114. Ambrose, *Eisenhower*, vol. II, p. 208.

115. Hoopes, *Devil and Dulles*, pp. 238–239.

116. Ibid., p. 239. Dulles, dissatisfied with some elements of the Geneva accords, refused to sign the Final Declaration, which in turn led all the other potential signatories to follow suit.

117. Ibid.

118. Ambrose, *Eisenhower*, vol. II, p. 209. Eisenhower, fearing that the loss of North Vietnam to the Communists would be viewed adversely by many Republicans, made a point of indicating at a news conference that "the United States has not itself been a party to or bound by the decisions taken."

119. Robert Dallek, *Lone Star Rising: Lyndon Johnson and his Times, 1908–1960* (Oxford University Press, 1991), pp. 459–460.

120. Ibid., p. 460.

121. Ibid., p. 461.

122. Clearly, Eisenhower's first two years in office had not given the electorate very great satisfaction.

123. Bundy, *World*, p. 273. Bundy, writing about both the 1954–1955 crisis over Quemoy and Matsu, and that of 1958, said: "To many critics at the time, and to most students in retrospect, what is most notable about these two crises is that Eisenhower and Dulles should have declared a major American interest in the defense of these islands. A lively prospect of open conflict with China, let alone a possibility of nuclear war, over these trivial bits of land struck many as preposterous."

124. Ambrose, *Eisenhower*, vol. II, pp. 285–286.

125. Ibid., pp. 227–228 and 340–341.

126. Ibid., p. 261.

127. Ibid., p. 267. Ambrose, always seeking to find cause to praise Eisenhower, writes: "As Dulles had warned would be the case, nothing had been settled at Geneva. But as Eisenhower had determined would be the case, Geneva produced an intangible but real spirit that was felt

and appreciated around the world. The year following Geneva was the calmest of the two decades of the Cold War."

128. Ibid., p. 264.

129. Ibid., p. 266.

130. Harold Macmillan, *Tides of Fortune, 1945–1955* (Macmillan, 1969), p. 622.

131. Ambrose, *Eisenhower*, vol. II, p. 266.

132. This may have been the most notable event of his first administration.

133. The introduction of the televised news conference, a major innovation, spelled the end of the more informal conferences made memorable by Roosevelt.

134. Leuchtenberg, *Shadow of FDR*, p. 59. The first "hundred days" had not been especially productive; as Joseph C. Harsch, a journalist, had written: "Dwight D. Eisenhower's public performance during the First Hundred Days of his Presidency has been so at variance with his adherents' more extravagant campaign forecasts of a 'new broom' sweeping out the 'rascals' in a vast purge of the personalities and policies of the past that the net result almost seems to be a man whanging golf balls at the White House back fence while history flows around him."

135. See David M. Oshinsky, *A Conspiracy So Immense: The World of Joe McCarthy* (Free Press, 1983), perhaps the best of the many accounts written of this sordid episode.

136. Ibid., p. 507. Oshinsky writes: "He [McCarthy] could have been stopped rather quickly. Robert Taft, J. Edgar Hoover, Dwight D. Eisenhower–any of them could have halted McCarthy, but all of them had reasons for remaining supportive or simply aloof."

137. This may have been the most important immediate political consequence of the televised hearings.

138. See James T. Patterson, *Grand Expectations: The United States, 1945–1974* (Oxford University Press, 1996), pp. 270–271. Eisenhower's domestic achievements were so minimal that liberals, in Patterson's words, "had a field day making fun of him," and some dubbed him "Eisen-Hoover."

139. Dallek, *Lone Star*, p. 463. Johnson argued for bipartisanship in domestic as in foreign policy, insisting only that Eisenhower pay for this cooperation by allowing the Democrats to have a voice in major decisions taken.

140. See Malcolm Moos, "Election of 1956" in Schlesinger, *Presidential Elections*, vol. viii, p. 3386. The Party's platform, quoting Abraham Lincoln, represented Eisenhower as following his wise dictum that "The legitimate object of Government is to do for a community of people whatever they need to have done but cannot do at all, or cannot so well do, for themselves in their separate and individual capabilities. But in all that people can individually do as well for themselves, Government ought not to interfere."

141. Ibid., p. 3419. Eisenhower, in his acceptance speech, said: "I am not here going to attempt a eulogy of Mr. Nixon. You have heard his qualifications described in the past several days. I merely want to say this: that whatever dedication to country, loyalty and patriotism can do for America, he will do–and that I know."

142. Ibid., pp. 3347–3348.

143. Ibid., pp. 3415–3416. Stevenson, in his own acceptance speech, said: "I say that what this country needs is not propaganda and a personality cult. What this country needs is leadership and truth, and that's what we mean to give it. What is the truth? The truth is that the Republican party is a house divided. The truth is that President Eisenhower, cynically coveted as a candidate but ignored as a leader, is largely indebted to Democrats for what accomplishments he can claim."

144. Eisenhower was never able to translate his popularity into gains for the Republicans in the House or Senate, a condition that testified to the continued repute of the Democrats, still profiting from public recollection of the accomplishments of the Roosevelt and Truman administrations.

145. See Patterson, *Expectations,* p. 309. While many American scholars doubted that Eisenhower and Dulles had demonstrated skill in their handling of Suez and Budapest, others, including James Patterson, were satisfied with their performance in those crises.

146. Ambrose, *Eisenhower,* vol. II, p. 315. Eden, meeting Eisenhower in Washington in January, had hinted that he thought Nasser would have to be removed. Ambrose wrote of the president's surprise at this. He wondered why Eden had lost confidence in Nasser.

147. Percy Cradock, *Know Your Enemy: How the Joint Intelligence Committee Saw the World* (John Murray, 2002), pp. 109–134. This chapter, entitled "Suez, 1956" must figure as one of the most imaginative analyses of that event.

148. Ambrose, *Eisenhower,* vol. II, p. 317.

149. Ibid., p. 318.

150. D.R. Thorpe, *Eden: The Life and Times of Anthony Eden, First Earl of Avon, 1897–1977* (Chatto and Windus, 2003), pp. 503–504.

151. Ambrose, *Eisenhower,* vol. II, p. 338.

152. Thorpe, *Eden,* p. 513.

153. Ibid.

154. Ambrose, *Eisenhower,* vol. II, pp. 340–341. U–2 flights over Eastern Europe had begun the previous spring.

155. Adam Ulam, *The Rivals: America and Russia Since World War II* (Viking, 1971), p. 265. Ulam wrote: "From the beginning of the disturbances, the United States made it clear that it would support the cause of the Hungarian people *solely* through action in the United Nations and through appeals to world opinion. At one level this was both humane and realistic: one ought not to arouse false hopes which could only lead more Hungarians to sacrifice their lives or freedom vainly. At yet another level, it was both impolitic and shameful."

156. Ibid., pp. 245–248.

157. William Taubman, *Khrushchev: The Man and his Era* (Norton, 2003), p. 284.

158. Ulam, *Rivals,* p. 244.

159. Andrew, *President's Eyes,* p. 231.

160. Ibid., pp. 233–238. Andrew writes: "Ike was so much in the dark that he speculated that 'the hand of Churchill' rather than of Eden, might be behind the British Suez adventure, since it was 'in the mid-Victorian style.'"

161. Piers Brendon, *Ike: The Life and Times of Dwight D. Eisenhower* (Secker and Warburg, 1957), p. 328. See also, Denis Healey, *The Time of my Life* (Michael Joseph, 1989), p. 171. Healey, opposed to the war, as all Labour Party politicians were, writes: "Among the many mysteries of Suez is how the Cabinet could allow Eden to remain Prime Minister during the most serious crisis which had faced Britain since the war, although they knew he was physically ill and mentally unbalanced. . . . "

162. Cradock, op. cit., p. 132. The vote was scarcely a surprise, given what Cradock writes of the "dramatic wastage of government resources through secrecy, duplicity, and sheer muddle."

163. Eisenhower lacked the strategic sense that might have told him that it was impossible for the Soviet leaders to pursue action in the Middle East when their troops were so heavily engaged in putting down the revolt in Hungary.

164. Thorpe, *Eden,* pp. 529–531.

165. Ambrose, *Eisenhower,* vol. II. pp. 316–317. Eisenhower never had in his entourage men able to claim an intimate acquaintance with the Middle East, and when he thought to engage in personal diplomacy, he chose to send Robert Anderson, a Texas oil tycoon, to try to make peace between Egypt and Isreal.

166. Hoopes, *Devil,* pp. 329–332 and 336–342. Dulles excused himself by claiming that he acted only in response to congressional pressures, that he refused to be "blackmailed" by Nasser. These explanations never satisfied his critics.

167. See Anthony Eden, *Memoirs: Full Circle* (Cassell, 1960), Book III, "Suez," pp. 419–584, especially p. 540, which offers his defense of a policy that saw the United States, not the Soviet Union or any Arab state take the lead in the UN Assembly debate.

168. Andrew, *President's Eyes,* pp. 224–225. Andrew writes: "At least for a time, Eden seems to have been attracted by the possibility of a covert action to assassinate Nasser. Eisenhower was not."

169. Kissinger, *Diplomacy,* p. 547. See, also, Cradock, *Enemy,* p. 132, who reports that Adenauer said the same thing to the French premier, Guy Mollet. The role of the Suez crisis in cementing Franco-German relations may have been one of its most important results.

170. Taubman, *Khrushchev,* p. 380.

171. Ambrose, *Eisenhower,* vol. II, pp. 381–383.

172. The Eisenhower Doctrine enjoyed a modest repute in its day, and has since been largely forgotten.

173. Ambrose, *Eisenhower,* vol. II, p. 372. Henry Cabot Lodge, the United States ambassador to the United Nations, told Eisenhower that "there is the feeling at the U.N. that for long years we have been exciting the Hungarians through our Radio Free Europe, and now that they are in trouble, we turn our backs on them," to which the president replied, "We have never excited anybody to rebel." Dulles, from his hospital bed, following major surgery, informed of the conversation, assured the president "we always said we are against violent rebellion."

174. Bundy, *Danger,* pp. 234–235. Sputnik persuaded many in the United States that the Soviet Union did indeed lead in long-range ballistic missile development, and that a "missile gap" existed.

175. Dallek, *Lone Star,* p. 529. Senator Symington of Missouri took the lead in proposing an inquiry, and Johnson joined him, understanding the potential advantage to himself and the Democratic Party in making the space issue central.

176. Ibid., pp. 531–532. The hearings served greatly to enhance Johnson's reputation.

177. Eisenhower found it always difficult to change course, and when he did almost always pretended that he had not done so.

178. His opposition reflected two of his fundamental political beliefs: the federal government ought not to involve itself in a field that traditionally fell within the jurisdiction of the states; economic prudence made novel federal appropriations always suspect.

179. Alistair Horne, *Macmillan, 1957–1986: The Official Biography* (Macmillan, 1989), vol. 2, p. 22. These are all Macmillan diary entries.

180. Ibid.

181. Ibid.

182. Ibid., p. 23.

183. Ibid. The pact made the United States the guarantor of the defense of states once protected by Great Britain.

184. Ibid.

185. Ambrose, *Eisenhower,* vol. II, pp. 469–471. These events in Iraq were to have the gravest consequences for the United States for the rest of the twentieth century, and to deal with them, Eisenhower chose not to summon the whole National Security Council, but to bring together "an informal group of key advisers" to meet in his office. Robert Cutler, present at this small meeting, described the president as "the most relaxed man in the room," knowing exactly what he wanted to do, which was to move into Lebanon, "to stop the trend toward chaos."

186. Ibid., p. 471. Ambrose wrote: "Thus did Eisenhower unleash the American military for the only time in his Presidency."

187. Taubman, *Khrushchev,* p. 402. Khrushchev, delighted by the Iraqi revolution, told Nasser, Egypt's president, visiting Moscow at the time, "The situation is highly dangerous, and I think the people with the strongest nerves will be the winners."

188. Horne, *Macmillan*, vol. 2, p. 98.

189. Ulam, *Rivals*, p. 280.

190. *New York Times*, June 5, 1958.

191. Taubman's biography of Khrushchev remains the absolutely essential source for the description of the Soviet Union's deteriorating relations with China, a matter that neither concerned nor preoccupied the president and his secretary of state.

192. This is but one additional proof of the innocence of the Eisenhower administration on issues relating to China.

193. Bundy, *Danger*, p. 527. Bundy's observations on this crisis are arresting; he wrote: "What was happening on both sides, we may now conclude, was that threatening words were used not so much to warn of action truly intended as to give the appearance of determination. The strong words on both sides were not so much a warning of action as a substitute for it. But if each side's rhetoric had a large role in stimulating the rhetoric of the other, there was an important difference in the eventual consequences. When one party has nuclear weapons and the other does not, exchanges of menace do not have equal weight. It is hard to avoid the conclusion that the precipitant of Mao's decision to have a bomb was a genuine perception of the Americans as nuclear bullies."

194. Taubman, *Khrushchev*, p. 403. Because U.S. relations with Germany were growing closer, Khrushchev's great fear was that Germany would be given nuclear weapons by the United States, causing his own prestige to fall dramatically.

195. Kissinger, *Diplomacy*, p. 513. The Rapacki Plan, in Kissinger's view, would have "traded German integration into the West for Soviet withdrawal from East Germany and parts of Eastern Europe which, unless coupled with guarantees against Soviet intervention to protect Communist regimes, would have led to a dual crisis: one in Eastern Europe, and another in finding a responsible international role for Germany, which had proved elusive since its unification in 1871."

196. Taubman, *Khrushchev*, pp. 361–395, a remarkable chapter entitled: "Alone at the Top, 1957–1960."

197. Ibid., pp. 397–339. Khrushchev made this announcement at the first press conference he ever convened on America's Thanksgiving Day. Eisenhower, learning of the statement, told his son that if he surrendered to Khrushchev, "no one in the world could have any confidence in any pledge we make." Should the efforts to defend West Berlin lead to war, he said, ". . . we are not going to be betting white chips, building up gradually. Khrushchev should know that when we decide to act, our whole stack will be in the pot." This was bravado, a threat substantially modified a few days later when he referred to the crisis as an "instance in which our political posture requires us to assume military positions which are wholly illogical," representing the American position on Berlin as a "can of worms."

198. Horne, *Macmillan*, pp. 121–128.

199. Lacouture, *De Gaulle, The Ruler, 1945–1970*, pp. 392–393.

200. While the creation of the Common Market was certainly not the result of the Suez crisis, the yearning for closer Franco-German unity became more salient with the return of de Gaulle to power.

201. Kissinger, *Diplomacy*, p. 581. This statement by Gray, injudicious in every respect, suggests why few remember him today. While Kissinger does not dwell on the weakness of Eisenhower's foreign policy team, it would be difficult to argue the contrary.

202. Ibid.

203. This was always a major Eisenhower concern.

204. Taubman, *Khrushchev*, p. 446. Khrushchev believed initially that Eisenhower was not personally responsible for the flight, and that "rogue elements in the military and the CIA were."

When he learned the truth he expected an apology from Eisenhower who would then "sit still for a show trial of the captured American pilot."

205. Michael R. Beschloss, *Mayday: Eisenhower, Khrushchev and the U-2 Affair* (Faber, 1986).

206. Horne, *Macmillan*, p. 221. Macmillan, reporting to the foreign secretary, Selwyn Lloyd, on his visit with Eisenhower told him that he clearly believed the position in Cuba "was becoming intolerable, but . . . realized the difficulties of *overt* action."

207. Andrew, *President's Eyes*, pp. 251–256.

208. This was one of the most acute observations Truman made of a man he knew had lost touch with his humble origins.

209. The British knew Eisenhower well, and though few were greatly impressed with his mind, almost all admired his genial personality. Macmillan, as aware of his weaknesses as Churchill, sought to wean him away from his excessive dependence on Dulles and never succeeded in that objective.

CHAPTER 13 (The Boy Wonder)

1. Kennedy's inaugural address, even more than Roosevelt's in 1933, filled with memorable phrases, contributed greatly to establish his reputation as someone who intended to bring new vigor and ideas into government.

2. The issue of age, like that of religion—Kennedy having finally broken the tradition that only Protestants could serve in the highest office—had great appeal for journalists, happy to see the end of the static rule of Eisenhower.

3. Robert N. Bellah, "Civil Religion in America" in William G. McLoughlin and Robert N. Bellah, editors, *Religion in America* (Houghton Mifflin, 1968), pp. 3–23. While religion often figured in inaugural addresses, in the ritualistic way common to men who knew that the public expected some mention of God, Robert Bellah recognized that Kennedy's references were of a different kind, promulgating a "civil religion" that all Americans could embrace.

4. Richard Nixon would not have thought to use such language, or employed speechwriters to produce it, had he won the closely fought 1960 election.

5. *New York Times,* January 21, 1961, p. 8.

6. No previous presidential father was ever so heavily involved in his son's political career; few, indeed, had lived to see their sons assume the presidency.

7. Doris Kearns Goodwin, *The Fitzgeralds and the Kennedys: An American Saga* (Simon and Schuster, 1987), pp. 441–444.

8. Ibid., p. 427.

9. Ibid., p. 447. Howe "complained that assigning Kennedy to police Wall Street was like setting a cat to guard the pigeons."

10. Ibid., p. 448.

11. Ibid., pp. 498–499.

12. When one considers that Andrew Mellon was the man Hoover chose to appoint to the London post following his more than decade-long service as secretary of the treasury under three Republican presidents, succeeding in a line of other socially prominent individuals, one has some sense of the radical nature of the Roosevelt appointment of an Irish American Roman Catholic.

13. Ibid., pp. 520–522.

14. Wealth, whatever its advantages in the years before World War II, did not provide admission to what many regarded as the preferred schools and clubs that had room for Protestants only.

15. No Catholic of his parents' generation was equally exempt from such prejudice, an experience common also to Jews, whether affluent or poor.

16. Goodwin, *Fitzgeralds*, pp. 605–606.

17. Kennedy's undergraduate thesis, deposited in the Harvard College Library, is the work of a not especially well-read youth, scarcely resembling what Theodore Roosevelt wrote decades earlier on the War of 1812.

18. John F. Kennedy, *Why England Slept* (Hutchinson, 1940), p. xx.

19. Ibid., p. 228.

20. Goodwin, *Fitzgeralds*, p. 606.

21. Ibid., p. 605.

22. Ibid., p. 606.

23. Ibid., pp. 614–617.

24. Robert Dallek, *John F. Kennedy: An Unfinished Life, 1917–1963* (Allen Lane, 2003), pp. 83–84. This excellent biography of Kennedy, written forty years after his assassination, is especially revealing on his private life, giving details on his sexual activities and medical problems only hinted at in the years immediately following 1963. Dallek portrays Inga as a great beauty, twice divorced, who "exuded sexuality," and whose affair with the young Kennedy was an "open secret," a relationship considered highly inappropriate by his Catholic parents.

25. Ibid., pp. 86–87. Kennedy was seriously ill before he accepted his Navy commission, suffering from back pain and intestinal problems, caused by colitis. These ailments were never hinted at in a Chelsea Naval Hospital record that spoke of his "general good health," and declared him "fit for duty."

26. Ibid., p. 95.

27. Ibid., pp. 95–98. Dallek, considering the very considerable newspaper publicity given to Kennedy's heroic exploit, avidly publicized by his father, recognizes that the tale acquired additional resonance from the fact that "it was not only ordinary G.I.s from local byways risking their lives for national survival and values but also the privileged son of a wealthy, influential father who had voluntarily placed himself in harm's way and did the country proud."

28. Goodwin, *Fitzgeralds*, p. 706.

29. Kennedy's Catholicism and war record helped him greatly.

30. Goodwin, *Fitzgeralds*, p. 720. Joseph Kennedy was said to have spent nearly $250,000 to secure Jack's election to the House. Goodwin suggests it was "probably higher."

31. Kennedy, as a freshman representative in a very safe seat, was in no way threatened by the 1946 Democratic Party debacle.

32. Goodwin, *Fitzgeralds*, pp. 756–757.

33. *New York Times,* November 4, 1952, p. 23.

34. Dallek, *Kennedy,* p. 173. Issues figured scarcely at all in the contest. Writing of Kennedy and Lodge, Dallek says: "They were both internationalist supporters of containment as well as conservatives with occasional bows to liberalism; they both favored sustaining labor unions, less government intervention in domestic affairs, and balanced federal budgets."

35. Ibid., p. 175. Kennedy made great efforts to attract Jewish voters, to "overcome allegations that his father had been anti-Semitic and even pro-Nazi."

36. Arthur M. Schlesinger Jr., *A Thousand Days: John F. Kennedy in the White House* (Houghton Mifflin), p. 13.

37. Ibid., p. 14.

38. Ibid., p. 76. Schlesinger notes that Mrs. Roosevelt changed her mind about Kennedy in the course of the 1960 election campaign, telling him shortly after his narrow victory, "I don't think anyone in politics since Franklin has had the same vital relationship with crowds."

39. Robert Dallek, *Lone Star Rising: Lyndon Johnson and His Times, 1908–1960* (Oxford University Press, 1991), p. 490.

40. Ibid.

41. Ibid., p. 491.

42. Ibid.

43. Dallek, *Kennedy,* p. 207.

44. Ibid. Joe Kennedy was furious with his son, and berated him "as an idiot who was ruining his political career."

45. Ibid.

46. James MacGregor Burns, *John Kennedy* (Harcourt Brace, 1959), pp. 259–276 is one of the most compelling portraits of the young Kennedy.

47. See Dallek, *Kennedy,* p. 208, for the words Arthur Schlesinger Jr. used, telling the senator, ". . . you clearly emerged as the man who gained the most during the Convention. . . . Your general demeanor and effectiveness made you in a single week a national figure. . . "

48. Dallek, *Lone Star,* p. 556.

49. *Congressional Record,* 85th Congress, First Session, vol. 103, part 8, July 2, 1957, p. 10784.

50. Schlesinger, *Thousand Days,* pp. 553–554. This view is not shared by Schlesinger who notes that though "the Algerian speech brought Kennedy more mail, both from the United States and abroad than any other address he made in the Senate," it was not greeted enthusiastically by "the foreign policy establishment in the United States—the Council on Foreign Relations, the *New York Times,* the Department of State."

51. Ibid., p. 18. Schlesinger, seeking to explain Kennedy's "diffidence" on McCarthyism, writes of "his exasperation with the ideological liberals of the day and what he regarded as their emotional approach to public questions."

52. Goodwin, *Fitzgeralds,* p. 795.

53. Theodore H. White, *The Making of the President, 1960* (Athenaeum, 1961), p. 108. This, the most authoritative book on the 1960 election despite its exaggerated pro-Kennedy bias, spoke of "the handsome, open-faced candidate on the TV screen, showing himself, proving that a Catholic wears no horns."

54. Goodwin, *Fitzgeralds,* p. 798.

55. Dallek, *Kennedy,* pp. 256–257. Kennedy indicated that "any discussion of the war record of Senator Humphrey was done without my consent, as I strongly disagree with the injection of this issue into the campaign."

56. Ibid., p. 258. Humphrey, always a good loser, refused to accept the *Newsweek* accusation that Kennedy had "stolen" the election, saying "I have no complaints about the election—Senator Kennedy won it and I lost it."

57. Dallek, *Lone Star,* pp. 571–573. Johnson's words were scarcely more scathing than those used by his supporters who challenged Kennedy for never resisting McCarthyism, his frequent absences from the Senate, alluding even to the health problems he persistently concealed.

58. Ibid., p. 577. Dallek considers many of the explanations for Johnson's decision to accept the vice presidency, including his realization that "his best days as Majority Leader had passed," but leans to the idea that he believed he "might use his political magic to convert the vice presidency, as with the Senate Leadership, into something more than it had been before."

59. Ibid., pp. 285–286. The most devastating comment on Nixon's appearance may have been made by Mayor Daley of Chicago who said: "My God! They've embalmed him before he even died."

60. Ambrose, *Eisenhower,* vol. II, p. 597.

61. Ibid. Ambrose wrote that "Eisenhower confessed he found the statement, which echoed Kennedy's charges, 'somewhat astonishing,' especially as it came from two men 'who had long been in Administration councils and who had never voiced any doubt—at least in my presence—of the adequacy of America's defenses.'"

62. Ibid., p. 600.

63. Dallek, *Kennedy*, p. 296. Dallek says: "In the final analysis, the most important question is not why Kennedy won but why his victory was so narrow. Harry Truman was amazed at the closeness of the race," and he adds: "What they missed was the unyielding fear of having a Catholic in the White House. Although about 46 percent of Protestants voted for Kennedy, millions of them in Ohio, Wisconsin, and across the South made his religion a decisive consideration. It was the first time a candidate had won the presidency with a minority of Protestant voters."

64. Kennedy, more than any of his predecessors, relied on a small team of talent scouts to identify the individuals he needed to consider for the major posts. It is significant that he so rarely appointed former Senate or House colleagues, and made so little effort to consult them.

65. Deborah Shapley, *Promise and Power: The Life and Times of Robert McNamara* (Little, Brown, 1993), pp. 82–84.

66. Ernest R. May and Philip D. Zelikow, editors, *The Kennedy White House During the Cuban Missile Crisis* (Harvard University Press, 1997), p. x.

67. Though Robert Kennedy had shown surprising ruthlessness, greatly distressing those Democrats who opposed his brother's presidential nomination, no one ever questioned his abilities as a campaign manager.

68. This is the only reasonable defense of his choice.

69. For other equally perceptive observations on the Kennedy presidency by James McGregor Burns, see his article, "Political Craftsman in the White House," *New York Times Magazine*, January 15, 1961, pp. 4–5; also, see his review of Theodore White's *The Making of the President*, in *New York Times Book Review*, July 9, 1961, p. 1.

70. David Halberstam, *The Best and the Brightest* (Random House, 1969), p. 41.

71. Andrew, *President's Eyes*, pp. 257–259. Few of those who joined Kennedy in the new administration knew much about intelligence. The president, suspicious of the State Department, portrayed it as "the Beast of Foggy Bottom" and he was reported to have said: "If I need some material fast or an idea fast, CIA is the place I have to go. The State Department is four or five days to answer a simple yes or no."

72. Kai Bird, *The Color of Truth: McGeorge Bundy and William Bundy, Brothers in Arms* (Simon and Schuster, 1998), p. 194. By February 8, McGeorge Bundy was telling the president, "Defense and CIA now feel quite enthusiastic about the invasion. . . . At the worst, they think the invaders would get into the mountains, and at the best, they think they might get a full-fledged civil war in which we could then back the anti-Castro forces openly."

73. Ibid., pp. 195–196. Bundy, though accepting the plan, was sufficiently wary to write Kennedy that if Richard Bissell, the CIA's deputy director of plans, whom the president greatly esteemed had any fault, "it is that he does not look at all sides of the question." Still, this did not lead Bundy to oppose the proposed invasion, and Rusk, perhaps equally uncertain about the wisdom of the operation, never expressed his doubts openly. Insofar as anyone did, it was Senator Fulbright who in a memo to the president said: "The Castro regime is a thorn in the flesh but it is not a dagger in the heart." When Fulbright expressed these views openly to the president in a meeting attended by his principal advisers, Bird writes, they were not impressed by his eloquence, and "closed ranks against the outsider."

74. Dallek, *Kennedy*, p. 361. Both Arthur Schlesinger and Dean Acheson, when told about the plans by Kennedy, expressed their skepticism. Learning that the Americans intended to disembark only 1,500 men and expected to meet resistance from 25,000 Cubans, Acheson said: "It doesn't take Price-Waterhouse to figure out that fifteen hundred aren't as good as twenty-five thousand."

75. Ibid., p. 364.

76. Ibid., pp. 366–369. Kennedy, mourning the dead and feeling responsible for those taken prisoner, described the Bay of Pigs as "the worst experience in my life."

77. Though never despairing in public, Kennedy was shattered by the experience, and while the Republicans held their fire, something they might not have done under Truman, the Republican Congressional Committee's newsletter included the very damaging words: "It is doubtful if any President has gotten the United States in so much trouble in so short a time."

78. Taubman, *Khrushchev*, pp. 492–493. Taubman notes that Kennedy in his despair over the failed invasion feared that his "Cuban mistake" would encourage the Soviet Communists to become "tougher and tougher," challenging him everywhere. The facts were otherwise. Though Khrushchev, in his first message to Kennedy before the outcome of the invasion was clear, issued a warning that seemed ominous, saying: "It is not yet too late to prevent what may be irreparable," his second message, in Taubman's words, "lapsed into angry clichés." Indeed, Khrushchev had taken for granted that Kennedy intended to follow up the initial invasion with a bombing campaign and the dispatch of U.S. Marines, and when that did not happen said to his son, "I don't understand Kennedy. What's wrong with him? Can he really be that indecisive?"

79. Lawrence Freedman, *Kennedy's Wars: Berlin, Cuba, Laos, and Vietnam* (Oxford University Press, 2000), pp. 151–152.

80. Ibid.

81. Ibid., p. 151.

82. Ibid., p. 152.

83. Ibid.

84. Taubman, *Khrushchev*, p. 495. Kennedy, traumatized by his encounter with Khrushchev, seemed a "shattered" man to Harriman; Macmillan found him "completely overwhelmed by the ruthlessness and barbarity" of the Soviet leader, and Johnson gleefully suggested that "Khrushchev scared the poor little fellow dead." Khrushchev, according to his son's testimony, found Kennedy a "serious partner" and his memoirs suggest that he thought him "a better statesman than Eisenhower," unlikely to "make any hasty decisions which might lead to military conflict." This, according to Taubman, led Khrushchev to believe that the weakness Kennedy had displayed at the Bay of Pigs could be "exploited," that the young president "could be pushed around."

85. Lacouture, *De Gaulle, 1945–1970*, pp. 371–372.

86. Ibid., p. 373.

87. Kennedy was not the only president who believed that America's interests, humane and generous, scarcely resembled those of France, a country neither he nor his principal foreign policy advisers knew at all well.

88. Dallek, *Kennedy*, p. 402.

89. It is interesting that neither de Gaulle nor Khrushchev felt the slightest awe for the president, at least when they expressed their views privately to their colleagues.

90. Taubman, *Khrushchev*, p. 500. Their last session in Vienna was especially stormy. When Kennedy suggested that the Soviet leader was offering a choice between American retreat and a confrontation, Khrushchev replied "if the U.S. wanted war, that was its problem," and insisted that the Soviet decision to sign a peace treaty was "firm and irrevocable."

91. Unlike de Gaulle and Adenauer, Macmillan never expressed fundamental reservations about Kennedy.

92. Dallek, *Kennedy*, p. 423. His words were bold; Kennedy said: "We cannot and will not permit the Communists to drive us out of Berlin, either gradually or by force. . . . We will at all times be ready to talk, if talk will help. But we must be ready to resist with force, if force is used upon us."

93. Andrew, *President's Eyes*, p. 269. See, also, Bundy, *Danger and Survival*, pp. 363–368. Bundy, in his discussion of "Khrushchev's nuclear threat," writes that "what I remember of 1961 and 1962 is that we thought it wise to take him seriously, as our predecessors had, and nothing

has changed my mind." As for the Berlin Wall, it was an abomination, Bundy wrote, but "no one in power in any major government believed in using force against the wall."

94. Bird, *Color of Truth,* pp. 212–214. Bundy's memorandum, in part inspired by one sent to him by his assistant, Carl Kaysen, giving his "instinctive reactions to the Berlin situation," expressed the opinion of others, but did not reflect Acheson's view at all. In a letter to a friend, Acheson wrote: "It seems to me interesting that a group of young men who regard themselves as intellectuals are capable of less coherent thought than we have had since Coolidge. They are pretty good at improvising. . . . But God help us . . . if they are given any time to think!"

95. Kissinger, *Diplomacy,* p. 587.

96. Ibid., pp. 587–588. Kissinger writes: "In effect, these conciliatory phrases cancelled each other out. Since the stated American and German positions were irreconcilable, and since Germany was totally dependent on the United States for the defense of Berlin, denying Bonn a veto could produce only one of two outcomes: risking war for a cause in which the Kennedy administration said it did not believe, or imposing views on Bonn that had been rejected by the German leaders. The former course could not have been sustained in the American Congress or in public opinion; the latter would have wrecked Germany's commitment to the West and the cohesion of the Atlantic Alliance."

97. Dallek, *Kennedy,* p. 428.

98. The Berlin crisis helped further to cement Franco-German relations.

99. Schlesinger, *Thousand Days,* pp. 545–547.

100. Halberstam, *Best and Brightest,* p. 172. Halberstam gives a devastating appraisal of the Taylor-Rostow report, saying that it showed "a complete misunderstanding of the war."

101. Ibid., p. 168.

102. Ibid., p. 170.

103. Ibid., p. 171. Taylor, Halberstam explains, was recommending "firmness," and the suggestion came from "the man the Kennedy Administration believed its foremost strategic planner; a cautious man who would understand wars like this."

104. Ibid., pp. 176–177. This statement reflected the thinking of both McNamara and Rusk, faithfully expressing the president's wishes in the matter.

105. Shapley, *McNamara,* pp. 146–149. McNamara's "inspection tour," of only forty-eight hours, might have led a more modest man to question his understanding of the situation, but he accepted that vast areas of the country were being made secure, and while the *New York Times,* with its access to the Vietcong told a different story, this was not one McNamara cared to hear.

106. Ibid., p. 260. According to Shapley, while the American press reported that McNamara and Taylor, together on their joint mission, found the war to be "going better," with the political turmoil having "no effect whatever" on military operations, in their reports to the president, they showed themselves more circumspect, fearing that U.S. pressures were unlikely to "move Diem and Nhu toward moderation."

107. Ibid., p. 262. Such statements by McNamara became commonplace, and John McNaughton, general counsel in the Defense Department told Daniel Ellsberg that McNamara had "an understanding with Kennedy that they would close out Vietnam by 'sixty-five, whether it was in good shape or bad."

108. Ernest R. May and Philip D. Zelikow, *The Kennedy Tapes: Inside the White House During the Cuban Crisis* (Harvard University Press, 1997), p. x.

109. Ibid.

110. Robert F. Kennedy, *Thirteen Days: A Memoir of the Cuban Missile Crisis,* with an afterword by Richard E. Neustadt and Graham T. Allison (Norton, 1971).

111. Ibid., p. 117.

112. Ibid.

113. Ibid., pp. 105–106. Robert Kennedy, in his account, giving credit to all his brother did to avert disaster, said: "After it was finished, he made no statement attempting to take credit for himself or for the Administration for what had occurred. He instructed all members of the Ex Comm and government that no interview should be given, no statement made, which would claim any kind of victory. He respected Khrushchev for properly determining what was in his own country's interest and what was in the interest of mankind. If it was a triumph, it was a triumph for the next generation and not for any particular government or people."

114. See also Abram Chayes, *The Cuban Missile Crisis* (Oxford University Press, 1974), p. 88. The crisis ended, in effect, when the president announced his determination not to allow the missiles to remain in Cuba.

115. Percy Cradock, *Know Your Enemy: How the Joint Intelligence Committee Saw the World* (John Murray Books, 2002), pp. 179–189.

116. Ibid., pp. 187–188.

117. Bundy, *Danger and Survival*, p. 436. Bundy, in his own account of this secret engagement, suggested that he initially opposed it, believing that NATO would see it as "trying to sell our allies for our interests." Twenty-five years later, less committed to that opinion, he believed that the president had been right in his "unwavering recognition that the basic interest of all concerned was to find a peaceful end to the crisis, and that the Turkish missiles, whatever the opinion of allies, did not justify bloodshed in Cuba."

118. May and Zelikow, *Tapes,* pp. 668–671.

119. Ibid., pp. 691–692.

120. Andrew, *President's Eyes*, p. 286.

121. Christopher Andrew and Vasili Mitrokhin, *The Mitrokhin Archive: The KGB in Europe and the West* (Penguin Books, 2000), p. 237.

122. Taubman, *Khrushchev*, p. 556.

123. Ibid., p. 691.

124. Kissinger, *Diplomacy,* p. 593.

125. Cradock, *Enemy,* p. 188.

126. Ibid.

127. Ibid.

128. Dallek, *Kennedy,* p. 528; also p. 671.

129. Ibid., pp. 672–681. Dallek describes admirably the president's hesitations during this period, knowing that the Diem regime could not win the war, fearing that if the generals in South Vietnam effected the coup they intended and failed, the administration would be blamed. As Dallek, in considerable detail explains, the problems seemed insoluble, and Kennedy never awarded them the attention he gave to the Cuban crisis, angry only at what U.S. journalists were saying about American policy in Vietnam.

130. Ibid., p. 681. Dallek writes: "Since the plotters promised to give Lodge only four hours notice, he saw no way that the United States could 'significantly influence [the] course of events.'"

131. Schlesinger, *Thousand Days,* p. 996. Schlesinger writes: "McNamara returned to Washington doubting whether Diem could last even if he took corrective action. But he also believed that the political mess had not yet infected the military situation and, back in Washington, announced (in spite of a strong dissent from William Sullivan of Harriman's staff who accompanied the mission) that a thousand American troops could be withdrawn by the end of the year and that the major part of the American military task would be completed by the end of 1965."

132. Ibid., p. 997. Schlesinger says: "It is important to state that the coup of November 1, 1963, was entirely planned and carried out by the Vietnamese. Neither the American Embassy nor the CIA were involved in instigation or execution. . . . What lay behind the coup was not the

meddling of Americans, quiet or ugly, but the long history of Vietnamese military resentment against Diem, compounded now by the fear that Nhu, with his admiration for totalitarian methods of organization, might try to transform South Vietnam into a police state. It was almost inevitable that, at one point or other, the generals would turn against so arbitrary and irrational a regime." See also David Kaiser, *American Tragedy: Kennedy, Johnson, and the Origins of the Vietnam War* (Harvard University Press, 2000), p. 275. Kaiser writes: "In subsequent decades some American policymakers and historians—including Eileen Hammer, William Colby, Frederick Nolting, and Lyndon Johnson and Richard Nixon—cited the coup against Diem as the American government's biggest mistake and, perhaps, the most important cause of full-scale American involvement in the war. Nixon went further during his presidency, undertaking unsuccessful attempts to prove—wrongly—that Kennedy had ordered Diem's assassination."

133. Dallek, *Kennedy*, p. 683.

134. Schlesinger, *Thousand Days*, pp. 997–998. Schlesinger reminds his readers that Kennedy, ". . . with his memory of the French in Indochina in 1951 . . . had always believed there was a point at which our intervention might turn Vietnamese nationalism against us and transform an Asian conflict into a white man's war." This was never in fact the problem, and Kennedy, imagining himself an expert on France but also on French colonial affairs, greatly exaggerated his understanding of both.

135. Schlesinger, Ibid., pp. 940–947.

136. Dallek, *Kennedy*, p. 493.

137. Schlesinger, *Thousand Days*, pp. 958–959. Receiving a group representing Americans for Democratic Action on the day after the TV airing of the police violence against the Birmingham demonstrators, Kennedy said that he had been made "sick" by what he had seen, but that there was nothing he was constitutionally able to do to change the situation.

138. Ibid., p. 964.

139. Ibid., p. 965.

140. Ibid.

141. Ibid., p. 966.

142. Ibid., p. 973. Though the president was delighted with the demonstration, and invited its leaders to the White House that evening, liberal Democrats in the House continued to believe his proposed civil rights legislation was too modest in its aims. Schlesinger wrote that "the administration feared a stronger bill would face trouble in the House Rules Committee and later in the Senate," and was therefore reluctant to press for such.

143. James T. Patterson, *Grand Expectations: The United States, 1945–1974* (Oxford University Press, 1996), p. 465. See, also, p. 461 where Patterson discusses the journalistic habit of "celebrating" the American presidency, never more fully displayed than in Theodore White's reverential treatment of Kennedy.

144. Ibid.

145. Peter H. Smith, *Talons of the Eagle: Dynamics of U.S.–Latin American Relations* (Oxford University Press, 1996), pp. 150–158 and pp. 162–163. This, an unusually sober and convincing account of the aspirations of the Alliance for Progress, documents both its accomplishments and its failures.

146. Bundy, *Danger and Survival*, pp. 419–420.

147. Cradock, *Enemy*, p. 190.

148. As two of the men who knew Kennedy well, and who observed him closely in the White House, the Schlesinger and Sorenson biographies are of course invaluable. Neither, writing so soon after his assassination, would have thought to compose the sort of critical assessment published decades later by Dallek. Still, even that book, for all the invaluable information it provides on Kennedy's illnesses, essential to an understanding of his presidency, fails to reflect adequately

on what may one day be recognized to have been his insufficient grasp of the complex foreign policy issues he confronted. That book remains to be written. It is vaguely hinted at by Patterson in his *Grand Expectations* where he says, on p. 517, "Contrary to the claims of his acolytes, he did not grow very much on the job."

149. Bird, *Color of Truth*, p. 403. Bird, given access to the unfinished Bundy manuscript, still unpublished today, noted that it acknowledged his participation in "a great failure," while insisting on the "centrality of presidential leadership." Bird writes: "In effect, he was blaming the war on Lyndon Johnson's determination to send in combat troops—a decision Bundy in retrospect thought John Kennedy would have avoided." McNamara, as quoted by Shapley, *McNamara*, pp. 605–606, is even more emphatic in this insistence, "I know for a fact that John Kennedy would have withdrawn from Vietnam." He has repeated that in his recent film, *Fog of War*.

150. Freedman, *Kennedy's Wars*, pp. ix–xii offers a very sympathetic though occasionally critical rendering of Kennedy's foreign policy. For a more searing critique, though essentially silent on foreign policy issues, consult the tendentious study written by Seymour Hersh, *The Dark Side of Camelot* (Little, Brown, 1997).

151. Niall Ferguson, editor, *Virtual History: Alternatives and Counterfactuals* (Picadon, 1997), p. 369.

152. The story of Kennedy's court waits to be written. The exaggerated tales told by Hersh scarcely do justice to that strange combination of men—there were no women of any prominence in the Kennedy administration—who basked in the rays that emanated from their gracious "sun king." Many of those in secondary positions, especially on the White House staff, were never destined again to enjoy any public prominence, finding no place in either the Carter or the Clinton administrations. They retired, some into academic obscurity, remembering always the glorious days of Camelot when they were regularly admitted to the presence. Some of Franklin Roosevelt's courtiers, no less avid in their recollections of the great days spent in the service of a remarkable leader, showed scarcely less modesty in telling all that they had done to make his administration a success, but their stories were on the whole more convincing and sometimes, as with Ickes, more entertaining.

CHAPTER 14 (The Texan)

1. Kennedy was always represented as an "intellectual," surrounded by intellectuals, a designation never used to describe his successor who in fact retained many of Kennedy's appointees.

2. Dallek, *Lone Star*, pp. 14–15.

3. Doris Kearns, *Lyndon Johnson and the American Dream* (Harper and Row, 1976), pp. 63–64. Kearns writes: "Lyndon Johnson never questioned that his was the best of all countries. The assumption of superiority imposed a moral obligation to share the American way with the world. And it was accompanied by a sense of justified outrage at the slightest criticism of America."

4. Johnson's war experiences were negligible, but gained from their telling by an accomplished creator of fictions about himself.

5. Texas, both a Southern and a Western state, in its politics resembled all the old states of the former Confederacy, reliable Democratic strongholds.

6. Dallek, *Lone Star*, pp. 20–21. Johnson's father and grandfather, ardent populists and active politicians, made the farmers' plight their chief concern.

7. Ibid., p. 96.

8. Because powerful chairmanships in both the House and Senate were awarded on the basis of seniority, a very large number were held by Southerners, Texans being very prominent among them.

9. Dallek, *Lone Star,* pp. 123–124.

10. Ibid., pp. 147–148. A very different perspective on Johnson is offered by Robert Caro in what must still be considered the most comprehensive work on his life. Robert A. Caro, in his three volumes on "The Years of Lyndon Johnson," *The Path to Power* (Random House, 1982), *Means of Ascent* (Random House, 1990), and *Master of the Senate* (Random House, 2002) gives a devastating account of Johnson's political career, recounting a tale of treachery and deceit. Robert Dallek, publishing his *Lone Star Rising* in 1990, speaks of Caro's first two volumes as having "sent his already tarnished reputation into a free fall."

11. Ibid., pp. 207–209.

12. Ibid., p. 223.

13. Caro, *Ascent,* p. 21. Caro, with his customary skepticism, writes: "Johnson did not go to the Pacific. He went to the White House—to ask for a job in Washington."

14. Dallek, *Lone Star,* p. 238.

15. Ibid., pp. 240–241. Caro's account of this episode is, not surprisingly, very different; in *Means of Ascent,* he writes, on p. 48, "Exaggeration is a normal aspect of war stories, only to be expected. With Johnson, however, exaggeration spilled over into something more—until the story of his wartime service bore little resemblance to the reality. . . . He had been in action for a total of thirteen minutes."

16. Dallek, *Lone Star,* p. 240.

17. Ibid., p. 241–242.

18. Caro, *Ascent,* pp. 99–105. Caro gives a full account of the circumstances that made it reasonable for the purchase to be made in Lady Bird's name.

19. Dallek, *Lone Star,* pp. 265–267. Dallek stresses Johnson's grief, describing him as virtually prostrate. Caro, in *Ascent,* p. 122, says that Johnson, speaking with one of his secretaries on the day following Roosevelt's death, considered only the political implications of his death, telling her: "There is going to be the damnedest struggle for power in this man's town for the next two weeks that anyone ever saw in their lives."

20. Caro, *Ascent,* p. 124.

21. Ibid.

22. Ibid., p. 125.

23. Ibid. Caro writes: "Speaking out as he had never before done in Congress, Lyndon Johnson in 1947 opposed most of Truman's 'Fair Deal.'"

24. Dallek, *Lone Star,* p. 346.

25. These could all be seen as "Fair Deal" extensions on policies that had their origin in Roosevelt's "New Deal."

26. Johnson, like Truman, did not believe that education, traditionally a prerogative of the states, should remain so.

27. Dallek, *Lone Star,* pp. 384–386. Johnson, an ardent supporter of the administration's policies in Korea, believed its earlier reluctance to press for higher defense appropriations had given the country only "50 percent of the military might" it needed to resist the North Korean aggression. His decision to create a "watchdog committee" similar to the one presided over by Truman during World War II, brought him into closer relations with the president, and no less important, made the party and the nation more aware of him.

28. Ibid., p. 401. Dallek writes: "Johnson gained considerable political capital from the MacArthur hearings and the work of his preparedness subcommittee."

29. Though Russell, a died-in-the-wool Southern conservative senator was one of Johnson's closest friends and collaborators, Johnson himself never made the mistake of ignoring the importance of the liberal elements in the Senate, and for a time enjoyed good relations with Hubert Humphrey and others of his political beliefs.

30. The president, by seeming to co-opt Johnson, made several prominent Senate liberals suspicious of the Texan senator, but Johnson never lost sight of his prime objective—to be the leader of all the Democrats in the Senate.

31. This massive majority against an exceedingly weak opponent was secured, of course, in the Democratic Party primary, the only election that counted in Texas, still a staunch Democratic state, but not destined to remain so for very long.

32. The position of Majority Leader, though important, never enjoyed the reputation it acquired in the next six years through Johnson's extraordinary capacity to persuade senators to vote in the ways he recommended.

33. Johnson, seeking to prove the Democratic Party fiscally prudent, finally laid to rest the ghost of the long-standing Republican charge that it was spendthrift and irresponsible.

34. Johnson's interest in securing the Democratic presidential nomination in 1960, increasingly apparent to everyone, made him suspect to liberals like Humphrey who recognized what he hoped to gain by propitiating Southern Democrats.

35. Dallek, *Lone Star,* p. 566.

36. Ibid.

37. Ibid., pp. 568–569.

38. Ibid., p. 571.

39. Ibid., pp. 571–572. Dallek writes: "Nothing incensed the Kennedys more than the Johnson revelations about Jack's health."

40. Johnson, knowing what he had accomplished as Senate Majority Leader, expected to be able to do the same with the vice presidency.

41. Johnson's abilities were never adequately appreciated by those who served Kennedy, little impressed by what they conceived to be his Texas crudeness, so different from the elegance and suavity of the man they had served.

42. Leuchtenburg, *Shadow,* p. 142. Leuchtenburg writes: "He was not satisfied to go down in the history books merely as a successful president in the Roosevelt tradition. He aimed instead to be 'the greatest of them all, the whole bunch of them.' And to be the greatest president in history, he needed not just to match Roosevelt's performance but to surpass it."

43. While Johnson had no great esteem for Kennedy, believing his political performance as president inadequate, he felt something approaching awe for a number of the intelligent and articulate men he had brought into his service, especially those deputed to handle military and foreign affairs.

44. Many, genuinely frightened of him, wished only to do his bidding, anxious to support him in the policies he favored.

45. No one has thought to make a serious study of the Kennedy court, comparing it with the one established by Johnson, as different one from the other as Roosevelt's was from Truman's.

46. Dean Rusk, *As I Saw It* (Norton, 1990).

47. Though biographies of both McNamara and Bundy exist, none to date has even hinted at how these incontestably able men, loyal to the president, viewed the strange leader they for a time agreed to serve. Clark Clifford, who joined Johnson's administration in 1968, wrote what must still be regarded as the most compelling portrait of Johnson by one of those who retained his affection for him. See Clark Clifford, with Richard Holbrooke, *Counsel to the President* (Random House, 1991), pp. 385–386. Clifford said: "Lyndon Johnson was the most complex man I ever met; he also may have been the most difficult. . . . I was always struck by his attitude toward his poor origins—his combination of pride, shame, and sensitivity. But he never forgot those origins, and their memory fuelled his genuine commitment to social progress. . . . In dealing with people, he could be astonishingly devious. . . . a terrible bully, especially to those closest to him. . . . He was uncommonly hurt by those who questioned his

motives, yet much of the time his behaviour raised unavoidable questions even in the minds of his closest friends."

48. In this early period, Johnson exploited the two conditions that favored him: the memory of the slain Kennedy that had such a powerful influence with the public; his own long experience in Congress, both in the House and in the Senate, that told him how to deal with legislative leaders he knew personally.

49. Patterson, *Grand Expectations,* p. 444. While poverty figured as a major issue for Johnson in great part because of his own life experience, Patterson is right to draw attention to the importance of the publication in 1962 of Michael Harrington's *The Other America* which did so much to "dramatize" the issue.

50. Johnson's concern to craft a social reform program with appeal to many social classes, greatly expanding the ranks of those who felt allegiance to the Democratic Party for what Franklin Roosevelt had accomplished, reflected his understanding of how much the country had changed since the depths of the Depression, nowhere more evident perhaps than in his own Texas.

51. *New York Times,* August 9, 1964, p. 58.

52. Eric Goldman, *The Tragedy of Lyndon Johnson* (MacDonald, 1969), p. 301. Goldman, the historian appointed by Johnson to serve him as Schlesinger had once served Kennedy, understood how much Johnson wished to exceed Roosevelt's record as president, and tells of Johnson's telephone call to him on election night before all the returns were in. His great concern was to discover whether his majority was indeed greater than the one Roosevelt had achieved in 1936.

53. This must certainly figure as one of the century's more inspired political slogans.

54. Johnson recruited a wholly new White House team to help press for the domestic legislation he deemed essential. This group of men accepted that their mission was never to question the president, but to carry out the orders he gave. In foreign policy and defense policy, where the principal Kennedy appointees were retained, there was comparable deference to the president, but few of those who consented to serve him doubted that they knew more about their subject than he did.

55. The size of the congressional majorities suggest how effective Johnson was in making education a matter of the highest national priority, with great appeal to all social classes. While the elementary and secondary school legislation served the impoverished principally, children in America's slums, the higher education bills were intended to have a social impact that would extend to the middle class as well.

56. The prospect of mass higher education, heralded by the GI Bill of Rights, became a reality with these additional large federal appropriations.

57. The extension of life for the aged became one of Johnson's principal aims.

58. Patterson, *Grand Expectations,* p. 573.

59. Ibid.

60. Ibid., pp. 573–574.

61. Ibid., pp. 574–575. Patterson notes that this legislation "fell short of national health insurance," and that most Americans "had to contribute to employer-subsidized group insurance plans, to pay for private insurance, or to do without," a situation exacerbated by the 15 percent who as late as the early 1990s had no medical insurance at all. This was the condition Clinton later sought to remedy.

62. *New York Times,* March 16, 1965, p. 30.

63. Ibid.

64. Kearns, *Dream,* pp. 304–305. The Watts riots, coming at the end of a week that saw Johnson sign the Voting Rights Act, described by him as "a triumph for freedom as huge as any victory that has ever been won on any battlefield" left him wholly bewildered, asking "How is it

possible, after all we've accomplished? . . . Is the world topsy-turvy?" As Kearns notes, "Watts was the precursor of more than one hundred riots that stretched out for three long summers, leaving 225 people dead, 4,000 wounded, and $112 billion in property damage."

65. Ibid., p. 308. "White backlash," a problem discernable even before Watts, became the major domestic political issue after the events of that long "hot" summer and undoubtedly contributed to the significant losses suffered by the Democrats in the 1966 off-year congressional elections.

66. Ibid., pp. 304–307.

67. These reforms, all accepted by a Congress dominated by the Democrats elected with Johnson in 1964, became the salient features of his early second term, redolent in many ways of the first administration of Franklin Roosevelt but also of Woodrow Wilson.

68. Lyndon Baines Johnson, *The Vantage Point: Perspectives of the Presidency, 1963–1969* (Holt, Rinehart, and Winston, 1971), pp. 232–241.

69. George W. Ball, *The Past Has Another Pattern* (Norton, 1982), p. 316. Unlike Humphrey who always maintained a certain reticence in speaking or writing about Johnson, Ball, who served as his undersecretary of state, felt no such constraints; he wrote in his memoirs: "He was of a breed I had known only from literature, legend, or at a distance. As a Stevenson Democrat, I had shared the prevailing stereotype of LBJ as a shrewd political manipulator—an 'operator' ready to make a deal even by compromising policies in which I strongly believed. I did not think of him as a 'liberal,' which for many of us was still the shibboleth of respectability, but as a Texan and a southerner—with the particular qualities those two words connoted in the stilted vocabulary of our parochial politics."

70. Johnson, *Vantage Point,* pp. 124 and 235.

71. The Munich analogy was the one most constantly used in this period, and it remained vital for the rest of the century.

72. The question of which individual colleagues recognized that the Maddox tale was false has never been clearly established.

73. Ball, *Past,* p. 380. Ball writes: "The Tonkin Gulf Resolution (a terrifyingly open-ended grant of power) disappointed me; I had counted on Congress to insert qualifying language, but Congress had abdicated."

74. Shapley, *Promise,* p. 457. Shapley, writing about McNamara in 1993, before he acknowledged his "error," guessed that he had lied.

75. Bird, *Color of Truth,* p. 316.

76. Johnson, *Vantage,* p. 134.

77. Kaiser, *American Tragedy,* p. 418.

78. Ibid., pp. 418–419. Kaiser writes: "The highest officials of the administration remained quite determined to conceal their plans for ground troops from the public. . . . On the same day, [April 1] administration sources told the *New York Times* they saw no change in the strategy of bombing the North." At an NSC meeting on April 2, Kaiser wrote, Bundy "laid down the law regarding statements to the press," saying that "Under no circumstances should there be any reference to the movement of U.S. forces or other courses of action."

79. Bird, *Color of Truth,* pp. 322–323. Johnson, immensely agitated by the Dominican situation, was reported to have consulted Bundy "no less than eighty-six times during the first days of the Dominican crisis," a telling comment on his excessive excitability.

80. Johnson, *Vantage,* p. 232.

81. Ball, *Past,* p. 398. The McNamara memorandum, which Ball found unsatisfactory, induced him to write his own memorandum, warning the president against any increase in the U.S. troop deployment.

82. Ibid., pp. 398–399. Ball writes: "Mac Bundy gave the President my memorandum, along with memoranda by his brother William Bundy and McNamara. In his transmittal note, he ad-

vised: 'My hunch is you will want to listen hard to George Ball and then reject his proposal.' Discussion could then move on to the narrower choice between my brother's course and McNamara's."

83. William Bundy became a more ardent advocate of the war than his brother, as is very evident in his passionate apologia, a criticism of Nixon and Kissinger, *A Tangled Web: The Making of Foreign Policy in the Nixon Presidency* (Hill and Wang, 1998).

84. Bird, *Color*, p. 338. Mac Bundy's comment the following day, according to Bird, was that "it was all terribly misinformed advice, but by playing the role of a beleaguered president, Johnson had manipulated, indeed, provoked these gray hairs into throwing their caution to the winds."

85. James Chace, *Acheson: The Secretary of State Who Created the Modern World* (Simon and Schuster, 1998), p. 410.

86. Ibid.

87. Johnson, *Vantage*, pp. 239–240.

88. Ibid., p. 240. Johnson expressed no feelings about Bundy's resignation in his autobiography, simply noting that Walt Rostow was appointed to take his place.

89. Johnson always paid great attention to public opinion polls, and this one, coming as late as the spring of 1967, following the disappointing results in the 1966 congressional off-year elections can only have encouraged him.

90. Kaiser, *Tragedy*, p. 490.

91. Shapley, *Promise*, p. 418

92. Ibid., pp. 418–419.

93. Ibid., pp. 420–421.

94. Ibid., p. 421.

95. Ibid., p. 428.

96. Ibid., p. 436.

97. Ibid., pp. 436–437. Shapley strongly implied that the president had pushed him out and that Bobby Kennedy wished for McNamara not to accept the World Bank appointment.

98. In his recent film, McNamara reveals that it was Katharine Graham, publisher of the *Washington Post*, who told him that of course he had been pushed out.

99. Clifford, *Counsel*, pp. 473–474. Clifford wrote: "As a military campaign the outcome of the Tet Offensive may remain in dispute, but there can be no question that it was a turning point in the war. Its size and scope made mockery of what the American military had told the public about the war, and devastated American credibility. Five of South Vietnam's six major cities, 36 of its 44 provincial capitals, and 66 of the 242 district towns were attacked. American losses were heavier than ever before, 3,895 killed in eight weeks."

100. Ibid., pp. 500–502. The first primary election almost coincided with the revelation by the *New York Times* that a great debate was taking place in the administration over whether to grant Westmoreland's request for an additional 206,000 troops. Clifford notes Johnson's fury over this revelation, "certain that it was a civilian in the Pentagon who had betrayed him. . . ."

101. Ibid., p. 507. Johnson, addressing the convention of the National Farmers Union in Minneapolis, made one of his more emotional speeches, saying: "Your President has come to ask you people, and all the other people of this nation, to join us in a *total national effort* to win the war. We will—make no mistake about it—win. . . . We are not doing enough to win it in the way we are doing it now."

102. Ibid., pp. 514–520. Though both Acheson and Vance had clearly changed their views about the war, Clifford refused to believe as Rostow and others did, that this meeting witnessed the end of the American establishment. Clifford wrote, "In fact, the men in the room were still strong supporters of policies to contain the Soviet Union and China, and almost half of them still supported the war; opposition to the war was based solely on the belief that Vietnam was weakening us at home and in the rest of the world. And they were right."

103. Ibid., p. 516. Bundy, in his summary, began by acknowledging that "there has been a very significant shift in most of our positions since we last met," and then went on to suggest that the hopes of "reasonably steady, slow, but sustained progress, especially in the countryside," was no longer believed by many of the Wise Men. Johnson was clearly shocked by what he heard.

104. Johnson, *Vantage*, p. 418.

105. Ibid., pp. 436–437.

106. Ibid., pp. 539–543.

107. Ibid., p. 543. This statement, revealing for what he chose to tell about his last meeting with Kennedy, suggested the deeper feelings Johnson harbored about the New Politics that he so clearly abominated.

108. Lacouture, *De Gaulle, The Ruler, 1945–1970*, p. 470.

CHAPTER 15 (The Villain?)

1. The negative portrayal of Nixon is still the most common one today, but it is important to note changes that are occurring, documented in David Greenberg, *Nixon's Shadow: The History of an Image* (Norton, 2003), pp. 304–337, in a chapter entitled "The Historians: Nixon as Liberal." The proposition that Nixon was in fact a "populist," seriously concerned with social reform, would have seemed outlandish three decades ago when he left the White House in disgrace.

2. Dallek, *Lone Star*, p. 5. Dallek, contrasting the "post-presidential reputations" of Nixon and Johnson notes the "measure of public redemption" that Nixon has won, suggesting there has been no equivalent tolerance for Johnson's "mistakes or wrongdoings."

3. Nixon received an excellent undergraduate education at this little-known Quaker college.

4. Not many who came from the impoverished family circumstances of the Nixon family would have thought such a career move possible, but Nixon's law degree from Duke made him eligible for law firms that generally preferred to recruit from Harvard or Yale. As a Protestant male with an excellent grade record, he could at least hope for an interview.

5. No one has adequately explained this early Nixon ardour for the Republican Party or his exaggerated antipathy for Roosevelt; his Southern California upbringing cannot wholly explain it.

6. Roger Morris, *Richard Milhous Nixon: The Rise of an American Politician* (Henry Holt, 1990), p. 243. Morris notes how his short service in the OPA confirmed his suspicions of "craven bureaucrats," and also his contempt for government regulation.

7. Ibid., p. 242. Morris quotes Thomas Harris, an OPA colleague who esteemed Nixon for his industry, as saying: ". . . among the liberals, the Eastern law school graduates, the Jews he rubbed shoulders with on the job. . . he lacked sophistication and the big-city graces."

8. Ibid., p. 336. Morris notes that Voorhis, broken-hearted by his defeat, left politics and wrote *Confessions of a Congressman* (Doubleday, 1947), which "contained few revelations about the circumstances of the campaign, though his files bristled with evidence, often from those who experienced at firsthand the whispering, the anonymous calls, and other smears."

9. Ibid., p. 330.

10. Ibid.

11. These were views common to liberal Democrats in the early years after the war.

12. Greenberg, *Nixon's Shadow*, pp. 29–30. Greenberg writes: "Nixon picked up an attack that had been used against her in the primary, comparing her votes to those of Vito Marcantonio [the only Communist member of the House of Representatives]. . . . He juxtaposed the two representatives' records on a pastel flyer that became known as the 'Pink Sheet.' Many liberals were outraged by this tactic; thereafter they fumed about Nixon's too-ready use of the communism issue and pronounced him a cheap-shot artist nonpareil."

13. Morris, *Nixon,* p. 617. Nixon's office denied in May 1958 that he had ever made such a statement to David Astor.

14. Greenberg, *Nixon's Shadow,* pp. 33–34. Greenberg writes: "Millions of letters and telegrams poured in—to Nixon, to Eisenhower, to the RNC [Republican National Committee], to NBC, to countless news outlets. Heavily pro-Nixon, they professed admiration that he had courageously bared his soul, and his finances, before the public; they praised him as honest, sincere, humble."

15. Richard Nixon, *Six Crises* (Doubleday, 1962), p. 107. Nixon explained the success of the Checkers speech by the fact that he chose "to tell [his] story directly to the people rather than funnel it to them through a press account."

16. Taubman, *Khrushchev,* p. 417.

17. Stephen E. Ambrose, *Nixon: The Education of a Politician, 1913–62* (Simon and Schuster, 1987), pp. 524–525.

18. Ambrose, *Eisenhower,* vol. ii, pp. 597–598.

19. *New York Times,* July 29, 1960, p. 9. See also Theodore H. White, *The Making of the President, 1960* (Athenaeum, 1961).

20. Nixon, because of these two TV successes, greatly exaggerated his command of the medium.

21. Sidney Kraus, ed., *The Great Debates* (Indiana University Press, 1962), pp. 142–150. Jeffery Auer, one of the contributors to this volume, raises in his chapter entitled "The Counterfeit Debates" whether these were debates at all, "confrontations. . . in any well-considered definition of the word," since they lacked "the element of direct mutual interrogation" and had "no clearly delimited focus of controversy."

22. Ambrose, *Eisenhower,* vol. ii, p. 604.

23. *New York Times,* November 8, 1962, p. 1.

24. *New York Times,* November 9, 1962, p. 34.

25. Greenberg, *Nixon's Shadow,* p. 136. A "new Nixon" was constantly being discovered or looked for, never more evident than after 1962 when Walter Lippmann, Theodore White, and Norman Mailer all imagined they had found one.

26. Theodore H. White, *The Making of the President, 1968* (Simon and Schuster, 1969), p. 70.

27. Ibid., p. 287. Also, *New York Times,* March 22, 1968, p. 32.

28. Ibid.

29. Ibid., p. 289. Also, *New York Times,* May 1, 1968, p. 30.

30. For Republican National Convention delegates, especially those not already pledged to a specific candidate, such poll findings were all-important.

31. White, *President, 1968,* pp. 311–312. Nixon scarcely knew Agnew, having met him only a few months previously, and seen him three or four times, but chose him because he wanted "a man he could trust, who could work with him for four years, and who understood the cities." He himself expected to handle foreign affairs, the prerogative of the president.

32. Stephen E. Ambrose, *Nixon: The Triumph of a Politician* (Simon and Schuster, 1989), p. 175.

33. Ibid., pp. 175–176. In addition to all he said about remedying the disordered conditions at home and abroad, Nixon spoke lovingly of his father who "had to go to work before he finished his sixth grade, sacrificed everything he had so that his sons could go to college." He spoke also of his Quaker mother who "quietly wept when he went to war but . . . understood why he had to go."

34. Carl Solberg, *Hubert Humphrey: A Biography* (Norton, 1984), p. 172. Solberg writes: "After the fiasco of Chicago, Humphrey floundered. He had failed to resolve his relationship with the president. He had not come to grips with what kind of campaign he would run against Nixon and Wallace."

35. Clifford, *Counsel,* p. 572. Clifford writes: "Although the speech was later remembered as a decisive break with the President, it was, in fact, a cautious proposal, almost identical to recommendations Ball, Harriman, Vance, and I had made unsuccessfully for weeks, and not very different from the Administration's negotiating position. Its tone, though, was unmistakably different from Lyndon Johnson's, and it was enormously important for the political signal it sent—Humphrey was setting out on his own for the first time."

36. Solberg, *Humphrey,* pp. 384–385. Humphrey, knowing what he was risking in making a pledge to stop the bombing, hoped to make it more palatable to Johnson, and added the phrase, "In weighing that risk—*and before taking action*—I would place key importance on evidence—direct or indirect, by deed or word—of Communist willingness to restore the demilitarized zone between South and North Vietnam."

37. Ibid., p. 386.

38. Indeed, by October, the Wallace campaign appeared to be almost in a free-fall.

39. *New York Times,* October 25, 1968, p. 1.

40. *New York Times,* October 26, 1968, p. 1.

41. Johnson, *Vantage Point,* pp. 554–555.

42. Clifford, *Counsel,* pp. 581–584. Clifford offered a fascinating account of the exchange of messages between Anna Chennault and those in the Nixon campaign, including John Mitchell, urging the Vietnamese not to enter negotiations till after the election when they fully expected to be in the White House.

43. Johnson, *Vantage Point,* pp. 548–549. The president, still smarting from Humphrey's Salt Lake City speech, though pretending to have accepted the vice president's explanation that he had not intended to depart from the president's policies, did nothing to help Humphrey, arguing that this simply confirmed his March 31 pledge to show no partisanship in the campaign.

44. Ibid., p. 548. Johnson made no specific mention of the Chennault intervention, preferring to say only that "people who claimed to speak for the Nixon camp began encouraging Saigon to stay away from Paris, and promising that Nixon, if elected, would inaugurate a policy more to Saigon's liking." The decision of the South Vietnamese not to go to Paris, in Johnson's view, cost Humphrey the election.

45. Clifford, *Counsel,* p. 594.

46. Ibid., pp. 594–595.

47. *New York Times,* January 21, 1969, p. 21.

48. Ibid.

49. Nixon always concealed his views about Eisenhower, and recognized the political advantages of not attacking Kennedy too openly. On Johnson, he showed similar discretion, perhaps recognizing that Johnson and he were birds of a feather, accomplished politicians and inveterate liars. Johnson, in his memoirs, spoke admiringly of Nixon, saying in 1971, "I never shared the intense dislike of Richard Nixon felt by many of my fellow Democrats. . . . I considered him a much-maligned and misunderstood man. I looked upon Nixon as a tough, unyielding partisan and a shrewd politician, but always a man trying to do the best for his country as he saw it." (pp. 547–548) Unwittingly, Johnson wrote the eulogy of a fallen president he might have wished someone would one day write about himself.

50. Any such comparison, while certain to offend Democrats loyal to the memory of Robert Kennedy, needs to be reflected on.

51. No one to date has compared the "court at Camelot" with Nixon's Victor Herbert court, distinguished for its *kitsch,* symbolized in the trumpets and gaudy uniforms designed to satisfy a president of little taste who yearned for grandeur.

52. Godfrey Hodgson, *The Gentleman from New York: Daniel Patrick Moynihan* (Houghton Mifflin, 2000), pp. 159–160. Hodgson writes: "That was a good, if minor, example of the role Moynihan played . . . as an 'ideas man.'"

53. Jeremy D. Mayer, *Running on Race: Racial Politics in Presidential Campaigns, 1960–2000* (Random House, 2002), pp. 91–95.

54. See Kevin Phillips, *The Emerging Republican Majority* (Arlington House, 1969). Phillips, dedicating his book to the attorney general, John Mitchell, was one of the first to understand how much American politics had changed since the time of Truman and Eisenhower, and what Nixon had contributed to that change.

55. Ambrose, *Triumph*, p. 294. The reaction to the plan was excellent, and Moynihan reported that the president was "euphoric" about its reception.

56. Greenberg, *Nixon's Shadow*, p. 306.

57. Ibid., p. 307. Greenberg writes: "Even if moved by reelection hopes, Nixon . . . acted boldly (if also, many thought in retrospect, ill-advisedly) to impose controls on wages, prices, and corporate profits."

58. While these measures proved temporary, of no great importance, Nixon's decision to allow the dollar to "float," no longer to be redeemed at a fixed rate, was a change that has survived from his day to the present.

59. Herbert S. Parmet, *Richard Nixon and His America* (Little, Brown, 1990), p. 551. Parmet writes: "Over the objections of most of his cabinet, welfare reform became the centrepiece of what he called a New Federalism, which he announced on August 8, 1969. It called for a massive reordering of the way government went about doing things, a pullback from the concentration of power that had been going on ever since New Deal days. It was not designed to do for the disadvantaged what the Great Society had failed to accomplish. That kind of objective had little support from the administration, the Republican party, or the American people."

60. Ibid., p. 554. Revenue-sharing, Arthur Burn's "pet plan," introduced together with Daniel Patrick Moynihan's Family Assistance Plan, called for the federal government, in the president's words, to "build a foundation under the income of every family with dependent children that cannot care for itself—and wherever that family may live."

61. Ambrose, *Triumph*, p. 330. Ambrose wrote: "What a strange man was Richard Nixon. Subtle and skillful in his approach to the Chinese, he was stubborn and spiteful in his approach to the Senate. He had vowed, when the Senate turned down his nomination of Judge Haynsworth, that he would 'show them.' He did. On January 19, he nominated Judge G. Harrold Carswell for the Supreme Court vacancy. . . . Carswell had everything going against him. As a candidate for the Georgia legislature in 1948, he had said: 'Segregation of the races is proper and the only practical and correct way of life. . . . I have always so believed and I shall always so act.'. . . Further, his qualifications for the high court were simply nonexistent. Bryce Harlow, always one to tell the truth, informed Nixon that the senators 'think Carswell's a boob, a dummy. And what counter is there to that? He is.'"

62. Mayer, *Race*, p. 97.

63. Ibid., pp. 98–99.

64. Ibid., p. 99. Mayer writes: "The chief policy adviser on urban affairs, and Nixon's most prominent liberal appointee, Daniel Moynihan, was the author of a memo that called for benign neglect of black problems by the administration. The memo caused a firestorm of criticism, and Moynihan unconvincingly claimed that he had only been suggesting neglect for black militants, not blacks generally."

65. Ibid., p. 100.

66. Ibid., p. 108.

67. Ambrose, *Triumph,* p. 364. Ambrose's observations are compelling; he wrote: "Nixon's wants were contradictory. He wanted voluntary compliance with the court orders, which was about as likely in the Deep South as an August snowstorm in Mississippi. He wanted the confrontations over and done with in 1970, so there would be relative peace on the racial front during his re-election in 1972. He wanted to expand his gains in the South, even as desegregation took place. He wanted to do what was right, without having to use force, and without having to pay a price."

68. Ibid., p. 523. Nixon, in this nationwide address, asked Congress to "impose a moratorium on the federal courts to prevent them from ordering any new busing to achieve racial balance," knowing such a proposal would gain him wide public support.

69. Johnson believed the same, arguing in his autobiography that had he chosen to run in 1968, he would have been reelected.

70. Richard Reeves, *President Nixon: Alone in the White House* (Simon and Schuster, 2001), p. 203. These themes, implicit in everything Nixon and Kissinger did at the time, providing their justification for bombing Laos and invading Cambodia, led to a remarkable interview that Kissinger had with Joseph Alsop, a journalist and friend he trusted. Alsop's notes on the conversation, as given by Reeves, are illuminating. Kissinger is reported to have said: "Our problem is that the whole establishment, which detests Nixon, has turned against him at the very moment that he is trying to save the establishment. Nixon is not a fool. He is perfectly aware that there is no way to leave South Vietnam with all the banners flying. 'But we have to get out as a matter of policy—American policy. We cannot be shoved out. If we are shoved out by the North Vietnamese this would have terrible effects abroad and it would tear this country apart, and hand it over to the hard hats. That is why Nixon is in the curious position of trying to save an establishment which despises him.'"

71. Ibid., pp. 192–193. In April 1970, the president, persuaded that the threat to Cambodia from the North Vietnamese would soon cause his policy of "Vietnamization" to collapse, decided on decisive action. Reeves, seeking to explain Nixon, writes: "He [Nixon] had been President for more than a year and a frustrated one for most of that time. The North Vietnamese had shelled Saigon early in 1969 and he had done nothing; the North Koreans had shot down the EC-121 and he had done nothing. The Soviets were moving into the Middle East and the United States had been unable to stop them. . . . [The] communists were having their way in Laos and were now threatening to take Cambodia, too. This was the time and this was the place to show the world that he could meet force with force. 'This is what I've been waiting for,' he told Kissinger."

72. Henry Kissinger, *Ending the Vietnam War: A History of America's Involvement in and Extrication from the Vietnam War* (Simon and Schuster, 2003). This is Kissinger's most elaborate explanation of what he and the president intended, where they agreed on policy and where they differed.

73. Ibid., pp. 591–600. Kissinger prints the transcript of his press conference on October 26, 1972, where he describes the negotiations with the North Vietnamese in greatest detail, making the statement, "We believe that peace is at hand."

74. Reeves, *Nixon,* p. 207. Nixon, speaking to the nation in a TV address, said: "This is not an invasion of Cambodia. The areas in which these attacks will be launched are completely occupied and controlled by North Vietnamese forces. Our purpose is not to occupy the areas. Once enemy forces are driven out of these sanctuaries and their military supplies are destroyed, we will withdraw."

75. Ibid., p. 208. See, also, Ambrose, *Triumph,* p. 351. Within days of making what the president and others believed was an immensely effective defense of his policy in ordering the invasion of Cambodia, the *New York Times* reported that both the secretary of state, Rogers, and the secretary of Defense, Laird, "had serious misgivings about the use of American troops in Cambodia," suggesting that the "war decisions in the last two weeks have been reached in an atmosphere of confusion as well as dissension." Nixon was "shocked and disappointed" by the leaks.

76. *Presidential Commission on Campus Unrest* (1970).

77. *Newsweek*, May 25, 1970, p. 30.

78. *The Vietnam War: An Almanac,* edited by John S. Bowman with an introduction by Fox Butterfied (Bison Books, 1985), p. 273. The chronology offered in this book makes it a uniquely valuable publication.

79. Ibid., p. 275.

80. Ibid.

81. Ibid.

82. Ibid., p. 276.

83. Ibid., p. 282. The report in the *Almanac* for May 3 to May 5 reads: "The militant antiwar demonstrations in Washington end as police arrest 12,614 protestors—a record high for arrests in a civil disturbance in the nation's history. With inadequate detention facilities, most of those arrested are held 24 hours and the charges against them are subsequently dropped."

84. Ambrose, *Triumph,* p. 428. Nixon reacted as he did in part because of the thousands of telegrams he had received, protesting the Army's treatment of Calley, in their view made a "scapegoat."

85. Ibid., p. 359. Ambrose wrote of the half-million letters and cards that flooded into the White House, mostly supporting the president, a record number seemed to confirm the Gallup Poll's finding that 50 percent supported his incursion into Cambodia with only 39 percent opposed.

86. *The Pentagon Papers* (Bantam Books, 1971).

87. Daniel Ellsberg, *Secrets: A Memoir of Vietnam and the Pentagon Papers* (Viking, 2002), p. 422. This, a biased but extremely useful analysis of the import of the *Pentagon Papers* revelations, expresses Nixon's reaction succinctly. Ellsberg writes: "On the one hand, Nixon's private reaction to the contents of the first installments of the Pentagon Papers—with their unflattering revelations about his Democratic predecessors—becoming known to the public was entirely positive. On the other hand, he was very concerned lest this revelation be a precedent for exposure of his own past and present secret actions and policies in Indochina."

88. Ibid., pp. 444–457. No words uttered by Nixon were more revealing than those he used in speaking to Haldeman when the trial against Ellsberg was collapsing because of the revelations that Gordon Liddy and Howard Hunt had burglarized the offices of Ellsberg's psychiatrist. The president said: ". . . on this national security thing, we have the rocky situation where the son-ofabitchief is made a national hero and is going to get off on a mistrial. And the *New York Times* gets a Pulitzer Prize for stealing documents. . . . They're trying to get us with *thieves. What in the name of God have we come to?"

89. Kissinger, as much as Nixon, provided the rationale for the "opening to China," but the president's own role in the matter cannot be sufficiently emphasized. It was the most important foreign policy achievement of his six years in office.

90. See Henry Kissinger, *Diplomacy* (Simon and Schuster, 1994), pp. 703–731. In these very revealing pages in a chapter appropriately titled "Foreign Policy as Geopolitics: Nixon's Triangular Diplomacy," Kissinger describes the advantages these novel foreign policy initiatives were expected to bring. Believing Nixon to be "the first president since Theodore Roosevelt to conduct American policy largely in the name of the national interest," he acknowledges that such a policy was unlikely to impress the American people.

91. *Foreign Affairs*, October 1967, pp. 111–125.

92. "Building for Peace," A report by President Richard Nixon to the Congress, February 25, 1971.

93. Kissinger, *Diplomacy,* p. 728.

94. Ibid., pp. 728–729. These earlier agreements had not touched the fundamental differences that separated the Communist powers, both China and the Soviet Union, from the

United States. Kissinger believed that within a year and a half of the signing of the Shanghai Communiqué, "Sino-American relations had moved from strident hostility and isolation to *de facto* alliance against the pre-eminent threat," in Mao's mind, the one posed by the Soviet Union.

95. In the 1950s and 1960s, a small group, principally of American academics, developed ideas that in time provided the rationale for the arms control policies pursued by successive administrations. Kissinger was prominent among these scholars, made so by his publication of *Nuclear Weapons and Foreign Policy* in 1956.

96. Jenn Newhouse, *Cold Dawn: The Story of Salt* (Holt, Rinehart, and Winston, 1973) pp. 140–141. The idea of "linkage" was born.

97. Kissinger, *Diplomacy,* p. 747. Kissinger writes: "Although he had been Nixon's first choice for Secretary of Defense, Jackson was to become the most implacable opponent of the administration's Soviet policy."

98. Bundy, *Danger and Survival,* p. 552. The phrase MAD originated with Donald Brennan who had been influential as a scholar in the field of arms control since the early 1960s. Brennan had written in the *National Review,* "The concept of mutual assured destruction provides one of the few instances in which the obvious acronym for something yields at once the appropriate description; for it, that is, a Mutual Assured Destruction posture as a goal is, almost literally, mad. MAD."

99. Ibid., p. 554.

100. Ibid., pp. 555–556.

101. *New York Times*, November 3, 1972, p. 1.

102. Bundy, *Danger and Survival.*

103. Henry Kissinger, *White House Years* (Little, Brown, 1979) pp. 1406–1407.

104. Ibid., p. 1407.

105. Ibid., p. 1448.

106. Ibid.

107. Ibid., p. 1449.

108. Ibid.

109. Ibid., p. 1452.

110. Ibid., pp. 1453–1454.

111. Johnson makes no reference to this taping system in his *Vantage Point,* and his principal biographer, Doris Kearns Goodwin, is equally silent.

112. Reeves, *Nixon,* p. 604. Reeves, while of course giving attention to the Butterfield revelation, made on July 16, 1973, so important in bringing Congress almost a year later to initiate impeachment proceedings against him, in his very succinct summary of the unravelling of the administration, notes that from April 30 when he announced the resignations of Haldeman and Ehrlichman to the end of November 1973, the president "spent only thirty-two days in Washington, ten of them as a patient, with pneumonia at Walter Reed Hospital."

113. Stanley I. Kutler, Edited with an Introduction and Commentary *Abuse of Power: The New Nixon Tapes* (Free Press, 1997), pp. 321–322.

114. Ibid., p. 321.

115. Ibid.

116. Ibid., p. 323.

117. Ibid.

118. Ibid., p. 350.

119. Ibid., p. 381.

120. Ibid.

121. Ibid.

122. Ibid., p. 382.

123. Ibid., pp. 382–383.

124. Ibid., p. 384.

125. Reeves, *Nixon*, p. 594. Dean, as early as April 20, had released a statement that greatly alarmed Nixon. Dean, through his secretary, had told the *Washington Post* that "Some may hope or think that I will become a scapegoat in the Watergate case. Anyone who believes this does not know me, know the true facts, nor understand our system of justice."

126. Henry Kissinger, *Years of Upheaval* (Little, Brown, 1982), pp. 294–299.

127. Bob Woodward and Carl Bernstein, *The Final Days* (Simon and Schuster, 1976), pp. 58–59. In response to this demand, Pat Buchanan suggested to the president that he destroy the tapes. The "bonfire" approach, he argued, would create a political "firestorm" that would quickly blow over. Neither the president's lawyer, J. Fred Buzhardt, nor his new chief of staff, General Haig, recommended that course of action. Haig believed that "destroying the tapes would look like an admission of guilt," and since the president insisted that "nothing in the tapes would hurt him," only "a few ambiguous statements that might be misconstrued if they were taken out of context," that approach seemed ill-advised. Leonard Garment, another of his lawyers, told him that in any case it was "too late."

128. Ibid., pp. 459–460. The chronology of the next two months, as given by Woodward and Bernstein, is enormously telling. On September 29, Rose Mary Woods, the president's secretary, began to transcribe some of the tapes. On October 10, 1973, Vice President Agnew resigned, the first man in his office to be ousted because of the crimes he had committed. Two days later, Nixon nominated Gerald Ford to succeed him. On October 20, the celebrated Saturday Night Massacre occurred, with the president firing the special prosecutor, Archibald Cox, and both the attorney general, Elliot Richardson, and the assistant attorney general, William Ruckelshaus, resigning in protest. In the next days, some 44 Watergate-related bills were introduced in Congress, including 22 that called for an impeachment inquiry.

129. These events would later come to haunt Kissinger, held responsible by some for what happened in Santiago.

130. Kissinger, *Upheaval*, pp. 414–449.

131. Ibid., p. 420.

132. Ibid., pp. 415–416.

133. Ibid., p. 417.

134. Ibid.

135. Ibid.

136. Henry Kissinger, *Crisis: The Anatomy of Two Major Foreign Policy Crises* (Simon and Schuster, 2003). This book, a collection of the conversations Kissinger had in connection with the Yom Kippur War, following the Egyptian surprise attack on Israel, and also those that took place in the last month before the final collapse of the U.S. effort to remain in Vietnam, is a telling account of two crises that coincided with the virtual eclipse of Nixon's presidential power, followed by Ford's humiliation at the hands of a Congress unwilling to support him in any effort to defeat the North Vietnamese in their advance on Saigon.

137. Ibid., p. 342. Kissinger gives a day-by-day account of the negotiations leading up to this very unwelcome message from Brezhnev, sent on October 24.

138. Ibid., pp. 347–357. Kissinger, without making additional comment, simply notes what Nixon, in his own memoirs, elected to say: "When Haig informed me about this message, I said that he and Kissinger should have a meeting at the White House to formulate plans for a firm reaction to what amounted to a scarcely veiled threat of unilateral Soviet intervention. Words were not making our point—we needed action, even the shock of a military alert."

139. Ibid., p. 353.

140. Ibid., p. 356.

141. Ibid., p. 357.

142. Woodward and Bernstein, *Final Days*, p. 95. Judge Sirica ordered a public hearing on the matter, and summoned Buzhardt, Haig, and Woods to testify, along with Secret Service agents and other White House aides.

143. Kissinger, *Upheaval*, p. 1198.

144. Ibid., p. 1200–1203.

145. Ibid., p. 1203.

146. Ibid.

147. Ibid.

148. Ibid.

149. The Kissinger autobiography, unique in many respects—a fact too rarely commented on—is different from all other such accounts in its unusual candor about the strange individual he chose to serve. Though there are numerous autobiographies written by those acquainted with the courts of twentieth-century presidents, few have illuminated the White House in the way Kissinger has. If, as some argue, he greatly exaggerated the president's abilities, he made no effort to deny his massive and disconcerting flaws.

150. Greenberg, *Nixon's Shadow*, pp. 338–347. Greenberg's Epilogue, along with many of his other chapters, is a compelling analysis of how Nixon "resurrected" himself, making it possible for some who have written about him in recent decades, together with those who attended his funeral, to praise him. As Greenberg says, the eulogies cannot be simply characterized as *de mortuis nil nisi bonum*, "of the dead say nothing that is unkind."

151. There is no way to demonstrate that the opinion about Nixon is still more negative than positive even in the twenty-first century, but it would be difficult to prove the contrary.

152. Bundy, *Danger and Survival*, pp. 522–524.

153. Ibid., p. 524.

154. Kissinger, *Upheaval*, pp. 979–1031, a chapter entitled "The Decline of Détente: A Turning Point," one of the most important in his autobiography.

155. Ibid. See especially pp. 981–985.

CHAPTER 16 (The Innocent)

1. Gerald R. Ford, *A Time to Heal* (W. H. Allen, 1969), p. 98. This presidential autobiography, so different from the less candid accounts so common of late, demonstrates Ford's readiness to write honestly about most issues, though not all.

2. Ibid., p. 173. Ford insists, contrary to the opinion and recollections of others, that his decision to pardon Nixon "had nothing to do with any sympathy I might feel for him personally or any concern I might have for the state of his health." He believed that "public policy demanded that I put Nixon—and Watergate—behind us as quickly as possible," and that this alone explained his decision.

3. Jerald F. ter Horst, *Gerald Ford* (W. H. Allen, 1975), pp. 236–238. ter Horst, appointed Ford's press secretary, felt compelled to resign his post, writing that he could not "in good conscience support your decision to pardon former President Nixon even before he has been charged with the commission of any crime."

4. Ford, *Time to Heal*, pp. 141–142. Ford, showing considerable daring, made his amnesty announcement before a convention of the Veterans of Foreign Wars.

5. Ibid., pp. 142–145. Ford suggests that he knew the Rockefeller nomination would leave conservative Republicans "sputtering," and writes that his only concern was to choose the most able and most experienced man.

6. It is curious that Ford, knowing Congress so well, should have ignored the opinion of the Democrats, dominant in both the House and the Senate, unlikely to take kindly to the nomination of a Rockefeller.

7. Ford never hinted that he understood this.

8. Richard Reeves, *A Ford, Not a Lincoln: The Decline of American Political Leadership* (Hutchinson, 1976), p. 119. Ford, questioned closely on the reported expenditure of some $8 million to upset the government of Salvador Allende, the elected president of Chile, a Marxist, replied, "I am not going to pass judgment on whether it is permitted or authorized under international law. . . . I think this is in the best interest of the people of Chile, and certainly in our best interest."

9. *New York Times,* December 22, 1974, p. 1.

10. Ford, *Time to Heal,* pp. 229–230. Commenting on the Hersh article, Ford writes: "Bill Colby [Director of the CIA] had warned me that Hersh was working on the story. He predicted that its publication would be embarrassing; but at the same time, he assured me that while the agency might have broken the law in the past, it had long since abandoned such practices. As firmly as I could, I told him that I simply wouldn't tolerate any violations of the law in my Administration. The Agency's charter clearly prohibited operations within U.S. borders, and I expected that charter to be upheld." It was only on January 3, Ford writes, that Colby told him of what higher CIA executives referred to as the "family jewels," the "highly classified documents that provided details about unsavory and illegal CIA practices. In the 1950s and 1960s, the CIA had plotted to assassinate foreign leaders, including Fidel Castro. Although none of these assassinations had been carried out, the fact that government officials had even considered them was distressing."

11. See Kissinger, *Years of Renewal,* pp. 310–343, a chapter entitled "The Intelligence Investigations," filled with explicit criticisms by Kissinger of those in Congress who stimulated the intelligence inquiries. He is especially critical of Colby who believed that his duties as director of the CIA obliged him to "cooperate with the investigations and educate the Congress, press, and public as well as I could . . . " Kissinger argued that no CIA director before Colby had ever believed that such duties inhered in his office. (p. 323).

12. Ford, *Time to Heal,* pp. 236–238. It is interesting to note that neither Ford nor Kissinger gave any attention to this serious presidential gaffe, almost pretending it was never made. Ford, after explaining the reasons for selecting Rockefeller to head the commission, turns in his memoirs to consider the new Cabinet appointments, especially the selection of Edward Levi to be his attorney general. Levi was recommended by Rumsfeld but suspect to both James Eastland, chairman of the Senate Judiciary Committee, and the ranking Republican on the Committee, Roman Hruska. Ford summoned both senators to the Oval Office to tell them that Levi was a "law-and-order man," not a "bushy-haired liberal. . . not another Ramsey Clark. . . not a liberal academic who is going to give the store away." Both senators came away persuaded that this was one academic they could support.

13. Ibid., p. 329. Kissinger, writing of the five "alleged" assassination plots, notes that all but one occurred during the Kennedy administration.

14. Since the most serious transgressions were made under Kennedy, it is strange that Ford made the same mistakes in treating the Senate investigations led by Senator Church that Nixon had committed in his violent reaction to the publication of the *Pentagon Papers* that dealt only with Democratic administration misdemeanors.

15. Ford, *Time to Heal,* p. 226. Ford signed the Foreign Assistance Act of 1974 only because it allowed the administration to continue its arms aid to Turkey, though only for a time. Still, he knew that "it reduced economic and military aid to both South Vietnam and Cambodia to levels that endangered their ability to survive as free nations."

16. Ibid., pp. 283–284. Ford mentioned these casualties, of course, and acknowledged that he "felt terrible about it"; much of his comment, however, had to do with those liberals in the press and Congress critical of the operation, including Tony Lewis of the *New York Times,* criticized for

his column entitled "Barbarous Piracy." See, also, McDonald, *American Presidency,* p. 417 where he discusses the War Powers resolution that required the president to "consult with Congress" before sending U.S. forces "into hostilities or into situations where imminent involvement in hostilities is clearly indicated." Roy Rowan, *Four Days of Mayaguez* (Norton, 1975) is an especially good appraisal of this incident.

17. Ford, even more than Nixon, by making this appointment, launched Bush on the road that led him eventually to the presidency.

18. *New York Times,* December 14, 1975, p. 1. This was the famous Seymour Hersh article on Angola and secret American aid.

19. Ford, *Time to Heal,* p. 345.

20. *New York Times,* January 20, 1976, p. 18.

21. Given Ford's long experience in Congress, it is striking that he showed so little sensitivity in knowing how to deal with legislative criticism.

22. *Covert Action in Chile 1963–1973* (US Gov't Printing Office, 1975).

23. These were all classic Republican remedies, as popular in the time of Harding and Hoover as in Ford's day.

24. McDonald, *Presidency,* pp. 354–355. McDonald notes that Kennedy, Johnson, and Carter, with their strong Democratic majorities most of the time, rarely felt any need to use the veto power. He depicts Eisenhower and Reagan as "essentially nonconfrontational," and though both faced large Democratic majorities during their sixteen years in office, "in the interest of keeping the doors open to successful negotiations they tried to avoid using the veto." This situation changed dramatically during the time of Nixon and Ford. McDonald writes: "Nixon and Ford, by contrast, wielded the veto as a weapon, but they met with little success against a Congress that was, by 1973, openly hostile. Of their seventy-one regular vetoes of public bills, more than a quarter were overridden—the worst records except for the hapless Andrew Johnson and Franklin Pierce."

25. Ford, *Time to Heal,* pp. 316–317.

26. Ibid., pp. 151–152. Ford claimed that the reasons for the economic crisis were clear. Johnson, in seeking to finance his domestic programs and the military build-up necessitated by the Vietnam War, doing both without raising taxes created a large federal deficit. Nixon, Ford acknowledged, only added to the fire by imposing wage and price controls in 1971, greatly disconcerting the business community. Finally, the Yom Kippur War of 1973 vastly increased the price of oil. All these events, preceding his accession, were made even more serious by the American drought in 1974 that caused food prices to rise appreciably.

27. John Osborne, *White House Watch: The Ford Years* (New Republic Books, 1977). Because Ford has not to date received attention from scholars, those who seek to learn more about him and his administration are necessarily led to his own memoirs and those of Kissinger, as well as the observations of major American journalists. Among these, none wrote more tellingly than John Osborne whose columns appeared almost weekly in the *New Republic.*

28. Ibid., pp. xxiv–xxv. Osborne wrote, in introducing his book, "My reports showed some awareness of the animosities and frictions that seethed behind the seemingly placid Ford façade. But it was only in the twilight weeks, when Ford people loosened up and were more willing to talk than they had previously been, that I began to comprehend the depth and ferocity of the animosities. Donald Rumsfeld, whom I respected during his term at the head of the White House staff and respect now, was the center and target of much of the distrust. Nelson Rockefeller was convinced that Rumsfeld deliberately frustrated his efforts to contribute to domestic policy formulation, engineered the pressures upon Rockefeller to withdraw from consideration for the 1976 vice presidential nomination, and beguiled Gerald Ford into firing Secretary of Defense James Schlesinger and CIA Director William Colby, replacing Schlesinger with Rumsfeld at De-

fense and Colby with George Bush at CIA, depriving Secretary of State Henry Kissinger of his White House base and status as assistant for national security affairs on November 2 and 3, 1975. Of the persons named, only Rockefeller asserted on the record that Rumsfeld did all this in the interest of placing himself in line for the 1976 vice presidential nomination. Kissinger, Schlesinger and Secretary of the Treasury William Simon, who detested the White House staff under Rumsfeld and his successor, Richard Cheney, as thoroughly as Rockefeller did, shared the suspicions of Rumsfeld and found them believable. But they did not speak of them as accepted fact in the way that Rockefeller did."

29. Kissinger, *Years of Renewal,* pp. 1059–1079.

30. These issues, treated extensively in Kissinger's book, recount a tale of accomplishment while also acknowledging failures, describing the rare moments of euphoria but also the more common times of disappointment and frustration.

31. Kissinger, like General Scowcroft, his deputy and successor as national security adviser, accept as incontestable that Ford inherited a discredited presidency, and that his great accomplishment was to re-create some semblance of order, making the country aware of its principles, effectively beginning to lead a distressed nation away from its fixation on the Vietnam War, Watergate, and Nixon.

32. Ibid., p. 1065. Kissinger issued the ultimate accolade when he wrote: "Most important in a period when passions still ran deep, Ford rescued a cohesive American policy from the carnage of Vietnam and Watergate. He made this contribution despite the handicap that, facing our only unelected President, Congress and the media felt freed of some of the shackles that normally place a limit on excessive self-will. Ford achieved all this without histrionics and visible emotional strain largely because he was so unlike the political leaders now brought into prominence by our normal electoral processes."

33. Mayer, *Race,* p. 126.

34. Ibid., pp. 133–136.

35. Osborne, *Ford Years*, p. 380.

36. The elevation of both Rumsfeld to head the Defense Department and Bush to direct the CIA must be considered the most important consequences of this "changing of the guard."

37. The Rockefeller suspicions about Rumsfeld's ambitions, reported by Osborne, have never been proved, but they continue to resonate for some of those who served Ford, still reluctant to say this publicly.

38. Bush was doing almost nothing in Beijing, and bringing him back to Washington to head the CIA gave him a prominence greater than any he had enjoyed previously, including the time he spent as ambassador to the United Nations when Nixon and Kissinger effectively determined what he was allowed to do or say.

39. Few Ford "loyalists" are prepared to acknowledge this even today; such is the fear of "mighty Don."

CHAPTER 17 (The New Georgia)

1. Jimmy Carter, *An Hour Before Daylight* (Simon and Schuster, 2001), pp. 270–271. In his old age, Carter has written a delightful sentimental account of his childhood and youth, portraying himself as a paragon of virtue, embodying all the values that a romantic America wishes to believe in. As in *Why Not the Best?* Carter's 1976 campaign autobiography, it is difficult to know when he is being sincere, and how much his concern to be "politically correct" encourages him to express a sentimentality calculated to have wide appeal.

2. Betty Glad, *Jimmy Carter: In Search of the Great White House* (Norton, 1980), pp. 58–68 and 123–228. This book, more than any other, explores Carter's early life critically, but his years

as governor are also exceptionally well treated. Glad devotes attention to the "series of emotional experiences" that led him to be "born again," to become a true Christian, able to shed his "Pharisee" past, prepared to spread the word to others still lost in darkness.

3. Mayer, *Race,* pp. 127–128.

4. Ibid., p. 128. It was important for Carter to avoid the issue of race, something he had done effectively in his campaign to become governor of Georgia.

5. Mayer, *Race,* pp. 130–131. In heavily Catholic Massachusetts, a state of ethnic and racial enclaves, Jackson's policies on busing had great appeal, especially in Boston where Wallace managed to win in many precincts.

6. Hadley, *Invisible Primary,* pp. 272–273. Hadley, a journalist writing before the results were known, recognized that Carter had to do well in Florida for his candidacy to remain alive.

7. Ibid., pp. 274–275. Again, writing before the New York results were known, Hadley believed that only Udall had to finish either first or a close second to maintain himself in the race, taking for granted that Jackson would do well.

8. Mayer, *Race,* pp. 132–133. Carter's Wisconsin victory was so small that the next Midwestern primary in Michigan was seen to be crucial. In that state, Carter was greatly helped by Coleman Young, the mayor of Detroit, who urged blacks to vote against Udall "because he was a Mormon, a faith that did not admit blacks to its priesthood."

9. Ibid., p. 131.

10. Ibid., pp. 131–132.

11. Ibid., p. 132.

12. Ibid.

13. Glad, *Carter,* p. 254.

14. Ibid., pp. 254–270. Glad notes the "rocks in the road" for Carter in the last weeks of the primaries, placed there principally by the late entry of two new men into the race, Senator Frank Church of Idaho and Governor Edmund G. (Jerry) Brown of California.

15. Kraus, *Great Debates,* p. 20. Harold Laswell, in his Introduction, poses the question few journalists care to ask: "Does direct debate foster enlightenment? Or does it contribute to public confusion by encouraging competitive declarations of devotion to traditional ambiguities, and by tolerating the confident reiteration of half-truths and self-serving prophesies?"

16. Betty Glad, "Election of 1976" in Schlesinger, *Presidential Elections,* Supplemental Volume, p. 101.

17. Ibid., pp. 147–149. Carter's most wounding statement may have been, ". . . that as far as foreign policy goes, Mr. Kissinger has been the President of this country."

18. Ibid., p. 102. Glad, in her comment on this gaffe, noted that Ford was initially perceived as having won the debate by a margin of 44 to 35 percent, but this changed to an adverse judgment of his performance, a loss of 61 to 19 percent when newspapers emphasized the mistake he had made in his reference to Eastern Europe. Indeed, by failing to acknowledge his error for a week, Ford only added to his problems with the media.

19. Zbigniew Brzezinski, *Power and Principles: Memoirs of the National Security Adviser 1977–1981* (Farrar, Straus, Giroux), pp. 9–10. Brzezinski writes: "On matters of substance, the debate was probably a standoff, but the combined effects of Ford's misstep on Poland and his defensive demeanor served to project Carter as genuinely Presidential, the dynamic and fresh leader that the country so badly needed after the crises of Watergate and Vietnam."

20. Carter pointed out that Ford had been in office for more than 800 days, "almost as long as John Kennedy," and asked what he had accomplished.

21. Glad, *Carter,* pp. 475–507. Glad, in two brilliant chapters, has given an incomparable portrait of Carter's mind and personality, showing him to be thorough but not creative, ambitious but not always as self-assured as he pretended to be, given to lying about himself and his

accomplishments, often on trivial matters, but laying great store on presenting himself as always truthful. Glad suggests that in Carter's concern to appear "the central actor in the political system" and "the sole spokesman for the public interest," he perpetuated the "Imperial Presidency" that Arthur Schlesinger Jr. had associated with Nixon. In a very searing indictment of Carter's rule, she writes: "This is what the 'Imperial Presidency' is about—not fancy uniforms or 'hails to the Chief' as the discussion during the 1976 campaign suggested it was. . . . Rather than acting as the moral and political leader of the nation, he [Carter] has used his position and his ability to command attention to promote a further trivialization of political dialogue in America and an obfuscation of the political alternatives before the nation. From the beginning of his presidency, Carter has used his public relations skill to focus on his own person rather than on these political alternatives. The agenda for the nation has been compiled out of a random list of promises he had made on the campaign trail and his *ad hoc* reaction to events in terms of his political interests." See, also, Richard M. Pious, *The American Presidency* (Basic Books, 1979), p. 4. Pious writes of Carter's appointment of his relative, Hugh Carter, nicknamed "Cousin Cheap," given "the assignment of 'depomping' the presidency."

22. *New York Times,* January 21, 1977, p. 25.

23. There is no comparable photograph of any previous president.

24. He knew less about the subject than he pretended, just as he greatly exaggerated his competence in defense matters, based on his brief experience in the Navy, serving on a nuclear-powered submarine.

25. Pious, *Presidency,* p. 135. Pious notes that Carter won by a very small margin, but that of the twenty-one senators elected or returned to the Senate, twenty had a greater margin of victory than his, and few came to Washington believing that the president had greatly helped them in their campaigns.

26. *New York Times,* April 12, 1978, p. A 1.

27. Brzezinski, *Power,* p. 124.

28. Ibid.

29. Sol Linowitz, *The Making of a Public Man* (Little, Brown, 1985), p. 210.

30. Hedley Donovan, *Roosevelt to Reagan* (Harper and Row, 1985), pp. 233–236.

31. Essay on Carter by Steven M. Gillon in Alan Brinkley and Davis Dyer, ed., *The Reader's Companion to the American Presidency* (Houghton Mifflin, 2000), pp. 482–483.

32. Jimmy Carter, *Memoirs of a President* (Collins, 1982), pp. 60 and 121. Carter never discusses the reasons for such a massive dismissal of key members of his Cabinet, but chooses instead to dwell on how long they had served him, writing: "With rare exception, I was well pleased with the original members of my administration. More than thirty months passed before I replaced a Cabinet member—which made my Cabinet the most stable in modern American history." Of the major Cabinet changes made in 1979, Carter writes briefly and, by his standards, self-critically, saying: "I handled the Cabinet changes very poorly. . . ."

33. Hamilton Jordan, *Crisis: The Last Year of the Carter Presidency* (Michael Joseph, 1982), pp. 46–47. Hamilton Jordan, Carter's chief of staff, wrote: "In organizing his foreign policy team, Carter saw no inherent conflict between the men and the institutions they represented. Zbig would sit at his side, stimulating new ideas, creating long-range plans, and sifting through the mountains of foreign policy papers that regularly came to the White House for the President. Vance would be the diplomat, meeting with ambassadors and foreign dignitaries, the manager, trying to control the sprawling State Department bureaucracy; and the implementer, responsible for making the policies work." A devastating comment on Brzezinski was made by Clark Clifford, *Counsel,* pp. 620–621, who expressed reservations about him when the president first mentioned his name, saying that he was "an articulate and combative academic. . . too much of an advocate and not enough of an honest broker. . . . " Those remarks gave no pleasure to Carter,

nor did he respond to Clifford's view that "he would clash with the gentle and collegial Vance." Clifford's misgivings about Carter went well beyond the doubts he expressed about some of the others he chose to appoint. The president's great failing, he wrote, was that having won the election "on his own," he believed he "could govern without Washington."

34. Carter, *Keeping Faith*, pp. 495–496. Carter recognized that Egypt and Israel interpreted the Camp David Accords differently, Sadat wanting "maximum autonomy for the Palestinians on the West Bank while Begin wanted just the opposite," contributing to their ultimate failure to achieve what he had himself hoped for. Clifford, while willing with most others to give credit to Carter for his Israeli/Egyptian negotiations, saw his inadequacies differently, saying: "He was always best in the pursuit of a single objective—whether it was the Democratic nomination, the election, or the historic agreements between Israel and Egypt. When confronted with the subtler tasks of sorting out the nation's priorities from a myriad of competing claims and leading the nation, he had more difficulty. To the end, his good intentions and genuine achievements were undermined by the inexperience of the people around him, and by his reluctance to widen his circle of advisers." Clifford, *Counsel,* p. 636.

35. Ibid., p. 496. It is doubtful that even had the events in Iran not intervened, requiring all of the president's attention, that much more would have been accomplished in the Israeli/Palestinian stand-off. Carter expected "both sides would mark time until the American election was over."

36. Brzezinski, *Power,* pp. 424–425. Brzezinski, exceedingly pleased with what he himself had done to cement American-Chinese relations, wrote with pride of the Chinese having adopted his theories about the Soviet Union, repeating them as if they originated with them.

37. Ibid., pp. 36–47. These pages, in their consideration of the major differences between Carter's national security adviser and the secretary of state, include a statement by Harold Brown, the secretary of defense, made to the *New York Times* on December 7, 1980, after Carter had lost the election. Brzezinski, insisting on his respect for Vance despite their differences, finds it convenient to quote Brown as having said: "Secretary of State Vance was persuaded that anything that involved the risk of force was a mistake." This, Brzezinski clearly sees as Vance's fundamental strategic flaw. As for Brown, while Brzezinski praises him for his own gradual shift to a harder line, resembling his own, this does not prevent his noting also that "out of both personal caution and intellectual agility Harold [Brown] tended to see every side of an issue, edge up to a firm view, and then quickly again hedge it." With both the secretary of state and the secretary of defense clearly lacking the requisite understanding of the world situation, who, then, could be relied on to give good advice to the president? Brzezinski avoided the question, but suggested that with Brown's help and his own advice, "President Carter was fashioning a policy truly responsive to our geopolitical and strategic dilemmas."

38. *New York Times,* January 21, 1977.

39. Brzezinski, *Power,* pp. 146–190. In this remarkable chapter, entitled "Salt Without Linkage," Brzezinski reveals unmistakably his perpetual preoccupation with Kissinger, concerned always to demonstrate his own superiority as a strategic thinker. Brzezinski, prepared to ask questions about relations with the Soviet Union that did not simply replicate those posed by Kissinger, led to conflicts with both Vance and Brown, but he finally brought the president to say in a major foreign policy speech at Wake Forest University that "Our strategic force must be—and must be known to be—a match for the capabilities of the Soviets. . . . Arms control agreements are a major goal as instruments of our national security, but this will be possible only if we maintain appropriate military force levels."

40. This was only the most startling of Carter's foreign policy and defense reversals.

41. Carter, *Keeping Faith*, pp. 184–185. In his very full account of the difficulties he faced in seeking to persuade Congress to accept the Panama treaties, Carter emphasizes the courage of

those in Congress who voted with him, men who resisted the arguments of their irresponsible colleagues.

42. *New York Times,* January 24, 1980, p. A 12.

43. Brzezinski, *Power,* pp. 426–469. Brzezinski, in his long chapter on the Carter Doctrine, documenting the differences within the administration on all the major steps taken to counter the Soviet aggression, ends with the kind of triumphal salute to himself and the president characteristic of his autobiography, saying: ". . . I felt we completed an important year during which we had fashioned a new geopolitical doctrine, a revised nuclear strategy, and a foreign policy in which our continued commitment to principle was reinforced by a more credible emphasis on the role of American power."

44. Andrew, *President's Eyes,* p. 455.

45. Ibid.

46. Brzezinski, *Power,* p. 506.

47. Yergin, *Prize,* p. 696.

48. See Brzezinski, *Power,* pp. 291–295. Neither Helmut Schmidt nor Valéry Giscard d'Estaing thought a great deal of Carter, and Brzezinski made no secret of his clashes with the German chancellor whom he found "rather haughty and distant." By comparison, he admired Callaghan for "cultivating Carter personally," and after a relatively few personal meetings becoming "Carter's favorite." See, in this connection, Robin Renwick, *Fighting with Allies: America and Britain in Peace and at War* (Times Books, 1996), p. 311 where he writes of the difficulties the British, French, and Germans had with the new administration on their sale of nuclear reactors to Brazil and Pakistan, and of the unsuccessful efforts they made to persuade Carter to do more to stabilize the dollar. On a lighter note, Renwick tells of Callaghan's entertaining Mondale in London, only to discover later that one of the vice president's staff members "had taken the wine list back to his hotel and priced it—then told the press that the Labour government lived in a state of decadent luxury that the president would never tolerate in Washington."

49. Denis Healey, *The Time of My Life* (Michael Joseph, 1989), p. 435.

50. Douglas Brinkley, *The Unfinished Presidency: Jimmy Carter's Journey Beyond the White House* (Viking, 1998).

51. Ibid., pp. 368–387.

52. Ibid., p. 433.

53. Richard Nixon, *The Real War* (Warner, 1980) pp. 169, 172.

CHAPTER 18 (The Actor)

1. Ronald Reagan, *An American Life* (Hutchinson, 1990). An extraordinary autobiography, more for what it reveals than for what it conceals.

2. Reagan, a city boy, was the son of a shoe salesman whose family moved about constantly. Dixon, Illinois, was the small town that came closest to being his boyhood home.

3. Lou Cannon, *President Reagan: The Role of a Lifetime* (Simon and Schuster, 1991), p. 225.

4. Ibid., pp. 91 and 227. Reagan's agent, anticipating his success with *King's Row,* negotiated a very favorable contract, giving him $1 million over seven years—a substantial sum at the time—making him independently wealthy after World War II.

5. Ibid., p. 225. Louella Parsons, the gossip columnist, also hailed from Dixon, Illinois, one of the bonds between these two very different Hollywood celebrities.

6. See Stephen Vaughn, *Ronald Reagan in Hollywood: Movies and Politics* (Cambridge University Press, 1994), p. 101.

7. See Reagan, *American Life,* p. 106. Reagan never denied his liberal past, saying "I joined just about any organization I could find that guaranteed to save the world, like the United World

Federalists and American Veterans Committee, which got me with their slogan, 'A Citizen First; a Veteran Afterward.' I really wanted a better world and I think I thought what I was saying would help bring it about."

8. Vaughn, *Reagan in Hollywood,* p. 143.

9. Cannon, *Reagan,* p. 74. Reagan cast his first vote for a Republican in 1952 when he voted for Eisenhower, and in 1960 presented himself as a "Democrat for Nixon."

10. Vaughn, *Reagan in Hollywood,* p. 209. See also Garry Wills, *Reagan's America, Innocents at Home* (Doubleday, 1987), pp. 241–258 for the most penetrating account of what led Reagan to be converted to anticommunism, how he came to believe that Hollywood was threatened with a Communist "takeover," and why the FBI, initially suspicious of him as a "Red," came to embrace him.

11. Kurt Ritter and David Henry, *Ronald Reagan: The Great Communicator* (Greenwood Press, 1992), p. 14.

12. William E. Pemberton, *Exit with Honour: The Life and Presidency of Ronald Reagan* (Armonk, 1997), p. 52.

13. Reagan, *American Life,* p. 137. Reagan's own account of the cancellation, more gratifying to his ego, is significantly different.

14. Robert Dallek, *Ronald Reagan: The Politics of Symbolism* (Harvard University Press, rev. edition, 1999), p. 28.

15. Ronald Reagan, *Where's the Rest of Me?* (Duell, Sloan and Pearce, 1965), p. 336.

16. Wills, *Reagan's America,* p. 311.

17. Ibid., p. 312.

18. Ibid., p. 330.

19. *Reagan in his Own Hand,* edited by Kiron K. Skinner, Annelise Anderson, and Martin Anderson (Free Press, 2001), p. 9–10. This collection of Reagan's radio talks, indicating the corrections he made, are as interesting for those things he chose to omit as for what he finally decided to say.

20. Ibid., p. 156. Reagan chided Carter for his hypocrisy in recognizing Communist China, showing no concern for "human rights," and betraying 17 million Chinese on Taiwan.

21. See Leuchtenberg, *Shadow,* pp. 209–210. While most commentators paid attention to the scathing comments Reagan made on Carter, Leuchtenberg, in his much more original interpretation of the acceptance speech, noted Reagan's frequent favorable mentions of Franklin Roosevelt. Leuchtenberg was not surprised that the *New York Times* the next day entitled its lead editorial, "Franklin Delano Reagan."

22. *New York Times,* January 21, 1981, p. B 1.

23. Reagan, *American Life,* p. 238.

24. Ibid., p. 239.

25. Ibid., p. 582.

26. Ibid., p. 263.

27. Reagan makes no mention of the opposition within his entourage to a second term for Volcker. Indeed, Volcker, who did as much for his administration as almost anyone, is mentioned only once in his autobiography.

28. *New York Times,* Feb. 6, 1983, p. 28.

29. Reagan, *American Life,* p. 270. The dispute over the letter allowed Reagan to make his first explicit criticism of Haig, saying: "He didn't want to carry out the president's foreign policy; he wanted to formulate it and carry it out himself."

30. Ibid., pp. 272–273.

31. Ibid., p. 273. Reagan described Brezhnev's response as "icy."

32. Ibid., p. 361.

33. Ibid. Reagan claimed that the Haig he had met at NATO was not the same man he came to know as secretary of state.

34. Ibid., pp. 360–361.

35. Ibid.

36. Alexander M. Haig Jr., *Caveat: Realism, Reagan, and Foreign Policy* (Macmillan, 1984), pp. 167–193. This is the most complete account available on what Haig imagined a U.S.-Middle East policy might be, the advantages it would bring.

37. *New York Times,* Oct. 28, 1982, p. A 7.

38. *Times* (London), June 9, 1982, p. 4.

39. Ibid.

40. Reagan, *American Life,* pp. 569–570. Reagan writes that he "made the 'Evil Empire' speech and others like it with malice aforethought," wanting "to remind the Soviets we knew what they were up to."

41. Ibid., pp. 575–576. Reagan publishes large segments of his correspondence with Andropov, saying that the latter's letters "were stiff and cold as a Siberian winter. . . ."

42. *New York Times,* May 10, 1984, p. A 16.

43. Reagan, *American Life,* pp. 473–477. Reagan complained of the unwillingness of Congress and public opinion to respond to his warnings that the Soviet Union and Cuba "were acting in concert to make the Caribbean a Communist lake." He was especially critical of the Speaker of the House, "Tip" O'Neill, and Representative Boland, chairman of the Intelligence Committee, who in his words were "battling to limit virtually everything the administration was trying to do in Central America."

44. Kissinger, *Diplomacy,* p. 774. Kissinger defined the Reagan Doctrine as a policy to "help anticommunist counterinsurgencies to wrest their respective countries out of the Soviet sphere of influence."

45. Andrew, *President's Eyes,* pp. 470–471. The administration, relying on CIA "covert action" in Nicaragua, was greatly embarrassed when *Newsweek* revealed on November 8, 1982, that the United States was engaged in a secret operation to overthrow the Nicaraguan government through "the training and organizing of Contra rebels."

46. On all issues relating to the Middle East, U.S. policy in respect to Israel, Iran, Iraq, Lebanon, and Syria during the Reagan administration, George Shultz, *Turmoil and Triumph, My Years as Secretary of State* (Scribner's, 1993) is one source that must be consulted. Very discreetly, Shultz acknowledges but never reveals the full extent of Reagan's "tilt," removing Iraq from the list of terrorism-supporting states, and urging its allies to help Saddam defeat the Iranians. For a more candid account of Reagan's policy vis-à-vis Iraq and Iran, a policy that Republicans in the age of George W. Bush would rather not recall, see Kenneth M. Pollack, *The Threatening Storm: The Case for Invading Iraq* (Random House, 2002), pp. 18–19. Pollack writes: "U.S. support for Iraq blossomed throughout the war. Starting in 1983, the United States provided economic aid to Iraq in the form of Commodities Credit Corporation guarantees to purchase U.S. agricultural products—$400 million in 1983, $513 million in 1984, and climbing to $652 million in 1987. This allowed Iraq to use money it otherwise would have spent on food to buy weapons and other military supplies. With Iraq off the terrorism list, the U.S. could also provide quasi-military aid. For example, Washington sold Baghdad ten Bell UH-1 Huey and sixty Hughes MD-500 Defender helicopters that were ostensibly in 'civilian configurations' but that Iraq quickly converted to military use. Iraq was also able to purchase large quantities of trucks that Washington knew would go to its war effort. Then, in March 1985, the United States began issuing Baghdad high-tech export licenses that previously had been denied. The sophisticated equipment Iraq bought with these licenses proved crucial to its weapons of mass destruction programs. In addition, the Reagan administration kept ratcheting

up its level of intelligence cooperation with Baghdad, eventually authorizing a liaison relationship between U.S. intelligence agencies and their Iraqi counterparts. Perhaps more than anything else, the high-quality intelligence the U.S. regularly furnished Baghdad regarding Iranian forces and operations proved vital to Iraq's conduct of the war. Finally, Washington encouraged its allies to similarly support Iraq against Iran."

47. As in later years, the greatest expectations were held of what such American intervention could do to resolve the problems between Israel and the PLO, and while Shultz never spoke of a "road map," he clearly imagined he was fashioning one, always disappointed by one or other of the parties.

48. Shultz, *Turmoil*, p. 233. Shultz writes that Begin, Israel's prime minister, at one time "envisaged the transformation of Lebanon into the second Arab nation, following Egypt's example, to make peace with Israel," but such hopes were dashed by the tragic massacres at Sabra and Shatila.

49. Neither the president nor his secretary of state felt any obligation to suggest how this task was to be accomplished.

50. Shultz, *Turmoil*, pp. 233–234. Both Reagan and Shultz, genuinely shocked by the incident, used it to press Israel to withdraw from Lebanon.

51. *New York Times,* September 21, 1982, p. A 1.

52. Shultz, *Turmoil*, p. 234.

53. Ibid., pp. 235–245. This chapter, entitled "Iraq, Iran, and Chemical Weapons," more than any other in Shultz's autobiography, expresses the self-righteousness but also the confusion that existed in the administration on Middle Eastern policy. Shultz, writing of the decision to resume diplomatic relations with Iraq, says: "There were no stars in my eyes or in Ronald Reagan's. I simply thought we were better off with diplomatic relations with Iraq. . . . After Israel's air attack in 1981 that disabled the Iraqi nuclear reaction under construction at Osirak, I felt sure that Iraq would not abandon its efforts to build a nuclear weapons capability. Iraq's ambitions and activities were not of a kind to breed confidence in Saddam Hussein. But the fact remained that a radical Iran now posed an immediate threat to the strategic Gulf area, and Iraq was the only military machine that could block the path of Khomeini's forces."

54. Weinberger, as Shultz knew, resisted any measure that might involve the country in active warfare in the Middle East.

55. This, the most serious terrorist attack on Americans, galvanized the president to speak out, but lacking any solution for the problem, and having no one in his immediate entourage prepared to reconceptualize Middle Eastern policy, nothing happened. Reagan's administration, bewildered by Middle Eastern events, never attempted anything that could be remotely thought a reappraisal of the situation, certainly nothing comparable to what Nixon sought to do with his China initiatives.

56. Political considerations seemed the paramount ones at this time for the president, and they dictated policy.

57. Thomas L. Friedman, *From Beirut to Jerusalem* (Anchor Books, 1990), p. 204.

58. Reagan, *American Life,* pp. 449–459. The dramatic account of this military operation, as given by Reagan, emphasizing his decisiveness in making the decision to invade the small island, thereby saving the Caribbean basin from communism, must be read by anyone who doubts that Reagan was an accomplished myth-maker, a story-teller with few rivals.

59. Margaret Thatcher, *The Downing Street Years* (HarperCollins, 1993), pp. 328–335.

60. See William V. Shannon, "Election of 1984" in Schlesinger, *Presidential Elections,* supplemental volume. Shannon, like others in this series who wrote of the U.S. elections beginning in 1972 did not find it necessary to publish the party platforms, thinking it more useful to publish the texts of the presidential debates.

61. Ibid., p. 293.

62. Ibid., p. 299.

63. Ibid., p. 303.

64. Ibid.

65. Ibid., p. 345.

66. Ibid., p. 305. Shannon, quoting from an article that appeared in the *New York Times* by Kevin Phillips noted that Reagan "drew from the same sources of strength as Nixon in 1972," emphasizing the "regional, Protestant fundamentalist, ethnic and racial contours of his victory."

67. *Washington Post*, September 25, 1984, p. A2.

68. Cannon, *Reagan*, pp. 229–230.

69. *New York Times*, October 28, 1983, p. A 10.

70. *New York Times*, July 9, 1985, p. A 12.

71. Andrew, *President's Eyes*, p. 481.

72. Ibid., p. 480. For the president, such questions scarcely existed. His only concern appeared to be the fate of the hostages.

73. Reagan felt only contempt for the Democrats who seemed bent on questioning and destroying these prized foreign policy initiatives.

74. Andrew, *President's Eyes*, p. 481. Andrew writes: "No record was made of his discussion with McFarlane, and it is uncertain whether at this meeting he agreed to the sale by Israel of Tow missiles to Iran for use in the war against Iraq."

75. Reagan, *American Life*, pp. 506–507. Reagan suggests that his sole purpose was to establish relations "with responsible people who might be the future leaders of Iran."

76. Shultz, *Turmoil*, pp. 808–840. This chapter, "A Battle Royal," may be the most interesting in the book, not least for its revelations about George Bush; playing the "loyal Lieutenant" role, Shultz knew, could get Bush into trouble. Shutlz and Weinberger were the only "voices of dissent"; all the others accepted the policy (p. 808).

77. Donald T. Regan, *For the Record: From Wall Street to Washington* (Harcourt Brace Jovanovich, 1988), p. 320.

78. Cannon, *Role*, p. 629.

79. Ibid.

80. Shultz, *Turmoil*, p. 700. Shultz, in the December 7, 1985, meeting, told the president that "arms for hostages and arms to Iran were both terrible ideas . . . a betrayal of our policies and would only encourage more hostage taking." Weinberger, who did not always agree with Shultz, expressed the same opinion, but everyone in the room knew where the president stood on the issue; he wanted the operation to go ahead. For the president's view on that crucial meeting, the last when he might have turned back, see his *American Life*, p. 512. The Arms Export Control Act required Congress to be notified of any sale that exceeded $14 million.

81. Cannon, *Reagan*, p. 630–631.

82. Andrew, *President's Eyes*, p. 481. Andrew writes: "Reagan was both deceived and humiliated by the allegedly moderate Iranians. . . . The fiasco was due partly to the gullibility of NSC staff—and, ultimately, of the President himself."

83. Reagan, *American Life*, pp. 517–518. Reagan, noting that "more than two hundred people, including at least fifty American servicemen, had been injured in the blast," knew that "we had to do something about the crackpot in Tripoli," and saw no alternative to a military response.

84. *New York Times*, November 14, 1986, p. A 8. Reagan claimed that the items were only "small amounts of defensive weapons and spare parts for defensive systems, and that the United States had not "swapped boatloads or planeloads of U.S. weapons for the return of American hostages."

85. See Reagan, *American Life,* pp. 536–537. Regan received slight recompense for his loyalty, believed by many, including Nancy, as well as members of the Cabinet, White House staff, and congressional leaders that he "had an oversized ego that made him difficult to deal with."

86. Reagan, *American Life,* pp. 529–531.

87. *The Tower Commission Report,* John Tower, chairman, Edmund Muskie and Brent Scowcroft, members. Introduction by R.W. Apple (Bantam, 1987).

88. *Washington Post,* March 5, 1987.

89. Reagan, *American Life,* p. 540. He wrote: "To this day, I still believe that the Iran initiative was *not* an effort to swap arms for hostages. But I know it may not look that way to some people."

90. See Daniel Deudney and G. John Ikenberry, "Who Won the Cold War?" in Alexander Dallin and Gail W. Lapidus, *The Soviet System: From Crisis to Collapse* (Westview, 1995), pp. 695–696. They write: "The Reagan victory school and the broader peace-through-strength perspectives are, however, misleading, both in their understanding of deeper forces that led to the end of the Cold War. It is important to reconsider the emerging conventional wisdom before it truly becomes an article of faith and comes to distort the thinking of policymakers in America and elsewhere."

91. The Reagan courtiers were never willing to acknowledge that the collapse of the Soviet Union owed more to Gorbachev and his policy of perestroika than to anything Reagan did or said. In the wake of that collapse, American scholars and journalists wrote remarkable analyses that scarcely support the "Reagan victory school." See, for example, Martin Malia, *The Soviet Tragedy: A History of Socialism in Russia, 1917–1991* (Free Press, 1994) or John B. Dunlop, *The Rise of Russia and the Fall of the Soviet Empire* (Princeton University Press, 1993). Among the more brilliant analyses produced by journalists, interestingly not replicated in recent years in journalistic analyses of Iraq, see Hedrick Smith, *The New Russians* (Random House, 1991) and David Remnick, *Lenin's Tomb* (Random House, 1993).

92. Reagan, *American Life,* p. 708.

93. Cannon, *Reagan,* pp. 320–333. Cannon represents Reagan as a sincere "nuclear abolitionist," wholly sincere when he said in his March 1983 speech, "I call upon the scientific community in our country, those who gave us nuclear weapons, to turn their great talents now to the cause of mankind and world peace, to give us the means of rendering these nuclear weapons impotent and obsolete."

94. Ibid., pp. 762–763.

95. Ibid., p. 774.

96. See Mikhail Gorbachev, *Perestroika: New Thinking for our Country and the World,* new edition (Fontana/Collins, 1987), pp. 251–252. It was impossible for the American public not to resonate to a Russian leader prepared to say: "Great work of historic importance lies in store for the Soviet Union and the United States. Neither of our countries alone will be able to do this work. I mean the issue of concern of our day—staving off the threat of humanity's destruction in a nuclear war. If this work is performed successfully, there are grounds to see a bloom in Soviet-American relations, a 'golden age' which would benefit the USSR and the USA, all countries, and the whole world community."

97. See Cannon, *Reagan,* p. 780. A very substantial right-wing campaign was launched against the treaty, with some 300,000 letters sent in protest, and a newspaper advertisement that compared Reagan to Chamberlain.

98. *New York Times,* December 4, 1987, p. A 1.

99. Reagan only very rarely showed such reliance on scholars for the speeches he delivered on the Soviet Union.

100. *New York Times,* June 1, 1988, p. A 12.

101. Cannon, *Reagan,* p. 788.

102. Ibid.

103. *New York Times,* June 4, 1988, p. 6.

104. See Richard Pipes, *VIXI: Memoirs of a Non Believer* (Yale University Press, 2003), pp. 163–68 and 176. Richard Pipes, one of the few academics who accepted to serve in the Reagan administration, has published one of the most telling accounts of his two years in Washington. In his representation of Reagan as having an "intuitive" rather than an "intellectual" grasp of the "big issues," by which he means essentially those matters that touched the Soviet Union, he makes a persuasive defense of the president's anticommunism, contrasting it with that of his wife, who "wanted her husband to win a place in history by ending the Cold War, by which she meant accommodating himself to communism rather than getting rid of it." His portrayal of Haig is devastating, representing him as vain, pompous, and superior, disliked by the president who seemed to avoid even looking at him when they sat together in the Cabinet Room. The unadorned quality of the Reagan court and of its courtiers is represented in a single sentence and a footnote where Pipes writes: "During the briefings which took place in the Oval Office, I was surprised to see how little deference Deaver and Baker showed Reagan—they seemed to treat him rather like a grandfather whom one humors but does not take very seriously." To this, he appended a footnote that reads: "They seemed to feel the need to tell Reagan amusing anecdotes, which they did so badly they did not even elicit a chuckle from him." On the vice president, Pipes was less severe, saying only ". . . I was repeatedly surprised by Bush's anti-Israeli attitude and his seeming lack of understanding for Israeli behaviour."

105. Cannon, *Reagan,* p. 831. Cannon, never wishing to underestimate Reagan's accomplishment, writes: ". . . it was Reagan, not his staff, who set the agenda and established the priorities for the major accomplishments of his presidency. It was Reagan who wanted the tax cuts and the military buildup. It was Reagan, although not Reagan alone, who wanted to negotiate with Mikhail Gorbachev. And it was Reagan, again not alone, who advocated the sale of U.S. arms to Iran in exchange for U.S. hostages." What he does not say, but is eloquently argued by Paul Pierson, *Dismantling the Welfare State?: Reagan, Thatcher, and the Politics of Retrenchment* (Cambridge University Press, 1994), is that the Thatcher claim to having changed "everything," like the claim of American conservatives that there was a "Reagan Revolution" was hyperbolic. While Pierson has no wish to claim that there was no "retrenchment," he is unprepared to buy into the theory of a "Reagan revolution."

CHAPTER 19 (The Connecticut Yankee in Disguise)

1. See Herbert S. Parmet, *George Bush: The Life of a Lone Star Yankee* (Scribner, 1997) for an uncritical but detailed account of George Bush's life through his years as vice president. For a more skeptical view of that political career, as well as that of his father, Prescott Bush, see Kevin Phillips, *American Dynasty* (Allen Lane, 2004).

2. See Charles Yost, *The Conduct and Misconduct of Foreign Affairs: Reflections on U.S. Foreign Policy Since World War II* (Random House, 1972), p. 192. Yost writes: "While I am not familiar in detail with the relations of my successor, George Bush, with the White House, he has the advantage of being an ardent and active Republican, and I understand, a favorite of the President's. Still, these assets do not seem, as far as one can judge from the outside, to have given him any substantial voice in policy-making in Washington, or even to avoid being obliged by the Administration to undertake foolish and impossible assignments at the United Nations on several occasions." Yost was correct in emphasizing the insignificance of Bush's involvement in foreign policy decisionmaking, but erred when he thought him an "intimate" or even a "favorite" of the president. Nixon simply used him.

3. Ibid., p. 193. Yost writes: "The tragic and, so far, decisive fact is that the U.S. government, like the governments of the other strongest nations, is not yet convinced that its major interests will be best served by being dealt with in and through the United Nations. Our Ambassador there will not be at the center of power in Washington until the United Nations is more nearly at the center of power in world affairs."

4. Ibid., pp. 138–140.

5. Phillips, *Dynasty,* p. 31. Phillips writes: "When he was chairman of the Republican National Committee in 1973–74. . . he covered the country 'like a Republican brush salesman for a total of 124,000 miles, giving 118 speeches and 84 press conferences. Wherever he went he passionately insisted that no White House hand had been in the Watergate jam pot.' Like his father, he was more charmer than thinker. By now his image had begun to suffer. In 1972, *New York* magazine included Bush in its list of 'The Most Over-Rated Men in New York.'"

6. Kissinger, *Upheaval,* pp. 1203—1204. Kissinger, in memorable passages, tells the story of Nixon's last Cabinet meeting, and of Bush's contribution, telling the president, in effect, that the time had come for him to go. Kissinger called the intervention "cruel" but "necessary." It is symptomatic of Bush's insignificant role in the Nixon administration that this is the only instance when Kissinger feels any obligation even to mention him.

7. Kissinger, *Renewal,* pp, 842–843. Kissinger prints the text of the cable Bush sent from Beijing explaining why he accepted the post of CIA director, knowing it would be "the total end of any political future" for him, but faithful to the principles of his father, wishing only to "serve his country and his President." Kissinger, with no hint of irony, suggests that Bush served "with great distinction and with no harm to his presidential prospects."

8. See John Prados, *Lost Crusader: The Secret Wars of CIA Director William Colby* (Oxford University Press, 2003), pp. 297–330, a chapter entitled "The Year of Intelligence," which discusses Colby's problems in the Ford administration. Prados, in defending Colby, writes: "Suspended between the past and future of intelligence, William E. Colby alone among the actors of the Ford administration understood that realities had changed. In post-Watergate America the mere assertion of a national security interest no longer sufficed to justify arbitrary actions."

9. Edmund Morris, *Dutch: A Memoir of Ronald Reagan* (Modern Library, 1999), p. 444. Morris, describing Bush as he saw the vice president at a state dinner given many years later for Anwar Sadat, writes: "I was surprised at Bush's bigness and *vigor di vita:* this was not the rumored wimp whom Dutch secretly despised." Did Reagan really "despise" Bush? Did Eisenhower really despise Nixon? Are we likely ever to know?

10. R.J. Cline, "The Cronkite-Ford Interview at the 1980 Republican National Convention: A Therapeutic Dialogue," *Central States Speech Journal,* vol. 49, pp. 43–56.

11. Bush, as we have seen, was never likely to deny a president's request, least of all one that gave him the second position in the federal government.

12. Mayer, *Race,* pp. 211–214. Susan Estrich, campaign manager for Michael Dukakis, described Bush's first TV advertisement on the Horton case, saying: "There's this big black dude in his prison cell with street clothes on, whistling softly as he packs his toothbrush and a few incidentals before setting out on a weekend of pillaging."

13. Reagan, *American Life,* p. 722.

14. Ibid.

15. Michael R. Beschloss and Strobe Talbott, *At the Highest Levels: The Inside Story of the End of the Cold War* (Little, Brown, 1993), pp. 3–4.

16. Ibid., p. 4.

17. Ibid.

18. Morris, *Dutch,* pp. 638–639.

19. *New York Times,* January 21, 1989, p. 10.

20. Ibid.

21. Ibid.

22. Parmet, *Bush,* pp. 371–374. Parmet writes: "Fidelity to Tower was a *sine qua non* for the political right. Reaganite conservative publications saw it as a test of Bush's need to stick to his principles," but Tower's "lifestyle clearly outraged religious conservatives. Paul Weyrich, chairman of the Coalition for America, told a public session of the committee about his personal encounters with a besotted and obviously lecherous Mr. Tower. There were clearly reasons for 'grave doubts' about his 'moral character.'"

23. Ibid., pp. 358–359. Parmet writes: "His [Baker's] relative inexperience in foreign affairs was widely viewed as counterbalanced by his brilliance as a negotiator and political cunning."

24. Beschloss and Talbott, *Highest Levels,* p. 29. Baker, on his first visit to London after his appointment as secretary of state, heard Margaret Thatcher say "that she was concerned about the policy review and 'apparent air of relaxation' in Washington, adding, 'And I'm sure Mr. Gorbachev is, too.'"

25. While some in the Republican Party were critical of what they interpreted as unnecessarily large "concessions" by the president to the Soviets, the Russians themselves were unimpressed with what the speech appeared to promise.

26. See Beschloss and Talbott, *Highest Levels,* p. 122. Quayle, worried that Baker might be a rival for the Republican Party's presidential nomination in 1996, warned a Los Angeles audience against those "who say the Cold War is over." In his view, improvements in Soviet-American relations were "neither inevitable nor irreversible."

27. Ibid., p. 123.

28. See Malia, *Soviet Tragedy,* pp. 445–489, a chapter entitled "From Perestroika to Collapse," an excellent narrative of the events of the years that witnessed the collapse of the Soviet Union. Malia writes: "Thus, by December 25, 1991, when the Red Flag came down over the Kremlin for the last time and Gorbachev read his farewell address over television, none of the key Soviet institutions remained. The process that had begun with the collapse of Leninism in Eastern Europe in 1989 was now completed with Leninism's collapse in the mother country. As one Russian commentator put it, the Soviet Union had suffered the structural equivalent of defeat in a major war. In fact, the Soviet catastrophe was worse, for it was self-inflicted. . . . And the only other comparable collapses in this century, those of the Axis and of Japan in 1945, were produced by crushing military defeat. But that an ostensibly advanced industrial nation and superpower should collapse without any large-scale military defeat, after forty-five years of peace, and essentially from internal causes, is unheard of in modern history."

29. Beschloss and Talbott, *Highest Levels,* pp. 182–193.

30. Philip Bobbitt, *The Shield of Achilles: War, Peace and the Course of History* (Allen Lane, 2002), pp. 630–636.

31. George Bush and Brent Scowcroft, *A World Transformed* (Knopf, 1998), p. 41.

32. Ibid., p. 42.

33. Ibid., pp. 293–294. While Kohl liked the American proposals, Thatcher was skeptical. Bush writes: "She argued that we were abandoning the fundamentals of solid military strategy for the sake of 'eye-catching propositions.' She supported the idea of changing NATO's emphasis, but she wanted no part of altering the long-established strategy of flexible response. That policy kept open the possibility that NATO would use nuclear weapons first in the event of a Soviet conventional attack and thus help deter it. She saw the move to declare nuclear weapons 'weapons of last resort' as undermining our short-range forces and as slipping us to a position of 'no first use of nuclear weapons,' leaving our conventional forces vulnerable. She thought the tone of the declaration would make people think that the Soviets no longer posed a threat. . . . She demanded an entirely new draft, to be prepared by the United States, France, West Germany, and Italy."

34. Andrew, *President's Eyes,* p. 518.

35. Ibid.

36. Ibid.

37. Ibid.

38. Ibid., p. 519.

39. Ibid., p. 515.

40. Ibid.

41. Ibid., p. 519.

42. Ibid.

43. Ibid.

44. Ibid., pp. 519–520.

45. Ibid., p. 520. Andrew writes: "The conflict in the gulf was to be George Bush's war. Powell was initially reluctant to go beyond sanctions against Iraq. Baker sought a compromise settlement. Bush was set on military victory."

46. Ibid., p. 521.

47. Beschloss and Talbott, *Highest Levels,* pp. 261–267.

48. Ibid., p. 265. The final sentences of the joint communiqué read: "It is essential to work actively to resolve all remaining conflicts in the Middle East and Persian Gulf. Both sides will continue to consult each other and initiate measures to pursue these broader objectives at the proper time."

49. Stephen R. Graubard, *Mr. Bush's War: Adventures in the Politics of Illusion* (Hill and Wang, 1992), pp. 111–112.

50. Ibid., p. 113.

51. *New York Times,* September 12, 1990, p. 20.

52. Graubard, *Bush's War,* pp. 113–114.

53. Ibid., p. 114.

54. Ibid.

55. These exaggerated estimates always figured in the thinking of prominent Democrats in Congress but were never believed by the president or his close associates; they had a much more realistic sense of the respective military strengths of the U.S. forces and those Saddam Hussein would be able to mobilize.

56. Parmet, *Bush,* pp. 394–395.

57. Ibid., pp. 429–435.

58. Ibid., pp. 439–440 and 468–470.

59. Bush and Scowcroft, *World Transformed,* p. 379.

60. Ibid., pp. 379–380.

61. Ibid., pp. 416–449. This chapter, entitled "Through a Cacophony" is filled with interesting observations by both Bush and Scowcroft on the events in November, December, and January that in their minds legitimated the actions taken on January 16.

62. *New York Times,* December 1, 1990, p. 6.

63. Ibid., January 14, 1991, p. 11.

64. Ibid.

65. Ibid., January 21, 1991, p. 17. See, also, James Reston, *Deadline: A Memoir* (Random House, 1991), p. 445. Reston writes: "It was a perfect American war: quick, flashy, and all on television. More Americans were killed at home during those four days than were killed in the war. President Bush called it, without undue modesty, the greatest military victory in the history of the Republic and scarcely mentioned the 150,000 Iraqis who were slaughtered in the process."

66. Ibid., p. 446. Reston writes: "No doubt the Gulf War served several useful purposes. It put future aggressors on notice that they could not assume American neutrality. It made clear that

the United States regarded the oilfields of the Middle East as vital to its security and would not permit them to come under the control of any hostile power. It put an end to the self-doubts that had plagued the nation after its defeat in Vietnam, but this Vietnam syndrome was followed by a kind of Iraq swagger of boasting that Uncle Sam was number one and would now at last redeem the optimistic visions of Woodrow Wilson and the other prophets of eternal peace."

67. *New York Times*, January 25, 1991, p. 1.

68. Ibid.

69. Ibid.

70. Ibid., January 30, 1991, p. 12.

71. Parmet, *Bush*, p. 481.

72. Bush and Scowcroft, *World Transformed*, p. 425. This, one of the most important revelations made by Bush, was intended to besmirch the reputations of those who had argued that the war would be another Vietnam. In fact, it simply confirms what is implicit throughout this book; that the wars the United States has engaged in since the time of Reagan have all been "fail/safe," that those like Cheney who have emphasized their difficulty and danger deliberately sought to deceive, making the guaranteed victories seem even more remarkable.

73. Colin Powell, with Joseph E. Persico, *My American Journey* (Random House, 1995), p. 525.

74. Ibid., pp. 525–526.

75. Ibid., p. 526.

76. Ibid., p. 527.

77. Ibid., p. 528.

78. Ibid., p. 542.

79. Ibid.

80. *New York Times*, March 7, 1991, p. 8.

81. See Graubard, *Bush's War*, pp. 162–166, for a full account of this speech, described there as "banal."

82. See Bobbitt, *Achilles*, pp. 609–663, a chapter entitled "The Peace of Paris," a reference to the thirty-four nation conference that met in Paris in late November 1990, as brilliant a summary of Baker's accomplishments as is to be found anywhere. Bobbitt sees Baker "as in some ways playing the role of Colonel House in a later era as the president's political manager, personal intimate, and international representative." All these facts, while true, ignore the larger possibility that Bush was no Wilson and Baker a substantially less considerable person than House.

83. Shultz, *Turmoil*, p. 5.

84. Ibid., pp. 5–6.

85. Bush and Clinton resembled each other in this respect, vastly exaggerating the importance of their personal relations with leaders abroad, never developing foreign policies that bore their distinctive signatures that would retain any resonance for a later generation.

86. Boris Yeltsin, *The Struggle for Russia* (Times Books, 1994), p. 136.

87. John Kampfner, *Blair's Wars* (Free Press, 2003), p. 8. The Scott inquiry showed that the British government under John Major, like the American government under George Bush, "armed Saddam before, during, and after the gassing of civilians."

CHAPTER 20 (The Rake's Progress)

1. The Clinton White House was always porous, but that condition has not contributed to the composition of biographies that compare with those written on Roosevelt, Truman, and Kennedy. Nor has it produced autobiographies that compare with those who served Nixon and Reagan.

2. Strobe Talbott, *The Russia Hand: A Memoir of Presidential Diplomacy* (Random House, 2002) must figure prominently as a work very complimentary to the former president. Not quite as unreservedly so, but still lauditory is Robert E. Rubin and Jacob Weisberg, *In an Uncertain World: Tough Choices from Wall Street to Washington* (Random House, 2003). George Stephanopoulos, *All Too Human: A Political Education* (Little, Brown, 1999) is the work of a disappointed man who expected more from a president he greatly admired; Robert B. Reich, *Locked in the Cabinet* (Vintage, 1998), is the autobiography of a former Cabinet colleague both disappointed and dismayed by his performance, perhaps the most critical of all the works written by those able to claim some closeness to the president. As for Hillary Rodham Clinton, *Living History* (Simon and Schuster, 2003), this is neither history nor memoir and may be best read as an early warning of her intention one day to return to the White House, and not as a guest.

3. Stephanopoulos, *Human*, pp. 3–6.

4. Ibid., p. 4.

5. Ibid., p. 3.

6. Ibid.

7. Joe Klein, *The Natural: The Misunderstood Presidency of Bill Clinton* (Doubleday, 2002).

8. Ibid., pp. 216–217.

9. Elizabeth Drew, *The Corruption of American Politics: What Went Wrong and Why* (Overlook Press, 2000).

10. Ibid., p. vii.

11. Ibid.

12. Ibid., pp. 151–152.

13. Ibid., p. 152.

14. Clinton, *History*, p. 63. Hillary Clinton, in her *History*, tells the standard tale of Bill defending his mother against her husband's attacks, and caring always for his younger brother.

15. Ibid. Bill's mother, we are told by Hillary, did not like her in the beginning, finding her style "baffling" and her Yankee ideas "strange," but they soon came "to respect each other's differences and developed a deep bond," anchored, we are told, in their love for the same man.

16. Why did a devout Baptist choose to enroll in a predominantly Catholic university, founded by the Jesuits, and why in the School of Foreign Service? Clinton's explanation, as given in his recent autobiography, Bill Clinton, *My Life* (Knopf, 2004), p. 66, suggests that he simply "wanted to go back to Washington."

17. This political "apprenticeship," though in superficial ways redolent of Lyndon Johnson's, never brought the young Clinton into touch with prominent Democrats.

18. Winning a Rhodes Scholarship from a state like Arkansas was substantially easier than acquiring the same from a state like New York, but such distinctions counted for little with someone who saw himself in an Arkansas succession that included one of the Senate's most illustrious members, William Fulbright.

19. It is interesting to note that Ambrose Evans Pritchard, *The Secret Life of Bill Clinton: The Unreported Stories* (Regnery, 1997), a book on Clinton analogous to the one Hersh wrote on Kennedy in *The Dark Side of Camelot*, never thought to explore his years at Oxford, perhaps suggesting there were few "unreported stories" in his two-year residence abroad. The chapter on Clinton's years at Oxford, as given in Roger Morris, *Partners in Power: The Clintons and Their America* (Holt, 1996), pp. 79–106, deals fully with Clinton's strategies for avoiding the draft, using "every string he could think of."

20. Bill Clinton, *Selected Speeches, 1974–1992,* compiled and edited by Stephen A. Smith (University of Arkansas Press, 1996), pp. 2–4.

21. *New York Times,* July 3, 1978, p. 41.

22. Clinton, *Speeches*, p. 22.

23. Ibid.

24. This speech, given in 1984, helped to establish Clinton's reputation among Democrats.

25. Ibid., p. 24.

26. Ibid., p. 25.

27. Ibid., p. 26.

28. Ibid.

29. Ibid., pp. 26–27.

30. Ibid., p. 27. Clinton instructed his New York audience in their prime obligation, "We must get middle class and upper middle class out to vote."

31. Clinton, *History,* p. 90. Hillary Clinton ascribes the loss to the advertisements put out by the White campaign, especially those relating to the use of the National Guard to suppress the Cuban riots at the neighboring military base. In her words, "The 1980 campaign, where truth was turned on its head, convinced me of the piercing power of negative ads to convert voters through distortion."

32. Ibid., pp. 92–93. Hillary Clinton makes no mention of her husband's TV advertisement, but dwells instead on her own decision, at the prompting of friends, to consent to use the name Hillary Rodham Clinton, explaining, "I decided it was more important for Bill to be Governor again than for me to keep my maiden name."

33. Morris, *Partners,* p. 287. Morris writes: ". . . Clinton waged in the 1982 general election . . . one of the most acrimonious campaigns in state politics."

34. Clinton, *History,* pp. 93–94. Hillary, dwelling not at all on the nature of the campaign and choosing not to emphasize the magnitude of her husband's victory, describes him as a "humbler, more seasoned Governor returned to the State House, though no less determined to get as much done as possible in two years." As she had helped him "tackle health reform in his first term," so now, he asked her to "tackle education," and though initially she refused, she finally agreed to do so.

35. Clinton, *Speeches,* p. 45.

36. Ibid., p. 46.

37. Ibid.

38. Ibid., p. 47.

39. Needless to say, the story of Gary Hart and Donna Rice do not figure in Hillary Clinton's *History.* Hart exists for her only as someone who had a role in the McGovern campaign.

40. Clinton, *History,* p. 98. Acknowledging that the nominating speech was a "fiasco," she writes: ". . . Dukakis and his staff had reviewed and approved every word of Bill's text ahead of time, but the speech was longer than the delegates or the television networks expected. Some delegates on the floor began yelling at Bill to finish. This was a humiliating introduction to the nation, and many observers assumed Bill's political future was over. Eight days later, though, he was on Johnny Carson's *Tonight Show,* making fun of himself and playing his saxophone. Yet another comeback."

41. It is significant, certainly, that Hillary Clinton mentions Dukakis only twice in her autobiography, a "loser" who scarcely merits attention.

42. Clinton, *Speeches,* p. 99.

43. Ibid. The character of this speech may be gleaned from any number of passages, but none more characteristic than where he spoke of the Reagan Revolution and the Bush Succession, saying: "During this administration, the economy has grown more slowly and fewer jobs have been created than in any administration since World War II. . . . Ten years ago, America had the highest wages in the world. Now we're tenth, and falling. Last year, Germany and Japan had productivity growth rates three and four times ours because they educate their people better, invest more in their future, and organize their economies for global competition, and we don't."

44. Ibid., p. 100.

45. Ibid.

46. Ibid. Clinton, pretending to have a new economic theory, told his audience: "The old economic answers are obsolete. We've seen the limits of Keynesian economics. We've seen the worst of supply-side economics. We need a new approach. For twelve years, we've had no economic vision, no economic leadership, no national economic strategy."

47. Ibid.

48. Ibid., pp. 102–104.

49. Ibid., p. 98. Stephen Smith, who edited the Clinton speeches, thought it appropriate to cite a *Washington Post* editorial accolade, seeing no need to mention the substantially more reserved opinion expressed by Bob Woodward, its star reporter.

50. Ibid., p. 112.

51. Ibid., pp. 112–114. Clinton chided Bush for deciding to "side with China's communist rulers after the democratic uprising of students," and also for his being "willing to leave the Kurds to an awful fate."

52. Ibid., p. 114.

53. Ibid.

54. Ibid., pp. 115–116.

55. Ibid., p. 116. In his words, "We need to clamp down on countries and companies that sell these technologies, punish violators, and work urgently with all countries for tough, enforceable, international non-proliferation agreements."

56. Ibid., pp. 118–121.

57. Ibid., p. 121. Clinton ended his speech with a telling reference to words Lincoln had used in 1862 when he said: "The dogmas of the quiet past are inadequate to the stormy present. The occasion is piled high with difficulty, and we must rise with the occasion. As our case is new, we must think anew, and act anew. We must disenthrall ourselves, and then we shall save our country. Fellow citizens, we cannot escape history."

58. Clinton, *History,* p. 106. Hillary learned about the story before it appeared, the president assuring her it was untrue.

59. Ibid., p. 107.

60. Ibid., pp. 107–108. Needless to say, there is no suggestion of this in the story Hillary gives in her autobiography, which dwells on the remark she made during the program: "You know, I'm not sitting here, some little woman standing by my man like Tammy Wynette. I'm sitting here because I love him and I respect him and I honor what he's been through and what we've been through together. And you know, if that's not enough for people, then heck, don't vote for him." In speaking of Tammy Wynette, she explained later, her reference was to her song, "Stand By Your Man," and not to her person, but the angry reactions of many listeners led her to apologize for her careless use of words.

61. Stephanopoulos, *Human,* p. 80.

62. Ibid.

63. Morris, *Partners,* p. 439. Morris, seeking to demonstrate how much journalists and politicians at one time associated Clinton's sexual proclivities with Hart's, tells of a 1988 skit at the Little Rock Gridiron Club which "brought down the house," with members impersonating Clinton and Hart all singing together: "To All the Girls We've Loved."

64. Clinton never adequately acknowledged his indebtedness to Carter for teaching him how to win primaries, just as he never admitted how much he learned from closely observing Reagan.

65. Parmet, *Bush,* p. 505. Parmet writes: ". . . while Perot was holding forth [in the second debate] Bush glanced at his wristwatch. One camera caught that, and the director put it on the air. The image seemed to confirm everything: he was impatient, bored, and uninterested in the job. The debates did even less good than the convention."

66. No one, to date, has thought to make an in-depth analysis of the political careers of Taft and Bush, both one-term presidents who rose without significant experience of elective office, and were universally thought to lack the charismatic qualities that had made the administrations of their immediate predecessors so memorable.

67. Reich, *Cabinet,* pp. 64–66. In this illuminating discussion of the early White House discussion of the deficit, Reich writes: "Bentsen, Panetta, and Rivlin [the President's principal economic advisers] want to cut the deficit by $500 billion over the next five years, mainly by cutting spending. If they have their way, the investment agenda is stone-dead. I argue that rather than aim for a specific amount of deficit reduction, we should aim for a reasonable ration of deficit to the nation's total output, perhaps a 2.4 or 2.5 percent. It doesn't help that Bill is exhausted. I don't think he's sleeping at night. He can barely stay awake at today's meeting. When I make my usual point—'Mr. President, at this rate we won't have money left for your investments'—his eyelids droop and his pupils move up under them, leaving nothing but a narrow sliver of white eyeball. My influence has reached a new low. I'm addressing a sleeping President."

68. Baird, like so many others, does not exist for Hillary Clinton in her autobiography. She, like Reich, is simply airbrushed out of the picture.

69. Stephanopoulos, *Human,* pp. 118–120. Stephanopoulos, more candid and considerably more forthcoming, writes: "Her [Baird's] selection, the ensuing controversy, and the way we responded were emblematic of our early troubles."

70. Ibid., p. 120. Stephanopoulos writes: "Christopher was dispatched to convince her to withdraw, but she relented only after we agreed to take the hit. Her letter to the president stressed that she had fully disclosed her situation to the transition team, and the letter we drafted for Clinton praised Baird and accepted full responsibility for the failed nomination."

71. Clinton, having never served in Congress, had no intimate friends in either the Senate or the House, and never succeeded in establishing close relations with any of the more prominent Democrats in either chamber.

72. Stephanopoulos, *Human,* p. 121. Stephanopoulos tells of a "tiff" with Moynihan in the very first week of Clinton's presidency, and writes: "Moynihan responded graciously, but he would remember this slight and exact his revenge many times over in the next few years."

73. Needless to say, Guinier is unmentioned in Hillary Clinton's autobiography.

74. Clinton, *History,* pp. 172–174. She suggests that the dismissals stemmed from the discovery that "a minimum of $18,000 of checks had not been properly accounted for," and that the office records were in a "shambles." She claimed that she "would wake up in the middle of the night worrying that the actions and reactions concerning the travel office [had] led Vince Foster to take his own life." In her words, "Vince Foster was stung by the travel office affair. A meticulous, decent, and honorable man, he felt that he had let down the President. . . and me by failing to understand and contain the drama."

75. Reich, *Cabinet,* pp. 121–122. Reich, joining the others in "celebrating" the victory, writes: "We've won the battle over the economic plan. But have we lost the war? No mistake, there's good in it: We've made the tax code a bit more equitable—partially making up for the regressive direction Reagan set us in. Those at the very top will pay more. Five million people working at the bottom will each get about $3,000 a year, in the form of an expanded Earned Income Tax Credit. Ten million others just above them will also have lower taxes. And surely the budget deficit had to be reduced. But what about public investment? It's now a tiny morsel of what we originally sought. . . . I *want* to celebrate tonight. I don't feel the thrill of victory. I raise my glass with the rest, but I don't feel celebratory. I look down the road, and much of what I hope for seems imperiled."

76. Klein, *Natural,* pp. 53–55. Klein regretted that Clinton would not be allowed to enjoy the traditional presidential "honeymoon," denied that privilege by both the Republicans and the

media. Worse, by making "tactical retreats," Clinton had "gained the reputation—in Washington at least—of being a weak President," who lacked "core values." In Klein's view, these charges were unjust, but he recognized what damage they did to his reputation.

77. Stephanopoulos, *Human,* pp. 198–199. Among the many revelations in the Stephanopoulos book, few are more interesting than the hyperbolic statements he attributes to the president and the First Lady. They imagined they would achieve something approaching immortality with their health plan. He writes: "The President was determined . . . to forge another New Deal, to succeed where FDR, Truman, Kennedy, Johnson, Nixon, and Carter had all failed, to be remembered as the president who made basic health care, like a secure retirement, the birthright of every American." Stephanopoulos describes Hillary as "Eleanor to his Franklin," making health care "her baby, a sweeping program that would save lives and prove to the world that a first lady could be a fully public presidential partner."

78. Clinton, *History,* pp. 143–155. This chapter, entitled "Health Care," does not begin to explain why the plan failed to commend itself to Congress. The subject is almost certainly too painful for the former First Lady to wish to dwell on it.

79. Stephanopoulos, *History,* p. 187.

80. *New York Times,* March 8, 1992, p. 1.

81. Clinton, *History,* pp. 165–181. In this lengthy chapter, simply entitled "Vince Foster," Hillary Clinton records her grief over Foster's death, and cites the torn note discovered in his briefcase that read: "I was not meant for the job in the spotlight of public life in Washington. Here ruining people is considered sport. . . . The public will never believe the innocence of the Clintons and their loyal staff. . . . The WSJ [*Wall Street Journal*] editors lie without consequence."

82. Stephanopoulos, *Human,* p. 322.

83. *New York Times,* January 24, 1996, p. 14.

84. Clinton, *History,* p. 369.

85. Not one of them, however, chose to resign. Only Peter Edelman, assistant secretary for health and human services did so, along with Mary Jo Bane, another assistant secretary.

86. Samantha Power, *"A Problem from Hell": America and the Age of Genocide* (Basic Books, 2002), pp. 247–329. The chapter entitled "Bosnia: 'No More Witnesses at a Funeral'" is incontestably the best study of the inadequacies of the Bush administration in dealing with these tragic events, but she is scarcely more sympathetic to what the Clinton administration tried to do, saying that though "they were far more attentive to the human suffering in Bosnia, they did not intervene to stop it." (p. 294) Power, critical of both the secretary of state and the president, recognizes that much of their reaction was rhetorical, empty of substance. Her sympathy is reserved for Marshall Harris, the Bosnia desk officer in the State Department who resigned in disgust, complaining, in her words, that "the administration refused to lead either the American people or its European allies and then complained that its policy was constrained by a lack of support from both."

87. See Talbott, *Hand.* Clinton's relations with Yeltsin, as recounted in this *apologia* for the president's Russian policies, are sometimes comic, though never intentionally so. Talbott was overwhelmed with being at the right hand of his old Oxford Rhodes Scholar "chum" in what he and the president saw as momentous negotiations. Both the courtier and the king greatly deceived themselves.

88. Power, *Problem,* pp. 304–305. While Power emphasizes the fears Clinton had of his domestic programs being jeopardized by too bold policies abroad, as Johnson's had been by his foreign interventions, she recognizes that the Pentagon's opposition to "humanitarian missions," and the wish of his foreign policy team to secure the "consent and active participation of their European partners" also played a role. So, also, did the president's concern that the Russians might take offense by any action taken against their fellow Orthodox Christian Serbs.

89. Ibid., pp. 305–306. Power writes: "Instead of leading the American people to support humanitarian intervention, Clinton adopted a policy of nonconfrontation. The administration would not confront the Serbs, and just as fundamentally, they would not confront opponents of intervention within the U.S. military or the Western alliance. Clinton's foreign policy team awaited consensus and drifted into the habits of its predecessor." The proposition that Clinton pursued the same hesitant policies characteristic of the Bush administration is made even more eloquently by Kenneth Pollack in his treatment of Clinton's failed policies in Iraq. See the invaluable discussion in Pollack, *Storm*, pp. 55–94.

90. Power, *Problem*, p. 306.

91. Ibid. Power notes how redolent these words were of those Neville Chamberlain used decades earlier in respect to Czechoslovakia.

92. Ibid.

93. See Stephanopoulos, *Human*, pp. 355–356. It is interesting to note that Stephanopoulos paid no attention to what Clinton or Gore said about the Balkans in this White House program celebrating Larry King's tenth anniversary on the air, but worried about the wisdom of the president agreeing to do an imitation of Marlon Brando kissing his host on the lips, afraid that this would be featured the next day on the morning news programs.

94. The full Larry King broadcast must be seen by anyone interested in considering Clinton's very substantial gifts as a TV star.

95. Power, *Problem*, pp. 436–437.

96. Ibid., p. 430.

97. Ibid.

98. Ibid.

99. Ibid., p. 440.

100. Ibid., pp. 329–389. Samantha Power's long chapter on Rwanda, subtitled "Mostly in a Listening Mode," is a no less severe indictment of the Clinton administration's failure to perceive the humanitarian catastrophe in that little-known African country. In this instance, it was impossible to blame the Bush administration for not attending to the problem. The crisis arose on Clinton's "watch," and Power's contempt for his inaction is rendered in one searing sentence; she writes: "Once the Americans had been evacuated from Rwanda, the massacres there largely dropped off the radar of most senior Clinton administration officials." (p. 364)

101. Ibid., p. 373.

102. Clinton, *History*, pp. 455–457. Hillary Clinton, telling of the president's visit to Rwanda, meeting with survivors of the genocide at the airport—the city was declared too unsafe by the Secret Service for him to venture in—writes: "No country or international force, including the United States, had intervened to halt the killings. It would have been difficult for the United States to send troops so soon after the loss of American soldiers in Somalia and when the Administration was trying to end ethnic cleansing in Bosnia. But Bill publicly expressed regret that our country and the international community had not done more to stop the horror." Later, in Senegal, she writes of his "moving apology for slavery," saying: "The statement was controversial among some Americans, but I believed it was appropriate. Words matter, and words from an American President carry great weight around the world. Expressing regret for genocide in Rwanda and our legacy of slavery sent a message of concern and respect to Africans who confront the intertwined challenges of poverty, disease, repression, starvation, illiteracy and war. But Africa needs more than words; it needs investment and trade if its economies are ever to develop. That requires both significant changes in most governments and a partnership with the United States. That's why the African Growth and Opportunity Act, which Bill proposed and Congress passed, is so critical. It creates incentives for American companies to do business in Africa." While it serves no purpose to mock either the presidential statements or his wife's exaggerated

praise for a very inconsequential congressional act, such were the apologies the president and his wife thought it necessary to make.

103. Richard Holbrooke, *To End a War* (Random House, 1998). This account, written by the American who deserves the lion's share of the credit for what he did to negotiate an accord on Kosovo, needs to be read in conjunction with a substantially more nuanced and historically sensitive account by a British observer, Tim Judah, *Kosovo: War and Revenge,* second edition (Yale University Press, 2002), p. 312. Judah writes: "While Albanians take their revenge today, the time may yet come when Serbs can take theirs. The way the Serbs have lost Kosovo means that, for the foreseeable future, they will have no chance to get it back. How could they while it is occupied by NATO troops? But what will happen in ten or twenty years?"

104. Talbott, *Russian Hand,* p. 133.

105. Ibid.

106. The Lewinsky affair, so salacious in its sexual detail, is treated principally by journalists concerned to describe how a political magician, Bill Clinton, met and defeated his political enemies. An equally interesting tale, unfortunately neglected, relates to how the affair affected the country's foreign policy. Kenneth Pollack, in his very compelling account, reminds his readers that the attacks on the U.S. embassies in Kenya and Tanzania occurred the day after Monica Lewinsky testified before the grand jury (Pollack, *Storm,* pp 90–92). For the next several months, as was obvious to journalists and all who read their accounts, the president spent most of his time preparing his defense against what he knew would be a Republican move to impeach him. Clinton lived the agony Nixon had known decades earlier, but few of his colleagues acknowledged that in these circumstances foreign policy necessarily took a very secondary place. Clinton, in his weakness, could do nothing but argue that the Iraqi problem was one the United Nations ought to handle as he had once argued that the Bosnian crisis was one for the Europeans to resolve.

107. Clinton, *History,* pp. 440–441. Hillary's account of that fateful day begins with the president waking her to tell her about news reports of his having had an affair with a White House intern. She writes: "I questioned Bill over and over about the story. He continued to deny any improper behaviour but to acknowledge that his attention could have been misread. I will never understand what was going on through my husband's mind that day. All I know is that Bill told his staff and our friends the same story he told me: that nothing improper went on. Why he felt he had to deceive me and others is his own story, and he needs to tell it in his own way. . . . For me, the Lewinsky imbroglio seemed like just another vicious scandal manufactured by political opponents. After all, since he had started running for public office, Bill had been accused of everything from drug-running to fathering a child with a Little Rock prostitute, and I had been called a thief and a murderer. I expected that, ultimately, the intern story would be a footnote in tabloid history."

108. Ibid., pp. 466–469. Clinton acknowledged his guilt to his wife two days before his grand jury appearance, claiming that what had happened was "brief and sporadic," that he had been unable to tell her the truth seven months earlier because "he was too ashamed to admit it and . . . knew how angry and hurt I would be." When he went to address the nation, Hillary writes, he knew that "the President of the United States couldn't afford to appear on television looking weak." Why not? In her words, "In the days before his confession to me, we had discussed the dangerous standoff looming in Iraq, precipitated on August 5 by Saddam Hussein's announcement of a ban on continued weapons inspections. And only Bill and I, along with his foreign policy team, knew that within hours of his statement about his personal transgressions, the United States would launch a missile strike against one of Osama bin Laden's camps in Afghanistan, at a time when our intelligence indicated bin Laden and his top lieutenants would be there, to retaliate for the embassy bombings in Kenya and Tanzania." She notes that Clinton was criticized for the attack. In her words, "He was accused of doing it to divert attention from

his own troubles and the growing talk of impeachment by both Republicans who still didn't understand the dangers presented by terrorism in general and bin Laden and al Qaeda in particular." In this very partial account, so different from the one that Pollack provides, we have no hint that the president came close to bombing the Iraqis earlier but pulled back at the last moment, leaving the vice president "livid"; Gore was one of those who urged military action (Pollack, *Storm*, p. 91).

109. Ibid., p. 132.

110. Rubin, *Uncertain World*, pp. 143–144. The president is unlikely to have many of his former colleagues write more appreciatively of him, going so far as to deny even the commonly held view that the administration got off to "a rocky start." Rubin writes: "For chaos was certainly not what I experienced. To the contrary, in the early months of the administration, I saw people working together in an effective, productive way. I used to make that point, and others would look at me as if I'd been spending time on another planet."

111. Ibid., pp. 3–38. The threat of Mexican default, which Rubin treats as "the first crisis of the twenty-first century," was one that the president understood perfectly; together with his deficit reduction plans (pp. 118–131) they figure as two of the more considerable evidences of his political genius, as interpreted by his secretary of the treasury.

112. Reich, *Cabinet*, pp. 22–23. Reich had recommended to the president-elect that he appoint Rubin to head his National Economic Council, saying: "Even though he's spent the last twenty-five yeas as an investment banker with Goldman, Sachs in New York, he seems genuinely concerned about the poor. He's bright and good-natured, and also a bit shy and self-effacing."

113. Rubin, *Uncertain World*, p. 152.

114. Ibid., pp. 20 and 229. He was, in fact, a leading economic expert in the Federal Reserve Bank, much esteemed by Rubin.

115. Ibid., p. 402. Rubin believes he understands this when he entitles his final chapter "A Declaration of Interdependence," but there is less geopolitical insight in this chapter than Rubin, a superb financier, imagines. Again, Pollack is the more reliable observer. It is he who notes that the administration began in 1999 to consider policies to overthrow Saddam, given his refusal to allow UN inspections, but that in the end it held back from pursuing a policy that seemed dangerous, that "had no better than a one-in-three chance of succeeding, even if the United States pressed it to the hilt." Without naming his source, Pollack writes of a senior administration official who told him in early 2000: "The President wants to finish his term by making peace between the Arabs and the Israelis, he doesn't want to start a war between us and the Iraqis." Pollack adds: "There were other things on the administration's plate that also had a higher priority, such as the opening to India and a new initiative toward Africa." (Pollack, *Storm*, p. 99)

116. Talbott, *Hand*, pp. 133–134.

117. Ibid., p. 10, for Talbott's representation of Clinton as a "hedgehog."

118. *The Sunday Telegraph*, Review, p. 11.

119. Clinton, *My Life* (Knopf, 2004), p. 957.

CHAPTER 21 (Reagan's Boy)

1. In 1877, the struggle was even more prolonged, and no less fractious.

2. A comparison of the Adams family and the Bush family, building on the information in Kevin Phillips, *American Dynasty: How the Bush Clan Became the World's Most Powerful and Dangerous Family* (Allen Lane, 2004) would make fascinating reading, suggesting how different politics in the eighteenth and early nineteenth centuries were from what became commonplace in the late twentieth century.

3. The nineteenth-century post–Civil War decline in the quality of those who came to occupy the presidency closely parallels the decline after the Vietnam War, but Congress was neither the beneficiary nor the cause of this decline. Indeed, the power of the presidency became again very substantial with the arrival of Reagan.

4. Another book that waits to be written, that would illuminate America's changing social and cultural scene would be a dual biography of Abigail Adams and Barbara Bush.

5. See Dexter Perkins, *The Monroe Doctrine, 1823–1826* (Harvard, 1927). In the vast literature on the subject, this remains the outstanding study.

6. Alexandra Robbins, *Secrets of the Tomb: Skull and Bones: The Ivy League and the Hidden Paths of Power* (Little, Brown, 2002), pp. 130–131.

7. Ibid., p. 162.

8. Ibid.

9. Ibid., p. 179.

10. Ibid., pp. 179–181.

11. Phillips, *Dynasty,* pp. 130 and 192. Phillips writes: "Harken was described in the *Texas Observer* as having 'direct links to institutions involved in drug-smuggling, foreign currency manipulation and the CIA's well-documented role in the destabilization of the Australian government.'" Whatever the truth of these allegations, Phillips, writing of the defense made by Bush's lawyers against the charge of "insider dealing," says: "George W. Bush had gotten his slice of Middle Eastern pie earlier through the help of the Saudis, Kuwaitis, and Bahrainis in financing Arbusto and Harken (as well as the Bahrain drilling contract awarded to Harken). . . . Rarely, if ever, has a U.S. President's family been so involved, both in commerce and high-level connections, in such a strife-ridden, high stakes part of the world."

12. Ibid., pp. 49–50. Writing of Bush's "conversion," Phillips says: "Taken together, his self-certainty, religious conviction touched with messianic hints, and a tendency to both doctrinal extremes and black-versus-white simplicities suggests a striking new pairing . . . *the aristocrat as fundamentalist.*"

13. It is sometimes forgotten that *A Charge to Keep* was Bush's election tract.

14. Kissinger was most often represented as a disciple of Metternich, but others, looking for an even more damaging association, thought of him as Bismarckian.

15. The speech was riddled with platitudes of this kind. This showed the Reagan influence unmistakably: Reagan had made comparable criticisms of Carter for abandoning Taiwan in favor of "Red" China.

16. Because journalists' accounts of the 2000 election have focussed primarily on the disputed outcome, few have given the same attention to the campaign itself, and even fewer to the fact that Bush ran as much against Clinton as against Gore. In this connection, see the admiring account by David Frum, *The Right Man: An Inside Account of the Surprise Presidency of George W. Bush* (Weidenfeld and Nicolson, 2003), pp. 12–30, a chapter entitled "The Un-Clinton."

17. Andrew J. Bacevich: *American Empire: The Realities and Consequences of U.S. Diplomacy* (Harvard, 2002), p. 203. Bacevich notes that despite Clinton's implicit and explicit denial, "most of the sentiments expressed could have been lifted directly from the Web site of the Clinton White House."

18. See Michael Lind, *Made in Texas: George W. Bush and the Southern Takeover of American Politics* (Basic Books, 2003), p. xi.

19. Ibid., pp. 80, 159, and 164.

20. Ibid., pp. 78–79.

21. Lewis Lapham, *Theater of War* (New Press, 2002), pp. 77–79.

22. Ibid., p. 79.

23. Bob Woodward, *Bush at War* (Simon and Schuster, 2002), p. 22.

24. Ibid.

25. Ibid. Neither Kissinger nor Rumsfeld have ever thought to record their true sentiments about the other, and one can only guess at what they are.

26. Ivo H. Daalder and James M. Lindsay, *America Unbound: The Bush Revolution in Foreign Policy* (Brookings, 2003), pp. 15–16. These authors, never doubting that Bush and his associates did indeed fashion a "revolution" in American foreign policy, are reluctant to give the "neo-cons" in the administration the importance others ascribe to them. They write: "Neo-conservatives—who might be better called democratic imperialists—were more prominent outside the administration, particularly on the pages of *Commentary* and the *Weekly Standard* and in the television studios of Fox News, than they were inside. The bulk of Bush's advisers, including most notably Dick Cheney and Defense Secretary Donald Rumsfeld, were not neocons. Nor for that matter was Bush. They were instead assertive nationalists–traditional hard-line conservatives willing to use American military power to defeat threats to U.S. security but reluctant as a general rule to use American primacy to remake the world in its image. . . . They placed their faith not in diplomacy and treaties, but in power and resolve." In short, though they emphasized their commitment to human rights and democracy, these were mere decorative fig leafs intended to conceal their Nietzschean will to power, something neither of these authors are prepared to say.

27. Bacevich, *Empire,* pp. 205–206.

28. James A. Baker III, *Global Challenges at the New Millenium* (Institute of United States Studies, 1998), pp. 7–9. Baker spoke of the threat posed by terrorism and the proliferation of weapons of mass destruction, saying: "The attack earlier this year against American embassies in Tanzania and Kenya served as grim reminders that terrorism remains an acute international menace. And I believe that the Clinton Administration's response to them was not just appropriate but, indeed, necessary. We should recall, however, that the war against terrorism is a truly protracted struggle, one that will take firmness of purpose and consistency of policy if the international community is to prevail. The threat arising from the proliferation of weapons of mass destruction is, if anything, even graver. While recent comments from New Delhi and Islamabad give us grounds for cautious hope, India and Pakistan's decision to 'go nuclear' has nonetheless made the world an immensely more dangerous place. With each additional nuclear power, the risk of war, if only by miscalculation or misunderstanding, rises dramatically. The spread of chemical and biological weaponry is hardly less fraught with danger. This is particularly true when it comes to rogue states like Iraq." Three years before the attack on the twin towers, Baker, so important in both the Reagan and first Bush administrations, outlined the policy George W. Bush adopted in its entirety. There is no evidence that Bush felt equal regard for the views of General Scowcroft, once so prominent in his father's administration.

29. See Paul Krugman, *The Great Unravelling: From Boom to Bust in Three Scandalous Years* (Allen Lane, 2003). This collection of articles by the *New York Times* columnist must figure as among the most damning of any written on the economic policies pursued by the George W. Bush administration.

30. Ibid., pp. 101–106 and 113–115. Krugman believed, in this instance incorrectly, that the Enron "scam," so obviously characterized by fraud and deception, would "mark a bigger turning point for America's perception of itself than September 11 did."

31. Bacevich, *Empire,* p. 206. Bacevich, glancing at the Bush administration's early foreign policy, makes the interesting observation that much less changed than the candidate had promised. He writes: "Like Eisenhower in 1953, George W. Bush in 2001 by and large embraced the policies of his predecessor. As in 1953, Republicans vigorously denied that such was the case, and Democrats found it expedient to minimize the similarities. But those similarities far outweighed the differences." A more devastating critique of the early Bush policy, documenting its essential passivity, especially on the issue of terrorism, is provided by Richard A. Clarke, *Against*

All Enemies: Inside America's War on Terror (Free Press, 2004), p. x. Clarke, noting the failures of earlier administrations, including that of Reagan, Bush, and Clinton, gives the last some credit for identifying "terrorism as the major post–Cold War threat." In his account, Clinton was weakened by "continued political attack," and "could not get the CIA, the Pentagon, and FBI to act sufficiently to deal with the threat." His most searing criticism is of George W. Bush "who failed to act prior to September 11 on the threat from al Qaeda despite repeated warnings and then harvested a political windfall for taking obvious yet insufficient steps after the attacks; and who launched an unnecessary and costly war in Iraq that strengthened the fundamentalist, radical terrorist movement worldwide."

32. Sir Michael Howard offered his opinion in a speech delivered to the Royal United Services Institute on October 30, 2001. The speech received wide publicity in the United Kingdom, reprinted in the widely read *Evening Standard* on October 31, but made little impression in the United States where public opinion joined the president in believing that this was war, and that Sir Michael's notion that it resembled Britain's age-long trials with terrorists in Ireland was "like trying to eradicate cancer cells with a blow torch."

33. Woodward, *Bush,* p. 101. On September 17, the president authorized the CIA to "disrupt the al Qaeda network and other global terrorist networks on a worldwide scale, using lethal covert action to keep the role of the United States hidden." Woodward, once a scathing critic of Nixon, had become an admirer of his Republican successor, as is evident in this book.

34. Ibid., p. 106. At a National Security Council meeting, according to Woodward, based on information he secured from one or more of those who participated, almost certainly Condoleezza Rice, the national security adviser, Rumsfeld "raised the possibility that weapons of mass destruction could be used against the United States," and asked the president to mention that threat specifically in his address to Congress that evening. Bush chose not to do so, lest he alarm the nation unduly so soon after the terrible events of September 11.

35. Ibid., p. 108. Woodward chose to emphasize the passage where the president said, "Americans should not expect one battle but a lengthy campaign, unlike any other we have ever seen. It may include dramatic strikes visible on TV, and covert actions, secret even in success. . . . I will not forget this wound to our country and those who inflicted it. I will not yield. I will not rest; I will not relent in waging this struggle for freedom and security for the American people." Woodward described the applause as "thunderous."

36. Bacevich, *Empire,* p. 234. The war, Bacevich explains, was largely fought with air power, but the most exaggerated claims were made of how "doggedly," the Taliban warriors were "hanging on," and how defeating them was going to require a "long, long campaign." This propaganda, so redolent of what was said in the Gulf War, would be used again when the attack on Iraq was launched.

37. One waits to see how many years elapse before the younger Bush chooses to acknowledge the truth of this, as his father did in respect to the Gulf War in the book he wrote jointly with General Scowcroft.

38. See David Cole, *Enemy Aliens: Double Standards and Constitutional Freedoms in the War on Terrorism* (New Press, 2003), pp. 57–69. Cole writes that this omnibus bill soon acquired the acronym USA Patriot Act, suggesting that to oppose the "many changes to criminal, immigration, banking, and intelligence law" was unpatriotic, in effect, un-American.

39. Daalder and Lindsay, *America Unbound,* pp. 84–85. Bush asked Congress to appropriate $9.8 billion for homeland security immediately after 9/11. In February 2002, he asked for an appropriation of $31.7 billion. "Counterterrorism," we are told, "became the priority number one at the CIA and the FBI."

40. Council on Foreign Relations, *Emergency Responders: Drastically Underfunded, Dangerously Unprepared,* Foreword, p. vii.

41. Noel Annan, *Changing Enemies: The Defeat and Regeneration of Germany* (HarperCollins, 1995).

42. John Dower, *Embracing Defeat: Japan in the Wake of World War II* (Norton, 1999).

43. Daalder and Lindsay, *American Unbound*, pp. 120–121. The authors write: "The key elements of this emerging strategy, which reflected the administration's hegemonist worldview, were American power and leadership, a focus on rogue states, and the need to act pre-emptively. A few weeks after Bush's axis of evil speech, Cheney made clear that responsibility for meeting this threat lay squarely on America's shoulders. 'America has friends and allies in this cause,' the vice president told a packed gathering at the Council on Foreign Relations, 'but only we can lead it. Only we can rally the world in a task of this complexity, against an enemy so elusive and so resourceful. The United States, and only the United States, can see this effort through to victory. This responsibility did not come to us by chance. We are in a unique position because of our unique assets—because of the character of our people, the strength of our ideals, the might of our military, and the enormous economy that supports it.'" See also Eliot A. Cohen, *Supreme Command: Soldiers, Statesmen and Leadership in Wartime* (Free Press, 2002), p. 192. Cohen says of Cheney, "the secretary of defense, a tough Wyoming politician, had, like many politicians of his generation, been of draft age during the Vietnam War and had never served, a fact that may have colored the attitude of some of the senior officers with whom he dealt."

44. Ibid., p. 122.

45. Ibid., pp. 122–126. In the authors' very sympathetic rendering of this message, they considered the arguments others made against the doctrine of preventive war but never suggested the criticism made in this book, too rarely noted, that George W. Bush and those who thought as he did showed no appreciation for what other presidents had done to counter more considerable threats, posed by Nazi Germany and the Communist Soviet Union. In the mythological history invented by Bush and his administration, they alone were prepared to take risks, were the sole heroes in this encounter with evil, a precise borrowing of the argument first used by Reagan's courtiers.

46. See *WMD in Iraq: Evidence and Implications* (Carnegie Endowment for International Peace, 2004), a remarkable report prepared by Joseph Cirincione, Jessica T. Mathews, and George Perkovich which throws substantial doubts on all the principal claims made by the administration in respect to weapons of mass destruction.

47. Another happy prospect, touted by Condoleezza Rice, the president's national security adviser that the *Financial Times* in London knew to be exaggerated, indeed illusory. Believing that her expert knowledge of the Soviet Union gave her some purchase on the new international realities, she saw the transformation of the Middle East as the "moral issue" of her age. See *Financial Times*, September 15, 2003, p. 17.

48. See Richard Clarke, *Against All Enemies: Inside America's War on Terror* (Free Press, 2004) and Ron Suskind, *The Prince of Loyalty: George W. Bush, The White House, and the Education of Paul O'Neill* (Simon and Schuster, 2004).

49. See Bob Woodward, *Bush at War* (Simon and Schuster, 2002) and Bob Woodward, *Plan of Attack* (Simon and Schuster, 2004).

50. Daniel Okrent, "Weapons of Mass Destruction? Or Mass Distraction," *New York Times*, May 30, 2004, "Week in Review," p. 2.

51. I choose to see the 1980s and 1990s as the "locust years," a portrayal that neither Republicans nor Democrats will welcome.

EPILOGUE

1. Paul Kennedy, *The Rise and Fall of the Great Powers: Economic Change and Military Conflict from 1500 to 2000* (Random House, 1987), p. 533.

2. Niall Ferguson, *Empire: How Britain Made the Modern World* (Allen Lane and Basic Books, 2003), p. 370. See also Niall Ferguson, *Colossus: The Price of American Empire* (Allen Lane and Penguin, 2004).

3. Ibid.

4. G.M. Young, *Portrait of an Age,* 2nd ed. (Oxford University Press, 1983), p. 164. The book was published originally by Oxford in 1936.

APPENDIX

1. The two texts most relied on for this chapter are Alexis de Tocqueville, *Democracy in America,* (University of Chicago Press, 2000) translated and edited by Harvey C. Mansfield and Delba Winthrop and James Bryce, *The American Commonwealth* (Macmillan, 1927 and 1928), a new edition published in two volumes.

2. An indication of the popularity of the Bryce text, especially in the United States, is suggested by Robert C. Brooks, editor, *Bryce's American Commonwealth* (Macmillan, 1939), p. 239. The sales for the book from 1888 through 1897–1898 were 71,378; between 1898–1899 through 1907–1908, they were 46,568; they rose to 56,097 between 1908–1909 through 1917–1918, and declined in the period 1918–1919 through 1927–1928 to 31,275; from 1928–1929 through 1937–1938 they were 6,970. The work, published in all editions by Macmillan, sold 212,288 copies in the half-century after its publication. Because there is no single publisher for Tocqueville, it is impossible to give figures for the English translations that appeared in this same period; they were never comparable. Tocqueville's major sales in the United States began with the edition, based on the Henry Reeve text published in 1945 by Alfred Knopf, edited by Phillips Bradley, that went through eight printings by 1960. Innumerable new translations have appeared since.

3. *The Letters of Theodore Roosevelt,* selected and edited by Elting E. Morison and John M. Blum, vol. 1 (Harvard University Press, 1951), p. 134. This document is wrongly dated in this otherwise commendable and extraordinarily valuable edition of TR's letters.

4. Look at Woodrow Wilson, "Bryce's American Commonwealth, A Review," printed originally in vol. 4. no. 1 of the *Political Science Quarterly* (1889), and more conveniently available in Brooks, *Bryce's American Commonwealth,* pp. 169–188. The Wilson review is an admirable scholarly essay, more intellectually compelling than the review published by Lord Acton in the *English Historical Review,* vol. 4 (April 1889).

5. Wilson, *Review,* in Brooks, pp. 170 and 180–181.

6. Theodore Roosevelt, "Machine Politics in New York City," *Century Magazine,* November 1886, pp. 74–82. Bryce virtually accepted all of Roosevelt's arguments, as given in this single article.

7. Ibid., p. 81. Roosevelt never expressed great enthusiasm for intellectuals who shunned politics. In this essay, he writes: "The boss knows every man in his district who can control any number of votes. . . . Of course this fact does not of itself make the boss a bad man; there are several such I could point out who are ten times over better fellows than the mild-mannered scholars of timorous virtue who criticize them."

8. This is the principal theme of Wilson's *Congressional Government.*

9. Wilson, *Congressional Government,* p. 42.

10. Ibid., p. 43.

11. Wilson, *Review* in Brooks, *Bryce's American Commonwealth,* p. 186.

12. Ibid.

13. Ibid., p 187.

14. Wilson, *Congressional Government,* pp. 79–96.

15. Bryce, *American Commonwealth*, vol. 1, see chapter xix, pp. 191–208, "General Observations on Congress." Also, p. 83. Bryce, contrasting the twenty presidents of the years between 1789 and 1900 with the British prime ministers of that age, ends by saying: "It would seem that the natural selection of the English parliamentary system, even as modified by the aristocratic habits of that country, had more tendency to bring the highest gifts to the highest place than the more artificial selection of America." As a footnote, he adds: "Of Presidents since 1900 it is not yet time to speak."

16. Tocqueville, *Democracy*, vol. 1, pp. 105–161. Chapter 8, "On the Federal Constitution," must be read by anyone who cares to appreciate Tocqueville's originality.

17. Ibid., pp. 377–378.

18. Ibid., p. 247.

19. Ibid., p. 121.

20. Ibid., p. 118.

21. Ibid., pp. 128–130.

22. Ibid., p. 130.

23. Ibid., pp. 328–329.

24. Ibid., vol. 2, pp. 617–618.

25. Ibid., p. 621.

26. Ibid.

27. Ibid.

28. Ibid., p. 661.

29. Ibid., pp. 662–663.

30. Ibid., p. 664.

31. Ibid., vol. 1, p. 241.

32. Ibid., p. 244.

33. Ibid., p. 227.

34. Patriotism, in its American form, has virtually disappeared in its more virulent forms from all the older democracies of Europe, especially members of the European Union. The patriotic expressions, commonplace in the United States during and after the Gulf War and also following George W. Bush's declaration of victory in the war against Iraq have almost no analogue in Europe.

35. Ibid., p. 279. Tocqueville, *Democracy*, p. 279, wrote: "In the United States religion not only regulates mores, but extends its empire over intelligence."

36. Ibid., p. 409.

37. While American fundamentalists emphasized the Calvinist doctrine of "original sin," and most members of the religious right were attached to the Republican Party, Reagan himself was never one to accept such a gloomy doctrine. See Garry Wills, *Reagan's America: Innocents at Home* (Doubleday, 1987), pp. 378–388, a chapter entitled "Original Sinlessness."

38. Tocqueville, *Democracy*, pp. 672–673.

ACKNOWLEDGMENTS

Kevin Phillips, in his recent book, *American Dynasty: How the Bush Clan Became the World's Most Dangerous Family* distinguishes between the books written about Presidents Lincoln, Washington, Jefferson, and FDR, contrasting them with those written about Clinton and the Bushes. Phillips suggests that "perhaps some day people will talk of Clinton and Bush scholars—but not for now." In writing about the American presidency since Theodore Roosevelt, I would describe the situation somewhat differently. While both Theodore and Franklin Roosevelt, among twentieth-century presidents, have been fortunate in their many biographers, only Woodrow Wilson, Harry Truman, and John F. Kennedy have claimed comparable attention from equally accomplished scholars. If other presidents in the first two-thirds of the century have not benefited from magisterial biographical studies, it would be a serious mistake to underestimate what American scholars have contributed to an understanding of these earlier twentieth-century presidents.

Beginning with Lyndon Johnson and continuing to this day, the situation is very different; journalism has indeed substituted for scholarship, with the massive autobiographies produced by Richard Nixon, Ronald Reagan, and Bill Clinton, together with those who served them, providing much of the information on which we are compelled to rely. These three complex and secretive dissemblers occupied the White House for more than twenty-two years in the last decades of the twentieth century, a period rife with what Kevin Phillips, speaking only of the Bush clan, characterizes as a time of "disinformation." If, as Phillips argues, the tendency of the Bush family has been to conceal itself "behind a facade thrown up over many decades," this is no less true of the presidencies of Nixon, Reagan, and Clinton. They, like their less illustrious presidential peers—Ford, Carter, and the two Bushes, together with the insufficiently appreciated Johnson—wait to be reexamined by a new generation of scholars, American and foreign. While it is impossible to guess as to what these scholars will discover, what secrets are contained in still-classified documents, the greatest surprises are likely to come from new interpretations of a century and a presidential office that has not conformed to what many, even a generation ago, believed to be impending.

My own interpretation of the presidency from Theodore Roosevelt to George W. Bush is informed, of course, by what I have read, but also from what I have heard in conversations in the United States, Europe, Latin America, Asia, and Africa, extending over more than half a century. How can I express my indebtedness to those individuals who have been most instrumental in sharing their opinions with me, about the United States, but also about its politics and its presidents? The company is diverse in every sense and includes many whose names will resonate even for the young in the twenty-first century while others will be unknown to them. I recall with gratitude all that I learned from Eleanor Roosevelt and Rex Tugwell, Roger Shugg and Lowell Ragatz, Charles McIwain and Michael Karpovich, John Conway and Klaus Epstein, Dorothy Thompson and Vincent Sheean, Harold Laski and R.H. Tawney, Cleo Noel Jr. and William Kontos, Raymond Aron and Eric Weil, Sinclair Weeks and Lyman Kirkpatrick, Fabio Luca Cavazza and Romano Prodi, Karl Dietrich Bracher and Michael Mertes, McGeorge Bundy and Daniel Patrick Moynihan, Gerald Holton and Paul Freund, Henry Kissinger and Brent Scowcroft, Roy Jenkins and Peter Hennessy, Jill Conway and Vartan Gregorian, Arthur Schlesinger Jr. and Kenneth Galbraith, John Hope Franklin and Kenneth Clark, Mark Medish and Jamie Metzl, Perry Miller and Ernst Gellner, Shmuel Eisenstadt and Talcott Parsons. Friends, teachers, colleagues, and students, they stimulated me to reflect about the United States in ways I would not otherwise have done. No one of them would subscribe to all that I have said in this book, but they, like many others, encouraged me to wander, to trespass into fields that were not my own, to edit a journal, *Daedalus,* the Journal of the American Academy of Arts and Sciences, that for almost four decades became a distinctively international publication, resembling no other. I must thank also Andrew Blick, my very able research assistant, who showed great patience and understanding with an admittedly difficult task.

My greatest debt is to my wife, Margaret, who more than a quarter of a century ago gave me new eyes with which to see the world. From our home in rural Northamptonshire, where this book has been largely written, I have gained new respect for those abroad, in the United Kingdom and in the European Union, who seek to understand what the United States so recently was, and what it appears to be today. It has been a rare privilege for me to be able to live for extended periods on both sides of the Atlantic, encouraging me in my faith that only reason and intellectual discourse can provide a viable exit from our present discontents.

INDEX

The following abbreviations are used: Bush (GHW) for Bush, George Herbert Walker; Bush (GW) for Bush, George Walker; Roosevelt (FD) for Roosevelt, Franklin Delano; Roosevelt (T) for Roosevelt, Theodore

Caribbean and, 137–38; childhood illness and, 121; declares war against Germany, 9, 150; Democratic National Convention, 129–30; as a diplomat, 9–10, 162; dispute with Harvey, 128; establishment of the Federal Trade Commission and, 136; Federal Reserve legislation and, 134–35; and foreign policy of, 162–63; Fourteen Points, 152–53, 156; legislation as New Jersey governor, 127; Mexico and, 138–40, 143, 144–45, 149; neutrality and, 142, 143–44; objection to separate Bolshevik peace terms, 151, 152; president of Princeton, 122–24; public opinion and, 155, 163; race and, 563; vs. Republicans, 167; Russian policy, 153; tariff legislation and, 133–34; wartime legislation and, 150–51, 154; wins New Jersey governorship, 125

Winchell, Walter, 325
Winning of the West (Roosevelt), 73
Wirtz, Alvin, 353–54
Wiseman, Sir William, 153
Wofford, Harris, 333
Wolfowitz, Paul, 540
Wood, Kimba, 512
Wood, Leonard, 168, 169
Woodcock, Leonard, 429
Woodward, Bob, 540, 548–49
Works Progress Administration, 215
World Bank, 18
World Court, 170, 176
World Economic Conference, 213
World Transformed, A (Bush/Scowcroft), 483, 488, 491
World War I, 9–10; American mediation and, 142; British blacklisting of American firms, 145–46; German U-boat warfare, 143, 148; Lloyd George and, 147, 153, 156, 157–58, 161; Wilson and, 9–10, 148–51, 155, 157–61; Wilson neutrality and, 142, 143–44; Wilson's Fourteen Points, 152–53, 156; as "Wilson's war," 154

World War II, 30, 31, 292; American industry and, 213, 229; American vs. British strategy, 287–88, 290, 293, 294; Churchill and Roosevelt (FD), 219–20, 222, 226–27, 229, 230–31; Churchill and Eisenhower, 293–94; De Gaulle vs. Roosevelt (FD), 231–34; Germany occupies Poland, 218–19; Japan attacks Pearl Harbor, 228–29; Moscow negotiations, 253–55; Nazis invade Soviet Union, 225; OVERLORD, 291; the Philippines and, 287; Potsdam Conference, 252–53; Tehran conference, 237–38; TORCH (North African campaign), 230, 235, 288–90; Truman and, 13, 57, 250, 252; Yalta conference, 238–41
Wyman, Jane, 443

Yale University, 103, 123, 413, 473, 499, 535
Yalta conference, 238–41
Yamamoto, Isoroku, 235
Year of Europe, 420
Year of Intelligence, 415
Years of Renewal (Kissinger), 420
Years of Upheaval (Kissinger), 406
Yeltsin, Boris, 483, 484, 485, 494, 525
Yergin, Daniel, 439
Yom Kippur War, 22, 407, 412, 413
Yost, Charles, 473, 474
Young, Coleman, 429
Young, G. M., 555
Yugoslavia, 224, 520; NATO bombing of Serbia, 523–24; Serb atrocities against Muslims, 521

Zapata, Emilio, 143
Zelikow, Philip, 339, 343, 349
Ziegler, Ron, 404, 407
Zimmermann, Arthur, 148–49
Zoellick, Robert, 540
Zwicker, Ralph, 308